Gun Digest

35th Anniversary
1981 Deluxe Edition

EDITED BY KEN WARNER

Follett Publishing Company / Chicago

T-1449

OUR COVER GUN

This revolver was once a common or garden variety Smith & Wesson Model 1917 in 45 ACP, designed and issued as a substitute for then-scarce 45 Model 1911 automatic pistols. Its owner, writer C. E. Harris, has had it reworked, and it now has two cylinders, one the original and the second in 45 Colt, as well as other touches, such as matted surfaces and sight inlays. For the story of this convertible revolver, and to find out how you could achieve the same result with a similar revolver, see pages 36-40 in this issue. Cover photo by John Hanusin.

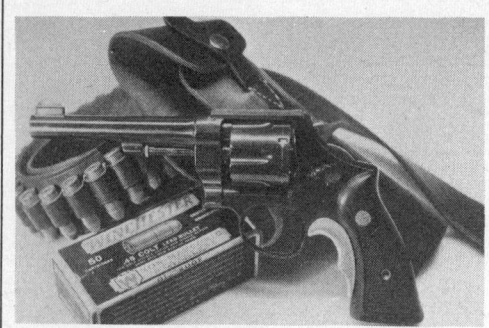

GUN DIGEST STAFF

EDITOR-IN-CHIEF
Ken Warner
ASSISTANT TO THE EDITOR
Lilo Anderson
SENIOR STAFF EDITOR
Harold A. Murtz
ASSOCIATE EDITOR
Bob Anderson
PRODUCTION MANAGER
Pamela J. Johnson

CONTRIBUTING EDITORS
Bob Bell
Ralph C. Glaze
Dean A. Grennell
Larry S. Sterett
Hal Swiggett
Ken Waters
J. B. Wood

EUROPEAN CORRESPONDENT
Raymond Caranta

EDITOR EMERITUS
John T. Amber
PUBLISHER
Sheldon L. Factor

DBI BOOKS, INC.

PRESIDENT
Charles T. Hartigan
VICE PRESIDENT & PUBLISHER
Sheldon L. Factor
VICE PRESIDENT — SALES
John G. Strauss
TREASURER
Frank R. Serpone

Copyright ©MCMLXXX by DBI Books, Inc., One Northfield Plaza, Northfield, Illinois 60093, a subsidiary of Technical Publishing, a company of the Dun & Bradstreet Corporation. All rights reserved. Printed in the United States of America.

No part of this publication may be reproduced, stored in a retrieval system, or transmitted in any form or by any means, electronic, mechanical, photocopying, recording, or otherwise, without the prior written permission of the publisher.

The views and opinions contained herein are those of the authors. The editor and publisher disclaim all responsibility for the accuracy or correctness of the authors' views.

Manuscripts, contributions and inquiries, including first class return postage, should be sent to the Gun Digest Editorial Offices, One Northfield Plaza, Northfield, IL 60093. All material received will receive reasonable care, but we will not be responsible for its safe return. Material accepted is subject to our requirements for editing and revisions. Author payment covers all rights and title to the accepted material, including photos, drawings and other illustrations. Payment is at our current rates.

Arms and Armour Press, London G.B., exclusive distributors in the United Kingdom of Great Britain, Northern Ireland, and Republic of Eire; Australasia; South Africa and Zimbabwe.

ISBN-0-910676-09-7   Library of Congress Catalog #44-3588

Townsend Whelen Award

D. C. Cole is the recipient of our $500 award, its 15th presentation, for his remarkable piece of Southwest history, "Firearms In Apache Tribal Use," which begins on page 98 of this issue. Cole's article is the very stuff of tough history; his background as a member of the Apache nation shows through every sentence.

This annual award is made to the writer who, in our judges' opinions, made the most outstanding contribution to arms literature as published in GUN DIGEST 35th.

We thank writer Cole and we congratulate him.

It would not be amiss to say that if there were Honorable Mentions, at least five other writers could be listed here.

NBRSA Gun Digest Heavy Varmint Trophy

Our GUN DIGEST Trophy was awarded to Ed Watson of Greenville, SC who shot a Grand Aggregate score of 0.2652" for the 100- and 200-yard matches. Watson's equipment consisted of a Remington XP-100 action, McMillan barrel in 6mm PPC and Lyman/Siebert scope. Dale McMillan did the gunsmithing work. Ed's handload was 25.0/4198 using his own 65-gr. bullets and Federal 205 primers. Best wishes, Ed!

IBS Gun Digest Heavy Varmint Trophy

The winner of the 1979 Heavy Varmint National Championships and the GUN DIGEST trophy was Larry Earp of Charlotte, NC. Larry's Grand Aggregate score (25 shots at 100 and 200 yards) was 0.2739". His 100-yard score went 0.2376", while the 200-yard was 0.3102". He used a sleeved Remington 40X action with McMillan barrel in 6mm PPC. The scope was a Redfield 3200. Earp did his own stock work and Fred Sinclair handled the rest of the gunsmithing chores. Earp's handload was 25.0/4198 with home-made 65-gr. bullets and Federal 205 primers. Congratulations, Larry!

Warnings For Wildfowlers ...

Hunters must use steel shot in ALL gauges when hunting waterfowl in steel-shot zones in fall, 1980, the U.S. Fish and Wildlife Service has reminded hunters. No exception will be made.

Waterfowl hunters had to use steel shot (the only approved nontoxic shot) in 12-gauge guns in the zones during the 1979 waterfowl season. Lead shot was then permitted in other gauges.

Supplies of steel shot in 10, 12, and 20 gauges are expected to be available in many areas. Hunters are urged to check sporting goods stores and other retail outlets in their areas for more specific information, including a list of steel-shot zones. (There is an extensive discussion of steel shot in this issue. See page 41.)

For Wildcatters ...

Remington warns wildcatters that there is a very good reason not to shoot their 7mm-08 Remington loads in wildcat 7mm-308 chambers.

To get a longer neck, factory 7mm-08 cartridge cases are .020" longer than the case you get when you simply neck down a 308 case. The necked-down 308 is OK, if made with a good die, in the factory chamber, but the factory cartridge in a tightly fitted wildcat chamber might be a different story, and a pressure increase might well result from the chamber neck crimping in on the extra length of brass.

Sensibly, since Remington has no control over wildcat chamber dimensions, they want people to know about the problem.

Milestones

Some highlights from events in the shooting world in 1980:

• SHOT SHOW, held the first time in January of 1979, becomes a runaway success in the world of trade shows. The 1981 Show has the Superdome in New Orleans filled to overflowing. There will be over 500 exhibitors in 105,000 square feet of space, drawing over 12,000 registrants. In broad terms those numbers just about double the impressive first show held in St. Louis. National Shooting Sports Foundation has a real winner here.

• On a different front, NSSF spent much time preparing 1980 as a year to begin to have a pro-shooting impact on schools nationwide. A first-cabin filmstrip entitled "Unendangered Species," all about game animals and hunting, was distributed free to 6000 schools as the 1980-81 school year opened.

• WINCHESTER-WESTERN named Jim Carmichel, gun editor of *Outdoor Life*, Outdoorsman of the Year, Carmichel, in achieving this distinction, follows such luminaries as Fred Bear, Jack O'Connor and Nash Buckingham.

IN THE BLACK

• NATIONAL RIFLE ASSOCIATION built itself bigger than ever, getting, at 1.75 million members, well within reach of the announced goal of two million members. It's more all along the front at NRA, with shooter programs, increased publication emphasis, heavier member services in areas like insurance options for members. It's still Harlon Carter, Neal Knox and Gary Anderson at the helms.

• OUTSTANDING AMERICAN HANDGUNNER of the year was Warren Center, named at the annual banquet during the NRA Annual Meetings. Center's principal contribution to handgunning is, of course, the Thompson/Center Contender pistol, a single-shot that makes new marks everytime someone comes up with a new game. It is a most versatile design; the tribute to its creator is fitting.

The Shot Show has international flavor: from left—Tom Turpin and Nick Winter, North American associates of Friedr. Wilh. Heym K.G., with Peter Bang, director of the German firm, with Herr Bang holding one of Heym's deluxe over-under cal. 458 double rifles. On the display wall is John Amber's very special Heym-Ruger rifle. Photo: Dan Werbe

CONTENTS

FEATURES

Walnut: Nonpareil For Gunstocks
    by Stuart Williams 6
The Afghan And His SMLE
    by Jack Lott 12
My Triumphs In Gun Collecting
    by John T. Amber 18
Frontier Firepower: 1836-1872
    by Rick Hacker 26
Shoot Your Own Convertible 45
    by C. E. Harris 36
Steel Shot 1980
    by Wallace Labisky 41
Handguns Today: Sixguns and Others
    by Hal Swiggett 44
Handguns Today: Autoloaders
    by Ralph C. Glaze 54
How Wide Are Shotgun Patterns?
    by Nick Sisley 59
The Truth About Bird Guns
    by Dave Duffey 62
The Savage Pocket Automatic Pistol Model 1907
    by Donald M. Simmons 68
The Cylindrical Bullet Kills Better
    by Robert K. Sherwood 86
Handloading To Date
    by Dean A. Grennell 90
The Remarkable Guns of M. K. Jurek
    by Jerry Evans 94
Firearms In Apache Tribal Use
    by D. C. Cole 98
Cop-Proof
    by Colin Greenwood 106
The Greatest of All Webley Collectors
    by R. Bretnor 109
Scopes and Mounts
    by Bob Bell 116
Shotgun Slugs At Long Range
    by Joe Krieger 126
Two-Gun Hunter Matches
    by Tom Turpin 134
Walther's P5 Pistol
    by James P. Cowgill 138
Blackpowder
    by Edward M. Yard 142
7mm-08 Remington: Gun and Cartridge
    by Layne Simpson 152
Accuracy In 22-Caliber Target Pistols
    by Kenneth L. Walters 158

Remington's XP-100 Silhouette Pistol
    by Hal Swiggett 167
The First Short Magnum: The 425 Westley Richards Magnum
    by Jack Lott 170
The Hunter In The 20th Century
    by Roger Barlow 178
Trends In The World Of Air Guns
    by J. I. Galan 184
Kimber Model 82
    by Robert A. Painter 192
The 32-20 Never Said Die!
    by Robert S. L. Anderson 195
The Buffalo and The Chapuis
    by Ken Warner 200
Long Guns In Review
    by Larry S. Sterett 204
Especially Good Books 210
Recall: How The Firearms Industry Responds
    by Jim Crossman 212
Custom Guns 218
Winchester's Model 70 XTR
    by Frank Marshall Jr. 222
The Sinistral Problem Solved
    by John T. Amber 224
Sporting Arms of the World
    by Larry S. Sterett 227
Spanish Doubles In Classic Style
    by John T. Amber 233
Art of the Engraver 236
FIE's Combo 20 ga./30-30
    by C. E. Harris 240
Testfire: Winchester's Model 94 Big Bore Carbine; Franchi's Model 530 Autoloading 12 Gauge Trap Gun
    by Larry S. Sterett 242
Bolt Action Brush Guns For Deer
    by Frank B. Petrini 246
Custom Knives Today 250
Shooter's Showcase 253
American Bulleted Cartridges
    by Ken Waters 258

DEPARTMENTS

Ammunition Tables 265
Handguns—U.S. and Imported 269
Rifles—U.S. and Imported 298
Shotguns—U.S. and Imported 337
Black Powder Guns 365
Air Guns 384
Chokes and Brakes 398
Metallic Sights 399
Scopes and Mounts 402
Arms Association in America and Abroad 409
Periodical Publications 411
Shooting Publications 412
Arms Library 413
Directory of the Arms Trade 431

WALNUT: NONPAREIL FOR GUNSTOCKS

JAZZY WOODS HAVE GONE AWAY LIKE JAZZY STOCK DESIGNS, THIS WRITER BELIEVES, AND WALNUT ABIDES.

by Stuart Williams

WITH THE RISE to popularity of the California gee-whiz stock, a number of exotic stockwoods came into vogue. Among them were curly and birdseye maple, myrtle and mesquite, monkeypod and madrone, rosewood and koa and yama and bubinga. At last, however, the California style stock is being perceived for the meretricious thing that it is, and it is fast falling from favor among the cognoscenti of fine firearms. With its passing, all the exotic stockwoods are falling into disfavor too. As Homer wrote somewhere in *The Odyssey:* "Dogs, you have had your day!"

At the same time the contemporary classic stock style is firmly in the ascendancy. It is, of course, unthinkable to make such a stock out of anything other than walnut. Consequently walnut is once again being recognized as the royalty and nonpareil of gunstock woods. Yes, the cream always comes to the top. Our very finest stockmakers will—to a man—refuse to work on anything else. Moreover, men like Al Lind, Jim Cloward, Bill Dowtin, and Dave Miller attribute much of their success in drawing and holding customers to their large inventories of fine walnut blanks. Why is this? Simply because walnut offers more of the desirable properties of gunstock wood—beauty, strength, stability, and workability—than any other wood.

In the Book of Judges in The Old Testament, Jothan recounts a parable of how all the trees convened to choose a king to reign over them. The walnut tree is not mentioned in the parable, but to my way of thinking it has more kingly qualities than any other tree. Its generic name—juglans, or nut of Jupiter—indicates its royal heritage.

The origins of walnut are lost in the dark of time. Walnut furniture from every century from the 5th century B.C. forward may be found in museums around the world. Dendrologists make an educated guess that the first walnut tree grew in China or Persia. In the 13th century, Marco Polo brought back the nuts from those countries to Italy, whence they spread to all of Europe. In the 16th century, the Spaniards brought them to the western hemisphere, where the industrious Spanish priests planted the nuts in northern California. Later on, when California became part of the United States, planting of walnuts and seedlings intensified greatly. A certain Colonel Bidwell was especially indefatigable in his zeal for planting walnuts.

All this planting activity was supplemented by the activity of settlers arriving from the East. They brought with them nuts and seedlings of the numberless varieties of walnut trees that were available in the eastern and midwestern states, and planted them or grafted them onto the local walnuts. The resulting clones and cultivars have produced some of the most interesting varieties of walnut for gunstocks—Mayette, Franquette, Hartley, Eureka, etc. These names will not mean anything to the casual gun buyer, but to real walnut freaks—and their numbers grow apace—they are the "stuff that dreams are made of."

During the days of the intense planting activity in California—the third quarter of the nineteenth century—the walnuts were planted exclusively for nuts rather than wood. When those trees stopped producing nuts they were no longer of interest for their original purpose. This happened during the years of the Great Depression. Thereupon, buyers from the big veneer-making factories of Italy, France, Switzerland, and Germany started making regular raids throughout the Sacramento Valley, and the sawing began in earnest. Bill English, a fine stockmaster who lived in that part of California at the time, tells me that there were groves of hundreds upon hundreds of trees, the smallest of which was 5 feet in diameter! Most—but fortunately not all—those trees were sold as veneer logs. Many of the most beautiful gunstock blanks have

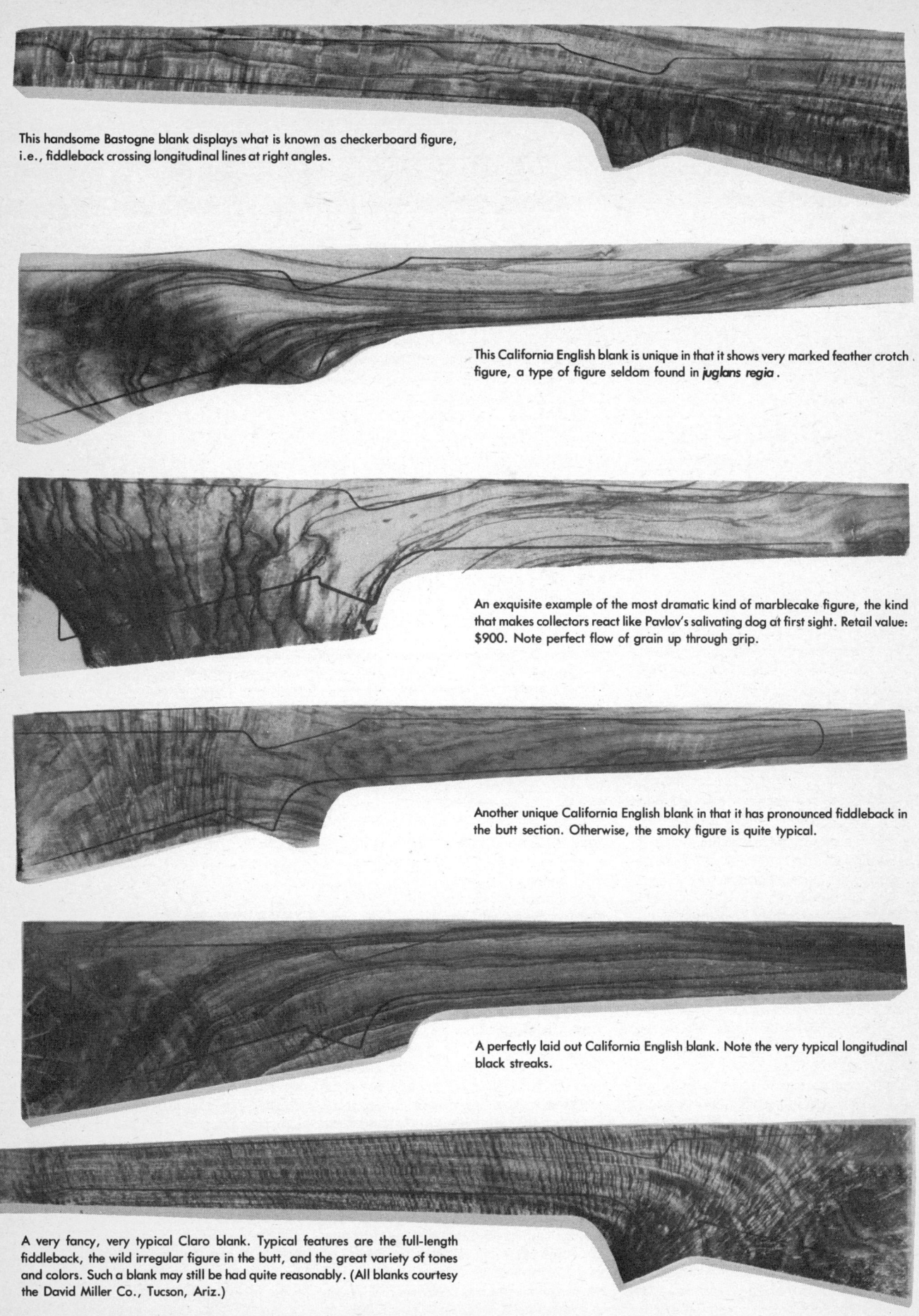

This handsome Bastogne blank displays what is known as checkerboard figure, i.e., fiddleback crossing longitudinal lines at right angles.

This California English blank is unique in that it shows very marked feather crotch figure, a type of figure seldom found in *juglans regia*.

An exquisite example of the most dramatic kind of marblecake figure, the kind that makes collectors react like Pavlov's salivating dog at first sight. Retail value: $900. Note perfect flow of grain up through grip.

Another unique California English blank in that it has pronounced fiddleback in the butt section. Otherwise, the smoky figure is quite typical.

A perfectly laid out California English blank. Note the very typical longitudinal black streaks.

A very fancy, very typical Claro blank. Typical features are the full-length fiddleback, the wild irregular figure in the butt, and the great variety of tones and colors. Such a blank may still be had quite reasonably. (All blanks courtesy the David Miller Co., Tucson, Ariz.)

come from those original plantings. In places where there were hundreds of enormous trees, however, there remain today but a few.

Yes, the stands of walnut trees in California—and across the nation—have fallen upon evil days. All the consumers of walnut—furniture-makers and veneer-makers and gunstock-makers—have been gobbling the stuff up ever more voraciously. To aggravate matters, there has been very little replanting and regrowth of walnut. In the first place, walnuts have not for years been an important part of the American diet. At the current price of walnuts it is hardly worth one's while to pick them up off the ground, let alone plant trees to grow more of them. In the second place, the huge wood products companies—which do most of the tree planting and growing in this country—are involved almost exclusively with softwoods. Yet the demand for walnut grows every year.

In post-war years the most aggressive foreign buyers of California walnut have been the Japanese. Whereas the European gunmakers have for years scorned American walnut as being inferior to European walnut (this trend is being reversed), the Japanese, having little native walnut, have been eager buyers of American walnut, and stock their guns almost exclusively with it. Roy Schaefer of Eugene, Oregon—one of the grand old men of the walnut sawing and selling business—tells me that he was recently approached by a Japanese gunmaker with an order for 10,000 blanks a year—and that was from one of the smaller Japanese gunmakers!

Recently Fabrique Nationale of Belgium—which owns the controlling interest in Browning, which in turn has most of its guns made in Japan—has been buying huge quantities of California walnut for the various Browning guns.

However, the great weight of demand being placed on California walnut by the Japanese—and by European and domestic buyers as well—is for veneer logs and not for gunstock wood. The Japanese veneer-making industry is a very interesting and impressive offshore operation. The Japanese veneer-makers load the logs on floating veneer factories in California ports and slice them into veneer on the way home. The ships are unloaded there, and then are loaded up with Toyotas and tapedecks, Kawasakis and Canons, shotguns and soy sauce, fishing reels and running shoes, and all the infinite other consumer goodies bound for the Land of the Great PX.

Veneer-making is an extremely profitable business—certainly much more profitable than sawing and selling gunstock blanks—so that the veneer makers can and do easily outbid the gunstock sawyers for the best trees. Bill English tells of an enormous tree cut in the Chico area for which a Swiss veneer-maker paid the unheard-of—for that time—price of $10,000—and then turned around and made a net profit of a quarter million dollars off the tree! Cloyce Davis, a tree surgeon and sawyer out of Liveoak, California, who saws out some magnificent gunstock blanks, sold two carloads of veneer wood at a profit of $8,000—but the veneer-maker made over $450,000

from the same wood. Obviously, then, the gunstock sawyers cannot compete against the veneer-makers for the best trees. The one thing that has kept the veneer-makers from pushing the gunstock makers entirely out of the market is the fact that much of the wood that is suitable for gunstocks is not suitable for veneer, and vice versa.

At any rate, the various sources of demand—foreign and domestic—have increased steadily over the years, so that the great walnut groves of northern California have just about been wiped out. One of the more pessimistic of the walnut sawyers—Roy Schaefer—predicts ominously that there will hardly be a walnut log left in California in five years if present trends continue. In an attempt to reverse these trends, the Fine Hardwoods Association and the Walnut Manufacturers Association have in the past decade attempted to introduce legislation that would restrict the volume of walnut exports, but have had very limited success.

The other great walnut-growing area of the world—the Rhone Valley of France—is also in serious decline. Two world wars destroyed many of the very finest trees, and walnut thieves, operating at night with tractors and chains, have stolen many others. Furthermore, the old French tradition of planting walnut seedlings on the birth of a baby girl to form part of her dowry has been gradually falling into neglect. During three visits to France in the past two years, I have inspected hundreds of rifle blanks and shotgun sets, and I must frankly say I saw none I consider outstanding.

If you listen to people like Roy

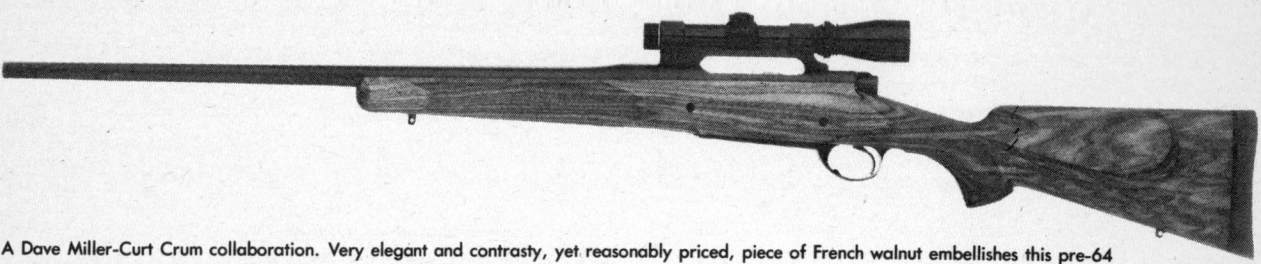
A Dave Miller-Curt Crum collaboration. Very elegant and contrasty, yet reasonably priced, piece of French walnut embellishes this pre-64 Model 70 with Marquart barrel in 375 H&H. Notice that the checkpiece side of the buttstock has much more interesting figure than the bolt side, hence the reasonable price. Very few pieces of walnut have equally good color and figure on both sides. Checkering is a 26 lpi point pattern.

Schaefer and Joe Oakley and Bill English—probably the three senior men in the country in terms of their professional involvement with walnut—they will tell you that the enormous old trees, the ones that produce the finest gunstock blanks, are just about all gone. Joe Oakley goes so far as to say that there isn't a walnut tree with gunstock wood in it left in the state of California. The way these men talk only wealthy men will be able to afford walnut stocks on their guns in another ten years.

Stumpers are felling smaller and smaller trees, and less and less desirable wood is being offered on the market. More and more sapwood is showing up on blanks and on completed rifles. (There are, of course, some people who like sapwood in their gunstocks.) Labor disputes in California have caused walnut growers to bulldoze and burn thousands of trees. As younger and younger trees are being cut, more blanks and completed stocks have nice figures on one side, but are plain on the other. In the middle 50's, the minimum acceptable log size for sawing into gunstock blanks was 16 inches in diameter. In the early 60's, the standard was reduced to 15 inches; then to 14 inches. Today it is 12 inches, and will inevitably go to 10 inches. Henry Pohl of E.C. Bishop and Son predicts that within 20 years all stocks on factory-made guns will be cut from such small trees that they will have to be laminated.

At the opposite extreme are some optimistic voices who say that the so-called walnut scarcity is like the gasoline scarcity—purely imaginary and contrived to line the purses of a few greedy hucksters. For example, Cloyce Davis—who cuts absolutely magnificent Bastogne and California English blanks on a regular basis—is confident that five years from now he will be cutting just as fine blanks—and just as many of them. Likewise, Henry Pohl is quite hopeful about the future of walnut in this country. He says that more trees are growing and more trees are available for sale now than when he began in the walnut business 22 years ago.

Farmers have gotten wise to the value of walnut and are letting trees grow rather than cutting them down when clearing land. They have even been planting trees on a modest scale. Moreover, forestry researchers have recently devised a method of doubling the growth rate of walnut trees.

Then there is a great neglected supply of walnut—the thousands upon thousands of standard-grade California English blanks that are cut and stockpiled to go unsold. California English is very much in vogue among the elite stockmakers and their mandarin clientele, but they are only interested in the cream of the crop—the top two or three per cent of the blanks. Meanwhile the plainer stuff goes completely without takers. Go into any large gun store and look up and down the rack. You will see that about 80% of the guns are stocked in American black walnut and the remainder in Claro. I daresay you won't see a single gun stocked in California English, even though in many ways it is superior to the other two species.

As for myself, I lean slightly toward the optimistic position if for no other reason than that I have great faith in the free enterprise system. When the price of a commodity goes high enough—and the price of walnut has reached that level and will certainly go higher—then Adam Smith's "invisible hand of the marketplace" will enter to supply that commodity. I foresee that the big wood products companies will become actively involved in planting and growing walnut. Some of them already are.

Moreover, I believe techniques and processes will be devised to enhance the desirability of some kinds of walnuts and softwoods that are not at present acceptable for gunstocks. For example, Robert Kleinguenther, president of Kleinguenther's Distinctive Firearms, has for several years been working on a process that will

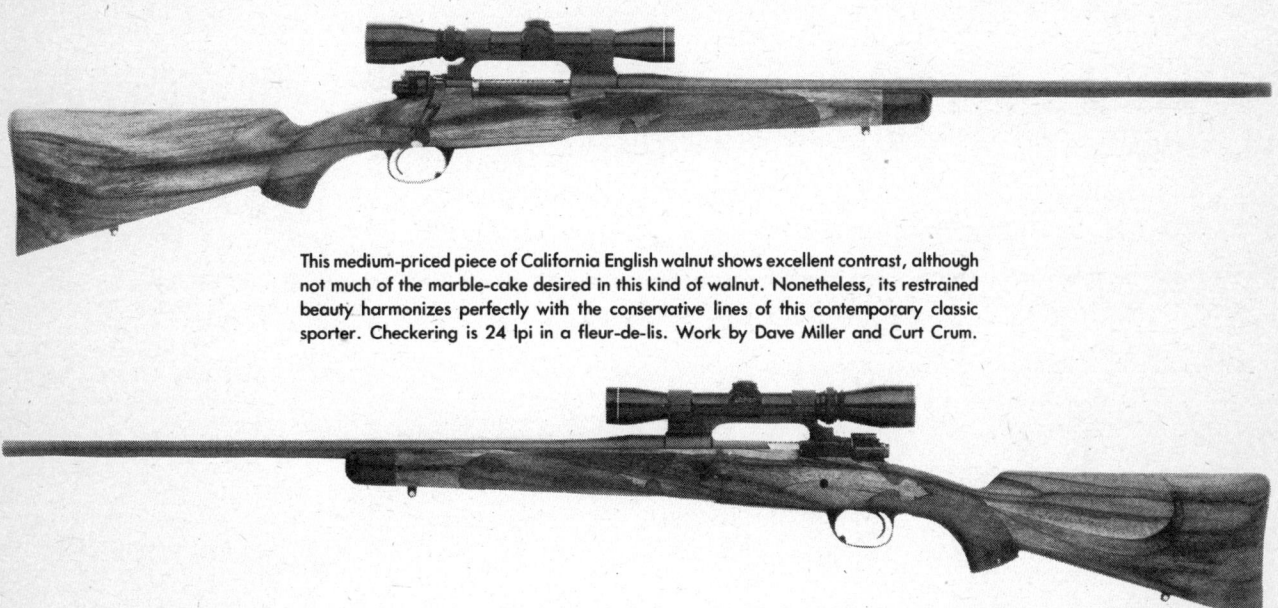

This medium-priced piece of California English walnut shows excellent contrast, although not much of the marble-cake desired in this kind of walnut. Nonetheless, its restrained beauty harmonizes perfectly with the conservative lines of this contemporary classic sporter. Checkering is 24 lpi in a fleur-de-lis. Work by Dave Miller and Curt Crum.

increase the shear strength and the tensile strength of softwoods six or eight times over, give them the stability of fiberglass—and make them look like fine walnut! I have not inspected any of the blanks so treated, but I have spoken with several knowledgeable people who have, and they are unanimously impressed. They say that it is just about impossible to drive a nail into the treated wood, and difficult, if not downright impossible, to distinguish it from walnut. Moreover, the treated wood has the workability characteristics of the finest French walnut. If this process is all that it is claimed to be, it could revolutionize the gunstock industry overnight.

At present and anticipated price levels, it will become increasingly feasible to seek out and exploit foreign sources of walnut. Several entrepreneurs are doing just that, and their numbers will increase. There are significant stands of mature walnut in the canyons of northern Mexico, and in scattered enclaves in lower Mexico and Central America; in Russia and Yugoslavia; in Israel and Oman and Yemen and Turkey and India. There are goodly numbers of trees in South America and New Zealand. I suspect that there are significant numbers of big old trees in Red China. Bill Dowtin, an outstanding young stockmaker from Celina, Texas, is gambling that there are. As I write these lines, he is en route to China to undertake an extensive exploratory expedition in search of walnut. Undoubtedly others will follow and others will discover new sources that we don't even suspect yet.

Ultimately, however, I do not think that we can expect to import large quantities of desirable gunstock walnut. Most of the major producing countries have erected barriers against log exports. The only major producing country that still allows such exports is New Zealand, and many blanks sawed there are improperly laid out.

There is plenty of room for upward movement of walnut prices to induce even more suppliers to enter the market. Consider that the average blank going on a regular production rifle costs about $9.50—yet the rifle is selling for about $300. Obviously the cost of the walnut is only a tiny component of the total cost. Even if the price of walnut were *doubled* the price of the rifle would only increase by about *12* per cent.

I am confident, then, that for many years there will be plenty of the standard-grade walnut that goes on the regular production-grade guns that most of us must content ourselves with. It is the fancy stuff that is in short supply, and will be just about extinct in a few years. This is an important distinction that must always be kept in mind in any discussion of the availability of walnut. The fancy stuff comes only from the very big, old trees that are fast following the way of the dodo, the kind that take 70, 80, or 100 years to grow. At the same time, however, demand for the very finest blanks is growing wildly. Connoisseurs of elegant guns are keeping the elite gunmakers of the country booked up for two, three, and even four years. Whereas a custom rifle was once considered a privilege reserved for the affluent, many working men can now afford custom rifles, and they have served to increase the demand for fine walnut.

Of course, the demand is vastly disproportionate to the supply. It has thus driven prices so high that exhibition and presentation grade blanks have almost become a precious substance such as gold, silver, ivory or rhinoceros horn. Such blanks will sell for at least $350, and range up from there—way up. At the 1979 NRA meetings and the 1979 Game Conservation International Conference I saw a number of fine blanks being offered in the $600-800 range, and several that were priced at $1000 and up. One of Holland and Holland's walnut scouts recently offered a friend of mine $1600 for a one-in-a-million quality blank. My friend refused; he is confident that he can get $2000.

With prices at such a stratospheric level, a lot of quick-buck artists have gotten into the game. The most bold and outrageous are the walnut rustlers, who operate at night with trucks and chain saws. Then there are wood dealers who pass off green blanks as dried blanks. There are also unprincipled walnut vendors who put green blanks in kilns and literally cook them to death—the quicker to pocket their profits. Then there was the case of the unscrupulous wood merchant who force-cured his blanks with salt. Problem was that he sold a large quantity of them to a major gunmaker. When they were made up into stocks and put on guns, the guns—some of them very expensive pieces—promptly rusted to ruination. The last I heard, that walnut merchant had forked over a very large settlement after a successful suit by the gunmaker. Most stockmakers and reputable wood-dealers agree that air-drying is the only proper method to

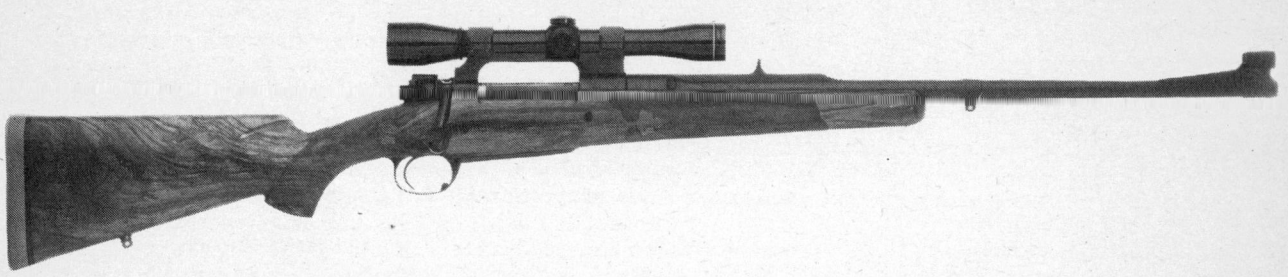

Dave Miller and Curt Crum teamed up to produce another. This rifle—a 338 built around a highly refined 1909 Argentine Mauser action with Douglas barrel—is adorned with very exceptional and very expensive California English walnut. This piece of wood displays an excellent example of the much-coveted marble-cake figure. Price for the blank: about $800.

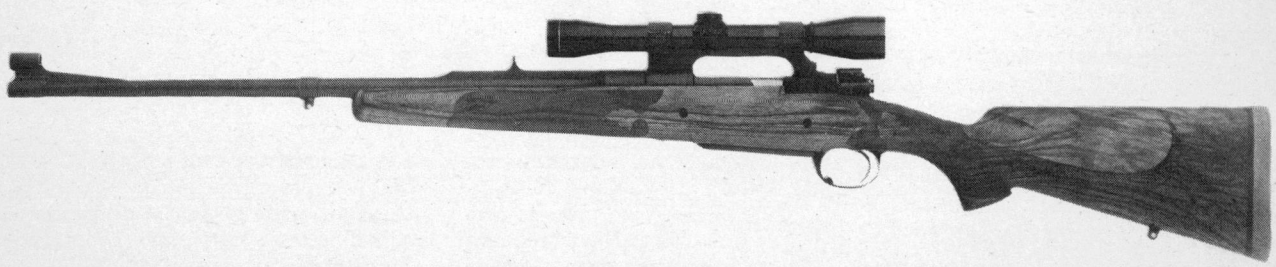

cure walnut blanks. It is also the slowest method. In buying walnut, the guideline is—more than when buying most other commodities—*caveat emptor.*

In buying a blank, one should first of all deal strictly with merchants of unimpeachable reputation. If you are dealing by mail, get it in writing that you have the right to return a blank and get another until you are satisfied. You should also have it stated in writing that if you can't get what you are looking for, you will receive a full and prompt refund. As far as the blank itself goes, make sure that the grain flows up through the grip area. Since fancy figure can be a Pandora's box of stresses and strains, all fancy figure should be confined to the buttstock. The grain in the fore-end of a blank to go on a light-barreled sporter should have a certain amount of upturn to help maintain upward pressure on the barrel. The wood should ideally be as close-grained and dense as ivory in order to take and hold fine checkering and to assure strength and stability. To further enhance stability and to show off figure to best advantage, the blank should be quarter-sawed, i.e., radially, or at right angles to the annular rings. Of the two considerations —stability and figure—the former is much more important. As far as weight goes, I prefer a light blank, even for a heavy-recoil rifle. You're going to carry the thing a whole lot more than you're going to shoot it.

Perhaps it would be appropriate at this point to give a brief description of the major varieties of walnut.

Most familiar, of course, is our own home-grown black walnut. Black walnut is found in virtually all the lower 48 states, but is found in commercial quantities only in the Midwest. The more elegant blanks that display pronounced feather crotch or irregular stump figure can be breathtaking stuff. Blanks with true feather crotch figure are rare indeed. Virtually all American mass-produced guns— Remington, Winchester, Ruger, Savage—are stocked with American black walnut, but it has some disadvantages for stocking fine custom rifles. Much of it is porous and open-grained, and therefore not very stable and not a good medium for accepting and holding fine-line checkering. Besides, fancy black walnut tends to be rather heavy. Since it is looked upon as second class stuff by most stockmakers and their clients, it may still be had at relatively moderate cost. E.C. Bishop, the nation's largest wood purveyor, and a specialist in black walnut, can still provide you a structurally sound, highly figured blank for $100-150. Roy Schaefer and Gilman Keasay of Oregon also offer very fine, reasonably priced black walnut blanks.

The second all-American type of walnut is Claro, or *juglans hindsi.* Most Claro grows in large walnut orchards in northern California. Much of it therefore is unsuitable for gunstocks. It forks too close to the ground and it forks too many times. It is grown in fertile soil in a temperate climate and receives plentiful moisture. Thus it grows rapidly and develops soft, porous wood. All these conditions militate against the growth of fine gunstock wood. Moreover, orchard trees are usually bulldozed out when they stop producing profitable quantities of nuts—at about 40 years of age— whereas a tree must grow at least twice that old to produce really superb gunstock wood.

It is unfortunate that most Claro does not have better structural properties, because it has unquestionably the most dramatic color and figure of all the varieties of walnut. Much of it has perfect fiddleback that reminds me of an accordion compressed. Much of it also has striking tiger-tail figure. Then there are often irregular kinds of figure that defy all description. Some of the characteristic colors of Claro are amber, ochre, auburn, gold, black, brown, and mahogany—in many instances all present in the same blank. Since it—like American black—is looked down upon by the custom stockmakers and the cognoscenti, it may still be had at reasonable prices. $80-120 will get you a dazzling chunk of the stuff. If you are fortunate enough to find a *hard* piece of Claro, the kind that Cloyce Davis frequently cuts, you have come upon something very special indeed. Grab it.

Because of its eye appeal, its availability, and its reasonable cost, Claro has become very popular for stocking many foreign-made guns. Guns stocked in Claro include the Weatherby rifles and shotguns, the Colt-Sauer, the Browning 78 and the Citori, and the Nikko Golden Eagle rifles and shotguns.

Next is a relatively rare type, Bastogne, which is a hybrid by pollination between English and black walnut. Generally, Bastogne is very dense, heavy stuff, ideally suited to stocking up rifles such as the 30-caliber magnums, the 338, 375, and 458. Because it is a hybrid, it has no recognizably distinctive features, but much of it has very attractive watermark and fiddleback, and much of it has a tawny or golden hue.

The Bastogne trees that are being cut today are mostly huge, old shade trees. Cloyce Davis of Liveoak, California has his antennae extended all over northern California for such trees, and he finds some that produce wood of extreme rarity and splendor.

Because of its rarity, Bastogne is seldom seen on commercially produced guns. The Browning BBR is the only such gun that I am aware of that is stocked in Bastogne walnut.

Then there is the final, the most celebrated and coveted species —*juglans regia,* or royal walnut, sometimes known as common walnut. This species includes all the walnuts known as French, English, Circassian, California English, etc., *ad infinitum.* This wood is the favorite of custom stockmakers and their clients because in general it is dense and hard, it works beautifully, it takes and holds fine checkering and sharp edges, and it is stable. Unlike black and Claro, it is usually not highly figured, but it offers two other features much more prized by the cognoscenti—color and contrast. Both these features are present in the much sought-after marble-cake figure displayed by the best blanks. Marble-cake consists of mineral deposits in the form of irregular smoky or jet-black streaks against a contrasting amber, ochre, honey, or gold background. The streaks may be thin—as in most California-grown wood of this type—or broad as in much of the New Zealand wood. The background may be quite light, as in the California wood, or rather reddish-brown or even gray, as in the best European-grown wood. Generally the California-grown stuff is more prized because of its greater contrast. The best of it is exquisite stuff indeed, and prices for it are so heady that it is reserved for "the few and the very few," to quote Benjamin Disraeli.

Fancy walnut has long embellished the world's most beautiful guns. How much longer it will continue to do so I cannot say, but I think that the really fine stuff will be just about extinct in another decade. All gun-lovers—not just the affluent connoisseurs—will be the poorer for its passing. Today walnut freaks are buying and hoarding the stuff as if it were topaz of Ethiopia or gold of Ophir. It makes an even better investment, appreciating by 20-30% a year. In the hands of a cunning craftsman an exquisite piece of walnut can become like a drawn bow, a wind-filled sail, or a horse in speed—a thing of rare beauty. •

When it comes time to fight, the Afghan likes to be looking down their throats, and the terrain helps. These three fighters all have SMLE's. Wide World photo.

The workman at the right, in Darrah, is stocking a hill-made Martini. His sidekick appears to have an early SMLE copy.

THE AFGHAN AND HIS SMLE

He likes the bolt gun, the old 303, and makes his own when he has to, and his tactics and riflery make the Afghan hills tough nuts to crack.

by JACK LOTT

As THE SUN crept from its place of ambush behind the sawtooth peaks lining the Khyber Pass, an eagle soared over the bone dry ridges flanking the little Afghan valley below, seeing all, including a herd of strange metal creatures groaning and whining up the camel track towards the watchtowers of a fortified tribal village. Malik Yousef Ali Khan, the village headman and chief of his clan's guerrilla band, awaits the approach of the Russian armored column with a deadly patience born of a two-thousand-year heritage of defending these hostile barren mountains against foreign invaders, including Alexander the Great, Genghis Khan and the Imperial British of Kipling's time.

Wearing coarse homespun baggy trousers and shirt under a sleeveless sheepskin coat, Ali Khan had swept the loose part of his turban over his face until only the fierce black eyes of the hawk-faced Pathan (pronounced "Ptahn") showed. His hands clutched an Afridi tribal-made copy of Britain's World War I battle rifle, the 303 Lee-Enfield Mark III (SMLE), its stock patina the result of years of handling and shoulder-slung rubbing against homespun. A bandolier of 303 Mk. VII ammo smuggled in from India crossed his chest, and in a homemade flap holster on his belt hung an original Webley Mk. VI 455 British Army revolver, the fruit of a trade with an Afridi involving a camel and the Webley, which the Afridi's father had taken from a fallen British subaltern in 1938. In deference to an older tradition, Ali Khan kept a 12-inch straight-bladed "Pesh-Kabz" dagger in his belt with its camel bone grip and heavy ridged back and reinforced point, originally for piercing chain mail. The dagger is quite useless for skinning ibex, but the thrifty Pathans do not waste expensive 303 ammo on wounded enemies.

Crouching behind Ali Khan are a dozen fierce-looking rangy bearded giants, type-cast by nature for the role they were born to and prefer to play. All watch and listen for the column of Russian T-62 tanks and BTR-60PA armored personnel carriers to round the rocky promontory just downhill on the torturous road of broken stones. The armor is on the way to the village to reduce it to rubble for spawning a series of successful raids on truck transports supplying a remote Afghan puppet troop garrison to the north. Unknown to the Russian column commander and his Russian and Afghan officers and men, the road behind them, their only escape route, was closed after they passed by an avalanche of boulders launched by Gul Mustafa's men, who are part of Ali Khan's "lashkar" (fighting group). What the Russians also cannot see is that in the track below Ali Khan's "Mujahedeeni" (holy warriors) a second roadblock, an appalling chaos of boulders, blocks the upward track to anything but ibex and the agile Pathans.

As the lead tank confidently approaches the place of ambush, it is killed by the blast of two captured Russian TM 57 anti-tank mines with their combined charge of thirty-one pounds of TNT. This is the signal for Ali Khan's men to attack the stalled column with Molotov cocktails and grenades quickly wedged in the treads. Two guerrillas are killed by automatic fire during this audacity, but the rest

There it is: In this man's face, you can read all you need to know about what the Russians face in the Afghan hills. Wilfred Thesiger photo.

are too quick, and in seconds three tanks at the rear are burning and immobilized, stalling the column.

The rear of the trapped column is under attack by Gul Mustafa's men. It takes but a brief interval for turret lids to open and for other tanks to lay down a withering fire, but the tribesmen provide few opportunities. The Russian tank commander in the lead tank emerges, Makarov pistol in hand, only to be killed instantly by a sniper's 303 from the hillside. He is quickly pulled down out of the way by the panicked Afghan and Russian crewmen whose raised hands obtain no mercy from the Pathans, who give no quarter and ask no quarter.

The fight lasts no more than 20 minutes. The mainly Afghan crews succumb to the compelling wisdom of fear – fear of an enemy and neighbor whose implacability and fighting skills were their childhood legendry. It is a case of familiarity which does not breed contempt. Those Afghani puppet troops who shout "Allahu Akbar" (God is Great) quickly enough are spared, quickly disarmed and tied and blindfolded, to be marched to a cave outpost and "encouraged" to join the "Mujahedeeni."

The Pathans waste little time and ammunition on the Russians, who are invariably killed with the "Pesh-Kabz" to save 303 ammo. Most tribesmen reload their SMLE copies for any encore, while other more old-fashioned types clean their soiled blades on Russian uniforms. The Russian prisoners all die bravely, but their eyes betray a stark animal fear of an enemy even more brutal than themselves. Even these Marxist-programmed peasant soldiers cannot refute the simple justice: In Afghanistan, it is bad manners to come to a war when you're not invited!

"Inshallah" (God is bountiful) and the tribesmen sling their 303's and begin the looting. Once more the old favorite had justified a faith forged in 50 years of Frontier warfare. The Soviet gunship arrives too late to save the armored column, as the Pathans bound up the rocky hillsides with their own rifles, captured AK's, RPK's and PKM's, ammo, grenades and a few rocket launchers and rockets. The gunship descends as low as possible for maneuvering within the narrow confines of the defile, its 6,000 r.p.m. electronically driven "Gatling" delivers a cloudburst of leaden rain, mainly to the boulders, but also to a few visible darting figures of Tenth Century men in homespun, clutching burdens of booty, like overloaded ants departing an untidy campground. Two overburdened tribesmen drop their prizes for an instant, fumble trying to save their loads, and die on the spot. Most work up into the giant rocks they know as the eagle knows his eyrie.

The gunship circles continuously to lay down a full measure of fire power, but bulletproof and visible rocks are many, and visible rebels few. Napalm and incendiary are ineffective when there is little but rock to burn. One tribesman in an outburst of elan and outrage fires his 303 impotently at the armored underbelly of the Russian pterodactyl, and for this instant of bravura is crumpled into a pitiful bloodstained heap of homespun.

From a natural "sangar" (rocky emplacement) a thousand or more feet above the still hovering and spitting gunship, Nazar, Ali Khan's younger brother, aims an old but still serviceable 303 Bren gun captured years before from the British by Afridis across the Durand Line in what was then India. Serving the Bren is his young cousin Ahmed, while Ahmed's brother Suleiman, 14, works his Lee-Enfield copy like a veteran. The gun-wise tribesmen hadn't forgotten to load some Indian tracers, and the Bren now spits them out at the gunship below. Suleiman empties his magazine in aimed rapid fire and clip reloads another ten Mark VII's. The faces of the three young Pathans, though adolescent, glare at the gunship with a hardness born of centuries of fighting heritage as they feed the ravenous Bren with spendthrift indifference. The deadly parabola of 303's arcs gracefully down at an angle of 50 degrees, the tracers catching up fast. Suleiman's SMLE finds the cockpit bubble in the copter's topside, its unarmored sticking place. Nazar's final burst completes the job begun by Suleiman's rifle, and in a blinding explosion, the gunship commits suicide with its own fuel supply. Obsidian Pathan eyes watch with grim satisfaction as the copter disintegrates.

Ali Khan and his men rendezvous and rest, then await nightfall for a final salvage operation for anything usable and unburned. The bodies of the five fallen comrades are removed for burial, the wounded handed over to the women for nursing. The Russians will not be returning for a while, and when they do, there is more weaponry available to repel them. So long as the Pathans do not try to defend fixed positions, drawing concentrated Russian air and ground firepower, the tribesmen retain the initiative, and as always, the night belongs to them.

The eagle circles above the smoking wreckage, uninterested in the inedible metallic creatures as it seeks marmots or a strayed village lamb. An ibex ram gives a haughty glance at the strange spectacle below, then casually turns and rounds the ridge, a hoof catching a stone which tumbles crazily down the canyon, loosening others in turn, until all reach bottom, where there is only death in a disorderly shambles of steel and blood. No other sound breaks the silence, and for a while, a peace of sorts returns to the valley and its people.

That's what's happening and here's some background:

Whether he's finishing a casting or has filed it all the way to shape, this Darrah worker shows that our frontier backwoods has its counterpart today. John Feyk photo.

The rebel tribesmen of Afghanistan prefer their Afridi-made 303 Mark III, Lee-Enfield copies to Soviet AK-47's. They are, by tradition and experience, mountain guerrilla snipers, relying mainly on aimed fire from strong natural positions. When surprise and ambush have immobilized an enemy for even a brief interval, the Pathan swiftly attacks with maximum ferocity, then breaks contact and fades into the rocky fastness.

This is "Jihad" (Holy War) in defense of the Moslem faith as much as of native mountains and a way of life combining feudalism and barbarism with the gentlest hospitality to friends who come in peace to share their humble fare. Loyalties are first to the family, clan and tribe, the law of blood feud, the Khyber knife and the 303, and criminal use of a gun is rare within the tribe.

The arrival of the British in the 19th Century meant some losses for the tribesmen, but they regarded that colonial warfare as "sport," and the British conceded the Pathan's independence in Independent Tribal Territory, and only reacted forcefully when raided outside that sanctuary. This war is different, and there is no respect or romantic aura such as inspired Kipling's poetry. There is only a bottomless hate for the invader.

Though obviously a "nation of riflemen," the Pathan is not exactly "the boy next door" with a turban and a 303! His love of freedom, family, tribe and land, finds a sympathetic understanding among Americans. Americans, however, do not think highly of beheading prisoners, of cutting off a wife's nose "to spite her face" when she has flirted, or flaying alive especially hated enemies, or wearing daggers, SMLE's and bandoliers like three-piece suits. They are not asking us to accept their sometimes frightful customs, only to understand their right to freedom, and their ability and determination to fight to the utmost with what they have—or can make, which includes rifles.

The Afridi tribal rifle industry began in 1910 in Independent Tribal Territory in Kohat Pass. A "Malik" (headman) of the Adam Khel tribe of Afridis disassembled a Martini-Enfield rifle he had taken from an Indian Sepoy (soldier) he had killed in a fierce skirmish between his lashkar (fighting group) and a withdrawing picket of British Colonial troops. The old Martini falling block action with a 303 Enfield barrel was issued to native troops then. Sher Din Shahabuddin, the Malik, admired the rifle's rugged simplicity and understood its working principles. He reasoned that its manufacture, aside from rifling, was no more difficult than that of a flintlock "Jezail."

In Bombay and Sialkot were work-

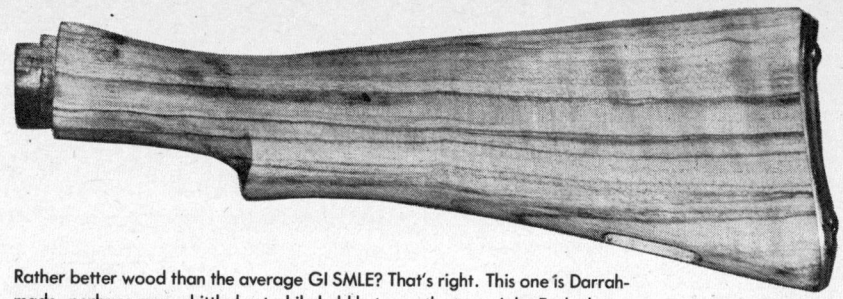
Rather better wood than the average GI SMLE? That's right. This one is Darrah-made, perhaps even whittled out while held between the toes. John Feyk photo.

men who had experience in British Indian arsenals, some retired, some unemployed. A tribal council gave tentative approval. At first railroad tracks were ripped up to make actions; eventually crude wooden lathes and rifling machines produced the barrels.

They make Mauser copies in Darrah, too, and now and then, someone shoots one and this fellow is doing just that.

Hillmen don't have much, but they do have essentials: sandals, headgear, a rifle and ammo, and doubtless a knife under there somewhere.

It is really custom gun work. If you want a handmade Luger, they'll do it and here is what the job looks like. It is not DWM, but don't bet it won't shoot. John Feyk photo.

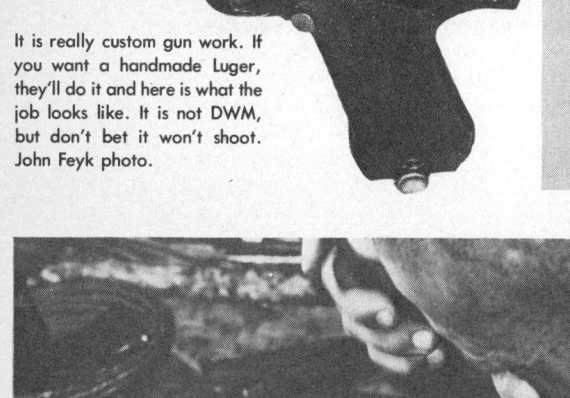
If it takes a cold chisel, that's what they use in Darrah, where this man is chiseling out a revolver frame. The gun will work, too. John Feyk photo.

Wind-toughened native walnut provided material for the stocks, inletted and shaped while held between the toes.

Later, more workers were imported from Sialkot and steel from Bombay. Gone was the day of ripping up railroad tracks. Ammo was now a problem, but there were British ammo convoys plying the Khyber and Kohat Passes. When ambushes of ammo convoys became expensive in men and rifles, Sher Din and his sons thought again.

The result of this thinking was a

This pile of rocks in a sangar, virtually invisible, and the three gentlemen within carry an SMLE, an AK-47, and RPK machine gun sans bipod. This is at Barikot in Kurnar Province late last year and these men had targets in sight. Wide World photo.

decision to experiment with reloading the empty fired cases. Ordinary wooden matches made in India used a simple fulminate, easy to make, so a similar compound was applied to the cups of fired Berdan primers with the indentations hammered out. Narrow punches were used to drive out the primers through a flash hole. Highly inflammable nitro-cellulose motion picture film was imported and shredded into a sort of unstable and vicious flake powder whose loading data would never grace a Lyman handbook or be sold by Bruce Hodgdon. By cut and try, fire and fly, the ammo improved until the 303's wounded or killed more enemies than firers.

A tribal industry had been born, and on Sher Din's death his five sons inherited a thriving business. They soon argued and with economic attrition were reduced to three separate firms from an original five. In 1925 a Darrah-made Martini-Enfield cost four hundred rupees ($128). Each year, production increased an increment or two and prices became more competitive with the British-made original, which was more expensive both in terms of money and the other terms which the British and their Colonial troops invariably demanded and received in "payment."

The Russian invasion of Afghanistan has now created a big boom in Darrah's small arms industry and a sympathetic reaction among related tribes in Pakistan. Sharing the same religious, ethnic and linguistic background, the Paks need no encouragement. Rebel groups filter across the border at night for resupply and to convey wounded and refugees to hospitals in Peshawar. Captured Russian AK's and other small and not so small arms are traded, bought and sold. Arab oil money pours into the Frontier, much of it going for the weaponry of Darrah.

Sajad Ahmed in his mid-twenties runs a factory in partnership with his three brothers, and produces 40 rifles a month, including fake SMLE's and '98 Mausers for $300 apiece. Waiting time is four days. The favorite rifle of the "Mujahedeeni," the 303 SMLE copy, sells in Darrah for between $200 and $300. It is difficult for any but the expert eye to distinguish the Darrah copy from the genuine. Earlier copies of the SMLE were softer and cruder, so that the tribesmen preferred the British product, but Darrah has come of age, and generally, the Darrah product is battle-worthy. Even their ammo is usually serviceable, but of course, imported arsenal ammo is preferred—and more expensive—up to $3 per round when supplies are tight, but cheaper when a new lot arrives by camel caravan.

One Darrah gunmaker stated the case thusly for the local product: "They serve us well (SMLE's) and every man with a gun is a free man. The Pakistani government offered to build us a textile mill and all kinds of other things a few years ago if we would give up our autonomy and our guns, but we value our freedom and our guns more than anything."

Indeed, there is little crime in Darrah and no police, since individual responsibility is the law as dispensed by tribal Jirga and the word of the Prophet Mohammed as written in the Koran.

My knowledge of Darrah-made rifles is first-hand, based on onetime ownership of a fine Martini-Enfield

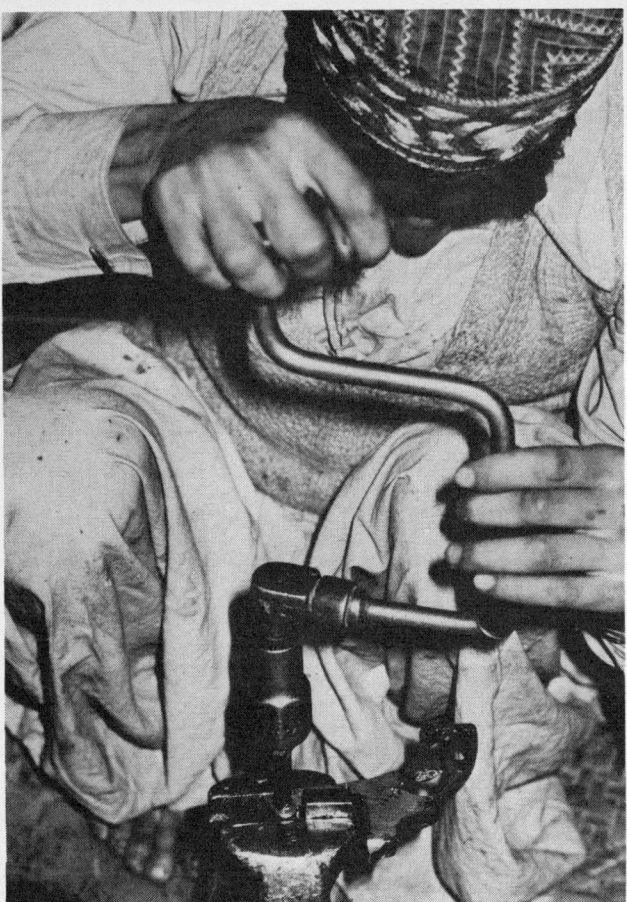

Tools from anywhere is the motto in Darrah. This one looks British and is being used to ream the hole for the hinge-pin in a Webley revolver look-alike. John Feyk photo.

The Afridi understand hot metal and with a hand-pulled bellows will forge-weld and harden drill bits and reamers. John Feyk photo.

Fat as he is, this is no underpriviledged child. He's playing with a purpose, learning the family business as his fathers before him in Darrah. John Feyk photo.

copy. Proof of its excellence is that the proprietor of the gunshop where I purchased it, an expert, didn't know it was a copy. The hand-engraved range markings on the elevator sight were, on close scrutiny, not the work of an Enfield artisan, and the stock walnut was simply too fancy and "Circassian" to be British issue.

The tribesmen produce a variety of heavier arms, including 20 mm anti-tank rifles, mines and grenades, and many thousands of rounds of 303 and other ammunition are produced from imported and fired brass.

The Russian invasion is unlikely to inspire such poetry as Kipling wrote, but a certain timelessness is apparent. A comment from the official British India yearbook of 1930 gives the British view of the Pathan:

"The trans-border tribes are in communication with each other from north to south, as well as with tribes beyond the Durand Line, and military operations against any one of them are apt to produce sympathetic effects among the others. And containing as they do some of the most magnificent fighting men in the world, it is only picked and highly trained troops who can compete with them on anything like equal terms in their own hills."

Indeed the Russians and their Afghan puppets have their work cut out for them, and they know it enough to remain in their bases at night. All hands are against them, and to stall a vehicle for more than a few minutes, or to be left wounded or to be in the wrong place for more than a few minutes means instant death. The Pathan equates freedom and the rifle with life and the air he breathes, and every Pathan man, woman, and child now knows why the textile mill and similar incentives to drop small arms production was a bad bargain.

> **Editor's Note:**
>
> *It may be, sadly, that the Soviets will succeed in the Afghan hills. If they do, it will be with weapons other than artillery, air power and small arms. With such, the hillmen can contend and even win.*
>
> *There are other weapons, noxious ones, in the Soviet arsenal. They have demonstrated their willingness to use them; what has not been demonstrated is the effectiveness of gas attack in the hills. No one knows if determined riflemen cannot figure a way to beat such weapons.*
>
> *It was thought until recently that helicopter gunships were a sure cure against guerrilla groups. It now appears that when the targets shoot back, accurately and quickly, gunships are vulnerable. Perhaps it will be so with other weapons.*
>
> *However it goes in the end, riflemen alone have shown the world, and most certainly the Soviets, they ought not be counted as other men.*
>
> *K.W.*

My Triumphs In GUN COLLECTING

The fun, the furor and the fantastic deals of 40 years.

by JOHN T. AMBER
PHOTOS: ROBERT S. L. ANDERSON

IMMEDIATELY after World War II, when Marshall Field & Company marketed antique and collectors' firearms—1944-1946—a woman came up to me one day and spoke about a large lot of 45-70 Springfield rifles she controlled. These 750-plus single shot military rifles, Models 1873 and later, were in storage at the Navy's Great Lakes Training Station, north of Chicago.

When the war broke out, she told me, the National 4-H Clubs, anxious to do their bit, had obtained these rifles from the Minnesota National Guard and delivered them to Great Lakes. Intended to supplant more modern rifles for sentry duties there, the 45-70s had not been used. The Navy wanted to get rid of them, and had asked the 4-H Club to remove them. "Would the Gun Shop," she asked, "be interested in buying them?" Thinking quickly about the amount of money that would be tied up if we bought them, and of how long it might take to sell them, I told the woman we would prefer to handle them on consignment. She agreed.

A week or so later we received the first shipment, some 200 45-70 rifles and their accoutrements. All, surprisingly, were in very good to excellent condition (most had never been fired, I was sure). The next Friday we ran a small illustrated ad in the Chicago *Daily News,* now defunct. Reaching a price had been difficult—we had no previous experience to go on, and some 750 rifles was a lot! We wanted to sell them quickly, if we could, so I set a price of $5.00 or $7.50 per rifle, including bayonet and scabbard, cartridge belt (blue-colored Mills web), sling strap and 25 rounds of blank cartridges—those were among the Great Lakes shipment, too.

We were not open on Saturday, but on Monday morning all hell broke loose. Hundreds of people, mostly men, were jammed against our street level doors, clamoring to get in, jostling for position. Our ad had not mentioned how many we had. Once the doors opened, our 5th floor was soon overflowing with customers for the 45-70 rifles. Men were packed 6 and 7 deep along our long counters, money waving in their hands, shouting to be waited on. I was aghast, as were my several fellow salesmen, not to mention the bevy of executives who had come over from their main store offices to investigate the near-riot.

I was severely criticized by the brass, but I wasn't taking any of that. Sure, we were faced with an unruly mob, but the sale was a success, a hell of a success. Gradually a semblance of order was achieved, and we moved out all the 200-odd rifles on hand. Advance orders were taken, pending delivery of the rest from Great Lakes. By the end of the day we had all but sold the entire lot, and the next morning saw those disposed of.

In the days and weeks following, mail orders for the 45-70s came in from all over the country, but the rifles were gone. The store returned checks

Amber and Ken Warner with an unbelievable gun: A three-barrel Lefever with the rifle barrel on top.

Perhaps the gun which comes closest to pleasing Amber most is his accidentally gold-inlaid Billinghurst buggy rifle.

to over 600 would-be buyers, so I'm certain we could have easily sold 1500 rifles had they been available.

I was kidded about that inept pricing job for a long time, but we had had a *sale!* I wonder—could we have got $10 and $15?

During the mid-1940s I managed Field's antique arms section, a part of their famed Gun Shop. Later on, a well-dressed man, 40 years old or so, approached me. Opening a large briefcase, he produced a pair of flintlock pistols, the like of which I'd never handled before, though I'd seen the type at the Metropolitan Museum in New York, and pictured in auction catalogs. What could I tell him about them—their origin, their current value?

Obviously of the late Renaissance period, these pistols were deeply carved—not engraved as such—in the rococo style typical of their time. Each had several grotesque masks (heads of gargoyles and other monsters), and the general theme was one of monkeys—another sign of their period. The metal was generally black or nearly so. They had never been cleaned, I felt—the chiseling was so sharp that an unwary grasping of them could cut the thumb. The barrels were Spanish, each showing the sunken mark in gold of Nicolas Bis, royal gunmaker to the Spanish court in 1690-1710 or so. Spanish barrels were famed for their quality at that period, so their use was not amiss on these Italinate pistols. In addition, both barrels carried the engraved symbols of two noble orders—the Knights of Malta and the Order of the Golden Fleece.

Gently removing one of the lockplates, I read inside the name: Pietro Manani. I knew something of that name; a superb craftsman, by all accounts, but relatively unknown and uncollected, perhaps because his output was limited. I told the gentleman before me most of what I've just put down here. He was, he told me, an ex-colonel of artillery, and he'd "found" the pistols in Europe during the late war. Were they for sale, I asked. No, not just now, he said—he might call me later. Reluctantly I handed the pistols to him; I'd never held such magnificent quality before. They were gone forever, I feared.

Some 18 months later the red-legged colonel called me. Did I remember him and did I still want the Manani pistols? I did—I'd thought about them endlessly. After a brief bit of haggling, I bought them. I won't say what the cost was, but it was more by far than I'd ever paid before. They remain my most valuable flintlocks, monetarily and otherwise.

Dr. Prentice D. Cheney, long since dead, was a charming and affable gentleman, a native of Jerseyville, Ill. Doc was, rumor had it, a devotee of John Barleycorn—his periodical benders, some lasting for weeks, it was said, were legend. We were long-time friends, if only casually so, and fellow members of the Ohio Gun Collectors

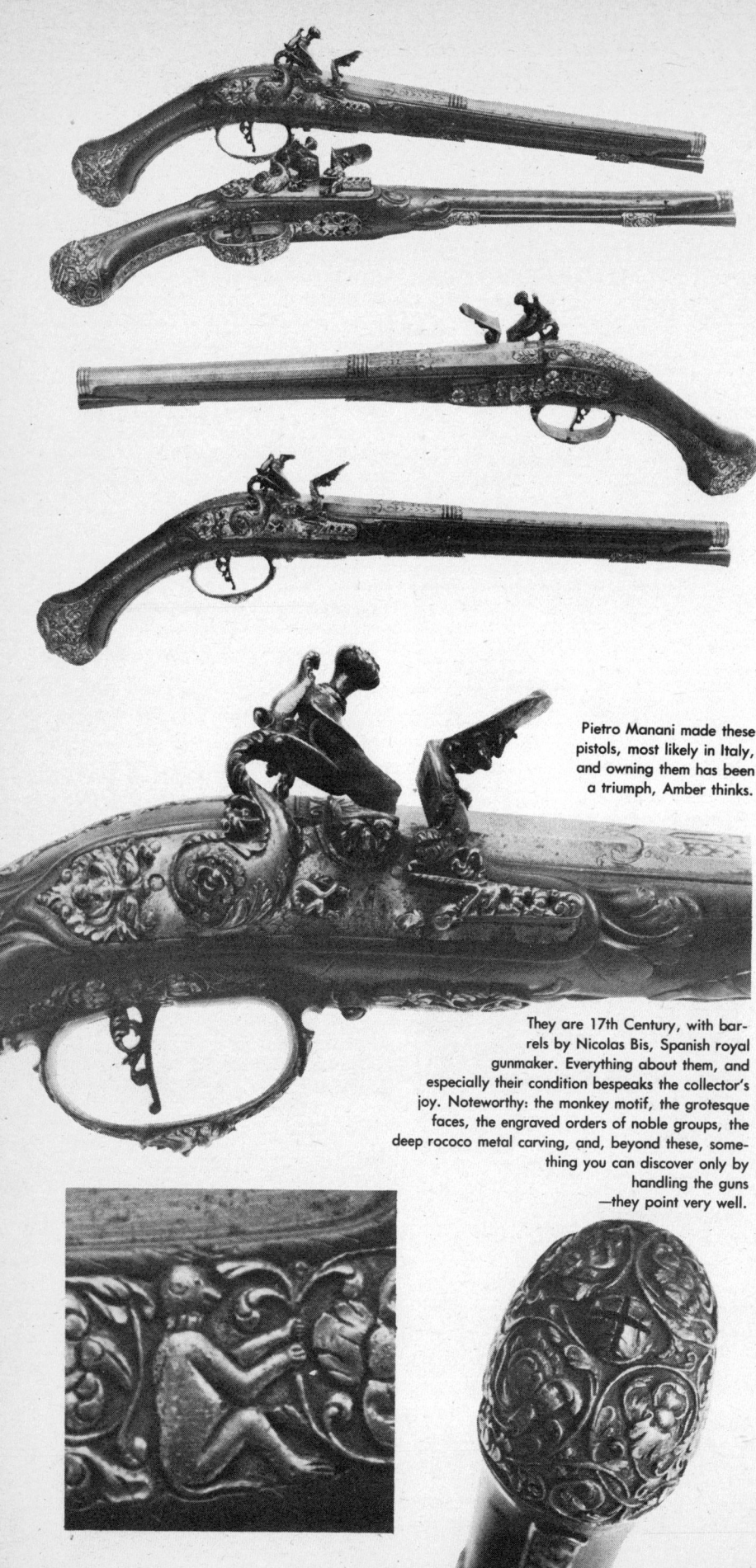

Pietro Manani made these pistols, most likely in Italy, and owning them has been a triumph, Amber thinks.

They are 17th Century, with barrels by Nicolas Bis, Spanish royal gunmaker. Everything about them, and especially their condition bespeaks the collector's joy. Noteworthy: the monkey motif, the grotesque faces, the engraved orders of noble groups, the deep rococo metal carving, and, beyond these, something you can discover only by handling the guns —they point very well.

Assn. Doc's collecting aims were catholic—no specialist whatever, he bought or traded for anything, as long as the guns were in mint condition, or nearly so, and of the very best quality.

One Friday night, in the mid-1950s, I went to a weekend OGCA meeting at Columbus, Ohio. Walking into the hotel's coffee shop on Saturday morning, there sat the amiable Dr. Cheney, across from him his latest wife—his third or fourth, I'd heard. It was also being bruited about that Doc was in need of cash—he spent money wildly when in his cups, and he was, reportedly, paying stiff alimony to his earlier wives.

Doc asked me to sit down. He then told me—confirming the current gossip—that he was going to sell "a lot of guns" that weekend, among them his Gatling gun. I hadn't known he owned one. That sparked a memory, for I'd long wanted to have a Gatling, though it wasn't a high-priority desire.

A year or so before I'd been one of a party of eight or nine hunters at a Maine camp. Among the gang was Herb Glass, then and now a well-known dealer in collectors arms. One evening during that hardly-successful whitetail hunt, Glass revealed that he had been quietly gathering together an array of Gatling guns. (All of us were in the gun world, one way or other—a younger Bill Ruger was there, Mike Walker of Remington, Warren Page, Harry Sefried, a Ruger designer, so gun talk was natural if not mandatory—after or before girls and fast cars I'm not sure.)

Glass had now, he told us, some 25 Gatlings stashed away. The late Lucian Cary, he said, had written a story on Gatlings that would soon appear in *True* magazine—which it did. I asked Herb if, in that many Gatlings, did he have duplicate models? Sure, he said, he'd several such on hand. Would he sell me one, I wanted to know? No way, he replied—the Cary piece would quickly elevate Gatling prices and he was going to cash in grandly. Gatlings, it was true, had not been widely traded, scarcity alone preventing that. There was, therefore, little solid price information available on them—they were, at that time, an unknown quantity.

All right, I said, you greedy S.O.B., or words to that effect, and I put Gatling guns out of my mind.

"Doc," I said, just as he rose to go upstairs, "how about giving me first refusal on the Gatling?"

"Of course," he told me, as I sat on and waited for my breakfast, "and I'll

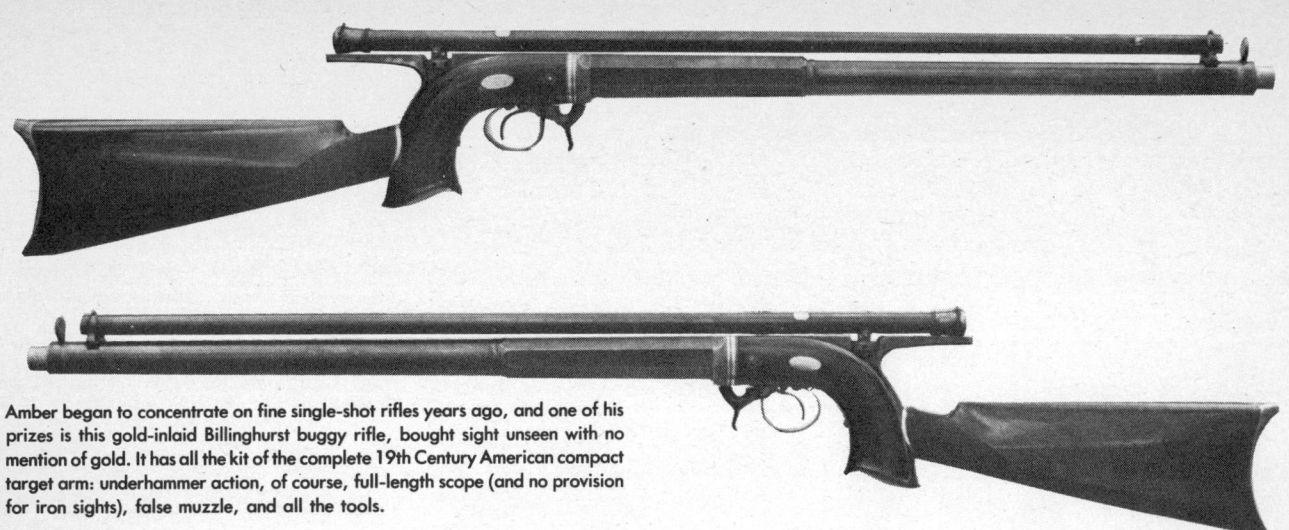

Amber began to concentrate on fine single-shot rifles years ago, and one of his prizes is this gold-inlaid Billinghurst buggy rifle, bought sight unseen with no mention of gold. It has all the kit of the complete 19th Century American compact target arm: underhammer action, of course, full-length scope (and no provision for iron sights), false muzzle, and all the tools.

Under the oaks at Creedmoor Farm, Amber can't help grinning over owning what is probably his favorite—an unexpected triumph.

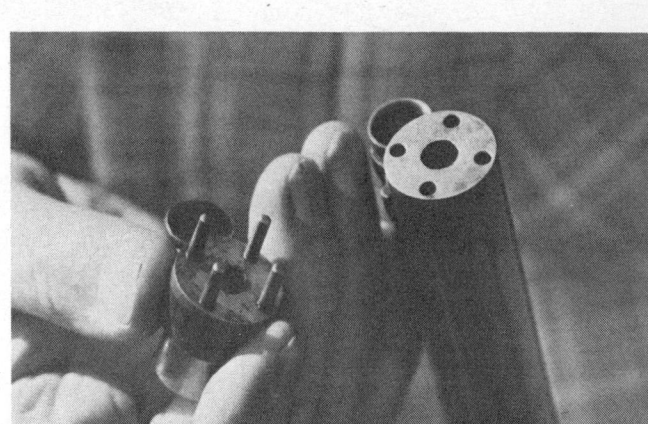

The Billinghurst false muzzle slides satisfyingly into place on its four pins. Note the blinder that blocks the scope view to ensure the muzzle is not shot off the gun by any aimed shot.

Packed in the case when Amber got the Billinghurst were bullets and patches and wound cotton cleaning bobs.

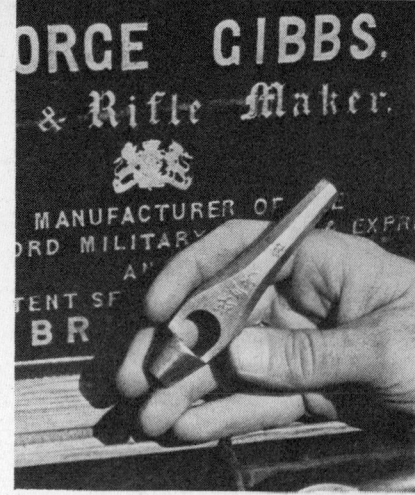

The 45-caliber arch punch in the Gibbs' kit is marked with Japanese ideograms. As can be seen, it is in new condition.

(Top) Regally gloating over a regal rifle, Amber handles what he regards as one of the pinnacles of the art of the long-range target rifle, his Gibbs Farquharson apparently built for or presented to the royal family of Japan 100 or more years ago. It is also shown above as it arrived, full-length in a case.

Gold on purple, Gibbs' proud label left no doubt of the source of Amber's remarkable possession—the label is as high as the case is wide.

Gibbs is fitted for the several sorts of sighting favored at long range, including this vernier heel sight for the supine position.

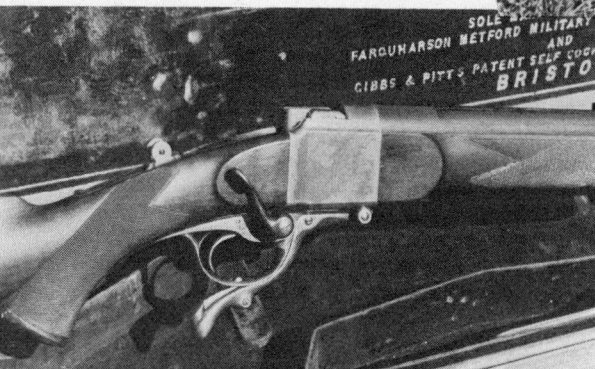

To add to Amber's joy, this Japanese Gibbs is a scarce version of the Farquharson action, the type with a separate side-cocking lever. Note the anchor for a tang sight.

see you later."

I walked into the display room, filled with gun-loaded tables already. Doc Cheney stood behind two tables, reaching down into assorted bags and cartons for the guns he'd brought to the show. Behind him stood the Gatling gun on its brass-and-steel tripod, the brass sleeve over its 6 barrels gleaming. Atop the breech was an 1883-patent Accles cartridge drum, its all-brass exterior also glowing warmly. I'd seen a photograph, I recalled, of a like small Gatling gun in Chinn's* book on machineguns—was this the same type? Inspection showed the typical "Colt Pat. F.A. Mfg. Co." marking, hand engraved in big bold letters, and—a thrilling shock—"No. 1" in equally big size.

Hurriedly, I tried to gain Doc's attention, tapping him on the back as he talked and bargained with the large group crowded in front of his tables—now loaded with guns.

He turned to me at last and I said "Doc, the Gatling—how much?"

He hesitated for a moment or two, then said "I've got to have $400 or I'll take it home."

At that very moment I could see Herb Glass approaching Doc's display, so I had to act *now*—yet I didn't know whether I was getting a bargain—"stealing it," as the jargon has it, or paying 'way too much.

"Doc," I said, folly or not, "you've just sold your Gatling. I'll give you a check later."

At that moment Glass had reached the edges of the crowd standing before Cheney. He stood on tiptoe, pointed at the small 45-70 caliber Gatling, and pantomimed "Mine," pointing at himself.

O frabjous day! Making no effort to conceal my glee and malice, I thumbed my nose at old friend Herb and silently mouthed "No, mine."

Herb Glass followed me all over the show floor that memorable weekend, cajoling me, pleading with me to sell him the Gatling. I think tears came to his eyes once—crocodile, of course.

"No," I said repeatedly, "I won't sell it to you," even though by this time he had raised his offer to well over my cost.

I was adamant Amber now, and I reminded Herb of our talk in Maine and his smug refusal to sell me a Gatling, even a fairly common 10-barrel Army type. I'm afraid I was a little sadistic. I hope so.

Giving Doc Cheney my $400 check

---
*Col. G.M. Chinn, *The Machine Gun* Vol. 1. (Washington, D.C. 1951).

later, I had a small but pleasurable shock. "John," he said, thanking me for the money, "I'll send the other 5 magazines to you later."

Harvey Brandt wrote about this baby Gatling and its shooting in the 1958/12th edition of GUN DIGEST, pages 20-29.

One of the most interesting and valuable pieces in my collection is the type commonly called, for some obscure reason, a buggy rifle. These are quite short-barreled (10 inches to 14 inches or so) "rifles," usually with detachable buttstocks. They often look like long-barreled pistols, and they're usually found cased, with an array of loading tools, sometimes with false-muzzled barrels. Calibers were, for their day—the 1850s-1870s—small; 30 or 32 caliber is a common size. They're caplock muzzleloaders, of course.

Mine is by Wm. Billinghurst of Rochester, New York, better known for his heavy-barreled match rifles, one of which I also have in "picket ball" form—conical lead bullets with no cylindrical section—with which I won several matches or was well-placed in them.

Billinghurst was partial to the understriker ignition system, which he pioneered, and justly so. Many modern made slug rifles used in the stiffest competitions use the same system—the trigger guard acts as main spring and sear, driving the hammer against the underside nipple of these front-loading rifles. The train of fire, obviously, runs directly and straight to the main charge of black powder.

Shortly after Marshall Field & Co. closed out the antique arms section I got a phone call from a man in Virginia. He had seen one of our brochures, in which were listed several cased sets of English duelling flintlock pistols. They were priced at about $250-$350, I recall, and my caller wanted to know if I would trade him a set for what he offered, a buggy rifle. I explained that all such sets had been sold, and that his buggy rifle—which I assumed to be the common, average type, then selling for $100 or so—could hardly be traded even for a pair of flint duellers in case.

What I'd said was true, he agreed, but he thought he might achieve his desire at less than the figures I'd cited. Well, I said, why not try that, and if he'd put a price on the Billinghurst pistol, I might buy it—I explained that rifled arms of any type interested me. "Give me $150, and it's yours," he told me.

Some two weeks later, after some correspondence between us, the heavy carton reached me. There, lying in its beautifully-figured rosewood veneer case, lay a buggy rifle the likes of which I'd never seen, never dreamed of, and in virtually new condition. This Billinghurst had to be truly unique, I felt.

Reverently picking up the pistol-gripped rifle, I started counting the several gold inlays and appliques—one lay athwart the full-length telescope sight, reading MALCOLM; two were let into the sides of the pistol grip and another—reading RAWSON—was on the S-curved bottom of the grip. Two gold bands lay around the barrel breech and, of all places, the top of the false muzzle carried a section of gold a sixteenth-inch thick! To ward off rust, I'd guess. The buttstock, of fancy reddish English walnut (as is the hand grip) is holed for a through-bolt, used to fit the butt to the rear of the grip. Yet another gold band surrounds the area of the joint.

Not *once*, during our phone talk or in his letters, did my Virginian mention the gold inlays—perhaps he thought they were all made that way. I was tempted to send him a few hundred more dollars, Confederate money, that is.

Postscript: I've said that I deemed this superb Billinghurst unique. A few years later I saw another Billinghurst buggy rifle almost identical with mine. Not a duplicate, but one of the same high quality with, again, numerous gold inlays.

The 1951 Meeting of the NRA was held in San Francisco. GUN DIGEST had a booth there and I went out to manage it. One day Elmer Keith came by, carrying a long-barreled rifle to show me. We were very busy at the time, and, hardly looking at the rifle, I told Elmer I'd see him later.

The next day, during a lull, I walked over to where it was displayed. There, now lying in its long oak-and-leather case, was a magnificent long range target rifle, with "George Gibbs, Bristol," emblazoned in big gold letters on the purple velvet covering the lid's interior. The action was a Farquharson of scarce form, a *cocking* lever along the side in addition to the normal underlever. The barrel, of Wm. Metford's patented design, was 36 inches long, its rich blue flawless. In fact, the rifle and the case's contents were in new condition. Two domed leather boxes held the sights—short and long Vernier tangs, an even 20 front sight apertures, etc. A false muzzle, which at the time I'd never seen before, was among the tools. Among

Magnificent Griebel-engraved, gold-inlaid Model 21 is a 16-bore marked "SKEET."

Amber explains on oval-bored nitro-proved Lancaster double rifle's working to colleague Harold Murtz.

Charles Lancaster made this 450 hammer double rifle, a most handsome Grade C, and proved it for 42-gr. Cordite and a 385-gr. bullet. How good was an A grade?

The Amber taste runs to more modern collectable guns, too, like this Griffin and Howe Mauser in 30-06, engraved by Rudolf Kornbrath, of course.

The single-shot target rifle in its infinite variety always attracted the Amber eye, and this Remington-Walker 32-40 Schuetzen Match rifle was no exception.

This is the Griebel-engraved, gold-inlaid 16-ga. Model 21 Skeet gun (top) and below a close-up view from the bottom. It is a magnificent achievement in the combined arts required to refine a good gun into a great gun.

these was an arch punch in 45 caliber, marked on both sides of its shank in Japanese ideographs.

The owner, one Capt. G., told me he had bought the outfit in Tokyo at the end of the war. He'd take the highest offer bid on it during the show—if sufficient. I wouldn't do that, I said, but if he would get in touch with me after the meeting I thought I might be able to top his best offer. I knew that all too frequently such bidding was used by the owner to successively raise each bidder's price.

I left for home, worried about who would get the rifle, convinced that I'd never hear from Capt. G. Elmer Keith, of course, was well known as a single shot rifle collector/shooter.

But my guardian angel prevailed.

A three-barrel gun is not so rare, and even one with the rifle bore centered at the top is understandable, but when it is marked Lefever and is this handsomely gotten up, one can truly marvel.

A splendid gold setter and a splendid woodcock grace the left side of the receiver of the Griebel-finished Model 21 16-ga. Skeet gun.

Apart from the fun of getting and shooting guns, Amber loves to talk of them and here does so with successor Ken Warner. Such talk can be heady stuff for a confirmed enthusiast.

About a month later Capt. G called me, and I bought the Gibbs-Farquharson-Metford rifle. Sure, I had to beat what he said was a firm, legitimate offer, but I've never regretted it.

Today, almost 30 years later, this remarkable rifle and its many fittings is, arguably, the best single shot rifle I own, perhaps the most valuable. A translation of the archaic Japanese characters reads, roughly: Corridor 3, Number XX of the Royal Household. I wrote about this rifle at length in the GUN DIGEST for 1954/12th ed., the story called "Tokyo Treasure."

Our 25th/1971 edition of the GUN DIGEST carried a splendid story by John T. Dutcher called "George Schoyen—Riflemaker Extraordinary." No one better deserved that praise; his barrels were the prime choice of numerous top level marksmen.

A few years before the article appeared I had received a letter from a man in Iowa. He had, he said, a muzzle-loading Schoyen rifle, caliber about 30—small indeed for a front loader. I was highly skeptical—Schoyen was known for metallic cartridge barrels, 32-40, 38-55 and the like. No, said the Iowan, the barrel was clearly marked Schoyen and it was indeed a muzzleloader. After a few phone talks and a couple of letters, the rifle was shipped to me. There, in a roughly-made but old pine case, was a profusely engraved, gold-inlaid Schuetzen rifle in excellent condition. As with the Billinghurst gold-embellished buggy rifle described earlier, my man in Iowa had failed to make any mention of the gold work or the engraving!

A careful inspection revealed several things. The rifle had been made originally by Edwin Phillips of New York City, sometime before 1868. A gold plaque, let into the buttstock, shows that it was a prize awarded at the "Third Union Shooting Festival," held in July, 1868 in New York. Sometime subsequently George Schoyen had rebarreled the rifle to 32-40 size, and had included the false muzzle and bullet starter normally supplied with his cartridge barrels; the original caliber was, most likely, 45 or larger.

The engraving and gold work was done by the famed L.D. Nimschke; the patterns (rubbings) of the work are shown in the Nimschke pattern book published by John J. Malloy.

I included detailed notes on this Phillips-Schoyen rifle, plus seven photographs of it, with the Dutcher story mentioned above. I'm glad my curiosity overcame my skepticism—very glad. •

FRONTIER FIREPOWER: 1836-1872

by Rick Hacker

A Century-Later Look at Myths and Methods of the First Pistoleros

IF THERE IS a single element that can be credited with perpetuating the continuing Romance of the Firearm, it is the saga of the sixgun on the American frontier. This one entity has transcended the boundaries of time, culture and geography to convince the entire world that not only were 19th Century Americans "straight shooters," but we were equally fast and deadly with our sixguns when confronted with evil.

The revolver has been a true American hero ever since 1836, when Sam Colt introduced his unique idea of firing a revolving cylinder of pre-loaded charges through a single barrel. The Colt Revolving Pistol revolutionized the entire concept of firepower from a single gun. And it came just in time; the West was still unknown and uncharted, and there was plenty of action in the South and Southwest regions of our continent. Later, the fast-firing sixguns would be carried by lawmen and desperados alike into the untamed reaches of the American Frontier, right on through the Civil War, and into the realm of the Far West, where the venerable cap and ball revolver gradually found itself firing against the cartridge gun, which eventually—and literally—shot it out of existence.

Heavy recoil made the 44 Dragoon awkward for follow-up shots, but the big gun was unchallenged as a powerhouse.

To be sure, it the cartridge gun that we hear and see most of when watching the mass media's depiction of the Old West. But in actual fact, it was the cap and ball revolver that began taming the country, blazing the way clear for more advanced guns to enter a more subdued stage. Men like Wild Bill Hickok, Jesse James, Buffalo Bill Cody and John Wesley Hardin all initiated their now-legendary careers with the single-action cap and ball pistol. Indeed, Colt and Remington front-loading handguns were in common usage well into the 1880's and early 90's, a good fifteen years after the metallic cartridge-carrying Colt Model 1873 Single Action Army and Remington New Model Army of 1878 made their debuts. For more than 40 years the cap and ball revolver was the mainstay of survival and protection for lawman and lawless alike. Carried in belts, boots, pockets, purses, holsters and saddlebags, it represented the last line of defense . . . or the first sign of offense.

From a historical standpoint, as well as a shooter's curiosity, how many of us have wondered: Just how good were the cap and ball revolvers of the 19th Century? Were they as accurate as their offspring, the cartridge wheelgun? And how fast could a skilled gunman actually be with Samuel Colt's renowned invention? These were the questions that were raised one night, during a conversation between the author and GUN DIGEST Editor Ken Warner. To the best of my knowledge, no writer in recent history had ever tried to determine the functional reliability of the early guns in

cepted word in the English language, antique meant junk, and the black powder replica revolution was still a few years away. I recall paying $15 for a battered and used Navy Colt, which I loaded with 000 buckshot, not having any local source for obtaining lead balls that would fit the .36 chambers. The buckshot was a little loose in the cylinders, as I recall, and I kept each projectile in place against a charge of 20 grains of black powder by using kleenex wads, covered over with Crisco to prevent chain firing. Later on, I also acquired an 1860 Army for $25 (the price was a little higher, I was told, because the gun was newer!); the gun was so worn that every few shots the wedge would drop out. I eventually employed my gunsmithing skills by shimming the wedge in with a piece of cardboard.

I perforated many a tin can and fencepost with those historic relics,

Shooting with sights wasn't easy, but "point shooting" as shown was accurate enough for small targets at close range, given enough practice.

terms of shooting performance, the job they were originally intended to do. Not a "pick-it-up-and-shoot-it" field test, but a modified form of black powder combat course. I also felt that perhaps the basics of this article could possibly serve as an impetus for a new shooting sport to give black powder fans even more variety—a series of contests designed to test cap and ball shooter's skills in rapid fire and 19th Century combat situations.

As a teenager growing up in Arizona, I was quite familiar with shooting original Colt Navies and 1860 Armies. The guns were relatively plentiful and cheap back in the early 1950's. Nostalgia had not yet become an ac-

The Dragoon's power was shown by penetrating a Los Angeles phone book and a 2" board backer.

35TH EDITION, 1981 27

but could never quite get their accuracy down to the point where they would have made reliable sidearms, their rifling and tightness having been shot away years ago. Later on, I traded both guns for an 1860 Army of impeccable credentials. The fact that I carried and shot that gun so much the original bluing wore off makes most of today's collectors—even myself—shudder. Those early Colts taught me two things: black powder shooting was fun, and with a sound, crisp gun, I suspected the cap and ball revolver could be as effective as today's beefiest magnum. Notice I said *as effective,* not as powerful. In any case, I was about to find out now, in 1980.

For this in-depth GUN DIGEST test, I selected seven of the most popular defense pistols of their day: the .36 caliber 1836 Paterson Colt, the heavy duty .44 caliber 1848 Dragoon, the 1849 31 Baby Dragoon, the 1851 .36 caliber Navy Colt, the .44 1858 Remington Army, the .44 caliber Colt 1860 Army and the .36 caliber 1862 Colt New Model Pocket Police. Although there were many other makes of cap and ball revolvers such as Manhattan, Beals, Smith & Wesson and LeMat in common use during the latter half of the 19th Century, it was predominantly the Colt and Remington revolvers which enjoyed the most popularity during the Victorian era. This was due primarily to a far better system of distribution by the two arms makers, and a more aggressive approach to marketing, of which Colt was far and away the leader.

Unlike the earlier days of my youth, it was no longer feasible to conduct my cap and ball shooting with original arms, as their collector's value has soared far above their shooting ability. That's sad, for these old guns were

The 1863 Police and the practiced author produced this 5-shot group from the hip in 5 seconds. At any range, that is good shooting and deadly accuracy.

originally made to shoot, not to be tucked away in a collector's case. However, American and Italian ingenuity have long since rallied to the cause, and an array of near-duplicate replicas have been supplying cap and ball needs for over two decades. Some of these guns are better than others, with the only deviation from the originals being in the screw threads used.

For my tests, I selected guns from three of the top replica firms: Navy Arms, Western Arms and Dixie Gun Works (all of whose products, including the guns tested here, can be found in the catalog section in the back of this book). Ironically, I was not able to obtain any authentic Colt re-issue black powder arms due to production problems existing at the time.

Wishing to duplicate the ballistics of the 19th Century as nearly as possible, all shooting was done with standardized loads of FFFG black powder (varying from 15 to 40 grains, depending on the gun tested) and cast, lead balls. Although my tests were conducted with all chambers fully loaded, in actual usage, the revolvers would normally be carried with the hammer resting on an unloaded or an uncapped chamber, to prevent an accidental discharge. Advertising literature of the time urged pistoleros to carry their fully charged revolvers with the hammer resting either on the pins (Colt) or in the cylinder notches (Remington) machined in between the chambers, for just that purpose. But the pins of the Colt were quickly battered or worn down until they were useless and the Remingtons often skipped out of time when carried in that manner. It was far safer to leave one chamber empty, unless knowingly going into a precarious situation.

During the cap and ball era, multiple discharges, wherein more than one chamber fired at the same time due to a crossover flash from the powder, were always unexpected and often spectacular. I've seen a number of these incidents occur, always due to the shooter failing to cover his loaded chambers with grease. Fortunately, I've never seen anyone injured, although I have seen one original 1860 Colt severely leaded... on the *outside!*

At best, a multiple discharge is a sinful waste of hard-to-get and costly powder and lead; at its worst, it could cost the shooter some fingers... or his life. Then, as now, the knowledgeable shooter always takes precautions to insure that the only chamber firing is the one directly lined up with the barrel. For this article, loaded chambers were covered with a mixture of mutton tallow and beeswax, the same material utilized over 125 years ago, and sold, at that time, under a variety of brand names. (This odorous but effective substance is still available today, from Dixie Gun Works, under the name of Old Zip.) Candle wax and even animal fat was used on the frontier when the commercial product could not be obtained, although the latter had a tendency to soften and leak into the powder during hot weather.

The problem of reloading, once the revolver was emptied, has been a perpetual one and in the muzzleloading era, there was no easy solution. There is just no fast way to reload a cap and ball revolver. I am, by nature, a meticulously slow loader; there is less

Hacker sets up for rapid-fire "unloading" run from the hip. Time variations were surprising.

The Dragoon of 1848 and the Pocket Model of 1853 were very different, but Hacker thinks the Pocket Model beat a derringer.

chance of making a mistake that way. On average, it takes me five minutes to load a six shot revolver. Even when rushing, which I don't like to do when shooting, my best time is a little under four minutes.

One hundred and fifty years ago there were many solutions to the empty cylinder, but few remedies. One technique was the use of pre-loaded paper cartridges, which were somewhat effective, especially during the War Between the States. But paper cartridges were difficult to obtain, expensive, and time consuming to make. Another popular method of fast follow-up shots was the practice of carrying an extra, pre-loaded *but uncapped* cylinder. The reason for not capping until the cylinder was assembled on the gun is obvious: multiple discharges are unnerving enough in the gun; in the hand, they might be disastrous.

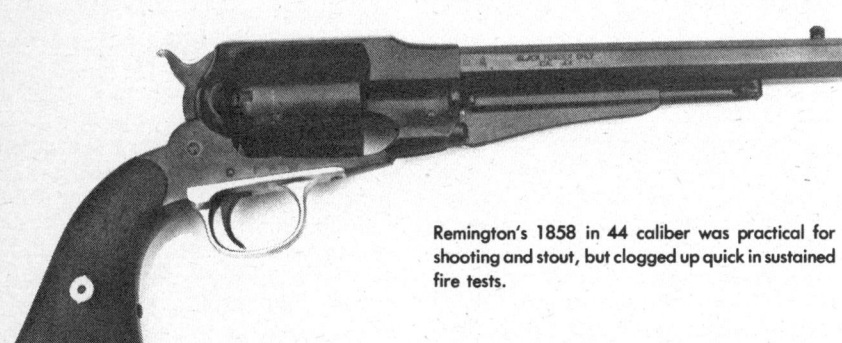

Remington's 1858 in 44 caliber was practical for shooting and stout, but clogged up quick in sustained fire tests.

I have often wondered why more replica cap and ball revolvers today aren't sold with extra cylinders. To my knowledge, there is only one black powder arm supplied in this manner, and that is the limited edition Butterfield 1860 Army offered by B. E. Hodgdon of Shawnee, Kansas. This gun, authentic as it may be, only exists in 500 sets, making it strictly a collector's item. Why not make one for shooters?

Of course, the best and most obvious answer for the individual who wants more than the customary cylinder-full of lead is to carry two guns of the same make and caliber. Not only is he assured of having spare parts to keep at least one gun operating, but the weapons balance better on the hip and firepower and survival opportunities are normally doubled. There are exceptions to the rule, however, as in the case of Wild Bill Hickok, whose brace of Navies could not stop a bullet in the back. In summary, the man with an empty gun was the same as a man with no gun at all, which is why the best technique has always been to make that first shot count.

Initially each gun was thoroughly cleaned and bench tested with a cylinder-full of powder and ball at a 25-yard target to determine its grouping capabilities. Then the practical shooting began, both rapid fire from the hip and then a slightly slower, semi-aimed fire . . . all at targets from 10 to 25 feet away, about the distance across a poker table or halfway down the bar. These are the practical ranges for which the single-action cap and ball revolvers were designed.

Without exception, every revolver fired from the rest shot high. This is exactly in keeping in character with the originals. It should be pointed out, however, that the sights are rudimentary at best, consisting, in the case of the Colts, of a shallow notch filed in the hammer or, as with the Remingtons, a groove milled down the center of the topstrap. Front sights are either a brass bead or a fixed blade. How worn the gun becomes, how far back the hammer can be cocked or how tightly the barrel wedge is driven in: these are all facts that can change the bullet's impact. It is for this reason that the best practical shooting with these fixed sight revolvers is always done from the hip. I don't believe the defense guns of the 19th Century were ordinarily aimed; they were pointed or "instinct shot," a technique whereby the eyes take in the tip of the barrel of the gun held at hip level or with the arm slightly extended. It is the same technique shotgunners and "Wild West" exhibition shooters use.

Another factor that will significantly affect the point of aim with a cap and ball gun is fouling. The more black powder burned in the barrel, the more the point of impact of the projectile will vary, just as in a muzzle-loading rifle. This was an important point to consider in our sustained fire tests.

This same "fouling factor" has another major effect on gun performance during extended firing. It tended to gum up the works of all our revolvers at various points, depending on the load used and the design of the gun. It is a little known fact in today's world, but generally speaking, black powder percussion revolvers cannot endure more than 10 to 12 shots without gumming up their cylinders, sometimes to a point where the guns become inoperative. Worst offender of this phenomenon was the 1858 Remington, which became difficult to cock after 10 shots. The larger-framed .36 and .44 caliber Colts went through 12 to 18 rounds (2 to 3 loadings) before becoming sluggish.

From the bench, the 1851 Navy grouped the best, firing an average six-shot string measuring 2¼ inches. From personal experience with originals, I suspect this grouping would open up slightly once the gun had become worn. Following close behind was the 1858 Remington, which shot solid 2½ inch groups consistently. The worst offender, in terms of benchrest accuracy, was the diminutive 1849 Colt. Its four-inch barrel left little sighting radius and the .31 caliber ball seemed difficult for me to group tightly. However, aimed fire was not the purpose of these guns, as we shall see. Ironically, the earliest of the revolvers, the .36 Paterson, shot surprisingly well. Aided by the narrow 9 inch octagon barrel, I was able to keep all

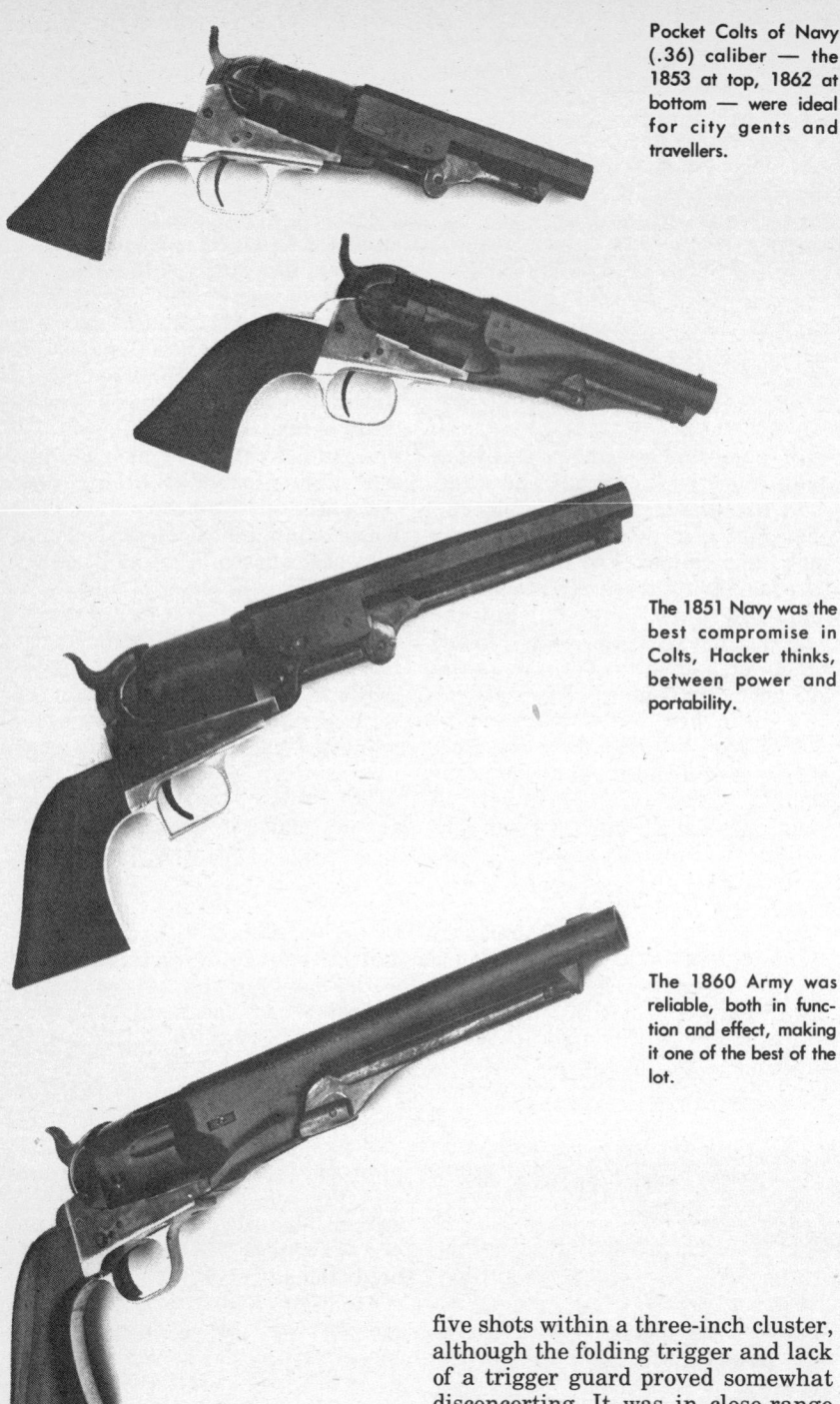

Pocket Colts of Navy (.36) caliber — the 1853 at top, 1862 at bottom — were ideal for city gents and travellers.

The 1851 Navy was the best compromise in Colts, Hacker thinks, between power and portability.

The 1860 Army was reliable, both in function and effect, making it one of the best of the lot.

five shots within a three-inch cluster, although the folding trigger and lack of a trigger guard proved somewhat disconcerting. It was in close-range rapid-fire hip shooting that most of the guns tested came into their own.

Rapid fire with the various cap and ball revolvers was hampered by the age old problem of split and spent caps falling off the nipples and becoming jammed between the hammer and frame, thereby stopping the hammer short, or cylinder and frame where they jammed the cylinder and hammer. The only sure remedies for this problem are to try and shake or pluck the cap out of its new-found crevice, or to completely disassemble the barrel and cylinder assembly from the frame and remove the culprit cap. Obviously, neither of these solutions is ideal in a combat situation.

Cap jams *were* partially eliminated by using the old-time trick of flipping the gun to one side as it was being cocked, theoretically tossing the cap off the nipple as the cylinder rotated. Although picturesque, this technique does not always work.

The cap jam, coupled with the fouling problem, served as a reminder that truly rapid, sustained fire did not become practical until the advent of the smokeless powder cartridge gun. In the era of the cap and ball, the man who could place his first few shots accurately and kept his gun cleaned and tuned usually had the upper hand in a life or death situation.

Although the Colt 1836 Texas Paterson was the first practical revolving pistol to appear on the firearms scene, it was, by all later standards, rudimentary. The folding trigger and lack of trigger guard made the Texas Paterson difficult to manipulate for fast repeat shots (it often required two hands to cock) and the trigger was located too far forward in the frame for accurate control. The slim nine-inch barrel of the 2½ pund "belt pistol" did aid in shot placement. Loaded with 22 grains of black powder, this .36 pioneer five-shot revolver took an average of 14 seconds to empty.

The Paterson was also the most difficult of all the percussion revolvers to load. It had to be broken into the barrel, cylinder and frame groups for reloading and on the early model (such as the one I tested for this article), there is no loading lever, which means that extra implements must be carried by the shooter. A standard practice of the old-timers was to use the base pin of the frame to ram home the ball in the cylinders—hard on the gun and hard on the shooter! Another disconcerting feature of the Paterson is the fact that the caps cannot easily be placed on the nipples unless the gun is at full cock—a dangerous practice under any situation, and especially so in the excitement of battle.

It should be noted that in 1841 famed mountain man and scout Kit Carson, aided by a brace of these awkward Texas Patersons, succeeded in defeating more than 100 Kiowa and Comanche Indians who had attacked a Santa Fe-bound wagon train he was with. And during the years he guided John C. Fremont's exploration party across the unknown Sierras, Carson always slept with his two Paterson Colts at half-cock (no doubt to free the folding triggers) next to him, under the covers of his bedroll. The famed explorer's attachment to and skill with these early percussion revolvers was not so much a testimony to the gun, as to the fact that the Patersons, even with their drawbacks, were the only half-way reliable multi-shot guns available at that time.

In 1848 the massive Colt Dragoon made its appearance and for the first time, the mounted frontiersman found himself with heavy-duty repeating firepower. Previously, Colt had produced a limited number of hefty Walker pistols, but they never enjoyed the mass-production and popularity of the 4 pound, 2 oz. .44 Dragoon. Due to its size and weight, this hefty hand cannon was not a practical belt gun. It was intended to be carried in pairs, slipped inside two saddle holsters draped over the pommel of a saddle. Prior to, and throughout the War Between the States, many riders, including Quantrill, carried their Dragoons in just that fashion. The Colt Dragoon was made in three models, each one demonstrating a slight improvement over its predecessor It was the first revolver to feature a locking latch to keep the loading lever from slipping down during recoil and jamming the cylinder. The Dragoon also sported a cut-away area on the right side of the recoil shield, which facilitated the time-consuming chore of capping.

For our GUN DIGEST article, I selected the Second Model, as it retains the best features of all three versions (square back trigger guard, improved lever latch, and simplified, more reliable mainspring). The six-shot cylinders were packed with 40 grains of FFFG, although some testing was conducted with 45 grains, all the chambers would hold with a 135 grain lead ball. However, I found the 40 grain charge of this hand cannon easier to control. The hefty size and heavy load of the Dragoon made fast-recovery repeat shots difficult, so it took an average of 12 seconds to fire six shots into lethal areas of a man-sized target. Most of this time was not spent in aiming but in recovering from recoil. I found the Dragoon to be extremely accurate. With its 7½ inch barrel and plow-handle grips, it is a natural "pointer." The weight of the Dragoon, which helped absorb the recoil, also made sustained fire a short-lived event. It was hard work. Although not a practical choice for fast-shooting, close-in defense, the "magnum" energy of this gun, the most powerful mass produced revolver of its day, would make repeat shots unnecessary, when a shooter was able to hit his mark the first time. Not the most comfortable belt gun to have

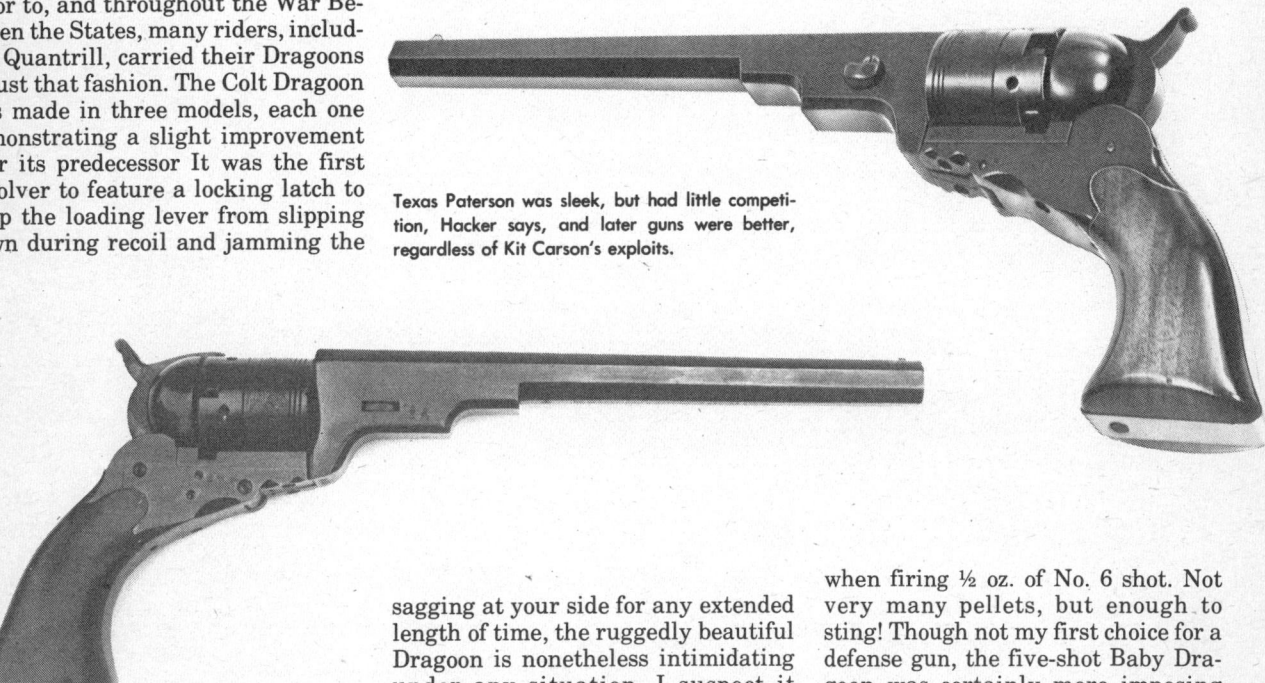

Texas Paterson was sleek, but had little competition, Hacker says, and later guns were better, regardless of Kit Carson's exploits.

sagging at your side for any extended length of time, the ruggedly beautiful Dragoon is nonetheless intimidating under any situation. I suspect it thwarted as many an argument in the holster as in the hand.

From the largest of the frontier's most popular revolvers we now go to the smallest, the diminutive Colt 1849 Baby Dragoon. This five shot, .31 caliber pipsqueak is sometimes referred to as the "Wells Fargo" model (without loading lever) but very few Pony Express riders carried it because of its questionable stopping power. Its small cylinder holds just 15 grains of black powder in each chamber, behind a 44-gr. lead ball.

The little guns came in 3 to 6 inch barrels and, despite their small size and limited power, were one of Colt's best selling products. Compactness and lightweight portability were their biggest attractions. They were the only alternative to the single and double derringers on the market at that time. In addition, the usefulness of the little .31's could be extended somewhat by loading the chambers with shot instead of a single lead ball. While not a lethal load (except at extremely close range), hits were certain.

Because of its small size, our four-inch barreled 1849 was easy to load and fun to fire. The lightweight 24 oz. gun easily emptied its chambers in less than six seconds, placing all five shots in a 2⅞ inch circle at a paced-off 10 feet. The short four inch barrel we used made it difficult to keep the shots tighter during rapid fire. Interestingly, this was about the same size of the pattern the short barrel threw when firing ½ oz. of No. 6 shot. Not very many pellets, but enough to sting! Though not my first choice for a defense gun, the five-shot Baby Dragoon was certainly more imposing than the single shot derringers of its day, and it didn't take up much more room in a coat pocket or saddle bag. Its concealability gave it an advantage of surprise that must have, more often than not, made up for its limited punch.

In 1851 Colt introduced their first practical revolver for self-defense, the 1851 Navy. Here at last was a pistol that encompassed all the desirable features for fast, effective shooting: a well porportioned, contoured grip, later to be duplicated on the immortal Single Action Army, a lethal and accurate .36 caliber, and a smooth, simplified action. It is a medium-frame, relatively light (2 lb., 10 oz.)

It wouldn't do to shoot C&B revolvers in a leisure suit, or at least not a 20th Century one. Here, Hacker charges the monster Dragoon, which is easier to load than the others. There is so much room to work.

six-gun that found instant acceptance throughout the country. Wild Bill Hickok was one of the most famous proponents of the famous pistols, and a Harper's Magazine article of 1867 stated that "... his waist was girthed by a belt which held two Colt's Navy Revolvers."

Hickok's use of his brace of Navies became legendary and he fired them with such speed and accuracy that on one notable occasion in Abilene, he not only killed his attacker with a single shot fired from the hip, but a split second later thumbed off a repeat shot which dropped a local townsman coming to his aid!

I found the Colt Navy to be a natural pointing gun and I was easily able to shoot—at 10 feet—tight 2¼ inch six-shot groups in 7.5 seconds. Both round and conical balls were available for the Navies. I prefer the 70 grain round ball, as it is easier to load and enabled me to pack in more powder. For our tests 22 grains of FFFG was used. This was the standard load of its day and proved to be an extremely comfortable charge to shoot.

Although powerful for a black powder revolver, the .36 caliber was never as lethal as famed Western artist George Catlin depicted, when he once painted a portrait of himself on horseback shooting a buffalo with a Navy Colt. This famous gun which once graced many a holster on both sides of the law is a graceful, reliable and accurate shooter, but it is definitely not a buffalo gun! The ultimate testimony to its classic design is that when Colt first decided to re-issue their line of black powder pistols in 1971, they first produced the 1851 Navy.

Although never quite achieving the Navy's fame, the .44 1858 Remington should have logically been the gunman's first choice. It sported many features that Colt did not: a solid frame with top strap, a more practical base pin arrangement for easy removal of the cylinder, and a tighter, cylinder-to-recoil shield design that helped prevent spent caps from becoming trapped inside the mechanism.

Remington's gun found favor with many, but it had two major drawbacks, the worst of which was the inability of the Remington to fire more than two cylinders full of black powder without becoming extremely difficult to cock due to fouling, while many of the open-top Colt designs can fire 18 to 24 shots before becoming so fouled as to be inoperative. In a first-one-out-of-the-holster situation, this drawback is negligible, but in any type of sustained fire situation it could be embarassing for the Remington owner. The other Remington problem was not tangible: it simply did not have the reputation of the Colt.

In our tests, I averaged one cap-jam per seven shots with the Remington, compared with one cap-jam per four shots with the Colts. With its solid design and 8-inch barrel. The Remington should have out-shot the Navy, but it didn't. The best I could do was 2½ inch groups at 10 feet, taking 8.5 seconds to empty six chambers loaded with 28 grains of FFFG behind a 128 grain lead ball. For my hands, the grip-trigger-hammer relationship is not quite right. It could be argued that I have small hands, which I do, but it should be remembered that these guns are replicas of 19th Century firearms and the men of the 1800's had smaller hands than most men do today. The guns should fit, but not all of them do and this may have been part of Remington's problem. It certainly was

Obviously, researching this article was fun for Hacker, but the tight group shown, produced from the hip at encounter range in 5 seconds, would be no laughing matter in a fight. The gun is the 1862 Colt Police in .36 caliber.

Hacker found the Texas Paterson exceedingly awkward and also hard to hold. Note the strained angle of the trigger finger and the obvious lack of anything to hold onto. Still, it shot five times without reloading.

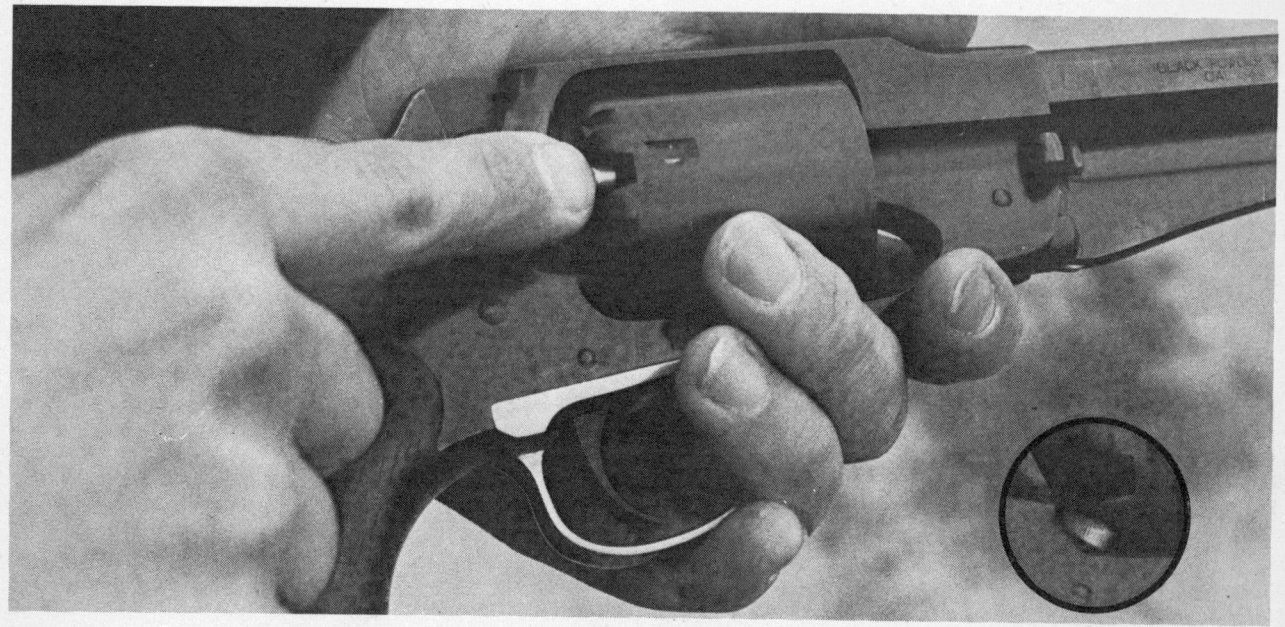

Careful cap seating in cramped quarters and careful choice of caps to fit the nipples still allow jams in cap and ball revolvers. This Remington jammed (see inset) about once in seven shots; Colts did it more often.

not its shooting ability or design, which the firm later carried on over into the cartridge era.

In 1860, Colt came out with their Army Model, which is the most graceful of all the cap and ball revolvers I tested. It sported an improved loading lever, 7½ and 8 inch .44 caliber barrel, and one of its most unique features, an elongated grip, supposedly to help the shooter control the gun during recoil. I have fired 1860 Armies fitted with the standard Navy grip and found them just as comfortable and controllable—even more so—than the long drop-grip normally encountered. I find the gun a pleasant one to shoot, but it is not as fast for rapid fire as the Navy, due to the fact that the grips place one's hand higher up on the backstrap; when the gun recoils, the thumb is closer to the hammer, making cocking more awkward, and difficulty is experienced bending the wrist to bring the gun back on target. It took eight seconds to empty all six shots into a 3-inch circle at ten feet, using 28 grains of powder. However, I much preferred the 1860's heavier 128 grain bullet and greater stopping power compared to the Navy's smaller 70-grain .36 caliber ball.

If any percussion revolver can be called "cute," the Model 1862 Police Pocket Pistol lays claim to that title. A continuation of that nomenclature should be "... and deadly." Originally designed for in-city police work, the

'62 Police Pocket was the final culmination of the Colt percussion arms. It employed the best of all features: compact design coupled with a medium-potent .36 caliber, controlled balance, a light 26 oz. weight (thanks to the incorporation of a five-shot, semi-fluted cylinder), and the streamlined albeit scaled-down appearance of the 1860 Army, complete with ratchet loading lever.

This small pistol can comfortably fire charges ranging up to 22 grains of black powder and is extremely accurate for its size. It fills the hand with almost as much controllability as the Colt Navy. During our test, I was able to fire 2½ inch groups within six seconds; it was the fastest shooting (though not the most accurate) of these guns. All shots hit within lethal areas. Group size, up to a point, becomes academic when firing for self defense. The main point to consider is: does the gun hit where it's being pointed? In the case of the 1862 Pocket, the answer is a definite "yes." This fact explains why this small five-shooter was adopted by the Pinkerton Detective Agency and a number of other law enforcement groups, not to mention businessmen and travelers.

Now that the testing is done and the sulfuric smoke has cleared, the ultimate question must be, "What was the optimum choice for an 19th Century individual desiring a pistol for self protection?" The answer is not a logical one, for logically, the Remington 1858 should be the choice. Part of the decision rests in the era in which you were born. You may not have liked the bulk of the big Dragoon, but in 1848, it was all you could get. Assuming, however, that we were alive in the late 1860's, when all the various cap and ball models had made their ultimate appearances, I would base my decision on two factors: stopping power and portability. Accuracy, especially at the close-in ranges we are considering for defense purposes, does not become a crucial factor. All of the guns tested proved that they can be fired with deadly rapidity.

If I had to pick one gun, it would be the 1860 Army, due to its combination of large caliber and advanced design. I would, however, swap those elongated grips for a Colt Navy's just as soon as I could work a deal with the local gunsmith. If, by some stroke of fortune, I was able to afford two guns, they would be the fast-handling, accurate Colt Navies with the 1862 Police Pocket as a concealed back-up. Both revolvers fire the same size bullet and have proved equally effective in rapid fire.

I would pass on the small .31 caliber, considering it too soft-hitting to be effective. The Paterson, while picturesque, would have been outdated by anyone's shooting standards. If I spent most of my time on horseback and traveled through high mountain country where animals larger than deer might be encountered, a mighty Dragoon would provide a multi-shot backup to my big bore rifle; it might also serve me well when I ventured into scattered and unpredictable outposts of civilization.

As for the Remington? The grips feel funny, the gun's action is prone to excessive fouling, and it doesn't have the Colt name. Designwise, it may be the most logical choice, but I wouldn't carry it around my hip. So you see, after all these years, the times and the guns still haven't changed. And neither has the romance, myths and methods of frontier firepower. •

Frontier Firepower Ballistics Comparison Chart

Compiled by Rick Hacker

Gun	Caliber	Ball Size (in.)	Bullet Wgt. (rd. ball, lead)	Load (FFFG for all cap & ball guns)	*Muzzle Velocity (ft. per sec.)	**Striking Energy (ft. lbs.)
Colt Baby Dragoon	31	.320	44 gr.	12 gr.	550	30
Colt Paterson & Navy	36	.376	70 gr.	22 gr.	710	78
Colt 1860 Army & 1858 Remington	44	.441	128 gr.	28 gr.	736	154
Colt Dragoon	44	.445	135 gr.	40 gr.	830	207

*Barrel length had a major impact on velocity in black powder guns; generally, the longer the barrel, the greater the velocity.

**In determining the effective stopping power of a firearm, muzzle velocity is not as important as striking energy. Thus, as the caliber increases, so does the striking energy, at a much greater proportion than the powder charge would indicate. For example, the difference of striking energy power between the .36 caliber Navy and the .44 caliber 1860 Army is more than doubled, even though the black powder load of the .44 is only 6 gains more than the .36. The larger diameter ball makes the difference.

The impact that the self contained cartridge loaded with modern smokeless powder had on Frontier Firepower is evidenced by the fact that today's modern 38 Special cartridge loaded with a 200 grain bullet and fired from a revolver with a 6" barrel, has a muzzle velocity of 730 f.p.s. (slightly less than a Colt 1860 Army) but achieves a striking energy of 236 foot pounds — greater than the mighty Colt Dragoon.

Safety Note: All cap and ball guns are made to be used with FFFG Black Powder or Pyrodex "P" ONLY! Never use smokeless powder in any of these guns — you will certainly blow up the gun and portions of yourself. Remember: BLACK POWDER or PYRODEX only.

SHOOTERS waited a long time before Smith & Wesson introduced the Model 25-5 for the .45 Colt, but S&W will not install .45 Colt cylinders on .45 ACP Model 1955 Target revolvers or convert the 25-5 to .45 ACP. If you have any ideas of installing a 1955 Target .45 ACP cylinder in your 25-5, you'd better forget it, since it is too short. Similarly, the .45 Colt 25-5 cylinder is longer than the one on the 1955 Target .45 ACP, and is not interchangeable with it.

If you want to shoot BOTH of these fine cartridges in a double-action revolver, it takes TWO guns, unless you let your Yankee ingenuity take over, as I did. All hope for a convertible .45 double-action is not lost. And there are several gunsmiths who can handle the job.

What follows is not a step-by-step procedure, since this job falls beyond the realm of hobby gunsmithing. I will describe the basic procedure, and this will give revolver mechanics worth their bluing salts enough information to get them on the right track, since they already have the skills and knowledge to fill in gaps not explained in detail here.

There are several ways you can go about this, with several guns, and the one you choose will affect the amount of work which must be done, its cost, and also the character of the finished revolver. I started with an old M1917 S&W military .45 ACP which was in generally good shape, though it needed some gunsmithing. While having its ills attended to, I had an extra cylinder and yoke for the .45 Colt fitted, and retained the original .45 ACP barrel. You can treat the Model 1950 Army the same way, ending up with a potent 38½ oz. package with 5½" barrel. The procedure for converting the Model 1955 Target .45 ACP is the same, though you have a lot heftier revolver, tipping the scales at 45 ozs. with its 6½" target barrel.

You can also convert smaller caliber N-frame S&W revolvers, such as the .38-44 Heavy Duty or Outdoorsman, the Model 27, or 28 .357 Magnums, the Model 57 .41 Magnum or Model 29 .44 Magnum. I'd not suggest converting pre-war revolvers having potential collector value. The M1917 military can be converted without permanent alteration, so please leave those beautiful .44 Special or .455 New Centurys, or early .357s alone. If you are going to buy a gun to convert, the best prospect is the Model 28 Highway Patrolman or the Model 1955 Target .45 ACP, the latter better than the former. For a beefy 4" barrel, fixed sight, holster gun, some think the Model 58 .41 Magnum Military and Police is a prime candidate. It weighs 40 ozs. after converting to .45 Colt.

All these smaller caliber guns require barrel replacement in addition to the cylinder work, using 1955 Target .45 ACP barrels for adjustable sight models, and 1917 or 1950 Army barrels for fixed sight guns. The .41 Magnum, or .44 Magnum heavy barrels can be rebored successfully, though .38 Special or .357 Magnum

SHOOT YOUR OWN CONVERTIBLE 45

Double-action revolvers for both 45 ACP and 45 Colt are only money and a gunsmith away.

by C. E. HARRIS

barrels of the contour used on the Outdoorsman, Model 27 or 28 don't have enough wall thickness to take out to .45 on a rebore.

Barrels for the .45 Colt made since World War II are of the same nominal specifications as those for the .45 ACP, with .442" bore, .451" groove and 16" twist. My M1917 S&W, current Ruger .45 revolver barrels, and the 1955 Target Model 25 all slug the same, so any of these will work OK. Such a barrel will handle .451" jacketed bullets very well, and gives fine results with swaged or cast lead bullets not over .454" diameter.

With all of these conversions you will require an extra cylinder and yoke assembly, unless you want to take a .357, .41 or .44 Magnum and simply convert to .45 Colt by rechambering and rebarreling, ignoring the .45 ACP convertible option. A lot of people are willing to do this and be content, but I feel that's missing half the possible utility, and much of the fun. New cylinders and barrels are available from parts suppliers advertising in *Shotgun News*, and some can be obtained from S&W. Getting yokes, .357, .41 or .44 Magnum barrels or cylinders for rechambering, fitting, and reboring is a problem, since S&W company policy is not to sell these parts, but only to fit them at the factory into guns returned to them for repair. It is my understanding, however, that .45 ACP barrels and .38 Special or .44 Special cylinders for N-frame guns, which are suitable for this conversion, can be purchased, while they last (which won't be long after this makes print).

If you are starting with a .45 ACP revolver such as a 1950 Army, M1917 or 1955 Target, you are ahead of the game, since you have one cylinder which fits, and a barrel with the right size hole in it already. You need only to make sure your revolver is mechanically correct to start with, and then rechamber and fit a .45 Colt cylinder and yoke assembly. My gun took more than the usual amount of work, and is worth explaining so you have an idea what you could run up against.

As 60-year-old guns go, my M1917 was in good shape, having a perfect bore and less than the usual amount of surface damage, but it had loose headspace from long use, and so much endshake in the cylinder that its forward movement was arrested by its striking the rear barrel face, which was out of square, instead of being supported by the gas shield of the cylinder and the fit of the yoke against the cylinder's internal shoulder as it should be. This required setting back the barrel one thread, to give enough shank length to permit refitting the cylinder. Correcting the endshake required building up the gas ring of the cylinder and the end of the yoke which bears against the internal shoulder of the cylinder by welding, then machining them oversize to allow surplus for refitting. The rear face of the barrel was made square and the original out-of-round forcing cone cleaned up; the original out-of-square cylinder face trued up; then everything was refitted and the cylinder gap adjusted to pass a .004" feeler gauge, but not .006". This all took a lot of gunsmith time, but turned out to be far better in fit and shooting performance than the original gun.

Now that the original cylinder and barrel were corrected and the re-

Author's converted M1917 S&W with .45 Colt cylinder installed, its original .45 ACP cylinder and the .45 Auto Rim and .45 Colt cartridges to which it is adapted.

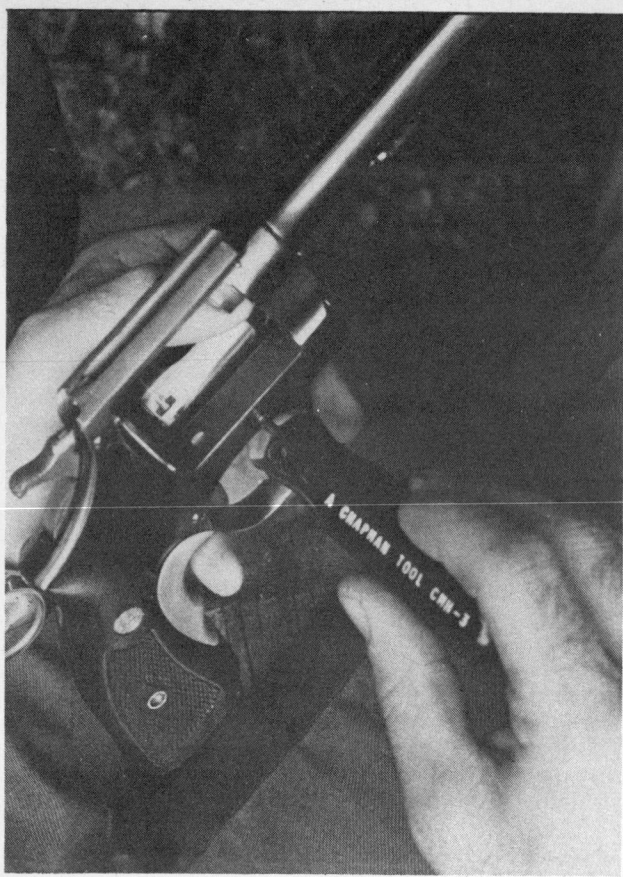 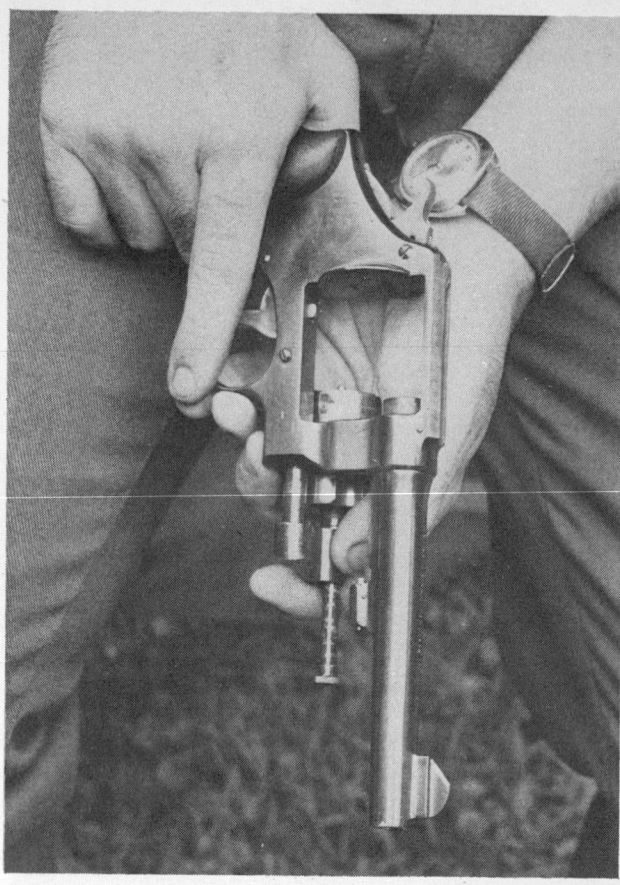

Converted M1917 with .45 ACP and auxiliary .45 Colt cylinder is a potent 38½ oz. package. With 250-gr. bullets and 8.2 grs. of Unique in .45 Colt or 6.2 grs. in .45 AR, the 5½" barrel delivers 840 f.p.s. and 392 ft.-lbs. Swapping cylinders takes only a minute, loosening one screw and interchanging the cylinder/yoke assemblies. This permits use of .45 Colt, .45 ACP and .45 Auto Rim in the same gun with equal accuracy.

volver's mechanical problems cured, we could start on the meat of the conversion—the .45 Colt cylinder. Mine was rechambered from one for a Model 28 .357 Magnum. A .45 ACP cylinder cannot be rechambered to .45 Colt because its rear is faced off to provide proper headspace for the combined .090" thickness of the .45 ACP case rim, plus the half-moon clip. The maximum rim thickness of the .45 Colt is .045", so such a cylinder, if rechambered, would have grossly excessive headspace. The rim thickness of the .45 Colt is .015" less than that of the .38 Special, .357, .41 or .44 Magnums, and .045" less than the .45 Auto Rim, so its cylinder must fit more closely against the recoil shield of the revolver frame than a .45 ACP cylinder.

Getting the .45 Colt cylinder positioned correctly, while at the same time permitting correct headspace and interchangeability of the .45 ACP cylinder requires some trickery. The cylinder limit stop on the frame locates the cylinder when it is swung open, and it is essential that this be correctly dimensioned to accommodate the shorter .45 ACP cylinder, if the dual-cylinder conversion is desired. This will require slight building up of the limit stop on .38 Special, .357 Magnum, .41 Magnum or .44 Magnum revolvers. After this is done, the rechambered .45 Colt cylinder is modified by lathe turning a step .040-.045" wide, just deep enough to clear the stop when the cylinder is swung open, permitting it to fit the correct distance from the recoil shield for proper headspace. The .45 ACP, M1917, 1950, or 1955 revolvers have stops that are correctly dimensioned for this conversion already, so don't fool with them; just get that step turned on the .45 Colt cylinder.

 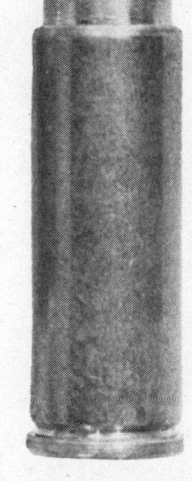

Using same 250 gr. bullet, .45 Auto Rim is crimped into crimp groove, whereas .45 Colt is crimped on front of first driving band, so as not to exceed 1.60" overall cartridge length, which is maximum for that cartridge.

After both cylinders are fitted for minimal end play, .004"-.006" cylinder gap and proper headspace, you will probably have to rework the extractor ratchet on one cylinder or the other to have both index correctly on all chambers with the same hand. This gets a bit tricky, and should be done by a qualified gunsmith, since it may require some parts swapping, patience and hand work.

Although we have dealt only with

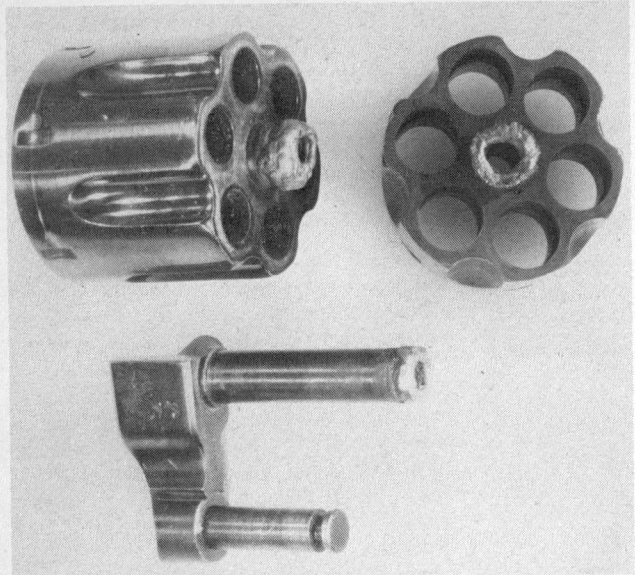

(Above left and right) Cylinder gas shields and bearing end of yokes were welded and then machined oversize to allow surplus metal to be removed for fitting, to eliminate excess headspace and endshake from long use. This technique works Gun has fired 1,000 rounds or more since fitting this way.

the S&W N-frame revolver here, the Colt New Service or M1917 military can be converted similarly, using slightly different techniques. The cylinder limit stop on Colt revolvers is part of the side plate. Suitable revolvers for conversion and extra barrels or cylinders aren't quite as readily available as they are for S&W guns. However, lacking an original Colt .45 DA barrel, the New Service is much easier to rebarrel from a blank than the S&W, since you don't have to install the lock plunger for the extractor rod. One such gun I know of was rechambered from a .38 Special Shooting Master, had an M1917 Colt .45 ACP cylinder as an auxiliary, and was fitted with a piece of barrel from a M3 sub-machine gun. The owner then put S&W adjustable sights on it and Jordan Trooper stocks, making an accurate, though large, .45 revolver. Sometimes you can find surplus cylinders for .455 Webley Colt New Service or S&W revolvers. These will readily rechamber to .45 Colt, but their chamber throats are somewhat oversize for best accuracy, being .456-.458", instead of the optimum .452"-.454".

My converted S&W M1917 isn't exactly a target gun, but is very comfortable to carry and shoots better than I can hold. It averages about 2½" from a Ransom Rest for 10-shot groups at 25 yds., with my standard handload of 8.2 grs. of Unique and 250 or 255-gr. cast Keith type bullets, such as the

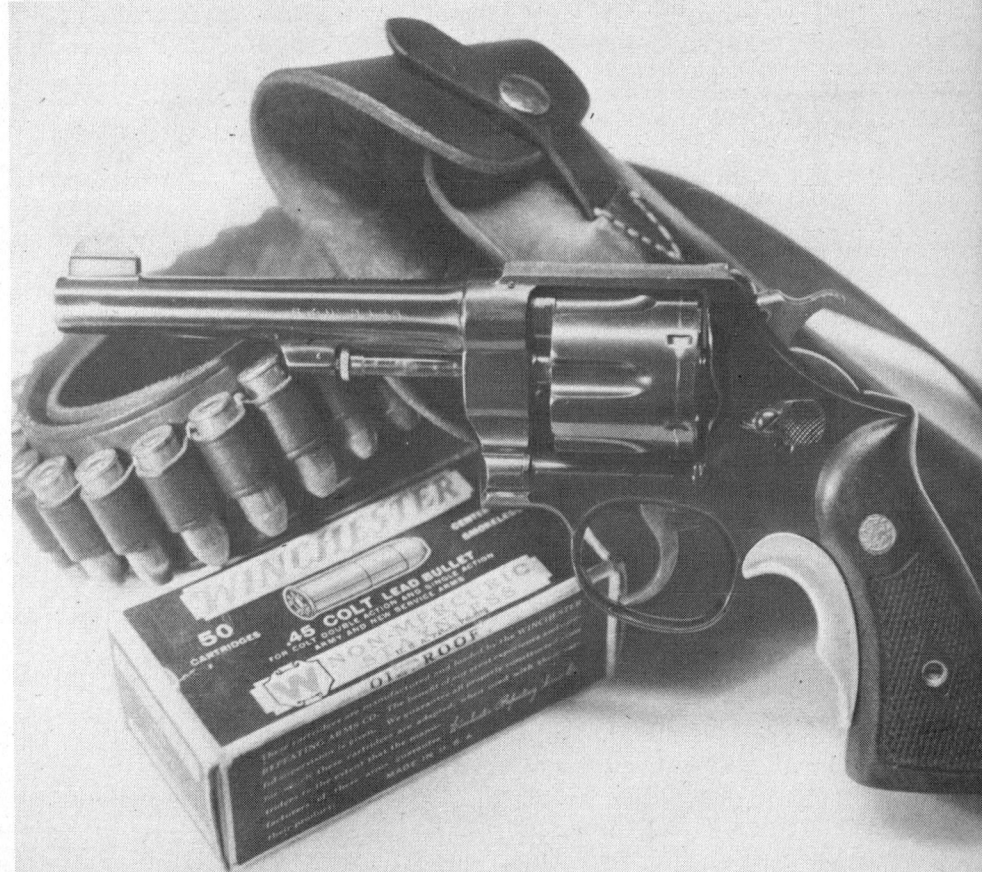

Finished M1917 .45 Colt/.45 ACP convertible makes a friendly holster gun which is lighter than *large frame* .357, .41, or .44 Magnums, yet it packs a suitable punch for game up to deer-size at short ranges.

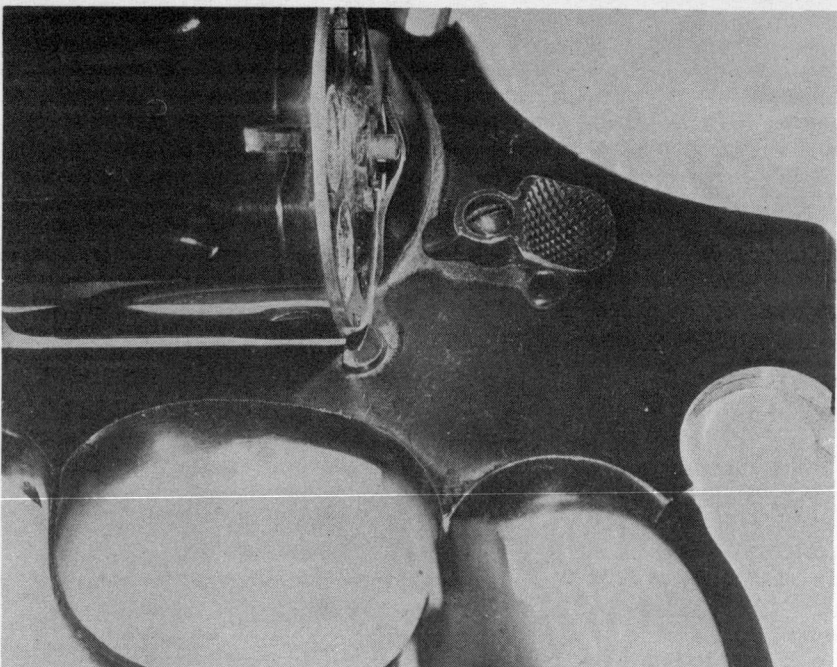

Closeup of 45 Colt cylinder, rechambered from a .357 Magnum one for an S&W Model 28, showing relief cut which permits it to fit back against the recoil shield when cylinder limit stop on the frame is correct to accommodate the interchangeable .45 ACP cylinder.

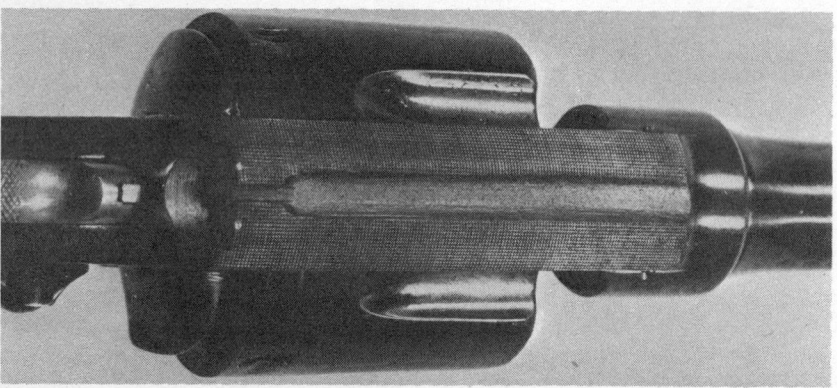

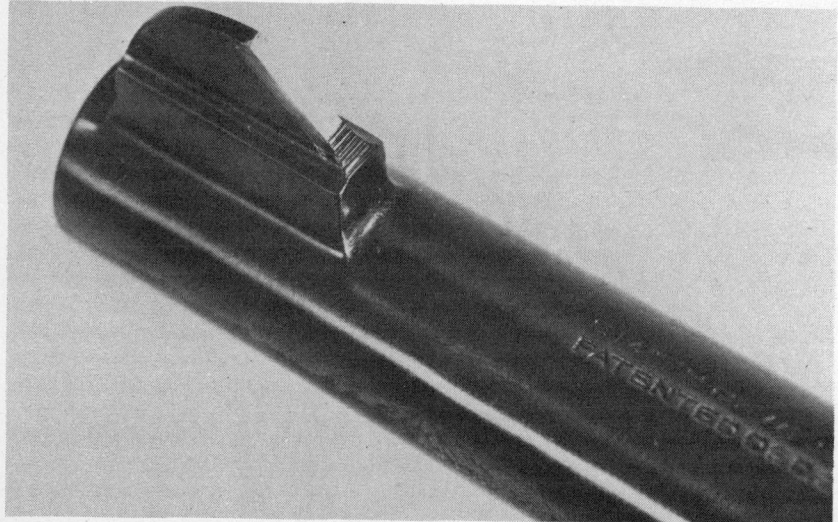

(Above and below) Author had burnished stainless steel inlay installed in front sight, gold outline around rear sight notch, and checkered topstrap to reduce glare. Combination is a custom touch that helps in field shooting.

NEI 250-451, Lyman #454424 or RCBS 45-255KT. This load gives 840 f.p.s. from my 5½" barrel of .451" groove diameter, with .005" cylinder gap. The bullets are sized .454" to fit the chamber throats of both cylinders for best accuracy.

My revolver is set up to shoot .45 ACP hardball ammunition to point of hold at 25 yds., and my 250-gr. .45 Colt handloads and factory ammunition shoot dead center in the black at 25 yds. with a six o'clock hold and to point of hold at 50 yds. My 250-gr. .45 Auto Rim handloads with 6.2 grs. of Unique or 8.6 grs. of Blue Dot shoot to the same points of impact. Wadcutters as light as 210-grs., shoot close enough to the sights to be useful for short range work with the fixed sights, but 185-gr. wadcutters or hollow-points shoot about 6" low at 25 yds. and strike even lower at longer ranges. This isn't a handicap for me, since I prefer the 225-260-gr. bullets. Of course, if you convert an adjustable sight gun, you can use whatever weight bullets you like and adjust the sights accordingly.

Converted guns like these are not suitable for buffalo stomper loads recommended for the Ruger Blackhawk or Thompson-Center Contender, but may be used with any standard .45 Colt loads from reliable data sources such as the *Lyman Pistol and Revolver Handbook* or *Speer No. 10 Handbook*. Over-all cartridge length must not exceed the 1.60" length for factory ammunition, because of the cylinder length. Keith bullets such as the #454424 must be crimped on the forward edge of the front driving band, rather than in the crimping groove. If you want more performance than you can get with standard loads in the .45 Colt, you should get a .44 Magnum. Overloading the .45 Colt cartridge to attempt Magnum velocity levels doesn't make good sense, really isn't needed; and it could be dangerous.

Realistically speaking, there is very little actual difference in the velocity and energy levels of .45 ACP, .45 Auto Rim or standard .45 Colt loads in these guns. The real result of this conversion is increased flexibility, not greater power. And you get it.

I have twice as much fun as any other .45 double-action shooter I know, since I can use my plentiful supply of .45 ACP brass or ammo to provide a bucket full of loads for a Saturday's practice at the iron critters, or stoke up some .45 Colts for hunting purposes. Any .45 ammunition I can find will fit this beast, which is one of my favorite handguns. That's the best thing.

LET'S SHOOT 1980

by WALLACE LABISKY

Ten gauge loads make a real killing difference

FEW WATERFOWL hunters seem to relish the fact, but steel shot is now firmly entrenched. Not only is it here to stay, but the loophole that existed in past years will be nailed shut for the 1980-81 season. No longer will duck and goose hunters be able to circumvent the steel-shot mandate legally by turning to guns of larger or smaller bore size than 12 gauge. It's now going to be a steel-or-nothing proposition in those so-called hotspot zones where non-toxic shot is required. So say the Feds.

Among those of us who have kept close watch on the development of steel-shot loads, the consensus has been that the 10-ga. Magnum appeared to be the most promising candidate of all. That cavernous 3½" shell, we've pointed out, would accommodate a relatively extra-heavy payload of steel, thus serving to keep the pellet count high (and the pattern more dense) with the more lethal and larger-sized shot, such as steel 2's and BB's. At the same time, the 10's larger bore diameter would serve to ease that vexing problem of chamber pressure, which severely limits the velocity of the heaviest 12-ga. steel loads (1½ ozs. at present). The gain, therefore, would be two-fold: more delivered energy on a per-pellet basis, and an improvement in target saturation.

The minds at Federal Cartridge Corporation were obviously in tune with all this, for early in 1980 came the announcement of a steel-shot load for the Big Ten. It is being assembled

New from Federal for 1980 is a steel-shot loading in 10-gauge Magnum with a 1⅝-oz. payload. Offered in two shot sizes—2's and BB's—the charges are fully contained in a tough wad of high-density polyethylene.

in FCC's brown-colored, Reifenhauser-type plastic shell and it contains 1⅝ oz. of steel. The pellet sizes offered are 2's and BB's, and the muzzle velocity is 1,345 fps (feet per second), as opposed to about 1,200 fps for the heaviest 3″ 12-ga. steel loads.

With lead pellets, a 1⅝-oz. charge in the Big Ten would be considered pretty mild medicine. But with steel pellets, this is a whopping big payload. When viewed in terms of pellet count, it's very nearly the equal of a 2⅜-oz. lead shot payload, assuming equal pellet size. That shows the large weight difference between lead and steel. Steel pellets are running much lighter.

FCC isn't trying to kid anybody about the charge weight. I've checked several rounds in both shot sizes and find that the charges not only run very uniform, but they're right on the nose at an honest 1⅝ oz. The No. 2 loads contain 202 pellets on the average; the BB's run 120 pellets.

Wadding is a unit-type combination powder-gas seal and shot pouch of high-density plastic that's plenty tough to prevent the very hard steel pellets from cutting through and making bore contact. There is a 20-ga. fiber wad insert for cushioning and crimp regulation, but the payload is still fully contained in the shot pouch. The pouch, of course, is divided into the usual four segments by fine-line slits.

My pattern testing was carried out at 40 yards using an Ithaca MAG-10 which was in the process of receiving a barrel "tune-up." The chamber's forcing cone was still original, but the very tight constriction at the muzzle had been relieved from 0.050″ to 0.037″. Additionally, the bore had been smoothed up somewhat by polishing with fine-grade steel wool.

The 5-shot string with steel 2's was exceptionally uniform, there being an extreme variation in efficiency of only 5.5 percent. Average efficiency for the 30″ circle was 73.1 percent, with the 20″ core catching an average of 88 pellets, while a fraction over 59 pellets registered in the 5″ annular ring. That figures out to a central thickening factor of 1.47.

With the steel BB's, the average efficiency climbed to 79.6 percent, but the extreme variation jumped to a rather excessive 14 percent. On the matter of pellet distribution, the core/annular breakdown was a fraction over 59 and 36 pellets, respectively, for a central thickening factor of 1.65.

Obviously, both shot sizes delivered patterns with rather strong center density from the choke-relieved barrel. I might also add that felt recoil with the 1⅝-oz. steel 10-ga. payload is markedly milder than it is with the much slower starting factory load containing 2 ozs. of lead pellets. It should be noted, too, that the steel loads have adequate gusto to provide reliable functioning in the Ithaca gas gun—at least this was true in regard to my testing which was carried out under an ambient temperature of 55 degrees F.

The new 10-ga. steel load contains only 1⅝ ozs. of shot, but that doesn't mean it's suitable for use in old, arthritic-ridden side-by-side guns with 2⅞″ chambers. The load is intended for use only in properly chambered guns of fairly recent manufacture.

That's not all that's been happening to steel shot at Federal. The company has been hard at work developing a steel-shot load for the 20-ga., and this one is expected to be ready in time for the 1980 waterfowling season. How's that for an encore?

The 20-ga. load will be in the 3″ shell and it will carry one ounce of steel shot in No. 4 size only. Those 192 pellets (approximately) will be contained in a special barrel-protecting wad of tough, high-density polyethylene. FCC is aiming for a muzzle velocity of about 1,335 fps, and the performance out to 40 yards has been calculated to be equivalent to that of a standard 1-oz. lead-shot load. In making this claim, it is assumed that FCC is talking about total energy within the shot cloud and not delivered energy on a single pellet basis. At any rate, this 20-ga. loading should serve adequately for taking ducks over decoys.

As for the existing 12-ga. steel-shot loads, there will be no basic changes for 1980. This holds true for all three manufacturers—Federal, Remington, and Winchester-Western. However, FCC will add steel BB's to the available shot sizes in its 2¾″ 1¼-oz. loading. Previously, BB's were offered only in the 3″ 1⅜-oz. loading.

BALLISTICS
Remington 12-Gauge Steel Shot Loads

		40 Yards		50 Yards		60 Yards	
Load/MV	Pellet Size	Pellet Energy Ft-lbs	Flight Time Sec.	Pellet Energy Ft-lbs	Flight Time Sec.	Pellet Energy Ft-lbs	Flight Time Sec.
2¾ Inch 1⅛ Ozs. 1,375 fps	4	2.16	.134	1.66	.183	1.27	.239
	2	3.71	.130	2.90	.176	2.28	.228
3-Inch Magnum 1¼ Ozs. 1,375 fps	1	4.72	.127	3.73	.172	2.96	.223

W-W likewise will offer BB's for the first time in both their 2¾" and 3" steel loads. In checking samples of these, I found the charge weights to be substantially lighter than stated. Those from the 2¾" shell, which is supposed to contain a 1¼-oz. charge, averaged one grain in excess of 1⅛ oz. And the stated 1½-oz. charges in the 3" load averaged only 1⁷⁄₁₆ oz. These weight shortages stem from the fact that, for a given charge weight, large-sized pellets bulk up more than those of a smaller size. In the above instances, there is neither room in the shell nor space in the shot pouch for heavier charges of steel BB's.

Remington will hold the line in 1980 with the two 12-ga. loads I discussed last year. These are a 2¾" loading with 1⅛ oz., and a 3-incher with 1¼ oz. The available shot sizes are Nos. 1, 2, and 4 in both loadings. Both the standard and magnum versions generate a muzzle velocity of 1,375 fps, which makes them the fastest of all steel-shot loads presently on the market. An appended table shows the individual pellet energy and time of flight (calculated) for these Remington loads at ranges of 40, 50, and 60 yards.

Since my last report, I've done some pattern testing, and also a bit of duck shooting, with the 12-ga. Remington 3" steel loads. The gun was a Breda Mark II magnum autoloader fitted with interchangeable choke tubes. Since steel loads pattern with higher efficiency than non-buffered lead loads (this due to practically no pellet deformation during load start and bore travel), I selected the modified-choke tube which provides .020" muzzle constriction.

At 40 yards, Remington's 1¼-oz. charge of steel 4's averaged a fraction over 72 percent for 5 shots, while the No. 2 steel averaged close to 77 percent. Center density was markedly strong with both shot sizes, the 20" pattern cores averaging 1.65 times as many pellet hits as the 5" annular area. The 4's (236 pellets per load) handled early-season ducks nicely, giving clean kills as far out as 40 to 45 yards on the smaller species such as teal, widgeon, and gadwall.

The possibility of gun barrel damage is still very much a matter of concern among waterfowlers, particularly those who have yet to try steel-shot loads. Rest assured, those horror stories that continue to circulate really have no basis in fact. The firing of steel loads WILL NOT leave the bore looking as though it has straight rifling. So long as the steel charge is totally contained within the high-density plastic shot pouch, there is no chance of pellet contact with the bore. All factory loads measure up fully in this respect.

But what about damage in the choke area? This, it seems, is much more than a remote possibility; it's a distinct probability after firing many hundreds of rounds of steel-shot loads. Winchester looked into this matter very carefully a few years ago (the Nilo Study) and found it then required about 5,000 rounds to produce a clearly visible "expansion ring" of 0.0057" to 0.0065" on the barrel exterior near that point where the muzzle constriction begins. It should be noted, however, that roughly half of the total "bulge" occurred during the firing of only 500 rounds.

Lead shot, being almost putty-soft in comparison with steel, yields easily as it squeezes through the barrel's choke. With steel pellets, it's a situation where hard meets hard, and the resulting interaction is what produces the expansion ring. Theoretically, at least, the tighter the choke, the more severe the interaction becomes.

However, choke design may also be a factor. A very tight choke having a long, gradual taper may not be any more susceptible to damage than a moderate choke with a short, abrupt taper. And, as Winchester pointed out, the type of steel used in manufacturing the barrel, as well as the barrel wall thickness at the muzzle, will also have a bearing on the matter. This suggests that many older guns, those barreled with a milder steel than what has been used in recent years, are likely to be more vulnerable to choke expansion.

The one thing that everybody seems to agree on is that steel loads are a no-no in twin-tube guns. *(Remington has produced some 3200 over-unders as duck guns with beefed up choke sections to handle steel shot, but that's the only exception to Labisky's statement I can take: KW.)* Most doubles and over-unders, because of their relatively "thin" muzzles, are truly prime candidates for developing that much-talked-about expansion ring. Not only that, but there is also the possibility that the barrel-joining ribs may, in turn, let go and permit a separation of the two tubes at their muzzle end.

My personal rule is to confine the use of steel shot to pump guns and autoloaders of fairly recent manufacture, and to select a choke that's less aggressive than maximum constriction. I can easily live with a minor expansion ring in the choke area, but to bring ruination to a fine double gun would break me up. ●

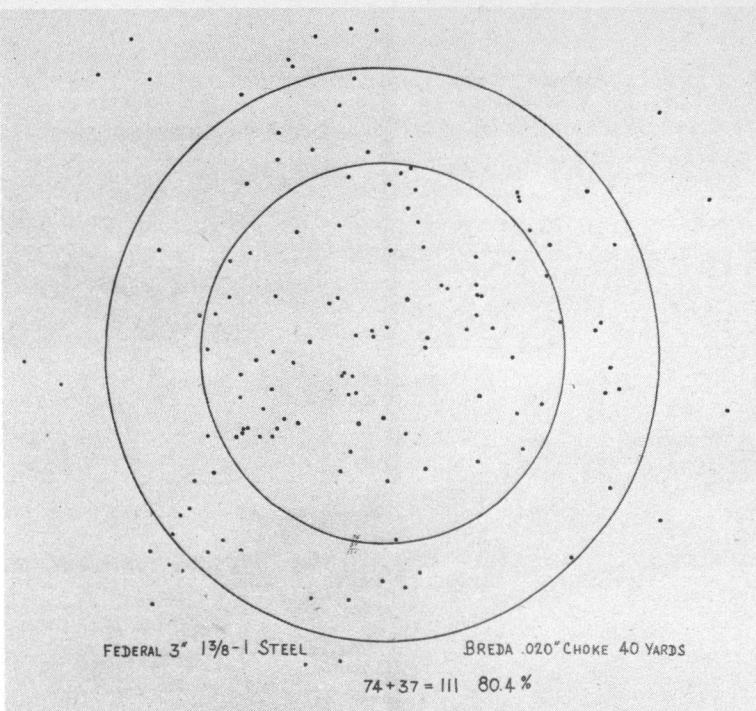

This pattern, which counted out to 80.4 percent, has twice as many pellet hits (74) in the 20" core as it does in the 5" annular ring (37). Dense cores seem to be pretty much the rule at 40 yards with both modified and full chokes, and with all sizes of steel shot.

HANDGUNS TODAY:
SIXGUNS AND OTHERS

by HAL SWIGGETT

Charter Arms Bulldog "Tracker" 357 Mag.

Burris 2x LER scope.

Charter Arms Undercover .38 SPL —2" Barrel, stainless steel.

Charter Arms Explorer II, 22 LR Pistol—8" barrel, black—Shur-Hold grips.

EACH YEAR there is a nagging thought in the back of my mind: "What's left for next year?"

Then comes next year and they show me.

This time they have shown a lot, even more than usual: new guns, new calibers in old guns, redesigned guns, custom guns, new and improved handgun scopes, better bullets, new and improved grips (or stocks, depending on whose they are) and improvements on ways to carry handguns. Not all can be listed, unfortunately. I hope you approve of my selection. I've tried to cover something for each type of shooting—and shooter.

In alphabetical order:

Burris Long Eye Relief Scopes

Don Burris has been in the scope manufacturing business a long time but only a few years under his own name. He toiled lots of years for one of the major scope makers, but then put his name on a complete line to which he's now added a couple of long eye relief (LER) scopes designed for lever action rifles, muzzle loaders and, of course, handguns.

The 2x weighs 6¾ ounces and is 8¾ inches long; the 3x weighs the same and is only ⅛-inch longer; they're designed to take the recoil of handguns as well as rifles. Burris also makes scope bases for the Virginian, Ruger Blackhawk and similar Rugers with adjustable rear sight, Thompson/Center Contender, Dan Wesson, Smith & Wesson handguns and the Winchester Model 94 lever action rifle.

Charter Arms

Still living up to their initial philosophy of offering well-made revolvers at down-to-earth prices Charter Arms has several new goodies this year. Foremost, possibly, is the Bulldog "Tracker" 357 Magnum. It's a 5-shot revolver sporting a 6-inch barrel that measures ¾-inch in diameter at the recessed muzzle. This heavier barrel shows up in the weight which hit 27.5 ounces on my postal scales.

The front sight is of ramp design. The back sight is all new, fully adjustable with a square notch, elevation reference lines and a definite click indication. Grips are hand checkered walnut in Charter's square butt design.

And it shoots. I ran only 150 rounds through my sample. One box each of Federal 110, 125 and 158 grain loads. My best groups were fired with Federal's 158-grain semi-wadcutter loads but then I sort of expected them to be. High performance ammo serves its intended purpose but calmer loads group better, at least in my hands.

This "Tracker" should be another winner for Charter Arms. Being a bit heavier than any other gun in their line it handles the potent 357 Magnum with a little less fuss, but it will never be mistaken for a full-sized magnum revolver, not when it goes off. Part of this comes from the extremely short grip. My hands are smaller than most, yet I still can't get a good solid hold on the tiny grip. To put it another way: one walnut tree must last Charter Arms a long, long time.

Also new in 1980 is a stainless steel Undercover 38 Special at 17 ounces. The 2-inch barrel doesn't take up much space in a pocket. Another new for the year is the stainless steel Pathfinder 22 LR. This one wears a 3-inch barrel and tips the scales at 20 ounces. Most stainless steel is very rust-resistant, so both of these little guns should prove popular. Peace officers and home protection for the 38 Special and outdoor oriented folks for the 22 LR—that's the market.

Just in case this one doesn't get mentioned in the autoloader coverage, Charter Arms now offers the Explorer II, semi-auto 22 LR 8-shot pistol. An off-shoot of the AR-7 Explorer, it will never win any beauty contests, and probably would never be allowed to enter, as a matter of fact. Resembling somewhat the ancient Mauser military pistol in all its ugliness, the Explorer II 22 LR is designed to sell inexpensively. It's much too large to ever be called a "Saturday Night Special" (whatever that is) because of the 8-inch barrel and will undoubtedly fill a need for the camper or weekend shooter wanting a "plinking" pistol.

Charter Arms Pathfinder .22 LR—3" barrel, stainless steel.

Colt Python with 8-inch barrel. Available in 357 Magnum and 38 Special.

Colt Trooper MK III.

Charter Arms adjustable rear sight has .140" notch, non-glare finish and ¼-turn elevation clicks.

Colt

The big news according to much of the firearms press is another two inches on the barrel of the Python. For silhouette shooters and hunters, they're appreciated, no doubt, but there are other and even greater accomplishments from this great firearms company.

First, the Python: The finest in the Colt line, this precision-made revolver leaves little to be desired in a handgun so far as workmanship and design are concerned. That extra barrel length does increase holding capabilities and that additional sight radius does aid in closer holding, especially for those longer shots in silhouette shooting and hunting. The 8-inch Python is in 357 Magnum, of course, and the usual 2½, 4 and 6-inch barrels are still available, and in blue or nickel plate finish.

The Trooper MK III is that "even greater accomplishment" referred to in the first paragraph. It, too, can now be had with an 8-inch barrel chambered for the 357 Magnum. Weighing in at 44½-ounces (8-inch barrel) as opposed to 48-ounces for the same length Python. For only 3½-ounces less weight, shooters can have Colt quality at a suggested list of $176.55 less money. The Python lists at $471.50 (blue, 8-inches) and the Trooper MK III at $294.95 (same finish, length). This is the "sleeper" in the Colt line in my opinion.

There is more. Not only is the Trooper MK III available in 8-inch barrels, it can now be obtained in 22 Long Rifle and 22 Winchester Magnum Rim Fire in all barrel lengths (4, 6 and 8-inches). And in blue or nickel plate finish.

I own and used to shoot constantly an Officers Model Match 22 WMRF. Only when I found out it was of somewhat rare extraction did I retire it to fondling only. It proved itself a jack rabbit handgun deluxe, so I'm looking forward to getting my hands on a 6-inch Trooper MK III which will match my retired gun in length and, hopefully, shooting capabilities. I see no reason why it won't. Many of us tend to

(Above and right) Swiggett found the 6-inch barreled Dan Wesson Model 22V—22 Long Rifle—very accurate and ideally suited to small game hunting.

5½-inch H&R Model 686.

belittle 22's and we are wrong. If only one gun could be owned we'd all find the 22 LR of the most all-round use. And don't ever think the 22 WMRF is not a killer for small game and varmints.

And now, the icing on the cake. Last year, on these pages, I suggested someone humor a bald-headed old handgunner by bringing out a good single action 44-40. I'm not so naive as to think I had anything to do with it but new for 1980 is the reintroduction of caliber 44-40 in the New Frontier Single Action Army.

This is the one with adjustable rear sight and the ramp front. The sixgun is available in 45 Colt with both 4¾ and 7½-inch barrels but in 44 Special and 44-40 in the 7½-inch length only.

Thank you, Colt!

Dan Wesson 22

And the name goes on. Dan Wesson went to his Maker November 24, 1978 but the revolver he invented will carry his name forever.

Known as the man who made interchangeable barrels on revolvers a practical thing, his Pistol Pac, a case with 2½, 4, 6 and 8-inch barrels for the same gun, soon became a popular item with handgunners. Then he added 10, 12 and 15-inch barrels for long range shooters, hunters and silhouette shooters to be specific. They, too, made a hit.

Collectors are going to have a ball, once Dan Wesson revolvers reach that stage, because he went through a continuing series of changes, none advertised particularly. As he could improve the revolver, he did it. Period.

Now there is a 22 Dan Wesson. If it looks big, it's because it is big. Made on the full 357 frame, the 22 weighs from four to seven ounces more than the bigger caliber because of the smaller bore. My test gun is the Model 22V with a 6-inch barrel and it's a shooter. The first six shots, with three witnesses, went into 2½-inches at 50 yards, off sand bags. The rangemaster was watching through a spotting scope. He said the first one was on the target so I elected to try for a group without changing the sights. The remainder of the cylinder was fired, six in all. The group was round, evenly spaced, and measured a conservative 2½-inches. This was with Federal Hi-Power maximum velocity long rifle ammunition, hunting stuff.

Haven't had a chance to try other brands or any of the "super" long rifle loads now available, but 200 rounds of the initial ammo haven't changed my mind that the 22 Dan Wesson is going to prove superbly accurate to all concerned.

It's a pleasure to shoot because of the weight which makes it easy to hold plus the wide trigger and serrated hammer spur designed for easy squeezing and cocking. Mine has a red insert in the front sight (standard), but both yellow and white are also available. The rear sight is click adjustable for both windage and elevation. The square notched blade is white outlined.

There are nine grip styles including an inletted walnut blank in case none of the other eight fit.

Still more—maybe not by the time you read this but in time for hunting seasons, there should be a 44 Dan Wesson. Unlike the 22 this one won't be with just a different sized hole. Completely redesigned, the 44 Magnum edition holds several new patents. It is planned for production with four interchangeable barrels of 4, 6, 8 and 10-inch lengths.

H&R Model 686

The second revolver I owned as a youngster growing up in Kansas was an H&R 999, purchased in 1935. I don't remember the price but it couldn't have been much or I wouldn't have been able to buy it. I was fourteen at the time. That gun stayed with me for two decades and I'm still sorry I traded it off. It was the basis for my first article sold as a gun writer in 1947—how I used it on my trap line.

Their catalog currently lists 22 (I think, but since it's more than I have fingers and toes I could be wrong) models. Most all are 22's with a few 32's thrown in. Several are new. The one singled out for this review is the Model 686 convertible 22/22 WMRF.

It has western styling with the loading gate and ejector rod, yet is modern double action. The front sight is H&R's new revolver ramp. The rear is called "Wind-Elv" and is fully adjustable for both windage and elevation to the tune of ¾-inch at 25 yards.

The frame, ejector rod housing and trigger show deep antique color casing; barrel, cylinder and trigger guard are blue. Other features include serrated hammer spur, wide target-type trigger, extended trigger guard and walnut finished grips.

Barrel lengths are 4½, 5½, 7½ and 12-inches. The 5½-inch length weighs 33 ounces loaded. Cartridge capacity is nine for the 22 LR cylinder and six in 22 WMRF.

Lawmen Leather

Big handguns are hard to carry in sizes used for hunting. Hip holsters are out of the question because of barrel length in most cases. I happen to like 6-inch barrels and these fit fine worn on the side. My problem is that only two of the guns I like for hunting have 6-inch barrels. The others vary from 7½-inches out to a foot long, a full 12-inches.

Shoulder holsters are the only way to go. There are several good makers on the market. I've used Bianchi and Safariland a good deal. In fact, three Bianchi shoulder rigs are in my stable at the moment along with one Safariland. All are good. It's a bit like Fords and Chevrolets. For one reason or another some like one—some like the other. And now there is a new one worthy of mention.

A young ex-cop from Chicago turns out a fine shoulder rig dubbed "Dirty Harry" from the movie of that same name. Originally designed for Clint Eastwood and the Model 29 S&W used in the movie, it has been increased in size, modified to use Jerry Ardolino's words (he's that ex-cop), so that 8⅜-inch barrels can now be accommodated.

I've been carrying one for more than a year switching back and forth between two guns. The Dan Wesson fitted with its 8-inch barrel and the Virginian with 7½-inch barrel. Aside from design features which are distinctly different from other lines, the "Dirty Harry" is cut out in the cylinder area to do away with some of the thickness caused by leather over that wider portion of the handgun.

Made from premium grade top-grain leather, the holsters are fully suede-lined. They are easily adjustable and very comfortable. I have mine on while typing this and have done so many times to remind myself of its ease of wearing. Some months back I was sitting here in the office with the "Dirty Harry" on and stuffed with the Virginian 44 Magnum when my wife phoned from the church (she's secretary) needing me there right away. Up and away I was getting out of my car when I realized the rig was still in place. Without a jacket on, it was too late then so I went on in and immediately took it off. Not too many shoulder holsters for big guns can be fitted out comfortably. Jerry Ardolino can be contacted at Lawmen Leather, P.O. Box 447, Katy, TX 77450.

Merrill Sportsman

Silhouette shooting has been a boon to this company as with other manufacturers of single shot pistols. Merrill has added three calibers of their own design to the line, all based on the 225 Winchester case and in 7mm, 6mm and 30 calibers, plus most conventional silhouette calibers. These are chambered in a 15-inch barrel to take full advantage of silhouette shooting rules. There is also a new 22 silhouette barrel, contoured to reduce weight since the legal limit is 54-ounces.

I've not shot one of the long barrels but have expended many hundreds of rounds through earlier 44 Magnum and 22 LR barrels and can testify to their accuracy. My 22 is topped with a Bushnell scope and will put most rifles through a severe test in matching its accuracy.

Standard length barrels are available and legal as Production guns for silhouette shooters competing in this category—and for hunting (R.P.M.—Rock Pistol Mfg., 704 E. Commonwealth, Fullerton, CA 92631).

Mossberg's Abilene

The 1980 GUN DIGEST, on these pages, listed the attributes of the Abilene single action revolver as

The "Dirty Harry" by Lawmen Leather.

Merrill 22 LR single shot pistol.

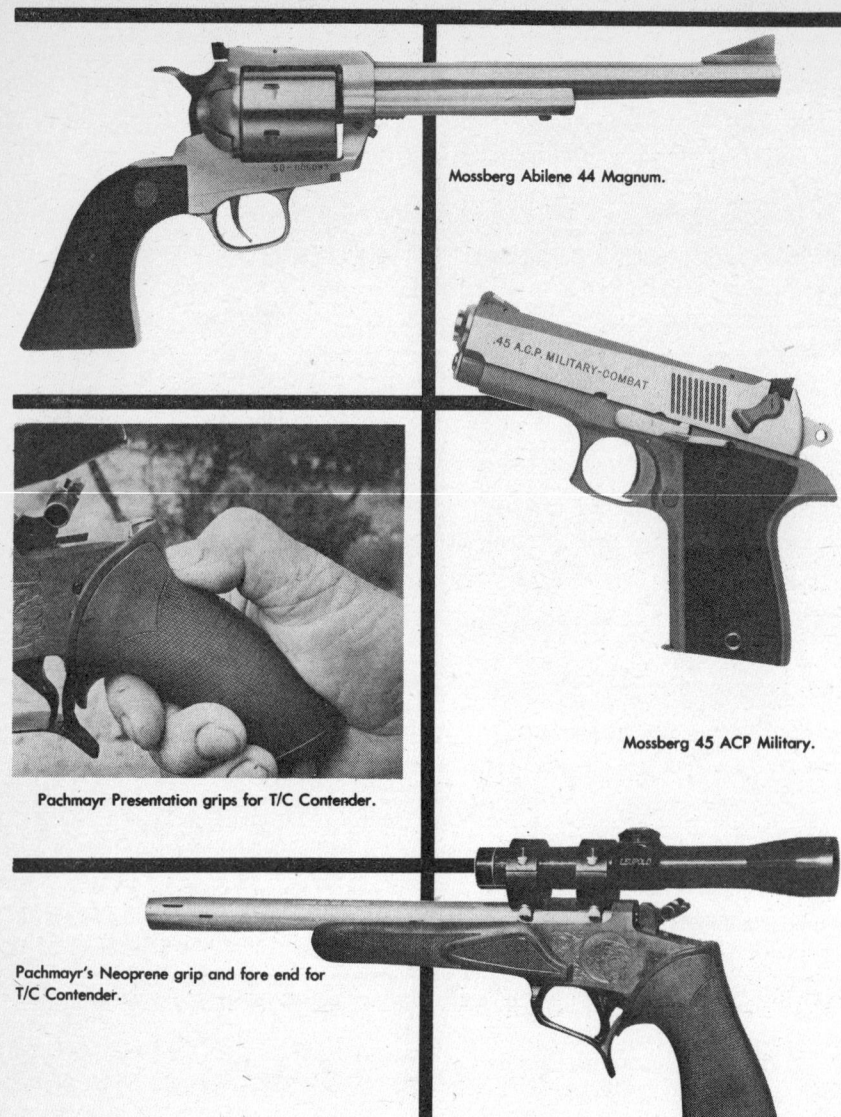

Mossberg Abilene 44 Magnum.

Mossberg 45 ACP Military.

Pachmayr Presentation grips for T/C Contender.

Pachmayr's Neoprene grip and fore end for T/C Contender.

manufactured by the United States Arms Corporation. At the time there was some discussion over the transfer bar in use on these single actions. There is a new owner and a new safety.

Mossberg, long famous for long guns, is in the handgun business since acquiring the U.S. Arms organization. The guns will be produced by U.S. Arms Division of A.I.G., Inc. and marketed exclusively by Mossberg.

Still called the transfer bar, the safety is unique and better described as the "Anvil" system. Its function is the same, however, in that it is safe to carry the new Abilene fully loaded, all six chambers, with the hammer down. There is no way it can be fired without the trigger being pulled to activate the Anvil and put it into position.

The Abilene retains old West tradition by permitting loading and unloading via the half-cock system.

Abilene single actions will be available in 357 Magnum, 44 Magnum and 45 Colt. Barrel lengths of 4⅝, 5½ and 6½-inches on 357's; 6½-inches on 45's and 7½, 8½ and 9-inches on the 44's. The handgun weighs 48 ounces in 44 Magnum with an 8½-inch barrel.

Sights are serrated ramp front and click adjustable rear. Both the hammer and trigger are wide target style and each is serrated. Grips are smooth walnut except the silhouette version wears target style walnut.

This is a well-made single action with a "name" company behind it. I would say the future looks good for the Abilene in all categories—hunting, plinking and silhouettes. Production is scheduled so the Abilene should be in dealers hands as you read this.

Following the single action by only a few months will be the PRO-38. A 5-shot 2, 3 or 4-inch barrel revolver for plain clothes or off-duty law enforcement use. Weighing in at 21 ounces with a 3-inch barrel the little five-shooter has a ⅛-inch serrated ramp front sight and the usual duty (fixed) rear. The finish is brushed satin stainless steel.

Hard on the heels of this little gun will be a 45 ACP Military—Combat autoloader. Read about it under coverage of self-loaders elsewhere in this GUN DIGEST.

Pachmayr Grips

It was a long time coming but now there is relief for Thompson/Center Contender shooters who favor those heavier calibers. Pachmayr Presentation grips are currently available for this bruiser of hands. The T/C's grip design offers no alternative other than to batter the hand that holds it, where big calibers are concerned. Many have tried, but this Los Angeles-based company came up with the answer.

Constructed of a special compound of Neoprene with a molded in light weight steel insert for stability, the grips are purely functional. Available for most double and single action guns as well as autoloaders, it's their newest that is of concern here.

Designed to take the hump off the back of the Contender there is also close to half an inch of cushion in the upper portion where it bears against the web of the hand. Like a recoil pad on a shotgun, it sure do work! I have one on a 30-30 T/C and another on a 45-70 (custom barrel) T/C.

Pachmayr is now offering, to match up the above, a forend for the Contender made of the same material. Though not made for looks, it doesn't look bad.

Redfield Pistol Scopes

Last year they gave us 1.5x and 2.5x handgun scopes. I prefer to call them by that designation because of my ingrown habit of separating pistols and revolvers even though Redfield refers to their product as Pistol Scopes. Autoloaders and single shots are pistols per my definition. Revolvers—self-explanatory. All are handguns. Sorry about that.

Through popular demand a 4x has been added to the Redfield line. The field of view is nine feet at 100 yards with eye relief of 12 to 22-inches. The 4x weighs one-half ounce more than the scopes of lesser magnification, has a slightly larger objective diameter (one-half inch) and is one-tenth inch shorter.

Listed as "magnum proof," Redfield officials describe this design as featuring two easily-adjustable, full radius ball sockets which fit the locking end of the erector tube and are in contact over a much larger bearing surface than any other system. Coupled with the well-known Redfield base featuring rotary dovetails for both front and back rings on which a recoil shoulder has been established. This takes the stress off mounting screws and absorbs it in metal-to-metal contact with the handgun.

Production models of these scopes on the Redfield recoil testing machine routinely withstand acceleration forces of over 1,000 g's more than 2,000 times without any change in point of impact.

I have long been a booster of scopes on handguns and through friendly heckling of Redfield's hierarchy maybe had a hand in the addition of handguns scopes to their line. My interest is solely in bullet placement. Handguns—true handguns and not the short rifles made popular by silhouette shooters—are short range firearms at best, so let's not kid ourselves in that respect. But let's do try to get our bullets in the proper spot especially when hunting game. Scopes can be a tremendous aid in this respect. I don't care who the shooter is or how good his eyes are.

Remington "XP-100"

Remington introduced the "XP-100" bolt action, single shot pistol and a new cartridge at the same time 17 years ago. Adjectives used in describing the handgun were "unique" and "innovative." The cartridge was designated the 221 'Fire Ball'. Unfortunately, neither made a big hit with the shooting public.

A bit on the order of Buck Rogers style, the gun was really only a shortened rifle as was borne out the following year when the Model 600 rifle was introduced. The nylon stock coupled with its contour didn't help any, but enough were sold to keep the XP-100 in the line.

Then came silhouette shooting. The first match, held in Tucson, was won by an XP-100 converted to a shortened 308. From then on it's been a downhill pull for the XP-100. In almost every instance, the gun has been converted to some other caliber. The 221 isn't exactly up to knocking over the heavy metal targets used in silhouette shooting, particularly rams at 200 meters. Calibers ranging from 6mm to 6.5, 7 and on up to the 30s have been chambered successfully in the XP-100 action.

Now, seventeen years after its introduction, Remington has the XP-100 Silhouette 7mm Bench Rest. Based on Remington's Bench Rest case, the 308

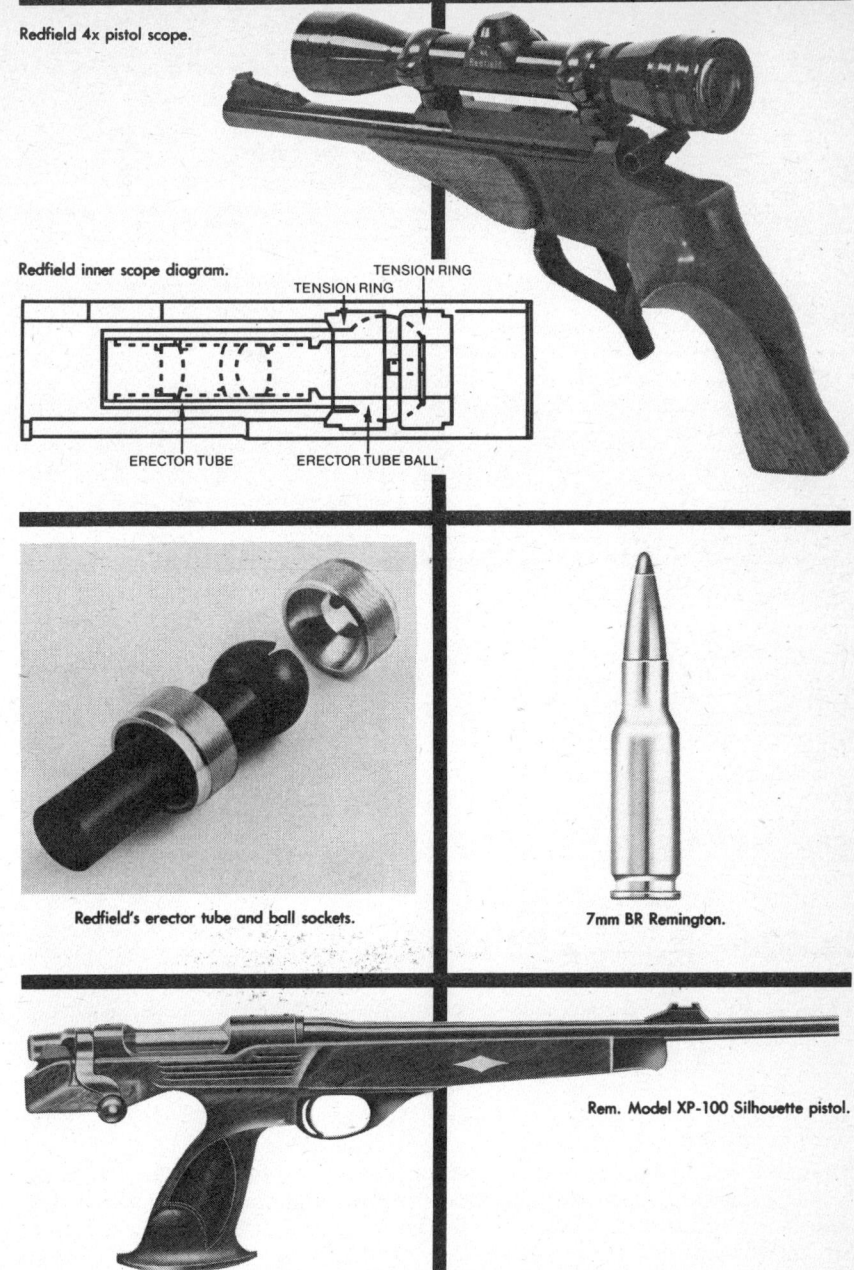

Redfield 4x pistol scope.

Redfield inner scope diagram.

Redfield's erector tube and ball sockets.

7mm BR Remington.

Rem. Model XP-100 Silhouette pistol.

drilled to accept small rifle primers and specially annealed for cutting off and forming, the 7mm BR is shortened to 1.520-inches, then necked down to 7mm.

At the moment there are no plans for factory brass. This is a handloaders handgun from the word "go." Cases are hard to make and that has to be done before the gun can be shot. Not really hard, I guess, but the task is a demanding one and time-consuming. Velocities of 2100 plus feet per second can be achieved with 140-grain bullets, which is enough oomph to knock over a ram at 200 meters.

The new silhouette version is fitted with 15 inches of barrel, the maximum allowed by silhouette shooting rules, and weighs in at a fraction under 4½-pounds to meet the weight limit. No sights are included. There is a front sight ramp and the receiver is drilled and tapped for any sight of the shooter's choice.

Then there is the icing on the cake: the XP-100 Silhouette is currently priced at $299.95, just a fraction of what custom silhouette guns cost. The unlimited class is now within reach of any shooter interested.

Ruger

The Redhawk, by Ruger, will one day be on dealers shelves. Touted by one and all for the past year or so, the

Ruger Redhawk DA 44 Magnum.

S&W 25-5 shot best groups with Federal 225-gr. load bullet.

S&W magnum belt buckle.

S&W Model 25-5 45 Colt.

big double action 44 Magnum has yet to be turned out on the production line. That it will be well received is a foregone conclusion. God willing, a few will be made available by fall but in nowhere near sufficient numbers to fill orders already in.

On the positive side this writer feels it's worth waiting for so don't cancel your order. Hang in there. Shooting a Redhawk, your own gun, once it's in hand will soon dispense with those frustrations brought on by the long wait.

In case some might not know, the Ruger Redhawk is 3¼-pounds of stainless steel double action 44 Magnum with 7½-inches of barrel and fully adjustable rear sight along with a colored insert (red or yellow) in the front sight. A blued chrome-molybdenum version with a 10-inch barrel is in the offing.

Of things for sure, the Ruger Super Blackhawk 44 Magnum, the big single-action, is available with a 10½-inch barrel. This seems oriented towards silhouette shooters though hunters will share at least an equal interest. Standard Super Blackhawk barrels are 7½-inches in length.

New from Ruger in their double action revolvers is the chambering of the 9mm autoloader cartridge. I'm not sure why, since it is even less potent than the proven inadequate 38 Special, but there must have been a need indicated or 9mm double action revolvers would not have been made available in both the Speed-Six and the Police Service-Six.

Smith & Wesson

Some things are inevitable. The S&W Model 25-5 proved to be one of them.

A few years back S&W came out with their Model 25 commemorative (celebrating their 125th anniversary). Gobbled up like ice cream at a kids party, they never really made the scene so far as the shooting public was concerned. And the reason wasn't really because of the word "commemorative." Caliber, I think, had the most to do with that popularity. Magic is still a factor when 45 Colt is mentioned. The Model 25, also known as Model 1955, had been singularly chambered for the 45 ACP cartridge up until that time.

Now all of us can own a S&W 45 Colt, reasonably priced. Why? Because that world-famous Springfield, Massachusetts firm is now producing the Model 25-5. If wondering what the Model 25-5 is, just think of it as a Model 29 (44 Magnum) with slightly bigger holes in the cylinder and barrel.

I own an ancient (in excellent condition) Triple Lock 44 Special that has been shot a good deal (by me). I also own, and shoot a good deal, a Model 1950 45 ACP that was recently rebarreled with the heavier Model 1955 barrel. It is a shootin' dude, along with assorted K-22s and K-38s, of course, plus my Model 29 44 Magnum. So I expected great things from my test Model 25-5 45 Colt.

Since the 45 Colt cartridge—and let me point out here that there is no such thing as 45 Long Colt, though some writers insist on that designation to set it off from the shorter 45 ACP cartridge—is an all-time favorite of mine, I had various and sundry loads on hand and Federal's great new 225-grain H.P. 45 Colt factory load. An hour after receiving the Model 25-5 it was at work.

All told, seven handloads consisting of three powders (H4227, AL-7 and Unique) and four bullets (185, 200 and 230 grain jacketed along with cast 454424s) were fired. My worst group, at 25 yards resting my wrists across sandbags, was five shots in 3½-inches. The best was 5-shots in 1½-inches and this feat was accomplished with the Federal factory 225-grain factory load. Most were consistent at 2 to 3 inches.

There was one problem. All of the loads, except one, printed from five to ten inches high with the back sight screwed down as tight as it would go. That one happened to be Hornady 185-grain jacketed hollow points loaded maybe hotter than they should have been with H4227. These put three 5-shot groups to the point of aim and averaged an even 2-inches.

From this limited experience I'd have to say handloaders have their work cut out for them in trying to equal the accuracy of Federal's factory load. Improving on it seems out of the

50 THE GUN DIGEST

question at the moment.

I'm looking forward to hunting with this gun and will probably be shooting a full charge of Unique under hardcast 454424s. This load has served well in several other 45 Colt guns so I see no reason to change now in spite of the better accuracy I got from the Federal load. Hunting game animals demands penetration. Penetration comes from heavy bullets *not* expanding. Bullets of almost a half-inch in diameter do not have to expand to kill cleanly. The sharp shoulder cuts clean. The weight (250-255 grains) gets it in deep. Animals are killed by getting a bullet in where they live.

Thank you, Smith & Wesson, for the Model 25-5 45 Colt.

More from S&W: A new belt buckle honoring the 357 Magnum. First tested in 1934, the 357 Magnum went on to make handgun history and lead the field in magnumitis. The new Magnum buckle is a dressy two-inch diameter for a 1½-inch belt. It is a replica of the rear view of an N-frame revolver cylinder loaded with S&W 357 Magnum cartridges, except that one is the distinctive S&W logo.

The copywrited design is die-struck in solid brass with a stainless steel-look finish.

SSK

Home of the "Big Boomers." I guess that is what SSK Industries (Rt. 1, Della Drive, Bloomingdale, OH 43910) could be called. They manufacture custom Thompson/Center Contender barrels with, and I quote them, "Power to effectively take very large game . . . ."

Available in calibers from 17 Remington to 50-70 much of SSKs emphasis is toward bores of 33 and larger. Necked down from a 444 Marlin case the 375 JDJ produces 2100 fps with 220-235-grain bullets and only 200 fps less with the heavier 270-300-grain bullets, J.D. Jones claims. I was privileged to fire one of these one time and since Mildred Swiggett didn't raise any idiots I quit while I was ahead.

Shooting with J.D. and his wife on the YO Ranch, Jones suggested I try a football sized rock, one I knew to be 225 yards since I was the guy who had placed it earlier for that purpose. Handing me the pistol J.D. said to hold up a specific amount of front sight. Shooting with two hands, I tried to do what I was told and hit the rock. Anyone who shoots again after an accident like that should have his head examined.

SSK's 338 CJMK is a necked down

Taurus bullets are coated with a dry film bonded lubricant designed to drastically reduce bore leading.

SSK's 14-inch barreled 45-70 produces craters in a lead block equal to those of a 308 180 grain factory load. The smaller holes are miscellaneous handgun hits.

Carol has no trouble at all handling this 375JDJ from SSK fitted with a Juenke brake.

Taurus Model 85 "The Protector" 38 Special.

35 Remington designed primarily for silhouette shooting. The 45-70 will safely produce 1500 fps with 400-grain bullets out of a 14-inch barrel. These custom barrels are straight bull configuration and can be had in any length up to 14-inches.

SSK also markets their own line of custom springs for T/C, Ruger, S&W and Colt along with custom dies for all their calibers.

Though these calibers might sound big for a pistol they really aren't all that hard to handle. I have been shooting a 45-70 for most of a year, both hunting and plinking, and have found it to be a real "fun" gun. Fitted with a 12-inch barrel and Mag-na-ported my

45-70 is probably only a little more punishing than the standard weight 44 Magnum with full loads.

Taurus Bullets

Coated with a dry film bonded lubricant Taurus bullets (The Alberts Corporation, P.O. Box 157, Franklin Lakes, NJ 07417) wear no grease grooves yet are said to drastically reduce bore leading. Since no additional lubing is required the chore of reloading is obviously both cleaner and faster.

I've shot several boxes of these bullets in my 45 Colt New Frontier and Ruger Blackhawk 45 Colt (250-grain SWC) along with an equal number in my Bob Day customized Mark IV 45

Steve Herrett's new standard (Target) stock for the Thompson/Center Contender. There is a long thumb rest on this right-hand model (on the other side). It's also available for left-hand shooters. There is a hunter version with only a slight thumb rest so it can be used in either hand.

T/C's new Recoil Proof 2.5 handgun scope.

Trapper Gun 44s-44-40 means what it says. Made from a New Model Ruger Blackhawk 357 Magnum this one has a 4-inch barrel and two cylinders. One for 44 Special and 44 Magnum and the other for the venerable old 44-40.

Virginian Dragoon 45 Colt with 7½-inch barrel.

autoloader (both 200- and 210-grain SWC) without any signs of leading. Neither was any leading encountered with my 44 Special loads (230-grain SWC-HP) fired in a Triple Lock. I have not tried any in 44 Magnum as I do not believe in lead bullets in this caliber.

None of my loads, by the way, are souped up as my life-long policy has been jacketed bullets for hot loads. Sensibly loaded, I do not believe anyone will have problems with these Taurus bullets. They are dry, round, and show practically no variation in weight: a pleasure to work with. They are available in six calibers and 16 weights or designs along with two conicals for black powder pistols.

Taurus "Protector"

Made in Brazil Taurus handguns are imported by International Distributors. Their new one is a cute little 5-shot, 3-inch barrel 38 Special. Designated Model 85 the name of record at the moment is "The Protector." There is a ramp front sight and the usual notch to line it up through.

The revolver is all steel, drop forged, and the cylinder is of 4140. With the small service grips the little revolver tips the scales at slightly over 21 ounces.

Thompson/Center

A new caliber, one dropped, an improved stock design and surging full-steam-ahead with their "Recoil Proof" handgun scopes is the story from Thompson/Center. Caliber 223 has been added in both 10 and 14-inch barrels. Velocity from the short edition is listed at 2,640 fps and at 2,849 fps from the longer tube. Two others not really so new but maybe you didn't know: Both 41 Magnum and 45 Winchester Magnum are also available in both 10 and 14-inch barrels. This makes a total of 19 calibers available in one form or another of the Contender.

The fine little 5mm Remington RFM has been dropped.

Contender stocks have long been noted for being hard on the hand. Various overtures have been made towards correction over the years and it would appear this is the best. Steve Herrett, stockmaker deluxe from Twin Falls, Idaho was the man behind this change and it looks mighty good. Available in both hunting and target format the new shape is considerably easier on the shooting hand. The foreend has been design-changed to go along with the "new look." Downright handsome is as good a way to describe it as any.

The Contender standard, or target, grip has a long flowing thumb rest and can be had for both right- or left-hand shooters. The "Hunter" is similar to the standard except that the thumb rest is more suggestive than real and the single model is for either right- or left-hand use. Both models are finger-grooved for aid in handling recoil.

T/C still lists their line of Lobo handgun scopes in 1½x and 3x but now they have a new one called "Recoil Proof." This is a rugged design in both 1.5 and 2.5 magnification. Before they purchased exclusive rights to market these long eye relief scopes Thompson/Center subjected them to extensive and punishing abuse. The design held up and it now wears the name of Thompson/Center.

Practical eye relief is 11 to 20 inches. Field of view is 28 feet at 100 yards for the 1.5 and 15 feet for the 2.5. Each offers 60 inches of maximum adjustment in either direction for both windage and elevation. Tube diameter is 1-inch. The 2.5 is offered only with the rail mount for use on standard T/C scope mounts. The 1.5 is to be used with conventional mounts made for the Contender by B-Square, Buehler, Conetrol, Leupold and Redfield.

The 1.5 can be had with either standard or target turrets. It weighs 5.1 ounces in the standard version and 6.0 ounces a la target. The 2.5 weighs in at 6.5 ounces.

And the punch line is revealed on their literature in red letters. Each Thompson/Center "Recoil Proof" scope is sold with a Lifetime Warranty.

Trapper Gun

Already referred to under Colt but last year, in talking about single action revolvers on these pages I said, and I quote, "Both 44s and 45s are lifelong favorites but if I had to choose between them, the 45 would win out, unless someone wants to humor an old bald-headed handgunner and bring back the 44-40 in a top quality handgun." Colt has done that but Trapper Alexiou beat them by several months, except that his is custom made and not so generally available.

Only a couple of months after the 34th Anniversary GUN DIGEST (1980) was published I received a box via UPS. In it was a sixgun, a beautiful sixgun. The ejector rod housing, trigger guard and backstrap are satin nickel. The hammer and trigger are engine-turned. Grips are stag and there is a red insert in the front sight. The barrel, cylinder and frame are blue. A thing of beauty for sure. Engraved on the left side of the barrel is "Trapper Gun 44-40." "Trail Blazer" is engraved on the flat of the top strap. The 4⅝-inch barrel makes it total perfection so far as I'm concerned.

Made up on a 357 Magnum New Model Ruger Blackhawk, Trapper (Trapper Gun, Inc., 28019 Harper, St. Clair Shores, MI 48081) removed the barrel and replaced it with a Douglas .429" barrel which conforms with the old guns which varied from .425" to .429". He used the original Ruger 357 cylinder and bored it out to accept the 44-40 case. And it shoots like it looks.

I've had a ball with it and have shot more lead bullets during these few months than I've shot in the past three decades. One of my idiosyncrasies is jacketed bullets since I'm not a great fan of loading down. But to enjoy the 44-40 one must load true 44-40 velocities which means lead bullets can be used freely. I'd forgotten, in fact, just how much fun they can be.

Two or three months after the first gun arrived another box was delivered. This one contained a 4-inch single action emblazoned, on the top strap, "Trail Boss." On the left side it read: "Trapper Gun 44s-44-40." A convertible it is and there was an extra cylinder in a little red bag. It shoots 44 Special and 44 Magnum in one cylinder and 44-40 in the other. Mighty cute it was, built on the Ruger 357 New Model Blackhawk, but I'm here to tell you no one had to be consulted as to whether or not the gun went off when stuffed with factory 240-grain ammo. When that hammer fell, things happened.

Factory loads in 44 Special and 44-40 were fine as were similar handloads but 4 inches of barrel is a mite short for full 44 Magnums, especially in such a light gun. Anyway, if you are interested in a well-made 44 Special or 44-40, Trapper can do a first class job on your Ruger or his.

Virginian

We talked about it on these pages last year. A delay was encountered but now it is available: Interarms Virginian 45 Colt.

Interarms had a fire. A big fire. It leveled the plant where the Virginian was made. Insurance people told them they would be out of business a long time before the mess could be cleaned up and a new plant built. One of the executives talked it over with employees. All were anxious to help. In a few short months the place was not only cleaned up but a new facility was on the spot and work again underway. The American way had again prevailed over bureaucracy. All it took was the willingness to work.

Of traditional single action design, basically, the Virginian is bigger than the Colt and feels bigger than the Ruger though it weighs in about the same.

The Virginian is traditional single action as there is no transfer bar and loading is accomplished by the half-cock system. There is a safety, however, though not of much practical use as I see it. Called "Swissafe" it features a lengthy cylinder pin which can be inserted to the degree it stops the hammer from hitting the floating firing pin.

The safest way to carry the Virginian is the time-honored "leave one empty under the hammer" method. And the Virginian is set up for this by a couple of marks on the cylinder alongside one of the chambers and so spaced that they can be seen on either side of the top strap. Leave this one empty and it's easy to find without looking down the dangerous end of the barrel.

Never intended to be a magnum, nevertheless the 45 Colt cartridge loaded fully in a gun built to stand such goings on can be a hunting handgun to be reckoned with. Frankly, it will do anything a 44 magnum will do so far as killing game is concerned and probably on a silhouette range. The trajectory maybe a bit loftier but of no real consequence to a real 45 Colt fan.

Barrel lengths of standard dimensions are available. And so is stainless steel. Now. In all calibers currently available.

Weatherby

Long famous for high quality rifles, Weatherby was quick to jump into handgun silhouette shooting since one of their actions needed only a handgun stock and a shorter barrel.

Developed from the Mark V Varmintmaster action, the Weatherby Mark V Silhouette Pistol is a single shot chambered in 308 Winchester for silhouette shooters and 22-250 for varmint hunters. The action features six precision locking lugs and a recessed bolt face which totally encloses the cartridge case head. The bolt body is fluted and has three gas escape ports for accidental flowback of gases.

As in the Mark V rifle, the 15-inch barrel is chrome moly steel and "hammerforged" so there are no reaming or rifling marks. Although it is necessary to remove the stock for access, the trigger is fully adjustable for creep, slack and weight of pull.

Sights are set at the 15-inch radius allowable in silhouette shooting and consist of a target-type rear peep and a front globe with inserts. The action is drilled and tapped for standard Varmintmaster scope mounts.

The thumbhole stock is of Claro walnut, hand selected, and fitted with the traditional Weatherby rosewood fore-end tip and pistol grip cap and finished the same as all Weatherby firearms.

Wichita

A top contender in the field of accuracy, Wichita Engineering & Supply, Inc. (333 Lulu, Wichita, KS 67211) turned their rifle-making skills towards the silhouette shooter when that sport grew worthy of note.

New to their line this year is the "Classic." It wears an 11¼-inch octagon barrel (other lengths optional) of chrome-moly material and finished in non-glare blue. The sights are Micro Open. The receiver can be drilled and tapped for scope mount on special order.

The bolt is of three-lug design, engine-turned, and with three gas escape ports.

Exhibition grade American black walnut checkered 20 lines to the inch is used for the stock (other woods available on special order). The trigger is of their design and fully adjustable. Calibers up to and including .308 Winchester can be had in this left-hand bolt single shot pistol.

The "Classic" is delivered in a fitted wooden case. Prices are on request.

Like I said, what's left for next year?

HANDGUNS TODAY: AUTOLOADERS

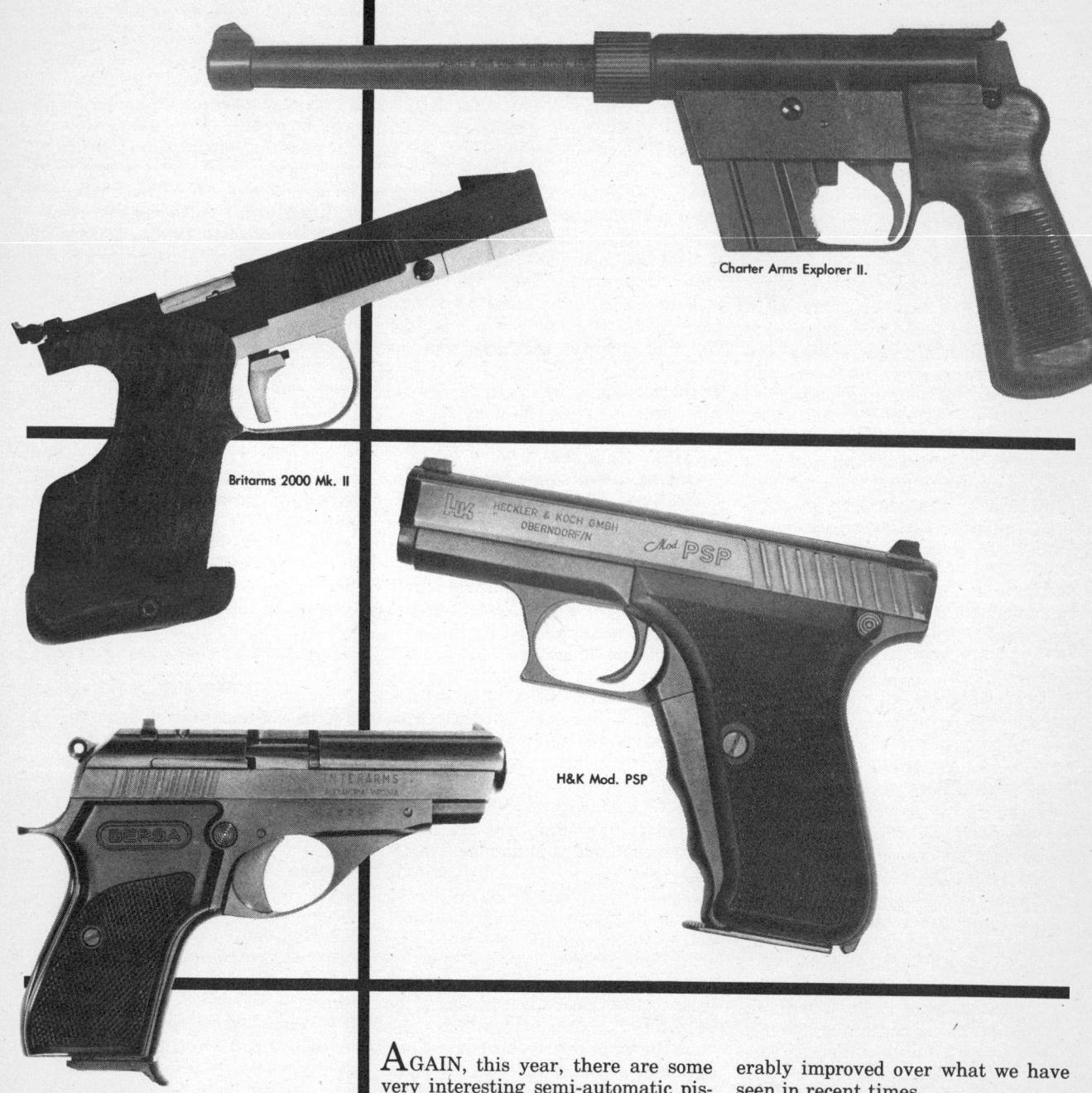

Charter Arms Explorer II.

Britarms 2000 Mk. II

H&K Mod. PSP

Bersa Model M644 22LR

AGAIN, this year, there are some very interesting semi-automatic pistols appearing in the market place. Apparently there is no end to the ingenuity of arms designers and manufacturers. Older designs are up-dated to improve accuracy and reliability, and new models have been introduced to take full advantage of modern materials and manufacturing methods. Emphasis seems to be once again on quality. The degree of precision and class of finish appear to be considerably improved over what we have seen in recent times.

If there is any sort of trend in semi-auto design, it follows the line of more exotic locking systems, such as are found in the use of gas pressure in the Heckler & Koch P7 and the Wildey systems, and in the adaptation of double action mechanisms to auto pistol design.

As semi-automatic pistols are engineered to fire ever more powerful cartridges, the utilization of gas-

by RALPH C. GLAZE

action unlocking systems is a natural choice of the arms designer. It is most probable that we will see others join the Wildey and the P7 in adopting some form of gas operated actions in the future. An exception to the use of gas actuation in very powerful autos is found in a large pistol under development by Coonan Arms of 570 S. Fairview, St. Paul, MN. The Coonan uses a Browning-type falling block locking system, and in fact closely resembles a Colt Model 1911. The difference lies mainly in the caliber for which it is chambered—the 357 Magnum. The author has not been able to test this hand cannon, but in handling it at the SHOT show was most impressed. This is a development that will bear watching.

A large proportion of pistol experts quite vehemently deplore the use of double action triggers, but we continue to see more of these devices on the market. There must be someone out there who likes them. It must be admitted there is some speed advantage in getting off a first shot with a double action auto—at least, in the hands of most shooters. That may explain the whole thinking.

Most of the new model semi-autos use modern, high strength steels to increase longevity and reliability. There is also a continuing tendency for arms makers to offer auto pistols made of stainless steel.

The 9mmx19 (9mm Luger or Parabellum) continues to be the most popular caliber, although the 45 ACP gets its share of attention, too. With the growth of the sport of silhouette shooting, we should see more powerful cartridges adapted to auto pistols. The Wildey, chambered for the mighty 45 Winchester Magnum, and the 9mm Winchester Magnum may be the first of many super calibers to come.

After a few fits and starts over the last several years, an increasing number of police departments are becoming interested in the adoption of auto pistols as their standard service arm. It is obvious that several manufacturers had the police, or military, in mind when preparing their most recent designs for production. Whether the auto will ever replace the revolver as a primary police sidearm is problematical. The revolver is too well entrenched, and has too many advantages to be cast aside by one and all. Nevertheless, automatics are gaining adherents in the police ranks, and it is almost a sure thing that we will be seeing more autos in everyday service.

A run-down of the most outstanding of the new semi-automatics follows. Most of these have been test fired by the author except where noted otherwise. The descriptions are presented as product reviews, and not necessarily as personal recommendations.

Britarms 2000 MkII

Innovative designs in high quality target pistols appear only rarely on the scene. There is not a mass market for handguns in this category, which is a shame. If more shooters had the opportunity to fire some of the world's truly great target pistols, there would surely be an increased demand for them in spite of their much higher cost. The results in terms of accuracy and satisfaction far outweigh the additional money involved.

The newest of the standard 22 rimfire semi-auto target pistols is made in England by Britarms, a small but progressive company dedicated to producing only the best in basic design and quality. The Britarms 2000 Mk II proudly joins the ranks of such famous makes as Hammerli, Walther, and Unique with no apologies to any of them.

The new model takes many of the better design points of older, established handguns, adds a few of its own, and comes out as what must stand as the very best target 22 auto made anywhere in the world today.

Steel is used for all parts of the Britarms pistol. The frame and trigger are satin chrome finished, while the rest of the pistol is conventional blue, which makes quite an attractive looking package. The grip is of the anatomic style, made by Wilhelm Hofman of Germany, who is one of the world's leading stockmakers. An adjustable palm rest assures a proper fit for a wide assortment of hand sizes.

The centerline of the bore lies as low above the shooting hand as is possible, resulting in minimum barrel bounce during recoil—a factor that contributes greatly to the overall stability and accuracy of the pistol. The action is simple blow-back, as is typical of all 22 autos.

Perhaps the most outstanding feature of the Britarms is the trigger action. The trigger itself is shaped so that the finger of the shooting hand lies in a natural position, and not against the side of the trigger. The trigger is adjustable for take-up, weight, sear engagement, and overtravel. In addition, the trigger may be moved fore and aft to accommodate larger or smaller hands. Let-off is crisp and clean, with virtually no movement during hammer fall. For anyone who is accustomed to the triggers generally found on production 22 autos, the trigger action of the Britarms will come as a true revelation of the gunmakers art. The trigger and hammer, together with all necessary springs, etc., are contained in a single unit that is readily removable from the frame for any required service or adjustment.

Takedown of the Britarms is accomplished by means of a single lever on the left side of the frame just ahead of the trigger guard. A flip of this lever allows the barrel to come off its dovetail attachment to the frame. Both the bolt and bolt cover may then be lifted off. Thorough cleaning of all parts is easily and quickly done.

Sights are Patridge type, with a very wide rear blade that is fully adjustable for windage and elevation. Each click of the rear sight moves the point of impact 5mm at 25 meters.

Barrel length is 6 inches, and overall weight is a bit short of three pounds. All dimensions comply with ISU regulations, and the pistol is legal for both NRA and ISU competitive events.

The Britarms magazine holds 5 rounds, and is similar to the magazine used on the Domino pistol in that it loads into the frame from the top when the bolt is held in the most rearward position. This sort of magazine placement makes for a small frame beneath the grip, allowing for any reasonable modification to the grip shape that may be required by the shooter to assure maximum comfort.

With its great weight and low boreline, the Britarms 2000 Mk II is as near to being recoilless as any usable 22 can be. The Britarms is chambered for the 22 Long Rifle cartridge, of course, and should not be confused with ISU rapid-fire guns that use the 22 Short.

Although admittedly expensive at $995.00, the Britarms 2000 Mk II represents an excellent value for a highly sophisticated, beautifully made target handgun. At the time this article was written, no distributor had been appointed for the United States, but information may be obtained from the manufacturer, Britarms, Ltd., Unit 1, Raban's Close, Raban's Lane Industrial Estate, Aylesbury, Bucks., England.

Charter Arms Explorer II

Charter Arms to date has offered only revolvers, but now produces a 22 caliber semi-automatic handgun. Known as the Explorer II, the new pistol is based on an action derived from the action of the AR-7 Explorer rifle.

right side of the receiver. A trigger blocking safety is located at the right rear of the receiver at the top of the grip.

Made from light alloy, the Explorer II is remarkably light for its size, tipping the scales at only 28 ounces. The standard version has an 8-inch barrel and an over-all length of 15½ inches, although 6-inch and 10-inch barrels are available as optional accessories. Barrels may be interchanged quite readily by means of a knurled nut that surrounds the barrel and screws onto the receiver.

The grip is of simulated walnut, in a design that the manufacturer calls the Shur-hold style. It is quite comfort-

The Explorer II is finished in black heat-cured enamel. Some shooters object in principle to firearms finished with paint, but it is a most practical method that offers better protection in many cases than a more traditional blued surface. In any event, the Explorer II has a pleasing appearance.

Accessories available for the Explorer II include a scope mount and long eye-relief scope, extra magazines, and a fitted black vinyl carrying case. Each pistol is covered by the Charter Arms one year full warranty.

Current list price for the Explorer II is $90.00, which is certainly a reasonable figure. For trail use, informal plinking target practice, or as a sur-

Wildey Auto Pistol
Smith & Wesson Model 439
Smith & Wesson Model 459

The AR-7 is the civilian version of the renowned AR-5 U.S. Air Force survival rifle. The AR-7 was originally designed and produced by Armalite, but it has been made by Charter Arms for some time. I have felt for many years that this neat lightweight action could be made into a practical handgun for hunters and backpackers. It is most gratifying to see that this has now been done.

The action of the Explorer II is a simple floating-bolt, blow-back type, fed from an 8-round detachable magazine located just ahead of the trigger guard. The bolt may be operated by a small handle that protrudes from the

able, and features a space within the grip for storage of an extra magazine. Magazines are fully interchangeable with those of the AR-7 rifle, making a combination of the two a very workable proposition.

Though the Explorer II is by no means a target pistol, accuracy is quite good—due in large part to sights that are somewhat better than might be expected in a handgun of this type. The front sight is mounted on a band around the muzzle and is both sturdy and relatively snag-free. The rear sight is adjustable and rugged enough to maintain settings under rough field conditions.

vival arm, the Explorer II is plenty good enough to warrant serious consideration.

Heckler & Koch P7

Heckler and Koch's P7, formerly known as the PSP (Police Self-loading Pistol) and originally developed for the West German police, is now beginning to reach these shores. The P7 is certainly one of the most advanced designs that has appeared in many years, and its unique features deserve a bit of explanation.

The action of the P7 must be described as a delayed blowback type, but the delay is more positive in action than usual. A small vent in the barrel immediately in front of the chamber allows high pressure gas to flow into a cylinder beneath the barrel, holding the slide closed. After the bullet has left the muzzle, and pressure has been considerably reduced, the slide can move to the rear. There is no complicated locking mechanism, and the barrel is stationary for added reliability and accuracy. The locking system is simple, positive, and compact.

Instead of a double action trigger, with all the faults of such a design, the P7 has a squeeze-cocker built into the front strap of the frame. The normal action of grasping the pistol depresses the squeeze cocker, which automatically cocks the striker-type firing pin. No conscious effort is required to hold the cocker in the shooting position—the ordinary pressure of the fingers is sufficient. As soon as the pistol is released, the cocker snaps forward and uncocks the firing pin. If the pistol is dropped, it is uncocked and safe before it hits the ground. After the last round is fired, the slide stays back. When a fresh magazine is inserted, a squeeze of the cocking lever lets the slide snap forward, loading a live round at the same time that the firing pin is cocked. Since there is no slide release on the side of the slide or frame, the P7 may be handled with equal ease by either right- or left-handed shooters. When the P7 is cocked, the tail of the firing pin protrudes from the rear of the slide, giving positive visual and tactile indication that the pistol is ready to fire. The P7 has no manual safety—the squeeze cocking device is all the safety required.

The grip angle is a more or less conventional 110 degrees but the magazine is almost vertical, which reduces the angle at which a cartridge is fed into the chamber. This feature makes it possible to feed all types of ammunition from hollow point to armor piercing with virtually no chance of malfunction. The P7 has a hardened steel slide and receiver, and the barrel is hammer forged with polygonal rifling. While polygonal rifling looks rather strange, it works very well indeed, giving an added bonus of slightly higher velocity than conventional rifling.

The P7 is smaller than most 9mm pistols, being just 6½ inches long and 5 inches high. The P7 weighs about 35 ounces, which is enough weight to insure good stability and recoil absorption.

The H&K P7 is beautifully made and superbly engineered. It should be an excellent choice as a police or defensive handgun. The more the P7 is handled, the more impressive it becomes.

In addition to this new pistol, the Heckler & Koch P9S in 45 ACP continues to find favor among pistol experts all over the world. This very fine handgun has been, or is being, accepted by many police departments in this country. The P9S is available in 9mm Luger caliber, of course, but it is the 45-caliber version that has aroused the most interest in the United States.

Interarms P5 and Bersa

New from Interarms this year is the Walther P5, a compact, light weight (28 ounces) 8-shot semi-auto in 9mm Luger caliber. The P5 was designed to meet the criteria stipulated by the West German military and police. It is in the same general category as the Heckler & Koch P7, but is differently engineered.

The P5 utilizes the time-tested P38 double action trigger mechanism, but otherwise bears only a vague resemblance to the venerable Walther design. It has a solid slide with side ejection port, similar in appearance to a conventional Browning pistol. Finish is satin black, with plastic grip plates. Workmanship is typically Walther, excellent in every way. It is reviewed in detail elsewhere in this issue.

Interarms has also introduced the PPK/S in stainless steel. The PPK/S is still offered in the good old-fashioned blue finish as well. Now known as the Walther American PPK/S, these fine little pistols are now made entirely in this country, not only for domestic sale, but for export to the rest of the world as well. There is no discernible difference in appearance or quality between the American and German versions of the PPK/S except for the barrel rib—there is a minor variation in the checkering that will allow the knowledgeable to spot the American model at a glance.

The best news about the PPK/S American is that the price is well under $300.00, little more than half the cost of its German counterpart. This tells us more than we probably want to know about what has happened to the value of the once mighty American dollar in world trade.

The PPK/S is chambered only for the 380 ACP at this time. Demand for the more anemic 32 ACP has fallen off to the point where it is no longer practical to manufacture pistols in this caliber, especially when Interarms can sell all the 380s they are able to produce.

One of the more interesting semi-autos imported by Interarms is the Bersa. This well made little pistol, in 22 Long Rifle caliber, is made in Argentina. Designated the Model 644, the Bersa has very clean lines, somewhat reminiscent of the Mauser HSc. It is a single action, blowback design, with molded plastic thumbrest grips, a button-release magazine, and three distinct safeties. There is a magazine safety, a firing pin safety, and a hammer safety. Sights are fixed, but windage adjustment may be effected by drifting the rear sight to one side or the other.

The Bersa has a 3½-inch barrel, is 6½ inches long over-all, and is 4¼ inches high. Weight is 27 ounces, which makes it a medium sized auto. Although the Bersa hardly qualifies as a defense handgun, it would make an excellent belt gun for the hunter, fisherman or backpacker. The current list price of $175.00 for the Bersa is entirely reasonable for a pistol of this quality.

S&W Models 439 and 459

Smith & Wesson has incorporated a number of long-needed changes into the basic Model 39 and Model 59 designs. The modifications are so extensive that the manufacturer has elected to rename these popular semi-autos so as to eliminate any confusion that might arise due to identification with the old model numbers. Henceforth, the Model 39 will be known as the Model 439, and the Model 59 becomes the Model 459.

In general outward appearance the new pistols are quite similar to the originals, but the later versions are readily identifiable by the new rear sight, which has "wings" that protect it from being accidentally jolted out of alignment through rough handling. The sight blade features a large square notch and is fully micrometer click adjustable for both windage and elevation. The sight mechanism and protective wings are parts of a rugged casting, making the new sight far better and more stable than the one on the older models. Some shooters think the large winged sight adds a racy appearance to the pistol, while others think it somewhat clumsy-looking. Regardless, the new sight is indeed strong, dependable, and accurate.

Internally, there is a new firing pin lock, actuated by the trigger, that locks the inertial firing pin regardless of the position of the manual safety. The lock will release only when the trigger is pulled to the nearly full back position. As the trigger approaches the limit of its rearward travel, positive action of the trigger lifts a plunger from its locking recess in the firing pin, releasing the firing pin just before the sear is disengaged.

There is a second firing pin lock that functions in the same manner as in the earlier pistols. When the manual safety is rotated to the "on" position, a block of steel shields the firing pin from the hammer. At the same time, the safety engages a notch in the firing pin that locks the pin in place. The function of the hammer is not affected. The manual safety has been improved by the use of a high-strength alloy casting.

Extractors on both the 439 and 459 have been modified so that they exert a direct, in-line force that results in a more positive grip on the cartridge case rim than the older simple lever design. The new pistols should not suffer from extraction or ejection problems.

For better or worse, a magazine safety is provided that prevents functioning of the hammer and trigger unless a magazine is inserted into the pistol.

Magazine capacity is eight rounds for the 439, and 14 rounds for the 459. Both pistols are available only in 9mm Parabellum caliber. Two magazines are furnished with each new pistol.

Barrel length of both models is four inches, overall length 7⁷⁄₁₆ inches, with a sight radius of 5¾ inches. The 439 weighs 27 ounces, empty, and the 459 is only a bit heftier at 28 ounces.

The Model 439 comes with checkered and monogrammed walnut grips, while the 459 has high-impact molded Nylon grip plates.

Firing impressions are much the same as with the Models 39 and 59, with the exception of the improved sight picture. The protective wings, or ears, on the rear sight seem to make it easier to center the ⅛-inch wide ramp front sight in the rear sight notch, which could speed up the aiming process in an emergency situation. No malfunctions were noted in firing a variety of ammunition through these pistols, although it was not possible to conduct a full field test. Workmanship seems to be a bit better than has been the case in the immediate past. It is hoped that reliability has been equally improved.

Although both models will not be generally available until later in the year, the announced prices are $286.00 for the 439, and $342.00 for the 459. These prices are for blue finish. Nickel finish is optional at about $25.00 additonal. Both pistols are of good quality, and are good buys for the money in today's wildly inflated market. The firepower of the Model 459, with its 14-round magazine will appeal to many shooters, as did the Model 59 of old.

Wildey Gas-action Semi-auto

Since its introduction a couple of years ago, the Wildey gas-operated semi-automatic pistol has received copious publicity, but to date no pistols have appeared on the general market. That is too bad, because the Wildey was a very good handgun. The past tense is used intentionally here, for the reason that the Wildey has been extensively re-designed to make it even better before placing it into full production.

The Wildey design utilizes a rotating bolt with locking lugs much like a bolt action rifle. In fact, the Wildey action is as strong as the actions on numerous rifles. It has to be to withstand the pressures generated by the Winchester Magnum cartridges for which it is chambered. Machining an action of this type involved a great degree of high precision that led to some difficulties when applied to volume production. It soon became obvious to Wildey Moore, the father of this unusual handgun, that changes would have to be made.

The design was altered to a considerable extend in order to facilitate ease of manufacture and, in the process, an even better-functioning pistol emerged. It is for this reason that the Wildey must be considered as a new handgun, even though the basic design has been around for a while.

The Wildey pistol is a gas-operated semi-automatic pistol. A cylinder surrounds the barrel just ahead of the receiver. An annular piston takes up the space between barrel and cylinder. Gas is vented from the barrel at a point immediately in front of the chamber. Upon firing, a small quantity of propulsive gas, under very high pressure, pushes against the operating piston to move the bolt into the unlocked position, allowing the action to continue to open under the pressure of residual barrel gases. A strong recoil spring then comes into play to return the bolt to battery. As the action opens, of course, the fired case is ejected; upon closing, a fresh round is picked up from the magazine and loaded into the chamber. This system works quite well. The vents and cylinder are more or less self-cleaning. In firing the prototype for several hundred rounds, the author found no problem with fouling of the gas system. Incidentally, the power of the operating piston may be varied to match the action to different loads by simply turning the outside cylinder sleeve to alter the timing of the piston stroke.

The trigger mechanism of the Wildey pistol is double action for the first shot, and single action after that. There is an outside hammer, making it possible to cock the pistol for the first shot if the shooter does not choose to use the double action mode. The firing pin is of the rebounding type that is not locked by the safety. The safety is a hammer blocking unit that effectively insulates the hammer from the firing pin when it is engaged. Stainless steel is used throughout the Wildey pistol.

There will be a choice of two superb cartridges, the Winchester Magnum in either 9mm or 45. The 45 Winchester Magnum is the world's most powerful auto pistol cartridge, delivering almost precisely 1,000 foot pounds of energy at the muzzle of a 5-inch barrel. The 9mm Winchester Magnum is the world's highest velocity auto pistol cartridge, leaving the muzzle of a 5-inch tube at 1475 feet per second. (The claims of "world's most powerful" and "world's fastest" apply only to commercial cartridges, since there are some wildcats or semi-production cartridges that can top these figures.)

The Wildey is a large handgun, topping 51 ounces with a 6-inch barrel, but it feels good in the hand and delivers outstanding accuracy. One of the reasons for its fine accuracy is that the barrel is fixed to the frame, and is therefore not subject to the same alignment problems that plague many semi-auto designs. Another factor contributing to accuracy is that the sights are of excellent target quality, being micrometer adjustable for both windage and elevation.

It is easy to think of two primary uses for the Wildey, hunting and silhouette shooting. It should be an excellent choice for both these purposes. Carrying the Wildey in the field could present some problems due to its size, but a major maker of leather goods is said to have designs prepared for making hip and shoulder holsters for it.

Workmanship displayed in the Wildey is of the highest order. It is a quality arm in the classic tradition. It looks good, feels good and, even better, it shoots well, too! It will be made with barrels of 5, 6, 7, 8, and 10-inch lengths—which should just about meet all reasonable requirements.

List prices for all models will be slightly under $500.00. Inquiries may be made to Wildey Firearms Co., P.O. Box 447, Cheshire, CT 06410. ●

HOW WIDE ARE SHOTGUN PATTERNS?

by NICK SISLEY

THE UPLAND GUNNER NEEDS SHOT SPREAD; HERE'S WHAT HE GETS

THE BIGGEST PART of my hunting time is spent in the uplands—battling through thick cover—after grouse, woodcock, quail, sometimes cottontails. My experience has always been that open chokes are far more effective in putting game in the larder than tighter borings. Few experts disagree with that premise, but the novices I meet afield are almost invariably armed with modified and full choked shotguns. Why they continue to keep making this mistake is puzzling.

Recently, thinking this over, I tried to figure out a scientific and mathematical method of proving—when taking shots in close cover, at short ranges—that one is far better off using Skeet or improved-cylinder borings.

The method I decided to use is, I believe, unique—at least I've not seen similar methods and results in print before. The basic idea is to fire loads from Skeet, improved cylinder, modified and full choke barrels at specified short ranges, then measure the pattern width of each. I also wanted to find out if there were any significant pattern-width differences in loads with varying amounts of shot, and between 12- and 20-gauge guns.

Remington provided the two guns. Model 1100 semi-automatics in 12 and 20. Each came with 4 barrels—full, modified, improved cylinder. and Skeet. I loaded all of the shotshells used on a Ponsness-Warren Duo-Matic 375, a tool on which it is easy to change gauges and loads.

Two loads were tested in 20 gauge —using all four barrels—⅞- and 1-oz. shot loads, both backed by 11.5 grains of Red Dot powder. The three 12-gauge loads follow, all with Red Dot: 1-oz./ 16.5 grains; 1⅛-oz./18 and 1⅜/18. Number 8 shot was used in all tests, avoiding any variables that might have resulted from different size shot. It was also felt that using shotguns and barrels of the same make and model would help eliminate variables.

I fired patterns at 10, 15, 20, 25, and 30 yards—with each barrel, each gauge, and each of the 5 loads. Shots beyond 30 yards are rare in the uplands. I then measured the width of each pattern, the results permitting easy mathematical conclusions.

Measuring effective pattern width takes some "Kentucky windage." Not much problem at the closer ranges, but increasingly difficult with open borings at 25 and 30 yards. The problem is flyers—pellets striking outside the circle of the effective pattern—and judging where the effective circle ends and the flyers begin.

It was soon apparent that No. 8s in a Skeet bore were only effective to about 25 yards. Beyond that enough holes existed to let small birds, say quail and woodcock, fly through unscathed. Improved cylinder borings were effective out to 30 yards, but not much beyond.

Once the reader digests the accompanying tabulated results, it will become readily apparent how much more

Shotgun Pattern Width Tables
(All with No. 8 Shot)

	No. I	No. II	No. III	No. IV	No. V	No. VI	No. VII	No. VIII
	20 Full	20 Mod.	20 IC	20 Skt.	20 Full	20 Mod.	20 IC	20 Skt.
	7/8 oz.	7/8 oz.	7/8 oz.	7/8 oz.	1 oz.	1 oz.	1 oz.	1 oz.
10 yds.	4.5"	6.0"	11.5"	14.5"	6.0"	8.0"	13.5"	15.5"
15 yds.	10.0"	11.5"	19.5"	23.0"	10.5"	12.0"	19.5"	22.5"
20 yds.	15.5"	18.5"	26.0"	26.0"	17.0"	18.5"	24.5"	30.0"
25 yds.	21.0"	20.5"	31.0"	35.0"	20.5"	24.5"	29.5"	35.0"
30 yds.	25.5"	23.5"	33.5"	40.0"	27.0"	26.0"	33.5"	40.0"
	av. 15.3	av. 16.0	av. 24.3	av. 27.7	av. 16.2	av. 17.8	av. 24.1	av. 28.6

	No. IX	No. X	No. XI	No. XII	No. XIII	No. XIV	No. XV	No. XVI
	12 Full	12 Mod.	12 IC	12 Skt.	12 Full	12 Mod.	12 IC	12 Skt.
	1 oz.	1 oz.	1 oz.	1 oz.	1-1/8 oz.	1-1/8 oz.	1-1/8 oz.	1-1/8 oz.
10 yds.	9.0"	8.0"	12.0"	14.5"	10.0"	8.0"	13.0"	15.0"
15 yds.	13.0"	11.0"	19.0"	21.5"	16.5"	12.5"	21.5"	22.5"
20 yds.	17.5"	17.5"	24.0"	31.0"	22.5"	20.5"	28.5"	30.0"
25 yds.	26.0"	22.5"	33.0"	37.0"	28.5"	29.5"	32.5"	37.0"
30 yds.	30.0"	31.5"	39.0"	42.0"	32.5"	33.5"	38.5"	42.0"
	av. 19.1	av. 18.1	av. 25.4	av. 29.2	av. 22.0	av. 20.8	av. 26.8	av. 29.3

	No. XVII	No. XVIII	No. XIX	No. XX
	1-3/8 oz.	1-3/8 oz.	1-3/8 oz.	1-3/8 oz.
10 yds.	9.5"	10.5"	13.0"	18.5"
15 yds.	14.0"	17.5"	27.0"	26.0"
20 yds.	21.0"	22.5"	32.0"	33.0"
25 yds.	31.5"	28.5"	37.0"	39.0"
30 yds.	36.0"	38.5"	43.0"	44.0"
	av. 22.4	av. 23.5	av. 30.4	av. 32.1

Table XXI
(10-yd. Pattern Diameters and Areas in Sq. Inches)

	Full	Mod.	IC	Skt.
20ga/7/8 oz.	4.5"	6.0"	11.5"	14.5"
20ga/1	6.0"	8.0"	13.5"	15.5"
12ga/1	9.0"	8.0"	12.0"	14.5"
12ga/1-1/8	10.0"	8.0"	13.0"	15.0"
12ga/1-3/8	9.5"	10.5"	13.0"	18.5"
	av. 8.0	av. 8.1	av. 12.6	av. 15.6
Area, Sq. Ins.*	50	55	130	190
% Avg. of Full	0	10	160	280

*To find area, square radius and multiply by 3.14(pi).

Table XXII
(15-yd. Pattern Diameters and Areas in Sq. Inches)

	Full	Mod.	IC	Skt.
20ga/7/8 oz.	10.5"	12.0"	19.5"	22.5"
20ga/1	10.0"	11.5"	19.5"	23.0"
12ga/1	13.0"	11.0"	19.0"	21.5"
12ga/1-1/8	16.5"	12.5"	21.5"	22.5"
12ga/1-3/8	14.0"	17.5"	27.0"	26.5"
	av. 12.8	av. 12.9	av. 21.3	av. 23.2
Area, Sq. Ins.*	130	130	360	415
% Avg. of Full	0	0	175	220

*To find the area, square radius and multiply by 3.14 (pi).

effective Skeet and IC chokes are at close ranges compared to modified and full borings. Perhaps my only task then will be to convince readers that most upland game is shot at very close range—closer than even many experienced upland shooters realize. Remember, I mean rabbits, woodcock, grouse and quail, all consistently found in close cover.

An ardent grouse hunter friend, a while back, killed one at what he thought was extreme range, so far away that he paced it off. Twenty-six long steps later the dead bird was at his feet.

Several years ago I paced every grouse kill. Of some 40 birds shot that year, the average was 22 paces (mine average about a yard) to where the bird struck the ground—*not* where he was hit. It is safe to say that the average grouse was hit at less than 20 yards—momentum then propelling them several yards farther before they hit terra firma. Not convinced yet? Start pacing off your kills.

Because "Kentucky windage" was a slight factor in measuring effective pattern width, I felt my results would be more accurate if I "averaged" them. I did this by adding up each individual test, then dividing by 5—the number of shots fired. This "average pattern width" is shown with each series of

Table XXIII
(20-yd. Pattern Diameters and Areas in Sq. Inches)

	Full	Mod.	IC	Skt.
20ga/7/8 oz.	17.0"	18.5"	24.5"	30.0"
20 ga/1	15.5"	18.5"	26.0"	26.0"
12ga/1	17.5"	17.5"	24.0"	31.0"
12ga/1-1/8	22.5"	20.5"	28.5"	30.0"
12ga/1-3/8	21.0"	22.5"	32.0"	33.0"
	av. 18.7	av. 19.5	av. 27.0	av. 30.0
Area, Sq. Ins.*	315	315	570	705
% Avg. of Full	0	0	80	124

*To find area, square radius and multiply by 3.14(pi).

Table XXIV
(25-yd. Pattern Diameters and Areas in Sq. Inches.)

	Full	Mod.	IC	Skt.
20ga/7/8 oz.	21.0"	20.5"	31.0"	35.0"
20 ga/1	20.5"	24.5"	29.5"	35.0"
12ga/1	26.0"	22.5"	33.0"	37.0"
12ga/1-1/8	28.5"	29.5"	32.5"	37.0"
12ga/1-3/8	31.5"	28.5"	37.0"	39.0"
	av. 25.5	av. 25.1	av. 32.6	av. 36.6
Area, Sq. Ins.*	500	500	825	1050
%Avg. of Full	0	0	65	101

*To find area, square radius and multiply by 3.14(pi).

patterns. See Tables I through XX.

By comparing these average pattern widths against the same choke constrictions, but with different loads and with both gauges, one can see a difference. Slight, yes, but there.

What do these differences mean? For those who haven't already guessed, it is that heavier shot loads give *wider* patterns than lighter ones! So, it pays to use maximum shot loads, no matter the choke used, for a better chance to hit game.

Note well—I don't increase the amount of powder when I increase the amount of shot. Numerous tests have shown me that my most even patterns result from standard or low velocity loads, but that pattern distribution is better as more shot is added. Now I've found, via these tests, that plenty of shot also gives *broader* patterns. At upland game ranges, high velocity isn't needed. Don't use more powder—use more shot!

Additionally, these results show that, in all instances, 12-gauge 1-oz. loads give wider patterns than 20/1-oz. loads, both with the same choke. Because more shot can be loaded in the bigger case—if you can find a 12 bore light enough to suit you for upland shooting—it would pay to use standard velocity 1⅛-oz. loads. A good handload with that shot charge uses Winchester AA cases and AA red wads plus 18 grains of Red Dot. This recipe results in a well-filled case and perfect crimps.

My next job is to *prove* how much more effective Skeet and IC chokes are at close ranges. Again to eliminate that "Kentucky windage" problem, I decided to "average" results. I did this by adding all pattern widths fired at 10 yards (as a first effort), and dividing by 5 (the number of loads tested), then computing the area in square inches of each "average" pattern.

Here is an example: At 10 yards, taking all the full choke patterns (See Table XXI), I added up their widths and divided that sum to find the average, which was 8 inches in this instance. As the table shows, that equals only about 50 square inches in total coverage at 10 yards!

Using that same formula, the modified choke area at 10 yards was 55 inches, the IC was 130, the Skeet choke 190 inches.

This means that at 10 yards one's chances of hitting a flushing bird are 10% better with a modified choke versus a full choke, 160% better with an IC, and an unbelievable *280%* better with a Skeet choke.

Agreed, every upland critter doesn't present a 10-yard shot. Let's move to 15 yards and go through the same exercise. As Table XXII shows, the mod and full chokes have about the same area, 130 square inches, but the IC choke shows over 360 and the Skeet over 415! This means that the shooter who can bag 10 out of 50 birds at 15 yards with a full choke will nail the same 10 with a modified, but he'll get some 27 of 50 with the IC and 32 birds with the Skeet barrel. The increase in success with an IC choke is 175%, with the Skeet barrel, 220%.

What about 20-yard shooting? As before, the full and mod patterns were alike, or 315 square inches, the IC went 570, the Skeet 705. The percentages for greater success aren't as high as at 10 or 15 yards, of course, but still impressive—80% for the IC, 124% for the Skeet choke. See Table XXIII.

Now let's shoot from 25 yards—which I'd found was the effective limit for the Skeet boring. At this range the FC and the modified cover about 500 square inches, the IC some 825 and the Skeet choke 1050. Thus the IC boring has a 65% edge over FC and modified, with the Skeet constriction showing a 101% better chance over full or modified.

By now some eyes should be opened. These figures show how much the shooter can improve his chances on game found in close cover, that his obvious choice for shots at 25 yards and closer is an open-bored gun, preferably one with a Skeet choke. In a double gun Skeet and IC would be an excellent choice, but how many gun companies offer that combination? Skeet and Skeet would be a far better choice than IC and modified.

Still not convinced? For proof, just step off your upland kills, and you'll quickly learn how close to the muzzle grouse, quail, woodcock, rabbits and other upland game falls. As veteran brushbusters have long known, no choke at all can be even better, though such wide bores often deliver uneven patterns. Skeet chokes have a few points of choke—they're not true cylinder.

My upland favorite is a light, short, fast 20 gauge side by side, bored cylinder and IC. Normally it carries 1-oz. loads in 2¾-inch cases, but I'm going to test soon some 1⅛-oz loads. No, not to put more shot into the game I shoot, but to increase effective pattern width. By doing that I'll bring down those birds that might otherwise be missed—on the fringe.

It might even be a better idea to find a 12 bore light enough to carry all day and feed it my low-velocity 1⅛-oz. loads. Such a team should offer the widest-possible patterns for thick cover shotgunning. •

THE TRUTH ABOUT BIRD GUNS

NO MAGIC, NO TRICKS, NO EASY WAY—ANY DECENT GUN AND A LOT OF PRACTICE MAKES A SHOOTER WHO HITS

by
DAVE DUFFEY

ABOUT any shotgun there is one absolute truth: When *you* consistently hit game birds with it, it *is* a bird-gun—a very fine one.

The only other near-truth about the shotgun chosen for your upland game forays is the distinct probability that a bird-getter that suits you won't satisfy anyone else, even your best hunting buddy.

All else about bird guns, whether based upon fact or speculation, is purely a matter of opinion. That goes a long way toward explaining why we have a bewildering variety of shotgun styles, gauges, chokes and loads.

Now, should the shotgun and loads you are banging away with also be scoring for you (like maybe three for four on pheasant, two out of three on bobwhite quail or you are batting .250 on ruffed grouse and better than .500 on woodcock) there's only one reason for you to read further. You might find out why you're doing so well.

If you modestly admit to being better than an average shot because you just know you are (despite the carefully expressed reservations of some polite gentlemen who have shot with you) you might be surprised to find you could do even better if you were using the right gun and a proper load.

You need some additional help if an honest evaluation of your shooting skills is on the discouraging side. If you seek out some competent instruction and frequently practice what you are taught, chances are good that you can adapt to your hitherto unsatisfactory gun. Good firearms are often unjustly maligned even though it's the man using them who's responsible for the misses. However, a fresh start with the right gun may boost your confidence.

If you've just left the starting blocks to get underway in a new recreational pursuit some facts and opinions, both biased and unbiased, may help in keeping you in the race. Once you hit your stride, whether or not you make the Olympics, you are sure to develop opinions of your own.

Get one thing straight about a good upland bird gun right from the start. It is a specialized item, be it a customized work-of-art or a work-a-day tool right off the rack in the local hardware store.

There is no all-round bird gun anymore than there is an all-purpose bird dog. But there are all kinds of workable compromises. If you are lucky enough to hunt a wide variety of game birds you may need more than one gun. In the interests of familiarity and economy, one or more extra barrels, each choked differently, can be the ticket to successful shooting.

As far as good shooting is concerned, familiarity is more important than cost. A bird gun should point like your finger. But no matter how well-designed or suitable, it won't point unless you are intimately at ease with it. Only with much practice does mounting and swinging a shotgun become a subconscious reflex.

When you become a truly good shot, you'll find that you can pick up virtually any shotgun and do a respectable job with it. But until that level is achieved, stick to the same style and action. When necessary, switch chokes and/or loads to increase your chances of knocking down the particular game bird you are after on a certain day.

Let's drive home the familiarity *requirement* and the sometime need for something special by noting that my favorite bird gun for some years now has been a 20-gauge Ithaca-SKB over-under with Skeet-bored 26-inch barrels. It serves beautifully in any situation on ruffed grouse, woodcock and bobwhite, on pheasants shot over points or flushed well within range by properly trained spaniels or retrievers.

But for most of *my* pheasant shooting it is unsuitable. While guiding and dog-handling at a private hunting club I carry a gun and shoot. Most of the shots I touch off at the big birds are distinctly long-range. It's not a matter of personal choice or timing. It is back-up shooting at missed birds guests have already fired at.

As a pump-gun addict, owning seven "corn-shuckers" in various gauges, to compensate for this handicap it seemed logical to tote along a 12-gauge Remington M-870 trap gun with its 28-inch full-choke barrel.

Resulting problems encountered had less to do with design and balance (and certainly not with familiarity) than with sometimes momentary hesitation or confusion about simple things like the location of safeties and differences in actions caused by shifting back and forth between dissimilar guns.

The solution? Purchase of a very specialized shotgun, which is fine for pass-shooting geese or jump-shooting ducks and the very antithesis of what can be recommended for upland bird gunning. With its 30-inch barrels bored improved-modified and full, this 12-gauge Ithaca-SKB matches the familiar 20-gauge over-under used most frequently for pleasure hunting and dog training.

This cannon is in keeping with the use to which it is put and, because

When handled right by an experienced pointer, even wily cock pheasants get up close and an open-bored 20 gauge over-under with light loads will do the job for Dave Duffey as he kicks a rooster out from under Stupido's point. (Erwin Bauer photo)

double-guns do not have the receiver required on pumps and autoloaders, its barrel length is not unwieldy. So it answers the need for familiarity and balance in a gun that must be easily mounted and swung to score on difficult shots.

The 3-inch chambers, however, have never hosted anything but 2¾-inch shells. The long rounds and even the 2¾-inch "baby magnums" have no place in upland bird shooting. They are questionable even for waterfowling when a barrel is choked tighter than modified because of resulting poor shot patterns. In over-simplified terms, too much shot is being crammed through too much restriction.

However, if "superloads" turn *you* on and you can grin and bear both the cost and brain-rattling recoil, when a shotgun is choked improved-cylinder the "overloads" will throw a deadly cloud of shot. Although unnecessary over decoys, out of open barrels the magnum loads are fine for waterfowling and high crow shooting, a sport that will give you off-season practice and better understanding and appreciation of your gun's capabilities.

If you insist upon mutilating upland game with more than 1¼ ounces of shot, refrain from serving it up to dinner guests who are finicky or nasty enough to sue for reimbursement of their dental bills.

While many shooters are not "into guns" to the extent that they are prepared to quibble about somewhat esoteric special applications of guns and loads to the game they are pursuing, most seek an "ideal" gun for upland shooting. A Skeet gun will provide the most simple and satisfactory bird-getting instrument for anyone who is not a firearms addict.

Any gun giving you a decent score at Skeet (the degree of decency is left to your judgment) will serve admirably in virtually any situation on any kind of upland game. Skeet is a game designed to simulate the kind of shooting upland birds afford: close-up with a variety of angles. The type of action, autoloader, pump, side-by-side or over-under, is unimportant. Choke, barrel length, balance and drop are.

However, for you the most popular gun for competitive shooting might not be the best bird gun. So before dealing with the cogent aspects of chokes and loads let's take a look at various shotgun types.

The most favored Skeet gun is Remington's M-1100 autoloader. Reliably free of malfunction as far as autoloaders go, it points and swings well and makes a fine upland gun. Despite personal aversion to autoloading shotguns, when I've borrowed an 1100 it did well for me. When the 1100 I gave my son on his 12th Christmas was stolen, as an adult and a good shot he replaced it with another. So much for personal testimonials.

This model hits good, particularly for the casual hunter, because it is heavy on the fore-end. That out-front weight tends to keep a gun swinging despite any inclination on the shooter's part to stop his swing. Along with failure to firmly "cheek" the stock, the most common cause of misses is failure to follow through when shots are touched off.

For any number of reasons, other brands of autoloaders will serve individual shooters as well or better. But practically all are rated in comparison to the 1100. Autoloaders lack the lines, the quick-handling and feel of a nice double-barrel and, except in lightweight versions, are comparatively heavy, a factor worth considering in a gun carried on all-day hikes. If recoil is a factor, the autos absorb more of it and are softer to shoot. Over-under scatterguns "kick" hardest.

Despite personal fondness for the mechanically reliable pump-action shotgun, it's farthest from what's ideal in an upland bird gun. Human malfunction can cause problems with this basically sound piece. Mastery of the coordination required to shuck expended shells and smoothly slide new rounds up into the chamber for repeat shots requires more practice and familiarization than is needed with other styles when a shooter is under pressure to get off quick second or third shots after an initial miss or when faced with a multiple flush of game.

Slide-actions, however, share with autoloaders, a capacity for holding two to five reserve rounds that permit more follow-up shots and chances on covey rises, where the law allows a full magazine. Also, "pumping" the action serves to pull down the barrel and may settle down a "shook up" shooter who may have touched off a hasty shot at a close-in bird.

The most reasonably priced of multi-shot firearms, pumps are all good buys and are available from virtually every major maker of firearms. The aforementioned Remington 870s and the classic Winchester Model 12 lead the pack in popularity. As far as the latter goes, if you can buy a second-hand Model 12 in good condition, manufactured prior to the early 1960s when the model was discontinued, you'll own a more valuable gun than the reintroduced version public demand forced the firm to bring back.

For the one-gun owner, the pumps and autoloaders rate as the most versatile shotguns, thanks to inter-

Handling a hunting Labrador in light cover during the winter snow time on a shooting preserve provides long, open shots on pheasant. Dave Duffey uses an Ithaca-SKB over-under in 12-gauge bored improved-modified and full choke for such work. (Irwin Gebhart Photo)

changeable barrels. For years the only gun I shot was a trap-grade 870. With different barrels, full choke, Skeet choke and rifled slug. I killed waterfowl, predators, upland game, deer and competed in both trap and Skeet. Although I seldom hunt with it anymore my best trap scores are still shot with it and if the trap stocking was unsuitable for Skeet I was unaware of it. That should serve as testimony to the versatility and durability of pump guns and the value of being "finger-pointing familiar" with a gun.

Traditionally the double-barreled shotgun has been the *beau ideal* of bird guns. Whether its barrels lay side-by-side or are stacked on top of each other, the double always has been considered a gentleman's sporting firearm. It still is and it's also practical, if expensive.

Doubles are the shotguns safest and most simple to operate. They've been on the sporting scene longer than any type of bird gun and have many advantages. In the recent past the steep cost of good double guns has mitigated against their general acceptance.

Clean and neat in appearance, double guns handle the same way. This crisp quickness is an asset in the uplands where shots are mostly reactive rather than deliberately calculating. Light weight and good balance makes them easy to tote all day.

Double triggers still are extolled by a few sportsmen. The two triggers do offer quicker barrel selection than do single, selective triggers. If you do acquire a twin-trigger gun, avoid a pistol grip. Straight stocks facilitate finger-shifting. But for the most part, double triggers are looked upon with disfavor by shooters and should actually be avoided if a switch is being made from autos or pumps in favor of a double. But most of the well-made heirloom guns that remain serviceable and lend tradition and prestige to a hunting day have two triggers.

Most modern doubles have a single selective trigger which will permit a shooter to take advantage of what has always been a "sales point" for twin-barreled shotguns, the choice of two different chokes mounted and ready to go. The idea being that a shooter can quickly select the barrel choked to match the distance the game flushes from him, using the more open choke for close shots and the tighter for those farther out.

Rarely, however, is a hunter this calculating when a bird gets up. And if he is thinking about which barrel might be best he can lose the concentration it takes to kill a bird, or a moment's indecision may mean a lost shooting opportunity.

So it is hard to fault less expensive doubles that have a non-selective single trigger that always fires the "close" barrel on the first shot and the "distance" barrel with the second pull, a normal shooting sequence in 95% of the shots taken at upland game.

Automatic ejectors also hike the cost of a double gun and except for providing for quick reloading may be less practical than simple extractors which present an expended shell so it can be pulled out of the chamber with the fingers. For hunters who reload, or those concerned with littering, who pocket the expended cases, automatic ejectors can be more pain than pleasure.

Savage Arms, with its durable, no-nonsense Fox Model-B side-by-side, for years provided about the only answer for the hunter who had limited bucks to spend on a "classic" upland gun. But with the advent of Japanese manufactured shotguns, the market has been flooded with both over-unders and side-by-sides at affordable prices. Good guns for the money include Winchester 101s, SKBs and Savages. Somewhat of a cost factor, compared to pumps and autos, remains.

Browning's Superposed has been

About The Author

Dave Duffey is best known in the hunting world for his involvement with gun dogs. Author of six books about dog training and upland hunting, he has been hunting dogs editor of *Outdoor Life* magazine for more than 20 years and as a free-lance outdoor writer has contributed to many national publications and anthologies.

While training dogs for others, on personal hunts across the country and while handling his dogs on guided hunting parties, he has shot at or watched others shoot at literally thousands of birds each year. Clients and guest shooters, annually numbering 200-300, have ranged from farmers to financial tycoons and included crack shots, duffers and beginners who needed instructions before they were taken afield. The guns they use to hit and miss with constitute as wide a variety as can be found on the gun rack in many sporting goods stores.

From these experiences, Duffey has formed some opinions and offers some suggestions the editor of GUN DIGEST hopes will bring other sportsmen nearer to "THE TRUTH ABOUT BIRD GUNS."

and still is the prestige over-under. But for some time it has been overpriced and over-rated. More than 15 years ago, when one could be purchased in field grade for about $300 my personal experience with that model soured me on it. Today when a hunter I'm guiding experiences some malfunction with an autoloader or an over-under, without looking I can make money betting it's a Browning. Other brands of guns at half the price will just as well serve most hunters who are purchasing a smoke-pole for hunting rather than as a speculative investment or a treasure to be handed their heirs.

Considering choke in an upland bird gun, the only absolutely wrong choice is full choke, the tightest boring available. A full choked gun will concentrate at least 70 per cent of the shot pellets fired from each cartridge within the confines of a 30-inch circle on a pattern-board 40 yards from the muzzle. It's terrific for those long shots, but upland gunning is not a long-range game.

A modified (half) choke should put about 50-55 percent of the shot in that two and a half foot circle at the same distance and the cylinder (open) choke about 25-30 percent. Improved-cylinder (quarter) choke ranks between cylinder and modified. Improved-modified (three quarter) choke is betwixt modified and full in delivering maximum shot concentration on 40-yard shots.

So it's not difficult to comprehend that the more open the boring the quicker it will deliver a pattern of maximum spread and killing density. Most upland birds are dropped 15 to 35 yards from the gun and more are shot at when 10 yards away than out at the 50 or 60 yard distances at which full-choked guns are capable of consistent killing if the operator is skilled enough to swing properly, which is seldom. The opposite extreme, cylinder bore, will lose birds shot at beyond 30 yards but that quick dispersion of shot makes a shooter look good on the common close-quarter shots.

Within the ranges at which most upland birds are shot, the concentrated full choke pattern will cause the so-so shooter to miss and mash up the birds a good shooter scores on. If there is an all-purpose choke for all people it has to be improved-cylinder which will knock down birds by compensating for sloppy holds and can kill cleanly out to 40 yards.

When selecting choke, a great deal depends upon your own evaluation of your gun handling techniques and the type of bird you most often hunt. A quick-reacting shooter whose game is bobwhite quail, ruffed grouse or woodcock will improve his scores with a short, "wide-open" cylinder barrel.

Even masters of the art of wingshooting have been known to tinker with their guns to open them up or get them stubbed off to less than the 26 inches available in stock-model guns.

Milo Mabie, a woodcock expert, has

Although he frequently shoots birds with a 410 while training bird dogs like this pointer, Stupido, Dave Duffey has a strong preference for 28-gauge performance when sportsmen turn to the lightweight sub-small bores for upland birds.

compensated for his slowed reflexes since retiring from his Neillsville, Wis. barbershop by opening up the barrels of his Fox Model B side-by-side. John Rukavina, a young salesman and transplanted Tennessee duck hunter, who finds Wisconsin's fall upland hunting compensates for its bitter winters, simply cut a couple inches off the muzzle of his light Franchi autoloader to better cope with ruffed grouse and woodcock.

Frank Woolner, the down-to-earth Massachusetts author of the classic books *Grouse and Grouse Hunting* and *Timberdoodle* made extensive modifications on a glass-barrelled Winchester M-59 autoloader to get a bird gun meeting his specs. Other inveterate uplanders may also consider experimenting with guns they buy over the counter, assured that a gun that will score on woodcock and partridge will also be deadly on bobwhite or any game bird species getting up in front of a dog's point.

There is hope even for the dedicated waterfowler who dabbles in upland bird hunting, short of ruining his favorite "long-gun" by chopping it off or opening it up.

For some, not bothered by appearance or complaints about the increased muzzle blast from other hunters sharing a duck blind, the familiar Cutts compensators, devices attached to the muzzle that can be quickly adjusted to change the degree of choke, are an obvious answer. Winchester makes available some production model shotguns complete from the factory, with a similar Win-choke.

But a most practical alternative to gun-alteration is a box of "brush" or "scatter" loads, which are hard to find, but nice to have. Shot wads are used in such a manner that these special shells will "open up" to produce somewhat spotty but much more widely dispersed patterns than regular rounds fired out of full or modified barrels. They permit practical use of a tight-choked gun in the uplands. In light of the advances in modern shotshell loading that result in patterns tighter than indicated chokes are supposed to deliver, scatter loads may be worth trying in more open bores as well.

Some very deliberate gunners, who may seem slow as they "ride out" a bird, run up very good bird scores. If that is your shooting form, or if the game is pheasant, prairie grouse or Hungarian partridge, modified choke in a single-barreled gun may be the best way to go.

Double-barreled guns, of course, permit two different chokes. Practical and easiest to obtain are doubles bored improved cylinder for the first barrel and modified for the second. That will do the job for you on everything from woodcock to pheasant. But, again for chopping down at close range, get cylinder and improved cylinder (or Skeet and Skeet) if you can. A combination that works well for any kind of pheasant hunting and will also get your ducks is improved cylinder and improved modified.

Unfortunately, the most recommended shot size for upland hunting is No. 6. That is a compromise load. As such it is unsatisfactory when extremes are encountered. If a hunter anticipates running into several species in the same cover, or wants to settle on a single shot-size, No. 7½ is his best all-purpose bet.

No. 4 or No. 5 does it best in long-range pheasant shooting as with birds flushing wild out of cornfields and No. 6 or No. 7½ gets the nod for prairie grouse and Hungarians, or for pheasant under 35 yards. Even for woodcock and quail, No. 9 shot is too light. The most effective load for those birds and ruffed grouse is No. 8 with No. 7½ not far behind. Depending upon the bird and the usual distance you take them, the decision rests with you as to whether the increased energy of coarse shot is needed to "break up" a tough bird or the increased number of fine shot ensures that a small bird won't slip through the pattern.

But because individual barrels do good, bad or indifferent jobs with different shot sizes, what your barrel does best should govern the shot size you select. Nor does every barrel deliver with every size shot the expected percentage pattern that a designated choke is supposed to.

Does this call for testing on a pattern board? Definitely so if you seek some clear answers about your shotgun's performance. There is an exception. If the gun-load match you are using satisfies you, forget about patterning your gun. What comes out on the pattern sheet may shake your confidence. That can play havoc with your shooting.

I've never patterned my favorite upland gun, the 20-gauge O&U bored Skeet and Skeet. It does so well with everything from No. 5 to No. 9 there's been no reason to. But when other guns were not doing the job on easy shots, patterning them revealed there were specific shot sizes those particular barrels did not deliver properly. A shift in size, one way or the other, resulted in even patterns.

For what it's worth, an unscientific conclusion of mine is that what's become an almost off-beat load now, No. 5, has some special affinity for full-choke barrels. In all three of the popular gauges I find No. 5 does a superior job out of full choke to either No. 4 or No. 6.

Reloaders experimenting with powder and shot combinations can come up with tailored loads more satisfactory for their special purposes than over-the-counter shells. But if you can find 12-gauge shells loaded with 1¼ ounces of No. 7 or No. 7½ shot, propelled by 3¼ drams equivalent of powder (rather than the customary 3¾ drams) you'll have found the nearest thing available to a hunter's Holy Grail—an all-purpose load giving beautifully even patterns. I suspect live pigeon and international trap shooters use similar loads. For dense, unholey patterns, which are more important to an uplander than super-power, the lightest powder load that will adequately propel the most shot is the answer.

In most instances, a 12-gauge is the best choice for upland shooters and certainly is the most popular. But aside from tough cock pheasants, in upland hunting the smaller gauges will serve any decent shot as well and may be preferred for their quickness and lighter weight.

By trying a 28, 20 or 16-gauge shooters of 12-gauge pumps and autos who find them slow and heavy compared to double guns will be encouraged to stick with the familiar style, discovering that both gun and shells are lighter and the smaller charges most satisfactory.

Even if he decides not to change gauges, experimenting with the smaller bores should teach the 12-gauger something. He can shoot "cheaper" if he "loads down." The light 12-gauge loads, often available as price leaders at discount stores, are all he needs on anything except wild-flushing pheasant and spooky prairie grouse.

Field loads containing 1 ounce of shot or the 1⅛ ounce trap-loads equal or surpass the amount of shot and the pattern composition hurled out by 16, 20 and 28-gauge guns. So a shooter may reckon it foolish to pay premium prices for high-brass shells with their 1¼ ounces of shot. Although not needed, the extra shot and powder can be handled by a 12-gauge. So, if a shooter believes added "power" will give him an edge he may use heavier loads to advantage. It's a psychological thing.

But it is idiocy to go the other way and attempt to soup-up a 20-gauge gun with available magnum loads in an effort to make the 20 "equal" 12-gauge performance. For 20 gauges with 3-inch chambers shotshells containing up to 1¼ ounces of pellets are offered true. But with identical shot charges, the larger the gauge the better it will deliver a proper pattern and the heavier gun will normalize recoil that is nasty in a lighter shotgun.

In 20-gauge, Skeet loads of ⅞-ounce do fine on small birds killed close, like quail and woodcock. The 20 also handles a full ounce of shot well and that's what pheasant should be pounded with. I think loads of 1⅛ or 1¼ ounces in 20-gauge are a waste of money and will rattle your teeth and give you a headache in a gun you picked for its easy carry, quick point, and light weight.

The 410-bore shotgun is something for an expert to show off with and requires the restraint to pass up shots at birds that are not easy shots. Patterns are consistently erratic. The 28-gauge is something else. Theoretically it should bear the same relationship to the 20-gauge as the 20 does to the 12-gauge, but the 28's ¾-ounce load, out of a *modified* barrel, seems to strike some sort of ballistic balance that makes it nearly equivalent to the 20-gauge. Shells containing ⅞-ounce of shot are also available. Good shots, willing to pay a premium price for shells and with finding them unavailable at cross-roads stores, will find the neat, quick 28-gauge a joy to tote and shoot in the uplands.

Reference to the advantages of a shotgun that points like a finger might lead to a dissertation on proper gun-fit. But that can be rather briefly dismissed. If you can afford the tab for a custom-fit scattergun, have at it. Unless you are built like a circus freak, however, you'll probably be better off to fit yourself to a production model of your choice than be concerned about made-to-order dimensions. Lots of shooting in the field and on clay birds will accommodate you to your gun.

Familiarity is more important than technically perfect fit, as my experience shooting Skeet with a trap-stocked, theoretically unsuited gun, illustrates. For the record, most guns best suited to field shooting come out today with a length of pull of about 14 inches, a 1⅝-inch drop at comb and a 2½-inch drop at heel.

The dead serious bird-gunner, who does some shopping around and experimenting with the wide variety of gun models (and loads) available is likely to find a certain model that comes up right, feels right and will really do the job for him.

If you are already doing well with what you have, be happy and enjoy. Don't change a thing, don't try to analyze what makes you and your bird gun click and ignore suggestions by anyone that haven't been borne out in your own experience. But if you haven't yet found that perfect-for-you piece of upland armament, hopefully what you've read here will put you on track and explain some questions about the selection of a suitable bird gun.

To repeat, the proof of the puddin', the one immutable truth about the quality of a bird gun, is that the man swinging it takes a fair share of whatever he touches off at. For men who can do that, all else is pasture pie.

Sportsmen dissatisfied with the ratio of birds bagged to shots fired may find it pays to switch rather than fight a shotgun not suited to them. Eventually, by shooting the newly acquired piece enough to gain proficiency, they'll soon be wedded to their own truths about bird-guns. •

THE SAVAGE POCKET AUTOMATIC PISTOL MODEL 1907

Cut from Savage's book by Bat Masterson "The Tenderfoot's Turn" showing the slanting of the copy toward women and the uninitiated.

IT WAS EASIER TO DELIVER 10 SHOTS QUICK — EVEN FOR HOUSEWIVES — THAN TO SORT OUT SAVAGE VARIATIONS

by DONALD M. SIMMONS

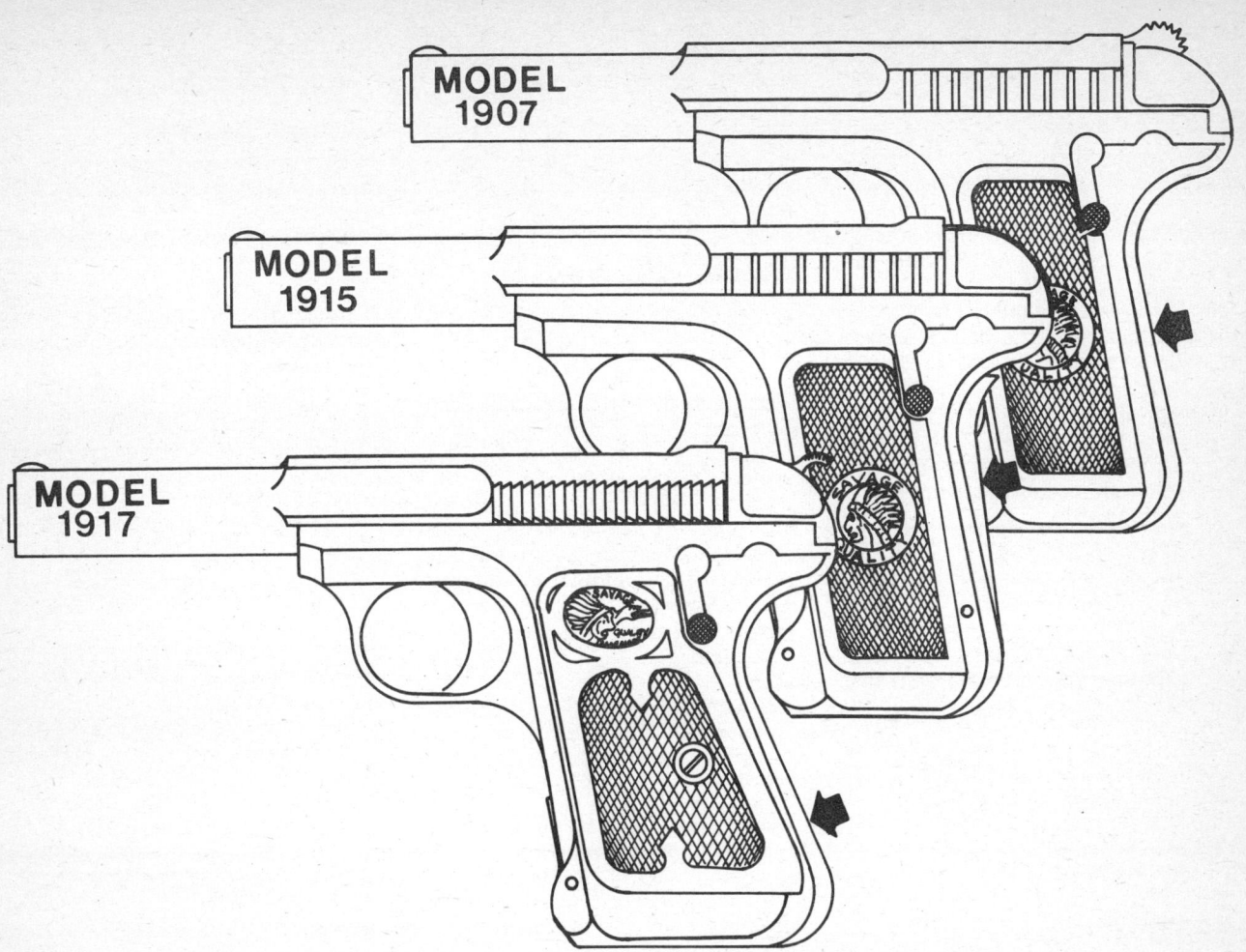

This sketch shows the points to look for in identification of the various Savage models. The slanted rear grip of the Model 1917, the cocking piece and straight grip of the Model 1907 and the lack of cocking piece, straight grip and grip safety of the Model 1915.

THE SAVAGE ARMS Corporation seems to be a young firm compared to most of the other well known gun manufacturing enterprises found in the United States today and yet today Savage is in its eighty-sixth year. It was founded on April 5, 1894 by Arthur W. Savage and was known as the Savage Arms Company. The factory was at Utica in the beautiful Mohawk valley region of upper New York state. The Savage Company was formed to manufacture Arthur Savage's patented lever action high powered rifle. This rifle, the model of 1899, is still made today and is now called the Savage 99.

In 1915, Savage Arms Company was sold to Driggs-Seabury Ordnance Company. In 1917 the name was changed to Savage Arms Corporation as it remains today. In 1926 Savage acquired the Page Lewis Company; in 1930, the Fox Gun Company, and also in that year, the Davis-Warner Arms Corporation; in 1931 the Crescent Firearms Company, and in 1936 the J. Stevens Arms Company. These other firms gave Savage a broad base in the manufacture of shoulder arms, both rifles and shotguns. In 1963 Savage Arms Corporation was merged into the American Hardware Corporation which changed its name to the Emhart Corporation in 1964. Savage Arms is today a division of that Emhart Corporation.

Savage, in late 1905 or early 1906, negotiated the right to manufacture an automatic pistol designed by Elbert Hamilton Searle of Philadelphia, Pa. Because of intense interest in an automatic pistol to replace the perennial revolver in the U.S. armed forces, both Savage and Searle devoted the initial effort into developing a pistol to compete against Colt's 45 automatic in the Government sponsored test to be held in January, 1907. In May of 1911, the U.S. military turned to Colt and Savage, the only other serious contender, was the loser.

During the years from 1907 until 1911 Savage, not content just to wait and see if their military pistol would be adopted, brought out a civilian pocket automatic (self-loading) pistol. The first Savage pocket automatic was made on March 22, 1908—it was in 32 ASP (Automatic Savage Pistol). The 32 ASP name never caught on and the cartridge is always referred to as the 32 ACP (Automatic Colt Pistol) or 7.65 mm Browning, abroad.

Savage also made this automatic in 380 ACP at a later date. They experimented with a vest pocket automatic in caliber 25 ACP but it never got off the ground. They also experimented with a 38 ACP automatic in prototype only.

These then, represent the automatic

pistols made by Savage.

The Savage Pocket Automatic pistols in caliber 32 ACP and 380 ACP were made in three different models. The Model 1907 (also called, wrongly, I believe, the Model 1905 and 1909 and 1910); the Model 1915 and the Model 1917. These are factory designated Model names and everything else should be classed as a variation. The production of the Model 1907 began in 1908 and was only offered in 32 ACP until 1913 when the 380 ACP was added to the line. The Model 1915's were made only in 1915-1916 and were in both 32 and 380 ACP. The Model 1917 was made from 1920 to 1928 in both calibers. The breakdown of quantities of each model is as follows:

Model	32 ACP	380 ACP
Model 1907	209800	9845
Model 1915	6520	3902
Model 1917	29671	15157
	245991	28904

A glance at these figures will show that by far the most common Savage pocket automatic is the 32 ACP Model 1907, all the rest are rare. Savage Arms was the only American manufacturer of pocket automatic pistols which even approached Colt Patent Firearms Company in quantity sold. Savage made a total of 274,895 in the three Models and two calibers; Colt made 572,214 32 ACP automatics and 138,000 380 ACP automatics for a total of 710,214. Thus Savage made a respectable 39% of the amount that the venerable Colt produced. One must also remember that Colt made pocket automatics from 1903 to 1945/46, over twice as long a time.

What makes a Savage Model 1907 different from a Model 1915 or 1917? There are two things to look for. Does the grip have no large swelling on the rear grip strap, toward the butt of the pistol? If not, the pistol must be a 1907 or a 1915. Now, is there an apparent hammer or cocking device? If present then the pistol is a 1907, if not a 1915. If the pistol has a grip safety it is also a Model 1915.

Here is the quick description found in Savage's own pamphlet, boxed with each pistol, called "It Banishes Fear."

"32 Caliber automatic"

Magazine Capacity 10 shots.

Barrel 3¾ inches. Weight 19 ounces. Length over all 6½ inches. Price $15.00. Extra Magazines, each 50 cents.

Note—Cartridges for the 32 automatic pistol may be obtained all over the world. Those adapted to it are the 32 Automatic SAVAGE, 32 Automatic Colt and 7.65 M.M. Browning. These are different names for the same cartridge.

"380 Caliber automatic"

Magazine Capacity 9 shots.

Barrel 4¼ inches. Weight 21 ounces. Length over all 7 inches.

Price $16.00 Extra Magazines each 50 cents.

Note—Cartridges for the 380 Automatic Pistol may be obtained throughout the world. Those adapted to it are the 380 Automatic SAVAGE, 380 Automatic Colt and 9 m.m. Browning Short. These are simply different names for the same cartridge.

Also in "It Banishes Fear," we find a section entitled "Strong Points of the 32 and 380 SAVAGE AUTOMATIC PISTOL"

Ejects empty shells, reloads and cocks hammer automatically.

Ten shots. Double the number in an ordinary revolver. Two more than other automatics.

Rapidity: Fires as fast or as slowly as you pull the trigger. Four to five shots a second if required.

Shoots straight without taking aim, because it fits the hand naturally, and you point it straight instinctively, as you point your finger.

Balance: Center of gravity is well to the rear, so pistol fits solidly and securely in the hand.

Handle is flat, a perfect handful; will not flinch on the trigger pull.

Weight, caliber 32, 19 ounces; caliber 380, 21 ounces.

Length over all, caliber 32, 6½ inches; caliber 380 7 inches. So compact and flat it can be easily carried in trousers watch pocket.

Appearance: Small, trim, well proportioned. No corners to catch in the pocket.

Accuracy: Automatic locking of the breech retains all the powder gases behind bullet until it leaves the barrel. This insures uniform bullet velocity and accuracy.

Reloads in a fraction of a second with a ten shot magazine for the 32 and nine-shot magazine for the 380. Empty magazine is released by catch on grip and drops out immediately.

Freedom from fouling. Powder gases cannot escape into the breech. Not of the blowback type.

Flat trajectory. Shoots where you hold it up to 100 yards.

Penetration: With full mantled bullet, penetration is seven inches in pine.

Energy: Has greater shocking energy than any other automatic of the same caliber, because locking breech retains all powder gases behind the bullet.

Fewer parts than any other automatic.

Dismounts completely by hand quickly, and goes together again without the aid of any tools.

Strong parts—because fewer and simpler.

No screws to work loose.

All springs are spiral and will not break.

Empty shells are ejected, with great uniformity, off to the right hand from twelve to twenty feet, according to how pistol is held when fired.

Safety: Will not discharge by striking hammer.

Safety: Firing pin is released only by pulling trigger.

Safety-catch under control of the thumb, positively locks the trigger, making it impossible to discharge the arm.

Most of the above statements are true. There has always been a great deal of debate about whether or not the Savage/Searle method of locking is really effective. I have always conceded that these Savage pistols are not blowback, and I think you can call them locked breech in that the barrel is locked to the breech piece and slide

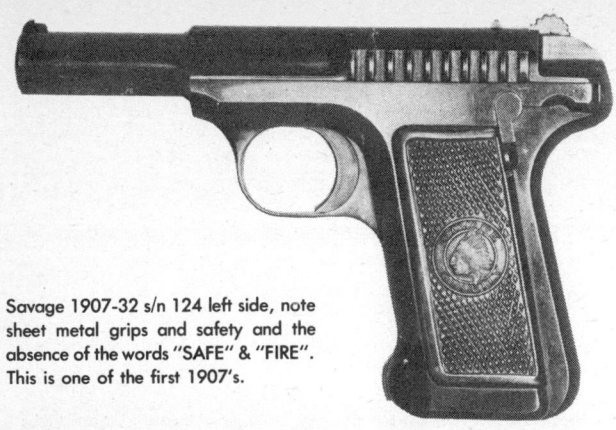

Savage 1907-32 s/n 124 left side, note sheet metal grips and safety and the absence of the words "SAFE" & "FIRE". This is one of the first 1907's.

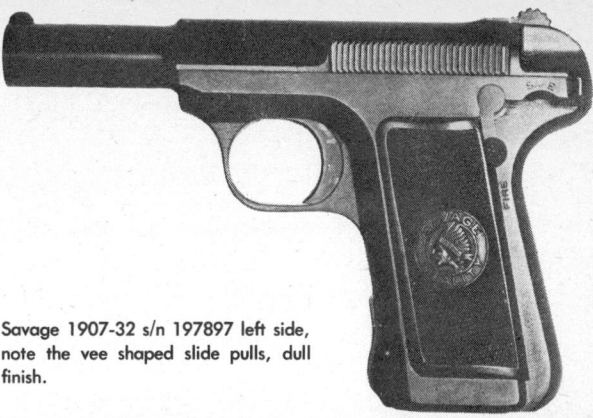

Savage 1907-32 s/n 197897 left side, note the vee shaped slide pulls, dull finish.

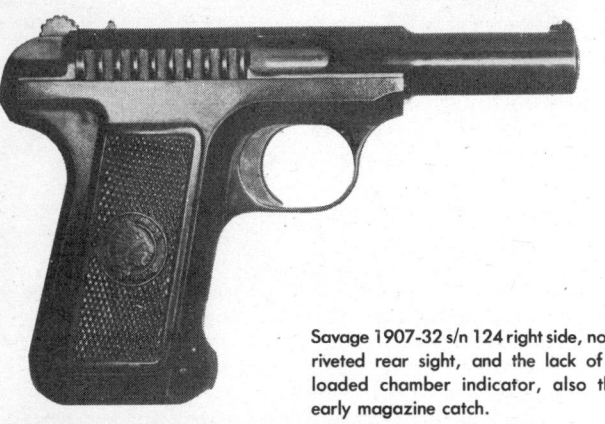

Savage 1907-32 s/n 124 right side, note riveted rear sight, and the lack of a loaded chamber indicator, also the early magazine catch.

Savage 1907-32 s/n 229221 right side, note spur cocking piece. This is one of the last 1907's.

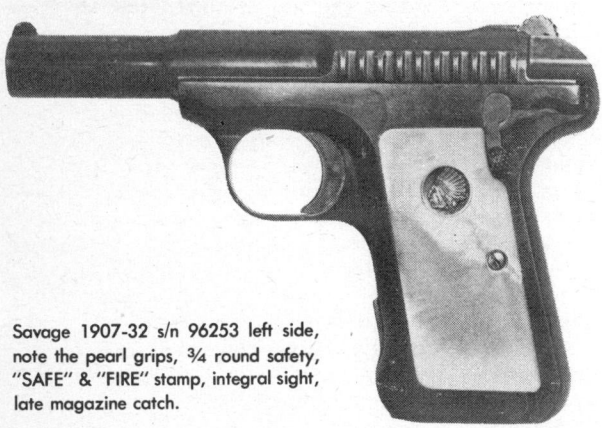

Savage 1907-32 s/n 96253 left side, note the pearl grips, ¾ round safety, "SAFE" & "FIRE" stamp, integral sight, late magazine catch.

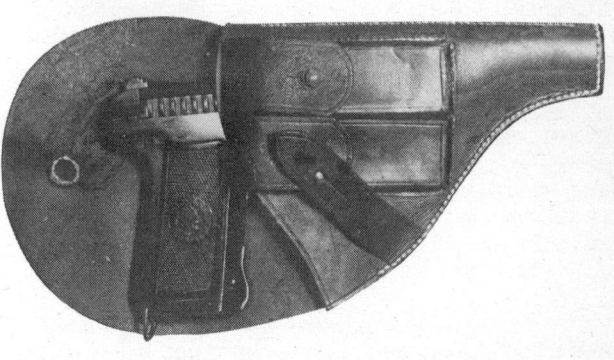

Savage 1907-32 s/n 166491 in military holster right side, note lanyard loop and the two extra magazines in holster. This is a Portuguese contract.

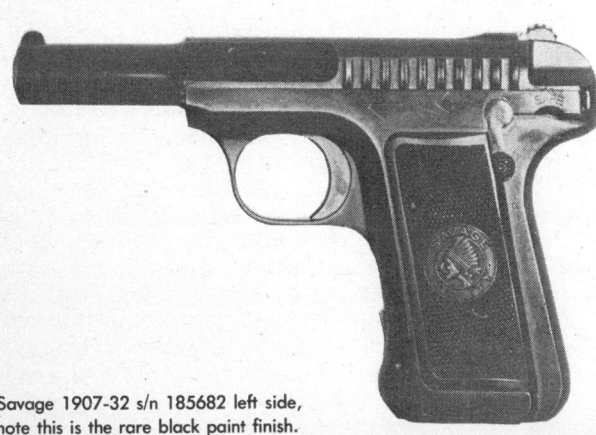

Savage 1907-32 s/n 185682 left side, note this is the rare black paint finish.

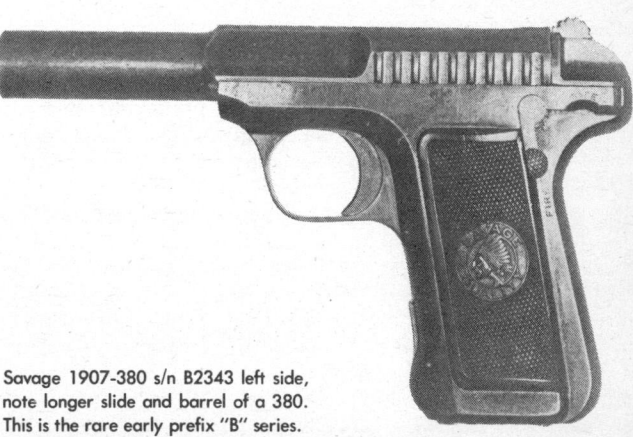

Savage 1907-380 s/n B2343 left side, note longer slide and barrel of a 380. This is the rare early prefix "B" series.

at the moment of firing. Let us look at what Elbert Searle has to say on the subject taken from his initial patent #804,985 of November 21, 1905:

"One object of my present invention is to provide a simple and effective positive locking means to prevent recoil of the breech-closure until after the projectile leaves the barrel, which locking means is prevented from unlocking by the passage of the projectile through the barrel, thereby preventing the premature opening of the breech. This feature of my invention is dependent upon the discovery that the inertia of the projectile or its resistance to rotation as it takes into the rifling of the barrel amounts to a very considerable force that can be utilized to perform work without materially detracting from the effect of the rifling on the projectile."

Several things point to the fact that Searle's system does delay the opening of the breech sufficiently for successful operation. Take the weight of Colt's blowback operated pocket automatics recoiling parts and we find they weigh 9 ounces. The Savage 32's equivalent parts weigh a scant 7 ounces yet the Savage even with its lower weight and consequent higher velocity of recoil is not plagued with shell cases blowing out or with parts beaten by the recoil associated with a too-low mass of recoiling parts. What I am saying is that Searle's system seems to work. Consider also that Searle was able to design a working 45 ACP using his principles.

In further exploring based on the claim often made by Savage that bullets fired from their pistols had more penetration and velocity than the same cartridges fired in blowback pistols, I set up a penetration test. Using telephone books and pistols with approximately the same barrel length as the Savage, I found that time after time Savage did penetrate more pages and also that the fully locked Frommer 32 ACP automatic as would be expected, penetrated more pages than either the blowback pistols or the Savage.

As a final test, the lug on the barrel of a Savage 32 was ground off so that there could be no interaction between the rotation of the barrel and the slide going rearward during recoil. First, ten rounds were fired with the lug on and then ten more were fired with it off. I could feel no difference in recoil and the pistol functioned just as well either way. However, I had no way to measure the velocity during this test and therefore can not say if it changed from barrel lug-on to lug-off. I did notice that in both cases there was powder residue in the magazine well and on the breech piece face, and on the highly polished surfaces of the trigger and sear trip, indicating an opening of the breech while some gas was still present.

I think it is significant that when Savage decided in 1913 to make a 380 Model, they increased the weight of the slide. This is how a well-designed *blowback* line should be enlarged to 380 caliber but with a locked breech, why would it be necessary? The recoiling parts in a 32 weigh 6.95 ounces while the longer 380's weigh in at 8.52 ounces, or almost two ounces more! Here is what Searle said in Patent 804,985:

"By using the automatic locking member (rotating barrel-slide lock) I am enabled to construct the receiver (slide) and its breech-block of lighter dimensions than when it is necessary to depend upon inertia of these parts to withstand the back pressure of powder gases. . ." The Savage pistol while not blowback, is so close to being such, that to all intents and purposes, it functions like a blowback and I feel that were it not for the mass of its recoiling parts, it would suffer from the premature opening of the breech.

Another point brought up in the advantages of the Savage automatic was easy toolless takedown. This is a very good feature if it becomes necessary to fully strip a gun in the field, i.e. if it were dropped in water. Savage 1907 pistols can be disassembled in 30 seconds into a frame with the magazine catch, safety and ejector assembled, two grip pieces, magazine assembly, barrel, recoil spring, slide, breech block assembly, trigger lock, trigger, and sear trip assembly, and all this is done without any tools. There are no screws in a Model 1907, therefore no screw driver is needed. This capability and coil springs are real pluses in the Savage.

The Savage pistol does point very well for me, and though the 1907 grips were changed in the Model 1917, I still prefer the old frame. The whole credo of the Savage was aimed at the inexperienced shooters being able to use the pistol for defense. In addition to "It Banishes Fear," Savage put out a book written by that Western hero, Bat Masterson, *The Tenderfoot's Turn*.

"The Savage Automatic Pistol is something entirely new and different in pocket arms. If we'd had the ten-shot Savage Automatic in the old days there wouldn't have been any tenderfeet, because you can't help but point it straight, just as you can't help but point straight instinctively with your finger. And when you pull the trigger you don't even throw your aim off, because the handle won't let you, being flat instead of round. It can't kick up like a revolver because the handle stops what little kick is left after the action has blown back and reloaded. And you don't need to worry about being quick, because the pistol attends to that too.

"A tenderfoot with a Savage Automatic and the nerve to stand his ground could have run the worst six-shooter man the West ever knew right off the range."

Later on Savage's advertising adopted the slogan which was always associated with the line—"10 shots quick" and most of their ads seemed to be pointed to women and inexperienced shooters.

This article deals with the Savage pocket automatic pistol called the Model 1907. You will also hear it called the Model 1905, 1909, or 1910—none of these are correct and none should be used. The factory called their pistol the Model 1907 and you can't beat City Hall. Here is one more point—even though the 380 wasn't introduced until 1913, it still is called the Model 1907. It is in the Model 1907 that we find so many variations.

Jim Carr, in his excellent book on Savages, attempted to sub-divide Savage's Model 1907 into sub-groups and then sub-sub-groups and finally modifications. I believe I will stay away from these divisions mainly because they tend to stultify the subject, allowing no room for additional variations if found and they pretend that some different variations occurred at the same time which may not be so. Finally, by using this system, Carr wound up with apparently similar guns in the two different calibers having different nomenclature, i.e., 32 issue 1907-13 modification 2 is the same as a 380 issue 1907-13 modification 4 which is confusing to say the least.

Savage Arms was not interested in what future generations of gun collectors would call their various modifications and variations—they were interested in selling guns. Carr's system, while well thought out, is not easy to remember and most collectors seem not to have adopted it. To illustrate, a "Late Model 1907 32 1907-19 Modification #1" would be a lot easier to describe as a Savage 1907-32 with vee slide pulls, s/n 185682 " and everybody who knows Savage knows what

Savage 1907-32 s/n 116051 left side, closeup of the special optional hammer spur and "SAVAGE" on frame.

Savage 1907-32 s/n 455-P33, a factory cut-a-way showing the earliest type of Savage 1907 with an A-1 safety. The frame is machined to show the action of the trigger and the cocking piece and the sear trip lever. This rare pistol also has a two way magazine catch—it can be pushed in as is normal or pulled out by the bottom knurled section.

Savage 1907-32 s/n 48048 showing the typical "crown" over "V" British proofs and the unusual engraved "Westley Richards & Co. London W." of the distributor.

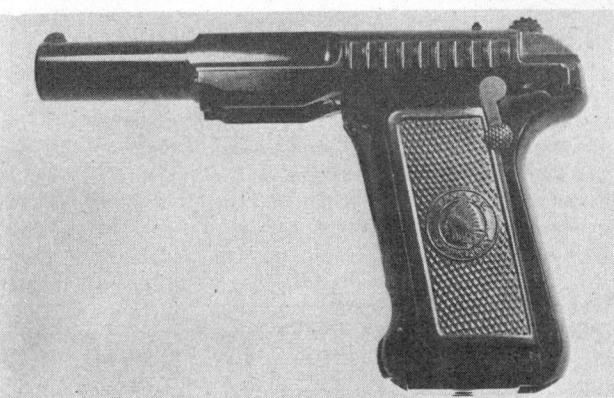

Savage 1907-32 s/n ? factory number P3 factory cut-a-way pistol in the serial range of 2500 to 8300, probably made at around s/n 6000 to show the action of the lower barrel lug which was to be thinned at that time.

Mondial s/n 10637, a 25 ACP Spanish copy of the Savage.

Savage 1907-32 s/n 455 factory number P33, top view showing the cuts in slide which show the upper barrel lug in its groove in the slide. The sear also shows in the bolt front face. This is the pistol ready to be fired.

Cut from a circa 1933 catalog of William R. Burkhard, St. Paul, Minn. This shows a 1907-32 of the last type mislabled "S. & W. AUTOMATIC", gives an idea of used prices back in the depression.

35TH EDITION, 1981 73

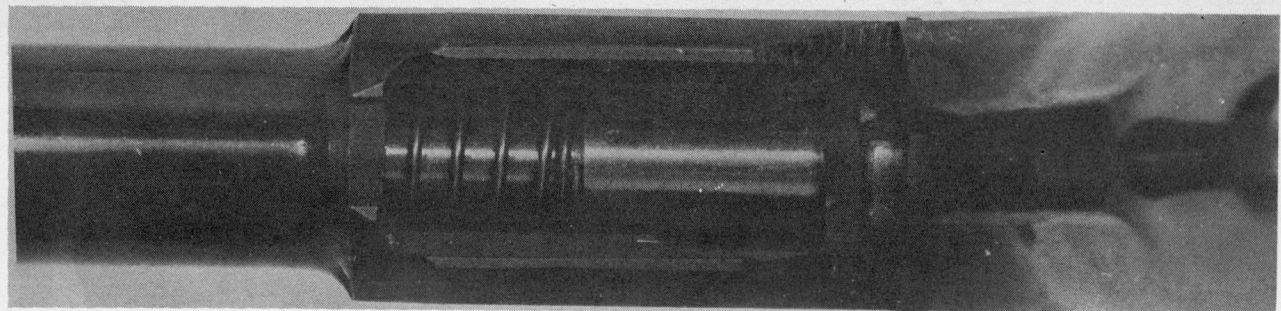

Savage 1907-32 s/n ? factory number P3, bottom view showing the lower barrel lug's motion during recoil.

you are describing.

This, then will be my way of discussing the variations found in the Savage 1907 pistol. I will graphically illustrate the variations and tell the serial number range where it will be found in both calibers. Then in the written description, I will suggest why the change was made by Savage. There is one more point to remember about the Savage Model 1907. You will find improvements that were instituted for a time and then taken off again, such as the "loaded chamber indicator" which was an obvious improvement, but which gave Savage such a fit, that they took it off and didn't replace it with a less fragile one.

I have a letter from W.H. McCrillis of Arms Service Division at Savage in answer to my questions back in July, 1955. I will rely heavily on it for the points where certain changes were made.

The Model 1907 Savage 32 started with a serial number 2 which was given to Savage Arms President, Colonel Benjamin Adriance, on April 22, 1908. The 1907 series went from there to serial number 129,999 at which point the concealed cocking piece Model 1915-32 began. A block of 20,000 was set aside for these pistols and the next Model 1907 was serial number 150,000 produced in 1916. The Model 1907-32 went from there to serial number 229,800 at which point it was discontinued in April, 1920, in favor of the Model 1917.

The 380 Model 1907 because of starting production later, does not have as many variations as does the 32. The first 1907-380 was serial number B2000 made May 23, 1913. The first 400 or so Model 1907-380s had a "B" preface to the serial number. After that the "B" always followed the serial number and is often mistaken for the number "8." The series proceeded to 9999B and there stopped for the Model 1915-380. The Model 1907-380 reestablished itself at the serial number 13903B and proceeded from there to the end of that Model, serial number 15748B. In both calibers, the Model 1907 is apparently continuous except for those numbers taken by the Model 1915. That is to say there are no numbers for which there are not guns. Both the Model 1915 and the later Model 1917 have this type of blank.

The following figures are approximate quantities of pistols made per year. As a basis for these yearly figures, I have used author James Carr's work resulting from detailed examination of Savage's records, but adjusted them to give the totals given by Savage Arms.

Quantities Made Per Year

Year	32	380
1908	2000	—
1909	12000	—
1910	15500	—
1911	20000	—
1912	30000	—
1913	19500	3998
1914	15750	2972
1915	14250	1028
1916	16752	none
1917	17748	none
1918	1346	none
1919	38004	729
1920	5950	1118
	208800	9845

I will discuss the many variations found in the Model 1907 by my own system. Each point at which a variation is found will be given a letter identification and the actual different variations will be given a unique number. For example, the manual safety will be called "A" and an "A-3" safety is that one illustrated in the sketch "A" number "3." There will be no other variation called 3, if some future variation is found it will be called "A-3a" using the lower case "a". This system lends itself to a complete identification of any Savage 1907 by just describing the gun as Savage Model 1907-32 S/N 19652, M-36 O-42 which is code for a "safe" and "fire" marked frame and a full serial numbered breech block.

The M-36 and O-42 are features which make this pistol interesting and are noted for that reason. The M-36 is a feature which will start around this serial number 19652, and will continue to the end of the Model 1907. On the other hand the O-42 is a feature found only on some pistols; it is not a continuous variation.

On the sketches accompanying this article, the serial number range is shown for each variation. When this number is not underlined, the actual number is not known or the change appears only to disappear and no fixed number can be assigned. If a serial number is underlined it was given to me by Savage Arms Corporation and was researched by them. It still may be wrong but it is better than anyone else's guess at this late date. If Savage uses a different nomenclature for a part, it is in brackets after the present part name. Now to take up the various variations found in the Model 1907 Savage:

EXTERNAL VARIATIONS

A: The safety lever (safety indicating thumb piece).

The original safety lever type 1, used on the Model 1907, had a dished-out upper section for finger manipulation. These are quite rare because field complaints must have come in immediately, that this type safety was hard to find to place in the "fire" position. The dished safety was replaced by the fully rounded knurled type number 2. Both the numbers 1 and 2 safety depended

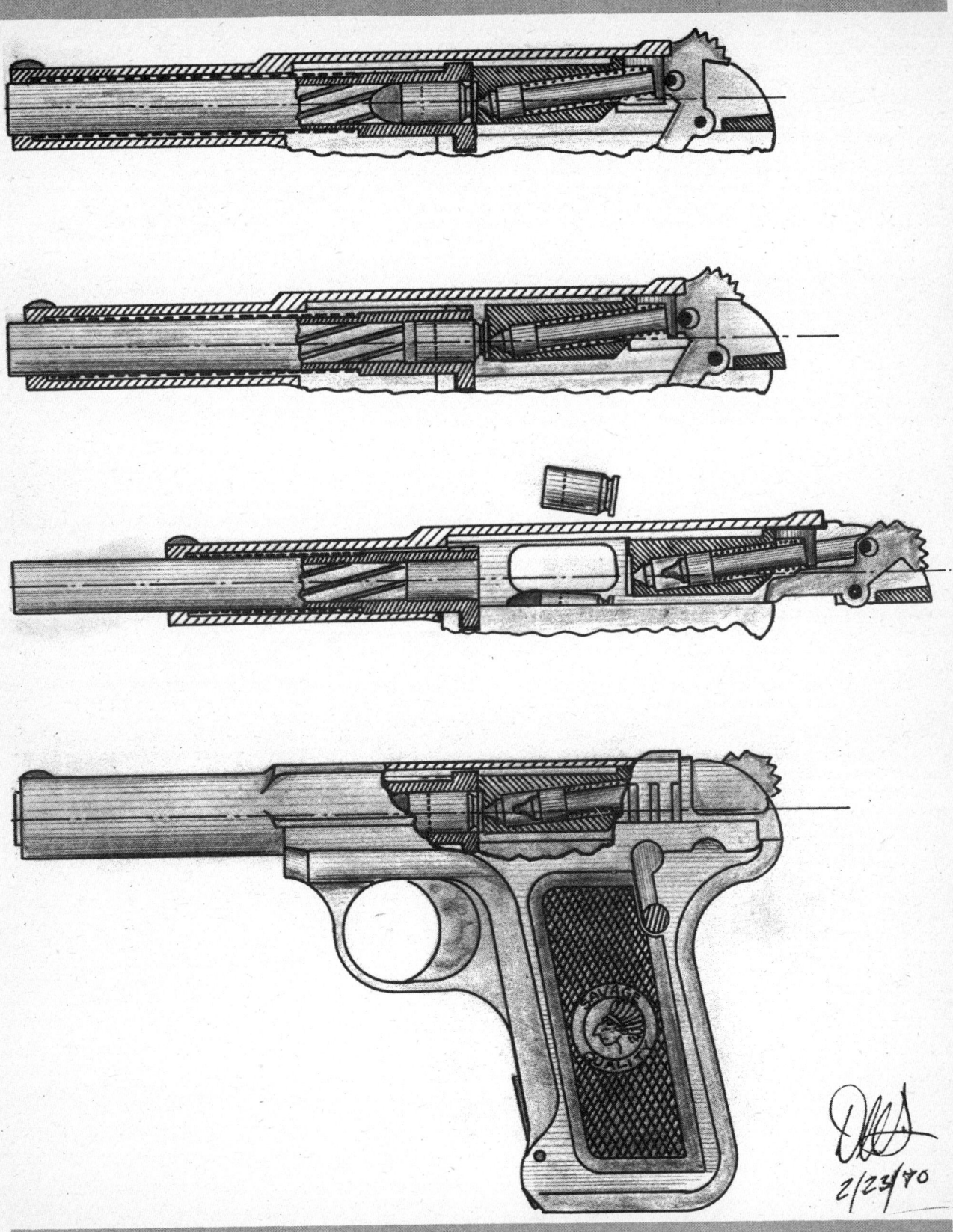

This sketch shows the successive steps of recoil from the moment the round is fired at the top to the final chambering of a new round at the bottom.

on their own springiness for staying in the "on" or "off" position and were found to be much too easily moved to be called a positive safety. They were replaced by number 3 which had a spring and later a plunger and spring to make the action positive. Externally, they are recognized by the fact that they have only a three quarter round knurled finger pad. The number 4 safety is like 3 except for a small hole in its side to receive the rearward end of the trigger lock bar. Apparently the two early safeties were very much disliked by shooters and long before Savage dropped them from production, pistols were being sent in for modification to the number 3 safety.

B: Location of serial number.

Early Model 1907-32s had the serial number on the front radius of the frames trigger guard which made the number readable when the pistol was upside down. This is a number 5 serial number location. The number 6 location which is on all later 1907-32s and all 1907-380s is on the forward edge of the frame and can be read by looking straight down the muzzle of, I hope, an unloaded pistol.

C. Slide (bolt) pull grooves.

The number 7 type of slide pull grooves have narrower peaks than do the later number 8, both are ten in number. Because both these types could slip, the more conventional sawtooth type was instituted and are called the number 9 type, there are twenty-eight teeth in this type.

D: Rear sight.

The original rear sight was a separate piece riveted to the slide (bolt). This is a number 10 sight. The later type rear sight, number 11, is integral to the slide (bolt). The number 10 sight had a "U" shaped aperture while number 11 had a square notch.

E. Magazine catch

The original magazine catch was operated by the third finger of the shooter's hand without a change from shooting position. Thus a magazine in an emergency could be dropped and the shooter's other hand could ram in a loaded magazine. This type catch and frame are called number 12. The later number 13 catch is operated from the bottom of the forward grip strap of the frame and requires a shifting of the pistol to operate. The reason for change was that number 12 catch could, I suppose, accidentally be depressed with the result of a dropped magazine.

F: Grip (stocks).

The grips of a Savage 1907 pistol are unique in that they are held to the frame by nothing more than the elasticity of their material. The original grips of the Savage 1907 were steel sheet metal which had the checkering and the Savage logo embossed on them. These are type 14 grips and require a long slot in the frame to lock. The later type 15 grips are made from black or sometimes dark brown baked rubber. They require a shorter locking notch in the frame. One pistol in my collection Model 1907-32 S/N 870 has a frame milled for the much later rubber grips and was so equipped when purchased. My feeling is that this gun was a rejected frame which, while serial numbered, was not finished until after 1910. A few of the pistols shipped by Savage to Portugal had special grips with the Portuguese crest on them instead of the Savage logo. They were also made of baked rubber, they are number 17. Savage also offered pearl grips with a gold Savage medallion on each side; these are very rare. These factory medallions are of two types. The early type 18a with the "SA" logo and the later 18b with the Indian head. Pearl grips with the Indian head medallion were held to the frame by a screw on each side.

G & H: Loaded chamber indicator and the cuts in slide (bolt) for same.

The loaded chamber indicator was an improvement designed by Savage designer Charles A. Nelson. Nelson's indicator was filed for patent in October of 1912 and granted on December 30, 1913, #1082969. Nelson's type of indicator also required an internal slot in the slide just forward of the ejection port, also the rear of the ejection port was relieved so that the trigger finger could feel even at night if the chamber was loaded. It was a great idea but the delicate two dimensional flat spring part was plagued with breakage so Savage discontinued the indicator, reverting back to the type 19 barrel. Slides with the two cuts for the indicator lasted for 10000 more 1907-32s and less than 1000 more 1907-38s.

J: Logo on top of slide (bolt).

The Savage logo stamped on the 32's slide went through several changes. The first logo was 23a. It was straight up letters followed by 23b which used the exact words but smaller straight up letters covering less of the slide's upper surface. The size of the words "CAL.32." is particularly noticeable. Both 23a and 23b have the word "MANUFACTURED BY" which is dropped in 24. Logo 24 also has the addition of the word "7.65 M-M," probably decided on because overseas sales were beginning. Also the letters are slanted and "NOV." is changed to "NOVEMBER" in the patent date. The last logo number 25 changes Savage from a company to a corporation.

The logo on the Savage 380s is different from the 32s because the 380s have a sighting groove running from the rear sight past the front edge of the ejection port and the logo is stamped on each side of this groove. Stamped logo 26 has straight up letters and only the caliber reference is "CAL." over ".380." The words "MANUFACTURED BY" are in the logo just like the early 32s. Logo 27 adds the "9 M/M" and also drops the "MANUFACTURED BY." Two trumpet like devices bracket the lower line's words "PATENTED NOV. 21 1905." The final logo 28 uses slanted letters and changes company to corporation. It also drops the trumpets by using the entire word "NOVEMBER" instead of "NOV.".

K: Magazine.

The magazines issued with the early 32s have only a lower hole for use with catch E-12. These are number 29 and they have no caliber identification and no company name. The second 32's magazine 30 has the characteristic two holes for either an E-12 or E-13 catch and still no identification marks. The 380's magazine has only one higher hole since they always used the E-13 catch; they are also marked "380 CAL" to identify them from the 32's mags. The rib on either side of a 32's magazine reaches 3/4 of the way from the top to the bottom, while the rib on a 380 goes less than half this distance. This is because Savage uses a double stacked magazine and these ribs control the different diameter cartridges into the lips at the top. The actual basic dimensions of the magazines are the same which allows the magazine wells in the frames of both calibers to be machined with the same tooling.

L: Cocking piece (cocking lever).

The Savage is a rather unique pistol in that it has a cocking piece (cocking lever) attached to a striker (firing pin). The usual automatic which can be manually cocked has a hammer which impinges on a firing pin. The majority of 1907 Savages have what is called a burred cocking piece. The burred cocker 32 worked well to cock the striker but woe unto he who tried to lower the striker with this device. Just at the least forward movement, the flesh of the thumb was pinched between the cocking piece (cocking lever) and the slide (bolt) causing the violent removal of the thumb which could allow the striker to impinge on a primer of a live round. After May 1914, it was possible for the buyer of a Savage to get a special spur cocking lever at no extra charge, these optional spur equipped pistols are quite rare. The owner could also send back to the factory a burr cocking piece and have it replaced by a spur cocker. The final type cocking piece is the number 34. It is different in one respect from both the optional spur and the burr 32 in that it has its upper section relieved so that the pistol may be sighted with the cocking piece in the down position. When the cocking piece is down on a Savage, the striker's forward end can be resting on a live primer. Were the pistol dropped and the cocking piece hit, Savage claimed there would be no accidental firing. This is because the hole in the striker is oversize to the pin holding it and therefore there can be no transfer of motion to the striker if the cocking piece is struck.

M: "Safe" and "fire" stamp on frame.

As originally made, the user of a 32 Savage automatic had to remember which was the safe position and which was the fire of the pistol's safety. This must have led to many complaints from the field and these unmarked frames are variation number 35. Number 36a had "S" & "F" markings on frame while 36b simply adds "SAFE" and "FIRE" to the frame, the word "FIRE" is stamped vertically. This addition made the Savage a lot safer in the hands of the uninformed. The 380s always had the stamping. When pistols were returned to the factory the stamping was added. Thus, these early 1907-32s serial numbers 163, 870, 2269, 4845, and 9995 all have the "SAFE" and "FIRE" stamp. Also S/N 3773 has "S" and "F" instead of the full words.

INTERNAL VARIATIONS

T: Ejector.
The original type of ejector had a short

A: Safeties

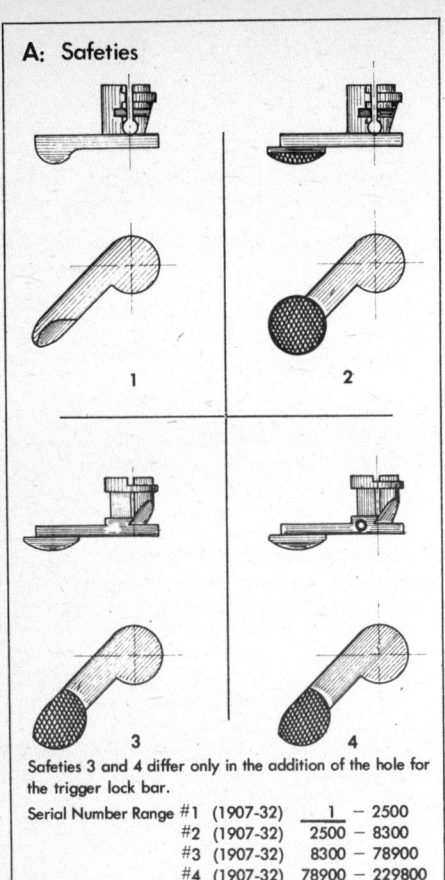

Safeties 3 and 4 differ only in the addition of the hole for the trigger lock bar.

Serial Number Range #1 (1907-32) 1 — 2500
#2 (1907-32) 2500 — 8300
#3 (1907-32) 8300 — 78900
#4 (1907-32) 78900 — 229800
(1907-380) B2000 — 15748B

C: Slide Pull Grooves

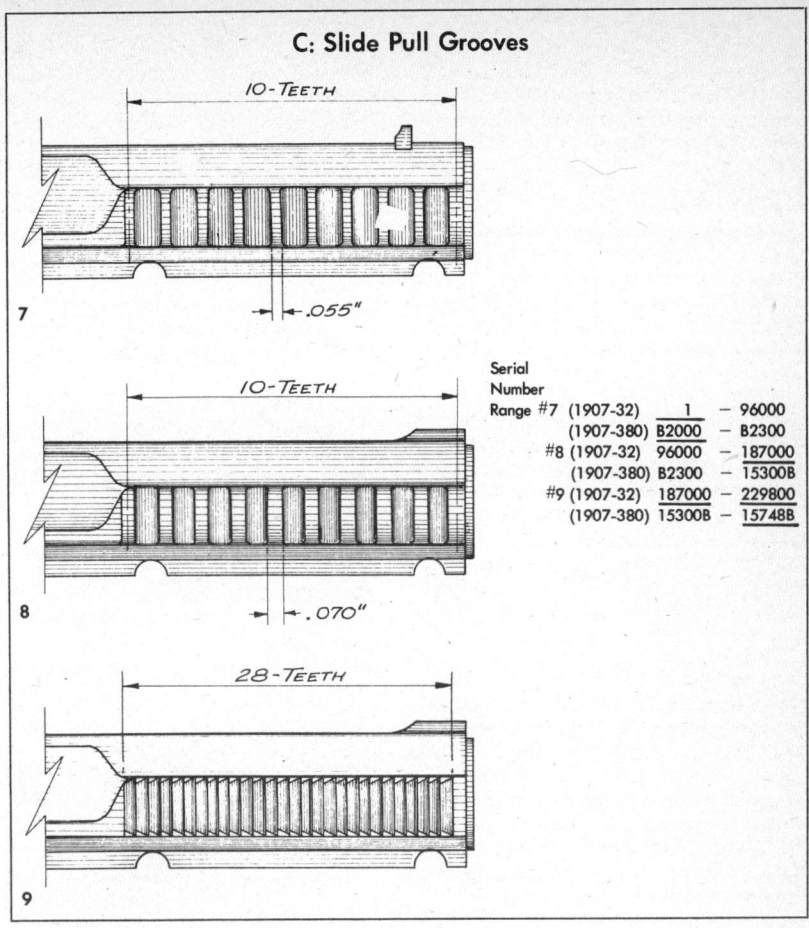

Serial Number Range #7 (1907-32) 1 — 96000
(1907-380) B2000 — B2300
#8 (1907-32) 96000 — 187000
(1907-380) B2300 — 15300B
#9 (1907-32) 187000 — 229800
(1907-380) 15300B — 15748B

B: Serial Number Location

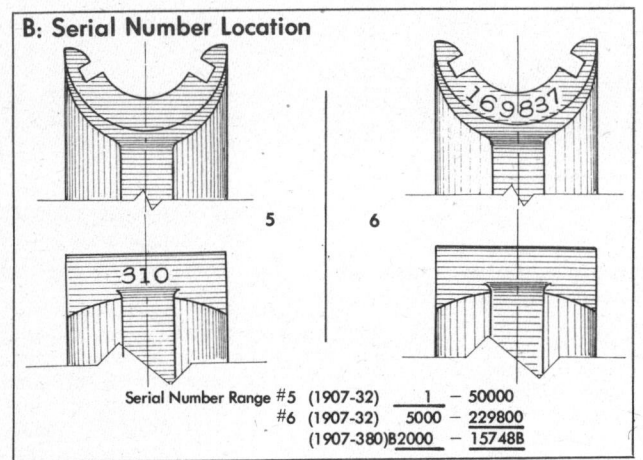

Serial Number Range #5 (1907-32) 1 — 50000
#6 (1907-32) 5000 — 229800
(1907-380) B2000 — 15748B

D: Rear Sight

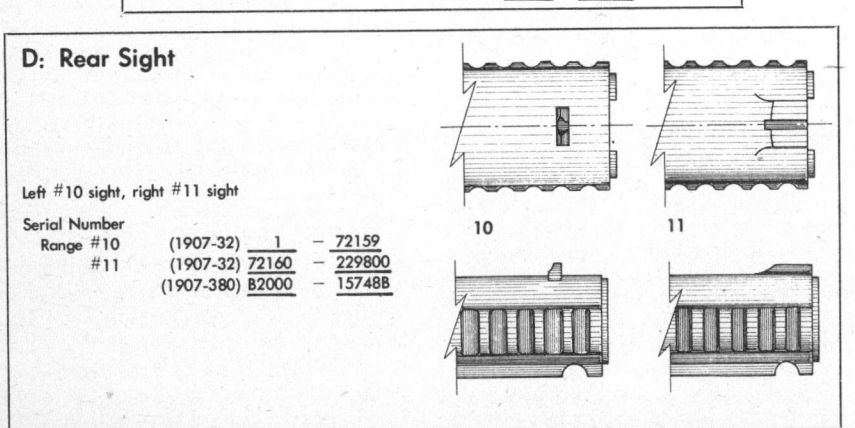

Left #10 sight, right #11 sight

Serial Number Range #10 (1907-32) 1 — 72159
#11 (1907-32) 72160 — 229800
(1907-380) B2000 — 15748B

E: Magazine Catch

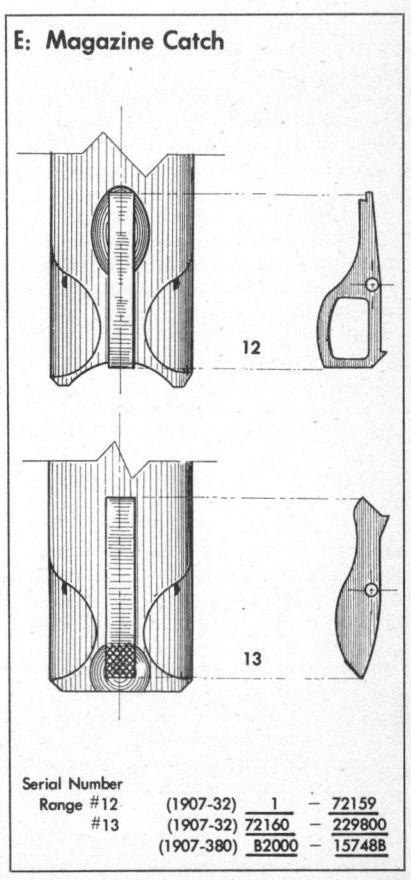

Serial Number Range #12 (1907-32) 1 — 72159
#13 (1907-32) 72160 — 229800
(1907-380) B2000 — 15748B

working arm and no hole for a safety spring. This is a number 56. The ejector arm was lengthened and drilled for the safety spring forming a number 57 ejector. A number 58 ejector has a small plunger added to the working end of the safety spring.

U: Sear.

There were three different sears used; the differences are all in the nose which engages the sear trip of the trigger group. Type 59 is found on early 32s; type 60 was rather short lived and gave way to type 61 which was used from then on.

V: Barrels, recoil springs, and slide (bolt) muzzles.

The barrel on the earliest 32s was very thin walled and had a large lower rear lug, a number 62 barrel. This was changed to the number 63 barrel which had a thinner lug. Next came the number 64 barrel which was greater in diameter than the two earlier barrels. It had a new recoil spring to fit over its increased girth. It also required a larger hole in the slide's muzzle. A 65 barrel was machined to take the cartridge loaded indicator. The 380's barrels started with a type 66 which had the loaded chamber indicator slot and had a rectangular cross-section recoil spring. 380 barrels were ½-inch longer than 32s. The 380's barrels were of greater diameter than the 32's and so had a larger hole in the slide's muzzle. Even with the larger thickness, I find many 380 Savages with bulged barrels. When the indicator was dropped there were still 380 barrels with the annular groove already machined on them so they were used for a time, these are type 67. The 1907-380s finally had a type 68 barrel with no machining for a loaded chamber indicator.

The 1907-32s start with the rifling twist of 1 turn in 16 inches (1 to 16). At about S/N 60000 they change to 1 to 12. The 1907-380 on the other hand being a later development, always was 1 to 12.

W: Breechblock (breech plug).

The first breechblocks were with one interrupted lug and are called number 69, they were used with a T-59 sear. The next breechblock 70 had two sets of lugs for greater strength and were used with a number T-60 sear. The 71 breechblock was just changed in the sear area and used a T-61 sear. The last breechblock 73 was changed in the bolt face only. Sketch W also shows a 72 block which has a small hole in the lower rear section for the cocking lever of the Model 1915. These blocks are included because it is possible when Savage discontinued the Model 1915 that some of the blocks were used on the continuing Model 1907. These would be in the 32s S/N 150000 or 380s in the S/N 13900B area.

X: Trigger.

To improve the operation of the sear trip's plunger, a small pin was added to the trigger. The pinless trigger is number 74 and the pinned trigger is 75.

Y: Sear trip and trigger locking bar.

The Savage sear trip went through several changes. The first type trip 76 had no slot for the trigger locking bar. The trigger locking bar was added by type 77. Type 78 is only used in the Model 1915, to my knowledge, but knowing Savage's policy of never scrapping anything, it is again possible that 1907 pistols in the 32 range of S/N 150000 and 380s of S/N 13900B may have these sear trips.

Z: Striker (firing pin).

To improve trigger pull and sear action in general, Savage changed from a simple lathe turned striker head number 80 to an additional milled head engaging slot, number 81.

VARIATIONS/ WITH NO SKETCHES

N: Left hand side of frame marking.

Originally, Savage had no identification marks on the frame; this would be a 38 frame. They added a large "SAVAGE" on the left side of the frame just over the grip, forming a 39 frame. They later discontinued this and went back to a 38 frame. It is interesting to note that had the same stamp done both the "safe" and "fire" and the "SAVAGE", it probably would have been left on but since stamping "SAVAGE" was an extra operation, it was deleted.

38 frames	(32)	1	– 78000
	(380)	B2000	– 7000B
and			
	(32)	180000	– 229800
	(380)	13900B	– 15748B
39 frames	(32)	78000	– 180000
	(380)	7000B	– 13900B

I also have in my collection, 1907-32 S/N 118749 with a 38 or no "SAVAGE" marked frame. I know of no reason for this since all the later Model 1915 (S/N 130000 to S/N 136500) have the stamp.

O: Serial number on the breechblock.

Dan K. Stern, author of the Savage Book, *10 Shots Quick*, believes that Savage marked their pistol's breechblock with the full serial number during the period when they went from sear U-60 to U-61. This is from Dan's examination of the Savage's shipping ledger. The lowest numbered was 85631 and continued sporadically up into 102000. This seems to me to be true in this particular number area but does not explain two pistols in my collection which fall way out of the above block. 1907-32 S/N 19652 has an etched full serial number on both its breechblock and its barrel. 1915-32 S/N 133854 has the full S/N stamped on its breechblock. I call the full serial numbered breechblocks variation 42 and those with no number, 41. There are still other variations that have to do with numbers. Pistol 1907-32 S/N 185682 has the last three digits on its breechblock "682" and this constitutes a 43 variation. The last thing is that on a nickeled pistol like my 1907-380 S/N 7197B, "138" is marked in the slide and on the frame under the grip; it is also marked "24" on the breechblock which I assume was a factory mismatch after the pistol was plated. These are assembly numbers and have no bearing on the later serial.

P: Pistol finish.

Savage Arms tried a lot of different finishes during the 20 years they made pocket automatic pistols. The first finish 44a was what is called flame blue. It was light and did not wear well as Savage soon found out. This was standard for (32s) 1 to 11000. The frame, safety, magazine, grips, breechblock are blue; the hammer, trigger and magazine catch are case-hardened or mottled; the barrel is polished only as it was always during the production of these pistols. At around S/N 11000, the finish 44b changed to a deep and much more durable blue; by this time the hammer is also blued and grips were baked rubber (32s) 11000 to 184609, (380s) B2000 to 14000B. The next finish tried by Savage is so rare that were it not for Mr. McCrillis' letter, it would have been unknown. Starting with 1907-32 S/N 184610, a black paint was applied to the pistols, finish 45. This made them look somewhat like the French Model 1935A of the World War II period and it went over like a lead balloon. It was quickly replaced by a blue/grey parkerized finish which is number 46 and went from (32) 186000 to 229800, (380) 14000B to 15748B.

Savage also offered nickel plating and silver and gold. Even nickel is rare and the other two I have seen only in 1907-32 silver plated and B engraved with 18a grips. Engraving in three grades was also available; Protector or A; Monitor or B; and Special or C. Engraved pistols are very rare, too.

AA: Disassembly aids.

From the day in 1908 when the first Savage was to be disassembled by its owner, trouble started. After pulling the slide rearward and locking it by the safety, the magazine had to removed; then the breechblock was twisted 90 degrees clockwise and removed and then the trigger had to be depressed to remove the slide. If the magazine was left in, its feed lips would be badly dented by the rear section of the slide. If the trigger was not pulled, the sear trip would hang up on the breechblock securing lug in the slide, shearing it off if force was used to disassemble. By machining the slide away, both the faults were corrected. AA-81 is the original way; 82 no trigger pull needed; 83 neither trigger nor magazine movement needed. Magazine removal is a good habit anyway.

This completes the variations as I know them. I am sometimes asked where the biggest number of changes occurred. I feel without doubt, that this would be in the Model 1907-32s between 60000 and 81000 for in those 21000 pistols, the following changes happened.

F: Grips

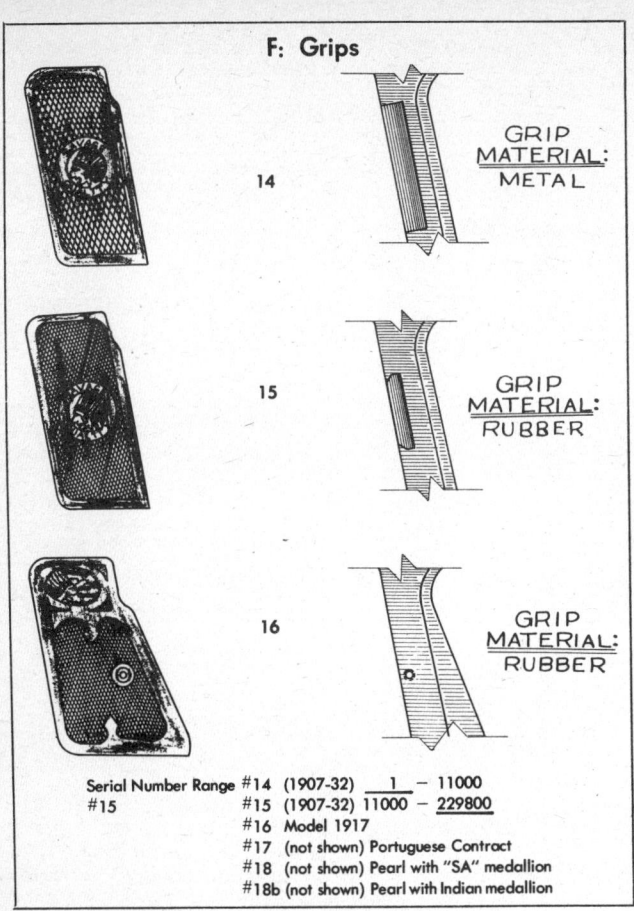

14 — GRIP MATERIAL: METAL
15 — GRIP MATERIAL: RUBBER
16 — GRIP MATERIAL: RUBBER

Serial Number Range #14 (1907-32) 1 – 11000
#15   #15 (1907-32) 11000 – 229800
#16 Model 1917
#17 (not shown) Portuguese Contract
#18 (not shown) Pearl with "SA" medallion
#18b (not shown) Pearl with Indian medallion

L: Cocking Piece

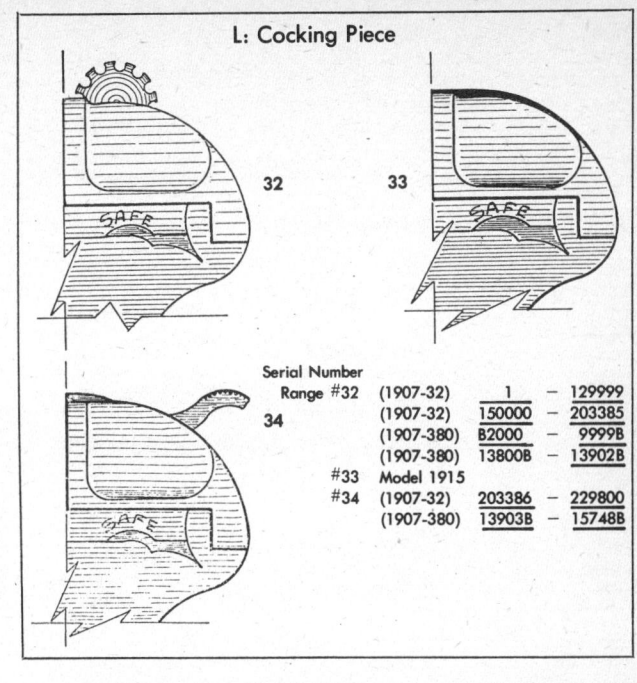

32   33   34

Serial Number
Range #32 (1907-32)   1   – 129999
      (1907-32)   150000 – 203385
      (1907-380) B2000 – 9999B
      (1907-380) 13800B – 13902B
#33 Model 1915
#34 (1907-32)   203386 – 229800
    (1907-380) 13903B – 15748B

Indicators: G-Loaded Chamber/H-Cut in slide

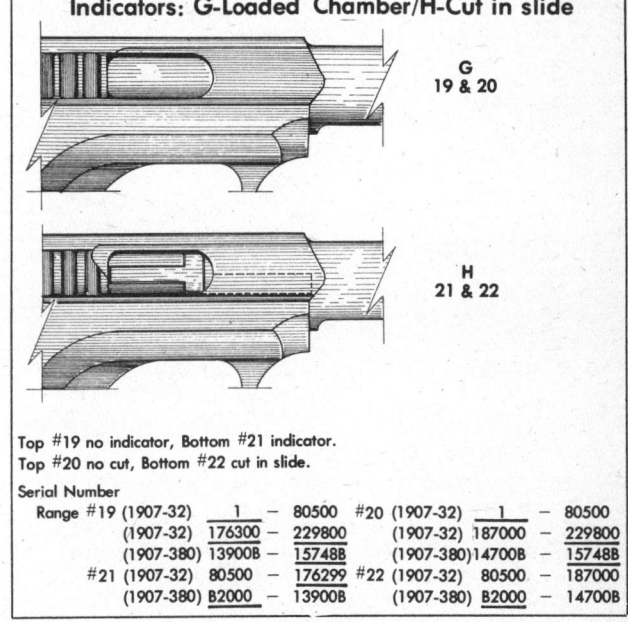

G 19 & 20
H 21 & 22

Top #19 no indicator, Bottom #21 indicator.
Top #20 no cut, Bottom #22 cut in slide.

Serial Number
Range #19 (1907-32)   1   – 80500   #20 (1907-32)   1   – 80500
      (1907-32)   176300 – 229800   (1907-32)   187000 – 229800
      (1907-380) 13900B – 15748B   (1907-380) 14700B – 15748B
#21 (1907-32)   80500 – 176299 #22 (1907-32)   80500 – 187000
    (1907-380) B2000 – 13900B   (1907-380) B2000 – 14700B

K: Magazines

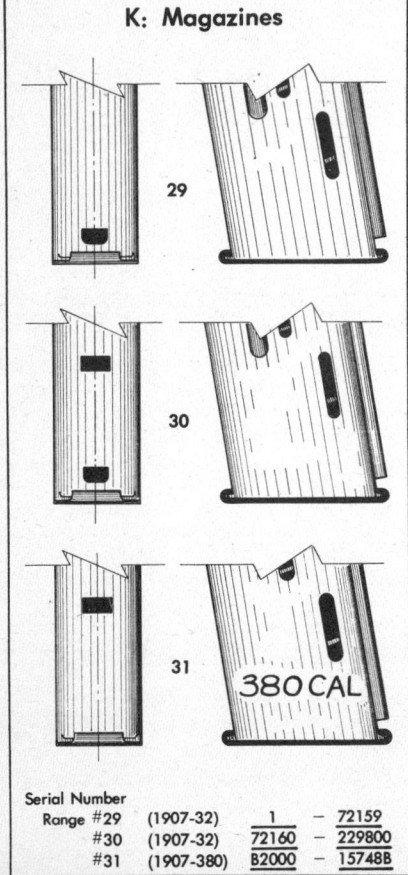

29
30
31 380 CAL

Serial Number
Range #29 (1907-32)   1   – 72159
      #30 (1907-32) 72160 – 229800
      #31 (1907-380) B2000 – 15748B

J1: Logo on Slide Top—32

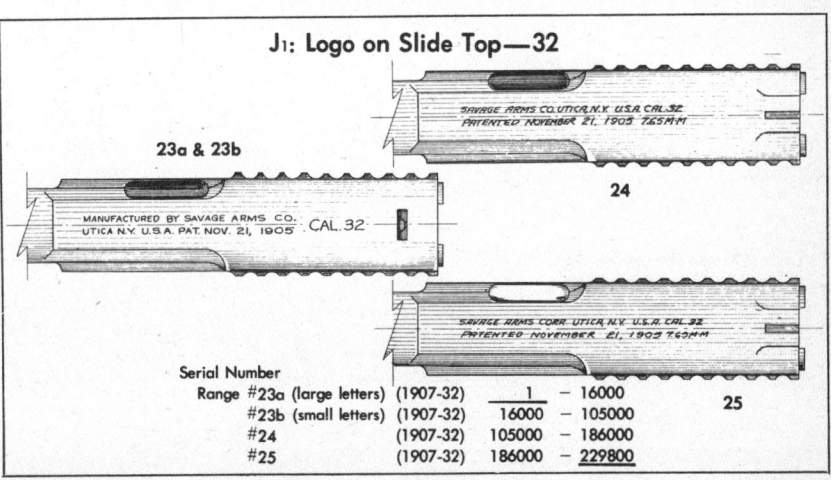

23a & 23b
24
25

Serial Number
Range #23a (large letters) (1907-32)   1   – 16000
      #23b (small letters) (1907-32) 16000 – 105000
      #24 (1907-32)   105000 – 186000
      #25 (1907-32)   186000 – 229800

J₂ Logo on Slide Top — 380

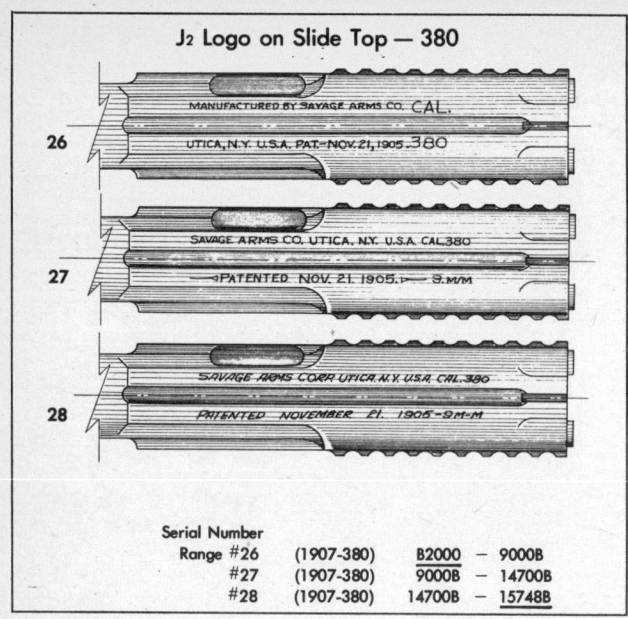

Serial Number
Range #26 (1907-380) B2000 — 9000B
#27 (1907-380) 9000B — 14700B
#28 (1907-380) 14700B — 15748B

M: "SAFE" & "FIRE" Stamp on Frame

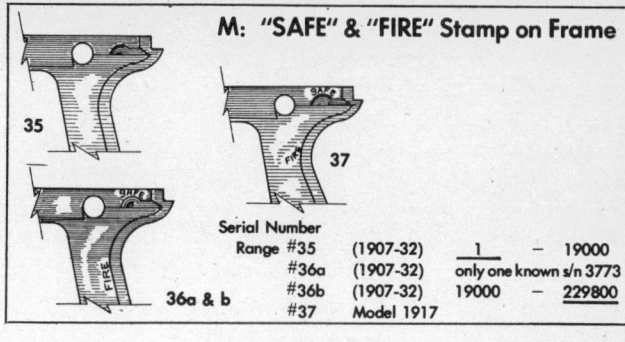

Serial Number
Range #35 (1907-32) 1 — 19000
#36a (1907-32) only one known s/n 3773
#36b (1907-32) 19000 — 229800
#37 Model 1917

T: Ejector

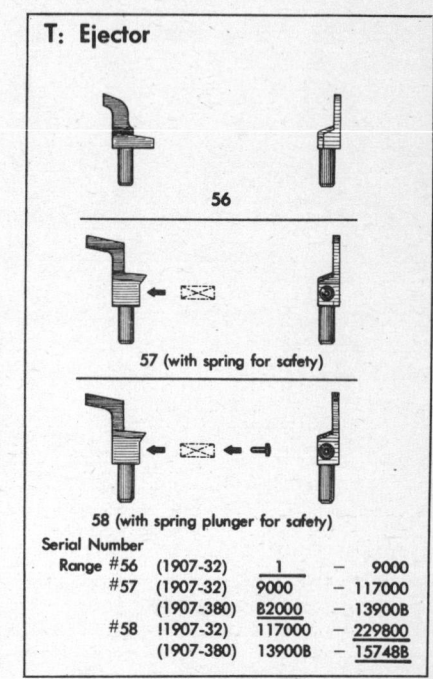

Serial Number
Range #56 (1907-32) 1 — 9000
#57 (1907-32) 9000 — 117000
(1907-380) B2000 — 13900B
#58 (1907-32) 117000 — 229800
(1907-380) 13900B — 15748B

U: Sear

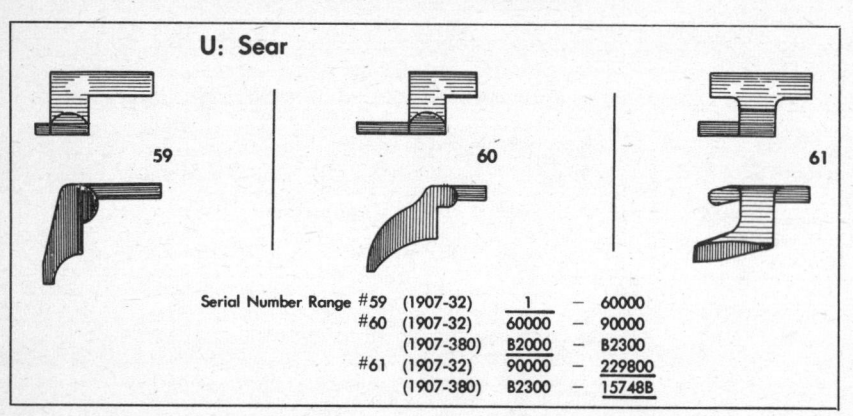

Serial Number Range #59 (1907-32) 1 — 60000
#60 (1907-32) 60000 — 90000
(1907-380) B2000 — B2300
#61 (1907-32) 90000 — 229800
(1907-380) B2300 — 15748B

V₁ & V₂: Barrels, Recoil Spring, & Slide Muzzle

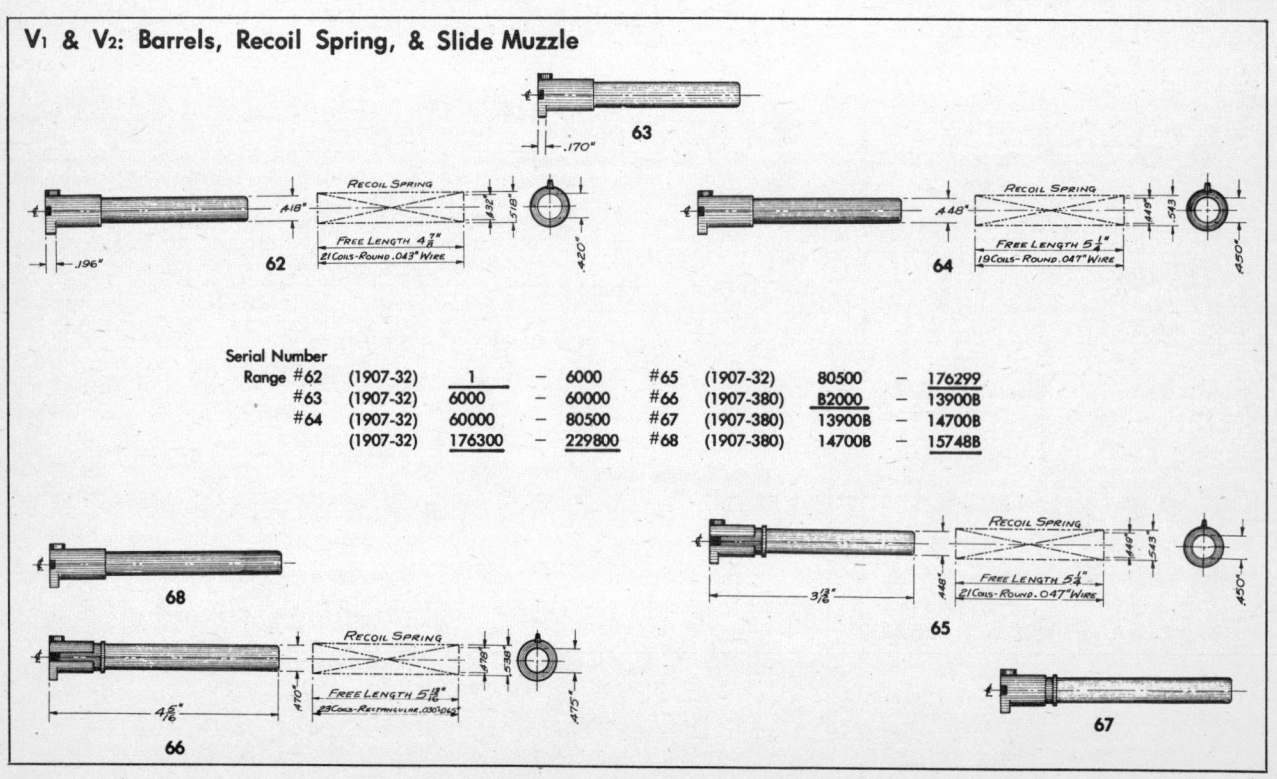

Serial Number
Range #62 (1907-32) 1 — 6000   #65 (1907-32) 80500 — 176299
#63 (1907-32) 6000 — 60000   #66 (1907-380) B2000 — 13900B
#64 (1907-32) 60000 — 80500   #67 (1907-380) 13900B — 14700B
(1907-32) 176300 — 229800   #68 (1907-380) 14700B — 15748B

W: Breechblock

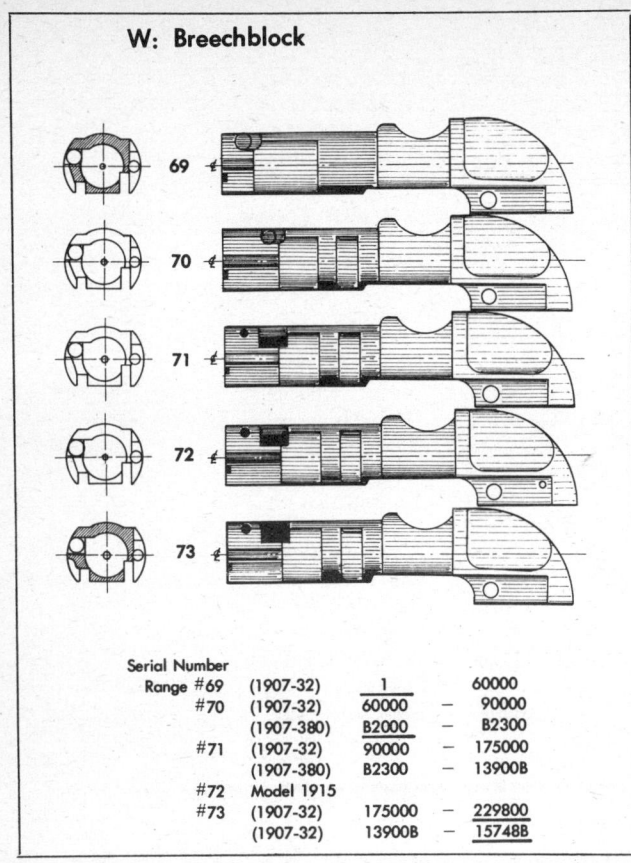

Serial Number
Range #69 (1907-32) 1 — 60000
#70 (1907-32) 60000 — 90000
(1907-380) B2000 — B2300
#71 (1907-32) 90000 — 175000
(1907-380) B2300 — 13900B
#72 Model 1915
#73 (1907-32) 175000 — 229800
(1907-32) 13900B — 15748B

X: Trigger

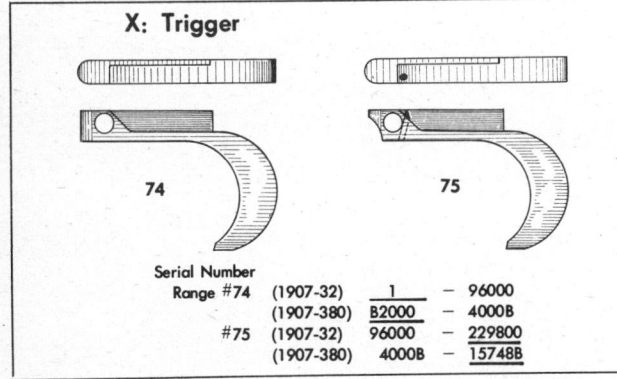

Serial Number
Range #74 (1907-32) 1 — 96000
(1907-380) B2000 — 4000B
#75 (1907-32) 96000 — 229800
(1907-380) 4000B — 15748B

Z: Striker

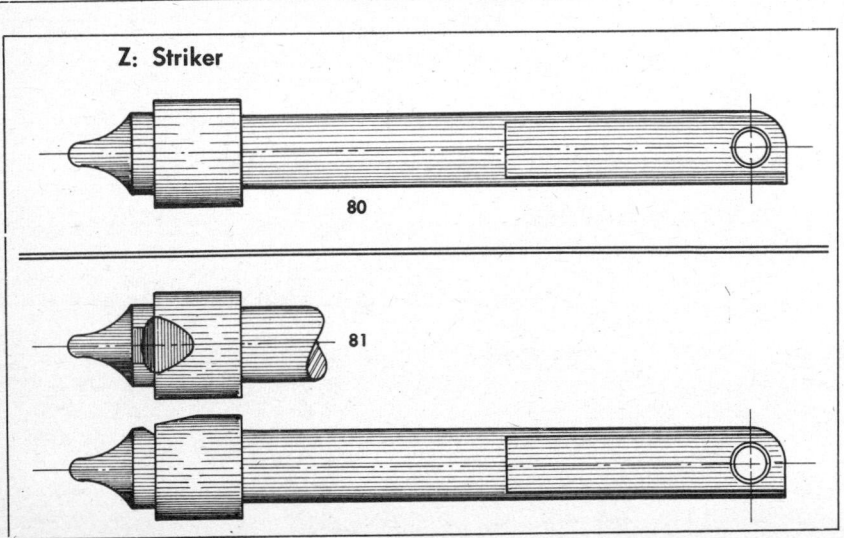

Y: Sear Trip & Trigger Locking Bar

#76 without trigger locking bar, #77 with trigger locking bar, #78 Model 1915, back to #77 again.

Serial Number
Range #76 (1907-32) 1 — 78900
#77 (1907-32) 78900 — 229800
(1907-380) B2000 — 15748B
#78 Model 1915

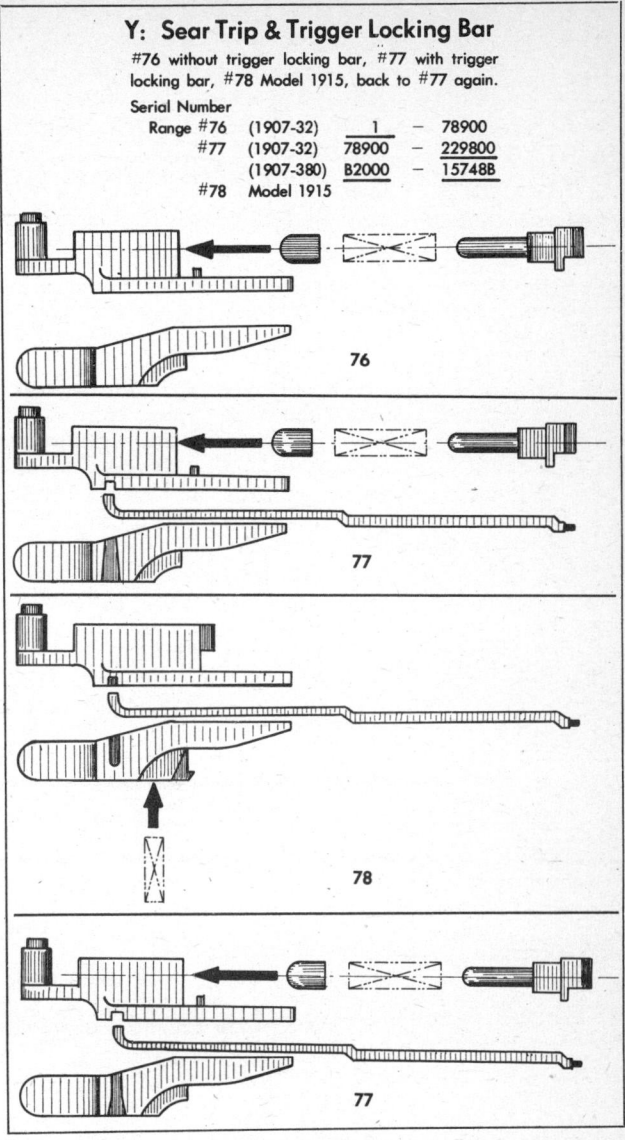

Safety	A-3 to A-4
Rear Sight	D-10 to D-11
Magazine Catch	E-12 to E-13
Load Chamber Indicator	G-19 to G-21
Slide	H-20 to H-22
Magazine	K-29 to K-30
Sear	U-59 to U-60
Barrel	V-63 to V-64 to V-65
Breechblock	W-69 to W-70
Sear Trip	Y-76 to Y-77
Disassembly	AA-81 to AA-82 to AA-83

Jim Carr in his book *Savage Automatic Pistols* calls this period the 1907-12 transitional. This is because of the number of changes and the fact that they appear only to disappear for a time.

There are those who note that final inspector's marks change from an L to R, but to me this is really not a variation.

Conclusion

The Savage 1907 was a good pistol comparing it to its peers; it had less sharp corners and more shots. On the negative side, it had a reputation for firing all the cartridges in its magazine with one pull of the trigger. This "machine gunning" usually happened when the owner tried to reduce the trigger pull which caused the pistol to "jar" fire, but so will other pistols so abused. No, my feeling is that treated right, the Savage was a good protection arm and I think that had they been made for the same number of years as were the Colt pocket automatics, they would have matched the Colts in sales. When an experienced arms manufacturer goes into a new field, we always find a quality product—the Savage Model 1907 was just that. Best of all from the collector's point of view, the prices on Savage Model 1907s are still very reasonable and there are lots of sleepers and variations to have a full collection.

Bibliography

Savage Automatic Pistol, James R. Carr, 1967. Privately published.

10 Shots Quick, Daniel K. Stern, 1967. Globe Printing Co., San Jose, CA 95150.

Textbook of Automatic Pistols, R.K. Wilson, 1943. Now published by Stackpole Books, Harrisburg, PA.

Pistols & Revolvers, W.H.B. Smith, 1946. Now published by Stackpole Books, Harrisburg, PA.

Firearms Identification Vol I, II, III, J. Howard Mathews, 1962. Now published by C.C. Thomas, Springfield, Ill.

U.S. Cartridges & Their Handguns, Charles R. Suydam, 1977. Beinfeld Publishing Inc., North Hollywood, CA 91605.

Acknowledgements

This article is dedicated to Sid Aberman who has always helped me so generously over the years.

Special thanks to those two who led the way; James Carr and Daniel Stern and extra special thanks to Robert A. Greenleaf of Savage's R&D department for working on his lunch hour to date most of the known serial numbers.

Thanks to fellow collectors: Richard Baker, Michel Carney, James Cottrill, the late Charles Engles, Richard Fern, Neils Hanson, Leonard Hunter, Ernie Lang, Douglas Lawrence, Fred Stegner, Winfred "Jr." Sumner, Larry Tieger.

Thanks also to those at Savage Arms Corporation, especially to one who helped twenty years ago, William H. McCrillis.

Thanks to my roommate, Doris S. Simmons, Editor and typist, to whom Savage is a mood after what she has been through.

Patents

The patents that have to do with Savage automatic pistols are as follows:

U.S. Patent #	Date issued	Patentee	Used on 1907	Notes
804984	Nov 12 1905	Searle	no	Target Length Pistol
804985	Nov 12 1905	Searle	yes	Basic Patent
936369	Oct 12 1909	Searle	no	45 Pistol
985847	Mar 7 1911	Searle	no	45 Pistol
1080364	Dec 2 1913	Nelson	yes	Positive Safety
1082961	Dec 30 1913	Lang	yes	Trigger Locking Bar
1082969	Dec 30 1913	Nelson	yes	Loaded Chamber Indicator
1085698	Feb 3 1914	Nelson	yes	Positive Safety
1168024	Jan 11 1916	Nelson	yes	Magazine Latch
1206892	Dec 5 1916	Nelson	no	Revised
1320572	Nov 5 1919	A. S. Savage*	no	Greatly Revised
1395455	Nov 1 1921	Searle	no	One Hand Cocking Pistol

*Arthur W. Savage's son

KNOWN SAVAGE MODEL 1907-32 PISTOLS

MODEL 1907 STARTED WITH S/N1 on APRIL 22, 1908

Serial Number	Date Accepted	Date Shipped	Features	Serial Number	Date Accepted	Date Shipped	Features
				110	?	10-21-08	A-1, B-5, C-7, D-10, E-12, F-14, G-19, H-20, J-23, K-29, L-32, M-35, N-38, O-41, P-44a, T-56, U-59, V-62, W-69, X-74, Y-76, Z-80, AA-81
P-3	?	?	factory cut-a-way				
0013	?	?	32/380 combo				
0013#2				124	?	11-2-08	as s/n 110
00004A	?	?	special contract	163	?	10-26-08	M-36, "safe" & "fire"
00038A	?	?	special contract	236	—	—	as s/n 124

KNOWN SAVAGE MODEL 1907-32 PISTOLS (cont'd)

Serial Number	Date Accepted	Date Shipped	Features
245	?	10-14-08	as s/n 124
267	—	—	as s/n 124
298	—	—	as s/n 124
310	—	10-21-08	A-2 safety
455/P-33	—	—	factory cut-a-way
626	?	1-27-09	as s/n 298
836	?	10-27-08	as s/n 298
867	?	11-2-08	as s/n 298
870	?	11-2-08 2-9-09	returned J-32 slide marks, A-3 safety reshipped F-15 grips, M-36 frame
1132	—	10-14-08	as s/n 867
1272	—	—	0-42 s/n on b/b
1397	—	11-18-08	as s/n 1132
1430	?	11-16-08	as s/n 1132
1678	—	—	0-42 s/n on b/b
1941	—	1-19-09	0-42 s/n on b/b
2177	—	—	as s/n 1430
2269	4-19-09	4-26-11	M-36 "safe" & "fire"
2707	—	—	0-42 s/n on b/b
2919	—	3-25-09	as s/n 1430
3081	—	—	A-2 safety, s/n stamped inside slide
3105	—	5-14-09	as s/n 2919
3363	—	3-9-09	as s/n 2919
3773	?	?	A-2 safety, M-36, "S" & "F"
4014	—	7-22-09	A-2 safety
4092	3-13-09	9-2-09	as s/n 3363
4478	2-24-09	6-10-09	as s/n 3363
4620	—	—	A-2 safety
4708	—	—	0-42 s/n on b/b & slide
4845	?	12-9-08	A-2 safety, M-36 "safe" & "fire"
6027	—	—	as s/n 4845
6044	—	—	as s/n 4845
6128	2-3-09	8-5-09	as s/n 4845
6786	4-16-09	7-13-09 9-20-09	returned reshipped V-63 barrel
7087	4-17-09	10-28-09	V-63 barrel
7095	5-13-09	7-13-09	V-63 barrel
8177	—	—	V-63 barrel
8253	—	—	Toronto Police
8311	5-4-09	10-30-09	A-3 safety
8378	5-5-09	8-16-09	A-3 safety
8807	—	—	consecutive
8809	—	—	serial numbers
8845	5-28-09	6-14-09	as s/n 8378
8853	5-15-09	10-30-09	as s/n 8378
9995	6-10-09	4-26-11	as s/n 8378
10103	6-15-09	8-10-09	T-57 ejector, shipped to Canada Bank of Commerce
10488	6-29-09	10-30-09	T-57 ejector
10704	6-30-09	10-30-09	T-57 ejector
10823	7-8-09	4-26-11	T-57 ejector
11942	8-12-09	12-1-09	F-15 grips, J-23 slide marks
12184	8-30-09	10-30-09	P-44b finish
13681	10-27-09	11-3-09	P-44b finish
14944	11-5-09	2-2-10	P-44b finish
15189	11-9-09	3-7-10	listed by Savage as a military! What country?
16303	12-20-09	2-16-10	as s/n 14944
16545	—	—	British proofs
17954	—	—	as s/n 16303
18885	3-16-10	3-30-10	as s/n 16303
19039	3-16-10	4-18-10	as s/n 16303
19301	3-21-10	4-19-10	as s/n 16303
19436	3-30-10	5-23-10	as s/n 16303
19579	4-15-10	4-26-10	as s/n 16303
19652	4-14-10	4-23-10	M-36 "safe" & "fire", 0-42 s/n on b/b and bbl
19709	4-15-10	4-28-10	M-36 "safe" & "fire"
22262	5-24-10	7-9-10	M-36 "safe" & "fire"
24537	—	—	M-36 "safe" & "fire"
24598	7-21-10	9-10-10	M-36 "safe" & "fire"
25543	8-4-10	10-3-10	M-36 "safe" & "fire"
25998	8-29-10	9-17-10	M-36 "safe" & "fire"
26454	9-6-10	11-25-10	M-36 "safe" & "fire"
27043	9-16-10	12-12-10	M-36 "safe" & "fire"
30561	12-12-10	1-18-11	M-36 "safe" & "fire"
30871	12-15-10	1-18-11	earlier pistol renumbered
31856	2-3-11	2-9-11	as s/n 30561
32111	—	—	as s/n 30561
32709	—	—	as s/n 30561
34875	3-20-11	3-22-11	as s/n 30561
37635	4-21-11	4-28-11	as s/n 30561
38400	—	—	as s/n 30561
38709	5-13-11	5-19-11	as s/n 30561
40762	—	—	P-47 nickel plated
41608	second hand stock	1-17-30	F-18b pearl grips
42648	7-18-11	9-5-11	as s/n 38709
42952	—	—	special long slide like 380
43357	8-11-11	11-3-11	C.A. Nelson's special long slide
43846	8-30-11	9-22-11	as s/n 42648
44512	—	—	as s/n 42648
44855	9-25-11	11-6-11	only marked on slide "32CAL"
48048	10-28-11	12-28-11	marked "Westley Richard & Co. London W."
48918	11-17-11	1-6-12	as s/n 44512
49216	11-23-11	1-9-12	as s/n 44512
49774	—	—	as s/n 44512
49946	12-6-11	1-18-12	as s/n 44512
51438	—	—	as s/n 44512
54-86	3-20-12	3-21-12	B-6 s/n location
54354	3-25-12	3-21-12	B-6 s/n location
57990	4-27-12	4-27-12	B-6 s/n location
60428	6-6-12	6-7-12	The beginning of changes finalized by s/n 81000
61247	6-3-12	6-3-12	Rifling 1 turn in 12 inches
62865	6-3-12	6-4-12	1912 Olympic presentation gun
70654	7-30-12	7-30-12	as s/n 60428
72528	8-19-12	8-31-12	factory list most of changes by s/n 72160
74011	9-12-12	10-9-12	A-3 safety, H-20 slide
74170	9-13-12	9-30-12	marked "SAP" Savage Arms Pistol
74461	7-24-12	9-25-12	as s/n 72528
74577	?	10-1-12	as s/n 72528
75267	10-30-12	10-31-12	as s/n 72528
75372	10-18-12	10-19-12	as s/n 72528
76275	10-29-12	12-4-12	as s/n 72528
76702	10-29-12	12-4-12	as s/n 72528
77931	11-12-12	11-15-12	as s/n 72528
78547	—	—	N-39 frame
78933	?	12-2-12	N-39 frame
80538	12-21-12	1-16-13	N-39 frame
80740	1-10-13	1-13-13	N-39 frame
81672	1-14-13	1-14-13	marked "K.P.D. 16" Kingston N.Y.
84053	—	8-11-13	A-4 safety, Y-77 trigger lock
84803	—	—	silver plated with 18a pearl grips
84835	—	—	blue-engraved
85094	2-24-13	2-25-13	as s/n 84053
86109	3-4-13	5-23-13	as s/n 84053
87255	—	—	as s/n 84053
88593	4-1-13	6-6-13	as s/n 84053
89370	5-5-13	5-8-13	as s/n 84053
91838	9-29-13	10-20-13	as s/n 84053
93631	9-10-13	9-11-13	as s/n 84053
94634	8-27-13	9-13-13	Z-81 striker
95124	—	—	as s/n 94634

KNOWN SAVAGE MODEL 1907-32 PISTOLS (cont'd)

Serial Number	Date Accepted	Date Shipped	Features
95669	—	—	as s/n 94634
95848	9-25-13	11-10-13	O-42 s/n on b/b
95905	8-27-13	9-25-13	N-38 frame
96253	6-15-14	6-20-14	U-61 sear, J-24 logo, W-71 breech, X-75 trigger, F-18b grips, engraved
96949	—	—	as above, not engraved
97044	10-21-13	1-20-14	as above, regular grips
98352	10-31-13	12-10-13	as s/n 97044
99249	12-2-13	12-29-13	as s/n 97044
100107	1-9-14	2-9-14	shipped to Peters Arms Co.
101728	4-13-14	4-27-14	as s/n 99249
101961	2-12-14	3-21-14	F-18b pearl grips
102107	6-5-14	6-8-14	O-42 s/n on b/b and slide
102145	2-12-14	3-19-14	as s/n 101728
102404	2-27-14	4-30-14	as s/n 101728
103255	—	—	as s/n 101728
103689			special spur cocking piece
103674	4-6-14	never shipped	as s/n 103255
105769			as s/n 103255
107259	7-22-14	8-1-14	French contract
107533	7-30-14	Never shipped?	J-24 logo, British proofs
107866	?	7-31-14	as s/n 103674
110036	10-1-14	10-16-14	as s/n 103674
112830	11-16-14	11-18-14	French contract
113252	11-20-14	11-20-14	as s/n 110036
114068			O-42 s/n on slide
114323	12-1-14	12-1-14	as s/n 113252
114780	12-15-14	1-27-15	as s/n 113252
115285	12-26-14	1-13-15	as s/n 113252
115300	12-30-14	1-16-15	as s/n 113252
115999	1-4-15	1-23-15	repaired 9-9-20
116051	4-24-15	6-28-15	special spur cocking piece, repaired 7-30-34
117479	—	—	as s/n 115999
118749	8-8-17	8-11-17	repaired 3-10-?
119473	3-24-15	8-3-15	as s/n 117479
120950	4-24-15	9-24-15	as s/n 117479
12142	—	—	French contract
121445	—	—	as s/n 120950
122735	3-25-15	9-28-15	French contract
123334	4-7-15	9-28-15	as s/n 122735
124593	9-17-15	10-25-15	as s/n 122735
126656	10-7-15	10-25-15	as s/n 122735
126706	10-6-15	10-25-15	as s/n 122735
127883	—	—	as s/n 122735
127939	—	—	as s/n 122735
129270	10-28-15	12-16-15	A-4, B-6, C-8, D-11, E-13, F-15, G-21, H-22, J-24, K-30, L-32, M-36, N-39, O-41, P-44b, T-58, U-61, V-65, W-71, X-75, Y-77, Z-81, AA-83

MODEL 1915 BEGINS WITH S/N 130000, ENDS S/N 136500
MODEL 1907 RESTARTS WITH S/N 150000

Serial Number	Date Accepted	Date Shipped	Features
150963	11-12-15	12-16-15	French contract
152514	11-29-15	12-16-15	as s/n 150963
152987	12-4-15	12-16-15	as s/n 150963
153273	12-7-15	12-16-15	as s/n 150963
153679	12-9-15	12-16-15	as s/n 150963
154168	—	—	as s/n 150963
157258	4-6-16	4-8-16	as s/n 150963
157976	4-15-16	5-15-16	as s/n 150963
158736	5-18-16	7-15-16	as s/n 150963
158823	—	—	as s/n 150963
161294	7-31-16	8-14-16	as s/n 150963
161807	—	—	Portuguese contract, most of the holsters found in the U.S. are Portuguese. They can be identified by the stamp "A.E."
162414	8-21-16	9-29-16	French contract
162655	9-6-16	9-29-16	as s/n 162414
162702	9-13-16	9-29-16	as s/n 162414
163448	9-20-16	9-29-16	as s/n 162414
163991	—	—	British proofed, round lanyard ring
164335	10-17-16	10-26-16	French contract
165282	12-18-16	12-23-16	F-17 Special Portuguese grips, Portuguese contract
166056			Portuguese contract
166056	12-9-16	12-13-16	F-17 special Portuguese grips, Savage Arms Co.
166227	12-18-16	12-23-16	F-15 grips, Portuguese contract
166387	2-1-17	2-2-17	as s/n 166227
166491	12-6-16		Portuguese contract, "Direccao Material Guerra de Marinna"
166501	12-13-16	12-23-16	as s/n 166387
166706	—	—	as s/n 166387
166742	12-8-16	12-23-16	as s/n 166387
167055	1-18-17	1-19-17	Commercial production
167205	1-4-17	1-9-17	as s/n 167055
167218	1-8-17	1-9-17	as s/n 167055
167674	2-28-17	3-1-17	as s/n 167055
167866	4-7-17	4-9-17	as s/n 167055
168456	—	—	as s/n 167055
168872	—	—	as s/n 167055
169837	4-11-17	4-12-17	N-38 frame
171085	5-14-17	5-15-17	as s/n 169837
171425	5-17-17	5-18-17	as s/n 169837
171585	7-5-17	7-6-17	as s/n 169837
173119	6-27-17	6-28-17	as s/n 169837
173898	—	—	as s/n 169837
174344	6-26-17	6-28-17	as s/n 169837
174879	7-21-17	7-23-17	as s/n 169837
174958	8-7-17	8-9-17	as s/n 169837
175528	—	—	as s/n 169837
175919	7-17-17	7-18-17	as s/n 169837
178912	—	—	as s/n 169837
178967	9-13-17	9-14-17	as s/n 169837
179547	12-20-17	12-20-17	as s/n 169837
180465	10-4-17	10-5-17	as s/n 169837
180892	—	—	as s/n 169837
183033	11-19-17	11-21-17	as s/n 169837
183442	11-30-17	12-1-17	as s/n 169837
183655	11-30-17	1-18	Dominion Express Co.
184353	1-16-18	1-22-18	as s/n 183442
184399	—	—	as s/n 183442
184971	?	?	F-18b pearl grips, P-47 nickel plated
185682	4-8-18	4-19-18	P-45 black painted finish
187725	—	—	P-46 finish, C-9 slide pulls
187742	1-16-18	1-22-18	as s/n 187725
188723	6-5-19	6-7-19	as s/n 187725
189962	—	—	as s/n 187725
190391	6-16-19	6-17-17	as s/n 187725
190438	6-27-19	7-3-19	as s/n 187725
191132	6-24-19	6-25-19	as s/n 187725
192429	7-10-19	7-18-19	as s/n 187725
192439	7-1-19	7-2-19	as s/n 187725
193767	7-11-19	7-12-19	as s/n 187725
194581	—	—	as s/n 187725
194795	7-17-19	7-18-19	as s/n 187725
194959	7-18-19	7-19-19	as s/n 187725
194965	7-25-19	7-28-19	as s/n 187725
195034	7-23-19	7-24-19	as s/n 187725
197897	8-12-19	8-13-19	as s/n 187725
198027	8-5-19	8-11-19	as s/n 187725

KNOWN SAVAGE MODEL 1907-32 PISTOLS (cont'd)

Serial Number	Date Accepted	Date Shipped	Features
199303	8-11-19	8-12-19	as s/n 187725
200704	8-18-19	8-25-19	as s/n 187725
201021	8-20-19	8-21-19	as s/n 187725
201551	8-29-19	8-30-19	as s/n 187725
201638	8-22-19	8-30-19	as s/n 187725
203078	9-3-19	9-5-19	as s/n 187725
203391	8-27-19	8-27-19	as s/n 187725
203976	9-10-19	9-11-19	L-34 cocking piece
204532	—	—	as s/n 203976
206808	9-25-19	9-26-19	as s/n 203976
206891	9-29-19	9-29-19	F-18b pearl grips
208490	10-11-19	10-13-19	as s/n 206808
209801	10-6-19	10-7-19	as s/n 206808
210150	10-17-19	10-18-19	as s/n 206808
211950	10-21-19	10-22-19	as s/n 206808
212544	10-21-19	10-21-19	as s/n 206808
212569	10-18-19	10-20-19	as s/n 206808
212685	—	—	star on slide
215921	11-26-19	11-26-19	as s/n 212569
220156	12-1-19	12-2-19	as s/n 212569
223199	12-27-19	12-31-19	as s/n 212569
223460	4-26-20	5-18-20	as s/n 212569
223617	1-6-20	1-14-20	as s/n 212569
224149	1-15-20	1-19-20	as s/n 212569
226141	—	—	as s/n 212569
226825	1-15-20	1-28-20	as s/n 212569
227211	1-13-20	2-18-20	as s/n 212569
228176	2-10-20	3-11-20	as s/n 212569
228283	1-23-20	3-2-20	as s/n 212569
228538	1-31-20	3-11-20	as s/n 212569
229221	2-10-20	3-9-20	as s/n 212569
229501	2-23-30	3-9-20	A-4, B-6, C-9, D-11, E-13, F-15, G-19, H-20, J-25, K-30, L-34, M-36, N-38, O-41, P-46, T-58, U-61, V-64, W-73, X-75, Y-77, Z-81, AA-83

MODEL 1917 BEGINS WITH S/N 229801

Serial Number	Date Accepted	Date Shipped	Features
B2091	4-7-13	5-27-13	A-4, B-6, C-8, D-11, E-13, F-15, G-21, H-22, J-26, K-31, L-32, M-36, N-38, O-41, P-47b, T-57, U-60, V-66, W-70, X-74, Y-77, Z-80, AA-81
B2100	—	—	as s/n B2091
B2140	1-27-13	4-4-13	as s/n B2091
B2343	1-23-13	5-23-13	as s/n B2091
2487B	4-14-13	5-24-13	U-61 sear, W-70 b/b
2638B	4-23-13	5-24-13	blued loaded chamber indicator
2835B	5-9-13	5-24-13	as s/n 2487B
3933B	6-3-13	6-4-13	as s/n 2487B
4094B	6-12-13	7-19-13	as s/n 2487B
4155B	6-5-13	7-16-13	as s/n 2487B
4208B	—	—	as s/n 2487B
4365B	5-29-13	6-10-13	as s/n 2487B
4714B	9-3-13	12-18-13	"#10" stamped on b/b
4742B	6-17-13	6-19-13	special spur cocking piece
4884B	6-14-13	9-18-13	as s/n 4365B
5024B	8-28-13	12-19-13	as s/n 4365B
5186B	8-20-13	8-28-13	as s/n 4365B
NOTE 1			
6003B	—	—	as s/n 4365B
6253B	—	—	as s/n 4365B
6466B	10-7-13	11-28-13	as s/n 4365B
6867B	4-7-14	5-13-14	as s/n 4365B
6984B	10-17-13	1-17-14	as s/n 4365B
7197B	3-31-14	2-15-16	N-39 frame, AA-82 takedown, P-47 nickel finish
7326B	1-23-14	2-4-16	P-47 nickel finish
7388B	6-5-14	6-25-14	same but P-44b finish
7702B	6-23-14	8-11-14	as s/n 7388B
7847B	9-3-14	9-11-14	has a stamped "C"
8039B	8-25-14	8-26-14	as s/n 7702B
8086B	—	—	as s/n 7702B
8511B	9-28-14	12-12-14	as s/n 7702B
8529B	—	—	as s/n 7702B
8690B	1-12-15	1-19-15	special spur cocking piece
8697B	10-5-14	11-7-14	as s/n 8511B
8702B	10-8-14	12-1-14	as s/n 8511B
8757B	—	—	0-42 s/n on slide
8794B	—	—	special spur cocking piece
8832B	10-14-14	12-1-14	as s/n 8702B
8896B	12-1-14	12-10-14	P-47 nickel finish
8961B	12-2-14	12-31-14	shipped to Iver Johnson Co.
9130B	?	3-20-16	J-27 slide markings
9563B	—	—	as s/n 8832B
9956B	4-23-15	4-28-15	J-27 slide markings

MODEL 1915 BEGINS WITH S/N 10000B, ENDS WITH S/N APPROX. 13500B
MODEL 1907 RESTARTS WITH S/N 13903B

Serial Number	Date Accepted	Date Shipped	Features
14678B	1-9-20	1-10-20	A-4, B-6, C-8, D-11, E-13, F-15, G-19, H-22, J-27, K-31, L-34, M-36, N-38, O-41, P-46, T-58, U-61, V-67, W-73, X-75, Y-77, Z-81, AA-83
14707B	1-9-20	1-10-20	as s/n 14678B
14709B	1-9-20	1-9-20	as s/n 14678B
14722B	1-14-20	1-14-20	as s/n 14678B
14727B	1-6-20	1-9-20	as s/n 14678B
15030B	1-9-20	1-9-20	C-9 slide pulls
15093B			F-18b pearl grips
15216B	1-13-20	1-14-20	P-47 nickel finish
15241B	1-15-20	1-16-20	same with P-46 finish
15245B	1-13-20	1-14-20	as s/n 15216B
15286B	1-31-20	1-31-20	as s/n 15216B
15370B	1-19-20	1-20-20	as s/n 15216B
15554B	—	—	as s/n 15216B
15656B	2-23-20	2-25-20	as s/n 15216B
15729B	1-20-20	1-21-20	as s/n 15216B

MODEL 1917 STARTED AT S/N 15749B

Serial Number	Date Accepted	Date Shipped	Features
22897B	1920	1907	18b pearl grips
22900B	1920	1907	18b pearl grips

These out of range numbered pistols were made up after the Model 1907 was terminated, probably because some people still liked the 1907 grip. They are always dressed-up pistols.

Note 1 A group of 250 pistols were sold to Columbia S.A. in this range

Note: The pistols which have no "accepted" and "shipping" dates were itemized after Bob Greenleaf of Savage had received my massive list for dates, and so could not be dated. A "?" means no entry in Savage books.

The Cylindrical Bullet Kills Better

Sherwood knows the round ball, and the reasons for it, but knows, too, there's a better killer.

by ROBERT K. SHERWOOD

IN THE WESTERN United States, muzzle-loader hunting is rapidly achieving a position of prominence. Increasing numbers of hunters are purchasing replica rifles, and several states have inaugurated muzzle-loader only hunts. By the very crowded condition of these hunts we are shown the need for more of them.

However, as with most new concepts, it meets with opposition, not nearly all of which is well-advised or very intellectual. (Yes, I realize that muzzle-loading firearms have been known to be around since 1388, but the concept of a hunt just for them in this day and age is, indeed a new thing.) The heaviest and most frequent argument leveled against muzzle loader hunting and special seasons is that they are wounders and lack adequate killing power for medium and big game hunting. At first this doesn't seem too logical; most of their bores will take a couple of marbles at once without much friction on the sides, and the idea of punching that size of hole in anything is easy to connect with sudden death.

But it doesn't always work that way. The sphere is the most difficult geometric form to deform or destroy. In the muzzle-loader the spherical round ball is not given enough velocity to deform it unless it hits a large bone. Otherwise, sufficient impact for bullet deformation and subsequent spreading is not there. And the roundball has a definite tendency to spread muscle fibers, rather than to cut them. The hole made by a roundball in any medium is not one of extreme damage. Examine, for instance, a roundball hole through a paper target. Nearly always you can put the paper edges of the perforation back together because the round ball tears rather than punches a hole, and no paper is actually destroyed or carried away. It follows that such a projectile can pass through flesh separating fibers rather than cutting them, arteries and veins can be dislocated and passed rather than cut by the ball, and the result is a wound of little shock value and not much bleeding effect.

There is an exception to this pattern. When the roundball makes a solid hit on a major bone, such as a humerus, a scapula or a vertebra, then it does deform and mushroom mightily. Then shock is adequate, bleeding frequent and copious, and death not far away at all. The path of the projectile may deviate markedly from the angle of entrance following impact with the bone, but it is a much more destructive path in terms of tissue damage.

Lest someone level the charge of daydreaming theoretician at me, it should be stated that I researched this rather thoroughly. As a Game Manager for the State of Idaho I had wide opportunity for contact with black-powder hunters and to examine their kills both in the field and through check stations.

Projectiles tested, from left, TC 45 Maxi Ball, RCBS 45 Minie, Ideal 454612, Ideal 575494, Lee 400-gr. 58 REALbullet, RCBS 500-gr. Minie Ball.

Table I
58 Caliber Rifles

Rifle	Bullet/Type	Wgt./Grs.	Charge/Grs. FFg	Best Group (in.) 100 Yds.
Parker-Hale Enfield 1858	RCBS Minie	500	70	3
	57494 Ideal	315	60	6
	Lee REALbullet*	400	70	4, one flier
	Roundball, Speer	285	70	3.5
Navy Arms Springfield 1863	RCBS Minie	500	70	3.5
	575494 Ideal	315	60	3.7
	Lee REALbullet	400	70	8
	Roundball, Speer	285	70	3
Lyman Plains Rifle	RCBS Minie	500	70	3.3
	575494 Ideal	315	60	9
	Lee REALbullet	400	70	6
	Round Ball, Speer	285	70	3
Navy Arms Zouave	RCBS Minie	500	70	6
	57594 Ideal	315	60	wild
	Lee REALbullet	400	70	9
	Round Ball, Speer	285	90	2.5

*Worth Noting: Did not have opportunity to try REALbullets in various diameters.

I watched Frank DeShon shoot a 45-cal. ball into the spine of a 4-point buck at the Magpie Spring. Death was instantaneous and the wound channel impressive. He hit the animal squarely in the spine immediately behind the withers. The resulting wound was impressive even when compared to like hits with modern rifles.

Robert Bottoms, a highly successful muzzle loader hunter of the area, has dropped three elk in or right near their tracks, using a 58-cal. Zouave loaded with a round ball. In every case he hit a major bone and the projectile behaved as was hoped. I watched several antelope hunters drop their animals on the spot with their 50s, and in every case the projectile struck a spine or a scapula.

I had accounts of other kills of this nature, and given those alone could have made an excellent case for traditional blackpowder hunting with the most acceptable traditional bullet, the round ball. But there were the other accounts, and the opposition used them to try to eliminate muzzle-loader hunting. Some of these horror stories of animals wounded and lost or nearly so came from the same careful hunters and good shots that made the excellent one shot kills.

Frank DeShon and his son collectively put seven round balls through a little buck out in Cedarville Canyon before they got him off his feet, and Bob Bottoms had to shoot a 3-point four times with his Zouave 58 before bringing him to bag. Bill McDonald took something like four or five shots to get a little buck down, using a 50 loaded with a round ball.

Frank Lawyer shot a 54-cal. round ball through a mature mule deer, end to end, and recovered the spent ball. It was as cast, no deformation, no dents and certainly no expansion. He shot it a second time through his rifle with accurate result. I watched two hunters

Chopper rides for Sherwood mean deer and elk surveys in Idaho. He works full time with Idaho's game population.

pelt a forkhorn liberally with 50-cal. roundballs, before I threw a Minie from my Parker-Hale Enfield through it to save it further suffering.

This last tells us that one can make a good case against the muzzleloader as a hunting weapon, especially if the audience doesn't know how many animals are crippled and lost through irresponsible shooting by modern centerfire users. And a point was well made by these sloppy kills. Not only must the muzzle-loader hunter place his shot exactly, he must have a thorough knowledge of animal anatomy and he must learn different rules of shot placement than he did to hunt with a centerfire.

All of the illustrative sloppy kills involved one or more bullets immediately behind the shoulder. They were good hits, by centerfire standards. They illustrated two very important facts. Deer flesh and deer bones so small as a rib will not by themselves disrupt the form of a sphere of lead; what is a killing shot right now with a humble 30-30 is not such with a roundball-charged musket. Secondly, any one of the many balls fired at the aforementioned deer would have been a killing round had they hit a major bone. The conclusion

The Sherwood family are consumers as well as managers of game. This is the Redoubtable Charlotte and a moose.

Sherwood gets to work on the ground, too, and in this case he's in wild country counting goose nests, another part of the job.

is that when using such a weapon and projectile, one should shoot for the shoulder rather than behind it in the ribcage. When the animal is coming on or going away, one should try for the biggest bone he knows he can hit to insure a good clean kill.

Now a lot of us are not that good as marksmen. A very great number of hunters can do beautifully on the target range and they royally get the buck fever when the real thing breaks cover. They are lucky to get a decent hit in the front end of the critter, somewhere between gut and shirtfront. On a running animal, a lot of us aren't much better than that. So if we all continue to hunt deer with muzzleloaders loaded with spherical projectiles, some of us are going to make our section of the sport liable to a lot of unwarranted criticism. And that criticism, if it gets heavy enough, can cost us things such as special muzzle-loader hunts. The ban-the-gun types are very quick to jump on muzzle loader and archery hunting as inhumane, witness Cleveland Amory. They say it is a pageant of savagery to go about wounding animals with primitive weapons, and if they do this effectively enough, they can cost us our sport.

I like primitive weapons hunting. If

Table II
45 Caliber Rifles

Rifle	Bullet/Type	Wgt./Grs.	Charge/grs. FFFg	Best Group (in.) 100 Yds.
Lyman Plains rifle	RCBS Minie	285	80	2.8
	454612 Ideal	300	80	3.0
	TC MaxiBall	220	70	6.5
	Roundball, Speer	127	80	2.5
Navy Arms Kentucky	RCBS Minie	285	60	3.0
	454612 Ideal	300	60	wild
	REALbullet, Lee	200	60	5.0
	TC Maxiball	200	60	3.0
	Roundball, Speer	127	60	2.0
Thompson-Center Seneca	RCBS Minie	285	60	3.0
	454612 Ideal	300	60	3.0
	TC MaxiBall	220	60	7.5
	Roundball, Speer	127	60	2.3

Putting together the facts for this article meant a lot of loading.

Sherwood hunkers down to touch off a Lyman Plains Rifle from the bench, part of his load development program.

The 58 caliber Plains Rifle, with a suitable bullet and not a ball, is one of author's choices for muzzle-loader hunting. It isn't primitive, perhaps, but it kills better, he feels.

I didn't own a single firelock and had I never flipped a stick, I would like it. I was a professional game manager and biologist for 20-odd years, and in that time I saw a lot of changes. In a lot of places and states, public hunting dwindled away or was severely curtailed, due to dwindling animal populations, increasing human populations and, in some cases, unwarranted human conservatism. Sometimes the uninformed but sincere doomsday criers had their way.

Now, nobody but the hunter and his appointed and paid representatives maintained the wildlife populations, game and non-game, of the United States. When the hunter goes, so does the wildlife, simply because no one other than the buyers of firearms, ammunition and hunting licenses ever financed protection and propagation of wildlife, and if he doesn't nobody else is going to. If we decrease his number we will decrease the resource proportionately. It therefore follows that the wildlife manager should and firstly protect and maintain the number of hunters through general hunting seasons.

Now, a centerfire hunter takes 12 hunting days to kill an animal of the deer class. A muzzle-loader hunter takes 32 hunting days. (Or if 32 muzzle-loader hunters hunt a day apiece, one will kill a deer, however you choose to break it down.) Obviously, you can be a lot more liberal with muzzle-loader seasons than you can with those for any weapon. There are many cases where you could have a much longer season, or an either-sex season if you limited the equipment to muzzle loaders; there are places where you can't in the interest of safety permit the use of flatshooting 270s, but where such short-range weapons as shotguns and Hawken rifles are quite acceptable; and there are some areas where you have a choice of a limited draw hunt with centerfires, or a general, everybody-can-hunt season with muzzle loaders. In summary, you can have a lot more general and liberal seasons with muzzle loaders than you can without them, and it is in the interests of outdoor writers and biologists to maintain them.

Now, as with most problems we face today, there are solutions. For the traditionalist of the baggy buckskins brigade who says that the only way he can feel that he is muzzle-loader hunting is to wear the clothing of and shoot the projectile of Boone and Bridger there can be but one answer: become an extreme degree expert marksman and hold only for a big bone, or the head or neck. Learn the anatomy of the quarry, so that you know what you are shooting for. Shoulders give the biggest margin for error which will still result in a killing shot on the spot. And do keep in practice.

There are a lot of us who enjoy hunting with muzzle loaders, and who aren't that choosy about the gear and gunnery of Osborne Russell. Perhaps the traditions of Chicamauga loom as large as do those of Old Vincennes to us. We use cylindrical bullets, and this is a whole new ball game.

There has never been any question over the destructive effect of a soft-lead cylindrical projectile. The black-powder cartridge guns, such as the 38-55 or the 45-70, have never been logically accused of lacking killing power for deer or even elk. I've killed deer and antelope with such rifles and witnessed a lot of kills with them by others. They are quite effective within their range limits, and these last were the only reason for their obsolescence.

It likely follows that a 300 grain cylindrical bullet propelled by 80 grains of FFFg from a 45 caliber muzzle loader will perform on game in a fashion identical to that of a 45-70 loaded the same way, and that a 500 grain Minie chucked out of a 58 by 100 grains of black exceeds most black-powder cartridge arms and some modern centerfires in killing wallop. Any rifle, from 45 caliber on up is adequate for elk and all smaller game when loaded with a good powder charge and a cylindrical bullet of 250 grains or more in weight. Furthermore, any good chest area hit will have the animal off his feet rather quickly. Or at least in a hundred or so yards. Nothing ancient or modern guarantees all kills to be immediate, on the spot and in tracks. Deer commonly run some small yardage half the time, even when heartshot with a 270. Expect to trail an animal now and then with the best of hits from the largest cannon.

It would appear that one is far better off with a cylindrical bullet and the sport can thereby reduce one serious criticism. There is a kicker as there is in all pat solutions. Cylindrical bullets do not shoot accurately in some guns. There are some types which do not shoot too accurately in any rifle that I have tried them in; there are some which shoot well in one rifle but not the one next to it, of the same make and caliber.

I have one rifle, a Parker-Hale Enfield, that shoots everything with hunting accuracy and some types of Minie quite as well as it throws a round ball. I have a Navy Arms Zouave which will not keep any Minies I have tried in it on a dishpan at 60 yards, although it will group roundballs tight enough to compete with modern lever actions at 100 yards.

In summary, the muzzle-loading rifleman who has achieved proficiency with roundball loadings has to learn all over again when he switches to one of the cylindrical types.

Recently I did this, gathering all the rifles I had and all I could conveniently borrow, and testing them with all the cylindrical projectiles I could fabricate or gather. I worked through countless powder-charge combinations with each bullet; I burned a couple of cans of Double-F and one of Triple-F, and ran about 20 pounds of lead through the various muskets in my rack and in Frank's. The results are tabulated in tables I and II. I fired swaged roundballs as a control; each weapon has originally been broken in with a roundball load and the best charge for such a projectile worked up for the weapon in each case.

I came to the conclusion that there was a cylindrical bullet load for most muzzle-loading rifles and for those rifles it was hardly ever the Lee REALbullet cast in the molds I had. The Zouave 58 was the least adaptable to any cylindrical bullet, but I am still trying. A friend has since advised me that I wasn't using enough powder with the Lee bullet; he killed his elk with it, using a 58 Kodiak loaded with 160 grains of FFFg. While he killed the elk at something over 100 yards, he has not fired the load for group nor for general practice. I do not believe this lack of shooting enthusiasm requires much explanation.

Rather moderate charges of powder gave the best cylindrical bullet accuracy. These coupled with the progressive depth rifling of the Parker-Hale, or the 1-turn-in-48 inches rifling of the Plains Rifles, made for excellent accuracy. Anything over a hundred grains of powder was likely to shred the skirt of the Minie ball.

There were some unexplainables produced with all the test firing. The Navy Arms Springfield did very well with both Minie balls tried in it, although it has neither tight twist rifling nor progressive groove depth. The Navy Arms Kentucky did better by far with the Maxi-ball than did the rifles for which it was explicitly designed. However some 45 and 50 TC users swear by the Maxi and shoot excellent scores with it.

My Parker-Hale Enfield has been used to take a moose, a deer and a bear. The moose was leveled by my wife and typist, the Famous Charlotte, using a 400-grain Lee REALbullet and 80 grains of Double-F. It folded him in his tracks, and she then shot him with an 1855 horse pistol replica, loaded with the same charge and ball. I got the pistol bullet back out of him, but could not find the one from the rifle. The bullet was shortened and compacted by the impact with moosemeat, but otherwise undeformed. Both wound channels were impressive, and the rifle bullet mangled his heart in the desired fashion.

The bear was shot over bait at about 30 yards with the RCBS 500 grain Minie. The bullet took him in the right cheek and penetrated through the neck vertebra, lodging in the muscles of the left side of his neck. It was well mushroomed back over the skirting, and the wound channel was indeed impressive. He was dead before he hit the ground.

The deer, a big 3-pointer, was facing me at about 100 yards. I shot him dead center through the neck with the 500 grain Minie, propelled by 80 grains of Double-F. He, like the bear, died on his way down. I found the beautifully mushroomed bullet in the skin just ahead of the withers.

These might have been expected to be killers, due to the bullet placement. I examined three elk taken in the Island Park muzzle-loader hunt, each with a single 50 caliber 370 grain Maxi-ball. All were shot through the ribcage at fairly close range and all of them went off their feet in twenty steps or less. Good clean kills, excellent damage patterns and impressive cutting of wound channels. All of these were propelled by 90 grains of Triple-F.

In summary, I have arrived at the following conclusions:

1. The roundball is a good killer only with exact bullet placement—at a place where it will expand.
2. The cylindrical projectiles are good killers with a neck or chest section hit.
3. One often is forced to a great deal of experimental shooting with the individual rifle, using different types and weights of cylindrical bullet before determining an accurate combination.

Finally, such a load is usually there, if one searches enough. The results from it are well worth the effort.

Parker-Hale Enfield and a 400-gr. REALbullet leveled this moose for the Famous Charlotte, shown approaching a still-breathing, heart-shot animal.

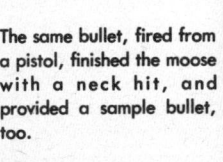

The same bullet, fired from a pistol, finished the moose with a neck hit, and provided a sample bullet, too.

HAND-LOADING TO DATE

by DEAN A. GRENNELL

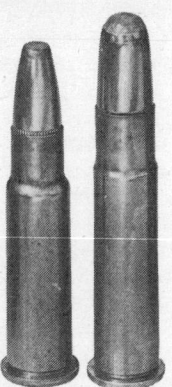
30 and 357 Herrett cases from Texas Contenders.

RCBS Competition Die Set.

Two new Hensley & Gibbs mould designs.

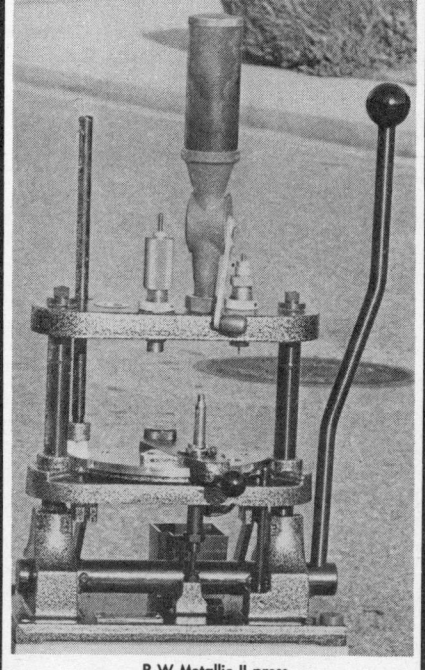
P-W Metallic II press.

RCBS "Little Dandy" powder measure can be used hand-held or mounted on a press. Rotors for 26 charge weights are available.

RCBS "Green Machine."

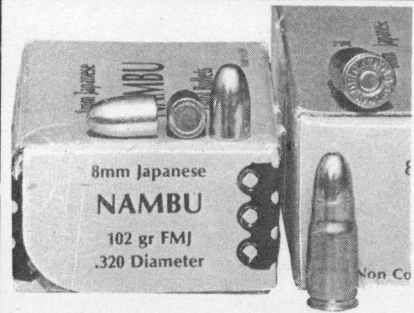
8mm Nambu bullets and loaded ammo.

WE'VE GOT A lot of new items to cover since last year's edition appeared, so let's get on with it in no particular order of going. I will, however, slug a line at the start of treating any one particular topic.

Accessible cases for reloading: Norma-Precision introduced loaded ammunition and unprimed cases in 44 Auto Mag to their line of cartridges and components. The ammo carries a 240-grain jacketed Power Cavity bullet, rated at 1350 fps/975 fpe out of the standard length Auto Mag barrel; index number 11105, it carried a suggested list price of $27.25 per box of fifty. The unprimed cases are index number 21102 and list at $13.30 for fifty. If you need 357 Auto Mag cases, it's an easy matter to run the 44 size into the full-length resizing die for the 357 AM and take it from there.

Two of the more popular of today's wildcats are the 30 and 357 Herretts, both based upon the venerable 30-30 WCF case and developer Steve Herrett suggests the use of Remington-Peters brass for best results. RCBS offers case-forming die sets in both sizes, but it's a bit of a chore to convert 30-30 cases. For those who prefer to avoid such efforts, Frank Kendricks, head of Texas Contenders (4127 Weslow Street, Houston, TX 77087) offers unprimed brass in both 30 and 357 Herrett, made up from Herrett's recommended Remington-Peters brass. Like all bullets, ammo or cases, it's available only through holders of FFLs so, if you're not of that group, check via your friendly local dealer.

Owners and custodians of 8mm Nambu auto pistols, as used by the Japanese forces in WWII, now can obtain loaded ammunition, Boxer-primed cases and suitable bullets for making up reloads. RCBS has the dies and shell holders for this project. The cases, bullets and loads are available from Midway Arms, Inc., Route 5, Columbia, MO 65201, through FFL holders, as noted.

New presses: We discussed the Ponsness-Warren P-200 Metal-Matic press in last year's edition, noting that it was designed primarily for straight-sided handgun cases. Since then, P-W has taken the obvious step of coming up with a companion unit for reloading the larger, bottleneck rifle cartridges, known as the Metallic II and it can be used on handgun cases as well as rifle ones, if desired. The Metallic II is supplied without dies or shell holders at a suggested retail of $325.00, or with automatic primer feed for $349.50.

The basic difference between the original P-200 and the Metallic II is that the former was designed around a central post, with a fixed turret at the top and a plate that moved up or down as the handle was actuated, with a shell holder carrier rotating around the plate to detented stops beneath the die stations; essentially a reverse of the old Hollywood turret presses. The new Metallic II is what is usually termed an H-type press, with a vertical post on each side supporting an upper crosspiece and a movable table hooked to the handle, again bearing a circular plate with detented rotating shell head carrier.

P-W's Glenn Jackson demonstrated the Metallic II to me at the SHOT Show in San Francisco in January and it certainly is a speedy device for turning dead ones into live ones. With this press, they're offering a bullet seating die of their own design, faintly akin to the old Vickerman dies or the ones once offered by Weatherby, with a window in the side through which the bullet is inserted. The P-W system incorporates a little collet for the various bullet diameters so that you only need the one seating die.

C-H Tool & Die Corporation came up with a very neat unit called their 444-X Pistol CHamp Reloader. Essentially, it's an upgrade of the firm's popular No. 333 H-type press, with its three die stations and matching three shell holders. The 444-X has four shell holders and four die stations. including one that carries their case mouth expander die with their neat little powder measure superposed above and coaxial with it.

In operation, you start the case at twelve o'clock and move it counter-clockwise through the steps. Rear/center is the tungsten carbide resizing and decapping die, with a thoughtfully-provided little plastic container to catch the spent primer. While you have the handle down and the table up for the size/deprime step, push the plunger of the primer feed to seat a fresh primer in the post. Remove the case from the first holder and transfer it to the one at nine o'clock, pushing the handle up to seat the primer, then down to expand the case mouth and push the plunger on the powder measure to drop a charge into the primed case.

Move the charged case on down to the six o'clock station and seat the bullet to the desired depth, then over to the three o'clock station for a neat taper crimp. C-H's Tony Sailer notes that the main motive for developing the 444-X was to please numerous customers who liked the Model 333 but preferred to seat the bullet as one step and then taper-crimp it as another. See?—pressmakers *do* listen to reloaders, sometimes!

Seventeen bushings are available for varying charge weights in the measure and the supplied bushing chart also lists charges for certain powders if no bushing is used. Suggested retail for the 444-X is $158.00, less dies, but with the four shell holders of your choice. It comes with both large and small diameter primer seating posts. Conversion die sets for popular handgun calibers go for $64.00 with the carbide sizer or $49.60 with a standard steel sizing die. Carbide sets are available for the 9mm Luger at $68.40, or for the 30 M1 Carbine at $81.40.

Lyman has a new O-type reloading press that they're calling the O-Mag, featuring a somewhat longer ram stroke for handling the more lengthy rifle cases such as the 8mm Remington Magnum. Carrying a suggested retail price of $49.95, less dies, it also has a flat work surface above and behind the die station so the owner can mount die racks, loading blocks or similar convenient accessories.

With the copy deadline for this edition of GUN DIGEST but days away, one of the new O-7 Pacific presses just arrived in time to be mounted and wrung-out for the comments that follow. From first impressions, it appears they have a winner on their hands and I am inclined to doubt that prolonged exposure is apt to mute down that evaluation to any great extent.

The O-7 at hand is number 53 of the first production run of five hundred and it was accompanied by a printed sheet requesting comments from the user as to suggestions for improvements. As is my usual custom, I mounted the O-7 to a small piece of two-inch plank, with the bolt heads countersunk flush with the lower side, so that it could be held to the edge of the bench with a pair of C-clamps. It's a good, practical approach, since it makes it easy to make minor adjustments of clearance for the toggle and changing the angle of the handle arc for maximum convenience.

The O-7 is supplied with a remarkably ingenious and handy priming arrangement that Pacific is calling the PPS, for Positive Priming System. The primer arm is a little, L-shaped affair that's easily removable when it's not in use and vastly more convenient than the usual pivoting primer arm found on so many presses. It comes with the punch for one primer size installed and a punch and collar to fit the other size. My suggestion to Pacific is that it would be a lot handier if they supplied two primer arms, one with a punch for each primer diameter, or at least made the arms available as an accessory, so that the operator would be spared the bothersome operation of changing punches and, even worse, of trying to keep track of the spare punch

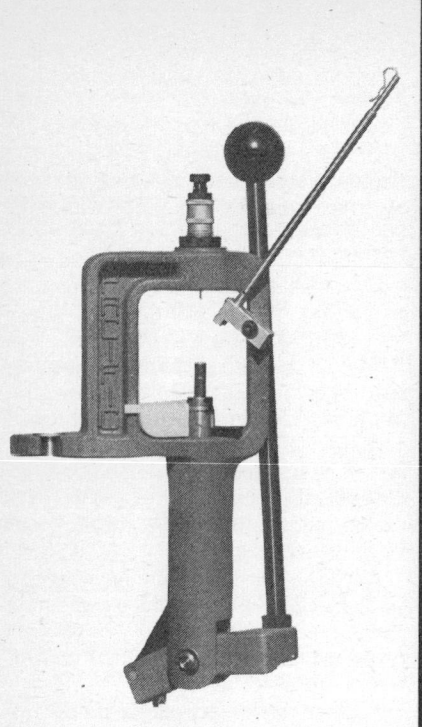
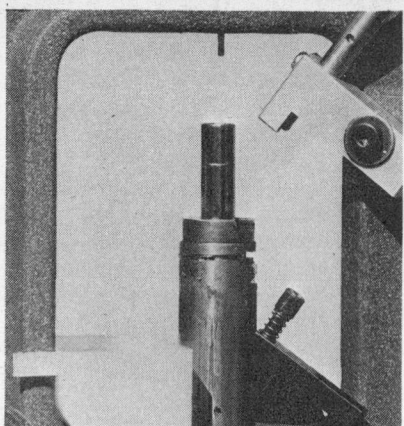

(Above and right) Pacific's Positive Priming System.

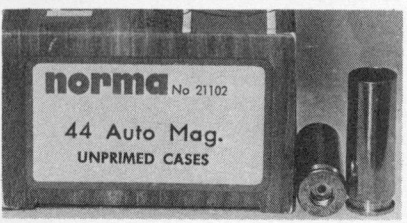

44 Auto Mag. brass from Norma.

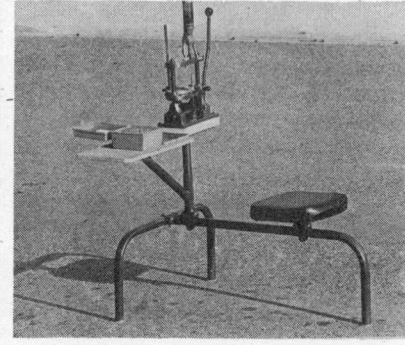

(Right) A remarkably neat and handy accessory called the "Reloading Horse," from Dave Weckwerth of D&D Enterprise, 1408 Dunham St., Albert Lea, MN 56007, at $89.95, plus $7.00 delivery: $96.95 in all. Shown with the P-W Metallic II press set up for loading .22-250 Rem.

and collar between times of need.

Press number 53 came with a neat little plastic catch-box for spent primers that clips to the rear frame member; not shown in the new Pacific catalog. This works quite well and seems to snare nearly all of the expelled primers—provided the priming arm is in place. If the priming arm is removed, the primers come out the front of the ram and make it to the floor.

The O-7 is a big, brawny-looking press, but it doesn't make your tendons creak to pick it up. The catalog says it's a special new strontium alloy, used for greater resistance to stress. The weight is given as nine pounds and they say it will stand up to stresses in excess of 8000 psi for more cycles than any reasonable usage is apt to entail. The suggested retail for the press is $59.95, plus another $10.00 for the O-7 automatic primer feed, if desired.

The test press came with the auxiliary primer feed and it proved not overly difficult to set up and get into troublefree operation, provided you have a hex-wrench measuring $5/32"$ across the flats. There are two brass feed-tubes, one for each primer diameter, and they jut out from the top of the press when installed. As a result, you'll probably want to remove the tube when it's not in use, to keep from snagging your shirt sleeve on it when walking past the bench. To remove a tube with primers still in it, use a toothpick or similar-sized item to poke the bottom few primers back up high enough to secure them with the spring clip that's provided.

Apart from the very minor quibbles noted here, the O-7 boasts numerous highly engaging features. The operating stroke has a remarkably good feel to it, with ample leverage for any reloading operation. Primer seating is likewise smooth and precise and the press is designed and angled so that it's extremely convenient to feed the raw cases in from the left and remove them from the right after processing, assuring a good rate of production.

RCBS has a progressive automated reloader for handgun cartridges under development and they were displaying it at the SHOT Show in San Francisco last January, where the accompanying photo was taken. Thus far, they refer to it as "The Green Machine," and, like the inventor's patent insect trap, it still has a few bugs in it. They're working to eradicate the last of the problems, up Oroville way, but it may take a bit of time yet before you encounter this latest RCBS goodie on the counter of your friendly neighborhood reloading equipment emporium.

Against their accountant's spluttering objections, RCBS continues to be the source of the exotic and unlikely in reloading dies and allied equipage. Their custom die shop can supply dies for a bewildering profusion of improbable and/or scarce cartridges and, if they don't have it, they're prepared to make them up. The individual dealer or retail customer can obtain details on such services, prices and deliveries by inquiring from Huntington Die Specialties, Box 991, Oroville, CA 95965.

Bullet moulds: Lyman's latest catalog trims the variety of their offering down to relatively small numbers for pistol and rifle use. Gone are a lot of the fondly-recalled designs of yesteryears, including some that were introduced quite recently. The ones that remain probably represent the best-selling numbers and certainly a lot of the best performers are still on the charts. New designs are conspicuous in their rarity, although I do not seem to recall the number 45468, an intriguing, Minie-like, hollow-base for the 45 Long Colt, with a catalog weight of 175 grains. Too, there is the 45266, which appears to be a bevel-base semi-wadcutter otherwise similar to the excellent 452460 that does so well in the 45 ACP cartridge.

An updated chart just turned up from Hensley & Gibbs, showing twenty-three new designs not illustrated before, as well as the rest of the ones offered previously. The brochure is available upon request for a business-length self-addressed stamped envelope from Hensley & Gibbs, Box 10, Murphy, OR 97533. Sales are strictly to retail customers, with no dealer discounts and the current rates, delivered within the contiguous forty-eight states, are $85.00 for a four-cavity, $125.00 for a six-cavity, and $210.00 for a ten-cavity. For diameters larger than 38, the ten-cavity is cut for eight cavities. The prices are as of February 1, 1980, and delivery time is quoted as approximately eight months.

Several of the H&G designs are available in a choice of bevel-base or plain-base and their literature offers a comment I find pertinent: "Accuracy appears to be the same, with proponents of either type base having excellent theories to back their favorite. In short, if you like to hear debates, ask a few people."

I'm afraid that's a controversy on which I'd have to declare myself a neutral. I have a few moulds with bevel-base configuration and I've yet to note a startling superiority of that type of bullets over the plain-base breed or, for that matter, vice versa.

The new H&G designs include their number 264, a bevel-base semi-wadcutter for the 9mm, rated at 119 grains in linotype metal and the number 265, a round-nose semi-wadcutter with bevel-base at 200 grains in the same alloy, for the 45 ACP. The number 264, designed by Charles Derbyshire, comes out of the mould large enough for sizing to .358" so that you can use it in 38 Specials or 357 Magnums, if you wish. The number 265, designed by John Adams, is intended to feed reliably in autoloaders, meanwhile cutting a clean hole in the paper for ease of scoring and, in my experience, it does both in a remarkably efficient manner.

Lee Precision recently added two-cavity moulds to their line, available for most handgun designs and two for use in rifles. The new double jobs are not available for casting hollow-points, of course. The Lee Precision single-cavity hollow-point moulds are extremely convenient to use, since the punch is integrally mounted and does not require removal and replacement from bullet to bullet. The new two-cavity moulds retail at $17.98 and the Lee Precision catalog quotes a typical production rate of 500-800 per hour.

New load data: The tenth Speer Manual rolled off the presses early in 1980, a bit over five years after the appearance of number nine, with 560 pages at a retail of $9.50 a copy. Nine new cartridges were listed and thirteen of the old ones were dropped. New listings included 22 PPC; 6mm PPC; 270 Weatherby Magnum; 7mm Weatherby Magnum; 358 Winchester; 375 Winchester; 30-30 (pistol); 357 Herrett and 45 Winchester Magnum. Dropped cartridges were the 17 Remington; 257 Improved; 25/284; 6.5mmx257; 7.62x39mm; 7.7mm Japanese; 7.65mm Mauser; 8mm/338; 22 Remington Jet; 256 Winchester Magnum; 32 S&W Long; 357 Auto Mag and 44 Auto Mag.

Comparing the tenth edition with the ninth, it appears that little if any data has been recycled from the previous edition. In some instances, identical charges for the same bullet in the same cartridge vary slightly. Energy figures no longer appear with the load data, but they're given in the 142-page Reference Section at the rear of the book, along with downrange data to 500 yards for each of the bullets at typical muzzle velocities.

Besides the new Speer Manual, there's a 12-page booklet available from dealers who handle the Thompson/Center Contender, or from Thompson/Center Arms, Box 2405, Rochester, NH 03867. The title is "Making Your Contender Perform!" The data was compiled by Bob Milek for cartridges used in the Contender with the exception of the 30 Carbine; 9mm Luger; 38 Super; 38 Special; 45 ACP and 45 Long Colt. The text clearly states that none of the eight should be loaded beyond the levels given in other manuals or handbooks. There is a note to the effect that the 45 LC data, such as listed in a separate section of the Speer Manual for use only in the Contender or Ruger Blackhawk, is acceptable for use in the Contender. The obvious objection to hotter loads in the eight cartridges is the hazard of their inadvertent use in guns other than the Contender.

It is noted that rifle data for cartridges such as the 222 Remington, 30-30 and 35 Remington as given in reloading manuals can be used, but the loads given in the Contender book are apt to perform better, being tailored to the shorter Contender barrel. Included are helpful tips on the slightly challenging operation of adjusting resizing dies for correct headspacing of the 30 and 357 Herrett cartridges, as well as data for certain cartridges out of both the ten-inch and fourteen-inch barrels.

Not listed in the first edition of the Contender booklet is the 223 Remington cartridge that recently became available as a Contender barrel. Thompson/Center had been a bit reluctant to offer barrels for that caliber, mindful of the pressures generated by some of the military loads for it. In a recent phone conversation with Warren Center, however, he reported that it is working out better than they had hoped, with accuracy that is generally encouraging.

Ballistic researcher W. L. Godfrey has produced a companion volume to his book of 30/06 loads that appeared about 1975. The new book covers the 243 and 6mm and, like the first, it's published by Elk Mountain Shooters Supply, 1719 Marie, Pasco, WA 99301, at $8.95 a copy, postpaid. Not really a reloading manual, in the usual sense of the term, it's more a mass of raw data of interest to the experienced reloader, on which to base further research. Included are reproductions of cathode ray tube traces from a strain gauge for typical powder charge/bullet combinations, as well as some others a far cry from typical. For but one remarkable example, data is cited for a 100-grain bullet with Alcan AL-5 powder, making it clear why that otherwise admirable propellant is used so rarely in 243 Winchester or 6mm Remington rifles!

There are several new bullets, including a number of boat-tail designs from Speer; a new shape for that maker. Hornady has modified the profile of some of their FMJ pistol bullets to a flat tip instead of the usual rounded configuration and the general observation is that the new shape feeds as well and groups better than the rounded ones. Sierra has a new 185-grain Match bullet for the 45 ACP that is a sort of JSP design, with no exposed lead at the tip. Listed as their index number 8810, the new Sierra bullet has been giving me some remarkably fine groups out of the various autoloaders in that chambering.

RCBS recently added competition reloading die sets in 222 Remington; 22-250 Remington; 243 Winchester; 270 Winchester; 30/06 Springfield and 308 Winchester calibers. The resizing die is fairly conventional except that its expander ball is located at the midpoint of the central rod, instead of at the lower end, to ease the effort of dragging the resized case neck across it. The bullet seating die has a micrometer top, with click stops for each .001" of seating depth and an open bullet port in front in somewhat the manner of the old Vickerman seating dies. The sets come in a sculptured mahogany case that's a work of art. •

The Remarkable Guns Of M. K. Jurek

Jurek displays two of his free pistols. One is for a right-hander; the other in left-hand persuasion. While not common, Jurek pistols are seen regularly in British shooting.

WORKING BY HIMSELF, THIS INDOMITABLE POLE CARVED HIS OWN FULL-SIZED NICHE IN THE FIREARMS WORLD

by JERRY EVANS

"A RARE AND FINE quality 22 LR single shot target pistol by the noted specialist maker Dr. M.K. Jurek of 180 Bradford Street, Birmingham, England," was the description that caught my attention. That item was a catalogue lot offered for sale by the leading specialist auctioneers, Weller & Dufty Ltd. of Birmingham, England. A telephone call entered my bid and a few days later an invoice arrived telling me that my bid was acceptable and when I paid the balance owing, the parcel would be airmailed to me. An international draft in pounds sterling was dispatched and I was really most anxious to see what I had bought.

I know very little about handguns, less about 22 single shot target pistols, and Jurek might be a noted specialist in Birmingham, England, but no one that I knew had ever heard of him, other than a collector friend who thought he was a retired dentist.

In due course my pistol arrived and I was very pleased with my purchase. The workmanship was excellent and it was truly a fine quality 22 single shot target pistol with a barrel length of nine inches. The hand-fitted grip was not exactly made for my right hand, but not being a competitive shooter, I was not bothered by the tight fit. The trigger pull, lock time and over-all mechanics of the pistol certainly exhibited expertise of workmanship and attention to detail not usually noted with backyard plumbers and pipe fitters. But who was Dr. M.K. Jurek? Did he design, make, command a shop, or was he a retired dentist? And was he still making pistols?

A letter sent to the Bradford Street address was not answered. The Birmingham telephone system did not have a listing for M.K. Jurek. Meanwhile, my collector friend acquired a Jurek 22 single shot target pistol that had a Birmingham address on St. Marys Row engraved on the color-cased action. A letter was sent to that address, but while it was not returned by the British postal system, no answer was received either.

A couple of years later, while wandering about London, I was able to buy another Jurek target pistol. This latest acquisition was also 22 Long Rifle, but had an interchangeable extra barrel chambered for 38 Special. The barrel fit was such that the firing pin adapted to the rimfire 22 or the 38 centerfire cartridge. Again, this was a manifestation of handwork at its best.

My schedule was such that I was able to take a train to Birmingham for the purpose of finding the elusive Dr. M.K. Jurek to talk with him and learn about his pistol making. Despite the help given me by Stuart Creswell of Westley Richards and Doug Nie from Weller & Dufty, both of whom had heard of Jurek, we could not find him. We found the shop on Bradford Street, but it was not open and a passerby allowed as how that was the pistol maker's shop, but he thought he was only there on Tuesday evening between 7 and 8 p.m. Unfortunately, my day in Birmingham was Wednesday, so back to the train and on to London, thence to Heathrow for the flight back to California.

During the next two years, Doug Nie was able to get the home address and telephone number of Dr. Jurek. A letter to his home address elicited a reply from Jurek and within a few days I arranged a visit with the "noted specialist maker," Dr. M.K. Jurek. This fine gentleman rode a series of buses from his apartment to my hotel and we talked far on into the night.

Jurek is a remarkable man. At the time of our conversation he was 75 years old, quiet and soft-spoken, yet maintaining an aura of staunch independence. It was immediately obvious that Dr. Jurek was the epitome of an all too rapidly declining breed of craftsmen, those for whom their work is a source of pride. There are not many such as Jurek and in this day to have the opportunity of meeting and talking with such a man is a rewarding and worthwhile experience, even though it took five years to find him.

Marien K. Jurek was born in Poland in 1904 and by 1919 he was scrounging and making parts for guns that he was building. He enjoyed shooting and was experimenting in gun making. Jurek continued his education at Krakow University in Poland and achieved his doctorate in chemical engineering, although he told me that it was mostly mechanical engineering that held his interest. By 1937 Dr. Jurek had advanced to head the research department of an ammunition factory in Warsaw. His interest in gun making was such that when using a weapon of his design his score of 529 points won a

Upper gun, with two barrels shown, is the 22 and 38 caliber Jurek Model S. The lower gun is the Jurek Popular model 22. Actions are closed in this photo. Obviously, the guns were built for different users, judging by the very different dimensions of the carved walnut grips. At what range author Evans fired the groups is unknown, but the guns obviously shoot well.

gold medal at Helsinki. Earlier, he had posted a score of 562 which was his best.

The Nazi war machine was sweeping through Europe and Jurek, who had been injured by grenade debris during the first World War, used devious routes through Rumania and France, and escaped to Great Britain. His brother, Karl, was less fortunate. He had a four-year stay at Buchenwald.

M.K. Jurek spent the war years in several branches of the British services, but while a member of the Parachute Regiment, found time to design and make his first free pistol. In October, 1946 his first of two 9mm SMG's were tested in Britain, but were rejected.

Action open, the Model S gun reveals it is solidly constructed, with deep and full fit in the length of the frame. Jurek guns, as target arms, do not eject the fired shell, but simply lift it partway out of the chamber.

A Dr. M. K. Jurek 22 LR single shot match rifle. This rifle incorporates his own design of bolt action operated by pulling the handle to the rear which retracts the bolt by means of a toggle action. The receiver is marked "patent pending". Floating heavyweight round barrel with sight dovetail at muzzle, rearsight dovetail at left of action, adjustable trigger and special walnut stock with dovetail slide for adjustable buttplate, large finger grooved pistol grip with thumb hole, cheekpiece and adjustable handstop, palm rest for offhand shooting, alloy hand stop, tunnel aperture foresight, fully adjustable rearsight with camera type adjustable iris diaphragm.

M. K. Jurek blinked his eyes for the camera in this photo made in the lobby of the Grand Hotel in Birmingham. He is holding the last pistol he made, shown below.

This narrow little building at 180 Bradford St., Birmingham, was the Jurek shop. It has now been demolished, following considerable disagreement with the U.K.'s Inland Revenue, and the machines and inventory sold off and, in short, Jurek makes pistols no more.

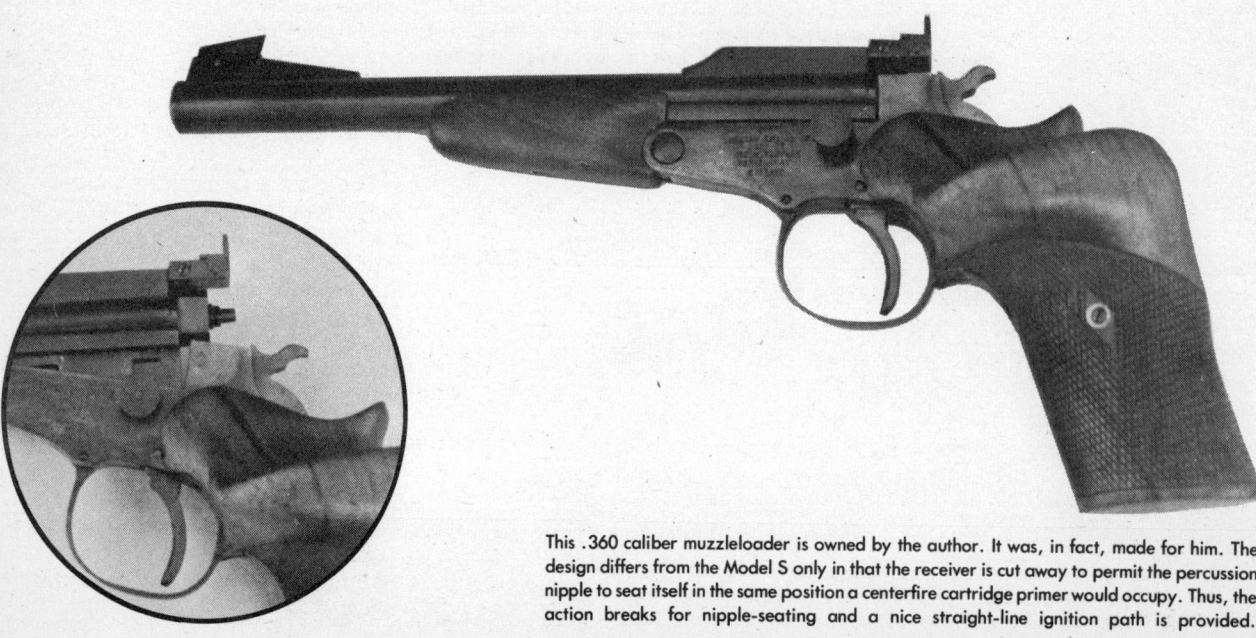

This .360 caliber muzzleloader is owned by the author. It was, in fact, made for him. The design differs from the Model S only in that the receiver is cut away to permit the percussion nipple to seat itself in the same position a centerfire cartridge primer would occupy. Thus, the action breaks for nipple-seating and a nice straight-line ignition path is provided.

Dr. Jurek doesn't think his guns were given a fair test. He feels the low cost of production and reliability would have made his machine gun a replacement for the Sten gun. He asserted, to me, that his SMG would fire at a rate of 350 RPM and with accuracy. This rather slow rate of fire was made possible by firing from a closed bolt and a separate hammer. Another feature was a small diameter recoil spring that was mounted on a guide rod that was removable and ran through the breech block. I nearly ended the interview at that point by remarking that I didn't think that accuracy of a machine gun was all that important. That got me a long, studious look and I was told, in a soft, slightly accented voice, that accuracy is important in all firearms.

During our conversation at the Grand Hotel in Birmingham, Jurek produced all of his shop drawings, working drawings and patent drawings for all his SMGs, free pistols, and automatic pistol designs and innovations. On a scale of 10, my mechanical knowledge and ability would rank about minus 5, but the good Ph.D. and engineer, Dr. M.K. Jurek, adroitly identified those areas that he felt were different, unusual, and worthy of note.

After the SMG rejection, Jurek made a prototype automatic pistol similar to the Colt-Browning. On the Jurek pistol, while the barrel and slide locking ribs are the same as Browning, the barrel movement is controlled by parallel twin linking systems. This method causes the barrel to return to exactly the same position for the succeeding shot, he said, and therefore results in greater accuracy.

Jurek then went to work for Webley and Scott as a pistol designer where his automatic pistols were remade and various additions and changes were redesigned by Jurek. As another project, while at Webley and Scott, he was able to create the beautiful color-case hardening that is so attractively a typical feature on the box lock actions of Webley and Scott shotguns today. The company was having some distortion problems and was not consistently attaining the colors desired. Delving back into his chemical engineering background, Jurek produced a bone-meal formula and established rigid temperature controls and the problems were solved. Very simple, he told me.

After several years of working for Webley, the quiet, soft-spoken Dr. Jurek decided that he was becoming something less than enamored with

Jerry Evans collects big game trophies as well as Jurek pistols, obviously. Here he is admiring his Jurek Popular 22.

the mass production of firearms. He had won the pistol championship of Great Britain three times, he said, and he had instructed and coached the crack shooting squads of Britain for years. Precision workmanship and accuracy were his goals so he quit and started his own business. He had designed and applied for a U.S. patent on a bolt action that was easily adaptable for left- or right-handed use and he had a British patent on a 22 rifle with a toggle trigger assembly.

During the years that Jurek operated his gun shop, he employed no one. Every part of the target pistols and rifles was made by him. He carved the grips on his target pistols from a mould of the shooter's hand so that the fit would be perfect. Jurek has records of two of his earliest 22 free pistols. One has fired slightly over 1,000,000 rounds and the other, serial #3, has had 600,000 rounds fired. There has not been a single malfunction nor parts breakage on either pistol. To me, that exemplifies precision workmanship at its finest.

Jurek's years of the one man gun shop produced 186 22-caliber Popular models, 13 Model S with two barrels (one 22 and the other 38 Special), 127 22 caliber slide action free pistols with various barrel lengths, 19 toggle action target rifles, 4 target rifles with left or right bolt actions called Universal models, and 3 muzzleloading target pistols, two of which were 360 caliber and one 45.

At some point in our talk, I asked Jurek if he had ever studied dentistry. That question got quite a chuckle and the story that he had been told by his dentist that he had a loose front tooth and it should be pulled. Jurek gave the dentist a negative shake of his head, left the chair and hiked himself to the gun shop. He wired his tooth up and it held up for a couple of years until he pulled it out with a set of gun barrel pliers. That was the extent of his knowledge of dentistry and he returned to the DDS for the fitting of a replacement.

Some years ago, Dr. Jurek decided that the British equivalent of our Internal Revenue Service was getting a bit too demanding and he would pay no more income tax. He wrote a letter to the Inland Revenue telling them that, "The Government has governed my business until I don't know who owns it any more. I have been enrolled, cajoled, required and commanded until I don't know where I am."

That august and authoritative body, Inland Revenue, took a rather dim view of such independent thinking and in 1978 revoked his gun maker's license, condemned the shop building he rented and demolished it. At the time of our conversation, he had sold his lathes and hand tools, and all that was left was a nearly complete serial #3, 360 caliber muzzleloading target pistol that he told me would be the last Jurek gun. He promised to complete it for me and send it to me. And he did so.

After that, Dr. Jurek thought he would visit his international banker son in Paris and then return to Poland to the wife he hadn't seen for twenty-five years. What he will be doing next he doesn't know. His letter to the British Inland Revenue ended with the statement, "The only reason I cling to life is to see what on earth happens next." •

EDITOR'S NOTE

Such solitary gunmakers as M.K. Jurek are fascinating. I have met and published articles on one or two Americans of similar bent and cannot resist getting the story told every time a new one comes along.

Jerry Evans has here produced a remarkable amount of information from a single interview. I know one such American well and we were friendly and I visited him off and on for a couple of years and over the whole time found out not much more than you can now know about M.K. Jurek.

There are only 352 guns bearing his mark. The survival rate will doubtless be high, but right here is most of what will ever appear in print. KW

This 1886 photo shows Geronimo at right with a 45-70 rifle; other warriors are his relatives, carrying 1873 Winchesters and a cavalry carbine. Geronimo also carries what appear to be shooting sticks to help make that first shot count.

FIREARMS IN APACHE TRIBAL USE

In this 1867 photo, a Jicarilla Apache fondles a Henry rifle, which according to the author would have been quite a prize at that time, even with its ammunition problems.

These are Tonto Apache, circa 1882. They had—at least for the photographer—no guns, but they were armed. Apparently, being armed is an Apache habit still in vogue.

How the Apache handled gun problems through 300 years of guerrilla war

by D.C. Cole

FEW NATIVE American peoples enjoyed such a fearsome reputation as fighters as did the Apache of the arid Southwest. For over 300 years the various divisions of the tribe prevented settlement of their mountains and deserts by Spanish, Mexican, and American colonists. During these centuries of warfare, the Apache became the acknowledged masters of the horse, the gun, and the tactics of mobile guerrilla warfare. Recent movies and books relate the activities of such remarkable leaders as Cochise, Geronimo, Ulzana, Chato, Mangas Coloradas, and Massai. Yet, very little has been written of the weapons they used or the sources of ammunition which sustained them in their years of combat.

Apache traditional history stresses the idea of a warrior people. According to the ancient stories, the people were hunters and raiders from the dim mists of their origins in forest Siberia. Part of the Athabascan group of peoples, the Apache were often known as the people of the knife, who also possessed the fearsome Asiatic compound-complex bow.[1] The arrival of these people in the Southwest in pre-European times triggered a 500 year war with the Aztecs and gained them the name Apache, "enemy people," from Zuni antagonists.

When the Spaniards arrived as heirs to the Aztec empire, they blundered into this ancient war and were caught up in it. Spanish viceroys and governors struggled for 250 years to subdue the area they called Apacheria. In the end they failed. The Spanish did, however, introduce the horse and the gun to the Apache.

The first Spanish guns into Apacheria were crude military firelocks (matchlocks); many of them rejects from European service.[2] Slow to load, unreliable, and hopelessly inaccurate, they were inferior as weapons to the bows of the Apache. During this time Apache ignored firearms, concentrating instead upon the speedy acquisition of horses, iron knives and lance tips, and, occasionally, pieces of Spanish armor. As one historian states, the Apache underwent a revolution in technology based on the horse and metal weapons.[3]

The advent of the miquelet lock in the early 16th century brought into being a relatively troublefree and reliable musket lock.[4] It became possible to make a musket of much lighter weight and shorter barrel, thus speeding reloading time without any loss in the weapon's questionable accuracy. By 1700, short-barrelled miquelet fusils became available to the plains dwelling Apache. These came at first by capture from Spanish sources and later through trade from the French colonies in Louisiana.[5] The French influence became a source of considerable worry to the Spanish who sought to end it by making alliances with the Comanche to attack the plains Apache. While this was in part successful, the Spanish were forced to supply their Indian allies with guns which fell frequently into Apache hands.[6] Warriors on horseback came to favor the fusil as the weapon for opening a fight, especially when the fusil was loaded with shot or gravel instead of a single ball.

Late in the 18th century, the Spanish were startled to discover the Apache engaged in manufacture of gunpowder.[7] Crude but functional powder was made from wet and ground willow charcoal, Texas sulphur, and nitrate from the bat-filled caves of New Mexico. Tribal legend holds that the secret of manufacture was learned by an Apache enslaved in Mexico who escaped his captors and returned to share the new knowledge with his people.

By 1779 Theodoro de Croix, the Spanish governor, went so far as to suggest that the Spanish themselves supply the Apache with guns and powder of inferior grade. This, it was hoped, would create dependency, wean the warriors from the bow, and cause them to give up the manufacture of powder on their own.[8] A Spanish expedition of 1780 penetrated to the Chiricahua Mountains for the first time since Spain's Apache wars began. There the Spanish discovered the Apache storing goods and weapons in sealed caves, a practice continuing to this day.[9]

The French had left Louisiana in 1763 and within a generation the supply of miquelet and flintlock fusils and muskets dried up. By 1800 few Apache warriors possessed working firearms. This situation changed suddenly in 1810.

The Mexican War for Independence threw the Southwestern frontier into a turmoil. Spanish officials, rebels, and English and American agents bid for Apache support.[10] These agents supplied the Apache with flintlock muskets, most of which were soon shortened for ease of use. Oddly these new muskets were almost all French. Americans tended to pass on superannuated muskets, 18th century types often called Charleville models supplied to patriots during the American Revolution. British agents passed on weapons captured from France during and after the 1760's. The Spanish, now under Joseph Bonaparte, brother of Napoleon, sent to the frontier French muskets declared unserviceable for use with Napoleon's troops.[11]

During this period a very few British Brown Bess muskets, Spanish fusils, and American-made rifles also fell into Apache hands. Still, the numbers of firearms remained low; few warriors had guns of any variety. After Mexican independence, more flintlock smoothbores came north from the settlements in trade and as spoils of war. These were now primarily British surplus, as England was supplying newly independent Mexico with military weapons.[12]

During the 1820s and '30s, American mountain men trapped in the southern Rockies. They brought with them the typical large bore mountain rifles, usually flintlocks by makers such as Hawken, J. Henry, Leman, and Golcher. The accuracy of the new weapons impressed the warriors of the Apache bands.

Some of these new weapons arrived in trade when James Ohio Pattie and James Kirker worked the Santa Rita, New Mexico, copper mines.[13] More were obtained after trappers turned to scalp hunting for the Mexican government in 1836. When James Gleason massacred friendly Apache at Santa Rita, the war bands virtually annihilated American trappers in Apacheria.[14] In this war of raid and ambush, many large bore, half-stock rifles fell into Apache hands. I remember seeing one of those mountain rifles as a boy. The flintlock still worked, but the bore of soft iron was worn out smooth to about .60 caliber.

It was still in use with shot and ball in the 1930s.

Various Texas adventurers entered Apache country during the late 1830s and early '40s. They brought with them rifles and rifled muskets of United States manufacture and issue. Some of these had been converted to percussion cap.

The first large influx of percussion guns came with the Mexican War of 1846-48. During the course of the war,

This is Naiche, an important Apache leader, sitting for a formal portrait, very likely with his wife, and almost certainly with a prop rifle not his own. Many contemporary Apache portraits show prop rifles and handguns—having a gun with them in their pictures apparently seemed fitting to warriors.

Apache fighting men and women noticed the Hall rifles with their effective, but brutal, detachable locks.[15] For the first time revolvers were seen. Previously, Apache had looked with contempt upon pistols and had refused even to take them as booty in raids. The big 44-cal. Walkers and Colt Dragoons with nearly four pounds of heft and deadly accuracy caught the warriors' fancy. It was several years before any Apache possessed one, but they were then treasured above all other firearms.[16]

The turmoil of the Southwest drew many adventurers carrying what seemed to the Apache to be an infinite variety of weapons. Many of these fell into tribesmen's hands. Most common were the converted flint percussion muskets and the newer U.S. percussion rifled muskets.

By this time the Apache had learned to make a sort of percussion cap out of match heads and hammered copper foil. These were marginally effective, giving frequent misfires and hang fires. Powder was readily available in trade. Much of it was supplied by Mexican traders at Janos and by Mormon traders from Utah. Each of these groups held grudges against the United States Army or settlers and gladly supplied tribesmen with weapons.[17] Lead was frequently scarce. On occasion warriors cast slugs from copper or hammered them out of gold and silver. General George Crook remarked in the 1870s that a sure way of predicting an Apache outbreak was to observe warriors gathering scrap cans in order to melt out the lead for bullets.[18]

For nearly twenty years after the Americans seized control of the Southwest from Mexico, the Apache relied on a wide variety of percussion firearms. Revolvers became somewhat more common with the big 44-cal. Dragoons being the weapon of preference. More common were ex-military rifled muskets in 69 or 54 caliber. The most frequently encountered firearms among Apache remained the converted flintlock smoothbore musket, usually shortened to about 44 inches over-all and fitted with crude sights.[19]

Civil War action brought both Union and Confederate forces into Apacheria. Control of the route to California gold fields was the great prize in the Southwest. Activities of Apache raiders effectively denied control of the routes to both sides. Arizona and New Mexico were nearly cleared of white settlement in the process.[20]

Apache leaders tried briefly to face down United States troops with massed forces. This had been successful against Spanish and Mexican soldiers. Zebulon Pike reported years earlier a conversation with a Spanish officer who stated, "Apache cavalry scattered our infantry and it was not to be thought that our cavalry could break a line of Apache infantry."[21] Such was not the case with the Americans, however. Cannon scattered the warriors at Apache Pass. Cochise, Mangas Coloradas, and others resumed guerrilla warfare, never to willingly mass against American troops again.

The battle of Apache Pass pointed up a major weakness in an Apache use of firearms which was never overcome. Due to lack of adequate ammunition

This is Dutchy, a Chiricahua scout, photographed in 1886 with his Mills belt and 45-70 Springfield carbine. Note also the considerable supply of ammunition this Apache on the Army side could carry.

for long range practice, the Apache marksmen tended to fire high. In spite of heavy fire in that battle, very few United States soldiers were injured.[22]

Following the Civil War, breech-loading rifles began to appear in Apache country in ever increasing numbers. Captain John C. Cremony, who had fought at Apache Pass, stated that Apache warriors were by 1868 well-equipped with the latest Spencer, Henry, and Sharps rifles.[23] This was not actually the case. Some rifles were at that time reaching tribesmen by way of traders from Salt Lake City, but numbers of trade guns were then quite small.

During the 1870s and '80s, increased numbers of lever action

Henrys, Winchester 1866s, and Winchester 1873s came into use by raiders. Most of these guns, likewise, were sold by Mormon traders who took payment in gold gathered from streams in the United States and Mexico.

While the light Winchester repeaters gave their user heavy firepower superiority, the warriors preferred the more powerful single shot rifles of the time.[24] The 1866 rifles with their brazed 50-caliber barrel inserts and Springfield 50-70s Model 1868 and 1870 were widely used. These trapdoor Springfield rifles with the later 1873 through 1884 Model 45-70 rifles and carbines became almost the standard of Apache armament for a generation. These were often obtained from battlefields, but also from traders who purchased the weapons of army de-

Handy guns with lever-actions still suit the Apache. Here the author's Winchester shows special practical touches: adjustable aperture sights and detachable sling swivels.

serters.[25]

Also encountered in the war bands were sprinklings of Marlin lever actions, usually Models of 1881 which used the 45-70 load similar to that of the U.S. cavalry carbine.[26] Remington arms were relatively scarce in Apache camps at this time, although a few rolling block sporting rifles were to be found and very rarely a Remington Keene in 45-70. Other repeaters included Colt pump action rifles in 44-40, a Colt Burgess lever action or two, and a few Bullard rifles obtained from Provo and Salt Lake traders.

In the canyon and chapparal country, shotguns were fairly popular with warriors. Cochise had favored a side-by-side silver inlaid gun which was buried with him. This particular gun may well have been a combination rifle/shotgun of German make. British doubles, such as Clayborough and Greener, were seen as were Colt, Remington, and other American doubles of assorted makes. Most were fitted with auxiliary rear sights and used with buck or ball as occasion demanded.[27]

Shot was obtained in raids or by crude manufacture. Lead was melted and poured out into flat sheets. The sheets were then cut into strips with a sharp knife. The strips cut into cubes were either used in that form or rolled round between blocks of mesquite. Alternatively, molten lead was poured into hollow reeds. The reeds were then cut into short strips and rolled round for use. Ten and twelve gauge brass cases were always available and Apache priming methods worked better for shotguns than rifle reloads.

Also favored, but rarely encountered, were the big Sharps cartridge rifles, especially when fitted with telescopic sights. Many Apache suffered from poor eyesight which they attempted to rectify with telescopic sights and good field glasses.[28] The preferred Sharps were all various 45 and 50 calibers. Massai preferred 50-cal. Sharps and Springfields. On occasion crude attempts were made to rebore a 40 or 44 Sharps to 45 or 50, usually with the result being ruined accuracy. Various attempts were also made to rebarrel weapons to 45 and 50 calibers. Some of these conversions were functional; others were not. A more useful expedient was to lengthen chambers to accommodate the longest case available in a given caliber. Thus most 45s were lengthened to accept all cases from 2.1 to 3.25 inches in length.

Toward the close of the Apache wars, the preferred repeater, when available, was the Winchester 1876, usually in 45-60 or 45-75 and often in carbine form. Naiche, Geronimo, and others favored this weapon for its sustained firepower and reasonable long-range accuracy.[29] The '76 was, however, a hard gun to keep functioning. Most saw only limited war use before parts breakage rendered them unserviceable.[30]

Throughout the 1870s and 1880s, many Apache scouts were enlisted by the United States Army. These were nearly all armed with standard issue Springfield trapdoor 45-70 rifles and carbines.[31] Some, acting as sergeants, were issued Colt single action army revolvers. The Colts were nearly all 7½ inch barrelled blued weapons rather than the nickel plated pistols issued to plains scouts and Indian police.[32]

Among hostiles any sort of pistol might appear. Geronimo favored a Remington Army 44 cap and ball.[33] Others stuck to Colt Dragoons, 1860 Armies, or Colt conversions. An occasional Smith & Wesson American, Schofield, or Russian might be seen, especially among southern Chiricahua Apache who raided in Mexico. Merwin and Hulbert revolvers, especially the open top single action model of 1876, were popular for a few years as cartridges interchanged with Winchester '73 rifles. Few Colt single action army revolvers came into Apache bands until the 1880's. They were highly regarded, but very scarce.

Many warriors preferred cap and ball weapons due to greater availability of ammunition. Blasting powder could be stolen from mines and railroads in 50 pound kegs. Coarse grained black powder was wet and ground down to smaller size. Fine powder was used as found or, on rare occasion, mixed with corn meal to reduce power.

Cartridge arms, on the other hand, demanded a steady supply of fixed ammunition. Due to the variety of arms in Apache camps, adequate munition supplies were almost impossible to obtain. Raids were often organized to obtain cartridges. Jason Betinez, who rode with Geronimo, told of a raid into the United States made necessary because the warriors were equipped with modern American breechloaders for which ammunition was unobtainable in Mexico.[34]

Traders were much more willing to sell rifles than ammunition. Raiders usually captured relatively few cartridges. Most warriors using cartridge firearms were forced to attempt reloading. Molds for bullets were cut from stone and proved effective. Cases were usually cut off rather than resized, but functioned well. Priming was a major problem. Copper foil and match head primers gave frequent misfires. Cases were often drilled out to accept percussion caps or primers. Even when ignition occurred, the primer was almost always blown and often jammed the action. Ammunition was such a problem that when Chali At Pun of the Mojave Apache surrendered to General Crook in 1873, he merely said, "Demasiados cartuchos del cobre." (You have too many copper cartridges.)[35]

The military was sometimes no better off. Lieutenant John Bigelow, Jr., wrote in *On the Bloody Trail of Geronimo* that soldiers of the U.S. cavalry stationed at Ft. Apache had gone six months without rifle practice.[36] He reported that several men could not shoot at all and that there was not one marksman or sharpshooter in the company.[37] Apache scouts, on the contrary, he reported, used their rifles as frequently as possible and hunted game at every opportunity.[38]

About 1900, these three Apache had Model 1894 and 1873 Winchesters, by then practically the standard article in the Southwest for Indian and white hunters and travelers alike.

What success the Apache enjoyed with firearms was usually based on hunting habits applied to war. A careful stalk to close range followed by a single well-aimed shot, or a single careful shot from ambush, brought the best results.[39] Subsequent shots were usually wild.[40] Very few Apache became long range marksmen; fewer still were capable of rapid fire hits on enemy personnel.

Apache wars with the United States ended before the 1886 Winchester, or the models of 1892 and 1894, became available in the Southwest. These rifles became favorites for the few reservation hunters who could afford them. Pictures showing warriors with these weapons sometimes are purported to be from the war era; this is in error. Another common error stems from salon pictures taken in 1884 and 1886 by a frontier photographer. Lieutenant Leonard Wood reported in *Chasing Geronimo* that General Nelson Miles and his captives stopped off for photographs.[41] These show many Apache notables against varied backdrops but using the same Frank Wesson single shot rifle as a prop. Field pictures taken during Geronimo's surrender negotiations show warriors with Springfield 45-70 rifles and carbines and Model '73 Winchester lever actions.[42]

This familiar pose and defiant expression is known to most Americans. It's Geronimo, of course, armed with another 45-70. In the end, Geronimo relaxed his fierce defiance sufficiently to ride in Theodore Roosevelt's inaugural parade.

Southern Chiricahua Apache in Mexico used many Remington rolling block 7x57mm rifles; the carbine was not favored. In later years the Mauser '93, '95, and '98 in 7x57mm came into wide use. Many of these were obtained from Mexican soldiers and revolutionaries; some were fitted with telescopic sights by their new users.

North of the border the Model '94 Winchester 30-30 was the weapon of choice through the 1950s. Those who could not afford Model '94s purchased Krag Jorgensen 30-40s at $1.50 to $3.50. Boys used Springfield 45-70s which often were loaded with 2½-inch .410 shells. Handloading the Springfield trapdoor was done in the same fashion as in an earlier generation.

Since the end of the Second World War, the guns in Apacheria have changed considerably. Pickup trucks, which have replaced horses, sport Model '70 Winchesters and Winchester Model 100 autoloaders. M1 carbines are seen frequently. Occasionally one encounters Rugers in Models 77 and No. 1. One deputy carries a chopped BAR in his jeep pickup. Pistols now run to Ruger in 357 and 44 magnums. A few Smith & Wesson 44 magnums are to be seen, as are a fair sprinkling of Browning 9mm Hi-Powers.

South of the border in the Sierra Madres, the Chiricahua Apache favor AK 47 in 7.62x39, and Czech M52 light machine guns. These are obtained at $400 to $700 from leftist guerillas who use the money to partake of capitalist luxuries in the cities.

Marksmanship had improved over the years. Two hundred to six hundred yard practice ranges have been marked out here and there. At least one two-thousand yard range is in use. Veterans of the United States Army practice regularly and some are interested in metal silhouette shooting. In both field hunting and guiding sportsmen, the Apache are recognized as first class hunters.[43]

At present many older weapons are being retrieved from arms caches which are in many cases over 100 years old. Numbers of these now adorn racks in modern cottages on the four United States reservations. Some will no doubt make their way into circles of trade and the hands of collectors. Many have seen hard service; others are nearly new. Unlike plains Indians' firearms, almost none of the Apache guns show any gaudy decorations of carving, tacks, beads, or feathers.

Show was never Apache style. Weapons were for use. They still are. Some things never change. •

BIBLIOGRAPHY

Interviews
Geronimo, Robert. ca1955

Documents
The National Archives. National Archives and Records Service. General Services Administration. *Letters Received by The Office of Indian Affairs, 1824-80*. Microcopy No. 234. Washington, D.C.: National Archives Microfilm Publications, 1966.

Books
Basso, Keith H., ed. From the notes of Grenville Goodwin, *Western Apache Raiding and Warfare*. Tucson: The University of Arizona Press, 1971.

Betinez, Jason, with Wilbur Nye. *I Fought With Geronimo*. New York: Bonanza Books, 1959.

Bigelow, John, Jr. *On the Bloody Trail of Geronimo*. Ed. by Arthur Woodward. Los Angeles: Western Lore Press, 1968.

Billington, Ray Allen. *Westward Expansion: A History of the American Frontier*. New York: Macmillan Publishing Company, Inc., 1974.

Chandler, David G. *The Campaigns of Napoleon*. New York: The Macmillan Company, 1966.

Cook, James H. *Fifty Years On the Old Frontier*. New Haven: Yale University Press, 1923.

Cremony, John C. *Life Among the Apaches, 1850-1868*. 1868 Rpt. Glorieta, N.M.: Rio Grande Press, 1969.

Crook, George. *General George Crook: An Autobiography*. Ed. by Martin F. Schmitt. Norman: University of Oklahoma Press, 1946.

Cruse, Thomas. *Apache Days and After*. Ed. by Eugene Cunningham. Caldwell, Ohio: Caxton Printers Ltd., 1941.

Dunn, J. P., Jr. *Massacres of the Mountains*. New York: Archer House, Inc., 1886.

Held, Robert. *The Age of Firearms*. New York: Harper & Row, 1957. Revised ed., Northfield, IL: DBI Books, 1970.

Horgan, Paul. *Great River: The Rio Grande In North American History*. New York: Rinehart & Co., Inc., 1954.

Jackson, Donald. *The Journals of Zebulon Montgomery Pike: With Letters and Related Documents, Vol. II*. Norman: University of Oklahoma Press, 1966.

John, Elizabeth A. H. *Storms Brewed In Other Men's Worlds: The Confrontation of Indians, Spanish and French In the Southwest, 1540-1795*. College Station: Texas A & M Press, 1975.

Kaywaykla, James, and Eve Ball. *In the Days Of Victorio: A Warm Springs Apache Remembers*. Tucson: University of Arizona Press, 1970.

Lamar, Howard Roberts. *The Far Southwest 1846-1912: A Territorial History*. New Haven: Yale University Press, 1966.

Lane, Jack C., ed. *Chasing Geronimo: The Journal of Leonard Wood, May-September, 1886*. Albuquerque: University of New Mexico Press, 1970.

Moorehead, Max L. *The Apache Frontier: Jacobo Ugarte and Spanish-Indian Relations In Northern New Spain, 1769-1791*. Norman: University of Oklahoma Press, 1968.

Opler, Morris E. *An Apache Life Way*. Chicago: University of Chicago Press, 1941.

Parsons, John E. *The First Winchester*. New York: Winchester Press, 1969.

Pattie, James Ohio. *The Personal Narrative of James O. Pattie Of Kentucky*. Chicago: R. R. Donnelley & Sons, Inc., The Lakeside Press, 1930.

Peterson, Harold L. *Pageant of the Gun*. Garden City, N.Y.: Doubleday and Company, Inc., 1967.

Thrapp, Dan L. *The Conquest of Apacheria*. Norman: University of Oklahoma Press, 1967.

_____. *Victorio and the Mimbres Apaches*. Norman: University of Oklahoma Press, 1974.

Utley, Robert M. *Frontier Regulars: The United States Army and the Indian, 1866-1891*. New York: Macmillan Publishing Company, Inc., 1973.

Wellman, Paul I. *Indian Wars of the West*. Garden City, N.Y.: Doubleday & Company, Inc., 1947.

Periodicals
Brady, Bruce. "Elk of the Mescalero," *Outdoor Life*, Vol. 156, No. 2, August, 1975.

Clum, John P. "The San Carlos Apache Police," *New Mexico Historical Review*, 1930.

Larson, E. Dixon. "Rarest Army S. A. Colt Was Nickeled," *American Rifleman*, Vol. 118, No. 5, May, 1970.

It will not be ancient revolvers should the Apache take up arms again. This is the author with his choice in a belt gun—the Model 1911 in 45 ACP.

FOOTNOTES

¹Morris E. Opler, *An Apache Life Way*. Chicago: University of Chicago Press, 1941, pp. 386-387.

²Robert Held, *The Age of Firearms*. New York: Harper & Row, 1957, rev. ed. Northfield, IL: DBI Books, 1970, pp. 38ff.

³Elizabeth A. H. John, *Storms Brewed In Other Men's Worlds: The Confrontation of Indians, Spanish and French In the Southwest, 1540-1795*. College Station: Texas A & M Press, 1975, pp. 19ff.

⁴Held, op. cit., pp. 74ff.

⁵John, op. cit., p. 698.

⁶Max L. Moorehead, *The Apache Frontier: Jacobo Ugarte and Spanish-Indian Relations In Northern New Spain, 1769-1791*. Norman: University of Oklahoma Press, 1968, pp. 157ff.

⁷John, op. cit., p. 530.

⁸Moorehead, op. cit., p. 122 and pp. 127-128.

⁹John, op. cit., p. 604, and Dan L. Thrapp, *Victorio and the Mimbres Apaches*. Norman: University of Oklahoma Press, 1974, p. 193.

¹⁰Paul Horgan, *Great River: The Rio Grande In North American History*. New York: Rinehart & Co., Inc., 1954, pp. 424-434.

¹¹David G. Chandler, *The Campaigns of Napoleon*. New York: The Macmillan Company, 1966, pp. 341-342.

¹²Ray Allen Billington, *Westward Expansion: A History of the American Frontier*. New York: Macmillan Publishing Company, Inc., 1974, pp. 484-494. Outlines British support to the Mexican government during this period.

¹³James Ohio Pattie, *The Personal Narrative of James O. Pattie Of Kentucky*. Chicago: R. R. Donnelley & Sons, Inc., The Lakeside Press, 1930, pp. 149ff.

¹⁴Paul I. Wellman, *Indian Wars of the West*. Garden City, N.Y.: Doubleday & Company, Inc., 1947, pp. 250ff, and J. P. Dunn, Jr., *Massacres of the Mountains*. New York: Archer House, Inc., 1886, p. 315.

¹⁵Harold L. Peterson, *Pageant of the Gun*. Garden City, N.Y.: Doubleday and Company, Inc., 1967, pp. 120-122.

¹⁶Keith H. Basso, ed., from the notes of Grenville Goodwin, *Western Apache Raiding and Warfare*. Tucson: The University of Arizona Press, 1971, p. 178.

¹⁷Howard Roberts Lamar, *The Far Southwest 1846-1912: A Territorial History*. New Haven: Yale University Press, 1966, pp. 342ff, and Thrapp, op. cit., p. 126.

¹⁸General Crook to General Schofield, Adj. General, Department of the Pacific, 25 January, 1872, *Letters Received by the Office of Indian Affairs 1825-1880* (Washington, D.C.: National Archives Microfilm Publications, General Services Administration, 1966), Microcopy No. 234. (This publication is hereafter referred to as LROIA.)

¹⁹John C. Cremony, *Life Among the Apaches, 1850-1868*. 1868 Rpt. Glorieta, N.M.: Rio Grande Press, 1969, p. 194.

²⁰Wellman, op. cit., p. 307.

²¹Donald Jackson, *The Journals of Zebulon Montgomery Pike: With Letters and Related Documents, Vol. II*. Norman: University of Oklahoma Press, 1966, p. 54.

²²Cremony, op. cit., p. 164.

²³Ibid., p. 194.

²⁴Jason Betinez, with Wilbur Nye, *I Fought With Geronimo*. New York: Bonanza Books, 1959, p. 77.

²⁵Robert M. Utley, *Frontier Regulars: The United States Army and the Indian, 1866-1891*. New York: Macmillan Publishing Company, Inc., 1973, p. 23. In 1891 the Adjutant General calculated ⅓ of enlisted men or 88,475 of 255,712 had deserted between 1866 and 1891.

²⁶Betinez, op, cit., p. 77.

²⁷Cremony, op. cit., p. 194.

²⁸Cremony, op. cit., p. 232. Also James Kaywaykla and Eve Ball, *In the Days Of Victorio: A Warm Springs Apache Remembers*. Tucson: University of Arizona Press, 1970, p. 13.

²⁹John E. Parsons, *The First Winchester*. New York: Winchester Press, 1969, p. 123. Parsons states that the .45-60 carbine only became available in 1885. Also Peterson, op. cit., pp. 171, 174-175, shows Model '76 .45-60 carbines surrendered by Naiche and Geronimo in 1886.

³⁰Parsons, op. cit., pp. 128-130, discusses the sort of damage common to the '76 in hard service.

³¹John P. Clum, "The San Carlos Apache Police," *New Mexico Historical Review*, 1930, p. 69. More than 300 Springfields were issued for the Chiricahua removal of 1876 alone.

³²E. Dixon Larson, "Rarest Army S. A. Colt Was Nickeled," *American Rifleman*, Vol. 118, No. 5, May, 1970, pp. 22-23.

³³Discussions with Robert Geronimo, ca 1955.

³⁴Betinez, op. cit., pp. 88-89.

³⁵George Crook, *General George Crook: An Autobiography*, ed. by Martin F. Schmitt. Norman: University of Oklahoma Press, 1946, pp. 173-179, and Wellman, op. cit., p. 356.

³⁶John Bigelow, Jr., *On the Bloody Trail of Geronimo*, ed. by Arthur Woodward. Los Angeles: Western Lore Press, 1968, pp. 104ff.

³⁷Ibid.

³⁸Ibid., p. 101.

³⁹James H. Cook, *Fifty Years On the Old Frontier*. New Haven: Yale University Press, 1923, p. 171.

⁴⁰Bigelow, op. cit., pp. 38-39, and Thomas Cruse, *Apache Days and After*, ed. by Eugene Cunningham. Caldwell, Ohio: Caxton Printers Ltd., 1941, pp. 115ff, discusses the Cibicu fight where hundreds of Apache fired for hours inflicting few casualties.

⁴¹Jack C. Lane, ed., *Chasing Geronimo: The Journal of Leonard Wood, May-September, 1886*. Albuquerque: University of New Mexico Press, 1970, pp. 111-112.

⁴²C. S. Fly, the Tombstone photographer, accompanied the 1886 expedition. See Dan L. Thrapp, *The Conquest of Apacheria*. Norman: University of Oklahoma Press, 1967, p. 343.

⁴³Bruce Brady, "Elk of the Mescalero," *Outdoor Life*, Vol. 156, No. 2, August, 1975, pp. 52ff.

COP-PROOF

by COLIN GREENWOOD

Sturm, Ruger's Police Service-Six.

Put down one reasoned British vote for the revolver and don't argue — he makes sense

THE NAME OF Walter Winans is not as well known as it should be amongst the shooters of today. Born of the Russian upper classes, he spent many years in the United States and in England as well as having strong connections with a number of other countries. He sponsored, promoted and took part in handgun competitions in many parts of the world. His shooting skill is well proven and many of today's better shots would find difficulty in improving on his performances.

In 1900 Winans became one of the first to write about handgun shooting techniques. His book *The Art of Revolver Shooting* can be read today with both interest and profit. A second book, *Hints on Revolver Shooting,* was followed by works on rifle shooting and, in 1919, by *The Modern Pistol and How to Shoot It*. Winans should be recognized as one of the father figures of both competitive and practical pistol shooting. But even Winans could be wrong. Chapter I of *The Modern Pistol and How to Shoot It* begins:

"There is now no use learning revolver shooting. That form of pistol is obsolete except in the few instances where it survives for target shooting, or is carried for defense; just as flintlock muskets even now survive in out-of-the-way parts of the world."

In the sixty years or so which have passed since Winans made his pronouncement, the revolver has gone from strength to strength. New manufacturers are in business and new models have come from both old and new makers. This obsolete old wheelgun keeps going and going. Its devotees claim it to be superior in some respects, or even in all respects, to the self-loading pistols (which we will call automatic in this article to conform with popular usage). Much as been written on the "revolver v. automatic" argument and it seems that little remains to be said. Unfortunately, there has been a lack of objectivity and logic and the debate has suffered from over-generalization. Perhaps there is *something* to be said.

It must be conceded at once that Winans' pronouncement was true as it relates to military sidearms. The British clung to the revolver longer than any other major power, but this arose more from a disregard for the handgun than from any conscious decision about the type to be used. No major power now uses the revolver as its standard military sidearm, though the wheel-gun often survives in specialized roles. The dictates of the military and the circumstances in which an army operates are not necessarily applicable in other spheres. With police forces the revolver finds strong supporters. The majority of police in the United States, Canada and many other countries, as well as England, still favor the revolver over the automatic. And there are very good reasons for this. In the context of the re-equipping of the British police, I was closely involved with this question at both local and national levels, and had to present and counter the various arguments raised. It might be worthwhile to study these arguments to see whether or not some further light can be shed on the controversy.

British Police

In the not too distant past the firearms used by the British Police were a weird mixture of long obsolete weapons. Some of the smaller forces had just a few handguns salvaged from confiscated weapons. Yorkshire's West Riding Constabulary, which I joined in 1954, had a small stock of 380 Webley Revolvers of the civilian Mark III pattern which had been

bought in the early 1920s. At a few major stations, four or six of these handguns would be securely locked in a safe in the Divisional Commander's office along with six shells per gun. Firearms training then consisted of sending a circular around the 3,000 man force asking who thought himself fit to carry a gun. If your name was on the list, you were officially trained. During my first twelve years of police service no one in the force was issued a gun and not one single round was fired in training. There was a very active and very successful pistol team, but shooting was a sport and not really connected with the business of policing.

This total ignorance of firearms was common throughout England. The best trained forces in the country allowed a very small number of men to fire up to twelve shots per year and one force—far and away the most lavish in this respect—allowed thirty rounds of ammunition per year to the very small number of "trained" men. The fact is that this level of weaponry and training was perfectly adequate for the needs of the day. In London in 1954 there were just *four* robberies in which a firearm was used. Records of such rare events were not kept outside London but there can be no doubt that in the whole of England the total number of robberies involving firearms would rarely exceed twenty per year. That situation has now deteriorated to the point where London expects robberies involving firearms to approach the one thousand mark per year. By international standards that is small stuff, but when compared to England in the 50s it represents an appalling decline. Add to that the growth in international terrorism and the British Police faced a new problem. Their small armories of obsolete weapons were not only inadequate, they were dangerous. The total lack of training created a situation in which armed police were probably a greater danger to the public than armed criminals.

Progressively from the mid-1960s police forces began to look to their armories and by 1970 the problem was receiving attention at national level. The advocates of the automatic pistol had their say and some autos were in use in a number of police forces. The general lack of experience within the English police meant that the few hobby shooters had a great deal of influence. Much of the argument advanced arose from the individual experience and personal preferences of committed enthusiasts who tried to

translate their ideas into policy recommendations. Arguments tended to be in abstract terms about which was the "best" weapon, but the arguers failed to establish the precise role which would be filled by a police handgun.

The Role

In police use, a handgun will be carried in its holster day in and day out, year after year. The officer will be involved in a wide range of activities during which he will not give his gun a second thought. Even in the most hectic parts of the world, the gun will rarely be drawn and even more rarely fired. The armed police officer will have many things on his mind and the mere fact of being armed will warrant little thought in his day to day routine. In most cases he will have ample warning of any need to use his gun, but occasionally he will have to bring it into play very quickly and with no warning.

Contrast this with the sportsman or hobby shooter, even with the practical pistolman. The period for which the latter will carry a gun is very limited and he will be well aware of the requirement to use it. The mere fact that he is carrying a gun will be uppermost in his mind. Contrast the policeman's

Author's grandfather (upper left) in 1904 knew little of guns in his time on the forces. The author (at left) as a village constable riding a bike in the 1950's also served in such a gunless era. By the mid-'70's, the author (below) as a Superintendent had official occasion to explain to HRH the Duke of Kent the reasons a short-barreled double shotgun had advantages for police use.

role with that of the soldier who, acting under orders, is committed to a combat situation in a state of preparedness. The police pistol will stay in its holster for every working day of perhaps thirty years, ready to go at any second but actually being fired only once or twice in that thirty year spell.

The police handgun will be carried by a working cop in any one of several branches of a force. He will not be a committed firearms enthusiast. He will not spend countless hours of his free time perfecting his shooting and weapon handling techniques. The odds are that he will be uninerested in his gun, regarding it as a necessary nuisance. He will undergo his training and then his periodic retraining.

During those periods he will be conscious of and interested in his gun, otherwise he will not. He will usually be working alone and unsupervised, with many complex problems on his mind. No matter what country he is from, his basic training will almost certainly be inadequate and his retraining too infrequent to maintain his weapon handling skills at a level where he will deal with all the problems rapidly and without conscious thought. Even in the few forces which provide really good firearms training, it is virtually impossible to keep a busy operational policeman at peak efficiency with his gun unless he is personally interested.

If the arguments about revolver v. automatic pistol are re-examined in this light, many aspects take on a very different complexion.

State of Readiness

The problem of carrying the gun in a holster, unused but ready for instant action, over a thirty year stretch militates against most automatics.

Single action autos carried with the hammer cocked for such a period might eventually suffer from a weakened spring and the less-than-interested cop may not recognize the fact until a fire fight is in progress. Despite the various systems of using holster straps as safety barriers, accidents are likely when cocked autos are drawn rapidly by men whose skills have rusted. Such handguns carried uncocked, or with an empty breech are much less likely to discharge accidentally but the average policeman in a panic situation can still wind up with an uncocked or unloaded gun after performing juggling feats which would mystify Houdini.

Double action autos have their own problems. They can be carried safely with a cartridge in the chamber and the hammer down, but the requirement which must cause most concern is that for drawing and firing a couple of shots at high speed. The first shot on a double action auto requires a long, heavy pull on the trigger; but the second requires much less effort. The average cop will not be able to cope with this rapid change in trigger pressures. In a series of tests it was found that this feature alone reduced the probability of hit by 20% when the subjects were officers with some experience of handguns.

The double action revolver can be fully loaded yet have all the working parts at rest. With no strain on any part, and with very low accident potential, it can be carried in a state of instant readiness for thirty years. When it has to be brought into action there is no fumbling with safeties and the like. The double action trigger pull will be constant from shot to shot and is relatively easily mastered. From the point of carrying in a state of readiness, the revolver is much safer and much more likely to prove effective for the average policeman.

Malfunctions

It is sometimes said that the automatic pistol is more prone to malfunction than a revolver and that malfunctions or misfires are more difficult to clear. In fact, modern automatics are very reliable and if the gun is well cared for, malfunctions are so rare as to merit little consideration. For the individual gun owner, this factor is of no consequence. But the less-than-interested policeman will not give his gun the sort of attention which the individual owner might lavish on it. One of the major causes of malfunctions with automatics in the field is distortion of the magazine lips caused by dropping a magazine on a hard surface. The knowledgeable gun handler will see the damage and correct it. The average cop will not. Clearing a malfunction in a revolver may not be as simple as the hobby shooter expects. Watching policemen struggling with the consequences of a raised primer does nothing to improve confidence. Despite that, it remains beyond question that the rapid clearing of a malfunction or misfire in an auto requires a degree of knowledge, dexterity and practice that police training rarely supplies. In terms of reliability the revolver scores over the auto for the average policeman.

In the hands of a competent shot whose mind is on his gun, the modern automatic pistol is a safe weapon; but the busy policeman with much on his mind can be less than totally attentive to his sidearm. The presence of a round in the breech after the magazine had been removed can and does cause accidents with autos. A magazine safety does not entirely remove this danger because of the chance of replacing an empty magazine without clearing the breech. In a perfect world there would be no accidents, but in the harsh and busy world of the operational policeman, the revolver is more "cop-proof."

Firepower

On magazine capacity the automatic must score. So many of the modern weapons have double column mags with more than a dozen shots in hand. In a military context this could be vital and combat competitions are often devised to give great advantage to the big magazine. The advantage is a dubious one for our average policeman whose average fire fight is likely to involve 2.6 shots. When reloading is required, there is usually plenty of time. The rare instances which indicate a need for rapid reloading in a police combat situation are usually a product of bad tactics. The marginal advantage given by the auto on this score does not balance its disadvantages. Police departments and those individuals who have to provide their own guns will also want to take account of the differences in effective lifetime. A self-loader shooting a serious man-stopping round will be unlikely to survive many more than 5,000 shots. A revolver will happily digest four times that number of cartridges without problems.

Cop-Proof

For the individual gun owner the revolver v. automatic pistol argument is academic and should be resolved on the basis of personal preference. Either type will serve him well if he looks after it, and each has its special features and advantages. For the military, the self-loader is unarguably superior to the revolver in a battle situation. For the average working policeman the revolver has the edge for simplicity, reliability, safety and the general ability to be more "cop-proof." In a service working under constant pressure these factors will allow for a higher standard of training in a given time scale. Overwhelmingly, the British police settled on revolvers in their re-equipping program. Though examined again and again, that decision still seems right. •

The Greatest of All Webley Collectors

By R. BRETNOR

The Royal Naval Club,
Portsmouth,
22nd May, 1968

My dear James,

Please accept my congratulations; you are a lucky young man. Kitty is not only my favourite granddaughter, she is, as you know, the loveliest girl in the world. Actually, when I first heard she was marrying a barbarian out of Montana—forgive me, but I know very well that you all wear hairy chaps and eat bear steaks for breakfast—I feared for her welfare. But when I found you in the pergola reading *The Webley Story*, that admirable book of Major Dowell's, and learned you were collecting Webleys yourself, I realised that civilization had penetrated further west than I had believed. Therefore now, instead of insulting you with my grandfatherly disapproval, all I can do is inflict on you my advice, which, because of my long and intimate acquaintance with Webley revolvers, the Webley works, and The Greatest of All Webley Collectors, will be absolutely invaluable to you.

You may recall that, at first, you had some idea of being what you called a "completist" Webley collector, but that you had sensibly given up this impossible goal even before meeting me, settling for one which seemed more practical to you—that of a complete collection of Webley-Fosbery automatic revolvers. I assure you, my boy, that the second goal is no more practical than the first, for reasons which I shall make clear to you. Though not more than 5000 of Colonel Fosbery's revolvers ever were made, it would be simply impossible to acquire one of each type, for of some types there weren't many more than that.

Let me give you an instance. A compatriot of yours in Louisiana, an avid collector, owns Number 5. It was retailed by Oakes & Co. in Madras, and sold to a Lt. Calthrop of the Essex Regiment. It is a .455, but it has a stepped cyclinder like the very scarce .38 ACP, and a few other features which, according to all the authorities, just can't be. And it was turned out long before The Greatest of All Webley Collectors came on the scene.

In 1913, you see, I was a very new junior officer, and I'd had a bout of pneumonia with some strange complications, and my Uncle Cosmo—Vice-Admiral Macnaughton, who I firmly believe could have won Jutland decisively—called me up and offered me this shore-side assignment at Webley's. Everybody knew everybody else in those days, and it made hush-hush matters ever so much easier to arrange.

We had luncheon together in London, and he told me all about The Greatest of All Webley Collectors, though of course we didn't then know that this was what he'd turn out to be. His name, by the way, was Rittmeister Graf Franz-Christian-Waldemar von und zu Hohenhaupt-Trohna, and he was a remarkable chap. He was no common cavalry captain; his commission was in one of their finest Guards regiments, and his family were as proud as the Hapsburgs and Hohenzollerns. They owned bleak castles and all sorts of dark forests with wolves in them. He was thirty years old, and he had an impressive higher degree in, of all things, mechanical engineering. He spoke English like a native of Ottawa, having spent several years in a Jesuit school there while his father was off exploring somewhere or other after a thundering great scandal involving a married Swedish princess.

Weapons were a hobby of his. You will not be surprised to hear that eventually we became very good friends.

Those were innocent days—pre-World War I. In Berlin we had in our pay a Roumanian Countess, as lovely as any king's mistress and with tastes as expensive. The nobleman to whom she was married was incredibly ancient and very broad-minded. Her lover was an Oberst-General von Krott, who not only had the amiable habit of talking in his sleep, but would actually answer her questions without waking up. As he was high in the Imperial General Staff, we rewarded the lady quite handsomely, and it was she, naturally, who put us onto Hohenhaupt-Trohna.

You see, some German officers on the technical side had noticed what you too have observed—that there seemed to be no end to minor variations in Webleys. A single model could have three or four different grips, barrels of assorted lengths and contours, differently fluted cylinders, and goodness knows what. There was no general purpose behind this; partly, I suppose, it was just the skilled British workman's way of kicking back at the machine age. But the Germans, being such logical people, realized only that someone was going to a great deal of bother for no immediately discernible reason, and began to suspect that there was hanky-panky, funny business, afoot. They presented their preliminary study to the appropriate section of the Imperial General Staff, and in due course Moltke the Younger and Falkenhayn and people like that became interested, and finally poor Hohenhaupt-Trohna was summoned before the top echelon.

Willie himself wasn't there, but the Crown Prince was, and everyone looked very stern and important. After Hohenhaupt-Trohna had saluted, bowed very formally, and reported his presence, von Krott apprised him of the high honour which was to be his.

Von Krott summarised the report of their technical people. Over a given number of months, Webley's had produced 74 unexplained variations in barrel dimensions, 16 in trigger-guard design, 188 in front- and rear-sight silhouette, et cetera, et cetera. Such and such a percentage of these had been observed on purely military types. And so on. The British were a practical people, ruling a vast and profitable Empire. No practical people would waste time and energy to no purpose. Therefore the purpose must be very deep, dark, and dangerous.

Obviously something was very wrong. It was a matter of maximum urgency.

Hohenhaupt-Trohna apparently tried to suggest that perhaps that was just the way the British did things—after all, he had grown up with our cousins in Canada, but he was promptly set down by von Krott. Then they issued his orders. He was given two weeks to die in—preferably in a hunting accident, which was plausible for a horseman. Then he was to endure a few months of training for his new job at Webley's—which, of course, they would have neatly arranged. Once settled in, he not only would report in detail on all the unexplained variations, but would ship a specimen of each one to Germany.

Uncle Cosmo, of course, thought the whole thing perfectly wonderful—especially the notion of employing one very junior officer (myself) and a few civilians to keep all sorts of German officers and technical experts expensively and uselessly busy, which was what we were now planning to do.

I used to like to imagine the poor fellow, stiff as a post in his full-dress cuirass and helmet, clicking his heels, saluting, bowing obediently, and going off to embark on his mission. Actually, except for the fancy dress, it was very much like that. He took leave of his regiment, broke off his engagement to a beautiful Baroness whose lineage was as long and involved as his own, and within two weeks he officially perished.

We talked about him occasionally, and made ready to welcome him; and sure enough, six months later he arrived. They were thorough, those Germans. They'd found him a marvellous cover—a chap named Adrian Higgins who'd died on his way back from Russia, where he'd worked a few years, and whose background included British Columbia and even some Jesuits. But I'll quote from my diary, entry of 12th May, 1913:

"Our spy finally arrived this a.m. Coulter and Mr. Whatman both vetted him backwards and forwards, and of course confirmed his employment. Coulter says he seems very competent. His friends have done a good job on him, I must say. Doesn't look a bit like his photograph. No monocle, no cavalry waist. They've fed him up by about forty pounds—probably with "all sorts of abominable sausages," as in Saxo Grammaticus.

"He has a moustache rather like Mr. Kipling's, only raggeder, and the same sort of spectacles. Speaks well, though like a Colonial. Perhaps too well; his manners show through. If we didn't know, I suppose we'd put it all on the Jesuits.

"I offered to help him find rooms, but he said he'd already found some—probably all arranged in advance. Uncle Cosmo tells me I have to be nice to him, and make sure he's happy and comfortable. Well, at least he's just a spy, not a *traitor!*"

During those first three or four months, I'm afraid we gave Mr. "Adrian Higgins" a rather hard time. After a few weeks of breaking in, Mr. L. W. Whatman, the works manager, and John Coulter, the foreman of the Revolver and Pistol Department, assigned him to work directly with me in my special project because "he had shown such aptitude for original design." I had one or two very good men under me, and whenever some county gunsmith sent in an order for two dozen of something just a bit different, Coulter brought it to us. Believe me, we solemnly turned out the damnedest things, like one lot of .297/.230 commercial Mark IV's with *triangular* lanyard rings, and three Fosberys with grip safeties like your .45 automatic.

Every day or so, Coulter would come around with Mr. Whatman or Uncle Cosmo or some army person in mufti,

110 THE GUN DIGEST

and they'd buzz about very mysteriously. Then we'd get busy designing something even more strangely nonfunctional. Uncle Cosmo had told me not to try to conceal my Royal Navy connection, but to act as though I were trying clumsily to conceal it—it probably would've been spotted immediately anyhow.

Hohenhaupt-Higgins fell in with all this very eagerly. He was a mechanical genius, and mad about weapons; when he was working, he put his whole heart into it. In fact, Coulter once told Uncle Cosmo, when one of our own men had botched half a day's output, that perhaps we ought to write to the German Emperor and ask for twenty such spies instead of trying to hire our workmen in Birmingham.

Before long, we'd conveyed the idea—without really telling him anything—that our business was fantastically hush-hush and *very* important. We knew we'd conveyed it successfully because our Countess informed us in detail after his reports had come in. The next step was obvious—as noted in my diary entry of 28th August, 1913:

"Well, we've promoted Hohenhaupt-Higgins. He's now, in effect, Chief Designer of the Odd and Unnecessary —without the title, of course. Besides the usual commercial jobs, he's been encouraged to give his imagination free rein, with a bonus for each new idea he gives birth to. We have sworn him to secrecy under pain of instant dismissal.

"Uncle Cosmo said yesterday that I mustn't refer to him as 'Hohenhaupt-Higgins' even *in camera;* if I do, I might say it aloud to him and blow the whole thing. I'm to address him as Adrian. 'Your association,' said Uncle Cosmo, 'must ripen into a beautiful friendship for King and for Country.'"

I must say that I didn't like the idea, for he *was* a spy after all. Besides, we were having a wonderful time egging him on. The more he invented, the harder it became for him to send one of each type back to Germany. They bought a lot on the open market through agents, but you simply can't do that when there may be only one or two of a type—and to make matters worse, they had him buying or locating a great many made before his arrival. The poor devil was really chasing his tail.

We gave him permission to work long hours overtime, and after everyone else had gone home he'd be down at the works copying whatever there happened to be only one specimen of. He began to get rather haggard after the first couple of months, and we heard that two or three times he'd failed to send them a specimen, and that the Kronprinz and von Krott were very annoyed with him. His sense of duty, of course, made him report all his failures. In spite of it all, he was always helpful and courteous, and as eager as ever; and the respect and affection with which the men treated him became almost fantastic.

It was then, I think, that I began to feel sorry for him. I'd been following Uncle Cosmo's instructions to the letter, and "Adrian" and I had taken to having a pint together whenever we could, or eating supper and playing chess afterwards. At first—because of the social distance between us, which of course was much more serious in those days—we only talked shop, but then we began to exchange reminiscences, mostly about shooting and life in the country. Somehow he fitted everything into Higgin's real background, shifting an incident from his family's forests to Russia's, or explaining how a friend of his father's in the R.C.M.P. had taught him to ride.

When he got on the subject of horses, he really came to life. His eyes flashed—even when he could barely keep their lids open. He laughed. He seemed to forget all his troubles. But these pleasant occasions became less and less frequent as he was forced to drive himself harder and harder, and finally I made up my mind to do something about it. Herewith my entry of 12th October, 1913:

"Today I spoke to Uncle Cosmo about Adrian, going to London just for the purpose. 'Sir,' I said 'I'm worried about him. We're pushing him too hard. He's likely to come apart on us.'

'I doubt that,' Uncle replied, doing ferocious things with his eyebrows. 'He's tough. Besides, if he breaks up it's their loss, not ours.'

" 'That's true, sir,' I said. 'But you told me that his activities here are tying up many of their best technical people, trying to puzzle out what we're up to. If he fizzles out, there'll be the end of it.'

"Uncle Cosmo just grunted. 'Next I suppose you're going to tell me he's really a very decent sort of chap and wonderfully helpful, is that it?'

"I nodded."

" 'Very well, what would you suggest?'

" 'Sir, couldn't we get that Countess of ours to whisper to General von Krott in his sleep that they don't really need specimens of every *minor* variation— that drawings would do just as well?'

"Uncle Cosmo objected that this might be too risky. He didn't know whether or not von Krott would follow such a suggestion. It would be up to the Countess; if she thought she could manage it safely, then well and good. But at least he agreed to ask her about it. Then he asked me whether I had planned anything else for my spy-pampering program?

" 'Nothing, sir' I told him, 'except to get Adrian some healthy outdoor exercise.'"

At that point, Uncle Cosmo chucked me out rather abruptly, so I had no chance to tell him how I proposed to accomplish this. What I wanted to do was to get Adrian onto the back of a horse, and—bearing in mind the social difficulties—there was only one way I could think of to do it. My Aunt Frances, my mother's and Uncle Cosmo's half-sister, had married beneath her. She had married Will Thacker, a well-to-do farmer who lived nearby, just a few miles from Coventry and scarcely an hour by train out of Birmingham, in some of Warwickshire's best hunting country. Like so many good men of that sort, he kept his own horses and hunted as keenly as Jorrocks. I knew that he'd welcome Hohenhaupt-Higgins without too many questions, especially after he found out how horsey he was.

I really planned it quite cleverly. I'd remembered that the real Adrian's mother had been a clergyman's daughter, and that she had married beneath her. (According to all our reports, she'd never let her husband forget it.) So I broached the subject with great delicacy one day at the pub, distorting the truth only a little. Without mentioning Uncle Cosmo, I spoke of Aunt Frances, and then started to talk about Uncle Will, explaining that he was really a wonderful fellow even if he wasn't quite out of the top drawer.

Actually, Hohenhaupt-Higgins's initial reaction was frosty—but this was because he was thinking like Hohenhaupt-Trohna instead of like Adrian Higgins; but as soon as I told him about Will's horses and hunting he began to thaw. I could see him wavering between the absolute discretion that his role seemed to demand and the born horseman's urge to go riding; and eventually the horseman won out, as I was sure it would.

I had hoped to get him up to Uncle Will's for the cub-hunting, but that was impossible, for it took the Countess eight weeks to make up her mind —at a cost to us of some hundreds of pounds—that she could risk whispering the message to von Krott in his sleep. Finally, a few days before Christmas, we heard that she'd managed it, and Hohenhaupt-Higgins learned the results almost as quickly as we did. The relief on his face was really a joy to behold. Thence-forward, he was to be allowed to forward drawings (with, of course, precise measurements) of all minor variations. Though this didn't stop him from being The Greatest of All Webley Collectors, it did cut down his collecting by about sixty percent, which made things much easier for him, and relieved my own mind.

It was easy enough to arrange an extra holiday, and off we went in the first week of January. Uncle Will and his daughter, my cousin Alice, met us at Brinklow Station, half a dozen miles this side of Rugby. The three of them took to each other immediately. I was quite pleased about it at the time, not being able to realise that, while it was perfectly genuine all the way round, the communion between Alice and Adrian was much stronger than one would expect even from the meeting of two such devoted horse-worshippers.

I had always thought Alice a rather strange person. Her nickname was Titmouse, which in those pre-James Bond days was not subject to vulgar misinterpretations. She was a tall girl, not quite twenty, dark blonde, with serious grey eyes and very dark lashes. In a way, I suppose, she was beautiful, and everyone said she was *lissome*, but I always thought of her as loose-jointed—a nice enough kid, but just not my sort.

She rode like a centaur, and one thing which may have prejudiced me was her insufferable habit of calling to me in the field, using more or less nautical terms: "I say matey, hadn't you better take a reef in those reins?" or "Hard a-port there, mate!" My seat wasn't perfect, but she was much too unkind about it, greeting me with such sallies as "Ah-ha! Here comes the bumboatman!" which I thought vaguely indelicate.

Adrian, however, did not see Titmouse through my eyes. Before we went back to Brummagem, she had obviously become one of the most wonderful things in the world—after Family Honour, Duty, the House of Hohenzollern, and horses, more or less in that order. After supper, on the night we arrived, she took him out to the stables and, by lantern-light, introduced him to every one of the horses. They must have whickered and neighed at each other out there for an hour at least; and when they came in,

Uncle Will was as pleased as punch. He remarked that my friend really knew horses, that he seemed an awfully nice chap, that he himself often wished that Titmouse might marry a Canadian or Australian and move out where there was still room for a decent gallop—the railways had spoiled everything around here, and the motor cars would inevitably work even more mischief.

But it was not until the next morning, when we joined the hunt at Snitterfield, that I really began to understand what had happened. Ordinarily, like most Europeans, Hohenhaupt-Trohna would probably have been appalled by how democratic the hunt was, with so many of those mounted up clearly not gentry—to say nothing of the strange crew of bumpkins following on foot. But he didn't notice a thing. Titmouse was usually surrounded by a crowd of ardent, more or less eligible, young men; everyone called them "Princess Alice's Own."

Now, however, taking one look at her with our Adrian, they simply melted into the background. He was really magnificent. Once in the saddle, those extra pounds they'd put on him vanished abruptly; his nearsighted stoop disappeared; even the Kipling moustache bristled with a new life of its own. Titmouse had put him aboard a wildeyed, vicious, iron-mouthed,

hammerheaded idiot of a horse who had thrown me twice and bitten me painfully and the brute was behaving as though Adrian was the patron saint of all horses.

It was a lovely morning, crisp and green and fast under a white-flecked canopy of blue—a huntsman's morning. Everything, I suppose, went wonderfully. All I remember of it, though, is a montage of Titmouse and Adrian flying over fences, hedges, ditches, almost hand in hand, and all sorts of people *ohing!* and *ahing!* at the sight, and asking me where I could ever have met such a splendid horseman. Then, as though that weren't bad enough, old Colonel Hetheringbotham began to imagine that he had seen Adrian—or Hohenhaupt-Trohna—somewhere before, which he very well may have, what with his stints as a military attaché and any number of manoeuvres and horse shows on the Continent. However, I told him about Adrian's travels, especially in Russia where he'd come under some strange foreign influences, and the Colonel finally persuaded himself that it wasn't the face, but the *seat* which was so familiar. Still, it disturbed me, and I decided to mention it when I made my report on the Adrian-Titmouse situation.

On the train, Adrian surprised me by mentioning her only in passing, usually in connection either with some horse he was interested in or some event of the hunt which he felt needed expert analysis. His manner was incredibly gay, light, and carefree, and he certainly didn't resemble a lover newly and hopelessly smitten. Nor, for that matter, did he resemble a Graf Rittmeister with a higher degree busily spying out a foreign land's supposed military secrets. All in all, I began to feel that perhaps my fears were unwarranted; and next day, when I lunched with my uncle, I told him as much.

"My lad," he chuckled, "you're right. We can judge neither Titmouse nor our Teutonic friend as though they were ordinary people. I doubt if he really sees her at all, or she him. They look *through* each other, but they *see* only horses. No doubt it's quite pleasant for them, but it's nothing for us to worry about. Besides, no *hochgeboren Offizier* in a German Guards regiment *can* fall in love with a farmer's daughter—even the well-brought-up daughter of a farmer as prosperous as Will. It iss *verboten*. It iss alzo against Regulations. Therefore, even if he did fall in love with her, he would not be aware of the fact, and no harm would be done. As for old Hetheringbotham, leave him to me. It'll work out nicely."

And, for a time, it certainly seemed he was right. The Colonel gave us no further trouble, ignoring Adrian completely. We went down to the farm for at least one day of hunting a week, and sometimes, when I could manage it plausibly, for two in succession. It did my heart good to see how happy he was. He and Titmouse continued to get along famously. Instead of whispering sweet nothings, they exchanged confidences about hooves and hocks. Instead of sighing and burning and clinging and yearning, they focussed their passion on fences and foxes. They were happy. Uncle Cosmo was happy. I was happy. Only Uncle Will, who had set his sights on a marriage, was a bit disappointed.

For more than two months, it was really idyllic. Von Krott and the Imperial General Staff were delighted with Hohenhaupt-Trohna, for their technical people had expressed great satisfaction with the enormous numbers of Webleys he had made available to them for study. So pleased were they that they even approved of his equine pursuits, which were necessary, Adrian explained, so that he might gain the full confidence not only of his imediate superiors at work, but of those mysterious authorities who were presumably pulling the strings.

That explanation was a terrible mistake.

It was mid-March when the blow fell, and it came without warning (my diary entry of 17th March, 1914):

"Today Uncle Cosmo sent for me, something he just never does. I caught the first train, and when I reported he really was wearing his Eve of Waterloo look. He had a bottle of brandy and a couple of glasses out on the table.

" 'Well, Gerald,' said he, 'the fat's in the fire.'

" 'Sir?'

"He poured the brandy, and pushed some my way. He had heard from the Countess. The technical people had rendered an impressive report, in three or four hundred pages. They'd analysed 1138 Webley revolvers, including some made as far back as the 'eighties, and nearly 200 self-loading pistols. They had documented all the measurements, all the variations, and had set forth their own speculations, giving the pros and cons for each one. And they had reached a conclusion—

"Uncle Cosmo swallowed his brandy, and I followed suit. The conclusion was simple: they could not solve the riddle. They had been denied materials for study; they had, in x many cases, received only drawings instead of the actual weapons involved!

"The report has been *accepted*, and an order has been written telling poor Adrian that he not only must go back to sending one of each kind, but that he'll have to find specimens of all those not previously sent!"

Well, my uncle agreed that we had to do *something*—not, he said gruffly, because of any consideration for the spy in our midst, but to keep the whole project from being washed down the drain; and he finally decided, after we'd thrashed it around, that von Krott needed another flea in his ear.

So he instructed the Countess to suggest to her lover that the riddle wasn't one for the technical people at all, that it involved the Empire and the psychological subtleties of its strange and assorted Native races, and that a really massive espionage effort by ethnologists and other such experts was called for.

"That," he said, "ought to do it, even if it does cost us money. They'll order our friend back to der Vaterland— then they'll start wasting even more men and energy than before."

"Titmouse will be awfully upset," I suggested.

"Nonsense, my boy. She may weep for a while, but then she'll find someone equally horsey, and British to boot."

Well, I wasn't so sure about that, but it was by no means the worst of my worries. The Countess was slow—I imagine there was a good deal of haggling—and I had to watch Adrian going to pot as he tried to obey the new orders. There was no question now of his taking any days off, and I'm sure it was only for appearances' sake that he managed to squeeze in a few dinners with me. Suddenly, all the ginger was out of him; once more, he looked haggard and drawn.

It was an odd situation. Ordinarily, because we were really on excellent terms, I would have felt free to enquire, to offer assistance—but that, naturally, was out of the question. Uncle Cosmo and I were both helpless; all we could do, unobstrusively, was to make it a little bit easier for him to get hold of some of the rarer specimens.

By the last week of May, he was worse than we'd ever seen him. His efforts to keep up a brave front were very depressing—and to make matters worse Titmouse started writing me notes asking what on earth we had done with him.

Then we heard from the Countess— and the second blow fell. She had done what we'd wanted, but von Krott had started to waken just after the Natives and before the ethnologists, so she'd had no chance to mention the latter part of it. As a consequence, next day he put up a very strong case for sacking the technical people, and then argued even more strongly for solving the problem by espionage. And who was the logical man for the job? Why, the man on the spot: Rittmeister Graf Franz-Christian-Waldemar von und zu Hohenhaupt-Trohna, the man who had cleverly galloped his way into the confidence, not only of his superiors at Webley's, but perhaps even of those shadowy behind-the-scenes military figures who without doubt were masterminding the plot!

Remember, the whole thing had been von Krott's baby, and he must have presented the case with considerable ardour. New orders were shelved, at least temporarily, and Adrian was informed that it was now *his* job to get to the root of the matter, to discover the reason for all the variations.

I was encouraged at first, thinking that things might come back to normal—but Uncle Cosmo soon shattered all such illusions.

"The trouble," he said, "is that Hohenhaupt-Trohna is an intelligent fellow. Up until now, he hasn't had to fret about the solution to the enigma; that's been up to the technical men. Now it's *his* problem—and I'm afraid he's going to see right through to the answer."

"But that means he'll write a report telling them the whole thing's a gull, a hoax! He's too honest to do anything else." Then the full import of it came home to me. "In effect he'll be saying that von Krott is an ass and that the Imperial General Staff has been incredibly stupid!"

"Precisely, Gerald—and I'm afraid that von Krott and his friends will reject the report out of hand."

"But he'll be *disgraced*, Uncle Cosmo."

"He will. And they'll tell him so very bluntly before they send him into the next room with a pistol and only one cartridge."

"Sir, we *can't* let that happen!"

My uncle wasn't as fond of Hohenhaupt-Higgins as I was, but he had taken a violent dislike to von Krott; and I suppose that decided him. "By God, we can't!" he growled. "That infernal von Krott shan't have a scapegoat. He'll pay for his own sins. Besides, it's better for us if an Oberst-General is disgraced than a Rittmeister. But what can we do? It's no good asking the Countess. His waking up frightened her, and she's said flatly that she'll make no more nocturnal suggestions."

We looked at each other, each of us thinking as hard as he could. Finally he said, "This is a damned strange situation. The only possible way we can help him, as I see it, is to find a solution ourselves."

"Of course, you young ninny—a solution to his problem. A really good reason for our doing what we've been doing, one he can feed to von Krott. In other words, the spied-upon are going to have to work like the devil to make sure the spy *succeeds* in his spying. It is not, I believe, a situation which occurs very often in history, and would usually be frowned on. Well, how shall we do it?"

I said the first thing that came into my mind. "Why not bring in the Natives? Sir, we could give him the same idea that the Countess was supposed to suggest to von Krott—about all those experts. We might even find some kind of ethnologist. He could talk learnedly about the effect of the wrong kind of rear-sight notch on the discipline of, say, Pathan noncoms."

Uncle Cosmo hoisted his pennant immediately. "We'll try it, by God!" he declared; and we sat there for a good hour thrashing out ways and means.

Hohenhaupt-Higgin's life changed after that. Though he no longer had to add to the Webley Collection, he seemed terribly depressed. Every Sunday, he would visit the farm, and he and Titmouse would go off on long, quiet rides. I often wondered what they said to each other, but I suppose they just talked rather unhappily about horses. I could tell that his sorrows were quite as prodigious as Werther's, though by no means as dramatic, and I would have been much more concerned had Uncle Cosmo not put our plan into action.

Our first Native visitors came in with an army type. They were a risaldar-major from Skinner's Horse, turban, shoulder-chains, and all, and a gloriously garbed, rather overweight pirate who commanded the Palace Guard of some maharajah. They got quite excited over a Fosbery with a swept-back Balkan grip, the risaldar-major booming away in his own language as though he were calling down either curses or blessings upon it.

After that, scarcely a day went by without one or two of them coming in—all sorts of Indians, and Gurkhas, Malays, Afghans, Egyptians, and everything else. The best of them all was the enthologist, a tall, craggy Scot who taught at St. Andrew's, and who proposed the most farfetched theories so solemnly even I almost came to believe them.

This went on all through June and into July, but Adrian's spirits failed to lift. Instead, his gloom deepened; his rides with Titmouse became longer and slower; she, herself, usually so buoyant, seemed wilted and worn, as though she'd contracted his sadness.

Then all was made clear—I quote from my entry of 8th July, 1914:

"Well, Uncle Cosmo heard from the Countess to-day, and Adrian's done it. He sent his final report in to von Krott a week ago. He stated that there was *no* military motive or plan behind what we were doing; that it had probably started out by being nothing more than the normal muddled way the British did things; that in all probability word of the German interest in it had leaked out; and that our Intelligence had apparently taken advantage of this.

"Lately, obvious attempts had been made—he described them—to attribute significance to the program. He recommended that he be recalled and that the whole operation be cancelled out.

"Von Krott hit the ceiling, and of course the report was rejected. Adrian's been told to get back as quickly as possible, and Uncle Cosmo says that his future looks very bleak. What can we do?"

Of course, there was nothing we *could* do. Even before we learned what had happened, he had seen Mr. Whatman and, pleading the suddenly critical illness of a close relation, had given him a month's notice. Mr. Whatman had sympathised with him, and had informed him that, under the circumstances, he could leave in a fortnight if he wished—they'd manage somehow. For this, Hohenhaupt-Higgins was genuinely grateful.

We talked it over together, Uncle Cosmo and I and Mr. Whatman and Coulter, and none of us was able to think of anything that would save him. However, Coulter suggested that, considering how hard he'd worked, we just couldn't let him go off without some token of our appreciation and friendship. He also suggested what that token should be, and, when we all agreed with enthusiasm, Mr. Whatman told him to get the men busy.

Well, those last days were strange ones. Hohenhaupt-Higgins now knew that we knew, and we knew that he knew that we knew, but naturally none of us gave any sign of it. Uncle Cosmo kept right on bringing in Natives, each more picturesque than the last, and we kept right on making new variations just as though nothing had changed.

Adrian was very subdued and withdrawn. He stayed much to himself, and did not again go to the farm. Uncle Cosmo and I both wondered how Titmouse would take it when she found out, but we decided that this was a problem better deferred.

Finally, his last day arrived. Mr. Whatman ordered the men to stop work half an hour early, so that there could be a small ceremony in the offices; and Adrian, on the way there, asked me to have dinner with him afterwards.

It was all very moving. Everybody was there, Uncle Cosmo included. Mr. Whatman said a few words, and John Coulter delivered a brief, but quite fervent address dealing with such subjects as True British Craftmanship and Devotion to Duty. Then we gave him the present we had made.

It was a beautiful thing—a *nine*-shot .32-20 Webley-Fosbery, the only one of its kind in the world, finished in that lovely dark blue you've seen on the WG target revolvers. It had ivory grips, and we'd had it put up in a handsome mahogany case, with all the accessories. The lid had a silver escutcheon on which was engraved: *To Adrian Higgins, With the Esteem and Affection of All at Webley's. 22nd July, 1914.*

We could see he was genuinely touched. He stood there ramrod-straight, holding it in his hands. "Thank you," he said. "You are very kind. Thank you." There were tears in his eyes.

Then the men gave him three rousing cheers, and everyone sang *For He's a Jolly Good Fellow*, and there was a great deal of handshaking, and wishing of good wishes, and bidding of good-byes.

Finally, he and I found ourselves out in the street, hailing a cab. We stopped at my quarters so that I could change, then at his so that he could do likewise, and finally we drove to the best restaurant in the city.

All through dinner—which, by the way, was superb—he was very much his old self. He talked about weapons; he talked about horses and hunting; he talked about Uncle Will and the farm. We drank toast after toast, all very tactfully vague. It was a splendid performance. Then, over the brandy, he became very serious.

"My friend," he began, placing the mahogany-cased Fosbery on the table between us. "I want you to know how

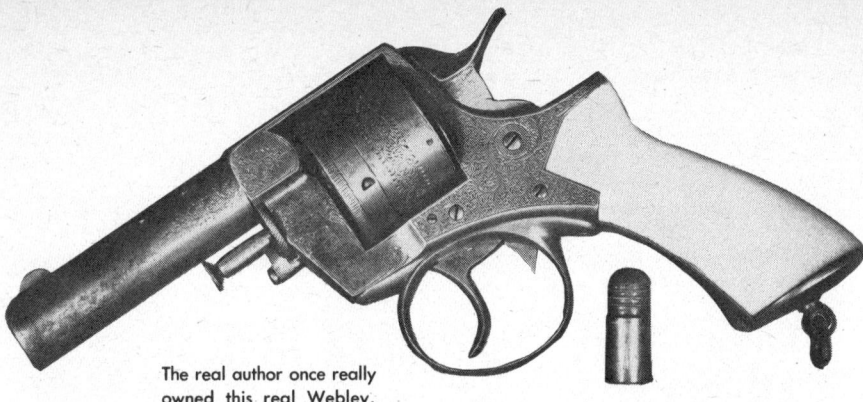

The real author once really owned this real Webley.

much I appreciate this. You've all been almost unbelievably generous." His smile, as he opened the case, was suddenly bitter. "It was decent of you to fill up the cartridge block. I know people who wouldn't have done that. They'd have thought one round was more to the point."

I could make no answer to that. Instead, as casually as I could, I said, "Adrian, old man, have you ever thought about emigrating? Out to New Zealand or—well, some place or other where there's room for a gallop, as Uncle Will puts it."

His manner chilled instantly, but for only an instant. "That was well meant, I know," he replied, "but you are an officer—no officer should ever suggest such a thing. If I were Adrian, I might very well emigrate. As I am Franz-Christian-Waldemar, we cannot discuss it."

Well, now it was out in the open, and besides he was perfectly right.

He asked very quietly, "Gerald, how long have you people known?"

"Several months," I replied, not telling the whole truth.

"One of our technical men informed you?"

I nodded; it would never have done to betray our Countess.

"And now," he said, under his breath, "now everything's over."

I knew what he meant by everything.

He drained his glass. "I'll have to go back, Gerald, but before we part company there are two things I will ask you to do for me." Out of his breast pocket, he took a rather thick envelope. "This letter is for your cousin Alice. Please deliver it into her hands."

I took it, and saw that he had addressed it to Titmouse, only more formally, and I assured him that I'd carry out his instructions.

Then he looked at the unique Fosbery once more, sighed, closed the case, locked it, and gave me the key. "I want you to have this," he said. "I—I do not want it to go with the—the rest of the Webley Collection."

We shook hands. There was really no more to say, and if there had been, I doubt if either of us could have said it.

I picked up the case and went home, leaving him—as I thought—to go back to Germany, suffer disgrace, and blow out his brains. I spent a sleepless night worrying about how much I ought to tell Titmouse.

Of course, it didn't work out quite that way. To start with, I took the letter to Titmouse next day, and watched her in silence while she read it and wept. After a bit, I tried to break the news gently. I told her, as tactfully as I could, that Adrian was suspected quite seriously of being a spy.

She flared up instantly. "The whole thing is absurd! There's nothing at Webley's worth spying on."

Although that was true enough, I was a little offended. "Oh?" I remarked. "And what makes you think so?"

"A-A-Adrian told me, you ass! B-besides, I think you're hateful—you and Uncle Cosmo and the whole l-l-lot of you. If England expects every man to do his duty, why shouldn't *Germany?*"

"Titmouse, that's *different*," I told her. But I decided to pursue the matter no further.

As for Hohenhaupt-Trohna, luck was with him. By the time he got back, August was almost upon us, and the Imperial General Staff was busy with more vital matters. But what I suppose really saved him was that the wretched von Krott, tiptoeing out of his mistress's bedroom full of champagne, caught his spur in the carpet at the head of her staircase and plunged to his doom. Uncle Cosmo learned of it from the Countess, and, even though it ended her usefulness, he celebrated the occasion by buying me dinner. We toasted Adrian any number of times, in the hope that things might work out for him.

In due course, they worked out very nicely. He was given some sort of reprimand, and, restored to life and his regiment, went off to the East to battle Samsonoff. He distinguished himself, naturally, winning the *Pour le Mérite,* and the Knight's Cross of the Iron Cross, and Lord only knows what else. He was wounded two or three times, and promoted two or three times, and finally was given a staff job on the Austrian front where, wounded again, he was captured by, of all people, the Italians, who treated him splendidly because he had been to their Cavalry School at Tordi Quinto.

After the war, he went back to Germany, but he didn't even stay long enough to watch his estates go down the drain under the Weimar Republic. There were no more Hohenzollerns. Everything was turned topsy-turvy. As soon as he could, he hurried to England, married Titmouse amid general rejoicing, and took her off to New Zealand, where they spent their lives raising horses. After one of their beasts won the Grand National two years running, Hohenhaupt-Trohna was actually knighted—and Titmouse referred to him as Sir Adrian to the end of his days.

He seemed to have lost all his interest in weapons, and he never did take back the Fosbery, which my boy, I am now sending to you as a wedding present. Be happy with it. But take the advice of your grandfather-in-law, and do *not* try to get one of each kind!

Affectionately yours,

Gerald Parringham
Captain, R.N., Retired

Editor's Note

Mr. Bretnor wrote this delightful story a decade ago when he was an active collector of Webley Fosbery automatic revolvers. Readers of GUN DIGEST are herewith warned that Mr. Bretnor's imagination has many figments and most of the Webley details and Webley arms described herein are among them. One of the guns does exist, but it is not the one–probably–with the triangular lanyard ring and—almost certainly —not the nine-shot 32-20. The Lt. Calthrop gun seems definitely an invention, but it is not. It exists; a friend of the author owned it.

Please do not trust anything in this story except the great fun and humanity revealed and do not expect anyone in the world, least of all me, to confirm or deny a word of it.   KW

SCOPES AND MOUNTS

Why is a scope?
by BOB BELL

Bob Bell with favorite long-range chuck outfit, a HB M700 Rem. 25-06, 12x Unertl 1½" target scope.

MY FIRST scope article appeared exactly 20 years ago in the 15th GUN DIGEST. In these Scopes and Mounts reviews in the years since, I've reported on hundreds of models, but most comment has been restricted to facts and figures about new scopes. Ken Warner thought it was time we gave some space to scopes in general—how they work, why we use them, etc.—and being the editor he tends to get what he wants. I'm not an optical engineer, so this won't be highly technical, but it might be interesting to hunters who have come to take glass sights for granted, and for young shooters who have given little thought to the basics of this gun accessory.

Viewed simply, a scope used as an aiming device on a gun (there are other kinds) is just a series of lenses fixed inside a metal tube, plus a reference point such as crosshairs which can be adjusted to coincide with the bullet's path at some desired distance from the gun's muzzle.

A scope is useful because it presents an enlarged image of the target to the shooter, allowing him to make out more detail (in a sense see better), and thus hit better—and hitting, of course, is the reason for shooting. However, magnification is not the only quality required of a scope. It also must have a field of view large enough to permit easy finding of the target, enough illumination to be functional under imperfect light conditions, and enough eye relief—that is, distance from the eye—so that it will not be dangerous to the shooter when the firearm recoils. Its size and weight must also be acceptable to the user, and it must be strongly enough constructed that it can withstand perhaps thousands of shots on a heavy-recoiling firearm.

It is a difficult chore to design and build such a scope, for many of the requirements are antagonistic. To get good illumination with a scope of high power requires large lenses, yet large lenses add weight, bulk and unhandi-ness, to say nothing of cost. High power also restricts field of view in any scope of reasonable size. And to increase strength in a conventional way, such as by beefing up metal thickness, would add significantly to weight. Ultimately, a good scope is a series of compromises, the best end product designers can come up with as they trade off a percentage of one desirable characteristic in order to get a reasonable percentage of another that's just as necessary.

My own interest in scopes stems from a statement some forgotten gunwriter made back in the mid-'30s. "When you look in the back end of a scope," he said, "you don't look out the front end." I was young then, and didn't own a scope, but that thought intrigued me. It wasn't until years later I realized that, strictly speaking, you don't even look into the back end of a scope. What we think of as sight is a phenomenon caused by light passing through the pupil of the eye and exciting the nerve ends on the retina at the rear of the eyeball, the impulses from this being interpreted by the brain as mental images. This points up the fact that the eye is an integral factor in any scope-sighting unit and actually determines many of the design features of the scope. We'll go into that later.

Meantime, let's note that it is light that makes seeing possible. We can see luminous objects—stars and light bulbs, for instance—because they create and give off light of their own, but everything else that's visible is seen by reflected light. That's how we see the world around us. From here on, any reference to light will be to reflected light.

The human eye is a marvelously efficient mechanism, but its ability to cuses it within the tube. However, the image is upside down and reversed left to right. It would be unnatural and distracting to try to aim with such an image, so an erector lens (usually a 2-lens system) is installed farther back in the tube. This uses the inverted image as a substitute for the real target, and when the light rays pass through it inverts them again to create a normal image behind it. This image appears in the focal plane of the ocular lens or eyepiece of the scope (so-called because it is the lens nearest the eye). The ocular lens acts as a magnifying glass to present an enlarged image to the eye, best seen, of course, from several inches behind the lens. And that is what I meant when I said we don't look into the back end of make the necessary measurements if he could. However, it's easy to determine true magnification by direct observation. Simply focus the scope on a brick wall or other area of repeated-unit design. While using the scope with one eye, look at the same area of the wall with the other. Then sort of relax both eyes so they go a little out of focus. Suddenly, you'll see two images, one magnified by the scope, the other normal. By adjusting the head slightly, you can overlap these. Count how many normal bricks fit into one magnified one, and this will be the true power of your scope.

Anything manufactured by man has certain tolerances of imperfection, but after checking enough scopes you'll find that most run awfully close to the

Bob Bell chuck hunting w/220 Swift, 112 Savage, 24x Redfield. Chuck rest by Jim Cravener, Ford City, Pa.

resolve detail decreases as distance increases significantly beyond 8 or 10 inches, the normal minimum at which it can perfectly focus. From the shooter's viewpoint, while the eye is adequate for aiming, unaided, at large targets at close range, it becomes progressively inefficient as targets get smaller and/or the range increases. A scope is useful because when interposed between a target and the eye it alters in a helpful way the light waves being admitted to the eye.

Let's give a little thought to how the scope does its job.

Light reflected from a target (bullseye, woodchuck, moose, or whatever, plus a restricted surrounding area) moves outward in all directions. A scope pointed at this target accepts the light which falls on its objective lens (so-called because it's the one toward the object of interest), and fo-

a scope. We look *at* this image on the focal plane of the ocular lens.

The ocular lens is not the only magnifying unit in most scopes. In a scope which does not have an erecting system, such as those used in some scientific work, magnification can be calculated by dividing the focal length of the objective lens (the distance behind the lens at which its image forms) by the focal length of the ocular. However, in some scopes with erecting systems, the erecting lenses contribute to magnification.

This information is of little practical use to the shooter who might wonder about the true magnification of his scope, a minor problem with American scopes but one that used to come up with foreign models as many were unmarked. He cannot readily dismantle the scope, and probably would not have the equipment and ability to

expected power, so close that the variation is unimportant. Most of the noticeable discrepancies come in the variable-power models, but this is usually due to the manufacturer mislabeling the magnification just to simplify things. A so-called 2-7x will turn out to be a 2.3-6.9x, for instance. Nevertheless, some guys want to know these things, and this is the way to find out.

Most of the light which falls on the objective lens of today's scopes is passed on through to the shooter's eye. Before the introduction of magnesium fluoride coating, as much as 4 percent of the light meeting each air-glass surface was reflected away, the total loss in the whole system being about one-third; however, this MF coating, only a few millionths of an inch thick on each appropriate surface, has recovered almost all of that loss, and also has eliminated much of the glare which used to make a scope unusable when aimed too near a bright light such as the setting sun.

Since the objective lens of any scope has much greater area than the pupil of the eye, far more light falls on it in any given situation than on the pupil. This light is compressed by the scope's design to a bundle of rays called the exit pupil—the small circle of light seen in the middle of the ocular lens when the scope is held at arm's distance. Thus a scope is said to "gather light." Mathematically, the diameter of the exit pupil, in millimeters, is equal to the unobstructed* diameter of the objective lens, also in millimeters, divided by the scope's magnification. Thus a 4x scope with a 32mm objective, a common size, has an exit pupil of $32/4$ or 8mm. A 2½x scope with a 20mm objective, which is about average in a scope with a one-inch tube and unenlarged objective, also has an 8mm exit pupil.

There's a good reason for this exit pupil size. Earlier, we mentioned that the eye was an integral part of the scope-sighting system, and here's where that ties in. The pupil of the eye is an amazing mechanism, one that alters its diameter according to the intensity of the ambient light. In bright light it squeezes down to almost a pinpoint; however, there's a limit as to how far it can open when the lighting is bad. Tests have indicated its maximum diameter under dark conditions is about 7mm, with a normal diameter under average conditions of about 5mm. This means that under no conditions can it utilize more light than can be transmitted through a scope exit pupil measuring 7mm. Any excess simply is wasted because it strikes outside the perimeter of the eye's pupil, thus is wasted insofar as illumination goes.**

For this reason, many straight-power scopes are designed to give an exit pupil of 8mm, with numerous variable-power models giving a 5mm pupil when set at top power, so they will transmit adequate light under any normal situation. At the lower powers, they of course will give larger exit pupils.

Some makers, notably Bausch & Lomb a few years back, have designed their straight-power scopes to give 5mm exit pupils, assuming this diameter will handle almost all shooting situations and permit smaller objectives, thus scopes of less weight and bulk that are neater looking on a gun. However, many shooters were bothered by this approach, believing these scopes did not transmit as much light as they should. This belief was fostered by an old term called relative brightness, which used to be listed in scope specification tables. This was a mathematical rating determined by squaring the diameter of the exit pupil in millimeters. Thus, a 5mm EP had a relative brightness of 25, compared with 64 for an 8mm pupil, or 144 for the occasional low power glass with a 12mm pupil. Many shooters looked at these numbers and automatically believed that the larger the exit pupil the better, not realizing much of that light went to waste because the eye couldn't absorb it.

That line of thinking also accounted for the belief, still held by many, that low power scopes are superior to high power ones when shooting under poor light conditions. Some hunters felt otherwise, arguing that the larger target image supplied by a higher power scope more than made up for some apparent light loss. This attitude has long been held in Europe, where medium power (6x-8x) large-lensed scopes have for generations been first choice for much of their hunting. A lot of their deer and boar shooting is done at dawn and dusk, and their field experience indicated such scopes were superior to the American-favored 2½x models, despite the higher relative brightness figures of the latter.

In an effort to develop a formula which would permit easy mathematical comparison of scopes of different power and lens size, the Europeans came up with a rating called the twilight factor. This is calculated by multiplying the unobstructed diameter of the objective lens, in millimeters, by the magnification, and taking the square root of the product. Running some conventional size scopes through this formula gives the following comparisons between relative brightness and twilight factors:

Bob Wise chuck hunting using 220 Swift, 112 Savage HB, and 18x Unertl.

Power	Objective Diameter	Exit Pupil	Relative Brightness	Twilight Factor
1½x	20mm	13.3mm	177	5+
2½x	20mm	8mm	64	7
4x	32mm	8mm	64	11+
6x	42mm	8mm	64	15+
8x	56mm	7mm	49	21+
12x	38mm	2.4mm	5.7	21+

The 1½x20mm was included because it is typical of a small variable set at bottom power, and the 12x38mm because it represents a traditional target scope with 1½-inch objective. The others are conventional size hunting scopes, the larger ones being typical of European design. Note that these four all have exit pupils of about the same size, which means they all have about the same relative brightness. Yet the far greater TF ratings of the higher power models indicate the importance of added magnification when shooting in dim light.

The accuracy of the twilight factor rating seems to be borne out by field experience. Yet if applied to all scope

---

* The diameter of a lens is not always what it seems to be. Viewed from in front, an objective might appear to measure 32mm, say—the diameter seen inside the metal tube. However, the mechanical units which hold the lens in place on the back side sometimes have a smaller aperture than that, thus decrease the effective diameter of the lens. Some makers also, for various reasons, install baffles inside the tube, with the same effect.

** One advantage of a large exit pupil is quicker scope alignment when aiming time is limited. One disadvantage is that aim taken along the outer edge of a large exit pupil introduces a trace of parallax, thus inaccuracy. Both of these effects are minor.

Fully adjustable chuck rest built by Jim Cravener. M700 Rem. 22-250, 12x Leupold, Redfield Jr. mount.

sizes, it can lead to some strange conclusions. For instance, if we built an 8x20mm scope, its TF would be 12+, exceeding that of the 4x32mm, and that doesn't seem reasonable. And as shown in the table above, the 12x38mm theoretically equals the 8x56mm, yet anyone who has tried to sort a chuck's head out of the grass with such a target scope in late evening knows that's highly unlikely. And so we believe that the twilight factor is most reliable when comparing scopes whose exit pupils equal the maximum diameter the eye's entrance pupil can attain—7mm. Obviously the Europeans feel the same way, for they build their scopes to that specification. But the formula for calculating the twilight factor makes no mention of it, at least in any literature I've seen, so it seems appropriate to bring it up.

This does not mean that a big 6x or 8x is the best scope for all hunting conditions. While excellent in dim light, we must remember that the fields of such scopes are comparatively small—on the order of 23 and 17 feet, respectively, at 100 yards, which means they would be far from ideal for targets at woods ranges. Eye relief also tends to be shorter and more critical than that of lower power models.

All of which means that there's good reason for the numerous sizes, styles and magnifications of scopes on the market. The small inexpensive 4x "22 scopes" are suitable for their market because they are matched to the guns they're used on. The rimfires don't have the recoil of big game cartridges, so these scopes don't have to be constructed so ruggedly. Ammo is cheap and the usual target is relatively unimportant, so adjustments don't have to be so precise. (If 4 shots don't get you zeroed, take 6; and if you miss a squirrel it's not as important as missing a Dall sheep.)

Big game hunters know in general what kind of cover they'll be hunting in and approximately what size their critters will be. For deer or elk in the timber, a 2½x or 4x will be ideal, as each has plenty of power for accurate aiming, enough field to catch a typical moving target, and each transmits plenty of light for most conditions. If the quarry is pronghorns, a 6x or 8x is top choice. Their fields are smaller than the 4x's at 100, but since field of view grows with range, you know it's going to be plenty big out where this critter is shot.

Some hunters, wanting to be prepared for all eventualities with one scope, opt for a variable. For most kinds of big game use, a 2-7x is ideal for it has plenty of field at 2x, plenty of power at 7x. Such a rig costs a bit extra in both money and weight, but a lot of hunters willingly pay the price. One caution: if you go for a variable, get the highest quality one you can afford. Most makes have improved over the years, but it's still possible to get a variable whose point of impact changes with every power switch, which means your chances of hitting with such a glass are not the best. Test 'em against a collimator's grid or by shooting a couple of shots from each power setting and seeing if the over-all group size is normal. If it isn't, send it back to the maker and get a better one. A good variable is highly adaptable, but a bad one is a bloody nuisance that nobody needs.

Varmint shooters have a wide selection of scopes, the 10x-16x action-mounted models being the most suitable for critters such as woodchucks and crows, the 4x-8x best for coyotes, jackrabbits, etc. Similar designs in higher powers take care of the bench-rest shooting with some individuals still preferring the older, long-tube target designs for both paper and field use.

The scope's reticle (aiming point) is important. As a general rule, the big game hunter wants something that's conspicuous in any light. Twenty years ago, medium-weight crosshairs (actually wires) were almost standard, having taken over from the flat-topped post. Now, the Duplex design, which consists of a post projecting into the field from each cardinal compass point and fine crosswires in the center, is top choice. The posts are visible in all light conditions, yet the crosswires allow precise aiming on a small target. A small but steady percentage still chooses the Lee Dot, and it's a fine reticle—but get it big enough. Four minutes of angle is about perfect in a 4x scope for average big game hunting.

No matter what scope is chosen, it's vitally important that it be mounted so the full field of view is immediately visible when the rifle is thrown to the shoulder. You don't have time to jerk your head frantically up and down and back and forth, trying to get your eye lined up with the scope so you can get the crosswires on a vanishing buck. So get it properly set up long before the season—and when trying it out, make certain you're wearing the kind of clothes you'll have on when hunting. A half-inch difference in thickness on the shoulder will make a helluva difference in where that scope has to be mounted.

As to mounts—well, that's another subject for another time. Meanwhile, here's a look at what's available in shooters' optics this year:

American Import continues to offer the extensive line of L.M. Dickson Signature scopes, from rimfire models up through the conventional-power big game models. New this year are a pair of Super Wide Angle 4x's. The M235 is a 4x20mm built on a one-inch tube. Both have 42-foot fields and internal quarter-minute clicks.

B-Square has a new handgun mounting system for all ribbed pistols, 45 autos, and the like. There's no drilling of the frame or removing of sights. Two base bolts screw into the barrel rib or slide and the B-Square rings lock to these bolts. Weight is only 2 oz. Studs (10x32) can be screwed in or out for elevation and shimmed for windage. This mount has been tested with over 10,000 rounds, according to the maker, including removal and re-installation every 1000 rounds, with no problems. It can also be used on some rifles. It's $32.95.

B-Square's big item for the moment is their mount for the Heckler & Koch M91 and M93 ($49.95), and of course they make models to fit numerous handguns and long guns, including the Charter Arms AR-7, Remington 600, 700, 788 and 1100.

Beeman: I don't have much experience myself with either airguns or scopes on them, but Beeman's does and they have developed their own line of scopes for these remarkably accurate guns for at least two reasons: I presume a sales organization makes a profit on the things it sells, which is one reason; the other is it takes something a little special to scope an airgun.

The regulation range at which airguns are used is 10 meters, or 33 feet, although some shooting runs all the way out to 50 meters. Ordinary scopes are factory-adjusted for minimum parallax error at more like 150 meters. In field use at either pest abatement or plinking, airguns can be stretched to perhaps 25 or 30 yards for most of us. Using the typical factory scope will therefore introduce error on an airgun, and so Beeman's has their scopes adjusted to the shorter distances. I am told this is useful at rimfire ranges as well as with the pump-up guns.

There is more. The new Beeman Blue Ribbon scopes are full 1" tube jobs which offer the special parallax setting and a few more airgun-oriented goodies. There is a fine-lined five-point aiming reticle, and two-way lens bracing, and a slight optical tilt to make high rimfire and airgun trajectories easier to deal with. The two-way lens bracing is a defense against the two-way snap of the typical airgun's action, which the shooter can hardly notice but which Beeman's believes can damage the usual scope over a period of time.

Prices run from $39.95 to $139.50 for these scopes. The highest priced model permits dial adjustment of the parallax error, all the way down to 4 meters

Buehler is now in their 35th year of scope-mount making, a fact that deserves mention. The basic design of this popular mount has not changed greatly through the decades—probably because it has been a good looking and extremely rugged design right from the first. (Remember the ads they used to run, showing Buehler-mounted hunting scopes on such fearful monsters as the 600 Jeffery Nitro

Beeman's Blue Ribbon.

Express and other African doubles? Any mount that can stand up to such loads has nothing to fear from an '06, obviously.) Well, the Buehlers are still machined from solid bar stock for strength and they're still good looking, and current models number upwards of a hundred.

New this year are the Mossberg RM-7, Code RM7, a 2-piece base to fit this rotary magazine rifle; Code M9, a one-piece base with short ring spacing to mount the new compact scopes on the Marlin 1894 lever gun; Code XP1 for the Remington XP-100 (also fits M600 and short M700) is a new one-piece base with recoil shoulder to accommodate most pistol scopes, including the Leupold M8 4x; Code 39, a one-piece base for the Marlin 39A rimfire which is now drilled and tapped for mounts; also, the Code R 2-piece Remington base will fit the new Smith & Wesson M1500 bolt action rifle which has the same receiver dimensions as the long 700.

Burris has added another scope to their Mini line, this one a 2-7x that is only 9½ inches long and weighs but 10½ oz. Despite its small size, this model has a 32-foot field at bottom power, which is enough for general big game hunting in the woods, and 14 feet at top magnification. Eye relief is 3.75 inches, which makes it usable even on magnum rifles—and it is built to take the recoil of such outfits.

This addition means Burris now has five scopes in this Mini series, fixed-power models in 4x, 6x and 8x, and variables in 2-7x and 3-9x. As a shooter who has long deplored the tail-wagging-the-dog appearance of over-size scopes on big game guns, I'm glad to see this development.

In another change, Burris now offers their 4-12x with the Safari finish, a low luster finish that gives a scope a "belonging" appearance on a hunting rifle. This finish is also available on the 4x, 6x, 2-7x and 3-9x Fullfield models.

I might say that for some years now I have been using a 2-7x Burris on a Remington 7mm Magnum with excellent results. This is the ideal magnification for this class of cartridge, in my opinion, as 7x is plenty of power for big game at any range where the load is effective, while at 2x the view is extremely large in this Fullfield model—50 feet— which makes it plenty fast for woods use. Yet at the same time, the scope's size is almost identical with a straight 4x, so it looks nice on a gun. It seems to me that any big game hunter who can own but one scope would do well to pick a 2-7x.

Bushnell has added a new feature to their new 10x40mm Banner Silhouette scope, and it's going to attract the attention of a lot of shooters who go for those distant metal critters. Beside the popular Bullet Drop Compensator which permits holding dead on via a simple elevation adjustment, and an adjustable objective lens unit to eliminate parallax at any range, this one Bushnell scope now has a Wind Drift Compensator to reduce the ancient "Kentucky windage" approach to the problem healthy breezes create for bullets.

A sample scope was not available at this writing, but, according to Ken Morris, the windage turret also has a window similar to the BDC unit in the elevation turret. It reveals a dial that's graduated to show inches at 100 meters (the range units of primary interest to MS shooters; for all practical purposes, of course, other shooters can consider these meters to be yards). The dial will show up to 7 inches left or right windage, which will accommodate for quite a breeze.

There's no all-out magic about this WDC unit. To use it, the shooter must estimate the amount of deflection the prevailing wind will give his bullet. He then dials the correction and holds center. Doubtless there will be human error involved, but it's helpful to be able to hold center rather than trying to get a shot off at some imaginary point of aim, so there could be some advantage to this arrangement.

New 3-9x Wide Angle and 4-12x Banner scopes are also offered with the Bushnell Prismatic Rangefinder feature, which uses for its basic reference a pair of horizontal wires with the usual 18-inch spacing for bracketing a deer's body. When adjusted to just touch the deer's withers and brisket, the range can be read in the top of the field. The shooter then turns the Bullet Drop Compensator to that range and aims directly at his target. For smaller animals such as woodchucks, there's a dot midway between the horizontal wires, to give a 9-inch reference.

Such features would seem to eliminate many of the problems inherent in long-range shooting. However it

distance—such as between 300 and 500 yards, which might be the guesses of two hunters looking at the same head of game. (If you think that's preposterous, you haven't hunted with many different guys in many different places.) So these RF gizmos can be helpful, but don't expect 'em to be infallible.

Bushnell also has a new Banner 22 scope this year, a 4x20mm built on a one-inch tube. It has 3-inch eye relief and comes complete with sturdy rings to fit grooved receivers.

And for the handgunners, there's a new Bushnell pistol scope built to take the recoil of today's goosed-up handgun loads. This is a 1.3x Wide Field which converts to 2.5x for long-range use by screwing a Power Booster onto the front end. Body tube is one inch in the low power, but the Booster has a 28mm objective, compared to the 1.3x's 21mm. Installing the Booster does not require re-zeroing. Eye relief is 21 inches, fields are 17 and 9 feet.

Clear View scope mounts, which raise the scope high enough, or offset it enough, to permit use of iron sights, has expanded its line to accommodate two popular lever actions. The M99 fits Savages of that number with serial numbers above 1,000,000, and the Winchester 94 Big Bore 375 Mount is adapted to that comparatively new rifle. This mount attaches to the left

Clear View Model SM-94.

Clear View models 101 (left) and 22 (right).

Conetrol's three-ring base and low rings in "Custum" grade for the Thompson/Center Contender pistol.

should be recognized that, in a practical sense, it isn't always possible to use these systems in the field. It's often impossible to hold the gun steadily on the game and still have a third hand to fiddle with the adjustments, etc., and of course deer and assorted other critters don't always measure that basic 18 inches in body depth. This is not a criticism of these Bushnell scopes or of any other make which uses a similar setup, but rather a reminder that no such rangefinder is completely accurate. One big benefit is their ability to reduce gross errors in estimating side of the action using existing holes, so no drilling and tapping is required. This mount accepts scopes up to 2-7x style, and the forward scope ring is adjustable for proper eye relief.

Clear View mounts are also made to fit the dovetails of 22 rimfires. Basically, these are designed to accept one-inch tubes, but they come with inserts to fit ⅞- and ¾-inch models also. The base design of the M101 fits Weaver-type bases, so can easily be adapted to many rifles already using that popular style.

Conetrol continues to expand its mount line—or maybe three lines would be more accurate, since there are three slightly different versions of this super-slick scope mount, the Hunter, Gunnur and Custum, for what might be called conventional installation on a base that screws to the receiver. There is also a DapTar base to fit actions with integral mounting units, such as the Sako and Ruger. The DapTar is now being built for the Heckler & Koch guns and will attach without drilling and tapping.

For scoping handguns, Conetrol makes a base that accepts three sets of rings, to absorb the vicious recoil put out by many of today's hotshot handgun loads. Cost of the 3-ring Custum base is the same as for 2-ring; however, the third ring must be purchased.

Speaking of costs, Conetrol allows its dealers a one percent discount on every sale made to an NRA member.

Davis Optical Co. still offers two Spot Shot target scopes with focusing via sliding objective lens units. The 1½-inch objective, in powers from 10x to 30x, now sells for $98.50, the 1¼-inch in 10x to 20x is $76.50. Davis also makes the Targeteer and Varmint Master attachments to convert hunting scopes to medium-power varmint glasses, and a long eye relief eyepiece to make a handgun scope out of a conventional hunting model. Increasing the eye relief cuts original power about in half.

Griffin & Howe's double lever side mount is possibly the most prestigious scope mount made. I won't say it's the best seller, for its comparatively high price has to have some effect in the marketplace, but an awful lot of hunters who have never even seen one in the flesh do know about it from their reading, and perhaps aspire to own one someday. It has been around for 40-plus years, used by many of the world's top hunters, and is deserving of its reputation.

Less known is the G&H top mount, an even more expensive version, which must be installed in their New York shop. Currently priced at $245 and up, it's a quality item which looks at home on a high-grade rifle.

S&K's stainless mounts on a Ruger Mini-14.

J.B. Holden Co. has expanded their Ironsighter See-Thru scope mounts to fit many of the readily available rifles plus an assortment of handguns, including the T/C Contender and XP-100, which do not require drilling and tapping, the Colt Trooper Mark III, and various Dan Wesson, Ruger and S&W's.

In another attempt to solve the problem of long-range hitting, Holden has developed a Bullet Drop Compensating Scope Mount. It is usable with any one-inch scope and any rifle fitted with a Redfield Dovetail or Weaver Detachable type base. After sighting in the rifle at 100 yards with its own adjustments, you dial the range you want, which tilts the scope up or down, aim and squeeze. Each mount comes complete with two dial and ring cap combinations for the two most popular bullet weights in each caliber, except in 223 and 22-250, where only units for the 55-gr. are offered. Other loads covered are: 243, 80 and 100-gr.; 25-06, 100, 120-gr.; 270, 130, 150-gr.; 30-06, 150, 180-gr.; 7mm Remington Magnum, 150, 175-gr.; 300 Winchester Magnum, 150, 180-gr.; 308 Winchester, 150, 180-gr.

Interarms markets three Mauser scopes and two types of mounts. Made in Japan to Mauser standards, the scopes have duralumin tubes with internal quarter-minute adjustments, are nitrogen filled, serially numbered and factory registered. Two 4x40mm models are offered, one a widefield, and a 3-9x variable. Choice of CH or Duplex reticle. Quick detachable steel ring mounts in two heights that fit tapered dovetail bases are available with windage adjustment, or aluminum alloy rings that use Weaver-type bases.

Paul Jaeger makes another excellent mount with bases for most popular rifles. A quick-detachable, lever-locked unit, no tools or coins are needed to remove or replace this side mount. Rings are available in three heights, one-inch diameter only. Weight with base, 5 oz., price $88.

Jaeger can also supply, on special order only, German claw mounts such as are typically used on drilling and combination guns, some to be fitted to American bolt actions. Approximate cost, $140.

Kahles scopes have been produced since 1898 in Austria, and for some time now have been imported into this country by Del-Sports, Inc. Steel tube or lightweight models are offered in the usual straight powers and 1½-4½x, 2-7x and 3-9x variables. All lightweight tubes are 26mm diameter, which limits the choice of mounts. Steel models are available with one-inch tubes.

The Germanic countries have long built large-objective scopes of medium power (6x, 8x) to make accurate aiming possible under poor light conditions, particularly from their shooting stands where it is often possible to use a rest. The Kahles 8x Helia-Super is typical of these. It has a 56mm objective lens, which gives the 7mm exit pupil traditionally used in night glasses, for an excellent 21.2 twilight rating (square root of the magnification multiplied by the clear diameter of the objective lens). It would be hard to top this performance under bad light conditions.

Kahles scopes offer a large selection of reticles, most of them variations on the design known in this country as the Duplex. Besides high visibility, these can be used as rangefinders when the hunter knows at what distance his game will fill the space between opposing posts.

Kahles prices range from $252 to $489.

Del-Sports also imports several models of EAW (Erzeugnisse in Aller Welt) mounts. The Pivot style is similar to Redfield's two-block dovetail system but also gives some vertical adjustment to eliminate stress on the scope tube when there is a slight variation in action contours—not unusual with military 98 Mausers, for instance. A version of this mount also accepts scopes with integral mounting rails on the bottom of the tube. Prices run $125 and up. EAW claw-type mounts also are available, as are QD slide-on rings in several diameters that attach to dovetail blocks.

Kris Mounts, another look-through design with an oval aperture for easy full-view seeing, has added a one-piece mount for the Marlin 336, number 263-1. KM's are offered in one- and two-piece top mounts and a side version, for one-inch or 26mm tubes.

Kesselring some time ago dropped their QD mount for the 7mm BRNO but continues to supply the Standard, See-Em-Under and Dovetail designs for a large number of rifles. Rings are made in ⅞ and one inch, 26mm, and an assortment of unusual diameters for foreign non-standard scopes.

Lee Tackhole Dot reticles have been favored by a certain percentage of shooters—including me—for a long time. I've always felt it was only their extra cost that kept more hunters from using them. Regardless, a significant number do, and will continue to. The important thing with a dot is not to get it too small. My own feeling, after using a good number of Tackhole Dot-equipped scopes over almost 35 years, is that for big game use the diameter should be 3 or 4 moa in a 4x, and proportionately bigger as power goes down, smaller as power goes up.

Leupold is taking a breather this year, insofar as new models go, and that's understandable, for it would be hard to find an unfilled slot in the Leupold line. They've got all the conventional powers in the popular M8 series, including Metallic Silhouette models, Extended Eye Relief handgun models, delightful Compacts in 2½x and 4x, action-mounted varmint and benchrest glasses, and two separate but similar switch-power lines, the Vari-X II and Vari-X III series.

In the variables, the 3-9x and 3½-10x are both offered with and without an adjustable objective lens unit. I prefer them with. At the lower powers this capability isn't needed, but it can be helpful at high magnification for it permits precise focusing at any range. If you happen to bed down for an afternoon of prairie dog shooting at long range, say, it is nice to get everything as sharp and parallax-free as possible. For quite a few years I've been using 10x and 12x Leupolds for a big percentage of my varmint shooting, and their adjustable objective has often been helpful.

It's especially satisfying to see the 2½x Compact featured on a customized M70 375 Magnum in the latest Leupold catalog. This little scope has plenty of magnification for

New B-Square mount.

Del-Sports Kahles scopes.

use on our biggest game at any reasonable range, and enough field for use on dangerous game under most conditions. Furthermore, it looks as if it really *belongs* on that beautiful Model 70. Obviously, there are occasions when high power (and thus a large scope) is needed to get the job done. But that's rarely the case on big game, and a large variable on a small carbine really gives me the galloping mugwumps. So I'm glad a trend in the other direction is developing.

Michaels of Oregon producer of many gun goodies, recently took over the Ka-Ram-Ba brand of scope covers.

 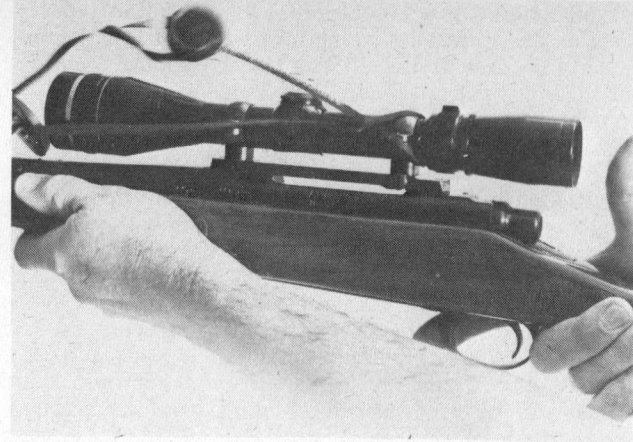

Michaels QD Scope Covers.

Renamed the QD Scope Covers, each set consists of a pair of lens covers attached by neoprene bands. Flipping the eyepiece cover off permits the tension in the bands to remove the objective cover. Made for most scopes. $6.95.

Pachmayr's most recent Lo Swing mount is the BBR model for the Browning bolt action and the RU-14-181/191 for Ruger's newer Mini-14 series. They have provided Lo Swings for most sporting rifles for many years, of course—and that reminds me, I used one on my latest elk-whomper, a 338 built on a pre-64 M70 action. Have had it shooting only a year or so, but it does fine.

Redfield will be offering, by the time you read this, a new 4x pistol scope to accompany the 1½x and 2½x models mentioned last year. The increasing interest in long-range handgun shooting made the earlier models immediately popular and created a demand for higher magnification. The 4xPS (actually 3.6x) is built on a one-inch tube with an enlarged objective, to give an 8mm exit pupil. This is large enough to make for easy scope alignment, even extended at arm's length, and transmits all the light the human eye can utilize. The 4xPS is 9.7 inches long, weighs 11.1 oz., and has .3 moa internal adjustments with a maximum movement of 45 minutes. Eye relief is 12-22 inches and field is 9 feet. Reticle is 4-Plex.

As with the earlier pistol scopes, this one is described as "magnum proof," and in tests has reportedly survived thousands of magnum rounds with no effect.

For added strength, the dovetail mounting system used in the front ring of Redfield's rifle mount is used with both rings for these handgun scopes. The bases incorporate recoil shoulders wherever practicable.

Mounts are available for Smith & Wesson's K and N frames, Remington XP-100, Colt J and I frames, T/C Contender, Colt 45 ACP, Ruger Super Blackhawk, Interarms Virginian, Hi-Standard Semi-Auto Heavy Barrel, and all octagonal-barrel black-powder rifles measuring ⅞ to one inch across the top barrel flat.

In the past I mentioned a 12x Metallic Silhouette Redfield I use on a heavy barrel M700 22-250. It has always

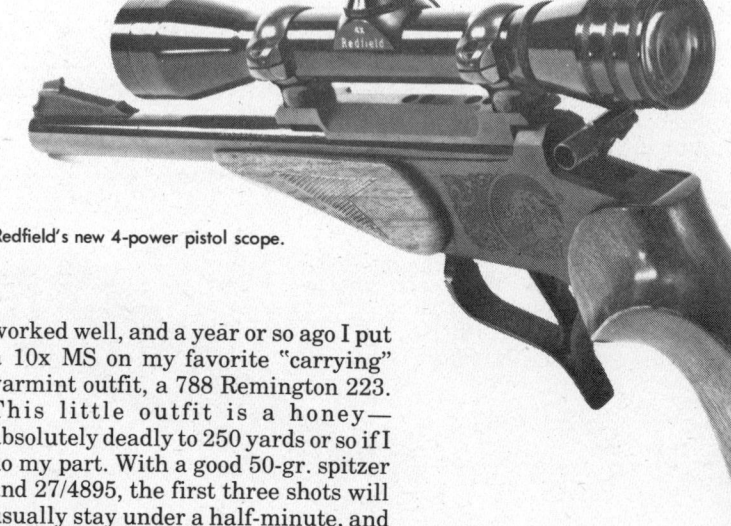

Redfield's new 4-power pistol scope.

worked well, and a year or so ago I put a 10x MS on my favorite "carrying" varmint outfit, a 788 Remington 223. This little outfit is a honey—absolutely deadly to 250 yards or so if I do my part. With a good 50-gr. spitzer and 27/4895, the first three shots will usually stay under a half-minute, and with a velocity of 3250 chronographed, trajectory is no problem over the ranges I use it. The 10x MS gives excellent definition in the back pastures, easily quartering a chuck's head at 200 yards and differentiating between such a head and the usual assortment of gray-brown rocks.

A few paragraphs back I mentioned building my second 338. The scope I installed on it is one of the older 1-4x Redfields, a Traditional model with the round eyepiece. I mention this because this model has been dropped, apparently due to lack of sales. I'm glad I'd been saving this one, as I personally can't get used to looking into a scope and not seeing a round field of view. Maybe I don't watch enough television. At any rate, the similar 1.8-4.6x Low Profile Widefield is still in the Redfield line, and hopefully will be for a long time to come. There are also full lines of LPW's and Traditional models, both straight powers and variables, plus the popular 3200 and 6400 target jobs.

S&K Mfg. Co., maker of the easily installed Insta Mounts, has no new models this year—they're going full blast just trying to keep up with the demand for the current line—but has added one variation on a mount already in production. This is a "stainless" version of the Ruger Mini-14 mount. The base is a clear anodized aluminum alloy, with chrome-alloy steel rings. $50 complete.

Wally Siebert's power-boosting conversions of medium-power action-mounted scopes continue to find favor with experienced benchresters, despite the availability of similar telescopes from various large manufacturers. In the 1979 Heavy Varmint Nationals, twelve of the top twenty competitors, including the first- and second-place winners, used Siebert-converted Lyman scopes. And as if that weren't enough, six of the top twenty in the 1979 Unlimited Nationals, where weight is no consideration, used Wally's conversions. Maybe there's something significant there, huh?

Thompson/Center Arms, as a result of their Contender's long range accuracy with numerous cartridges, has long sold the 1½x and 3x Lobo handgun scopes, compact, internally adjustable, aluminum-tubed models. However, these are recommended only for loads of light to medium recoil. For the heavy kicking cartridges—and Lord knows there are plenty available in the Contender—several "Recoil Proof" designs are now offered. A 1½x can be had with either standard or target-type adjustments, and has eye relief of 11-20 inches, a 28-foot field, 7½-inch length, weight under 6 oz., and Duplex reticle. A 2½x model is a whisper bigger and heavier with an integral mount base, and field is 15 feet. It has a CH reticle. A 3x is available with either type of adjustment, Duplex reticle, 13-foot field. All models have 60 minutes of adjustment, either direction, and each sells for $89.50 less mounts.

T/C also offers a small non-magnifying optical unit called the Insta-sight. Only 2¾ inches long and 1¼ inches high, it contains interacting optical units which display a set of "crosshairs" to the user who shoots with both eyes open, thus has essentially unlimited field and eye relief. Adjustable for w. and e. $73 plus $9.75 for base to fit numerous handguns.

Unertl Optical Co. has long manufactured an extensive line of target scopes, variations of these for varmint use, several hunting scopes, and an action-mounted 10x varmint glass.

In recent years, benchrest shooters have favored short, high-power scopes which can be mounted entirely on the action or the action's heavy sleeve, as they prefer to get all the scope's weight off the barrel. It's hard to dispute that concept. However, it's also hard to create a short, high-power scope with the optics of the more traditional design target scope; in fact, I'm not sure it's ever been done. Younger bench shooters who grew up using the short models might find it interesting to try one of these "old style" Unertls, say the 1½-inch 20x, and the long-range varmint hunters might find the same model in 12x or 14x a surprise in the chuck pastures. I've used several 1½ inchers for many years, and have a 12x latched to my HB 25-06 because I can't find anything that does a better job or presents a more detailed image.

Weatherby's Premier scopes are offered in 2¾x, 4x and 3-9x, with a choice of wide angle versions in the latter two. They have binocular-type focusing to suit the user's eye, quarter-minute clicks, and can be had with a Lumi-Plex reticle which lightens against dark backgrounds.

New this year in the 3-9x is the Tra-Com (trajectory compensating) system, which uses a calibrated elevation drum that permits setting the scope for a specific distance and then holding directly on, rather than placing the aiming point somewhere above the desired impact point with the intention of dropping a bullet into it.

Weaver has long had one of the most extensive scope lines, with over two dozen models, mostly K's (the big game glasses), V's (the variable power versions of the K's), KW's and VW's (the wide field version of each), T's (for Target), and D's (for 22 rimfires).

Added to the line this year, at least on a national advertising level, are five Marksman scopes, a lower-price line with some interesting features. These are steel-tube units with centered reticles (Dual-X in the inch-tube scopes, CH in the ¾-inch rimfire models), and come with mounts.

The M34 and M34W (widefield version) are 4x's for rimfires, priced at $13.25 and $17.15.

The M1 might be called a utility version of the popular K4; it lists at $57, as does the M1-SF-TO, which has a short focus (40 yds.) so that it's parallax-free at normal squirrel ranges. It comes with tip-off mounts to fit most rimfire rifles, and is an excellent choice for a high quality bushytail bushwacker. Fact is, we've had one around for the past year or so and can report from personal experience that it does the job. The full inch tube and enlarged lenses transmit plenty of light even in dark woods—a decided advantage for anyone who takes his squirrel hunting seriously.

The last Marksman is the M39V, a 3-9x variable with field that varies from 32 to 11 feet through the power range; 4-5 inches of eye relief, which means it can safely be mounted on any magnum, and quarter-minute ad-

Weatherby premier 3x to 9x variable scope.

justments, as on the other one-inch Marksman models. Price, $81.

We've often discussed the K's, V's and last year covered the T's, so won't go into them further here except for one comment on the old V4.5 that's been on my 284 Mauser so many years. My luck ran out last deer season—didn't get a shot, for the first time in years. But I'd like to mention the weather. On opening day, November 26, it literally poured rain throughout most of Pennsylvania, from before dawn till late afternoon. And I was out in it all that time, on the ridgetop facing Conrad, in Potter County. Anyone with a lick of sense would have stayed in bed, but you know how it is. At this writing in mid-March, I'm still coughing from the soaking I got. But that old V4.5, which I've been using for what seems forever now, went through the whole thing without shipping a drop of water or fogging up in the slightest. A lot of scopes did, that day—more than a couple hunters grumpily showed me completely unusable ones as they slopped past on their way out of the woods—but Ol' Faithful just ignored the rain and humidity, so I've nothing to blame for my unused deer tag except my own ineptitude.

•

SHOTGUN SLUGS

AT LONG RANGE

In His Country, This Writer Needs 200-Yard Slug Accuracy — One-Minute-Of-Deer — And Gets It.

by Joe Krieger

THE MORNING of November 20th, 1967, brought a brilliant glare over the rolling hills south of Franklinville in Western New York. Bright blue skies allowed the sun to broadcast its rays over the freshly-fallen snow.

Franklinville produces near-record whitetail bucks each season, and that morning, thirteen years ago, a record-class head was what the red-clad hunter had in mind as he walked out to his stand. This particular buck, which several other hunters claimed could have passed for an elk, had been sighted on three different mornings during the preceding two-week bow season.

The young hunter posted himself within 60 yards of the trail the animal had been using. Equipped with a Mossberg 500 Slugster, and Peters factory loads, he waited.

As if materializing from the mist, the buck arrived, but not exactly where the hunter had expected.

It was 175 yards uphill from his stand to the huge 12-pointer. For the next few moments, the hunter and the deer stared at one another. Several times, the hunter even sighted down the barrel of the Mossberg pump, but the buck was beyond the 75 yard limit he had imposed upon himself and his gun, and the buck silently disappeared into a stand of apple trees 50 yards from where he had first been seen.

Though the '67 season ended successfully, the hunter—me—was determined not to let such a magnificent trophy escape again. I was unsure how to solve the problem, though.

The winter of '68 was spent gathering every bit of information on slugs and slug-shooting that could be found. One fact became quite obvious as the reading progressed: each and every fall, a few articles appeared and continued to appear, dealing with shotguns and their use on big game. The types of shotguns to be used were usually dealt with, choice of sighting equipment discussed, slight reference made to the projectiles; in the final summary, the authors would state emphatically what the maximum range for this weapon should be.

The maximums varied in these analyses, from a low of 40 yards out to 100 yards or so. Seventy-five yards seems to be the accepted maximum range chosen by the majority of experts.

Yet I questioned the information and the advice given after constantly seeing the words "considered to be," and "usually" in the texts of these articles. It's quite easy to place the maximums at 50 or 60 or 70 yards, but I wondered "considered to be" by whom, and "usually," but when?

Often, the shotgun was belittled as a big-game weapon, said to be useful only at short range. But few skeptics offered range, or actual field experience, to back up their opinions. It was as if we were hearing words, spoken by some unknown or forgotten sage, repeated again and again, to be followed without question.

Through actual use on whitetails since, I have found the regular factory slug, or Foster handload of similar power, to have sufficient energy and the accuracy to drop the intended target out to 150 yards or so. The limitations in most cases are neither the performance of the gun, nor that of the slug, but the inexperience and inability of the shooter.

Since more game than not will be sighted within 150 yards, a hunter choosing the factory slug will find it to be an effective load in the majority of situations. But think how devastating it can be when a buck, carrying a trophy rack, appears beyond your self-imposed maximum range, as was my experience in 1967.

The search for the added yardage I desired continued. I hoped for a weapon useful out to 225 to 250 yards, and since the New York Conservation Department demanded the use of the shotgun in my end of the state, it seemed that another bullet would have to be found. I found it.

An article by Alfred J. Goerg, provided a great deal of hope, the article appeared in the 1964 edition of *Sports Afield's Hunting Annual*, under the title "Slugging for Hoofed Game."[1]

Mr. Goerg detailed some interesting occurrences that had taken place on several hunting trips. On each hunt, the author carried an Ithaca Deerslayer, firing 12-gauge factory loads. The shotgun was equipped with a Bausch & Lomb 2.5-8x, Balvar variable.

The information supplied is unique for several reasons. Mr. Goerg stated his belief that the 12-gauge slug would be sufficiently powerful for all North American hoofed game and the remark was backed up with some actual experience. An Alaskan bull moose was downed by the author in the Susitna River area, on the Gulf of Alaska. The task was accomplished with two shots from the Deerslayer, at 120 yards. The author also took several Hawaiian feral sheep, feral goats and a number of wild pigs, at ranges out to 150 yards. No animal traveled far after being hit, nor did any escape. The gun did a remarkable job for a "short-range weapon."

Slug Selection

Mr. Goerg's accomplishments provided the basic information that aided me in the selection of slugs for my own use. To reach out, a slug other than the standard Foster would have to be used. While Mr. Goerg used factory-loaded Brennekes, my own

[1] Alfred J. Goerg, "Slugging For Hoofed Game", *Sports Afield Hunting Annual*, (1964) pp. 44-46.

A Remington 870 with Weaver 1100/870 mount, and the 2.5x scope that comes from the factory. While better than open sights, an increase in power can make the rig more effective.

A Mossberg 500 Slugster and the highly efficient Bushnell 3 to 9x, Custom M scope. The rear open sight was removed to allow for the base. The box, assembled by myself to serve as shooting rest, carries equipment, too.

range-time and experience shows currently available Brenneke factory loads to be rather weak, in both velocity and energy, when compared to the levels the handloader can achieve using the same Brenneke slug. The fact that a great many hunters may be firing these slugs in doubles and drillings may account for the mild factory loadings. Velocity out of a 28" barrel averaged just 1330 to 1360 fps with factory loads, compared to the 1550 to 1575 fps that was achieved using Hercules data in Federal Hi-Power cases.

Since the Brenneke is the only other factory load available, at least in my area, long-range slugging is a handloader's game. Aside from the Foster slug, my own experience is limited to three slugs, with which I have worked extensively; these are the BRI Shotgun Bullet, the Brenneke, and the Vitt Aerodynamic.

BRI Bullet

The very best slug ever offered the shotgunner was the Ballistic Research Institute's 12 ga./.50 saboted bullet. The BRI slug could safely be loaded to 1550 fps at the muzzle, and combined this with the highest sectional density (.251) and ballistic coefficient of any slug ever available. It attained previously unheard-of down-range ballistics.

As many probably know, this slug used a two-piece plastic sabot, a holder of sorts, that carried it down the bore and fell free of the slug as the unit exited the barrel. The 50-caliber slug then made its way to the target in near-perfect condition. Its aerodynamic shape helped put the slug very near to where the hunter had aimed it, in many cases with rifle-like accuracy.

One load I have used, consisting of 29.0 grains of SR 7625, a Federal 209 primer in a Federal Hi-Power case, produced two 6" groups at 200 yards. The average group size for 5 three-shot groups ran to 10" over the same distance. These groups were fired through a Remington 870 Wingmaster, which was equipped with a Weaver 2-7x variable, over a *measured* 200-yard range.

While the slug can be found from time to time, BRI no longer markets it. Smith & Wesson purchased the rights to the slug, but stopped production a number of years ago. I continue to search for BRI slugs, but as the years roll by, stocks are disappearing. It still seems unusual that so many years after manufacture a few are still around; it may well have been the average shooter's ignorance that caused the producer to end the manufacture of these slugs.

The Brenneke

This slug remains one of the best commercially available slugs, and by far the oldest. Though not widely available in component-form, it can be ordered through sporting goods stores and other FFL holders.

Once again, I would like to state that due to the factory's underloading, I see only the handloaded variety as an adequate bullet for ranges beyond 150 yards. Trajectory is flattened, and the increase in energy is appreciated as the range increases.

Vitt's Aerodynamic, 12 gauge

The Vitt slug is once again available in quantity. Ray Boos has begun production of the slugs he and Eleanor Vitt market. The reloader has to work with an FFL dealer to get them, as is the case with the Brennekes.

The Vitt is, without question, capable of transmitting more energy to the target than anything that has yet come along for the 12-bore. Its accuracy, while not as good as the BRI slug, is all a shooter will need to keep all his shots in the chest cavity of an animal the size of a whitetail, even at extreme range.

George Vitt provided invaluable data concerning the handloading of slugs in general, and his creation in particular, in correspondence prior to his death. The loading information Mr. Vitt worked up made it relatively easy to achieve muzzle energy in excess of 2800 ft. lbs. These figures, plus the tremendous bulk of the slug provides the hunter with a very good game stopper. A chart, (No. 1) shows the relative differences between the Vitt slug, a heavily loaded Brenneke, the standard Foster slug, and two rifle cartridges, the 30-06 Springfield, and the 35 Remington. The rifle cartridges are universally acclaimed to be very good loads.

Note that the energy listed for the factory slug falls short of the published 2485 ft. lbs. The actual energy of 2274 ft. lbs. is based on the advertised velocity, but at the corrected, true weight of the slug. The Vitt betters the Foster round's energy by 25% at the muzzle. The weight of the Vitt slug (575 grs.) brings about a tremendous increase in sectional density, when compared with the factory slugs. At 100 yards, the Vitt retains more than 80% of its muzzle velocity. This produces 2024 ft. lbs. of energy at that range; the factory round carries less than 900 ft. lbs. The Brenneke falls short of the Vitt, but it shows drastic improvement over the Foster, beating it by 12% at the muzzle, and 61% at 100 yards.

Gun Selection

The nature of the slugs that should be used for long-range dictates a certain powder type. This in turn dictates a change in the slug shooting gun. Many succumb to advertising claims. We have been led to believe that short, cylinder-bored barrels will not only shoot more accurately, but are a joy to handle in the woods.

Prior to my using Brennekes and the Vitt slugs, I, too, carried a buck special, and was very happy with its performance. Though I had other 12 gauge guns in my rack, a Hi-Standard Brush King was my primary slug gun. With light Foster slugs, its 20-inch barrel performed as well as any, but when firing heavily-loaded Vitts and Brennekes, this gun failed to make it. Velocity was lower than anticipated with all loads fired, and accuracy was poor. The slow burning powders prescribed for use with these slugs failed to burn completely, and the resulting muzzle-blast was enlarging group size beyond acceptable limits, I felt.

I followed George Vitt's recommendation, and went to a longer barreled gun. The longer barrel would allow complete combustion of the heavy powder charge, give higher velocity, and reduce muzzle-blast. I began using a Remington 870 and a Mossberg Slugster for these heavy slugs. Definite improvement was immediately evident, both in velocity and accuracy. The same loads that worked poorly in the short barrel were excellent in the longer barrels of the 870 and the Slugster.

The Remington pump was equipped with a 28" barrel, originally choked modified; the barrel had been reamed to remove any sign of the choke, resulting in a 28" cylinder bore. The Mossberg was equipped with a 24" slug barrel, also cylinder-bored. The use of cylinder boring allows slugs to pass through the barrel with a minimum of bore-scuffing to the lead portion of the slug. The screw-attached wads center the slug in the barrel, and take the abuse. I have never found the longer barrels to cause any sort of problem I couldn't handle in the field.

Both the guns worked out well, with only the minor choke-modification to

Velocities & Energies: Chart No. 1

Projectiles	Load #	Muzzle Vel./Energy[2]	100 yds. Vel./Energy[2]	200 yds. Vel./Energy[2]
Factory/Foster	(note 1)	1600/2274	960/819	(NA)
Vitt, 12 ga.	#6	1490/2835	1259/2024	950/1153
Brenneke, 12 ga.	#2	1570/2562	1080/1324	880/803
30-06 Spring.[3]	165 gr.	2900/3082	2672/2613	2467/2236
35 Rem.[4]	200 gr.	2000/1777	1647/1206	1337/795

1. Factory velocity based on manufacturer's advertised velocity.
2. Energy figures computed using formula: Energy = weight (in grains) x velocity^2 ÷ 450240.
3. Springfield data based Speer data, Speer Handbook #8.
4. Figures for 35 Remington based on Hornady Ballistics Tables, Hornady Handbook #2.

Ballistic Information: Chart No. 2

Slug	Diameter	Weight	Sectional Density	Ballistic Co-efficient
Foster/Factory[1]	.684	405 gr.	.121	.064
Vitt, 12 ga.	.728[2]	575 gr.[3]	.155	.125
Brenneke, 12 ga.	.732[2]	468 gr.[3]	.124	.0965
308/165[4]	.308	165 gr.	.247	.416
35 rn./200[5]	.358	200 gr.	.223	.201

1. Factors for factory slugs are the average of 15 each; Remington, Winchester & Federal.
2. Vitt and Brenneke slugs, average lead portion, 25 slugs each brand.
3. Average weight 25 slugs per brand, with wads attached.
4. Data for Speer, 165-gr. spire point.
5. Data for Hornady, 200-gr. round nose.

the Wingmaster. Other hunting companions have had to go to more expense in coming up with adequate long-range guns. When spread over the years the gun will be carried afield, the cost is slight. This is especially true when compared to the other hunt-related costs like gasoline, for instance.

Sighting Equipment

Few rifle hunters would consider shooting at ranges beyond 100 yards without the aid of a scope-sight, but few shotgun hunters go to the added expense and trouble of mounting scopes on their shotguns. A great many have not even progressed beyond the original front bead. This is probably due, in part, to the erroneous belief that the slugs cannot be accurate beyond short-range.

Many hunters grumble and feel a hit may be more a matter of luck than accuracy as the yardage increases. However, those 70 caliber bullets have proven accurate enough over the years I've been using them, and at ranges out to 250 yards. This last comment concerns the Brennekes and the Vitt slugs. The lighter Foster slugs seem to demand a lot of trial and error loading and shooting to get effective loadings.

Scopes under 4x are normally considered to be compatible with the shotgun. After firing thousands of rounds at paper targets, woodchucks and red squirrels, I began to disagree with that advice. By increasing the magnification to an 8 or 9x maximum, I've been able to increase the slug-rig's effective range. The increased clarity and definition provided by the higher magnification makes for more accurate shooting and shot placement.

A variable power scope is the obvious choice, as this selection does not limit where the weapon can be used. At 7, 8, or 9x, the rig would be totally useless in a brushy draw or a thicketed orchard. A simple adjustment, however, matches the magnification to the area being hunted.

I have used two variables on my shotguns so I will limit my comments to them. Both scopes, a Bushnell 3-9x, Custom M, and a Weaver 2-7x, have performed flawlessly. The Bushnell has been mounted on the Mossberg Slugster, and has survived 200 heavy-load Vitts, in addition to hundreds of lighter slug loads. Once an accurate load was developed, the load continued to be accurate; point of aim remained constant throughout the load testing.

The Weaver base was attached to the gun's receiver using four 8-40 bolts, rather than the smaller 6-48's usually used. Some years back, I had used Bushnell's two-stud mounting system, and had those studs pull out of the alloy receiver of the Mossberg after firing a number of rounds. Only a little damage occurred to the scope and the shooter, but that range session made me decide on the use of the #63B base, for fit, and the larger bolts.

The Weaver 2-7x was mounted on the Remington 870 using Weaver's new 1100/870 side-plate mount. This combination has tolerated an equal number of loads. My only complaint about the Weaver system is the fact that rust has a tendency to form between the mount's side-plate and the receiver. After a hunt in wet weather, removal is a must, in order to wipe up the water that has accumulated there. This mount was developed for easy removal, so this point may not be that

Slug Loads: Chart No. 3

Load #	Slug	Case[1]	Primer	Powder/gr.	Muzzle Velocity	Group[2] Size/Range
1.	Vitt	Rem. SP	Rem. 57*	Herco/36.0	(NA)	6" /100 yd.
2.	Brenneke	Fed. Hi.	Fed. 209	Herco/37.0	1570	10" /150 yd.
3.	Brenneke	Rem. All-Am.[3]	CCI 109	Herco/35.0	1510	5" /125 yd.
4.	BRI/Bullet	Fed. Hi.	Fed. 209	SR7625/29.	(NA)	10" /200 yd.
5.	Vitt	Fed. Hi.	Fed. 209	AL8/44.0	(NA)	11" /125 yd.
6.	Vitt	Rem. SP	CCI 157	AL7/39.5	1490	9" /175 yd.
7.	Vitt	Rem. SP	CCI 157	AL5/36.0	1485	12" /175 yd.
8.	Vitt	Fed. Hi.	Fed. 209	AL120/31.	1505	14" /175 yd.
9.	Brenneke	Rem. All-Am.[3]	Rem. 97*	PB/28.5	1320	9" /125 yd.
10.	Vitt	Fed. Hi.	Win. 209	Bl.dot/48.5	1525[5]	8" /100 yd.
11.	Vitt	Rem. SP	Rem. 57*	SR4756/35.	1375	10" /100 yd.
12.	Brenneke	Win. Comp.	Win. 209	SR4756/31.	1350	12" /125 yd.
13.	Brenneke	Rem. SP	CCI 157	SR7625/27.	1385	10" /125 yd.
14.[4]	Vitt	Rem. SP	CCI 157	AL7/39.5	1490	11" /175 yd.
15.[4]	Vitt	Rem. SP	CCI 157	AL5/36.0	1485	14.5"/175 yd.
16.[4]	Brenneke	Fed. Hi.	Fed. 209	Herco/37.0	1570	15" /150 yd.

1. Unless otherwise noted, all cases once-fired, factory slug or buckshot shell.
2. Average group size, minimum of five 3-shot groups.
3. Loads #3 & 9, fold-crimped, using Stoeger slug spacers above slug.
4. Loads #14, 15, & 16, fired in Mossberg 500, with Bushnell 2.5 Custom M. Same loads as #'s 6, 7, & 2, respectively, but these were fired, same gun, with a Bushnell 3-9x, Custom M, set at 9x. Note smaller groups fired with higher power scope.
5. Load #10 was not fired at longer ranges as supply of Fed. roll-crimped cases ran out. Due to the power produced by the load, it may prove to be more suitable than load #6, if the accuracy can be improved upon.

DATA SOURCES:

Loads #1&8 —Ray Boos and Eleanor Vitt.
Loads #2 —Hercules Powder Inc.
Loads #5,6,7 —George Vitt.
Loads #3&9 —Stoeger Arms Corp.
Loads #10&11—Lyman Shotshell Handbook, 2nd. ed.
Loads #12&13—DuPont Handloader's Guide, 1975-76 ed.

Trajectory Chart No. 4

Projectile	50	75	100	125	150	175	200	225	250
Vitt, @ 1490 200 yd. zero	+8.5	+12.	+12.	+9.3	+6.7	+4.	+	− 9.5	
Vitt, @ 1490 150 yd. zero	+6.3	+ 8.6	+ 7.6	+3.7	+	−4.	− 9.	−19.6	−25.5
Brenneke @1570	+6.	+ 7.	+ 6.8	+4.	+	−7.	−16.		
35 Rem. 200 gr.				+ 2.6	+1.5	−	−3.3	− 6.5	−12.2 −18
30-06 165 gr.			+ 2.			+		− 1.8	− 3.5

big a problem for most hunters, but I dislike fiddling around with the scope once it has been mounted and sighted-in. The Wingmaster will continue to put the shots where they are aimed after such a disassembly; I feel that I must check out the zero at the range in order to be absolutely sure. I feel this system developed by Weaver is an excellent unit, but I plan to have a rifle-type base attached to the Wingmaster's receiver in a more permanent fashion before the next season comes around.

Prior to firing, I had really expected to dislocate a base or reticle, or shear off a screw or two, but no such problem surfaced. A total of 925 shots were fired this past summer through the two scoped shotguns without so much as a loose screw, an excellent accomplishment when one takes into account the tremendous recoil developed by the loads used. Borden's two-part epoxy was liberally applied to the receiver, base and screws on the Mossberg, and to all the ring screws on the Wingmaster. This probably had something to do with keeping things together.

At ranges out to 100 yards or so, there was little difference in the group size the two combinations produced. Several scopes were tried, and the accuracy remained about the same as when using the higher power settings on the variables at 100 yards. As the yardage increased, the low-powered scopes produced the larger group; see chart No. 3, note 4.

Not everyone will be inclined to go out and get a scope with the higher magnification I advocate, and I expect many to disagree with my selections, but the fact remains that these rigs produced what I consider to be the ultimate in accuracy. It's all a matter of choice, and I'm sure the disagreements help make shooting so interesting a sport.

Load Development

I've been working with loads for slug shooting for many years, but I made some real progress this past summer. With the Vitts again available, I felt confident longer range could be achieved. I assembled data for the Brennekes from an information sheet that Stoeger Arms Corporation packed with the slugs that company imported into the U.S., and from the 1978 Hercules Reloader's Guide. Mr. Vitt supplied the original data for his slugs, with some additional loads supplied by Ray Boos and Eleanor Vitt this summer.

I've listed the loads that produced

This collection of slugs is probably all the shooter will be able to find: The Vitt, (#1), and the Brenneke, (#5), produce the best results at ranges beyond 150 yards. Inside that yardage, the Lyman cast slug, (#2), and the Winchester, (#3), and Remington, (#4), offerings will do an effective job. Federal's factory load is somehow absent, but OK.

The Brenneke, (#1), and the Vitt, (#2) provided the handloading hunter with a vastly superior projectile, especially so, when loaded to maximum velocity. The Remington, (#3), and the Winchester, (#4), factory loads are the type normally carried by the slug-hunter.

This Vitt handload shows perfect turnover applied by the Lyman press. Some minor scuffing to the nose of the slug had no adverse effect on the slug's ability to group, and at ranges out to 250 yards.

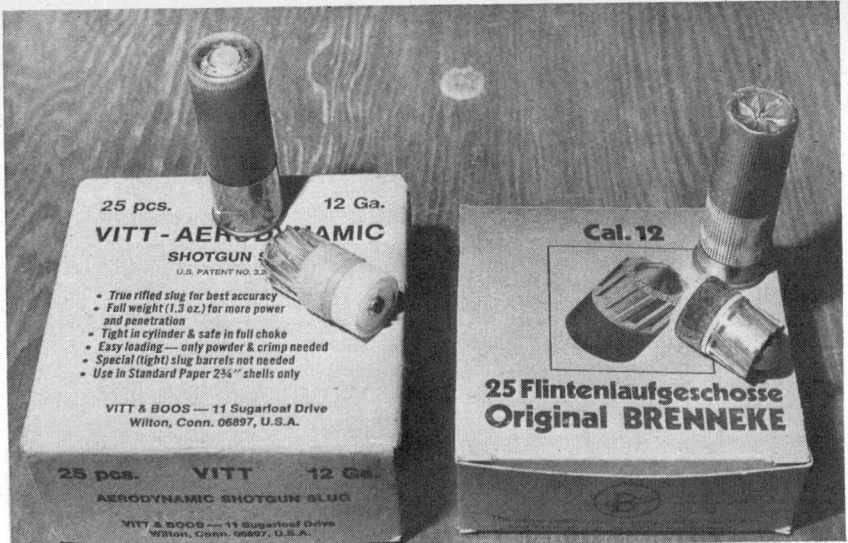

These slugs, the Vitt Aerodynamic, and the Brenneke, proved to be an excellent choices for longer-than-normal slug shooting, as detailed in the article. Both show a great increase in sectional density and ballistic coefficient, when compared to the standard shotgun slug.

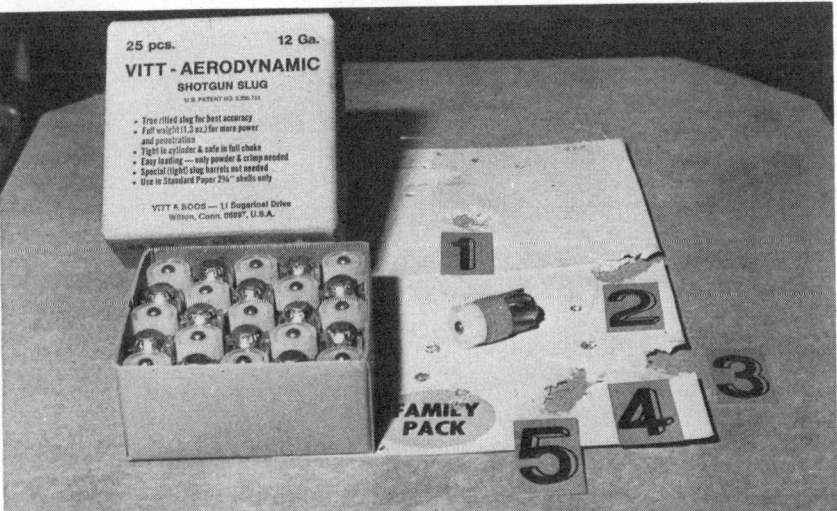

The first group fired using Vitt slugs at 100 yards would prove to be mediocre, though at first glance would seem more than sufficient. The first shot through a clean barrel hit 4.5" above the next four shots; these four grouped within 5", center-to-center.

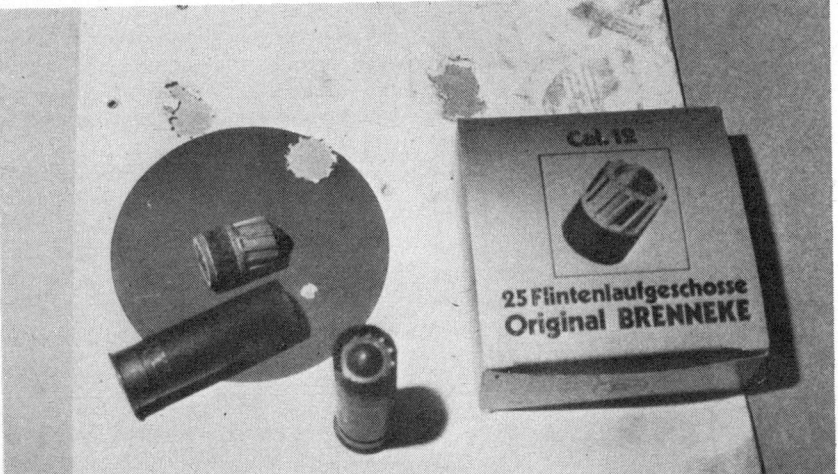

While not as good ballistically as the Vitt at long range, the Brenneke produced some outstanding groups out to 175 yards. Shown is a 3.5" group, fired at 125 yards in the Wingmaster. The upright RXP case is shown prior to the crimp-application.

the best in accuracy in chart No. 3. Several loads listed gave excellent accuracy, but velocity is a bit low. These would be load #11 for the Vitt, and loads 9, 12, and 13, for the Brennekes. This causes problems in regard to trajectory; hold-over estimation becomes worrisome. Holdover is something the hunter should not have to worry about as a shot is touched off at a distant whitetail.

The loads were provided by the source listed, and can be assembled using readily available components. As is the case with all reloading information, it is to be used as a guide, at your own discretion. No load listed caused any major problem, but extended reloading of the case may cause the case head to split at the rim. I would definitely suggest the use of shooting glasses to protect one's eyes from any permanent damage.

As firing test groups started, an unusual situation was encountered. Various Vitt loads showed a tendency to group a little tighter as the range increased. There was no pattern to this, and I could find no reason for it. I questioned Ray Boos on the matter and he detailed why this happened on such a regular basis. It seems that the Vitt, exiting the barrel at 0 rpm., is forced by atmospheric contact to rotate at an increasing rate the further it travels. The increasing rotation causes the slug to become more stable in flight, thereby making the tighter grouping a welcome "problem." The ribs on the Vitt cause the rotation. When fired in a cylinder bore, they remain relatively undamaged. This can aid the handloader in the search for accuracy.

The Vitt slug has another unusual tendency, that being the yaw of the slug as it travels down-range. This will be evident by the elongated impression left by the slug on various targets. After first noting this, I feared poor accuracy. Continued firing soon proved the yaw would have no detrimental effect on the accuracy produced by the slugs. The Brennekes also had a tendency to yaw in flight. Again, this did not seem to affect the accuracy potential of the slug; the condition does not appear as often as with the Vitt slug.

In all cases, the yardage was measured, not estimated prior to firing. The actual firing was done from benchrest, or with the shooter assuming a prone position. The size of the groups may not impress the average rifle shooter; they are absolutely fantastic when one considers what has been written about the accuracy potential of the shotgun slug.

Energy

In his recent book, *A Complete Guide To Handgun Hunting*, Bob Milek makes a very interesting comment concerning a handload developed for the 30 Herrett. While in no way related to shotgun hunting, the comment lends some credence to my own claim concerning the shotgun's effectiveness in regard to energy. The statement reads, "Pushed at 2269 fps., . . . it would be effective, I knew, out to at least 200 yards or more."[2]

Milek is referring to a 125-grain load in the statement, and to its use on big game. When compared to the Vitt, the 30 Herrett, so loaded, produces less energy from the muzzle, all the way out to 200 yards, and beyond. If the 890 ft. lbs. produced by the handgun cartridge at 200 yards can be considered effective, then the 1153 ft. lbs. churned-up by the Vitt has to be more so, at least that is the way I see it. The Vitt will also hold together better than will the 30 caliber slug, and also cause a much larger wound. The possible blood loss should be greater than a similar hit with the pistol slug.

Some additional information is provided in chart No. 1. Note that the Vitt will also out-perform the 35 Remington, yet in the 1974 edition of GUN DIGEST, this rifle cartridge is said to be ". . . effective on larger game such as moose at moderate ranges . . ."[3] Now I am not saying that you should use the shotgun slug on moose, but it would seem entirely adequate, at least based on a paper evaluation and comparison. The 35 Remington looks like a dwarf when compared to the Vitt, heavily loaded.

The point is the 12-gauge slug can and does pack all the power necessary to drop an animal the size of a whitetail, no matter what has been said to underrate it. In all fairness to those who have written such unflattering statements about the shotgun slug, it should be noted that the majority of this information has dealt with the more common Foster slug, and not such specialized slugs as the Vitt or the Brenneke.

For those who choose to use momentum as the measurement in comparing projectiles, I've assembled a list comparing the Vitt and the Brenneke with some pretty strong

---

[2]Bob Milek, *A Complete Guide To Handgun Hunting*, (Los Angeles, Cal.: Petersen Publishing Company, 1979) p. 36.

[3]Kenneth L. Waters, "American Bulleted Cartridges," *Gun Digest*, 28 ed., John Amber, editor, (Northfield, Illinois: Digest Books, Inc., 1973) p. 303.

---

competitors. Listed, are the factors for momentum at the muzzle, at 100 yards, and at 200 yards.

	Muzzle	100 yd.	200 yd.
Vitt, 12 ga.	122	103	78
Brenneke, 12 ga.	105	72	59
.30-06 Sp., 165 gr.	68	63	58
.35 Rem, 200 gr.	57	47	38
.375 H&H., 300 gr.	111	97	84
7mm Rem., 175 gr.	72.5	67	62
.338 Win., 225 gr.	93.6	86	80

Based on the momentum figures, the Vitt looks good, beyond my own expectations. At 200 yards, the Vitt exceeds the 7mm Remington Magnum, and falls only two pound-feet short of pacing the 338 Winchester Magnum. At the muzzle, and out to

The author firing at the target (arrow) positioned 200 yards down-range. Only through trajectory determination, and actual firing can the shooter hope to make his shots count at such extreme range, using the shotgun.

100 yards, it exceeds the 375 H&H. How can the slug possibly be considered weak?

The slugs *will* lose a higher percentage of their power than the rifle bullets, but out to 250 yards or so, they've still enough energy to do their intended job. And no matter what energy formula you use, you'll find the Vitt and the Brenneke near the top of any of these lists. Those huge 70 caliber chunks of lead will produce the kills for the hunter who takes the time to develop the loads and the know-how needed to use them. The next step is to see that the slugs hit the target.

Accuracy-Trajectory

In coming up with the average group sizes listed in chart No. 3, a great many handloads were fired, at 25-yard increments, from 25 yards to 250 yards.

I had determined from the start that accuracy would be considered adequate when all the shots from the individual groups would hit within the area afforded by a 14x12 inch target. The target size represents the heart/lung area of an average-size whitetail, the most sought-after target of the slug hunter. When the slugs were unable to stay within the target area, that, and that alone would determine the maximum range for that particular load combination.

I soon found that the majority of load combinations were more than equal to the task; the groups of many of the loads were hitting within half the area provided. The few loads that gave ineffective accuracy were not listed.

It became evident trajectory and not accuracy would be the deciding factor in coming up with the effective maximum range for the various loads. As long as I could estimate the correct hold-over at the various ranges, I would consider the weapon adequate out to that range.

Load 6 provided the best accuracy with the Vitt slugs out to 200 yards; velocity and energy were also near the top with this load. Only one other load exceeded this combination, load 8, using 31.0 grains of AL120, but the group size was not quite as good. With load 6, trajectory was relatively flat for a shotgun slug; out to 200 yards, using a 150-yard zero, the shooter can hold point-blank. At 225 to 250 yards, the shooter will have to allow for drop in order to keep the slug within the chest cavity of the animal. With practice, and actual firing over the extended range, the hunter can *teach* himself exactly where to hold.

The best accuracy with the Brenneke came when using load 2. This combination of a Federal Hi-Power case, primed with a Federal 209 primer and 37.0 grains of Herco, also gave the highest velocity and energy of any load combination used with the Brenneke. While its lighter weight makes it less suitable beyond 200 yards than the Vitt, this slug is a dramatic improvement over the standard slug load carried by the vast majority of hunters.

Table 4 on trajectories shows how the slugs perform in relation to the 30-06, and the 35 Remington.

With both the Vitt slug and the Brenneke being available, I would choose the Vitt for my smoothbores, based on the accuracy I've been able to get from this slug and the power it carries. With the trajectory it provided, it is the better choice of the two slugs.

Chart No. 3 gives the accuracy potential that can be had at relatively long-range. But in order to provide the reader with an idea as to how the Vitt can group at various distances, I've assembled the following information. It represents the averages gained by firing 3 or 4 3-shot groups at each distance, and is shown in terms of vertical dispersion and horizontal dispersion, rather than center-to-center distances.

The loads fired were load 6, using 39.5 grains of AL7, in a Remington SP case, and load 7, which also used the Remington case, with 36.0 grains of AL5. Firing was done in August, using my Mossberg pump. At that time, the Bushnell Variable, which I have spoken of so highly, had been mounted on a Winchester 88. (I had hoped to use the rifle on an upcoming Canadian hunt which never materialized.) In its place, a Bushnell 2.5x, Custom M was attached. Though I would have preferred the variable, I did not have the range time to make the switch prior to the actual firing of these rounds. As it turned out, the lower-powered scope worked out well, and was carried during the fall deer season. In addition to sighting in this combination, I wanted to check these two loadings, assembled with a new run of slugs Ray Boos had just sent; these slugs proved to be of the same excellent quality that was evident in all the Vitt slugs I have ever used.

Here's how it went:
Slug: Vitt Aerodynamic, 12 ga.
Case: Remington, SP, once-fired, factory.
Primer: CCI 157.
Powder: AL7, 39.5 grains, and AL5, 36.0 grains.

	25 yd.	50 yd.	75 yd.	100 yd.	175 yd.
vertical dispersion	3/8"	1/2"	1/2"	1¾"	3¾"
horizontal dispersion	3/8"	1 5/8"	4"	3¼"	9"

I would like to believe that the horizontal dispersion would have been similar to the vertical dispersion had it not been for a strong wind, which was gusting at 30 mph. But again, certain time limitations made firing on a calm day impossible. I'll have to wait for a more convenient time to prove this belief, right or wrong. Note that all the shots fired, (50-60 rounds) in achieving these results would have hit within the chest cavity of the life-size targets I use. A hunter can ask little more from any projectile.

Field Experience

I had originally expected to submit this article to Ken Warner, based on a paper evaluation, dealing with loading data, velocity and energy figures, and other relevant ballistical information, but a recent hunt supplied some all-important field experience.

The hunt took place in western New York, in Rattlesnake Hills Game Management Area. After six hours afield, I had failed to sight a single whitetail on this particular day. The first good snowfall of the season had come the night before; with this added advantage, I had expected to score on my regular New York tag, on the deer management permit I was carrying. But by afternoon, I had my doubts.

Heading west over a steep rise, I came upon 10 to 12 whitetails bedded in a stand of pines. All were off without offering a shot, most headed downhill. Knowing they would work their way uphill after a short dash, I crossed a narrow saddle that led to another deep gully. I got to the rise overlooking the gully and waited; only moments passed before three deer appeared. They were unhurried as they browsed near a stream in the bottom of the gully.

The three, all does, were about two hundred yards across the gully. Having glassed the area sufficiently, I found no bucks. My watch helped me decide to take one of the does on the party permit in my pouch.

As I laid down the monocular, and brought the Mossberg to my shoulder, I experienced some doubts. The animals looked further away at 2.5x, than they had through the 7x monocular. I thought of the 900-plus rounds I had fired over the past three months as I followed the largest of the three, walking among numerous oaks and birches. My confidence returned and, holding several inches over her chest, I moved ahead to an opening in her path. Before she hit the opening, the shot was touched off; recoil from the shot obscured the animal's reaction. All three deer rushed downhill, running till they were out of sight.

It is at this point in the hunt many deer are wasted. Many hunters, seeing their target rush off seemingly unhurt, assume a miss. Few will take the time to check out the area thoroughly and be sure of that miss they grumble about.

After sliding more than 100 feet into the gully, a climb uphill, brought me to the area where the animals had been browsing fifteen minutes ago. First, a bit of brown hair and a drop or two of blood; 25 yards further, additional droplets.

On this hunt, the snow made the tracking easy, as did the frequency of red droplets. One hundred yards away, lay the doe. A neck shot ended the day's hunt.

The Vitt slug had hit the deer just below the spine, at the diaphragm, ripping a 1" hole in the liver; blood loss was tremendous and fatal. The slug continued through the animal, taking out two ribs on the opposite side. The Vitt had done its job, though it now seems I did not lead her sufficiently, since the chest had been my target. The exact distance was measured at 210 yards, not paced off, but measured with an accurate tape. Knowing how the slug would react after leaving the barrel brought success to this hunt. And while I feel I may be more dedicated than the average hunter, the techniques used are easily duplicated, and make it possible to reach out a great deal further than you may have in the past using your shotgun. ●

Editor's Note

Sources for the special projectiles Mr. Krieger mentions are:

Lyman Products Corp., Rte. 147, Middlefield, CT 06455, for Foster slugs.

Stoeger Industries, 55 Ruta Ct., S. Hackensack, NJ 07606 or Interarms Ltd., 10 Prince St., Alexandria, VA 22313, for Brenneke slugs.

Vitt & Boos, 2178 Nichols Ave., Stratford, CT 06497, for Vitt slugs.

BRI slugs are no longer available.

IN GERMANY THEY SHOOT...

Two-Gun Hunter Matches

by Tom Turpin

German hat shows four distinctions. From the left: Badge of DJV for Rheinland-Pfalz; badge of American Rod and Gun Clubs — Europe; silver DJV medal, won by shooting; and the *gamsbart*, a trophy from the chamois, also won by shooting.

I THINK THERE is a need in this country for a shooting sport for hunters. By that, I mean one that is restricted to guns that are suitable for hunting, one that combines both rifle and shotgun competition, and one that has some degree of realism to it.

It appeared for awhile that silhouette shooting might be at least a partial response to that need. Unfortunately, as with so many other shooting sports today, that form of competition has turned into another equipment race, rather than a concentration on the hunter and hunting guns. The word *unfortunately* is used from the point of view of a hunter's shooting sport. The competition offered by silhouette shooting is desirable, but there is no denying it has changed.

As I understand the original concept of silhouette shooting, only rifles suitable for hunting were used in the competition. The game has now evolved to such a degree, at least in this country, that a participant armed with a normal hunting rifle has about as much chance of winning a match as the proverbial snowball. In the absence of highly specialized equipment, one is simply not competitive.

There is a shooting game in the world today that is designed specifically for the hunter, and that has doggedly resisted all efforts to change it into a more equipment-oriented sport. I first encountered this shooting sport in 1961, when I made my first trip to Europe, more specifically, West Germany. This competition for hunters is simply called the DJV matches. The full name is the Deutschen Jagdschutzverbandes matches, which explains why it is referred to simply as DJV. The DJV is a national organization in Germany, similiar to the NRA in the United States, but oriented specifically to hunting.

DJV matches are conducted across a course that includes both rifle and shotgun competition, and restrictions are such as to eliminate highly specialized competition firearms. Only those firearms suitable for hunting are allowed to be used. This is not to say that only serious hunters participate in this shooting sport. There are many highly competitive shooters who spend far more time competing in DJV matches than they ever do in the field. Of course, there is nothing wrong with that, if that is what they prefer to do. On the other hand, many, many hunters do participate in DJV matches, primarily to hone their shooting skills in anticipation of opening day. In the DJV shooting sport, there is no real head-to-head competition. Instead, the DJV shooter is competing against the course, rather than against other competitors. In a way, it can be said that each shooter competes against himself.

The shotgun portion of a DJV match consists of 15 targets at trap, and 15 targets at Skeet. The trap targets are more or less conventional, with two significant differences from the ATA variety. First, the shooter is allowed two shots at each target, and a missed first shot, so long as the second connects, is still scored as a hit. Secondly, the shooter must call for the target with the butt of the gun at his hip. The gun cannot be shouldered until the target appears.

The 15 Skeet targets consist of singles from stations 1,3,4,5 and 7, again with two shots allowed at each target, and the low gun position required until the target appears. Doubles are shot from stations 2 and 6, with only one shot per target, and the low gun position required. The 15th target is shot at station 4.

In keeping with the hunting spirit, and knowing that the hunter in the field must take crossing as well as straight-away game with the same gun, in DJV shooting the competitor must use the same gun in both the Skeet and trap competition. Changing barrels is not allowed, and neither are adjustable choke devices.

These thirty targets make up the shotgun portion of the competition, and count 5 points per target. The maximum possible scores in the shotgun competition is 150 points.

In the rifle portion of the match, a total of 20 shots are taken, as follows: 5 shots at a standing roebuck target at 100 meters distance (approximately 110 yards), standing position with a pole rest allowed; 5 shots at a standing wild boar target at 100 meters distance, standing position, no rest allowed; 5 shots at a sitting fox target at 100 meters distance, prone, sitting, or kneeling position; and finally, 5 shots at a running boar target at 60 meters distance, standing position, no rest allowed. The moving boar target crosses an opening 6 meters wide in approximately two seconds. In the running boar portion of the rifle competition, the shooter must have his rifle in the low gun position, with the gun butt on his hip, when calling for the target.

Each of the 20 shots with the rifle count up to 10 points each, or a maximum possible score of 200 points. Therefore, a perfect score in both the rifle and shotgun portions of the match would be 350 points.

As previously stated, DJV shooting is designed as a hunters shooting sport, and not another form of competitive shooting where the shooters equipment is often as much a determinant of the outcome as is the skill of the shooter. In DJV shooting, specialized equipment not suitable for hunting is specifically prohibited. Even the ammunition used is carefully monitored. Handloads are not normally allowed, so only commercially available ammunition is permitted. Solid bullets are not allowed in the rifle competition, and the shot size for shotgun shooting cannot be larger than number 7 shot.

Any gauge up to 12 is allowed for use in the Skeet and trap shooting, although practically speaking, rarely is anything but a 12 or 16 gauge ever seen in competition. Rifle calibers are also rather freely allowed, with most any caliber suitable for hunting permitted in the competition. Most participants use the smaller calibers however, with the 222 seen very frequently.

All firearms are inspected for suitability by match officials prior to a match. In the case of the shotgun, the barrels are marked in some way, to insure they are not changed. The normal manner of marking is to place a

Reflecting field practice, the sitting fox DJV shooter may elect sitting position for five shots at 100 meters. Author shoots a scoped small-caliber centerfire for the shoot.

Prone or kneeling are also permitted on the sitting fox in DJV shooting. Choice of position at a given shoot might be dictated by how wet the ground is, which makes field sense, too.

Shooting the roebuck target at 100 meters is permitted with a pole rest, but only from standing position. This reflects much field shooting on small buck shot from high seats.

The DJV standing boar shot, however, has to get his five rounds in without benefit of rest. It's easy to tell — check the butt position — that this is not a 30-caliber rifle.

There are 15 birds in the DJV Skeet course, and each shot or pair of shots starts from a low-butt position as shown. On singles, shooters may shoot twice, so 25 shots may be fired.

The bird is in the air in the trap phase and the shot about to go. Even in trap, the low-gun position is held until the bird appears. Also, the same gun used in Skeet must be shot.

seal in the sling swivel. In Europe, the hunter attaches a sling to his shotgun as well as his rifle.

Scopes are almost universally used on the hunting rifle and so are permitted. Open sights, if they are desired by the shooter, may also be used. The weight of the rifle, up to 6.5 caliber and without scope, cannot exceed 8 pounds. If the rifle being used in the match is of a larger caliber than 6.5 (rare today), the maximum allowable weight is determined by the official in charge of the match. His determination is based on the caliber of the rifle, and the type of rifle it is. In all cases, if the rifle to be used in the match is unsuitable for hunting, its use will not be permitted.

In DJV shooting, there is no individual winner, *per se*. Prizes are awarded in these matches based on each individual's score. The prize is a small metal pin, designed to be worn on the hunting hat. An appropriate certificate, suitable for framing and hanging in the den, is also awarded.

For a score of 220 points or better, a bronze award is presented. For 260 points or better, a silver one is awarded. At 300 points or better, the award is made of gold, and the ultimate prize, the "grosse gold," literally translated meaning great or magnificent gold, is awarded for a score of 320 points or better. Again, there are no individual winners; every shooter that amasses the necessary points is awarded the appropriate prize. The awarded prize can then be worn on the hunting hat for all to see.

Not all prizes can be awarded at every match however. The German thoroughness is far too suspicious for that. The "grosse gold," for example, is far too prestigious an award to be presented at just any match. This special gold award can only be attained at the highest level of matches, the "meisterschaft," which is the equivalent of Camp Perry and the National Matches. Bronze, silver, and gold awards can be made at each of the state matches, and only the bronze award can be presented at the regional matches. In this respect, it is not unlike the U.S. shooter in pursuit of the Distinguished Marksman badge, and the "leg" matches leading up to it.

All in all, for the hunter, DJV shooting seems to me to be the best game in town. Before letters start flying to the Editor, let me add that this writer is not condemning anyone's sport. I personally enjoy, and participate in, numerous different shooting sports. I enjoy Skeet, trap, small and large bore rifle competition, plinking away at beer cans with any available firearm, whatever. I have not yet had the opportunity to participate in silhouette shooting, nor in benchrest competition. I am certain however, that I would enjoy both. As a pure hunting style shooting game however, nothing I have seen so far equals DJV shooting, in my opinion.

To be truly competitive in any of the popular shooting sports in the United States today, highly specialized equipment, often quite expensive, is a must. One simply does not grab his hunting rifle off the rack and hold any hope of winning the Wimbledon Cup. Neither does one have much of a chance of winning the Grand American with his field shotgun. I suppose it could happen, but it is highly unlikely.

I do recall having my clock cleaned by a young lad in bib overalls from the hill country of eastern Kentucky though. We were both participating in a turkey shoot, and when the dust cleared, he and I were the only remaining shooters in the match, tied for the turkey. It was decided that a shoot-off would be held, consisting of doubles from station 4 on the Skeet field, miss and out.

I was shooting a lovely Browning O/U, with 26-inch barrels, choked improved cylinder and modified. My opponent, not realizing the handicap he faced, was armed with an ancient Model 97 Winchester pump. It looked as though it had been put to hard use for many years as a boat anchor! Naturally, it was equipped with a 32-inch barrel, choked as full as they come. From the sound of the old Model 97 going off, I suspect my young opponent was also using magnum loads of #4 shot. Neither of us were ideally equipped for station 4 doubles: I had far the more appropriate gun.

At any rate, and at the risk of further embarrassment, I will only say that the turkey I took home for Thanksgiving came from the local A&P, and not from the matches. I shudder to think what that kid could have done on the Skeet field if armed with an appropriate Skeet gun.

The point of all this is that in DJV shooting, the shooter can successfully utilize his field guns to win awards. They must be capable of good accuracy, to be sure, but highly specialized equipment is neither necessary nor allowed.

Further, the course of fire is designed with the hunter in mind. In Europe, most hunters are armed with a double gun of one form or the other, when taking to the field after upland game. If, by chance, the hunter misses a rising pheasant with the first shot, he will surely let fly with the second. Hence, realistically, two shots are allowed at clay targets, from most stations. If two pheasants rise at the same time, naturally the hunter will try for

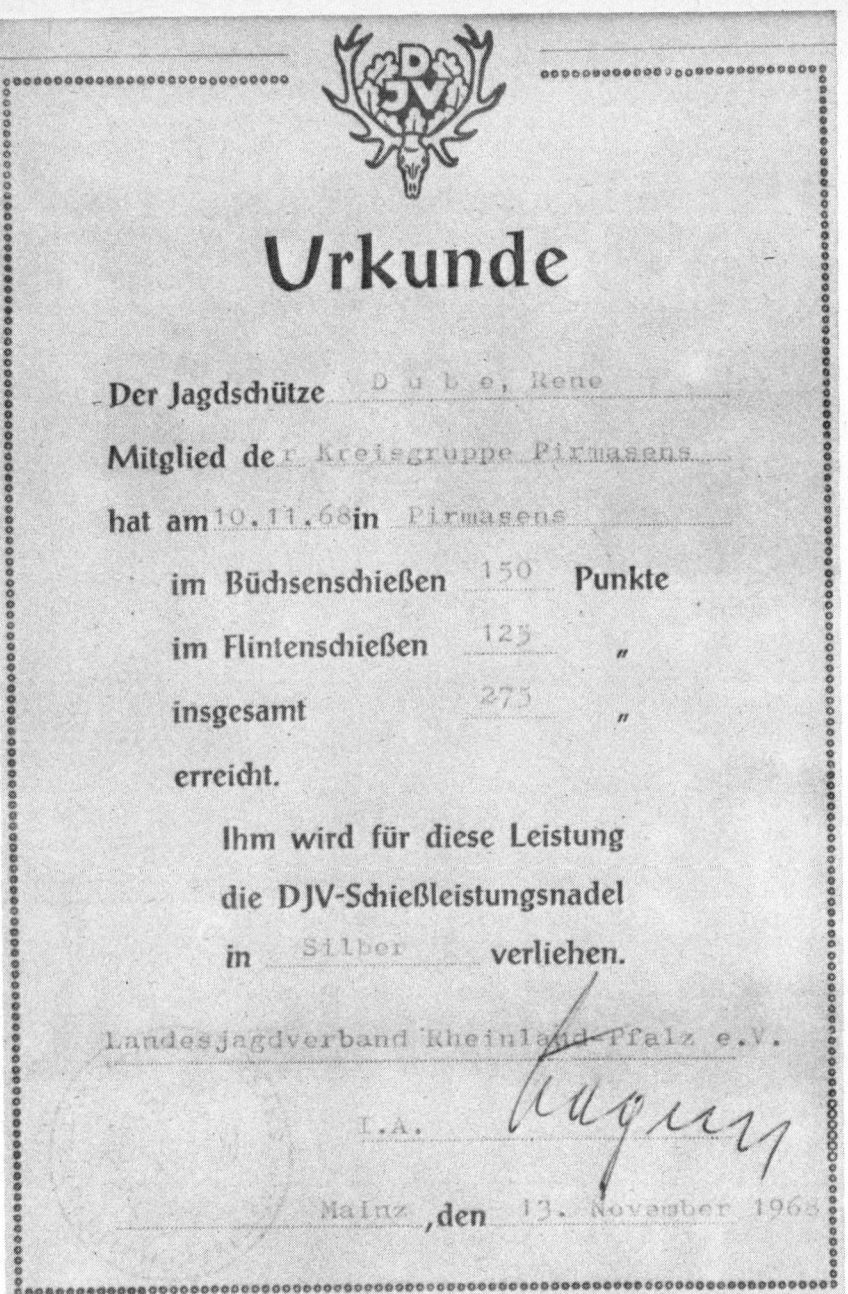

Besides the badges awarded in this shoot where each shooter competes against the course, there is also a certificate for the good shooter's wall. This one gives the author the silver for 275 points out of 350.

each, one shot per bird. At stations 2 and 6 on the Skeet field in DJV shooting, this is simulated by shooting doubles. As the hunter does not normally walk through the hunting fields with his gun shouldered (at least not if he hunts with me!), it is likewise not allowed in DJV shooting, until the target appears.

In the rifle shooting, the targets used look like game animals, and the positions allowed for shooting are, by and large, those that would appropriately be used on those animals on an actual hunt. Particularly realistic is the running boar shooting. This is designed to simulate drive hunting for the wild boar. The 6 meter wide opening for the target just happens to be the width of the normal forest road in Germany. During boar drives, about the only chance a hunter will have at a boar will be as it crosses a forest road, heading for another thicket. It takes a real, live boar about 2 seconds to cross such an opening, unless closely pursued.

There is no doubt that if the rules were changed to permit the switching between specialized Skeet and trap guns for the shotgun competition, and specialized target rifles, with plumbobs, gyroscopes, and spirit levels were allowed, scores would rise appreciably. Laced into a leather International shooting coat would also help a great deal, especially in the standing position. Under those circumstances, the "grosse gold" would most probably be frequently encountered and not rarely, as it is today.

If all this were allowed, the scores would rise greatly, but then the game would not be a hunters' contest. I, for one, hope they never change the rules.

I would like to see this style of shooting contest introduced into the United States. It seems to me that it would be of interest to far more shooters, and require no great outlay of cash for equipment, to be competitive.

The only remaining question is, does it work? That is, do hunters who regularly participate in DJV shooting do better in the field after game than those who do not? I think I have to answer yes. While any practice contributes to success in the game fields, be it Skeet, trap, or shooting balloons with a BB gun, the DJV style of shooting is particularly effective at preparing the hunter for the coming season. It provides fairly realistic shooting conditions and targets, and generally the participant uses the same sporting arms that he will use in the field. That has great merit, and is better preparation than using specialized guns for shooting Skeet, trap, etc.

It is not to be implied that all German hunters are great game shots; they are not! Some of the very best, and the very worst, shots at game I have ever hunted with were German hunters. Of course, all German hunters do not participate in DJV matches either. Those that do actively participate in DJV shooting that I personally know do very well in the field. I do not know a single German hunter who does well in DJV shooting who does not do equally well in shooting game.

I cannot attribute that totally to DJV shooting. I think that practice with one's hunting guns, whatever form it takes, makes one a far better game shot in the field. The business of cleaning the hunting guns as soon as the season is over, and sticking them away in the gun cabinet until the next opening day, is the cause of most of the lousy game shooting. However, DJV shooting does provide a realistic vehicle for practicing for opening day, competing for recognition of your prowess with rifle and shotgun, and having a hell of a lot of fun doing it. It is a great shooting game for the hunter, and perhaps one day it or something like it will catch on here in the U.S. •

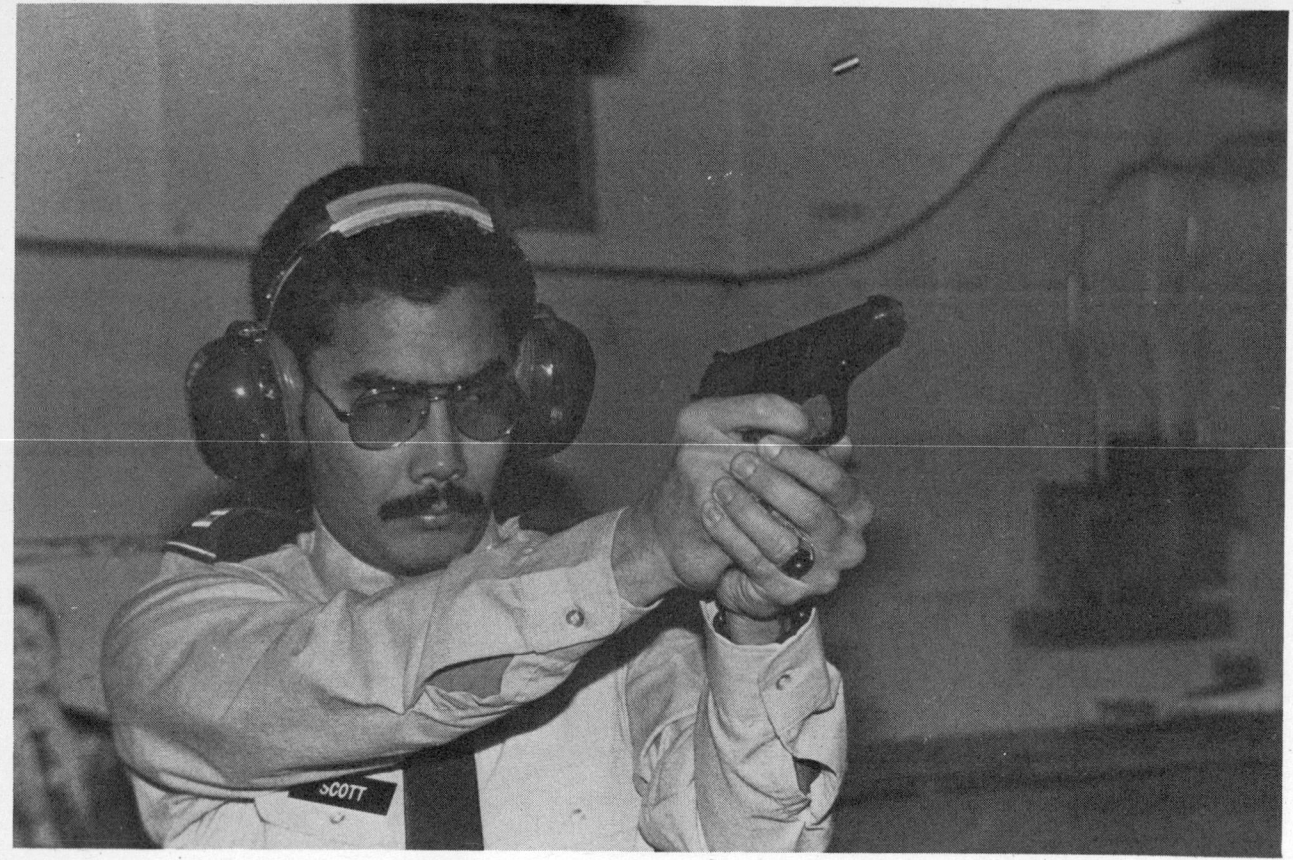

Sam Scott didn't find the leftward pitch of the empty brass bothering him as he worked with Walther's newest cop gun in 9mm.

WALTHER'S P5 PISTOL

by JAMES P. COWGILL

The new generation in police handguns takes new tacks. Or are they?

IMAGINE an autoloading service pistol with no safety lever.

"No way," one might say. "It wouldn't be safe to carry loaded."

But wait. Is your typical service revolver safe to carry loaded?

"Of course," one thinks. "Modern double-action revolvers can be safely carried, hammer down, with all chambers loaded."

Then where is the safety lever on your revolver?

"There is none. A safety lever on a revolver is unnecessary because the firing pin cannot contact a primer unless the trigger is pulled all the way to the rear."

Exactly. But the West German firm of Carl Walther has produced a new autoloading service sidearm, the P 5, with no safety lever. This pistol, however, is safe to carry with hammer down and a round in the chamber.

The P 5 was developed in response to a German government competition to standardize police handguns and ammunition. Federal police and the military use the 9mm Parabellum Walther P 1, the lightweight-alloy framed version of the famous P 38 double-action autoloader. State and local departments use a variety of pistol types with .32 autoloaders probably the most popular. The *Polezei* are very big on submachineguns, universally issued in 9mm caliber. The different calibers in use cause some logistics problems in ammo interchangeability, procurement, and stockage.

A committee drafted specifications for their concept of the ideal European law enforcement handgun, including these criteria:

Caliber: 9x19 mm Parabellum (Luger)

Magazine capacity: 8 rounds minimum

Muzzle energy: 369 ft.-lb. minimum

Over-all length: 7 in. maximum

There are no operating controls on the right side of the P5 and no ejection port either. German police and the Dutch government like the gun.

From this angle, the P-38 ancestry can be seen, although the inside isn't all ancient history. The "safety" is actually an operating lever; see text.

Over-all height: 5⅛ in. maximum
Width: 1¹⁵⁄₁₆ in. maximum
Weight: 2 lb., 3 oz. maximum

The specifications also stated that the pistol would be safe to carry with a round in the chamber, ready to fire instantly without the necessity of operating cocking or safety levers. In testing, the pistols were required to fire 10,000 service rounds without major failure.

The surviving three of four candidates were:
* Heckler & Koch's Model PSP (P 7) with its unique gas-delayed blowback action.
* Sig-Sauer's Model P 225, an abbreviated P 220 (BDA).
* Walther's Model P 5, which improves upon the P 38's (P 1's) safety features.

The P 5 bears a strong family resemblance to the P 38. Both have double-action triggers and steel slides. The P 5 shares the P 1's lightweight alloy in its frame. Unlike its predecessors, however, the P 5 has no safety lever.

Obviously, neither its designers nor the German committee felt it needed one. The P 5 has four independent working safety features:

First, the firing pin is, as translated from the German operating manual, "arrested from longitudinal axis motion" at all times, except when the trigger is pulled fully rearward. That is, the firing pin is blocked in a safety rest position until the trigger is pulled. Thus the weapon will not fire if dropped muzzle-down on a hard surface.

Second, there is a cavity cut in the striking surface of the hammer. When the trigger is forward, the firing pin rotates downward so that the base of the pin is aligned with the cavity. Even if the hammer should fall, it would not strike the firing pin.

Third, the hammer, in its uncocked resting position, is held by a hammer latch at a stand-off distance from the firing pin, even if the pin were rotated into the path of the hammer striking surface.

Fourth, a disconnector mechanism prevents firing unless the slide is fully closed in battery.

A unique feature of the P 5 is the operating lever on the left side of the frame. This lever has two functions: to close the open slide, and to uncock the weapon.

Gun closes when operating lever is depressed, chambering round and leaving hammer cocked. To uncock, depress the operating lever a second time.

Nothing mysterious here. P5 breaks easily into the usual slide, frame, barrel and magazine groups. The barrel is a little more complicated, true.

How big is a service pistol? Here are three: the P1 (P-38), the Colt M1911 and the new P5, which is much the smallest.

Magazines for the P-1 (P'-38) and P5 look alike, but they are not. Each holds eight rounds, though.

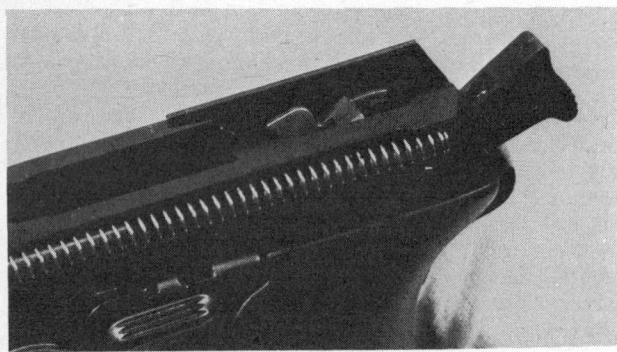

Left— The bright-metal projection in the center of the frame is the disengagement lever, shown in the raised position it reaches only when the trigger is fully to the rear. This lever lifts the firing pin into firing position.

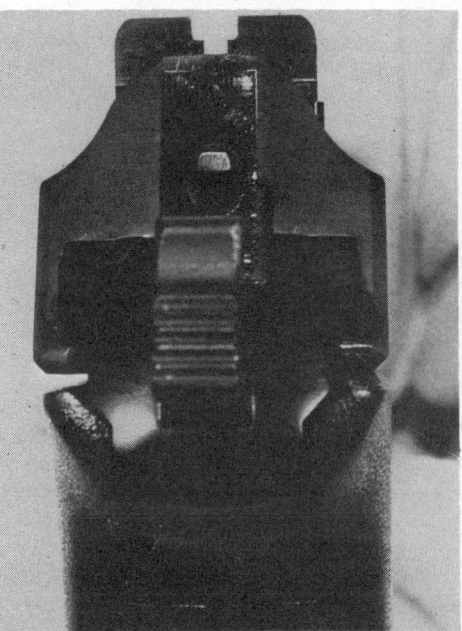

At left, the base of the firing pin rests in the safety position. Only pulling the trigger will lift it into line so the striking surface of the hammer can hit it. This is one of four basic safety mechanisms in the new Walther P5.

To load the pistol, the slide is pulled to the rear and the slide stop engaged either manually or automatically by the follower of an empty magazine. A loaded straight box magazine (8-round capacity) is inserted. The operating lever is pushed downward with the thumb of the shooting hand (right-handers), which closes the slide, chambering a round. The weapon is now cocked and ready to fire. Releasing the operating lever and depressing it once more safely lowers the hammer. The pistol is now safe to carry but ready to fire by either pulling the trigger for double-action, or by thumb-cocking the hammer for a single-action first shot.

The recoil of the slide cocks the hammer for subsequent shots, but the operating lever can be used to lower the hammer at any time.

With proper familiarity and training, the P 5 can be as safe to carry as a revolver—and just as ready to fire. The firing pin cannot strike the primer unless the trigger is pulled all the way. But, since the weapon is double-action, the firing pin will be struck by the hammer *every time* the trigger is pulled.

The P 5 has a typical German grip-heel magazine catch. Takedown into four major groups (magazine, slide, frame, barrel) is done simply by rotating a "barrel-stop lever" located on the left front of the frame.

The P 38-type locked breech is of proven reliability and accuracy potential. Locking lugs connect the barrel to the slide in battery. Upon firing, the slide and barrel recoil together for about an eighth of an inch, when a shaft on the bottom of the locking lug assembly hits the frame and cams the locking lugs away from the slide, freeing it to recoil fully rearward. Spent brass is extracted and ejected. Dual slide springs return the slide which picks up a round from the magazine and chambers it.

Double-action trigger pull is a lot heavier than that of a PPC revolver, but the single-action trigger feels much better than that of other double-action autoloaders. After taking up the slack characteristic in this type of action, there was no mush in the test auto's single-action trigger. Very economical movement fired off each shot.

When the slide is in battery, two things happen at the trigger's rear-most travel—the trigger bar forces a disengagement lever upwards moving the firing pin off its safety rest and into the path of the hammer; and the hammer latch is pulled from the rear notch on the hammer, allowing it to fall and strike the firing pin.

A recess is cut in the slide for the disconnector. The recess is aligned with the disconnector only when the slide is fully closed. If the slide is partially open, the disconnector nose on the trigger bar contacts the slide, forcing the bar downward and out of position to release the hammer latch, preventing firing from an open breech.

When the pistol is uncocked, the hammer latch holds the hammer away from the slide so that it cannot contact the firing pin base even if the firing pin were moved off its blocked position in the slide.

Thus there are multiple, independent, and redundant safety features incorporated into the P 5's design. However, even the safest weapon can be dangerous through improper operation. Training remains the ultimate key to safety for all firearms.

Test firings, using factory-loaded Federal 123-grain full-metal-case bullets and handloads with Sierra 90- and 115-grain jacketed-hollow-point projectiles, had no stoppages at a local range (300 rounds fired). NRA target ten-ring accuracy at 25 yards from bench rest was no problem, surely adequate for a service pistol.

The Patridge sights are highlighted with a white dot on the front post and a white square immediately under the rear notch. This arrangement helps in low-light and dark-background shooting situations (the white surfaces do not glow in the dark). The rear sight is adjustable in windage.

The P 5 has been adopted as the duty sidearm for several German police jurisdictions. The Netherlands government, after extensive competitive tests, has ordered 35,000 P 5's. The U.S. importer is Interarms, 10 Prince Street, Alexandria, VA 22313.

The P 5 is a safe, reliable, and accurate service autoloading pistol. Now the mystery: The ejection port is on the left side of the slide, and ejected brass caroms high over the shooter's left shoulder. Why is the port on the left, when conventional industry practice puts it on the right side? Is this feature designed for left-handers? Or does the port position make inspection of the chamber easier for right-handers? Did a blueprint get reversed in reproduction at the factory? If you know the answer, please tell me!

Author found the pull smooth though heavy; recoil with Federal 125-gr. loads mild; accuracy good. He must like the gun—he bought one.

Walther Model P 5
Technical Data

System: Locked-breech, recoil-operated, self-loading
Breech: Locking toggle, slide-to-barrel
Caliber: 9mm Parabellum (Luger)
Dimensions: 7" long, 5" high, 1¼" wide. 3½" barrel; 5¼" sight radius.
Frame: Lightweight alloy
Weight: 28 oz. unloaded
Magazine capacity: 8 rounds
Manufacturer: Carl Walther, Ulm (Do), West Germany
Importer: Interarms, Inc., 10 Prince St., Alexandria, VA 22313

BLACKPOWDER

THERE'S MORE TO KNOW THAN YOU THINK

BY EDWARD M. YARD

BLACKPOWDER shooting is popular. Despite hitches in powder supply, switches in source and regulation uncertainties, muzzleloading has been the fastest growing segment of shooting sport. The growth of the Thompson/Center plant in New Hampshire over the last ten years is simply startling. Old style guns have grown on the market from a few handfuls to proliferating resurrection of designs even your granddad doesn't remember.

Gadgets and accessories for shooting the old front loaders abound. There are fiberglass ramrods, neat little cappers and rotary sawed flints. Why I don't know, but there is even a nipple substitute so you can use centerfire cartridge primers instead of caps. Makers and brands of percussion caps have come and gone. The game is still booming.

Shelves bulge with books ranging from mere pamphlets to tomes that will inform and regail you about stuffing in a portion of powder, placing a soaked patch and ramming a ball down the bore. Of these Lyman gives good tables of loading data listing breech pressure, which is important

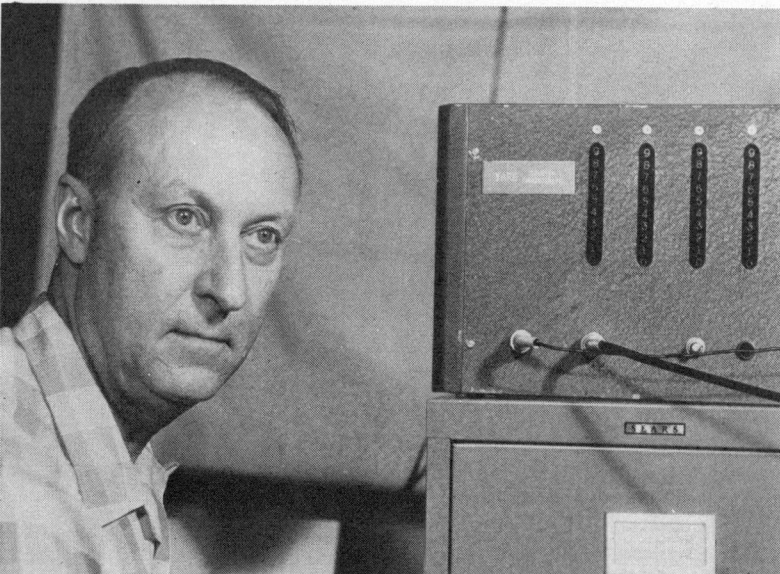

Ed Yard with his chronograph, the essential tool of ballistic testing. He made this photo himself.

.00312 is the time in seconds it took the bullet to pass through two screens 5 feet apart. A table, a calculator or slide rule will show about 1603 fps.

142 THE GUN DIGEST

and valuable. The author has contributed quite a bit to blackpowder load data with measured breech pressures preceding Lyman's handbook and published in GUN DIGEST.

Blackpowder pressure is an important, possibly crucial, point. It has been, at least among many shooters, common to assume that blackpowder does not produce high pressure. With proper loading, it certainly need not. But blackpowder *is* a gunpowder. We now call it blackpowder because we have other and more modern gunpowders that are only dark in color if dyed, but that does not mean that it does not generate quite effective pressures to kick those balls and bullets out the front of your gun.

Blackpowders are not all the same. Those available over a century have been made with different machinery and processes. Because they do, necessarily, produce respectable chamber pressures in guns, they must be treated with respect. The characteristics of a powder should be understood if it is to be used safely.

On this point the guides we have had have failed. One and all they fail to convey the characteristics of blackpowders. They differ, depending upon who made them, when, and for what purpose. There never has been a report of variations. A few opinions have been expressed; a few measurements have been reported; no correlations have been made.

The author is not going to pretend that he will answer every question about blackpowder. It is the purpose of this article to reveal the chronograph and pressure gun test data the author has produced in testing many varieties of it. All of the powders reported on are sporting grades or military types usable in small arms.

Blackpowder is an effective propellant producing good firearm ballistic results. It is the only entirely satisfactory gunpowder for all muzzleloading guns. Sometimes referred to as "soft coal" because of its sulfurous smell, it does a good job. It should be understood.

Because it is old fashioned, there never was much measured information about it. There was little instrumentation. The ballistic pendulum of Benjamin Robins allowed Capt. Mordecai to measure military gun velocities. General Rodman's pressure measuring methods came so late that I have never seen any U.S. military small arms blackpowder loads listed with pressure. I realize that Nobel and Abel, Sarrau, Berthelot, and Charbonnier in Europe did

A lead crusher is snugged up to a piston directly entering the gun powder chamber. Powder burning slams the piston against the crusher and how much it is compressed indicates the breech pressure.

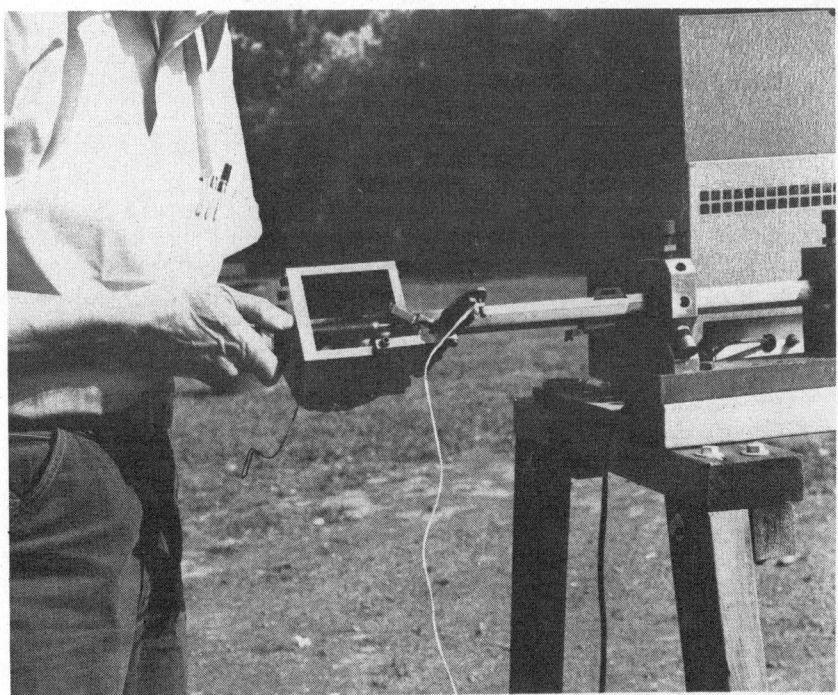
The test gun is loaded. The lanyard is in place. A lead crusher is being put in the breech. Next—cap and fire.

do such testing. You will never find it. And it will not relate to your needs if you do.

Nobel and Abel of England measured English blackpowder pressure as high as 96,000 pounds per square inch. I hope I have your attention. There is something to learn about blackpowder characteristics.

During the turmoil in supply after Du Pont stopped making it, many other sources sold powder through the dealer channels. Motley could be the term for it. It did vary. Some was leftover Du Pont, including one incredible lot. Then for a while it was ICI powder, though not that clearly identified. Few knew what the stuff

Each shot yields a breech pressure, impressed on the lead crusher, and a muzzle velocity for the bullet as it clips through the chronograph screens. It is now beyond that powder smoke puff.

was, not really much about it. Labels were Hodgdon, Meteor (C-I-L of Canada), Austin, and ICI. Briefly, Green River and West-Tech powders reached limited markets.

The author bumped into this by becoming involved in load data testing for Thompson/Center in July, 1971. Du Pont had had an accident in their Belin plant June 6th and decided to stop making Superfine Black Rifle Powder.

The first tests were made using Du Pont powder still on dealers' shelves. Du Pont informed the author that ICI of Great Britain would supply "equivalent" powder under labels as above. There was not enough volume for Du Pont to continue. The best account of all this is in GUN DIGEST, 1972, by the author.

ICI powder, when it came along, was tested. It produced less velocity and less pressure in equal charges than Du Pont had, but not always. Some unexpected high pressures were encountered. These were so *unanticipated* that minor damage to the pressure gun occurred. A test range accident nearly resulted.

All of these events—a change in powder source, discovery of real differences in powder behavior, uncertainty of supply—prompted the author to look into the whole situation. By phone, by letter, by chronograph and pressure test, he tried to learn and to understand why the powders differed. It seemed reasonable to suppose that the makers would know. This proved unfounded.

A search of reference books (bibliography appended) turned up much comment about the importance of (the) charcoal in the performance of blackpowder. Correspondence also lent some credence to this view. Four actual makers—Du Pont, C-I-L, ICI and Gearhart-Owen—did not know. All of these makers had experienced changes in their charcoal supply in relatively recent years, this century and this decade.

Gunpowder has been known by published reports in the western world for over 700 years. The composition of it has varied. Basically it has been and is a mechanical mixture of potassium nitrate (saltpeter, nitre), charcoal and sulfur. This is the only composition we will be concerned with here. Ingredients have been changed or substituted, but what has been used consistently and traditionally in military and sporting arms is the above mixture. It has varied in proportion and purity and consistency during its history.

For 200 years the formula has standardized to about (a nominal) 75% potassium nitrate, 15% charcoal, 10% sulfur by weight. Today the chemical purity of KNO_3, and S are assured, but charcoal, the product of partial combustion of wood, while mainly carbon, is not an inherently pure material. There has been comment over hundreds of years by many sources that it does affect the properties of blackpowder, the original gunpowder.

Before going further with charcoal, the role of the ingredients of this historic mixture should be examined. Potassium nitrate, (saltpeter, KNO_3) has three oxygen atoms that release readily to combine with the carbon of charcoal to form two gases, carbon dioxide and carbon monoxide. The chemical combination of carbon and oxygen, generally termed combustion, releases considerable heat energy. Heating a gas causes it to expand. What was a teaspoon of powder suddenly becomes a rather large amount of hot gas. This is what makes a gun work.

The sulfur in the mix burns partially, about one half, forming mostly solids. Some hydrogen sulfide results, hence the soft coal or rotten egg smell.

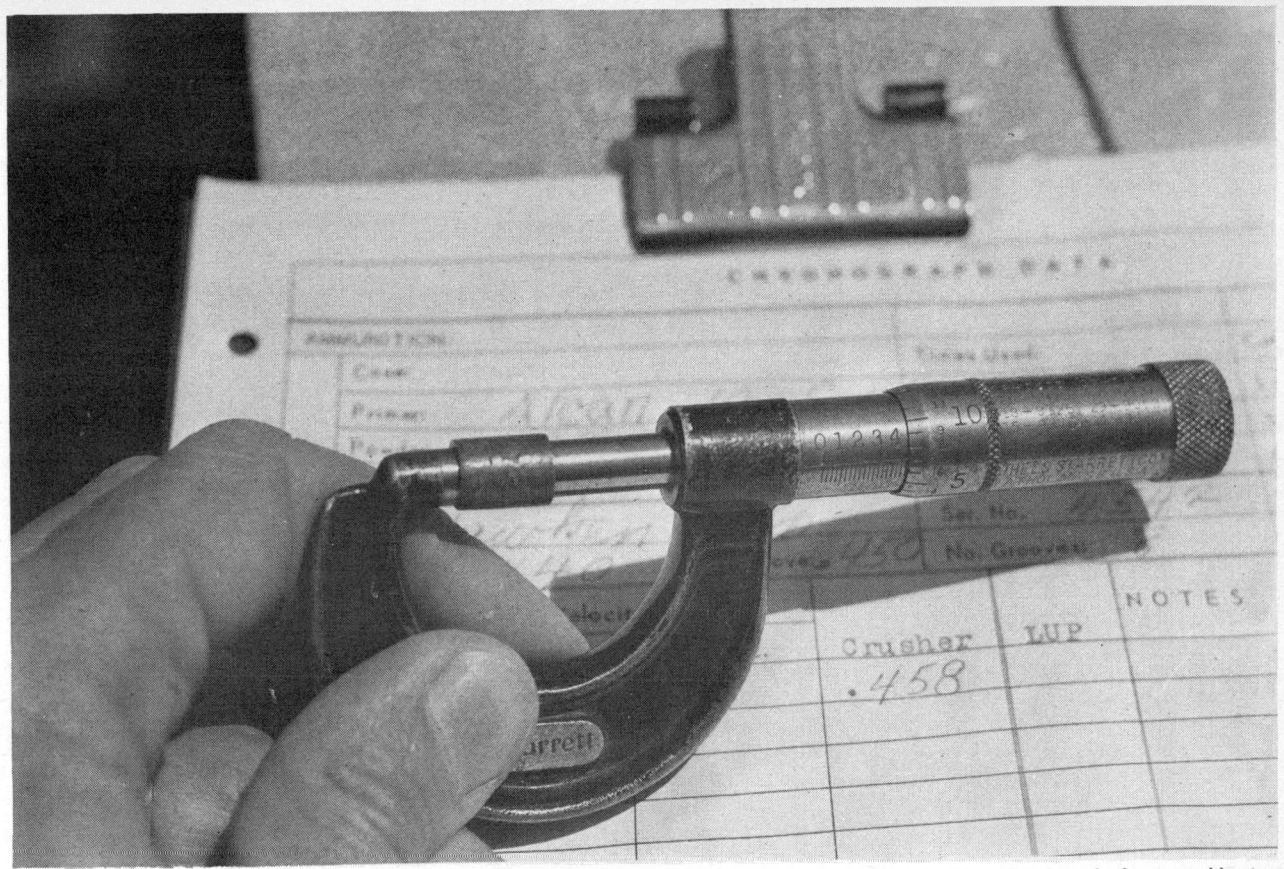

The lead crusher's remaining length is measured by micrometer and the corresponding pressure is read from an international standard tarage table.

The exact role of the sulfur is not clearly stated in references. It is generally considered to provide a catalyst and to bind the materials into grains, serving as a cement.

The nitrogen in the KNO_3 comes out as a gas, one third of the gases produced. The net result, though, is that 56 to 57 percent of the products of burning blackpowder are solids. That fact does have an effect on its performance as a propellant. Chronograph tests show that bullet velocity levels off and then diminishes with powder charges that approach and then exceed bullet weight. This is because the powder energy must propel its own mass.

The chamber pressure does, however, go up with each increase in charge, even after bullet velocity, as stated before, drops. That is because more energy is released quickly within the gun chamber and causes a gas pressure before the bullet moves, even though later movement is less efficient.

When the author found by chronograph and pressure gun tests of samples of ICI black gunpowder made in Stevenston, Ayrshire, Scotland, that it gave lower bullet velocity and lower breech pressure than the then available late lots of Du Pont, he recalled the reference book statements about the importance of the charcoal used.

The *Encyclopedia Brittanica*, 13th Edition, relying on Nobel and Abel, Hime, Smith and others says: "Dogwood is mainly used for small-arm powders. Powders made from dogwood charcoal burn more rapidly than willow &c." *Military Explosives* says: "The type of charcoal used in the manufacture of blackpowder is reflected in the burning rate of the powder .... much more rapidly when made from willow or alder .... than oak .... " *Chemistry of Powder And Explosives* by Davis says: " ... grapevine or willow, ... with black alder .... are preferred .... for slow burning." There is not real concurrence here.

The writer then contacted those who might have direct knowledge of this. Mr. George Swenson, London, England reported: "The supply of Spanish Dogwood charcoal has run out .... the strength of the powder (Curtis and Harvey) is notably decreased."

Mr. Cullen of ICI replied that Nobel used charcoal from alder or dogwood. Du Pont responded that they used commercially available hard wood charcoal. Gearhart-Owen managers have said that they use commercial hard wood charcoal. C-I-L indicates the same. One contact said that oak was not acceptable. Another said maple was preferred. Another said they preferred willow.

Charcoal has been made by two processes (at least) over the years. One chars in a retort out of contact with air and the other burns it in a kiln with air contact. The only direct information in this respect is that Du Pont going over to Gearhart-Owen went through a switch from retort charcoal to another source making it by kiln. They managed to maintain all military specifications during the change which was brought about by air pollution regulations.

There are subjective reactions to the fouling of different blackpowders. This may be results of the use of different

35TH EDITION, 1981 **145**

charcoals, since saltpeter and sulfur are now chemically distinct and pure materials. Such differences would get into fringe chemistry and be about impossible to evaluate. To me ICI powder fouling left a greenish oily film on my hands when firing the pressure test gun. C-I-L (Canada) and Du Pont, Goex do not.

C-I-L Ammunition Inc. of Canada became interested in manufacturing blackpowder for our U.S. market because, after the Du Pont accident caused their drop-out, Nobel had problems at their plant and then shipping problems to U.S. ports developed. C-I-L used essentially Du Pont methods to make a few lots of blackpowder practically identical to recent Du Pont production using commercially available hardwood charcoal.

A close cooperation with the Canadians in Montreal and Beloeil developed and more information came in from them than from reference books. Powders from other sources were also showing up as samples. Gearhart-Owen reactivated the Belin plant and information from them began to help. By feeding back chronograph and pressure gun test information to powder sources, a lot of reverse data was obtained. A pressure gun and a chronograph can't analyze powder, but they do fingerprint it.

Once a dialogue was established, much of mutal benefit resulted. A lot of this filters down to those who shoot blackpowder. That is because of what has been mutually learned and that there is an awareness of consumer concern and testing ability. Lyman's extensive testing of blackpowder ballistics, paralleled by the author's work for Thompson/Center and GUN DIGEST probed the product.

The author questioned why ICI powder differed from the Du Pont it replaced for a time and had rivaled as an import. Sound ballistic measurements showed it was not the same. Gearhart-Owen looked at our test results and came up with better powder than Du Pont. As you will see from tests to be cited ICI, while inferior to Du Pont and Goex in many areas, performs quite well in specific applications. Similar observations are made about other powders.

Table I
Comparison of Du Pont And ICI Powder

Du Pont Granulation Designation	Sieve	ICI Granulation Designation	Sieve
Fg	12x16	T.P. Cannon	8x20
FFg	14x30	F	18x24
FFFg	20x40	FFF	24x70
KNO$_3$	74.0 +/−1.5%		75.0 +/−1.5%
Charcoal	15.6 +/−1.0%		15.0 +/−1.0%
Sulfur	10.4 +/−1.0%		10.0 +/−1.0%
Moisture	0.85% Max.		1.2% Max.
Spec. Gravity	1.72-1.80		1.70 Min.
Burning Speed lead fuze	75-85 sec./yd.		90-100 sec./yd.

This data was supplied to the author by Mr. J. M. Cullen of ICI, Nobel House, Stevenston, Ayrshire, Scotland.

Powders differ. Blackpowders differ. Unfortunately the total demand for black sporting powder does not warrant multiple sources to insure competition. It is not my intent to criticize those who have been in the market, but to point out that where a sales volume is limited, diversity is curtailed.

Pyrodex

In 1976 a rival to black powder was put on the market. Not very much reached shooters as a plant accident cut off production until 1979. As blackpowder is very flammable, Dan Pawlack, an explosive and pyrotechnic expert, sought to make a similar propellant. He formulated his powder, Pyrodex, with ingredients like those of our old gunpowder. He hoped that his formula would be less hazardous to store and to ship.

Whether or not this is true is not known. Dan Pawlack lost his life with two other men in an inflammatory accident in the Pyrodex plant in Issaquah, Washington. Investigation is still going on about its relative safety in transportation.

Dan Pawlack told me that his powder was not fully oxidized, a reference to the fact that it contained more than one oxygen bearing material but, like black powder, does not have enough oxygen to consume all of the carbon in it.

Current production of Pyrodex is much finer in grain size than Goex black powder. This would suggest that it may burn faster and so produce higher pressure in equal charge weights. Tests made in 1976 with production Lot No. 57616, RS grade (Rifle and Shotgun), ran somewhat higher than usually found with a Du Pont or Goex FFg charge. A 1979 test with new plant Lot No. 175179, RS

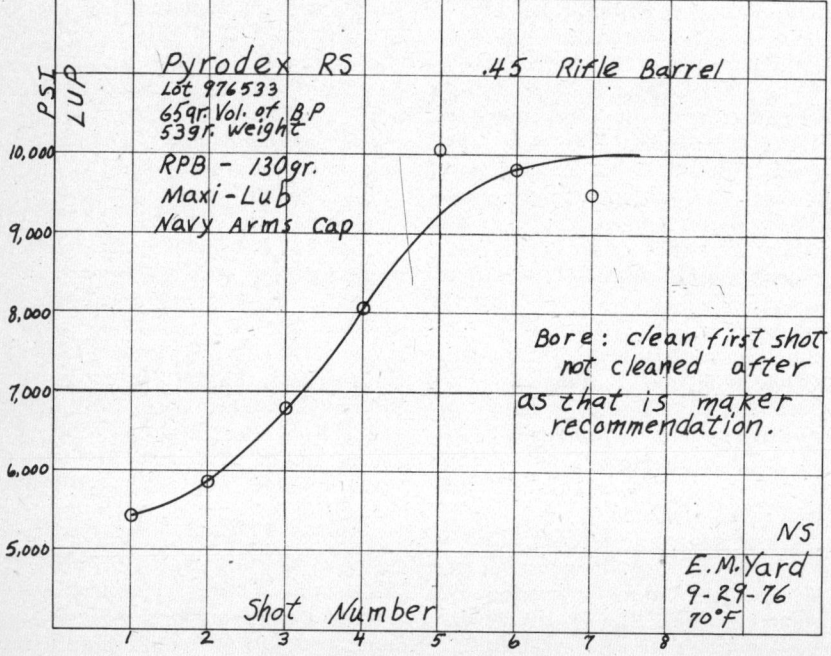

Pressure Change in a Fouled Bore

grade, also indicated higher LUP, (lead units of pressure) than FFg.

Tables of ballistic results for Pyrodex measured by the author are included. It should be understood that in the lead crusher pressure measuring system, an industry standard method, the gases in the gun chamber force a piston against a lead cylinder. There is illustration of this with the article. The force that crushes the lead cylinder is simultaneously acting on the gun.

Rusting of the gun bore is the worst problem, in the author's opinion, with Pyrodex. Apparently, corrosive salt products of combustion are driven into barrel crevices and with air moisture quickly start corrosive action—rusting. Then it is difficult to halt. Many shooters have reported to me that this has caused them to abandon using Pyrodex.

The author has not found a foolproof means of bore clean-up to avoid rusting. Even heroic scrubbing procedures and supposedly smart chemical treatments fail. The most successful procedure tried was an instant (within five minutes of cease-fire, not ten) thorough swabbing with WD-40, patch after patch after patch until they come clean, then drench the bore with WD-40. I will not guarantee that this or another water dispersant petroleum product might work.

There has been suggestion that fouling does not build up in the bore as much when using Pyrodex. A look at the graph of sequential shots made in 1976 will show that a series of firings gave progressively higher pressures, the bore not being cleaned between shots, following the Hodgdon recommendation. 1979 tests show the same pattern.

It has also been recommended that Maxi-Lub be used when shooting Pyrodex and that a beeswax base lubricant should not be used. Actual test results show that the beeswax lubricants give lower LUP breech pressures than Maxi-Lub and there is less build up of pressure with continued shooting in a fouled bore.

The reader should understand that test results are what happen at that time with the equipment and materials in use. The author is reporting only his test observations and his opinions about what was measured, seen or felt.

Pyrodex raises another "difference." It is harder to ignite than regular blackpowders. Hotter caps would help, but tests show that hotter caps raise blackpowder pressure. Special nipples are offered to improve both Pyrodex and blackpowder ignition but pressure data is not provided. It is inevitable that if by any means muzzle velocity of the bullet is increased the mean effective gun barrel pressure was raised and this normally means a higher peak pressure.

It was during the sole reign of black gunpowder that shaped grains were devised. Every shooter knows that blackpowder comes in different granulations. Most know that the finer grained is for smaller bores, the coarser for the bigger. They do not always use this knowledge. More will be said.

The tables that accompany this article are the essence of it. Test results speak a language even powder companies can hear and understand. The shooter should listen as well. He does not control the market, but if shooters understand the product, they can ask for what they need.

It would be nice to think that every question about blackpowder could be answered here. It is not possible. This book could not hold it all. More important to me is that no person could ever assemble it all.

We have tested and will compare those blackpowders recently available in the U.S. Not all of those to be found somewhere in the world are included. Transportation regulations make that impossible. It is also practically irrelevant as they are not on the shelf.

What is of interest to any U.S. blackpowder shooter is how their powder supply could vary in performance even though made to the same nominal specifications by similar methods, using equivalent raw materials. It is observable from the results in the tables that are part of this article that powders originating in three comparable plants with four managers do differ. All of this variation took place in less than ten years. These plants have all been involved in our supply picture in this decade.

Should there by any upset in our supply in the future, it is of interest to note the results obtained with powders from quite different sources that, in their time, loomed as alternatives, indicated differences can be resolved. If we have this information, and know how to view it, then we may have a

Pyrodex Ballistics With Breech Pressures

Caliber & Bullet	Pyrodex Grade	Charge Weight Grains	Muzzle Velocity FPS	Breech Pressure LUP	
.45					
128 RPB	P	70	2000	12,300	
	RS	60	1885	8,300	Velocity
		70	1810	8,600	variation was
		80	1910	11,500	110 to 175 FPS
		90	1725	9,500	
		100	1685	10,000	All Remington
		110	1670	20,000	No. 11 caps
	RS	60	1882*	8,900	RWS Cap
.45					
230 Maxi	RS	60	1590	9,200	
		70	1700	10,200	
.50					
174 RPB	RS	70	1730	9,000	
		80	1785	10,500	
346 Minie	RS	80	1420	9,900	
.58					
530 Minie	RS	60	950	7,000	
Primer Ignition Of Pyrodex					
.45					
128 RPB	RS	60	1880	8,900	Winchester 108
		70	2000	11,000	Primers in Adapter
		80	2005	12,600	100-150 FPS
		90	1880	13,800	Variation.

*This was a comparison firing with another cap and the last digit is allowed to show to emphasize the close check.

RPB means round patched ball and very tight patching lubricated with Bee Bullet Lube was employed though Crisco works well.

Where no cap make is shown both Navy (RWS) and Remington were tried with no noticeable difference.

LUP means lead units of pressure showing that standard Lead Pressure Crushers were used to determine pressure.

Edward M. Yard, 1976

guide to help us adjust.

There has been darn little information about blackpowder characteristics from the past. Even as little as 25 years ago no pressure data was available for muzzleloading guns. Meager muzzle velocities provided scant information of real ballistic use. Fortunately that era is over for any who will look for the information. Articles by the author give it; starting with GUN DIGEST 26th Ed. 1972, breech pressures for all blackpowders have been published.

Many blackpowder shooters know that the same charge of FFFg will give more velocity to the bullet than FFg in many guns. What they do not know is what the pressure may be. Neither do they know if, and that, there is a break-over point in pressure, nor with what powder or loads it may occur. Quite equally unknown is if powders nominally stamped as the same "F" granulation are, indeed, the same even their specifications are equal and held to.

The average-to-experienced muzzleloader shooter has little or no concept of the effect of black powder granulation upon ballistic performance. If they have the word that 70 grains of FFFg will give more bullet velocity than the same amount of FFg, this will sway them. It will not matter that 80 grains of FFg will give the same or a better velocity at less pressure.

Smokeless powder cartridge reloaders think nothing of putting 15% more powder in to eke out 4% more velocity while just squeaking below a case-stretching pressure. They do know, as well they must, that they are using a slower burning powder. Our centerfire brothers are adept at sifting just one more grain into a cartridge for a fraction of a percent more MV, even using magnum primers to make it work.

It is fortunately true that blackpowder pressures usually are not so high that they cause a problem. Note, though, that muzzle-loading guns show no cartridge case extraction difficulty to warn of high pressures.

Blackpowder can produce about 100,000 PSI. Nobel and Abel measured 96,000 in the 1880s. Today, blackpowder is stronger. The author has only been brave enough to hang around the test gun while pressures range up mid-50,000s PSI. Even a pressure gun comes unglued at some point. Muzzleloading guns are blown up with blackpowder every year by gross overloads or failure to seat the ball tightly on the charge.

Black Powder Ballistic Tests

Table 361 (36-cal.)

Bullet	Powder	Charge	MV fps	Pressure lup	ME fp	r
58 RB	ICI FFF	30	1520	3,700	300	12-21-71
Patched		40	1690	4,550	370	12-8-71
		50	1860	5,100	445	
		60	2000	7,900	515	12-28-71
		65	2095	7,400	565	
		70	2095	7,700	565	
Double Ball		60	1715	12,300	755	12-29-71
	G-O FFFg 03-06	60	2230	9,000	640	8-18-75
128 Maxi Ball		60	1845	13,000	970	7-12-74
58 RB	Navy Stick	31	1315	3,700	220	12-21-71
Patched	RWS	24.7	963	3,400	120	
		21.6	1320	4,600	225*	
	ICI FFF	31	1570	4,800	320	

*Bullet seated into breech plug giving bullet start resistance.

Table 401 (40-cal.)

Bullet	Powder	Charge	MV fps	Pressure lup	ME fp	r
93 RB	ICI FFF	50	1795	6,500	665	11-26-71
Patched		60	1865	6,600	720	
		70	1970	8,250	805	
	ICI F	50	1550	4,900	495	11-30-71
		60	1665	5,100	570	
		70	1770	5,500	650	
		80	1870	6,000	725	
	G-O FFFg 03-06	60	1965	9,500	800	8-18-75

Table 451 (45-cal.)

Bullet	Powder	Charge	MV fps	Pressure lup	ME fp	r
128 RB	Du Pont FFFg	50	1570	5,150	700	9-7-71
Patched		55	1620	5,450	745	
		60	1720	5,700	840	
		65	1785	6,500	905	
		70	1825	6,700	950	
		75	1855	7,100	975	
		80	1925	8,600	1055	
		85	1955	9,100	1085	
	ICI FFF	65	1660	5,100	785	10-1-71
		70	1680	6,200	800	
		75	1730	6,100	850	
		80	1750	6,300	870	10-4-71
		85	1835	7,400	955	
		90	1860	7,400	985	
		95	1865	7,800	990	
		100	1875	6,300/14,300		11-8-71
		110	1810	20,000 (1 shot)		11-9-71
	ICI F	80	1550	4,700	680	11-5-71
		90	1765	6,300	885	12-9-71
		100	1845	6,400	965	11-8-71
230 Maxi Ball	ICI F	80	1330	6,100	860	11-17-71
		100	1505	7,000	1100	
	Du Pont FFg	100	1660	8,500	1330	11-21-72
128 RB	Brazilian 3F	70	1475	4,300	620	1-17-73
Patched	" 2F	70	1510	4,400	650	
	Du Pont FFg Old Lot	70	1700	6,400	820	
	Du Pont FFFg Lot 03-123	70	1600	12,700	730	
	Brazilian #3	70	1315	4,200	490	3-9-73
	" #1	70	1820	9,100	940	
	CIL #7 Fuse	70	1820	7,000	940	
	CIL #42 "	70	1650	5,700	775	
	" "	70	1700	8,000	855	3-27-73
	CIL 7AF	70	1760	6,100	880	3-12-73
	CIL #37 Fuse	70	1770	9,100	890	3-27-73
	Brazilian 3F	70	1535	6,000	670	4-6-73
	" 2F	70	1540	5,500	675	
	King FFFg	70	1600	4,600	730	5-16-73

Table 452 (45-cal.)

Bullet	Powder	Charge	MV fps	Pressure lup	ME fp	r
128 RB	CIL 7FA	70	1600/2000	7,000/12,000		6-6-73
Patched	CIL 4FA 4-5-73	70	1750	7,450	870	7-23-73
	CIL 4FA 9-5-73	70	1775	6,300	895	
	CIL 4FA	70	1960	6,850	1090	
	CIL Spl. FFg	70	1610	6,450	740	7-24-73
	CIL Spl. FFFg	70	1855	8,700	980	
	G-O FFg 02-02	80	1880	8,200	1005	8-20-73
	G-O FFFg 03-02	70	1880	9,300	1005	
	G-O FFg 02-03	70	1810	7,400	935	8-30-73
	G-O FFFg 03-03	70	1925	9,700	1055	
	G-O FFFg	70	1890	8,600	1015	11-12-73
		80	1975	10,100	1110	
	CIL FFFg	70	1800	8,000	920	11-26-73
		80	1950	10,300	1080	12-10-73
	Du Pont FFg 02-18	110	2020	9,200	1160	4-17-74
	G-O B	70	1233	5,300	430	8-16-74
2 Balls	"	350		23,000		
	G-O Mil. Class 5	70	1910	8,900	1035	8-20-74
	Green River FF	70	1600	4,800	730	8-8-74
		100	2015	6,800	1170	
	43-3/16-inch barrel					
	ICI FFF	70	1950	6,100	1080	8-23-74
	DuPont FFFg 03-19	70	1950	7,300	1080	
	ICI F	70	1635	3,600	760	

The tables of blackpowder ballistic tests that accompany this article report chronograph and pressure gun firing of 75-15-10 formula blackpowders made by the wheel mill process and for King Semi-Smokeless, Pyrodex, Green River, and Brazilian powders. How the latter powders were made isn't known. The Green River and Brazilian powders are of the 75-15-10 type, but not from a wheel mill. King semi-smokeless is said to be a mixture of blackpowder and nitrocellulose. Pyrodex is a patented formula that is suitable for use in muzzleloading guns. Pyrodex is much cleaner burning than King semi-smokeless.

During an interim period between the use of blackpowder and smokeless powders as we now know them, nitrocellulose bulk powders were introduced. They were sometimes used in muzzleloading guns and in cartridges into the 1930s. I used Du Pont No. 80 myself for pistol loads. Schultze was a nitrated wood pulp powder of this era.

To use any nitrocellulose powder in a muzzleloader is a misapplication of the powder. It is much worse than that. Nitrocellulose can burn quite rapidly, much faster than blackpowder despite anything you may have heard or read, and it burns well only under high pressure. If smokeless powder is used in muzzleloaders the pressures required to burn it properly are beyond their normal range. A bullet that can be seated by pushing it into the muzzle of a gun does not offer enough resistance to build up pressure to burn nitrocellulose. If enough of a fast burning smokeless powder is fired in a muzzleloading gun, the pressure will destroy it. About 40 to 50 grains of a shotgun type smokeless powder, about the amount usually loaded in two shotshells, will split a muzzleloader barrel.

During this investigation of blackpowder the often mentioned importance of the kind of charcoal has faded away. Dogwood, alder, willow are now old terms. Recent makers buy commercial charcoal. They say they prefer maple, then hickory or cherry, but how do they know what wood was burned? It is all carbon when it gets to them.

Other anomalies include a report of the products of combustion by Davis showing more hydrogen gas than is accounted for in the ingredients. The only hydrogen in blackpowder, if it is made from the stated materials, is that in the moisture. Another is that the graphite used to apply a glaze to the powder surface in the finish tumbling stage is not accounted for chemically, nor is the graphite which is carbon, differentiated from the carbon of the charcoal. The full effect of the sulfur in blackpowder is not disclosed. Sulfur vaporizes at about 445°C which is also about the ignition point of carbon and where gunpowder starts to burn. It is suggested that the vaporized sulfur adds to the other gases, carbon dioxide, etc., and carries the hot gas through the charge.

Sulfur, nominally 10% by weight of the composition, is 8.74% of the solid products of combustion according to Davis quoting Nobel and Abel. Multiplying .57 by 8.74 gives 4.98. Just about half of the sulfur does not burn, is not chemically combined when blackpowder burns. The author has tested blackpowder in a bomb calorimeter. The inside of the bomb is as yellow as an egg yolk, coated with the unburned sulfur.

Opinions of the Author About Blackpowder

It isn't easy to decide when to start calling what you say opinion rather than fact. It is hard to determine a fact. The reporting of observations and the recitation of published information, often mere opinion, heretofore cited in this article, qualifies for the distinction of not being the opinion of the writer. There are a few spots where I have presumed to have thought something.

From here on I am looking at my own tests of blackpowder and saying what I think about the results. I will refer to or rely on another source of information, but now I will be saying how I interpret the results.

The bottom line of this article is the tables of data to report what the chronograph and pressure gun revealed, not what I say about these figures. The results are tabulated here for all to read and evaluate for themselves.

An analysis of ICI and Du Pont black gunpowder with grain sizing is given in Table 1. Referring to later tables of load results, you will note that each load of ICI powder grades gave a lower velocity and a lower pressure for the same charge weight *except for exceptions!*

ICI powder had a higher specified moisture content than Du Pont, 1.2% maximum compared to 0.85%. This information was furnished by ICI. All references concur that higher moisture content slows the burning rate and weakens the powder.

The tables of load test results are labeled for my convenience by a number: two digits for the caliber, then one for the sheet.

In table 451 you can see that ICI FFF comes unglued at 100 grains. That single 110 grain shot bent the piston of the pressure gun because the lead crusher was flattened. A copper crusher breech would have measured this pressure, had the result been expected. The piston diameters are not the same for LUP and CUP (Lead Units of Pressure and Copper Units of Pressure) so that the pressure level has to be anticipated to be using the correct breech.

You may note in table 452 that 110 grains of Du Pont FF gave 2020 FPS at 9200 LUP which is 210 more FPS at less than half the pressure of the FFF ICI. 100 grains of Green River FFg produced 2015 FPS at only 6800 LUP, which is essentially the same velocity at 26% less pressure. That seems to be a material difference.

Going back to table 451, 70 grains of Du Pont Lot 03-123 measured only 1600 FPS at 12,300 LUP, while an old Du Pont (pre-serial numbers) FFFg gave 1700 MV for 6400 LUP. Another Du Pont bought in 1971 went 1825 for 6700.

You had better believe it. Blackpowder does differ depending upon who made it and when. I have not dug through every line of my own tests to see all that may lurk in there. The tables are given to you, the reader, for what you may glean from them if I have failed to call something to your attention.

Other things affect blackpowder burning rate and its ballistic effect, based on one hell of a lot of chronograph and pressure gun shooting plus information from ICI, C-I-L, Du Pont and Gearhart-Owen. Increasing moisture content will slow the burning and eventually inactivate the powder. The granulation is important.

Water vapor is a gas, moisture in a powder must be evaporated, and that takes energy from the powder. In some cases this detracts from the effectiveness of a powder. Note that Table 1 shows ICI has a spec for water much higher than Du Pont but in Table 581 gives more FPS for the same 60 grains. The other variations in that table are not, from my information, accountable except that C-I-L and Gearhart-Owen powders are drier.

Granulation affects the burning rate of blackpowder just as it affects the combustion speed of smokeless. The French compressed big chunks of it for their artillery. Our General Rodman developed shaped grains of powder to control its burning. Dust-size bits fizz off in an instant, larger chunks have to burn through like a log.

Small arm blackpowder is not formed into grains, it is broken and then sieved. By grade all pieces will shake through a large mesh and all will be contained on a smaller mesh. Du Pont, ICI, C-I-L, and Gearhart-Owen have used different sieve specs from time to time. Similar sounding grades, even those "said" to be the "same," or at least "equivalent," are not necessarily equal.

In working with C-I-L Ammunition Inc., Canada, to develop a replacement for Du Pont powder, a trial lot was

Table 501 (50-cal.)

Bullet	Powder	Charge	MV fps	Pressure lup	ME fp	r
174 RB Patched	Du Pont FFFg	80	1770	6,700	1210	10-15-71
		100	1860	7,100	1335	11-9-71
	ICI FFF	75	1540	4,700	915	10-14-71
		80	1560	4,900	940	
		85	1610	5,200	1000	
		90	1600	5,000	985	
		95	1660	5,500	1060	
		85	1595	5,000	980	11-2-71
		110	1790	6,200	1240	11-8-71
	ICI F	80	1440	4,350	800	11-4-71
		90	1500	4,550	870	
		100	1550	4,700	925	
		100	1585	4,500	975	10-14-71
		100	1610	5,100	1000	12-9-71
		110	1610	4,900	1000	11-5-71
		110	1680	5,600	1090	12-9-71
450 Mini T/C	ICI F	80	1010	5,400	1020	7-17-72
		90	1135	6,300	1285	
		100	1180	6,800	1390	
388 Maxi Ball		80	1050	6,300	950	10-27-72
		90	1130	6,800	1110	
		100	1215	7,300	1270	
	Du Pont FFg	100	1350	8,800	1570	11-21-72
174 RB Patched	G-O FFg	80	1850	9,800	1320	11-12-73
	G-O FFFg 03-06	70	1700	8,600	1110	12-6-73
	CIL FFFg	70	1665	7,500	1070	11-26-73
		80	1715	7,700	1140	12-6-73
	CIL FFg	70	1525	7,000	900	11-16-73
		100	1760	7,400	1195	12-6-73
	Du Pont FFg 02-18	110	1845	7,000	1315	7-17-74
	Green River FF	80	1365	4,100	720	8-12-74
		100	1625	5,000	1020	8-9-74

Table 581 (58-cal.)

Bullet	Powder	Charge	MV fps	Pressure lup	ME fp	r
315 Minie	Du Pont FFg	56	950		630	6-15-72
	ICI F	56	970		655	
505 Minie	Du Pont FFg	60	810		740	6-15-72
	ICI F	60	835		795	
	CIL FFg	60	980	3,600	1080	8-9-73
		60	990	3,600	1095	12-10-73
	G-O FFg	60	1010	4,300	1145	12-10-73
	Green River FF	60	765	3,100	655	8-12-74

made, one milling, as customary, and sieved into FFg and FFFg for test. The FFg was as close to Du Pont FFg as you could get. The 3F was hot. 85% of it would pass a 40 mesh. Shooting what held on the 40 screen gave results quite equivalent to Du Pont.

Of the factors affecting blackpowder performance today, it is my opinion that the source of the charcoal is minor if the ash in it is minimal (and the references do not help). A small increase in the saltpeter gives a bit more energy, but where the over-all effect of energy and burning rate culminate for best results is not known. Of the powders supplied to me with a stated moisture content, the driest were the strongest and, in the right granulation, do best in a pistol. Regarding moisture, some is necessary to obtain a good glaze from the graphite coating.

Blackpowder fouling is not particularly corrosive. Goex is made of quite pure ingredients and the residues are not particularly hygroscopic or are they oxidizers. The materials left in and on a blackpowder gun are easily washed away with soapy water. Your author has long used a slightly more sophisticated solution of detergent, soluble oil, isopropyl alcohol, and ammonia diluted with cold water. Since it works, I keep on using it.

In bygone days when paper caps and metallic ones contained chlorates, these formed chlorides on ignition and caused corrosive action. This led to the idea that blackpowder itself is corrosive. Rusting will develop on ferrous metal surfaces exposed to the atmosphere whether or not coated with modern black powder fouling (residues).

If cleaning of a blackpowder gun is taken care of with a water solution within two to eight hours, the gun dried and oiled, there is little likelihood of corrosion. A good precaution is to spray the gun lightly with a low viscosity water dispersant rust inhibiting lubricant, WD-40 or its equal. Years of experience prove this true. ●

Bibliography

The Encyclopedia Brittannica, 13th Edition, Volume 12, Gunpowder.
Hatcher's Notebook, Julian S. Hatcher, Major General, U.S.A.
Ordnance And Gunnery, Lieutenant Colonel Earl McFarland.
Chemistry Of Powder And Explosives, Tenney L. Davis, Ph.D.
Military Explosives, TM 9-1910/TO 11A-1-34.
A History of Gunpowder, Partington.
Ordnance And Gunnery, Lt.-Col. William H. Tschappat.

45-Cal. Rifle 28" Barrel

Bullet	Powder	Charge	MV fps	Pressure lup	ME fp
128 RB Patched	Du Pont FFFg Lot 03-108	60	1720	5,700	840
		70	1825	6,700	950
		80	1925	8,600	1055
	ICI FFF	70	1680	6,200	800
		80	1750	6,300	870
		90	1860	7,400	985
	CIL FFFg	70	1800	8,000	920
		80	1950	10,300	1080
	G-O FFFg Lot 03-06	70	1890	8,600	1015
		80	1975	10,100	1110
	Du Pont FFg Old Lot	70	1700	6,400	820
	ICI F	80	1550	4,700	680
		90	1765	6,300	885
		100	1845	6,400	965
	Du Pont FFg Lot 02-18	110	2020	9,200	1160
	CIL FFg	70	1610	6,400	740
	G-O FFg Lot 02-03	70	1810	7,400	935
	CIL #7 Fuse	70	1820	7,000	940
230 Maxi Ball	ICI F	80	1330	6,100	860
		100	1505	7,000	1100
	Du Pont FFg Lot 02-88	100	1660	8,500	1330

Data Report 5-7-76

All Tests Performed By: Edward M. Yard, P.E.

PISTOLS

45-Cal. 9" Bbl.

Bullet	Powder	Charge	MV fps	Pressure lup	ME fp	r
128 RB Patched	ICI FFF	20	645	3,550	120	8-18-72
		25	765	3,700	165	8-15-72
		30	845	3,950	200	
		35	890	4,200	230	
		40	945	4,400	255	
		45	985	4,600	275	8-18-72
		50*	980	4,600	270	
		*Unburned powder blows back				
155 Conical	ICI FFF	25	710	3,400	175	9-5-72
		30	755	3,700	195	
		35	820	3,900	230	
		40	840	4,000	240	
128 RB Patched	03NS	30	1005	4,900	350	5-16-73
	CIL FFFg	30	955	3,900	260	8-9-73
	G-O FFFg	20	1000	5,100	285	9-7-73
	03-03	30	1245	6,300	440	
		35	1380	7,000	540	

36-Cal 9" Bbl.

Bullet	Powder	Charge	MV fps	Pressure lup	ME fp	r
58 RB Patched	G-O FFFg	20	1110	5,200	160	7-12-74
	03-06	30	1350	7,800	235	

Ruger OLD ARMY Revolver

45-Cal 7½" Bbl.

Bullet	Powder	Charge	MV fps	Pressure lup	ME fp	r
143 RB .457"	ICI FFF	20	545		95	12-14-72
		25	630		125	
		30	750		180	12-19-72
		35	815		210	
		30	750		180	1-25-73
		35	800		200	
		40	890		250	
	03NS	30	825		215	5-17-73
		40	870		240	

7mm-08 Remington: Gun and Cartridge

It adds up to a modern 7x57mm Mauser, and that ain't bad.

by LAYNE SIMPSON

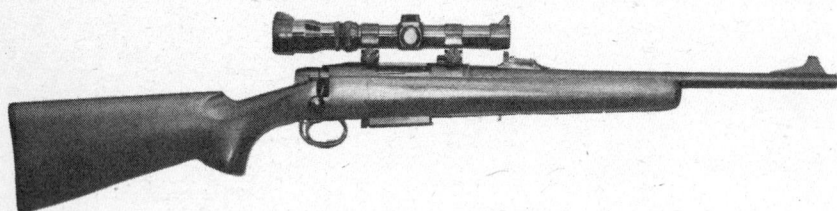

Remington Model 788 bolt action centerfire rifle with 18½-inch barrel, available in 6mm Remington, 243 Winchester, 308 Winchester, and 7mm-08 Remington calibers.

Shown on extreme left; 120-gr. Hornady seated backward to show throat length in author's 7mm-08 Remington. Cutaway cases illustrate seating depths. From left; 115-gr. Speer, 120-gr. Hornady, 130-gr. Speer, 140-gr. Sierra, 150-gr. Remington, 160-gr. Sierra, 175-gr. Hornady. Author contends bullets over 154 grains aren't needed, that lighter bullets will take any big game animal in North America with exception of big bears.

THE TRUTH is, an accurate description of the new 7mm-08 Remington has to say that this medium-capacity cartridge represents somewhat of a departure from what we have come to expect from the arms and ammunition giants. It really is medium. And that's good.

Hitherto, Winchester has maintained somewhat of a design monopoly on the 308 Winchester and its derivatives. Beginning in 1952 when they dressed the 7.62 NATO in civvies and introduced it as the 308 Winchester; again in 1955 by squeezing down the neck and bringing forth the 243 Winchester; and finally during the same year when they opened up the neck and introduced the excellent but now sadly neglected 358 Winchester.

In late 1979, Remington broke that monopoly by simply necking down the 308 Winchester case to 7mm and changing the headstamp to read 7mm-08 Remington. And so we have four cartridges based on the parent 7.62mm case, all dimensionally identical except in caliber and length of neck. Case bodies of the 243, 308, 358 and 7mm-08 measure 1.560 inches in length and all have shoulder angles of 20 degrees. Compared to many, the 308 Winchester could be called a youngster but no other American cartridge can boast of three commercial offspring that so favor their parent.

Remington now chambers the 7mm-08 in two rifles, one the Model 700 BDL Varmint Special, with 24-inch barrel. This combination is aimed at the silhouette shooting market where the cartridge has already enjoyed good popularity for several years in wildcat form. The name of the game in this battle with the steel animals is to push a precision bullet of high ballistic coefficient at a moderate speed from an accurate rifle without getting kicked too hard in the process.

Push a bullet too slow and the 500-meter rams will refuse to topple over. Push a bullet too fast and you'll burn holes in targets and receive an invitation to leave the match. Standard cartridges such as the 308 Winchester, 30-06, 7x57mm Mauser, 7mm Express Remington and the 7mm-308 wildcat handle silhouette chores quite well and since Remington's new 7mm cartridge is identical to its wildcat predecessor, both the 7mm-08 and the Model 700 silhouette rifle should be welcomed by iron-clangers.

However, Remington refers to their new offspring as a hunting cartridge and it is also available in their "economy sleeper" the Model 788 bolt action rifle. In fact, I didn't get too excited about the new cartridge until I learned of the new slicked-up version of the Model 788, replete with 18½" barrel. There are no rifle silhouette ranges in my neck of the woods, but timber-dwelling whitetails abound, so the 788 carbine was good news.

The Model 788 has features both good and bad. On the plus side, (other than its price) are 8-40 holes tapped in the receiver for scope mounting, a short, 68-degree bolt lift made possible by the interrupted, thread-type locking lug arrangement and the rigid tubular receiver, with thick guide rails and small ejection port. The bolt face is recessed ala Model 700 and the bolt releases by pushing the safety to its extreme forward position for takedown.

The Model 788 is fed via a three-round clip, which is fine if you like detachable magazines but I don't. The two vertical ribs pressed into the inside walls of the magazine about an inch back from the front appeal to me. The shoulders of loaded cartridges bear against these ribs and keep bullet tips unbattered during recoil. The trigger pull was crisp and without a trace of backlash but far too heavy at 76 ounces. It can be tuned by someone who knows his stuff or the trigger can be replaced, but doing so tends to defeat the purpose for purchasing an economy-priced rifle in the first place.

The 1980 version of the Model 788 has a new shape to its stock, or as Remington puts it, "the new stock reflects a more traditional straight-line styling." The rear sight sits lower on the barrel and the polish and bluing on the bolt handle and trigger guard have been improved. The bolt knob is shaped similar to the pre-64 Model 70 Winchester, but the shank is curved more toward the rear. Model 788s chambered for the 223 Remington and in 22-250 still sport 24-inch barrels but the 243, 308 and 7mm-08 versions are available only with the 18½" tube. Some will surely say that the 7mm-08 should have a longer barrel but I disagree. With cartridges such as the 7mm Express and the 270 Winchester available in longer barrels, I see no need for it but I do see a need for a quick handling, accurate and compact bolt action carbine, chambered for a flat-shooting cartridge.

Remington bills their 7mm-08 as the first modern 7mm round designed for use in short-action rifles, which overlooks the fact that the 284 Winchester beat them to that punch over seventeen years ago. The 284 case is longer by 0.155 inch and it requires the heavier bullets to be seated deep into the powder space when loaded for short-action rifles. Even at that, its powder capacity is over 20 percent greater than that of the 7mm-08.

Although the 7mm-08 is a new commercial offering, handloading the cartridge is old hat to me. Back in 1974 I put together a short wildcat by necking down the 308 Winchester case to 7mm, fireforming it out to a 0.005-inch body taper and increasing the shoulder angle to forty degrees. "Improving" the case brought its powder capacity to about ninety percent of the 280 Remington. Called the 7mm SGLC (Simpson's Good Little Cartridge), the reason behind this crea-

The Model 788 carbine is short and handy in timber and the 7mm-08 ideal for the hunter who is occasionally offered long shots. Author is shown in good whitetail country, later mounted a Weaver 1.5-4.5x scope on the rifle, making it a near-perfect outfit for his neck of the woods.

tion was to design a big game cartridge that would work in the little Weatherby Varmintmaster rifle.

I have two rifles chambered for this wildcat, the other being a Brown Precision 600SL, with fiberglass stock and 19-inch barrel. Thus far, these two rifles have accounted for sixteen big game animals such as moose, deer, pronghorn and greater kudu, with the expenditure of nineteen cartridges. I'm saying all of this to say that I know what a short 7mm cartridge will do on big game and am no stranger to handloading the efficient little rascal.

For accuracy testing the Model 788 carbine, I installed a Weaver 16x Model T scope, utilizing Weaver mounts. Weaver bases are available in both one and two-piece style and I chose the latter. The rear base only has one hole for mounting to the receiver but after staking all screws with Loc-Tite, the scope remained secure through over 500 test loads.

The 16x Weaver was a strange sight on the little carbine, since it is almost as long as the barrel but that's my method of testing a rifle from the bench. Afterwards, I switched the Model T for a Weaver 1.5-4.5x variable making the carbine a near-perfect whitetail outfit for most of my hunting.

The first order of business was to test the 140-grain factory load. Or I should say 139-grain, as I'll explain later. The Remington factory round is loaded with an average of 48 grains of ball powder which appears identical to WW-760, in both grain size and burning rate. It is a non-canister powder but I substituted my lot of WW-760 in several factory cartridges and these trials yielded velocities within 20 feet per second of the factory load.

The advertised velocity of this load, out of a 24" barrel, is 2860 fps (feet per second) and I could hardly believe the Oehler 33 when it clocked 2804 fps for the first three rounds out of an 18½" barrel. Running 12 more rounds through the Sky Screens I came up with an average of 2816 fps. To make sure, I dug out my old Oehler Model 11 which clocked almost identical readings. This load should gain at least 25 fps for each additional inch of barrel which would put it at 2950 fps out of the Model 700 silhouette rifle. That's close to 100 feet per second faster than Remington's claim.

In all my years of load testing, I have rarely seen domestic factory loads that even approach advertised velocities and this is the first cartridge that has ever exceeded those claims. In fact, as can be seen in my load data, only one of

Shown with a Bonanza Benchrest seating die are the bullet weights used in the author's tests. From left, 115-gr. Speer, 120-gr. Hornady, 130-gr. Speer, 140-gr. Sierra, 150-gr. Remington, 160-gr. Sierra, 175-gr. Hornady.

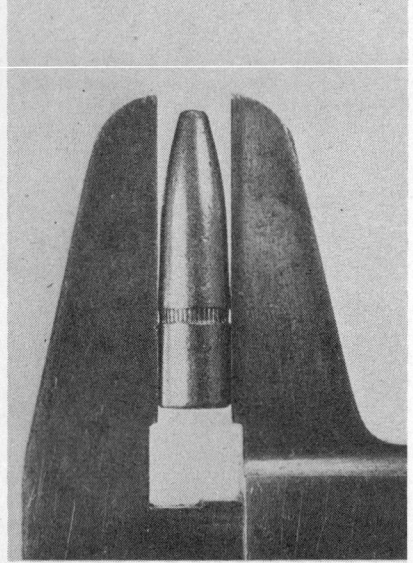

The 7mm 150-gr. Remington bullet has two-diameter design. For this reason, it can be driven almost as fast as the 140-gr. bullet, since its bearing surface is only about half that of other bullets of comparable weight.

The 7.62mm NATO round shown on the extreme left is the parent case for the 308 Winchester, 243 Winchester, 358 Winchester and the 7mm-08 Remington.

my loads with the 140-grain Sierra bullet exceeded the factory fodder's velocity and not by much at that.

I'm not sure how much value can be placed on my factory load test results since to get test rifles and ammunition to gun writers, Remington loaded up a batch of the latter with 139-grain Hornady bullets. Now that's what I call cooperation. The story I get is that rifle production outran the development of their new 140-grain bullet but by the time rifles and ammunition reach the dealer's shelves you will see the 140-grain Core-Lokt sticking out of the cases. Anyhow, Remington has stated that the new ammo will be loaded to the same pressures as the test rounds.

Assuming that the 7mm-08 will someday be chambered in 22-inch barrels, the factory load should do about 2900 fps at the muzzle, as compared to 2800 feet per second for the 150-grain 7mm Express Remington load and 2900 feet per second for the 270 Winchester. These velocities are what I get out of factory loads and not what I read in advertisements.

For load testing the 7mm-08, I selected bullet weights that blanket any varminting or big game hunting that is likely to be taken on with the cartridge. The 7mm-08 is a far cry from your ideal varmint cartridge but its medium-size case capacity does offer the added flexibility of taking to the lighter bullets. Both the 115-grain Speer and the 120-grain Hornady bullets showed acceptable accuracy for woodchuck-size varmints, out to about 200 yards. The little carbine should well serve the needs of the casual varmint hunter, such as the farmer who needs an accurate rifle to rid the cabbage patch of a pesky chuck once in a while.

The Speer bullet is a bit more explosive on varmints, due to its awesome hollow point, while the trim Hornady projectile has a slight edge in trajectory and wind buckability. No holdover would be necessary on woodchucks out to 250 yards when starting these bullets at 3100 fps and zeroing one inch high at a hundred yards.

The 130-grain Speer bullet was extremely accurate in the test rifle and at 2900 fps, is made-to-order for the carbine, on deer-size game. This bullet when loaded to 3200 fps in my 7mm SGLC, drops whitetail, mule deer and pronghorn like a lightning bolt and holds together all out of proportion to its diminutive appearance. I have taken pronghorn out to 400 yards and whitetail at ten paces with this bullet and it has yet to let me down. I have also found it to be one of the best in my 7x57mm Mauser and 7mm Express.

For heavier or tougher game, such as black bear, the 139-grain Hornady, 140-grain Sierra and the 145-grain Speer might be better choices. Either of these bullets will perform out to a good 400 yards when started at 2800 fps from the shorty carbine.

Although there are rifles better suited for the task, there is little doubt that the 7mm-08 carbine will be used by some for taking elk-size game. For such an occasion, I would suggest the 150-grain Remington or 150-grain Nosler. A long-range elk rifle it ain't, since it only packs about 1250 foot pounds of energy out at 400 yards, but limit your shots to 200 yards and the 7mm-08 will kill elk very dead.

After testing the 160- and 175-grain bullets in the short barrel, I concluded that they simply can't be driven fast enough to be of more than limited use in the 7mm-08 for big game hunting. Both the Hornady and Sierra were accurate enough but accuracy alone does not a big game cartridge make. This is

LOAD DATA: 7mm-08 REMINGTON

Remington Model 788, 18½″ barrel, 1-9¼″ twist; Remington cases, Remington 9½ primers; Velocity instrumental at fifteen feet, converted to muzzle velocity; Oehler Model 33 Chronotach, Temp., 35 degrees F. Rel. Humidity 76%

Bullet	L.O.A.	Powder	Charge	Velocity	Groups	Remarks
Rem. 140 factory	2.775	————	48.0	2816	1.220	39 fps velocity spread
115 Speer	2.672	WW-760	52.0	3042	1.342	Mild
		N-204	52.0	3137	0.604	Good 200 yard varmint load
		H-414	48.5	2912	0.980	Maximum, good varmint load
		IMR-4064	47.0	3155	1.269	Fastest load tested
		IMR-3031	43.0	3041	1.488	61 fps velocity spread
		H-335	42.0	3088	1.172	Too warm, drop back one grain
120 Hornady	2.722	WW-760	50.0	2908	1.015	19 fps velocity spread
		N-204	50.0	3053	0.821	Good 150 yard varmint load
		H-414	48.0	2864	1.225	Mild, 22 fps velocity spread
		IMR-4064	46.0	3091	1.016	36 fps velocity spread
		IMR-3031	42.0	2954	1.266	Maximum
		H-335	41.0	3056	0.904	Excellent load, 2488 fp muzzle energy
130 Speer	2.700	WW-785	55.0	2806	1.130	26 fps velocity spread
		N-MRP	54.0	2896	0.922	Deadly on deer and pronghorn
		H-450	49.0	2822	1.219	Maximum
		WW-760	49.0	2849	0.887	1400 fp energy at 300 yards
		N-204	49.0	2861	0.360	Most accurate load tested
		H-414	47.0	2738	0.820	Maximum, very accurate
		H-335	40.0	2817	1.294	Mild, 34 fps velocity spread
140 Sierra	2.780	WW-785	54.0	2719	1.117	Mild and accurate
		N-MRP	53.0	2744	1.211	Mild, good mule deer load
		H-450	51.5	2760	0.874	Very accurate, good for mule deer
		IMR-4350	50.0	2862	1.460	15 fps velocity spread
		WW-760	48.0	2772	1.236	2400 fp muzzle energy
		N-204	48.0	2754	0.595	Very accurate
		H-414	46.0	2736	1.306	Maximum, 28 fps velocity spread
150 Remington	2.865	WW-785	53.0	2674	0.800	Best load with this bullet
		N-MRP	52.0	2660	0.780	Good black bear load
		H-450	51.0	2661	1.201	Mild
		IMR-4831	50.0	2702	1.322	Lightly compressed
		IMR-4350	47.0	2668	1.484	Mild
		WW-760	45.0	2433	0.940	Accurate but burning rate too fast
		N-204	45.0	2485	1.128	Burning rate too fast with heavier bullets
160 Sierra	2.740	WW-785	51.0	2529	1.243	Mild
		N-MRP	49.0	2634	0.826	Silhouette load, 1.32 P-S momentum, 500 yds
		H-450	49.0	2672	0.919	Maximum, good for silhouettes
		IMR-4831	49.0	2685	1.685	Heavily compressed
		IMR-4350	46.0	2625	1.229	Mild
		WW-760	44.0	2479	1.113	Accurate but slow
		N-204	44.0	2490	1.317	Maximum
175 Hornady	2.748	WW-785	50.0	2472	1.120	Mild
		N-MRP	48.0	2511	1.206	Best load, this bullet
		H-450	48.0	2586	1.266	Maximum
		IMR-4831	45.0	2497	1.333	Heavily compressed
		IMR-4350	44.0	2541	1.325	Maximum, erratic pressures, 51 fps spread
		N-204	40.0	2270	1.217	Maximum, burning rate too fast

NOTES

For beginning loads, reduce all charges shown by ten percent.
Group sizes shown are averages of three, three-shot groups per load.
Velocity shown for each load is an average of nine rounds.
Test rifle accuracy: Smallest composite group, 0.360 moa. (9 shots)
Largest composite group, 1.685 moa. (9 shots)
Aggregate accuracy for 144, three-shot groups, 1.115 moa.

not to say that the 175-grain bullet would ricochet off an elk's rib but it *is* to say that most heavy 7mm bullets are constructed to hold together at magnum velocities. Start the 175-grain Hornady spire point at 2600 fps and at 300 yards it's loafing along at just over 2000 fps, with about the same retained energy as a 30-30 carbine at the muzzle. Bullet expansion at this velocity would probably leave a bit to be desired. For this reason, I consider the 150 Remington and 154 Hornady bullets as the heaviest useful in the

fact that most Remington bullets are two-diameter designs and can be seated farther out of the case than bullets with long, full-diameter shanks. However, when loading for the Model 788, the magazine prohibits loading any cartridge with an over-all length greater than 2.870 inches. Seating the 150-grain Remington bullet to just clear the lands brings it to an over-all length of 2.865 inches and the base only barely encroaches on the powder space. I consider neither the Model 788's short throat nor short magazine a

115-grain bullet is Norma 204, hands down, and it's a toss-up between that powder and H-335 behind the 120-grain Hornady. WW-785 and N-MRP started turning in good performance with the 130-grain bullet and accuracy was excellent but not quite up with H-414, WW-760 and N-204. Actually, no powder tried turned in poor performance with this bullet and for this reason it would be tough to pick a favorite without additional load testing.

With the 140-grain bullet, IMR-4350 took the laurels in velocity and showed uniform shot to shot velocity spread but I just couldn't get it to shoot tight groups in the M788 carbine. Both WW-785 and N-204 consistently turned in small groups at good velocities and WW-760 and N-MRP were not far behind. If pinned down to two choices in powder for the 140-grain Sierra, I would go with WW-760 and WW-785.

The highest velocities recorded with the 150-grain bullet were with IMR-4831 but it averaged the largest groups of any powder tried. Previous to my tests, I had assumed that this powder would be hard to beat in the 7mm-08, especially with the heavier bullets but my test results did not bear this out. H-450 really came into its own with this bullet, as did N-MRP and WW-785, with N-204 up to snuff in accuracy but falling back in velocity. WW-760 also started losing ground fast when this bullet weight was reached and like N-204 proved to be too fast burning for the heavier bullets.

The author has had quite a bit of experience with short 7mm cartridges. Shown here with a warthog taken in Rhodesia in 1977 with his 7mm SGLC wildcat designed for the Weatherby Varmintmaster rifle he's holding.

carbine and even they are more limited in usefulness than bullets in the 130- to 145-grain range.

It's a different story when steel silhouettes are the prey. One should have no problem in loading match grade bullets, such as the Hornady 162-grain boattail and the Sierra 168-grain Matchking in the 2700 to 2800 feet per second bracket, *if a 24 inch barrel is used.* The 175-grain Sierra spitzer boattail should also do the trick on steel rams as it retains 1.42 pound-seconds of momentum at 500 meters.

Possibly, the heavier and slower bullets will be preferred by some for hunting big game in the timber but the short magazine and throat require that they be seated deeply into the case, thus taking up valuable powder space at the expense of velocity. I, along with others, have long complained about short throats in factory rifles but many of us often overlook the

handicap since bullets weighing from 130 to 150 grains will handle any big game that should be hunted with the carbine.

Before selecting powders for testing in the cartridge, I compared the 7mm-08's case capacity with a few other cartridges. It holds about ten percent less than my 7mm SGLC and a couple of grains less than the 7x57mm Mauser. I figured powders that had worked in these two would do likewise in the 7mm-08 but my assumption was only partially correct. In my two 7mm SGLCs and my 7x57, Norma MRP and WW-785 are the best powders with all but the varmint-weight bullets and they worked fine behind some bullets in the 7mm-08 but they did not prove to be greatly superior to some of the other powders tried.

IMR-4064 was the fastest with the 115- and 120-grain bullets but accuracy was not up to varmint shooting par. My choice of propellant for the

Little can be said about the powders tried behind the 160-grain Sierra bullet except that H-450 did an excellent job. Again, neither of the IMR powders made a good showing in accuracy although IMR-4350 did do a bit better than with the lighter bullets.

The 175-grain Hornady was not impressively accurate in the carbine but was plenty accurate for big game hunting at ranges which it will expand satisfactorily. H-450 pegged the highest velocities but WW-785 held a slight edge in accuracy.

All handloads for my tests were prepared with a Bonanza Co-Ax press and their bench rest dies, the latter being a stock item long before Remington decided to domesticate the 7mm-308. For a major company to manufacture reloading dies for a wildcat as a stock item is a good indication of its popularity as a hunting and competition cartridge. Dick Lee's Auto-Prime tool proved most valuable since deadlines caused a mad rush in testing all of the loads. This little gadget is one of the best inventions since the wheel.

A characteristic I have found common among many of the 7mm cartridges is their habit of placing all bullet weights close to the same point of impact at 100 yards. Both of my 7mm SGLCs do it; ditto for my 7mm Express and 280 Remington; likewise for my Ruger Number One in 7x57mm and my John Towle XP-100 in 7mm T-N-T and ditto for the 7mm-08 carbine. As can be seen by perusing the groups listed herein, all bullets from the 115-grain Speer to the 175-grain Hornady show a composite group of about five inches at 100 yards.

I'll hop up on a limb by saying that the Model 788 rifle I shot is one of the most consistently accurate off-the-shelf sporter weight rifles I have ever tested. Doubtless, the 16x Weaver helped squeeze groups down a bit but it takes more than a good, powerful scope to make a rifle perform. The carbine's barrel is short, stiff and heavy, tapering to a muzzle diameter of 0.635 inch and its bore is minus tool marks and shines like a preinflation silver dollar. The receiver is massive, measuring 7½ inches long by 1.310 inch in diameter. This compares to 7⅞ by 1.365 inch in diameter for the Model 700 long action.

Beyond those facts, it's hard to find a bad 7mm bullet nowadays. This coupled with an underbore capacity case adds up to a cartridge with plenty of accuracy potential. Doubtless, Remington will soon add the 7mm-08 to their 40X target rifle. In fact, I'll even ease out on the limb's very tip by stating that a carefully bedded Model 788, in 7mm-08, with a trigger equal to the Model 700, fed handloads that are put through the benchrest loading routine and with match bullets, will crowd one half minute of angle all day long.

Understand, however, that the characteristics that help the carbine's accuracy actually weigh against it as a lightweight hunting rifle. It looks and feels light and well-balanced, but looks are deceiving as the carbine pegs my postage scale at seven pounds, nine ounces. Add the Weaver scope, Weaver mounts, sling and a clip full of cartridges and she goes one ounce under nine pounds. Ah, such a pity.

While I'm feeling critical, the magazine has a lip for grasping which will take small but painful chunks of flesh from one's hand. Five minutes with a file and a bottle of cold bluing remedy it, but it should be done at the factory. The rear sight has sharp corners that dish out the same treatment and should be shaped to a smoother contour. I like the front blade-type sight but would like to see a gold insert added, ala Sourdough. These are paltry complaints considering the carbine's performance and price. On the positive side, the bolt glides smoothly to and fro, with minimum wobble and I like pushing the safety forward to release the bolt. The stock is shaped nicely with a comfortable fore-end but the grip could stand a couple of minutes with a good, sharp wood rasp—it's a little thick for me.

Where does the 7mm-08 Remington fit into the scheme of things? I see the cartridge as one of the best for silhouette shooting and equally as good for hunting deer-size game. It's also a likely candidate for a lightweight custom rifle with shortened and lightened '98 Mauser action and 22-inch barrel.

Chambering the 7mm-08 in a rifle with longer throat and magazine would allow the heavier bullets to be seated farther out of the case, thus improving its performance but that would be wasted effort since we already have the 7mm Express. One of the best homes for the short cartridge would be in the dainty little Weatherby Varmintmaster rifle but to date Weatherby hasn't seen fit to utilize that action for anything other than varmint cartridges, and his silhouette pistol. My Varmintmaster in 7mm SGLC weighs seven pounds, one ounce complete with 2-7x scope, sling and three cartridges and I believe if not for Weatherby's prices the Varmintmaster in 7mm-08 would sell like aspirin tablets.

I expect to see the cartridge chambered in the Model 99 Savage and the Browning BLR lever actions because the 7mm-08 like the 284 Winchester would have no peer as a high intensity cartridge for lever action rifles. I suspect the 7mm-08 will prove to be more popular in lever guns, at least when applied to hunting, than in the bolt actions, but then, I predicted the same fate for the 308 Winchester, a cartridge that presently enjoys a considerable following in bolt action hunting rifles. I'm sure we will soon see the 7mm-08 offered in the Savage 110S and the Ruger Model 77 silhouette rifles, in the very near future.

As a big game cartridge, the 7mm-08 will aptly handle about anything within the capability spectrum of the 308 Winchester. It can be said that the cross sectional base area favors the larger caliber and bullets of the same weight can be driven faster from the 308. On the other side, the higher sectional density of the 7mm bullet gives the 7mm-08 a slight trajectory advantage for shooting at the longer ranges.

When bullets of near-equal sectional densities are loaded in both cartridges, the 308 pushes a bit ahead. Good examples are the Hornady 308-caliber 165-grain bullet versus the 7mm, 139-grain Hornady, both exiting the muzzle at 2800 feet per second. At 300 yards the heavier bullet strikes less than a half inch lower than the 7mm and it packs almost 250 foot pounds more energy at that range. All conditions being equal, the 7mm bullet will penetrate as deep, probably deeper, into game but on the other hand, the fatter 308 bullets will expand to a larger frontal area thus causing more tissue damage.

When either bullet is placed into the lungs of an animal, the result will be the same—it would die very quickly. With the proper load and in the hands of a good hunter and rifleman who understands the importance of proper bullet placement, the 7mm-08 will handle anything in North America that grows horns or antlers. In fact, it will do just as good a job as some of our more glamorous rounds. For example, at 300 yards, the 7mm-08 carbine delivers more retained energy than any load that can be safely squeezed out of the 25-06 Remington, although the latter cartridge does have an advantage in trajectory.

Equipped with a good scope, such as the 1.5-4.5x Weaver or the 1-4x Leupold, the shorty rifle is tough to beat as a timber rifle for hunting deer and black bear especially for those who hunt from tree stands or in thick brush yet are occasionally offered longer shots across clearings. Neither can I think of a better combination for the lady or youngster looking for an easy-on-the-shoulder deer rifle.

There will be wild claims about the amazing performance of the 7mm-08, and others that label it just short of useless for big game shooting. Somewhere between these two extremes sits the mild-mannered 7mm-08. Like any other cartridge, it contains no magical properties in its powder charge and it will always eat the dust of the bigger-jugged 7mm cartridges but take my word, the 7mm-08 will handle tasks all out of proportion to its appearance.

Perhaps the 7mm-08 Remington can be called a modern, souped-up version of the excellent old 7x57mm Mauser as it certainly lives up to that name in performance. That's not a bad pedigree to hang on the runt in Remington's 7mm litter.

ACCURACY IN 22-CALIBER TARGET PISTOLS

EXTENSIVE TESTING—REALLY EXTENSIVE TESTING—PROVIDES NEW FACTORS TO CONSIDER

by KENNETH L. WALTERS

IN HIS ARTICLE entitled "Selecting A .22 Target Gun," Gil Hebard presented an evaluation of some 22-caliber target pistols of the early '60s. This work was important because it was the first systematic attempt in popular literature to evaluate pistol performance on a large scale.

I became interested in examining 22 target pistol accuracy since there were new and better techniques available for analyzing results, newer, better machine rests on the market, and several new guns had appeared. Using nearly 50 handguns and tens of thousands of rounds of ammunition, the accuracy of autoloaders, and to a limited extent revolvers, was examined. From this information it was possible to develop a reasonably simple explanation of gun, muzzle brake, and counterweight performance. It is important, I think, to have at least a feel for the extent of the work. Between one and two hundred hours were spent at the shooting range and hundreds of hours were spent analyzing the data.

All tests involved considerable duplication. In almost every case, each firearm was tested not once but usually four or five times. Where meaningful, duplicate identical guns were tested. Duplication didn't stop, however, with just duplicate testing of a particular gun or set of nominally

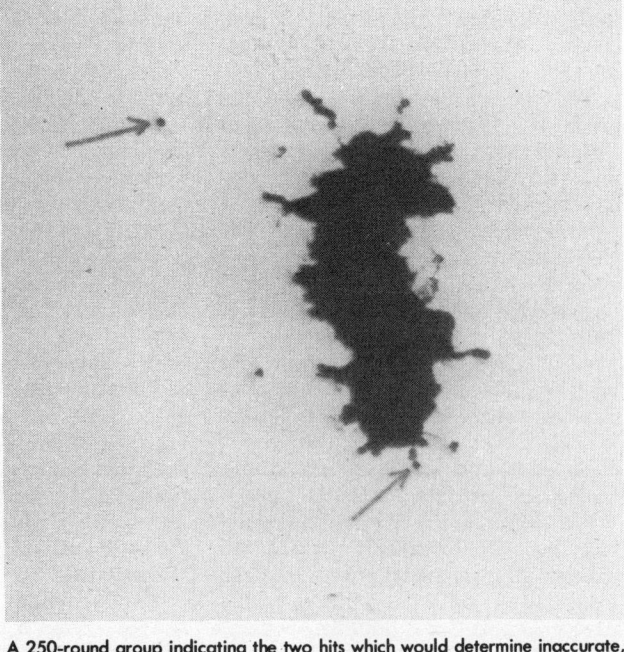

A 250-round group indicating the two hits which would determine inaccurate, conventional group size.

(Left) Lee machine rest. Considered for possible use in these experiments but rejected.

identical guns. Similar guns of different barrel lengths also supplied a form of duplication. When, for instance, guns with 4½", 5", 5½", and 6" barrels were tested, a single accuracy dependence on barrel length was observed. That a particular gun in this series was performing properly could be judged not only by comparison to its own duplicate testing and that of nominally identical pieces but also by comparing its performance to similar firearms of slightly different barrel lengths. These extensive studies showed that two phenomena largely determine handgun accuracy: barrel length and type.

To understand the effects of barrel type, two definitions had to be developed. A flexible barrelled handgun has a circular cross-sectioned barrel. A rigid barrelled handgun has a barrel with a non-circular cross-section or a very heavy barrel, one of sufficient strength to eliminate any barrel flexibility.

Since shooter involvement might cause variations that would make seeing small differences in gun performance difficult, machine rests were used throughout the testing. There were two such rests on the commercial market, the Lee and Ransom, so one of each type was purchased. While the Lee might be quite good for the average shooter, tests of both units showed that the Ransom (1978 GUN DIGEST article) was clearly superior and hence it was used herein.

As Table I indicates, the machine rest tests showed that barrel length was one of the most important considerations in firearm performance. Proof can also be seen from the corresponding graph, Figure I.

Perhaps the most interesting result shown by this data, however, is the importance of barrel rigidity. Note in the series with a constant 6.75" barrel length accuracy increases substantially as the barrels become progressively more rigid. This, I think, is an original observation.

Another interesting observation is the degree to which total barrel length affects accuracy. Above eight inches or so, little improvement is gained. It is almost as if the added two inches between the eight and ten-inch Citations increased potential gun accuracy at the same time it increased barrel flexibility and the two effects almost cancelled each other out.

If this rigidity concept is correct, i.e. guns with more rigid barrels shoot better than pistols with flexible ones, then guns with bull or heavy barrels should have a much higher accuracy for the same barrel length than the flexible barrelled weapons discussed thus far. To test this theory the guns listed in Table II, whose results are plotted in Figure II, were tested. The barrel length effect is clearly shown, and, as a comparison of the two graphs will indicate, so is the increase in accuracy due to increased barrel rigidity.

As one inspects the actual gun results listed in Table II, several interesting aspects of the individual pieces can be spotted. The results clearly show, for instance, that guns of the same barrel length and rigidity, perform pretty much alike. It should be noted also that the Rugers as a family of guns yield another interesting observation. These guns all performed as rigid barrelled arms, even though they visually would appear to be of the flexible barrel style. This proves, as did the series of 6.75" guns, that circular cross-sectioned barrels can be made rigid and indicates that a pistol does not necessarily require a bull or rectangular cross-section for top accuracy. Normal relatively thin and flexible barrels, however, are just not the top choice in target guns.

In addition to testing guns, accessory barrel weights were also the subject of experimentation. Primarily this arose because several of the weapons were supplied with these devices and testing of the initial ones yielded such unusual results as to capture attention.

The first such gun was the Unique DES-69. Although it was shown to be a normal rigid barrelled weapon, its performance became truly erratic when the counterweights were attached. Given this unusual circumstance, the examination of counterweights was expanded. While many of these studies were interesting and all are reported in the tables, the results from the Hammerli Walther were so fantastic that they will be discussed at length below.

Using the front counterweight which clamps directly to the barrel not only increased the accuracy of the gun, it essentially altered it from a flexible barrel to a rigid barrel in grouping. Now since the shooting characteristics of a pistol could be reproducibly and repeatedly altered from performance as one type of barrel to the other, absolute proof of the barrel rigidity concept was available. Its flexible style was apparently capable of slight movement at the end of the bore which uniformly decreased its inherent accuracy. The counterweights strengthened the barrel and reduced the movement. Any counterweight which increased the rigidity of a flex-

Front view of Ransom rest showing method of securing baseplate to shooting bench.

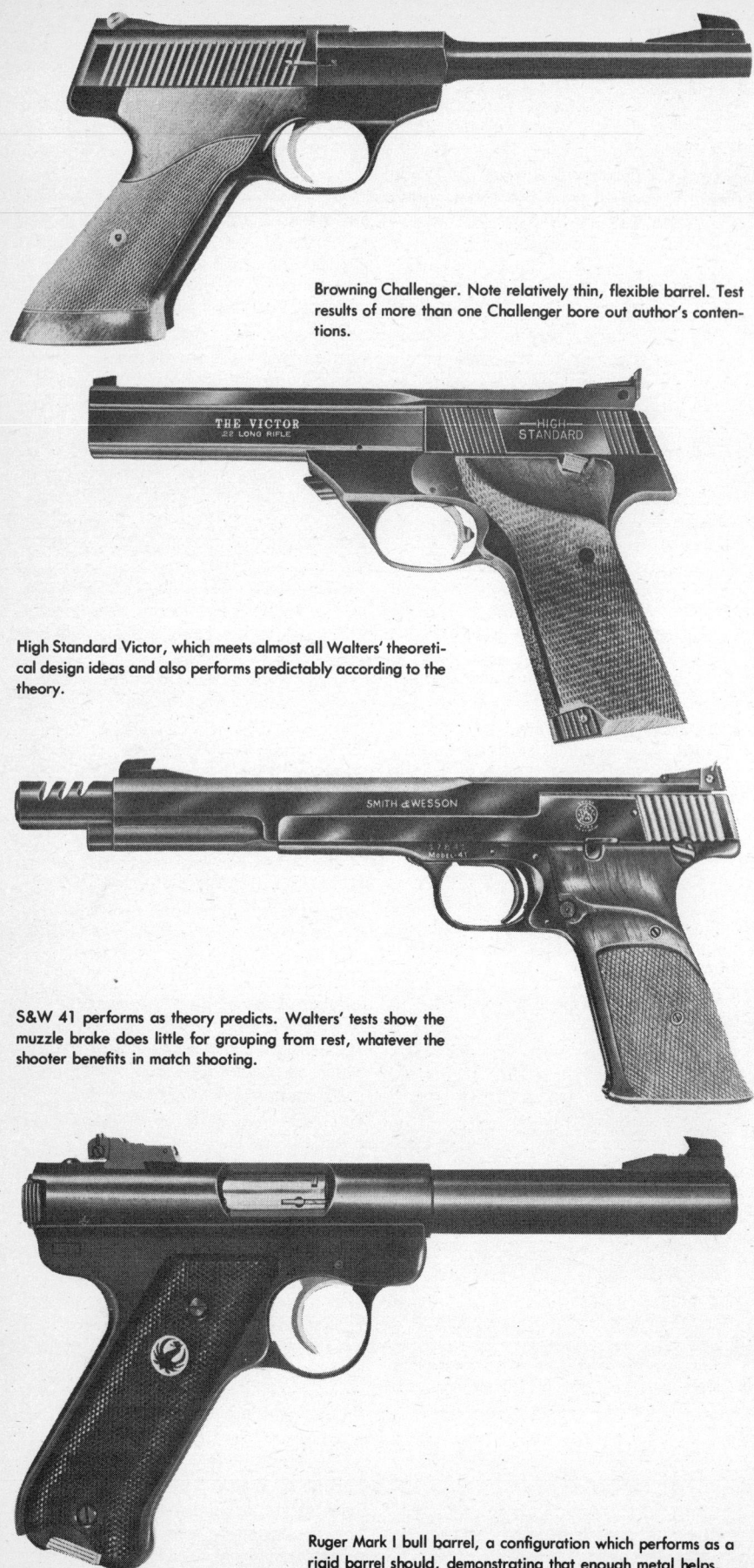

Browning Challenger. Note relatively thin, flexible barrel. Test results of more than one Challenger bore out author's contentions.

High Standard Victor, which meets almost all Walters' theoretical design ideas and also performs predictably according to the theory.

S&W 41 performs as theory predicts. Walters' tests show the muzzle brake does little for grouping from rest, whatever the shooter benefits in match shooting.

Ruger Mark I bull barrel, a configuration which performs as a rigid barrel should, demonstrating that enough metal helps.

ible barrel would improve the gun's inherent accuracy, not necessarily to that of the corresponding heavy barrel, but at least toward it. To the extent that the barrel was stabilized by the proper use of counterweights, the gun's performance would approach the corresponding (in length) rigid barrel's inherent accuracy level.

This discovery changed drastically all my experiments, causing not only a much greater examination of counterweights but adding several non-counterweighted guns to the list of guns studied.

Counterweighted High Standard Victors were located as well as High Standard Tournaments and two H-D Militaries. These older High Standards were chosen to see if a thick flexible barrel would essentially approximate a rigid or bull barrel. A quick comparison of the data shows that at least the Tournament came very close to doing just this. Indeed with just the addition of a counterweight, conversion to a rigid barrel performance was possible. I had hoped that both H-D's would essentially duplicate this effect but the one had just seen too much use. Their failure to live up to expectations was, I believe, brought on by years of hard use.

Every flexible barrel counterweight system which increases barrel rigidity also increases firearm accuracy. While the Hammerli Walther is the prime or first example, a Walther PP Sport and a High Standard Tournament also clearly showed this trend. That all these guns from different manufacturers would repeatedly and reproducibly convert between barrel types due to the increase in barrel rigidity thru the proper use of counterweights, seems undeniable proof of my barrel rigidity theory. Counterweighting systems, like the High Standard Citation's which don't increase rigidity, however, do little good. As Table III shows, for the experiments with the eight and ten-inch versions of this gun, both large accuracy decreases and improvements were obtained. Getting good results with such a system is thus just a matter of blind luck.

The Hammerli Walther tests showed another interesting aspect of counterweight usage. Unlike any other flexible barrel system tested, these could shift position during use due to gun recoil. Tests clearly proved that if the counterweights finally shifted due to extensive use to the point where the front and rear weights touched, the shooting characteristics, but not the inherent accuracy, of the weapon changed instantaneously.

The last interesting item about these weights was that rear counterweights which bolt directly to the gun and not to the barrel at all also increased gun accuracy. This improvement can be explained, I think, by simple mechanical dampening. Increasing the mass of the gun changes the way it vibrates during firing and in this case that change led to better accuracy.

When counterweights were applied to the High Standard Victor, accuracy increased very significantly, though the counterweights in question were the least massive of all tested, despite the fact that the gun was already performing as an excellent rigid barrelled pistol. The merit of this excellent system lies in its shape. By being both securely bolted to the gun and contoured to mate to the gun's barrel, this system provided the needed barrel rigidity increase more through shape than physical strength.

The Victor's counterweighting system is important for another reason. If a comparison is made of all the 5½" bull barrelled guns, there is no clear cut choice, at least as far as accuracy is concerned. All the guns tested shot, statistically speaking, equally well. Thus if the counterweight effect isn't to be considered, the best buy would be the Ruger Mk I since it clearly has the best price. When counterweights are considered, however, things change. Through the use of the Victor's counterweight the inherent accuracy of the weapon is significantly increased. Thus from an accuracy standpoint, at least, in either the 4½" or 5½" versions, the Victor simply can not be beat, regardless of cost.

One last point should be noted about the Victor. Of the guns studied, only the Victor seems to have all the attributes necessary to reach maximum theoretical accuracy. Its barrel, for instance, could be easily extended to almost any length and a longer barrel plus the excellent counterweights would allow it to pass the S&W or counterweighted Hammerli Walther as the most accurate handguns. Although 10" barrels would probably be unmanageable, 6½" or 7½" versions would, I think, make excellent additions to the line. The counterweights would have to be one-piece, contoured construction running the full length of the barrel, of course. Incidentally, the sight rib for this gun is just such a counterweight though we don't normally think of it as such.

In addition to counterweights, muzzle brakes were also examined. In only one case did these little devils do anything but decrease performance. They

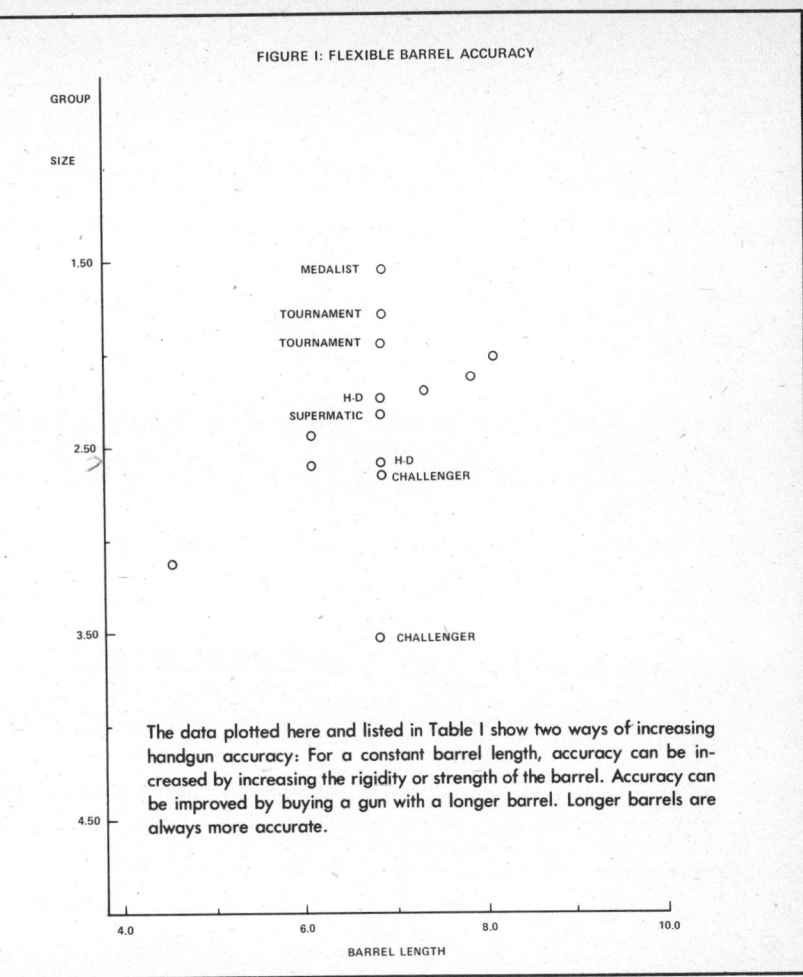

FIGURE I: FLEXIBLE BARREL ACCURACY

The data plotted here and listed in Table I show two ways of increasing handgun accuracy: For a constant barrel length, accuracy can be increased by increasing the rigidity or strength of the barrel. Accuracy can be improved by buying a gun with a longer barrel. Longer barrels are always more accurate.

Table 1
Flexible Barrel Handgun Accuracy*

	Barrel Length	Group† Size
Barrel Length Effect		
High Standard Citation	10.00	1.97 (7)
High Standard Citation	8.00	2.01 (5)
Hammerli Walther	7.75	2.12 (8)
High Standard Fluted	7.25	2.20 (5)
High Standard Supermatic	6.75	2.31 (2)
Colt Challenger	6.00	2.44 (4)
Colt Challenger	6.00	2.60 (4)
Browning Challenger	4.50	3.12 (4)
Barrel Rigidity Effect**		
Browning Medalist	6.75	1.54 (4)
High Standard Tournament††	6.75	1.77 (4)
High Standard Tournament	6.75	1.93 (3)
High Standard H-D Military	6.75	2.23 (6)
High Standard H-D Military	6.75	2.59 (4)
Browing Challenger	6.75	2.63 (5)
Browning Challenger	6.75	3.51 (3)

ALL DIMENSIONS IN INCHES

*Flexible barrels have slim circular cross-sections

**As the rigidity of a barrel increases, the accuracy improves. For flexible barrelled guns, two ways are available to improve performance: greater length or greater thickness.

†The numbers in parentheses indicate the number of 50-round 50-yard tests done with each pistol.

††Counterweights which increase barrel rigidity improve handgun accuracy. This particular pistol's excellent performance is due to the use of its excellent counterweights.

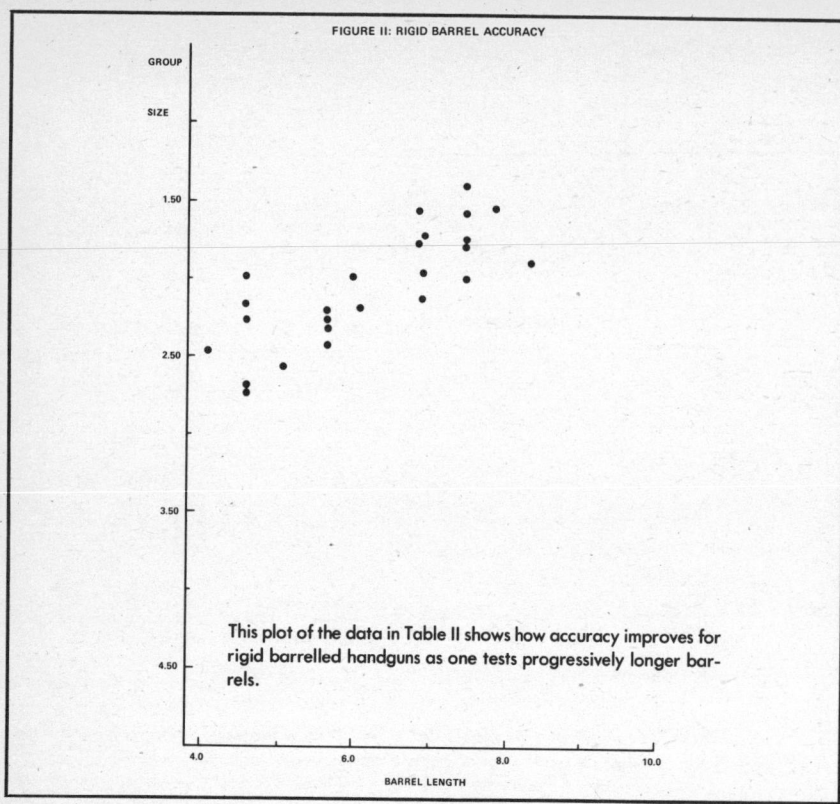

FIGURE II: RIGID BARREL ACCURACY

This plot of the data in Table II shows how accuracy improves for rigid barrelled handguns as one tests progressively longer barrels.

Table II
Rigid Barrel Handgun Accuracy*

	Barrel Length	Group† Size
Walther PP Sport**	8.250	1.87 (3)
Hammerli Walther**	7.750	1.53 (5)
Smith & Wesson††	7.375	1.38 (3)
	7.375	1.57 (4)
	7.375	1.74 (5)
	7.375	1.78 (4)
	7.375	1.99 (8)
Ruger Mk I	6.875	1.71 (3)
	6.875	1.96 (2)
	6.875	2.11 (3)
Browning Medalist	6.750	1.54 (4)
High Standard Tournament**	6.750	1.77 (4)
Colt Match Target Woodsman	6.000	2.19 (5)
Unique DES-69	5.900	1.98 (4)
High Standard Victor	5.500	2.20 (3)
Ruger Mk I	5.500	2.25 (4)
High Standard Supermatic	5.500	2.31 (5)
Smith & Wesson	5.500	2.42 (5)
Smith & Wesson	5.000	2.56 (3)
High Standard Victor**	4.500	1.98 (3)
Colt Match Target Woodsman	4.500	2.68 (17)
High Standard Victor	4.500	2.71 (4)
Walther GSP	4.500	2.17 (5)
	4.500	2.25 (4)
Ruger Standard Model	4.000	2.46 (3)

ALL DIMENSIONS IN INCHES

* Rigid barrelled handguns have barrels of non-circular cross-section or very heavy round barrels of sufficient strength to eliminate barrel flexibility. Note that no rectangular cross-sectioned barrel tested performed in a class with flexible barrelled guns.

** Counterweighted pistols.

† The numbers in parentheses indicate the number of 50-round 50-yard tests done with the various pistols.

†† Only the first, most accurate results shown were obtained by the use of counterweights. Since Smith's weights don't strengthen the entire barrel, they don't always improve performance.

also lead to another interesting problem—barrel obstructions.

Obviously few people would knowingly fire a gun with a barrel obstruction. Since, however, I managed to do this once during these tests with rather interesting results, it's worth discussing. During one of the testing series using a muzzle-braked 8" High Standard Citation, the group suddenly moved several inches straight up. This new, unexplained second impact point was every bit as consistent as the first and, as later calculations showed, every bit as accurate. As soon as a complete fifty round group had been fired at the new impact point, the gun and rest were examined minutely. The cause of the problem was finally found, though overlooked repeatedly.

As a one-time chemist, perhaps my first impression of the High Standard Citation's muzzle brake was how much it resembled a gas condensing chamber. Indeed, in the case in point, a small paper-thin amount of material had condensed on the face of the barrel in a mere 150 or so rounds. This finger-like growth had grown right into the path of the oncoming bullet. To see if this was indeed the cause of the trouble, the growth was removed and the muzzle brake resecured. All the remaining bullets hit the target at the first impact point. No other change whatsoever was made in the gun or the rest setup so it almost had to be due to this small growth. In addition to indicating how important it is to keep these devices clean and how fast dirt buildup can occur, this indicates how easily a bullet can be significantly deflected from its normal trajectory.

Deflections from normal trajectory can arise for other reasons. Temperature is one possibility:

"It is well known, from practical experience, that a shot from a cold gun usually falls short . . . (Also) Fairly consistent shifts in deflection after the initial round, have been observed in the case of some guns, and it is probable that such shifts occur for all guns, though they may often be small enough to escape notice."

This quote, from the discussion of cold gun errors in the 1940 edition of the Naval Academy textbook on exterior ballistics, so intrigued me that I had to see if I could detect it in standard velocity 22 ammunition, even though the original comments were concerning 16" 2600 f/s naval weapons at far greater ranges.

For these experiments, sighting shots were obviously out, and uncomfortable if not severe weather required. Thus, I set out on a cold

Christmas Eve to see what weather effects might be detectable on a 5½" High Standard Victor. Gun performance showed no change in accuracy but the groups moved slowly but progressively upward throughout the tests. To insure that this was not just a fluke, six more testing series were run between the day after Christmas and New Years using various configurations of the ten-inch High Standard Citation and a 5½" Ruger Mk I. Although these tests were eventually stopped because of the daily drop in temperature and increasing levels of snow cover, in each and every case, the noted cold gun effect was clearly present with *no* change in gun accuracy. The groups did not change, but they moved.

This last point is quite important. All guns had previously been tested in warm, summer weather so that their inherent accuracy had already been determined. When this testing series was performed, it not only was possible to look for horizontal or vertical group movement, the latter being typical of the Cold Gun Effect, but also to see if the accuracy characteristics of the firearm changed. The most interesting aspect to me as a pistol shooter is that this effect was most clearly noted on the gun with the most massive barrel, the High Standard Victor.

In retrospect, I think it very fortunate that my tests were performed in a sheltered area not subject to direct sunlight for while it has been proven to my satisfaction that a cold barrel loses no statistically detectable inherent accuracy, I don't know, and indeed don't believe, that an overheated barrel would be as accurate.

Another subject studied was that of revolver performance. The initial interest stemmed not from a desire to study these guns but rather from a need to get all possible duplication for the flexible style barrels discussed earlier. It was hoped that my 8⅜" K-22 could be useful in supplying at least a form of duplication for the longer barrelled High Standards. Since revolver accuracy could be a function of the particular chamber, each was fired one hundred times, two 50-yard 50-round groups, to pinpoint this problem should it be present. As Table IV indicates, no chamber effect was noted.

While not really interested in testing revolvers, since this new K-22 had done so poorly, I decided to test the two other S&W revolvers listed. This would allow for three comparisons to ensure that these guns were in no way similar to autoloaders accuracy wise. Additional duplication, like say test-

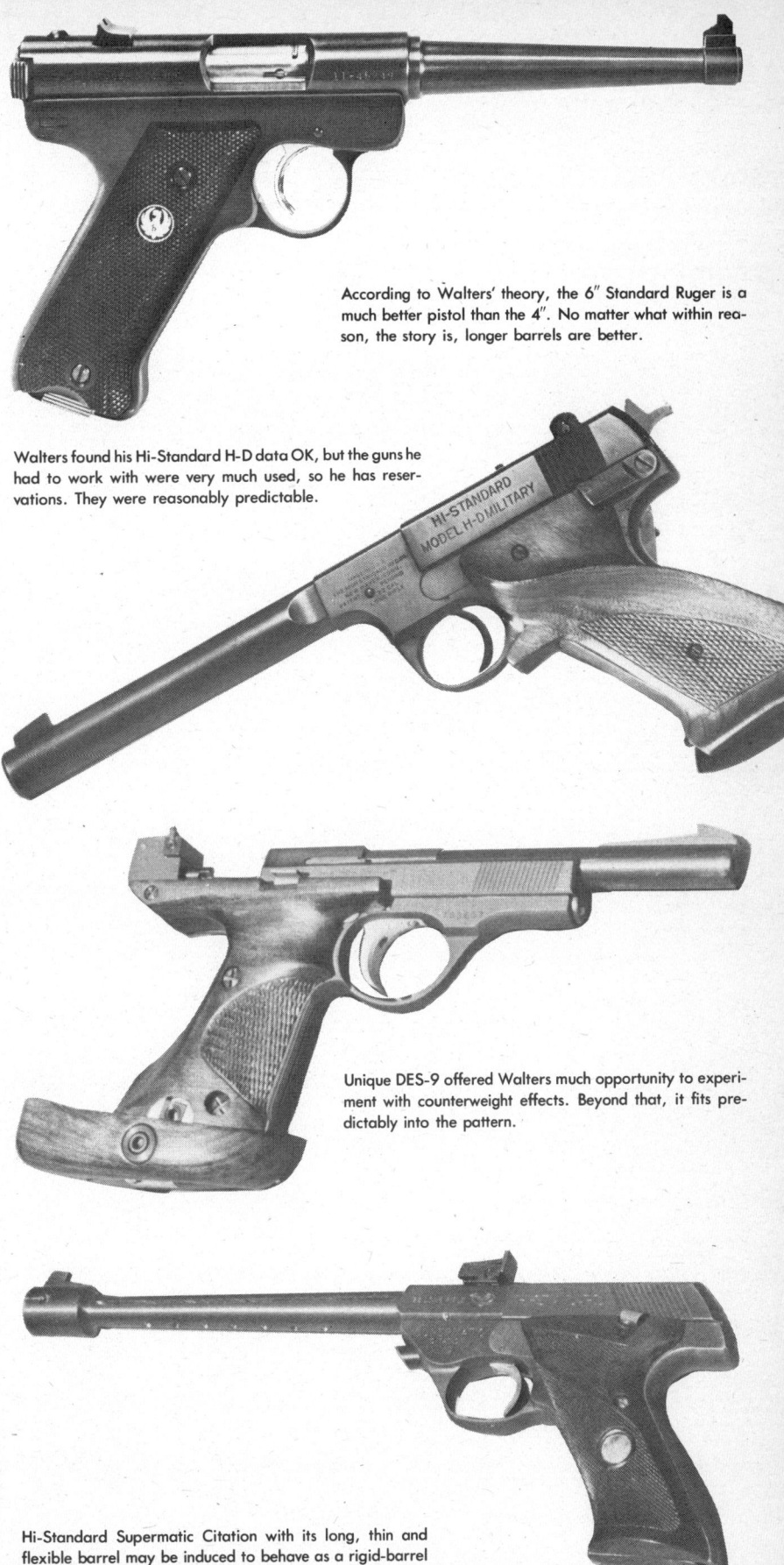

According to Walters' theory, the 6" Standard Ruger is a much better pistol than the 4". No matter what within reason, the story is, longer barrels are better.

Walters found his Hi-Standard H-D data OK, but the guns he had to work with were very much used, so he has reservations. They were reasonably predictable.

Unique DES-9 offered Walters much opportunity to experiment with counterweight effects. Beyond that, it fits predictably into the pattern.

Hi-Standard Supermatic Citation with its long, thin and flexible barrel may be induced to behave as a rigid-barrel arm with properly installed counterweights.

35TH EDITION, 1981 **163**

Table III
Counterweight & Muzzle Brake Effects

Firearm	Barrel Length	Gun	Group Size* CW	MB	Both
High Standard Citation	10.00	1.97 (7)	2.47 (5)	2.09 (5)	2.64 (5)
Walther PP Sport	8.25	2.41 (3)	1.87 (3)		
High Standard Citation	8.00	2.01 (5)	1.72 (4)	2.21 (4)	
Hammerli Walther	7.75	2.12 (8)	1.85 (5)**		
			1.53 (5)***		
			1.83 (6)†	2.00 (5)	1.92 (5)
Smith & Wesson	7.375	1.78 (4)	1.38 (3)		
High Standard Tournament	6.75	1.93 (3)	1.77 (4)		
Browning Medalist	6.75	1.54 (4)	1.65 (4)		
Unique DES-69	5.90	1.98 (4)	2.31 (2)††		
			1.50 (2)		
High Standard Victor	4.50	2.71 (4)	1.98 (3)†††		

* The numbers in parentheses indicate the number of 50-round 50-yard testing series that were done with the pistols. Test done using counterweights are shown in the CW column while results obtained with muzzle brakes are listed under the MB heading. The column marked "Both" contains data obtained when using both counterweights and muzzle brakes.

** Full set of counterweights.

*** Front counterweights only.

† Rear counterweights only.

†† Note the erratic performance. Although the same gun and weights were used, the performance changed from 2.31" to 1.50" just by removing and reattaching the weights. It was, in fact, never possible to know how the gun would perform when the weights were attached except by testing.

††† Note how dramatically even a rigid barrelled pistol's performance can be improved when good counterweights are used. The weights on the Victor were the best design studied.

ALL DIMENSIONS IN INCHES

Table V
Ammunition Effect

Firearm	Ammunition Lot Number	Barrel Length	Group Size
High Standard Citation	W29R1D	10.0	1.79 (3)
	W26T2A	10.0	2.40 (9)
			2.32 (5)*
			2.87 (5)**
			2.29 (3)***
	Y29R1A	10.0	1.97 (7)
			2.47 (5)*
			2.09 (5)**
			2.64 (5)***
High Standard Citation	W26T2A	8.0	2.45 (4)
	Y29R1A	8.0	2.01 (5)
Smith & Wesson	W29R1D	7.375	1.48 (5)
			2.09 (1)*
			1.71 (1)**
	Y29R1A	7.375	1.78 (4)
			1.38 (3)*
Smith & Wesson	W29R1D	7.375	1.63 (8)
			1.79 (4)*
			2.02 (4)**
	Y29R1A	7.375	1.99 (8)
Smith & Wesson	W29R1D	7.375	1.81 (4)
	W26T2A	7.375	2.08 (5)
	Y29R1A	7.375	1.74 (5)
Smith & Wesson	W29R1D	7.375	1.65 (3)
	W26T2A	7.375	2.11 (3)
	Y29R1A	7.375	1.57 (4)
High Standard Fluted Miltary	W29R1D	7.25	2.20 (5)
	W26T2A	7.25	2.65 (3)
High Standard Victor	W29R1D	5.50	2.20 (5)
	Y29R1A	5.50	2.20 (3)
Ruger Mk I	W29R1D	5.50	2.05 (8)
	Y29R1A	5.50	2.25 (4)
High Standard Supermatic	W26T2A	5.50	2.80 (4)
	Y29R1A	5.50	2.31 (5)
Colt Match Target Woodsman	W26T2A	4.50	3.63 (5)
	Y29R1A	4.50	2.68 (17)

* Counterweights used.

** Muzzle brakes used.

*** Both counterweights and muzzle brakes used.

ALL DIMENSIONS IN INCHES

---

ing two 6" K-22s wasn't done since a single revolver test required three times the ammunition necessary for a single autoloader. Then too, few still use revolvers for serious target work.

The results seem straightforward. First, revolver chamber effects, like those noted for the six-inch K-22 do occur, but clearly not in every case. This means that over-all gun performance could be different, though perhaps only slightly, from the accuracy of a given chamber. Second, revolvers, at least these 22-caliber revolvers, are significantly less accurate than autoloaders. Figure III shows the revolver results. Here, unlike the first two graphs, you'll notice that a line has been added to indicate the dependence of group size on barrel length. Done using a curve fitting technique called linear regression, this type of line can be of considerable value.

If the results for the flexible and rigid barrelled guns are similarly analyzed, one gets the accuracy to barrel length dependence shown in Figure IV. Using this graph it becomes possible to estimate with reasonable precision the accuracy of guns other than those tested. For instance, to determine the accuracy of an 8" revolver, one would draw a line up from the 8 on the bottom of the figure until it hit the revolver accuracy line. Then by drawing a line from this intersection to the group size axis, we see that such a revolver should shoot 2.58 inch groups. Similarly a 8" rigid barrelled automatic would yield 1.58 while a flexible barrelled auto would yield 2.15.

Another factor which can affect revolver or autoloader performance has to be ammunition. Although this effect was deliberately eliminated from these tests by using one large ammo lot so that other factors like barrel length and rigidity could be studied, ammunition experiments were also performed.

Three lots of Remington ammunition were used in the first ammunition series whose results are presented in Table V. The first two, W29R1D and W26T2A, were both standard velocity 6122 Kleanbore. The third, Y29R1A, was standard velocity 6100 Target. Extensive cross-checking was done on the results obtained from these three. While I fully expected some minor differences, the experiments clearly showed that W26T2A was far worse and statistically poorer than the other two. Fortunately Y29R1A was the one used throughout the main body of this work.

One last facet of the ammunition effect should be considered. Hebard's

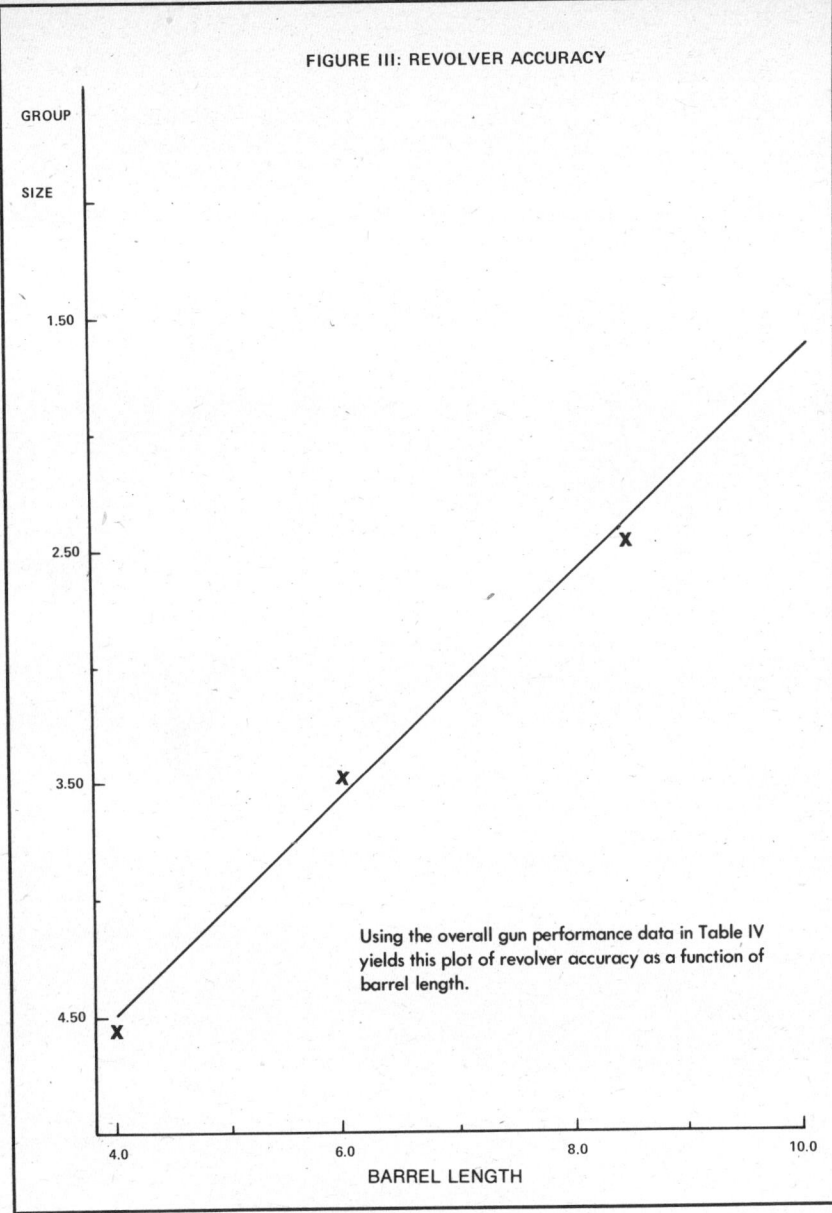

FIGURE III: REVOLVER ACCURACY

Using the overall gun performance data in Table IV yields this plot of revolver accuracy as a function of barrel length.

Table IV
Revolver Accuracy

Arbitrary Chamber #	Kit Gun 4 inch	S&W K-22 6 inch	S&W K-22 8⅜ inch
1	4.21	2.51*	2.44
2	4.73	3.49	2.49
3	4.78	3.77	2.52
4	4.99	3.69	2.43
5	4.47	3.82	2.38
6	4.13	3.54	2.30
Over-all Gun Performance	4.55	3.47	2.43

*This was the only documented case where the performance of one chamber differed from the others. Odd that it indicated an unusually accurate chamber since normally we assume that if a chamber is unique that it is uniquely bad.

ALL DIMENSIONS IN INCHES

work showed a better level of accuracy than those I've reported. Hebard, however, used "match ammo" which for the volume of shooting I did was just too expensive. If by match ammo, however, he meant something like Remington Match Long Rifle cartridges or Western Super-Match III, then, of course, an additional improvement might be gained. To try and gauge this effect, one S&W long barrelled automatic was fired with 250 rounds of not only Y29R1A but also identical amounts of two lots of Western Super-Match. The results, while only perhaps suggestive, showed the group size of Y29R1A to be 1.57″ while the other lots yielded values of 1.24″ and 1.35″. Clearly accuracy can improve with the use of such ammunition.

To summarize, several key features of this study are significant. First, the most important factor in a target 22 is barrel length. Clearly length can be made so long as to be foolish, but within reason the longer the barrel the better the gun will shoot regardless of barrel style. I see absolutely no reason, for instance, to purchase a 22 target gun with a barrel under 5½″ and would prefer one in the 7″ to 8″ range.

Second, there are clearly two styles of barrels, flexible and rigid. Though not absolutely determinable on sight, no rectangular cross-sectioned barrel was ever found that performed as if it was a flexible barrel. The advantage of the rigid barrels is a significant increase in gun accuracy. Tables I and II delineate the classification as to type of all the barrels tested. I see no reason for purchasing a flexible barrelled target pistol unless it's appropriately counterweighted, as they simply don't provide the best, most accurate barrel design.

Third, it is possible to alter the performance of a gun in either direction, by using counterweights. Any system that increases barrel rigidity also improves accuracy. This, of course, means that you could buy an old High Standard Citation, design a contoured counterweight, and then have an excellent gun for a modest investment.

Fourth, little if any good is obtained by the use of muzzle brakes. Though studied extensively, none of the types that can be purchased today seem to increase gun accuracy reliably.

Finally, ammunition can significantly affect gun performance. I believe that the results suggest that barrel length and type are more important than the ammunition effect but since exceptionally poor lots are known to occur, this effect should not be overlooked by shooters.

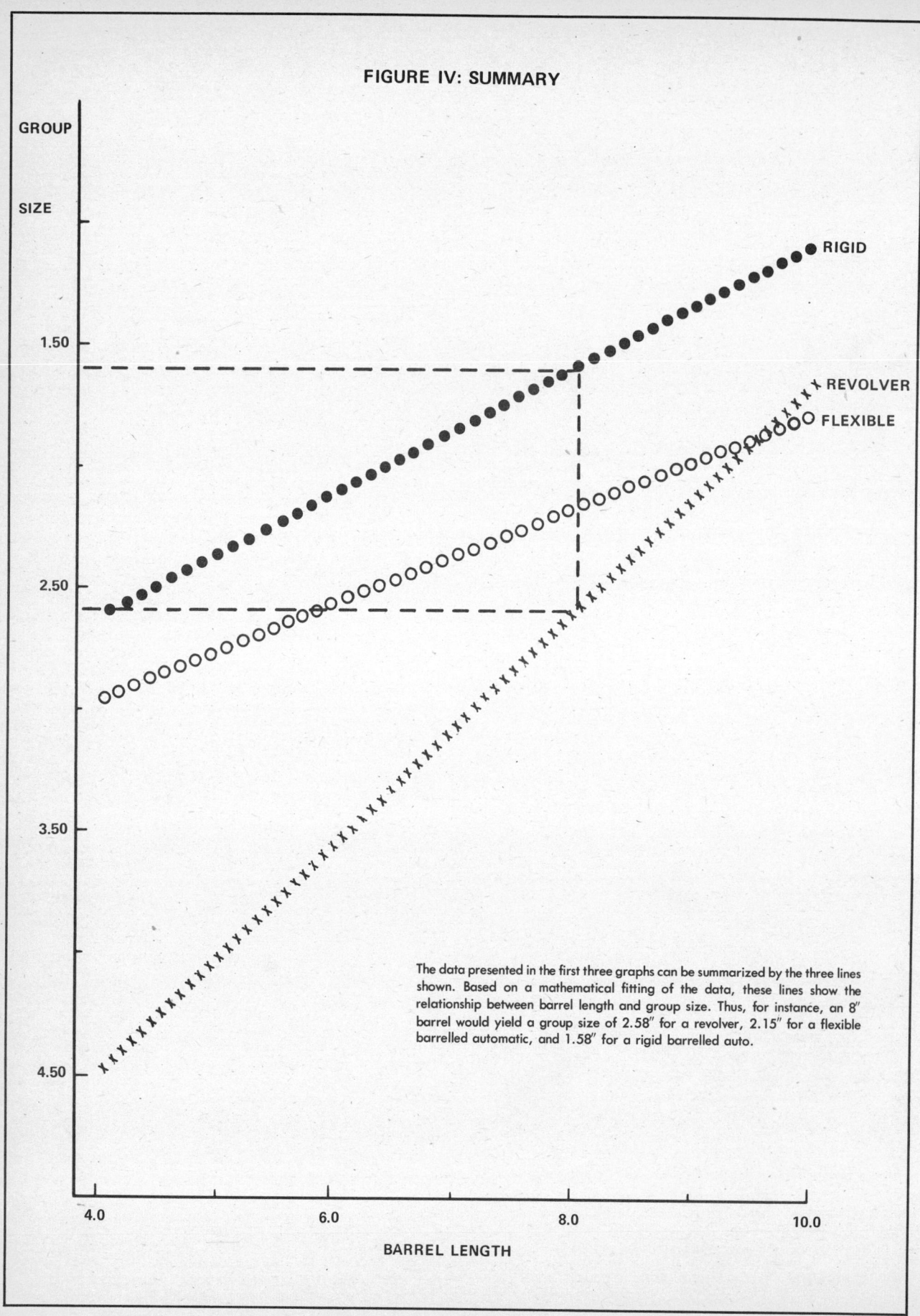

REMINGTON'S XP-100 SILHOUETTE PISTOL

YOU HAVE TO MAKE THE CASES, BUT IT'S WORTH IT

by HAL SWIGGETT

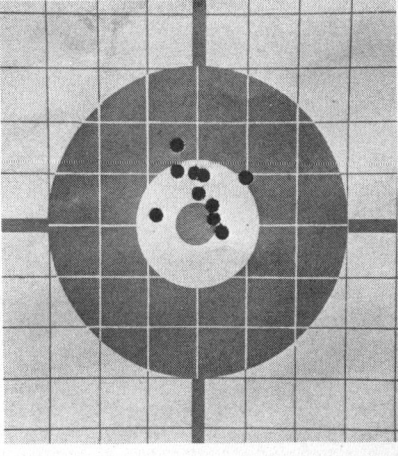

Swiggett's best group. Ten shots. One hundred yards. One and fifteen-sixteenths inches. With 139-grain Hornady bullets over 27.5 grains of H-322 set off with Remington Bench Rest No. 7½ primers.

(Below) The prototype Remington "XP-100" Silhouette 7mm Bench Rest bolt action single shot pistol.

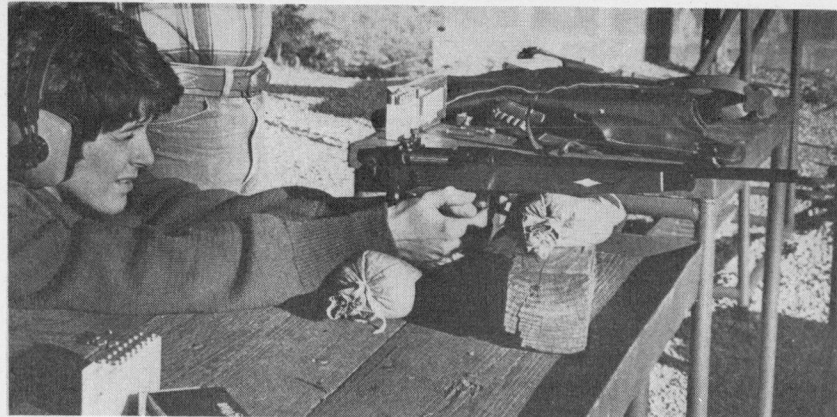
Debbie Mitchell goes after, and gets, a turkey silhouette at 375 yards on the YO Ranch range.

MY BEST GROUP was 1¹⁵⁄₁₆-inches for ten shots at 100 yards. I'm confident a better shooter can keep this to an inch and maybe even a half or three-quarters. The gun shoots good.

I have been field testing the new Remington "XP-100" Silhouette 7mm Bench Rest bolt action single shot pistol. These tests were conducted with the prototype that was shown to writers and editors at Remington's annual seminar. There will be one minor difference. This prototype had only a 14-inch barrel. Production XP-100 Silhouette 7mm BR guns will wear one measuring 15-inches to take full advantage of the rules.

There is nothing new about the "XP-100." It was introduced in 1963 with a 10½-inch barrel as a single shot bolt action chambered for the 221 Fire Ball. Fitted with a Du Pont "Zytel" nylon stock it was a bit far out in appearance though super accurate. It never made any great impression on the shooting fraternity except that enough guns were sold to keep it in their catalog.

Then came silhouette shooting. The second international match, in 1976, was won by Jose Porras with an XP-100 converted to a shortened 308 Winchester wildcat cartridge. Since then, XP-100's have been converted into everything from hotter 22's through full-blown 30's.

Remington officials decided to hop on the silhouette bandwagon. Since they were already marketing a specially annealed 308 Bench Rest case drilled to take small rifle primers and had in the past two or three years developed both a 22 and 6mm BR cartridge made from that brass the only step necessary was to develop a 7mm round and chamber for it. And add the longer barrel.

So the XP-100 Silhouette 7mm BR was born.

That basic brass has to be trimmed to 1.520-inches and neck reamed. It's a bit of a chore but a careful workman could make 100 cases in a long evening. I made 80 at one sitting. RCBS makes the forming and loading dies.

The gun I tested, as mentioned, was used at the seminar so it was finely tuned. The trigger broke beautifully at 32-ounces. It was fitted with Williams sights. Production guns will be delivered minus sights but with a ramp in front ready for whatever sight the shooter desires. The receiver is drilled and tapped for most any sight that might be wanted, from iron to glass.

The brass and Bench Rest No. 7½ primers arrived early, as did the dies from RCBS. I had 20 cases made before the gun was ever in hand. This was precautionary. I wanted to be sure they fit before making more. Soon as the gun arrived it was determined the brass fit perfectly so they were loaded that evening.

Remington's prescribed loads were 27.5 grains of H-322 under Sierra's 140-grain bullet at 2140 fps and 28.5 grains of the same powder under Sierra's 120-grain at 2200 fps. I didn't have any Sierra bullets so used Hornady's 139-grain. Same deal for the 120-grain load.

This was on Wednesday evening, after church. I was scheduled for a South Texas deer hunt the next day so the XP-100 went along. I tried the 139-grain Hornadys on a rock at about 75 yards. Three shots printed a nice group but too far right. Moving the sight, two more shots were fired. Another slight adjustment and then three more shots to verify the setting. We went hunting.

Never did get a shot at a deer but just before lunch a small herd of javelina was spotted. At 60 yards, a bullet ripped through both shoulders with no, or at least little, expansion and dropped the animal in his tracks. That little pig was maybe the first wild animal killed with the 7mm BR.

Eighty more cases were made and we did a lot of shooting. Jimmy and Debbie Mitchell, both of silhouette handgunning fame, were on the YO Ranch hunting. I got them involved. The YO's silhouette range doesn't conform to anything but YO standards. It features regulation chicken targets at 250 yards, turkey at 375 yards and 18-inch squares at 500 yards. All are across a canyon from the shooting point.

Between us we rather easily knocked off chickens and even the turkey targets, from sandbags, but we didn't do any real damage to those 18-inch squares. We did not change the sight setting but used Kentucky windage all the way.

All this was before the gun was ever seriously put on paper. The paper proved very revealing. I learned right away the gun would shoot a lot better than I could.

My eyes aren't the best—I've been totally blind in both—but each was repaired by a fine Christian opthalmologist, Dr. Tom Hogan of San Antonio. The left was first to go and wears a permanent soft contact for 20-20 vision most of the time. Any contact lens wearer knows what I'm talking about. The right one came late enough that it was repaired with an implant. It performs at 20-15 and is my shooting eye. Its only handicap is that it does not have the elasticity of a young eye in going from near to far so trifocals are in order. Each eye needs a bit of astigmatism correction.

At 50 yards I use the trifocal (intermediate) segment which gives me a clean rear sight and a distinguishable target. Groups of ½-inch were common for five shots and a few were even

Swiggett with javelina killed at 60 yards with Hornady's 139-grain bullet over 27.5 grains H-322.

Hornady's Load Data

Powder			Velocity			
120 gr. H.P.	2000	2100	2200	2250	2300	2350
H-322	24.7	25.9	27.0	27.6	28.2	—
IMR 3031	26.2	27.3	28.4	28.9	29.5	30.0
IMR 4895	27.6	28.9	30.3	30.9	31.6	—
Win. 748	—	29.2	30.6	31.2	31.9	32.6
BL-C2	29.8	31.2	32.6	33.2	33.9	—
139 gr. S.P.	1900	2000	2050	2100	2150	2200
H-322	24.0	25.2	25.8	26.4	26.9	—
IMR 3031	25.4	26.5	27.0	27.6	28.1	—
IMR 4895	26.8	28.0	28.7	29.3	29.9	—
Win. 748	27.2	28.4	29.0	29.6	30.2	30.8
BL-C2	28.6	30.0	30.7	31.4	—	—
154 gr. S.P.	1800	1900	1950	2000	2050	2100
H-322	23.1	23.9	—	—	—	—
IMR 3031	23.8	25.0	25.5	26.1	26.7	—
IMR 4895	25.5	26.9	27.6	28.2	—	—
Win. 748	—	26.9	27.6	28.3	29.0	29.7
BL-C2	27.7	28.9	29.5	30.0	30.6	—
162 gr. BTHP	1700	1800	1900	1950	2000	2050
H-322	21.6	22.7	23.9	24.5	—	—
IMR 3031	22.7	23.7	24.8	25.4	25.9	—
IMR 4895	23.7	25.2	26.6	27.3	28.0	—
Win. 748	—	25.6	26.9	27.6	28.2	28.9
BL-C2	—	26.9	28.3	29.1	29.8	30.6

tighter. Doubling the distance forces me to go to that upper portion of the glasses which means the target is clear but the rear sight only somewhat so. Groups were more than doubled because of this eye situation but one, and admittedly it's my best, fell in pretty good.

Ten shots nicely spaced in 1$^{15}/_{16}$-inches. Not bad, but not good for an expert. Close enough though to convince me the gun and load will produce in the hands of that expert. For me, the 120-grain loads never printed quite so tight as the heavier bullet.

The only fault I found was that the chamber wasn't throated far enough out in my opinion. I had to seat 139-grain bullets deeper than I thought necessary.

However, what I thought a short throat causing my chambering problems turned out to be true in part only. My ream die was .002" over-size. In RCBS' hurry to get a set of dies to me this one slipped out. Hornady technicians who got gun and dies, simply turned the cases down to correct dimensions in a lathe to complete their testing. Ron Rieber did confirm part of my thinking, however. They did find that the heavier bullets had to be seated so deeply as to decidedly take up powder space. Though, I hasten to add, Ron didn't consider that fact of any consequence.

Hornady used five powders and four bullet weights—all set off with Remington #7½ BR primers—and the loads that will appear in their next manual are shown here.

To quote Rieber's letter, "Winchester 748 proved to be the best for accuracy and velocity." Since his letter didn't put any figure on the accuracy I called him and learned that 120-grain h.p.'s were consistent at groups of less than one-inch. The heavier bullets, 139-grain and up, printed groups close to one-inch, sometimes better, but as bullet weight went up group size also widened.

Ron's letter giving me this loading information closed with, "By the way, I liked the combination so much I ordered one."

The XP-100 Silhouette 7mm BR will readily be accepted, of that I'm sure, but it would be even more so if Remington could see their way clear to providing ready-made brass. Forming dies are expensive, the work a bit demanding and definitely time consuming.

The XP-100 Silhouette 7mm BR is a fine cartridge/gun combination. One I think handgun hunters will like at least as much as silhouette shooters. •

THE FIRST SHORT MAGNUM:

THE 425 WESTLEY RICHARDS MAGNUM

by JACK LOTT

In 1908, the virtues of a standard action in a big sporter were already recognized.

THE FIRST DECADE of the 20th Century was in many ways a continuation of the Victorian era (which in effect continued to WW I's beginning in 1914) and the flowering of its creative genius. Nowhere was this truer than in the development of military and sporting arms and ammunition, which became a design revolution ignited by the earlier advent of smokeless powder. By 1900, the armies of all modern powers used the new powder in recently developed repeaters, mostly Mausers, shooting small caliber high-velocity bottle-necked cartridges using cupro-nickel or cupro-nickel plated steel jacketed bullets.

The velocities of these first small bore military rifle cartridges hovered around a then-high plateau (2,000 to 2,200 fps) until some years later when technical developments permitted another pace-setting increase within those pressure limits of around 48,000 psi. Barely 15 years after introduction, those 2,000 to 2,200 fps velocities became pedestrian with Imperial Germany's introduction in 1905 of the "S" load for the 8x57 JS round of their Gewehr 98. This was a "spitzer" bullet of 153 grains at a then ultra-high velocity of over 2,800.

One year later the United States adopted the 1906 cartridge for its 1903 Springfield modified Mauser, which produced 2,700 fps with a 150-grain spitzer. In Britain, Sir Charles Ross with his Canadian-produced straight-pull action and his 280 Ross with its 140-grain copper-capped spitzer at over 2,900 fps startled shooters with hitherto unknown velocities in a sporting rifle.

Tradition is supposed to die hard in Britain, but veterans of the Boer War with their sobering experience at the hands of Boers and their accurate 7x57 Mausers embraced the Mauser action in its Model 98 guise. Ivory hunters like "Karamoja" Bell and Dennis D. Lyell preferred military calibers such as the 7x57 and 8mm Mausers and the 303 Lee-Enfield, but with the older style heavy, slower round-nose parallel-sided "solids." These, they discovered, would penetrate an elephant's skull for the brain shot at any angle when employed with superior skill of aim and anatomical expertise, to say nothing of more open country.

Others less skilled, in trying to use the same armament in thick bush, failed when the pachyderms charged and the pencil-like bullets failed to produce a stopping effect. Though such a mixed result provoked a furious debate between small and large bore ad-

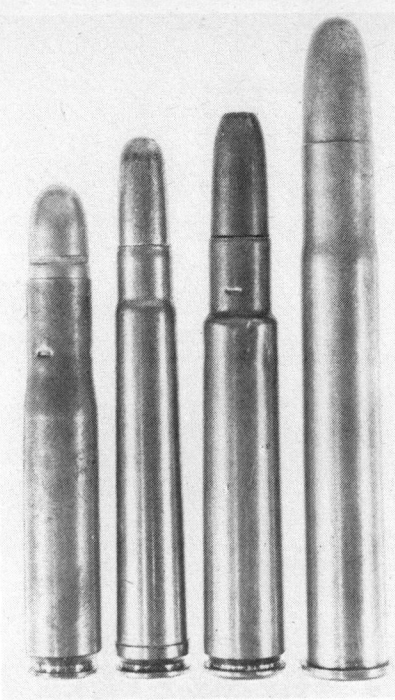

The 425 at left offers fair ballistic comparison to the 375 H&H Magnum, the 416 Rigby and (at right) the 475 No. 2 (Jeffery), and the 425 fits the standard length Mauser. FACING PAGE: Selous on campaign during World War I; the rifle probably a 275 H&H Magnum.

vocates that rages unabated today, the demand for the small bores continued, somewhat lessened for heavy game, while spurring the introduction of large-medium bore Mausers. What was wanted were cartridges more compact than the big cordite nitro-expresses but with essentially their energy minus the inefficient rimmed blackpowder cases unsuited to the Mauser.

The prestigious old Birmingham firm of Westley Richards headed by its Managing Director, Leslie Taylor, never slow to innovate, introduced its 425 Westley Richards Magnum around 1908. Around the same time Taylor introduced his 318 "Accelerated Express," named after an express train running from London up-country. Taylor obtained a sort of "immortality" for having also introduced the Westley Richards capped bullets, including one named the "L.T." pattern, a semi-pointed capped bullet for rapid expansion on lighter game. The round-nose form was for use on heavier thin-skinned dangerous and non-dangerous game such as lions, tigers and large antelope.

The 425 was soon followed by Rigby's famous 416 which achieved the same ballistics with a smaller diameter bullet (.416″) and a much longer case requiring the long and ex-

pensive Magnum Mauser action. W.J. Jeffery's 404 (10.75x73) was slightly shorter than the 416 but the basic case was that of the 425, slightly longer, and without the 425's rebated rim. Since the 425 used a smaller case than either the 404 or the 416, its pressure was higher, but held to 18½ Long Tons by the larger bore (.435″) in combination with that rule of internal ballistics that says "the larger the case, the more powder it takes to obtain a given velocity for an equal bullet in a smaller case." This is the same principle that requires more powder in a 300 magnum to push an equal bullet the same velocity as in a 30-06. The .435″ diameter bullet of the 425 also gave more base area for powder gasses to push on while reducing sectional density insignificantly under that of the 416 or 404. It also had more frontal striking area which gave a slightly greater "knockdown" on frontal elephant head shots with solids, according to John Taylor's "Knockdown" formula.

Like most shooters knowing of the 425's rebated (reduced diameter) rim, I originally assumed this was done to avoid the cost and effort of machining the bolt face to accept a larger rim. With a bit of time and thought I concluded that so facile a reason was hardly logical. In fact, the rebated rim permitted use of Mauser charger clips, exactly the same as those made for the Gewehr 98 except longer to hold five of the fatter 425s. It also combined a larger diameter case body than that of the 8x57 with an 8x57 sized rim for reduced base area to thrust against the lugs. Since pressure is in pounds per square inch, the pressure against the bolt face is substantially less with the 8x57-sized rebated rim than it would be with a full diameter rim equal to that of the 404. In those pre-WW I days there was also concern about the added rearward thrust cracking receivers or shearing off bolt lugs. Action body cracking with early nitro double rifles led to the reinforcement of action bodies at the angle of the standing breech, such as Holland's famous contoured bulges on either side of their sidelock actions.

Of course, money was saved by not having to machine open those standard bolt faces and utilization of the existing receiver bridge clip lips. It was also cheaper to use the standard length Mauser action than the Magnum Mauser action despite having to produce a special hinged five-shot magazine for the short but fat 425.

There were difficulties with the rebated rim because the bolt sometimes failed to catch the rim. The rebate set lower in the magazine than a full-sized rim. The bolt would tend to cam over the cartridge if the underside of the receiver rails were not properly relieved to permit a higher rise of the 425 case and offer a normal amount of rim engagement. This work was done by careful hand grinding and fitting by individual smiths, and the quality varied. The perfunctory shop testing of feed with dummy rounds fed deliberately, usually with rifle in the padded jaws of a vise, could easily conceal a field disaster with the same rifle when the action was worked with the slam-bang urgency of a professional hunter in a running, jumping thornbush bash with a Cape buffalo! However, such problems were uncommon in the earlier years of careful hand production of the 425 or it never would have attained its outstanding reputation.

This was all before WW I took its toll of an entire generation of craftsmen and apprentices in the mud of Passchendael and Ypres, a toll that would not be made up until the advent of the Great Depression. Despite talk about the "quality" of pre-war British guns, that truth did not apply to the immediate post WW I production during the great dearth of craftsmanship from the war's attrition.

Aside from problems of feed with individual rifles, the only other problem or criticism was the presence of a 28-inch barrel to attain full velocity. Given the Mauser's four-inch longer overall length compared to a double rifle of the same length barrel, the 425 appeared at a distance as one of those 32-inch barreled bolt action "Long Tom" goose shotguns so dear to Iowa farm boys. However, despite the current unpopularity of such long-barreled rifles, many then enjoyed their steadiness in offhand shooting and advantage in taming muzzle jump. In addition, most African hunting was done in the open, either on the plains or in semi-open bushveld where a few inches extra length meant nothing. Of course, if the 28-inches bothered, it was easy for a gunsmith in Nairobi, Salisbury or Johannesburg to shorten it, and it could be made to order at 24 inches in the first place. Like the 416 Rigby, the 425 Westley Richards Magnum was never a standard cartridge, open to the trade, as Holland's 375 Magnum or Jeffery's 404 became.

In 1912, the great English hunter Frederick Courtenay Selous put the 425 through extensive field tests in British East Africa. Selous also took along a Holland & Holland 275 Belted Magnum, the first small-bore belted magnum and a near look-alike of today's 7mm Remington Magnum. That was also a Mauser and Selous warmed quickly to the new cartridges and their Mauser-actioned rifles. Between 1896 and 1915 when he went to war, Selous tested over a dozen new rifles and cartridges in the game fields of East Africa, Asia Minor, Europe and North America. He had become the leading British big game rifle expert of the day and wrote up his results in the *Field* and other publications. No hunting and firearms authority would achieve Selous' breadth of experience, from 4-bore muzzle-loaders to belted magnums, the age of the ox wagon to that of the tank and pursuit plane. Selous' battery of a 425 Westley Richards Magnum and a 275 H&H Magnum would still be a fine choice for Africa today, so little has the basic rifle and ammo changed in these 68 years since 1912!

According to Selous' biographer and friend, the artist-naturalist, J.G. Millais, Selous was ready to leave for Africa in 1912 and had called a cab from his Regent's Park home. It was his custom to test the sights of a rifle before departing from Britain, where any additional work could be done beforehand. One hour before his departure to the railway station en route to the port, the 425 arrived with its cartridges. Asking the maid to see that his coat, hat and kit was ready by the door, Selous went to his second story bedroom and opened the window. He made a hasty rest on the sill and selecting a chimney some 100 yards off, fired five shots in quick succession at a particular pattern of brick. Examining the tight group with his Zeiss glasses, Selous carefully cleaned his 425 with hot water and Rangoon oil, put rifle and glasses in their cases and went below to enter the waiting cab. Outside were a frightened group of neighbors and a bewildered London Bobby. When asked if he had heard the shots, Selous replied calmly, "Yes, they seemed to have come from a nearby room," then gravely entered the cab.

Selous was impressed with the stopping power of the 425 on Cape buffalo, which, not elephant or rhino, is the real test of a heavy game rifle. Accompanied by two Somali gun bearers, Selous wounded a bull and followed with his gun bearers into thick bush, finding the bull dead from a heart shot. A second bull was shot and wounded, running off into medium bush. They caught a glimpse of it as it ran off and crossed a dry watercourse

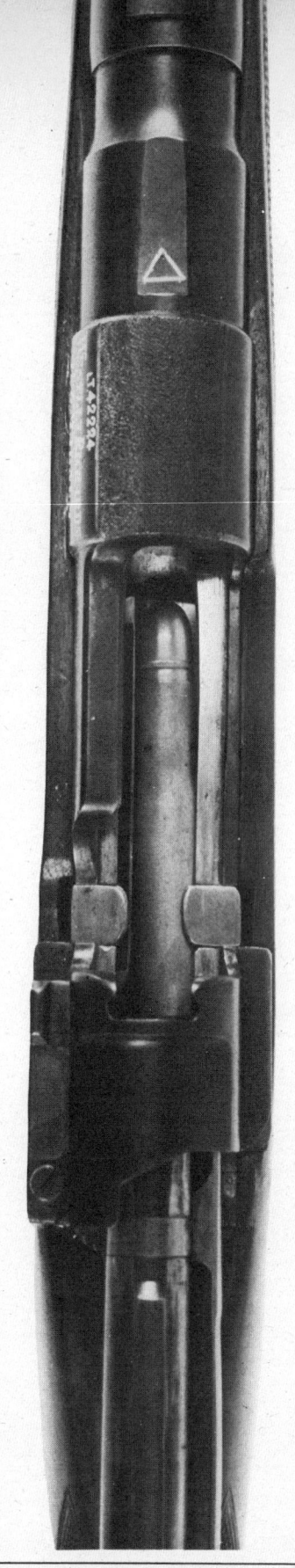

This pre-war best quality 425 shows the cartridge clips added to hold high-rising rounds in place. Triangle on barrel flat would face to rear were this a takedown rifle.

172 THE GUN DIGEST

with steep banks. Selous carried his 425 and the gunbearer the 275 Magnum. The gunbearer made a lot of noise with his hobnailed boots as he glissaded down the rocky sides of the donga and scrambled up its other side. Selous, 425 at the ready, climbed out of the donga just as the unmmistakable angry grunts of a charging buffalo were heard.

He wrote of it:

"Look out! I shouted, and took one step sideways, and in another instant the buffalo was on us. As I fired, the muzzle of my rifle was almost touching it, and my bullet caught it in the neck, fortunately damaging one of the vertebrae and causing it to drop on its knees as if struck by lightning. I put a second shot into it as it slid past me, breaking its back before it could do more damage.

"The Somali never fired the rifle he held in his hands and never moved, and at the same moment that my bullet struck it, the buffalo, as it fell on its knees, hit him with either one of its horns or its outstretched nose. I am inclined to think the latter, as the man fell beneath it and was carried down the slope and under its throat and in front of its knees.

"Whichever part of the buffalo's head it was which struck my man, the blow fell full on the strong leather case containing my Zeiss glasses, which was hanging at his side. These glasses were broken in two and squeezed out of the case, and my Somali had four ribs broken. We had to send him to the hospital at Meru where I am glad to say he made a very quick recovery from his injuries. He now undoubtedly knows more about the nature of a wounded buffalo than he used to." *(British Sports and Sportsmen,* London, 1914)

The late John "Pondoro" Taylor, famous ivory poacher and author of *African Rifles and Cartridges,* its English predecessor, *Big Game and Big Game Rifles* and others, became an admirer of the 425 but disliked its usual 28-inch barrels. Taylor of course, preferred double rifles and therefore wanted a 425 in that guise, which Westley Richards produced in limited quantities, using their patent rimless extractors. I have examined a few of these 425 doubles and have never heard anything negative about them as I have about individual 425 Mausers, but there is no point in such a rimless double when so many good rimmed chamberings were available with their more positive extraction and larger bullet weights and diameters.

Taylor held a common misconception about 425 Mausers, saying "five-shot magazines were customary, and it was found that the springs had a habit of weakening and were unable to press up the last shell sufficiently for the bolt to get hold of." This is Taylor's interpretation of the problem of the rebated rim with its lower position in the magazine relative to the bolt face, sometimes causing the bolt to cam over the rim, causing a jam. Naturally this spring was more limp with one round left in the magazine and surely some Mauser magazine springs do weaken, but this complaint rarely occurred with other calibers using identical springs.

Its success as a game control rifle in Uganda, Rhodesia, and other African colonies clinched the 425's reputation as a rifle for large, dangerous game, and all native hunters of Uganda's famous Elephant Control staff were once equipped with it. Using the 425, three such hunters were especially commended for killing 300 elephant marauders in seven months. Another killed 90 in nine months. In the 1960s 425 ammo became scarce when existing stocks dried up and Rhodesian Control hunters switched to 458s, 375s and double 470s and 500s.

By 1963 most of Rhodesia's 425 ranger control rifles were stored in the Department of National Parks & Wildlife Conservation's Salisbury Armory or had been issued to the Tsetse Control staff hunters in the Zambesi Valley and Southeastern lowveld. One Tsetse Control hunter threatened to resign if he was not issued another rifle to replace the 425 that jammed when he was charged by a buffalo. This was a post-war "Game Ranger" 425 with F.N. Series 300 action, a plain grade rifle with inadequate hand work to insure elimination of the aforementioned tendency to jam when the bolt face cams over the rebated rims.

I have never hunted with a 425 despite having owned three in best quality and still owning two, including one obtained recently in Johannesburg, probably a surplus Rhodesian Control rifle with barrel cut to 26-inches. My other 425 is a takedown, cased with a

Those who bought big magazine rifles pre-World War I wanted firepower and got it with clip-loading, even such large rounds as the 425 Westley Richards Magnum, which were accommodated by a magazine extension in this model.

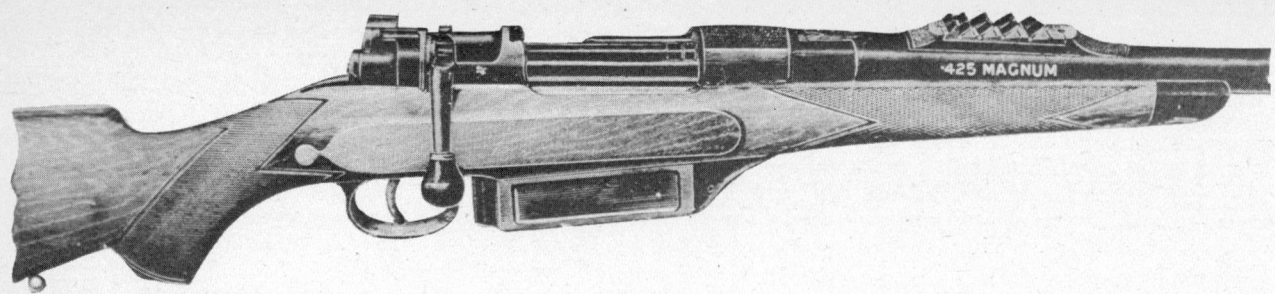

This catalog cut shows a number of the original Westley Richards customary or patented features, including the five-round extended magazine, five-leaf express sights, side-paneled stock and buffalo horn bolt knob.

Holland-Schoenauer 375 "Velopex" Belted (not magnum) express.

A few years ago the Rhodesian Game Department sold off their 425s and the safari guide John Kingsley-Heath told me that he had obtained a batch and had them rebored to 458. In Johannesburg I met Hugh MacNeil, a Director of Safari South, and saw his favorite Mauser, a 458 rebored from 425 with a 20-inch barrel for close combat with Botswana's Okavango Swamp buffalo. Though too short in the barrel for me, it was a good conversion, very reliable according to MacNeil and good looking, too. I will however, retain my 425s as original since I have a good supply of all types of ammo, and if I need handloads I have RCBS dies and can use R.W.S. or Jim Bell's B.E.L.L. Boxer-primed 404 brass and Barnes .435" bullets.

I invented my own version of the 425 which offers no "improvement" since it uses a standard 425 chamber. I call it the 425 Lott, which is simply a 425 without a rebated rim as made from shortened, neck-reamed 404 brass. To accommodate the larger diameter rim I use an extra 98 Mauser bolt with face opened up to accept the 404 and then I have both eliminated the problem of jams (which do not occur with my 425s) but mainly I do not have to turn down the rims (rebate) which is a big saving of time and effort.

Of course, anyone wanting to do this must first obtain a bolt which headspaces properly with factory

Post-World War II, the firm offered this version, the Game Ranger.

WESTLEY RICHARDS GAME RANGER MAGAZINE RIFLE

.425 MAGNUM
.404
.375 MAGNUM

NOTE THESE SPECIAL FEATURES IN THIS NEW HEAVY CALIBRE RIFLE.

THE GAME RANGER is a modern Big Game rifle of medium price incorporating features designed by Westley Richards for Government Game Departments throughout British Africa and now adopted by them. The materials and workmanship are identical to those used in the famous Best Quality Rifle, and functioning and accuracy are guaranteed equal. Costs have been kept to a minimum by providing strong, simple but practical fittings such as sights, etc., and omitting all unessential features of more expensive rifles such as engraving, fore-end tip, grip-cap, etc.

BARREL — Finest quality nickel or chrome molybdenum steel barrels precision rifled and chambered to highest standards. Barrel length 25". An extra strong sling-eye is fitted. Barrel is engraved "Westley Richards & Co. London," and bears Government Proof Marks, including calibre, bullet weights, etc.

STOCK — Seasoned French walnut stocks are used to avoid any warping and are inletted by hand to give consistent accuracy. The full pistol grip and fore-end are checkered and sling-eyes are fitted to barrel and butt.
In addition to the normal action screws, the stock is bolted through the fore-end to a steel lug brazed to the underside of the barrel. (5). In view of the extra recoil forces, the stock is inletted with a steel recoil-plate on which the action fits and which insures against the stock splitting or alteration of the action seating (6).

SIGHTING — Both rear and front sight bases are secured to the barrel by a new screwing process which absolutely guarantees that they will not be knocked off (4).
The New Game Ranger backsight—a strong standard open sight, vertical to avoid reflection and filed with a wide shallow V. It is engraved with the maximum range depending on calibre. (A standard and 2-flush-folding-leaf backsight can be fitted at an extra charge).
The foresight is a medium-large silver tipped bead, mounted on a short stem to avoid being knocked out of alignment. Spare foresights can be supplied at any time which are interchangeable. The ramp of the foresight bases is file-cut and a slip-on protector is supplied.
A receiver-type aperture sight, as illustrated, is available for fitting to this rifle. It is made in England by Parker Hale and has both horizontal and vertical adjustments. When this sight is fitted the open barrel-sight is removed and the dovetail filled with a blank. The V sight can be marked for zero and supplied separately.

ACTION — Mauser Bolt action with low swept-back bolt handle and pre-war type full turn-over safety—commercially made (1), not converted military. Bolt cam is specially hardened for smooth loading. A strong steel magazine (2) is fitted with a thumb-button release for the bottom plate.
Magazine Capacities .425 .404 and .375 3 ctgs.
Extra Capacity Magazines (3): An extension magazine, as illustrated, can be fitted to give a capacity of 4 ctgs. in .425 and .404 calibres and 5 ctgs. in .375.
Note: In all cases an extra round can be placed in the chamber by hand, but this causes undue strain to the extractor and is not recommended as regular practice.
WEIGHTS .425 and .404 — 9½ lbs.
.375 — 8½ to 8¾ lbs.

ammo unless only handloads with proper headspace built into them are used. I say this because although the original 425 rounds won't extract with the opened-up bolt face, they could be fired singly. The rifle is then original and ready for any older or future production factory ammo. If clip loading is desired, surplus 8x57 JS Mauser clips can be used, but only for four rounds.

I was fortunate in obtaining in Rhodesia almost every style of 425 ammo including box and label styles, steel, cupro-nickel and gilding metal solids and old and new capped bullets, both round-nose and the pointed "L.T." pattern. I was very lucky to get a box of clip-fitted solids, five to a clip. With these it is possible to reload a five shot 425 with great rapidity which in the case of a wounded or charging buffalo or a second animal attacking could be a lifesaver. I could have used such an arrangement when I was charged and tossed by a wounded buffalo during a three-month Mozambique safari in 1959.

With one in the chamber and five in the magazine, there are three times as many rounds as in a heavy double, and with adequate skill one has considerably more firepower than a double user, particularly when reloading with five-shot charger clips. To suggest that even a skilled double user, even with a second double and skilled loader, could compete with a skilled 425 Mauser man working the bolt from the shoulder is to believe in the supernatural. At best it is stretching the romance and undoubted appeal of doubles (which I share to a point) beyond reality. The shortness of the 425's standard length Mauser bolt throw enhances this superiority.

Whereas the original 425 "solid" used a cupro-nickel jacket, a tough alloy of about 80% copper and 20% nickel, it was a fairly effective bullet on buffalo, rhino and elephant. This was due to an excellent combination of toughness and hardness in that alloy. Fortunately for users of the large bore British nitro-expresses, that lumpy metal fouling associated with cupro-nickel only occurs with velocities well over the 2,000-2,350 fps range of these large bores. Our old Krag-Jorgensen 30-40 Army with its cupro-nickel 220-grain solid at 2,200 fps did not foul in this manner as did the original 150-grain 2,700 fps 30-06 load. Despite this, it is unwise to fire that old cupro-nickel jacketed 425, or any other nitro-express ammo thusly bulleted, for fear of case splitting and head separations, to say nothing of corrosive and possibly mercuric priming.

If you have some copper-colored "solids" in your 425 Kynoch ammo supply, be sure to test with a magnet since the early post-war "solids" with thin gliding metal jackets are useless for anything but targets or non-dangerous game. This criticism does not apply to Barnes .049″ copper tubing jacketed "solids" with their soft but tough characteristics.

Bullet styles available for the 425 were conventional round-nose solids in cupro-nickel, then gilding metal, (immediately post WW II) then steel with gilding metal plating, W.R. patented round-nose capped and "L.T." pointed capped, all in 410-gr. weight. Later, the capped bullets had copper caps or copper caps and gilding metal bodies. A special 300-grain "L.T." pointed copper capped bullet with 2,450 fps velocity was available to appeal to those customers impressed by such ineffective loads with their dif-

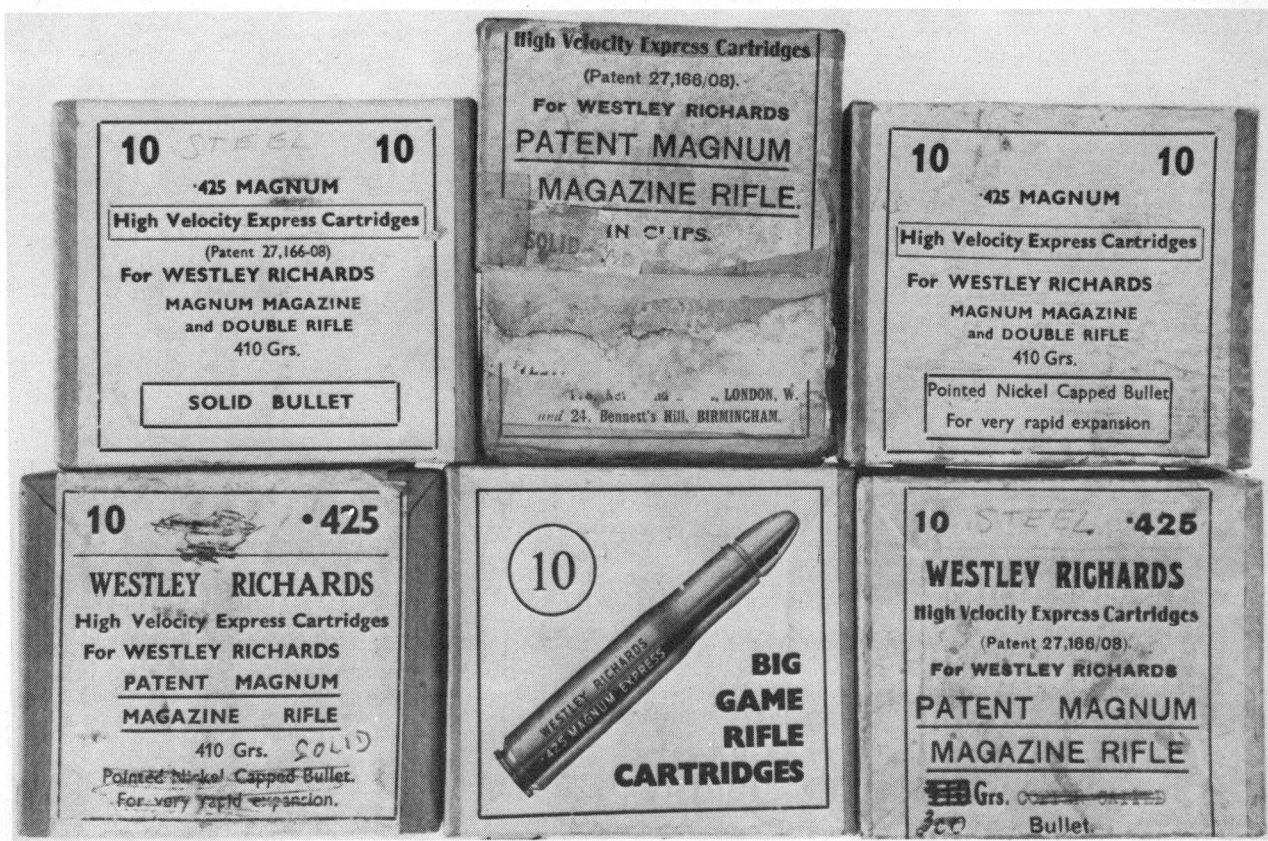

Author's collection of original cartridge boxes picked up during Rhodesian safaris. The style changed from time to time, obviously, but there wasn't much change in the cartridges, sold ten at a time, almost always with 410-gr. bullets, solid or patent expanding.

Westley Richards
•425 Magnum Express Magazine Rifle

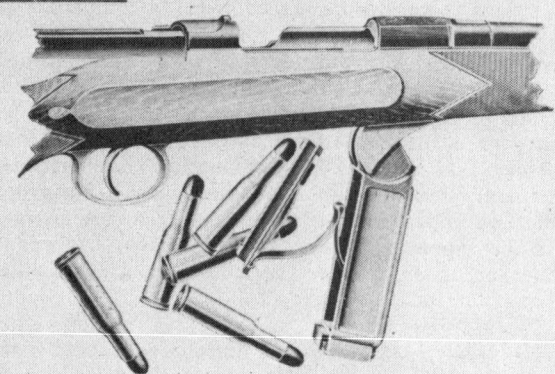

The Westley Richards •425 Magazine Rifle is fitted with five-loader extending magazine, but is also supplied with magazine plate flush with the Stock, holding three cartridges in the magazine.

Price Best Quality - £38 . 0 . 0
       Second ,,   - £33 . 0 . 0

Weight about 8½ lbs.

Showing quick method of emptying the Magazine.

All Westley Richards Magazine Rifles are strengthened at the points where Rifle Stocks have the greatest strain by a special process of their own and are the strongest Rifle Stocks made.

"A short time ago I purchased one of your •425 bore Magazine Rifles, with only 25 cartridges—12 solid nose and 13 L.T. ones—and with the former I have up to date shot four Bison and one Elephant, and with the latter a fine leopard. The first time I tried this Rifle at a live target was a Bison over 200 yards and the first shot rendered him *hors-de-combat*. Its execution is a subject of high praise amongst my friends, and a week ago one of them told me that he had heard an aspirant to hunting fame remarking that it was his ambition in life to shoot with my Westley Richards. It is more like a trusty friend than a piece of cold steel."

R.V., June 30, 1925.

Catalog pages from the 1930's tell the story of this combination as Westley-Richards and a number of customers saw it. These pages are virtually stereotypes of the sales mode for British big bore rifles in the old days.

Westley Richards
Improved Magnum Express Magazine Rifle, •425 bore
For Large Game.
Patented and introduced by Westley Richards.
**Shooting the 410 grain Solid and Capped Bullets.
The •425 Solid Bullet is constructed so as to ensure
: : : deadly effect**

Everything depends upon the bullet. For penetrating the hardest and toughest substances the Solid Nickel bullet is requisite, and the essential of a Solid bullet is a hard envelope thick enough to maintain the bullet whole.

The •425 bore Solid Bullet.

"I killed the Rhinoceros and one of the Buffalo Bulls with one bullet each (•425 bore). It is a very powerful weapon and very accurate."
The late F. C. SELOUS.

"Had I only possessed such a rifle in my old Elephant hunting days I am sure I should have killed three or four times as many Elephants as I actually laid low."
(Signed) F. C. SELOUS.

The •425 bore Solid (fired) Bullet extracted from clay.

From Dr. D. W. McMILLAN,
Pensacola, Fla.
"I am well pleased with the remarkable performance of your •425 Rifle . . . . I have shot Bear and Elk with it. It is beyond doubt the most powerful firearm in the world. If you ever make any improvement upon it let me know."

From J. A. COWIE.
"My partner and self killed forty-nine Elephants on the trip, besides Rhino., Buffalo, Lions, Leopards, and all the larger Antelope. At one meeting I killed eight Elephants out of a troop of nine, on another occasion a troop of seven, and later, five out of a troop of six. These bags I attribute solely to the excellence of my •425 . . . . In conclusion, I have to thank you for bringing these Rifles to my notice. Out of some fifty parties who were in the Sehungwe, I understand that our bag was a long way the largest, and to our Rifles much of the credit must lie."

R.A.J.M., of Tanga.   February, 1925.
"You will be interested to hear that since writing you last I have shot yet another Elephant, 2 Rhino., and a Lion with the •425 Rifle."

From T. A. JENKIN.
Fort Johnston, Nyasaland.   November 6th, 1912.
"I have just returned from a hunting trip on the Rovunia river, where I have been using your •425 Magnum Magazine Rifle. You may be pleased to know that I have found it perfect in every way and one of the finest Rifles I have ever used, it is deadly accurate and the striking power is tremendous. I have used pretty nearly every Rifle from an 8 bore to a •303, but consider this •425 far ahead of them all . . . . With regard to the cartridges, the "L.T." Bullet is great for everything from Buffalo to Hartebeeste. I have cut bullets out of Eland and Koodoo and found them hang together well and *so set up that they wouldn't go down an 8 bore*."

The Capped and Solid Bullets ensure easy action. They do not jamb in the magazine.

PAGE FORTY SEVEN

ferent sighting and the risk of mistakenly or stupidly using them on lion or leopard. This trend was popular to some extent throughout England's gunmaking trade as evidenced by Jeffery's 300-gr. 404 and Holland's 365-gr. 465 bullets. Such freaks with their inferior accuracy and penetration, poor sectional density and mediocre improvement in velocity died an early death, but not before some amount of injuries and deaths of hunters, gun bearers and lost game occurred due to misuse.

One important advantage, to me the main advantage, of Westley Richards capped bullets, was that they did not mushroom in the magazine from recoil as do conventional soft nosed bullets. This is a serious problem which causes many jams, as any user of 375 Magnum or 458 conventional round-nose lead tipped bullets can testify. One derivation of the Westley Richards capped bullet appears to be Winchester-Western's "Silvertip," my favorite expanding bullet for the 375 Magnum.

During the immediate post-WW II years Kynoch produced its worst "solids," those thin-jacketed, fragile, gilding metal versions I've already mentioned. Beginning around 1955, Kynoch, doubtless influenced by John "Pondoro" Taylor's eloquent pleas for all dangerous game solids to be steel jacketed like those of Rigby's famous 416 and 350 Magnum, began offering steel solids. Gilding metal in America is usually called "Lubaloy," a registered name of Winchester, but in Britain, the same alloy, roughly 90% copper and 10% zinc, is known as "Nobeloy," in honor of Alfred Nobel, the inventor of Dynamite.

Comments by professional hunters serve to illustrate the reputation of the 425 in its pre-war heyday. The Uganda Game Department reported as follows. "The new rifle is a magnificent weapon from the point of view of killing. The 425 Westley Richards magazine rifles have proved wonderfully efficient weapons, fully capable of standing up to the constant hard usage in all weathers. Up to date—one ranger has killed 58 elephants and 8 buffaloes with one of these weapons. All are now armed with Westley Richards 425 bore magazine rifles. There is no doubt this weapon has greatly increased their efficiency..."

J. F. Muirhead, a professional hunter, had this to say on Dec. 17, 1920:

"I am a professional hunter, and have had this particular 425 rifle for the last ten years, and have shot elephants, lions and practically all other game. My last trip with this same rifle I shot 19 elephants, some I shot dead with one shot each. I have been shooting in the Congo, German East Africa, Northern and Southern Rhodesia, etc. The rifle, although I have had it for ten years and done a lot of shooting with it, I would not part with it. It has never failed me, and I have been charged by both elephant and lion. I enclose some photographs, and among them one of myself seated upon one of five elephants shot in one afternoon in Central Congo with a 425 Westley Richards rifle. This can be proved correct by the Belgian Administrator if necessary. Two of the elephants were taken with one shot each. Yours faithfully, J.F. Muirhead, Big Game hunter, South Africa."

The comments of F.C. Selous are of interest and are reproduced as published in the pre-war Westley Richards catalogs. Americans have also been among the many satisfied users of the 425, including Lyle Corcoran, founder of the Hollywood Gun Shop and manufacturer and designer of the famous Hollywood loading tools, Robert Lee of New York, who also developed the 424 Lee Magnum, an "improved" 425 with straighter sidewalls and a 30 degree shoulder. Lee achieved around 2,450 fps using American IMR powders, but the original case could also achieve such a velocity with our powders. A former American Ambassador to South Africa also preferred the 425, this time a double with which he did achieve an outstanding bag. Lyle Corcoran was very successful with his 425 on buffalo and other large game in the eastern Congo.

Being substantially lighter than a double rifle of equal power, the 425 was a more versatile and handy rifle, particularly when it is also used for a general purpose rifle to feed the hunter and his African staff. For shots over 50 yards it is superior to, say, a 470 and having a flatter trajectory and closer grouping than the combined left and right patterns of a double over 100 yards, it is more versatile. In competition with its ballistic twin (leaving out slightly inferior sectional density) the 416, it was a cheaper rifle using cheaper ammo. In best quality guise, the 425 offered more firepower with its clip loading, a superior front sight protector, shorter bolt stroke and slightly greater "knockdown" on frontal shots at elephant due to its .019-inch larger diameter.

Though its appearance is strangely awkward to Americans with their current role models of the belted magnums with their sharp shoulders and short necks, the 425 with its very long neck and gradual shoulder gave an extra grip to the heavy bullets during recoil. There is no truth to the view that the slight shoulder interfered with headspacing. There was plenty of increased diameter in the case body over that of the neck to prevent the firing pin from driving the case forward. This form of case with rebated rim and long neck was also used by the German firm of Schuler with their 11.2x72 and 12.7x70 Schuler (500 Jeffery) as well as the Mauser 11.2x60.

I once criticized the 425 Westley Richards Magnum as a bad design on account of its rebated rim, but this was before I had owned one and worked with it. I was then younger and more inclined to depend on theory, a tendency I have suppressed after some further years of experience, oftimes sad, in Africa's game fields. I now look forward to field testing my latest 425 acquisition, the 26-inch barreled best quality Mauser with commercial Oberndorf action. I will try all of the various bullet styles in my ammo chest, with maybe a batch of .049" copper tubing jacketed Barnes solids and Boxer primed R.W.S. re-formed, trimmed and neck reamed 404 brass.

Most pre-war 425s have serial numbers beginning with "L.T." commemorating the inventor, Westley Richards' late Managing Director, Leslie Taylor, whose initials also preceded the serial numbers of pre-war 318s, another Leslie Taylor development along with capped bullets. Taylor insisted that the 318s use elliptical Metford rifling, but all 425s I've examined used conventional Enfield rifling like our rifles.

If you own a 425 Westley Richards Magnum in good working order, don't rebore or rebarrel it. It is an excellent choice as-is for African dangerous game, Asian dangerous game or even large Alaskan bears and moose. If done properly, there is no objection to reducing the length of barrel from 28 to, say, 24 inches, but of course you will then have to refit the front sight. If the 28 inches doesn't bother you, it can be left alone for reduced recoil, muzzle flip, blast and for full velocity and steady holding on offhand shots. Long barrels shoot nicely by not wobbling around on offhand shots so much and by not bucking as much as shorter ones. Install a Pachmayr solid "Old English" pad if you will, (without a white line, if you please) and then load up some Boxer-primed ammo with Barnes bullets. You will then be ready for the "big uns." ●

THE HUNTER IN THE 20th CENTURY

The Daily Life Is Different; The Hunter, The Philosopher Said, Is The Same As Always

by Roger Barlow

Hunters through the ages have been more alike than different...

EVERY HUNTER has at some time had the enjoyment of his dinner disrupted when his host or hostess, overhearing some reference to a hunting trip or hunting dogs, asks, in one way or another, "How can you kill poor defenseless animals that can't shoot back?"

Now, except for a fund-raising dinner for the Vegetarian Party with Vegechops as the entre, effective response exists because the hostess has no doubt served, or is planning to serve, a main course of some type of meat. That permits an answer in this vein: "Dear lady, the only difference between us is that I hunt in field and wood, killing some of the meat my family eats, while you do your hunting in supermarkets; thereby, in effect, *hiring* someone to do your killing for you!"

We hunters know our problem with most non-hunters is basically one of hypocrisy and a refusal to face reality. While condemning *us* they are quite willing to have someone else slaughter the animals that provide much of the protein in their diets and the leather for their shoes and bags.

Unfortunately, one can't very well call one's host, hostess or acquaintances out-and-out hypocrites. We must try to make our points a bit more indirectly and without merely trading insults.

You can lay good odds that your hostess is now going to try to establish her moral superiority over hunters by such illogical logic as, "But I couldn't *bear* to kill anything ... while you seem to *enjoy* killing things. ... I think that's terrible!"

This is certainly one of the non-hunters greatest misconceptions about hunters and hunting: that our enjoyment is mainly or entirely derived from the act of killing.

Other than the usual sense of triumph a hunter experiences after a successful stalk or an effective shot, almost every sportsman feels somewhat saddened by the death of his quarry, whether lordly moose or lowly rabbit. So tell your hostess (or whoever) that if it was the *killing* that gave you pleasure you'd spend your vacations working in a slaughter house instead of climbing mountains after bighorn sheep or freezing in a duck blind.

Jose Ortega y Gasset, the great Spanish philosopher, had the insight to understand the true essence of our sport. He wrote in his *Meditations On Hunting:* "To the sportsman the death of the game is not what most interests him; that is not his sole purpose. What interests him is everything he has to do to achieve that death—that is, the *hunt*. The killing of the animal is the natural end of the hunt

... And today's hunter shares their skills and heritage.

and the goal of hunting itself, not of the hunter. The hunter seeks this death because it is no less than the sign of reality for the whole hunting process. To sum up, one does not hunt in order to kill; on the contrary, one kills in order to have truly hunted."

Nevertheless, our detractors will continue to belabor their favorite theme, "But there's no *need* for modern man to be a hunter, is there now?"

As it happens, we have some fairly good answers to this too:

"Dear lady, what you mean is that *you* have no need to be a hunter . . . you can't very well speak for *my* needs, can you? Remember, man, and I mean *man* and not *woman*, was a hunter long before he was a farmer, a herdsman and certainly before he was a lawyer or accountant. Even though part of early human diet included fruit, berries, nuts, etc., primitive groups prospered almost in direct relation to the success of their hunters of animals and fish."

No woman in the families of early mankind ever asked, "Why do you have to kill things?" Everyone knew from sad experience that bellies would be uncomfortably empty if the hunters failed to kill things.

So for millions of years of our prehistoric existence and for all the thousands of years of our recorded history, until less than about 50 years ago, the hunter was one of the most respected members of the community. Hunting has been one of man's main efforts and important social respon-

Others hunt, too, on this planet . . .

Editor's Note: About these drawings: They were made expressly by Lewis Brown for Roger Barlow's motion picture *Meditations on Hunting*. Brown also illustrated the English translation of Jose Ortega y Gasset's book of the same title, published in English by Scribner. The film, which visually melds the current hunting scene with Brown's drawings and Ortega y Gasset's words, is available from the National Rifle Association. The NRA commissioned Barlow to do the film. K.W.

... And we join them, possibly because we must. Today, of course ...

sibilities. That it has also entertained us in no way denigrates its importance in mankind's history any more than the enjoyment of sex invalidates the importance of the procreative drive.

Consider, too, the seriousness with which children play hunting games and the eagerness with which boys welcome the opportunity to go on a real hunt with adults. There *are* no more enthusiastic hunters than boys, perhaps simply because they are basically a bit closer to the cave than most adults.

What brought about the change in the attitude toward hunting in so many Americans?

Certain major changes in our national way of life come to mind, such as the population shift from rural to urban living. People who lived on farms both hunted and butchered their livestock with their own hands to put the meat dish on their tables.

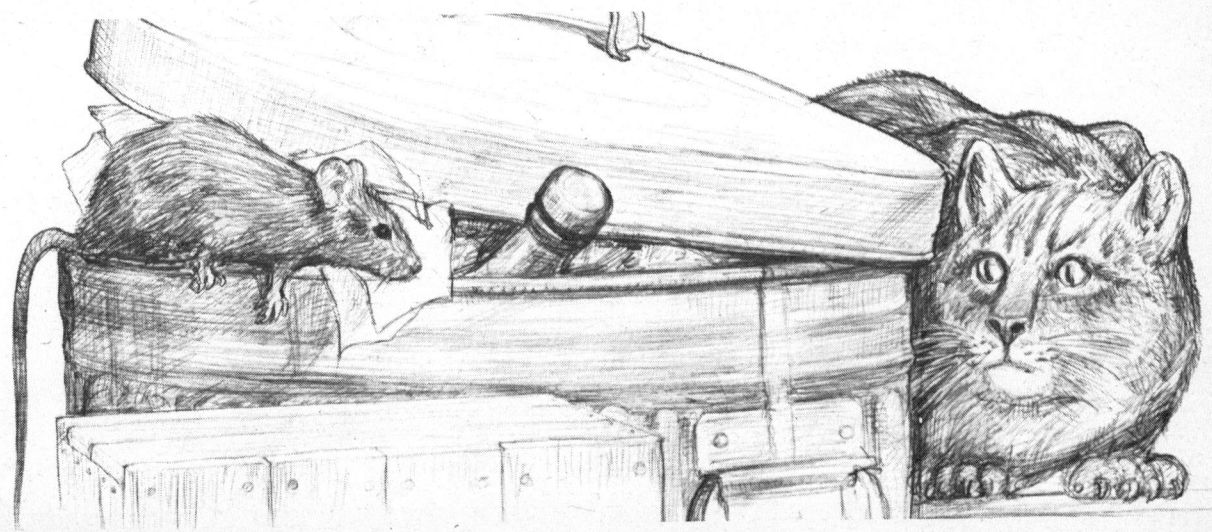

... many hunters endure the city to make the hunt possible.

Women (and girls) usually took on the task of selecting a chicken from the flock, catching it, carrying it to the chopping block, lopping off the head with a well-placed hatchet blow and then, when the bird ceased its convulsive flapping about, removing the steaming entrails before cutting it up for the pot or pan.

Even in the cities up to 25 years or so ago, many housewives bought poultry at the local butcher which had been freshly killed but not dressed out.

What was, not so long ago, simply part of the normal preparation of a meal would today reduce the average teenager to hysterics and terminal retching! And do the same for most housewives, I suspect.

However, this squeamishness hasn't reduced our young people's appetite for hamburger or caused us to accept soybean meal, molded into the appropriate shape, as a substitute for the Thanksgiving turkey. No, indeed. Too many just pretend the meat we crave never came from a living creature that *someone* had to kill in cold blood. As I said, hypocrisy is the operative word when most people strive to put down the hunter.

Supermarkets today display meat so neatly cut up and packaged as to look *manufactured,* giving little or no indication that the material being purchased and consumed has ever had any relationship to a once living animal. Small wonder that the lady of the house can serve roast lamb without her mind ever registering the image of the woolly little creature that was actually killed to provide that meal.

Another factor working against an understanding and acceptance of we modern hunters by so many urban dwellers is that hunting is largely carried out with *firearms*. For the past 20-25 years we have been subjected to a barrage of anti-firearm propaganda by forces seeking to control crime by the misguided disarming of the law abiding citizen, by making the *gun* itself responsible for crimes committed by our criminal element. Thus, increasingly, anyone who uses a gun for any legitimate sporting or utilitarian purpose is now guilty by association . . . with guns.

At some point your hypothetical (but all too real) hostess is almost certain to glare accusingly at you as she seeks to cut the ground out from under you, "I suppose you're a member of that awful gun lobby, the NRA!" It's quite as though NRA was a front for the PLO terrorists or the Mafia instead of an organization just possibly made up of the most law abiding citizens of this country.

Then, too, many of the active conservationists are strongly antihunting despite the founder of the conservation movement being Theodore Roosevelt, a lifelong shooter and hunter.

Remind your hostess of this fact and also point out that the majority of hunters are not slobs . . . that we are doctors, lawyers, musicians, teachers, priests and preachers, artists and poets as well as truck drivers, farmers, miners, shopkeepers and, yes, sometimes housewives! The ranks of past and present hunters include such notables as Winston Churchill (a person of some undeniable stature), the composer Verdi, who was an ardent duck hunter, Bernard Baruch, advisor and confidant of Presidents and a quail hunter along with Presidents Eisenhower and Jimmy Carter. And if your hostess could ever have had Ernest Hemingway, Clark Gable, Bing Crosby and Gary Cooper as dinner guests she would have sat at table not only with four of the most handsome and entertaining guests any hostess could have dreamed, but four serious and passionate hunters. CBS to the contrary, hunting men and women are *not* depraved louts!

However, I think we must consider at least one other aspect of our predicament as hunters in a society that regards us with such suspicion, loathing and total lack of understanding. It seems to me we are the victims of a new attitude toward people whose views or way of life differs. Despite seeming strides in reducing various forms of discrimination, intolerance has only become more selective. How often have you heard anyone angrily demand of a churchgoer why he or she attends a Catholic rather than a Lutheran church? When have you, a good Democrat, denounced someone for voting Republican? I have never heard a devoted watcher of TV football take someone to task because they prefer to watch Masterpiece Theatre. I've never had a Jewish friend chide me for not eating kosher food.

In the midst of all this civilized tolerance for the rights and foibles of others, it would never occur to me to suggest to a vegetarian that some meat in his or her diet might be a good thing. Nor have many hunters ever suggested to a so-called conservationist that he or she ought to do some quail or turkey hunting with them. Knowing their attitudes on these matters, few hunters would be so ill mannered as to call them seriously into question unless they raised the matter themselves.

But although I've never asked anyone why they don't eat meat or hunt pheasants I have all too often been discourteously and arrogantly upbraided for eating meat or being a 20th century hunter. When you hear the question, "Why do you kill things?", just remember the intent is never to probe your mind, your needs or motivations. No, indeed, that question is merely rhetorical and an answer is not invited. It is primarily a launching pad for an all-out verbal offensive against a way of life your "questioner" does not approve.

We like to think of our democratic society as a place to live in which one is free to do what one pleases as long as it is legal and does not intrude upon the life-style of others. Increasingly we are at the mercy of people who have assumed the right to demand that certain activities be condemned and *made* illegal simply because they run counter to their own beliefs and prejudices.

We must respect the vegetarian's aversion to the taking of animal life to provide food just as we must respect the various ways in which our fellow men and women chose to worship the various concepts of God. But we should *not* have to be guided or restricted by our detractors' totally unrealistic, Disney-like conception of animal life.

Hunting is the basic way of life (and death) in the animal kingdom. The cat hunts mice, the shark hunts smaller fish, the hawk hunts the dove, the lion hunts the zebra, the spider hunts flies, the wolf hunts caribou.

If we Americans were to give up hunting for meat or for sport it would have no appreciable effect upon today's wildlife except to deprive that wildlife of the benefits made possible by the millions of dollars contributed by hunters through various special taxes and licenses. The draining of ponds and swamps by farmers and developers is far more harmful to waterfowl than are the shotguns of we hunters, as just one example.

Nevertheless, no bird or animal in the U.S. had been put on the endangered list by sports hunters. The market hunters of many years ago are a different matter (often overromanticized by many writers) for they were basically butchers, no matter how skilled they were with shotgun or rifle, and they would have killed the last buffalo or antelope for $1.25 or the last prairie chicken for a quarter. Sports hunters, however, long before most of today's "conservationists" were even born, had saved our pronghorn antelope and wild turkey and had demanded lowered bag limits and shorter hunting seasons.

All these are points to remember when you are called upon to defend yourself as a 20th century hunter.

Let Ortega y Gasset, the philosopher, have the last words:

"This is the reason men hunt. When you are fed up with the troublesome present, with being 'too twentieth century', you take your gun, whistle for your dog, go to the mountain, and, without further ado, give yourself the pleasure during a few hours or a few days of being 'Paleolithic'. And men of all eras have been able to do the same without any difference except in the weapon employed. 'Natural' man is always there, under the changeable historical man. We call him and he comes — a little sleepy, benumbed, without all his early instincts, but, after all, still alive. When modern man sets out to hunt, what he does is not a fiction, not a masquerade it is, essentially, the same thing that Paleolithic man did. The hunter is, at one and the same time, a man of today and one of ten thousand years ago. Hunting alone permits us the greatest luxury of all, the ability to enjoy a vacation from the human condition (of today) through an authentic immersion in Nature."

Ortega is saying, in effect, that of all modern men and women only the hunter is fortunate enough to be able to walk away from the 20th century and emotionally be once again a man of primitive times. The gun in our hands can be, in reality, man's only functioning Time Machine!

Perhaps the animosity we encounter is born of envy. •

TRENDS IN THE WORLD OF AIR GUNS

MAGNUMS AND MATCH GUNS AND VARMINT RIFLES – THESE ARE ADULT AIRGUNS

by J. I. GALAN

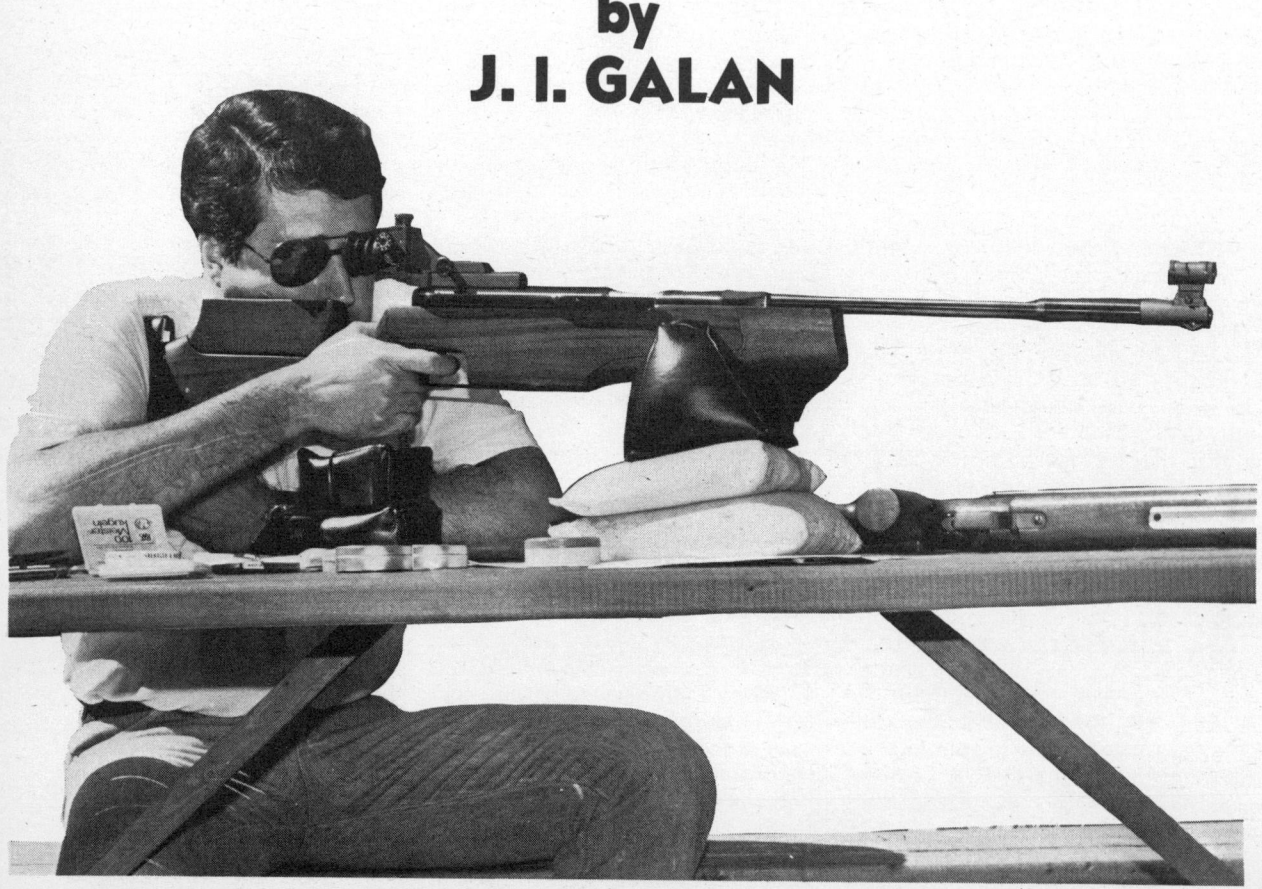

Author test-fires the FWB 300S Universal. Notice the raised sights and high cheekrest.

THE FASCINATING world of airguns is in a state of unprecedented growth. A staggering variety of models are streaming forth from factories in the U.S., Western Europe, Eastern Europe, and even in the Far East. Just about everybody wants a piece of this fast-expanding worldwide market, which is on its way to becoming one of the principal pillars of the shooting sports as restrictions on the ownership and use of firearms continue to increase. This new "age of the airgun," however, has not been brought about solely as a result of repressive firearms legislation. Technological advancements in the aerospace and related fields during the past decade have had a significant impact on airgun technology. New materials and specially new lubricants—such as the molybdenum disulfide family—have generally upgraded airgun design concepts and the "life expectancy" of certain airgun types.

As with most other large-scale industries, product diversification seems to be a definite trend in today's airgun market. Diversification can be interpreted, in a sort of round-about way, as *specialization*, which in reality appears to be where we are headed with airguns. Thus, we now find an increasing number of airguns that, while retaining an overall purpose—recreational shooting—are specially designed for certain specific applications. The net result of all this is a "buyer's market" situation where we can pick and choose the airgun that best meets our specific needs and budget.

This is the case with match air rifles. The current generation of these incredible tack-drivers is composed of several models, each of which has its own special use. In contrast, less than a decade ago, all of the European match air rifle producers had a couple of models, at best. Westinger & Altenburger, makers of the world-famous Feinwerkbau line, for instance, used to have just one model, the F-150, temporarily joined by a simplified version called the F-120. Walther had just one basic model back in the late 60s and early 70s, the LGV. And so on. At the present time, the Feinwerkbau line is made up of *five* different models. Some are intended for "general purpose" match and target shooting, while others fulfill a more restrictive role in the lofty world of competition. The Feinwerkbau 300S Match, for instance, is the mainstay of the Feinwerkbau line and, as its name implies, it is generally meant to be used in formal competition. The FWB 300S Universal, on the other hand, lends itself to a variety of uses, from shooting at moving targets to Olympic-grade matches. The FWB-300S Junior, a reduced-size, lighter weight version of the Universal for shooters of slight build, is just

The Beeman 6 (now superceded by the Model 800), shown here with optional shoulder rest, scope and custom walnut stock.

Italian-made RO72 air pistol is available in a 13" barrel version with shoulder stock extension. Sights are match-grade and it also comes with a scope sight ramp.

as versatile. The FWB-300S Running Boar model, on the other hand, is quite specialized. It comes without iron sights, ready to accept a telescopic sight. Its adjustable thumbhole stock—in the latest version—is designed for a comfortable hold while swinging at a moving target in the rapidly growing Running Boar airgun event. Finally, the FWB-300S Tyrolean is also a general purpose match rifle with the supreme elegance that only a Tyrolean-style stock can provide.

Walther still offers its LGV match-grade air rifle, which utilizes a spring-piston powerplant. In the early 70s, the Walther LGR model was introduced. Instead of a spring-piston system, the LGR went to a single-stroke pneumatic powerplant. Thus Walther began a new trend in airgun powerplant design that combines the complete absence of recoil and vibration of a pneumatic gun with the convenience of single-stroke operation, hitherto found only in spring-piston airguns. This now proven system was simultaneously used in Walther's LP-II and in the current LP-3 match air pistols. The Daisy Mfg. Co., incidentally, has recently picked up on that same powerplant concept and is now producing a couple of single-stroke pneumatic models. More on that later.

In the mid-seventies, Walther further diversified the LGR by introducing the LGR Special Match model, which differs from the standard LGR only in having a stock with a higher profile and higher sights. At present, there is also a third version of the LGR, the Running Boar model, with thumbhole stock and adjustable cheekpiece.

Another area in which we are witnessing an increasing level of specialization is in sporting air rifles. This category encompasses just about any air rifle of acceptable quality and power that is not classed as a true match rifle. At the very top of this group we find the so-called "magnum" models, which are truly high-performance powerhouses. A common trait to all members of this select group is a muzzle-energy of at least 9.5 ft.-lbs. Unlike the match air rifle category, this field is not the sole domain of German products. American, British, and German air rifles are found here, with their relative prices increasing in the same order.

Most of the models in the "magnum" group are really intended for small-game hunting. Some of the British models, in particular, are specifically

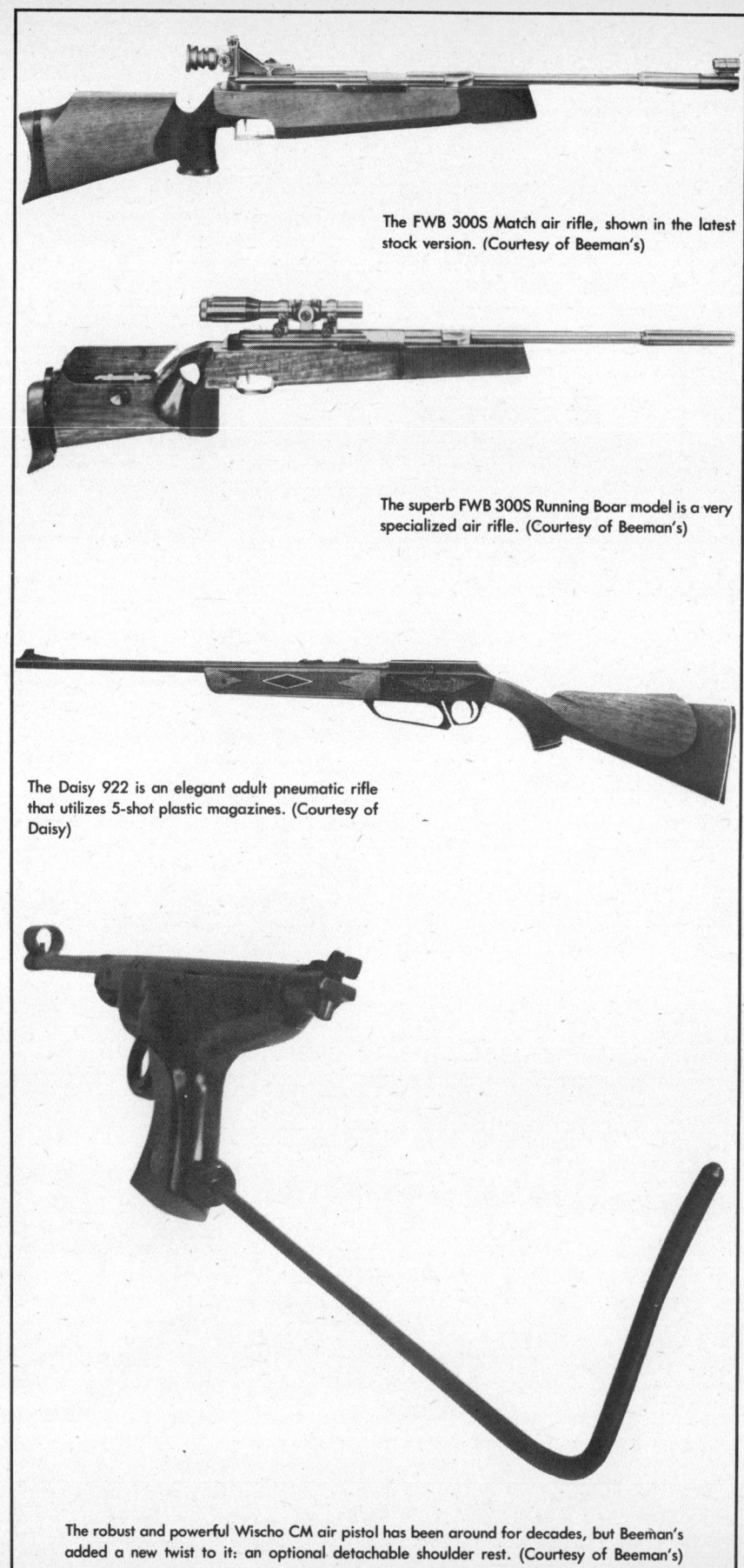

The FWB 300S Match air rifle, shown in the latest stock version. (Courtesy of Beeman's)

The superb FWB 300S Running Boar model is a very specialized air rifle. (Courtesy of Beeman's)

The Daisy 922 is an elegant adult pneumatic rifle that utilizes 5-shot plastic magazines. (Courtesy of Daisy)

The robust and powerful Wischo CM air pistol has been around for decades, but Beeman's added a new twist to it: an optional detachable shoulder rest. (Courtesy of Beeman's)

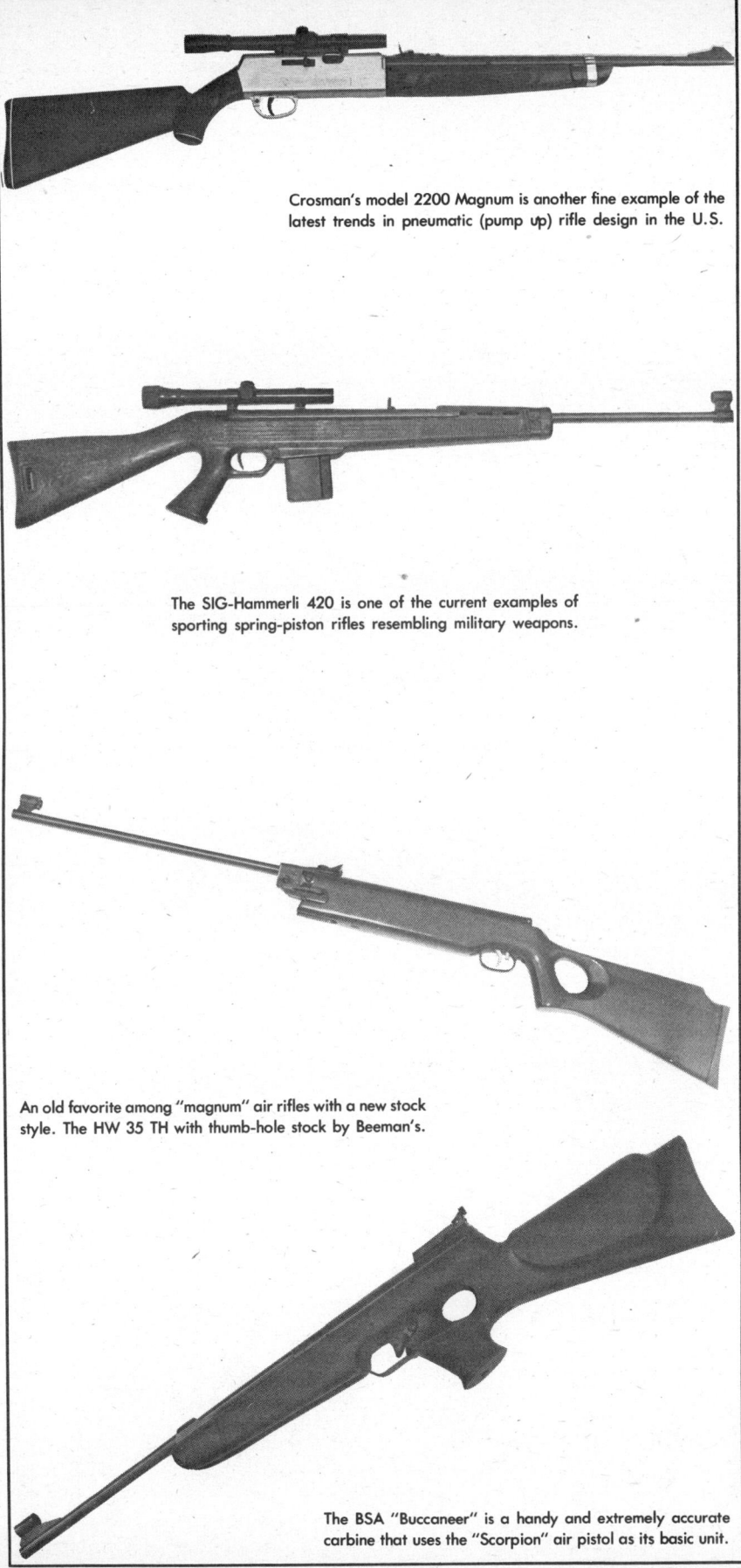

Crosman's model 2200 Magnum is another fine example of the latest trends in pneumatic (pump up) rifle design in the U.S.

The SIG-Hammerli 420 is one of the current examples of sporting spring-piston rifles resembling military weapons.

An old favorite among "magnum" air rifles with a new stock style. The HW 35 TH with thumb-hole stock by Beeman's.

The BSA "Buccaneer" is a handy and extremely accurate carbine that uses the "Scorpion" air pistol as its basic unit.

advertised with hunting and/or "vermin control" as their main applications. The Jackal models AR-7 and 2300, distributed by the Sussex Armoury, for instance, are prime examples. Rugged and extremely powerful, those models were not designed to punch holes through paper targets. Everything about them indicates that they are meant for field use, pure and simple.

Some of the German "magnum" models are going to be in even greater demand now that Silhouette shooting has been adapted to airguns. The Weihrauch HW 35, Feinwerkbau 124 and 127, and the recently introduced Beeman 250 all combine more than enough power and accuracy for the demanding "Siluetas Metálicas." Of course, there are quite a few other models that *could* be used successfully in this new airgun event, but I suspect that the aforementioned German models will emerge as the top contenders.

The HW 35 comes in various stock configurations, including a slick thumbhole version sold by Beeman's. A long-time favorite, the HW 35 has a muzzle velocity (in 177 cal.) of approximately 730 fps. It is also available in 22 caliber, with a MV of approximately 580 fps. The Feinwerkbau F-124 (177 cal.) and F-127 (22 cal.) is another spring-piston "magnum" of the highest quality. Muzzle velocity in 177 cal. is 800-plus fps, while in 22 cal. it can reach as high as 680 fps. The latter translates into a muzzle energy of more than 14 ft.-lbs.—indeed a "magnum" by modern air rifle standards! Finally, the recently introduced Beeman 250 is also right up there, producing an average MV of 820 fps (in 177 cal.) with H&N match pellets. All of the models deliver excellent accuracy too, with an average center-to-center group spread capability of approximately 3/16" at 25 ft.

These rifles represent a definite trend toward more powerful airguns, not only in some countries abroad, but in the good old U.S.A. as well. Fortunately, the power of airguns is not subject to control in this country—yet. Let's hope that our elected representatives and their cohorts have enough common sense to refrain from interfering in this particular arena. British airgunners, on the other hand, must abide by their current laws which limit the power of air rifles to a maximum of 12 ft.-lbs. of ME (6 ft.-lbs. maximum for air pistols). Any airgun exceeding those particular levels is classed as a firearm and cannot be bought legally, unless the intended buyer first secures a (horrors!) firearms certificate from the local constabulary. Still in all, the Britons manage to turn out some pretty zippy airguns that fall within the parameters allowed by their Home Office by the proverbial whisker.

Crosman scrapped its classic Model 1400 22-cal. pneumatic rifle a couple of years ago, substituting it with the Model 2200 Magnum. The latter is not only a sleek and beautifully proportioned 22-cal. pneumatic rifle, but it also produces up to 620 fps of MV, which is an improvement over the MV of the old Model 1400.

Daisy has also joined the trend toward better and more powerful pneumatic rifles with its Powerline series. A fairly recent addition has been the Daisy 922 pneumatic rifle with 5-shot clip. Elegant and relatively powerful, the Model 922 and the 177-cal. Model 881 incorporate decagon-rifled brass barrels and easy pumping mechanisms that even at peak pressure demand only about 18 lbs. of effort.

These Crosman and Daisy models are, without question, part of the ongoing effort by the American airgun manufacturers to compete with the growing multitude of quality airguns from Europe. Competition at all levels is stiff and consumers often prefer to pay a much higher price for an imported *adult* airgun rather than spend less money on a so-called (sometimes mistakenly) *youth oriented* domestic model. That, it appears, is what the American airgun companies are working hard to dispel: the notion that most American-made airguns are little more than toys, not suitable for serious adult use. Slowly but surely they are succeeding in this worthwhile endeavor and we can expect to see more tangible proof of this as American airguns become increasingly sophisticated.

A recent example of what I've just said is the Daisy 717/722 pellet pistol. This is one of the new models which I made reference to earlier, that utilizes

The recently introduced Daisy 717/722 pellet pistol (top) utilizes a single-stroke pneumatic powerplant concept similar to that of the superb Walther LP-3 (bottom).

a single-stroke pneumatic powerplant, "a la Walther".

The Daisy 717 (177-cal.)/722 (22-cal.) pistol is intended for use by adults. This is evident not only in the outward features of the gun, but in the internal design as well. The match-style grips, for instance, are large and have an ample thumb-rest. With an over-all length of 13⅛ inches, and a weight of 2.8 lbs., this Daisy is definitely out of the youth class. The fully adjustable rear sight sports a wide notch in order to pick up the square target-grade front blade. The sights alone should be sufficient to convince anyone that this is not kid's stuff!

Internally, there is a computer-optimized, single pump pneumatic powerplant. This means that the muzzle velocity output is supposed to be very consistent from shot to shot. The 717 (177-cal.) produces a MV of 360 fps, while the 722 (22-cal.) rates at a more conservative 290 fps. The single pump demands a pressure of 17 lbs. on the part of the shooter. This pistol is a commendable effort indeed, because it offers match-grade profile and precision for under $50, making it an excellent buy in our inflationary times.

There are other exciting developments going on currently in the air pistol field. Again, the Europeans have the jump on us here. Furthermore, it appears as if the idea that "bigger is better" has taken a firm hold in the minds of those who are responsible for setting trends in the world of air pistol design over there. Those of us who thought that the British had "taken the cake" with the huge BSA "Scorpion" pistol—18¼" long, with muzzle piece, and weighing 3½ lbs.—were in for a surprise. Millard Brothers, Ltd. of Scotland, a world-famous airgun producer, came out with an even bigger and more versatile air pistol less than two years ago. Called the "Cougar," this giant measures 19" over-all and weighs nearly 4 lbs. Its most striking feature, however, is a detachable, skeletonized shoulder rest that turns the Cougar into a 28" long multipurpose fun carbine. The micrometer-adjustable open sights can be removed and a ramp base installed that will accept either a telescopic sight or Milbro's own excellent peep sight. The Cougar comes in both, 177 and 22 calibers. In the former, it churns up approximately 450 fps and in the latter, approximately 350 fps. As such, the Cougar is a wee bit less powerful than the BSA Scorpion but definitely more versatile.

The trend to add shoulder extensions to air pistols seems to be catching on, by the way. The Italian-made RO72 "Artillery Carbine" is a 20¼" spring-piston air pistol (13" barrel) that comes with a 14" detachable shoulder extension. This interesting model comes with a really fine open rear sight and hooded front sight that accepts various inserts, plus an integral scope sight ramp. While not overly powerful—only around 350 fps in 177-cal.—the RO72 carbine is quite accurate and pleasant to shoot.

Both the Cougar and the RO72 are, unfortunately, not yet available in the U.S. I have mentioned them solely to illustrate a particular trend in air pistols abroad. Nevertheless, the idea of adding shoulder extensions to air pis-

A trio of the best British pistols (Top) The Milbro "Cougar" with shoulder rest and match-grade aperture sight installed. (Center) The powerful BSA "Scorpion" and (bottom) the Webley "Hurricane" with telescopic sight.

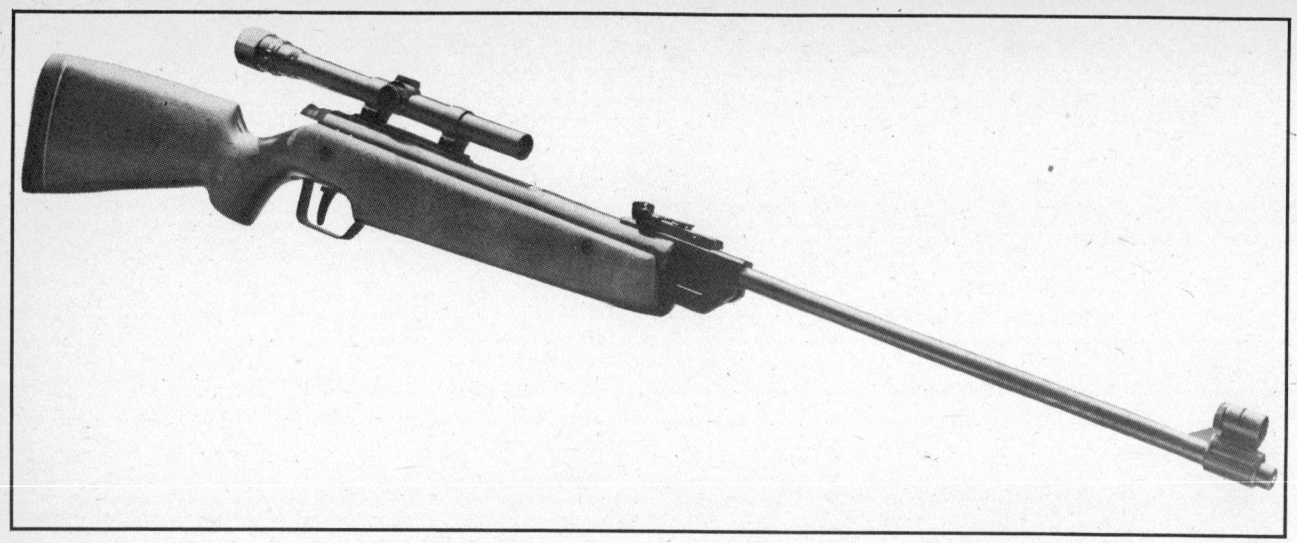

The hot new Beeman model 250 is one of the most powerful spring-piston air rifles available.

tols, while not new by any means, seems to be practical, specially since it does not fall under the severe restrictions that apply to shoulder extensions on cartridge handguns. Versatility alone is sufficient justification for this trend, due to the fact that a lot of people—myself included—like to take an air pistol along in the car. An air rifle is generally just too bulky for those circumstances, whereas a pistol with shoulder stock and even scope sight can be easily carried in a small briefcase or pouch, with an ample supply of pellets, targets, etc. This way, I know that I am equipped to handle anything from a regular air pistol match to dispatching a small pest at up to 25 or 30 yards—plus all sorts of plinking applications—if the occasion arises. Also, let's not forget that there is a romantic fascination attached to shoulder-stocked handguns which many of us find hard to resist. This new trend certainly fills a definite need, if not a void, in the world of air pistols.

American air pistol manufacturers have yet to come up with a production pistol/shoulder extension combo, but I hope that in the near future a couple of models so adapted will be marketed. Beeman's Precision Airguns have offered for the past couple of years a detachable shoulder extension that can be installed on some of the air pistols which they sell.

It can then be stated, perhaps conclusively, that air pistol producers are finally being responsive to the needs and wants of the shooting public. Not only in the matter of shoulder stocks but as far as the adaptation of telescopic sights to air pistols as well. Air Rifle Headquarters pioneered the latter concept some years ago by marketing a 1.5x Tasco handgun scope specially parallax-corrected for air pistol use. A bit later, Beeman's also picked up on this idea. No doubt seeing the "handwriting on the wall," Webley & Scott decided to provide a novel telescopic sight base as a standard item when the Webley "Hurricane" air pistol was first marketed some three years ago. A bit before that, BSA had decided to add receiver grooves for telescopic sight use to their Scorpion air pistol.

BSA, however, apparently wanted to go a different route on the matter of shoulder-stocked pistols. They came up with a full carbine outright, rather than add a removable stock to the Scorpion. The result is called the "Buccaneer." In essence, it consists of a Scorpion powerplant and trigger system, with a longer barrel and a molded thumbhole stock. Quite handy and *very* accurate to boot, with a MV of around 510 fps in 177-cal. and 400 fps in 22-cal. The BSA Buccaneer measures 35¼" over-all and weighs 6 lbs. Its thumbhole stock gives the Buccaneer a somewhat rakish look commonly associated with the current generation of short military rifles, both here and in Europe.

However, there are other air rifle models that follow the modern military rifle profile far more closely than the BSA Buccaneer. A case in point is the earlier mentioned Jackal AR-7, a British-made spring-piston air rifle that looks as deadly as an M-16, with its black ABS "straight line" stock and dummy magazine that doubles as a pellet storage compartment. The AR-7 measures only 35" over-all but weighs nearly 8 lbs. It comes in 22-cal. only, producing a MV of around 580 fps. The "Parabellum" is a longer-barreled version of the AR-7 that comes in both 177- and 22-calibers. One noteworthy aspect of the AR-7 is that it is intended for shooting at moving targets, mainly rats and other such pests. It comes without iron sights, but a Single-Point sight is usually supplied (and recommended), as an extra, with this rifle. Telescopic sights can also be installed. The Jackal line of air rifles may already be available in the U.S. by the time you read this.

Another military-style air rifle that made its appearance not too long ago is the SIG-Hammerli Model 420. This German-made spring-piston rifle bears a close resemblance to the Jackal air rifles in powerplant design. The 420, however, looks more like an FN/FAL assault rifle. It sports a simple, although adjustable, open rear sight and a post-with-hood front sight. Its full accuracy potential, however, can only be realized when a scope is used. This particular model *is* available in the U.S. through both Fanta Air Rifles and Mandall Shooting Supplies.

It would be necessary to write a book in order to go in greater detail into the recent design and production trends that have helped to mold the world of adult airguns at present. I have tried to touch upon all of those developments which I consider important enough to warrant attention, either as new plateaus or as stepping stones that will eventually lead to new plateaus. Some ergonomic trends that apply to firearms are certainly (and finally) beginning to apply to airguns. A case in point is the modernization of some of the models we have discussed that are offered with straightline military style plastic stocks. We will probably see more of this in the near future. The airgun, as old as it is, has at last come out of the closet to claim a large stake in the shooting sports. As such, it needs all the trappings that modern technology can give it. This picture is by no means complete, nor can it be when brevity, on one hand and a rapidly expanding industry on the other, are juggled together for some sort of comprehensive report on the latter.

As for the airgun's future, if the present trends are any indication, it most assuredly is here to stay and it may even be called upon to play the central role in preserving the shooting sports for coming generations. •

The Sussex Armoury's Jackal AR-7 with Single-Point sight is intended primarily for "vermin" control and plinking at moving targets. It is a first-rate rat buster that offers ample power, ruggedness, and is easily serviced by the average owner.

Kimber Model 82

After the problems: A handsome 22 that shoots

Handsome clean pre-war (any war) styling of the Kimber 82 is the reason Model 52-lovers like it. It has all that and shoots very well, which is why Painter likes it. It's not a copy, but it surely is near it.

by Robert A. Painter

THE KIMBER Model 82 Rifle is an American-made bolt-action 22 Long Rifle repeater. It comes with a plain barrel and 5 shot box magazine at a list price of $365.00. Optional at extra cost are: open sights, scope rings, 5 and 10-shot magazines, and even a Leupold 4x compact scope. Barreled actions are also available.

Kimber of Oregon, the manufacturer of the Model 82, is located in Clackamas, a suburb of Portland. Kimber is run by Greg Warne, whose father, John, designed the rifle and is a vice-president with Omark. Both have many years experience in gun manufacturing both here and abroad.

I first saw the Kimber at the 1980 Shot Show in San Francisco, and thought enough of it to buy one for myself. As a firm believer in Col. Townsend Whelen's dictum, "Only accurate rifles are interesting," I set out to see if it would hold my interest. And honestly, it didn't. The first five-shot group covered 6 inches at a range of 50 yards. The rifle didn't group much better, no matter what ammunition I used. The rifle was re-bedded, the barrel free-floated, and the groups were reduced to about 2½ inches. This accuracy was not good enough for a rifle at this price, so I contacted the manufacturer.

Big gun details in a man-sized 22 are revealed beneath — two screws hold it together, trigger guard and buttplate are steel, and the magazine is flush. This is the first Kimber — second gun had north-south timing on screws, to boot.

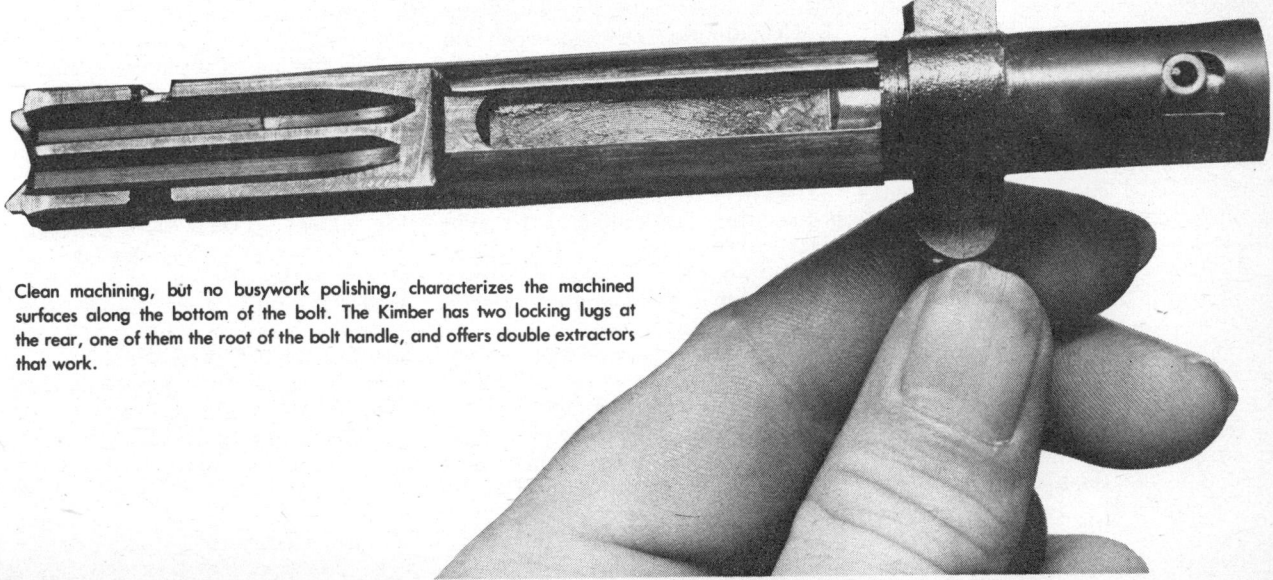

Clean machining, but no busywork polishing, characterizes the machined surfaces along the bottom of the bolt. The Kimber has two locking lugs at the rear, one of them the root of the bolt handle, and offers double extractors that work.

I didn't tell them I was writing a test report, but they sent me a complete new rifle, and a two page typewritten explanation, apparently because I was an unhappy customer.

I quote from their letter: "The most serious problem we encountered was related to the accuracy. We pinpointed the cause as oversized diameters at the front end of the chambers which was causing poor accuracy and blow-back of powder in some extreme cases. Originally we had been getting our barrel manufacturer to chamber the barrels to SAAMI "Sporting" specifications. He was doing this to the outside of the tolerances and some early rifles were even out of tolerance on the high side. Subsequently, we have tightened the chamber dimensions significantly and they are now closer to the SAAMI "Match" specifications. I am confident that you will find the rifle we have air freighted you today shoots well for an out-of-the-box 22 rimfire sporter."

The second gun, Kimber Model 82 Rifle serial number 654, is the gun tested for this report. The rifle was taken from the box, and following the instructions in the manual the bore was cleaned, scope mounted and I set out for the range with this second gun and various brands of 22 Long Rifle ammunition.

The rifle was tested with a Leupold scope in Kimber rings on an overcast day with wind gusting to an estimated 30 MPH. Control groups were shot with a 22 target rifle of known capabilities. Fourteen types of ammunition were used. At 50 yards, most brands would group under 1", with the best five-shot groups staying in ⅝". At 100 yards the Model 82 grouped ⅞" with CCI Mini Mag. I decided I was definitely interested in the Kimber. Although it shot well with standard velocity and match ammunition, this particular rifle shot best with various brands of high velocity ammo.

The Kimber functioned well. Bolt travel and throw on the new rifle were initially stiff, but not objectionably difficult. The action movement smoothed up rapidly during shooting. It feels slick with no slop or play. All test firing was done with ammunition fed from the magazines. Feeding was flawless. Ejection was good and controllable by the amount of force used in pulling the bolt back. Again, no failures.

Trigger pull was light and crisp initially, about 2½ pounds. Later the pull seemed to occasionally have a slight amount of creep and at the same time the weight of pull increased. A trigger pull gauge showed that the trigger pull was varying between 2½ and 4 pounds. Removing the action from the stock and putting a couple of drops of oil on the sear surfaces (easily done through access holes in the trigger housing) brought consistent trigger pull that measured 2 to 2⅛ pounds.

Showing the effects of much firing, this bolt face is cleanly machined, like the rest of the bolt. It looks as if the twin extractors are file-fitted, too.

I like the looks of the Kimber; the lines are classic. My gun had good wood to metal fit, excellent for a production gun. The checkered steel buttplate, steel grip cap, and steel trigger guard all add to the classic look, and polishing and blueing on all metal parts were as good as I've seen on a production gun. Also, all screws were timed; that is, the screw slots all lined up with the long axis of the stock, which is a sign of craftmanship and careful assembly. (Most of the pictures for this article are of the first rifle.)

The Kimber is modeled after a classic, the Winchester Model 52 Sporter. The action of the Kimber resembles a 52 action with the addition of scope grooves and a bolt shroud, although it retains the distinctive vertical bolt handle. The bolt has two rear locking surfaces 180 degrees apart. One is the bolt handle, the other is an opposing lug. There are two extractors on the bolt which, as I've mentioned worked perfectly.

The safety is unique. It is a flat topped rotating disc located at the right rear of the receiver. The disc rotates through an arc of 45 degrees with a positive stop at either end of its travel. It is connected by a rod to an assembly and locks the trigger and sear, but not the bolt. The disc has a red dot that is exposed when rotated forward to the firing position. It works well. Also unique were the steel scope rings. They are beautifully made and fit the gun perfectly. These rings are one of the really impressive things about this gun.

The barreled action is held in the stock with two screws as in center fire rifles. On the bottom of the barreled action is a large housing which holds the trigger mechanism, the safety assembly, and also serves as a magazine guide and retainer. Adjusting screws for trigger pull and overtravel are located on this housing. On the bottom of the barrel is a round recoil lug.

The stock is good, dense, plain, straight-grained, American black walnut. The finish is satin with all pores well filled. Checkering is 18 lines per inch with double borders and good coverage. Most diamonds were sharp in the center, but flat at the edges of the pattern. There were slight runovers. The execution and quality of wood and checkering strongly reminded me of vintage Winchesters. I should mention in passing that the stock bedding surfaces were rough.

The rifle without scope weighs 7 pounds 5 ounces. Length of pull is 13⅝ inches. The barrel is 22 inches long with a 1 in 16 inch twist. The Kimber stock was comfortable with a scope. The rifle and scope with five cartridges in the magazine balanced near the middle of the front receiver ring.

The Kimber Model 82 Rifle is a new product, and when you buy a new product you have to worry about three things. The first is whether or not you get what you're paying for. The second is whether or not the manufacturer will stand behind his product. The third is whether or not the company will remain in business. From my experience with Kimber, I feel I got my money's worth. Kimber also proved that they stand behind their product. I feel that a company that is as honest as they've been with me, and has a solid well made product, will prosper. Here is someone that is making a high quality rifle.

This gun may cost a bunch of money, but it's been years since you could go out and buy a gun like this. Three weeks ago a friend and I went to the Houston gun show to buy him a Winchester Model 52 Sporter. We found 17 52s for sale. Prices were generally $1000.00 and over. We judged that the quality of the Kimber was at least as good as the 52 Sporter. Granted, the 52 has collectors value. When the 52 went out of production over 20 years ago, it cost around $200.00, which was more than a Model 70 at the time. Allowing for inflation, the quality of the Kimber makes it a real bargain in today's economy. My friend did not buy a 52 Sporter. He now shoots a Kimber. Another friend ordered a barreled action. It's a good 22 rifle. ●

The 32-20 NEVER SAID DIE!

Maybe nobody likes this elegant light-recoil revolver round but people

by ROBERT S. L. ANDERSON

IN 1882 THE West was being won, the wounds left by the Civil War were healing slowly, and the 32-20 W.C.F. made its debut in Mr. Winchester's Model 1873. The cartridge must have been warmly received as its popularity grew to a point where it could be said that just about every American arms maker had a rifle or handgun chambered for it. At least that's the way Frank Barnes sees it in his book CARTRIDGES OF THE WORLD.

In handguns, the 32-20 has been chambered in revolvers made by Colt, Smith & Wesson and Bayard—the latter offering not nearly as popular in the U.S. as Colt or S&W products. In order to achieve its considerable popularity, the 32-20 had to offer the turn-of-the-century shooting public a benefit or two. Certainly, the opportunity to have a rifle/pistol combo was an inducement. The 32-20 was accurate, light in recoil, economical to load and was (with a rifle in the right hands) capable of handling medium-sized game out to 100-yards-plus.

Today the 32-20 is everything but 100 years old; it has been 30 years since a firearm was commercially chambered for that round; but it won't give up the ghost.

My own interest in 32-20 handguns came about five years ago when a friend offered me one—an old, 6-inch S&W, M&P (4th change). The gun was in good shape except for very light and evenly distributed pitting in the bore. I thought the $100 price tag was a bit stiff; however, the gun came with an original Heiser holster and cartridge loop belt—besides, my wife liked it. What's a fella to do?

So, I picked up a set of RCBS dies and started to roll my own. If you've seen the pictures accompanying this piece of prose you know the story doesn't end here. Six months ago I did a friend a favor. My friend then did me a favor. He gave me a S&W, M&P (4th change) 32-20 revolver. (Sound familiar?) The only difference between the "new" M&P and the old one was the new gun was, in fact, *as new*. At this point I figured I was the only guy in the Midwest to possess a pristine pair of M&P 32-20 popguns. Well, a couple of shooting buddies seemed to feel the 32-20 was a pretty fair cartridge and I had been incredibly lucky. Two other shooting chums proffered up condolences and advised they wouldn't want their daughters to marry one! Again, what's a fellow to do??

At the local range, the comments among the old-timers were more uniform. To a man, the experienced shooters advised that my M&P could

(Left) The internal working mechanisms of most pre-war M&Ps are nicely polished, providing a smooth single or double action trigger pull.

(Below) With the one exception mentioned by the author, all the test loads exhibited normal pressure signs and extracted freely.

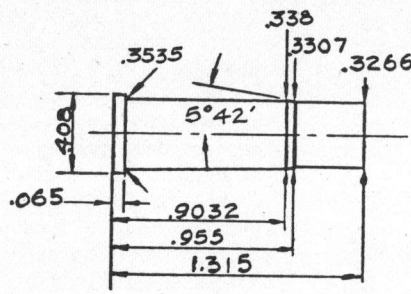

A rimmed cartridge, the 32-20 was chambered in a number of Colt revolvers and only one model Smith & Wesson, the Hand Ejector (M&P) in all its variations.

The author's pair of S&W 32-20s sport 6-inch barrels and fixed sights. In general, fixed sights can be adjusted by thinning, raising or lowering the front sight blade once the shooter has selected the load that best suits his purposes.

be an accurate and powerful S.O.B. ("Sweet Old Blaster") in the right hands.

It became apparent to me the 32-20 indeed had a following, a somewhat aging and/or underground coterie of believers. I decided to see just how popular this cartridge really was. After doing a little checking, I came up with some interesting ammo/brass figures. It appears Remington and Winchester collectively sell somewhere in the neighborhood of 100,000 empty brass cases every year. Where Winchester is concerned, the brass is a standard catalog item; however, no bullets are available. With Remington the brass availability is on a special-order basis; but, also on special order, Remington offers 100- and 80-grain lead bullets at a suggested retail of $7.10 and $6.41, respectively, per 100. It should be noted that the Remington 100-grain .310", and 80-grain .310" lead slugs are the only 32-20 bullet offerings from the major manufacturers. In terms of jacketed 32-20 ammo alone, Remington does offer a 100-gr. JSP loading for those who're interested.

When it came down to the sale of loaded ammo neither Winchester nor Remington would comment directly other than to say (in the case of Winchester), "We sell a good amount of loaded ammo."

Major reloading houses sell 500-plus sets of 32-20 dies a year with RCBS marketing the lion's share. In fact, sales figures for the 32-20 dies have remained surprisingly constant at RCBS for many years now. (When it comes to dies, look to RCBS or Pacific as Lyman no longer offers them in this caliber.)

All these sales figures say the 32-20 is indeed alive and breathing at a rather steady pace. No, the figures don't tell us that the 32-20 is a barn-burner. They simply tell us that the ammo, components and dies sell at a very steady rate. Winchester's positive comments on loaded 32-20 ammo sales leads me to believe that a lot more guys *should be* reloading it, considering the number of handguns still floating around.

How many might there be? Lots.

Let's take a look at what was actually turned out by Colt and S&W:

A call to Roy Jinks at Smith & Wesson confirmed that only the Hand Ejector revolvers were chambered for that round by S&W. (The Hand Ejector series of 32-20 is mechanically identical to the 38 Special M&P series that was introduced in the same year—1899. Being identical, both guns are commonly called "M&P;" a designation we'll use for the 32-20 S&Ws mentioned in this article.) A total of 144,677 S&W 32-20s in M&P persuasion were produced between 1899 and 1940 according to Norm Flayderman's *Guide to Antique American Firearms*.

In Colt's single-action line-up the following represents the 32-20 production:

1. Single Action Army 29,812
2. SAA Target 30
3. Bisley 13,291
4. Bisley Target 131
   Total 43,264

Beyond this, Colt manufactured a total of about 1,500,000 other double action revolvers, in which the 32-20 chambering could be ordered. This total production was spread out among the following models: Official Police, Officer's Model, Police Positive Special, New Police, Army Special.

If we assume only 5 percent of the total Colt D/A production was for the 32-20, then we have an approximation of 75,000 D/A 32-20 Colts.

Altogether then, the total known 32-20 handgun production is slightly over a quarter million pieces. If we further assume 50 percent of those guns have survived, then we can estimate there are around 130,000 single- and double-action 32-20s still available for shooters to enjoy.

Most 32-20's have fixed sights. Lest you feel hesitant about a handgun that doesn't come with everything but radar, pick up an S&W Model 10 M&P in 38 Special. I've owned three, from the snub-nose on up, and have found the sighting equipment to be well regulated right out of the box. There's little question, therefore, that a handloader has the latitude and economy to shop for a load that suits his 32-20.

If you're lucky enough to own an adjustable-sighted Colt, you've got a wider range handloading potential to play with; however, don't knock those fixed sights till you've tried 'em. A lot of combat pistol shooters are heading for fixed sights on expensive guns. Such sights are rugged, fumble-free and regulated for one, good, reliable load.

Elmer Keith once told me the Western adage that goes, "Beware the man with one gun—he knows how to use it." The modern combat shooter might be saying, "Beware the man with one load—he knows where it hits."

My own 32-20 M&P's tell me you'll shoot to the point of aim with bullets in the 100- to 120-grain range. I'm not

Bottom left box is 30 years old, others are current.

TWO 32-20's?

As a pistol cartridge, our round got short-changed with the advent of smokeless powder. With light bullets, rifle velocities could be counted on to surpass the 2,000 fps mark; however, 32-20 revolvers with thin chamber walls had to be down-loaded considerably. In fact, much of the commercial ammo made for the 32-20 carried labeling information indicating the ammo inside was or was not suitable for pistol use. To some extent that probably created a small amount of confusion in the transition days of black to smokeless powders. As a result, current 32-20 commercial ammo is made for *both* rifle/pistol consumption and it so states on the end flap of a box of Remington ammo sitting in front of me.

I will be the first to admit that ammo label confusion alone doesn't spell the demise of a particular cartridge or the guns chambered for it. It's my personal opinion that handgunners in 1930's found themselves one hell of a lot more interested in the then-new 357 S&W Magnum (and a host of other still-popular handgun rounds) than they were in a cartridge that was almost 70 years young and yawning its way into oblivion. The 32-20 yawned, true enough, but it never went to sleep.

Old label shows smokeless load and suitable guns. The back panel of this old box of Western 32-20s clearly advises the buyer that the ammo in this box is loaded with *smokeless* powder. It also spells out what guns the ammo is suitable for and the fact that it *can* be used in revolvers.

saying that, for instance, an 88-grain slug *won't* print to point of aim in your own gun, I'm simply saying it's not likely to.

Before you go running for the reloading manual, save yourself some steps. Unless you have *Cartridges of the World* by Frank Barnes, or P.O. Ackley's *Pocket Manual for Shooters and Reloaders,* you won't find a whole hell of a lot. In fact, the reloading-manual boys don't offer much in the way of handgun loading data—they don't make bullets for 32-20.

Cartridges of the World shows two loads for revolvers:

Bullet	Powder/Grs.*	MV/fps	ME/ft. lbs.
115 Gr. Lead	Unique 5**	980	248
115 Gr. Lead	Bullseye 3	840	185

*(Start your loads at 10% below these figures and work up to—and do not exceed—the powder charge listed.)
**Start at 3.5 grains and work up a tenth of a grain at a time.

P.O. Ackley's 32-20 loads are as follows:

Bullet Weight	Powder Charge*	Powder Type	MV/fps
80	4.2 grs.	Bullseye	1180
80	5.0 "	Unique	1220
90	3.6 "	Bullseye	1060
90	5.8 "	Unique	1160
115	3.1 "	Bullseye	850
115	4.5 "	Unique	925

*(Start your loads at 10% below these figures and work up to—and do not exceed—the powder charges listed.)

In working up a load that would shoot to point of aim in my oldest S&W M&P, I turned to Unique. Unique behind the right bullets in my K-38, a Model 39 and a Browning High Power consistently provide 1¼-inch or *under* groups when fired from a bench at 25 yards. For bullets, I cranked up the SAECO melting pot and got out my moulds. Lee, Lyman, SAECO and RCBS all offer suitable .312" moulds; however, I had the Lee and Lyman varieties on hand and chose among them. In order of use, they were: an 88-grain Lyman (#311419), a 100-grain Lee (#311-1002R), a 115-grain Lyman (#3118) and a 120-grain Lee (#311-1202R). The bore on my older M&P slugged out at .312" and all sizing was done on a SAECO Lubrisizer with a .3110 sizing die.

The 88-grain Lyman, backed by 4.5 grains of Unique shot decidely low and left. A called flyer opened the 10-shot group up to a shade under two inches; 8 of those rounds landed inside ⅞ of an

Recoil with the 32-20 S&W is more than manageable considering the fact that, when using light bullets (under 100 grains), you can churn up a muzzle velocity in the neighborhood of 1200 fps.

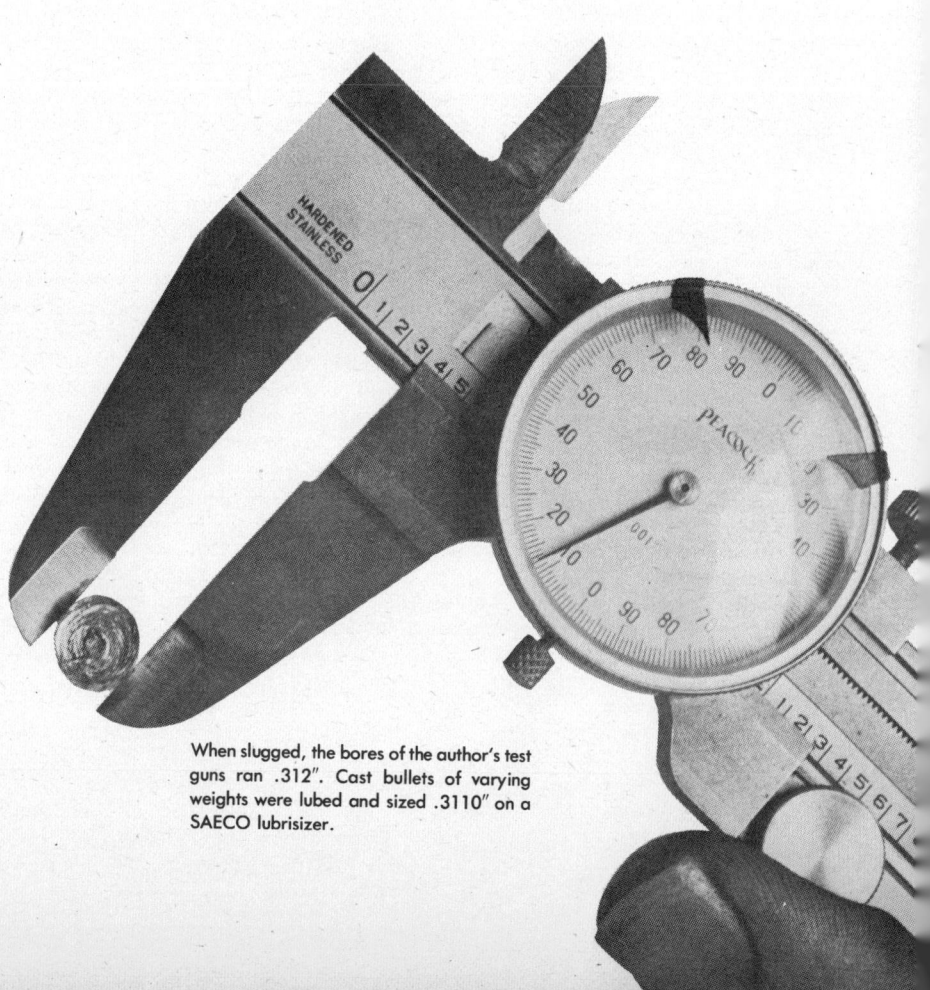

When slugged, the bores of the author's test guns ran .312". Cast bullets of varying weights were lubed and sized .3110" on a SAECO lubrisizer.

From left to right: Lyman 88-grain, Lee 93-grain, Lee 100-grain, Lee 119-grain, Lee 120-grain and the Lyman 115-grain. The heavier cast bullets—115 to 120 grains—tend to shoot more to the point of aim in handguns.

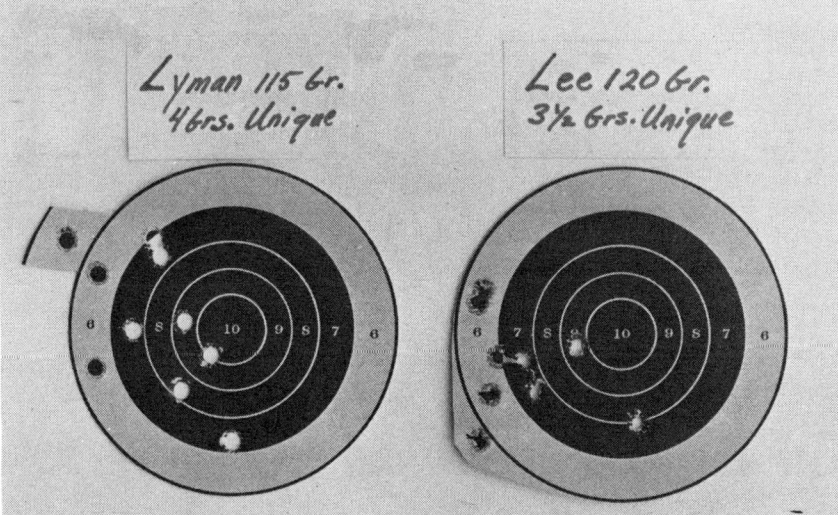

In terms of accuracy among the heavier cast bullets, the Lee 120-grain was the winner with a 2½-inch group with 3.5 grains of Unique.

This turn-of-the-century 32-20 round features a 110-grain lead bullet and 18½ grains of blackpowder—about 1½ grains shy of the "20" grains called for. If you happen to run across a batch of the old loads save 'em to look at, not shoot.

inch (center to center). Primer indentation on this load was light, extraction was easy; this is excellent accuracy.

The 100-grain Lee backed by 4.9 grains of Unique delivered a 10-shot group just below the point of aim. Primers were well flattened and extraction was a shade stiff—*I do not recommend this load.* Further loads will be reduced a grain and worked up a tenth at a time.

The 115-grain Lyman slug with 4 grains of Unique shot just to the left and an inch and a half high over the point of aim. Primer indentation was normal, no pressure signs, and the 10-shot group was 3¼-inches center to center. I intend to do some more shooting with this load.

Finally, the 120-grain Lee was given its chance at the bench. Using 3.5 grains of Unique, the 10-shot group hit on the money and slightly to the left. Group size ran 2½-inches center to center with 9 rounds going into 1¾ inches. This is a light load with excellent accuracy potential.

The 115- or 120-grain slugs shoot more closely to point of aim than lighter weights. I was after accuracy more than anything else in the initial shooting sessions. I will try some more shooting before settling on a particular bullet/powder combination. For instance, the 88-grain Lyman bullet has excellent grouping potential, and it can possibly be loaded to the point where it edges the 1200 fps mark. At the other end of the weight spectrum, there is good potential with the 120-grain Lee.

What it comes down to is a matter of personal choice. I won't make up my mind without more shooting. Adjustments to the fixed sights on my own gun may eventually amount to little more than thinning out the right side of the front sight blade and adding a bit of metal to the top of the blade itself.

If you're lucky enough to have a 32-20, and it's in good shooting condition, get a set of dies, some small rifle primers, a mould or two and give it a go. The 32-20 is, for my money, high on accuracy, low on recoil and potential dynamite on small game or varmints under 50 yards. Those S&W and Colt revolvers were all cranked out before WW II and many exhibit superb fit and finish. They aren't just for collecting, however, they are for shooting.

By the way, if you ever happen to learn that Smith & Wesson is reintroducing the 32-20 in their K-frame series of wheelguns, please call me—as fast as you can!

A few buffalo on a 7,000-acre pasture aren't always easy to find, once they figure out what's happening. This is Las Abros, Box 176, McQueeney, TX 78123.

THE BUFFALO AND THE CHAPUIS

Swatting an American bison is easy to arrange, but not so easy to do neatly, even with enough gun.

by KEN WARNER

THIS HAS to be a shooter's report, because there wasn't a whole lot of romance connected with killing a buffalo for meat down in Texas at the tag end of winter. For my Chapuis 9.3x74mm rifle and for me it was just a job of work, truth to tell.

We got it done, but neither of us covered ourselves with glory.

First, a little bit about buffalos and modern harvesting and about Chapuis rifles:

Today, except for a big herd in the wild around Great Slave Lake in Canada, the buffalo is a meat animal and a curio. In place of the teeming herds of the 19th Century, there are a surprising number of small bunches spread around the West. It takes either an awful strong fence or something over 5,000 acres to keep buffalo in one place, so they're not really cramped for space, whoever keeps them, most places.

Buffalo being bovines, they tend to increase. They are valuable in the first place and hardy in the second place and there are hardly any predators in the third place, so anyone with a herd gets into the surplus animal business pretty quick. Something has to be done because crowded buffalo turn mean or start busting fences. In a couple of weeks in, for instance, Texas, a buffalo with an urge to be elsewhere can burst through every fence he comes to in a 40-mile walk. (I talked to a fellow who watched a buffalo walk up to a five-strand barbed wire fence, a nice, tight fence, set his chest against it and look around for a minute. Then, without apparent effort or a change of expression, the buffalo started walking. Everything leaned and stretched and pretty soon it broke. Wires twanging about him, the buffalo just marched off into the fresh, new bushes.)

So what is done is harvest them—that is, kill, skin, butcher and use them. Since they can't really be herded, they are normally shot, and sometimes a dude does the shooting, impelled, no doubt, by thoughts of how a buffalo head will look on the wall, but mostly by an intense curiosity over his reaction and the animal's. Killing a buffalo is one old-time experience that can be achieved today. One need only do it to know what it was like.

Therefore, one can find a buffalo to shoot should he want one, under circumstances not so different from the genuine 19th Century meat-shooting. That is, there will be some rambling around looking for them, and a certain amount of indecision about which one is the one, and some shenannigans and fast walks to get a clear shot at the right place, and what with one thing and another it could take all day to get the right shot. Sometimes it might take more than a day, in fact.

A surprising number of those who shoot a buffalo now and again choose to use the old Sharps-type cartridges for the experience. Inevitably, muzzleloaders get a play from the buckskin brigade. Of course, a lot of buffalo are poked with whatever big rifle the shooter happens to own, and some are simply and economically slain with high-velocity bullets in the ear by fellows who really like buffalo meat and find this the quickest, cheapest way to get it.

You can read the literature on the subject 'til the lamp goes dim and you'll find few who ever called the buffalo a sporting beast. Ornery and sometimes dangerous, yes, but never a challenge to a rifleman. That is, given a good firearm, the buffalo hunter walked or rode into range, taking moderate care not to spook the beasts, and popped the one—or the 20—he wanted. After a suitable period, the beast or beasts died.

Well, it isn't a lot different today. And that's what we did.

We is that Chapuis rifle and me. I wanted to shoot something big with it and Hal Swiggett and Phil Koehne had these buffalo and a couple needed killing for the meat. It was a little late in the year, but we all figured if we worked fast, the meat wouldn't spoil nor the hair slip.

Koehne's Las Abras ranch is between San Antonio and Laredo and amounts to—just lately—some 7000 acres with only a few longhorns and buffalo on it. He sets up a kill now and again and was most gracious about this one. April is an awkward time to shoot a buffalo—it might be 95° that day, and the hides are mostly rubbed. On the other hand, buffalo meat customers who ran out of meat in March could be happy. So, anyway, we did it.

When John Amber got so interested in the Chapuis guns for last year's edition, I got pretty interested, too. The Chapuis system has technical interest, the guns feel elegant, and seemed likely to work pretty well. In the end, I bought the cheapest and plainest boxlock gun in 9.3x74R, together with a leather case and a pair of 3" 20-gauge barrels.

Then, there turned out to be lots of editing to do, so finally we had to accomplish a lot of shooting in a rush. Arranged-for ammunition didn't show up, but some dies and bullets did, enough to scrabble together jacketed loads that shot to the sights pretty well. That permitted some practice which went well and so with one 10-round box of RWS 285-gr. TUG cartridges I went off to Texas.

It was there I learned firsthand what everyone says is true—the American bison does not die easily. Now, all the experts say the 9.3x74R is a good cartridge, and all the numbers say it is a good cartridge, and my more experienced friends say the way my buffalo died indicates it was a good cartridge. However, I laced that creature behind the leg for one, and through the liver for another, and through the shoulders for another and it still took him 10 minutes or more to die.

Double rifles are, to my mind, built to deliver two shots quick to relatively large targets. That doesn't mean pachyderms exclusively. A deer at 50-60 yards is a large target, for instance. So is a buffalo. Anyway, for me, they're for open sights and quick shooting and that's why I picked the 9.3x74R chambering and the buffalo for a target. Having fooled with the gun a while, I think I picked the right rifle. I don't know about the target.

My Chapuis weighs just 7 pounds, 6 ounces. The model can be had in 375 H&H as well as several smaller cartridges. I can handle the relatively

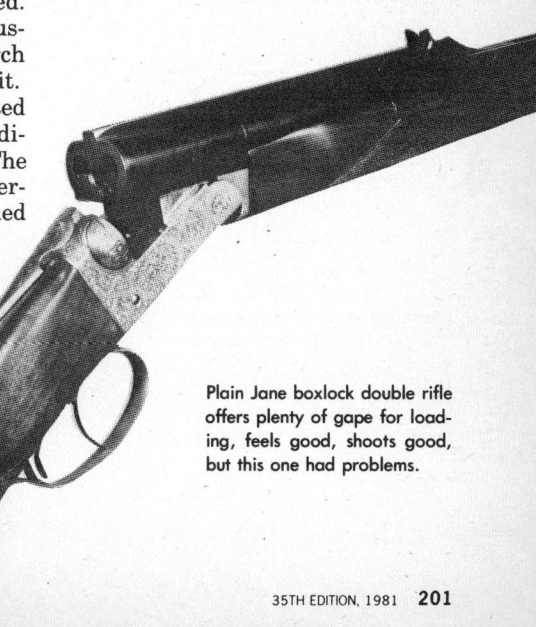

Plain Jane boxlock double rifle offers plenty of gape for loading, feels good, shoots good, but this one had problems.

35TH EDITION, 1981 **201**

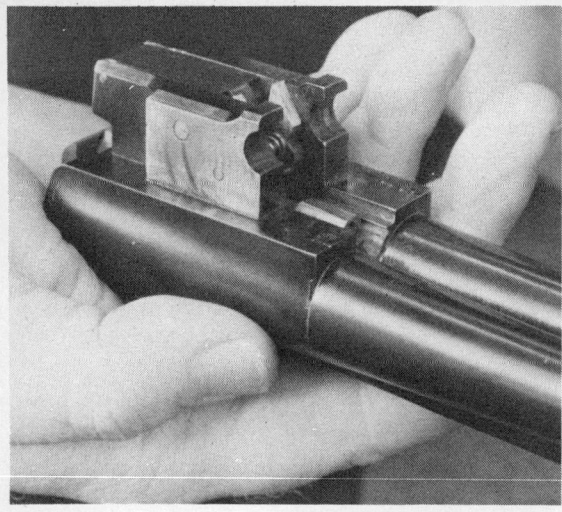

Chapuis system is different, offers big squared-off surfaces to help take the high-power rifle strain and house the ejector system.

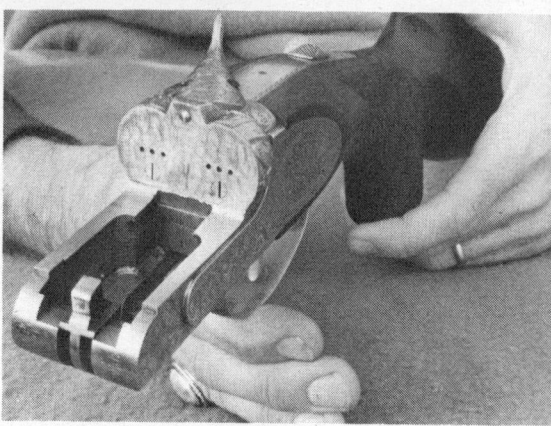

Wide and shallow, the Chapuis receiver gets its strength differently than most double guns. It's quality stuff—note bushed firing pins, screw-locked.

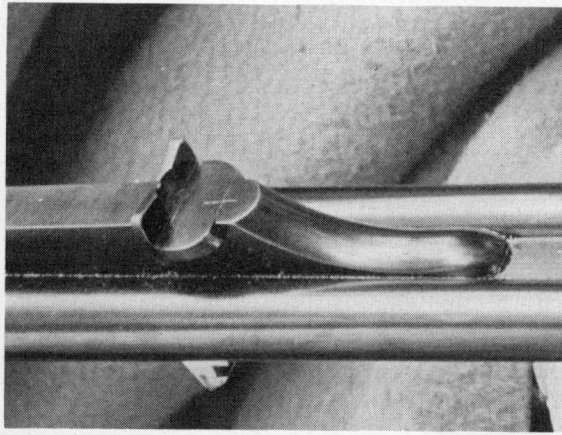

One appreciates elegance in a rear sight, and this one has strength and high visibility to offer as well. At the end of a nice quarter-rib, it's the right distance from the eye.

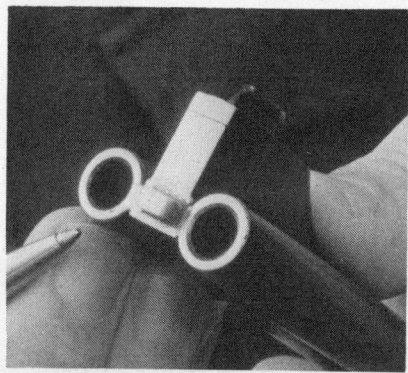

It isn't exactly correct to call this little block of metal a gadget, but that is what it is. With it sticking out, you'd have to try hard to damage the barrel muzzles.

mild recoil of the 9.3x74, but the 375 shades it a little and I think the recoil, even though Chapuis makes 375s heavier, would get strenuous enough to affect the shooting. I figured a 285-gr. .366" bullet at about 2200 fps would handle most any shooting problem. I still think so, but I may give up shooting buffalo with it.

Here's how it went:

After a lot of backing and filling, a fair-sized bull with horns, it turned out, over 16" long got situated about right and they said "Go" so I went, at about 60 yards or so. The first shot went in low behind his foreleg, which is where I promised to shoot him. He jumped and broke into a run and the second shot hit farther back, quartering up through the liver. After a few jumps, he stopped, and didn't travel anymore after that.

I popped the lever over and the two empty shells sailed away over my shoulder. Two more went in and I ran over to where the bull stood, bleeding from the mouth. I waited, but he didn't go down, so I shot for the shoulder. That one went through and busted up the off shoulder, and down he went.

I pushed the lever again and popped the gun open, and that fired case didn't sail away. So I shut the gun, waited a while which seemed a long time, and went for his neck and apparently missed. And I opened the gun again and neither case budged.

Well, that was a surprising development in a gun that hadn't bobbled any of the first 60 or 70 rounds. I certainly was glad the buffalo wasn't going anywhere. I was even gladder it was not a Cape buffalo or any of the more belligerent beasts toward which one might carry a double rifle. I was, in fact, excited.

The buffalo slowly and quietly died eventually, demonstrating a phlegmatic temperament and considerably more dignity than had I. It was a wonder to me. I just had not ever slammed anything that hard before without near instantaneous results.

Two days later I talked with Elmer Keith about it and he knew exactly how I felt. He knew because he had had substantially the same experience both times he had tried the job. He says they're tough. I agree.

I might say that a buffalo isn't much fun once he's dead, either. There's a lot of meat and blood there. David Nowotny, however, strove both manfully and productively and I wish I had a taxidermist along for all my shooting.

The next difficult thing I had to do was tell Bob Painter, who imports the Chapuis, the following three things:

1. His gun had failed. 2. It had failed while hunting. 3. It had publicly and conspicuously malfunctioned for the Editor of GUN DIGEST. It was an unpleasant experience for me and was even more so, I believe, for Mr. Painter.

The problem was not high-pressure or stuck cases or shooter mismanagement. It was in the ejector-extractor mechanism. Had I done what I know one should do, it would have been discovered under less embarrassing circumstances. What should one do? Well, you really ought not use a new gun for serious work before you've fired it several hundred times. That is particularly true of double rifles and shotguns, revolvers, autoloading guns of all kinds, and any new design, and less true for bolt-action rifles and other less complicated guns.

You won't believe this. Mr. Painter hardly could. The French workman who buttoned up the gun—the mechanism has a cover over the ejector springs and things—forgot to sweep up before shutting the door and going home. That is, he left lots of oil and grinding dust down there. It hadn't ground off any important surface, but it had all packed in a sear and nothing was happening.

Painter is going to some trouble to make the situation right. In fact, the gun, some hot letters, and Mr. Painter himself may be going to France over the matter. Painter says he's not treating me any differently than any other customer and I believe him.

So I am going to cut Mr. Painter and the Chapuis some slack right here: I'm going to keep the gun. It is not a test gun, remember. I bought and paid for it. And I assure you I could return the gun and get the money with no questions asked. I think this is just one of those things.

Why bother? Well, I like the Chapuis. It's a friendly piece to have around. It shoots well and carries easily. Remember that with all my shortcomings and with all the toughness of the target, the buffalo was out of business in just a few seconds, regardless how long it took to get to the end. That gun can do what it's supposed to do.

Should it prove otherwise, I'll let you know. And I believe I'll stick the next buffalo I shoot in the ear with a good fast bullet out of an accurate scoped rifle. Since there's not a whole lot of point in that, perhaps I'll just retire from buffalo before I lose any more ground. •

HUNT PHOTOS: HAL SWIGGETT

There was some wading about in the thornbushes on this shoot, some of it plenty high enough and thick enough to hide a bull. The quick handy double was comforting the while.

There just isn't much visible target, even with all this hair to shoot at. Next time, I believe I will go for the shoulder first shot, regardless of what I'm told to do.

This one will put him down by breaking a shoulder. The medium bull you see has already absorbed two good 9.3x74 hits. He isn't going anywhere, but he isn't falling down yet, either.

Not exactly triumphant, your writer and the Chapuis pose for the trophy shot. One thing about it: Even a less-than-gigantic buffalo is a pretty big animal.

LONG GUNS

by LARRY S. STERETT

IT'S GOING to be a good year for shooters. While few larger sporting arms manufacturers have introduced entirely new models—Remington's Model 870 "Competition" Trap Gun is really just a much changed 870—some new designs and some new manufacturers have appeared on the long gun scene, such as the Alpha I bolt action centerfire rifle from Texas, the Holmes Supertrap and Ljutic's Olympic Mono Gun with tubes, for trap shooters, and Mossberg's new Model 5600 gas-operated 12 gauge field gun. And, there's more in the following pages. It's going to be a good year for shooters.

Alpha Arms

Remember the Ranger Arms Magnum and Omega III rifles, and the current Snake Charmer shotgun? Now there's a new lightweight bolt action rifle by the same designer—Homer Koon. Measuring only 40¼ inches in over-all length with a 21-inch barrel, the Alpha I is a "no frills" rifle intended to be carried by a hunter for hours, if necessary, without tiring. It weighs approximately 6¼ pounds. Chambered for the new 7mm-08 Remington cartridge (also available chambered for the 243 Winchester) the Alpha I has several unique features, including a Teflon-coated trigger guard and floorplate assembly, a shrouded cocking piece, three locking lugs, each measuring .335-inch wide, a 60-degree bolt lift, plus a round receiver of 4130 steel measuring 7.875 inches in length and bedded in an aluminum V stock insert, to name a few. The receiver is drilled and tapped for those two-piece scope mounts designed to fit the Savage M110 rifle.

The walnut stock features a slim forearm, Monte Carlo cheekpiece, rubber butt pad, sling studs swivel, no checkering, and three point glass bedding of the barreled action—tang, receiver ring, and forearm. The walnut stock has a polyurethane satin finish, while the metal surfaces of the barrel action have a non-glare matte finish. The barreled action is retained in the stock via two screws into the receiver bottom—both through the aluminum V blocks—with one behind the magazine well and the other just ahead of the magazine well — with no screw into the rear tang or into the recoil lug. The recoil lug is .245-inch

(From top to bottom) The Alpha I rifle with a Leupold 2½x-7x scope. The Holmes Supertrap 12 gauge shotgun in the straight-pull design and a Morgan adjustable recoil pad. Note the straight line design of the Supertrap barrel, receiver, and buttstock. The Mossberg Model 380 semi-automatic rifle has a 20-inch barrel and is chambered for the 22 Long Rifle rimfire cartridge. Mossberg's new Model 5600 Slugster is a gas-operated autoloader featuring a 24-inch barrel with rifle-type sights for rifled slug use. The Anschutz/Savage Model 64-MS is designed for 22 rimfire metallic silhouette shooting.

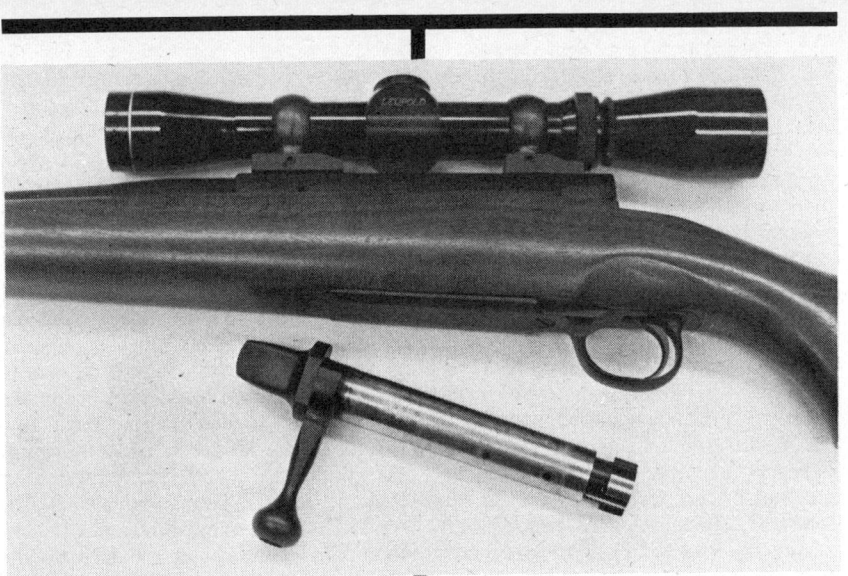

The Alpha I rifle is trim, with very few projections to catch on brush or hunting clothing. Note the bolt stop at the rear of the receiver, and the trim appearance of the bolt with its shrouded cocking piece.

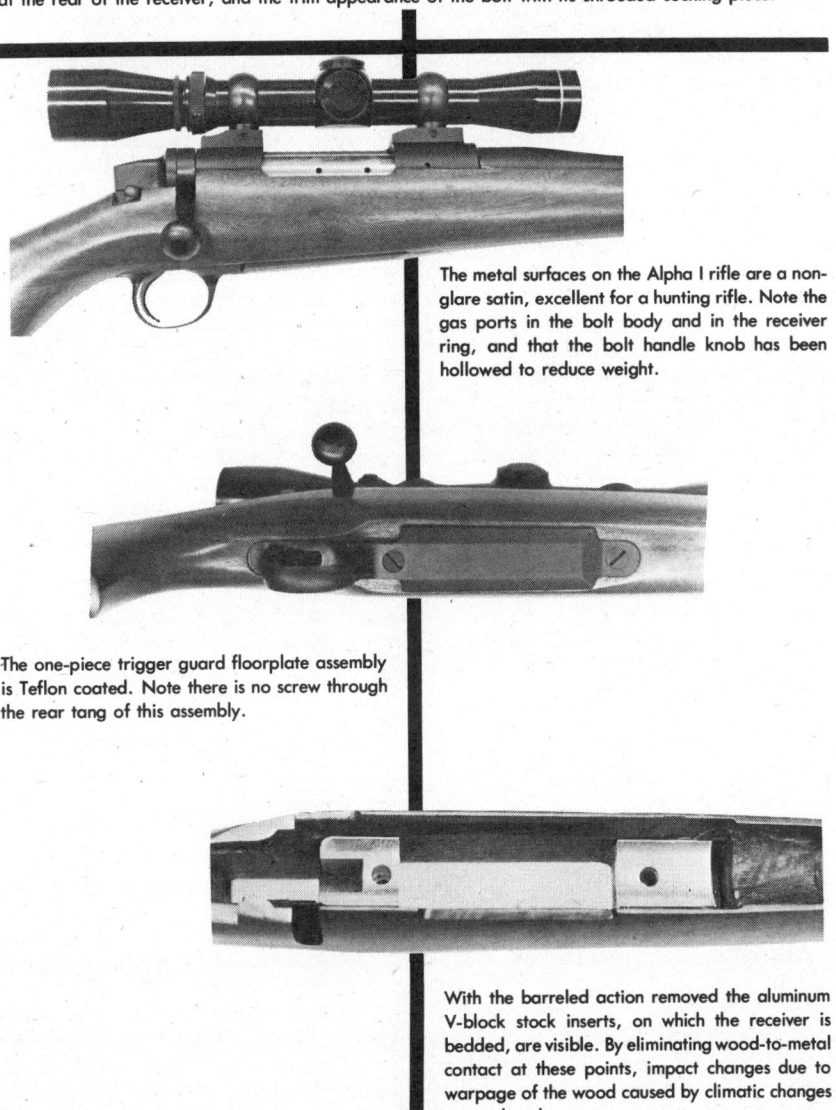

The metal surfaces on the Alpha I rifle are a non-glare satin, excellent for a hunting rifle. Note the gas ports in the bolt body and in the receiver ring, and that the bolt handle knob has been hollowed to reduce weight.

The one-piece trigger guard floorplate assembly is Teflon coated. Note there is no screw through the rear tang of this assembly.

With the barreled action removed the aluminum V-block stock inserts, on which the receiver is bedded, are visible. By eliminating wood-to-metal contact at these points, impact changes due to warpage of the wood caused by climatic changes are reduced.

thick, and measured outside to outside, the two guard screws are 4.075 inches apart. The bolt body is 5.458 inches long, with a diameter of .870-inch, the same as the locking lugs. When Alpha I is cocked and locked, the bolt locking lugs lock directly into the barrel extension, rather than into the receiver ring, in somewhat the same manner as some pump or autoloading shotgun designs.

Having already carried an Alpha I rifle for a couple of days, this writer can vouch for the fact it's a handy rifle for whitetail deer, or similar size game. It's short and handy, well balanced, accurate, and it looks good, all for about $300.00.

Bortmess Gun Company

Featuring the Voere 2145 action from West Germany, Bortmess rifles are available in two styles—Classic and Big Horn—and in chamberings from the 22-250 to the 375 H&H Magnum, plus most wildcats. The 375 Weatherby Magnum and the 458 Winchester Magnum are available as options for an additional $100.00. Both rifles use Shilen Match Grade barrels. The Big Horn has a unique Bortmess-designed stock of maple or Claro walnut with a Monte Carlo, while the Classic, naturally, has a classic stock design with cheekpiece, and a steel Niedner grip cap. Either rifle lists at $1150.00. The Big Horn model can also be purchased in a left-handed version.

Browning

Last year the over-under ST-100 with adjustable impact-point ventilated rib was introduced, and it's still available at $3250.00, with 30-inch barrels and a choice of three different choke combinations. New for 1980 is the Grand Liege 12 gauge over-under shotgun with a choice of 28- or 30-inch barrels having standard length chambers. A mechanical single selective trigger is standard, as are automatic ejectors, and a silver-grey receiver engraved with scroll designs and three different game scenes. Weighing between 7½ and 7¾ pounds, the Grand Liege is a field gun priced to sell at $995.00.

For double rifle fans, the Browning Express rifle is now available in a choice of 270 Winchester or 30-06 calibers for $3400.00, complete with fitted carrying case. The Express is an over-under design, with 24-inch barrels and open sights. The Express is identical to the Superposed Centennial with straight grip oil-finished stock, and single selective trigger, except for not having the extra set of over-under shotgun barrels.

Rimfire riflemen have not been forgotten. Both the BAR-22 and the BPR-22 Magnum rifles are available with Grade II receivers, a squirrel scene on the right side and a rabbit scene on the left side. The Grade II receivers have a grey satin finish. Naturally, this decoration adds $100.00 to the basic cost of the Grade I rifles.

Charles Daly

Last year the Charles Daly line of over-under shotguns was introduced by Outdoor Sports Headquarters in Dayton, Ohio, and this year the line has been expanded to include the Superior and Field Grade autoloaders. The two models differ mainly in the receiver finish—antiqued engraved silver or gunmetal—and are available only in 12 gauge. Gas-operated with a "floating piston," these shotguns resemble the Weatherby Centurion and Supermatic Shadow designs, but without the frills. Barrel lengths range from 26 inches to 30 inches, with the Superior version being available in a choice of chokes from Skeet to full. The Charles Daly name has been appearing on shotguns for over 50 years, but the current shotguns do not resemble the original models bearing the Daly name, or even the New York distributed over-under models of a decade ago.

Harrington & Richardson

The prices of the economical H&R arms have increased, although seldom more than $10.00 per model. No actual new models were introduced in 1980, but two additional barrel lengths—30 inches and 32 inches—were added to the Model 088 single shot 12 gauge shotguns; chokes on both are full. The sad news is the discontinuance of the Model 175 and 175 Deluxe muzzle-loading rifles in both the 45 and 58 chamberings, and the Model 171 Standard Cavalry Carbine in 45-70 Gov't. The balance of the long arm line remains the same, but there have been several additions to the revolver line.

Holmes Supertrap

One of the most unusual single-shot trap guns to appear in many years is manufactured in Fayetteville, AR, by gunsmith Bill Holmes. Available in three versions—straight-pull, turn bolt, and self-opening, the Supertrap barrel is directly in line with the tubular receiver and buttstock. With a Thompson-style grip beneath the receiver, the over-all appearance is somewhat along the lines of the military M16 rifle. Available with, or without, choke tubes, similar to the Winchoke, Accu-Choke, and Baker choke tube designs, the Supertrap was designed from the ground up as a trap gun, rather than as field gun modified to shoot trap.

Since the Supertrap is custom built, there are many options available. However, an average model would have a fancy walnut stock, forearm and pistol grip with excellent hand checkering at 24 lines-per-inch. If the straight-pull design was selected, rearward and forward movement of the cocking/charging handle would extract the fired case (eject if requested on original order), cock the hammer, chamber a 12-gauge shell, assuming one had been dropped into the loading/ejection port, and lock into battery via the crossbolt engaging both receiver walls. The trigger is adjustable, and turning a single screw will produce an adjustable release trigger out of it, should the customer prefer this type of trigger.

The straight-line design of the barrel/receiver/stock requires the use of a high ventilated rib, and beneath this rib—1.590 inches high at the muzzle—but above the barrel, is a gas-operated counter recoil mechanism that is guaranteed to make the Supertrap recoil less than any other 12 gauge shotgun on the market, at least as this is written. Barrel length may range from 26 to 36 inches, and the weight will be slightly more or less than 10½ pounds, depending on the density of the wood, style of forearm—slim, medium, or full—and the length of barrel. This weight in itself will aid in reducing recoil, and the recoil pad—customer's choice—will do a bit more.

Considering the customer has a choice of action type, three stock woods—maple, walnut, or myrtle—barrel length, stock dimensions, checkering pattern, chokes, point-of-impact, sights, recoil pad, ejection or extraction of fired shells, and forearm style, the $2,000-plus price is well within reason. There are a good many other non-custom shotguns on the market today which sell much higher, and while the Supertrap may look different, it breaks targets the same way.

Ithaca Gun

Back in operation again, and celebrating its Centennial as this is written, the Ithaca Gun Company is concentrating on production of four different designs—the pump action Model 37 Featherlight, the autoloading Model 51 Featherlight, the autoloading Mag 10, and the Single Barrel Trap. The Model 37 is available in a choice of 12 or 20 gauge chamberings, as is the Model 51, depending on the particular grade, but the Single Barrel Trap is available only in 12 gauge, choked full, in a choice of 32- or 34-inch barrel and 5E or $7500 grades. Naturally, the Mag 10 is available chambered only for the magnum 10 gauge shells, with 32-inch full choke barrel, but it is available in four grades—Standard, Standard Vent, Deluxe, and Supreme—with a top retail price of $725.00 in early 1980. Ten grades of the Model 37 are available, ranging from the Basic Standard at $242.00 to the Supreme at $450.00, while the 51 is available in six grades from the Standard at $319.00 to the Deluxe Trap with Monte Carlo at $460.00.

Kimber of Oregon

One of the brightest new sporting arms in years—the Kimber Model 82—is being manufactured in Clackamas, OR, on the outskirts of Portland. Chambered for the rimfire 22 Long Rifle cartridge, the Model 82 is a bolt action design in the classic tradition. Featuring a steel receiver measuring 1.156 inches in diameter, and a bolt locked by two horizontally opposed lugs, the Model 82 has a barrel length of 22 inches, and a weight of approximately 7 pounds, depending on the density of the hand-checkered walnut stock. The receiver is machined to accept special Kimber scope mount rings, available as an option, but the rifle can be obtained with open sights if desired, including a Williams' rear and a ramp-mounted front sight with hood. A checkered steel buttplate and a steel grip cap are standard on the walnut stock, which features a satin sheen finish, and studs for detachable sling swivels are installed. The action assembly is a solid unit containing the trigger mechanism, safety catch mechanism, and the magazine mount; the safety locks the trigger and sear, but not the bolt. The detachable box magazine holds 5 rounds, but a 10-round magazine is available as an option; a one-piece steel trigger guard and floorplate give the Model 82 an appearance of quality equal to that of an expensive centerfire sporting rifle, and with today's rush to synthetics, the Model 82's classic blend of walnut and blued steel is quality at its best. There is an extensive review of this important new rifle elsewhere in this issue of GUN DIGEST.

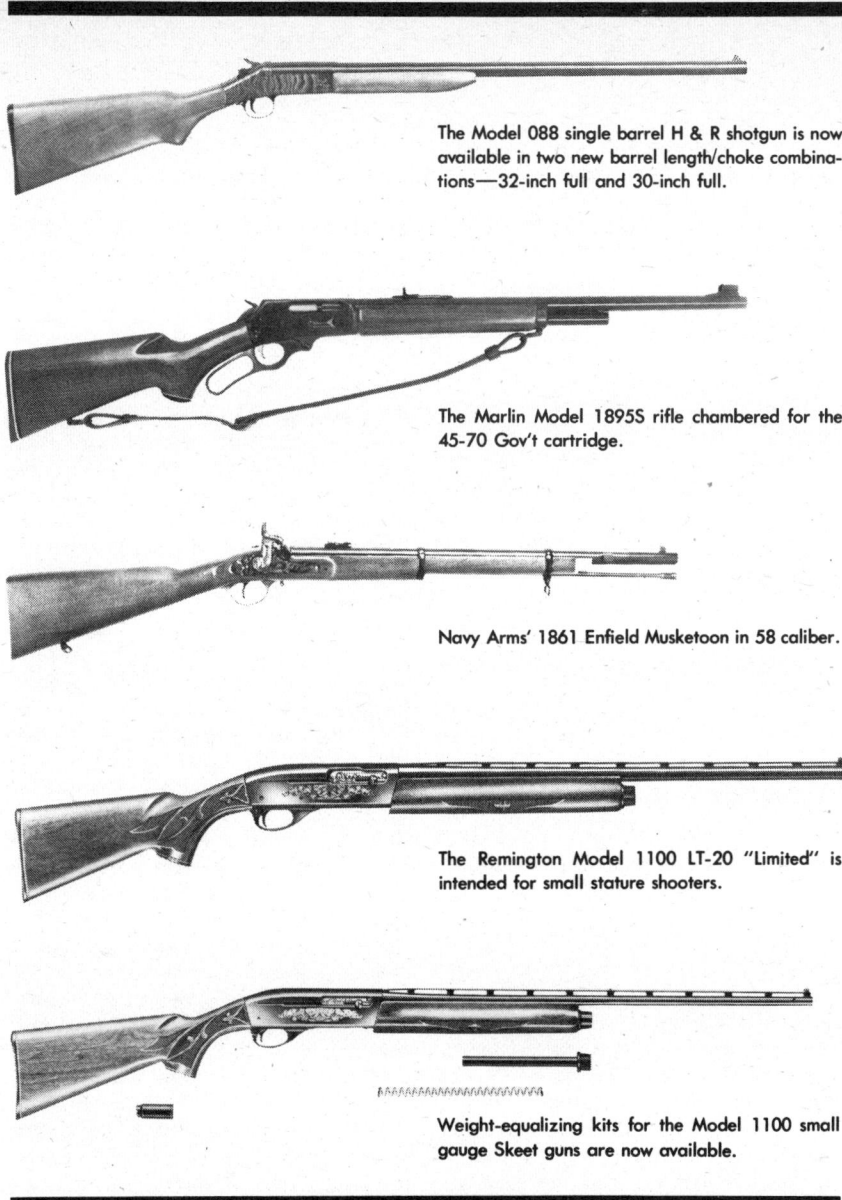

The Model 088 single barrel H & R shotgun is now available in two new barrel length/choke combinations—32-inch full and 30-inch full.

The Marlin Model 1895S rifle chambered for the 45-70 Gov't cartridge.

Navy Arms' 1861 Enfield Musketoon in 58 caliber.

The Remington Model 1100 LT-20 "Limited" is intended for small stature shooters.

Weight-equalizing kits for the Model 1100 small gauge Skeet guns are now available.

Ljutic Intl./Lambert

All Ljutic shotguns are now distributed by Tony Lambert from Carmel, Indiana, and the basic design is the Mono Gun. (Models such as the X73 and Dyn-A-Trap are no longer in production, although the Bi-Gun and Bi-Matic will be manufactured on special order, and some Dyn-A-Trap models may still be in stock.)

The standard Mono Gun lists at $3795.00 with regular ventilated rib, or at $3995.00 with the Hi-Rib and without choke tubes, or at the same price with the Olympic Rib and choke tubes. Engraved models are available, with the price depending on the amount and style of engraving. There is also the Live Pigeon Bi-Gun at $6500.00, complete with short Hi-Rib and Paternator choke tubes.

The Mono Gun features a 34-inch heavy trap barrel, push button opening in front of the trigger guard, a solid steel receiver with sand-blasted finish to prevent glare, a removable trigger guard assembly, and selected walnut in the stock and forearm. All Mono Guns are available with either pull or release triggers at no extra charge. Weight of the Mono Gun is approximately 8⅝ pounds, depending on the density of the walnut, and extra fancy wood is available at additional cost. Considered by many trap shooters as the world's finest shotgun, the Mono Gun has only eight parts in the entire firing operation, and a trigger movement of .005-inch; the hammer fall is only .0025-inch. Each Mono Gun comes in a John Hall hard case with combination lock, a lifetime warranty, and a spare parts kit, including lubrication.

Marlin Firearms

Sticking to traditional designs already in production, the big news at North Haven is the Model 375 chambered for the 375 Winchester cartridge. Based on the regular Model 336 side-ejecting lever action, the latest version features a 20-inch Micro-Groove barrel, and a half magazine that holds five of the rimmed 375 cartridges. The Model 1895 chambered for the 45-70 cartridge has been upgraded to the 1895S with a pistol grip stock, rubber butt pad and a hooded front sight, while the autoloading rimfire Model 990 rifle has a new checkering pattern, and the Model 995 has had the barrel band and swivels removed and the plain stock given an impressed checkering design. Even the 780 series of bolt action rifles have been given a new checkering pattern on the grip and forearm areas. Other changes include discontinuance of the Model 55S 12 gauge slug gun, the Glenfield 50 bolt action shotgun and the Glenfield 40 rimfire 22 autoloading rifle.

Mossberg

Although this North Haven firm is branching out into the handgun field after a lapse of many years, it is not resting on its laurels in the long gun field. A new rimfire autoloader—the Model 380—is now available in a "no frills" grade. Featuring a 15-round tubular magazine in the buttstock, the 380 has a 20-inch Ac-Kro-Gruv barrel, and a walnut-finished hardwood stock with pistol grip. Available with open sights, and with an optional 4x scope, the 380 weighs approximately 6¼ pounds unloaded.

New for shotgunners will be the gas-operated Model 5600. Available only in 12 gauge at first, the 5600 will be introduced in a field grade, to be followed by a trap grade. Mossberg jumped into the trap shooting arena a couple of years back by introducing the pump action Model 500 Hi-Rib, complete with Accu-Choke barrel and interchangeable choke tubes. With a stainless steel magazine tube, stainless steel piston rings, a dual buffering system, self-locking magazine tube cap, and a top safety which blocks both the trigger and the firing pin, the 5600 will weigh around 7¾ pounds. The field gun barrel will be available with or without a ventilated rib (the trap

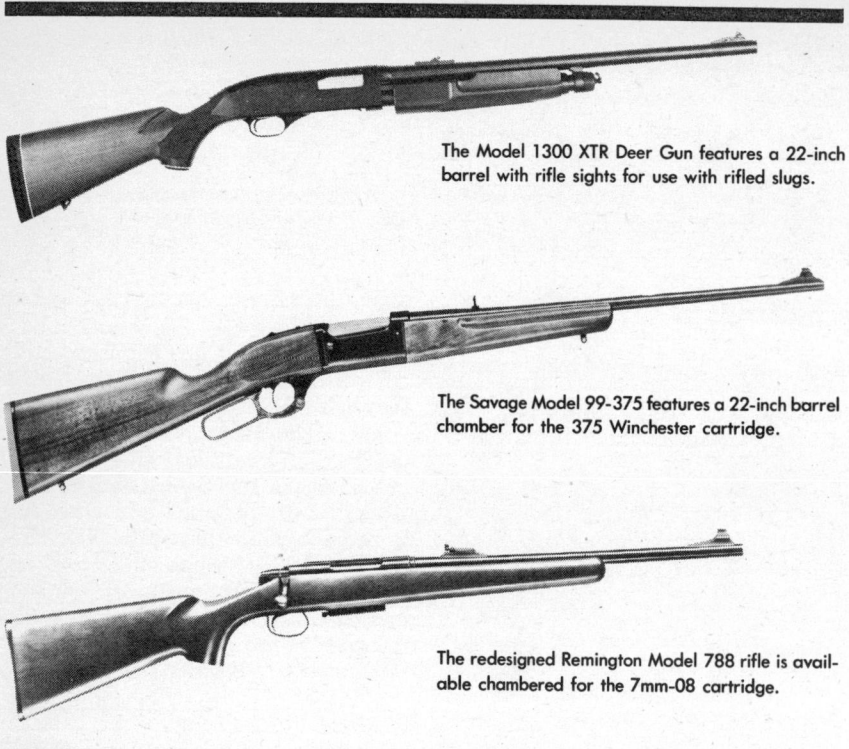

The Model 1300 XTR Deer Gun features a 22-inch barrel with rifle sights for use with rifled slugs.

The Savage Model 99-375 features a 22-inch barrel chamber for the 375 Winchester cartridge.

The redesigned Remington Model 788 rifle is available chambered for the 7mm-08 cartridge.

gun will have such a rib), and in addition, a magnum barrel for 3-inch shells, and a slug barrel with rifle sights will be available. Barrel length will be from 26 to 30 inches, and chokes include improved cylinder, C-Lect-Choke, modified and full; possibly the Accu-Choke will be available on the trap gun early in 1981. Examination of a couple of the early 5600 models indicated Mossberg is still dedicated to providing shooters with a lot of value for their money; the Model 5600 should be a real winner.

Navy Arms

The Henry carbine is again available in either the original 44 rimfire chambering, or chambered for the 44-40 centerfire cartridge. Magazine capacity is the same—nine rounds—for both versions, which feature 21-inch octagonal barrels and brass or iron frame. Approximate weight of the Henry is 8¼ pounds for the brass frame version, and 9¼ pounds for the iron frame model, of which only 500 standard grade and 50 engraved grades are being manufactured. Anticipated price for the brass frame Henry is $500.00 and $750.00 for the iron frame version, with the engraved carbines going at $1500.00 each. Navy Arms also has their own version of the Enfield rifle, in a choice of 1853, 1858, or 1861 models, all in .58 caliber, featuring three-groove rifling and color case hardened lockplate.

Remington

The boys at Ilion didn't spring many radically new designs for 1980, but there are a number of modifications and upgradings, starting with the unpretentious Model 788, which has been on the market for thirteen years. The stock has been redesigned along classic lines, including a fluted comb, recessed floorplate and more hand-filling pistol grip and forearm. The rear sight and barrel bracket have been lowered, the metal parts given a more lustrous bluing, the bolt polished and the bolt handle reshaped, in addition to shortening the barrel to 18½ inches on the heavier calibers, leaving the 24-inch barrels for the varmint calibers. The all-steel trigger guard has been given a new contour to complement the reshaped stock, and a new caliber—the 7mm-08 Remington—has been added to the available chambering. Yet, the whole package carries a suggested retail of only $209.95, making it one of the best values on the market, considering the excellent record for accuracy, durability and dependability the 788 has achieved in the past.

The shotgun line has seen the most changes, starting with the Model LT-20 "Limited," a modified version of the 1100 LT-20 designed for the shooter of smaller stature. Weighing approximately 6¼ pounds, this latest 1100 has a buttstock which is one-inch shorter than the standard version, plus a choice of improved cylinder or modified choke in a 23-inch ventilated rib barrel. The 23-inch barrel may be purchased separately for use on regular 1100 LT-20's, if desired. Suitable for smaller adults or youths, the Model 1100 LT-20 "Limited" lists for $378.95.

Although not a new sporting arm, Remington has introduced a set of three weight-equalizing kits for use on 20, 28, and 410-bore Model 1100 Skeet guns, so they'll balance and swing like the regular 12 gauge Model 1100. The kits will fit older 1100's or newly-purchased ones, and both the regular SA and "Tournament" Skeet Model 1100's.

The 30-year old Model 870 pump action shotgun has been given a face-lifting for 1980. The redesigned checkering patterns on the stock and forearm, and deeper bluing on the barrel and receiver make the 870 more attractive, but the strength and dependability for which this model is known are still there. In addition, to the face-lifting, there is a new "Competition" 870, featuring a unique, gas-assisted, recoil absorbing system that bleeds gas off the barrel against a spring-buffered inertia piston housed in the "magazine tube" which makes the latest 870 a single shot, pump action trap gun. For this reason regular 870 barrels cannot be used on the "Competition" 870, which has no shell latch cuts in the receiver. A target-type trigger, step-up ventilated barrel rib, extended forearm and special stock designed for trap, deluxe quality wood and highly polished bluing are among the other visible features of the Model 870 "Competition," which sells for $518.95, ready to shoot.

There's a Collector's Edition Model 1100 available to celebrate Remington's Diamond Anniversary of Autoloading shotgun production. (The first Remington autoloading shotgun was introduced in 1905.) Carrying a suggested retail price of $1125.00, this limited edition will be serial numbered from LE-80-0001 through LE-80-3000, and each shotgun will feature specially selected, distinctive figured high-grade American walnut in stock and forearm, plus cut checkering, a rosewood grip cap, and brown rubber butt pad. The steel receiver will have etched scrollwork, with a hunting scene and Diamond Anniversary on the left side, and Model 11 and

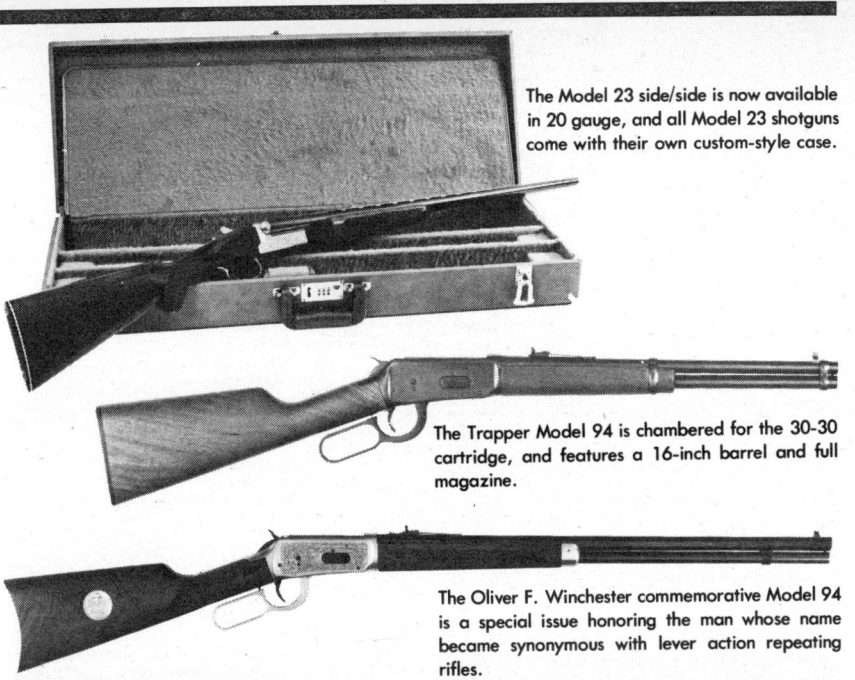

The Model 23 side/side is now available in 20 gauge, and all Model 23 shotguns come with their own custom-style case.

The Trapper Model 94 is chambered for the 30-30 cartridge, and features a 16-inch barrel and full magazine.

The Oliver F. Winchester commemorative Model 94 is a special issue honoring the man whose name became synonymous with lever action repeating rifles.

Model 1100 on the right side in addition to "1905 - 1980 Remington Arms Company - Limited Edition - One of Three Thousand." As a further enhancement, the left side of the receiver will feature the Model 1905 and Model 1100 shotguns in 14K gold, plus an outline of the special markings, also in 14K gold. It's a fitting tribute to 75 years of autoloading shotguns.

Savage Arms

For 1980 two additional chamberings—22-250 and 25-06—are available in Savage's Model 110-C rifle with 24-inch barrel, in the right-hand models only, plus the Model 99 is now chambered for the 375 Winchester cartridge as the Model 99-375. Featuring an uncheckered straight grip stock with recoil pad, and a semi-beavertail grooved forearm, the latest 99 has a 22-inch barrel, and comes complete with swivel studs and open sights for just under $300.00. Other changes in the Savage line are basically cosmetic, with the Models 99-CD, 99-C, 110-C and 110-CL rifles, plus the Fox Model B, BE. and B-SE shotguns having cut checkering replacing the impressed designs previously used. The Models 340 and 170 rifles now sport hooded ramp front sights, and the Model 24-V combination gun is chambered for the 22 Hornet cartridge over a 20 gauge barrel.

In the Anschutz rifle line the Models 1413, 1411, and 1407 have been given left-hand counterparts for 1980 as the 1813-L Super Match 54 rifle, 1811-L Match 54 Prone, and the 1807-L ISU Match 54. There's even a 6720-L International Sight Set which is designed for the left-handed rifles. The left-handed rifles are a bit more expensive than the right-handed versions, with the maximum amount being the top-of-the-line Model 1813-L at $1107.95 for 1980.

The big news in the Anchutz line is the Model 64-MS chambered for the 22 Long Rifle rimfire cartridge. Designed for rimfire metallic silhouette shooting, the Model 64-MS weighs just over eight pounds, is drilled and tapped for a top-mounted scope, features a barrel length of 21¾ inches, a two-stage adjustable trigger, and a silhouette-type walnut stock with Wundhammer swell and contoured thumb groove, all for $310.90, as this is written.

Smith & Wesson

A 20 gauge slug barrel for the Model 1100 autoloading shotgun is now available, for less than $100.00. Chambered for standard length rifled slug loads, the 22-inch cylinder bore barrel is equipped with rifle-type sights—the rear is adjustable for both windage and elevation.

Also new for 1980 is a Model 1000 Pump gun in 12 gauge, listing at $278.95 for the plain barrel version. Chambered to accept all standard and magnum length 12 gauge shells, the 1000 Pump features dual action bars, a choice of three barrel lengths—26 to 30 inches—without or with ventilated rib, a machined steel receiver, a crossbolt safety, and American walnut stock and beavertail forearm, with hand checkering.

The Model 1500 Standard and Deluxe bolt action rifles have two additional chamberings—25-06 and 300 Winchester Magnum. In addition, both should be more readily available due to increased production rates.

Winchester

New from the Red W boys will be a 20 gauge Model 23, and all of the 23's will now be shipped with a custom crafted case. The 23 is an excellent field gun, and with the 26-inch barrels it handles well; it is not a Model 21, but for under $1000.00, it's a lot of value. Other changes in the shotgun line include a full five-year warranty on the Models 1300 XTR and 1500 XTR, and the 1300 XTR is available in a Deer Gun version with 22-inch rifle-sight barrel, sling swivels, and a recoil pad. With a price tag of $270.00, it should find favor in those states in which deer hunting is permitted only with shotguns.

A new "Grand European" over-under trap gun will be available, possibly by the time you read this. It was introduced last year in Europe in a lot of 1000, in two grades, and sold so well it will be available to U.S. shooters. The Grand European is manufactured in Japan. Featuring 30-inch barrels topped with a tapered ventilated rib carrying the words "Grand European," this shotgun has a schnabel-style forearm and a choice of straight grip or Monte Carlo stock of American walnut. English-style scroll engraving gives the new over-under a touch of elegance.

The Model 94 rifle/carbine has to be the mainstay of the Winchester line, and for 1980 it's available in two additional versions—the Trapper and the Oliver F. Winchester commemorative. The Trapper will feature a 30-30-chambered 16-inch barrel to provide a handy over-all length of 33¾ inches, a full-length magazine tube holding five rounds, a weight of approximately 6⅛ pounds, and a price of $176.00 to start. The O.F. Winchester commemorative will be chambered for the 38-55 cartridge in an octagonal barrel. Only 20,000 such rifles will be manufactured, and the cost will be around $500.00, depending on the price of the gold used on the forearm tip, receiver, and underlever. A full-length magazine, deluxe cut checkering on the forearm and stock grip, and a traditional metal buttplate are among the other features of this commemorative.

ESPECIALLY GOOD BOOKS

Of the recent year's crop, these are books you shouldn't miss. They are either virtually standard references, or particularly well-done.

Eli Whitney and the Whitney Armory

This 96-page book, published by the Eli Whitney Museum, was written by Carolyn Cooper and Merrill K. Lindsay, with L.F. Beach and J.B. Smith. It is a historical update of interest to scholars and laymen, and deals explicitly with a number of matters of specific interest to collectors and to historians.

Whitney, of course, created, according to lore, interchangeability in industrial manufacture of firearms. Perhaps of more direct interest to collectors are specific chapters on the identification of Whitney flintlock muskets, a list of New Haven gunmakers, and a particularly informative chapter on Simeon North, called herein the "patriarch of United States pistolmakers." Price is $4.95 in soft covers, or $8.95 in hard covers; available from bookstores and some selected sporting goods stores, or by direct mail from Eli Whitney Museum, Whitney Ave. at Armory Street, Whitneyville, CT 06511. K.W.

The British Shotgun Volume 1, 1850-1870

Ian Crudgington and D.J. Baker here provide 256 handsome pages, including some color plates, to explain the mass of inventions which greeted the arrival in Great Britain of the breechloading systems, which made their first appearances in public at the Great Exhibition in the Crystal Palace in 1851.

The story and the developments were hectic from that point forward and in 20 short years, the hammer gun had reached a high degree of development, and hammerless systems were beginning to appear.

Crudgington and Baker seem reliably to explore all the highways and the byways of this very miscellaneous set of developments. Splendid care has been taken in the illustrations, which include good drawings, excellent modern photographs and a serious attempt to use only the cleanest of the 19th century photographs available.

The British Shotgun was published by Barry and Jenkins, 24 Highbury Crescent, London N51 RX at £10, or something approaching $25. It is worth it. K.W.

Yours Truly, Harvey Donaldson

One of the best-loved features of *Handloader* magazine for all too short a time was a column made up of letters from Harvey A. Donaldson, one of the fathers of modern handloading, the founder of organized benchrest shooting and probably the last of the old-time schuetzen shooters.

Now, Wolfe Publishing has gathered together all that material, and found more by talking to Mrs. Donaldson, and it now may be found in hard covers at $19.50 for a clothbound edition and at $35 for a leather-bound gold-embossed edition.

The book enlarges the scope of Donaldson's published thinking considerably. It is possible to trace back and forth between old writings and new writings and catch threads that never appeared when the different items were seen singly.

This book belongs in the library of

anyone interested in 20th century rifle work. K.W.

Contemporary American Stockmakers

Ron Toews undertook "to do the first serious study of stockmakers in America." With this publication he has accomplished that.

Toews believes custom guns to be a visual art and so his book is a picture book in which each gun discussed is studied photographically in considerable detail.

Contemporary American Stockmakers is not intended to be encyclopedic, but rather representative. The work of thirteen craftsmen is shown in considerable detail. These include Jerry Fisher, Al Biesen, Lenard Brownell, Earl Milliron—many of those craftsmen whose work has been enjoyed in Custom Guns published in GUN DIGEST every year.

There are 200 pages of photographs examining 40 different rifles and shotguns, together with a foreword by Jim Carmichel, gun writer for *Outdoor Life*. The book is 9 by 12 inches, and all photographs are 8" by 10" size. This limited first edition of 2000 copies, individually numbered and signed by the author, priced at $75 each from Dove Press, P.O. Box 3882, Enid, OK 73701. K.W.

Modern Firearm Engravings

Mario Abbiatico's new book on the art of gun embellishment is easily the finest work of its type to be offered to the English speaking world. It has hundreds of monochrome illustrations and numerous (60%) full color plates—all of them large, the details easily seen and appreciated.

However, Mario's text is at least equally important. He tells the reader in clear and simple language about the history of engraving, about the tools and techniques used in the work, and describes those methodologies in detail—scroll work, small and large; lightly and deeply chiseled design in rococo and baroque styles; the inlaying of precious metals and, as the ultimate, the game and other scenic motifs created by the small, single point graver or *bulino* tool.

Almost all of the work pictured is by Italian artists, and most of them living somewhere in the Brescian-Gardone Valtrompia area of northern Italy. And rightly so—with some notable and worthy exceptions, in the U.S. and Europe, Italy is where this magnificent art thrives mightily.

282 pages, 9x11¾ inches, about $60. J.T.A.

Cartridges of the World, 4th Edition

The standard general-purpose reference work on cartridges for which scientists, technicians and laymen alike reach first. It is once again updated by Frank Barnes. This basic book on the subject does its job for over 1000 different cartridges, with clarity and good organization. It is more than a catalog, it is an encyclopedic reference work. It goes 384 pages and its retail price is $9.95. K.W.

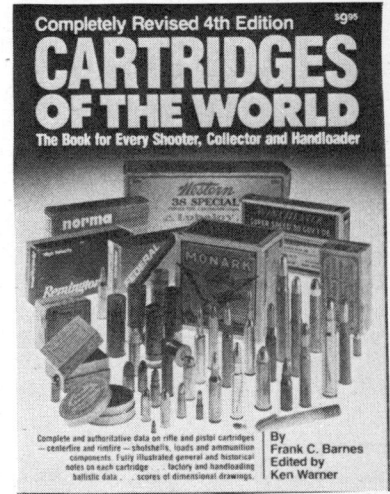

Flayderman's Guide to Antique American Firearms

Sooner than everyone thought, *Flayderman's Guide,* which became an instant best-seller and standard reference, is now out in a fully reworked second edition.

The prices are all new, and with this edition Flayderman introduces the "Flayderman Number," which may well become the book's most-used attribute. Every entry in it—and it covers all American firearms up until World War I—has a unique number, and using that number in place of all the descriptions will provide everyone concerned with an accurate description of a given gun. There are 608 pages in the second edition and its retail price is $15.95. K.W.

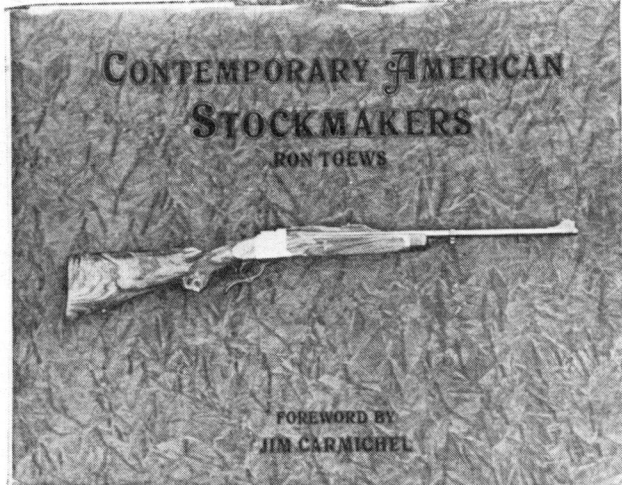

RECALL!

Whatever its other problems, our firearms industry has a fine record in dealing with safety-related product problems. Here's the recent history.

by JIM CROSSMAN

RECALL! That word strikes terror to the heart of a manufacturer! A recall means that someone has goofed. There is a mistake of some kind in the product, which makes it unsatisfactory or even dangerous in some degree. Perhaps there is some mistake in the basic design of the item. Or perhaps the design is okay, but someone made a mistake in manufacturing the part. Perhaps the dimensions are slightly off, or perhaps the heat-treatment is wrong, so that the part is too hard or too soft.

Sometimes a product which seems to be just great when made in prototype quantities, develops bugs when the manufacturing guys get their hands on it. In order to sell the thing, the factory people have to cut costs wherever possible. If the manufacturing planner doesn't thoroughly understand how the item works, and the relative importance of the dimensions and heat-treatment of each part, he could make a slip. The designer has to keep a close eye on the production man to see that he pays proper attention to the critical things.

Even after the designer has given the thing his loving care, and the factory people have done their best, when the gadget gets out in the hands of the consumer, things happen no one ever thought of.

Back in the Big War (WW II for you late-comers) I spent four years at the Infantry Board in Fort Benning. One of our main functions was to test equipment used by or proposed for use by the Infantry to see if it was suitable or if modifications were needed. I was sent there because of a strong background in guns, shooting and testing. For this reason, when I wanted to see how a thing would behave in the hands of the average soldier, I couldn't trust my own reactions. Instead, I would get a detail of soldiers from one of the units, teach them a bit about the weapon, and then sit back and watch how they used it. It was a very educational experience.

If you want to know how a product is going to work in the hands of the consumer, put it in his hands! But for a manufacturer, this may be too late—leading to a recall!

Careful testing by the manufacturer after the item is in production may show up some unexpected bugs. If they are bad enough—recall!

The U.S. arms and ammunition industry has been mighty good about the whole thing. There are no government agencies looking over the industry's shoulder and nit-picking everything it does with guns. There have been a number of recalls in the industry, all voluntary and many of them discovered in-house, as a result of follow-up inspection and testing.

I have recently written to most of the gun and ammunition people in this country, asking what items they had recalled (if any) and why. Some of these have been well publicized, while others have received little or no attention.

In some cases I got rather indignant replies back, "Who, me? We've never had a recall." Others ignored the letters, until I phoned them: "Hey, man! How could we answer your letter? We've never had a recall!"

Among those who sent along this happy answer were: Ron Walther of Ithaca Gun Company, George Sodini of Stoeger Industries, Tom Hoagland of Richland Arms Co., Howard Walzer of Beretta Arms, Dave Ecker of Charter Arms, Bill Bach of Sheridan Products, Bill Storck of Universal Firearms, Bob Gustafson of Thompson/Center Arms, and Ed Stark of Savage-Stevens.

Alex McDaniel of Valcartier Industries (Imperial ammunition), says VI has never had a public recall on their ammunition. They bought the old Imperial Ammunition Division of ICI in Canada but have no records of ICI recalls.

Glen Collier of High Standard says the present company has not had any recalls in the 2 years of its existence. He didn't know anything about the old company.

Arlen Chaney, from Omark Industries up in Lewiston, Idaho, says, "We have never had a 'full blown' advertised recall of any of our products. For-

Just the first 800 Browning BDA 380 autos carried a potential fault. Browning caught it and recalled them all.

tunately, in a couple of instances we were able to correct our mistakes through lot number tracing and several phone calls to dealers and jobbers. No 'critical defects' were involved, and only small quantities had been shipped."

A short while ago a couple of people who are not even in the gun or ammunition-making business found themselves the experts on recall in this field. It all came about the hard way.

Ed Davies and Rod Keep found themselves in the unenviable position of knowing more about recalls than anyone else in the gun industry. They are the head people in International Distributors, a Miami-based firm which makes no guns but imports the Taurus line of handguns from Brazil. A few years ago they had a report from a firm of security guards that one of their Taurus guns had been dropped and it had fired. This was more than passing strange, as the design of the gun wouldn't permit this! So the International Distributors people got on the next airplane and went up to look at the gun. And whaddya know? It would fire when dropped! Careful disassembly and examination showed that a couple of parts had been fitted incorrectly. Many revolver makers spend a lot of time hand-fitting the essential parts. Space is mighty limited inside and it is necessary to have each part function smoothly, and with exactly the right timing, which calls for hand-fitting.

This one gun caused the Taurus people some worry, but when they found another gun a few days later, this made up their minds—RECALL!

But now what? They couldn't find any precedent so they had to feel their way. Not wanting to have guns butchered by jackleg mechanics, they composed a letter which pointed out the danger, but not the defect or its cure. This was sent to 6,000 FFL license holders with whom they had done business at one time or another. Then, as jobbers sent in lists of dealers to whom they had sold Taurus revolvers, the International Distributors people wrote to all the dealers, asking for names and addresses of their Taurus customers. Each of the customers got a letter, as did all the people who had sent in warranty cards. More than 40,000 letters were sent out.

As the guns came back in to Miami, the numbers had to be checked with the names and addresses, so that the right gun was sent back to the right man. Each gun was carefully tested, and those which had bugs—of any kind—were fixed and sent back. And all this without cost to the customer, of course.

This problem was one of those really tough ones—only a relatively few guns were found bad, but all guns had to be checked, since it was a fitting problem, not one of design. They weren't sure which fitter at the factory was causing the problem, since the trouble was intermittent. It took a lot of time and effort and money to straighten the matter out.

And this was all done voluntarily, not with the threat of Federal action, not with a lawsuit forcing them. This is not to say that the possibility of a lawsuit wasn't considered—in these days almost anything you do, or don't do, is likely to end you up in a suit for a few million bucks.

Among the people who said they had made recalls was the Marlin Firearms Company, one of the biggest gun makers in this country. William S. Brophy, the Senior Technical Manager, said that recently a few M62 center-fire rifles got out without serial numbers, through a weird fluke. The rifles were called back and properly serial numbered. Even if a rifle didn't get back to be numbered, it would hardly be hazardous for the customer to use it.

The other Marlin recall was different, but again it posed no particular hazard to the user. On some Marlin Model 120 and Glenfield Model 778 pump shotguns, made in early 1979, the crossbolt safety wasn't hard enough. After considerable use, the safety button could develop a burr which would make the safety hard to operate. Word was sent to all Marlin distributors, to the dealers who bought from those distributors, and to all individuals who bought guns from the dealers. They were all asked to return the specified guns, so that Marlin could replace the safety. In the case of individuals, Marlin invited them to ask for packing and shipping material. Marlin paid all shipping expenses.

Marlin's neighbor in North Haven, Connecticut, is O. F. Mossberg & Sons. Ron Fine, Vice president, Sales/Marketing, tells me they did have a recall on their model RM7 bolt action rifle in caliber .30-'06. It really wasn't much of a recall—not that it wasn't a serious matter—but there were only a few hundred guns out all shipped to one mail-order house, so they were able to get the guns back without much trouble. The problem was found in testing at Mossberg, and involved accidental firing of a cartridge in the magazine. A sharp corner in the magazine lined up with the primer of the top cartridge, and sometimes would fire it on recoil. The problem was easily solved by modifying the sharp corner.

Problems usually arise when you bring out a new product, when you make a change in the old item, or when

Marketing Remington's 591 and 592 rifles for the 5mm Remington Magnum rimfire cartridge was delayed—after some had been shipped—while the company solved an extractor breakage problem.

you change factory procedures. After you've made a product for a while, you and your public should have found any bugs there are. But here's a firm that was founded after WW II, and is therefore only a bit over 30 years old. So all they have done in the past years is bring out new products, including single action revolvers, double action revolvers, under-and-over shotguns, auto pistols, semi-auto rifles, single shot rifles, and more.

I speak of Sturm, Ruger & Company, of course. A note from Bill Ruger says:

"In reply to yours of October 4th, I want to tell you that we have not, as yet, had a recall on any of our products. We would, of course, recall any product identifiable as containing a recognizable defect, but as yet that situation has not arisen, nor is it likely to in the future, because in addition to the traditional standard of safety, which we have always exceeded, we now also assume that the user is only slightly responsible for his own safety. This has not had any practical effect on our product design philosophy, but we are certainly working to tighten quality control standards to avoid manufacturing defects that could be safety related. We have never had many such defects reported in the past and you can be sure we want to keep it that way in view of the present circumstances."

That's a pretty good record for a firm with so many new things on the market! It speaks well of their engineering and quality control plus an active rabbit's foot for luck! Everyone needs a bit of that kind of luck.

Another rather new firm that has brought out a lot of new stuff in recent years is Weatherby, Inc. A letter from Roy Weatherby says:

"I can only think of one recall in the last thirty-four years of any consequence, and it was perhaps fifteen or eighteeen years ago. The factory was using the wrong type of lubricant in the bolt mechanism. If someone were hunting in temperatures down around the freezing point the lubricant congealed and retarded the firing pin so it would oftentimes cause a misfire. We sent out information to all of our dealers notifying them what could be done to eliminate the problem. It was necessary to rinse the bolt in kerosene. We also informed all of our dealers that if there were any questions to return the rifles and we would disassemble the bolts and put in the correct lubricant. There were probably only 100 rifles that left our place with the incorrect lubricant, and we only got complaints from three or four people. Naturally, they sent the rifles to us, and we took care of the problem. We also notified all of the consumers who had sent in their warranty cards. We explained to them how to make the correction themselves or to return the rifle to us for the correction.

"I don't mean by this that we are so perfect that we can't make mistakes. We do make mistakes, but we generally catch them before the product gets in the hands of the public. We do a tremendous amount of testing before we ever release them.

"I remember one time we had to hold up shipment on one model of shotgun in order to make up a new part that was causing us problems. Occasionally the gun would malfunction and not extract the spent shell. Fortunately, only a few of those got into the hands of the public, and they were taken care of immediately by our warranty policy.

"Jim, in the thirty-four years that I've been in business, I've always been extremely careful never to let anything get on the market that could possibly cause any type of problem. However, no matter how cautious we are, sometimes guns get out that have to be sent back for repair. As an illustration, if the metal part of a rifle isn't properly bedded to the stock wood, it can cause a crack back of the top tang. We feel this is our problem, and we generally replace the stock. Occasionally we have a broken extractor or other mechanical problems, but we generally take care of them free of charge unless the gun is very old. We have an extremely liberal warranty arrangement.

"We never had what is known as a recall."

Not a bad record!

The Browning Arms Company, which has guns made in Belgium, Portugal, Japan, Korea, and the U.S., would seem to have a tough time keeping things straightened out. But Harmon Williams, the President, says:

"We have had just two recalls in recent years, Jim, both of which occurred in the spring of 1979.

"One was a production series of about 12,000 of our bolt action center fire rifles in which we determined that the firing pin sear had been improperly heat treated. It was determined that galling could commence in 3000-4000 rounds and cause the sear to hang at times on the pull of the trigger. Then, of course, a sound jar, release of the safety, or lifting of the bolt could cause an inadvertent firing. We had no reports to this effect; our own Q.C. caught the problem, and of course, its seriousness necessitated a recall without a second thought.

"The other recall pertained to the first 800 of our BDA .380 caliber semi-auto pistol which were shipped. Again, from our Q.C. we discovered that with the magazine removed and the hammer in the half cock notch, that a sharp pull on the trigger would drop the hammer. This was not supposed to happen, of course, and to further magnify the problem we found that with some makes of ammunition, in about one time out of 20, a hammer fall from half-cock could cause ignition."

Harm Williams mentioned "Q.C." in his letter. This means Quality Control. Generally any factory of any size has a Quality Control Department. Q.C. techniques have been worked out over the years, both theoretically and practically, and are recognized worldwide. No one can afford to carefully inspect every part that is used in a gun. If you're a gun maker, you probably will buy your pins, screws, and springs, and perhaps other parts, from a firm which specializes in such things. The Quality Control people will not look at every one of those items but will take random samples and inspect them. If they are okay, the chances are high that the batch of parts is okay. If something is found wrong, additional samples are taken, and the defect is carefully examined to see if it is of consequence. If the dimension is way off, that can be important. But if the blueing has some bum spots, that probably isn't of any consequence to the gun functioning.

Critical parts are often inspected 100 percent. Proof testing, for example, is generally conducted on all finished guns or barrels, followed by careful inspection of the gun and checking of headspace.

Q.C. people constantly watch the output of the various machines, to try to spot trends before they become serious. They randomly check parts. And they may go into the warehouse and pull out guns that are all ready for shipment, to give them careful inspection and testing.

But once in a while, something gets away from everyone, which is the reason for this article.

Winchester has only been making guns for 110 years, more or less, so they've hardly had time to make a mistake worth a recall. But they did manage to have a gun problem three years ago. It wasn't too much of a problem, and they found it through their own Q.C. internal checking and testing. They found that after much use of the M490 .22 autoloader it was possible for the sear to wear. On some guns this might lead to the gun doubling—firing two shots with a single pull of the trigger. It was widely publicized in various magazines and papers, in interviews, in tapes, and in notices to everyone they could think of. Winchester believes that they got most of the guns back for replacement of the bad parts. While many guns

Winchester's Model 490 would, the company found, eventually acquire a worn sear and start doubling. The company widely broadcast an appeal to get the guns back and thinks they got virtually all of them. They fixed them, naturally.

were sent to the Winchester factory, many others were handled in the authorized repair stations scattered over the country. There were no injuries caused by the problem.

The other Winchester recall came from the East Alton ammunition plant rather than the New Haven gun plant. This involved some millions of rounds of "Wildcat" .22 Long Rifle ammunition. In a very small percentage of the cartridges there was an excessive powder charge, which could result in a burst cartridge head. This resulted from a change in the manufacturing procedure.

While a burst head isn't something that you want, it does not usually cause any serious trouble. I believe Winchester had a few complaints, but only of minor non-serious injury. Although the percentage of bad rounds was extremely small, it was necessary to call in millions of good cartridges to get the few bad ones.

Finding an occasional problem in something like ammunition can be a terrible job. The only way you can really test ammunition for an intermittent problem is to shoot it all. While this may solve that particular problem, it brings up some practical difficulties. One year when I was Director of the National Rifle and Pistol Matches at Camp Perry, we had a few cartridges of our special National Match lot of ammunition show up with no powder in 'em. It was something like a half-dozen out of a million rounds, not a high percentage, but it caused us some concern, because it couldn't happen! Every cartridge finally went through a gage-and-weigh machine, which would have tossed out any without powder. But there we were, with powderless cartridges! We finally guessed that a few bad cartridges had somehow gotten tossed into a tote box after the gage and weigh station. The manufacturing procedure was changed so that the identifying waterproof lacquer was put around the primer just as the cartridge successfully passed the final gage-and-weigh machine. The problem went away, but we were never sure of the original cause. Trying to solve an intermittent or sporadic problem can be really tough.

Somewhat the same problem exists in trying to find an intermittent problem in a gun. You may have to shoot thousands of rounds before the problem shows up. And it may never show up on some guns, no matter how much they are fired!

If you have a problem with a gun, as a rule you can change some parts or make an alteration or two and the gun will be as good as new—or even better. But if you have an ammunition problem, there isn't much you can do except destroy the whole batch, perhaps trying to salvage some of the components as you go. Generally there is no way you can repair ammunition, especially in those usual cases where only a small percentage of the stuff is likely to be bad.

The Daisy people have built over 20 million BB guns of one model. And, of course, they have built many other models. They have only had one recall. That was a bug found early in 1979 in a new rifle, which had been in production only a month. Internal testing by their Q.C. people showed that after several thousand shots, there was a possibility that the trigger mechanism would be so worn that the safety could be over-ridden.

Richard I. Daniel, President of Daisy says, "The recall was voluntary on our part, based upon our own internal testing. The guns as produced had no problems whatsoever. The problem only developed after several thousand shots, and then only developed on a percentage of the guns. Our recall of the gun was primarily to be supercautious with regard to the quality of the product."

The Daisy customers were notifed of the problems and how many guns had been shipped to each. News releases were given to news services. Three months after Daisy started their recall, the Consumer Products Safety Commission (a Federal agency) issued the same recall, but this was after most of the guns had already been sent back.

Recently the Daisy people had their hearts gladdened when the Arkansas Attorney General's Consumer Protection Division gave Daisy the Attorney General's "Gold Star" award for their voluntary recall.

As Dick Daniel said in a note, "I was pleased that the Attorney General's Office felt we deserved recognition. I am particularly pleased because today business gets all kinds of criticism and it's a welcome relief to have someone recognize that you are trying to be responsible."

Another airgun maker with some problems was Crosman (Nope, no relation—those poor guys don't even know how to spell the name correctly!). In '77 and '78 they found two separate problems, one with the CO_2 powered Model 454 semi-auto pistol and one with the M322-1377 pump-up air pistols. In the case of the 454, during a design change, an improper tolerance on a vendor part would, in some few instances, allow the pistol to be fired with the safety "on." Correction consisted of replacing three parts. On the other models, failure to properly tighten some screws (or loosening of them during use) could result in accidental firing. These problems were found in time, and no injuries were reported.

Unlike other recalls in guns and ammunition field, Crosman chose to go through the Consumer Products Safety Commission once the Crosman people had found the problem. The CPSC officially closed these matters in early 1980.

Up in Minneapolis, the home of the Federal Cartridge Corporation, Charles McKusick gathered together a file on the only two Federal ammunition recalls.

One of them brought back interesting memories. More than a dozen years ago I was retained by an attorney as an expert in the case involving the death of a hunter. The man had been using an old British .303 surplus rifle with Federal ammunition. His companions heard a shot, followed by some shouting, which they assumed meant that he had shot a deer and was letting the world know about it.

Some time later when they went back to the car, they were shocked to find their partner lying on the ground, dead! Further examination by the state police showed that the rifle had "blown up" and that the man had died from bleeding caused by metal fragments which hit him in the chest.

The poor guy's widow hired a lawyer, who got in touch with me. When I had a look at all the material, it was evident that there had been very high pressure, as the back of the .303 rifle chamber had bulged somewhat, the locking surfaces showed some upsetting, and the head of the cartridge case was separated from the body of the case. The whole thing could have been written off as "High pressure—cause unknown" except for two things. The first was the state police had found an obstruction in the bore just ahead of the chamber, and had driven it out. The obstruction turned out to be a bullet jacket! The front end was damaged where it had been pounded but the rear end had a big hole, turned inward. But this was a solid base bullet! The bore of this old rifle was very rough from years of having been shot with corrosive ammunition.

I finally concluded that, for some reason, the jacket of this bullet had "seized" in the rough bore surface and had seized so firmly that the building gas pressure on the base of the bullet had blown a hole in the base of the bullet and had then blown the lead core right out of the rifle! Meanwhile, all this had caused the pressure to skyrocket, bursting the head of the case. In this old rifle, the chamber had a rather thin section on the right rear, and the side walls of the case are not well supported in other areas.

Many years earlier I had heard about cores being blown out of military bullets and jackets sticking where the front of the bullet had been cut off for hunting and I had tried to duplicate it. But my upbringing was all wrong. As I was growing up, back in the days of corrosive ammunition, I was shooting, my mother was shooting, and my father was shooting. Guess whose job it was to clean all those guns after each shooting session? And guess who got a licking if a gun was found with a rusty barrel?

So my earlier experiments were with guns having good, bright bores. And that certainly wasn't true of the gun in this case.

To make things more difficult, the seizing and/or high pressure problems were not consistent. I shot some of the same ammunition in the same rifle, as well as in many other old .303 rifles, with no trouble.

The other thing that really bothered me about this case, and which I never did solve to my satisfaction, was how the man got hurt. According to the coroner's report, he was hit in the right side of the chest with fragments, which turned out to be part of the extractor assembly, as well as a couple of big brass fragments.

With the rifle at the shoulder in the normal fashion, these fragments should have been blown out to the right and upward from the rifle. There did not appear to be any way these pieces could have hit the man in the chest, unless they did a "U" turn in mid air. The other markings, from powder, brass, gas, etc., were not in the right place for him to have been shooting the rifle from his shoulder. Oh, yeah, he was a right-handed shooter. I never did figure out how he was holding the rifle when it went off.

While I was puzzling over all this, I spotted a most interesting advertisement in one of the gun magazines: "ATTENTION .303 BRITISH RIFLE SHOOTERS. We have found that because of the poor condition of some .303 British surplus military rifles, the use of certain lots of .303 rifle cartridges manufactured by our company in 1963 may give unsatisfactory performance. Damage to the rifle may occur, with risk of personal injury."

The ad went on to give lot numbers involved, which included the ammunition in my case. They asked folks who had ammunition from those lots to get in touch with Federal Cartridge Corporation. The ad pointed out that only .303 British ammunition was involved, and only .303 British of certain specific lots.

This was a full-column ad, which appeared in most of the gun and hunting magazines over a period of time. In addition, of course, Federal got in touch with their jobbers and dealers.

While the ad confirmed my feeling that there was some unusual combination of circumstances in my case, it came as quite a shock: This was the first time I could remember of any firm in the shooting field publicizing a recall in this fashion! It took a lot of courage and public awareness by Federal to so openly admit a problem.

Smith & Wesson fixed—for free—many Model 59's to improve extraction and feeding. This was not, of course, a recall, but it was very responsible behavior.

The Federal recall campaign went on for some time and they thought they had gotten the word to everyone concerned. But almost 10 years later, more trouble appeared, with the same lot! Apparently, quantities had been stored somewhere and had not been turned in during the recall.

So a second big campaign was begun, with notification to the dealers and jobbers and more big magazine advertisements, again specifying the lot number, but also pointing out that the stuff might be under various names: Federal, Hawthorne, Revelation, Sears-Roebuck, and American Eagle. The lot numbers were for .303 British ammunition only and included lots with numbers starting with 36 or a letter and 36.

While we're picking on Federal, we might as well have a look at their other recall, back in 1976. Again they had a tough intermittent problem to find and solve. A small fraction of one percent of several million .30-30 cases turned up with a defect which could give problems on occasion. Sometimes the defect would result in a head separation, which often jammed the rifle, and on occasion could cause some injury from loose gas. Although there had been no report of serious injury at the time of the recall, Federal felt there was a possibility and so recalled the stuff.

This involved .30-30 ammunition and empty primed cases with lot numbers ending in -5289 through -6285, stamped on the back of the box. Brand names involved were Federal, Revelation, Wards, and Hiawatha. Federal asked that the ammunition be sent back or destroyed. If you destroyed it and sent them the carton, or at least the back and end flap, they would send you a check!

Joyce Hornady and his Frontier Cartridge Company got caught in the same recall, as Frontier was using .30-30 cases bought from Federal. The Frontier lot numbers were 6-38-76-9, 6-42-76-9, 9-68-76-9, and 9-71-76-9. The Frontier lot numbers were stamped on the inside and end flap of each carton.

Lot numbers—I have used that phrase a great deal. What does it mean? It varies from factory to factory, and perhaps even within a factory, depending on the type of ammunition. But, in general, a "lot" of ammunition is loaded from identical components, on a particular machine during a particular period. The lot number is normally stamped on the individual ammunition box or carton, on the back, bottom, end flap, or somewhere. The box is, then, a critical item in any ammunition problem.

With the lot number, the ballistics people can dig into their files and determine on what date the ammunition was loaded, on what shift, on what machine, and can give the pressure, velocity, powder weight, powder lot, and many other things about that batch. Lot numbers are used for in-house checking and control. The competition shooter often will find that one lot shoots better than another in his particular gun, so he will buy quantities of the better batch. It may happen that another shooter's gun may perform better with a different lot.

And on those rare occasions when something goes wrong, the lot number is invaluable in bracketing the problem and in solving it.

Joyce Hornady goes on to say of Frontier ammunition and Hornady bullets:

"This is the only recall we have had and the only one, hopefully, that we expect to have.

"We were, of course, unsuccessful in getting all of the above ammunition recalled. Some of it was already in the hands of consumers and they did not get the word. However, we never received a single complaint from anyone due to a head separation of this ammunition.

"We have never had any recalls on bullets and none have been necessary, but a time or two a few bullets somehow got in the wrong box which was no fault of the bullets. These, of course, were returned to us by our dealers for replacement.

"Considering the sensitive nature of ammunition and the fact that it stands storage for such a long time would indicate that practically all of the factory manufactured ammunition on the market is remarkably reliable."

Over at Colt, Richard L. Brown, Vice President for Engineering, says that, due to the Federal regulations regarding control of handguns, "we anticipate that if we had a recall, it would be handled on a customer-by-customer basis."

With over 160 years in the business, Remington has brought out many new guns and new cartridges. Although the gun-making plant has been in Ilion, New York, for most of the time, the plant and its facilities have been rebuilt many times over the years. The predecessor of the Remington ammunition plant was set up in Bridgeport, Connecticut, more than 100 years ago, as the Union Metallic Cartridge Company. It was later joined with Remington as Remington-UMC, with only the "U" headstamp on rim fire ammunition now left as a memory. But a few years ago Remington decided to move most of their ammunition production out of the old plant.

They built a whole new factory in Lonoke, Arkansas, and went through the painful process of shifting machinery and people, buying new machinery, and training new people, in addition to modernizing the Bridgeport plant.

During the years, Remington has had a few problems serious enough to warrant recalling the item. The most famous—or notorious—was the recent recall of the Model 600 rifle and some XP-100 target pistols, both of which use the same trigger scheme. These guns had been built for many years before it was found that on some guns, a tolerance build-up could cause some trouble with the trigger and safety mechanism. This recall has been widely publicized. Check of the guns, and any necessary parts replacement, are being handled at the Remington Ilion plant, as well as through their authorized repair stations, scattered around the country.

This recall has been covered by radio and television announcements, as well as newspaper and magazine articles and advertisements. In addition, Remington circularized holders of Federal Firearms Licenses, asking for lists of customers who may have bought these guns.

Another rifle recall of a few years ago, but on a very limited scale, involved the M591 and 592 bolt action rifles, chambered for the now-nearly-dead 5mm rim fire cartridge. Shortly after shipment began, they ran into a problem with broken extractors. This was found early enough so that few guns got out.

In the ammunition field, Remington had a few small recalls involving problems which were caught early enough so that all, or practically all of the stuff was easily gotten back.

The only problem of any consequence involves a recent recall of some .30-'06 ammunition made late in 1978. This stuff gave somewhat higher pressure than normal, not enough to cause a problem with good modern rifles, but which might give some difficulty in older guns. As far as I know, there were no problems in the field with this, but it was found during in-house testing. Distribution was in a rather limited geographical area, but the matter has been given wide publicity anyhow. Ammunition concerned is the .30-'06 180-grain Soft Point "Core-Lokt," lots K21D and K22D.

Smith & Wesson haven't had any actual "recalls" of their handguns, but have suggested publicly that three guns have some changes made. In the medium-frame revolvers with target sights, they found that, on occasions, the trigger stop could loosen and turn so as to block the trigger, making the gun somewhat unuseful, particularly if you were a police officer pulling it for self-defense! The stop normally limited trigger travel during single action shooting. But if there was any chance you might use the gun for self-defense, S&W recommended you remove the trigger stop completely. Or if you wanted the trigger stop, send the gun to an S&W service station, where they would put in new parts and return the gun, without cost.

A couple of years ago, S&W found a way to reduce "spitting" between the barrel and frame on the big M29 .44 Magnum revolver. This change had to be done at the factory. This change cost $5, including return shipping.

Three years ago S&W offered to modify three parts to improve the functioning of the 14-shot 9mm Model 59. The parts were the extractor, magazine follower, and slide stop lever. If the gun was sent to one of five approved service centers, the job would be done and the gun returned for free!

While these weren't really "recalls" according to the S&W people, they have had to call back some shotgun barrels, due to a problem with the 12 gauge barrels of their takedown "Eastfield" pump shotguns. I haven't been able to find out just what the problem is, but their wide advertising of the recall says, in part, "Under certain conditions, the original barrel of the 12 gauge M916T, shipped with the gun, could rupture." All of which does not sound like something you would like to be shooting! New barrels have the letter "O" stamped on the top edge of the barrel near the breech end. The problem exists with the Smith and Wesson or "Eastfield" brand M916T 12 gauge pump guns. Only the barrel needs to be sent back to S&W for replacement, not the whole gun. You folks who have the M916 with fixed barrel, don't worry about how you're going to get the barrel off, because that model is okay, according to S&W people.

I was surprised the other day to see a notice of a recall of a gun by a maker I didn't recognize—AMF Voit, Inc. The story goes on to say that nearly 100,000 carbine models are being recalled because they "may accidentally fire even though the safety catch is engaged."

But then I look more closely and find that these are spearguns, used by divers, and not firearms! But it all goes to show that other people have gun trouble, too!! •

35TH EDITION, 1981 **217**

CUSTOM GUNS

TOP
MIKE YEE
Browning 20-ga. stocked in claro with grip fillet; engraved, diamond inlaid, by O'Brien.

DON ALLEN
Fox Sterlingworth stocked in Russian Circassian, checkered 24 lpi. Metal: Mark Lee.

J. J. JENKINS
Holland & Holland Grade 3 was rebuilt, new case color, French walnut stock by J. P. Mazur.

BOTTOM
H. D. WALLACE
Winchester M24, 16 ga. "ultimate camp gun," 30" o.a., has etched high life also.

JERRY FISHER
W & C Scott from "basket case"—Miller trigger; Warren engraving, Fisher walnut.

THOMAS McCANN
"Cherry Stick" has Siler locks, Douglas barrel, leather buttplate, cherry stock.

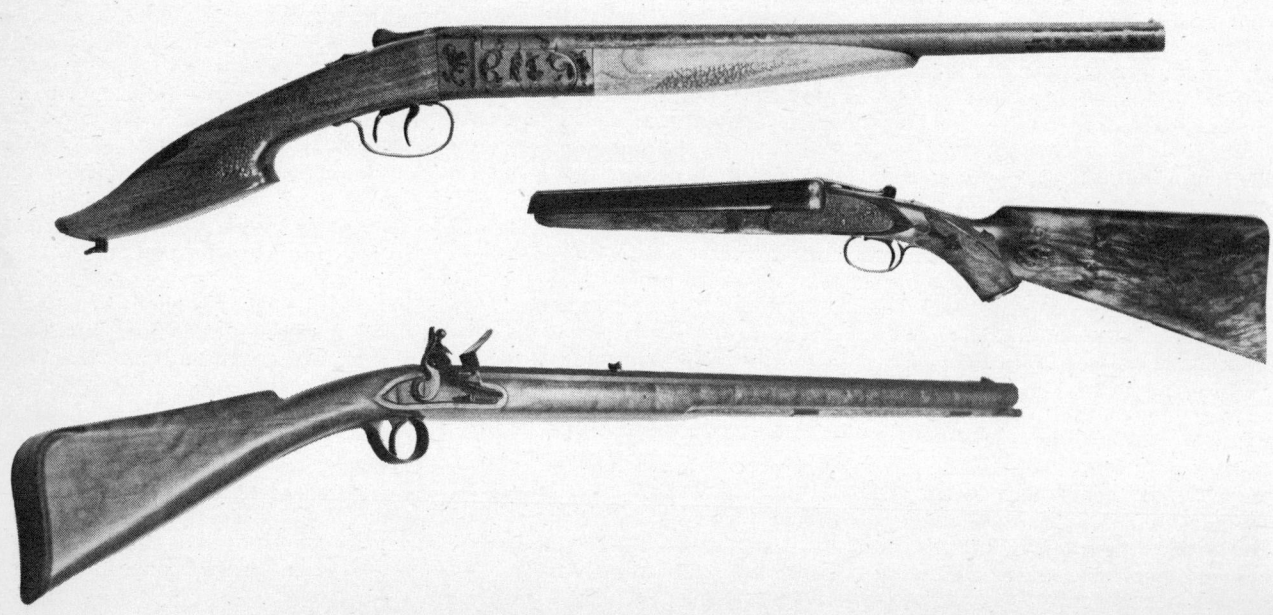

TOP
LARRY MROCK
Presentation flinter shows maple with brass; fire-blue lock; silver touches. It's a 45.

MARK CHANLYNN
Ruger #3 now in 30-06 has taper octagon barrel, integral rib and ramp, American walnut.

R. D. WALLACE
Restocked Ruger #3 has a new lever and engraving. Rifle is a 45-70, original.

JOE HOLLINGSWORTH
Cadet Martini in 218 Bee has tiger maple wood, Brownell and Neidner furniture.

BOTTOM
JOHN VEST
Husky in 270 has Bastogne walnut, M70-type safety by Jantz, Pachmayr swivels.

AL LIND
Sako L579 has Titus 7x57 barrel, tang safety, in New Zealand Circassian walnut.

H. L. GRISEL
Husqvarna 280 has Sherer stainless barrel, claro stock, tang safety, trap butt plate.

FRED D. SPEISER
Ruger M77 270 has Douglas barrel, English walnut from Miller, ironwood tip.

JOHN E. MAXSON
Sako L579 in 257 Roberts has Shilen tube, California English stock and custom safety.

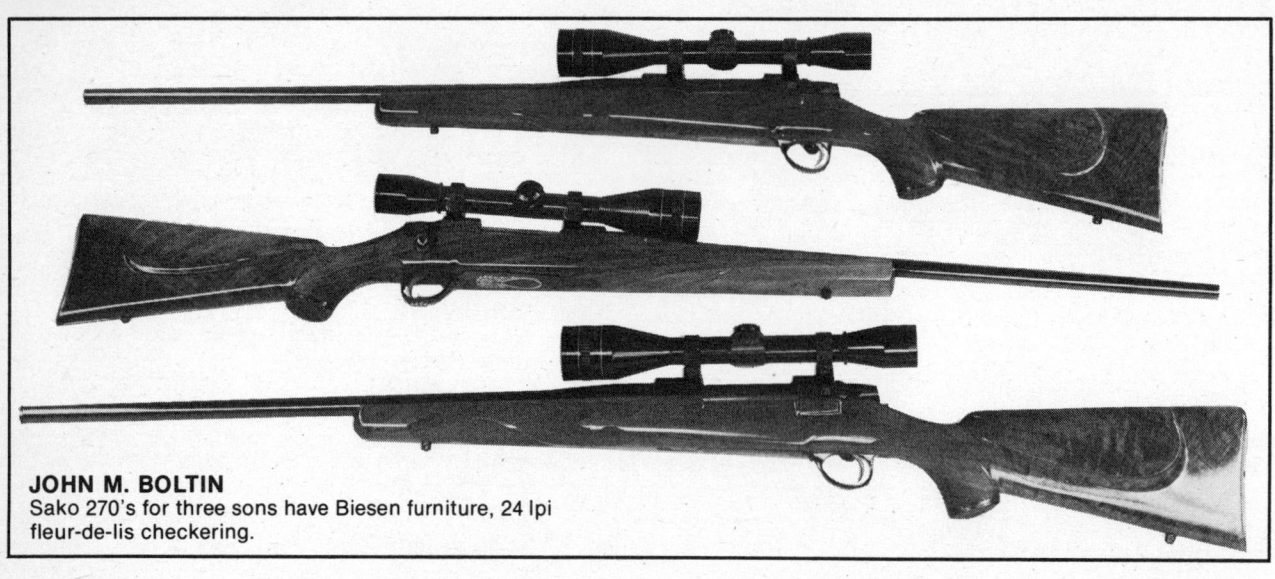

JOHN M. BOLTIN
Sako 270's for three sons have Biesen furniture, 24 lpi fleur-de-lis checkering.

FRANK R. WELLS
Wells magnum action, barrel, stock shape make 350 Wells Express manageable.

HARRY LAWSON
Weatherby Mark V, "Apache" stock and trimmings, make this a Lawson "650 Series."

HAL HARTLEY
Mauser 98 Hartley doesn't like—the customer picked the tip and the Monte Carlo.

STANLEY KENVIN
Model 70, with Blackburn, Brownell, Biesen and Jaeger touches has fine American walnut, too.

JACK DEVER
FN Mauser has Burgess work, Shilen 7x57 tube, French walnut with ebony, and a trap butt.

PAUL JAEGER INC.
Signature Grade Sako has Douglas tube, French walnut, by Apel; Willig engraving.

STEPHEN L. BILLEB
Mauser 98 in 6mm Remington has Biesen cap, Jantz safety in claro walnut, cut 24 lpi.

DALE GOENS
Model 70 30-06 Featherweight has new guard bow, California English wood, solid butt pad.

R. H. DEVEREAUX
Sako has feather crotch claro, with American walnut tip and cap, Bill Johns engraving.

ROBERT WINTER
BRNO has Douglas 270 barrel at 22", English walnut stock, metalwork by Ron Lampert.

WINCHESTER'S design department has obviously burned beaucoup midnight oil on this one and probably consumed gallons of coffee accompanied by desperate desk pounding trying to decipher the riddle of reviving the old faith in the renowned Model 70.

Three-quarters of a generation ago, as the crow flies, the Winchester jockeys were confronted with the universal American capitalist idea known as competition in the marketplace and at the same time the spiral of inflation was well on its way. Further confused by the big show on the gun scene of the gaudy cosmetic California rock-and-roll, white line, high heels and tight jeans hustler house sporters, I suspect the boys in staid old Connecticut were about ready to go back into the shirt business.

However, at this point of wind doping and hoping to stay in the V-ring for their share of the gold, they committed the cardinal sin: they changed a winning combination. Alas, poor Yorick, the poet said, and rightly.

Of course, hindsight is a universally accepted method of formulating corrective recommendations and this is known as learning by experience to not repeat the same mistake twice.

However, some benefit and some don't and in the riflery arena one good hard example is the Ruger 77 design which stuck to the straight conservative classic concept and I hear they do well at the fairgrounds and all the way to the bank with the wampum beads.

All Winchester has to do is get out the old plans discarded to the file basket in 1964, shake the Madison Avenue branch of the family tree, admit to having pulled a boo-boo and make first the old Model 70 Featherweight version which was the last of the front line and this will be a record for the earliest reproduction revival of the greatest sporting rifle.

The leader of the band over a vat of vintage stated simply that he only wanted to know: "Is the rifle known as the Model 70 XTR, in faith and fact, a rifle from the free-thinker, unbiased, non-partial viewpoint?" He said this with carefully calculated knowledge that I have a reputation as a full-rack pre-64-Model 70-or-bust rifleman.

So, with that said, as Ken would say, let's see what Winchester hath wrought:

First off, it is full and favorably functional according to plan, tuned to the modern man's concept of a sporter. The whole complete rifle, stem to stern in a durable high gloss finish, features the Monte Carlo cheek scope-mate stock as aesthetically as is possible in this style.

As the 70 XTR for show, as now usual, is drawn from the case in camp, with the card game pausing momentarily while the comraderos judge your choice of weaponry, the black composition non-steel buttplate with white line spacer comes to view first, followed by the harsh sheen of fair-figured dark walnut and if the setting sun is allowed to play a part here as it slants in the lodge cabin window, you will note provision for detachable sling swivels also. It will reveal a fair-grained piece of wood under the high lustre finish for a blended splendid effect just for this important status symbol style show. Madison Avenue exploits man's every weakness and there ought to be a law about that.

Furthermore, now is revealed a knurled, nicely rearward-swept pear-shape bolt handle of super polished unsullied dark gun blue denoting instantly that the new dude in camp is a hip bolt gun man and has done his homework with ballistics books.

The very sophisticated rear flipup rain sight then is revealed as the mesmerized card sharpies reluctantly tear their eyes away from the flashy damascened dazzling bolt body which the dude has immediately slick-slacked to the open "Look Ma, no cartridges" position, as the way to keep 'em in camp and gain friends.

The compromise, not square, not round, forearm of ample girth for fair holdability next sparkles in the slanting sun's rays revealing cut checkering of very fair form nicely matching same on pistol grip along with a black, also shiny, forearm tip with pistol grip cap to match and also both set off such as foxy tails on a hot rod Caddy with white line spacers. The finale of the "tease" is the sleek, high luster, dark blue-black 22″ slim barrel terminating with the eye and twig-catching high front sight and sight cover, to match, hopefully the high rear sight as is now established that iron lookers are mainly for in case you break your glass sights.

This Model 70 XTR from the showoff

Winchester's Model 70 XTR

...safe and sane, sturdy, nicely done sporting rifle...with old-time adequate accuracy

by FRANK MARSHALL JR.

Frank Marshall is that class of old-timer who is at home with new guns and old. Here he is with one of his favorites, a Lee Speed—you might call it a British deer gun.

222 THE GUN DIGEST

facts of camp life fulfills all the latest fashion requirements plus, but, then there is always the old "sage brush Sam" in every camp who asks loudly "Will it shoot?" Many dudes now go to sight-in days and invariably very thankfully after this almost always fun festivity, preferably prior to the hunt.

So of course, did I and with this 70 XTR, not to sight it in, as I'd done that, but for noting reaction to this creation by the average man of the woods type that are also found there.

Flatly and firstly, they liked it. They liked the medium weight, how it held in hand for hills hiking and how it pointed as pertinent to the target when thrown quickly to the shoulder as is the first thing done by average gun evaluators as this is what you do with guns come the bottom line moment of truth and Winchester knows that, too.

One above average curioso asked what it shot and where and how often, as he had been very hot at the bench. Now, I had a couple of wallet size cutouts with target rifle-size groups. I pointed out satisfaction with Winchester 170-gr. bobtailed match bullet handloads, but the factory Federal 165-gr. spitzer soft nose, all-purpose, best compromise 30-06 load, which I was then showing some to the lookers, gave me a couple of 1.6" groups, right out of the box, with no tightening, shimming, or stretching of anything this with an old tried-and-true 2½x Weaver scope on their bases as the 70 XTR is tapped for all popular scope bases for hunting type glassware.

Putting out an accurate hunting weight rifle is no trick with Winchester as this fact of firearms fidelity is not a superficial problem of saleability such as the overall appearance is on today's market. Winchesters, regardless of vintage, shoot pretty good most of the time. My man in the big manor house did not ask me to compare this with anything from the past or the present so I won't, except to note this about that as pertinent.

This latest from the big red "W" boasts all the best known bolt gun fea

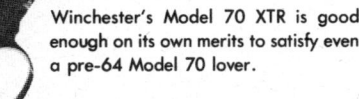

Winchester's Model 70 XTR is good enough on its own merits to satisfy even a pre-64 Model 70 lover.

tures considered worthy, dependable and safe along with established accuracy principles. Some features, such as the flat bottom receiver and floating barrel are best, according to many authorities on accuracy. The bolt head fully enclosing the rear of the cartridge coupled with the ample extractor and ejector pin also in the bolt face, using this super safe system, is all in accord with most modern ideas. The magazine floorplate is of the easy to unload latch-lid type and nicely engineered and works every time tried as did the positive magazine feed and extraction/ejection along with a slick running bolt well-fit to the nice lines sturdy receiver.

Notable and superior to most is the three-way safety conveniently positioned on the rear of bolt sleeve. It acts directly on the firing pin without depending on lever linkage separate from the bolt assembly and subject to malfunction under unusual circumstances. This M70 XTR three way safety is plain, simple, sturdy and safest over the long haul in many opinions. The third or middle position is to allow opening or closing of bolt while firing pin is locked and also is to expedite bolt disassembly without resort to tricky pin placement through hard-to-find tiny holes and such primitive and absurd methodology to dismantle a bolt for cleaning or inspection. Since the firing pin at the rear of the bolt is fully enclosed by the bolt sleeve for full gas protection, a red warning indicator protrudes from the bottom rear of bolt sleeve if rifle is cocked.

The 70 XTR is chambered for most popular current centerfire cartridges with a magazine capacity of five rounds for the regular rimless cartridges and three rounds for the belted magnum lineup. The magazine function was flawless using factory or handloaded spitzer form bullets.

All in all, the 70 XTR is a safe and sane, sturdy, nicely done sporting rifle tuned in to modern tastes, but with old-time adequate accuracy up to anything expected of a medium weight handy piece.

Altogether, it will undoubtedly appeal to the majority of today's market and that is the main idea. Still, the Winchester designers have managed a miraculous compromise blending of lines inoffensive to the old aesthetic classic standard by being functionally correct, but still dressy enough for the fashion nimrod who must have that look or he don't put down his dough. ●

With the rifle here and the shotgun below, John Amber manages to shoot from his right shoulder left-eyed.

THE SINISTRAL PROBLEM SOLVED

You can shoot off the right shoulder with no right eye—yes, you can.

by JOHN T. AMBER
PHOTOS: ROBERT S.L. ANDERSON

I LAY IN the hospital, after eye surgery, thinking about the happy past and about the bleak future and my spirits were low. I'd been told vision in my right eye was gone, that all I could expect from it would be to tell light from dark. Depressed as I was then, I wondered if my old zest for life, my enthusiasm for the new and interesting in firearms, would return.

If I've been anything, I've been a rifleman, bar a minor excursion into handgunning many years ago. My collecting interest lay in rifles; my hunting over much of the world had been for big game; and I'd hoped during my retirement years to write about many of my rifles—some of them genuinely unique, others of special interest or background. Now such projects were endangered—shooting from the left shoulder would be, I knew, awkward, clumsy—and so it has proven.

Moreover, such left-eye shooting wouldn't be fair to my rifles—or to my readers. A beginning retinal detachment had been found in my left eye, too, and its repair had left my far vision impaired. Targets 50 yards and beyond, unless I use a scope of quite high power, are fuzzy. Would these story projects be unfulfilled? I had to find a solution, at least a partial one.

My misgivings were, I was delighted to see, unfounded. Within a few weeks of my release I was again feeling good, my curiosity as strong as ever, my interest in guns and shooting restored.

I began writing to friends in the field, asking about means or ways to let me shoot from the right shoulder.

My first scheme was to obtain a scope with an offset eyepiece. That was looked into by the Weaver people, but to no avail. They gave up. Then I appealed to old friend Dick Hodgson, a custom gunmaker in Colorado. It took a long time, a couple of years, but one day I received from Dick a Weaver scope with the eyepiece in line with my left eye. Dick had used two 90° surface mirrors, via a new tube section, a cross tube and a standard eyepiece to do the trick. It worked, but not on bolt action rifles! The extra tubing made it too long, bringing the ocular end much too close to my eye. That was dangerous. I did use it, with fair success, on a Ruger No. 3 carbine and on an old Winchester single shot. As constructed, it wasn't the answer, but I'm still exploring the basic idea.

In the meantime, I'd not been idle. I'd talked to George Miller, head of Conetrol Mounts, about making an offset base—one that attaches to a bolt rifle normally but is wide enough to accept a pair of bases. George sent me, within a week, a trial sample, made from quarter-inch alloy and about 2 inches wide by 5 inches long. I told George it worked fine—which it did on a Model 70 rifle—and I soon had it back, now filled with nickel-sized holes to lighten it, nicely blackened, and usable on M700 Remington bolt

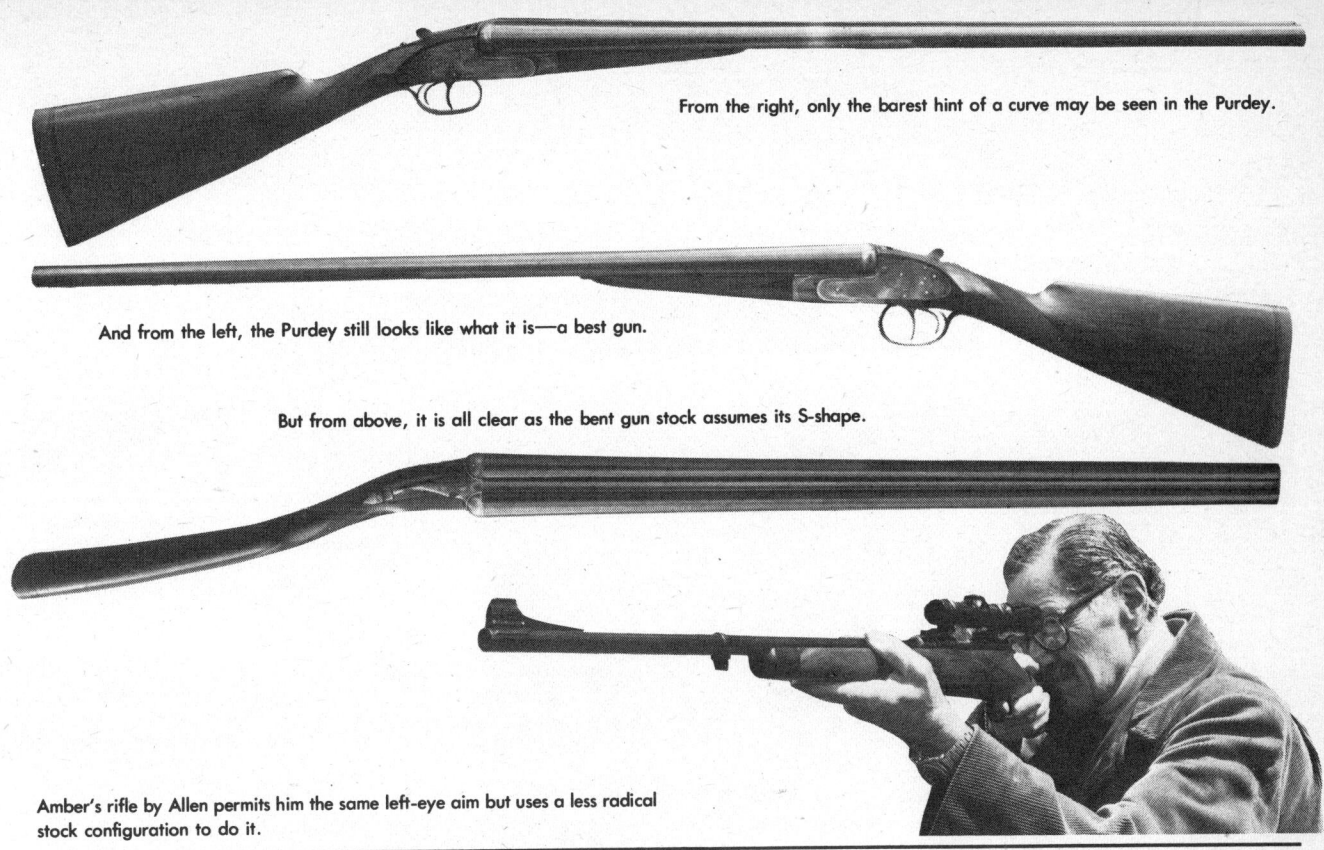

From the right, only the barest hint of a curve may be seen in the Purdey.

And from the left, the Purdey still looks like what it is—a best gun.

But from above, it is all clear as the bent gun stock assumes its S-shape.

Amber's rifle by Allen permits him the same left-eye aim but uses a less radical stock configuration to do it.

rifles as well.

True, it worked well at the bench, and it still does. But it was unhandy and cumbersome hunting—the offset mass of the wide base, the scope mounts and the scope unbalanced it badly. On those occasions when I could manage a prone or sitting position, I had little trouble, but otherwise . . .

During this same time something really nice happened. Don Allen and David Brown, a man I'd not met before, walked into my office. Mr. Brown was carrying a well-used but sound English-style trunk case. Nothing unusual in that, of course; I expected to be shown a nice double gun and, perhaps, to be asked about it.

Nothing of the sort—Don had told his friend about my eye problem and, as the case was opened, my eyes bugged! Sorry, my "eye." There lay a hammerless shotgun, used but in beautiful condition, its stock bent well to the right, and—all rise—a James Purdey, I became, almost in a trice, the new owner, and at a price both low and high. I paid well under what Purdeys then brought, and considerably less than they fetch today. Yet I paid more than I'd previously ever spent for a used shotgun.

I've written about the useful if unhandsome Purdey in GUN DIGEST 32/ 1972 ed. (p. 167), but for those without that issue, a few notes: I'd not closely examined a crosseyed stocked double gun before, certainly not a Purdey, so I was surprised indeed to see that no pains had been spared to make this heaven-sent gun as efficient as possible. To keep the bend in the wood close to the action, and at the same time to let the user grasp it normally —or nearly so—both lockplates had also been bent, as had both tangs and the top lever! More than that, imagine the special work required on the lock's working parts to make it function normally.

Shooting the Purdey showed that, unless I cheeked the stock very firmly, that I couldn't quite align my left eye, the rear of the rib and the front sight. Consequently the patterns at 40 yards from both barrels—improved cylinder right and full choke left—printed about 10-12 inches to the left. Short of removing some wood, how could that problem be fixed?

Recalling that Gough Thomas* had written about the flexing of buttstocks at the moment of firing, with notes on flexing bent stocks, I reread the article. He wrote that crosseyed stocks

*Shooting editor of the English weekly *Shooting Times and Country Magazine*.

were particularly subject to such movement, and that the muzzles of guns so made were thereby deflected laterally by some X amount. How could I alter that foot or so of leftward muzzle movement at the target? The testing had been done with standard 2¾-inch loads, 2¾ and 3 dram types holding 1⅛ ounces of shot. The gun is Nitro proved for such length chambers and loads.

Thinking that low-velocity loads might change the picture for the better, I called Mike Bussard, then with Federal Cartridge, and he graciously agreed to make up some factory loads for me, 2¾/1-oz./6s at about 1050-1075 fps muzzle velocity. My reasoning had been that the reduced velocity would mean a longer barrel time for that load, thus permitting the muzzles to move to the right. Happily, that's just about what happened, the new patterns, still nicely overlapping, printing dead on.

The Purdey has performed well—or well for me and my low-average skill with the smoothbore—on grouse, quail and pheasants, most shots taken at 20-25 yards, and virtually all with the I.C. barrel.

The Allen Bentstock 280

With the Purdey a success and the

The cross-eyed rifle combines an offset scope with a scooped and slanted butt, neither apparent in profile.

From either side, the Allen rifle in 280 Remington is the sort of American classic Amber is used to and prefers to shoot.

The Allen-made rifle is engraved as well, of course, and Amber and Ken Warner here look over the job.

The Purdey starts bending almost at the chambers. All action parts are curved and the wood then fitted.

Hodgson/Miller scope efforts not the answer I'd hoped for, I wondered anew—could a bentstock bolt rifle be made and would it work if produced?

I called that same Don Allen. He lives in Northfield, Minn., and is a pilot with Northwest Airlines, and also an excellent custom gunmaker. He employs an equally good metalsmith, Mark Lee. Allen designed and is marketing a high-precision stock carving machine, too, and examples of it are in use throughout North America and Europe.

I talked at length with Don about my idea, a crosseyed stock on a Model 70 Winchester, say. He wasn't enthusiastic—he'd never made one, he'd never seen or heard of one being done, nor had I, for that matter.

Still, the challenge of the unknown intrigued Allen, so he said he'd try it—misgivings or not. As with so many things we fear to undertake, he found the task quite easily done. First, he handmade a model, using an overthick blank of plain wood to allow for the bend. This was assembled to an old M70 action, *circa* 1949, which carried a Dave Huntington barrel in 280 Remington, and it was sent to me for trial. Metalsmith Herman Waldron had made and installed a set of custom bases and rings, offset to the left about a half-inch. That obviated the need to bend the wood the full amount it would otherwise need (like the Purdey), so the bend isn't highly obvious. Viewed in profile from the right side the stock looks normal. Shooting the sample stock—unfinished and the metal unblued—I found I'd need another ⅛-inch deeper depression for my cheek—where a cheekpiece might ordinarily be found there's a recess. That also aided in keeping the bend minimal.

Back in Don's hands, he put what was now the master model in his precision pantograph and copied it, using a fancy piece of New Zealand walnut. The completed rifle was sent to Tommy Kaye of Beaumont, Texas, for engraving—which he did in great style.

Besides the scope mounts, Waldron made a new floorplate (of straddle type) and guard, the latter narrower and rounded nicely; he also checkered the bolt knob, top and bottom, to teardrop-shaped patterns, fitted his all-but-invisible sliding floorplate release and added fine checkering to the bolt-release button.

Tommy Kaye engraved the floorplate, the pattern a handsome combination of small and medium scroll work, well laid out. In the center is a moufflon on all fours, relief inlaid in gold—I'd shot one of these in Czechoslovakia a few years ago. Kaye also engraved the scope rings/bases, the barrel breech and the steel grip cap, then put gold bands around the barrel muzzle and breech, around the bolt checkering, the grip cap and, a final touch, he set my initials in gold on the guard.

So I have, at last, a handsome rifle I can shoot left-eyed and an equally nice Purdey—an elegant classic despite its bent stock. The few groups I've fired so far with the rifle, using factory 150-grain cartridges, shoot into about 1.5 minutes of angle—not too bad for an old party.

Now, as I sit here, I'm seeing another spring unfold, the days getting longer and warmer, a blossoming and burgeoning I'd looked forward to during the long winter nights. I'm grateful to a divine Providence and grateful also to the understanding friends who have been so kind and helpful. I can shoot again. My cup runneth over indeed.

•

SPORTING ARMS OF THE WORLD

by LARRY S. STERETT

Action Arm's Uzi

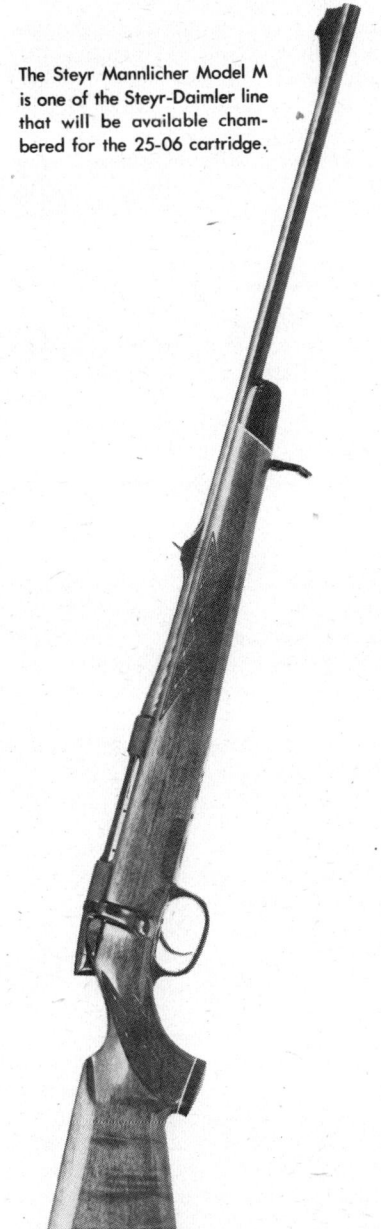
The Steyr Mannlicher Model M is one of the Steyr-Daimler line that will be available chambered for the 25-06 cartridge.

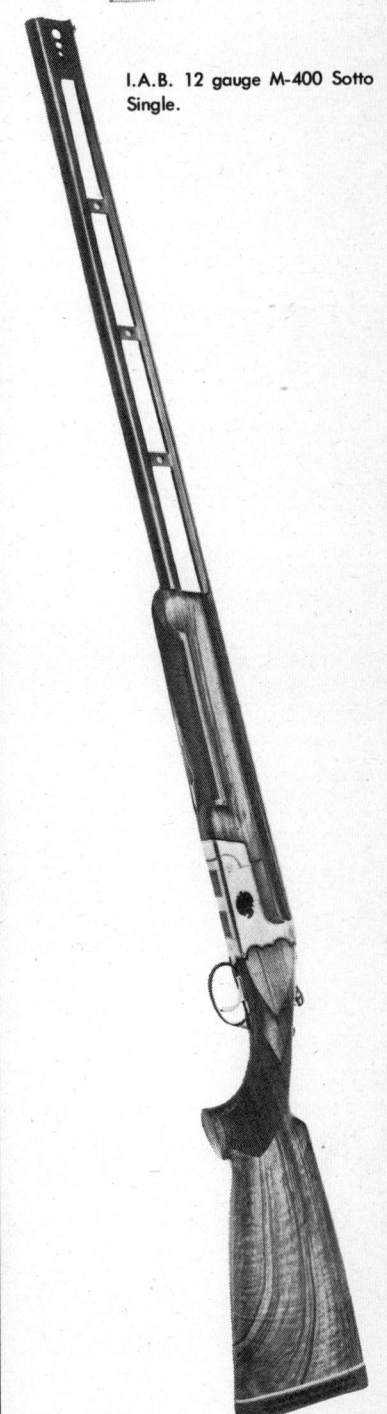
I.A.B. 12 gauge M-400 Sotto Single.

Introduction

Inflation has hit everyone and everything, large and small, American, European, Asian, consumer, manufacturer, raw material, and finished product alike. Yet, the sporting arms industry has not come to a standstill, but only raised the prices. One importer told this writer that a brand of shotgun he was importing cost $1300.00 just over a year ago, and as this is written the cost for the same shotgun to the importer has gone to $3800.00 f.o.b. Italy, or nearly triple what it was.

In some instances the radical increases are unwarranted, but there are new arms available, more with modifications, many older models with new higher prices, and even models on the drawing board to look forward to in the future, such as a stainless steel 22 rimfire rifle with a 50-round drum magazine. Other examples include: the Israeli Uzi is now available in a semi-automatic version; the 50-year-old Cosmi autoloading shotgun is now being imported into the U.S. (hopefully in quantities); there's a new Krieghoff-designed over-under and unsingle trap gun; and Valmet has introduced a "shooting system." Thus it goes. The years 1980-81 should be good ones for shooters interested in sporting arms of the world.

Action Arms

It may not look like a sporting arm, but a semi-automatic version of the legendary Israeli Uzi is now available. With a 16.1-inch barrel length, the Uzi fires the 9mm Parabellum cartridge from a closed breech with a floating firing pin, unlike the regular Uzi which fires from an open breech with a fixed firing pin. Empty weight of the new Uzi is 8.58 pounds, and over-all length with the stock folded is 24.2 inches. The magazine capacity is 25 rounds, and each Uzi comes with a car-

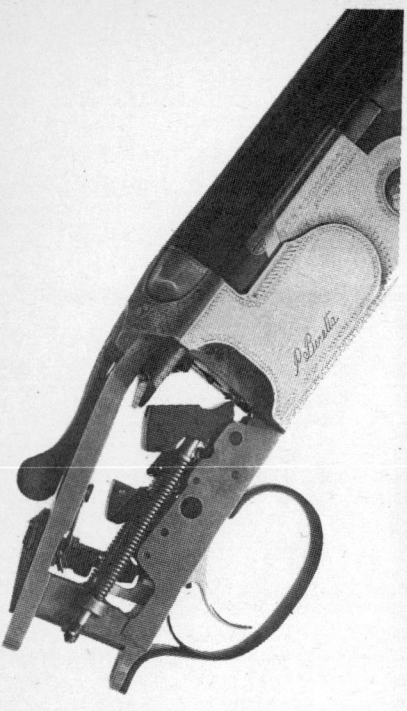

The Beretta 680 over-under features a sculptured receiver, coil spring powered hammers, and a barrel selector button which is located within the safety on the upper tang.

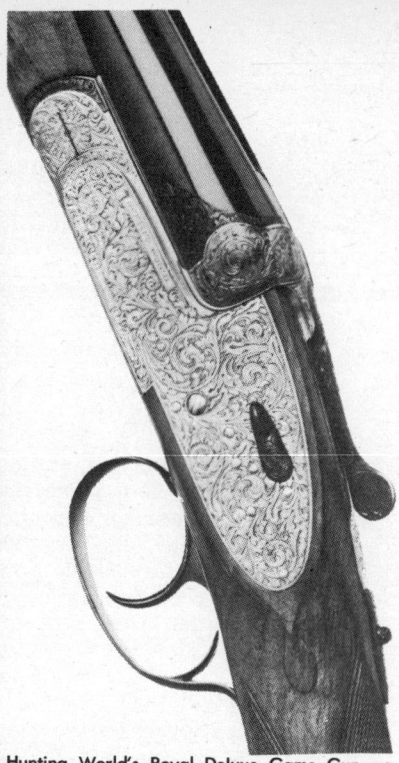

Hunting World's Royal Deluxe Game Gun—a side lock in the finest tradition.

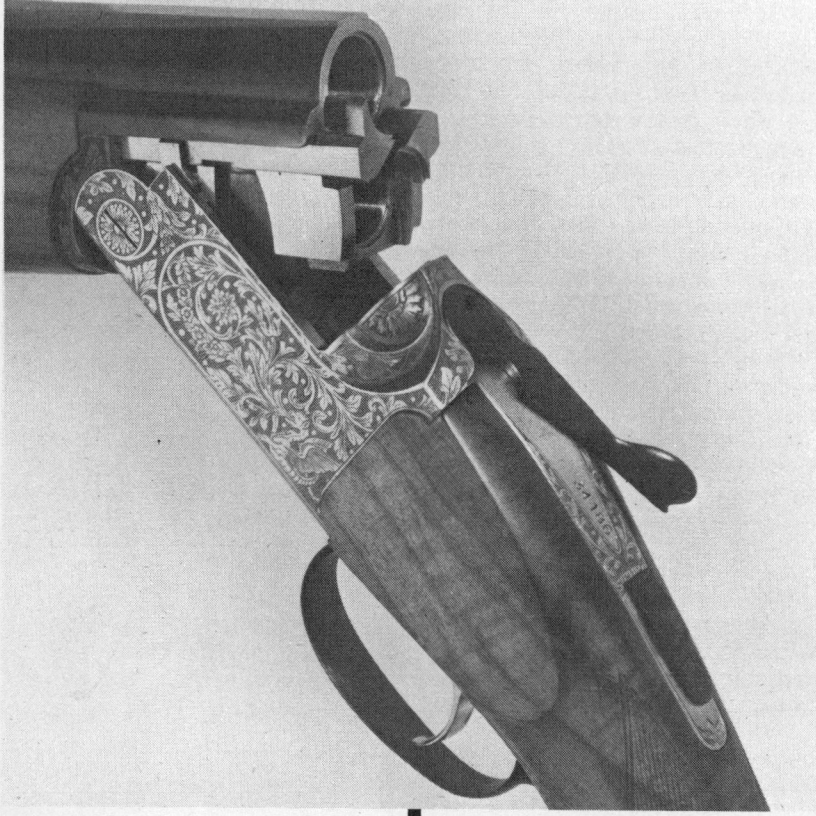

Ventura Imports' Contento over/under 12 gauge.

rying sling, an instruction manual, and a solid display (unfireable) barrel which can be used to replace the 16.1-inch barrel in order to duplicate the appearance of the regular Uzi, if desired.

Armsport

Several new models are available, including Finnish Tikka bolt action rifles in six chamberings from the 243 Winchester to the 300 Winchester Magnum, plus the Tikka Turkey Gun in 12 gauge and 222 Remington. Both were previously distributed by Ithacagun, and are now priced at just under $500.00 and $700.00 respectively. There are also six new black powder long arms, including 10 gauge and 12 gauge side/side percussion shotguns, and a 50-caliber rifle called the "Hawkentucky."

The really big news is the 12 gauge Premier Mono Trap Unsingle manufactured by Castellani of Italy. This Mono features an under barrel with high ventilated rib, an interchangeable trigger assembly, a choice of 32- or 34-inch barrel, and a walnut stock with Monte Carlo and Wundhammer swell on the grip. Underbolt locking is the basic design, but the trigger assembly uses coil springs, and the trigger is the mechanical-set single non-selective design, always firing the under barrel first. (The unsingle can be obtained with a set of over-under barrels in 30- or 32-inch length as the Competition Trap.)

Each Mono Trap or Competition Trap set comes with an extra interchangeable trigger assembly, and a hand-crafted Italian leather fitted luggage-style case, at a price of $2795.00 for the Mono Trap, or $3650.00 for the Mono with extra over-under barrels. The quality of craftsmanship on the Mono Trap examined was excellent.

For Skeet shooters there's a new 12 gauge Zoli-manufactured over-under Premier Competition Skeet Gun, with a choice of 26- or 28-inch barrels, all for $1750.00, complete with pistol grip swell and engraved action.

Beretta Arms

The Model 680 over-under trap and Skeet guns were introduced early in 1979, and for 1980 the line has been expanded to include an unsingle model with a choice of 32- or 34-inch barrel. Featuring a high rib (over one-inch) the unsingle barrel 680 carries a suggested retail price of $1340.00, or the same as the regular 680 over-unders. In addition, the single barrel can be purchased as a part of a set with over-under barrels at $1850.00 for the combination. Also available is a new 12 gauge black powder side/side shotgun with double triggers and exposed hammers. Designed more or less as a commemorative to celebrate the 300th Anniversary of the Beretta firm (1680 to 1980), the black powder shotgun will go for $650.00.

During mid-1979, detachable choke tubes became available for the A-301 autoloading shotgun. The A-301 comes in field, Skeet and trap models, and the only barrel length for the tubes is 28 inches. The standard A-301 trap barrel is a 30-inch full choke version, but the detachable choke barrel is interchangeable, and it has a ventilated rib. Unlike many of the other screw-in detachable choke tubes, the Beretta tubes slip into the muzzle and are retained by a cap or ring which screws onto the outside of the barrel muzzle. It may not be quite as trim, or as pleasing to the eye as other designs, but it works.

Bernardelli

Vincenzo Bernardelli introduced their Model 110 approximately five years ago in Skeet, pigeon and trap grades. For 1980, to celebrate 115 years of continued gun manufacturing, there's the Model 115 in two grades—Modello Caccia (hunting) and Modello Tiro (trap and pigeon)—available in 12 gauge only. Featuring select quality walnut stock and forearm, with hand checkering, the 115 is available with a choice of straight grip or pistol grip, and the Tiro stock is fitted with a recoil pad. Barrel construction is via a monobloc and the Tiro barrels are separated except at the muzzle and breech, while the Caccia model has side ribs. The standard trigger on the Tiro is a single non-selective design, while the Caccia model may be obtained with double triggers, single non-selective, or single selective trigger. Four different barrel lengths are available on the Caccia, ranging from 25.6 inches to 29.1 inches, while the Tiro is available only with 28-inch or 29-inch barrel. The ventilated barrel ribs are 9mm wide on the Caccia and 11mm wide on the Tiro grade. Weight of the 115 is approximately 7½ pounds, depending on the grade and the density of the walnut used for stocking.

BRNO

Excellent shotguns manufactured in Czechoslovakia have been imported into the U.S. at various times in the past by at least two firms, one in Florida and one in Massachusetts. Now the entire Brno line is being brought into North America by Pragotrade, a division of Motokov Canada, Inc., Rexdale, Ontario. Included in the line is the ZKM Series of rimfire rifles, two bolt action models and one semi-auto, the ZKB 680 Fox—a miniature Mauser-type rifle in 22 Hornet or 222 Remington, with detachable 4-round box magazine—and the ZKK Series of high powered rifles.

The ZKK Series is available in three action lengths: 600 for 270 and 30-06 length cartridges, 601 for 243 and 308 length cartridges, and the 602 for the 375 H&H and 458 Winchester Magnum cartridges. Features of the ZKK Series of rifles include a pop-up peep sight on the receiver bridge, two triggers—a set trigger with adjustable pull, and a single state replaceable trigger—hand checkering, "touch-release" magazine floorplate, and an improved Mauser-type action.

In the shotgun line there is the ZP side/side 12 gauge, without or with ejectors, a true sidelock design. The ZH over-under in 12 gauge is available in field, Skeet, or trap grades, or with an interchangeable rifle/shotgun barrel. This design has been around for many years and it is excellent, with one feature being the special double trigger mechanism that can fire either barrel. The CZ Series over-under shotgun is available as a 581 Field in 12 gauge, or as the 584 Combination with a 12 gauge barrel over a rifle barrel, such as the 270 Winchester.

One of the latest models from Brno is the Super Over-Under, a true Holland & Holland-type sidelock shotgun available in field, Skeet, and trap grades, a combination shotgun/rifle, or as the Super Express over-under rifle for such cartridges as the 375 H&H. The Super is a beauty, with engraving on the sideplates, and skipline checkering on the forearm and pistol grip.

Pragotrade also has a line of Slavia air rifles and pistols, the CZ autoloading pistols, including the CZ 75, considered to be the top autoloading pistol design in the world today by many informed handgunners, and Drulov Target Pistols, plus Zeiss Jena riflescopes, and Sellier & Bellot ammunition—metallic and shotshell.

The major problem is the customs duty on bringing the sporting arms into the U.S. Uncle Sam will collect a 60 percent tax when your rifle or shotgun crosses the border. Figuring transportation, etc., a dealer would have to pay nearly double the original cost of the shotgun, and then add on his profit. For example, a $400.00 shotgun would cost the dealer approximately $800.00 by the time it reaches his store, and you can figure from there. The Czech rifles and shotgun, and handguns, are of excellent quality, at least all this writer has worked with were, but they are not inexpensive, because of the U.S. Customs duty.

Hunting World

This New York based firm has only one shotgun—the side/side Royal Deluxe Game Gun. Listing at $6500.00 as this is written, and available only in 12 gauge with standard length chambers (2¾ inches) or 20 gauge with 3-inch chambers, the Game Gun is manufactured in Spain, but is equal to the "Best London Gun" or the Italian Fabri in quality, according to Bob Lee, the head of Hunting World. Barrel lengths range from 25 inches to 30 inches, with 26-inch barrels and a "Churchhill" rib being standard. John Amber reviews the gun elsewhere in this issue.

I.A.B.

The Puccinelli Company imports the I.A.B. line of shotguns, and for 1980 the emphasis is on the 300 series, including the C-300 with over-under barrels and a high rib model called the Sotto Single (unsingle), or the SC-300 with two such unsingle barrels. For 1981, if all goes well, there should be a 400 version available. Shown in prototype form at the Shot Show in San Francisco this new model will resemble the Sotto Single, but the high ventilated rib will be an adjustable impact-point design, permitting the pattern center to be raised or lowered relative to the actual target. The prototype had lots of merit, but it will be the production models that will prove the usefulness.

Incor Inc.

The Cosmi autoloading shotgun has been around for 50 years, but never in any quantity in the United States. Now a Texas firm is importing this unique Italian-manufactured recoil-operated hinge-action autoloader in 12 or 20 gauge. Priced at $3850.00 in the standard grade, the Cosmi has a weight of approximately 7½ pounds, unloaded, and a total magazine capacity in the buttstock of eight rounds. (Yes, that's eight rounds.) It's the only autoloading shotgun in the world that looks like an autoloader, but opens like a single barrel trap gun, via the use of a top lever.

Incor is also importing a line of over-under shotguns in field, Skeet,

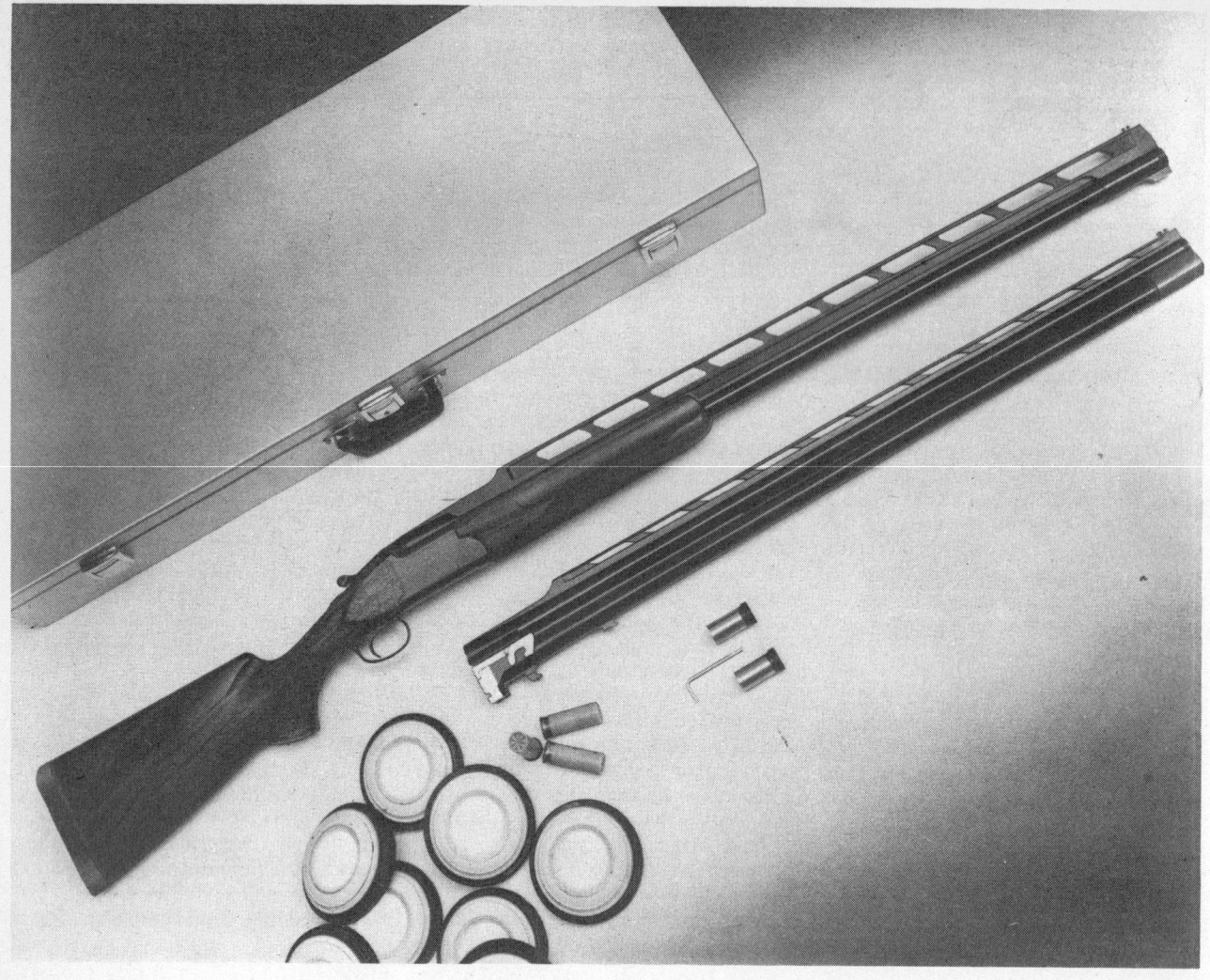

Note the high ventilated rib on the Franchi Trap '80 3000/2 underbarrel.

and trap grades in 12 and 20 gauge, a side/side model in 12 gauge, and a single barrel folding model. The over-under, labeled the SL-55, is a conventional design retailing at $619.95 in the trap grade with a Monte Carlo stock, while the single barrel folding model in a choice of 12, 16, 20, 28, or 410 lists at $139.95.

Perazzi

Following the original shutdown of the Ithaca Gun Company, the Winchester group of Olin Corporation took over distribution of Perazzi shotguns and rifles. As of the time of the San Francisco Shot Show in January 1980, a total of 57 different models and grades were catalogued, ranging from the Model TM1 single barrel trap gun at $2650.00 to the $20,000.00 Combination Gun (9.3x74R/20 gauge) and the Model DHO/O sidelock side/side shotgun. Many of the models are special order only, although many of the trap and Skeet models are stock items.

Newest of the trap guns are the Grand American I and II over-under combo guns. The Grand American I has a set of over-under barrels in a choice of lengths—29½ inches or 31½ inches—with the over barrel choked full and the under barrel fitted with an interchangeable choke tube. (Five choke tubes are provided.) The "ungun" single barrel on the Grand American I has a high tapered ventilated rib, interchangeable choke tube, and a choice of 32- or 34-inch length. Except for having a conventional top single barrel instead of the under single barrel, the Grand American II is the same as the Grand American I, plus it is supplied with an additional detachable trigger assembly. Trigger mechanisms are interchangeable on both Grand American models, as are the buttstocks, plus the over-under barrels on both models have ventilated side ribs.

Every Perazzi is shot for point-of-impact, the barrels are chrome-plated, chokes are hand honed, and all checkering is hand cut. Among the many variations, there are five different rib styles—broad straight, high broad, low taper, medium taper, or high taper—a dozen different chokes from Skeet to cylinder to extra full, and seven different interchangeable stock styles—from straight grip to trap with Monte Carlo—and a choice of over 30 engraving styles.

Rottweil

In 1979 Rottweil introduced the AAT with the raised adjustable ventilated rib. Available in a single barrel version with a choice of 32- or 34-inch length at $4062.50, the AAT can also be obtained with an extra set of over-under barrels for $5362.50, or with two sets of over-under barrels for $7275.00, plus there's a wide assortment of interchangeable stocks, forearms, and trigger assemblies available. Now a less expensive single barrel trap gun—the Rottweil 720

Trap Single—has joined the line. Priced at $2750.00, the 720 is a conventional design with a 34-inch full choke over barrel, and a non-removable single selective trigger. A raised .433-inch wide ventilated rib graces the top of the barrel. A French walnut Monte Carlo stock and hand-filling forearm complete the assembly.

Shotguns of Ulm

The Krieghoff Model 32 over-under shotgun has been discontinued, but there's a newer and much improved version—the K80—available, and it's manufactured in the same factory. Available in a variety of grades and finishes, the K80 features a finger-fitting adjustable-position stainless trigger, choice of five interchangeable forearms, five interchangeable stocks with a palm swell on each side of the pistol grip, an adjustable impact-point for the under barrel of the over-under, and an adjustable rib on the unsingle barrel that permits an impact-point change of from 7 to 35 inches, using only a coin. In addition, there's a factory built-in release trigger activated by the easy replacement of a few parts.

Skeet grade K80 shotguns are available in 12 gauge only, or with three extra barrels in 20 gauge, 28 gauge, and 410, or as an International Skeet version with Tula-type chokes and ventilated lower barrel. The trap guns are available as an over-under, a conventional single, or an unsingle, in addition to the K80 Trap Combo, which features a choice of 30- or 32-inch over-under barrels, and an extra over or unsingle barrel in 32- or 34-inch length, all fitted into a special luggage-style carrying case. The K80 should be available about the time you read this.

SKB

In 1979 SKB introduced the XL900MR gas-operated autoloader in trap, Skeet, and slug grades, and in 12 and 20 gauge sizes, to compliment the Model 7300 and 7900 pump guns. At the 1980 Shot Show the prototype of a new trap combination set was shown, although production will not start until about the time you read this, with delivery slated in early 1981. Based on the Model 5600 over-under action, and featuring a non-selective single trigger mechanism which will always fire the under barrel first, the Combo will be available with a set of 30-inch over-under barrels and a choice of 32- or 34-inch unsingle barrel. Price is anticipated to be around $2000.00 for the set, or about $1250.00 for the unsingle gun without the over-under barrels, complete with fitted hard case. The over-under barrels will be topped with a 12mm wide ventilated rib, while the unsingle will feature a raised ventilated rib tapering in width from 12mm at the breech to 8mm at the muzzle. Weight of the shotgun, with either the unsingle barrel or the over-under set, will be about 8¼ pounds, depending on the density of the fancy grade French walnut used for the stock and forearm.

W & C Scott

Webley & Scott ceased shotgun manufacture in 1979, but some 30 craftsmen with over 600 years of gunmaking skills between them have decided to pick up the pieces, and turn out a small number of superbly finished side/side shotguns each year from their Birmingham, England. shops. Two models—the Bowood and the Chatsworth—are being built in a choice of 12, 16, 20 or 28 gauge. Both guns are hammerless ejector game guns with double triggers, Anson & Deeley actions, and a choice of barrel lengths from 25 to 30 inches, with concave or flat Churchill rib. Chokes are as needed, and the stock and forearm are of deluxe walnut to order, with hand checkering at 24 lines-per-inch. Prices are dependent on the time of order, but consider around $5000.00 for the basic gun, and the options available are many, each of which must be counted to arrive at the final cost. A full pistol grip, for example, will add approximately $50.00 to the cost, while a beavertail forearm will add approximately $250.00.

Steyr-Daimler/Gamba

The Gamba line of shotguns has remained basically the same, with the Oxford, London, and Ambassador side/side models equal in quality to some of the best that came out of England, plus the Edinburgh over-under and mono models for Skeet and trap. In the Steyr Mannlicher rifle line the 25-06 cartridge has been added to the list of chambering available, and brings the possible choices to a total of 30 calibers. The 25-06 will be available in all five models. All Mannlicher rifles feature cold hammer forged barrels with a spiral tapered profile in the sporting line.

Stoeger Industries

In the Franchi shotgun line the 520 Deluxe autoloader and the Model 400 Peregrine Series over-under have been dropped. Neither is catalogued for 1980, although the 520 is illustrated. The top of the Franchi Trap '80 line of shotguns is the 12 gauge

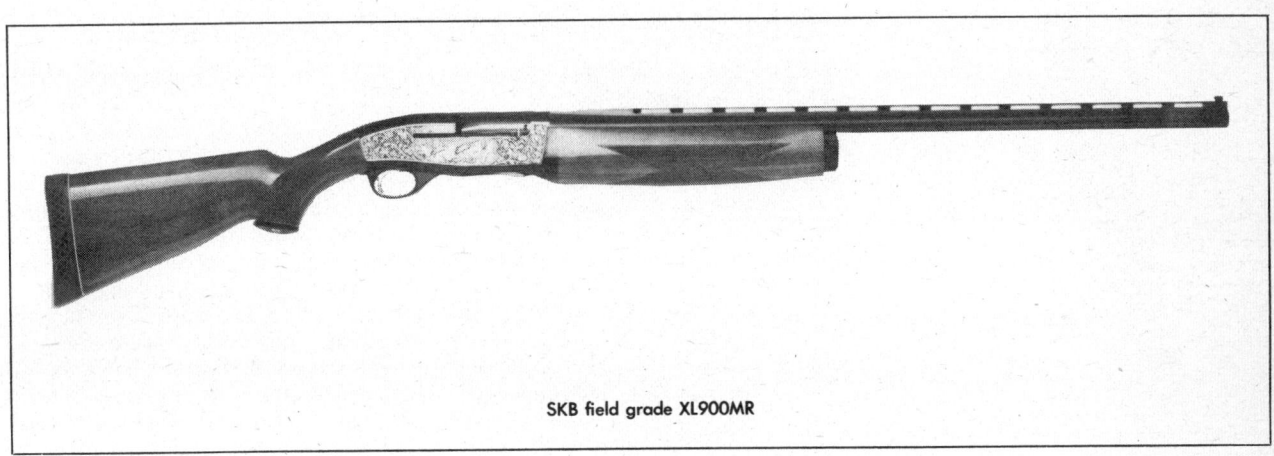

SKB field grade XL900MR

3000/2, featuring a choice of 30-inch over-under barrels with a 32-inch underbarrel, or 32-inch over-under barrels with a 34-inch underbarrel. Weight of the 3000 is approximately 8¼ pounds, and it comes with three choke tubes—interchangeable with either barrel set, and a choice of six different cast-off buttstock assemblies, each of which is drilled for installation of a recoil reducer. Currently $2995.00, the 3000 comes with carrying case.

In the Sako rifle line an entire series—the 3500 Series—has been added, covering three different grades, starting with the Classic. Available in medium, and long action models, the Classic features a hand-rubbed oil finish classic-design American walnut stock, without Monte Carlo or forearm tip, and a blued, satin-finished barreled action without sights; it's available chambered for the 243, 270, 30-06 and the 7mm Remington Magnum cartridges, for just under $600.00. The Safari Grade rifle at $1400.00 features the long action in a classic-style French walnut stock, with stepped-based cheekpiece and a recoil pad. The magazine is the extended design to allow the loading of four magnum cartridges, plus one in the chamber, and the caliber choices include the 7mm, 300, 338 and 375 H&H. Express-type rear sight, hooded front, and a barrel-mounted front swivel to prevent bruising the off hand, are other features of the Safari Grade rifle. The third addition to the 3500 Series of Sako rifles is the Super Deluxe, available only on special order at $1400.00 for regular cartridges and $1500.00 in the magnum calibers. (Caliber choices range from the 222 Remington in the short AI action to the 375 H&H in the long AIII action.) Features of the Super Deluxe rifles include extra select wood with a combination of carving, checkering, and stippling on the grip and forearm areas, plus high polished bluing and engraving on the floorplate and trigger guard.

Valmet

Shotguns from this Finnish firm have been around for a long time, but now the firm has its own distribution from Elmsford, New York, and has introduced what it calls a "shooting system." Using the same basic over-under action based on the time-tested Remington Model 32 design, and changing only the barrel assemblies, it is possible to have an over-under shotgun in 12 or 20 gauge, a combination shotgun/rifle with 12 gauge barrel over a choice of 222, 308, or 30-06, or an over-under rifle in 308 or 30-06. On the shotgun barrels a choice of extractors or automatic ejectors is available. The barrel selector is located on the trigger, and a special feature of the latest Valmets is an indicator located to the rear of the automatic tang safety to show which barrel has been fired, an excellent feature.

Prices on the Valmet shooting system, labeled the 412 Series, are in the $500.00 to $600.00 range, depending on which barrels are selected; the exception is the double rifle, which currently lists at $679.00; considering side/side rifles cost well up into four figures, the 412 over-under rifle is a real value. The quality of Valmet arms has always been good, and a selection of chokes is available on the shotguns. So, if distribution of the Series 412 arms is good, there should be a lot of Valmets showing up in the game fields and on the target ranges.

Ventura Imports

This Seal Beach, CA, firm imports shotguns from Italy in three designs—Piotti, Contento, and Ventura. The Piotti and Ventura models are side/side guns, while the Contento is an over-under design featuring Woodward/Boss side lugs for an exceptionally low center of gravity. The Piotti guns are available in two grades—Val Trompia Crown and Gardone. The first is a sidelock gun of the Holland & Holland type, with Florentine hand engraving and traditional English stocking, while the Gardone is an Anson & Deeley boxlock of the Westley Richards pattern. The Ventura side/side shotguns are available in four boxlock designs of the Anson & Deeley type, including the Models 51, 51 XXV-BL, 52 and 53, plus four Holland & Holland sidelock versions based on the Purdey designs, including the Models 62, 64, 64 XXV-SL, and 66. The majority of the side/side shotguns are available in 12 or 20 gauge models. The Contento over-under design is available in field, Skeet, trap, and pigeon styles, and Standard, Lusso, or Extra Lusso grades in 12 gauge only. Prices range from $1195.00 for a field grade Contento Standard, to $5160.00 for a 20 gauge Val Trompia Crown grade Piotti. Optional features, such as single selective trigger, threading O-U barrels for screw-in choke tubes, and extra barrels will up the cost, but not excessively. In addition, other shotguns, including a complete line of Merkels, is supposed to be available by the time you read this. •

The London grade Gamba side/side available from Steyr-Daimler is available in a choice of 12 or 20 gauge models, with single or double triggers.

Spanish Doubles In Classic Style

These two from Spain are not plain; but not fancy either: Just very nice.

by JOHN T. AMBER
PHOTOS: ROBERT S. L. ANDERSON

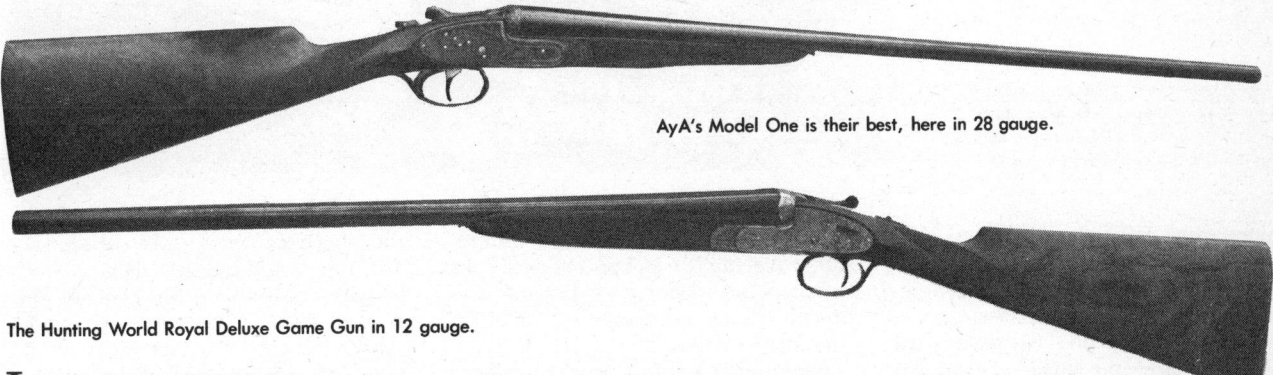

AyA's Model One is their best, here in 28 gauge.

The Hunting World Royal Deluxe Game Gun in 12 gauge.

I NEVER thought the day would come when a Spanish-made shotgun would carry a list price of $5200 or more, but it's here now! Bob Lee, long-time head of Hunting World, (a New York City shop catering to sportsmen*) recently sent me a shotgun that does, I think, justify the price range noted. But I'll describe the gun and you be the judge. With inflation being what it is, Lee's Royal Deluxe Game Gun—as he modestly calls it—will probably be more costly in 1981 and after.

The new side-by-side double, the first gun to be marketed by Bob's company, is certainly a delight to the eye—even to my jaundiced and critical one. Because of the outrageous prices asked for "best" London-made guns these last few years, Lee decided to find and offer a double gun closely comparable to London's finest sidelocks in "style, balance, mechanical design, engraving and finish . . ."

Has he succeeded? Well, if not perfectly, pretty damn close—and the minuses are quite minor.

The maker of this Lee double is Pedro Arrizabalaga of Eibar, a highly-regarded gunmaker in Spain and elsewhere. Bob told me he'd made some half-dozen trips to the factory in 1979 alone, making sure the guns he's importing would meet the demands of a particular and demanding clientele.

First, some general notes: This straight-stocked 12 gauge (No. 12834) has 26-inch barrels, the weight empty 6⅛ pounds. Stock dimensions are, nominally, 15¼x1½x2", though the sample gun has only a 1⅜-inch comb drop. Chambers are 2¾ inches.

The wood in stock and fore-end—a semi-beavertail—is nicely figured Spanish walnut, dull oil-finished—very dull, which I'll fix with some Lin-Speed soon. The hand checkering, 28 to the inch, carefully done in long-aspect diamonds (I found only a couple of imperfections), is cut to a multi-point pattern that covers well—the fore-end is almost fully cut, the grip area extensive and well back behind the hand. The heel of the butt is also checkered, so if the 15¼-inch pull is too long on these "Early Delivery" guns the stock can be readily shortened. Made-to-order guns, which I'll get into later, can be had with any stock dimensions. An 18K gold initial plate is set into the stock bottom.

Wood-to-metal fit is excellent indeed, snug and clear everywhere. I took off both lockplates and found the inletting for them equally crisp and smooth.

The lockplates, of hand-detachable style via an H&H-type lever, have intercepting safety sears, I'm pleased to see. The single non-selective trigger *must* be pulled to fire this double; a fall or a jar, no matter how hard, won't touch the sears off. The interior flats of the lockplates are engine turned, as are the flats of the barrel breeches and the action. The safety is automatic, the words *SAFE* inlaid in gold. Gold-lined cocking indicators show on the lockplates.

The action-lockup system closely matches the H&H design; double underbites are used, plus a Purdey-type third fastener—a lug on the barrel breeches, above the ejectors, mates with a recess in the standing breech. Purdey-type side clips are forged integral with the breech and carefully fitted. A plunger button, of Anson type, lies atop the fore-end for releasing it.

The firing pins are housed in two-pin removable bushings, a system that should be followed whenever possible,

*16 East 53rd St., NYC 10022.

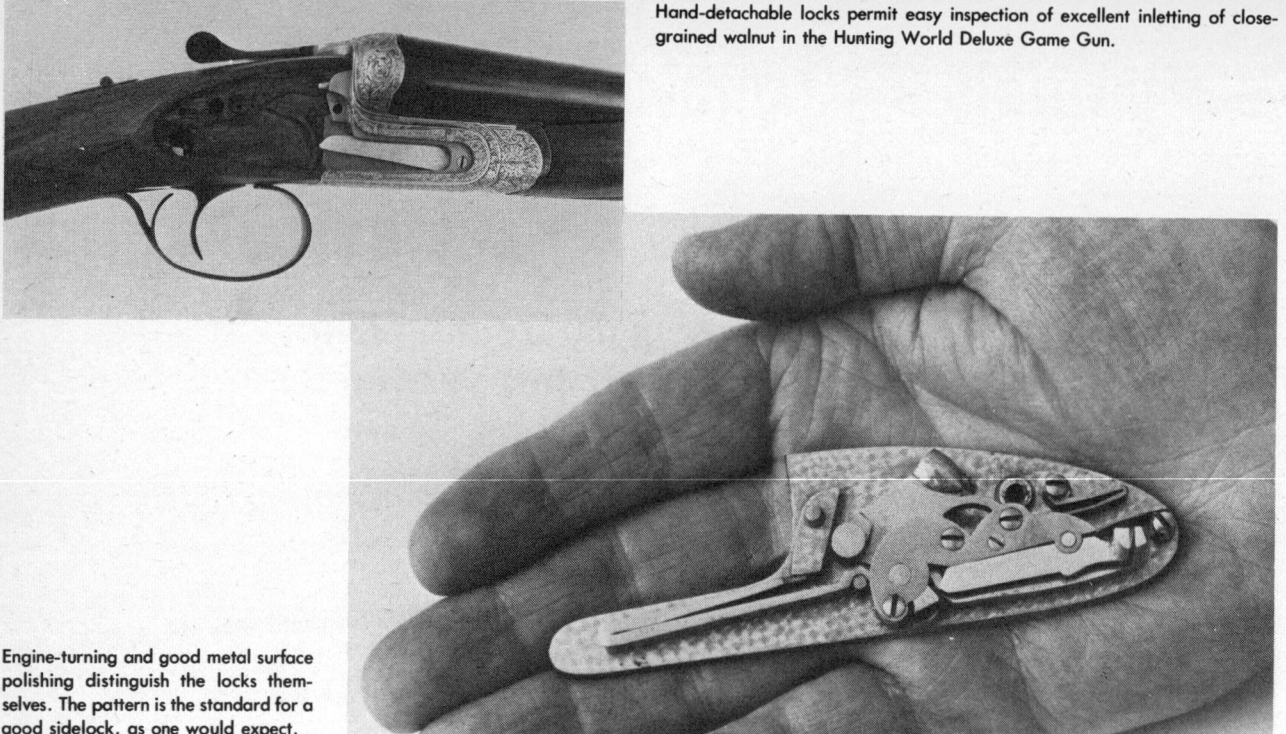

Hand-detachable locks permit easy inspection of excellent inletting of close-grained walnut in the Hunting World Deluxe Game Gun.

Engine-turning and good metal surface polishing distinguish the locks themselves. The pattern is the standard for a good sidelock, as one would expect.

in my view. Broken or damaged firing pins are a rarity these days, but they can occur. How very much easier, then, to remove the bushing and replace the faulty pin. No pulling the stock, no tiresome bother of grappling with the innards. By the same token, *no* maker I'm aware of furnishes a proper spanner to remove such two-holed—and sometimes three-holed—bushings. I wonder why?

The single trigger, London shaped and crisp at 4 pounds, is non-selective—the right barrel always fires first. That has its advantages—one needn't fuss or fiddle switching a selective trigger for that rarely-needed left-barrel long shot.

The true chopper lump barrels are polished inside to a mirror finish. The right one is choked improved cylinder, the left modified, if the stamped stars on them (3 on the left, 4 on the right) are a reliable indication. More on this later. A tapered narrow rib, of Churchill style, is fitted, the top dull matted. The rib's rear end is engraved to match the rest of the gun's embellishment. The exterior of the barrels shows no rippling or wavy condition; they have been well draw polished fore-and-aft to achieve that. A small gold bead at the muzzle is the only barrel sight.

The engraving is as good as any seen by me on Spanish guns, and much better than many of them. Bob Lee calls it "large scroll," but I'd term it of medium size. It's excellently done, fully covering the lockplates—old coin finished, or moderately bright—the breech fences, the tangs and a bit of the barrels. Nice.

As described, these "early delivery" guns are available now from Hunting World, though only some 40 of them will be made in 1980-1981. Their cost is $6500 for 12s or 20s; $7000 for the 28-gauge, FOB New York City. Your local dealer may have them—see him first. A few may be available with select, fancy wood at extra cost.

However, if you want or need a custom-made Royal Deluxe double, read on. These bespoke versions, much like the guns described, can be virtually anything you like—stocks and chokes to your desire, as are barrel lengths (25" to 30"), and so on. The basic custom gun lists at $5200, but certain options are extra: a Churchill rib is $125 (a concave rib is standard), a single trigger is $525, side clips are $525, the BT fore-end is $85 and the gold name plate is $145. The case for one gun is $300. Total, $6380. Fine English ribboned scroll engraving, a la Purdey, and the action case-colored, can be had without added cost.

As already noted, this Hunting World gun arrived here only recently, so there's been little time for an extended shooting test. Some patterning was done, though, six shots averaging about 70% with the modified barrel, some 61% with the improved cylinder tube—both rather tighter than the markings would indicate. Not all that unusual, of course—other loads might easily alter those percentages, made with Federal 3/1¼/6 cartridges at 40 yards. The ejectors are well-timed, the empties landing closely together some 15 feet behind the shooter.

Handling and mounting is excellent—the weight is much between the hands, and the muzzles are light—a recipe I like a lot. The "gape" is ample—the breeches rise well above the action top for easy loading.

Bob Lee says these are *self* openers on the H&H system, but I'd call them "easy" openers. They snap open when cocked and empty, but not when fired and ready for ejection. As with all such types a little more effort is needed to close them when loaded, but that's easily got used to. Certainly the extra effort on this new and somewhat stiff gun isn't burdensome.

Harry Lawrence, many years with Purdey, said to a man objecting to the closing effort, "Surely, old boy, you don't open your own guns?"

AyA 28-Gauge Model One

Don Garraldo, world sales manager for Aguirre y Aranzabal, and I are old friends. The late Seymour Ziebert and I once visited the AyA plant in Eibar, spending several hours looking over their wide range of shotguns and seeing the shops at work. The type that attracted me most was the Model One

The top of the line AyA Model One sidelock gun comes handsomely scroll-engraved, offers selective ejectors, and genuinely fancy European walnut.

sidelock, about at the top of their line. An appealing price was offered and, about 18 months later, the gun reached O'Hare. I reported on that trip in Gun Digest 30/1976 ed., the account called "Hunting in the Rain."

At the first S.H.O.T. show, held in St. Louis in 1979, AyA guns were on view, Don G. in attendance. He told me that they were then in good shape to deliver 28 gauge and .410 doubles, and he felt I ought to have one. What could I do but agree? I had two 28s, but neither was a classic double, nor had they been made for me. I passed on the .410.

As I've said, the Model One is AyA's "best" gun except for the same gun in fancier dress—game scene engraving, gold inlays as ordered and better wood. Well, I'd have had to wait even longer for one like that, and my poke is flatter than it used to be, too. I'm not in the IRS bracket I was in 1978.

On the other hand, I'm pleased indeed with the chaste beauty of this little, light and lively 28. It weighs a hair under 5 pounds empty, virtually all the weight seems to lie between the hands, and it should perform excellently in brush and brambles situations. It leaps into position!!

Tightly scaled down to fit the gauge, the action area is only 1¾ inches at its widest; across the lockplates it measures 1⅝ inches, and greatest depth is 1¾ inches. Grasping the gun ahead of the guard I can easily touch my thumb to my fingers.

The lockplates are readily detachable by means of the left-side lever. Made with chopper lump barrels, lockup is achieved through two sturdy under bites, excellently polished and fitted. Two triggers are present—which I'd asked for—the front one adequately hinged. Selective ejectors are standard on the Model One AyA, of course; these are not over strong, the empty cases flying together to land about 10 feet behind. The safety is automatic. A fairly simple adjustment alters the ejectors into simple extractors, benefitting the handloader. The guard is roll-edged on the right side—always a nice touch.

The lock system is essentially H&H, too, and intercepting safety sears are an integral part—no danger of accidental firing. The plate wall inside is nicely engine turned and all of the lock parts are heavily gold plated, except for the springs—a rust defeating measure that's been used for over a hundred years on top quality guns. Inletting for the plates is well and crisply done, as is the mating of wood to metal everywhere.

As I've hinted at above, I've been gradually moving away from the over-engraved gun—I admit I liked them a lot at one time—so this quite dark finished, almost somber AyA has its own appeal—a conservative, unobtrusive one. It is fully engraved, certainly, but the design is fine English scroll and roses, laced with curling open ribbons, much in the traditional Purdey fashion. Very well done, too, but because the lockplates and other action parts are darkly case colored, the effect is subdued. Only the pins and the gold-barred cocking indicators gleam. The rest of the metal is engraved to the same small design—action bottom, hinge areas, top tangs, guard, fences, top lever, safety and the fore-end bits. The barrels and the guard/tang are nicely rust blued to a soft sheen.

The 26-inch barrels, topped by a concave, swamped rib, are bored full and modified. Made of chrome-nickel steel, they're proofed at 100 Kgs/cm² or about 14,223 pounds per square inch—ample. Only one sight is fitted, a small gold-colored bead. The bores, very brightly polished, are chrome-lined up to but not including the choke area, so the chokes can be opened or worked on without problems.

Only two negatives appear, both affecting the wood, and both remediable. I can see, barely, that there's good figure in the walnut, but the brown stain applied hides it. I'll remove that, then apply Lin-Speed, probably, or some similar oil finish. The wood is nicely smooth. The checkering is, generally, well done at 24 lines per inch, but the diamonds are flattened here and there and they're not as well cut along some border areas as they ought to be. A re-cutting will soon fix that.

Both faults—flat-topped checkering and over-staining—are all too common European practices, and I'm not put off that they occur on this AyA 28. They'll learn one day.

Shooting was limited to W-W ¾-oz. of 9s—all I had and no larger shot sizes in the Marengo area. There's little call for 28s of any size. I shot at 25 yards instead of the usual 40 because I'll use this AyA at short ranges; a ¾-oz. charge doesn't offer high density at best. I'll try some ⅞- and 1-oz. loads later, when and if.

The 9s shot quite well at the reduced yardage, the modified choke showing a 6-round average of 67%, with good distribution; only a few open patches appeared, and those only in 3 shots. The full-choke tube was, for me, too tight; I'd miss a lot with that barrel! Six shots averaged about 76%, with pretty dense central concentration; dead-on hits would pulverize birds using these 9s. Sixes and 7½'s should do better.

I wasn't surprised when the pattern center printed about 6-8 inches high. Both barrels merged well (centers were a few inches apart at that range), but we'll probably have to cut the comb down a trifle. As it is, fast-rising birds should be nailed well.

The importers* price on the AyA Number One/28 gauge is $2650. The same gun in 410 is $2750, whereas 12s, 16s and 20s are $2450. To these prices add $300 for the case, and $325 for a two-barrel set case. Other options are: single trigger, $100; beavertail fore-end, $30; a spare set of springs and firing pins is $35, and a fitted recoil pad is also $35. •

*IGI-Domino Corp., 200 Madison Ave., New York, NY 10016
William Larkin Moore & Co., 31360 Via Colinas, No. 109, Westlake Village, CA 91361.

The Art of The Engraver

We selected for this issue the best photos of the best engravings we could get and here try to show each piece to its best advantage.

HANK BONHAM

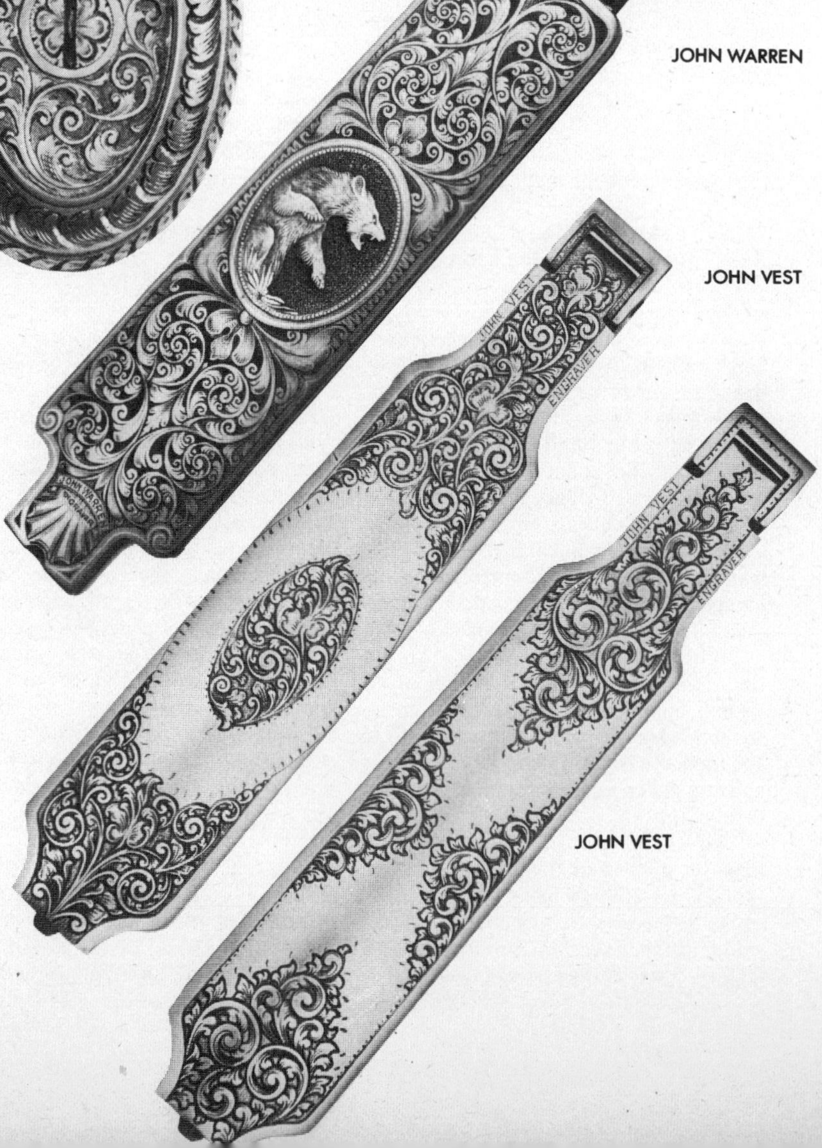

JOHN WARREN

JOHN VEST

JOHN VEST

HEIDE HIPTMAYER

H. V. GRANT

SAM WELCH

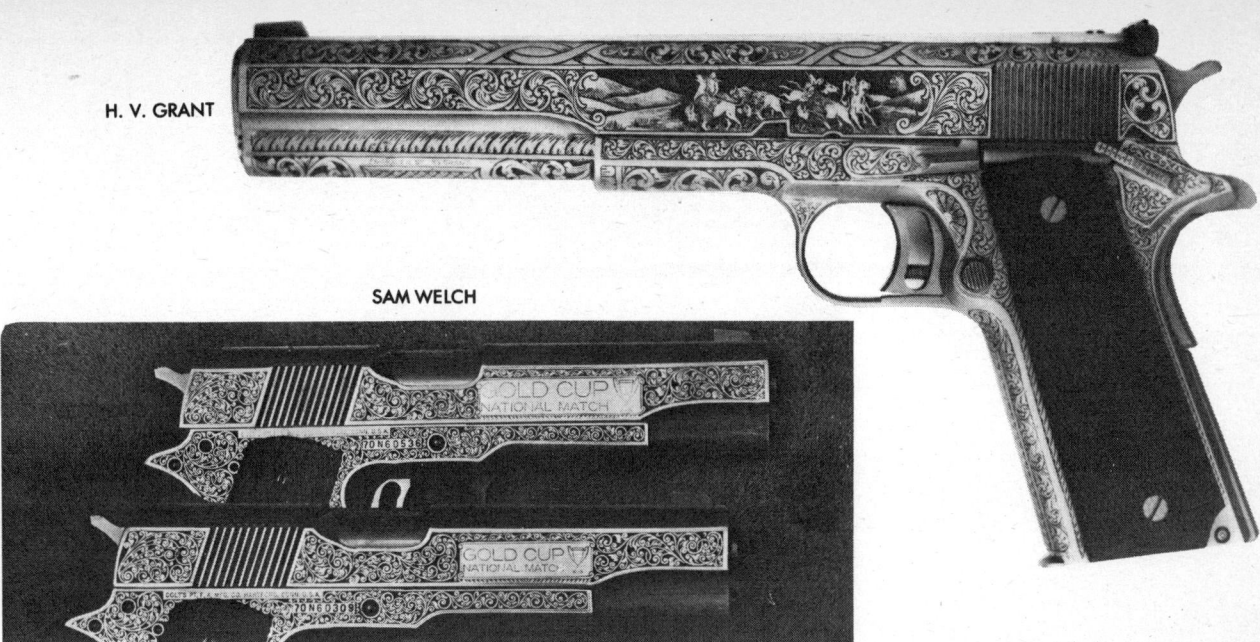

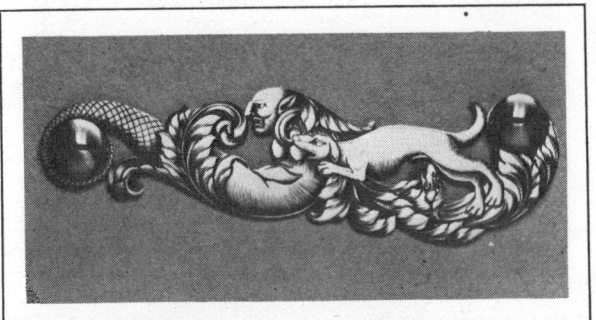

D. GOODWIN

WAYNE RENO/BLACKHAWK MTN.

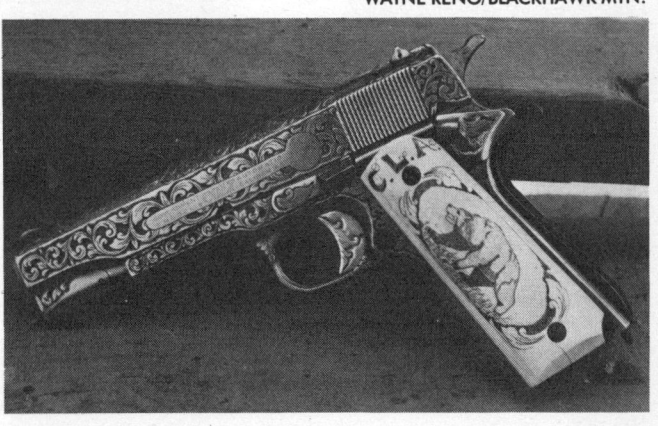

PAUL JAEGER, INC./CLAUS WILLIG

T. J. KAYE

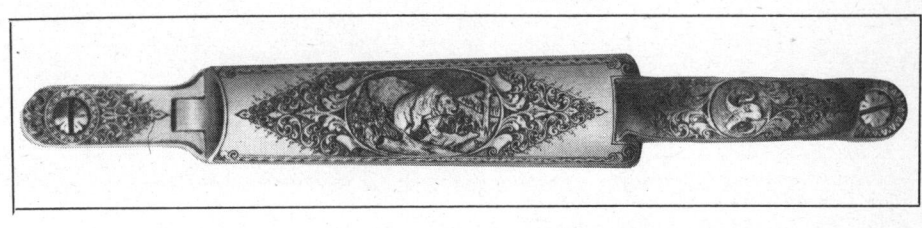

PAUL JAEGER, INC./CLAUS WILLIG

35TH EDITION, 1981

CARL BLEILE

GEORGE SHERWOOD

BRYAN BRIDGES

DWAIN WRIGHT

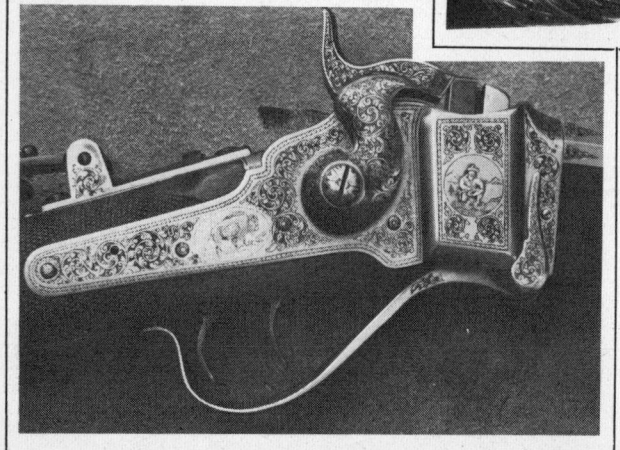
JOHN ROHNER

GERALD R. DESQUESNES

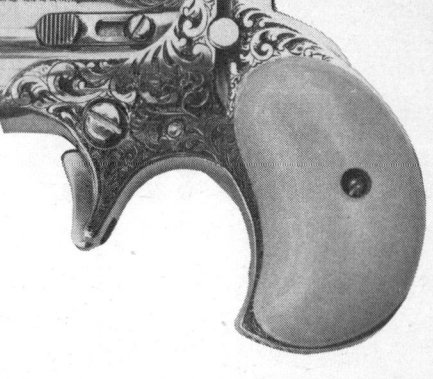
RALPH W. INGLE

BILL JOHNS

BEN SHOSTLE/THE GUN ROOM

MARTIN RABENO

LANCE KELLY

JIM KELSO

WINSTON CHURCHILL
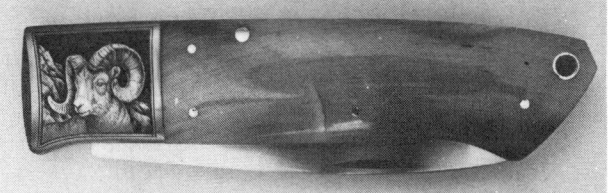

35TH EDITION, 1981 **239**

FIE'S Combo 20 ga./30-30

Big and heavy it is, but potentially useful because it shoots well.

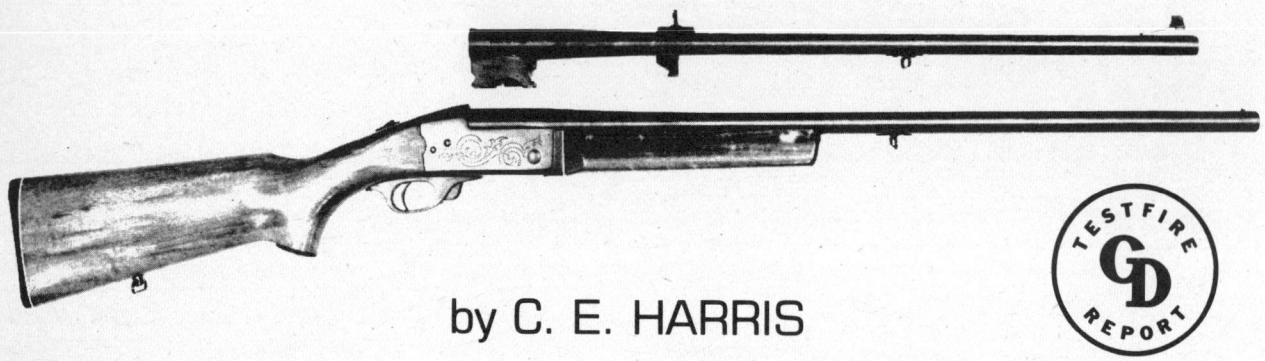

by C. E. HARRIS

SINGLE-BARREL shotguns are often scorned by fanciers of their more sophisticated cousins, but where firearms are working tools, the break-open, single-barrel shotgun outnumbers all the others. In South America, the utility of the lowly single shot is well appreciated, and factories there produce a variety. Most such South American guns have simple design rugged enough for rough use and can be produced for a moderate price. While sporting purists will disparage their lack of refinements and inferior finish, they are nearly always serviceable and satisfactory.

The CBC HL-41 is a typical example of the utility rifle/shotgun combo. It is made in Sao Paulo, Brazil by Campanhia Brasileira de Cartuchos, the largest manufacturer of ammunition in that country. The CBC firm makes a variety of shotguns for domestic consumption, some of which are imported into the U.S. This one imported by FIE Corp., of Opa Locka, Fla., has interchangeable 20-ga. shotgun and 30-30 rifle barrels for the same receiver.

The mechanism is a conventional break-open hammerless, automatic ejector design, with automatic top tang safety. A plastic latch in front of the trigger guard disengages the locking bolt from the barrel underlug so the action may be broken open. The 20-ga. shotgun barrel is 28" long, with 2¾" chamber, full choke, and brass front bead. The 30-30 rifle barrel is 25¾" long with a .1" wide blade front sight dovetailed into a broad ramp, and a folding open rear sight dovetailed into a base attached to the barrel with two screws. The buttstock, and both rifle and shotgun barrels have sling swivels, a useful idea.

Comparing the CBC combo gun with its U.S. equivalent, the H&R Topper, you are struck by its size. Its steel receiver is big enough for a 12-ga. gun. The manufacturer makes a 12-ga. gun on this receiver, but no 12-ga. combo guns are available. The sides of the receiver are roll engraved and nicely polished; the interior is quite rough. This didn't affect function however, and the gun worked easily. The barrels are quite heavy, so the gun weighs more than its U.S. counterpart, being 6¾ lbs. with the 28" shotgun barrel installed, and 8¼ lbs. when the 30-30 rifle barrel is substituted. While this weight is noticeable if you must carry it a great deal, it makes the shotgun swing more steadily, and the rifle barrel hold more solidly, contributing to better marksmanship. It also reduces recoil considerably.

It's interesting to speculate what could be done with this gun. At 6¾ lbs., it is heavy enough to make a useful 3" Magnum 20-ga., and that would greatly enhance its potential as a meat getter. The receiver is substantial enough to permit a physically larger rifle cartridge than the 30-30. It couldn't handle high-pressure rounds, but it would be truly interesting to have such a gun for rounds like the 45-70 or 444 Marlin.

The buttstock and fore-end are a close-grained Brazilian hardwood with unusual grain, pleasing color and interesting smell. The finish is somewhat slippery, though it is applied evenly. The fore-end is held securely to the barrel lug by a snap fastening with coil spring. To take down the gun or change barrels, make sure it is unloaded, then close the action and grasp the fore-end, pulling it down and away from the barrel to remove it. Then press the latch at the front of the trigger guard rearward, and simply open the gun to dismount the barrel.

The stock design leaves a bit to be desired, but plenty of scope for work. The fore-end is wide, flat bottomed and somewhat triangular in cross-section, giving it a boxy feel. There's enough wood there for two normal fore-ends. The buttstock is very thick through the wrist, more than is needed for strength, and could also be slimmed somewhat, but the butt itself is small, being only 4½" high from heel to toe. It really needs to be about ½" deeper than that, and it wouldn't hurt if it were a wee bit wider than its present 1½". Length of pull is 14".

Functioning was reliable with both factory loads and handloads. After firing about 100 rounds of factory loads in each barrel, I shot a quantity of reloads. Empties from the 20-ga. factory loads were reloaded using a Lee Loader with 2.2 cc charge cup, throwing 20 grs. of SR-4756, using Federal Gameload cases, 1 oz. of 7½s, the Remington PP23678 Wad and Federal 209 primers. The 30-30 cases also worked fine when reloaded with a Lee Loader, using the same 2.2 cc charge cup from the Lee Powder Measure Kit to throw 28.9 grs. of IMR-3031. I used this charge with both 150-gr. Hornady spire point and 170-gr. flatnose jacketed bullets with good success. With cast bullets best results were had using the RCBS 30-180FN cast of quenched wheelweights, using this same measure to throw 33 grs. of W-W 760, giving about 2000 fps in this long barrel. All these are good hunting loads.

I suspected there might be extraction or ejection troubles with the rifle barrel because of its narrow .09" wide ejector, compared to the broad one which engages a full 1/6th of the cartridge rim on the shotgun tube, but my suspicions were groundless. Empties from both barrels were reliably thrown 4-6 ft. from the gun. What did give some trouble were the iron sights, since they couldn't be satisfactorily zeroed with factory 30-30 loads. The folding leaf rear sight furnished was .65" high, and even when bottomed out as far as it could be adjusted, the rifle shot about a foot high at 100 yards. Substituting a Lyman No. 16C, which is .5" high, and elevates to .6" maximum did the trick. Of course, as it came from the box it also shot about a foot to the right, but there was more than ample range of adjustment available to drift the front or rear sights in their barrel dovetails to compensate for that. Once I got a satisfactory iron sight zero, however, I decided a Weaver K3 in Tip-Off mounts would be a better arrangement, and this proved to be the case. I had no trouble getting a good zero with the scope, and once snugged down it stayed put for over 300 rounds.

Accuracy of the rifle barrel, and patterning of the shotgun tube were entirely satisfactory. Groups with the 30-30 barrel using factory loads averaged around 3" with the scope and about 4½" with the open sights. Best accuracy requires you hold the fore-end in your hand, using the front sandbag only to support your arm with no rear bag under the butt. If you hunker down on the bags with the CBC as you would with your favorite bolt-action varmint rifle, your groups will probably string vertically as much as 6-8". Shooting off the shoulder, though, it will do a lot better than you can. I could approach 2" groups with handloads, but not consistently. On the whole, you'll shoot this rifle as well or a little better than your typical 30-30 lever gun, which isn't all that bad.

Although the shotgun barrel is supposed to be full choke, with field loads of 7½'s it gave patterns closer to modified, which is really about optimum for a utility gun. I didn't have any shot bigger than 6's to shoot but I'd expect you'd get good tight turkey killing patterns with high base No. 4's. Over-all, the shotgun barrel gave good game-killing patterns which were well distributed and only slightly above point of hold at 40 yards.

The 30-30 barrel has real potential because its 25¾" length permits you to realize the catalog, test-barrel ballistics which you never come within 120 fps of in a typical 20" lever-gun. Chronographing factory loads in the CBC showed no real difference between the velocities obtained and the factory numbers. Another bonus with the CBC, compared to the lever-guns is that you can safely use pointed bullets, and therefore retain a bit more velocity and energy down-range. This doesn't mean the CBC is a long-range gun, but it does insure you get the full potential out of it in making that one shot count.

Looking at the CBC combo objectively, it appears to be a highly serviceable, utilitarian firearm. It's not fancy, but it works. ●

Harris is not actually turkey-hunting here, but test-firing has led him to conclude the FIE combo gun is just what it is advertised to be—an inexpensive and reliable gun for both deer and birds.

TESTFIRE

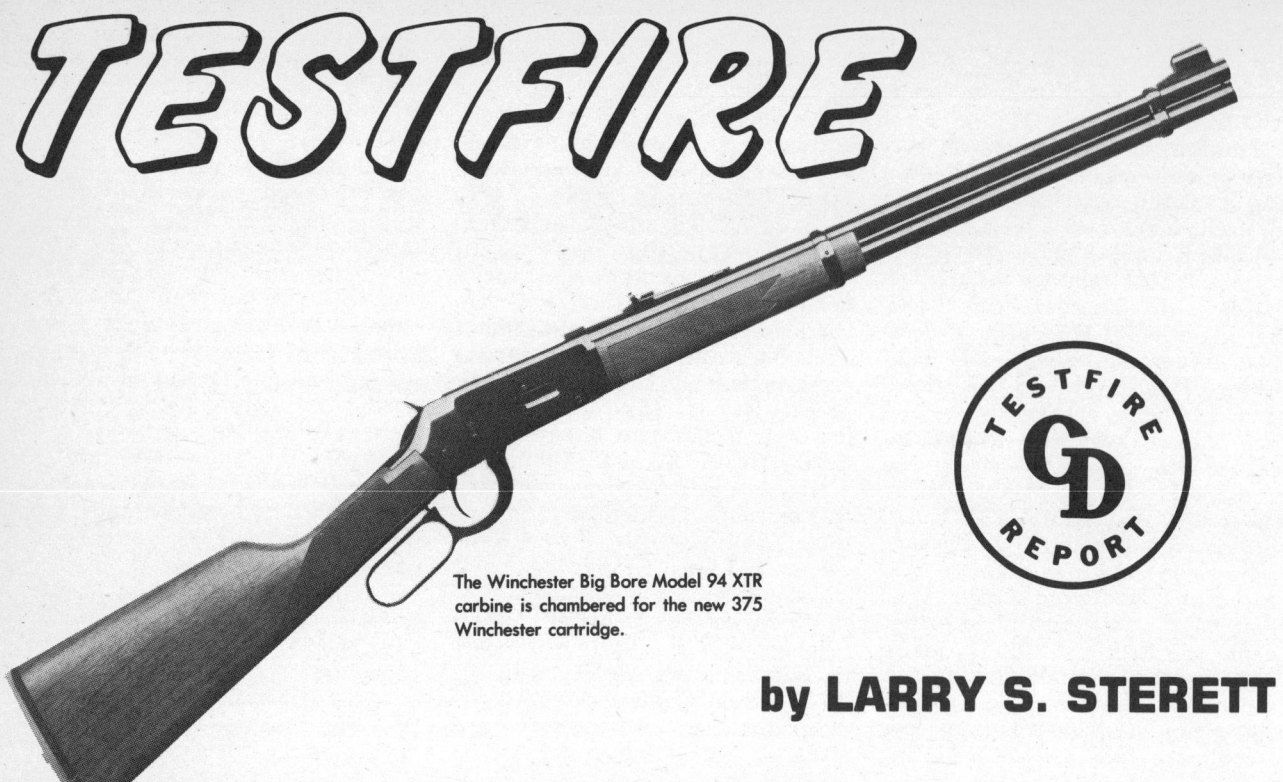

The Winchester Big Bore Model 94 XTR carbine is chambered for the new 375 Winchester cartridge.

by LARRY S. STERETT

Winchester Model 94 Big Bore Carbine

The Winchester Model 94 needs no introduction, nor a lengthy explanation on how it works. Well into its fourth quarter century of production, it has been chambered for a variety of cartridges, the most famous of which has been the 30 W.C.F., or 30-30 Winchester. Now it has been given an update and a new cartridge in the form of the Big Bore Model 94 XTR chambered for the 375 Winchester cartridge.

The XTR naturally stands for "extra" quality finish of the metal—it has the appearance of highly polished black chrome—and wood—the forearm has wraparound cut checkering at 16 lines-per-inch, and the grip has similar checkering on the grip sides. The checkering is good quality, with straight lines that are straight, and no borders or runouts. To handle the additional pressures of the new cartridge, the rear of the receiver has been beefed up in the lockup area. This additional metal on the side panels gives the Model 94 XTR a slightly different and more massive appearance, but it isn't really that noticeable, and it is necessary.

Note the beefed up side panels at the rear of the Model 94 XTR receiver and the good quality cut checkering on the grip.

The test gun weighed in at 6½ pounds, and measured 38⅛ inches in over-all length, with a barrel length of 20 inches. The barrel has a right-hand twist with one turn in 12 inches, and muzzle diameter .715-inch. Topping the barrel was a hooded ramp front sight having a .072-inch silver bead, in addition to an open rear sight with a shallow "V" having a small (.070-inch wide) "U" at the junction. The rear sight is adjustable for elevation via the elevator, and for windage by drifting with a punch. (Sight radius is 16⅞ inches.) In sunlight, this sight combination proved satisfactory, but near dusk, or in heavy timber, it proved close to worthless. The small "U" simply disappeared. Removal of the hood on the front sight is a must in heavily shadowed areas, such as thick brush or heavy timber.

The hammer on the Big Bore is a handy .358-inch in width, and grooved for non-slippage, while the trigger has been contoured for use with either hand. The hammer is powered by a coil spring to reduce the force needed to cock it. Two different Big Bore 94's were checked for trigger letoff, and both measured 3½ pounds, with no noticeable creep, providing a pleasant surprise.

The 375 Winchester cartridge has a rimmed straight case, and is available with a 200-grain Power Point bullet or

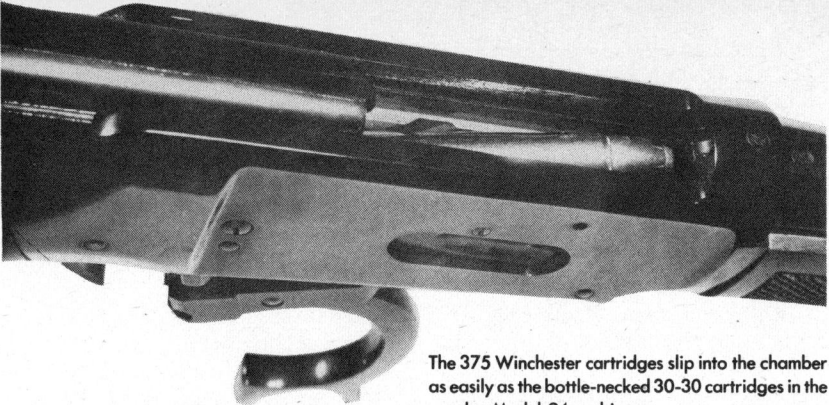

The 375 Winchester cartridges slip into the chamber as easily as the bottle-necked 30-30 cartridges in the regular Model 94 carbine.

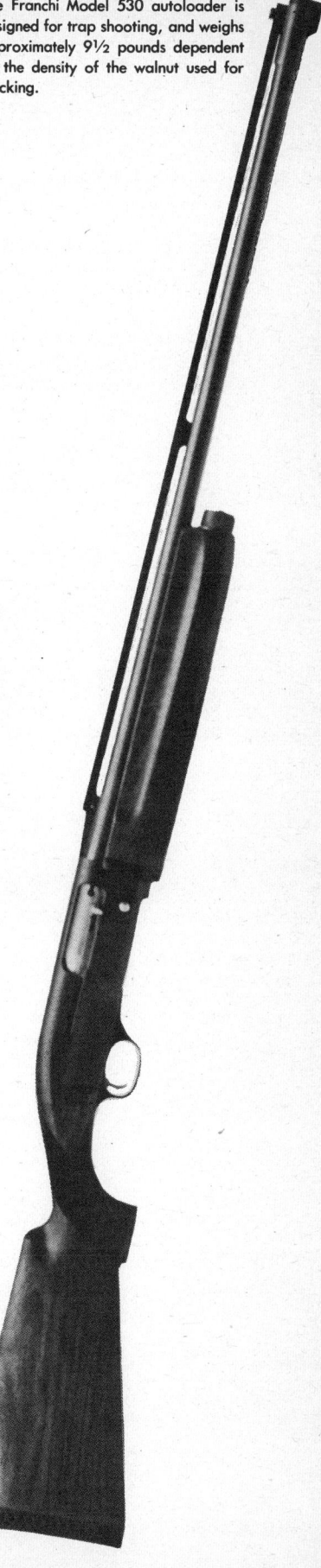

The Franchi Model 530 autoloader is designed for trap shooting, and weighs approximately 9½ pounds dependent on the density of the walnut used for stocking.

with a 250-grain Power Point. The 200-grain load has the same velocity at the muzzle as the 170-grain 30-30 Winchester factory load, but at 100 yards the 375 Winchester has 150 foot-pounds more energy than the 30-30 at the same distance, though the 30-30 does have a slightly flatter trajectory.

At the 100-yard range, firing consisted of 10 three-shot groups from the bench with each load, using sandbag forearm and butt rests. All cartridges were fed directly from the magazine, and no problems were encountered in feeding or firing. Fired cases ejected up and slightly to the rear: several cases actually landed in this writer's left breast shirt pocket. Accuracy was not as good as expected, with groups averaging around four inches with the open sights; such accuracy is good enough for deer hunting at short ranges, and the Big Bore is a short range carbine, but smaller groups would improve the chances of a solid hit.

Some additional firing was done at random targets, since no game was in season for a hunt. The 375 does pack a wallop at the muzzle, although the recoil on the shoulder did not seem as great as with the regular 30-30 Model 94, even when fired from the bench. Among the targets were sections of cured five-inch Osage Orange (commonly called hedge) posts set into a sand hillside. At 100 yards the 375-caliber bullets would penetrate the posts completely, blasting out the backside so it looked like matchwood, and slamming on into the sand backstop. The 250-grain bullet created more damage than the lighter 200-grain version, but the 375 Winchester cartridge does have penetration capabilities.

It's doubtful the 375 Winchester cartridge will ever replace the 30-30 Winchester cartridge, but the new Big Bore Model 94 XTR carbine is an excellent choice for use on game of whitetail and mule deer proportions, plus black bear. Thus, for the hunter favoring the Model 94 carbine, but wanting a bit more bullet weight, the Big Bore Model 94 XTR chambered for the 375 Winchester cartridge is the answer.

Franchi Model 530 Autoloading 12 Gauge Trap Gun

The basic design of the Model 530 is similar to U.S.-manufactured gas-operated autoloading shotguns, differing only in minor details. However, the 530, unlike many autoloading shotguns, was designed for trap use from the ground up, whereas most autoloading shotguns used for trap are field guns modified with a higher or wider ventilated barrel rib and a straighter buttstock.

The 530 receiver is steel, 1.45 inches wide at its maximum, and milled away slightly to a width of 1.09 inches above the trigger guard. Over-all weight of the 530 is 9½ pounds, and it has an over-all length of 50⅝ inches, with a barrel length of 29⅞ inches. Finish on the receiver, barrel, ventilated steel rib, and alloy trigger guard, is a nonglare matte blue, which resembles military Parkerizing; it's durable and definitely worthwhile on a trap gun. Polished chrome surfaces on the 530 include the bolt charging handle, bolt, bolt release button, carrier and trigger, plus the barrel bore, and all such surfaces are smooth.

A .394-inch wide raised ventilated rib, supported by forward sloping .10-inch-thick posts, tops the barrel, milled with concentric arcs to break up light reflections. The muzzle portion of the rib, where it aligns with the choke tube housing, is milled away in a "duckbill" to support the fluorescent plastic bead. A silver-colored center bead is located 14¾ inches behind the front bead.

Unlike the Perazzi and most American interchangeable choke tube designs, the 530 uses slip-in tubes. They weigh one ounce each, and are 1.767 inches long. The muzzle of the 530 barrel is fitted with a choke tube housing measuring 2¾ inches in length, and having lugs on the top and bottom—180 degrees apart. The choke tubes slip into this housing and are retained by two M4 socket head screws threaded into the lugs; so installed the choke marking on each tube is visible in the form of a letter—M for modified, IM for improved modified, and F for full—and those three tubes are provided, along with a hex wrench. Measurements of the breech and muzzle of the choke tubes indicated the

Carlo, is comfortable. A ventilated ¾-inch thick wide rubber recoil pad graces the butt. The forearm, rounded on the bottom with wide finger grooves along the upper edge, measured 11⁷⁄₁₆ inches in length, and it and the buttstock are oil finished and hand checkered at 20 lines-per-inch, without a border. Checkering on the test gun was very good, and the wood-to-metal fit was also very good.

At 40 yards, using Remington light RXP loads (2¾, 1⅛, 8), the five-shot pattern average was 62.5 percent with the improved modified tube installed. The pattern centers were eight inches high, and slightly to the right of the aiming point. However, distribution

might produce patterns averaging above 70 percent.

One accessory of the 530 is a spring steel clip-on shell saver, which snaps into position on the receiver quickly, and prevents fired shells from being completely ejected. (Without the shell saver installed, ejection of fired cases is downward and approximately two paces to the right of the 530.) With the shell saver installed, the 530 cannot be loaded through the loading port on the bottom of the receiver, nor can a shell be dropped into the ejection port. Instead, the shell must be loaded base first into the ejection port ahead of the shell saver, and tipped to slide rearward. Releasing the shell and pushing

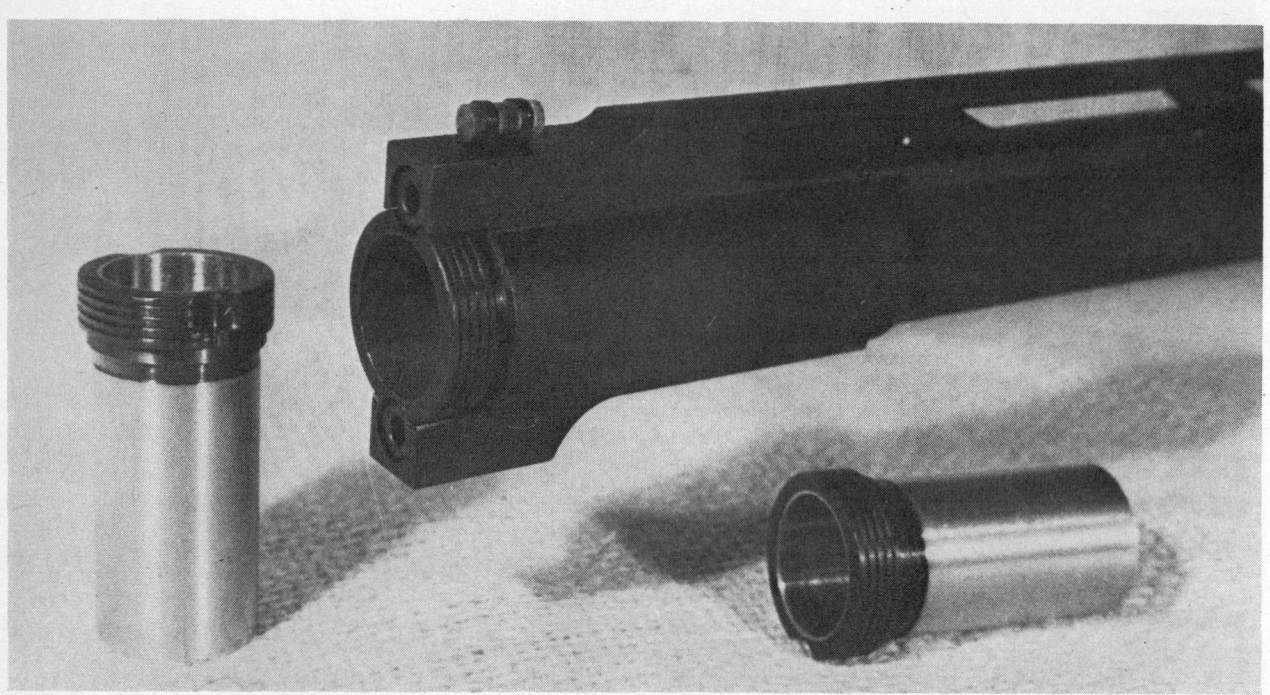

The Model 530 uses slip-in interchangeable choke tubes, which are retained in the choke tube housing by two socket head screws.

chokes to be tighter than corresponding U.S. chokes, as was the bore of the Franchi barrel, which measured .720-inch in diameter.

Choke Tube Bore Diameters

Choke Tube	Breech (inch)	Muzzle (inch)
Modified	.731	.708
Improved Modified	.727	.696
Full	.730	.688

The full pistol grip buttstock and forearm on the 530 are large and hand-filling, and the wide comb with slight forward slope, but no Monte

was good with only slightly dense centers. This average is closer to modified choke than to improved modified. The IM tube was also used to pattern Winchester-Western's AA heavy (3, 1⅛, 7½) load at 40 yards. With this load the average for five shots was 53.87 percent with the 30-inch circle, or less than expected.

Changing to the full choke tube, the same AA load was again patterned, and this time the five shot average was 59.4 percent, or over ten percent lower than is normally expected from a full choke tube. Every shotgun barrel and choke is different, and what works well in one may not work well in another. With a different factory load, or handload, even this particular 530

the bolt release will cause the bolt to chamber the shell. To recover a fired shell, slide it forward until the head clears, and lift it out. The process is simple, and fast.

Later, the 530 was used during several clay pigeon sessions to check functioning and ease of handling. During the firing of over 500 assorted factory and handloaded rounds, no feeding, extraction, or functioning problems were experienced. The trigger letoff measured just over four pounds, or about perfect for a trap gun. Although the pattern percentages were lower than expected, the 530 did break birds well from the 16-yard line, as long as this writer did his part.

Field-stripping of the 530 is a simple

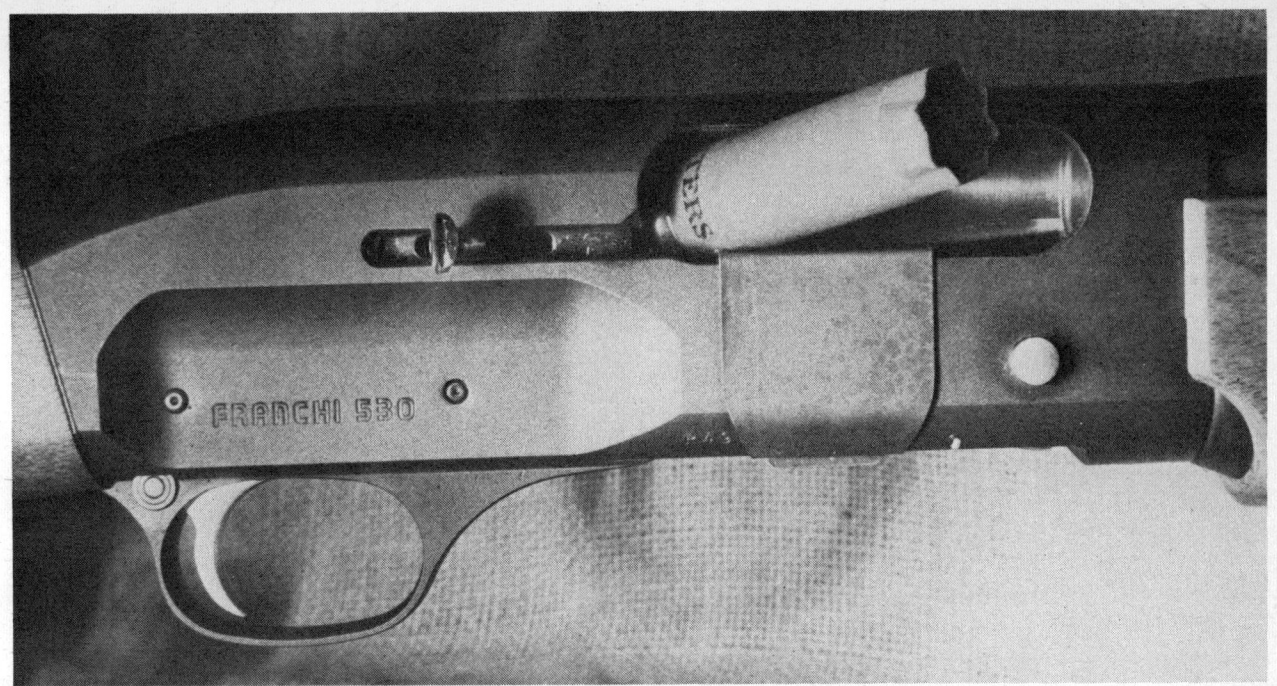

The clip-on shell saver prevents complete ejection of fired shells from the Model 530. Note the sculptured section of the 530 receiver; it reduces weight and breaks up an otherwise plain surface.

procedure, but care must be taken when replacing the breech bolt and barrel assemblies. Unscrew the magazine cap and remove the forearm, followed by unlocking the bolt slight in order to pull the barrel forward off the magazine tube. To remove the charging or cocking handle, it must be centered in the slot of the bolt and pulled sharply out to the right, after which the bolt assembly and piston may then be drawn forward out of the receiver and off the magazine tube, being careful not to lose the neoprene "O" ring. Finally, the trigger guard assembly can be removed by drifting out the two pins and carefully pulling downward on the trigger guard. Reassembly is in reverse order, taking care not to force any part into position.

The Franchi Model 530 is a solidly constructed autoloader, designed for reliability during extended firing sessions. The wood and metal finishes on the test gun were good, as was the wood-to-metal fit. As with all Franchi shotguns, the receiver of the 530 is guaranteed for the lifetime of the original purchaser as long as he remains the owner. The rest of the gun is guaranteed against defects in material or workmanship for one year from the date of purchase, and parts and service are available at Stoeger Firearms Service Centers. Mid-1980 retail price is $695.

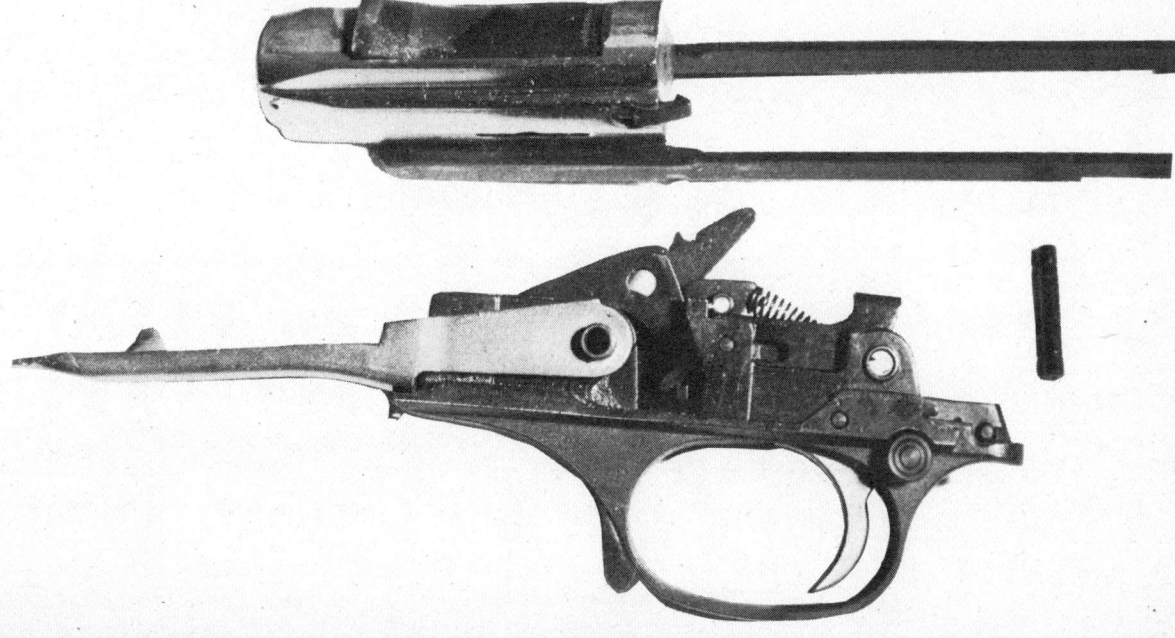

The trigger guard assembly is removable by drifting out the two retaining pins. The crossbolt safety at the rear of the trigger guard blocks movement of the trigger; the hammer is shown in the cocked position.

LIGHTER AND QUICKER SPORTERS MAKE THE DIFFERENCE FOR UP-CLOSE VENISON
by FRANK B. PETRINI

BOLT ACTION BRUSH GUNS FOR DEER

THE YOUNG hunter had been leaning casually against a large oak, rifle cradled in the crook of his arm, when he heard the slightest of sounds behind him. Slowly turning his head to peer under a low-hanging limb, he came face-to-face with the largest buck he'd ever seen in the woods. The man's pulse surged, blood pounded in his temples. The deer, alerted by the movement of the hunter's head, stiffened. For a fraction of a heartbeat their eyes locked over a 10-yard interval; then both exploded into action.

Adrenalin surged through the hunter's body as he side-stepped the tree, swung clear of the lower branches and shouldered the bolt action 30-06. Simultaneously, the buck's sinewy form twisted, turned and shot back into the thick entanglement.

Once, twice ... the deer bounded majestically away through the thick clumps of laurel and, on the third leap, countered to the left. The scope crosshairs followed, caught up and began to pass the fleeing animal when the rifle fired. The blast shattered the cool morning air just as the buck disappeared behind a thick copse of pines.

It took a few minutes for the man's heartbeat to return to normal; then he halfheartedly left his stand to search through the laurel, certain his shot had done nothing more than perforate a pine tree. Yet on the far side of the evergreens he stumbled over the buck, piled up on the tough vines. A blood-moist patch of hair revealed where the 150-gr. soft point bullet had broken the shoulder, killing the deer almost instantly.

To this young fellow, his first buck in tow, the incident was the final examination in his introduction to brush hunting. He'd passed with flying colors.

Now he understood the days his father had spent with him, searching gunshops and sporting goods stores for a rifle that would at least come close to fitting him, and, after finding one, the hours with rasp and sandpaper reducing the stock to a perfect fit for his short stature.

The reason for the many summer and autumn Saturdays when his father took him to the local range to fire handloads, first from the bench at formal targets, then offhand at stationary and moving targets, also was clear now. Yes, now he understood.

Gun "Feel"

The brush hunter seldom has any control over the situation when a whitetail appears unexpectedly in thick cover. But experts go to great lengths to lessen the element of chance through pre-season preparation. Perhaps the most important step in this preparation is choosing the right brush rifle.

The serious brush hunter should pick a rifle with which he can react instinctively. This is no easy task. He must consider his physical attributes, his preferred hunting methods, even his mental attitudes. When he finds the rifle which meets his requirements, he must practice diligently until his reactions become so deeply rooted that the hunter-rifle combination functions almost instinctively.

"Feel" is, assuredly, the most important attribute of a good brush gun. Balance, fit—call it what you like, without it you can't develop the rapport with your rifle that's necessary for accurate, instinctive brush-shooting.

When you first spot that trophy whitetail at short woods ranges you mustn't dawdle; there's no time for detailed thinking. Unless the rifle you use feels like an extension of your arm and jumps into action accordingly, you'll be without venison at the end of most seasons.

In the East, where I hunt, I've found each year more and more hunters using lightweight bolt action sporters in the thick stuff. This, I think, represents a significant change in thinking among the brush-hunting fraternity which for generations favored lever and slide action models.

Why the rising popularity of brush bolt guns? It's not feasible to interview every bolt gun advocate, or even a representative sample, but my own experiences lead me to make a few deductions.

Today's hunter is much more sophisticated than his father and grandfather before him. Better educated, better read, he thinks for himself. Most important to this topic, he

Author likes the Ruger 77 as-is—almost—as a bolt gun in the brush. It has the right mix of weight, easy-handling stock, barrel length and choice of calibers.

hasn't fallen for the "rapid fire" idea that occupied the old-timers for decades. One need only consider the number of scope sights currently in use to be sure today's hunter is interested more in precision shooting than lead spraying.

A good bolt action rifle is a practical tool. As mentioned earlier, the serious brush hunter should practice relentlessly until his rifle-handling is second nature to him, shooting that same rifle all year round if possible. Bolt rifles have the precision, reliability, and accuracy to permit their use not only for hunting varmints in the off-season but also for long-range big game species, should the opportunity arise. Today's hunter takes this into account.

Certainly personal quirks must be considered. Take me for example. No matter how much I've tried, I can't get accustomed to the wobbly fore-end on most pump rifles, and all lever action carbines are stocked too short for me. Both types lack the muzzle weight I like for steady swinging on moving game. It would seem I've been forced to accept the bolt action by default alone, but fortunately it has many other virtues as a woods gun.

Before going any further into the bolt gun's good points, let's get by the

Author slimmed the stock, floated the barrel, mounted a K2.5 on his FN Mauser 270 and got enough brush rifle to take this seven-pointer with one shot.

big stumbling block which still bothers many, that of action speed in close-in hunting situations.

Action Speed

For years the relative slowness of the bolt gun has been so exaggerated that, until now, it's taken for granted by many that a "fast" repeater, such as the slush-pump, is the ticket to brush-hunting success. Let's examine this more closely.

When a big bore rifle is fired, recoil and muzzle jump dictate a certain time interval before the sights can be brought back on target. This time lapse is sufficient for a practiced rifleman to chamber the next round with any of the manual actions, be it pump, lever or bolt.

Here we're talking about "aimed" firepower, not just rapidity of fire. In this context there's no discernible difference even with a semi-automatic; any discrepancy that exists is directly related to the amount, or lack, of practice on the part of the shooter in familiarizing himself with his own rifle.

Admittedly, there are times when more than one shot is required to put a deer down quickly. In the East, where the brushlands teem with hunters during the short seasons, you can't afford to have a hit deer run 50 yards or more before cashing in. By then he's someone else's target and trophy. Here aimed firepower is the answer and the action type is far less important than the man behind the buttplate.

Brush Cartridges

This is not the place to expound on the infinitesimal advantages of one

Author's favorite brush cartridges: 244 Remington with 90-gr. Speer; 308 Winchester with 150-gr. Sierra; 270 Winchester with 130-gr. Speer.

chambering over another. It's enough to say that any cartridge-bullet combination that can put down a large whitetail (maximum of about 250 pounds) with consistency and decent shot placement will do an adequate job in the brush. There are many cartridges, old and new, that qualify; most are available in bolt action rifles.

I've seen virtually all of the popular calibers in the 24 to 35 range used with success in the brush. While my own experience is limited to the 244, 270 and 308, I can attest to the efficiency of the 243, 250-3000, 257, 7x57mm, 30-30, 30-06, 8x57mm and 35 Remington, as I've seen them used by companions. All these cartridges are proven deerslayers in the brush and, in quite a few cases, on the plains. Which brings us back to a previous point.

Commercially available and relatively lightweight bolt action sporters are chambered for just about every cartridge that'll do the deed for both long-range and close-in hunting, a strong argument for the one-gun hunter.

My personal favorite for putting venison on the table is the 308 Winchester. It's never failed me and I'll argue its superiority as an all-round deer rifle, even over the 30-06. Strong stuff? Let me explain.

In the light- to medium-bullet weights, which are best for the small whitetail, the 308 approximates 30-06 ballistics so closely as to be indistinguishable, at least under woods and field conditions. Too, the newer round is available in short-length actions which, in turn, make lighter, more compact rifles. Sure, the difference is slight, but it's enough to give a subtle shift in balance that makes the rifle just a mite handier. I'll take every edge I can get.

My favorite hunting load is a 150-gr. soft nose in front of 47.5 grains of 4320, in Winchester cases. Velocity is about 2800 fps and pressure is moderate. Both of my 308s, equipped with 2.5 power scopes, will group this load within 1.25 MOA and they'll do this every day of the week. Most important, with either rifle there's no change in accuracy or point of impact at woods ranges with changes in temperature or season. This performance may not be up to bench rest standards, but it is still remarkable, if not for accuracy then for consistency, in 6½-lb. rifles with 2.5X scopes.

Bullet Deflection

Many shooters don't consider high velocity numbers such as the 6mms and the 270 to be good brush cartridges. They argue that such small-caliber hotshots don't buck brush well. As with the rapid fire idea, this is a myth, too.

Actually, few, if any, bullets sway branches or whip through limbs without being deflected. And while it's common to blame high velocity when bullets fly apart on small limbs, it's neither high velocity nor small caliber that's the culprit.

If your bullets disintegrate in the brush, look at the bullet you're using. It's probably too lightly constructed for the job. In the under-30 calibers, stick to heavily constructed and, if possible, blunt bullets such as the 100-gr. semi spitzers or 105-gr. round nose soft points in the 6mms and the 150-gr. round nose slugs in the 270.

In 30 caliber I use the 150-gr. soft point for deer. In my experience, 180-gr. and heavier bullets in this diameter are too stoutly built for the small whitetail. They sometimes bore right through the animal with little or no expansion. And while it's generally true that the 150-gr. bullet is too light for raking shots, it is just the ticket for frontal hits, which, in my opinion, are the only ones a sportsman should attempt anyway.

Experimentation

Bolt actions offer additional advantages for the handloader and workshop experimenter. Few will argue against the bolt gun's superiority for handloading. It's strongest among the repeating actions. In addition, bolt rifles, have the little-mentioned advantage of allowing stock modification and customizing for personal fit and preference.

Two of my rifles, a 270 FN Mauser and a Model 722 Remington 244, were upgraded from mediocre target punchers to prized brush guns through just a little work on my part. Previously, both rifles, with sporterweight 22-inch barrels, just couldn't cut it for serious target work.

I went to work on both, reducing and shaping the stocks to fit me for snapshooting. I practiced flipping each to my shoulder to identify and then remove high spots that hindered quick handling and sighting. It should be noted that during this procedure I wore my regular hunting clothing, including gloves, to approximate real hunting conditions.

When finished shaping the stocks, I sealed them with filler and then applied Linseed oil per instructions. Finally, I mounted a Weaver K2.5 on each. Completed, the 270 weighed in at 6¾ pounds, the 244 at 6½. In finished form, each rifle felt very good, at least for me.

My notebooks showed that the 270 had been, at best, a mediocre performer, a 2.5 MOA rifle. (Perhaps I'd not spent the time or effort to fully exploit the rifle's potential. It's been my experience that most off-the-shelf bolt action sporters will better 2 MOA if fed the right ammo.) I wanted to beat that.

The diet I worked up for the 270 used H-4831 powder, Federal brass, CCI 200 primers and Hornady 150-gr. soft point bullets. At first the groups were wide. Removing the metal from the stock revealed some points in the barrel channel where the wood had blackened from barrel contact. Sandpaper removed these uneven pressure points but accuracy still was not great. Finally I inserted a piece of an index card between the barrel and fore-end tip. This free floated the barrel except for the last two inches of the barrel channel. The groups immediately settled down, 57 grains of the old military propellant driving those Hornadys consistently into 1.5 inches at 100 yards. My Oehler chronograph clicked off 2900 fps for this load.

Finding a brush load for the little 244 was another problem. With a 1-in-12 twist, the rifle couldn't stabilize long-pointed bullets. The 100-gr. spire points keyholed on me. However, I didn't experience this problem with Speer's 105-gr. round-nose bullet.

The big Speer bullet and 47 grains of H-4831 were good enough for 3000 fps and a little under 2 MOA. This has become my main brush load for the little rifle.

Because it's borderline for the barrel twist, this 105-gr. bullet load doesn't compare in accuracy with the 47 grains of 4831 with the 90-gr. Speer or the 87-gr. Hornady or Sierra's 85-gr. spitzer. These lighter loads trip the Oehler at about 3100 fps and consistently group under 1.5 inches at 100 yards.

Did this experimentation pay off? You bet. Both rifles have performed well in the brush. When the big moment arrives, these rifles seem to act of their own accord in my hands, swinging smoothly and steadily, like extensions of my arms.

All deer taken so far have been one-shot kills, which speaks well for the loads I've developed. Of course, we can't overlook one major point. With each rifle I expended at least 300 practice rounds before taking them into the brush for serious hunting.

By this time, it should be obvious to everyone that the perfect brush gun doesn't exist. If you are content with your pump, lever or autoloading rifle, far be it for me to argue with success. But if you aren't happy with your present outfit, don't overlook the bolt rifle. For many it may be the only answer. •

Good Brush Loads

Cartridge	Bullet (Gr.)	Load**	Velocity (fps)
244 Rem.	90	47/4831	3100
	90	45/4350	3100
	90	41/4320	3100
	100*	47/4831	3050
	100*	45/4350	3050
	100*	41/4320	3010
	105†	47/4831	3000
270 Win.	130	58/4831	3000
	130	54.5/4350	3020
	150	57/4831	2900
	150	53.5/4350	2900
	170	56/4831	2800
	170	52/4350	2675
7 x 57mm	140	45/4320	2800
	140	53/4831	2750
	140	42/4895	2750
	150	44/4320	2700
	150	53/4831	2700
308 Win.	150	47.5/4320	2800
	150	48/H380	2750
	150	47/BC-2	2810
	150	44/3031	2820
	150	46/4064	2800
30-06	150	61.5/4831	2900
	150	53/H380	2950
	150	60/4350	2980
	150	48/3031	2900
	165	61.5/4831	2850
	165	57/4350	2800
8 x 57mm	150	53/4064	2900
	150	53/4320	2850
	150	56/H380	2825
	170	47/3031	2650
	170	51/4064	2700
	170	51/4320	2700
	170	53/H380	2625

Comments: All bullets seated to base of case neck, friction tight. Cases neck-sized only. CCI primers. All loads capable of 2 MOA or better accuracy in author's rifles. Velocities taken on Oehler Model 10 chronograph.

*100-gr. pointed bullets won't stabilize in 1:12 twist.
†105-gr. RN will stabilize in 1:12 twist.
**All 4831 loads shown used Hodgdon's older 4831 powder. Reduce such loads at least 3 grains if current-production IMR 4831 is used instead.

CUSTOM KNIVES TODAY

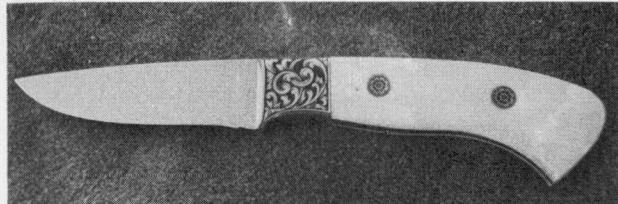
JAMES L. HARDENBROOK

HAROLD CORBY
WEYER PHOTO

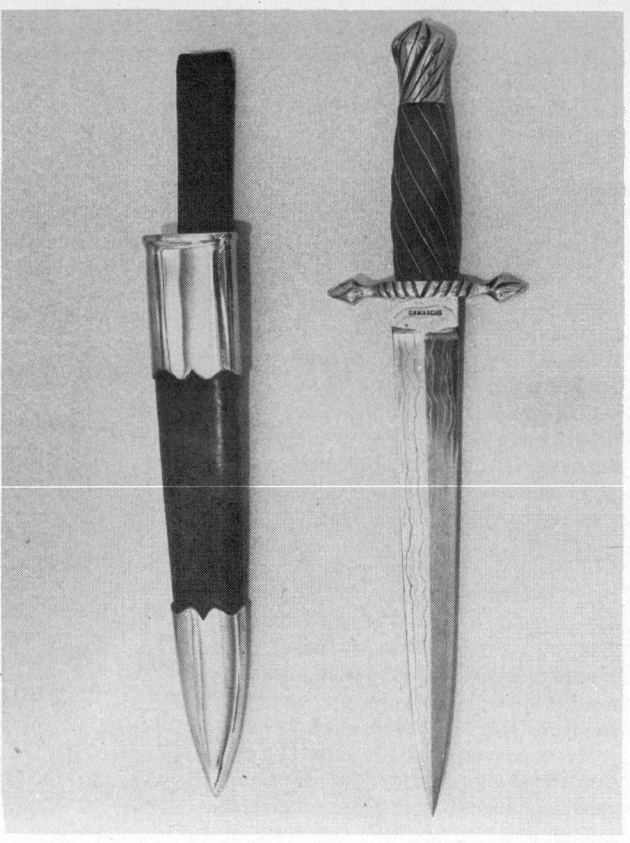
WM. F. MORAN JR.

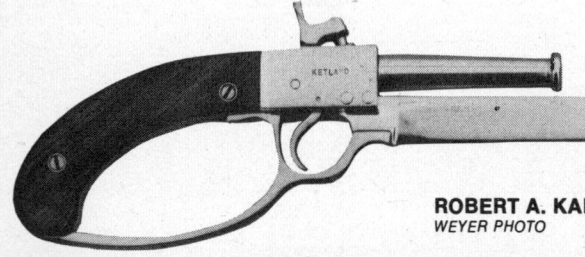
ROBERT A. KAPELA
WEYER PHOTO

SOME FANCIES

D'HOLDER CUSTOM KNIVES
WEYER PHOTO

JIMMY LILE

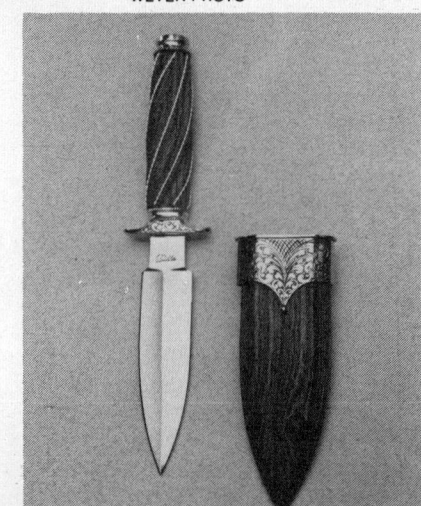

H. H. FRANK

FOLDERS

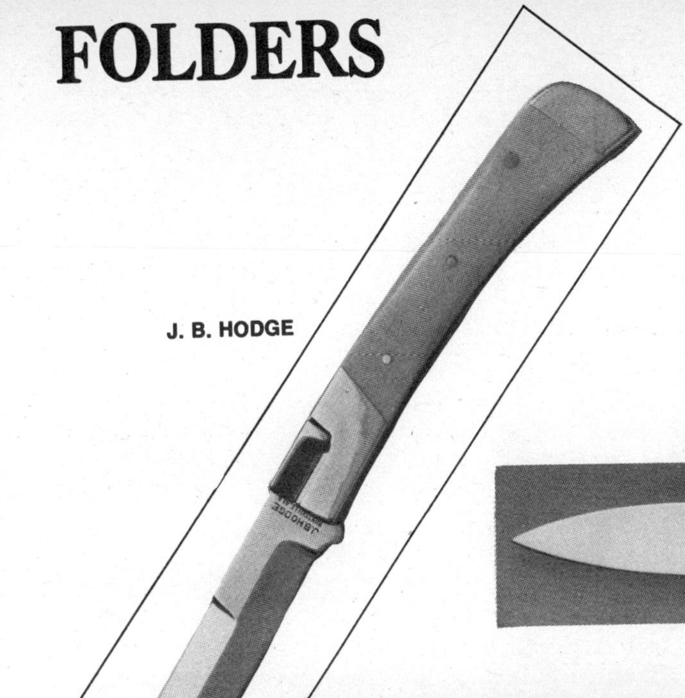

J. B. HODGE

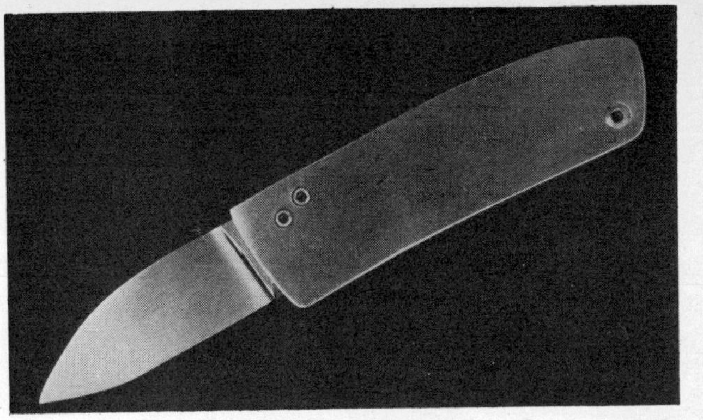

DENNIS BROOKER

MELVIN M. PARDUE

HARVEY McBURNETTE

L. R. HENDRICKS

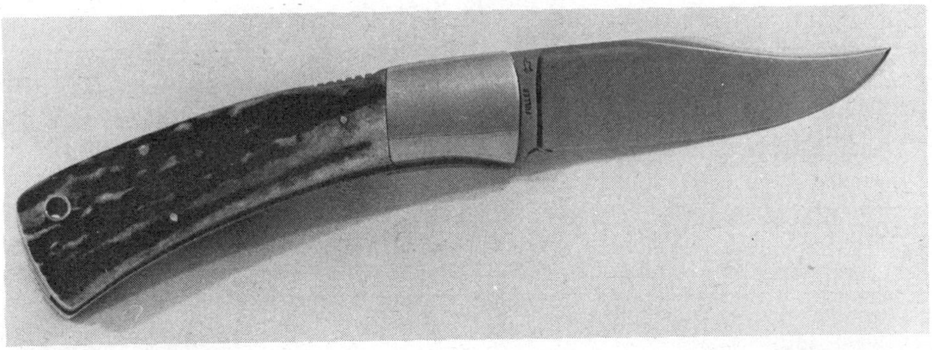

W. T. FULLER JR.

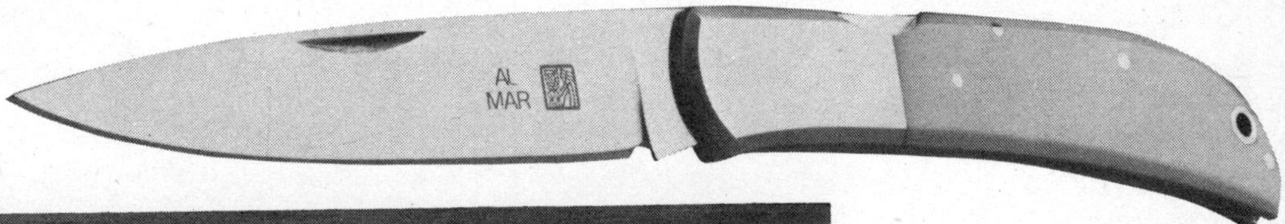

AL MAR

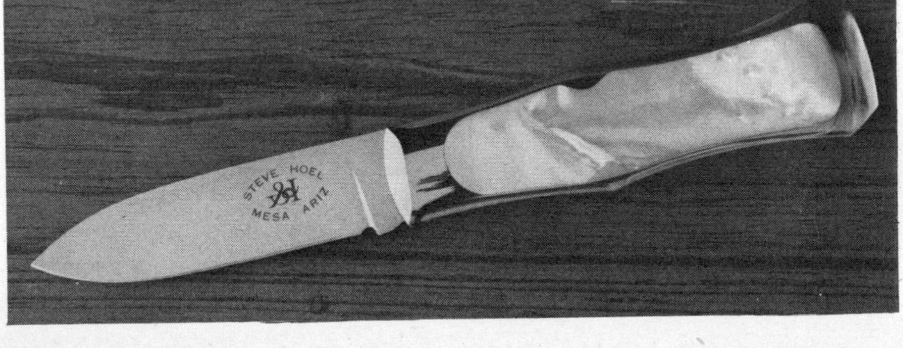

STEVE HOEL

35TH EDITION, 1981 **251**

HUNTERS

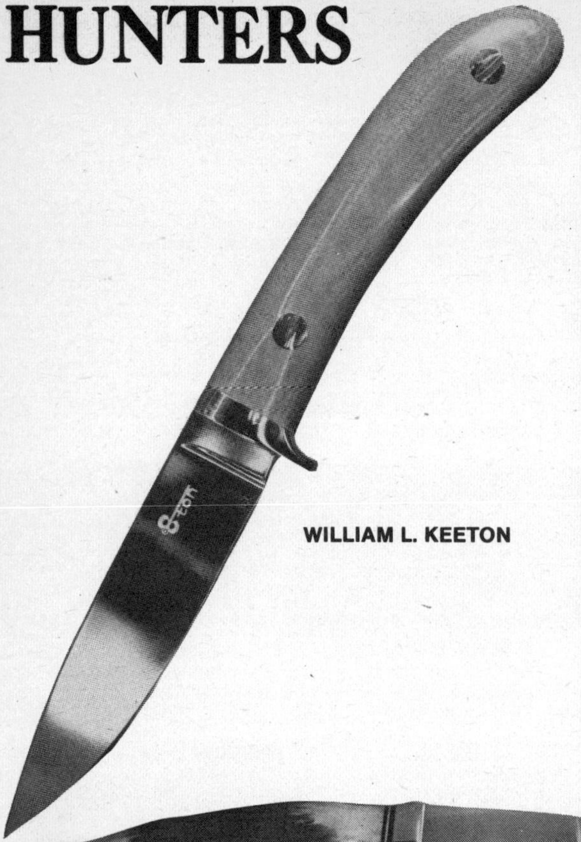

WILLIAM L. KEETON

G. M. (TIM) BRITTON

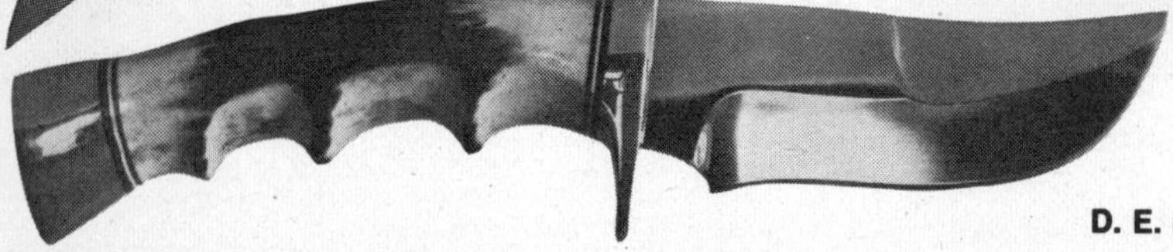

D. E. (LUCKY) CLARK

RUFFIN JOHNSON
WEYER PHOTO

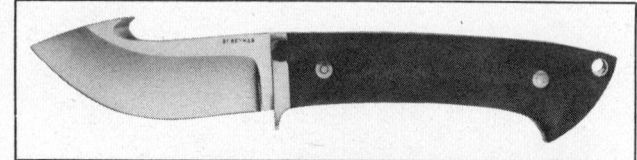

LESLIE L. BERRYMAN

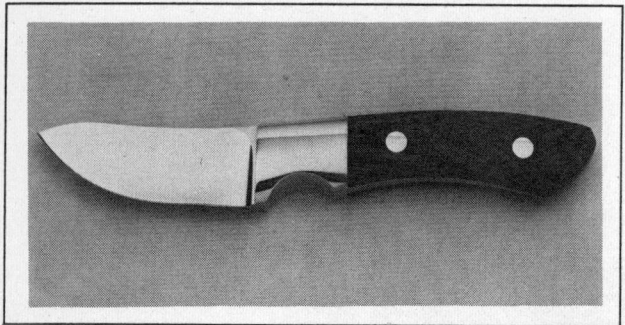

JIM HAMMOND
WEYER PHOTO

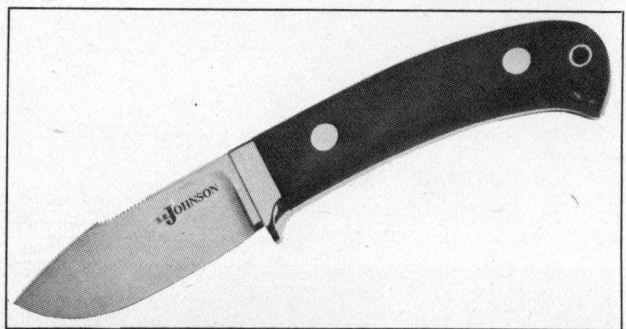

S. R. JOHNSON

WAYNE G. HENSLEY
WEYER PHOTO

SHOOTER'S SHOWCASE

Trius Still Makes Them

"Nothing extra to buy, make or borrow" is Trius' boast about their traps, the same good traps they've been making for years and years and years. Actually, it is not quite so. That is, if you want to throw high angles or to throw cans, you have to buy attachments for the Model 73, but you need not buy anything extra to throw doubles.

Trius traps are American-made and guaranteed not only because they say so but because they have a history of performance. K.W.

Essex M1911 Parts

Essex Arms up in Vermont is still offering receivers and frames for Model 1911-A1 45 pistols. The frames and slides will accept GI or commercial parts, Essex says, but no doubt a certain skill in fitting would be useful. They're unconditionally guaranteed to meet or exceed original U.S. government specifications and they are available in blued steel or stainless steel. The stainless steel receiver is $55, and a stainless steel slide is $60. Write for their brochure. K.W.

Break-Free Does It Better

There's no doubt about it. All the experts, including the military experts, agree that Break-Free CLP is a cleaner, a solvent, an oil, and a coating. It has solved all sorts of problems for everybody, and looks like replacing 30 different solutions in the military service, and more expected. It does not, however, smell like the old stuff. K.W.

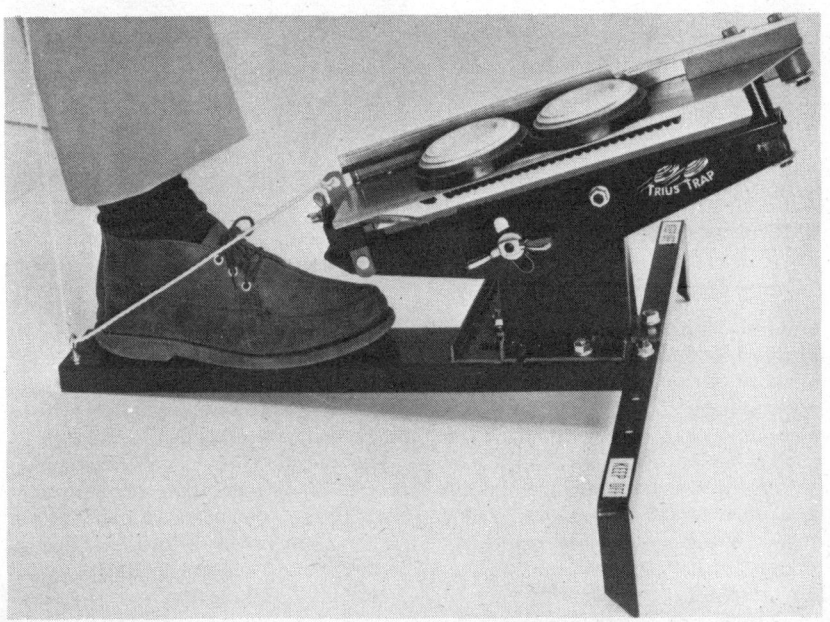

Ruger T-Grip

You can now get a Tyler T-grip for your Ruger double-action revolver, as well as for the newly popular round-butt Model 10-12-19 Smith & Wesson revolvers. For the Smith & Wesson guns order No. 3R. T-grips for the Ruger are size No. 8. They come in polished aluminum, black and a gold anondized color. K.W.

Jet-Away's 10-Bore

You don't hear of Arms Ingenuity Co. and their Jet-Away shotgun choke very often, but now they have a 10-gauge which they will sell for $50 plus shipping. They sell 20- and 16-gauge chokes for $40 plus shipping. There are not many 10-gauge choke attachments out there.   K.W.

Vault Between the Studs

This Model HW vault is 24 inches tall and designed to fit between wall studs to be thereafter concealed behind a picture or panel. The unit is 3½ inches deep and made of 14-gauge steel, lined with acrylic pile. It sells at its suggested retail price of $79 from Stowline, Inc.   K.W.

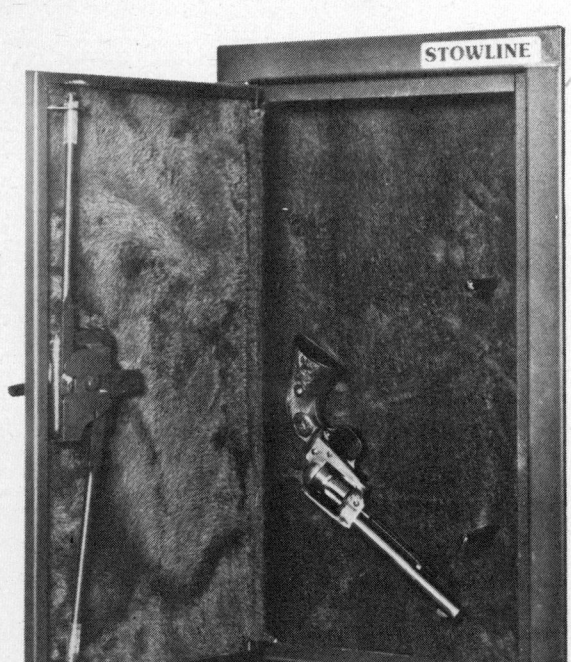

The Rex Is Reborn

Lenz Firearms is now producing a copy of the Rex engine turning fixture, which positively indexes longitudinally and around the entire circumference of the rifle bolt. The Lenz version is made with high strength alloy instead of cast iron, but retains the needed strength, Lenz says. Complete with arbors for Mauser 98, Winchester 70, and 1903 Springfield the jig is $75 and can be ordered directly. It is the Lenz ETF.   K.W.

B-Square Rifle Rest Folds

At $49.95 (plus $2.50 shipping) B-Square's new rifle rest looks good. It will fit into a 4x4x10-inch box, but the legs unfold to a 13-inch diameter and provide 4 to 8 inches of height adjustment. It is available in a Heavy model at 8 lbs., in a Standard model at 5 lbs.   K.W.

Curly Maple Stock Blanks

Golden Age sells a lot of items through their $2 catalog, but the principal part of their business is selling curly maple gun stocks. And they offer pre-carved stocks in a wide variety of blackpowder styles as well as in the blank. A full-stock blank in their best grade will cost $100. A half-stock blank in the lowest grade ordinarily offered is $15, both prices plus postage. They also offer pistol blanks and blanks in cherry and walnut.   K.W.

Reamers for Accuracy

Geo. M. Fullmer specializes in precision chambers and now has over 300 different chambers available using reamers by Elliott, Keith Francis or Hugh Henriksen. Fullmer tests all actions he rebarrels with his Rockwell hardness tester. He is not yet making extractors for Model 70 pre-'64 rifles, but he is making set triggers for Sharps Borchardts and Winchesters. Fullmer's letterhead says "Bench rest and varmint rifles take precedence over other work," which betrays a certain attitude.   K.W.

Edwards Snap Caps

The fellow who makes the Recoil Reducer offers these caps in 12, 20, 28 and 410 gauges. They are made of solid material, have a cavity filled with moisture-absorbent compound, and offer a nylon surface to the firing pin. Jesse B. Edwards says this snap cap is made to last a lifetime. They are $4 each.   K.W.

Personal Steel Stamps

David Woodruff in Delaware is offering a service for gun owners—or gunsmiths—who could use a hardened tool steel stamp with 1/16-inch letters or numbers with which to mark jobs or guns in a professional manner.

Delivery is four weeks for these custom-made steel tools and cancellations and returns aren't allowed. Up to 10 letters or numbers is $17.50; up to 15 letters or numbers if $22.50; and a 3-letter monogram, 3/16" high, is $17.50. All prices are post-paid. K.W.

No Options on These Holsters

Belt Slide, Inc. makes a line of standard design holsters, headed by their own version of the belt slide with safety strap, but do not offer custom modifications. They have a high ride for autoloaders, a thumb snap for revolvers, and plain heavy-duty belt rigs for sportsmen for both double-actions and single-actions. Prices from $8.50 to $15.95 in early 1980.   K.W.

Poly-Choke Handgun Ribs

Some are ventilated and at least one is not, but Poly-Choke has easily installed ribs for many popular handguns. Current catalog shows ribs for the Ruger Blackhawk, Super Blackhawk and Super Single Six, the Colt New Frontier, Ruger Security Six and the Smith & Wesson Model 19, which is the solid one. Rib comes in a kit to install yourself for $14.95 plus $1 postage and handling. From Poly-Choke.   K.W.

Oil for Old Stocks

Old World Oil Products has a linseed rubbing oil they feel answers a real need for fine guns. For $2.50 plus 50¢ postage, you can get either a natural color for American walnut, or a red oil for European wood, packed in 4-oz. plastic bottles. The oil is intended to reproduce the old original oil finishes, and Wayne Cowette seems to favor the red oil.

Not content with furnishing an oil, Old World has opened a new department which offers a stock polishing service in the old hand rubbed method on a custom basis.   K.W.

All-Out Portable Shooting Bench

Centrum Industries Inc. is introducing their Shooters Porta-Bench this year. Made up of patent saw-horse parts, with accessories adapted to shooters' needs, the unit is said to be both sturdy and steady. It does show interesting hinging and good foldability, along with neoprene-covered working surfaces. It may well be worth the price of $179.95, although that does not buy you the optional carrying case, accessory table, seat cushion, and the like.   K.W.

Cannon for the Masses

South Bend Replicas, Inc., is in the business of furnishing enthusiasts with authentic scale and full-size muzzle-loading cannon barrels or complete units. To fully understand their business, and doing business with them, takes a careful reading of their catalog, which is $4 postpaid in 1980. To our best ability to figure it out, 6-pounder barrel which weighs 860 lbs., would cost $1850, ready to be fitted with a carriage, and, of course, when so fitted would be shootable. It is possible to get into the scaled-down cannon business cheaper, of course.   K.W.

Job-Coded Screwdrivers

Grace Metal Products now provides set No. HG-8, hollow ground spring steel screwdrivers to fit sight guard screws and the like. The set sells for $28. Grace also provides marked special hollow ground screwdrivers to fit English and other extra fine screw slots, such as the Belgian Browning tang screw.   K.W.

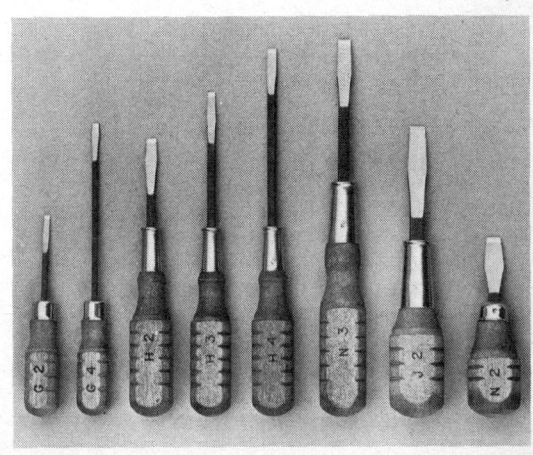

Handgun Shooting Rest

Jim Cravener has been making one kind and another of a portable shooting stand for rifle shooters for some time now, and here is his handgun rest. It is all steel and aluminum, with rubber padding for the barrel and on the aluminum hand plate, so no sandbags are required. The rest weighs 1¾ lbs., and has a 3-point leg setup so that it is extremely wobble-free, Cravener says. The Cravener rest offers a 3-inch height adjustment, which is plenty for testing on a range, or even for field-shooting. $32 buys the rest, the shipping and a 3-year warranty. K.W.

Muzzleloader Care Kit

With an intriguing name like Totally Dependable Products, Inc., a kit for taking care of blackpowder guns ought to be reliable. This one includes TDP's SS1 solvent, SS2 lubricant protector and their Stock Slick wood reconditioner. K.W.

One-Step Chamber Cleaner

Robert W. Hart & Son now offer, in two sizes, a tool to clean action locking lug recesses, barrel face and chamber in one operation. The tool is adjustable to fit action length and chamber, 222 through magnum sizes. Their #1 fits Remington, Hart, Shilen, Ruger, Winchester, Mauser, etc. In the future they plan their #2 to fit the Wichita Benchrest. The tool is furnished with long lasting felts for fast cleaning and may be washed in solvent. Retail price is $12.50. K.W.

Benchrester's Measure

The 20-year-old Lyman 55 powder measure design is preserved today for those willing to pay $85 for it to Neal A. Jones of Custom Products in Meadville, Pennsylvania. Of course, there are some special touches, such as custom-fitted inserts called the micro measuring drum and a baffle.

Jones' other products include a simple and elegant decapper, floating sizer dies and extra-fine cleaning rods. K.W.

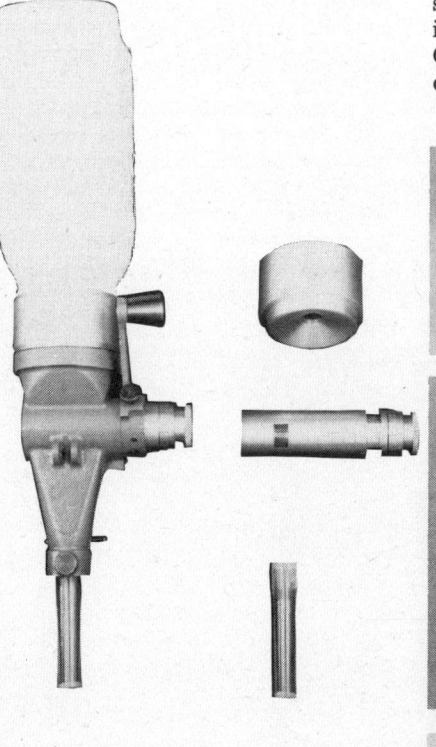

Neat Competition Stuff

Shooters Specialty in Tucson offers the Binkley aluminum buttplate assembly at $25. Furnished as a basic unfinished unit for gunsmith installation, the assembly requires no screwdrivers or Allen wrench for adjustment while shooting.

A set of stripper clips is important to the serious NRA competitor and they may be had from Shooters Specialty at $2.50 for 10. Another, more complicated gadget is their Champion front sight, with integral bubble level and inserts .080 to .120 plus a post. The Champion fits all standard front dovetail blocks, and lists at $22. K.W.

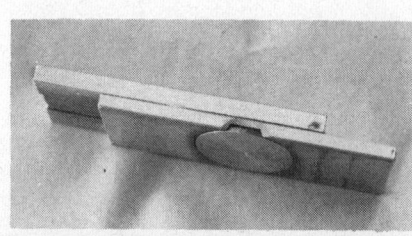

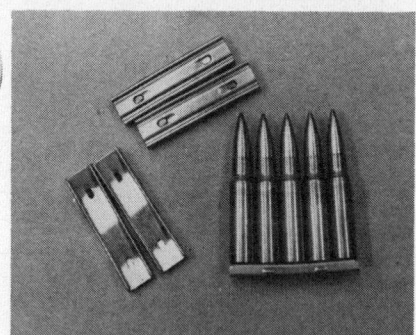

Scope Mount for H&K

Robert Medaris now offers a sight mount for H&K Models 91 and 93. The steel unit requires no drilling or tapping of the receiver or barrel. Rings are not included because the new mount's rail comes in Weaver detachable 1" scope rings. According to Medaris, the mount does not interfere with the iron sights and does not need to be removed for iron sight use. It is $76.50, including shipping and insurance. K.W.

Blackpowder Quick Loader

Butler Creek makes these plastic units to hold pre-measured powder up to 200 grains, patch and ball up to and including 58-cal., plus two caps. It shouldn't surprise anybody to learn that these work particularly well with Butler Creek's Poly Patch caps. A set of 3 loaders is $4.50 with pocket clip, $5.65 with belt clip, plus $1 per set for postage and handling. K.W.

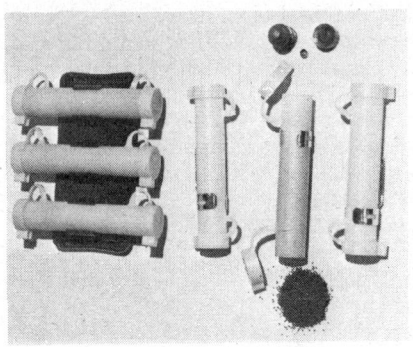

$510 Motorcase

Huey Gun Cases makes a turn-of-the-century compact case for double guns which permits the storage of a generous amount of cartridges or larger items, besides the gun, cleaning rod and small parts. It is made with solid brass corner braces, double locks, luggage straps and sewn leather grip, with overlapping lid and hand-stitched end covers.

Huey makes a number of similarly constructed cases for fine guns including trunk cases for take-down guns, flat cased or chest style for carbines and rifles, pistol cases and cartridge boxes. K.W.

Muzzleloader Scopes

Flintlock Muzzleloading Gun Shop in Anaheim, California, is offering an old-timer's scope for front-stuffers. It fits most octagonal barrels, the makers say. It has a 15mm objective lens, coated optics and brass construction in 4 power. Mounting hardware and dust caps are included. The price is $44.95 plus $2 postage and handling. K.W.

Butterfield Commemorative

B.E. Hodgdon is paying tribute to the Butterfield Overland Despatch by producing a limited edition 1860 Army revolver through Colt's custom shop. The Butterfield Despatch has a 5½-inch barrel, and is provided with a spare cylinder in a presentation case. All cylinders are Colt engraved in stagecoach scenes. Just 500 of this Limited Edition are to be made. They are to sell for $995. K.W.

New Seecamp Design

Sile Distributors Inc. reports they are getting along toward marketing the Seecamp-Sile Model IISS, a stainless 25 automatic, with 7-round magazine, double-action only, and all the modern appurtenances of such a tiny engine, weighing empty 10 ounces, more or less.

Nothing about availability yet for this blow-back autoloader, but samples have been seen. It is stainless steel throughout, Sile says. They hope to retail it at $149.95. K.W.

British Blackpowder Accessories

Ken Steggles, whose address is 17 Bell Lane, Byfield, Nr. Daventry, Northants NN11 6US, England, offers any number of British-type muzzleloader accessories, up to and including a rifle case with almost everything in it but the rifle. There are loading mallet and hammer and nipple cleaning tool sets, what is called "a wallet of turnscrews"—screwdrivers, of course—as well as combination tools for military and match rifles, flint wallets and shot flasks, powder measures, and doubtless even more. It all looks of good quality; prices are doubtless commensurate. K.W.

Bo-Mar Holsters

Pictures aren't available, but Bo-Mar says holsters for guns with their ribs are. They come in natural color, black or black basket weave and are soft lined. Either 4- or 6-inch are the same price—$29.50. K.W.

Lexan Trigger Lock

Central Specialties Company has replaced their former metal trigger lock with a plastic model in tough lexan. At a price of $3 retail, Cresco's TLR-P will hide the trigger on practically every domestic and foreign firearm, except lever-action guns.

The standard or consumer model is unlocked with a furnished 2-prong key. For dealers and not available to the public, there is a Cesco gun trigger lock for store displays which uses a single-prong key. K.W.

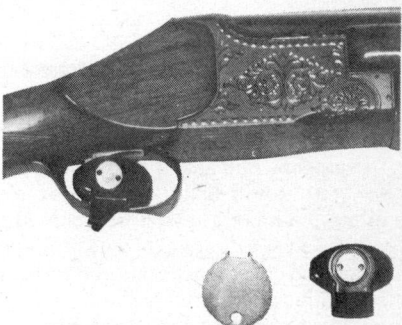

Durable Carry Straps

Michaels of Oregon has a line of gun carry straps made of nylon webbing, including both padded "Ultra" types in black and brown and black only "Utility."

Blued steel buckles permit instant adjustment, easy folding when removed from the gun and, of course, nylon's extreme durability make these real utility items. K.W.

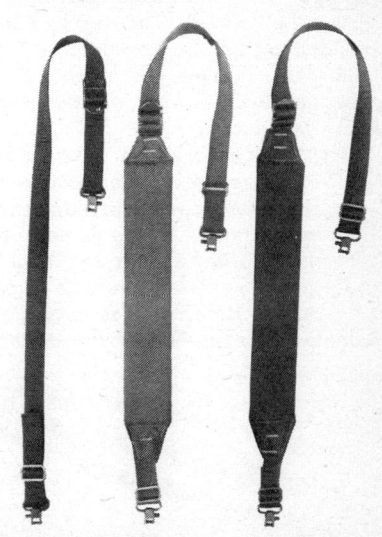

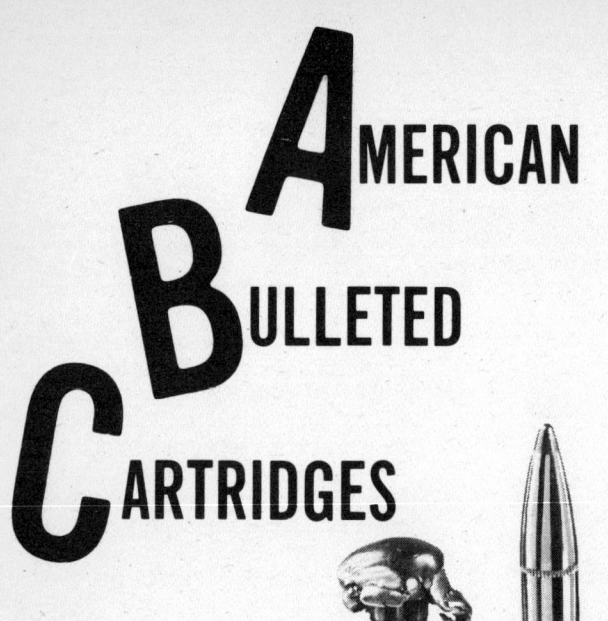

American Bulleted Cartridges

A detailed and comprehensive review of newly developed and introduced metallic cartridges and components.

by KEN WATERS

Latest Developments In Metallic Cartridges

If someone had asked me to make a prediction as to what this year would bring in the way of new cartridges and bullets, I'd have guessed that considering the economy as well as last year's spate of new items, we could look forward to a period of retrenchment. I'd likely have predicted some new bullet offerings for handloaders, particularly in the handgun line, but I'm reasonably sure I wouldn't have anticipated any new rifle cartridges.

How wrong can you get? With the year only started (as this is written), it appears we're likely to out-do even last year! So let's have a look at what's cooking.

Remington-Peters

Were we to name our years as the Chinese do, this could appropriately be called the Year of Remington, what with two totally new factory cartridges, a new cartridge case, and three new loadings for existing metallic cartridges.

Outstanding in the view of this firearms writer is Remington's latest big game hunting round for short-action rifles—the 7mm-08. The past two decades have witnessed the phenomenal rise to eminence of the 7mm bore amongst American riflemen, challenging even that venerable institution, the 30-caliber, and through it all Remington has been the leader.

First to appear was the 280 Remington, one of the finest all-round cartridges that ever came down the pike. Then in 1962, the belted case 7mm Magnum arrived and has ever since been taking the big game hunting world by storm. Even that bearded oldster, the 7mm Mauser cartridge, has undergone a surprising rebirth of popularity. And finally last year saw Remington re-introduce the 280 under a new headstamp as the 7mm Express Remington, about which I'll have more to say further along.

But all of those cartridges had one thing in common; they required a "standard" (that is, 30-06 length) action. The R-P line-up still lacked a 7mm round that would function in a rifle with a short action. Now that gap has been filled by necking down the enormously popular 308 case without any other changes to hold 7mm bullets, and once again the folks at Bridgeport have come up with what is practically dead-certain to be a winner.

The 7mm-08, so-called because of its 308 parentage, features a single loading (at least to start) with a 140-grain 7mm pointed soft-point bullet that bids fair to qualify as a highly efficient as well as effective combination.

The official Remington ballistic figures show the 140-grain bullet starting out at 2860 fps and reaching 300-yards with 2189 fps remaining, as compared to 2820- and 2009 fps for the 150-grain 308, or 2910- and 2083 fps for the 150-grain PSP in R-P's 30-06.

With a remaining energy of 1490-ft.lbs. at 300-yards in contrast to the 308's 1344 f.p. and the '06's 1445 f.p., it is alleged to be harder hitting than the 308-150 grain at that range, even equalling the 30-06.

And as for trajectory, when sighted to strike center at 200 yards, the new 140-gr. 7mm-08 will be hitting 8.1″ low at 300. This is 1″ less drop than the 150-gr. 308, and 0.4″ less than a 150-gr. PSP from the 30-06, or about the same as the more streamlined 150-gr. Bronze Point from that cartridge.

From this we must conclude that it betters the 150-gr. 308 in all respects, and is about equal ballistically to Remington's 150-gr. PSP loading for the 30-06. Quite a billing, wouldn't you say?

Following is a more complete listing of the 7mm-08's ballistics as provided by Remington, based upon use of a 24″ barrel:

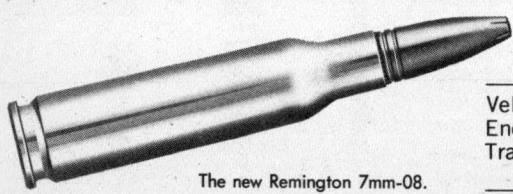

The new Remington 7mm-08.

	Muzzle	100 yds	200 yds	300 yds	400 yds	500 yds
Velocity (fps)	2860	2625	2402	2189	1988	1798
Energy (f.p.)	2542	2142	1793	1490	1228	1005
Trajectory	—	+2.1″	— 0 —	−8.1″	−23.5″	−47.7″

Judging from the above data, it is fairly evident that the 7mm-08 is a 300-yard cartridge when sighted-in at 200. On deer-size game, the range could conceivably be extended to around 400 yards if sighted to strike 3" high at 200 yards.

But of course it mustn't be expected to show up that well in short barrels, which inevitably mean lower velocity, less remaining energy and increased bullet drop. This will be especially true in the stubby 18½" barrel that Remington is (mistakenly, I believe) fitting to their redesigned Model 788 rifle in this caliber. I dislike seeing a fine cartridge's ballistics handicapped by a too-short barrel, and am old fashioned enough to still want my high velocity rifles to have 24" barrels.

Now if you're prepared for a real surprise, let me point out what a good cartridge in combination with a 24" barrel can do. I'll bet it's been quite a spell since you've run across a cartridge whose actual performance exceeds the advertised claims for it. Well, the 7mm-08 is one that does—in a 24" barrel, that is.

You can imagine my surprise when the Oehler Skyscreens reported velocities for the 7mm-08 with factory ammunition running better than 2950 fps! Frankly, I was dubious and immediately ran another 5-shot string with almost identical results. Still not convinced, I retired to our test tunnel where we have a second chronograph and permanently mounted pair of electronic screens.

Well, to make a long story short, the Skyscreens hadn't lied. The second chronograph confirmed that velocities were above 2950 fps; in fact, averaging all the readings from both chronographs together, gave us an instrumental velocity of 2956 fps, which converted back to muzzle velocity looks like 2972 fps. Some cartridge!

Accuracy of the new round in our Model 700 Varmint test rifle was likewise excellent. Look for this cartridge to go places.

The 7mm Express Remington cartridge was so new I hadn't been able to run trials with it at the time last year's report was written. Since then however, it's seen plenty of use on our test range, so here are a few of our findings on that cartridge:

(1) In general, the 7mm Express Remington is everything that the 280 Remington was and is, which is to say that it is one of the best calibers in existence for all-round hunting in the original 48 states, combining good sectional density and flat trajectory with fine accuracy and reasonable recoil in a standard non-belted case.

(2) Having said that however, I must admit to being chagrined on finding that ballistics are no better than those of the 280, and not as good as the smaller 7mm-08, strange as it may seem. I had hoped that this new round would be loaded up to the ballistics levels practicable in a bolt action rifle. Chronographed velocities ranged from 11 fps faster than Remington 280 factory loads with same 150-gr. bullet weight, to 51 fps slower; that is to say, from 2778 fps to 2840 fps M.V. from a 22" barrel. Advertised ballistics for the 7mm Express Remington had called for a muzzle speed of 2970 fps from a 24" barrel. I'm reasonably certain this cartridge could be factory loaded to reach the designed velocity without exceeding safe pressure limits. That it is being done successfully with the smaller case 7mm-08 is adequate proof.

(3) Uniformity of powder charges in the factory loads is excellent, as is accuracy from the Remington Model 700 ADL sporter without benefit of any accurizing whatsoever, and this despite a noticeable variation in case neck tension on bullets.

As an admitted devotee of the 280 Remington (and now of the 7mm Express as well), I sincerely hope velocities will be boosted. That's what is needed to make a good cartridge even better.

Yet another new "7," this one supplied as unprimed empty brass only, is Remington's 7mm Bench-Rest case intended for their XP-100 bolt action pistol. In previous years there have been the 22 Rem. B-R and 6mm Rem. B-R specifically for bench-rest shooters. Now the 7mm Rem. B-R makes it a trio, this one with metallic silhouette shooters in mind.

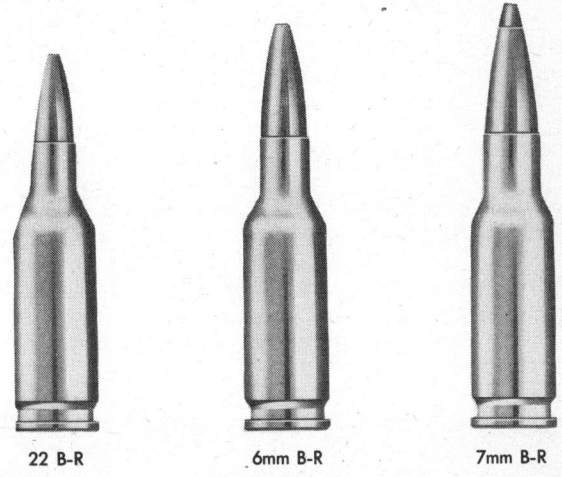

22 B-R   6mm B-R   7mm B-R

The 7mm Bench-Rest case, like the 22 and 6mm, is based on a special version of the 308 Winchester case with thinner, annealed walls and a smaller primer pocket taking the No. 7½ Remington *Small* Rifle primer. Case length has been shortened to 1.520" by the factory, but necking down to 7mm and final forming is left to the shooter. I believe this last point to be a mistake and have attempted to persuade the boys at Remington that they should go at least one step farther and fully form the case. This could be much more easily done at the factory, probably with more uniformity as well, and would almost surely increase the popularity of the little case.

Judging from our experience with the 308x1.5" wildcat, this should be an amazing little round with more punch than a 30-30, coupled with fine accuracy. Personally, I'd very much like to try chambering a short-short action rifle for this new round.

While I'm not aware that Remington has published any ballistic data for the 7mm B-R, I might note that we were able to obtain muzzle velocities of better than 2600 fps with 125-grain spitzers in the 308x1.5", and 2500 fps with 150-grain, so would anticipate somewhere in the neighborhood of 2500-2600 fps as being possible with 140-grain bullets in a 24" barrel chambered for the 7mm B-R.

The other new cartridge from Remington to which I referred is again the third in a series known as the "Accelerators," the name standing for a conceptual arrangement in which a 55-grain 22-caliber jacketed bullet is encased in a plastic 30-caliber sabot to enable the undersize projectile to be fired from a 30-caliber barrel. The sabot drops off a short distance from the muzzle after imparting the necessary stabilizing spin to the small bullet.

The objective, of course, is to make it possible for the owners of 30-caliber rifles to transform their big game hunting piece into a 22-caliber varmint rifle merely by changing ammunition (and readjusting the sights, I might add).

These Accelerators are factory-loaded only, no individual components being offered handloaders. First to appear was the 30-06 Accelerator in 1977. Then last year a second

Accelerator cartridge for 30-30 rifles was offered. Now in 1980 we have the third member of the family, this one for the 308 Winchester.

Starting a 55-grain .224" pointed soft point at a muzzle velocity of 3800 fps (from 24" barrels), the tiny slug is said to be still traveling 3242 fps at 100 yards, 2749 at 200, and 2307 fps at 300 yards, with a drop of 3.2" at 300 yards from a 250 yard zero, thereby equaling the ballistics of a 55-grain PSP from a 22-250.

Not having as yet had an opportunity to try these latest Accelerators, I can't say how they'll do, but can, however, report on my tests of last year's 30-30 Accelerators.

In our Winchester Model 54 bolt action, 5-shot groups at 100 yards ran approximately 1½" larger than the average with standard factory 30-30 ammo, but in a Winchester 94 Wells Fargo carbine groups ran only some ½" to ¾" larger. Chronographed velocity from the 20" carbine barrel averaged 3269 fps, more nearly like a 222 Magnum or 223 Remington. A third 30-30 produced key-holes and thus no measurable groups. Once again, as with the 30-06 Accelerators, performance varied from poor to quite good depending upon the individual rifle. I know of no way to tell in advance how well they'll do in your rifle. You'll just have to try 'em to find out.

Another Remington cartridge tested over the past year has been the 22 Long Rifle "Yellowjacket." These hot little numbers chronographed averages of 1530 fps from a Winchester 52-C sporting rifle, and 1248 fps from a Colt Official Police revolver with 6" barrel. Quite as important though, they displayed unusually good accuracy for this type of high velocity ammo; among the best in their class, in fact.

Now about those three new Remington loadings of existing calibers I mentioned earlier. First and foremost, they have at last heeded shooters' demands for a heavier bullet loading with thicker jacket in the 444 Marlin, designed for larger than deer-size American big game. The new round has a 265-grain soft point bullet of tougher construction, loaded to a muzzle velocity of 2120 fps. Remington characterizes it as being similar in power to the faster but lighter bullet 300 Savage. Most particularly, it should provide the deeper penetration sought by hunters of the larger big game.

The second new loading consists of a 180-grain semi-jacketed hollow-point bullet at 1610 fps in the 44 Remington Magnum cartridge. Essentially intended for use in revolvers of this caliber where it offers flatter trajectory *and lessened recoil,* there is, of course, no reason why it can't be used in 44 Magnum carbines as well. Despite the reduction in weight, this new bullet should be adequate for deer-size and smaller game with well placed shots.

Finally, there's a factory loading for the 223 Remington with 55-grain Metal Case (Full Metal Jacketed) bullet. The maker points out that this ammunition will be useful for police departments possessing automatic weapons of this caliber, and for hunters of fur-bearing animals desiring to minimize pelt damage.

While this writer will go along with the law enforcement application, together with the unmentioned added reliability in feeding advantage such FMJ ammo offers all users of automatic and autoloading 5.56mm (223 Remington) arms, I still have trouble in accepting the idea of reduced pelt damage. While I've never hunted American game with full-metal-jacketed bullets, I have seen what happens when a soft point bullet fails to expand (thus acting like an FMJ), and the resultant serious wounding that occurs in such situations is something most hunters hate to see happen. We'd rather have a torn pelt than cause unnecessary suffering.

Following are abbreviated ballistic tables on these three new Remington loadings:

The Remington Accelerator in 308 Win.

Remington's new 444 Marlin loading with 265-gr. SP.

444 Marlin 265-gr. S.P.

	Muzzle	100-yds	150-yds	200-yds
Velocity (fps)	2120	1733	1561	1405
Energy (f.p.)	2644	1768	1433	1162
Trajectory	—	— 0 —	−3.6"	−10.8"

44 Rem. Magnum 180-gr H.P.

	Muzzle	50-yds	100-yds
Velocity (fps)	1610	1365	1175
Energy (f.p.)	1036	745	551
Trajectory	—	— 0 —	−3.8"

223 Remington 55-gr. M.C.

	Muzzle	100-yds	200-yds	300-yds
Velocity (fps)	3240	2759	2326	1933
Energy (f.p.)	1282	929	660	456
Trajectory	—	+1.9"	— 0 —	−8.4"

It is worthy of note that kinetic energy figures can be misleading as to a cartridge's game killing ability. For example, although the new 223 round shows a greater remaining energy at 100 yards than does the 44 Magnum 180-gr. load at only 50 yards, field experience shows that the 44-caliber bullet is a far more reliable game stopper.

Winchester-Western

Troubled by a prolonged strike, the folks at Winchester-Western understandably haven't brought out any totally new cartridges this past year, but deserve high marks nonetheless for coming up with a trio of new factory loadings in existing calibers that will add to the versatility of guns with those chamberings.

Most interesting to this writer is Winchester's recognition of the resurgent popularity of the 45-70 and a consequent acknowledgment of the need for a higher velocity loading with increased bullet expansion probability while holding chamber pressures to safe levels.

Achievement of these goals in one of the old big bores with straight-sided case inevitably requires reducing bullet weight, which is what Winchester has done. The new 45-70 loading features a 300-grain jacketed hollow-point bullet with muzzle velocity listed as 1880 fps (presumably from 24" barrels), which compares most favorably to the old standard 405-grain loading's muzzle speed of only 1330 fps.

This looks like a sensible revival of the old "Express" cartridge concept wherein bullet weight is exchanged for higher velocities in a near-equal trade-off. My old 1914 Winchester catalog listed just such a 45-70 high velocity loading way back then, said to develop 1888 fps M.V. with 300-grain bullet! How much closer could they come?

Today's load should be even better, because we have the advantage of superior powders, primers and bullet construction. A fact not always mentioned about these Express loads is that shooter-felt recoil is less than with the heavier bullets. Also, they will usually give quicker kills on deer-size animals, for which the 45-70 is being increasingly used these days.

Here's how the new 300-gr. W-W 45-70 loading compares ballistically with the standard 405-grain rounds from the same maker:

Winchester's 338 Magnum has a new loading—the 225-gr. soft point. This is in addition to their presently available 200 (shown), 250 and 300 grain loadings.

least of which considerations being its reduced drop, requiring less accurate range estimation.

Another offering from Winchester-Western I find interesting is their new loading of the 338 Magnum with 225-grain soft point bullet at a rated muzzle velocity of 2780 fps from a 24" barrel.

The motivation behind this addition to the three bullet weights (200, 250 and 300 grain) presently available for the 338, is to provide a factory loading that offers greater retained velocity and energy at ranges from 350 yards and beyond. At those longer ranges the new round will also shoot flatter than any of the previous loads in this caliber.

Thus, in addition to its well established reputation as a powerful cartridge for the larger big game, the 338 Magnum is now able to compete directly with the hot 300 Winchester Magnum, having less drop than the 220-grain 300 Magnum, and only 3.1" more drop than the popular 180-grain 300 Magnum at 400 yards!

Upon first learning of this new 225-grain loading for the 338 Magnum, I was reminded of that great old African cartridge—the 350 Rigby Magnum. That worthy earned its enviable lustre with a 35-caliber bullet likewise weighing 225 grains, at a muzzle velocity of 2600 fps and energy of 3400 ft.lbs. From this it at once becomes apparent that the 225 grain 338 Magnum with an additional 180 fps velocity and 462 f.p. of energy is practically certain to prove an excellent prescription for big game hunting, assuming proper bullet construction. Everything considered, it sounds like an excellent choice for elk.

Just look at these ballistics:

	338 Win. Magnum 225-gr.	300 Win. Magnum 220-gr.	375 H&H Magnum 270-gr.
Muzzle Velocity (fps)	2780	2680	2690
Velocity at 200-yds.	2374	2228	2166
Velocity at 400-yds.	2003	1823	1707
Muzzle Energy (f.p.)	3862	3508	4337
Energy at 200-yds.	2816	2424	2812
Energy at 400-yds.	2005	1623	1747
Drop from 200-yd. Zero			
— at 300-yds.	−8.3"	−9.5"	−10.0"
— at 400-yds.	−24.0"	−27.5"	−29.4"

45-70

	Velocity		Energy		Trajectory	
	300-HP	405-SP	300-HP	405-SP	300-HP	405-SP
Muzzle	1880	1330	2355	1590	—	—
100-yds.	1559	1168	1619	1227	—0—	—0—
200-yds.	1294	1055	1116	1001	−13.5"	−24.6"

Newest handgun cartridge from Winchester-Western is a 210-grain jacketed hollow-point loading for the 41 Magnum, intended to give better bullet expansion than their soft point of same weight. Ballistics remain the same as for the soft point at 1300 fps M.V. and 788 f.p. M.E. from 4" barrels. Handgunners who use this caliber for big game

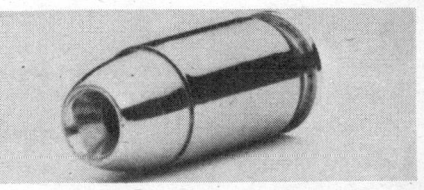

Winchester has discontinued listing bullets as separate components. Their rightfully famous Silvertips will be missed.

For all practical hunting purposes, the 45-70 is limited to around 200 yards with either bullet, with its greatest usefulness at under 150 yards. Within that muzzle-to-150 yards range, the new load is clearly more effective, not the

hunting are expected to favor this hollow-point loading, at least for deer and other lighter species.

Although we haven't yet been able to test the new round, six-gunners may find interest in our trials with the Winchester soft points in a 6½" barrel Ruger Blackhawk. From that longer barrel, velocity averaged 1434 fps, with bullets expanding to some .55"-.60". If the new hollow-points better this performance, they will indeed be excellent hunting rounds.

I only wish I could conclude my report on Winchester-Western activities on a cheerful note with these advances in metallic cartridges. Unfortunately though, we must include the depressing announcement that this maker of the world famous Silvertip bullets has discontinued listing of *all* bullets as separate components for handloaders. While continuing to offer empty cases, primers and canister Ball powders, there will be no more bullets!

Looking back over the many rewarding experiences this writer has had in past years with Winchester bullets, this is a most saddening event, and I for one remain hopeful that they will one day see fit to reverse their decision.

Frontier

Joyce and Steve Hornady have been busy again this past year and have filled what seemed like an obvious gap in our American rifle factory cartridge line-up. Their Frontier Division of Hornady has come forth with a pair of factory loadings for the great 220 Swift.

Still the highest velocity commercial cartridge and a top-flight long range varmint round, its potential was and is such that it never should have been dropped, but it had received some adverse press reports in its early years, many unfairly, and was handicapped by a too-light ballistically deficient 48-grain bullet.

What the Swift always needed was an aerodynamically shaped bullet of 55-grains or heavier with good sectional density to better retain its initial velocity and buck cross winds more effectively. Now it has not one but two such loadings from Frontier, one with 55-grain Hornady spire-point having a muzzle velocity of 3630 fps, and the other a 60-grain Hornady hollow-point at 3530 fps. This latter bullet is a special favorite of mine, as it will withstand being driven hard without losing its accuracy. These loads will make the 220 Swift into the cartridge it should have been from the beginning.

Frontier has also announced the addition of the 25 Automatic pistol cartridge to their line-up, bringing to 58 the total number of offerings. The new 25 Auto is loaded with a 50-gr. round-nose full-metal-jacketed bullet designed by Hornady specifically for this cartridge.

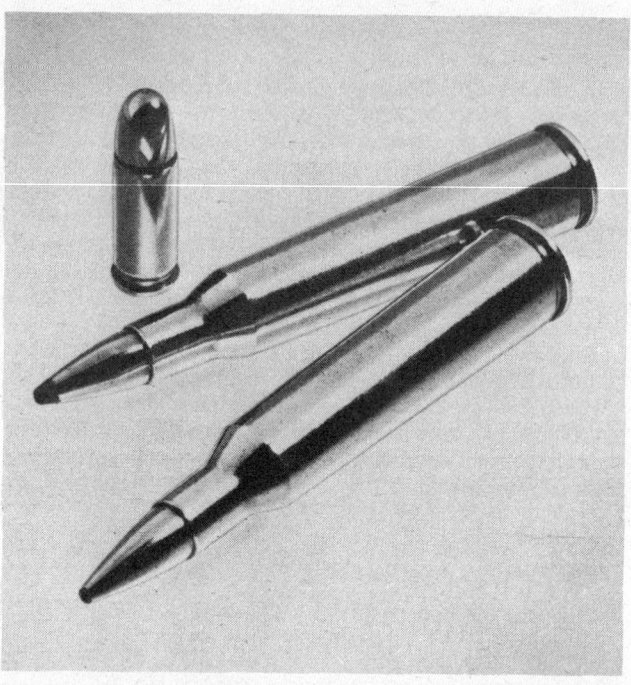

Latest centerfire cartridges from Frontier: A factory loading for 25 Automatic pistols with 50-gr. RN-FMJ Hornady bullet, plus a pair of much needed rounds for the 220 Swift, the upper with 55-gr. Hornady spire-point and the lower with 60-gr. Hornady hollow-point bullet.

Federal

The Federal Cartridge Company is unique among the larger ammunition manufacturers in that they have seen fit to load bullets produced by other makers when shooters' requests appear to indicate the desirability of certain combinations of components.

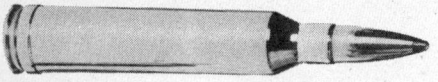

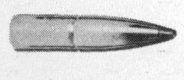

Federal's Premium brand now includes this 7mm Remington Magnum with a 160-gr. Nosler Partition bullet.

Most recently they have extended their offering of Federal cartridges loaded with the proven-effective Nosler Partition game bullets by adding the 7mm Remington Magnum cartridge loaded with 160-gr. Noslers. Apparently last year's introduction of 30-06 and 270 Winchester caliber cartridges featuring these controlled expansion Nosler bullets met with success, inducing Federal to repeat the procedure with the 7mm Magnum as part of their Premium ammo line.

Even though somewhat more costly than Federal's standard loading of the 7mm Magnum, I think it's a safe bet that big game hunters will be willing to ante up the difference in order to have these world famous bullets in factory cartridges. This is a real break for the non-reloader who can now have the same bullets formerly available only to handloaders.

Following are the ballistics released by Federal on this new loading of the 7mm Remington Magnum:

	Muzzle	100-yds	200-yds	300-yds	400-yds	500-yds
Velocity (fps)	2950	2730	2520	2320	2120	1940
Energy (f.p.)	3090	2650	2250	1910	1600	1340

A comparison with other bullet loadings in this caliber will show that out to around 300 yards, residual velocity of the new 160-grain load is somewhat lower than that of most 150-grain loadings, but beyond 300 yards remaining velocity is higher, adapting it for long range big game hunting.

CCI-Speer

After last year's enlargement of the Speer bullet line with the addition of nine spitzer boat-tail bullets in popular rifle calibers from 6mm to and including 30 caliber, plus a pair of handgun cartridges in the CCI "Lawman" series with flat-nosed full-metal-jacketed bullets, the Lewiston, Idaho firm has been consolidating their offerings.

Commonly, such a process involves the discontinuance of one or more items, and this appears to be no exception. Gone from the 1980 Speer bullet listing is their 70-grain semi-spitzer soft point in .228" diameter for the 22 Savage High Power and other 22-caliber centerfire rifles with that old oversize bore, most likely due to a decrease in popularity and therefore orders. I'll admit to some disappointment here, as I had hoped to see at least a modest re-birth of interest in the Savage High Power.

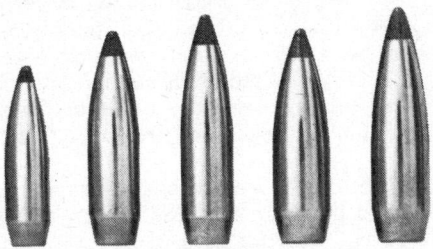

Speer's boat-tail bullet line includes the bullets above: (from left) 85-gr. 6mm, 130-gr. 270, 145-gr. 7mm, 150-gr. 30, and 165-gr. 30.

Helping to ameliorate this loss however, has been the excellent performances we've experienced with Speer's "Grand Slam" bullets. Most recent was the hunt for a trophy moufflon ram on the Evans ranch in the hill country outside of Kerrville, Texas.

Veteran guide Ray Krauss located a handsome full-curl ram for us amidst the brushy, rock strewn slopes, and there was just time enough for a quick off-hand shot before the departing game disappeared in the thick stuff at what later proved to be around ninety-four paces.

I had loaded 165-grain Grand Slams ahead of 57 grains of IMR 4350 in 30-06 cases—a combination that chronographed 2827 fps. The bullet entered behind the right shoulder and angled through the rib cage and up into the neck of the ram for an almost instantaneous kill. More could not have been asked of any bullet. These bullets are also accurate, grouping in under an inch at 100 yards from a target test rifle. Speer people know how to make game bullets, and the Grand Slams are among their best so far.

Although cartridges and bullets are the primary concerns of these columns, I can't refrain from mentioning the new Speer Reloading Manual No. 10 because of the tremendous assistance it offers those of us who reload. As a patron of the Speer manuals from the No. 1 edition, I've watched this publication grow in both content and quality. Each issue has something different, such as this year's chapters on "Siluetas Metalicas" and "Pressure and The Handloader," making for interesting as well as informative reading and reference material. No handloader or amateur ballistician should be without a copy.

Sierra

Sierra added five new bullets to their line-up for 1980, skillfully adapted to the several use groups, including a 55-grain 22-caliber spitzer boat-tail for varmint hunters; a 110-grain 30-caliber round-nose with full-metal-jacket for law enforcement and sport shooters with M-1 carbines; a 300-grain hollow-point for 45-70's and 45-90's replacing the older soft point of same weight as a still better big game hunting bullet; and for handgunners, whether police or silhouette shooters, a pair of full-metal-jacketed bullets—one a 220-grain flat-nose for 44 Magnums, and the other a 230-grain round-nose in 45 caliber for the Colt Auto, the new Winchester Magnum, or Long Colt revolvers. I plan to report on these new bullets after I've had sufficient opportunity for testing them. I'll be surprised if they aren't accurate; Sierras usually are, thanks in no small part to their maker's insistence on quality control.

A particularly interesting Sierra innovation in this year's catalog is what they refer to as "our categorization of bullets by use and/or type." Explaining that their segregations according to probable uses is intended only as a generalized grouping, the objective seems to be to help reloaders select the right bullets for the particular uses they may have in mind.

First, there are the famous Sierra "Match King" hollowpoints for match target competition—ten different bullets in calibers from 22 to 30. Then comes a selection of nineteen hollow- and soft-point boat-tail bullets from 22 to 375-caliber designated "Game King" for long range hunting varmints to big game. Next are what Sierra calls the "Pro Hunter"—twenty-eight flat base bullets for general hunting purposes, 6mm (or 24-caliber) to 45, and here I wish they'd put the pair of round-nose bullets for the 30 Carbine in another category, the one they refer to as "Sports Master" with target and law enforcement applications, including another thirteen bullets from 9mm to 45-caliber.

Sierra's twenty-one varmint bullets are appropriately called "Varminters" and cover the entire range from 22 to 30 caliber in both hollow and soft points. And finally there are the four "Tournament Masters"—38, 44 and 45 caliber full-metal-jacketed pistol and revolver bullets intended for target and silhouette competition. We think this is a novel approach with much to commend it.

Hornady

Last year we reported Hornady's introduction of a trio of flat-nosed full-metal-jacketed pistol and revolver bullets, one of .357" diameter for 38 Specials and 357 Magnums; the second for 44 Magnums and Specials; and a third for the 45 ACP. Said to have been developed by Hornady engineers in conjunction with a U.S. Air Force ballistics unit, they have several things going for them, amongst which are greater reliability of feeding and function in autoloaders, increased accuracy, and a more damaging impact effect.

Since then, a fourth Hornady bullet of this type has been

Hornady's new 9mm 124-gr. flat-point bullet with full metal jacket.

introduced, this one a 124-grain flat-nose in 9mm caliber. The maker claims tests have proven this new 9mm "more accurate than any other available 9mm bullet."

For bench-rest riflemen and long range varmint hunters, Hornady has introduced a new 22 caliber match bullet of hollow-point design with boat-tail base. Weighing 52 grains, this is the first Hornady .224" bullet to be given a boat-tail base, and I might note that it has a conservative, short-taper base. Also, its hollow point is extremely small—a second factor in its favor. If this new precision slug betters the accuracy performances of its predecessor, the 53 grain H.P. Match bullet, it will have to go some!

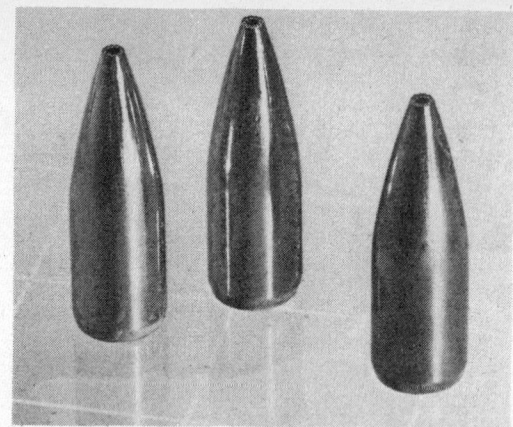

The 22 caliber Hornady 52-gr. BTHP (Boat-Tail Hollow Point) Match bullet.

Smith & Wesson

Recognizing the need to reduce airborne lead contamination that pollutes the air of indoor firing ranges, Smith & Wesson is out with a new type lead bullet protected by a nylon jacket that materially reduces the emission of lead oxide fumes—by more than 60%, according to S&W claims.

S&W's Nyclad ammunition—(from left) wadcutter, round nose, semi-wadcutter bullets.

Utilizing a coating of inert nylon capable of resisting the hot gases and friction to which a bullet is subjected, S&W engineers have been successful in causing the nylon jacket to remain affixed to the bullet throughout its travel, as proved by examination of recovered bullets. A bonus has been the reduction of smoke and bore fouling when using these bullets.

Accordingly, Smith & Wesson has initiated a new line of factory-loaded handgun ammunition under the trade name of "Nyclad," starting with calibers 38 Special, 38 Special +P, and 357 Magnum. In 38 Special, both wadcutter and round-nose bullet forms are offered; in 38 Special +P there are semi-wadcutters and SWC hollow-points; and the same in 357 Magnum. Listed velocities are 850 fps for 38 Special wadcutters, 890 fps for 158-grain round-nose, 1085 fps for both +P loads, and 1550 fps for the 357 Magnums, all velocities taken from a 6" test barrel.

The company states that "additional high performance loads for revolvers and semi-automatics will be added to the Nyclad line in the near future."

Taurus

A new firm, The Alberts Corporation in Franklin Lakes, New Jersey, is marketing a line of swaged lead bullets under the name of "Taurus" for handgun reloaders in calibers from 9mm to 45, featuring no less than sixteen designs, plus a pair of conical bullets for black powder revolvers, one each in 36 and 44 calibers.

Stressing accuracy as a major objective, quality control is emphasized starting with laboratory analysis of the lead with 3% antimony wire used, and followed by an allowable diameter tolerance held to .0002". They also seek to eliminate or at least minimize bore leading through the use of a special lubricant and system of lubricant applicant.

You'll perhaps be surprised at the absence of grease grooves on Taurus bullets. The new lubricating method doesn't require them, and the maker claims the omission of the usual grooves helps to maintain perfect roundness.

With the number of handgunners increasing daily, along with spiraling costs of factory ammunition, there would seem to be a growing demand and market for quality lead bullets.

Pyrodex

Pyrodex, the "Replica Black Powder," is back. The new plant at Herington, Kansas, is in operation producing this unique powder that smokes and smells like black powder, but is safer to ship and handle, and doesn't produce a build-up of fouling the way black powder does.

Available in four grades: "P" for pistols and revolvers (also, small caliber rifles); "RS" for shotguns and muzzle-loading rifles; "CTG" for cartridge rifles; and "C" for cannons, Pyrodex is distributed solely by the Hodgdon Powder Company of Shawnee Mission, Kansas and has been approved for shipping by UPS and other common carriers to dealers throughout the United States.

Although most references to Pyrodex are concerned with its use in muzzle-loading arms for which it is indeed excellent, I've found it especially useful for handloading metallic cartridges for the old black powder rifles, in particular those with huge cases wherein smokeless charges are almost lost to sight. And with the better ignition given by our modern large rifle primers, velocities generally run somewhat higher than with equal-weight charges of black powder.

With plenty of new goodies to work with in the year ahead, we shouldn't have any difficulty finding something that will add to the pleasure of our favorite sport. Good shooting!

CENTERFIRE RIFLE CARTRIDGES—BALLISTICS AND PRICES

Winchester-Western, Remington-Peters, Federal and Speer-DWM

Most of these centerfire loads are available from Winchester-Western and Remington-Peters. Loads available from only one source are marked by a letter, thus: Winchester (a); Western (b); Remington (c); Peters (d); Federal (e). Those fewer cartridges also available are not necessarily uniform, hence prices are approximate.

Cartridge	Bullet Wt. Grs.	Bullet Type	Velocity (fps) Muzzle	Velocity (fps) 100 yds.	Velocity (fps) 200 yds.	Velocity (fps) 300 yds.	Energy (ft. lbs.) Muzzle	Energy (ft. lbs.) 100 yds.	Energy (ft. lbs.) 200 yds.	Energy (ft. lbs.) 300 yds.	Mid-Range Trajectory 100 yds.	Mid-Range Trajectory 200 yds.	Mid-Range Trajectory 300 yds.	Price for 20*
17 Remington	25	HP, PL	4020	3290	2630	2060	900	600	380	230	—	1.5	7.3	**$ 9.75**
218 Bee*	46	HP	2860	2160	1610	1200	835	475	265	145	0.7	3.8	11.5	**26.50**
22 Hornet*	45	PSP	2690	2030	1510	1150	720	410	230	130	0.8	4.3	13.0	**17.95**
22 Hornet* (c, d)	45	HP	2690	2030	1510	1150	720	410	230	130	0.8	4.3	13.0	**17.95**
22 Hornet*	46	HP	2690	2030	1510	1150	740	420	235	135	0.8	4.3	13.0	**17.95**
222 Remington (a, e)	50	PSP, MC, PL†	3200	2660	2170	1750	1140	785	520	340	0.5	2.5	7.0	**7.65**
222 Remington Magnum (c, d)	55	SP, PL†	3300	2800	2340	1930	1330	955	670	455	0.5	2.3	6.1	**8.70**
222 Remington Magnum (c, d)	55	HP, PL†	3300	2830	2400	2010	1330	975	700	490	0.5	2.3	6.1	**9.30**
223 Remington (a, c, d, e)	55	SP, PL†, PSP	3300	2800	2340	1930	1330	955	670	455	0.5	2.1	5.4	**8.40**
223 Remington (e)	55	MCBT	3240	2880	2540	2230	1280	1010	790	610	0.7	1.9	9.9	**8.40**
22-250 Remington (e)	55	PSP	3810	3270	2770	2320	1770	1300	935	655	0.3	1.6	4.4	**8.40**
22-250 Remington (c, d)	55	HP, PL†	3810	3330	2890	2490	1770	1360	1020	760	0.4	1.7	4.3	**9.00**
225 Winchester (a, b)	55	PSP	3650	3140	2680	2270	1630	1200	870	630	0.4	1.8	4.8	**9.15**
243 Winchester (e)	80	PSP, PL†	3420	3020	2620	2310	2180	1690	1320	1030	0.4	1.8	4.7	**10.45**
243 Winchester (c, d)	80	HP, PL†	3450	3050	2675	2330	2115	1650	1270	965	0.4	1.9	4.9	**11.10**
243 Winchester (e)	100	PP, CL, PSP	2960	2700	2450	2220	2090	1730	1430	1190	0.5	2.2	5.5	**10.45**
6mm Remington (a, c, d)	80	PSP, HP, PL†	3450	3130	2750	2400	2220	1740	1340	1018	0.4	1.8	4.7	**10.45**
6mm Remington (a, c, d)	100	PCL, PSP	3190	2920	2660	2420	2260	1890	1570	1300	0.5	2.1	5.1	**10.45**
6mm Remington (e)	80	SP	3450	3130	2756	2400	2220	1740	1340	1018	—	—	—	**10.45**
6mm Remington (e)	100	SP	3190	2920	2660	2420	2260	1890	1570	1300	—	—	—	**10.45**
25-06 Remington (c, d)	87	HP	3500	3070	2680	2310	2370	1820	1390	1030	0.4	2.0	5.1	**11.35**
25-06 Remington (e)	90	HP	3440	3040	2680	2340	2360	1850	1440	1100	0.6	1.7	8.8	**11.35**
25-06 Remington (e)	117	SP	3060	2790	2530	2280	2430	2020	1660	1360	0.8	2.0	10.3	**11.35**
25-06 Remington (c, d)	120	PSP, CL	3120	2850	2600	2360	2590	2160	1800	1480	0.5	2.2	5.6	**11.35**
25-20 Winchester*	86	L, Lu	1460	1180	1030	940	405	265	200	170	2.6	12.5	32.0	**17.00**
25-20 Winchester* (c)	86	SP	1460	1180	1030	940	405	265	200	170	2.6	12.5	32.0	**17.00**
25-35 Winchester	117	SP, CL	2300	1910	1600	1340	1370	945	665	465	1.0	4.6	12.5	**11.65**
250 Savage (a, b)	87	PSP, SP	3030	2660	2330	2060	1770	1370	1050	820	0.6	2.5	6.4	**10.60**
250 Savage	100	ST, CL, PSP	2820	2460	2140	1870	1760	1340	1020	775	0.6	2.9	7.4	**10.60**
256 Winchester Magnum* (b)	60	HP	2800	2070	1570	1220	1040	570	330	200	0.8	4.0	12.0	**21.40**
257 Roberts (a, b)	100	ST, CL	2900	2540	2210	1920	1870	1430	1080	820	0.6	2.7	7.0	**11.70**
257 Roberts	117	PP, CL	2650	2280	1950	1690	1820	1350	985	740	0.7	3.4	8.8	**11.70**
6.5mm Remington Magnum (c)	120	PSP, CL	3030	2750	2480	2230	2450	2010	1640	1330	0.5	2.3	5.7	**17.00**
264 Winchester Magnum	100	PSP, CL	3700	3260	2880	2550	3040	2360	1840	1440	0.4	1.6	4.2	**14.65**
264 Winchester Magnum	140	PP, CL	3200	2490	2700	2480	3180	2690	2270	1910	0.5	2.0	4.9	**14.65**
270 Winchester	100	PSP	3480	3070	2690	2340	2690	2090	1600	1215	0.4	1.8	4.8	**11.35**
270 Winchester (e)	130	PP, PSP	3110	2850	2600	2400	2850	2390	2000	1660	0.5	2.1	5.3	**11.35**
270 Winchester	130	ST, CL, BP, PP	3140	2850	2580	2320	2840	2340	1920	1550	0.5	2.1	5.3	**12.00**
270 Winchester (c, d)	150	CL	2800	2440	2140	1870	2610	1980	1520	1160	0.6	2.9	7.6	**11.35**
270 Winchester (a, b, e)	150	PP, SP	2900	2550	2230	1930	2800	2290	1890	1550	0.6	2.5	6.3	**11.35**
280 Remington (c, d)	150	PCL	2900	2670	2450	2220	2800	2370	2000	1640	0.6	2.5	6.1	**11.50**
280 Remington (c, d)	165	CL	2820	2510	2220	1970	2910	2310	1810	1420	0.6	2.8	7.2	**11.35**
7mm Exp. Rem. (c)	150	PSP, CL	2970	2699	2444	2203	2937	2426	1989	1616	1.9	0.0	7.8	**11.35**
284 Winchester (a, b)	125	PP	3200	2880	2590	2310	2840	2300	1860	1480	0.5	2.1	5.3	**13.15**
284 Winchester (a, b)	150	PP	2900	2630	2380	2160	2800	2300	1890	1550	0.6	2.5	6.3	**13.15**
7mm Mauser (e)	139	SP	2660	2400	2150	1910	2280	1850	1490	1190	0.7	3.0	7.8	**11.60**
7mm Mauser	175	SP	2470	2170	1880	1630	2410	1830	1400	1100	0.8	3.7	9.5	**11:60**
7mm-08 Remington	140	SP	2860	2625	2402	2189	2542	2142	1793	1490	0.9	2.3	11.6	**11.35**
7mm Remington Magnum	125	CL	3430	3080	2750	2450	3260	2630	2100	1660	0.6	1.8	4.7	**14.10**
7mm Remington Magnum	150	PP, CL, SP	3110	2830	2570	2320	3540	2940	2430	1990	0.4	2.0	4.9	**14.10**
7mm Remington Magnum	175	SP	2860	2650	2440	2220	3660	2870	2240	1750	0.5	2.4	6.1	**14.10**
7mm Remington Magnum (c, d)	175	PCL	3070	2860	2660	2460	3660	3170	2740	2350	0.5	2.1	5.2	**14.10**
30 Carbine*	110	HSP, SP	1990	1570	1240	1040	950	575	370	260	1.4	7.5	21.7	**16.45**
30 Carbine (e)	110	MC	1990	1600	1280	1070	970	620	400	280	0.0	13.0	47.4	**7.30**
30-30 Winchester (e)	125	HP	2570	2090	1660	1320	1830	1210	770	480	0.0	7.3	28.1	**8.90**
30-30 Winchester (c, d)	150	CL	2410	1960	1620	1360	1930	1280	875	616	0.9	4.5	12.5	**8.90**
30-30 Winchester (e)	150	SP	2390	2020	1700	1430	1930	1360	960	680	0.9	4.2	11.0	**8.90**
30-30 Winchester (a, b)	150	PP, ST, OPE	2410	2020	1700	1430	1930	1360	960	680	0.9	4.2	11.0	**8.90**
30-30 Winchester	170	SP, HP, CL, ST, MC	2220	1890	1630	1410	1860	1350	1000	750	1.2	4.6	12.5	**8.90**
30-30 Accelerator (c)	55	PSP	3400	2693	2085	1569	1412	885	531	301	2.0	0.0	10.2	**9.90**
30 Remington	170	ST, CL	2120	1820	1560	1350	1700	1250	920	690	1.1	5.3	14.0	**11.50**
30-06 Accelerator	55	PSP	4080	3485	2965	2502	2033	1983	1074	764	1.0	0.0	5.0	**12.60**
30-06 Springfield (a, b)	110	PSP	3370	2830	2350	1920	2770	1960	1350	900	0.5	2.2	6.0	**11.35**
30-06 Springfield (e)	125	PSP	3140	2780	2450	2140	2840	2190	1710	1340	0.5	2.2	5.6	**11.35**
30-06 Springfield (c, d)	150	BP	2970	2710	2470	2240	2930	2440	2030	1670	0.5	2.4	6.0	**11.35**
30-06 Springfield (e)	150	SP	2910	2620	2340	2080	2930	2280	1760	1340	0.6	2.5	6.5	**11.35**
30-06 Springfield	150	ST, PCL, PSP	2970	2670	2400	2130	2930	2370	1920	1510	0.6	2.4	6.1	**11.35**
30-06 Springfield (c, e)	165	PSP, CL	2800	2534	2283	2047	2872	2352	1909	1534	2.3	0.0	9.0	**11.85**
30-06 Springfield	180	PP, CL, PSP	2700	2330	2010	1740	2910	2170	1610	1210	0.7	3.1	8.3	**12.00**
30-06 Springfield	180	ST, BP, PCL, SP	2700	2470	2250	2040	2910	2440	2020	1660	0.7	2.9	7.0	**11.35**
30-06 Springfield (e)	200	SPBT	2550	2400	2260	2120	2890	2560	2270	2000	0.0	6.0	18.8	**11.85**
30-06 Springfield	220	PP, CL	2410	2120	1870	1670	2830	2190	1710	1360	0.8	3.9	9.8	**11.35**
30-06 Springfield (a, b)	220	ST	2410	2180	1980	1790	2830	2320	1910	1560	0.8	3.7	9.2	**12.00**
30-40 Krag	180	PP, CL	2470	2120	1830	1590	2440	1790	1340	1010	0.8	3.8	9.9	**11.95**
30-40 Krag	180	ST, PCL	2470	2250	2040	1850	2440	2020	1660	1370	0.8	3.5	8.5	**11.95**
300 Winchester Magnum (a, c, e)	150	PP, PCL	3400	3050	2730	2430	3850	3100	2480	1970	0.4	1.9	4.8	**14.85**
300 Winchester Magnum (a, c, e)	180	PP, PCL	3070	2850	2640	2440	3770	3250	2790	2380	0.5	2.1	5.3	**14.85**
300 Winchester Magnum (a, b)	220	ST	2720	2490	2270	2060	3620	3030	2520	2070	0.6	2.9	6.9	**15.65**
300 H&H Magnum (a, b)	150	ST	3190	2870	2580	2300	3390	2740	2220	1760	0.5	2.1	5.2	**15.65**
300 H&H Magnum	180	ST, PCL	2920	2670	2440	2220	3400	2850	2380	1970	0.6	2.4	5.8	**15.25**
300 H&H Magnum (a, b)	220	ST, CL	2620	2370	2150	1940	3350	2740	2260	1840	0.7	3.1	7.7	**16.05**
300 Savage	150	SP	2630	2350	2100	1850	2370	1840	1410	1080	0.7	3.2	8.0	**11.45**
300 Savage	150	ST, PCL	2670	2390	2130	1890	2370	1900	1510	1190	0.7	3.0	7.6	**11.45**
300 Savage (c, d)	150	CL	2670	2270	1930	1660	2370	1710	1240	916	0.7	3.3	9.3	**11.45**
300 Savage (e)	180	SP, CL	2350	2140	1940	1720	2240	1660	1240	920	0.9	4.1	10.5	**11.45**
300 Savage	180	ST, PCL	2370	2160	1960	1770	2240	1860	1530	1250	0.9	3.7	9.2	**11.70**
303 Savage (c, d)	180	CL	2140	1810	1550	1340	1830	1310	960	715	1.1	5.4	14.0	**11.45**
303 Savage (a, b)	190	ST	1980	1680	1440	1250	1650	1190	875	660	1.3	6.2	15.5	**13.55**
303 British (e)	180	PP, CL	2540	2300	2090	1900	2580	2120	1750	1440	0.7	3.3	8.2	**11.70**
303 British (c, d)	215	SP	2180	1900	1660	1460	2270	1720	1310	1020	1.1	4.9	12.5	**11.70**
308 Accelerator	55	PSP	3770	3215	2726	2286	1735	1262	907	638	0.5	1.5	8.2	**12.60**
308 Winchester (a, b)	110	PSP	3340	2810	2340	1920	2730	1930	1340	900	0.5	2.2	6.0	**11.35**
308 Winchester (a, b)	125	PSP	3100	2740	2430	2160	2670	2080	1640	1300	0.5	2.3	5.9	**11.35**
308 Winchester (e)	150	SP	2820	2530	2260	2010	2730	2120	1630	1240	0.6	2.7	7.0	**11.35**
308 Winchester	150	ST, PCL	2860	2570	2300	2050	2730	2200	1760	1400	0.6	2.6	6.5	**11.35**
308 Winchester	180	PP, CL	2610	2250	1940	1680	2720	2020	1500	1130	0.7	3.4	8.9	**11.35**
308 Winchester	180	ST, PCL	2610	2390	2170	1970	2720	2280	1870	1540	0.8	3.1	7.4	**11.35**
308 Winchester (a, b)	200	ST	2450	2210	1980	1770	2770	2170	1750	1400	0.8	3.6	9.0	**12.00**
32 Winchester Special (c, d, e)	170	HP, CL, SP	2250	1920	1630	1370	1960	1390	1000	750	1.0	4.8	12.5	**9.50**
32 Winchester Special	170	PP, ST	2280	1870	1560	1330	1960	1320	920	665	1.0	4.8	13.0	**9.50**
32-20 Winchester*	100	SP	1290	1060	940	840	370	250	195	155	3.3	15.5	38.0	**17.10**

CAUTION: PRICES CHANGE. CHECK AT GUNSHOP. 35TH EDITION, 1981 **265**

CENTERFIRE RIFLE CARTRIDGES — BALLISTICS AND PRICES (continued)

Cartridge	Wt. Grs.	Bullet Type	Velocity (fps) Muzzle	100 yds.	200 yds.	300 yds.	Energy (ft. lbs.) Muzzle	100 yds.	200 yds.	300 yds.	Mid-Range Trajectory 100 yds.	200 yds.	300 yds.	Price for 20*
32-20 Winchester*	100	SP, L, Lu	1290	1060	940	840	370	250	195	155	3.3	15.5	38.0	13.85
8mm Mauser	170	PP, CL	2510	2110	1740	1430	2380	1670	1140	770	0.8	7.0	25.7	11.70
8mm Remington Magnum	185	PSP	3080	2761	2464	2186	3896	3132	2494	1963	1.8	0.0	7.6	16.65
8mm Remington Magnum	220	PSP	2830	2581	2346	2123	3912	3255	2688	2201	2.2	0.0	8.5	16.65
338 Winchester Magnum (a, b)	200	PP	3000	2690	2410	2170	4000	3210	2580	2090	0.5	2.4	6.0	17.80
35 Remington (c, d)	150	CL	2400	1960	1580	1280	1920	1280	835	545	0.9	4.6	13.0	10.50
35 Remington (c, d, e)	200	PP, ST, CL	2080	1700	1380	1140	1950	1300	860	605	1.2	6.0	16.5	10.50
350 Remington Magnum (c, d)	200	PCL	2710	2410	2130	1870	3260	2570	2000	1550	0.7	3.0	7.7	16.35
351 Winchester Self-Loading*	180	SP	1850	1560	1310	1140	1370	975	685	520	1.5	7.8	21.5	29.05
358 Winchester (a, b)	200	ST	2530	2210	1910	1640	2840	2160	1610	1190	0.8	3.6	9.4	16.60
375 Win. Big Bore (a)	200	FNPP	2200	1841	1526	—	2150	1506	1034	—	1.1	5.2	—	13.55
375 Win. Big Bore (a)	250	FNPP	1900	1647	1424	—	2005	1506	1126	—	1.4	6.4	—	13.65
375 H&H Magnum	270	PP, SP	2740	2460	2210	1990	4500	3620	2920	2370	0.7	2.9	7.1	17.65
375 H&H Magnum	300	ST	2550	2280	2040	1830	4330	3460	2770	2230	0.7	3.3	8.3	17.65
375 H&H Magnum	300	MC	2550	2180	1860	1590	4330	3160	2300	1680	0.7	3.6	9.3	17.65
38-40 Winchester*	180	SP	1330	1070	960	850	705	455	370	290	3.2	15.0	36.5	21.65
44 Magnum* (c, d)	240	SP	1750	1360	1110	980	1630	985	655	510	1.6	8.4	—	8.65
44 Magnum (b, e)	240	HSP	1760	1360	1090	950	630	970	635	480	1.8	9.4	26.0	8.65
444 Marlin (c)	240	SP	2400	1845	1410	1125	3070	1815	1060	675	1.0	5.4	16.5	12.65
44-40 Winchester*	200	SP	1310	1050	940	830	760	490	390	305	3.3	15.0	36.5	22.90
45-70 Government (e)	300	HSP	1810	1410	1120	970	2180	1320	840	630	2.5	22.0	69.0	12.95
45-70 Government	405	SP	1320	1160	1050	990	1570	1210	990	880	2.9	13.0	32.5	12.95
458 Winchester Magnum	500	MC	2130	1910	1700	1520	5040	4050	3210	2570	1.1	4.8	12.0	36.10
458 Winchester Magnum	510	SP	2130	1840	1600	1400	5140	3830	2900	2220	1.1	5.1	13.5	23.80

*Price for 50   HP—Hollow Point   SP—Soft Point   PSP—Pointed Soft Point   PP—Power Point   L—Lead   Lu—Lubaloy   ST—Silvertip   HSP—Hollow Soft Point   MC—Metal Case   BT—Boat Tail   MAT—Match   BP—Bronze Point   CL—Core Lokt   PCL—Pointed Core Lokt   OPE—Open Point Expanding   FN—Flat Nose   †PL—Power-Lokt (slightly higher price).

WEATHERBY MAGNUM CARTRIDGES — BALLISTICS AND PRICES

Cartridge	Wt. Grs.	Bullet Type	Velocity (fps) Muzzle	100 yds.	200 yds.	300 yds.	Energy (ft. lbs.) Muzzle	100 yds.	200 yds.	300 yds.	Mid-Range Trajectory 100 yds.	200 yds.	300 yds.	Price for 20*
224 Weatherby Magnum	50	PE	3750	3263	2814	2402	1562	1182	879	640	0.3	1.6	4.3	$18.95
224 Weatherby Magnum	55	PE	3650	3214	2808	2433	1627	1262	963	723	0.3	1.7	4.4	18.95
240 Weatherby Magnum	70	PE	3850	3424	3025	2654	2305	1823	1423	1095	0.3	1.4	3.8	18.95
240 Weatherby Magnum	85	Nosler	3500	3106	2739	2398	2313	1821	1416	1085	0.4	1.8	4.6	25.95
240 Weatherby Magnum	87	PE	3500	3165	2848	2550	2367	1935	1567	1256	0.3	1.7	4.4	18.95
240 Weatherby Magnum	100	PE	3395	3115	2848	2594	2560	2155	1802	1495	0.4	1.8	4.4	18.95
240 Weatherby Magnum	100	Nosler	3395	3068	2758	2468	2560	2090	1690	1353	0.4	1.8	4.6	25.95
257 Weatherby Magnum	87	PE	3825	3470	3135	2818	2827	2327	1900	1535	0.3	1.4	3.1	19.95
257 Weatherby Magnum	100	PE	3555	3256	2971	2700	2807	2355	1960	1619	0.3	1.6	4.1	19.95
257 Weatherby Magnum	100	Nosler	3555	3242	2945	2663	2807	2335	1926	1575	0.4	1.6	4.1	26.95
257 Weatherby Magnum	117	SPE	3300	2853	2443	2074	2830	2115	1551	1118	0.4	2.1	5.7	19.95
257 Weatherby Magnum	117	Nosler	3300	3027	2767	2520	2830	2381	1990	1650	0.4	1.9	4.7	26.95
270 Weatherby Magnum	100	PE	3760	3341	2949	2585	3140	2479	1932	1484	0.3	1.5	4.0	19.95
270 Weatherby Magnum	130	PE	3375	3110	2856	2615	3289	2793	2355	1974	0.4	1.8	4.4	19.95
270 Weatherby Magnum	130	Nosler	3375	3113	2862	2624	3289	2798	2365	1988	0.4	1.8	4.4	26.95
270 Weatherby Magnum	150	PE	3245	3012	2789	2575	3508	3022	2592	2209	0.4	1.9	4.7	19.95
270 Weatherby Magnum	150	Nosler	3245	3022	2809	2604	3508	3043	2629	2259	0.4	1.9	4.6	26.95
7mm Weatherby Magnum	139	PE	3300	3037	2786	2546	3362	2848	2396	2001	0.4	1.8	4.6	19.95
7mm Weatherby Magnum	140	Nosler	3300	3047	2806	2575	3386	2887	2448	2062	0.4	1.8	4.6	26.95
7mm Weatherby Magnum	154	PE	3160	2928	2706	2494	3415	2932	2504	2127	0.4	2.0	4.9	19.95
7mm Weatherby Magnum	160	Nosler	3150	2935	2727	2528	3526	3061	2643	2271	0.5	2.0	4.9	26.95
7mm Weatherby Magnum	175	RN	3070	2714	2383	2082	3663	2863	2207	1685	0.5	2.4	6.0	19.95
7mm Weatherby Magnum	175	PE	3070	2845	2630	2425	3663	3146	2689	2286	0.5	2.1	5.2	26.95
300 Weatherby Magnum	110	PE	3900	3465	3057	2677	3716	2933	2283	1750	0.3	1.4	3.7	19.95
300 Weatherby Magnum	150	PE	3545	3248	2965	2696	4187	3515	2929	2422	0.3	1.6	4.0	19.95
300 Weatherby Magnum	150	Nosler	3545	3191	2857	2544	4187	3392	2719	2156	0.4	1.7	4.3	26.95
300 Weatherby Magnum	180	PE	3245	3010	2785	2569	4210	3622	3100	2639	0.4	1.9	4.6	19.95
300 Weatherby Magnum	180	Nosler	3245	2964	2696	2444	4210	3512	2906	2388	0.5	2.0	5.0	26.95
300 Weatherby Magnum	200	Nosler	3000	2740	2494	2262	3998	3335	2763	2273	0.5	2.3	5.7	26.95
300 Weatherby Magnum	220	SPE	2905	2578	2276	2000	4123	3248	2531	1955	0.5	2.6	6.7	19.95
340 Weatherby Magnum	200	PE	3210	2947	2696	2458	4577	3857	3228	2683	0.4	2.0	4.9	20.95
340 Weatherby Magnum	210	Nosler	3180	2927	2686	2457	4717	3996	3365	2816	0.5	2.0	5.0	32.95
340 Weatherby Magnum	250	SPE	2850	2516	2209	1929	4510	3515	2710	2066	0.6	2.7	7.1	20.95
340 Weatherby Magnum	250	Nosler	2850	2563	2296	2049	4510	3648	2927	2331	0.6	2.6	6.7	32.95
378 Weatherby Magnum	270	SPE	3180	2796	2440	2117	6064	4688	3570	2688	0.5	2.2	5.8	38.95
378 Weatherby Magnum	300	SPE	2925	2564	2234	1935	5700	4380	3325	2495	0.6	2.7	6.9	38.95
460 Weatherby Magnum	500	RN	2700	2395	2115	1858	8095	6370	4968	3834	0.7	3.0	7.8	36.95
460 Weatherby Magnum	500	FMJ	2700	2416	2154	1912	8095	6482	5153	4060	0.7	3.0	7.6	36.95

Trajectory is given from scope height. Velocities chronographed using 26" bbls. Available with Nosler bullets.
SPE—Semi-Pointed Expanding   RN—Round Nose   PE—Pointed Expanding   FMJ—Full Metal Jacket.

RIMFIRE CARTRIDGES — BALLISTICS AND PRICES
Remington-Peters, Winchester-Western, Federal & Omark/CCI

All loads available from all manufacturers except as indicated: R-P (a); W-W (b); Fed. (c); CCI (d). **All prices are approximate.**

CARTRIDGE	BULLET WT. GRS.	BULLET TYPE	VELOCITY FT. PER SEC. MUZZLE	100 YDS.	ENERGY FT. LBS. MUZZLE	100 YDS.	MID-RANGE TRAJECTORY 100 YDS.	HANDGUN BARREL LENGTH	BALLISTICS M.V. F.P.S.	M.E. F.P.	PRICE FOR 50
22 Short T22 (a, b)	29	C, L*	1045	810	70	42	5.6	6"	865	48	$1.70
22 Short Hi-Vel. (c)	29	C, L	1125	920	81	54	4.3	6"	1035	69	1.70
22 Short HP-Hi-Vel. (a, b, c)	27	C, L	1155	920	80	51	4.2	—	—	—	1.80
22 Short Std. Vel. (a, b, c)	29	L*	1045	870	70	49	8.7	—	1045	870	1.70
22 Short (a)	15	D	1710	—	97	—	—	—	—	(per 500)	13.00
22 Stinger	32	C, HP	1686	1047	202	78	2.61	—	—	—	2.55
22 Xpediter	29	HP	1680	—	182	—	2.5	—	—	—	2.55
22 Long Rifle Yellow Jacket	33	HVTCHP	1500	1075	185	85	2.8	—	1500	165	2.37
22 Long Hi-Vel. (c)	29	C, L	1045	870	70	49	8.7	—	1045	70	1.80
22 Long Rifle T22 (a, b)†1	40	L*	1145	975	116	84	4.0	6"	950	80	1.91
22 Long Rifle (b)†2	40	L*	1120	950	111	80	4.2	—	—	—	3.82
22 Long Rifle (b)†3	40	L*	—	—	—	—	—	6¾"	1060	100	4.21
22 Long Rifle (d)†4	40	C	1165	980	121	84	4.0	—	—	—	1.92
22 Long Rifle Hi-Vel.	40	C, L	1285	1025	147	93	3.4	6"	1125	112	1.92
22 Long Rifle HP Hi-Vel. (b, d)	37	C, L	131	1020	142	85	3.4	—	1255	140	2.10
22 Long Rifle HP Hi-Vel. (a, c)	38	C, HP	1280	1020	138	88	6.1	—	1280	138	2.10
22 Long Rifle (b, c)	No.	12 Shot	—	—	—	—	—	—	—	—	3.93
22 WRF (Rem. Spl.) (a, b)	45	C, L	1450	1110	210	123	—	—	—	—	5.64
22 WRF Mag. (b)	40	JHP	2000	1390	355	170	1.6	6½"	1550	213	5.32
22 WRF Mag. (b)	40	MC	2000	1390	355	170	1.6	6½"	1550	213	5.32
22 Win. Auto Inside lub. (a)	45	C, L	1055	930	111	86	—	—	—	—	6.19
5mm Rem. RFM (a)	38	PLHP	2100	1605	372	217	Not Available				9.66

†Target loads of these ballistics available in: (1) Rem. Match; (2) W-W, Super Match Mark III; (3) Super Match Mark IV Pistol Match; (4) CCI MiniGroup.
C—Copper plated   L—Lead (Wax Coated)   L*—Lead, lubricated   D—Disintegrating   MC—Metal Case   HP—Hollow Point   JHP—Jacket Hollow Point
PLHP—Power-Lokt Hollow Point   HVTCHP—Hyper Velocity Truncated Cone Hollow Point.

NORMA C.F. RIFLE CARTRIDGES — BALLISTICS AND PRICES

Norma ammunition loaded to standard velocity and pressure is now available with Nosler bullets in the following loads: 270 Win., 130-, 150-gr.; Super 7x61 (S&H), 160-gr.; 308 Win., 180-gr.; 30-06, 150-, 180-gr., all at slightly higher prices. All ballistic figures are computed from a line of sight one inch above center of bore at muzzle. Write for their latest prices.

Cartridge	Bullet Wt. Grs.	Type	Velocity, feet per sec.				Energy, foot pounds				Max. Height of trajectory, Inches			Price for 20
			V Muzzle	V 100 yds.	V 200 yds.	V 300 yds.	E Muzzle	E 100 yds.	E 200 yds.	E 300 yds.	Tr. 100 yds.	Tr. 200 yds.	Tr. 300 yds.	
220 Swift	50	SP	4111	3611	3133	2681	1877	1448	1090	799	.2	.9	3.0	$16.55
222 Remington	50	SPSP, FMJ	3200	2660	2170	1750	1137	786	523	340	.0	2.0	6.2	7.60
	53	SpPSP	3117	2670	2267	1901	1142	838	604	425	.0	3.5	14.0	8.25
22-250 Remington	53	SpPSP (Match Spitzer)	3710	—	—	—	—	—	—	—	—	—	—	9.25
22 Savage Hi-Power (5.6x52R)	71	SP, FMJ	2788	2296	1886	1558	1226	831	651	383	.0	4.8	18.06	19.85
243 Winchester	100	SP, FMJ	3070	2790	2540	2320	2093	1729	1433	1195	.1	1.8	5.0	10.20
Carcano	139	PPDC	2576	2379	2192	2012	2046	1745	1481	1249	.0	4.7	16.6	19.55
	156	SPRN	2000	1810	1640	1485	1386	1135	932	764	Not Available			19.20
6.5 Japanese	139	SPSPBT	2428	2280	2130	1990	1820	1605	1401	1223	.3	2.8	7.7	19.20
	156	SPRN	2067	1871	1692	1529	1481	1213	992	810	.6	4.4	11.9	19.20
6.5x55	77	SPSP	2725	2362	2030	1811	1271	956	706	562	.0	4.8	18.1	19.20
	139	PPDC	2789	2630	2470	2320	2402	2136	1883	1662	.1	2.0	5.6	19.55
	156	SPSP	2493	2271	2062	1867	2153	1787	1473	1208	.3	2.9	7.9	19.20
270 Winchester	130	SPSPBT	3140	2884	2639	2404	2847	2401	2011	1669	.0	1.6	4.7	11.05
	150	SPSPBT	2802	2616	2436	2262	2616	2280	1977	1705	.1	2.0	5.7	11.05
7.5x55 Schmidt Rubin (7.5 Swiss)	180	SPSBT	2650	2450	2260	2060	2792	2350	1990	1665	Not Available			19.75
7x57	150	SPSPBT	2756	2539	2331	2133	2530	2148	1810	1516	.1	4.2	6.2	12.05
7x57R	150	SPSPBT, FJPBT	2690	2476	2270	2077	2411	2042	1717	1437	.0	5.2	15.2	19.85
7mm Remington Magnum	150	SPSBT	3260	2970	2700	2450	3540	2945	2435	1990	.4	2.0	4.9	15.05
7x64	150	SPSPBT	2890	2598	2329	2113	2779	2449	1807	1487	.0	3.3	12.5	19.85
280 Remington	150	SPSP	2900	2683	2475	2277	2802	2398	2041	1727	.0	3.4	12.4	12.20
30 U.S. Carbine	110	SPRN	1970	1595	1300	1090	948	622	413	290	.8	6.4	19.0	7.15
308 Winchester	130	SPSPBT	2900	2590	2300	2030	2428	1937	1527	1190	.1	2.1	6.2	11.25
	150	SPSPBT	2860	2570	2300	2050	2725	2200	1762	1400	.1	2.0	5.9	11.25
	180	PPDC	2610	2400	2210	2020	2725	2303	1952	1631	.2	2.5	6.6	11.25
7.62 Russian	180	SPSBT	2624	2415	2222	2030	2749	2326	1970	1644	.2	2.5	6.6	20.35
.308 Norma Magnum	180	PPDC	3100	2881	2668	2464	3842	3318	2846	2427	.0	1.6	4.6	25.40
30-06	130	SPSBT	3281	2951	2636	2338	3108	2514	2006	1578	.1	1.5	4.6	11.15
	150	SPSPBT	2972	2680	2402	2141	2943	2393	1922	1527	.0	1.9	5.7	11.15
	180	SPRN	2700	2494	2296	2109	2914	2487	2107	1778	.1	2.3	6.4	11.15
	180	PPDC	2700	2494	2296	2109	2914	2487	2107	1778	Not Available			11.15
30-30	150	SPFP	2410	2075	1790	1550	1934	1433	1066	799	.0	7.0	26.1	11.35
	170	SPFP	2220	1890	1630	1410	1860	1350	1000	750	.0	8.1	29.2	11.35
7.65 Argentine	150	SPSP	2920	2630	2355	2105	2841	2304	1848	1476	.1	2.0	5.8	19.55
303 British	150	SPSP	2720	2440	2170	1930	2465	1983	1596	1241	.1	2.2	6.5	12.85
	180	SPSPBT	2540	2340	2147	1965	2579	2189	1843	1544	.2	2.7	7.3	12.85
7.7 Japanese	130	SPSP	2950	2635	2340	2065	2513	2004	1581	1231	.1	2.0	5.9	19.55
	180	SPSPBT	2493	2292	2101	1922	2484	2100	1765	1477	.3	2.8	7.7	19.95
8x57J (.318 in.)	196	SPRN	2526	2195	1894	1627	2778	2077	1562	1152	.0	5.8	21.4	20.25
8mm Mauser (.323 in.)	196	SP	2526	2195	1894	1627	2778	2097	1562	1152	Not Available			13.25
358 Norma Magnum	250	SPSP	2790	2493	2231	2001	4322	3451	2764	2223	.2	2.4	6.6	25.75
9.3x57	286	PPDC	2067	1818	1595	1404	2714	2099	1616	1252	.0	9.1	32.0	20.65
9.3x62	286	PPDC	2362	2088	1815	1592	3544	2769	2092	1700	.0	6.5	23.5	20.65

P—Pointed SP—Soft Point HP—Hollow Point FP—Flat Point RN—Round Nose BT—Boat Tail MC—Metal Case DC—Dual Core SPSP—Soft Point Semi Point
SPSBT—Soft Point Semi Pointed Boat Tail FJPBT—Full Jacket Pointed Boat Tail SpPSP—Spire point Soft Point PP—Plastic Point

CAUTION: PRICES CHANGE. CHECK AT GUNSHOP.

CENTERFIRE HANDGUN CARTRIDGES— BALLISTICS AND PRICES

Winchester-Western, Remington-Peters, Norma and Federal

Most loads are available from W-W and R-P. All available Norma loads are listed. Federal cartridges are marked with an asterisk. Other loads supplied by only one source are indicated by a letter, thus: Norma (a); R-P (b); W-W (c). Prices are approximate.

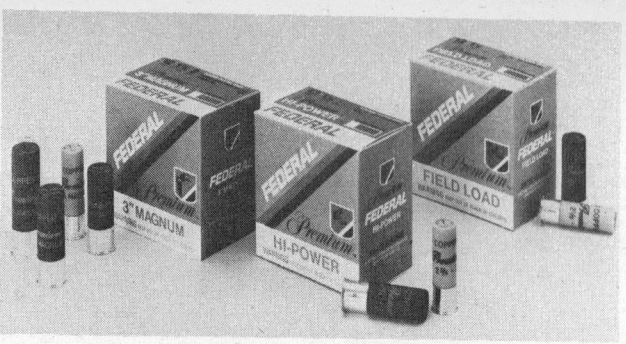

Cartridge	Bullet Gr.	Bullet Style	Muzzle Velocity	Muzzle Energy	Barrel Inches	Price Per Box
22 Jet (b)	40	SP	2100	390	8⅜	$18.95
221 Fireball (b)	50	SP	2650	780	10½	8.75
25 (6.35mm) Auto*	50	MC	810	73	2	11.05
256 Winchester Magnum (c)	60	HP	2350	735	8½	19.20
30 (7.65mm) Luger Auto	93	MC	1220	307	4½	17.75
32 S&W Blank (b,c)	No bullet		—	—	—	10.55
32 S&W Blank, BP (c)	No bullet		—	—	—	10.95
32 Short Colt	80	Lead	745	100	4	10.60
32 Long Colt IL (c)	82	Lub.	755	104	4	11.05
32 (7.65mm) Auto*	71	MC	905	129	4	12.60
32 (7.65mm) Auto Pistol (a)	77	MC	900	162	4	12.00
32 S&W	88	Lead	680	90	3	10.65
32 S&W Long	98	Lead	705	115	4	11.05
32-20 Winchester	100	Lead	1030	271	6	13.85
32-20 Winchester	100	SP	1030	271	6	17.10
357 Magnum*	110	JHP	1295	410	4	16.60
357 Magnum	110	SJHP	1295	410	4	16.60
357 Magnum*	125	JHP	1450	583	4	16.60
357 Magnum*	158	SWC	1235	535	4	14.05
357 Magnum (b)*	158	JSP	1550	845	8⅜	16.60
357 Magnum	158	MP	1410	695	8⅜	16.35
357 Magnum	158	Lead	1410	696	8⅜	14.05
357 Magnum	158	JHP	1450	735	8⅜	16.60
9mm Luger (c)	95	JSP	1355	387	4	15.70
9mm Luger (c)	100	JHP	1320	387	4	15.10
9mm Luger (c)	115	FMC	1155	341	4	15.70
9mm Luger (c)	115	STHP	1255	383	4	16.45
9mm Luger*	115	JHP	1165	349	4	15.70
9mm Luger*	123	MC	1120	345	4	15.70
9mm Winchester Magnum (c)	115	FMC	1475	556	5	16.80
38 S&W Blank	No bullet		—	—	—	12.75
38 Smith & Wesson	146	Lead	685	150	4	11.85
38 S&W	146	Lead	730	172	4	11.85
38 Special Blank	No bullet		—	—	—	12.85
38 Special, IL +P (c)	150	Lub.	1060	375	6	13.25
38 Special IL +P (c)	150	MP	1060	375	6	15.15
38 Special	158	Lead	855	256	6	11.95
38 Special	200	Lead	730	236	6	12.75
38 Special	158	MP	855	256	6	15.15
38 Special (b)	125	SJHP	Not available			15.15
38 Special	158	SJHP	Not available			14.85
38 Special WC (b)	148	Lead	770	195	6	12.45
38 Special Match, IL	148	Lead	770	195	6	12.45
38 Special Match, IL (b)	158	Lead	855	256	6	12.50
38 Special (a)	158	RN	900	320	6	11.95
38 Special*	158	SWC	755	200	4	12.20
38 Special Match*	148	WC	710	166	4	12.45
38 Special +P (b)	110	SJHP	1020	254	4	15.15
38 Special +P	125	JSP	945	248	4	15.15
38 Special +P	158	LRN	915	294	4	14.85
38 Special +P (b)	158	LHP	915	294	4	12.45
38 Special +P*	158	SWC	915	294	4	12.20
38 Special +P*	158	SWCHP	915	294	4	12.90
38 Special +P*	110	JHP	1020	254	4	15.15
38 Special +P*	125	JHP	945	248	4	15.15
38 Special Norma Mag. (a)	110	JHP	1542	580	6	24.85
38 Short Colt	125	Lead	730	150	6	11.65
38 Short Colt, Greased	130	Lub.	730	155	6	11.65
38 Long Colt	150	Lead	730	175	6	17.50
38 Super Auto +P (b)	130	MC	1280	475	5	13.65
38 Super Auto +P (b)	115	JHP	1300	431	5	14.20
38 Auto, for Colt 38 Super (c)	125	JHP	1280	475	5	14.10
38 Auto	130	MC	1040	312	4½	14.10
38 Auto +P	130	FMC	1280	475	5	13.65
380 Auto*	95	MC	955	192	3¾	12.90
380 Auto	88	JHP	990	191	4	9.70
380 Auto*	90	JHP	1000	200	3¾	12.90
38-40 Winchester	180	SP	975	380	5	21.70
41 Remington Magnum	210	Lead	1050	515	8¾	18.65
41 Remington Magnum	210	SP	1500	1050	8¾	21.85
44 S&W Special	246	Lead	755	311	6½	16.70
44 Remington Magnum*	180	JHP	1610	1045	4	19.65
44 Remington Magnum (b)	240	SP	1470	1150	6½	8.65
44 Remington Magnum	240	Lead	1470	1150	6½	21.20
44 Remington Magnum	240	SJHP	1180	741	4	8.65
44 Remington Magnum (a)	240	JPC	1533	1253	8½	13.00
44 Auto Mag (a)	240	JPC	1350	976	6½	42.50
44-40 Winchester	200	SP	975	420	7½	22.90
45 Colt*	225	SWCHP	900	405	5½	16.00
45 Colt	250	Lead	860	410	5½	16.95
45 Colt, IL (c)	255	Lub., L	860	410	5½	16.45
45 Auto (c)	185	STHP	1000	411	5	7.25
45 Auto	230	MC	850	369	5	17.30
45 ACP	230	JHP	850	370	5	18.95
45 Auto WC*	185	MC	775	245	5	17.85
45 Auto*	185	JHP	950	370	5	17.85
45 Auto MC (b)	230	MC	850	369	5	17.85
45 Auto Match (c)	185	MC	775	247	5	17.85
45 Auto Match*	230	MC	850	370	5	17.30
45 Winchester Magnum (c)	230	FMC	1400	1001	5	18.50
45 Auto Rim (b)	230	Lead	810	335	5½	18.45

IL—Inside Lub.   JSP—Jacketed Soft Point   WC—Wad Cutter
RN—Round Nose   HP—Hollow Point   Lub—Lubricated
MC—Metal Case   SP—Soft Point   MP—Metal Point
LGC—Lead, Gas Check   JHP—Jacketed Hollow Point
SWC—Semi Wad Cutter   SJHP—Semi Jacketed Hollow Point

SHOTSHELL LOADS AND PRICES

Winchester-Western, Remington-Peters, Federal

In certain loadings one manufacturer may offer fewer or more shot sizes than another, but in general all makers offer equivalent loadings. Sources are indicated by letters, thus: W-W (a); R-P (b); Fed. (c). Prices are approximate, list is a random sampling of offerings.

GAUGE	Length Shell Ins.	Powder Equiv. Drams	Shot Ozs.	Shot Size	PRICE PER BOX
MAGNUM LOADS					
10 (a¹, b)	3½	Max	2	2	$18.75
12 (a, b, c)	3	4	1⅞	BB, 2, 4	13.85
12 (a¹, b)	3	4¼	1⅝	2, 4, 6	12.80
12 (a¹)	3	Max	1⅜	2	11.60
12 (a¹, b)	2¾	Max	1½	2, 4, 5, 6	11.00
16 (a, b, c)	2¾	3¼	1¼	2, 4, 6	11.00
20 (a, b, c)	3	3	1¼	2, 4, 6, 7½	10.70
20 (a¹)	3	Max	1⅛	4, 6, 7½	9.55
20 (a¹, b, c)	2¾	2¾	1⅛	4, 6, 7½	9.55
LONG RANGE LOADS					
10 (a, b)	2⅞	Max	1⅝	4	12.30
12 (a¹, b, c)	2¾	3¾	1¼	BB, 2, 4, 5, 6, 7½, 8, 9	8.90
16 (a¹, b, c)	2¾	3¼	1⅛	4, 5, 6, 7½, 9	11.00
20 (a¹, b, c)	2¾	2¾	1	4, 5, 6, 7½, 8, 9	7.85
28 (a, b)	2¾	Max	¾	6, 7½	7.90
28 (c)	2¾	2¼	⅞	4, 6, 7½, 9	7.90
410 (b)	2½	Max	½	6, 7½	6.25
410 (b)	3	Max	11/16	4, 5, 6, 7½, 8	7.35
FIELD LOADS					
12 (a, b, c)	2¾	3¼	1¼	7½, 8, 9	8.40
12 (a, b, c)	2¾	3¼	1⅛	4, 5, 6, 7½, 8, 9	7.60
12 (a, b, c)	2¾	3	1	4, 5, 6, 8	6.60
16 (a, b, c)	2¾	2¾	1⅛	4, 5, 6, 7½, 8	7.60
16 (a, b, c)	2¾	2½	1	6, 8	6.55
20 (a, b, c)	2¾	2½	1	4, 5, 6, 7½, 8, 9	6.95
20 (a, b, c)	2¾	2½	⅞	6, 8	6.00
SCATTER LOADS					
12 (b)	2¾	3	1⅛	8	8.10
TARGET LOADS					
12 (a, b, c)	2¾	3	1⅛	7½, 8, 9	7.30
12 (a, b, c)	2¾	2¾	1⅛	7½, 8, 9	7.30
16 (a, b, c)	2¾	2¾	1⅛	8	7.10
20 (a, b, c)	2¾	2½	⅞	9	6.35
28 (a, c)	2¾	2	¾	9	7.70
410 (a, b, c)	2½	Max	½	9	6.30
SKEET & TRAP					
12 (a, b, c)	2¾	3	1⅛	7½, 8, 9	7.05
12 (a, b, c)	2¾	2¾	1⅛	7½, 8, 9	7.95
20 (a, b, c)	2¾	2½	⅞	9	6.35
BUCKSHOT					
10 (c)	3½	Sup. Mag.	—	4 Buck—54 pellets	4.25
12 (a, b, c)	3 Mag.	4½	—	00 Buck—15 pellets	3.20
12 (a, b, c)	3 Mag.	4½	—	4 Buck—41 pellets	3.20
12 (b)	2¾ Mag.	4	—	1 Buck—20 pellets	2.80
12 (a, b, c)	2¾ Mag.	4	—	00 Buck—12 pellets	2.80
12 (a, b, c)	2¾	Max	—	00 Buck— 9 pellets	2.80
12 (a, b, c)	2¾	3¾	—	0 Buck—12 pellets	2.50
12 (a, b, c)	2¾	Max	—	1 Buck—16 pellets	2.50
12 (a, b, c)	2¾	Max	—	4 Buck—27 pellets	2.50
16 (a, b, c)	2¾	3	—	1 Buck—12 pellets	2.50
20 (a, b, c)	2¾	Max.	—	3 Buck—20 pellets	2.50
RIFLED SLUGS					
12 (a, b, c)	2¾	3¾	⅞	Slug 5-pack	2.90
16 (a, b, c)	2¾	3	⅘	Slug	2.90
20 (a, b, c)	2¾	Max	⅝	Slug	2.65
410 (a, b, c)	2½	Max	⅕	Slug	2.50
STEEL SHOT LOADS					
12 (c)	3	Max	1⅜	BB, 1, 2, 4	14.95
12 (c)	2¾	3¾	1⅛	1, 2, 4	11.15
12 (a, c)	2¾	Max	1¼	1, 2, 4	13.45
12 (a)	3	Max	1½	1, 2, 4	15.50
12 (b)	3	Max	1¼	1, 2, 4	14.50
12 (b)	2¾	Max	1⅛	1, 2, 4	11.20

W-W 410, 28 and 10-ga. Magnum shells available in paper cases only, as are their scatter and target loads; their Skeet and trap loads come in both plastic and paper.
R-P shells are all of plastic with Power Piston wads except: 12 ga. scatter loads have Post Wad: all 10 ga., 410-3" and rifled slug loads have standard wad columns.
Federal magnum, range, buckshot, slug and all 410 loads are made in plastic only. Field loads are available in both paper and plastic.
[1]—These loads available from W-W with Lubaloy shot at higher price.

CAUTION: PRICES CHANGE. CHECK AT GUNSHOP.

HANDGUNS—TARGET AUTOLOADERS

BERNARDELLI MODEL 100 PISTOL
Caliber: 22 LR only, 10-shot magazine.
Barrel: 5.9".
Weight: 37¾ oz. **Length:** 9" over-all.
Stocks: Checkered walnut with thumbrest.
Sights: Fixed front, rear adj. for w. and e.
Features: Target barrel weight included. Heavy sighting rib with interchangeable front sight. Accessories include cleaning equipment and assembly tools, case. Imported from Italy by Interarms.
Price: $350.00

BERETTA MODEL 76 PISTOL
Caliber: 22 LR, 10-shot magazine.
Barrel: 6".
Weight: 33 ozs. (empty). **Length:** 8.8" over-all.
Stocks: Checkered plastic.
Sights: Interchangable blade front (3 widths), rear is fully adj. for w. and e.
Features: Built-in, fixed counterweight, raised, matted slide rib, factory adjusted trigger pull from 3 lbs. 5 ozs. to 3 lbs. 12 ozs. Thumb safety. Blue-black finish. Wood grips available at extra cost. Introduced 1977. Imported by Beretta Arms Co.
Price: With plastic grips $285.00
Price: With wood grips $320.00

BROWNING INTERNATIONAL MEDALIST
Caliber: 22 Long Rifle, 10-round magazine.
Barrel: 5¹⁵⁄₁₆".
Weight: 46¾ oz. (with counterweight). **Length:** 11¾" overall.
Stocks: Target-type; French walnut with adjustable palm rest.
Sights: Fixed, non-reflective front; rear is click-adjustable for w. and e.
Features: Target-grade pistol that meets standards of the I.S.U. Heavy barrel with sliding counterweight. Gold plated trigger is adjustable. All metal parts finished in non-reflective blue. Made by FN in Belgium. From Browning.
Price: $575.00

COLT GOLD CUP NAT'L MATCH MK IV Series 70
Caliber: 45 ACP, 7-shot magazine.
Barrel: 5", with new design bushing.
Length: 8⅜". **Weight:** 38½ oz.
Stocks: Checkered walnut, gold plated medallion.
Sights: Ramp-style front, Colt-Elliason rear adj. for w. and e., sight radius 6¾".
Features: Arched or flat housing; wide, grooved trigger with adj. stop; ribbed-top slide, hand fitted, with improved ejection port.
Price: Colt Royal Blue $399.95

DOMINO MODEL SP-602 MATCH PISTOL
Caliber: 22 LR, 5-shot.
Barrel: 5.5".
Weight: 41 oz. **Length:** 11.02" over-all.
Stocks: Full target stocks; adjustable, one-piece. Left hand style avail.
Sights: Match. Blade front, open notch rear fully adj. for w. and e. Sight radius is 8.66".
Features: Line of sight is only ¹¹⁄₃₂" above centerline of bore; magazine is inserted from top; adjustable and removable trigger mechanism; single lever takedown. Full 5 year warranty. Imported from Italy by Mandall Shooting Supplies.
Price: $899.50

DOMINO O.P. 601 MATCH PISTOL
Similar to S.P. 602 except has different match stocks with adj. palm shelf, 22 Short only, weighs 40 oz., 5.6" bbl., has gas ports through top of barrel and slide to reduce recoil, slightly different trigger and sear mechanisms.
Price: $899.50

CAUTION: PRICES CHANGE. CHECK AT GUNSHOP.

HANDGUNS—TARGET AUTOLOADERS

HAMMERLI MODEL 120-1 FREE PISTOL
Caliber: 22 LR.
Barrel: 9.9".
Weight: 44 oz. **Length:** 14¾" over-all.
Stocks: Contoured right-hand (only) thumbrest.
Sights: Fully adjustable rear, blade front. Choice of 14.56" or 9.84" sight radius.
Features: Trigger adjustable for single- or two-stage pull from 1.8 to 12 oz. Adjustable for length of pull. Guaranteed accuracy of .98", 10 shots at 50 meters. From Mandall Shooting Supplies.
Price: Model 120-1 .... $725.00
Price: Model 120-2 (same as above except has walnut target grips with adjustable palm-rest. RH or LH; illus.) $795.00

HAMMERLI MODEL 150 FREE PISTOL
Caliber: 22LR. Single shot.
Barrel: 11.3".
Weight: 43 ozs. **Length:** 15.35" over-all.
Stock: Walnut with adjustable palm shelf.
Sights: Sight radius of 14.6". Micro rear sight adj. for w. and e.
Features: Single shot Martini action. Cocking lever on left side of action with vertical operation. Set trigger adjustable for length and angle. Trigger pull weight adjustable between 5 and 100 grams. Guaranteed accuracy of .78", 10 shots from machine rest. From Mandall Shooting Supplies.
Price: $1,450.00
Price: With electric trigger $1,695.00

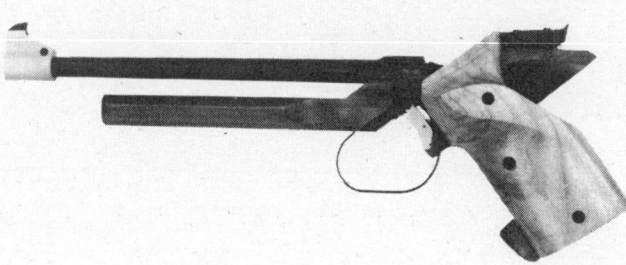

HAMMERLI STANDARD, MODELS 208 & 211
Caliber: 22 LR.
Barrel: 5.9", 6-groove.
Weight: 37.6 oz. (45 oz. with extra heavy barrel weight). **Length:** 10".
Stocks: Walnut. Adj. palm rest (208), 211 has thumbrest grip.
Sights: Match sights, fully adj. for w. and e. (click adj.). Interchangeable front and rear blades.
Features: Semi-automatic, recoil operated. 8-shot clip. Slide stop. Fully adj. trigger (2¼ lbs. and 3 lbs.). Extra barrel weight available. Mandall Shooting Supplies, importer.
Price: Model 208, approx. .$1,095.00   Model 211 approx. $1,025.00

HAMMERLI MODEL 230 RAPID FIRE PISTOL
Caliber: 22 Short.
Barrel: 6.3", 6-groove.
Weight: 43.8 oz. **Length:** 11.6".
Stocks: Walnut.
Sights: Match type sights. Sight radius 9.9". Micro rear, click adj. Interchangeable front sight blade.
Features: Semi-automatic. Recoil-operated, 6-shot clip. Gas escape in front of chamber to eliminate muzzle jump. Fully adj. trigger from 5¼ oz. to 10½ oz. with three different lengths available. Designed for International 25 meter Silhouette Program. Mandall Shooting Supplies, importer.
Price: Model 230-1 .... $1,025.00
Price: Model 230-2 .... $1,095.00

HI-STANDARD SUPERMATIC CITATION MILITARY
Caliber: 22 LR, 10-shot magazine.
Barrel: 5½" bull, 7¼" fluted.
Length: 9¾" (5½" bbl.). **Weight:** 46 oz.
Stocks: Checkered walnut with thumbrest.
Sights: Undercut ramp front; frame mounted rear, click adj.
Features: Adjustable trigger pull; over-travel trigger adjustment; double acting safety; rebounding firing pin; military style grip; stippled front- and back-straps; positive magazine latch.
Price: 5½" barrel $262.35
Price: 7¼" barrel $278.85

HI-STANDARD SUPERMATIC TROPHY MILITARY
Caliber: 22 LR, 10-shot magazine.
Barrel: 5½" bull, 7¼" fluted.
Length: 9¾" (5½" bbl.). **Weight:** 44½ oz.
Stocks: Checkered walnut with thumbrest.
Features: Grip duplicates feel of military 45; positive action mag. latch; front- and backstraps stippled. Trigger adj. for pull, over-travel.
Sights: Undercut ramp front; frame mounted rear, click adj.
Price: 5½" barrel $278.85
Price: 7¼" barrel $296.45

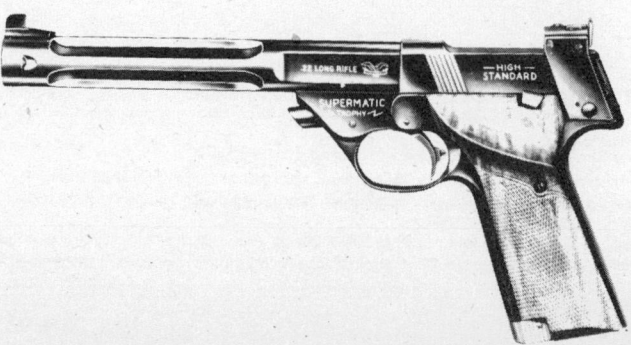

HANDGUNS—TARGET AUTOLOADERS

HI-STANDARD VICTOR
Caliber: 22 LR, 10-shot magazine.
Barrel: 5½".
Length: 9⅝" over-all. **Weight:** 47 oz.
Stocks: Checkered walnut with thumb rest.
Sights: Undercut ramp front, rib mounted click adj. rear.
Features: Vent. rib, interchangeable barrel, 2 - 2¼ lb. trigger pull, blue finish, back and front straps stippled.
Price: $319.00

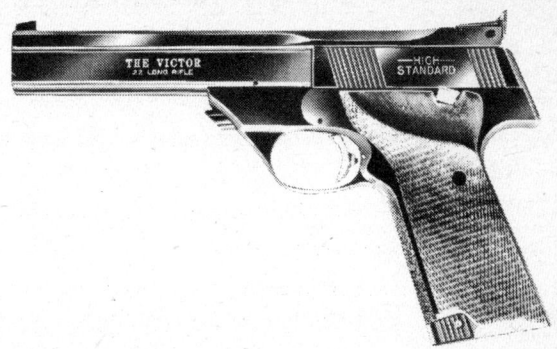

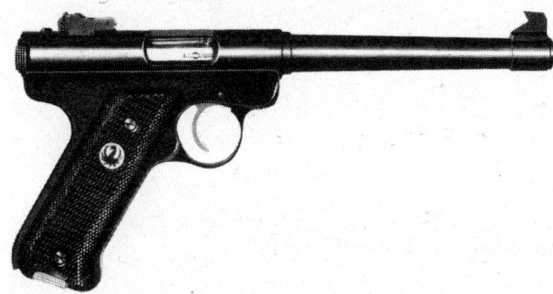

RUGER Mark 1 TARGET MODEL AUTO PISTOL
Caliber: 22 LR only, 9-shot magazine.
Barrel: 6⅞" or 5½" bull barrel (6-groove, 14" twist).
Length: 10⅞" (6⅞" bbl.). **Weight:** 42 oz. with 6⅞" bbl.
Stocks: Checkered hard rubber.
Features: Rear sight mounted on receiver, does not move with slide; wide, grooved trigger.
Sights: ⅛" blade front, micro click rear, adjustable for w. and e. Sight radius 9⅜" (with 6⅞" bbl.).
Price: Blued, either barrel length $140.00

SIG/HAMMERLI P-240 TARGET PISTOL
Caliber: 32 S&W Long.
Barrel: 6".
Weight: 4¼ oz. **Length:** 10" over-all.
Stocks: Walnut, target style, unfinished.
Sights: Match sights; ⅛" undercut front, ⅛" notch micro rear click adj. for w. and e.
Features: Semi-automatic, recoil operated; meets I.S.U. and N.R.A. specs for Center Fire Pistol competition; double pull trigger adj. from 2 lbs., 15 ozs. to 3 lbs., 9 ozs.; trigger stop. Comes with extra magazine, special screwdriver, carrying case. From Mandall Shooting Supplies.
Price: $1,450.00
Price: 22 cal. conversion unit $750.00

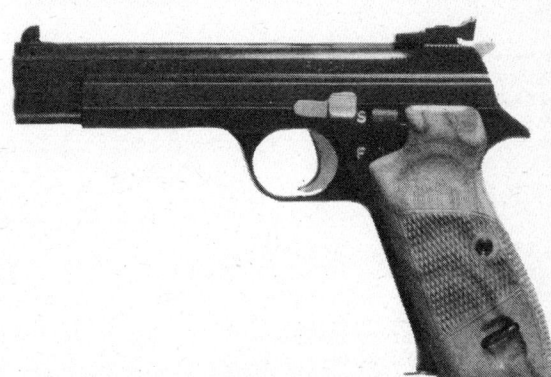

SIG P-210-6 AUTO PISTOL
Caliber: 9mm Para., 8-shot magazine.
Barrel: 4¾".
Weight: 37 oz. **Length:** 8½" over-all.
Stocks: Checkered black plastic.
Sights: Blade front, micro. adj. rear for w. & e.
Features: Adjustable trigger stop; ribbed front stap; sandblasted finish. Conversion unit for 22 LR consists of barrel, recoil spring, slide and magazine. Imported by Mandall Shooting Supplies.
Price: P-210-6 .... $1,450.00
Price: 22 Cal. Conversion unit $650.00

SIG P-210-1 AUTO PISTOL
Caliber: 22 LR, 7.65mm or 9mm P., 8-shot magazine.
Barrel: 4¾".
Weight: 31¾ oz. (9mm) **Length:** 8½" over-all.
Stocks: Checkered walnut.
Sights: Blade front, rear adjustable for windage.
Features: Lanyard loop; polished finish. Conversion unit for 22 LR available. Imported by Mandall Shooting Supplies.
Price: P-210-1 .... $1,450.00
Price: 22 Cal. Conversion unit $650.00

SMITH & WESSON 22 AUTO PISTOL Model 41
Caliber: 22 LR or 22 S, 10-shot clip.
Barrel: 7⅜", sight radius 9 5/16" (7⅜" bbl.).
Length: 12", incl. detachable muzzle brake, (7⅜" bbl. only).
Weight: 43½ oz. (7⅜" bbl.).
Stocks: Checkered walnut with thumbrest, usable with either hand.
Features: ⅜" wide, grooved trigger with adj. stop; wgts. available to make pistol up to 59 oz.
Sights: Front, ⅛" Patridge undercut; micro click rear adj. for w. and e.
Price: S&W Bright Blue, satin matted bbl., either caliber $294.00

HANDGUNS—TARGET AUTOLOADERS

SMITH & WESSON 22 MATCH HEAVY BARREL M-41
Caliber: 22 LR, 10-shot clip.
Barrel: 5½" heavy, without muzzle brake. Sight radius, 8".
Length: 9". **Weight:** 44½ oz.
Stocks: Checkered walnut with modified thumbrest, usable with either hand.
Features: ⅜" wide, grooved trigger; adj. trigger stop.
Sights: ⅛" Patridge on ramp base. S&W micro click rear, adj. for w. and e.
Price: S&W Bright Blue, satin matted top area $294.00

SMITH & WESSON 38 MASTER Model 52 AUTO
Caliber: 38 Special (for Mid-range W.C. with flush-seated bullet only). 5-shot magazine.
Barrel: 5".
Length: 8⅝". **Weight:** 41 oz. with empty magazine.
Stocks: Checkered walnut.
Sights: ⅛" Partidge front, S&W micro click rear adj. for w. and e.
Features: Top sighting surfaces matte finished. Locked breech, moving barrel system; checked for 10-ring groups at 50 yards. Coin-adj. sight screws. Dry firing permissible if manual safety on.
Price: S&W Bright Blue $471.00

UNIQUE D.E.S. 69 TARGET PISTOL
Caliber: 22 LR.
Barrel: 5.91".
Weight: Approx. 35 oz. **Length:** 10.63" over-all.
Stocks: French walnut target style with thumbrest and adjustable shelf; hand checkered panels.
Sights: Ramp front, micro. adj. rear mounted on frame; 8.66" sight radius.
Features: Meets U.I.T. standards. Comes in a fitted hard case with spare magazine, barrel weight, cleaning rod, tools, proof certificate, test target and two year guarantee. Fully adjustable trigger; dry firing safety device. Imported from France by Solersport.
Price: Right-hand $675.00
Price: Left-hand $705.00

UNIQUE DES VO 79 TARGET PISTOL
Caliber: 22 Short.
Barrel: 5.85", Four gas escape ports, one threaded with plug.
Weight: 44 oz.
Stocks: French walnut, target style with thumb rest and adj. palm shelf. Hand stippled.
Sights: Low, .12" front, fully adj. rear.
Features: Meets all UIT standards; virtually recoil free. Four-way adj. trigger; dry-firing device, all aluminum frame. Cleaning rod, tools, extra magazine, proof certificate and fitted case. Imported from France by Solersport.
Price: Right hand $675.00
Price: Left hand $705.00

WALTHER GSP MATCH PISTOL
Caliber: 22 LR, 32 S&W wadcutter (GSP-C), 5-shot.
Barrel: 5¾".
Weight: 44.8 oz. (22 LR), 49.4 oz. (32). **Length:** 11.8" over-all.
Stock: Walnut, special hand-fitting design.
Sights: Fixed front, rear adj. for w. & e.
Features: Available with either 2.2 lb. (1000 gm) or 3 lb. (1360 gm) trigger. Spare mag., bbl. weight, tools supplied in Match Pistol Kit. Imported from Germany by Interarms.
Price: GSP $1,100.00
Price: GSP-C $1,250.00
Price: 22 LR conversion unit for GSP-C $700.00
Price: 22 Short conversion unit for GSP-C $750.00

WALTHER OSP RAPID-FIRE PISTOL
Similar to Model GSP except 22 Short only, stock has adj. free-style hand rest.
Price: $1,100.00

272   THE GUN DIGEST

HANDGUNS—TARGET REVOLVERS

COLT PYTHON REVOLVER
Caliber: 357 Magnum (handles all 38 Spec.), 6 shot.
Barrel: 2½", 4", 6" or 8", with ventilated rib.
Length: 9¼"(4" bbl.). **Weight:** 38 oz. (4" bbl.).
Stocks: Checkered walnut, target type.
Sights: ⅛" ramp front, adj. notch rear.
Features: Ventilated rib; grooved, crisp trigger; swing-out cylinder; target hammer.
Price: Colt Blue, 2½" ...... **$444.50**   Nickeled, 4" **$473.50**
Price: 4" .... **$454.50**   6" **$475.50**
Price: 6" .... **$461.50**   8" **$485.50**
Price: 8" **$471.50**

SMITH & WESSON MASTERPIECE TARGET MODELS
Model: K-22 (M17).   K-22 (M48).
Caliber: 22 LR, 6 shot.   22 RF Magnum, 6 shot.
Barrel: 6", 8⅜".   4", 6" or 8⅜"
Length: 11⅛" (6" bbl.).   11⅛" (6" bbl.).
Weight: 38½ oz. (6" bbl.).   39 oz.(6" bbl.).
Model: K-32 (M16). (Illus.)   K-38 (M14).
Caliber: 32 S&W Long, 6 shot.   38 S&W Special, 6 shot.
Barrel: 6".   6", 8⅜".
Length: 11⅛".   11⅛". (6" bbl.)
Weight: 38½ oz. (loaded).   38½ oz. (6", loaded).
Features: All Masterpiece models have: checkered walnut, Magna stocks; grooved tang and trigger; ⅛" Patridge front sight, micro. adj. rear sights. Swing out cylinder revolver. For 8⅜" barrel add **$10.00**; for M-17, **$11.00** for M-48.
Price: Blued, all calibers M-17, 6" bbl. **$222.50**
Price: Blued, all calibers M-48, 4", 6" bbl. **$237.00**

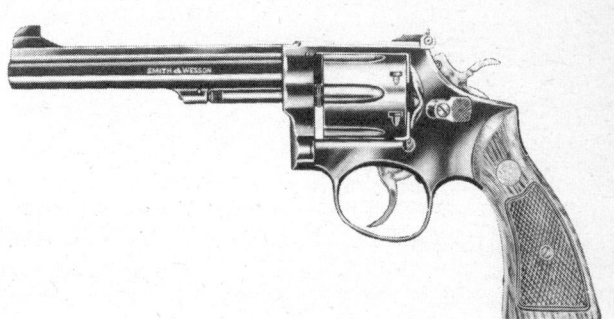

SMITH & WESSON COMBAT MASTERPIECE
Caliber: 38 Special (M15) or 22 LR (M18), 6 shot.
Barrel: 2" or 4" (M15) 4" (M18)
Length: 9⅛" (4" bbl.). **Weight:** Loaded, 22 36½ oz, 38 30 oz.
Stocks: Checkered walnut, Magna. Grooved tangs and trigger.
Sights: Front, ⅛" Baugham Quick Draw on ramp, micro click rear, adjustable for w. and e.
Price: Blued, M-15 .... **$169.50**
Price: Nickel M-15 .... **$182.50**
Price: Blued, M-18 .... **$205.00**

SMITH & WESSON 1955 Model 25, 45 TARGET
Caliber: 45 ACP and 45 AR, 6 shot.
Barrel: 6" (heavy target type).
Length: 11⅞". **Weight:** 45 oz.
Stocks: Checkered walnut target.
Sights: ⅛" Patridge front, micro click rear, adjustable for w. and e.
Features: Tangs and trigger grooved; target trigger and hammer standard, checkered target hammer. Swing-out cylinder revolver. Price includes presentation case.
Price: Blued **$356.00**

Smith & Wesson Accessories
Target hammers with low, broad, deeply-checkered spur, and wide-swaged, grooved target trigger. For all frame sizes, **$8.50** (target hammers not available for small frames). Target stocks: for large-frame guns, **$16.90** to **$19.00**; for med.-frame guns, **$14.25** to **$17.20**; for small-frame guns, **$12.65** to **$16.60**. These prices applicable only when specified on original order.
As separately-ordered parts: target hammers **$18.00** and triggers, **$15.42**; stocks, **$19.60** to **$25.35**.

> Consult our Directory pages for the location of firms mentioned.

TAURUS MODEL 86 TARGET MASTER REVOLVER
Caliber: 38 Spec., 6-shot.
Barrel: 6" only.
Weight: 41 oz. **Length:** 11¼" over-all.
Stocks: Over size target-type, checkered Brazilian walnut.
Sights: Patridge front, micro. click rear adj. for w. and e.
Features: Blue finish with non-reflective finish on barrel. Imported from Brazil by International Distributors.
Price: About **$156.00**
Price: Model 96 Scout Master, same except in 22 cal, about **$156.00**

HANDGUNS—AUTOLOADERS, SERVICE & SPORT

AMERICAN ARMS TP-70
Caliber: 22 LR, 25 ACP
Barrel: 2.6"
Weight: 12.6 oz. **Length:** 4.72" over-all.
Stocks: Checkered, composition.
Sights: Open, fixed.
Features: Double action, stainless steel. Exposed hammer. Manual and magazine safeties. The 22 cal. version will be available late 1980. From M & N Distributors.
Price: 25 ACP, about $180.00
Price: 22 LR, about $200.00

AMT 45 ACP HARDBALLER
Caliber: 45 ACP.
Barrel: 5".
Weight: 39 oz. **Length:** 8½" over-all.
Stocks: Checkered walnut.
Sights: Adjustable combat-type.
Features: Extended combat safety, serrated matte slide rib, loaded chamber indicator, long grip safety, beveled magazine well, grooved front and back straps, adjustable target trigger, custom-fitted barrel bushing. All stainless steel. From AMT.
Price: $450.00
Price: 45 Skipper (as above except 1" shorter) $450.00

AMT 45 ACP HARDBALLER LONG SLIDE
Caliber: 45 ACP.
Barrel: 7".
Length: 10½" over-all.
Stocks: Checkered walnut.
Sights: Fully adjustable Micro rear sight.
Features: Slide and barrel are 2" longer than the standard 45, giving less recoil, added velocity, longer sight radius. Has extended combat safety, serrated matte rib, loaded chamber indicator, wide adjustable trigger, custom fitted barrel bushing. From AMT.
Price: About $595.00

AMT COMBAT GOVERNMENT
Caliber: 45 ACP.
Barrel: 5".
Weight: 38 oz. **Length:** 8½" over-all.
Stocks: Checkered walnut, diamond pattern.
Sights: Combat-style, fixed.
Features: All stainless steel; extended combat safety, loaded chamber indicator, beveled magazine well, adjustable target-type trigger, custom-fitted barrel bushing, flat mainspring housing. From AMT.
Price: $395.00

ASTRA CONSTABLE AUTO PISTOL
Caliber: 22 LR, 10-shot; 32 ACP, 8-shot; and 380 ACP, 7-shot.
Barrel: 3½".
Weight: 26 oz.
Stocks: Moulded plastic.
Sights: Adj. rear.
Features: Double action, quick no-tool takedown, non-glare rib on slide. 380 available in blue or chrome finish. Imported from Spain by Interarms.
Price: Blue $300.00
Price: Chrome $325.00

BAUER AUTOMATIC PISTOL
Caliber: 25 ACP, 6-shot.
Barrel: 2⅛".
Weight: 10 oz. **Length:** 4".
Stocks: Plastic pearl or checkered walnut.
Sights: Recessed, fixed.
Features: Stainless steel construction, positive manual safety, magazine safety.
Price: Satin stainless steel, 25ACP $117.00

BERNARDELLI MODEL 80 AUTO PISTOL
Caliber: 22 LR (10-shot); 32 ACP (8-shot); 380 ACP (7-shot).
Barrel: 3½".
Weight: 26½ oz. **Length:** 6½" over-all.
Stocks: Checkered plastic with thumbrest.
Sights: Ramp front, white outline rear adj. for w. & e.
Features: Hammer block slide safety; loaded chamber indicator; dual recoil buffer springs; serrated trigger; inertia type firing pin. Imported from Italy by Interarms.
Price: Model 80 .... $200.00

Bernardelli Model 100 Target Pistol
Similar to Model 80 except has 5.9" barrel and barrel weight; heavy sighting rib; checkered walnut thumbrest grips; 22 LR only (10-shot). Comes with case, cleaning equipment and tools. $350.00

HANDGUNS — AUTOLOADERS, SERVICE & SPORT

BERETTA MODEL 92 DA PISTOL
Caliber: 9mm Parabellum (15-shot magazine).
Barrel: 4.92".
Weight: 33½ ozs. **Length:** 8.54" over-all.
Stocks: Smooth black plastic.
Sights: Blade front, rear adj. for w.
Features: Double-action. Extractor acts as chamber loaded indicator, inertia firing pin. Finished in blue-black. Introduced 1977. Imported by Beretta Arms Co.
Price: $470.00
Price: With wood grips $495.00

BERETTA MODEL 70S PISTOL
Caliber: 22 LR, 380 ACP.
Barrel: 3.5".
Weight: 23 ozs. (Steel) **Length:** 6.5" over-all.
Stocks: Checkered black plastic.
Sights: Fixed front and rear.
Features: Steel frame in 32 and 380, light alloy in 22 (wgt. 18 ozs.). Safety lever blocks hammer. Side lever indicates empty magazine. Magazine capacity is 8 rounds (22), 7 rounds in 380. Introduced 1977. Imported by Beretta Arms Co.
Price: $235.00

Browning Louis XVI Hi-Power 9mm Auto
Same as Browning Hi-Power 9mm Auto except: fully engraved, silver-gray frame and slide, gold plated trigger, finely checkered walnut grips, with deluxe walnut case.
Price: With adj. sights $1,250.00
Price: With fixed sights $1,200.00

BERETTA MODEL 81/84 DA PISTOLS
Caliber: 32 ACP (12-shot magazine), 380 ACP (13-shot magazine)
Barrel: 3¾".
Weight: About 23 oz. **Length:** 6½" over-all.
Stocks: Smooth black plastic (wood optional at extra cost).
Sights: Fixed front and rear.
Features: Double action, quick take-down, convenient magazine release. Introduced 1977. Imported by Beretta Arms. Co.
Price: M-81 (32 ACP) $335.00
Price: M-84 (380 ACP) $335.00
Price: Either model with wood grips $355.00
Price: M-82B, 8-shot 32 ACP $299.00
Price: M-85B, 8-shot 380 ACP $299.00

BERSA MODEL 644 AUTO PISTOL
Caliber: 22 Long Rifle, 10-shot magazine.
Barrel: 3½".
Weight: 26½ oz. **Length:** 6½" over-all.
Stocks: Contoured black nylon.
Sights: Blade front, rear drift-adj. for windage.
Features: Has three safety devices: firing pin safety, hammer safety and magazine safety. Button release magazine with finger rest. Introduced 1980. Imported from Argentina by Interarms.
Price: $175.00

BROWNING BDA-380 D/A AUTO PISTOL
Caliber: 380 ACP, 12-shot magazine.
Barrel: 3¹³⁄₁₆".
Weight: 23 ozs. **Length:** 6¾" over-all.
Stocks: Smooth walnut with inset Browning medallion.
Sights: Blade front, rear drift-adj. for w.
Features: Combination safety and de-cocking lever will automatically lower a cocked hammer to half-cock and can be operated by right or left-hand shooters. Inertia firing pin. Introduced 1978.
Price: $314.95

BROWNING HI-POWER 9mm AUTOMATIC PISTOL
Caliber: 9mm Parabellum (Luger), 13-shot magazine.
Barrel: 4²¹⁄₃₂ inches.
Length: 7¾" over-all. **Weight:** 32 oz.
Stocks: Walnut, hand checkered.
Sights: ⅛" blade front; rear screw-adj. for w. and e. Also available with fixed rear (drift-adj. for w.).
Features: External hammer with half-cock and thumb safeties. A blow on the hammer cannot discharge a cartridge; cannot be fired with magazine removed. Fixed rear sight model available.
Price: Fixed sight model $409.95
Price: 9mm with rear sight adj. for w. and e. ... $449.00
Price: Nickel plated, fixed sight $469.95

HANDGUNS — AUTOLOADERS, SERVICE & SPORT

BROWNING BDA AUTO PISTOL
Caliber: 45 ACP only (7-shot).
Barrel: 4¹³⁄₃₂".
Weight: 29 ozs. (9mm) **Length:** 7²⁵⁄₃₂" over-all.
Stocks: Checkered black plastic
Sights: Blade front, drift adj. rear of w.
Features: Double action. De-cocking lever permits lowering hammer onto locked firing pin. Squared combat-type trigger guard. Slide stays open after last shot. Introduced 1977. Imported by Browning.
Price: 45 ACP $349.95

BROWNING CHALLENGER II AUTO PISTOL
Caliber: 22 LR, 10-shot magazine.
Barrel: 6¾".
Weight: 38 oz. **Length:** 10⅞" over-all.
Stocks: Smooth impregnated hardwood.
Sights: ⅛" blade front on ramp, rear screw adj. for e., drift adj. for w.
Features: All steel, blue finish. Wedge locking system prevents action from loosening. Wide gold-plated trigger; action hold-open. Standard grade only. From Browning.
Price: $199.95

CHARTER EXPLORER II PISTOL
Caliber: 22 LR, 8-shot magazine.
Barrel: 8".
Weight: 28 oz. **Length:** 15½" over-all.
Stocks: Serrated simulated walnut.
Sights: Blade front, open rear adj. for elevation.
Features: Action adapted from the semi-auto Explorer carbine. Introduced 1980. From Charter Arms.
Price: .... NA

COONAN ARMS 357 AUTO PISTOL
Caliber: 357 Mag., 7-shot magazine
Barrel: 5".
Weight: 40 oz. **Length:** 8.3" over-all.
Stocks: Smooth walnut.
Sights: Serrated blade front, low profile open rear.
Features: All stainless steel. Non-glare finish on slide top. Design follows that of the Colt autos. Introduced 1980. From Coonan Arms.
Price: $450.00

COLT SERVICE MODEL ACE
Caliber: 22 LR, 10-shot magazine.
Barrel: 5".
Weight: 42 ozs. **Length:** 8⅜" over-all.
Stocks: Checkered walnut.
Sights: Blade front, fully adjustable rear.
Features: The 22-cal. version of the Government Model auto. Based on the Service Model Ace last produced in 1945. Patented floating chamber. Original Ace Markings rolled on left side of slide. Introduced 1978.
Price: Blue only $324.95

COLT GOV'T MODEL MK IV/SERIES 70
Caliber: 9mm, 38 Super, 45 ACP, 7-shot.
Barrel: 5".
Weight: 40 oz. **Length:** 8⅜" over-all.
Stocks: Sandblasted walnut panels.
Sights: Ramp front, fixed square notch rear.
Features: Grip and thumb safeties, grooved trigger. Accurizor barrel and bushing. Blue finish or nickel in 45 only.
Price: Blue $299.95
Price: Nickel $319.50

Colt Conversion Unit
Permits the 45 and 38 Super Automatic pistols to use the economical 22 LR cartridge. No tools needed. Adjustable rear sight; 10-shot magazine. Designed to give recoil effect of the larger calibers. Not adaptable to Commander models. Blue finish $174.95

COLT COMMANDER AUTO PISTOL
Caliber: 45 ACP, 7 shot; 38 Super Auto, 9 shot; 9mm Luger, 9 shot.
Barrel: 4¼".
Length: 8". **Weight:** 36 oz.
Stocks: Sandblasted walnut.
Sights: Fixed, glare-proofed blade front, square notch rear.
Features: Grooved trigger and hammer spur; arched housing; grip and thumb safeties.
Price: Blued $299.95

Colt Lightweight Combat Commander
Same as Commander except high strength aluminum alloy frame, wood panel grips, weight 27 oz. 45 ACP only.
Price: Blue $295.50

HANDGUNS—AUTOLOADERS, SERVICE & SPORT

DETONICS 45 PISTOL
Caliber: 45 ACP, 6-shot clip.
Barrel: 3¼" (2½" of which is rifled).
Weight: 29 ozs. (empty). **Length:** 6¾" over-all, 4½" high.
Stocks: Checkered walnut.
Sights: Combat type, fixed; adj. sights avail.
Features: Has a self-adjusting cone barrel centering system, beveled magazine inlet, "full clip" indicator in base of magazine; standard 7-shot (or more) clip can be used. Throated barrel and polished feed ramp. Introduced 1977. From Detonics.
Price: Blue $369.00
Price: Nickel $390.00
Price: Hardchrome $488.00
Price: Polished blue with adj. sights $499.00
Price: Stainless steel $579.00

ERMA KGP22 AUTO PISTOL
Caliber: 22 LR, 8-shot magazine.
Barrel: 4".
Weight: 29 ozs. **Length:** 7¾" over-all.
Stocks: Checkered plastic.
Sights: Fixed.
Features: Has toggle action similar to original "Luger" pistol. Slide stays open after last shot. Imported from West Germany by Excam. Introduced 1978.
Price: $178.00

ERMA KGP32, KGP38 AUTO PISTOLS
Caliber: 32 ACP (6-shot), 380 ACP (5-shot).
Barrel: 4".
Weight: 22½ ozs. **Length:** 7⅜" over-all.
Stocks: Checkered plastic. Wood optional.
Sights: Rear adjustable for windage.
Features: Toggle action similar to original "Luger" pistol. Slide stays open after last shot. Has magazine and sear disconnect safety systems. Imported from West Germany by Excam. Introduced 1978.
Price: Plastic grips $215.00

ERMA-EXCAM RX 22 AUTO PISTOL
Caliber: 22 LR, 8-shot magazine.
Barrel: 3¼".
Weight: 21 ozs. **Length:** 5.58" over-all.
Stocks: Plastic wrap-around.
Sights: Fixed.
Features: Polished blue finish. Double action. Patented ignition safety system. Thumb safety. Assembled in U.S. Introduced 1980. From Excam.
Price: $155.00

F.I.E. "THE BEST" A27B PISTOL
Caliber: 25 ACP, 6-shot magazine.
Barrel: 2½".
Weight: 13 ozs. **Length:** 4⅜" over-all.
Stocks: Checkered walnut.
Sights: Fixed.
Features: All steel construction. Has thumb and magazine safeties, exposed hammer. Blue finish only. Introduced 1978. From F.I.E. Corp.
Price: $109.95

> Consult our Directory pages for the location of firms mentioned.

F.I.E. TITAN II E32, E380 PISTOLS
Caliber: 32 ACP, 380 ACP, 6-shot magazine.
Barrel: 3⅞".
Weight: 25¾ ozs. **Length:** 4" over-all.
Stocks: Checkered nylon, thumbrest-type.
Sights: Fixed.
Features: Magazine disconnector, firing pin block. Standard slide safety, available in blue or chrome. Introduced 1978. From F.I.E. Corp.
Price: 32, blue $95.95
Price: 32, chrome $99.95
Price: 380, blue $109.95
Price: 380, chrome $114.95

F.I.E. TITAN 25 PISTOL
Caliber: 25 ACP, 6-shot magazine.
Barrel: 2⁷⁄₁₆".
Length: 4⅝" over-all. **Weight:** 12 oz.
Stocks: Checkered nylon.
Sights: Fixed.
Features: External hammer; fast simple takedown. Made in U.S.A. by F.I.E. Corp.
Price: Blued .... $49.95   Chromed $59.95

CAUTION: PRICES CHANGE. CHECK AT GUNSHOP.

HANDGUNS — AUTOLOADERS, SERVICE & SPORT

FTL 22 AUTO NINE PISTOL
Caliber: 22 LR, 8-shot magazine.
Barrel: 2¼", 6-groove rifling.
Weight: 8¼ oz. **Length:** 4⅜" over-all.
Stocks: Checkered plastic.
Sights: U-notch in slide.
Features: Alloy frame, rest is ordnance steel. Has barrel support sleeve bushing for better accuracy. Finish is matte hard chrome. Introduced 1978. From FTL Marketing.
Price: $199.95

HK P9S DOUBLE ACTION AUTO PISTOL
Caliber: 9mm Para., 9-shot magazine.
Barrel: 4".
Weight: 33½ oz. **Length:** 5½" over-all.
Stocks: Checkered black plastic.
Sights: Open combat type.
Features: Double action; polygonal rifling; sliding roller lock action with stationary barrel. Loaded chamber and cocking indicators; un-cocking lever relaxes springs. Imported from Germany by Heckler & Koch, Inc.
Price: P-9S Combat Model $519.00
Price: P-9S Target Model $591.00

HECKLER & KOCH HK-4 DOUBLE ACTION PISTOL
Caliber: 22 LR, 25 ACP, 32 ACP, 380 ACP, 8-shot magazine (7 in 380).
Barrel: 3¹¹⁄₃₂".
Weight: 16½ oz. **Length:** 6³⁄₁₆" over-all.
Stocks: Black checkered plastic.
Sights: Fixed blade front, rear notched drift-adj. for w.
Features: Gun comes with all parts to shoot above four calibers; polygonal (hexagon) rifling; matte black finish. Imported by Heckler & Koch, Inc.
Price: HK-4 380 with 22 conversion kit $376.00
Price: HK-4 in 380 only $348.00
Price: HK-4 in four cals. $477.00
Price: Conversion units 22, 25 or 32 cal., each $87.00

HECKLER & KOCH P9S DOUBLE ACTION 45
Caliber: 45 ACP, 7-shot magazine.
Barrel: 4¹⁄₃₂".
Weight: 32½ oz. **Length:** 7½" over-all.
Stocks: Checkered black plastic.
Sights: Open, combat type.
Features: Double action; polygonal rifling; delayed roller-locked bolt system. Imported by Heckler & Koch, Inc.
Price: $519.00
Price: With adj. trigger, trigger stop, adj. rear sight $591.00

HI-STANDARD SHARPSHOOTER AUTO PISTOL
Caliber: 22 LR, 10-shot magazine.
Barrel: 5½".
Length: 10¼" over-all. **Weight:** 42 oz.
Stocks: Checkered walnut with thumb rest.
Sights: Fixed, ramp front, square notch rear adj. for w. & e.
Features: Military frame. Wide, scored trigger; new hammer-sear design. Slide lock, push-button take down.
Price: Blued $232.10

IVER JOHNSON MODEL X300 PONY
Caliber: 380 ACP, 6-shot magazine.
Barrel: 3".
Weight: 20 oz. **Length:** 6" over-all.
Stocks: Checkered walnut.
Sights: Blade front, rear adj. for w.
Features: Loaded chamber indicator, all steel construction. Inertia firing pin. Thumb safety locks hammer. No magazine safety. Lanyard ring. From Iver Johnson's.
Price: Blue $170.00
Price: Nickel $180.25
Price: Military (matte finish) $170.00

HECKLER & KOCH VP '7OZ DOUBLE ACTION AUTO
Caliber: 9mm Para., 18-shot magazine
Barrel: 4½".
Weight: 32½ oz. **Length:** 8" over-all.
Stocks: Black stippled plastic.
Sights: Ramp front, channeled slide rear.
Features: Recoil operated, double action. Only 4 moving parts. Double column magazine. Imported by Heckler & Koch, Inc.
Price: $345.00

HANDGUNS—AUTOLOADERS, SERVICE & SPORT

L.E.S P-18 AUTO PISTOL
Caliber: 9mm Parabellum, 30 Luger, 18-shot magazine; 45 ACP, 10-shot.
Barrel: 5½", stationary; polygonal rifling.
Weight: About 36 oz.
Stocks: Checkered resin.
Sights: Post front, V-notch rear drift adj. for w.
Features: Gas-assisted action; all stainless steel; inertia firing pin Made in U.S.A. Both single and double action models offered, in two finish grades. From L.E.S.
Price: Std. D.A. (matte finish) 9mm or 45 .... $299.95
Price: Deluxe D.A. (polished) 9mm or 45 .... $389.95
Price: Std. DA, 30 Luger $339.95
Price: Std. S.A. (matte finish) 9mm or 45 .... $279.95
Price: Deluxe S.A. (polished) 9mm or 45 .... $369.95
Price: Std. SA, 30 Luger $319.95

LLAMA 9mm LARGE FRAME AUTO PISTOL
Caliber: 9mm Para.
Barrel: 5".
Weight: 38 oz. **Length:** 8½".
Stocks: Moulded plastic.
Sights: Fixed front, adj. rear.
Features: Also available with engraved, chrome engraved or gold damascened finish at extra cost. Imported from Spain by Stoeger Industries.
Price: Blue only $316.95

LLAMA LARGE FRAME AUTO PISTOLS
Caliber: Super 38, 45 ACP.
Barrel: 5".
Weight: 30 oz. **Length:** 8½".
Stocks: Checkered walnut.
Sights: Fixed.
Features: Grip and manual safeties, ventilated rib. Engraved, chrome engraved or gold damascened finish available at extra cost. Imported from Spain by Stoeger Industries.
Price: Blue $316.95
Price: Satin chrome, 45 only $369.95
Price: Blue, engraved, 45 only $379.95
Price: Satin chrome, engraved, 45 only $399.95

LLAMA SMALL FRAME AUTO PISTOLS
Caliber: 22 LR, 32 ACP and 380.
Barrel: 3^{11}/₁₆".
Weight: 23 oz. **Length:** 6½".
Stocks: Checkered plastic, thumb rest.
Sights: Fixed front, adj. notch rear.
Features: Ventilated rib, manual and grip safeties. Model XV is 22 LR, Model XA is 32 ACP, and Model IIIA is 380. Models XA and IIIA have loaded indicator; IIIA is locked breech. Imported from Spain by Stoeger Industries.
Price: Blue $244.95
Price: Satin chrome, 22 & 32 only $299.95
Price: Blue, engraved, 380 only $309.95
Price: Gold damascened, 380 only $1,500.00

NAVY ARMS "MAMBA" PISTOL
Caliber: 9mm Parabellum, 15-shot magazine.
Barrel: 5".
Weight: 42 ozs. **Length:** 8.58" over-all.
Stocks: Hard, checkered composition
Sights: Ramped front, rear drift-adjustable for windage.
Features: Double action. Made of stainless steel with matte finish. Ambextrous safety. Squared, combat-type trigger guard. Introduced 1979. From Navy Arms.
Price: $325.00

HANDGUNS—AUTOLOADERS, SERVICE & SPORT

RG 26 AUTO PISTOL
Caliber: 25 ACP, 6-shot magazine.
Barrel: 2½".
Weight: 12 ozs. **Length:** 4¾" over-all.
Stocks: Checkered plastic.
Sights: Fixed.
Features: Blue finish. Thumb safety. Imported by RG Industries.
Price: $49.95

RAVEN P-25 AUTO PISTOL
Caliber: 25 ACP.
Barrel: 3".
Weight: 12 oz.
Stocks: Smooth walnut or Pearl-O-Lite.
Sights: Ramped front, fixed rear.
Features: Available in blue, nickel or satin nickel finish. From EMF Co.
Price: $55.95

RUGER STANDARD MODEL AUTO PISTOL
Caliber: 22 LR, 9-shot magazine.
Barrel: 4¾" or 6".
Length: 8¾" (4¾" bbl.). **Weight:** 36 oz. (4¾" bbl.).
Stocks: Checkered hard rubber.
Sights: Fixed, wide blade front, square notch rear adj. for w.
Price: Blued $109.00

SILE-BENELLI B76 DA AUTO PISTOL
Caliber: 9mm Para., 8-shot magazine.
Barrel: 4¼", 6-groove. Chrome-lined bore.
Weight: 34 oz. (empty). **Length:** 8 1/16" over-all.
Stocks: Walnut with cut checkering and high gloss finish.
Sights: Blade front with white face, rear adjustable for windage with white bars for increased visibility.
Features: Fixed barrel, locked breech. Exposed hammer can be locked in non-firing mode in either single or double action. Stainless steel inertia firing pin and loaded chamber indicator. All external parts blued, internal parts hard-chrome plated. All steel construction. Introduced 1979. From Sile Dist.
Price: $349.95

SILE-SEECAMP II STAINLESS DA AUTO
Caliber: 25 ACP, 8-shot magazine.
Barrel: 2", integral with frame.
Weight: About 10 oz. **Length:** 4⅛" over all.
Stocks: Walnut with fine cut checkering.
Sights: Smooth, no-snag, contoured slide and barrel top.
Features: Aircraft quality 17-4 PH stainless steel. Inertia operated firing pin. Hammer fired double action only. Hammer automatically follows slide down to safety rest position after each shot—no manual safety needed. Magazine safety disconnector. Introduced 1980. From Sile Distributors.
Price: $149.95

SMITH & WESSON 9mm MODEL 39 AUTO PISTOL
Caliber: 9mm Luger, 8-shot clip.
Barrel: 4".
Length: 7 7/16". **Weight:** 26½ oz., without magazine.
Stocks: Checkered walnut.
Sights: ⅛" serrated ramp front, adjustable rear.
Features: Magazine disconnector, positive firing pin lock and hammer-release safety; alloy frame with lanyard loop; locked-breech, short-recoil double action; slide locks open on last shot.
Price: Blued .... $245.50   Nickeled $270.50

SMITH & WESSON MODEL 59 DOUBLE ACTION
Caliber: 9mm Luger, 14-shot clip.
Barrel: 4".
Length: 7 7/16" over-all. **Weight:** 27½ oz., without clip.
Stocks: Checkered high impact moulded nylon.
Sights: ⅛" serrated ramp front, square notch rear adj. for w.
Features: Double action automatic. Furnished with two magazines. Blue finish.
Price: Blued $294.00
Price: Nickel $321.00

SMITH & WESSON MODEL 439 DOUBLE ACTION
Caliber: 9mm Luger, 8-shot clip
Barrel: 4"
Weight: 27 ozs. **Length:** 7 7/16" over-all.
Stocks: Checkered walnut
Sights: ⅛" square serrated ramp front, square notch rear is fully adj. for w. & e.
Features: Rear sight has protective shields on both sides of the sight blade. Frame is alloy. New trigger actuated firing pin lock in addition to the regular rotating safety. Magazine disconnector. New extractor design. Comes with two magazines. Introduced 1980.
Price: Blue $286.00
Price: Nickel $309.00

HANDGUNS — AUTOLOADERS, SERVICE & SPORT

SMITH & WESSON MODEL 459 DOUBLE ACTION
Caliber: 9mm Luger, 14-shot clip.
Barrel: 4"
Weight: 28 ozs. **Length:** 7 7/16" over-all.
Stocks: Checkered high-impact nylon.
Sights: 1/8" square serrated ramp front, square notch rear is fully adj. for w. & e.
Features: Alloy frame. Rear sight has protective shields on both sides of blade. New trigger actuated firing pin lock in addition to the regular safety. Magazine disconnector; new extractor design. Comes with two magazines. Introduced 1980.
Price: Blue $342.00
Price: Nickel $367.00

STAR MODEL PD AUTO PISTOL
Caliber: 45 ACP, 7-shot magazine.
Barrel: 3.94".
Weight: 25 oz. **Length:** 7" over-all.
Stocks: Checkered walnut.
Sights: Ramp front, fully adjustable rear.
Features: Rear sight milled into slide; thumb safety; grooved non-slip front strap; nylon recoil buffer; inertia firing pin; no grip or magazine safeties. From Interarms.
Price: Blue $330.00

STAR BM, BKM AUTO PISTOLS
Caliber: 9mm Para., 8-shot magazine.
Barrel: 3.9".
Weight: 25 oz.
Stocks: Checkered walnut.
Sights: Fixed.
Features: Blue or chrome finish. Magazine and manual safeties, external hammer. Imported from Spain by Interarms.
Price: Blue, BM and BKM $275.00
Price: Chrome, BM only $300.00

STERLING MODEL 302
Caliber: 22 LR, 6-shot.
Barrel: 2½".
Length: 4½" over-all. **Weight:** 13 oz.
Stocks: Black Cycolac.
Sights: Fixed.
Features: All steel construction.
Price: Blue $104.95
Price: Stainless steel $124.95

STERLING MODEL 300
Caliber: 25 ACP, 6-shot.
Barrel: 2½".
Length: 4½" over-all. **Weight:** 13 oz.
Stocks: Black Cycolac.
Sights: Fixed.
Features: All steel construction.
Price: Blued $104.95
Price: Stainless steel $124.95

STERLING MODEL 450 D.A. AUTO
Caliber: 45 ACP, 8-shot magazine.
Barrel: 4¼".
Weight: 35 ozs. **Length:** 7½" over-all.
Stocks: Checkered walnut.
Sights: Blade front, rear adj. for w. & e.
Features: All steel, reversible safety, inertia firing pin. Introduced 1977.
Price: Blue only .... N.A.

CAUTION: PRICES CHANGE. CHECK AT GUNSHOP.

HANDGUNS—AUTOLOADERS, SERVICE & SPORT

STERLING MODEL 400 MK II DOUBLE ACTION
Caliber: 380 ACP, 7-shot.
Barrel: 3¾".
Length: 6½" over-all. Weight: 18 oz.
Stocks: Checkered walnut.
Features: All steel construction. Double action.
Price: Blued $209.50
Price: Stainless steel $259.95

STOEGER LUGER 22 AUTO PISTOL
Caliber: 22 LR, 10-shot
Barrel: 4½"
Weight: 30 oz.
Stocks: Checkered walnut.
Features: Action remains open after last shot and as magazine is removed. Grip and balance indentical to P-08.
Price: $148.95
Price: Kit includes extra clip, charger, hoister $186.95
Price: Combo (includes extra clip, holster, charger and carrying case) $194.95

TDE "BACKUP" AUTO PISTOL
Caliber: 380 ACP, 5-shot magazine
Barrel: 2½".
Weight: 17 oz. Length: 5" over-all.
Stocks: Smooth wood.
Sights: Fixed, open, recessed.
Features: Concealed hammer, blowback operation; manual and grip safeties. All stainless steel construction. Smallest domestically-produced pistol in 380. From AMT.
Price: About $250.00

TARGA TA380XE, GT32XE PISTOLS
Caliber: 32 ACP or 380 ACP, 12-shot magazine.
Barrel: 3.88".
Weight: 28 ozs. Length: 7.38" over-all.
Stocks: Smooth hardwood.
Sights: Adj. for windage.
Features: Blue or satin nickel. Ordnance steel. Magazine disconnector, firing pin and thumb safeties. Introduced 1980. Imported by Excam.
Price: 32 cal., blue $179.00
Price: 32 cal., nickel $185.00
Price: 380 cal., blue $179.00
Price: 380 cal., nickel $185.00

VEGA STAINLESS 45 AUTO
Caliber: 45 ACP, 7-shot.
Barrel: 5".
Weight: 40 oz. Length: 8⅜" over-all.
Stocks: Checkered walnut, diamond pattern.
Sights: Choice of fixed high combat-type or adjustable rear.
Features: Made completely of stainless steel and matches the original 1911A1 Colt almost exactly. Has both grip and thumb safeties. Slide and frame flats are polished, rest sand blasted. From Pacific International Merchandising Corp.
Price: With fixed sights $349.95
Price: With Accro-Adjustable sights $379.95

WALTHER PP AUTO PISTOL
Caliber: 22 LR, 8-shot; 32 ACP, 380 ACP, 7-shot.
Barrel: 3.86".
Weight: 23½ oz. Length: 6.7".
Stocks: Checkered plastic.
Sights: Fixed, white markings.
Features: Double action, manual safety blocks firing pin and drops hammer, chamber loaded indicator on 32 and 380, extra finger rest magazine provided. Imported from Germany by Interarms.
Price: (22 LR) $525.00
Price: (32 and 380) $500.00
Price: Engraved models .... On Request

Walther PPK/S Auto Pistol
Same as PP except bbl. 3.27", length 6.1" o.a.
Price: 22 LR $525.00
Price: 32 or 380 ACP $500.00
Price: Engraved models .... On Request
Price: Walther American PPK/s, 380 only $265.00

TARGA MODEL GT27 AUTO PISTOL
Caliber: 25 ACP, 6-shot magazine
Barrel: 2⁷⁄₁₆".
Weight: 12 oz. Length: 4⅝" over-all.
Stocks: Checkered nylon.
Sights: Fixed.
Features: Safety lever take-down; external hammer with half-cock. Assembled in U.S. by Excam, Inc.
Price: Blue $58.50
Price: Chrome $64.00

TARGA MODELS GT32, GT380 AUTO PISTOLS
Caliber: 32 ACP or 380 ACP, 6-shot magazine
Barrel: 4⅞".
Weight: 26 oz. Length: 7⅜" over-all.
Stocks: Checkered nylon with thumb rest. Walnut optional.
Sights: Fixed blade front; rear drift-adj. for w.
Features: Chrome or blue finish; magazine, thumb, and firing pin safeties; external hammer; safety lever take-down. Imported from Italy by Excam, Inc.
Price: 32 cal., blue $112.50
Price: 32 cal., chrome $118.00
Price: 380 cal., blue $132.50
Price: 380 cal., chrome $138.50
Price: 380 cal., chrome, engraved, wooden grips $183.50
Price: 380 cal., blue, engraved, wooden grips $177.50

HANDGUNS — AUTOLOADERS, SERVICE & SPORT

WALTHER P-38 AUTO PISTOL
Caliber: 22 LR, 30 Luger or 9mm Luger, 8-shot.
Barrel: 4$^{15}/_{16}$" (9mm and 30), 5$^{1}/_{16}$" (22 LR).
Weight: 28 oz. **Length:** 8½".
Stock: Checkered plastic.
Sights: Fixed.
Features: Double action, safety blocks firing pin and drops hammer, chamber loaded indicator. Matte finish standard, polished blue, engraving and/or plating available. Imported from Germany by Interarms.
Price: 22 LR **$750.00**
Price: 9mm or 30 Luger **$660.00**
Price: Engraved models .... **On Request**

Walther P-38IV Auto Pistol
Same as P-38K except has longer barrel (4½"); over-all length is 8", weight is 29 ozs. Sights are non-adjustable. Introduced 1977. Imported by Interarms.
Price: **$690.00**

WALTHER P-5 AUTO PISTOL
Latest Walther design that uses the basic P-38 double-action mechanism. Caliber 9mm Luger, barrel length 3½"; weight 28 oz., over-all length 7".
Price: **$860.00**

Walther P-38K Auto Pistol
Streamlined version of the P-38; 2¾" barrel, 6⅜" over-all, weight 26 ozs. Strengthened slide (no dust cover), recoil bearing cross-bolt. Rear sight adj. for windage, both front and rear sights have white accents. Hammer decocking lever. Non-reflective matte finish. Imported from Germany by Interarms. Introduced 1977.
Price: **$690.00**

WILDEY AUTO PISTOL
Caliber: 9mm Win. Mag. (14 shots), 45 Win. Mag. (8 shots).
Barrel: 5", 6", 7", 8", or 10"; vent. rib.
Weight: About 51 oz. (6" bbl.).
Stocks: Select hardwood, target style optional.
Sights: Adjustable for windage and elevation; red or white inserts optional.
Features: Patented gas operation; selective single or autoloading capability; 5-lug rotary bolt; fixed barrel; stainless steel construction; double-action trigger mechanism. Has positive hammer block and magazine safety. From Wildey Firearms.
Price: 9mm Win. Mag., 5" bbl. **$489.95**
Price: 45 Win. Mag., 8" bbl. **$499.95**

HANDGUNS — REVOLVERS, SERVICE & SPORT

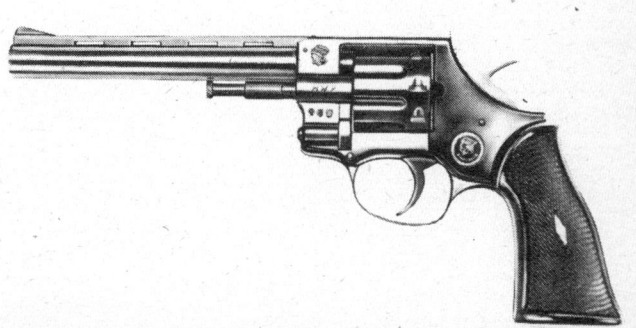

ARMINIUS REVOLVERS
Caliber: 38 Special, 357 Mag., 32 S&W (6-shot); 22 Magnum, 22 LR (8-shot).
Barrel: 4" (38 Spec., 357 Mag., 32 S&W, 22 LR); 6" (38 Spec., 22 LR/22 Mag., 357 Mag.); 8⅜" (357 Mag.).
Weight: 35 oz. (6" bbl.). **Length:** 11" (6" bbl. 38).
Stocks: Checkered plastic; walnut optional for $14.95.
Sights: Ramp front, fixed rear on standard models, w. & e. adj. on target models.
Features: Ventilated rib, solid frame, swing-out cylinder. Interchangeable 22 Mag. cylinder available with 22 cal. versions. Also available in 357 Mag. 3", 4", 6" barrel, adj. sights. Imported from West Germany by F.I.E. Corp.
Price: .... **$89.95 to $170.95**

HANDGUNS — REVOLVERS, SERVICE & SPORT

ASTRA 357 MAGNUM REVOLVER
Caliber: 357 Magnum, 6-shot.
Barrel: 4", 6", 8½".
Weight: 40 oz. (6" bbl.). **Length:** 11¼" (6" bbl.).
Stocks: Checkered walnut.
Sights: Fixed front, rear adj. for w. and e.
Features: Swing-out cylinder with countersunk chambers, floating firing pin. Target-type hammer and trigger. Imported from Spain by Interarms.
Price: 4", 6" $300.00
Price: 8½" $305.00

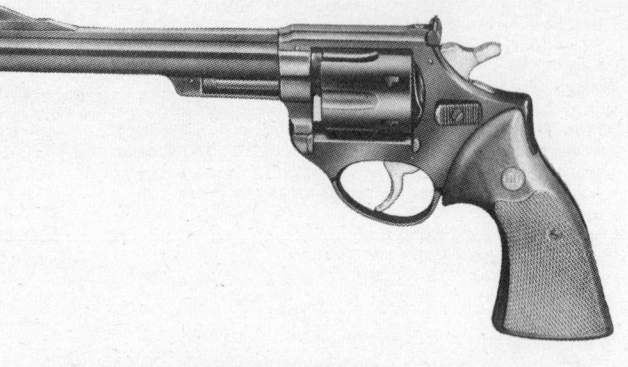

ASTRA MODEL 44 DOUBLE ACTION REVOLVER
Similar to the 357 Mag. except chambered for the 44 Magnum. Barrel length of 6" or 8½" only, giving over-all length of 11⅜" or 13⅞". Weight is 2¾ lbs. Introduced 1980.
Price: $390.00

CHARTER ARMS BULLDOG
Caliber: 44 Special, 5-shot.
Barrel: 3", 6".
Weight: 19 oz. **Length:** 7½" over-all.
Stocks: Hand checkered walnut; Square butt.
Sights: Patridge type 9/64" front, square notch rear.
Features: Wide trigger and hammer, chrome-moly steel frame, unbreakable firing pin, transfer bar ignition.
Price: 44 Spec., 3" $168.00
Price: In 357 Mag. as Tracker model, 6" $179.00

CHARTER ARMS POLICE BULLDOG
Caliber: 38 Special, 6-shot.
Barrel: 4".
Weight: 20½ oz. **Length:** 8½" over-all.
Stocks: Hand checkered American walnut; square butt.
Sights: Full length ramp front; fully adj. combat rear.
Features: Accepts both regular and high velocity ammunition; enclosed ejector rod; full length ejection of fired cases.
Price: Blue only, ... $175.00

CHARTER TARGET BULLDOG
Caliber: 357 Mag., 44 Spec., 5-shot.
Barrel: 4".
Weight: 20½ oz. **Length:** 8½" over-all.
Stocks: Checkered American walnut, square butt.
Sights: Full-length ramp front, fully adj., milled channel, square notch rear.
Features: Blue finish only. Enclosed ejector rod, full length ejection of fired cases.
Price: 357 Mag., 4" $189.00
Price: 44 Spec., 4" $193.00

CHARTER ARMS UNDERCOVER REVOLVER
Caliber: 38 Special, 5 shot; 32 S & W Long, 6 shot.
Barrel: 2", 3".
Weight: 16 oz. (2"). **Length:** 6¼" (2").
Stocks: Smooth walnut or checkered square butt.
Sights: Patridge-type ramp front, notched rear.
Features: Wide trigger and hammer spur. Steel frame.
Price: Polished Blue $149.00
Price: With checkered square butt grips, blue, 3" $166.50
Price: 32 S & W Long, blue, 2" $149.00
Price: Stainless, 38 Spec. 2" .... N.A.

Charter Arms Pathfinder
Same as Undercover but in 22 LR caliber, and has 3" or 6" bbl. Fitted with adjustable rear sight, ramp front. Weight 18½ oz.
Price: 22 LR, blue, 3" $168.00
Price: 22 LR, square butt, 6" $177.00
Price: 22 Mag., square butt, 3" $182.00
Price: 22 Mag, square butt, 6" $182.00
Price: Stainless, 22 LR, 3" .... N.A.

COLT DIAMONDBACK REVOLVER
Caliber: 22 LR or 38 Special, 6 shot.
Barrel: 4" or 6" with ventilated rib.
Length: 9" (4" bbl.). **Weight:** 24 oz. (2½" bbl.), 28½ oz. (4" bbl.).
Stocks: Checkered walnut, target type, square butt.
Sights: Ramp front, adj. notch rear.
Features: Ventilated rib; grooved, crisp trigger; swing-out cylinder; wide hammer spur.
Price: Blue, 4" bbl., 38 Spec. or 22 .... $307.50
Price: Blue, 22-cal. or 38 Spec. 6" bbl. $314.50

COLT LAWMAN MK III REVOLVER
Caliber: 357 Mag., 6 shot.
Barrel: 2" or 4", heavy.
Weight: 33 oz.
Length: 9⅜".
Stocks: Checkered walnut, service style.
Sights: Fixed, glare-proofed ramp front, square notch rear.
Price: Blued $245.50
Price: Nickel $260.95

284 THE GUN DIGEST   **CAUTION:** PRICES CHANGE. CHECK AT GUNSHOP.

HANDGUNS—REVOLVERS, SERVICE & SPORT

COLT DETECTIVE SPECIAL
Caliber: 38 Special, 6 shot.
Barrel: 2".
Length: 6⅝" over-all. **Weight:** 22 oz.
Stocks: Full, checkered walnut, round butt.
Sights: Fixed, ramp front, square notch rear.
Features: Glare-proofed sights, smooth trigger. Nickel finish, hammer shroud available as options.
Price: Blue $259.95
Price: Nickel $279.95

COLT TROOPER MK III REVOLVER
Caliber: 22 LR, 22 WMR, 38 Spec., 357 Magnum, 6-shot.
Barrel: 4" 6" or 8".
Length: 9½" (4" bbl.). **Weight:** 39 oz. (4" bbl.), 42 oz, (6" bbl.).
Stocks: Checkered walnut, square butt. Grooved trigger.
Sights: Fixed ramp front with ⅛" blade, adj. notch rear.
Price: Blued with target hammer and target stocks, 4", 357 ...... $288.95
Price: Nickeled 38/357 Mag. 4" $306.50
Price: 22 LR, blue, 4" $288.95
Price: 22 LR, blue, 8" $294.95
Price: 22 WMR, Nickel, 8" $317.50

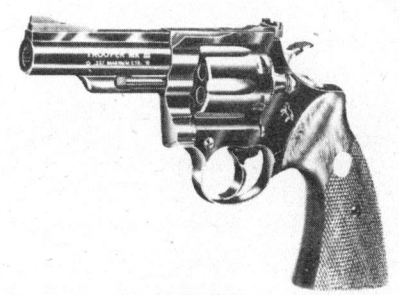

F.I.E. MODEL F38 "Titan Tiger" REVOLVER
Caliber: 38 Special.
Barrel: 2" or 4".
Length: 6¼" over-all. (2" bbl.). **Weight:** 27 oz.
Stocks: Checkered plastic, Bulldog style. Walnut optional ($10.95).
Sights: Fixed.
Features: Swing-out cylinder, one stroke ejection. Made in U.S.A. by F.I.E. Corp.
Price: Blued 2" or 4" ..... $87.95   Nickel, 2" or 4" bbl. $109.95
Price: Blue/Gold combo $114.95

H&R MODEL 940 ULTRA "SIDE-KICK" REVOLVER
Caliber: 22 S, L or LR, 9 shot.
Barrel: 6" target weight with ventilated rib.
Weight: 36 oz.
Stocks: Checkered walnut-finished hardwood with thumbrest.
Sights: Ramp front; rear adjustable for w. and e.
Features: Swing-out, safety rim cylinder.
Price: H&R Crown-Lustre Blue $110.00

H&R Model 939 Ultra "Side-Kick" Revolver
Like the Model 940 but with a flat-sided barrel.
Price: H&R Crown-Lustre Blue $110.00

HARRINGTON & RICHARDSON M622 REVOLVER
Caliber: 22 S, L or LR, 22 WMR, 6 shot.
Barrel: 2½", 4", round bbl.
Weight: 20 oz. (2½" bbl.).
Stocks: Checkered black Cycolac.
Sights: Fixed, blade front, square notch rear.
Features: Solid steel, Bantamweight frame; pull-pin safety rim cylinder; non-glare finish on frame; coil springs.
Price: Blued, 2½", 4", bbl. $69.50
Price: Model 632 (32 cal.) $74.50
Price: Model 642, 22 WMR 79.50

HARRINGTON & RICHARDSON M929 "SIDE-KICK"
Caliber: 22 S, L or LR, 9 shot.
Barrel: 2½", 4" or 6".
Weight: 26 oz. (4" bbl.).
Stocks: Checkered, black Cycolac.
Sights: Blade front; adjustable rear on 4" and 6" models.
Features: Swing-out cylinder with auto. extractor return. Pat. safety rim cylinder. Grooved trigger. Round-grip frame.
Price: Blued, 2½", 4" or 6" bbl. $89.50
Price: Nickel (Model 930), 2½" or 4" bbl. $94.50

HARRINGTON & RICHARDSON M732 GUARDSMAN
Caliber: 32 S&W or 32 S&W Long, 6 shot.
Barrel: 2½" or 4" round barrel.
Weight: 23½ oz. (2½" bbl.), 26 oz. (4" bbl.).
Stocks: Checkered, black Cycolac.
Sights: Blade front; adjustable rear on 4" model.
Features: Swing-out cylinder with auto. extractor return. Pat. safety rim cylinder. Grooved trigger.
Price: Blued, 2½" bbl. .. **$89.50**   Nickel (Model 733), 2½" bbl. $94.50
Price: Blued, 4" bbl. .. **$89.50**   Nickel, 4" bbl. $94.50

CAUTION: PRICES CHANGE. CHECK AT GUNSHOP.

HANDGUNS—REVOLVERS, SERVICE & SPORT

HARRINGTON & RICHARDSON M949 FORTY-NINER
Caliber: 22 S, L or LR, 9 shot.
Barrel: 5½" round with ejector rod.
Weight: 31 oz.
Stocks: One-piece, smooth frontier style wrap-around, Walnut-finished hardwood.
Sights: estern-type blade front, rear adj. for w.
Features: Contoured loading gate; wide hmmer spur; single and double action. Western type ejector-housing.
Price: H&R Crown-Luster Blue 89.50
Price: Nickel (Model 950) $94.50

Harrington & Richardson Model 976 Revolver
Similar to the Model 949 except has 7½" barrel, has color case-hardened frame, ejector rod housing and trigger. Has 9-shot cylinder. Standard model has blade front sight and windage-adjustable rear sight; Deluxe model has ramped blade front and fully adjustable "Wind-Elv" rear.
Price: Standard model $105.00
Price: Deluxe model $135.00

Harrington & Richardson Models 603, 903
Similar to 604-904 except has flat-sided barrel.
Price: $135.00

HARRINGTON & RICHARDSON M676 REVOLVER
Caliber: 22 LR/22 WMRF, 6-shot.
Barrel: 4½", 5½", 7½" or 12".
Weight: 31 oz. (4½"), 41 oz. (12").
Stocks: One piece smooth walnut-finished hardwood.
Sights: Western type blade front, adj. rear.
Features: Blue barrel and cylinder, "antique" color case-hardened frame, ejector tube and trigger. Comes with extra cylinder.
Price: 4½", 5½", 7½" bbl. $115.00
Price: 12" bbl. $135.00

Harrington & Richardson Model 686 Revolver
Similar to the Model 676 except has a ramp and blade front sight and fully adjustable "Wind-Elv" rear sight. Same barrel lengths and chamberings.
Price: 4½", 5½", 7½" barrel $135.00
Price: 12" barrel $160.00

HIGH STANDARD DOUBLE-NINE CONVERTIBLE
Caliber: 22 S, L or LR, 9-shot (22 WRM with extra cylinder).
Barrel: 5½", dummy ejector rod fitted.
Length: 11" over-all. **Weight:** 32 oz.
Stocks: Smooth walnut, frontier style.
Sights: Fixed blade front, rear adj. for w. & e.
Features: Western styling; rebounding hammer with auto safety block; spring-loaded ejection. Swing-out cylinder.
Price: Blued $200.20

High Standard Long Horn Convertible
Same as the Double-Nine convertible but with a 9½" bbl., adjustable sights, blued only, Weight: 38 oz.
Price: With adjustable sights $204.05

H&R SPORTSMAN MODEL 999 REVOLVER
Caliber: 22 S, L or LR, 9 shot, 32 S&W Long, 6-shot.
Barrel: 4", 6" top-break (16" twist), integral fluted vent. rib.
Length: 10½". **Weight:** 34 oz. (6", 22 cal.).
Stocks: Checkered walnut-finished hardwood.
Sights: Front adjustable for elevation, rear for windage.
Features: Simultaneous automatic ejection; trigger guard extension. H&R Crown Lustre Blue.
Price: Blued, 4", either caliber $140.00
Price: Blued, 6", either caliber $140.00

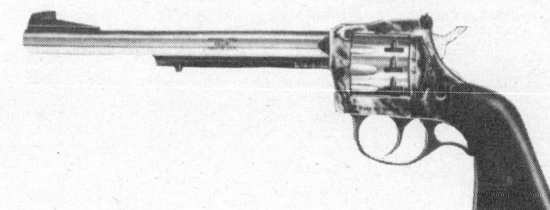

HARRINGTON & RICHARDSON MODELS 604, 904
Caliber: 22 LR, 9-shot (M904), 22 WMR, 6-shot (M604)
Barrel: 6".
Weight: 38 oz.
Stocks: Smooth walnut.
Sights: Blade front, fully adjustable "Wind-Elv" rear.
Features: Swing-out cylinder design with coil spring construction. Single stroke ejection. Tanget-style bull barrel has raised solid rib giving a 7¼" sight radius.
Price: M604 or 904 .... $135.00

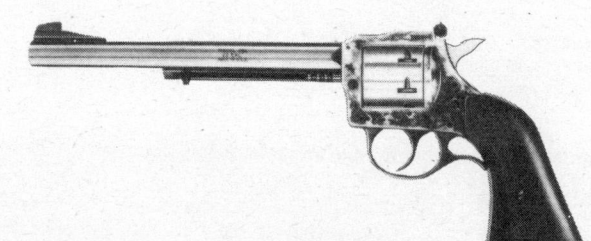

286   THE GUN DIGEST   CAUTION: PRICES CHANGE. CHECK AT GUNSHOP.

HANDGUNS—REVOLVERS, SERVICE & SPORT

HIGH STANDARD HIGH SIERRA DOUBLE ACTION
Caliber: 22 LR and 22 LR/22 Mag., 9-shot.
Barrel: 7" octagonal.
Weight: 36 oz. **Length:** 12½" over-all.
Stocks: Smooth walnut.
Sights: Blade front, adj. rear.
Features: Gold plated backstrap and trigger guard. Swing-out cylinder.
Price: Adj. sights, dual cyl. $204.05

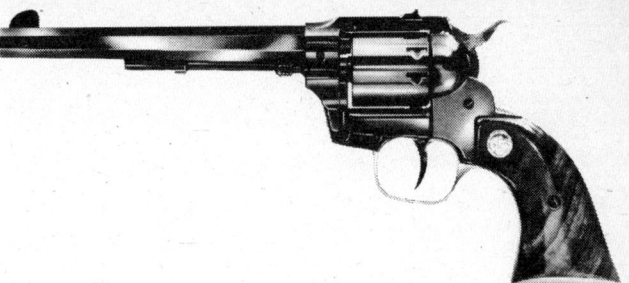

HIGH STANDARD CRUSADER COMMEMORATIVE REVOLVER
Caliber: 44 Mag., 45 Long Colt.
Barrel: 6½", 8⅜".
Weight: 48 oz. (6½").
Stocks: Smooth Zebrawood.
Sights: Blade front on ramp, fully adj. rear.
Features: Unique gear-segment mechanism. Smooth, light double-action trigger pull. First production devoted to the commemorative; later guns will be of plain, standard configuration.
Price: .... N.A.

LLAMA COMANCHE REVOLVERS
Caliber: 22 LR, 38 Special, 357 Mag.
Barrel: 6", 4" (except 22 LR, 6" only).
Weight: 22 LR 24 oz. 38 Special 31 oz. **Length:** 9¼" (4" bbl.).
Stocks: Checkered walnut.
Sights: Fixed blade front, rear adj. for w. & e.
Features: Ventilated rib, wide spur hammer. Chrome plating, engraved finishes available. Imported from Spain by Stoeger Industries.
Price: Blue finish $266.95
Price: Satin chrome, 357 only $341.95
Price: Gold damascened finish, 357, 4" $1,500.00

Llama Super Comanche Revolver
Similar to the Comanche except: 44 Mag., 6" barrel only; 6-shot cylinder; smooth, extra wide trigger; wide spur hammer; over-size walnut, target-style grips. Weight is 3 lbs., 2 ozs., over-all length is 11¾". Blue finish only.
Price: $414.95

RG 14 REVOLVER
Caliber: 22 LR, 6-shot.
Barrel: 1¾" or 3".
Weight: 15 ozs. (1¾" bbl.) **Length:** 5½" over-all.
Stocks: Checkered plastic.
Sights: Fixed.
Features: Blue finish. Cylinder swings out when pin is removed. Imported by RG Industries.
Price: $39.95
Price: Model 23 (central ejector, no pin to remove) $52.00

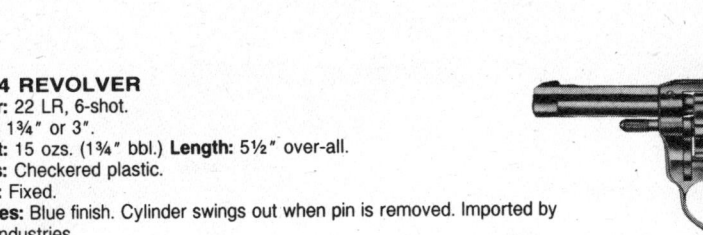

RG 31 REVOLVER
Caliber: 32 S & W (6-shot), 38 Spec. (5-shot).
Barrel: 2".
Weight: 24 ozs. **Length:** 6¾" over-all.
Stocks: Checkered plastic.
Sights: Fixed.
Features: Cylinder swings out when pin is removed. Blue finish. Imported by RG Industries.
Price: 32 cal. $68.00
Price: 38 cal. $68.00

HANDGUNS—REVOLVERS, SERVICE & SPORT

RG MODEL 74 REVOLVER
Caliber: 22 LR, 6-shot
Barrel: 3".
Weight: 21½ oz. Length: 7¾" over-all.
Stocks: Checkered plastic.
Sights: Fixed
Features: Swing-out cylinder with spring ejector. Introduced 1980. Imported by RG Industries.
Price: Blue only .... N.A.

RG 40 REVOLVER
Caliber: 38 Spec., 6-shot.
Barrel: 2".
Weight: 29 ozs. Length: 7¼" over-all.
Stocks: Checkered plastic.
Sights: Fixed.
Features: Swing-out cylinder with spring ejector. Imported by RG Industries.
Price: $88.00

RG 38S REVOLVER
Caliber: 38 Special, 6-shot.
Barrel: 3" and 4".
Weight: 3", 31 oz.; 4", 34 oz. Length: 3", 8½"; 4", 9¼".
Stocks: Checkered plastic.
Sights: Fixed front, rear adj. for w.
Features: Swing out cylinder with spring ejector. Imported from Germany by RG Industries.
Price: Blue $91.95

RG MODEL 39 REVOLVER
Caliber: 32 S&W, 38 Spec., 6-shot.
Barrel: 2".
Weight: 21 oz. Length: 7" over-all.
Stocks: Checkered plastic.
Sights: Fixed.
Features: Swing-out cylinder with spring ejector. Introduced 1980. Imported by RG Industries.
Price: Blue only .... N.A.

ROSSI MODELS 68, 69 & 70 DA REVOLVERS
Caliber: 22 LR (M 70), 32 S & W (M 69), 38 Spec. (M 68).
Barrel: 3".
Weight: 22 oz.
Stocks: Checkered wood.
Sights: Ramp front, low profile adj. rear.
Features: All-steel frame. Thumb latch operated swing-out cylinder. Introduced 1978. Imported by Interarms.
Price: 22, 32 or 38, blue $130.00
Price: As above, 38 Spec. only with 4" bbl. as M 31 .... $130.00
Price: Model 38 (adj. sights) $150.00
Price: Model 51 (6" bbl., 22 cal.) $150.00
Price: M68, M69, M70 in nickel $135.00

> Consult our Directory pages for the location of firms mentioned.

RUGER POLICE SERVICE-SIX Models 107, 108
Caliber: 357 (Model 107), 38 Spec. (Model 108), 9mm (Model 109), 6-shot.
Barrel: 2¾" or 4" and 4" heavy barrel.
Weight: 33½ oz (4" bbl.). Length: 9¼" (4" bbl.) over-all.
Stocks: Checkered American walnut, semi-target style.
Sights: Patridge-type front, square notch rear.
Features: Solid frame with barrel, rib and ejector rod housing combined in one unit. All steel construction. Field strips without tools.
Price: Model 107 (357) $148.00
Price: Model 108 (38) $148.00
Price: Mod. 707 (357), Stainless, 4" & 4" HB $162.00
Price: Mod. 708 (38), Stainless, 4" & 4" HB $162.00

RUGER SECURITY-SIX Model 117
Caliber: 357 Mag. (also fires 38 Spec.), 6-shot.
Barrel: 2¾", 4" or 6", or 4" heavy barrel.
Weight: 33½ oz. (4" bbl.). Length: 9¼" (4" bbl.) over-all.
Stocks: Hand checkered American walnut, semi-target style.
Sights: Patridge-type front on ramp, rear adj. for w. and e.
Features: Music wire coil springs throughout. Hardened steel construction. Integral ejector rod shroud and sighting rib. Can be disassembled using only a coin.
Price: 2¾", 4", 6" and 4" heavy barrel $192.50
Price: 4" HB, 6" with Big Grip stocks $208.00

HANDGUNS—REVOLVERS, SERVICE & SPORT

RUGER STAINLESS SECURITY-SIX Model 717
Caliber: 357 Mag. (also fires 38 Spec.), 6-shot.
Barrel: 2¾", 4" or 6".
Weight: 33 oz. (4 bbl.). **Length:** 9¼" (4" bbl.) over-all.
Stocks: Hand checkered American walnut.
Sights: Patridge-type front, fully adj. rear.
Features: All metal parts except sights made of stainless steel. Sights are black alloy for maximum visibility. Same mechanism and features found in regular Security-Six.
Price: 2¾", 4", 6" and 4" HB $212.00
Price: 4" HB, 6" with Big Grip stocks $227.50

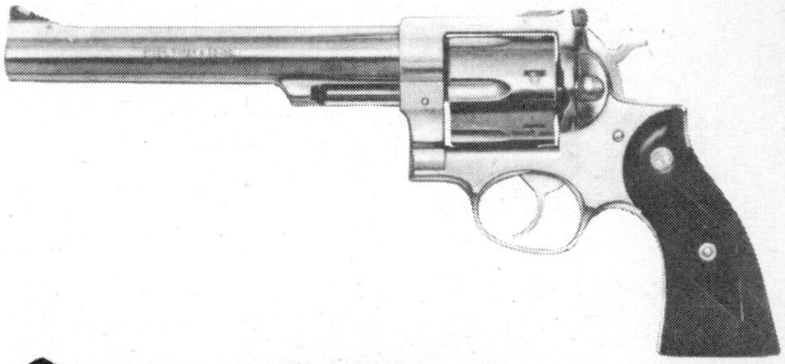

RUGER REDHAWK
Caliber: 44 Rem. Mag., 6-shot.
Barrel: 7½".
Weight: About 3¼ lbs. **Length:** 13" over-all.
Stocks: Square butt. American walnut.
Sights: Patridge-type front, rear adj. for w. & e.
Features: Stainless steel, brushed satin finish. Has a 9½" sight radius. Introduced 1979.
Price: $325.00

SMITH & WESSON M&P Model 10 REVOLVER
Caliber: 38 Special, 6 shot.
Barrel: 2", 4", 5" or 6".
Length: 9¼" (4" bbl.). **Weight:** 30½ oz. (4" bbl.).
Stocks: Checkered walnut, Magna. Round or square butt.
Sights: Fixed, ⅛" ramp front, square notch rear.
Price: Blued .... $143.00   Nickeled $154.50

Smith & Wesson 38 M&P Heavy Barrel Model 10
Same as regular M&P except: 4" ribbed bbl. with ⅛" ramp front sight, square rear, square butt, wgt. 34 oz.
Price: Blued .... $143.00   Nickeled $154.50

SMITH & WESSON 38 M&P AIRWEIGHT Model 12
Caliber: 38 Special, 6 shot.
Barrel: 2 or 4 inches.
Length: 6⅞" over-all. **Weight:** 18 oz. (2" bbl.)
Stocks: Checkered walnut, Magna. Round or square butt.
Sights: Fixed, ⅛" serrated ramp front, square notch rear.
Price: Blued .... $185.00   Nickeled $210.00

SMITH & WESSON Model 13 H.B. M&P
Caliber: 357 and 38 Special, 6 shot.
Barrel: 4".
Weight: 34 oz. **Length:** 9¼" over-all.
Stocks: Checkered walnut, service.
Sights: ⅛" serrated ramp front, fixed square notch rear.
Features: Heavy barrel, K-frame, square butt.
Price: Blue only, M-13 .... $156.50
Price: Nickel $171.00
Price: Model 65, as above in stainless steel $173.00

SMITH & WESSON Model 14 K-38 MASTERPIECE
Caliber: 38 Spec., 6-shot.
Barrel: 6", 8⅜".
Weight: 38½ oz. (6" bbl.). **Length:** 11⅛" over-all (6" bbl.)
Stock: Checkered walnut, service.
Sights: ⅛" Patridge front, micro click rear adj. for w. and e.
Price: 6" bbl. $221.50
Price: 8⅜" bbl. $232.50

RUGER SPEED-SIX Models 207, 208, 209
Caliber: 357 (Model 207), 38 Spec. (Model 208), 9mm P (Model 209) 6-shot.
Barrel: 2¾" or 4".
Weight: 31 oz. (2¾" bbl.). **Length:** 7¾" over-all (2¾" bbl.).
Stocks: Round butt design, diamond pattern checkered American walnut.
Sights: Patridge-type front, square-notch rear.
Features: Same basic mechanism as Security-Six. Hammer without spur available on special order. All steel construction. Music wire coil springs used throughout.
Price: Model 207 (357 Mag.) $148.00
Price: Model 208 (38 Spec. only) $148.00
Price: Model 209 (9mmP) $164.50
Price: Mod. 737 (357), Stainless $162.00
Price: Mod. 738 (38), Stainless $162.00
Price: Model 739 (9mm P), Stainless $178.50

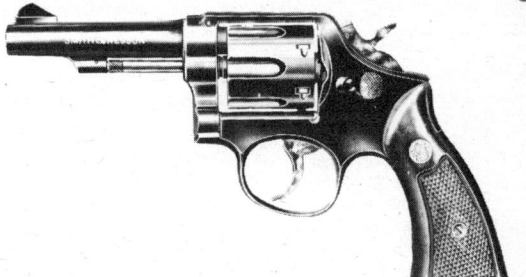

CAUTION: PRICES CHANGE. CHECK AT GUNSHOP.

HANDGUNS—REVOLVERS, SERVICE & SPORT

SMITH & WESSON 357 COMBAT MAGNUM Model 19
Caliber: 357 Magnum and 38 Special, 6 shot.
Barrel: 2½", 4", 6".
Length: 9½" (4" bbl.). **Weight:** 35 oz.
Stocks: Checkered Goncala Alves, target. Grooved tangs and trigger.
Sights: Front, ⅛" Baughman Quick Draw on 2½" or 4" bbl., Patridge on 6" bbl., micro click rear adjustable for w. and e.
Price: S&W Bright Blue or Nickel $216.50

SMITH & WESSON 357 MAGNUM M-27 REVOLVER
Caliber: 357 Magnum and 38 Special, 6 shot.
Barrel: 4", 6", 8⅜".
Length: 11¼" (6" bbl.). **Weight:** 44 oz. (6" bbl.).
Stocks: Checkered walnut, Magna. Grooved tangs and trigger.
Sights: Any S&W target front, micro click rear, adjustable for w. and e.
Price: S&W Bright Blue or Nickel, 4", 6" $344.00
Price: 8⅜" bbl. $356.00

SMITH & WESSON HIGHWAY PATROLMAN Model 28
Caliber: 357 Magnum and 38 Special, 6 shot.
Barrel: 4", 6".
Length: 11¼" (6" bbl.). **Weight:** 44 oz. (6" bbl.).
Stocks: Checkered walnut, Magna. Grooved tangs and trigger.
Sights: Front, ⅛" Baughman Quick Draw, on plain ramp. micro click rear, adjustable for w. and e.
Price: S&W Satin Blue, sandblasted frame edging and barrel top . $222.00
Price: With target stocks $238.50

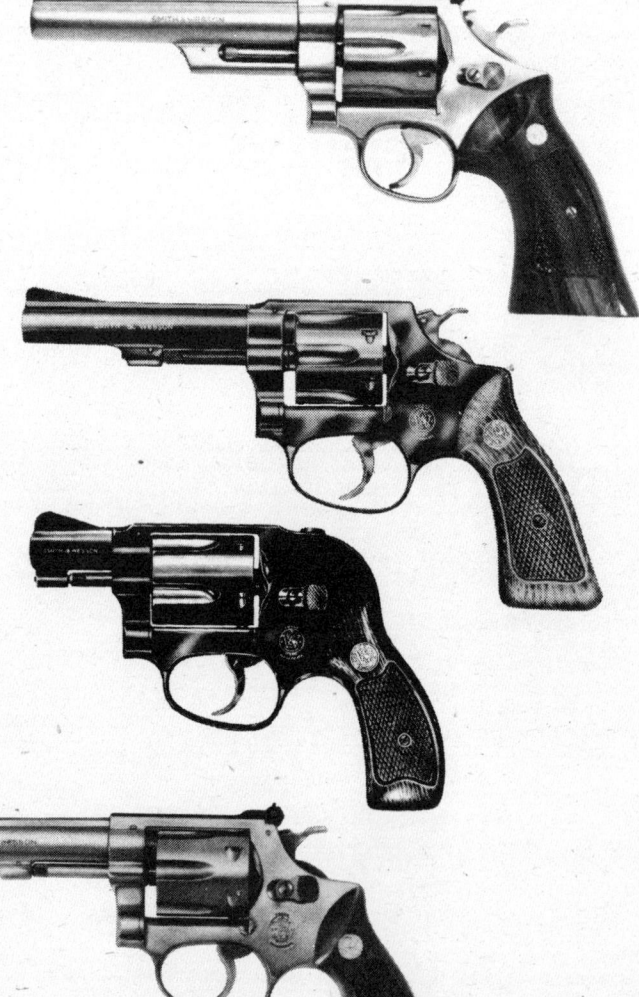

SMITH & WESSON 44 MAGNUM Model 29 REVOLVER
Caliber: 44 Magnum, 44 Special or 44 Russian, 6 shot.
Barrel: 4", 6", 8⅜".
Length: 11⅞" (6½" bbl.). **Weight:** 47 oz. (6" bbl.), 43 oz. (4" bbl.).
Stocks: Oversize target type, checkered Goncala Alves. Tangs and target trigger grooved, checkered target hammer.
Sights: ⅛" red ramp-front, micro. click rear, adjustable for w. and e.
Features: Includes presentation case.
Price: S&W Bright Blue or Nickel 4", 6" $376.00
Price: 8⅜" bbl., blue or nickel $388.00
Price: Model 629 (stainless steel) $421.00

SMITH & WESSON 32 REGULATION POLICE Model 31
Caliber: 32 S&W Long, 6 shot.
Barrel: 2", 3".
Length: 7½" (3" bbl.). **Weight:** 18¾ oz. (3" bbl.).
Stocks: Checkered walnut, Magna.
Sights: Fixed, 1/10" serrated ramp front, square notch rear.
Price: Blued $179.00

SMITH & WESSON BODYGUARD MODEL 38
Caliber: 38 Special; 5 shot, double action revolver.
Barrel: 2".
Length: 6⅜". **Weight:** 14½ oz.
Features: Alloy frame; integral hammer shroud.
Stocks: Checkered walnut, Magna.
Sights: Fixed 1/10" serrated ramp front, square notch rear.
Price: Blued .... $197.50   Nickeled $223.00

Smith & Wesson Bodyguard Model 49 Revolver
Same as Model 38 except steel construction, weight 20½ oz.
Price: Blued .... $183.50   **Price:** Nickeled $199.50

SMITH & WESSON 1953 Model 34, 22/32 KIT GUN
Caliber: 22 LR, 6 shot.
Barrel: 2", 4".
Length: 8" (4" bbl. and round butt). **Weight:** 22½ oz. (4" bbl.).
Stocks: Checkered walnut, round or square butt.
Sights: Front, 1/10" serrated ramp, micro. click rear, adjustable for w. & e.
Price: Blued .... $185.50   Nickeled $201.50
Price: Model 63, as above in stainless, 4" $216.00

HANDGUNS—REVOLVERS, SERVICE & SPORT

SMITH & WESSON 38 CHIEFS SPECIAL & AIRWEIGHT
Caliber: 38 Special, 5 shot.
Barrel: 2", 3".
Length: 6½" (2" bbl. and round butt). **Weight:** 19 oz. (2" bbl.); 14 oz. (AIRWEIGHT).
Stocks: Checkered walnut, Magna. Round or square butt.
Sights: Fixed, 1/10" serrated ramp front, square notch rear.
Price: Blued std. M-36 ... $170.50   Standard weight Nickel ... $184.50
Price: Blued AIR'W M-37 . $189.50   AIRWEIGHT Nickel $214.50

Smith & Wesson 60 Chiefs Special Stainless
Same as Model 36 except: 2" bbl. and round butt only.
Price: Stainless steel $207.50

SMITH & WESSON MODEL 64 STAINLESS M&P
Caliber: 38 Special, 6-shot.
Barrel: 4".
Length: 9½" over-all. **Weight:** 30½ oz.
Stocks: Checkered walnut, service style.
Sights: Fixed, 1/8" serrated ramp front, square notch rear.
Features: Satin finished stainless steel, square butt.
Price: $162.50

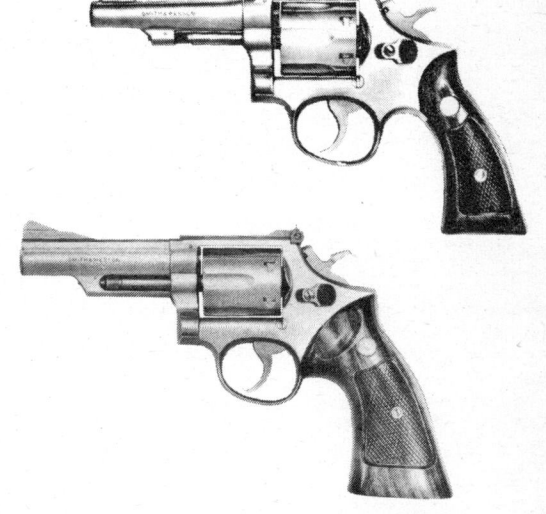

SMITH & WESSON MODEL 66 STAINLESS COMBAT MAGNUM
Caliber: 357 Magnum and 38 Special, 6-shot.
Barrel: 2½", 4", 6".
Length: 9½" over-all. **Weight:** 35 oz.
Stocks: Checkered Goncala Alves target.
Sights: Front, 1/8" Baughman Quick Draw on plain ramp, micro click rear adj. for w. and e.
Features: Satin finish stainless steel, grooved trigger with adj. stop.
Price: $231.50

SMITH & WESSON MODEL 67 K-38 STAINLESS COMBAT MASTERPIECE
Caliber: 38 special, 6-shot.
Barrel: 4".
Length: 9⅛" over-all. **Weight:** 34 oz. (loaded).
Stocks: Checkered walnut, service style.
Sights: Front, 1/8" Baughman Quick Draw on ramp, micro click rear adj. for w. and e.
Features: Stainless steel. Square butt frame with grooved tangs, grooved trigger with adj. stop.
Price: $212.50

SMITH & WESSON 41 MAGNUM Model 57 REVOLVER
Caliber: 41 Magnum, 6 shot.
Barrel: 4", 6" or 8⅜".
Length: 11⅜" (6" bbl.). **Weight:** 48 oz. (6" bbl.).
Stocks: Oversize target type checkered Goncala Alves wood and target hammer. Tang and target trigger grooved.
Sights: 1/8" red ramp front, micro click rear, adj. for w. and e.
Price: S&W Bright Blue or Nickel 4", 6" $376.00
Price: 8⅜" bbl. $388.00

TAURUS MODEL 66 REVOLVER
Caliber: 357 Magnum, 6-shot.
Barrel: 3", 4", 6".
Weight: 35 ozs.
Stocks: Checkered walnut, target-type. Standard stocks on 3".
Sights: Serrated ramp front, micro click rear adjustable for w. and e.
Features: Wide target-type hammer spur, floating firing pin, heavy barrel with shrouded ejector rod. Introduced 1978. From International Distributors.
Price: Blue, about $184.00
Price: Satin blue, about $199.00
Price: Model 65 (similar to M66 except has a fixed rear sight and ramp front), blue, about $161.00
Price: Model 65, satin blue, about $175.00

HANDGUNS—REVOLVERS, SERVICE & SPORT

TAURUS MODEL 73 SPORT REVOLVER
Caliber: 32 S&W Long, 6-shot.
Barrel: 3", heavy.
Weight: 22 oz. **Length:** 8¼" over-all.
Stocks: Oversize target-type, checkered Brazilian walnut.
Sights: Ramp front, notch rear.
Features: Imported from Brazil by International Distributers.
Price: Blue, about $122.00
Price: Satin blue, about $141.00

TAURUS MODEL 80 STANDARD REVOLVER
Caliber: 38 Spec., 6-shot.
Barrel: 3" or 4".
Weight: 31 oz. (4" bbl). **Length:** 9¼" over-all (4" bbl).
Stocks: Checkered Brazilian walnut.
Sights: Serrated ramp front, square notch rear.
Features: Imported from Brazil by International Distributers.
Price: Blue, about $117.00
Price: Satin blue, about $131.00

TAURUS MODEL 82 HEAVY BARREL REVOLVER
Caliber: 38 Spec., 6-shot.
Barrel: 3" or 4", heavy.
Weight: 33 oz. (4" bbl). **Length:** 9¼" over-all (4" bbl).
Stocks: Checkered Brazilian walnut.
Sights: Serrated ramp front, square notch rear.
Features: Imported from Brazil by International Distributers.
Price: Blue, about $122.00
Price: Satin blue, about $137.00

TAURUS MODEL 84 SPORT REVOLVER
Caliber: 38 Spec., 6-shot.
Barrel: 4".
Weight: 30 oz. **Length:** 9¼" over-all.
Stocks: Checkered Brazilian walnut.
Sights: Serrated ramp front, rear adj. for w. and e.
Features: Imported from Brazil by International Distributers.
Price: Blue, about $120.00
Price: Satin blue, about $133.00

TAURUS MODEL 83 REVOLVER
Caliber: 38 Spec., 6-shot.
Barrel: 4" only, heavy.
Weight: 34½ ozs.
Stocks: Over-size checkered walnut.
Sights: Ramp front, micro. click rear adj. for w. & e.
Features: Blue or nickel finish. Introduced 1977. From International Distributors.
Price: Blue, about $125.00
Price: Satin blue, about $138.00

TAURUS MODEL 85 REVOLVER
Caliber: 38 Spec., 5-shot.
Barrel: 3".
Weight: 21 oz.
Stocks: Smooth walnut.
Sights: Ramp front, square notch rear.
Features: Blue or Satin blue finish. Introduced 1980. From International Distributors.
Price: .... N.A.

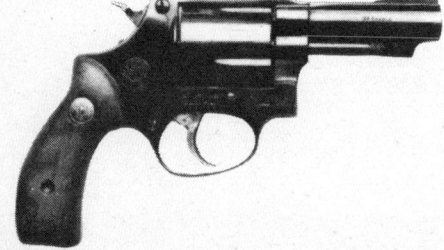

DAN WESSON MODEL 9-2, MODEL 15-2 & MODEL 22
Caliber: 22 LR, 38 Special (Model 9-2); 357 (Model 15-2), both 6 shot.
Barrel: 2", 4", 6", 8", 10", 12", 15". "Quickshift" interchangeable barrels.
Weight: 36 oz. (4" bbl), 40 oz. (4" rimfire). **Length:** 9¼" over-all (4" bbl).
Stocks: "Quickshift" checkered walnut. Interchangeable with three other styles.
Sights: ⅛" serrated blade front with red insert (Std.), white or yellow insert optional, as is Patridge. White outline, rear adj. for w. & e.
Features: Interchangeable barrels; four interchangeable grips; few moving parts, easy disassembly; Bright Blue finish only. Contact Dan Wesson for additional models not listed here. 10", 12" and 15" barrels also available with vent. rib. Rimfire specs. essentially the same as 357 models.
Price: 9-2H, 15-2H (bull barrel shroud) 2" $255.45
Price: 9-2H, 15-2H, 6" bbl. $273.10
Price: 9-2V, 15-2V (vent. rib) 8" $286.50
Price: 9-2V, 15-2V, 10" $315.60
Price: 9-2VH, 15-2VH (heavy vent. shroud) 12" $368.05
Price: Pistol Pac, VH $606.80
Price: 9-2, 15-2 (Std. shroud) 2" $232.90
Price: 9-2, 15-2, 6" $250.20
Price: 9-2, 15-2, 8" $258.90
Price: 9-2, 15-2, 15" $339.05
Price: 9-2, 15-2, Pistol Pac $444.90
Price: 22-cal. same as 357 models.

DAN WESSON MODEL 8-2 & MODEL 14-2
Caliber: 38 Special (Model 8-2); 357 (Model 14-2), both 6 shot.
Barrel: 2", 4", 6", 8". "Quickshift" interchangeable barrels.
Weight: 34 oz. (4" bbl.) **Length:** 9¼" over-all (4" bbl.).
Stocks: "Quickshift" checkered walnut. Interchangeable with three other styles.
Sights: ⅛" serrated ramp front, rear fixed.
Features: Interchangeable barrels; 4 interchangeable grips; few moving s, easy disassembly.
Price: 2" barrel $180.95
Price: 4" barrel $187.60
Price: 6" barrel $194.30
Price: 8" barrel $201.05
Price: Pistol Pac (cased with all above bbls.) $375.40

HANDGUNS—SINGLE ACTION REVOLVERS

ABILENE SINGLE ACTION REVOLVER
Caliber: 357 Mag., 44 Mag., 45 Colt, 6 shot.
Barrel: 4⅝", 6" (all cals.), 7½" (44 Mag. only).
Weight: About 48 oz.
Stocks: Smooth walnut.
Sights: Serrated ramp front, click adj. rear for w. and e.
Features: Transfer bar ignition, wide hammer spur. Blue or stainless steel. From Mossberg.
Price: Blue, 357, 4⅝", 6", 7½" $274.95
Price: Blue, 44 Mag., 7½", ... $274.95
Price: Either cal., Magnaloy (hard chrome) $312.95
Price: 10" barrel, 44 Mag. $356.95
Price: 45 LC, blue $267.95

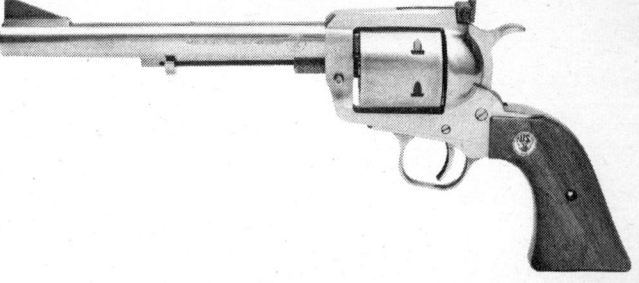

COLT SINGLE ACTION ARMY REVOLVER
Caliber: 357 Magnum, 44 Spec. or 45 Colt, 6 shot.
Barrel: 4¾", 5½", 7½" or 12".
Length: 10⅞" (5½" bbl.). **Weight:** 37 oz. (5½" bbl.).
Stocks: Black composite rubber with eagle and shield crest.
Sights: Fixed. Grooved top strap, blade front.
Features: See Colt catalog for variations and prices. Only basic models and prices listed here.
Price: Blued and case hardened 4¾", 5½" bbl. $399.95
Price: Nickel with walnut stocks $462.95
Price: With 7½" bbl. $409.95

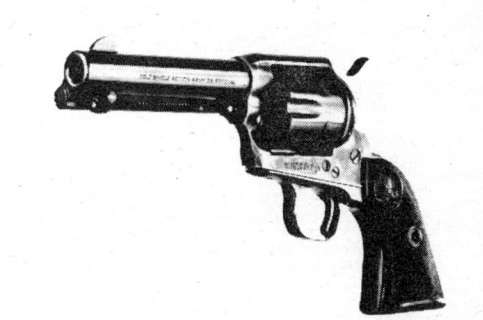

Colt Single Action Army—New Frontier
Same specifications as standard Single Action Army except: 44 Spec., 44-40 or 45 Colt; flat-top frame; high polished finish, blue and case colored; ramp front sight and target rear adj. for windage and elevation; smooth walnut stocks with silver medallion.
Price: 45 Colt, 4¾", blue $399.95
Price: Either cal., 7½", blue $475.95

F.I.E. "HOMBRE" SINGLE ACTION REVOLVER
Caliber: 357 Mag., 44 Mag., 45 LC.
Barrel: 5½" or 7½".
Weight: 45 oz. (5½" bbl.).
Stocks: Smooth walnut with medallion.
Sights: Blade front, grooved topstrap (fixed) rear.
Features: Color case hardened frame. Bright blue finish. Super-smooth action. Introduced 1979. From F.I.E. Corp.
Price: $159.95

F.I.E. "LEGEND" SINGLE ACTION REVOLVER
Caliber: 22 LR/22 Mag.
Barrel: 4¾".
Weight: 32 oz.
Stocks: Smooth walnut or black checkered nylon. Walnut optional ($14.95).
Sights: Blade front, fixed rear.
Features: Positive hammer block system. Brass backstrap and trigger guard. Color case hardened steel frame. From F.I.E. Corp.
Price: 22 LR $84.95
Price: 22 combo $99.95

F.I.E. E15 BUFFALO SCOUT REVOLVER
Caliber: 22 LR/22 Mag., 6-shot.
Barrel: 4¾", 7", 9".
Length: 10" over-all. **Weight:** 32 oz.
Stocks: Black checkered nylon.
Sights: Blade front, fixed rear.
Features: Slide spring ejector. Blue, chrome or blue with brass backstrap and trigger guard models available.
Price: Blued, 22 LR $39.95
Price: Blue, 22 combo $50.65
Price: Chrome, 22 LR $44.95
Price: Chrome, combo $54.95
Price: Blue/brass, combo $53.95

Consult our Directory pages for the location of firms mentioned.

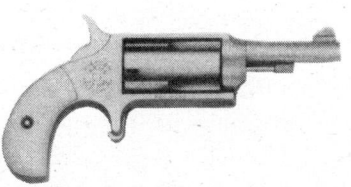

FREEDOM ARMS MINI REVOLVER
Caliber: 22 Short, Long, Long Rifle, 5-shot, 22 WMR, 4-shot.
Barrel: 1", 1¾".
Weight: 4 oz. **Length:** 4" over-all.
Stocks: Black ebonite or simulated ivory.
Sights: Blade front, notch rear.
Features: Made of stainless steel, simple take down; half-cock safety; sheathed trigger; cartridge rims recessed in cylinder. Comes in presentation case.
Price: 22 LR, 1" barrel $124.75
Price: 22 LR, 1¾" barrel $129.50
Price: 22WMR, 1" barrel $144.75
Price: 22 WMR, 1¾" barrel $149.50

HANDGUNS — SINGLE ACTION REVOLVERS

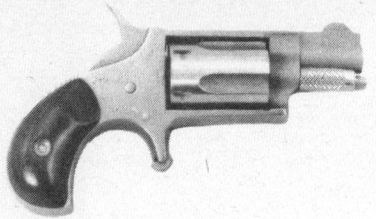

NAM MINI REVOLVER
Caliber: 22 LR, 5-shot.
Barrel: 1".
Weight: 4.5 oz. **Length:** 3.8" over-all.
Stocks: Smooth plastic.
Sights: Blade front only.
Features: Stainless steel, single action only. Spur trigger. The 22 WMR version will be available late 1980. From M & N Distributors.
Price: About $119.95

MITCHELL SINGLE ACTION REVOLVERS
Caliber: 357 Mag., 44 Mag., 45 Colt.
Barrel: 4¾", 5½", 6", 7½", 10", 12", 18".
Weight: About 36 oz.
Stocks: One-piece walnut.
Sights: Ramp front, rear adj. for w. & e.
Features: Color case-hardened frame, grip frame is polished brass. Hammer block safety. Introduced 1980. From Mitchell Arms Corp.
Price: 357, 44, 45, 4¾", 5½", 7½", fixed sights $179.97
Price: As above, adj. sights $194.95
Price: 44 Mag. 45 Colt, 10", 12", 18" bbl. $229.00

RUGER NEW MODEL CONVERTIBLE BLACKHAWK
Caliber: 45 Colt or 45 Colt/45 ACP (extra cylinder).
Barrel: 4⅝" or 7½" (6-groove, 16" twist).
Weight: 40 oz. (7½" bbl.). **Length:** 13⅛" (7½" bbl.).
Stocks: Smooth American walnut.
Sights: ⅛" ramp front, micro click rear adj. for w. and e.
Features: Similar to Super Blackhawk, Ruger interlocked mechanism. Convertible furnished with interchangeable cylinder for 45 ACP.
Price: Blued, 45 Colt $179.75
Price: Convertible $196.90

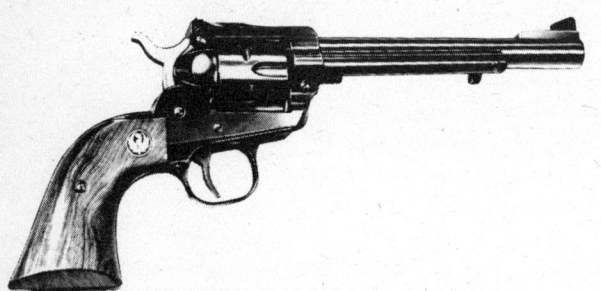

RUGER NEW MODEL SUPER SINGLE-SIX CONVERTIBLE REVOLVER
Caliber: 22 S, L, LR, 6-shot. 22 WMR in extra cylinder.
Barrel: 4⅝", 5½", 6½" or 9½" (6-groove).
Weight: 34½ oz. (6½" bbl.) **Length:** 11¹³⁄₁₆" over-all (6½" bbl.).
Stocks: Smooth American walnut.
Sights: Improved patridge front on ramp, fully adj. rear protected by integral frame ribs.
Features: New Ruger "interlocked" mechanism, transfer bar ignition, gate-controlled loading, hardened chrome-moly steel frame, wide trigger, music wire springs throughout, independent firing pin.
Price: 4⅝", 5½", 6½", 9½" barrel $141.50
Price: 5½", 6½" bbl., stainless steel $201.00

RUGER NEW MODEL BLACKHAWK REVOLVER
Caliber: 357 or 41 Mag., 6-shot.
Barrel: 4⅝" or 6½", either caliber.
Weight: 42 oz. (6½" bbl.). **Length:** 12¼" over-all (6½" bbl.).
Stocks: American walnut.
Sights: ⅛" ramp front, micro click rear adj. for w. and e.
Features: New Ruger interlocked mechanism, independent firing pin, hardened chrome-moly steel frame, music wire springs throughout.
Price: Blued $179.75
Price: Stainless steel (357) $225.00

Ruger New Model 357/9mm Blackhawk
Same as the 357 Magnum except furnished with interchangeable cylinders for 9mm Parabellum and 357 Magnum cartridges $196.90

RUGER NEW MODEL SUPER BLACKHAWK
Caliber: 44 Magnum, 6-shot. Also fires 44 Spec.
Barrel: 7½" (6-groove, 20" twist).
Weight: 48 oz. **Length:** 13⅜" over-all.
Stocks: Genuine American walnut.
Sights: ⅛" ramp front, micro click rear adj. for w. and e.
Features: New Ruger interlocked mechanism, non-fluted cylinder, steel grip and cylinder frame, square back trigger guard, wide serrated trigger and wide spur hammer. Deep Ruger blue.
Price: $207.00

Ruger New Model 30 Carbine Blackhawk
Specifications similar to 45 Blackhawk. Fluted cylinder, round-back trigger guard. Weight 44 oz., length 13⅛" over-all, 7½" barrel only.
Price: $179.95

HANDGUNS—SINGLE ACTION REVOLVERS

SMITH & WESSON K-38 S.A. M-14
Caliber: 38 Spec., 6-shot.
Barrel: 6".
Length: 11⅛" over-all (6" bbl.). **Weight:** 38½ oz. (6" bbl.).
Stocks: Checkered walnut, service type.
Sights: ⅛" Patridge front, micro click rear adj. for w. and e.
Features: Same as Model 14 except single action only, target hammer and trigger.
Price: 6" bbl. .... Special Order only

TANARMI S.A. REVOLVER MODEL TA22S LM
Caliber: 22 LR/22 Mag., 6-shot.
Barrel: 4¾".
Weight: 32 oz. **Length:** 10" over-all.
Stocks: Walnut.
Sights: Blade front, rear adj. for w. & e.
Features: Manual hammer block safety; color hardened steel frame; brass backstrap and trigger guard. Imported from Italy by Excam.
Price: 22/22 Mag., target sights $105.00

TANARMI SINGLE ACTION MODEL TA76
Same as TA22 models except blue backstrap and trigger guard.
Price: 22 LR, blue $60.00
Price: Combo, blue $75.00
Price: 22 LR, chrome $67.00
Price: Combo, chrome $82.00

THE VIRGINIAN DRAGOON REVOLVER
Caliber: 357 Mag., 41 Mag., 44 Mag., 45 Colt.
Barrel: 44 Mag., 6", 7½", 8⅜"; 357 Mag. and 45 Colt, 5", 6", 7½".
Weight: 48 ozs. (6" barrel). **Length:** 11⅞" over-all (6" barrel).
Stocks: Smooth walnut.
Sights: Ramp-type Patridge front blade, micro. adj. target rear.
Features: Color case-hardened frame, spring-loaded floating firing pin, coil main spring. Firing pin is lock-fitted with a steel bushing. Introduced 1977. Made in the U.S. by Interarms Industries, Inc.
Price: 5", 6", 7½", 8⅜" $250.00
Price: 12" Buntline $340.00
Price: Stainless steel, 41, 44, 45, only $280.00
Price: Stainless Buntline, 44, 45 only $370.00

HANDGUNS—MISCELLANEOUS

CLASSIC ARMS TWISTER
Caliber: 22 LR or 9mm Rimfire.
Barrel: 3¼".
Weight: 18 ozs.
Stocks: Pearlite.
Sights: None.
Features: Over-under barrels rotate on an axis for two separate shots. Spur trigger. 9mm Rimfire ammunition available. Available from Navy Arms.
Price: Either caliber $75.00

C. O. P. 357 MAGNUM
Caliber: 357 Mag., 4 shots.
Barrel: 3¼"
Weight: 28 oz. **Length:** 5.5" over-all.
Stocks: Checkered composition.
Sights: Open, fixed.
Features: Double-action, 4-barrels, made of stainless steel. Width is only one inch, height 4.1". From M & N Distributors.
Price: About $250.00

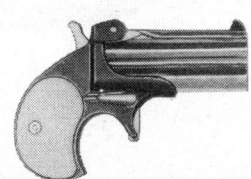

F.I.E. MODEL D-38 DERRINGER
Caliber: 38 Special or 38 S&W.
Barrel: 3".
Weight: 14 oz.
Stocks: Checkered white nylon.
Sights: Fixed.
Features: Chrome finish. Spur trigger. Tip-up barrel, extractors. Gun is made in U.S.A.
Price: $64.95

HANDGUNS—MISCELLANEOUS

HI-STANDARD 9194 AND 9306 DERRINGER
Caliber: 22 Rimfire Magnum. 2 shot.
Barrel: 3½", over and under, rifled.
Length: 5" over-all. **Weight:** 11 oz.
Stocks: Smooth plastic.
Sights: Fixed, open.
Features: Hammerless, integral safety hammerblock, all steel unit is encased in a black, anodized alloy housing. Recessed chamber. Dual extraction. Top break, double action.
Price: Blued (M9194) .... **$109.18**   Nickel (M9306) **$126.23**

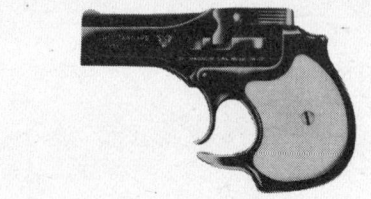

MERRILL SPORTSMAN'S SINGLE SHOT PISTOL
Caliber: 22 LR, 22 WMR, 22 Hornet, 256 Win. Mag., 357 Mag., 357/44 B & D, 30-30 Win., 30 Herrett, 35 Herrett, 41 Mag., 44 Mag., 375 Win., 7mm Merrill, 30 Merrill.
Barrel: 9" or 12", semi-octagonal; .450" wide vent. rib, matted to prevent glare; 14" barrel in 7mm and 30 Merrill only.
Weight: About 54 ozs. **Length:** 10½" over-all (9" bbl.)
Stocks: Smooth walnut with thumb and heel rest.
Sights: Front .125" blade; rear adj. for w. and e.
Features: Polished blue finish. Barrel is grooved for scope mounting. Cocking indicator visible from rear of gun. Has spring-loaded barrel lock, positive thumb safety. Wrist rest attachment (optional) is adjustable, can be swung out of way for holster carry. Scope and mount shown are not included.
Price: 9" barrel **$380.00**
Price: 12" barrel **$405.00**
Price: Extra barrel, 9" .... **$130.00** 12" **$165.00**
Price: Extra 14" bbl. (with RCBS dies) **$300.00**
Price: Wrist rest attachment **$30.00**

MITCHELL'S DERRINGER
Caliber: 38 Spec.
Barrel: 2¾"
Weight: 11 oz. **Length:** 5¼" over-all.
Stocks: Walnut, checkered.
Sights: Fixed, ramp front.
Features: Polished blue finish. All steel. Made in U.S. Introduced 1980. From Mitchell Arms Corp.
Price: **$129.95**

Remington XP-100 Silhouette Pistol
Similar to standard XP-100 except chambered for 7mm BR Remington caliber; 15" barrel gives 21¼" over-all length; 4⅛ lbs.
Price: **$299.95**

REMINGTON MODEL XP-100 Bolt Action Pistol
Caliber: 221 Fireball, single shot.
Barrel: 10½ inches, ventilated rib.
Length: 16¾ inches. **Weight:** 60 oz.
Stocks: Brown nylon one-piece, checkered grip with white spacers.
Features: Fits left or right hand, is shaped to fit fingers and heel of hand. Grooved trigger. Rotating thumb safety, cavity in fore-end permits insertion of up to five 38 cal., 130-gr. metal jacketed bullets to adjust weight and balance. Included is a black vinyl, zippered case.
Sights: Fixed front, rear adj. for w. and e. Tapped for scope mount.
Price: Including case **$274.95**

ROLLING BLOCK SINGLE SHOT PISTOL
Caliber: 22 LR, 357 mag.
Barrel: 8".
Weight: 2 lbs. **Length:** 12".
Stocks: Walnut.
Sights: Front adj. for w., buckhorn adj. for e.
Features: Polished brass trigger guard. Imported by Navy Arms.
Price: **$150.00**

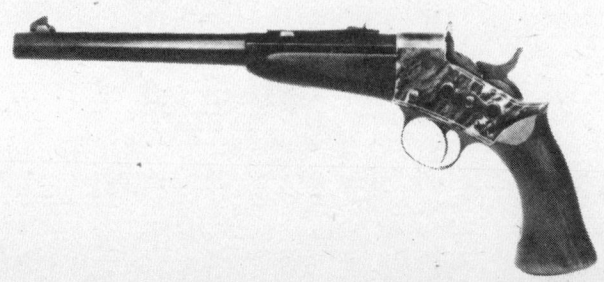

HANDGUNS — MISCELLANEOUS

SEMMERLING LM-4 PISTOL
Caliber: 45 ACP.
Barrel: 3½".
Weight: 24 ozs. **Length:** 5.2" over-all.
Stocks: Checkered black plastic.
Sights: Ramp front, fixed rear.
Features: Manually operated repeater. Over-all dimensions are 5.2" x 3.7" x 1". Has a four-shot magazine capacity. Comes with manual, leather carrying case, spare stock screw and wrench. From Semmerling Corp.
Price: Complete $645.00
Price: Thin Version (blue sideplate instead of grips) $645.00

TANARMI O/U DERRINGER
Caliber: 38 Special.
Barrel: 3".
Weight: 14 oz. **Length:** 4¾" over-all.
Stocks: Checkered white nylon.
Sights: Fixed.
Features: Blue finish; tip-up barrel. Assembled in U.S. by Excam, Inc.
Price: $72.00

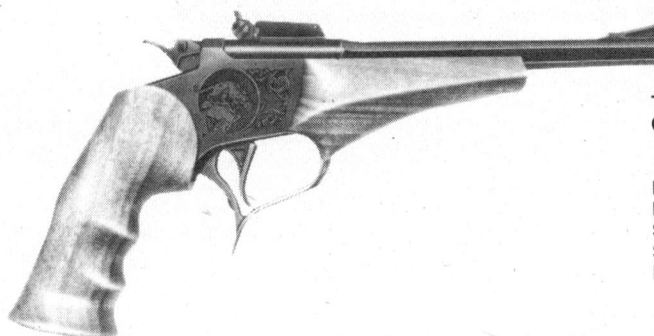

THOMPSON-CENTER ARMS CONTENDER
Caliber: 218 Bee, 221 Rem., 25-35 Win., 7mm T.C.U., 30-30 Win., 22 S, L, LR, 22 WMR, 22 Hornet, 256 Win., 357 Mag., also 222 Rem., 45 ACP, 44 Mag., 45 Long Colt, 45 Win. Mag.
Barrel: 10", tapered octagon, bull barrel and vent. rib.
Length: 13¼" (10" bbl.). **Weight:** 43 oz. (10" bbl.).
Stocks: Select walnut grip and fore-end, with thumb rest. Right or left hand.
Sights: Under cut blade ramp front, rear adj. for w. & e.
Features: Break open action with auto-safety. Single action only. Interchangeable bbls., both caliber (rim & center fire), and length. Drilled and tapped for scope. Engraved frame. See T/C catalog for exact barrel/caliber availablity.
Price: Blued (rimfire cals.) $225.00
Price: Blued (centerfire cals.) $225.00
Price: Extra bbls. (standard octagon) $90.00
Price: Bushnell Phantom scope base $8.75
Price: Fitted walnut case $45.00
Price: 357 and 44 Mag. vent. rib, internal choke bbl. $99.00

Thompson-Center Super 14 Contender
Similar to regular Contender except has 14" barrel with fully adjustable target-type sights. Available in 30 Herrett, 357 Herrett, 222 Rem., 223 Rem., 30-30 Win., 35 Rem., 41 and 44 Mag., and 45 Win. Mag. only. Introduced 1978.
Price: $245.00
Price: Extra barrels $99.00

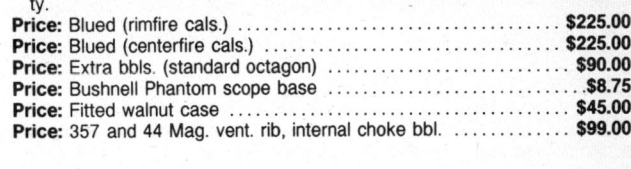

WEATHERBY MARK V SILHOUETTE PISTOL
Caliber: 22-250, 308 (full length), single-shot.
Barrel: 15".
Weight: 4½ lbs.
Stock: Thumbhole design of selected Claro walnut. Rosewood fore-end tip and grip cap.
Sights: Globe front with inserts, target-type peep rear.
Features: Single shot bolt action pistol uses a modified Weatherby Mark V Varmintmaster action. Drilled and tapped for standard Varmintmaster scope mounts.
Price: About $899.95

WICHITA SILHOUETTE PISTOL
Caliber: 7mm PPC, 308x1½, 308 (full length). Other calibers available upon request. Single shot.
Barrel: 14¹⁵⁄₁₆", (shorter lengths available).
Weight: 4½ lbs. **Length:** 21⅜" over-all.
Stock: American walnut with oil finish, or fiberglass (yellow or black). Glass bedded.
Sights: Lyman globe front with inserts, Lyman or Williams peep rear.
Features: Comes with either right- or left-hand action with right-hand grip. Fluted bolt, flat bolt handle. Action drilled and tapped for Burris scope mounts. Non-glare satin blue finish. Remington-type trigger (with Canjar set shoe optional at extra charge). Introduced 1979. From Wichita Arms.
Price: $595.00
Price: As above except with Rear Position Stock and target-type Lightpull trigger. (Not illus.) $661.45

> Consult our Directory pages for the location of firms mentioned.

WICHITA CLASSIC PISTOL
Caliber: Any, up to and including 308 Win.
Barrel: 11¼", octagon.
Weight: About 5 lbs.
Stock: Exhibition grade American black walnut. Checkered 20 lpi. Other woods available on special order.
Sights: Micro open sights standard. Receiver drilled and tapped for scope mount on special order.
Features: Receiver and barrel octagonally shaped, finished in non-glare blue. Bolt has three locking lugs and three gas escape ports. Completely adjustable Wichita trigger. Introduced 1980. From Wichita Arms.
Price: $1,295.00
Price: With fitted case $1,750.00

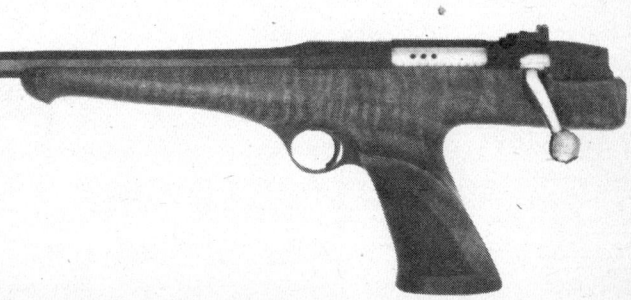

CAUTION: PRICES CHANGE. CHECK AT GUNSHOP.

CENTERFIRE RIFLES—AUTOLOADING & SLIDE ACTION

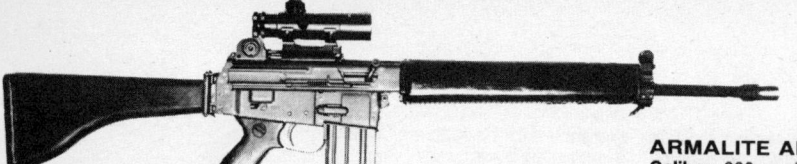

ARMALITE AR-180 SPORTER CARBINE
Caliber: 223 semi-automatic, gas operated carbine.
Barrel: 18¼" (12" twist).
Weight: 6½ lbs. **Length:** 38" over-all.
Stock: Nylon folding stock, phenolic fiber-glass heat dissipating fore-end.
Sight: Flip-up "L" type sight adj. for w., post front adj. for e.
Features: Safety lever accessible from both sides. Flash hider slotted to prevent muzzle climb.
Price: $389.00
Price: 3x (2.75 x 20mm) scope with quick detachable side-mount. $119.95
Price: Extra 5-round magazine $9.95
Price: Extra 20-shot magazine $15.95
Price: Extra 40-shot magazine $29.95

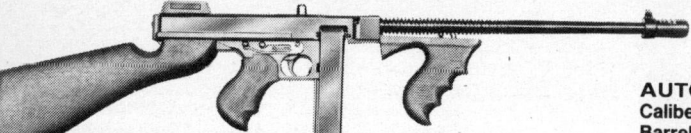

AUTO-ORDNANCE MODEL 27 A-1
Caliber: 45 ACP, 30-shot magazine.
Barrel: 16".
Weight: 11½ lbs. **Length:** About 39½" over-all (Deluxe).
Stock: Walnut stock and vertical fore-end.
Sights: Blade front, open rear adj. for w.
Features: Re-creation of Thompson Model 1927. Semi-auto only. Deluxe model has finned barrel, adj. rear sight and compensator; Standard model has plain barrel and military sights. From Auto-Ordnance Corp.
Price: Deluxe $449.65
Price: Standard $409.65
Price: 1927A5 Pistol (M27A1 without stock; wgt. 7 lbs.) $409.65

Auto-Ordnance 1927A-3
A 22 caliber version of the 27A-1. Exact look-alike with alloy receiver. Weight is about 7 lbs., 16" finned barrel, 10, 30- and 50-shot magazines and drum. Introduced 1977. From Auto-Ordnance Corp.
Price: $449.65

BERETTA BM 62 AUTO RIFLE
Caliber: 308 (7.62mm), 20-shot magazine.
Barrel: 17.5".
Weight: 9¼ lbs. **Length:** 38.5" over-all.
Stock: Walnut.
Sights: Blade front, peep rear fully adjustable for w. & e.
Features: Civilian sporting version of the BM-59 military rifle used by Italian armed forces. Has a bolt hold-open device, clip guide, rotary bolt, semi-auto only. Folding bipod, sling, 5-shot magazine, cleaning kit, bayonet and scope mount available. Introduced 1980. From Beretta Arms Co.
Price: $985.00

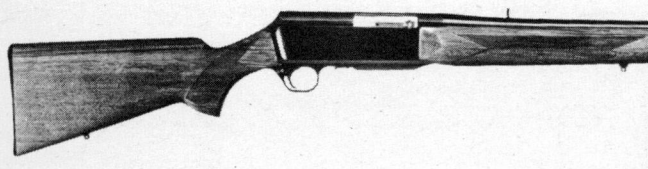

BROWNING HIGH-POWER AUTO RIFLE
Caliber: 243, 270, 30-06, 308.
Barrel: 22" round tapered.
Weight: 7⅜ lbs. **Length:** 43" over-all.
Stock: French walnut p.g. stock (13⅝"x2"x1⅝") and fore-end, hand checkered.
Sights: Adj. folding-leaf rear, gold bead on hooded ramp front.
Features: Detachable 4-round magazine. Receiver tapped for scope mounts. Trigger pull 3½ lbs. Gold plated trigger on Grade IV.
Price: Grade I $479.95
Price: Grade III $900.00
Price: Grade IV $1,700.00

Browning Magnum Auto Rifle
Same as the standard caliber model, except weighs 8⅜ lbs., 45" over-all 24" bbl., 3-round mag., Cals. 7mm Mag., 300 Win. Mag.
Price: Grade I .... $529.95   Grade III $950.00
Price: Grade IV $1,750.00

COLT AR-15 SPORTER
Caliber: 223 Rem.
Barrel: 20".
Weight: 7¼ lbs. **Length:** 38⅜" over-all.
Stock: Reinforced polycarbonate with buttstock stowage compartment.
Sights: Post front, rear adj. for w. and e.
Features: 5-round detachable box magazine, recoil pad, flash suppressor, sling swivels.
Price: $424.95

CENTERFIRE RIFLES—AUTOLOADING & SLIDE ACTION

Colt AR-15 Collapsable Stock Model
Same as standard AR-15 except has telescoping nylon-coated aluminum buttstock and redesigned fore-end. Over-all length collapsed is 32", extended 39". Barrel length is 16", weight is 5.8 lbs. Has 14½" sight radius. Introduced 1978.
Price: $466.00

COMMANDO ARMS CARBINE
Caliber: 9mm or 45 ACP.
Barrel: 16½".
Weight: 8 lbs. **Length:** 37" over-all.
Stock: Walnut buttstock.
Sights: Blade front, peep rear.
Features: Semi-auto only. Cocking handle on left side. Choice of magazines—5, 15, 30 or 90 shot. From Commando Arms.
Price: Mark 9 or Mark 45 .... $195.00
Price: Nickel plated $225.00

F.N.-F.A.L. COMPETITION AUTO
Caliber: 308 Win., 10-shot magazine.
Barrel: 21" (24" with flash hider).
Weight: 9 lbs., 7 oz. **Length:** 44½" over-all.
Stock: Black composition butt, fore-end and pistol grip.
Sights: Post front, aperture rear adj. for elevation.
Features: Optional 20-shot magazine available. Has sling swivels, carrying handle, rubber recoil pad. Consecutively numbered pairs available at additional cost. Imported by Steyr Daimler Puch of America.
Price: $2,000.00

HECKLER & KOCH HK770 AUTO RIFLE
Caliber: 243 and 308 Win., 3-shot magazine.
Barrel: 19.6".
Weight: 7½ lbs. **Length:** 42.8" over-all.
Stock: European walnut. Checkered p.g. and fore-end.
Sights: Vertically adjustable blade front, open, fold-down rear adj. for w.
Features: Has the delayed roller-locked bolt system and polygonal rifling. Magazine catch located at front of trigger guard. Receiver top is dovetailed to accept clamp-type scope mount. From Heckler & Koch, Inc.
Price: $470.00

HECKLER & KOCH HK-91 AUTO RIFLE
Caliber: 308 Win., 5- or 20-shot magazine.
Barrel: 19".
Weight: 9½ lbs. **Length:** 40¼" over-all.
Stock: Black high-impact plastic.
Sights: Post front, aperture rear adj. for w. and e.
Features: Delayed roller lock bolt action. Sporting version of West German service rifle. Takes special H&K clamp scope mount. Shown with light bipod and Zeiss scope. Imported by Heckler & Koch, Inc.
Price: HK-91 with plastic stock $568.00
Price: HK-91 with retractable metal stock $769.00

HECKLER & KOCH HK-93 AUTO RIFLE
Similar to HK-93 except in 223 cal., 16.13" barrel, over-all length of 35½", weighs 7¾ lbs. Slight differences in stock, fore-end.
Price: HK-93 .... $553.00
Price: HK-93 with retractable metal stock $763.00

IVER JOHNSON'S PLAINFIELD CARBINE
Caliber: 30 U.S. Carbine.
Barrel: 18" four-groove.
Weight: 6½ lbs. **Length:** 35½" over-all.
Stock: Glossy finished hard wood.
Sights: Click adj. open rear.
Features: Gas operated semi-auto carbine. 15-shot detachable magazine.
Price: $149.50
Price: Paratrooper model—with telescoping wire stock, front vertical hand grip $181.00
Price: Super Enforcer (9" bbl., full p.g.) $193.00

Consult our Directory pages for the location of firms mentioned.

CAUTION: PRICES CHANGE. CHECK AT GUNSHOP.

CENTERFIRE RIFLES—AUTOLOADING & SLIDE ACTION

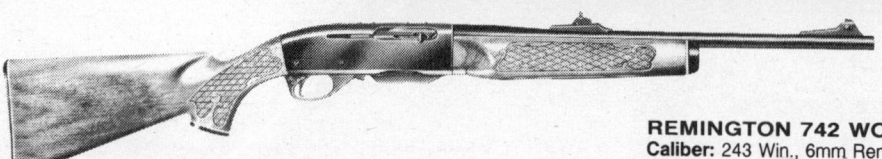

Remington 742 BDL Woodsmaster
Same as 742 except: "stepped" receiver, Monte Carlo with cheekpiece (right or left), whiteline spacers, basket-weave checkering on p.g. and fore-end, black fore-end tip, RKW finish (13 5/16"x1 5/8"x1 13/16"x2 1/2"). Cals. 30-06, 308 .... $382.95

Remington 742 Carbine
Same as M742 except: 18 1/2" bbl., 38 1/2" over-all, wgt. 6 3/4 lbs. Cals: 30-06, 308 Win. $352.95

REMINGTON 742 WOODSMASTER AUTO RIFLE
Caliber: 243 Win., 6mm Rem., 7mm Exp. Rem., 308 Win. and 30-06.
Barrel: 22" round tapered.
Weight: 7 1/2 lbs. **Length:** 42" over-all.
Stock: Walnut (13 1/4"x1 5/8"x2 1/4") deluxe checkered p.g. and fore-end.
Sights: Gold bead front sight on ramp; step rear sight with windage adj.
Features: Positive cross-bolt safety. Receiver tapped for scope mount. 4-shot clip mag.
Price: $352.95
 Extra 4-shot clip magazine $9.95
 Sling strap and swivels (installed) $17.95
 Peerless (D) and Premier (F) grades .... $1,400.00 and $2,800.00
 Premier with gold inlays $4,200.00

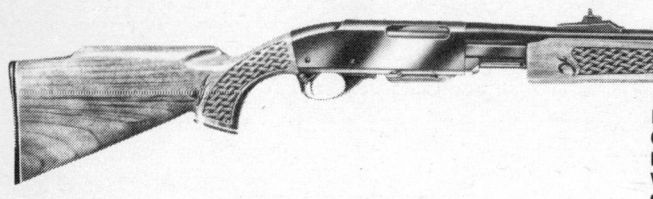

Remington 760 BDL Gamemaster
Same as 760 except: "stepped receiver," Monte Carlo stock with cheekpiece (right or left), whiteline spacer, basket-weave checkering on p.g. and fore-end, black fore-end tip, RKW finish. (13 5/16"x1 5/8"x1 13/16"x2 1/2"). Cals. 270, 30-06, 308 .... $339.95
Also in Peerless (D) and Premier (F) grades ... $1,400.00 and $2,800.00
(F), with gold inlay $4,200.00

REMINGTON 760 GAMEMASTER SLIDE ACTION
Caliber: 6mm Rem., 243, 270, 308 Win., 30-06.
Barrel: 22" round tapered.
Weight: 7 1/2 lbs. **Length:** 42" over-all.
Stock: Checkered walnut p.g. and fore-end (13 1/4"x1 5/8"x2 1/8") RKW finish
Sights: Gold bead front sight on matted ramp, open step adj. sporting rear.
Features: Detachable 4-shot clip. Cross-bolt safety. Receiver tapped for scope mount.
Price: $309.95
 Sling strap and swivels (installed) $17.95
 Extra 4-shot clip $9.25

Remington 760 Gamemaster Carbine
Same as M760 except has 18 1/2" barrel. Wgt. 7 1/4 lbs., 38 1/2" over-all. Cals: 308 Win. and 30-60 .... $309.95

RUGER 44 AUTOLOADING CARBINE
Caliber: 44 Magnum, 4-shot tubular magazine.
Barrel: 18 1/2" round tapered.
Weight: 5 3/4 lbs. **Length:** 36 3/4" over-all
Stock: One-piece walnut p.g. stock (13 3/8"x1 5/8"x2 1/4")
Sights: 1/16" front, folding leaf rear sight adj. for e.
Features: Wide, curved trigger. Sliding cross-bolt safety. Receiver tapped for scope mount, unloading button.
Price: $240.00

RUGER MINI-14 223 CARBINE
Caliber: 223 Rem., 5-shot detachable box magazine.
Barrel: 18 1/2".
Weight: 6.4 lbs. **Length:** 37 1/4" over-all.
Stock: American hardwood, steel reinforced.
Sights: Ramp front, fully adj. rear.
Features: Fixed piston gas-operated, positive primary extraction. 10 and 20-shot magazines available from Ruger dealers, 30-shot magazine available only to police departments and government agencies.
Price: $227.50
Price: As above except in stainless steel $277.50

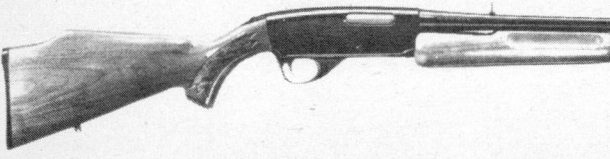

Savage Model 170-C Slide Action Rifle
Same as Model 170 except 30-30 only, has 18 1/2" barrel, no Monte Carlo on stock. Silent-Lok feature eliminates slide handle rattle. $159.71

SAVAGE MODEL 170 SLIDE ACTION
Caliber: 30-30 or 35 Rem., 3-shot mag.
Barrel: 22" round tapered.
Weight: 6 3/4 lbs. **Length:** 41 1/2" over-all.
Stock: Walnut (14"x1 1/2"x2 1/2"), with checkered p.g. Hard rubber buttplate.
Sights: Hooded ramp front, folding-leaf rear.
Features: Hammerless, solid frame tapped for scope mount. Top tang safety.
Price: $188.75

CENTERFIRE RIFLES—AUTOLOADING & SLIDE ACTION

SIG-AMT AUTO RIFLE
Caliber: 308 Win., 20-shot detachable box magazine.
Barrel: 18¾".
Weight: 9½ lbs. **Length:** 39" over-all.
Stock: Walnut stock and fore-end, composition vertical p.g.
Sights: Adj. post front, adj. aperture rear.
Features: Roller-lock breech, gas-assisted action; right-side cocking handle; loaded chamber indicator; no-tool take-down. Winter trigger (optional) allows firing with mittens. Spare parts, magazine, etc. available. From Mandall Shooting Supplies.
Price: $2,000.00

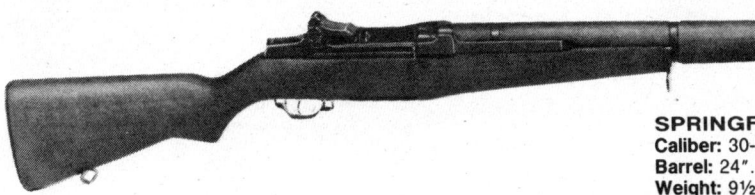

SPRINGFIELD ARMORY M1 GARAND RIFLE
Caliber: 30-06, 8-shot clip.
Barrel: 24".
Weight: 9½ lbs. **Length:** 43½" over-all.
Stock: Walnut, military.
Sights: Military square blade front, click adjustable peep rear.
Features: Commercially-made M-1 Garand duplicates the original service rifle. Introduced 1979. From Springfield Armory.
Price: Standard $420.00
Price: National Match $564.00

SPRINGFIELD ARMORY M1A RIFLE
Caliber: 7.62mm Nato (308), 5-, 10- or 20-round box magazine.
Barrel: 25 1/16" with flash suppressor, 22" without suppressor.
Weight: 8¾ lbs. **Length:** 44¼" over-all.
Stock: American walnut or birch with walnut colored heat-resistant fiberglass handguard. Matching walnut handguard available.
Sights: Military, square blade front, full click-adjustable aperture rear.
Features: Commercial equivalent of the U.S. M-14 service rifle with no provision for automatic firing. From Springfield Armory. Military accessories available including 3x-9x2 ART scope and mount.
Price: Standard M1A Rifle $420.00
Price: Match Grade $540.50
Price: Super Match (heavy Premium barrel) $650.00

UNIVERSAL ENFORCER MODEL 3000 AUTO CARBINE
Caliber: 30 M1 Carbine, 5-shot magazine.
Barrel: 10¼" with 12-groove rifling.
Length: 17¾". **Weight:** 4½ lbs.
Stocks: American walnut with handguard.
Sights: Gold bead ramp front. Peep rear adj. for w. and e. 14" sight radius.
Features: Accepts 15 or 30-shot magazines. 4½-6 lb. trigger pull.
Price: Blue finish $232.95
Price: Nickel plated finish (Model 3010N) $283.95
Price: Gold plated finish (Model 3015G) $274.95
Price: Black or olive Teflon-S finish (3020TRB, 3025TCO) $298.95

UNIVERSAL 1003 AUTOLOADING CARBINE
Caliber: 30 M1, 5-shot magazine.
Barrel: 18"
Weight: 5½ lbs. **Length:** 35½" over-all
Stock: American hardwood stock inletted for "issue" sling and oiler, blued metal handguard.
Sights: Blade front aperture rear. With protective wings, adj.
Features: Gas operated, hammerless. Cross lock safety. Receiver tapped for scope mounts.
Price: $166.95
Price: Model 2560 "Ferret" in 256 Win. $166.95

CENTERFIRE RIFLES—AUTOLOADING & SLIDE ACTION

Universal Model 5000PT Carbine
Same as standard Model 1003 except comes with "Schmeisser-type paratrooper" folding stock. Over-all length open 36"; folded 27".
Price: Blue only $208.95

Universal Model 1005 SB Carbine
Same as Model 1003 except has "Super-Mirrored" blue finish, walnut Monte Carlo stock, deluxe barrel band. Also available finished in nickel (Model 1010N), 18K gold (Model 1015G), Raven Black Du Pont Teflon-S (Model 1020TB) or Camouflage Olive Teflon-S (Model 1025TCO).
Price: Model 1005SB $211.95
Price: Model 1010N $224.95
Price: Model 1015G $331.95
Price: Model 1020TB, 1025TCO $298.95

VALMET M-71S
Caliber: 223, 15- and 30-shot detachable magazines.
Barrel: 16⅝".
Weight: 8¾ lbs. **Length:** 36⅝" over-all.
Stock: Walnut (standard).
Sights: Open tangent rear sight adjustable for elevation. Post front sight with protectors, adjustable for windage.
Features: Finnish semi-automatic version of AK-47. Imported by Interarms.
Price: Walnut stock $695.00

UZI CARBINE
Caliber: 9mm Parabellum, 25-round magazine.
Barrel: 16.1".
Weight: 8½ lbs. **Length:** 24.2" (stock folded).
Stock: Folding metal stock.
Sights: Post-type front, "L" flip-type rear adj. for 100 meters and 200 meters.
Features: Adapted by Col. Uzi Gal to meet BATF regulations, this semi-atuo has the same qualities as the famous submachine gun. Made by Israel Military Industries. Comes in molded Styrofoam case with sling, magazine and a short "display only" barrel. Imported by Action Arms Ltd. Introduced 1980.
Price: $595.00

WILKINSON "TERRY" CARBINE
Caliber: 9mm Para., 30-shot magazine.
Barrel: 16³⁄₁₆".
Weight: 7 lbs. 2 ozs. **Length:** 28½" over-all.
Stock: Black P.V.C. plastic stock, grip and fore-end.
Sights: Williams adjustable.
Features: Closed breech, blow-back action. Bolt-type safety and magazine catch. Ejection port has spring operated cover. Receiver dovetailed for scope mount. Semi-auto only. Introduced 1977. From Wilkinson Arms.
Price: $315.00
Price: Extra magazine $18.95

CENTERFIRE RIFLES—LEVER ACTION

BROWNING B-92 LEVER ACTION
Caliber: 44 Rem. Mag., 11-shot magazine.
Barrel: 20" round.
Weight: 5 lbs., 8 oz. **Length:** 37½" over-all.
Stock: Straight grip stock and classic fore-end in French walnut with high gloss finish. Steel, modified crescent buttplate. (12¾" x 2" x 2⅞").
Sights: Post front, classic cloverleaf rear with notched elevation ramp. Sight radius 16⅝".
Features: Tubular magazine. Follows design of original Model 92 lever-action. Introduced 1979.
Price: $264.95

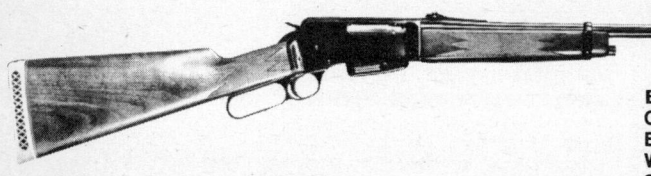

BROWNING BLR LEVER ACTION RIFLE
Caliber: 243, 308 Win. or 358 Win. 4-shot detachable mag.
Barrel: 20" round tapered.
Weight: 6 lbs. 15 oz. **Length:** 39¾" over-all.
Stock: Checkered straight grip and fore-end, oil finished walnut (13¾"x1¾"x2⅜").
Sights: Gold bead on hooded ramp front; low profile square notch adj. rear.
Features: Wide, grooved trigger; half-cock hammer safety. Receiver tapped for scope mount. Recoil pad installed.
Price: $329.95

CENTERFIRE RIFLES — LEVER ACTION

DIXIE ENGRAVED MODEL 1873 RIFLE
Caliber: 44-40.
Barrel: 23½", octagon.
Weight: 7¾ lbs. **Length:** 43" over-all.
Stock: Walnut.
Sights: Blade front, adj. rear.
Features: Engraved and case hardened frame. Duplicate of Winchester 1873. Made in Italy. From Dixie Gun Works.
Price: $395.00
Price: Plain, blued carbine $359.00

GLENFIELD 30GT LEVEL ACTION RIFLE
Caliber: 30-30, 6-shot tubular magazine.
Barrel: 18½".
Weight: 7 lbs. **Length:** 36¾" over-all.
Stock: Walnut-finished hardwood. Straight grip.
Sights: Brass bead front, adjustable rear.
Features: Checkering on p.g. and fore-end. Receiver top sand blasted to prevent glare. Introduced 1979.
Price: $174.95

MARLIN 336C LEVER ACTION CARBINE
Caliber: 30-30 or 35 Rem., 6-shot tubular magazine
Barrel: 20" Micro-Groove®.
Weight: 7 lbs. **Length:** 38½"
Stock: Select American black walnut, capped p.g. with white line spacers. Mar-Shield® finish.
Sights: Ramp front with Wide-Scan™ hood, semi-buckhorn folding rear adj. for w. & e.
Features: Gold plated trigger, receiver tapped for scope mount, offset hammer spur, top of receiver sand blasted to prevent glare.
Price: Less scope $187.95

Glenfield 30A Lever Action Carbine
Same as the Marlin 336C except: checkered walnut finished hardwood p.g. stock, 30-30 only, 6-shot. $174.95

Marlin 336A
Same action as the 336C with 24" round barrel, ½-magazine tube with 5-shot capacity. Blued fore-end cap and sling swivels. Available in 30-30 Win. only $195.95

Marlin 336T Lever Action Carbine
Same as the 336C except: straight stock; cal. 30-30 only. Squared finger lever, 18½" barrel, weight 6¾ lbs. $187.95

MARLIN 1894 LEVER ACTION CARBINE
Caliber: 44 Magnum, 10 shot tubular magazine
Barrel: 20" Micro-Groove®.
Weight: 6 lbs. **Length:** 37½"
Stock: American black walnut, straight grip and fore-end. Mar-Shield® finish.
Sights: Hooded ramp front, semi-buckhorn folding rear adj. for w. & e.
Features: Gold plated trigger, receiver tapped for scope mount, offset hammer spur, solid top receiver sand blasted to prevent glare.
Price: $193.95

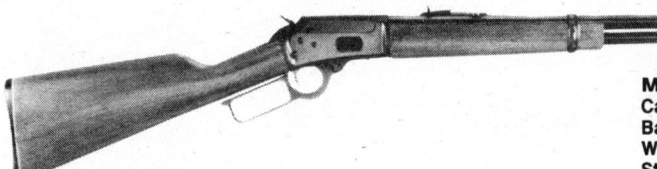

MARLIN 1894C CARBINE 357
Caliber: 357 Magnum, 9-shot tube magazine.
Barrel: 18" Micro-Groove®.
Weight: 6 lbs. **Length:** 35½" over-all.
Stock: American black walnut, straight grip and fore-end.
Sights: Bead front, adjustable semi-buckhorn folding rear.
Features: Solid top receiver tapped for scope mount or receiver sight; offset hammer spur. Gold plated steel trigger; receiver top sandblasted to prevent glare.
Price: About $193.95

MARLIN 1895S LEVER ACTION RIFLE
Caliber: 45-70, 4-shot tubular magazine.
Barrel: 22" round.
Weight: 7½ lbs. **Length:** 40½".
Stock: American black walnut, full pistol grip. Mar-Shield® finish.
Sights: Bead front with Wide-Scan hood, semi-buckhorn folding rear adj. for w. and e.
Features: Solid receiver tapped for scope mounts or receiver sights, offset hammer spur.
Price: $266.95

CENTERFIRE RIFLES — LEVER ACTION

MARLIN 444S LEVER ACTION SPORTER
Caliber: 444 Marlin, 4-shot tubular magazine
Barrel: 22" Micro-Groove®.
Weight: 7½ lbs. **Length:** 40½"
Stock: American black walnut, capped p.g. with white line spacers, rubber rifle butt pad. Mar-Shield® finish.
Sights: Hooded ramp front, folding semi-buckhorn rear adj. for w. & e.
Features: Gold plated trigger, receiver tapped for scope mount, offset hammer spur, leather sling with detachable swivels.
Price: $210.95

Marlin 375 Rifle
Similar to 444S except chambered for 375 Win., 5-shot magazine; 20" barrel; over-all length of 38½"; weight of 6¾ lbs. Comes with adj. leather carrying strap and q.d. swivels $210.95

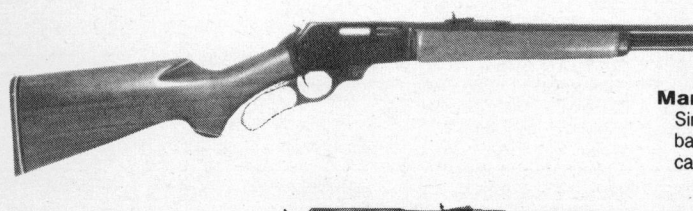

MOSSBERG MODEL 479 PC LEVER ACTION
Caliber: 30-30 or 35 Rem., 6-shot magazine.
Barrel: 20".
Weight: 7½ lbs. **Length:** 38½" over-all.
Stock: Walnut, fluted comb, p.g., composition buttplate and p.g. cap.
Sights: Ramp front, rear adj. for e.
Features: Trigger moves with lever on opening, hammer-block safety. Solid top receiver with side ejection. Also available with straight grip stock, either cal., same price
Price: $186.95

MOSSBERG 479 SC LEVER ACTION
Same as 479 PC except straight grip stock, composition buttplate, hammer block safety $186.95

NAVY ARMS MODEL 66 LEVER ACTION RIFLE
Caliber: 38 Special, 44-40.
Barrel: 16½", 19", 24".
Weight: 9¼ lbs. **Length:** 39½".
Stock: Walnut.
Sights: Fixed front, folding rear.
Features: Replica of Winchester Model 1866 "Yellowboy." Available with three grades of engraving, selected stock and fore-end at additional cost. Imported by Navy Arms.
Price: Trappers Carbine $250.00
Price: 24" octagon bbl. (illus.) $295.00

NAVY ARMS HENRY CARBINE
Caliber: 44-40 or 44 rimfire.
Barrel: 21".
Weight: About 9 lbs. **Length:** About 39" over-all.
Stock: Oil stained American walnut.
Sights: Blade front, rear adj. for e.
Features: Reproduction of the original Henry carbine with brass frame and buttplate, rest blued. Will be produced in limited edition of 1,000 standard models, plus 50 engraved guns. From Navy Arms.
Price: Standard $500.00
Price: Engraved $1,500.00
Price: Iron frame, standard $750.00
Price: Iron frame, engraved $1,500.00

ROSSI SADDLE-RING CARBINE
Caliber: 38 Spec. (9 rounds), 357 Mag. (8 rounds).
Barrel: 20".
Weight: 5¾ lbs. **Length:** 37" over-all.
Stock: Walnut.
Sights: Blade front, Buckhorn rear.
Features: Re-creation of the famous lever-action carbine. Handles 38 and 357 interchangeably. Introduced 1978. Imported by Interarms.
Price: $310.00

Consult our Directory pages for the location of firms mentioned.

CAUTION: PRICES CHANGE. CHECK AT GUNSHOP.

CENTERFIRE RIFLES — LEVER ACTION

NAVY ARMS "1873" MODEL RIFLE
Caliber: 44-40.
Barrel: 24" (rifle, octagon); 20" (carbine, round), 16½" (trapper).
Weight: 9 lbs. (rifle); 7½ lbs. (carbine).
Stock: Walnut.
Sights: Blade front, step adj. rear.
Features: Available in blue, case-hardened or nickel (44-40 only) finish. Sliding dust cover, lever latch. Imported by Navy Arms Co.
Price: Rifle $275.00
Price: Carbine $235.00
Price: Trapper $235.00

SAVAGE 99E LEVER ACTION RIFLE
Caliber: 300 Savage, 243 or 308 Win., 5-shot rotary magazine.
Barrel: 22", chrome-moly steel.
Weight: 7 lbs. **Length:** 39¾" over-all.
Stock: Walnut finished with checkered p.g. and fore-end (13½x1½x2½).
Sights: Ramp front with folding leaf sporting rear. Tapped for scope mounts.
Features: Grooved trigger, slide safety locks trigger and lever.
Price: $251.35

Savage 99A Lever Action Rifle
Similar to the 99E except: straight-grip walnut stock with schnabel fore-end, top tang safety, no magazine window. Folding leaf rear sight. Available in 250-3000 (250 Savage), 243 or 308 Win. $284.00

Savage 99C Lever Action Clip Rifle
Similar to M99A except: Detachable staggered clip magazine with push-button ejection. Cut checkering on stock and fore-end. Wgt. about 6¾ lbs., 41¾" over-all with 22" bbl. Cals. 243, 308 .... $291.75

Savage 99 CD Lever Action Rifle
Similar to Model 99C except: removable bead ramp front; removable adjustable rear sight; white line recoil pad and p.g. cap; weight 7 lbs., Monte Carlo stock and grooved fore-end; skip-line cut checkering; q.d. sling with swivels. Comes in 243 or 308.
Price: $322.95

Savage Model 99-358 Lever Action Rifle
Similar to Model 99 CD except has straight-grip stock, no checkering, chambered for 358 Win., 6-shot rotary magazine with cartridge counter, no Monte Carlo, weight 7 lbs., removable ramp front sight, folding leaf rear. Has vent. recoil pad, swivel studs. Introduced 1977. .... $299.00
Price: Model 99-375 in 375 Win. caliber. Same as above except has solid recoil pad. $299.00

WESTERN FIELD 79 LEVER ACTION CARBINE
Caliber: 30-30, 6-shot magazine.
Barrel: 20".
Weight: 7½ lbs. **Length:** 38½" over-all.
Stock: Walnut finished hardwood.
Sights: Ramp front, adj. rear.
Features: Trigger moves with lever on opening, cross-bolt hammer-block safety. Solid top receiver with side ejection. Scope not included. Ward article No. 10792.
Price: Standard Model $159.99

CAUTION: PRICES CHANGE. CHECK AT GUNSHOP.

CENTERFIRE RIFLES — LEVER ACTION

WINCHESTER MODEL 94 BIG BORE XTR
Caliber: 375 Win., 6-shot magazine.
Barrel: 20".
Weight: 6⅛ lbs. **Length:** 37¾" over-all.
Stock: American walnut with fine cut checkering, warm rich color. Satin finish.
Sights: Hooded ramp front, semi-buckhorn rear adjustable for w. & e.
Features: All external metal parts have Winchester's new deep blue high polish finish. Stock measurements are: 13¼" x 1¾" x 2½". Rifling twist 1 in 12". Rubber recoil pad fitted to buttstock. Introduced 1978.
Price: $253.00

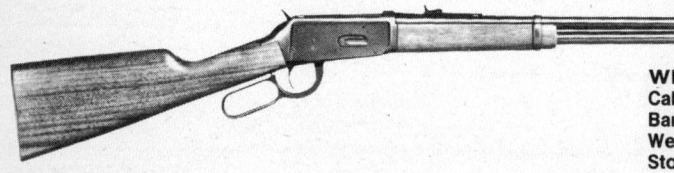

WINCHESTER 94 LEVER ACTION CARBINE
Caliber: 30-30, (12" twist). 6-shot tubular mag.
Barrel: 16", 20"
Weight: 6½ lbs. **Length:** 37¾" over-all
Stock: Walnut straight grip stock and fore-end (13"x1¾"x2½").
Sights: Bead front sight on ramp with removable cover; open rear. Tapped for receiver sights.
Features: Solid frame, top ejection, half-cock hammer safety.
Price: $176.00
Price: Trapper model, 16" barrel $176.00

Winchester Model 94XTR Carbine
Same as standard Model 94 except has high-grade finish on stock and fore-end with cut checkering on both. Metal has highly polished deep blue finish.
Price: $198.00

Winchester 94 Antique Carbine
Same as M94 except: color case-hardened and scroll-engraved receiver, brass-plated loading gate and saddle ring. 30-30 only $188.00

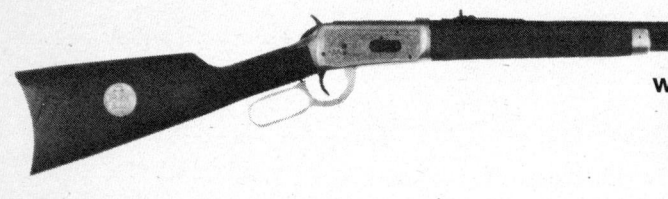

Winchester Oliver F. Winchester Commemorative
Similar to standard Model 94 except has a satin gold plated receiver with distinctive engravings; gold plated lever link, lower tang and fore-end tip; stock and fore-end are of semi-fancy American walnut with high grade cut checkering on authentic 19th century designs of highly finished Winchester rifles; specially blued octagonal barrel; barrel inscription reads, "Oliver F. Winchester 1810-1880". Comes in 38-55 caliber. Special packaging sleeve.
Price: $485.00

CENTERFIRE RIFLES — BOLT ACTION

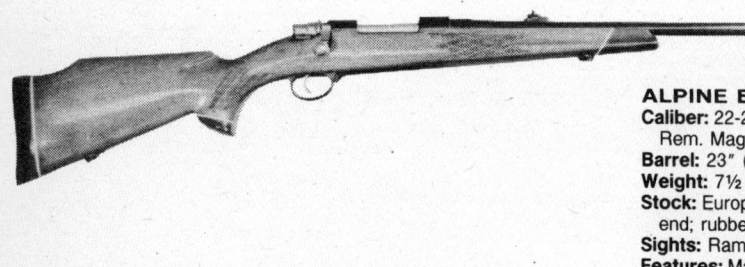

ALPINE BOLT ACTION RIFLE
Caliber: 22-250, 243 Win., 264 Win., 270, 30-06, 308, 308 Norma Mag., 7mm Rem. Mag., 8mm, 300 Win. Mag., 5-shot magazine (3 for magnum).
Barrel: 23" (std. cals.), 24" (mag.).
Weight: 7½ lbs.
Stock: European walnut. Full p.g. and Monte Carlo; checkered p.g. and fore-end; rubber recoil pad; white line spacers; sling swivels.
Sights: Ramp front, open rear adj. for w. and e.
Features: Made by Firearms Co. Ltd. in England. Imported by Mandall Shooting Supplies.
Price: Standard Grade $375.00
Price: Custom Grade $395.00

BSA CF-2 BOLT ACTION RIFLE
Caliber: 222 Rem. 22-250, 243, 6.5x55, 7mm Mauser, 7x64, 270, 308, 30-06, 7mm Rem. Mag., 300 Win. Mag.
Barrel: 24".
Weight: 7¾ lbs. **Length:** 45" over-all.
Stock: European walnut with roll-over Monte Carlo, palm swell on right side of pistol grip, skip-line checkering. High gloss finish.
Sights: Open adjustable rear, hooded ramp front. Removable.
Features: Adjustable single trigger or optional double-set triggers, side safety, visible cocking indicator. Ventilated rubber recoil pad. Introduced 1980. From Precision Sports.
Price: Standard calibers $444.95
Price: Magnum calibers $459.95
Price: Double-set triggers $45.00

CENTERFIRE RIFLES — BOLT ACTION

BROWNING BBR BOLT ACTION RIFLE
Caliber: 25-06, 270, 30-06, 7mm Rem. Mag., 300 Win. Mag.
Barrel: 24" medium sporter weight with recessed muzzle.
Weight: 8 lbs. **Length:** 44½" over-all.
Stock: Select American walnut cut to lines of Monte Carlo sporter with full p.g. and high cheek piece; 18 l.p.i. checkering. Recoil pad on magnums.
Sights: None fitted. Drilled and tapped for scope mounts.
Features: Short throw (60°) bolt with fluted surface, 9 locking lugs, plunger-type ejector, adjustable trigger is grooved and gold plated. Hinged floorplate with detachable box magazine (4 rounds in standard cals, 3 in mags). Convenient slide safety on tang. Special anti-warp aluminum fore-end insert. Low profile swivel studs. Introduced 1978.
Price: $399.95

CHAMPLIN RIFLE
Caliber: All std. chamberings, including 458 Win. and 460 Wea. Many wildcats on request.
Barrel: Any length up to 26" for octagon. Choice of round, straight taper octagon, or octagon with integral quarter rib, front sight ramp and sling swivel stud.
Length: 45" over-all. **Weight:** About 8 lbs.
Stock: Hand inletted, shaped and finished. Checkered to customer specs. Select French, Circassian or claro walnut. Steel p.g. cap, trap buttplate or recoil pad.
Sights: Bead on ramp front, 3-leaf folding rear.
Features: Right or left hand Champlin action, tang safety or optional shroud safety, Canjar adj. trigger, hinged floorplate.
Price: From $3,200.00

COLT SAUER GRAND AFRICAN
Caliber: 458 Win. Mag.
Barrel: 24", round tapered.
Length: 44½" over-all. **Weight:** 10½ lbs.
Stock: Solid African bubinga wood, cast-off M.C. with cheekpiece, contrasting rosewood fore-end and p.g. caps with white spacers. Checkered fore-end and p.g.
Sights: Ivory bead hooded ramp front, adj. sliding rear.
Price: $989.95

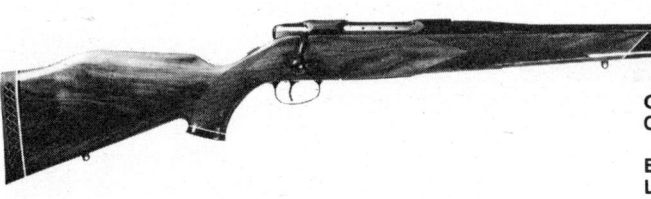

Colt Sauer Short Action Rifle
Same as standard rifle except chambered for 22-250, 243 and 308 Win. 24" bbl., 43" over-all. Weighs 7½ lbs. 3-shot magazine. $889.95

COLT SAUER RIFLE
Caliber: 25-06, 270, 30-06, (std.), 7mm Rem. Mag., 300 Wea. Mag., 300 Win. Mag. (Magnum).
Barrel: 24", round tapered.
Length: 43¾" over-all. **Weight:** 8 lbs. (std.).
Stock: American walnut, cast-off M.C. design with cheekpiece. Fore-end tip and p.g. cap rosewood with white spacers. Hand checkering.
Sights: None furnished. Specially designed scope mounts for any popular make scope furnished.
Features: Unique barrel/receiver union, non-rotating bolt with cam-actuated locking lugs, tang-type safety locks sear. Detachable 3- and 4-shot magazines.
Price: Standard cals. ...... $889.95   Magnum cals. $919.95

Du BIEL ARMS BOLT ACTION RIFLES
Caliber: Standard calibers 22-250 thru 458 Win. Mag. Selected wildcat calibers available.
Barrel: Selected weights and lengths. Douglas Premium.
Weight: About 7½ lbs.
Stock: Five styles. Walnut, maple, laminates. Hand checkered.
Sights: None furnished. Receiver has integral milled bases.
Features: Basically a custom-made rifle. Left or right-hand models available. Five-lug locking mechanism; 36 degree bolt rotation; adjustable Canjar trigger; oil or epoxy stock finish; Presentation recoil pad; jeweled and chromed bolt body; sling swivel studs; lever latch or button floorplate release. All steel action and parts. Introduced 1978. From Du Biel Arms.
Price: Rollover Model, left or right-hand $2,250.00
Price: Thumbhole left or right-hand $2,250.00
Price: Classic, left or right hand $2,250.00
Price: Modern Classic, left or right hand $2,250.00
Price: Thumbhole Mannlicher, left or right hand $2,250.00

Consult our Directory pages for the location of firms mentioned.

CENTERFIRE RIFLES—BOLT ACTION

DUMOULIN BOLT ACTION RIFLE
Caliber: All commercial calibers.
Barrel: 25".
Weight: 7 lbs. **Length:** 43".
Stock: French walnut with rosewood p.g. cap and fore-end tip, standard or skip line checkering, recoil pad.
Sights: Optional, available at extra cost.
Features: Made to customer requirements using Sako or FN action, with or without engraving (3 grades available). Imported from Belgium by Firearms Center.
Price: From $1,750.00

GOLDEN EAGLE MODEL 7000 RIFLE
Caliber: 22-250, 243, 25-06, 270 Win., 270 Wea. Mag., 7mm Rem. Mag., 30-06, 300 Win. Mag., 300 Wea. Mag., 338 Win. Mag., 375 H&H, 458 Win. Mag.
Barrel: 24" or 26".
Weight: 7¾ lbs. (8¾ lbs. in 338 and 375, 10½ lbs. in 458) **Length:** 43½" over-all (24" barrel).
Stock: American walnut, Monte Carlo, hand checkered p.g. and fore-end. Vent. recoil pad.
Sights: None furnished (except on 375 and 458). Drilled and tapped for scope mounting.
Features: Tang safety, five bolt locking lugs, grip cap with Golden Eagle head. Four-shot capacity in standard calibers, three-shot in magnums. From Golden Eagle Firearms.
Price: Std. cals. $599.00
Price: Mag. cals. $599.00
Price: African cals. $649.00
Price: Grade II, standard and magnum cals. $699.00
Price: Grade II African $749.00

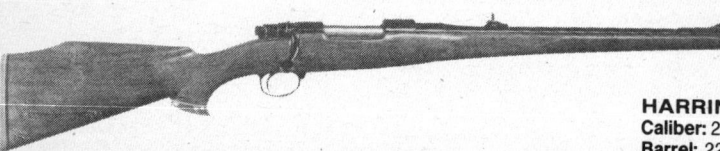

HARRINGTON & RICHARDSON M-300 BOLT ACTION
Caliber: 22-250, 243, 25-06, 270, 30-06, 308, 7mm Rem. Mag., 300 Win. Mag.
Barrel: 22" round, tapered.
Weight: 7¾ lbs. **Length:** 42½" over-all.
Stock: American walnut, hand checkered p.g. and fore-end, Monte Carlo, roll-over cheekpiece.
Sights: Adjustable rear, gold bead ramp front.
Features: Hinged floorplate; sliding side safety; sling swivels, recoil pad. Receiver tapped for scope mount. Commercial Mauser action.
Price: $395.00

H&R Model 301 Bolt Action Carbine
Same as Model 300 except has 18" barrel, full length Mannlicher-style stock with plain cheekpiece and blued nose cap. Not available in 22-250.
Price: $495.00

HEYM MODEL SR-20 BOLT ACTION RIFLES
Caliber: 5.6x57, 243, 6.5x57, 270, 7x57, 7x64, 308, 30-06 (SR-20L); 9.3x62 (SR-20N) plus SR-20L cals.; SR-20G—6.5x68, 7mm Rem. Mag., 300 Win. Mag., 8x68S, 375H&H.
Barrel: 20½" (SR-20L), 24" (SR-20N), 26" (SR-20G).
Weight: 7-8 lbs. depending upon model.
Stock: Dark European walnut, hand-checkered p.g. and fore-end. Oil finish. Recoil pad, rosewood grip cap. Monte Carlo-style. SR-20L has full Mannlicher-style stock, others have sporter-style with schnabel tip.
Sights: Silver bead ramp front, adj. folding leaf rear.
Features: Hinged floorplate, 3-position safety. Receiver drilled and tapped for scope mounts. Adjustable trigger. Options available include double-set triggers, left-hand action and stock, Suhler claw mounts, deluxe engraving and stock carving. Contact Heym for more data.
Price: SR-20L $864.00
Price: SR-20N $782.00
Price: SR-20-G $839.00
Price: Left-hand action and stock, add $127.00

CENTERFIRE RIFLES – BOLT ACTION

KLEINGUENTHER K-15 INSTA-FIRE RIFLE
Caliber: 243, 25-06, 270, 7x57, 7mm Rem. Mag., 30-06, 300 Win. Mag., 308 Win., 308 Norma, 375 H&H, 458 Win., 270-300 Wea. Mag.
Barrel: 24", 26".
Weight: 7 lbs., 13 ozs. **Length:** 43½" over-all.
Stock: Available in light, medium or dark European walnut. Monte Carlo, hand checkered, cheekpiece, rosewood fore-end tip, rosewood p.g. cap with diamond inlay.
Sights: None furnished. Drilled and tapped for scope mounts. Iron sights optional.
Features: Ultra fast lock/ignition time. Imported from Germany by Kleinguenther's.
Price: Std. cals. . . . . $699.00   Mag. cals. $699.00

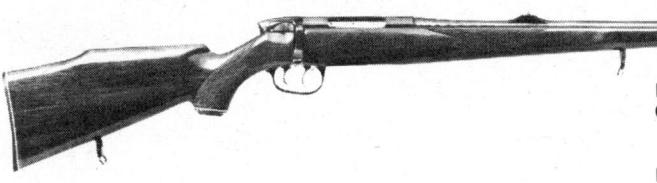

MANNLICHER MODELS L & SL
Caliber: M-SL—222, 222 Rem. Mag., 223; SL Varmint—222; M-L—22-250, 6mm, 243, 308 Win.; M-L Varmint—22-250, 243, 308 Win.; M-L optional cal.—5.6x57.
Barrel: 20" (full stock); 23.6" (half stock); 25.6" (Varmint).
Weight: 6 lbs. (full stock); 8 lbs. (Varmint). **Length:** 38¼" (full stock); 44" (Varmint).
Stock: Hand checkered walnut.
Sights: Ramp front, open U-notch rear.
Features: Choice of interchangeable single or double set triggers. Five-shot detachable "Makrolon" rotary magazine, 6 rear locking lugs. Drilled and tapped for scope mounts. Imported by Steyr Daimler Puch of America.
Price: Full Stock $602.70
Price: Half-stock $554.00
Price: Varmint $575.75
Price: Optional caliber, add $32.00

Mannlicher ML 79 (Model M)
Similar to Model M except chambered for 7x57, 7x64, 270, 30-06 (6.5x57, 6.5x55, 7.5x55 optional). European hand-rubbed oil finish or high gloss lacquer on stock. Has ramp front sight adj. for elevation, U-notch rear adj. for windage. Single-set trigger. Detachable 3-shot steel magazine (6-shot optional).
Price: Full stock $780.00
Price: Half stock $730.00
Price: Optional cals., add $32.00

MANNLICHER MODEL M
Caliber: 7x64, 7x57, 270, 30-06. Left-hand action cals.—7x64, 270, 30-06. Optional cals.—6.5x57, 8x57JS, 9.3x62, 6.5x55, 7.5x55.
Barrel: 20" (full stock); 23.6", 25.5" opt. (half stock).
Weight: 6.8 lbs. to 7.5 lbs. **Length:** 39" (full stock); 43" (half stock).
Stock: Hand checkered walnut. Full Mannlicher or std. half stock with M.C. and rubber recoil pad.
Sights: Ramp front, open U-notch rear.
Features: Choice of interchangeable single or double set triggers. Detachable 5-shot rotary magazine. Drilled and tapped for scope mounting. Available as "Professional" model with parkerized finish and synthetic stock (right hand action only). Imported by Steyr Daimler Puch of America.
Price: Full stock $663.56
Price: Half stock $613.75
Price: For left hand action add $54.00
Price: Professional model $440.95

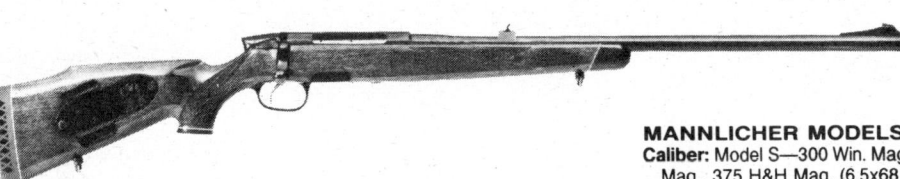

MARK X VISCOUNT RIFLE
Caliber: 22-250; 243; 25-06; 270; 7x57; 7mm Rem. Mag.; 308 Win.; 30-06; 300 Win. Mag.
Barrel: 24".
Weight: 7½ lbs. **Length:** 44".
Stock: Genuine Walnut stock, hand checkered with 1" sling swivels.
Sights: Ramp front with removable hood, open rear sight ajustable for windage and elevation.
Features: One piece trigger guard with hinged floor plate, drilled and tapped for scope mounts and receiver sight, hammer-forged chrome vanadium steel barrel. Imported by Interarms.
Price: With adj. trigger, sights, from $279.00
Price: With adj. trigger, no sights, from $267.00

MANNLICHER MODELS S & ST
Caliber: Model S—300 Win. Mag., 338 Wln. Mag., 7mm Rem. Mag., 300 H&H Mag., 375 H&H Mag. (6.5x68, 8x68S, 9.3x64 optional); M-S/T—375 H&H Mag., 458 Win. Mag. (9.3x64 optional).
Barrel: 25.6".
Weight: 8.4 lbs. (Model S). **Length:** 45" over-all.
Stock: Half stock with M.C. and rubber recoil pad. Hand checkered walnut. Available with optional spare magazine inletted in butt.
Sights: Ramp front, U-notch rear.
Features: Choice of interchangeable single or double set triggers. Detachable 4-shot magazine. Drilled and tapped for scope mounts. Imported by Steyr Daimler Puch of America.
Price: Model S or S/T $715.35
Price: With optional butt magazine $764.25
Price: Optional cals., add $32.00

CAUTION: PRICES CHANGE. CHECK AT GUNSHOP.

CENTERFIRE RIFLES—BOLT ACTION

MARK X RIFLE
Caliber: 22-250; 243, 270, 308 Win.; 30-06; 25-06; 7×57; 7 mm Rem. Mag; 300 Win. Mag.
Barrel: 24".
Weight: 7½ lbs. **Length:** 44".
Stock: Hand checkered walnut, Monte Carlo, white line spacers on p.g. cap, buttplate and fore-end tip.
Sights: Ramp front with removable hood, open rear adj. for w. and e.
Features: Sliding safety, quick detachable sling swivels, hinged floorplate. Also available as actions or bbld. actions. Imported from Europe by Interarms.
Price: With adj. trigger and sights, from $319.00
Price: With adj. trigger, no sights, from $304.00

MARK X MARQUIS MANNLICHER-STYLE CARBINE
Caliber: 270, 7x57, 30-06, 308 Win.
Barrel: 20".
Weight: 7½ lbs. **Length:** 40" over-all.
Stock: Hand checkered European walnut.
Sights: Ramp front with removable hood; open rear adj. for w. and e.
Features: Quick detachable sling swivels; fully adj. trigger; blue steel fore-end cap; white line spacers at p.g. cap and buttplate. Mark X Mauser action. Imported by Interarms.
Price: With adj. trigger and sights $369.00

MARK X CAVALIER RIFLE
Caliber: 22-250; 243; 25-06; 270; 7×57; 7mm Rem. Mag.; 308 Win.; 30-06; 300 Win. Mag.
Barrel: 24".
Weight: 7½ lbs. **Length:** 44".
Stock: Checkered Walnut with Rosewood fore-end tip and pistol grip cap, Monte Carlo cheek piece and recoil pad.
Sights: Ramp front with removable hood, open rear adjustable for windage and elevation.
Features: Contemporary-styled stock with sculptured accents; roll over cheek piece and flat bottom fore-end. Adjustable trigger and quick detachable sling swivels, standard. Receiver drilled and tapped for receiver sights and scope mounts. Also available without sights. Imported by Interarms.
Price: With adj. trigger and sights $369.95
Price: Adj. trigger, without sights $354.00
Price: 300 Win. Mag., 7mm Rem. Mag., with sights $379.00
Price: As above, without sights $364.00

MARK X ALASKAN MAGNUM RIFLE
Caliber: 375 H&H, 458 Win. Mag.; 3-shot magazine.
Barrel: 24".
Weight: 8¼ lbs. **Length:** 32" over-all.
Stock: Select walnut with crossbolt; hand checkered p.g. and fore-end; Monte Carlo; sling swivels.
Sights: Hooded ramp front; open rear adj. for w. & e.
Features: Hinged floorplate; right-hand thumb (tang) safety; adj. trigger. From Interarms.
Price: $389.00

MOSSBERG MODEL RM-7A, B BOLT ACTION RIFLE
Caliber: 30-06, 7mm Rem. Mag.
Barrel: 22" (30-06), 24" (7mm Rem. Mag.), tapered, AC-KRO-GRUV.
Weight: 7½ lbs. **Length:** 44" over-all (30-06).
Stock: American walnut, classic-style, with checkered p. g. and fore-end. Decorative p.g. cap, non-slip rubber buttplate with black spacer.
Sights: Gold bead front on ramp, adjustable folding leaf rear.
Features: Rotary magazine; 3-position bolt safety; sling swivel studs. Receiver drilled and tapped for scope mounting. Introduced 1978.
Price: $286.95

MARK X CONTINENTAL MANNLICHER-STYLE CARBINE
Caliber: 243, 270, 7x57, 308, 30-06.
Barrel: 20".
Weight: 7½ lbs. **Length:** 40" over-all.
Stock: Hand checkered European walnut. Straight European-style comb with sculptured cheekpiece.
Sights: Ramp front with removable hood; open rear adj. for w. and e.
Features: Similar to Mannlicher-Style except for stock differences noted above, single adjustable or double-set triggers, classic "butter-knife" bolt handle. Button release hinged floorplate. Imported by Interarms.
Price: Double-set triggers, with sights $389.00
Price: Single adj. trigger, with sights $350.00

NAVY ARMS 45-70 MAUSER
Caliber: 45-70 Govt.
Barrel: 18", 24", 26".
Weight: 9¾ lbs. (24") **Length:** About 43" over-all (24" barrel).
Stock: Checkered walnut. Pistol grip on 24" and 26" models, straight grip on 18" gun.
Sights: Bead on blade front, rear adj. for e.
Features: Action taken from Siamese Mauser. Straight bolt handle. Magazine holds 3 rounds. From Navy Arms.
Price: Rifle or carbine $180.00

CENTERFIRE RIFLES — BOLT ACTION

PARKER-HALE SUPER 1200 BOLT ACTION RIFLE
Caliber: 22-250, 243 Win., 6mm Rem., 25-06, 270 Win., 30-06, 308 Win., 7mm Rem. Mag., 300 Win. Mag.
Barrel: 24".
Weight: 7¼ lbs. **Length:** 45".
Stock: 13.5" x 1.8" x 2.3". Hand checkered walnut, rosewood p.g. and fore-end caps, fitted rubber recoil pad with white line spacers.
Sights: Bead front, folding adj. rear. Receiver tapped for scope mounts.
Features: 3-way side safety, single-stage adj. trigger, hinged mag. floorplate. Varmint Model (1200V) has glass-bedded action, free-floating bbl., avail. in 22-250, 6mm Rem., 25-06, 243 Win., without sights. Imported from England by Jana.
Price: .... $299.95 ($312.50, mag. cals.)
Price: 1200V $312.50

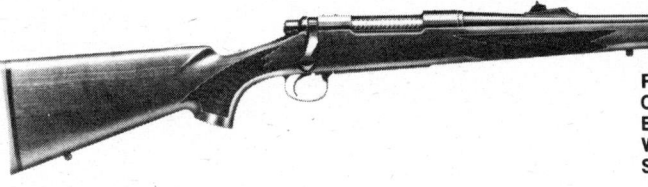

REMINGTON 700 "CLASSIC" RIFLE
Caliber: 22-250, 6mm Rem., 243, 270, 30-06, 7mm Rem. Mag.
Barrel: 22" (6mm, 243, 270, 30-06), 24" (22-250, 7mm Rem. Mag.).
Weight: About 7 lbs. **Length:** 43½" over-all (22-250).
Stock: American walnut, 20 l.p.i. checkering on p.g. and fore-end. Classic styling. Satin finish.
Sights: Hooded ramp front with gold bead, sliding-ramp rear adjustable for w. & e.
Features: A "classic" version of the M700ADL with straight comb stock. Fitted with rubber butt pad on all but magnum calibers, which has a full recoil pad. Sling swivel studs installed.
Price: All cals. except 7mm Rem. Mag. $327.95
Price: 7mm Rem. Mag. $342.95

REMINGTON 788 BOLT ACTION RIFLE
Caliber: 22-250, 223 Rem., 7mm-08 Rem., 243, and 308 (4-shot).
Barrel: 18½" round tapered (24" in 223 and 22-250).
Weight: 7-7½ lbs. **Length:** 41⅝" over-all.
Stock: Walnut-finished hardwood with Monte Carlo and p.g. (13⅝"x1⅞"x2⅝").
Sights: Blade ramp front, open rear adj. for w. & e.
Features: Detachable box magazine, thumb safety, receiver tapped for scope mounts.
Price: $209.95
  Sling strap and swivels, installed $10.95
  Model 788 with Universal Model UE 4x scope, mounts and rings in cals. 243 Win., 7mm-08 Rem., 308 and 22-250 .... $244.95

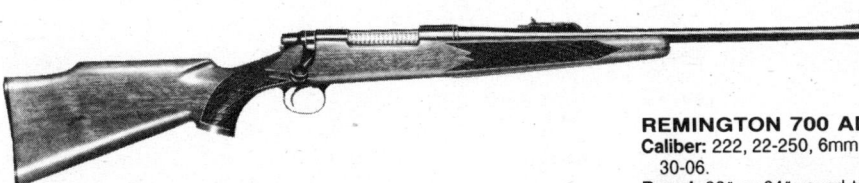

REMINGTON 700 ADL BOLT ACTION RIFLE
Caliber: 222, 22-250, 6mm Rem., 243, 25-06, 270, 7mm Exp. Rem., 308 and 30-06.
Barrel: 22" or 24" round tapered.
Weight: 7 lbs. **Length:** 41½" to 43½"
Stock: Walnut, RKW finished p.g. stock with impressed checkering, Monte Carlo (13⅜"x1⅝"x2⅜").
Sights: Gold bead ramp front; removable, step-adj. rear with windage screw.
Features: Side safety, receiver tapped for scope mounts.
Price: $279.95
Price: 7mm Rem. Mag. $312.95

Remington 700 BDL Bolt Action Rifle
Same as 700-ADL, except: skip-line checkering; black fore-end tip and p.g. cap, white line spacers. Matted receiver top, quick release floorplate. Hooded ramp front sight. Q.D. swivels and 1" sling **Price:** $357.95
Available also in 17 Rem., 7mm Rem. Mag. and 300 Win. Mag., 8mm Rem. Mag., caliber. 44½" over-all, weight 7½ lbs. $372.95
Peerless Grade .... $1,100.00   Premier Grade $2,200.00

Remington 700 C Custom Rifle
Same as the 700 BDL except choice of 20", 22" or 24" bbl. with or without sights. Jewelled bolt, with or without hinged floor plate. Select American walnut stock is hand checkered, rosewood fore-end & grip cap. Hand lapped barrel. 16 weeks for delivery after placing order $675.00

Remington 700BDL Left Hand
Same as 700 BDL except: mirror-image left-hand action, stock. Calibers 270, 30-06 **$372.95; Price:** 7mm Rem. Mag. $387.95

Remington 700 Safari
Same as the 700 BDL except 375 H&H or 458 Win. Magnum calibers only. Hand checkered, oil finished stock with recoil pad installed. Delivery time is about five months. $579.95

Remington 700 BDL Varmint
Same as 700 BDL, except: 24" heavy bbl., 43½" over-all, wgt. 9 lbs. Cals. 222, 223, 22-250, 6mm Rem., 243, 7mm-08 Rem. and 308. No Sights. $377.95

CENTERFIRE RIFLES — BOLT ACTION

Ruger Model 77 Magnum Round Top
Same as Model 77 except: round top receiver, drilled and tapped for standard scope mounts. Open sights are standard equipment. Calibers 25-06, 270, 30-06, 7mm Rem. Mag.
Price: All cals. $297.50

RUGER 77 BOLT ACTION RIFLE
Caliber: 22-250, 220 Swift, 243, 6mm, 308, 358 Win. (5-shot).
Barrel: 22" round tapered (24" in 220 Swift).
Weight: 6¾ lbs. Length: 42" over-all.
Stock: Hand checkered American walnut (13¾"x1⅝"x2⅛"), p.g. cap, sling swivel studs and recoil pad.
Sights: Optional gold bead ramp front, folding leaf adj. rear, or scope rings.
Features: Integral scope mount bases, diagonal bedding system, hinged floorplate, adj. trigger, tang safety. Scope optional.
Price: With Ruger steel scope rings (77R) $297.50
Price: With rings and open sights (77RS) $313.75
Price: 458 Win. Mag. $402.00

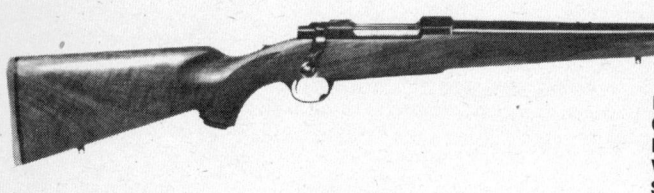

RUGER MODEL 77 VARMINT
Caliber: 22-250, 220 Swift, 243, 6mm, 25-06, 280, 308.
Barrel: 24" heavy straight tapered, 26" in 220 Swift.
Weight: Approx. 9 lbs. Length: Approx. 44" over-all.
Stock: American walnut, similar in style to Magnum Rifle.
Sights: Barrel drilled and tapped for target scope blocks. Integral scope mount bases in receiver.
Features: Ruger diagonal bedding system, Ruger steel 1" scope rings supplied. Fully adj. trigger. Barreled actions available in any of the standard calibers and barrel lengths.

Ruger Model 77 Magnum Rifle
Similar to Ruger 77 except: magnum-size action. Calibers 25-06, 270, 280, 7x57, 30-06 (5-shot), 7mm Rem. Mag., 300 Win. Mag., 338 Win. Mag., 458 Win. Mag. (3-shot). 270, 7x57, 280 and 30-06 have 22" bbl., all others have 24". Weight and length vary with caliber.
Price: $297.50

Price: $297.50
Price: Barreled action, 338, with open sights $235.00
Price: Barreled action only all cals. except 338, 458, open sights $252.00
Price: Barreled action, all cals. except 338, 458, no sights ... $235.00
Price: Bbld. action, 338, no sights $235.00
Price: Bbld. action, 458, with open sights $330.00

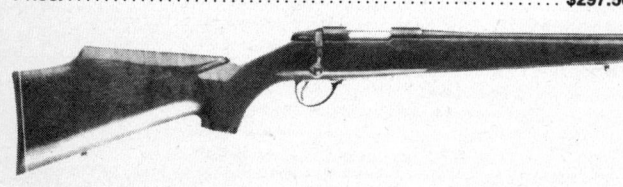
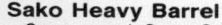

SAKO STANDARD SPORTER
Caliber: 17 Rem., 222, 223 (short action); 22-250, 220 Swift, 243, 308 (medium action); 25-06, 270, 30-06, 7mm Mag., 300 Mag., 338 Mag., 375 H&H Mag. (long action).
Barrel: 23" (222, 223, 243), 24" (other cals.).
Weight: 6¾ lbs. (short); 6¾ lbs. (med.); 8 lbs. (long).
Stock: Hand-checkered European walnut.
Sights: None furnished.
Features: Adj. trigger, hinged floorplate. 222 and 223 have short action, 243 and 22-250 have medium action, others are long action. Imported from Finland by Stoeger.
Price: Short action $499.95
Price: Medium action $499.95
Price: Long action $499.95
Price: Magnum cals. $549.95
Price: 17 Rem. $549.95

Sako Heavy Barrel
Same as std. Super Sporter except has beavertail fore-end; available in 222, 223 (short action), 220 Swift, 22-250, 243, 308 (medium action); 25-06, 7mm Mag. (long action). Weight from 8¼ to 8½ lbs. 5-shot magazine capacity.
Price: 222, 223 (short action) $584.95
Price: 22-250, 243 (medium action) $584.95
Price: 25-06, 7mm Mag. (long action) $584.95

Sako Classic Sporter
Similar to the Standard Sporter except: available in 243 (medium action), 270, 30-06 and 7mm Rem. Mag. (long action) only; straight-comb "classic-style" stock with oil finish; solid rubber recoil pad; recoil lug. No sights furnished—receiver drilled and tapped for scope mounting. Introduced 1980.
Price: $599.95

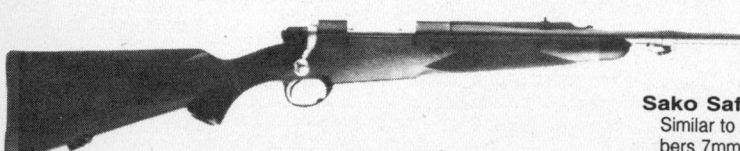

Sako Safari Grade Bolt Action
Similar to the Standard Grade Sporter except available in long action, calibers 7mm Rem. Mag., 300 Win. Mag., 338 Win. Mag. or 375 H & H Mag. only. Stocked in European walnut, checkered 20 l.p.i., solid rubber butt pad; grip cap and fore-end tip; quarter-rib "express" rear sight, hooded ramp front. Front sling swivel band-mounted on barrel.
Price: $1,400.00

CENTERFIRE RIFLES — BOLT ACTION

Sako Carbine
Same action as the Standard Sporter except has full "Mannlicher" style stock, 20" barrel, weighs 7½ lbs. 243, 270 and 30-06 only, medium or long action. Introduced 1977. From Stoeger.
Price: 243, 270, 30-06 only $599.95

Sako Deluxe Sporter
Same action as Standard Sporter except has select wood, Rosewood p.g. cap and fore-end tip. Fine checkering on top surfaces of integral dovetail bases, bolt sleeve, bolt handle root and bolt knob. Vent. recoil pad, skip-line checkering, mirror finish bluing.
Price: 222 or 223 cals. $716.95
Price: 220 Swift, 22-250, 243, 308 .... $716.95
Price: 25-06 270, 30-06 .... $716.95
Price: 7mm Rem. Mag., 300 Win. Mag., 338 Mag., 375 H&H $769.95

Sako Super Deluxe Sporter
Similar to Deluxe Sporter except has select European Walnut with high gloss finish and deep cut oak leaf carving. Metal has super high polish, deep blue finish.
Price: $1,400.00

SAKO MODEL 78 BOLT ACTION
Caliber: 22 LR or 22 Hornet.
Barrel: 22½".
Weight: 6¾ lbs.
Stock: Hand checkered European walnut.
Sights: None furnished; receiver has rail-type scope mount bases.
Features: New action design with tapered sporter weight barrel, adjustable trigger, detachable box magazine (5 shots in 22 LR, 4 shots in Hornet). Shrouded bolt, silent sliding safety, low bolt uplift. Introduced 1977. Imported by Stoeger.
Price: 22 LR $324.95
Price: 22 Hornet $391.95
Price: 22 LR Heavy Barrel $366.95
Price: 22 Magnum $366.95

SAVAGE 110C BOLT ACTION RIFLE
Caliber: 243, 270, 30-06, 4-shot detachable box magazine, 7mm Rem. Mag. (3-shot).
Barrel: 22".
Weight: 7 lbs. Length: 43" over-all.
Stock: Select walnut with Monte Carlo, skip-line cut checkered p.g. and fore-end.
Sights: Removeable ramp front, open rear adj. for w. & e.
Features: Tapped for scope mounting, free floating barrel, top tang safety, internal box magazine, hard rubber buttplate. Right hand only in 25-06, 22-250 with 24" barrel.
Price: Right hand 110C $273.15
Price: Left hand 110CL $281.80
Price: Right hand, mag. cals. $290.10
Price: Left hand, mag. cals. $299.50

SAVAGE 110S, SILHOUETTE RIFLE
Caliber: 308 Win., 5-shot.
Barrel: 22", heavy tapered.
Weight: 8 lbs., 10 ozs. Length: 43" over-all.
Stock: Special Silhouette stock of select walnut. High fluted comb, Wundhammer swell, stippled p.g. and fore-end. Rubber recoil pad.
Sights: None. Receiver drilled and tapped for scope mounting.
Features: Receiver has satin blue finish to reduce glare. Barrel is free-floating. Top tang safety, internal magazine. Available in right-hand only. Introduced 1978.
Price: $274.75

SAVAGE 340 CLIP REPEATER
Caliber: 22 Hornet, 222 Rem., 223 (4-shot) and 30-30 (3-shot).
Barrel: 24" and 22" respectively.
Weight: About 6½ lbs. Length: 40"-42"
Stock: Walnut, Monte Carlo, checkered p.g. and fore-end white line spacers.
Sights: Hooded ramp front, folding-leaf rear.
Features: Detachable clip magazine, sliding thumb safety, receiver tapped for scope mounts.
Price: $176.60

CENTERFIRE RIFLES—BOLT ACTION

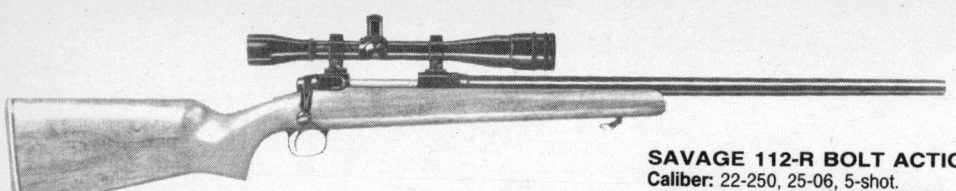

SHILEN DGA SILHOUETTE RIFLE
Caliber: 308 Win., 7x308 recommended. Others available. Single shot or magazine.
Barrel: 25", #5 contour.
Weight: 8 lbs., 11 ozs.
Stock: Select walnut. Competition-developed pattern for Silhouette shooting. Free-floated action, bedded action. Recoil pad installed with 13¾" pull.
Sights: None furnished. Drilled and tapped for scope mounting.
Features: Shilen DGA action. Fully adjustable trigger with side safety. Available with left-hand cheekpiece. Chrome-moly steel barrel; bore and chamber held to target tolerances. Available with Benchrest trigger (2-6 oz., $40.00) or Electric trigger ($150.00). Base and ring options same as Shilen Sporter and Varminter.
Price: Silhouette rifle $883.00

SAVAGE 112-R BOLT ACTION RIFLE
Caliber: 22-250, 25-06, 5-shot.
Barrel: 26" tapered, 13/16" at muzzle.
Weight: 9¼ lbs. **Length:** 47" over-all.
Stock: Walnut. Free floating varmint stock with high, deeply fluted comb, Wundhammer swell at p.g. White spacer at recoil pad, 1¼" q.d. swivels.
Sights: None. Drilled and tapped for scope mounting.
Features: Designed expressly for varmint shooting. Recessed bolt face; 2 gas ports; top tang safety; chrome moly steel barrel. Stock measures 13½", drop at comb and heel 9/16" (measured from barrel centerline).
Price: $299.00

SHILEN DGA BENCHREST SINGLE SHOT RIFLES
Caliber: 22, 22-250, 6x47, 308.
Barrel: Select/Match grade stainless. Choice of caliber, twist, chambering, contour or length shown in Shilen's catalog.
Weight: To customer specs.
Stock: Fiberglass. Choice of Classic or thumbhole pattern.
Sights: None furnished. Specify intended scope and mount.
Features: Fiberglass stocks are spray painted with acrylic enamel in choice of basic color. Comes with Benchrest trigger. Basically a custom-made rifle. From Shilen Rifles, Inc.
Price: DGA Benchrest Rifle $1,060.00

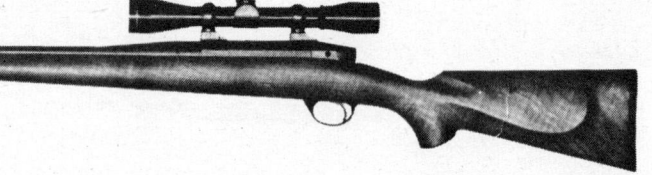

SHILEN DGA RIFLES
Caliber: All calibers.
Barrel: 24" (Sporter, #2 Weight), 25" (Varminter, #5 weight).
Weight: 7½ lbs. (Sporter), 9 lbs., (Varminter).
Stock: Selected Claro walnut. Barrel and action hand bedded to stock with free-floated barrel, bedded action. Swivel studs installed.
Sights: None furnished. Drilled and tapped for scope mounting.
Features: Shilen Model DGA action, fully adjustable trigger with side safety. Stock finish is satin sheen epoxy. Barrel and action non-glare blue-black. From Shilen Rifles, Inc.
Price: Sporter or Varminter rifle $927.00

Smith & Wesson Model 1500 Deluxe Rifle
Similar to Standard model except comes without sights, has engine-turned bolt; floorplate has decorative scroll. Stock has skip-line checkering, pistol grip cap with inset S&W seal, white spacers. Sling, swivels and swivel posts are included. Magnum models have vent. recoil pad.
Price: Deluxe, std. cals $335.00
Price: Deluxe, magnum cals $350.00

SMITH & WESSON M1500 BOLT ACTION RIFLE
Caliber: 243, 270, 30-06, 7mm Rem. Mag.
Barrel: 22" (24" in 7mm Rem. Mag.).
Weight: 7½-7¾ lbs. **Length:** 42" over-all (42½" for 270, 30-06, 7mm).
Stock: American walnut with Monte Carlo comb and cheekpiece; 18-line-per-inch checkering on p.g. and fore-end.
Sights: Hooded ramp gold bead front, open round-notch rear adj. for w. & e. Drilled and tapped for scope mounts.
Features: Trigger guard and magazine box are a single unit with a hinged floorplate. Comes with q.d. swivel studs. Composition non-slip buttplate with white spacer. Magnum models have rubber recoil pad. Introduced 1979.
Price: Standard cals $297.95
Price: Magnum cals $312.95

STEVENS 110E SUPER VALUE BOLT ACTION RIFLE
Caliber: 30-06, 243, 4-shot.
Barrel: 22" round tapered.
Weight: 6¾ lbs. **Length:** 43" (22" barrel).
Stock: Walnut finished hardwood with Monte Carlo, checkered p.g. and fore-end, hard rubber buttplate.
Sights: Gold bead removable ramp front, step adj. rear.
Features: Top tang safety, receiver, tapped for peep or scope sights.
Price: .... N.A.

CENTERFIRE RIFLES — BOLT ACTION

TIKKA MODEL 55 STANDARD RIFLE
Caliber: 17 Rem., 222 Rem., 22-250, 6mm Rem., 243, 308.
Barrel: 23".
Weight: About 6½ lbs. **Length:** 41½" over-all.
Stock: Hand checkered walnut, Monte Carlo, palm swell on p.g.
Sights: Bead on ramp front, removeable rear adj. for w. & e.
Features: Detachable 3-shot magazine, 5- and 10-shot magazines available. Receiver drilled and tapped for scope mounts. From Ruko Sporting Goods.
Price: About, ... $348.00

TIKKA MODEL 55 SPORTER
Caliber: 222, 22-250, 243, 308.
Barrel: 23" heavy target.
Weight: About 9 lbs. **Length:** 41½" over-all.
Stock: Walnut. Varmint/target-type with Monte Carlo, checkered p.g. and fore-end.
Sights: None furnished. Drilled and tapped for scope mounts.
Features: Detachable 5- or 10-shot magazine. Oil finished stock. Trigger pull is adjustable from 4 to 6 lbs. Introduced 1979. From Ruko Sporting Goods.
Price: About, ... $385.00

Tikka Model 65 Rifles
Same as Model 55 except chambered for 25-06, 6.5x55, 7x57, 7x64, 270, 308, 30-06, 7mm Rem. Mag., 300 Win. Mag. Barrel length 22", 5-shot magazine, adjustable trigger.
Price: Model 65 Standard, about, ... $350.00
Price: Model 65 Deluxe, about, ... $385.00
Price: Model 65 Deluxe American (gloss lacquer wood finish, no sights), about, ... $470.00

Tikka Model 55 Deluxe Bolt Action
Same as the standard rifle except has rollover cheekpiece, fore-end tip and pistol grip cap of rosewood with white spacers. From Ruko.
Price: About, ... $385.00
Price: Model 55 Deluxe American (gloss lacquer wood finish, no sights), about, ... $385.00

TIKKA MODEL 65 SPORTER
Caliber: 25-06, 6.5x55, 270, 308, 30-06.
Barrel: 22", heavy target.
Weight: About 9½ lbs. **Length:** 39" over-all.
Stock: Walnut. Target-type.
Sights: None furnished.
Features: Stock designed to meet ISU Standard Rifle match requirements. Stippled fore-end and palm swell. Large black composition bolt knob. Introduced 1979. From Ruko Sporting Goods.
Price: About, ... $525.00

TRADEWINDS HUSKY MODEL 5000 BOLT RIFLE
Caliber: 270, 30-06, 308, 243, 22-250.
Barrel: 23¾".
Weight: 6 lbs. 11 oz.
Stock: Hand checkered European walnut, Monte Carlo, white line spacers on p.g. cap, fore-end tip and butt plate.
Sights: Fixed hooded front, adj. rear.
Features: Removable mag., fully recessed bolt head, adj. trigger. Imported by Tradewinds.
Price: $345.00

WEATHERBY VANGUARD BOLT ACTION RIFLE
Caliber: 25-06, 243, 270, and 30-06 (5-shot), 7mm Rem. and 300 Win. Mag. (3-shot).
Barrel: 24" hammer forged.
Weight: 7⅞ lbs. **Length:** 44½" over-all.
Stock: American walnut, p.g. cap and fore-end tip, hand inletted and checkered, 13½" pull.
Sights: Optional, available at extra cost.
Features: Side safety, adj. trigger, hinged floorplate, receiver tapped for scope mounts.
Price: $399.95

CENTERFIRE RIFLES—BOLT ACTION

WEATHERBY MARK V BOLT ACTION RIFLE
Caliber: All Weatherby cals., 22-250 and 30-06.
Barrel: 24" or 26" round tapered.
Weight: 6½-10½ lbs. **Length:** 43¼"-46½"
Stock: Walnut, Monte Carlo with cheekpiece, high luster finish, checkered p.g. and fore-end, recoil pad.
Sights: Optional (extra).
Features: Cocking indicator, adj. trigger, hinged floorplate, thumb safety, quick detachable sling swivels.
Price: Cals. 224 and 22-250, std. bbl. $639.95
With 26" semi-target bbl. $649.95
Cals. 240, 257, 270, 7mm, 30-06 and 300 (24" bbl.) $659.95
With 26" No. 2 contour bbl. $669.95
Cal. 340 (26" bbl.) $669.95
Cal. 378 (26" bbl.) $799.95
Cal. 460 (26" bbl.) $919.95

Weatherby Mark V Rifle Left Hand
Available in all Weatherby calibers except 224 and 22-250 (and 26" No. 2 contour 300WM). Complete left handed action; stock with cheekpiece on right side. Prices are $10 higher than right hand models except the 378 and 460WM are unchanged.

WESTERN FIELD MODEL 765 BOLT ACTION RIFLE
Caliber: 30-06 (5-shot).
Barrel: 22".
Weight: 8½ lbs. (30-06). **Length:** 43½" over-all.
Stock: Walnut-finished hardwood, Monte Carlo cheekpiece.
Sights: Ramp front, adj. folding leaf rear.
Features: Recessed bolt head; hinged floorplate. Receiver drilled and tapped for scope mounts. 1" sling swivels. Top receiver safety. Wards catalog number 10765.
Price: 30-06 .... $199.99

WESTERN FIELD CENTERFIRE RIFLE MODEL 78
Caliber: 30-06 (5-shot), 7mm Rem. Mag. (4-shot).
Barrel: 22" (30-06), (7mm Rem. Mag.).
Weight: About 7½ lbs.
Stock: American walnut; p.g. cap; hand checkering.
Sights: Bead front, adj. rear.
Features: Rotary magazine; 3-position safety; swivel studs; drilled and tapped for scope mounts. Scope shown not included. From Montgomery Ward.
Price: 30-06 (Wards #10786) $249.95
Price: 7mm Rem. Mag. (Wards #10787) $249.95

WHITWORTH EXPRESS RIFLE
Caliber: 7mm Rem. Mag., 300 Win. Mag., 375 H&H; 458 Win. Mag.
Barrel: 24".
Weight: 7½-8 lbs. **Length:** 44".
Stock: Classic English Express rifle design of hand checkered, select European Walnut.
Sights: Three leaf open sight calibrated for 100, 200, 300 yards on ¼-rib, ramp front with removable hood.
Features: Solid rubber recoil pad, barrel mounted sling swivel, adjustable trigger, hinged floor plate, solid steel recoil cross bolt. Imported by Interarms.
Price: $525.00

WICHITA MAGNUM STAINLESS RIFLE
Caliber: From 270 Win. through 458 Win. Mag.
Barrel: 22" or 24".
Weight: Not over 8½ lbs. **Length:** 44¾" over-all (24" barrel).
Stock: AAA fancy walnut; hand inletted; glass bedded; steel grip cap; Pachmayr rubber recoil pad.
Sights: None. Drilled and tapped for Burris scope mounts.
Features: Stainless steel barrel and action, round contour. Target grade barrel. Available as a single shot or with a blind magazine. Fully adj. trigger. Bolt is ⅞" in diameter with recessed face. Hand rubbed stock finish, checkered 20 lpi. Shipped in a hard case. Introduced 1980. From Wichita Arms.
Price: $1,750.00

CENTERFIRE RIFLES—BOLT ACTION

WICHITA VARMINT RIFLE
Caliber: 17 Rem. thru 308 Win., including 22 and 6mm PPC.
Barrel: 20⅛", Atkinson chrome-moly.
Weight: 9 lbs. **Length:** 40⅛" over-all.
Stock: AAA Fancy American walnut. Hand-rubbed finish, hand-checkered, 20 l.p.i. pattern. Hand-inletted, glass bedded steel grip cap, Pachmayr rubber recoil pad.
Sights: None. Drilled and tapped for scope mounts.
Features: Right or left-hand Wichita action with three locking lugs. Available as a single shot or repeater with 3-shot detachable magazine. Checkered bolt handle. Bolt is hand fitted, lapped and jeweled. Side thumb safety. Firing pin fall is ³⁄₁₆". Non-glare blue finish. Shipped in hard Protecto case. From Wichita Arms.
Price: $895.00

WICHITA CLASSIC RIFLE
Caliber: 17 Rem. thru 308 Win., including 22 and 6mm PPC.
Barrel: 21⅛", Atkinson chrome-moly.
Weight: 8 lbs., 2 oz. **Length:** 41" over-all.
Stock: AAA Fancy American walnut. Hand-rubbed and checkered (20 l.p.i.). Hand-inletted, glass bedded, steel grip cap. Pachmayr rubber recoil pad.
Sights: None. Drilled and tapped for scope mounting.
Features: Available as a single shot or repeater. Octagonal barrel and Wichita action, right or left-hand. Checkered bolt handle. Bolt is hand-fitted, lapped and jewelled. Adjustable Canjar trigger is set at 2 lbs. Side thumb safety. Firing pin fall is ³⁄₁₆". Non-glare blue finish. Shipped in hard Protector case. From Wichita Arms.
Price: $1,295.00

WINCHESTER 70 XTR STANDARD RIFLE
Caliber: 222, 22-250, 25-06, 243, 270, 308 and 30-06, 5-shot.
Barrel: 22" swaged, floating. 10" twist (222 & 22-250 have 14" twist, 308 is 12").
Weight: 7½ lbs. **Length:** 42½" over-all.
Stock: Walnut, Monte Carlo, (13½"x1¾"x1½"x2⅛") checkered p.g. and fore-end.
Sights: Removable hooded bead ramp front, fully adj. open rear flips down for scope mounting.
Features: Sling swivels installed, steel p.g. cap, hinged floorplate, receiver tapped for scope mounts. Has new streamlined rear sight base, new Winchester blue finish. Stock has new color and finish.
Price: $354.00

Winchester 70 XTR Magnum Rifle
Same as M70 Standard except with recoil pad and in these magnum cals.: 7 Rem., 264, 300, 338 Win., 375 H&H (not XTR), 3-round mag. capacity. Wgt. 7¾ lbs. (8½ lbs. in 375), 24" bbl., 44½" over-all. R.H. twist: 9" in 264, 9½" in 7mm, 10" in 300, 338. .... $373.00
Cal. 375 H&H (not XTR) $547.00

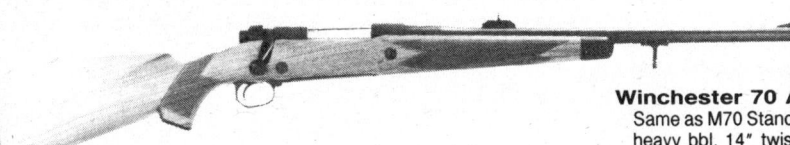

Winchester 70 African
Same as M70 Standard except: 458 Win. Mag. only, 3-shot. 22" non-floating heavy bbl. 14" twist. Stock measures 13½"x1⅜"x1¾"x2⅜", has ebony fore-end tip and grip cap; wgt. 8½ lbs., recoil pad and special rear sight.
Price: $607.00

WINCHESTER 70A XTR BOLT ACTION RIFLE
Caliber: 222, 22-250, 243, 25-06, 270, 30-06, 308.
Barrel: 22" (25-06, has 24").
Weight: 7⅛ to 7½ lbs. **Length:** 42½" (22" bbl.).
Stock: Monte Carlo, checkering at p.g. and fore-end.
Sights: Removeable hooded ramp front, adj. open rear.
Features: Sling swivels installed, three position safety, deep cut checkering.
Price: $313.00

Winchester 70 XTR Varmint Rifle
Same as M70 Standard except: 222, 22-250, and 243 only, target scope blocks, no sights, 24" heavy bbl., 14" twist in 22-250, 10" twist in 243. 44½" over-all, 9¾ lbs. Stock measures 13½"x⁹⁄₁₆"x¹⁵⁄₁₆"x⅜" from bore line.
Price: $373.00

Winchester 70A XTR Magnum Rifle
Same as 70A except with black recoil pad and in these cals.: 264, 7mm Rem., 300 Win., 3-round mag. capacity. Wgt. 7¼ lbs. 24" bbl., 44" over-all. R. H. twist: 9" in 264, 9½" in 7mm Rem. 10" in 300 Win. $333.00

Winchester Model 70A Police
Same as Model 70A except: 30-06 or 308 only, stock is tung oil finished.
Special order only $301.00

CENTERFIRE RIFLES – SINGLE SHOT

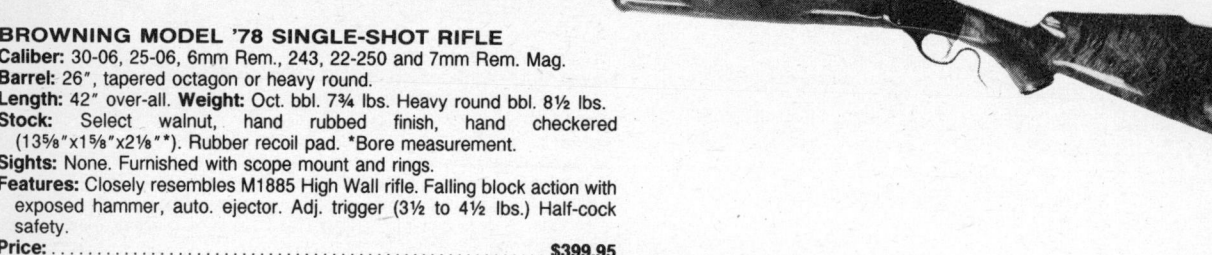

BROWNING MODEL '78 SINGLE-SHOT RIFLE
Caliber: 30-06, 25-06, 6mm Rem., 243, 22-250 and 7mm Rem. Mag.
Barrel: 26", tapered octagon or heavy round.
Length: 42" over-all. **Weight:** Oct. bbl. 7¾ lbs. Heavy round bbl. 8½ lbs.
Stock: Select walnut, hand rubbed finish, hand checkered (13⅝"x1⅝"x2⅛"*). Rubber recoil pad. *Bore measurement.
Sights: None. Furnished with scope mount and rings.
Features: Closely resembles M1885 High Wall rifle. Falling block action with exposed hammer, auto. ejector. Adj. trigger (3½ to 4½ lbs.) Half-cock safety.
Price: $399.95

BROWNING B-78 45-70 RIFLE
Caliber: 45-70.
Barrel: 24" heavy octagon; 6-groove, 1-in-20" twist.
Weight: About 8¾ lbs. **Length:** 40¾" over-all.
Stock: Straight grip French walnut with semi-schnabel fore-end, hand checkered. Measures 13¼"x2"x2¾".
Sights: Blade front, step-adj. rear. Drilled and tapped for scope mounts.
Features: Curved, blued steel buttplate; low profile recessed swivel studs (swivels provided).
Price: $399.95

HARRINGTON & RICHARDSON Model 155 "SHIKARI"
Caliber: 44 Rem. Mag. or 45-70, single-shot.
Barrel: 24" or 28" 45-70, 24" (44 Mag.).
Weight: 7-7½ lbs. **Length:** 39" over-all (24" bbl.).
Stock: Walnut finished hardwood.
Sights: Blade front, adj. folding leaf rear.
Features: Blue-black finish with color case hardened frame. Exposed hammer. Solid brass cleaning rod with hardwood handle included.
Price: Either caliber $110.00

HARRINGTON AND RICHARDSON 158 TOPPER RIFLE
Caliber: 30-30 and 22 Hornet.
Barrel: 22" round tapered.
Weight: 6 lbs. **Length:** 37".
Stock: Walnut finished hardwood stock and fore-end.
Sights: Blade front; folding adj. rear.
Features: Side lever break-open action with visible hammer. Easy takedown.
Price: 22 Hornet or 30-30 .... $85.00

Harrington & Richardson Model 157 Single Shot Rifle
Same as Model 158 except has pistol grip stock, full length fore-end, and sling swivels. Scope not included; drilled and tapped for mounts. 22 Hornet or 30-30 cals.
Price: $99.50

Harrington & Richardson Model 058 Combo Gun
Same as Model 158, except fitted with accessory 20-ga. barrel (26", Mod.).
Price: 22 Hornet or 30-30 Win. plus 20-ga $99.50

HEYM-RUGER Model HR 30/38 RIFLE
Caliber: 243, 6.5x57R, 7x64, 7x65R, 270, 308, 30-06 (standard); 6.5x68R, 300 Win. Mag., 8x68S, 9.3x74R (magnum).
Barrel: 24" (standard cals.), 26" (magnum cals.).
Weight: 6½ to 7 lbs.
Stock: Dark European walnut, hand checkered p.g. and fore-end. Oil finish, recoil pad. Full Mannlicher-type or sporter-style with schnabel fore-end, Bavarian cheekpiece.
Sights: Bead on ramp front, leaf rear.
Features: Ruger No. 1 action and safety, Canjar single-set trigger, hand-engraved animal motif. Options available include deluxe engraving and stock carving. Contact Heym for more data.
Price: HR-30N, round bbl., sporter stock, std. cals. $2,056.00
Price: HR-30G, as above except in mag. cals. $2,112.00
Price: HR-30L, round bbl., full stock, std. cals. $2,546.00
Price: HR-38N, octagon bbl., sporter stock, std. cals. $2,350.00
Price: HR-38G, as above, mag. cals. $2,420.00

Consult our Directory pages for the location of firms mentioned.

CENTERFIRE RIFLES — SINGLE SHOT

HYPER-SINGLE RIFLE
Caliber: All calibers, standard and wildcat.
Barrel: Choice of maker, weight, length (std. twist and contours).
Length: To customer specs. Weight: To customer specs.
Stock: To customer specs. AA fancy American black walnut is standard.
Sights: None furnished. Drilled and tapped for scope mounts.
Features: Falling block action. Striker rotates on bronze bearing and is powered by dual coil springs. Trigger adj. for weight, pull and travel. Tang safety. Octagon receiver on special order (same price).
Price: Complete Rifle .....$1,750.00 Barreled action $1,100.00
Price: Action only (blank extractor) $850.00
Price: Stainless steel barrel (extra) $75.00
Price: Fluted or octagon barrel (extra) $125.00

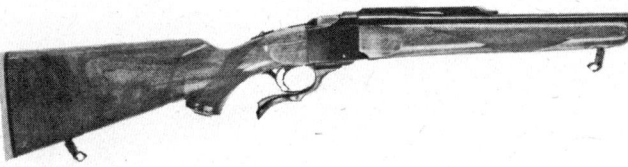

RIEDL SINGLE SHOT RIFLE
Caliber: All calibers, standard and wildcat.
Barrel: Lengths from 22" to 30", weights from 2½ lbs to 12 lbs.
Weight: About 6 lbs. (Light Weight rifle).
Stock: Deluxe Calif. Claro walnut standard. Other woods available.
Sights: None. Furnished with bridge scope mount or target bases.
Features: Rack and pinion action operation. Choice of chrome moly or stainless steel. Fully adj. trigger. Basically a custom-made rifle made to customer specs. Base prices listed. From Riedl Rifle Co.
Price: Chrome moly rifle......................................$439.00
Price: Stainless steel rifle....................................$499.00

RUGER NUMBER ONE SINGLE SHOT
Caliber: 220 Swift, 22-250, 243, 6mm Rem., 25-06, 270, 7x57mm, 30-06, 7mm Rem. Mag., 300 Win., 338 Win. Mag., 45-70, 458 Win. Mag., 375 H&H Mag.
Barrel: 26" round tapered with quarter-rib (also 22" and 24", depending upon model).
Weight: 8 lbs. Length: 42" over-all.
Stock: Walnut, two-piece, checkered p.g. and fore-end (either semi-beavertail or Henry style).
Sights: None, 1" scope rings supplied for integral mounts. 3 models have open sights.
Features: Under lever, hammerless falling block design has auto ejector, top tang safety. Standard Rifle 1B illus.
Price:..$348.00
Available also as Light Sporter, Medium Sporter, Special Varminter or Tropical Rifle..$348.00
Price: Barreled action, blued only $229.50

RUGER NO. 3 CARBINE SINGLE SHOT
Caliber: 22 Hornet, 223, 375 Win., 45-70.
Barrel: 22" round.
Weight: 6 lbs. Length: 38½".
Stock: American walnut, carbine-type.
Sights: Gold bead front, adj. folding leaf rear.
Features: Same action as No. 1 Rifle except different lever. Has auto ejector, top tang safety, adj. trigger.
Price:..$225.00

CENTERFIRE RIFLES — REPLICAS

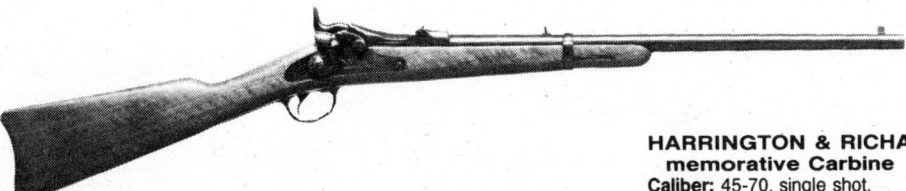

HARRINGTON & RICHARDSON Model 174 L.B.H. Commemorative Carbine
Caliber: 45-70, single shot.
Barrel: 22".
Weight: 7 lbs., 4 oz. Length: 41".
Stock: American walnut with metal grip adapter.
Sights: Blade front, tang mounted aperature rear adj. for w. and e.
Features: Replica of the 1873 Springfield carbine. Engraved breech block, side lock and hammer. Action color case hardened. Each comes with book entitled "In the Valley of the Little Big Horn".
Price:..$325.00

CENTERFIRE RIFLES—REPLICAS

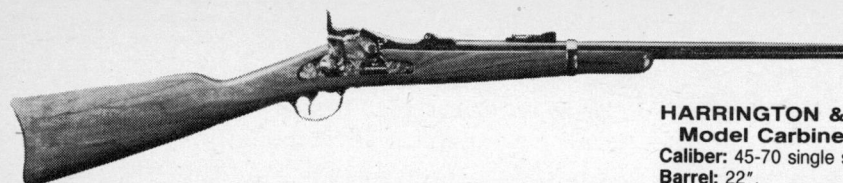

HARRINGTON & RICHARDSON Model 171 Cavalry Model Carbine
Caliber: 45-70 single shot.
Barrel: 22".
Weight: 7 lbs. **Length:** 41".
Stock: American walnut with saddle ring and bridle.
Sights: Blade front, barrel mounted leaf rear adj. for e.
Features: Replica of the 1873 Springfield Carbine. Blue-black finish. Deluxe version shown has engraved breech block, side lock & hammer.
Price: $325.00
Springfield Model 172 Silver Plated Carbine $1,500.00

HARRINGTON & RICHARDSON Officers Model 1873
Caliber: 45-70, single shot
Barrel: 26" round.
Weight: About 8 lbs. **Length:** 44" over-all
Stock: Oil finished walnut, checkered at wrist and fore-end white metal tipped.
Sights: Blade front, vernier tang rear adj. for w. & e.
Features: Replica of the 1873 Springfield has engraved breech block, side lock and hammer.
Price: $375.00

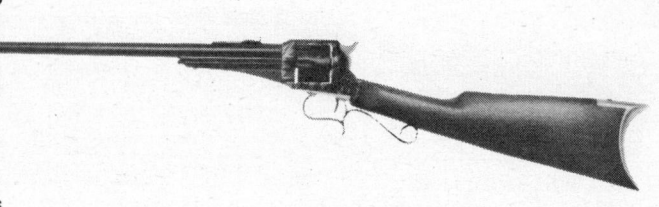

MODEL 1875 REVOLVING RIFLE
Caliber: 357 Mag., 44-40, 45 L.C.
Barrel: 20".
Weight: 5 lbs. **Length:** 38".
Stock: Walnut, brass butt plate.
Sights: Front blade adj. for w., buckhorn rear adj. for e.
Features: Action resembles Remington Model 1875 revolver. Polished brass trigger guard. Imported by Navy Arms and EMF.
Price: $215.00

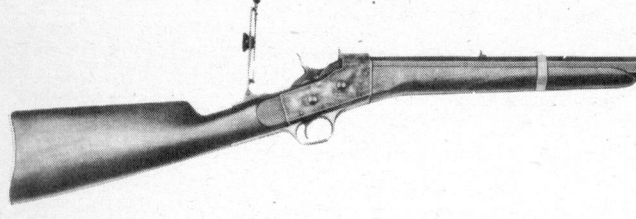

NAVY ARMS ROLLING BLOCK RIFLE
Caliber: 45-70.
Barrels: 26½".
Stock: Walnut finished.
Sights: Fixed front, adj. rear.
Features: Reproduction of classic rolling block action. Available in Buffalo Rifle (octagonal bbl.) and Creedmore (half round, half octagonal bbl.) models. From Navy Arms.
Price: 26" full octagon barrel $190.00
Price: Creedmore Model, 30" full octagon $210.00
Price: 18", 26", 30" half round $190.00
Price: Half-round Creedmore $210.00

ROLLING BLOCK BABY CARBINE
Caliber: 22 LR, 357 Mag.
Barrel: 20", octagon.
Weight: 4¾ lbs. **Length:** Approx. 35" over-all.
Stock: Walnut.
Sights: Blade front, rear adj. for e.
Features: Small rolling block action is color case hardened with blue barrel. Trigger guard and buttplate polished brass. Imported by Navy Arms.
Price: 22 LR $175.00
Price: 357 Mag $175.00

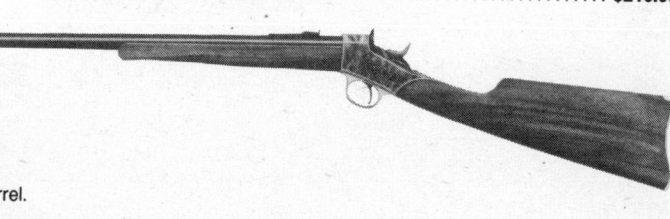

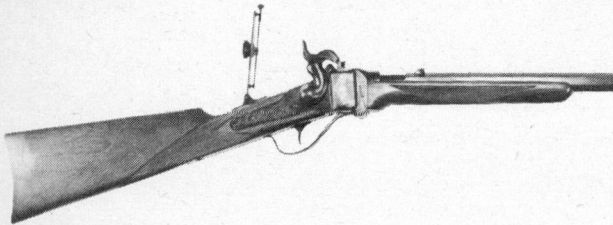

SILE SHARPS "OLD RELIABLE" RIFLE
Caliber: 45-70, 45-120-3¼" Sharps.
Barrel: 28", full octagon, polished blue.
Weight: 9½ lbs. **Length:** 45" over-all.
Stock: Walnut with deluxe checkering at p.g. and fore-end.
Sights: Sporting blade front, folding leaf rear. Globe front, vernier rear optional at extra cost.
Features: Falling block, lever action. Color case-hardened hammer, buttplate and action with Sile's automatic safety. Seven models of the Sharps are available from Sile, two in M/L configuration. All are available with engraved action for **$97.25** extra. From Sile Distributors Inc., Shore.
Price: Old Reliable $377.50
Price: Sporter Rifle $362.50
Price: Military Carbine $345.00
Price: Sporter Carbine $362.50

CENTERFIRE & RIMFIRE RIFLES—TARGET

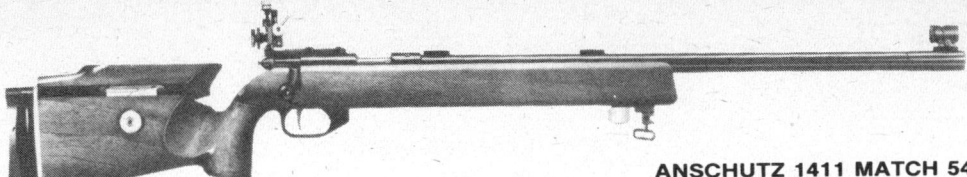

ANSCHUTZ 1411 MATCH 54 RIFLE
Caliber: 22 LR. Single shot.
Barrel: 27½ round (15/16" dia.)
Weight: 11 lbs. **Length:** 46" over-all.
Stock: French walnut, American prone style with Monte Carlo, cast-off cheekpiece, checkered p.g., beavertail fore-end with swivel rail and adj. swivel, adj. rubber buttplate.
Sights: None. Receiver grooved for Anschutz sights (extra). Scope blocks.
Features: Single stage adj. trigger, wing safety, short firing pin travel. Available from Savage Arms.
Price: Right hand, no sights $699.75
Price: M1811-L (true left-hand action and stock) $737.10
Price: Anschutz Int'l. sight set $161.60

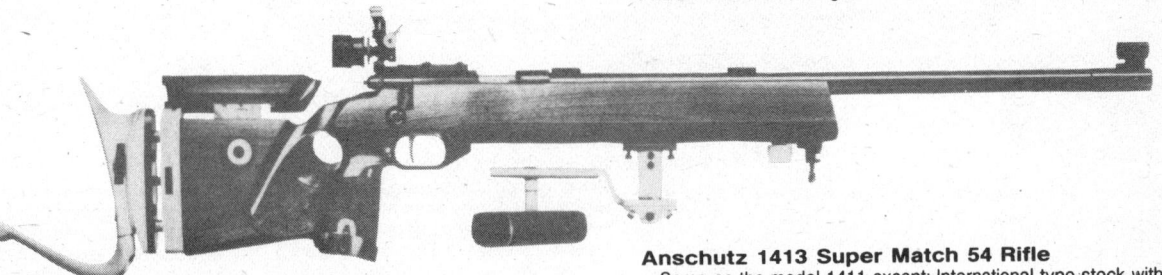

Anschutz 1413 Super Match 54 Rifle
Same as the model 1411 except: International type stock with adj. cheekpiece, adj. aluminum hook buttplate, weight 15½ lbs., 50" over-all. Available from Savage Arms.
Price: Right hand, no sights $1,006.95
Price: M1813-L (left-hand action and stock) $1,107.95

Anschutz 1407 Match 54 Rifle
Same as the model 1411 except: 26" bbl. (⅞" dia.), weight 10 lbs., 44½" over-all to conform to ISU requirements and also suitable for NRA matches. Available from Savage Arms.
Price: Right hand, no sights $616.60
Price: M1807-L (true left-hand action and stock) $678.75
Price: Int'l sight set $161.60
Price: Match sight set $110.25

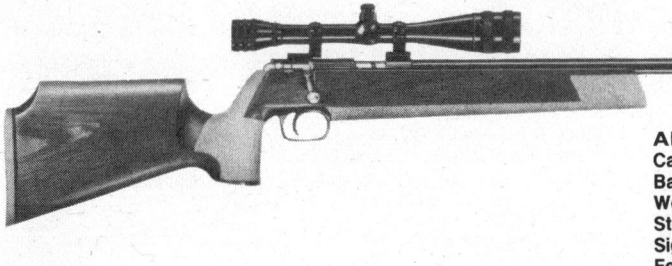

ANSCHUTZ MODEL 64-MS
Caliber: 22 LR, single shot.
Barrel: 21¾", medium heavy, ⅞" diameter.
Weight: 8 lbs., 1 oz. **Length:** 39½" over-all.
Stock: Walnut-finished hardwood, silhouette-type.
Sights: None furnished. Receiver drilled and tapped for scope mounting.
Features: Designed for metallic silhouette competition. Stock has stippled checkering, contoured thumb groove with Wundhammer swell. Two-stage trigger is adj. for weight of pull, take-up, and over-travel. Slide safety locks sear and bolt. Introducted 1980. Imported by Savage Arms.
Price: $310.90

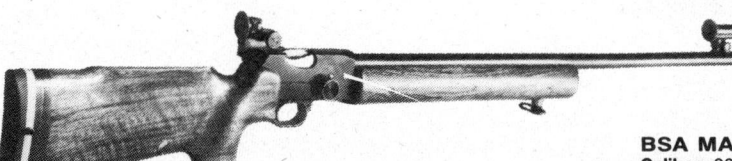

BSA MARTINI ISU MATCH RIFLE
Caliber: 22 LR, single shot.
Barrel: 28".
Weight: 10¾ lbs. **Length:** 43-44" over-all.
Stock: Match type French walnut butt and fore-end; flat cheekpiece, full p.g.; spacers are fitted to allow length adjustment to suit each shooting position; adj. buttplate.
Sights: Modified PH-1 Parker-Hale tunnel front, PH-25 aperture rear with aperture variations from .080" to .030".
Features: Fastest lock time of any commercial target rifle; designed to meet I.S.U. specs. for the Standard Rifle. Fully adjustable trigger (less than ½ lb. to 3½ lbs.). Mark V has heavier barrel, weighs 12¼ lbs. From Freelands Scope Stands.
Price: I.S.U., Standard weight $700.00
Price: Mark V heavy bbl. $735.00

CENTERFIRE & RIMFIRE RIFLES—TARGET

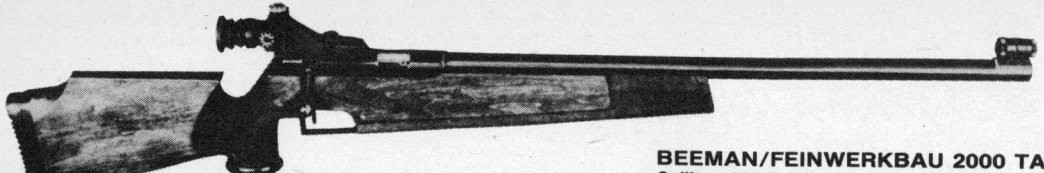

BEEMAN/FEINWERKBAU 2000 TARGET RIFLE
Caliber: 22 LR.
Barrel: 22" (Junior), 26¼" (Standard).
Weight: 9 lbs. 12 oz. (Standard), 9 lbs. 2oz. (Junior) **Length:** 43¾" over-all (Standard), 39" (Junior).
Stock: Standard match. Walnut with stippled p.g. and fore-end.
Sights: Globe front with interchangeable inserts; micrometer match aperture rear.
Features: Meets ISU standard rifle specifications. Extremely short lock time. Trigger fully adjustable for weight, release point, length, lateral position, etc. Comes in Junior or Standard form. Introduced 1979. Imported by Beeman's Inc.
Price: About $795.00

FINNISH LION STANDARD TARGET RIFLE
Caliber: 22 LR, single-shot.
Barrel: 27⅝".
Weight: 10½ lbs. **Length:** 44⁹⁄₁₆" over-all.
Stock: French walnut, target style.
Sights: Globe front, International micrometer rear, p.g. or thumbhole style.
Features: Optional accessories: palm rest, hook buttplate, fore-end stop and swivel assembly, buttplate extension, 5 front sight aperture inserts, 3 rear sight apertures, allen wrench. Adjustable trigger. Imported from Finland by Mandall Shooting Supplies.
Price: $499.50
Price: Thumbhole stock model $535.00
Price: Heavy barrel model (either stock) $570.00

MANNLICHER SSG MARKSMAN
Caliber: 308 Win.
Barrel: 25.6".
Weight: 8.6 lbs. **Length:** 44.5" over-all.
Stock: Choice of synthetic half stock or walnut. Removable spacers in butt adjusts length of pull from 12¾" to 14".
Sights: Hooded blade front, folding leaf rear.
Features: Parkerized finish. Choice of interchangeable single or double set triggers. Detachable 5-shot rotary magazine (10-shot optional). Drilled and tapped for scope mounts. Imported by Steyr Daimler Puch of America.

Mannlicher SSG Match
Same as Model SSG Marksman except has Walther target peep sights and adj. rail in fore-end to adj. sling travel. Weight is 11 lbs.
Price: Synthetic half stock $753.50
Price: Walnut half stock $804.65

Price: Synthetic half stock $557.45
Price: Walnut half stock $612.50
Price: Synthetic half stock with Kahles sniper scope $1,225.00
Price: Optional 10-shot magazine $57.75

MOSSBERG MODEL 144 TARGET RIFLE
Caliber: 22 LR only. 7-shot clip.
Barrel: 27" round (¹⁵⁄₁₆" dia.)
Weight: About 8 lbs. **Length:** 43" over-all.
Stock: Target-style walnut with high thick comb, cheekpiece, p.g., beavertail fore-end, adj. hand stop and sling swivels.
Sights: Lyman 17A hooded front with inserts, Mossberg S331 receiver peep with ¼-minute clicks.
Features: Wide grooved trigger adj. for wgt. of pull, thumb safety, receiver grooved for scope mounting.
Price: $138.95

REMINGTON 40-XC NAT'L MATCH COURSE RIFLE
Caliber: 7.62 NATO, 5-shot.
Barrel: 23¼", stainless steel.
Weight: 10 lbs. without sights. **Length:** 42½" over-all.
Stock: Walnut, position-style, with palm swell.
Sights: None furnished.
Features: Designed to meet the needs of competitive shooters firing the national match courses. Position-style stock, top loading clip slot magazine, anti-bind bolt and receiver, bright stainless steel barrel. Meets all I.S.U. Army Rifle specifications. Adjustable buttplate, adjustable trigger.
Price: $689.95

CENTERFIRE & RIMFIRE RIFLES—TARGET

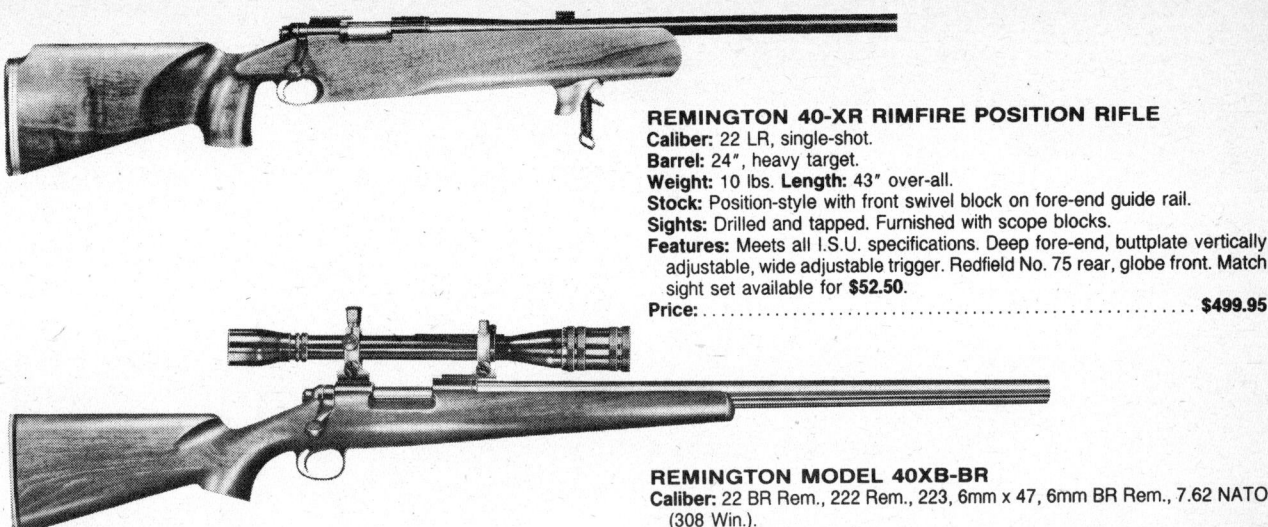

REMINGTON 40-XR RIMFIRE POSITION RIFLE
Caliber: 22 LR, single-shot.
Barrel: 24", heavy target.
Weight: 10 lbs. **Length:** 43" over-all.
Stock: Position-style with front swivel block on fore-end guide rail.
Sights: Drilled and tapped. Furnished with scope blocks.
Features: Meets all I.S.U. specifications. Deep fore-end, buttplate vertically adjustable, wide adjustable trigger. Redfield No. 75 rear, globe front. Match sight set available for **$52.50**.
Price: **$499.95**

REMINGTON MODEL 40XB-BR
Caliber: 22 BR Rem., 222 Rem., 223, 6mm x 47, 6mm BR Rem., 7.62 NATO (308 Win.).
Barrel: 20" (light varmint class), 26" (heavy varmint class).
Length: 38" (20" bbl.), 44" (26" bbl.). **Weight:** Light varmint class, 7¼ lbs., Heavy varmint class, 12 lbs.
Stock: Select walnut.
Sights: None. Supplied with scope blocks.
Features: Unblued stainless steel barrel, trigger adj. from 1½ lbs. to 3½ lbs. Special 2 oz. trigger at extra cost. Scope and mounts extra.
Price: **$669.95**

REMINGTON 540-XR RIMFIRE POSITION RIFLE
Caliber: 22 LR, single-shot.
Barrel: 26" medium weight target. Countersunk at muzzle.
Weight: 8 lbs., 13 oz. **Length:** Adj. from 43½" to 46¾".
Stock: Position-style with Monte Carlo, cheekpiece and thumb groove. 5-way adj. buttplate and full length guide rail.
Sights: None furnished. Drilled and tapped for target scope blocks. Fitted with front sight base.
Features: Extra-fast lock time. Specially designed p.g. to eliminate wrist twisting. Adj. match trigger. Match-style sling with adj. swivel block ($10.50) and sight set ($52.50) available.
Price: **$264.95**

REMINGTON 40-XB RANGEMASTER TARGET Centerfire
Caliber: 222 Rem., 22-250, 6mm Rem., 243, 25-06, 7mm Rem. Mag., 30-338 (30-7mm Rem. Mag.), 300 Win. Mag., 7.62 NATO (308 Win.), 30-06. Single shot.
Barrel: 27¼" round (Stand. dia.-¾", Hvy. dia.-⅞").
Weight: Std.—9¼ lbs., Hvy.—11¼ **Length:** 47"
Stock: American walnut with high comb and beavertail fore-end stop. Rubber non-slip buttplate.
Sights: None. Scope blocks installed.
Features: Adjustable trigger pull. Receiver drilled and tapped for sights.
Price: Standard s.s., stainless steel **$634.95**
Price: Repeating model **$676.90**
Price: Extra for 2 oz. trigger **$69.95**

Remington 540-XRJR Junior Rimfire Position Rifle
Same as 540-XR except fitted with 1¾" shorter stock to fit the junior shooter, Over-all length adjustable from 41¾" to 45". Length of pull adjustable from 11" to 14¼".
Price: **$264.95**

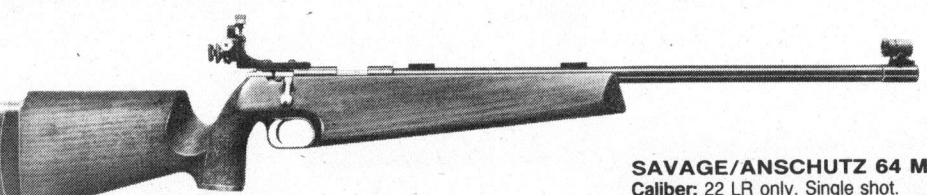

SAVAGE/ANSCHUTZ 64 MATCH RIFLE
Caliber: 22 LR only. Single shot.
Barrel: 26" round (¹¹⁄₁₆" dia.).
Weight: 7¾ lbs. **Length:** 44" over-all.
Stock: Walnut finished hardwood, cheekpiece, checkered p.g., beavertail fore-end, adj. buttplate.
Sights: None (extra). Scope blocks.
Features: Sliding side safety, adj. single stage trigger, receiver grooved for Anschutz sights.
Price: .... **$305.70**   64L (Left hand) **$318.65**
As above but with Anschutz 6723 Match Sight Set:
Price: Model 64S (Right hand) **$418.63**
Price: 64SL (Left hand) **$447.00**
Price: Anschutz Match sight set **$110.25**

CENTERFIRE & RIMFIRE RIFLES—TARGET

SAVAGE/ANSCHUTZ MARK 12 TARGET RIFLE
Caliber: 22 LR, single-shot.
Barrel: 26", heavy. 7/8" diameter.
Weight: 8 lbs. **Length:** 43" over-all.
Stock: Walnut finished hardwood.
Sights: Globe front (insert-type), micro-click peep rear.
Features: Action similar to the Anschutz Model 64. Stock has thumb groove, Wundhammer swell p.g., adjustable hand stop and sling swivel.
Price: $140.75
Price: Mark 12 Target Sling $16.50

UNIQUE T-66 MATCH RIFLE
Caliber: 22 LR, single shot.
Barrel: 25.6".
Weight: 11 lbs., 6 oz. **Length:** 43.5" over-all.
Stock: Straight grained French walnut, fore-end and p.g. hand stippled.
Sights: Interchangeable globe front; fully adj. Micro-Match rear; 8 inserts for front sight.
Features: Meets both NRA and UIT standards. Extremely fast lock time. Comes with proof certificate, two year guarantee, test target of 10-shot 50 meter group. True left hand model available. Imported from France by Solersport.
Price: Right hand $575.00
Price: Left hand $605.00

WALTHER U.I.T. SUPER
Caliber: 22 LR.
Barrel: 25½".
Weight: 10 lbs., 3 oz. **Length:** 44¾".
Stock: Walnut, adj. for length and drop; fore-end guide rail for sling or palm rest.
Sights: Globe-type front, fully adj. aperture rear.
Features: Conforms to both NRA and U.I.T. requirements. Fully adj. trigger. Left hand stock available on special order. Imported from Germany by Interarms.
Price: $950.00

Walther U.I.T. Match
Same specifications and features as standard U.I.T. Super rifle but has scope mount bases. Fore-end has new tapered profile, fully stippled. From Interarms.
Price: $1,050.00

Walther GX-1 Match Rifle
Same general specs as U.I.T. except has 25½" barrel, over-all length of 44½", weight of 15½ lbs. Stock is designed to provide every conceivable adjustment for individual preference and anatomical compatibility. Left-hand stock available on special order. From Interarms.
Price: $1,400.00

WALTHER RUNNING BOAR MATCH RIFLE
Caliber: 22 LR.
Barrel: 23.6".
Weight: 8 lbs. 5 oz. **Length:** 42" over-all.
Stock: Walnut thumb-hole type. Fore-end and p.g. stippled.
Features: Especially designed for running boar competition. Receiver grooved to accept dovetail scope mounts. Adjustable cheekpiece and butt plate. 1.1 lb. trigger pull. Left hand stock available on special order. Imported by Interarms.
Price: $900.00

DRILLINGS, COMBINATION GUNS, DOUBLE RIFLES

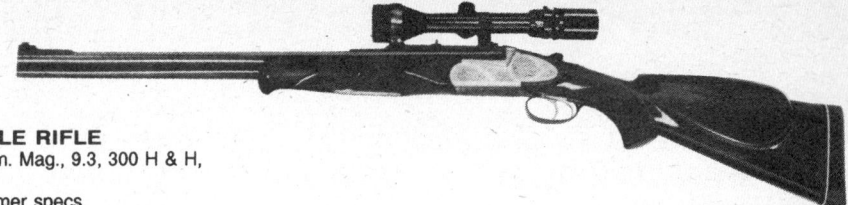

ARMSPORT "EMPEROR" 4000 DOUBLE RIFLE
Caliber: 243, 270, 284, 7.65, 308, 30-06, 7mm Rem. Mag., 9.3, 300 H & H, 375 H & H; Shotgun barrels in 16 or 20-ga.
Barrel: Shotgun barrel length and chokes to customer specs.
Stock: Dimensions to customer specs. Stock and fore-end of root walnut.
Sights: Rifle barrels have blade front with bead, leaf rear adj. for w.
Features: Receiver and sideplates engraved. Gun comes with extra set of barrels fitted to action. Packaged in a hand-made, fitted luggage-type leather case lined with Scotch loden cloth. Introduced 1978. From Armsport.
Price: Complete $9,250.00

ARMSPORT "EMPEROR" 4010 DOUBLE RIFLE
Side-by-side version of the Model 4000 over-under rifle. Available in 243, 270, 284, 7.65, 308, 30-06, 7mm Rem. Mag., 9.3, 300 H&H, 338 Win. and 375 H&H. Shotgun barrels in 16 or 20 ga., choice of length and choke. Comes in fitted luggage-type case.
Price: $12,000.00

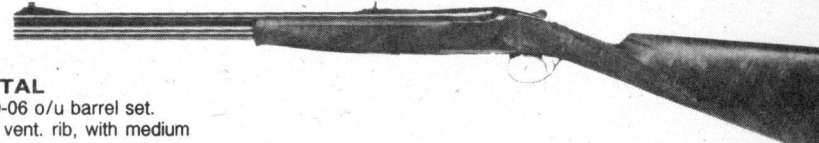

BROWNING SUPERPOSED CONTINENTAL
Caliber/Gauge: 20 ga. x 20 ga. with extra 30-06x30-06 o/u barrel set.
Barrel: 20 ga.—26½" (Mod. & Full, 3" chambers), vent. rib, with medium raised German nickel silver sight bead. 30-06—24".
Weight: 6 lbs. 14 oz. (rifle barrels) 5 lbs. 14 oz. (shotgun barrels)
Stock: Select high grade American walnut with oil finish. Straight grip stock and schnabel fore-end with 26 l.p.i. hand checkering.
Sights: Rifle barrels have flat face gold bead front on matted ramp, folding leaf rear.
Features: Action is based on a specially engineered Superposed 20-ga. frame. Single selective trigger works on inertia; let-off is about 4½ lbs. Automatic selective ejectors. Manual top tang safety incorporated with barrel selector. Furnished with fitted luggage-type case. Introduced 1979.
Price: $4,650.00

CHAPUIS EXPRESS RIFLE
Caliber: 7x57R, 7x65R, 30-06, 9.3x74R, 444 Marlin, 45-70, 375 H&H. Set of extra 20-ga. barrels optional.
Barrel: 23.6" for rifle except 444 and 45-70 which are 21½"; 26½" or 27½" for shotgun.
Weight: 7¼ to 8½ lbs. **Length:** 44" over-all (std. cals.).
Stock: Select French or American walnut, oil finish. Fine checkering on p.g. and fore-end. Right or left-hand stock. Deluxe wood, accessories optional.
Sights: Express sights; blade on ramp front, fixed shallow-V rear. Optional rear sight with folding leaves available.
Features: Single joining rib between barrels. Auto ejectors standard. Game motif and scroll engraving on receiver and sideplates. Rifle comes with regulation target for 75 meters. Available in three models: RG boxlock; R Deluxe false sideplates, and President with blued sideplates and receiver with gold inlays. From R. Painter Co.
Price: RG boxlock $2,803.00
Price: R Deluxe $3,329.00
Price: President $3,860.00
Price: Extra set of 20-ga. barrels with fitted leather case $868.89
Price: Extra set of rifle barrels .................................P.O.R.

> Consult our Directory pages for the location of firms mentioned.

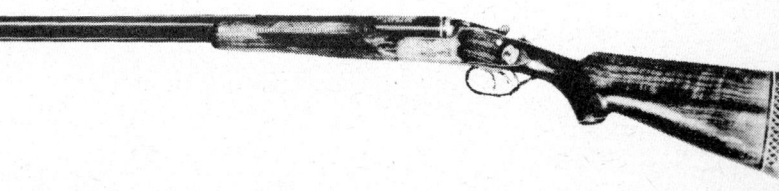

COLT SAUER DRILLING
Caliber: 12 ga., over 30-06, 12 ga. over 243.
Action: Top lever, cross bolt, box lock.
Barrel: 25" (Mod. & Full).
Weight: 8 lbs. **Length:** 41¾" over-all.
Stock: American walnut, oil finish. Checkered p.g. and fore-end. Black p.g., cap, recoil pad. 14¼"x2"x1½".
Sights: Blade front with brass bead, folding leaf rear.
Features: Cocking indicators, tang barrel selector, automatic sight positioner, set rifle trigger, side safety. Blue finish with bright receiver engraved with animal motifs and European-style scrollwork. Imported by Colt.
Price: $2,995.00

DRILLINGS, COMBINATION GUNS, DOUBLE RIFLES

FERLACH DOUBLE RIFLE
Caliber: Any caliber desired; metric, English or American.
Action: Boxlock or sidelock, side-by-side or over-under.
Barrel: Any length desired.
Weight: To customer specs. **Length:** To customer specs.
Stock: Custom or standard dimensions.
Sights: Any desired, including folding, night sights and scopes.
Features: Any desired, including highly figured wood, auto ejection, folding sights, extra barrel sets, night sights. Imported by Ferlach (Austria) of North America.
Price: Base, boxlock action $2,900.00
Price: Base, sidelock action $4,900.00

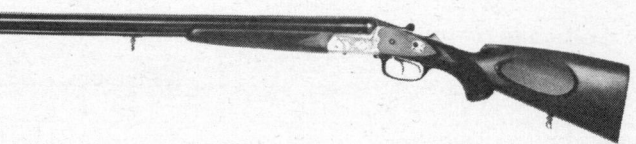

HEYM MODEL 33 BOXLOCK DRILLINGS
Caliber/Gauge: 5.6x50R Mag., 5.6x57R, 6.5x57R, 7x57R, 7x65R, 8x57JRS, 9.3x74R, 243, 270, 308, 30-06; 16x16 (2¾"), 20x20 (3").
Barrel: 25" (Full & Mod.).
Weight: about 6½ lbs. **Length:** 42" over-all.
Stock: Dark European walnut, checkered p.g. and fore-end; oil finish.
Sights: Silver bead front, folding leaf rear. Automatic sight positioner. Available with scope and Suhler claw mounts.
Features: Greener-type crossbolt and safety, double under-lugs. Double set triggers. Plastic or steel trigger guard. Engraving coverage varies with model. Contact Heym for more data.
Price: Model 33 .... $3,906.00

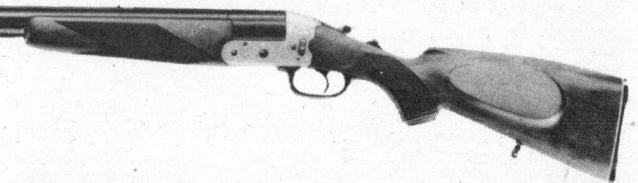

HEYM MODEL 22S SAFETY COMBO GUN
Caliber/Gauge: 16 or 20 ga. (2¾") over 22 Hornet, 22 WMR, 222 Rem., 222 Rem. Mag., 223, 22-250, 243 Win., 5.6x50R, 6.5x57R, 7x57R.
Barrel: 24", solid rib.
Weight: About 5½ lbs.
Stock: Dark European walnut, hand-checkered p.g. and fore-end. Oil finish.
Sights: Silver bead ramp front, folding leaf rear.
Features: Tang mounted cocking slide, separate barrel selector, single set trigger. Base supplied for quick-detachable scope mounts. Patented rocker-weight system automatically uncocks gun if accidently dropped or bumped hard. Contact Heym for more data.
Price: Model 22S $1,407.00
Price: Cals. 6.5x57R, 243, and 7x57R $1,596.00
Price: Factory fitted scope mounts, add $130.00

Heym Model 55BF/77BF O/U Combo Gun
Similar to Model 77B/55B o-u rifle except chambered for 12, 16 or 20 ga. (2¾" or 3") over 5.6x50R, 222 Rem., 5.6x57R, 243, 6.5x57R, 270, 7x57R, 7x65R, 308, 30-06, 8x57JRS, 9.3x74R, or 375 H&H. Has solid rib barrel. Available as boxlock or sidelock, with interchangeable shotgun and rifle barrels.
Price: Model 55BF boxlock $3,158.00
Price: Model 55BFSS sidelock $5,338.00

HEYM MODEL 37 DOUBLE RIFLE DRILLING
Caliber/Gauge: 7x65R, 30-06, 8x57JRS, 9.3x74R; 20 ga. (3").
Barrel: 25" (shotgun barrel choked Full or Mod.).
Weight: About 8½ lbs. **Length:** 42" over-all.
Stock: Dark European walnut, hand-checkered p.g. and fore-end. Oil finish.
Sights: Silver bead front, folding leaf rear. Available with scope and Suhler claw mounts.
Features: Full side-lock construction. Greener-type crossbolt, double under lugs, cocking indicators. Contact Heym for more details.
Price: Model 37 double rifle drilling $6,552.00
Price: Model 37 Deluxe (hunting scene engraving) from, ... $7,702.00

Heym Model 37 Side Lock Drilling
Similar to Model 37 Double Rifle Drilling except has 12x12, 16x16 or 20x20 over 5.6x50R Mag., 5.6x57R, 6.5x57R, 7x57R, 7x65R, 8x57JRS, 9.3x74R, 243, 270, 308 or 30-06. Rifle barrel is manually cocked and uncocked.
Price: Model 37 with border engraving $5,006.00
Price: As above with engraved hunting scenes $5,834.00

HEYM MODEL 77B/55B O/U DOUBLE RIFLE
Caliber: 5.6x50R, 222 Rem., 5.6x57R, 243, 6.5x57R, 7x57R, 7x65R, 308, 30-06, 8x57JRS, 300 Win. Mag., 9.3x74R; 375 H&H, 458 Win. Mag.
Barrel: 25".
Weight: About 8 lbs., depending upon caliber. **Length:** 42" over-all.
Stock: Dark European walnut, hand-checkered p.g. and fore-end. Oil finish.
Sights: Silver bead ramp front, open V-type rear.
Features: Boxlock or full sidelock; Kersten double crossbolt, cocking indicators; hand-engraved hunting scenes. Options available include interchangeable barrels, Zeiss scopes in claw mounts, deluxe engravings and stock carving, etc. Contact Heym for more data.
Price: Model 55B boxlock $3,875.00
Price: Model 55BSS sidelock $6,000.00
Price: Interchangeable shotgun barrels $1,757.00

Consult our Directory pages for the location of firms mentioned.

DRILLINGS, COMBINATION GUNS, DOUBLE RIFLES

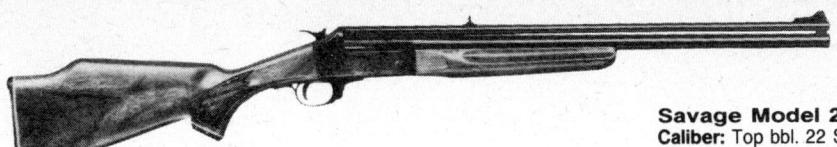

Savage Model 24-D O/U
Caliber: Top bbl. 22 S, L, LR or 22 Mag.; bottom bbl. 20 or 410 gauge.
Action: Bottom opening lever, low rebounding visible hammer, single trigger, barrel selector spur on hammer, separate extractors, color case-hardened frame.
Barrel: 24", separated barrels.
Weight: 6¾ lbs. **Length:** 40".
Stock: Walnut, checkered p.g. and fore-end (14"x1½"x2½").
Sights: Ramp front, rear open adj. for e.
Features: Receiver grooved for scope mounting.
Price: **$156.20**

SAVAGE MODEL 24-F.G. O/U
Same as Model 24-D except: color case hardened frame, stock is walnut finished hardwood, no checkering or M.C.
Price: **$124.70**

KRIEGHOFF RIFLE-SHOTGUN COMBO
Caliber: Top-12, 16, 20 (2¾"), 20 ga. 3"; lower-all popular U.S. and metric cartridges, rimless and rimmed.
Action: Sidelock—Ulm; Boxlock—Teck.
Barrel: 25", solid rib.
Weight: 6¼ lbs. **Length:** 41" over-all.
Stock: 14¼"x1¼"x2¼", European walnut.
Sights: Sourdough front, express rear.
Features: Interchangeable rifle barrels in 22 Hornet, 222 Rem., 222 Rem. Mag. priced at $250.00. Scope optional. Imported by Creighton & Warren.
Price: .... **Prices on request**

SAVAGE MODEL 24-C O/U
Caliber: Top bbl. 22 S, L, LR; bottom bbl. 20 gauge cyl. bore.
Action: Take-down, low rebounding visible hammer. Single trigger, barrel selector spur on hammer.
Barrel: 20" separate barrels.
Weight: 5¾ lbs. **Length:** 35" (taken down 20").
Stock: Walnut finished hardwood, straight grip.
Sight: Ramp front, rear open adj. for e.
Features: Trap door butt holds one shotshell and ten 22 cartridges, comes with special carrying case. Measures 7"x22" when in case.
Price: **$140.25**

Savage Model 24-V
Similar to Model 24-D except: 22 Hornet, 222 Rem. or 30-30 and 20 ga., 223 or 357 and 20 ga.; stronger receiver; color case-hardened frame; barrel; band; folding leaf rear sight; receiver tapped for scope **$186.25**

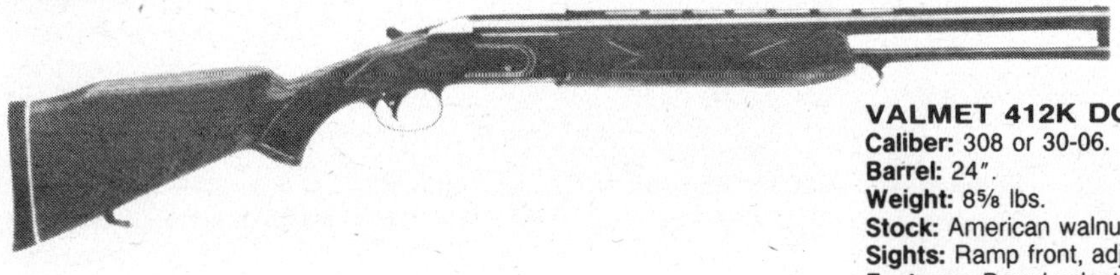

VALMET 412K DOUBLE RIFLE
Caliber: 308 or 30-06.
Barrel: 24".
Weight: 8⅝ lbs.
Stock: American walnut with Monte Carlo style.
Sights: Ramp front, adjustable open rear.
Features: Barrel selector mounted in trigger. Cocking indicators in tang. Recoil pad. Valmet scope mounts available. Interchangeable barrels. Introduced 1980. From Valmet.
Price: Either caliber **$679.00**

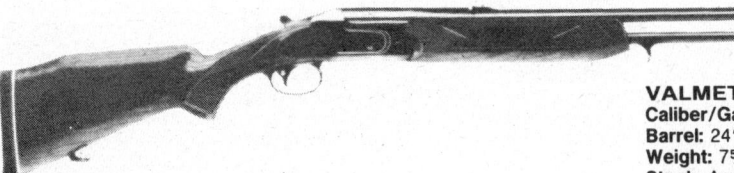

VALMET 412KE COMBINATION GUN
Caliber/Gauge: 12 over 222, 308, 30-06.
Barrel: 24" (Imp. & Mod.).
Weight: 7⅝ lbs.
Stock: American walnut, with recoil pad. Monte Carlo style. Standard measurements 14"x1⅜"x2"x2⅗".
Sights: Blade front, flip-up-type open rear.
Features: Barrel selector on trigger. Hand checkered stock and fore-end. Barrels are screw-adjustable to change bullet point of impact. Barrels are interchangeable. Introduced 1980. From Valmet.
Price: **$589.00**

TIKKA MODEL 07 COMBINATION GUN
Caliber/Gauge: 12 (2¾") over 222 Rem., 5.6x52R, 5.6x50R Mag. or 12 (3") over 222 Rem. only.
Barrel: Shotgun—24½" (Full), rifle 22¾".
Weight: About 7½ lbs. **Length:** 41" over-all.
Stock: Walnut, Monte Carlo-style with roll-over cheekpiece. Palm-swell on p.g.
Sights: Bead front, open rear adj. for windage.
Features: Exposed hammer; sling swivels; rosewood p.g. cap; ventilated rib. Introduced 1979. From Ruko Sporting Goods.
Price: About, ... **$510.00**

Tikka Model 77K Hammerless Combo
Similar to Model 07 except has hammerless shotgun-type action. Double triggers. Available in 12ga. (2¾") over 222 Rem., 5.6x50R Mag., 5.6x52R, 7x57R, 308 Win. Shotgun barrel choked Mod.
Price: About **$775.00**

A. ZOLI RIFLE-SHOTGUN O/U COMBO
Caliber: 12 ga./308 Win., 12 ga./222, 12 ga./30-06.
Barrel: Combo—24"; shotgun—28" (Mod. & Full).
Weight: About 8 lbs. **Length:** 41" over-all (24" bbl.).
Stock: European walnut.
Sights: Blade front, flip-up rear.
Features: Available with German claw scope mounts on rifle/shotgun barrels. Comes with set of 12/12 (Mod. & Full) barrels. From Mandall Shooting Supplies.
Price: With two barrel sets, without claw mounts **$1,295.00**
Price: With two barrel sets, with claw mounts **$1,495.00**

CAUTION: PRICES CHANGE. CHECK AT GUNSHOP.

RIMFIRE RIFLES—AUTOLOADING & SLIDE ACTION

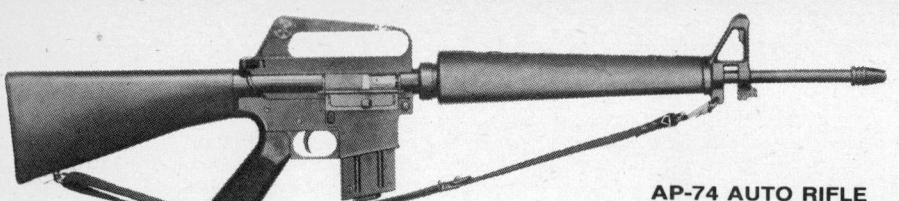

AP-74 AUTO RIFLE
Caliber: 22 LR, 32 ACP, 15 shot magazine.
Barrel: 20" including flash reducer.
Weight: 6½ lbs. **Length:** 38½" over-all.
Stock: Black plastic.
Sights: Ramp front, adj. peep rear.
Features: Pivotal take-down, easy disassembly. AR-15 look-alike. Sling and sling swivels included. Imported by EMF.
Price: $198.00
Price: With walnut stock and fore-end $220.00
Price: 32 ACP $210.00
Price: With wood stock and fore-end $230.00

AMERICAN 180 AUTO CARBINE
Caliber: 22 LR, 177-round magazine.
Barrel: 16½".
Weight: 5¾ lbs. (empty), 10 lbs. (loaded). **Length:** 36" over-all.
Stock: High impact plastic stock and fore-end.
Sights: Blade front, peep rear adj. for w. and e.
Features: Available in selective fire version for law enforcement or semi-auto only for civilians. Laser-Lok laser beam sight available at extra cost. Manufactured by American Arms International, Inc.
Price: $395.00
Price: Laser-Lok sight system $695.00
Price: Extra magazine and winding mechanism $115.00

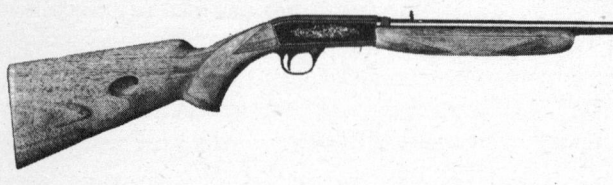

BROWNING AUTOLOADING RIFLE
Caliber: 22 LR, 11-shot.
Barrel: 19¼".
Weight: 4¾ lbs. **Length:** 37" over-all.
Stock: Checkered select walnut (13¾"x1^{13}/₁₆"x2⅝") with p.g. and semi-beavertail fore-end.
Sights: Gold bead front, folding leaf rear.
Features: Engraved receiver is grooved for tip-off scope mount; cross-bolt safety; tubular magazine in buttstock; easy take down for carrying or storage.
Price: Grade I .... $214.95 Grade II .... $314.95 Grade III $699.95
Also available in Grade I, 22 S (16-shot) $214.95

BROWNING BAR-22 AUTO RIFLE
Caliber: 22 LR only, 15-shot tube magazine.
Barrel: 20¼".
Weight: About 6¼ lbs. **Length:** 38¼" over-all.
Stock: French walnut. Cut checkering at p.g. and fore-end.
Sights: Gold bead front, folding leaf rear. Receiver grooved for scope mounting.
Features: Magazine tube latch locks closed from any position. Cross bolt safety in rear of trigger guard. Trigger pull about 5 lbs. Introduced 1977. From Browning.
Price: Grade I $209.95
Price: Grade II $309.95

BROWNING BPR-22 PUMP RIFLE
Caliber: 22 LR, 22 Mag. (15 shots, 11 shots).
Barrel: 20¼".
Weight: About 6¼ lbs. **Length:** 38¼" over-all.
Stock: French walnut. Cut checkered p.g. and fore-end.
Sights: Gold bead front, folding leaf rear. Receiver grooved for scope mount.
Features: Short, positive pump stroke, side ejection. Magazine tube latches from any position. Cross bolt safety in rear of trigger guard. Introduced 1977. From Browning.
Price: 22 LR, Grade I $209.95
Price: 22 Magnum, Grade I $229.95
Price: 22 Magnum, Grade II $329.95

CAUTION: PRICES CHANGE. CHECK AT GUNSHOP.

RIMFIRE RIFLES—AUTOLOADING & SLIDE ACTION

CHARTER AR-7 EXPLORER CARBINE
Caliber: 22 LR, 8-shot clip.
Barrel: 16" alloy (steel-lined).
Weight: 2½ lbs. **Length:** 34½"/16½" stowed.
Stock: Moulded grey Cycloac, snap-on rubber butt pad.
Sights: Square blade front, aperture rear adj. for e.
Features: Take-down design stores bbl. and action in hollow stock. Light enough to float.
Price: $98.00

ERMA ESG22 GAS-OPERATED CARBINE
Caliber: 22 WMR, 12-shot magazine, 22 LR, 15-shot magazine.
Barrel: 18".
Weight: 6 lbs. **Length:** 35½" over-all.
Stock: Walnut-stained beech.
Sights: Military post front, peep rear adj. for w. & e.
Features: Locked breech, gas-operated action. Styled after M-1 Carbine. Also available as standard blowback action. Receiver grooved for scope mounting. Introduced 1978. From Excam.
Price: Gas, 22 WMR $278.00
Price: Blowback, 22 LR $169.00

GLENFIELD MODEL 75C AUTOLOADER
Caliber: 22 LR, 14-shot magazine.
Barrel: 18".
Weight: 5 lbs. **Length:** 36¾" over-all.
Stock: Walnut-finished hardwood; Monte Carlo with full p.g.
Sights: Ramp front, adj. open rear.
Features: Bolt hold-open device; cross-bolt safety; receiver grooved for scope mounting. Introduced 1980. From Marlin.
Price: $74.95

GLENFIELD 60 AUTOLOADER
Caliber: 22 LR, 18-shot tubular mag.
Barrel: 22" round tapered.
Weight: About 5½ lbs. **Length:** 41" Over-all.
Stock: Walnut finished Monte Carlo, checkered p.g. and fore-end.
Sights: Ramp front, open adj. rear.
Features: Chrome plated trigger, matted receiver is grooved for tip-off mounts. Has new tube magazine closure system.
Price: Less scope $74.95

GLENFIELD 70 AUTO
Caliber: 22 LR, 7-shot clip magazine.
Barrel: 18" (16-groove rifling).
Weight: 4½ lbs. **Length:** 36½" over-all.
Stock: Walnut-finished hardwood with Monte Carlo, full p.g., checkered p.g. Sling swivels included.
Sights: Ramp front, adj. open rear. Receiver grooved for scope mount.
Features: Receiver top has serrated, non-glare finish; chrome plated trigger; cross-bolt safety; bolt hold-open; chrome plated magazine. Scope shown not included. Introduced 1978.
Price: Less scope $74.95

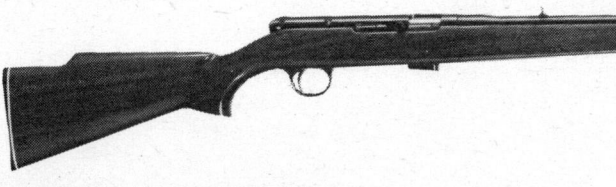

HARRINGTON & RICHARDSON Model 700 Auto Rifle
Caliber: 22 WMRF, 5-shot clip.
Barrel: 22".
Weight: 6½ lbs. **Length:** 43¼" over-all.
Stock: Walnut, Monte Carlo, full p.g., composition buttplate.
Sights: Blade front, folding leaf rear.
Features: Drilled and tapped for scope mounting. 10-shot clip available. Made in U.S. by H&R.
Price: $179.00

H&R Model 700 Deluxe Rifle
Same as Model 700 except has select walnut stock with cheekpiece, checkered grip and fore-end, rubber rifle recoil pad. No iron sights; comes with H&R Model 432 4x, 1" tube scope, with base and rings.
Price: $295.00

CAUTION: PRICES CHANGE. CHECK AT GUNSHOP.

RIMFIRE RIFLES—AUTOLOADING & SLIDE ACTION

HECKLER & KOCH MODEL 300 AUTO RIFLE
Caliber: 22 Mag., 5-shot box mag.
Barrel: 19¾".
Weight: 5¾ lbs. **Length:** 39½" over-all.
Stock: European walnut, Monte Carlo with cheek rest; checkered p.g. and Schnabel fore-end.
Sights: Post front adj. for elevation, V-notch rear adj. for w.
Features: Hexagon (polygonal) rifling, comes with sling swivels; straight blow-back inertia bolt action; single-stage trigger (3½-lb. pull). HK-05 clamp scope mount with 1" rings available at extra cost. Imported from Germany by Security Arms.
Price: HK300 .... $336.00
Price: Scope mount with 1" rings $98.00

HECKLER & KOCH HK270 AUTO RIFLE
Caliber: 22 LR, 5-shot magazine.
Barrel: 19¾".
Weight: 5.5 lbs. **Length:** 38.2" over-all.
Stock: European walnut with Monte Carlo cheek rest.
Sights: Post front adj. for elevation, V-notch rear adj. for windage.
Features: Straight blow-back action; 3½ lbs. trigger pull. Extra 20-shot magazine available. Receiver grooved for scope mount. Introduced 1978. From Heckler & Koch.
Price: $279.00

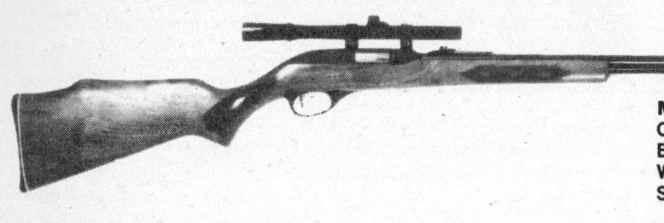

MARLIN MODEL 990 AUTOLOADER
Caliber: 22 LR, 18-shot tubular magazine.
Barrel: 22" Micro-Groove®.
Weight: About 5½ lbs. **Length:** 40¾" over-all.
Stock: American black walnut, Monte Carlo style with fluted comb and full pistol grip; checkered p.g. and fore-end.
Sights: Ramp bead front with Wide-Scan™ hood, adjustable folding semi-buckhorn rear.
Features: Receiver grooved for tip-off mount; bolt hold-open device; cross-bolt safety. Introduced 1979.
Price: $93.95

MARLIN MODEL 995 AUTOLOADER
Caliber: 22 LR, 7-shot clip magazine
Barrel: 18" Micro-Groove®.
Weight: 5½ lbs. **Length:** 36¾" over-all.
Stock: American black walnut, Monte Carlo-style, with full pistol grip. Checkered p.g. and fore-end.
Sights: Ramp bead front with Wide-Scan hood; adjustable folding semi-buckhorn rear.
Features: Receiver grooved for tip-off scope mount; bolt hold-open device; cross-bolt safety. Introduced 1979.
Price: $87.95

MOSSBERG 377 PLINKSTER AUTO RIFLE
Caliber: 22 LR, 15-shot tube magazine
Barrel: 20" AC-KRO-GRUV.
Weight: 6¼ lbs. **Length:** 40" over-all.
Stock: Straight line, moulded one-piece thumbhole.
Sights: No iron sights. Comes with 4x scope.
Features: Walnut texture stock finish, checkered fore-end. Tube magazine loads through port in buttstock. Has bolt hold-open.
Price: With 4x scope $90.95

MOSSBERG MODEL 353 AUTOLOADING RIFLE
Caliber: 22 LR, 7-shot clip.
Barrel: 18" "AC-KRO-GRUV".
Weight: 5 lbs. **Length:** 38" over-all.
Stock: Walnut, checkered at p.g. and fore-end. Black Tenite two-position fold-down fore-end.
Sights: Open step adj. U-notch rear, bead front on ramp.
Features: Sling swivels and web strap on left of stock, extension fore-end folds down for steady firing from prone position. Receiver grooved for scope mounting.
Price: $99.95

RIMFIRE RIFLES—AUTOLOADING & SLIDE ACTION

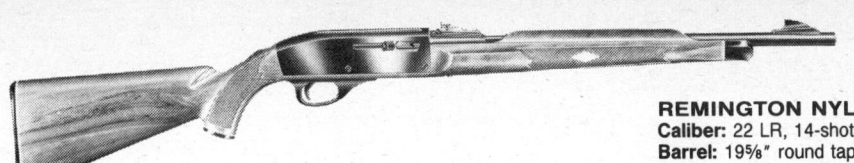

REMINGTON NYLON 66MB AUTO RIFLE
Caliber: 22 LR, 14-shot tubular mag.
Barrel: 19⅝" round tapered.
Weight: 4 lbs. **Length:** 38½" over-all.
Stock: Moulded Mohawk Brown Nylon, checkered p.g. and fore-end.
Sights: Blade ramp front, adj. open rear.
Features: Top tang safety, double extractors, receiver grooved for tip-off mounts.
Price: $99.95
Price: Model 66GS (22 Short only) $115.95
Price: Model 66MB With Universal UA 4x scope $107.95

Remington Nylon 66AB Auto Rifle
Same as the Model 66MB except: Apache Black Nylon stock, chrome plated receiver.
Price: $105.95

Remington Nylon 66BD Auto Rifle
Same as the Model 66AB except has black stock, barrel, and receiver cover. Black diamond-shape inlay in fore-end. Introduced 1978.
Price: $99.95
Price: Model 66 BD with 4x scope $107.95

REMINGTON 552A AUTOLOADING RIFLE
Caliber: 22 S (20), L (17) or LR (15) tubular mag.
Barrel: 21" round tapered.
Weight: About 5¾ lbs. **Length:** 40" over-all.
Stock: Full-size, walnut-finished hardwood.
Sights: Bead front, step open rear adj. for w. & e.
Features: Positive cross-bolt safety, receiver grooved for tip-off mount.
Price: $129.95

Remington Model 552BDL Auto Rifle
Same as Model 552A except: Du Pont RKW finished walnut stock, checkered fore-end and capped p.g. stock. Blade ramp front and fully adj. rear sights.
Price: $145.95

REMINGTON 572 FIELDMASTER PUMP RIFLE
Caliber: 22 S(20), L(17) or LR(14). Tubular mag.
Barrel: 21" round tapered.
Weight: 5½ lbs. **Length:** 42" over-all.
Stock: Walnut-finished hardwood with p.g. and grooved slide handle.
Sights: Blade ramp front; sliding ramp rear adj. for w. & e.
Features: Cross-bolt safety, removing inner mag. tube converts rifle to single shot, receiver grooved for tip-off scope mount.
Price: $134.95
Price: Sling and swivels installed $14.95

Remington Model 572 BDL Deluxe
Same as the 572 except: p.g. cap, walnut stock with RKW finish, checkered grip and fore-end, ramp front and fully adj. rear sights.
Price: $149.95
Price: Sling and swivels installed $14.95

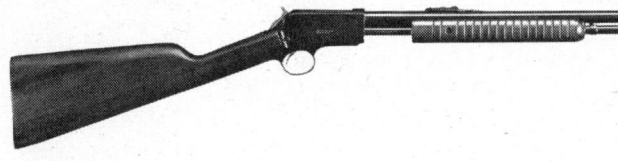

ROSSI 62 SA PUMP RIFLE
Caliber: 22 S, L or LR.
Barrel: 23".
Weight: 5¾ lbs. **Length:** 39¼" over-all.
Stock: Walnut, straight grip, grooved fore-end.
Sights: Fixed front, adj. rear.
Features: Capacity 20 Short, 16 Long or 14 Long Rifle. Quick takedown. Imported from Brazil by Interarms.
Price: Blue $147.00
Price: Nickel $160.00

ROSSI 62 SAC CARBINE
Same as standard model except has 16¼" barrel. Magazine holds slightly fewer cartridges.
Price: Blue $147.00
Price: Nickel $160.00

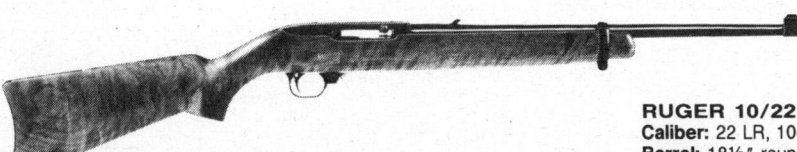

RUGER 10/22 AUTOLOADING CARBINE
Caliber: 22 LR, 10-shot rotary mag.
Barrel: 18½" round tapered.
Weight: 5 lbs., 12 oz. **Length:** 36¾" over-all.
Stock: American walnut with p.g. and bbl. band.
Sights: Gold bead front, folding leaf rear adj. for e.
Features: Detachable rotary magazine fits flush into stock, cross-bolt safety, receiver tapped and grooved for scope blocks or tip-off mount. Scope base adapter furnished with each rifle.
Price: $107.50

Ruger 10/22 Auto Sporter
Same as 10/22 Carbine except: Hand checkered p.g. and fore-end with straight buttplate, no bbl. band, has sling swivels.
Price: $128.50

CAUTION: PRICES CHANGE. CHECK AT GUNSHOP.

RIMFIRE RIFLES—AUTOLOADING & SLIDE ACTION

SQUIRES BINGHAM M16 SEMI AUTO RIFLE
Caliber: 22 LR, 15-shot clip.
Barrel: 16½".
Weight: 6 lbs. **Length:** 38½" over-all.
Stock: Black painted mahogany.
Sights: Post front, rear adj. for e.
Features: Box magazine, muzzle brake/flash suppressor. Imported by Kassnar Imports.
Price: $99.95

SAVAGE MODEL 80 AUTO RIFLE
Caliber: 22 LR, 15-shot tube magazine.
Barrel: 20".
Weight: 6 lbs. **Length:** 40" over-all.
Stock: Select walnut, checkered p.g. and fore-end.
Sights: Blade front, open rear adj. for w. & e.
Features: Adult-sized rifle. Monte Carlo stock with white spacers at p.g. and buttplate. Receiver grooved for scope mounting.
Price: $104.35

Consult our Directory pages for the location of firms mentioned.

SQUIRES BINGHAM M20D SEMI AUTO RIFLE
Caliber: 22 LR, 15-shot clip.
Barrel: 19½".
Weight: 6 lbs. **Length:** 40½" over-all.
Stock: Pulong Dalaga wood with contrasting fore-end tip.
Sights: Blade front, V-notch rear adj. for e.
Features: Positive sliding thumb safety. Receiver grooved for tip-off scope mount. Imported by Kassnar Imports.
Price: $79.95

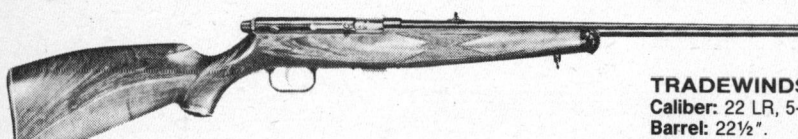

TRADEWINDS MODEL 260-A AUTO RIFLE
Caliber: 22 LR, 5-shot (10-shot mag. avail.).
Barrel: 22½".
Weight: 5¾ lbs. **Length:** 41½".
Stock: Walnut, with hand checkered p.g. and fore-end.
Sights: Ramp front with hood, 3-leaf folding rear, receiver grooved for scope mt.
Features: Double extractors, sliding safety. Imported by Tradewinds.
Price: $185.00

UNIVERSAL 2200 LEATHERNECK CARBINE
Caliber: 22 LR, 10-shot.
Barrel: 18".
Weight: 5½ lbs. **Length:** 35¾" over-all.
Stock: Birch hardwood with lacquer finish.
Sights: Blade front, peep rear adj. for w. & e.
Features: Look-alike to the G.I. Carbine except in rimfire. Recoil operated. Metal parts satin-polish blue. Flip-type safety. Optional 30-shot magazine available. Receiver drilled and tapped for scope mounting. Introduced 1979. From Universal Firearms.
Price: $166.95

WEATHERBY MARK XXII AUTO RIFLE, CLIP MODEL
Caliber: 22 LR only, 5- or 10-shot clip loaded
Barrel: 24" round contoured.
Weight: 6 lbs. **Length:** 42¼" over-all.
Stock: Walnut, Monte Carlo comb and cheekpiece, rosewood p.g. cap and fore-end tip. Skip-line checkering.
Sights: Gold bead ramp front, 3-leaf folding rear.
Features: Thumb operated side safety also acts as single shot selector. Receiver grooved for tip-off scope mount. Single pin release for quick takedown.
Price: $279.95

Weatherby Mark XXII Tubular Model
Same as Mark XXII Clip Model except: 15-shot tubular magazine. **$289.95**
Extra 5-shot clip .... **$6.95**   Extra 10-shot clip **$7.95**

RIMFIRE RIFLES—LEVER ACTION

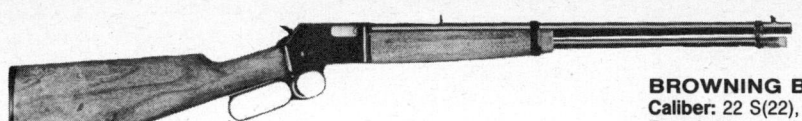

BROWNING BL-22 LEVER ACTION RIFLE
Caliber: 22 S(22), L(17) or LR(15). Tubular mag.
Barrel: 20" round tapered.
Weight: 5 lbs. **Length:** 36¾" over-all.
Stock: Walnut, 2-piece straight grip western style.
Sights: Bead post front, folding-leaf rear.
Features: Short throw lever, ½-cock safety, receiver grooved for tip-off scope mounts.
Price: Grade I **$189.95**
Price: Grade II, engraved receiver, checkered grip and fore-end .. **$214.95**

ERMA EG73 LEVER ACTION CARBINE
Caliber: 22 WRM, 12-shot magazine.
Barrel: 19¼".
Weight: 6 lbs. **Length:** 37⅜" over-all.
Stock: Walnut-stained beech.
Sights: Hooded ramp front, Buckhorn rear. Receiver grooved for scope mounting.
Features: Tubular magazine, side ejection. Introduced 1978. Imported by Excam.
Price: **$226.00**

Erma Lever Action Carbines
Model EG712. Similar to Magnum model except chambered for 22 S, L, LR with magazine capacity of 21, 17 and 15 respectively. Barrel length is 18½", weight is 5½ lbs. Introduced 1978 .... **$198.75**
Model EG712 L. As above except has European walnut stock, engraved nickel silver receiver, heavy octagonal barrel. Imported by Excam. Introduced 1978 .... **$325.00**

MARLIN GOLDEN 39A LEVER ACTION RIFLE
Caliber: 22 S(26), L(21), LR(19), tubular magazine.
Barrel: 24" Micro-Groove®.
Weight: 6½ lbs. **Length:** 40".
Stock: American black walnut with white line spacers at p.g. cap and buttplate.
Sights: Bead ramp front with detachable "Wide-Scan"™ hood, folding rear semi-buckhorn adj. for w. and e.
Features: Take-down action, receiver tapped for scope mount (supplied), gold plated trigger, sling swivels, offset hammer spur. Mar-Shield® stock finish.
Price: **$181.95**

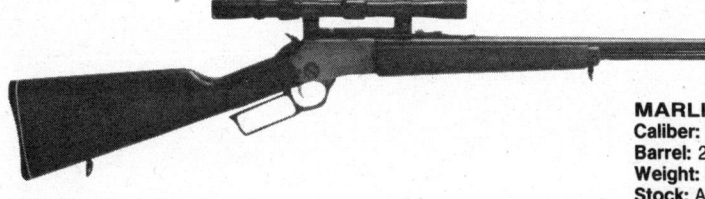

MARLIN GOLDEN 39M CARBINE
Caliber: 22 S(21), L(16), LR(15), tubular magazine.
Barrel: 20" Micro-Grove®.
Weight: 6 lbs. **Length:** 36".
Stock: American black walnut, straight grip, white line buttplate spacer. Mar-Shield® finish.
Sights: "Wide-Scan"™ ramp front with hood, folding rear semi-buckhorn adj. for w. and e.
Features: Squared finger lever. Receiver tapped for scope mount (supplied) or receiver sight, gold plated trigger, offset hammer spur, sling swivels, take-down action.
Price: **$181.95**

WINCHESTER 9422 XTR LEVER ACTION RIFLE
Caliber: 22 S(21), L(17), LR(15). Tubular mag.
Barrel: 20½" (16" twist).
Length: 37⅛" over-all. **Weight:** 6½ lbs.
Stock: American walnut, 2-piece, straight grip (no p.g.).
Sights: Hooded ramp front, adj. semi-buckhorn rear.
Features: Side ejection, receiver grooved for scope mounting, takedown action. Has new XTR wood and metal finish.
Price: **$236.00**

Winchester 9422M XTR Lever Action Rifle
Same as the 9422 except chambered for 22 WMR cartridge, has 11-round mag. capacity **$230.00**

RIMFIRE—BOLT ACTION & SINGLE SHOT

GLENFIELD MODEL 15 BOLT ACTION RIFLE
Caliber: 22, S, L, LR, single-shot.
Barrel: 22".
Weight: 5½ lbs. Length: 41" over-all.
Stock: Walnut-finished hardwood with Monte Carlo and full p.g.
Sights: Ramp front, adjustable open rear.
Features: Receiver grooved for tip-off scope mount; checkering on pistol grip; thumb safety; red cocking indicator. Introduced 1979.
Price: $67.95

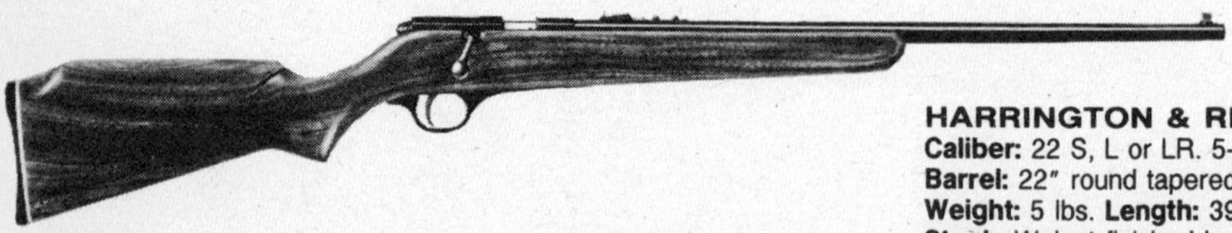

HARRINGTON & RICHARDSON 865 PLAINSMAN RIFLE
Caliber: 22 S, L or LR. 5-shot clip mag.
Barrel: 22" round tapered.
Weight: 5 lbs. Length: 39" over-all.
Stock: Walnut finished hardwood with Monte Carlo and p.g.
Sights: Blade front, step adj. open rear.
Features: Cocking indicator, sliding side safety, receiver grooved for tip-off scope mounts.
Price: $79.50

HARRINGTON & RICHARDSON MODEL 750 PIONEER
Caliber: 22 S, L or LR. Single-shot.
Barrel: 22" round tapered.
Weight: 5 lbs. Length: 39" over-all.
Stock: Walnut finished hardwood with Monte Carlo comb and p.g.
Sights: Blade front, step adj. open rear.
Features: Double extractors, feed platform, cocking indicator. sliding side safety, receiver grooved for tip-off scope mount.
Price: $69.50

KIMBER MODEL 82 BOLT ACTION RIFLE
Caliber: 22 Short, Long, Long Rifle, 5-shot detachable magazine.
Barrel: 24", 6-groove.
Weight: About 6¼ lbs. Length: 41" over-all.
Stock: Select walnut. "Classic" style stock. Checkered p.g. and fore-end.
Sights: Blade front on ramp, open rear adj. for w. & e.
Features: High quality adult-sized bolt action rifle. All steel construction. Rocker-type silent safety. All metal parts finished in high polish blue. Available with or without sights. Made in U.S.A. Introduced 1980. From Kimber of Oregon.
Price: Without sights $388.00
Price: With sights $395.00
Price: Scope mounts and rings $32.50
Price: Extra 5-shot magazine $8.50
Price: Extra 10-shot magazine $10.00

MARLIN 780 BOLT ACTION RIFLE
Caliber: 22 S, L, or LR; 7-shot clip magazine.
Barrel: 22" Micro-Groove.
Weight: 5½ lbs. Length: 41"
Stock: Monte Carlo American black walnut with checkered p.g. and fore-end. White line spacer at buttplate. Mar-Shield® finish.
Sights: "Wide-Scan"™ ramp front, folding semi-buckhorn rear adj. for w. & e.
Features: Gold plated trigger, receiver anti-glare serrated and grooved for tip-off scope mount.
Price: $86.95

Marlin 781 Bolt Action Rifle
Same as the Marlin 780 except: tubular magazine holds 25 Shorts, 19 Longs or 17 Long Rifle cartridges. Weight 6 lbs. $91.95

Marlin 782 Bolt Action Rifle
Same as the Marlin 783 except: 22 Rimfire Magnum cal. only, weight about 6 lbs. Sling and swivels attached. $96.95

Marlin 783 Bolt Action Rifle
Same as Marlin 782 except: Tubular magazine holds 12 rounds of 22 Rimfire Magnum ammunition. $99.95

Glenfield 20 Bolt Action Repeater
Similar to Marlin 780, except: Walnut finished checkered p.g. stock, adjustable open rear sight, ramp front.
Price: $71.95

RIMFIRE—BOLT ACTION & SINGLE SHOT

MOSSBERG MODEL 340B RIFLE
Caliber: 22 LR, 7-shot clip.
Barrel: 24" "AC-KRO-GRUV".
Weight: 6½ lbs. **Length:** 43½" over-all.
Stock: Walnut finish with p.g., Monte Carlo and cheek piece, sling swivels.
Sights: Mossberg S331 receiver peep with ¼-minute adjustments for w. and e. S320 Mossberg hooded ramp front.
Features: Front sight offers choice of post or aperture elements. Receiver grooved for scope mount.
Price: $96.50

MOSSBERG MODEL 341 RIFLE
Caliber: 22 S, L, LR, 7-shot clip.
Barrel: 24" "AC-KRO-GRUV".
Weight: 6½ lbs. **Length:** 43½" over-all.
Stock: Walnut, checkered p.g. and fore-end, Monte Carlo and cheek piece. Buttplate with white line spacer.
Sights: Bead front, U-notch rear adj. for w. and e.
Features: Sliding side safety, 8 groove rifling.
Price: $89.95

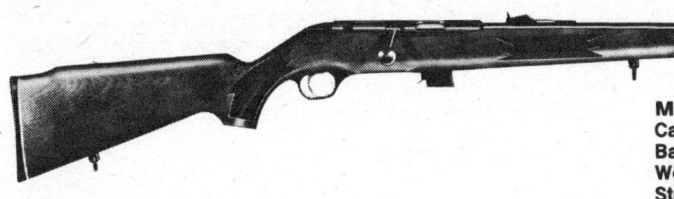

MOSSBERG MODEL 640K CHUCKSTER
Caliber: 22 WMR. 5-shot clip mag.
Barrel: 24" AC-KRO-GRUV.
Weight: 6¼ lbs. **Length:** 44¾" over-all.
Stock: Walnut, checkered p.g. and fore-end, Monte Carlo comb and cheek-piece.
Sights: Ramp front with bead, fully adj. leaf rear.
Features: Grooved trigger, sliding side safety, double extractors, receiver grooved for tip-off scope mounts and tapped for aperture rear sight.
Price: $101.50

MOSSBERG MODEL 321K
Caliber: 22 S, L, LR, single shot.
Barrel: 24".
Length: 43½" over-all. **Weight:** 6½ lbs.
Stock: Walnut finish, cheekpiece, checkered p.g. and fore-end.
Sights: Ramp front, adj. rear.
Features: Hammerless bolt action with drop-in loading platform and automatic safety, black buttplate.
Price: $78.95

REMINGTON MODEL 541-S
Caliber: 22 S, L, LR; 5-shot clip.
Barrel: 24"
Weight: 5½ lbs. **Length:** 42⅝".
Stock: Walnut, checkered p.g. and fore-end.
Sights: None. Drilled and tapped for scope mounts or receiver sights.
Features: Clip repeater. Thumb safety. Receiver and trigger guard scroll engraved.
Price: $294.95
Price: Extra 10-shot clip $6.00

REMINGTON MODEL 581 RIFLE
Caliber: 22 S, L or LR. 5-shot clip mag.
Barrel: 24" round.
Weight: 4¾ lbs. **Length:** 42⅝" over-all.
Stock: Walnut finished Monte Carlo with p.g.
Sights: Bead post front, screw adj. open rear.
Features: Sliding side safety, wide trigger, receiver grooved for tip-off scope mounts. Comes with single-shot adapter.
Price: $115.95
Price: Left hand action and stock $119.95

Remington Model 582 Rifle
Same as M581 except: tubular magazine under bbl. holds 20 S, 15 L or 14 LR cartridges. Wgt. 5½ lbs.
Price: $115.95

SAKO MODEL 78 BOLT ACTION
Caliber: 22 LR, 22 WMR or 22 Hornet.
Barrel: 22½".
Weight: 6¾ lbs.
Stock: Hand checkered European walnut.
Sights: None furnished; receiver has rail-type scope mount bases.
Features: New action design with tapered sporter weight barrel, adjustable trigger, detachable box magazine (5 shots in 22 LR, 4 shots in Hornet). Shrouded bolt, silent sliding safety, low bolt uplift. Introduced 1977. Imported by Stoeger.
Price: 22 LR $324.95
Price: 22 Hornet $391.95
Price: 22 LR Heavy Barrel $366.95
Price: 22 Magnum $366.95

Consult our Directory pages for the location of firms mentioned.

CAUTION: PRICES CHANGE. CHECK AT GUNSHOP.

RIMFIRE—BOLT ACTION & SINGLE SHOT

SAVAGE/ANSCHUTZ MODEL 54 SPORTER
Caliber: 22 LR. 5-shot clip mag.
Barrel: 23" round tapered.
Weight: 6¾ lbs. **Length:** 42" over-all.
Stock: French walnut, checkered p.g. and fore-end. Monte Carlo roll-over comb, schnabel fore-end tip.
Sights: Hooded ramp gold bead front, folding-leaf rear.
Features: Adj. single stage trigger, wing safety, receiver grooved for tip-off mount, tapped for scope blocks.
Price: $576.10
Price: Model 54M (22 WRM) $590.40

SAVAGE/ANSCHUTZ 164 BOLT ACTION RIFLE
Caliber: 22 LR. 5-shot clip mag.
Barrel: 24" round tapered.
Weight: 6 lbs. **Length:** 40¾" over-all
Stock: Walnut, hand checkered p.g. and fore-end, Monte Carlo comb and cheekpiece, schnabel fore-end.
Sights: Hooded ramp gold bead front, folding-leaf rear.
Features: Fully adj. single stage trigger, sliding side safety, receiver grooved for tip-off mount.
Price: $326.40
Price: Model 164M in 22 WRM (4-shot) $333.50

Savage/Anschutz Model 1432 Sporter
Same as Model 54 except chambered for 22 Hornet, 24" barrel, 5-shot capacity, over-all length 43⅝" $632.95

SAVAGE/ANSCHUTZ 1418-1518 SPORTERS
Similar to Model 164 except has European Mannlicher stock with inlays, hand-cut skip-line checkering, double set or single stage trigger.
Price: 1418 (22 LR) $462.95
Price: 1518 (22 Mag.) $471.10

Savage/Stevens Model 34 Rifle
Same as the Model 65-M except: 22 LR, walnut finished hardwood stock, bead post front sight.
Price: $73.90

SAVAGE MODEL 65-M RIFLE
Caliber: 22 WRM, 5-shot.
Barrel: 20" lightweight, free floating.
Weight: 5 lbs. **Length:** 39" over-all.
Stock: Walnut, Monte Carlo comb. checkered p.g. and fore-end.
Sights: Gold bead ramp front, folding leaf open rear.
Features: Sliding side safety, double extractors, receiver grooved for tip-off scope mount.
Price: $94.05

SAVAGE STEVENS MODEL 72 CRACKSHOT
Caliber: 22 S, L, LR.
Barrel: 22" octagonal.
Weight: 4½ lbs. **Length:** 37".
Stock: Walnut, straight grip and fore-end.
Sights: Blade front, step adj. rear.
Features: Falling block action, color case hardened frame.
Price: $94.50

SAVAGE-STEVENS MODEL 89
Caliber: 22 LR, single-shot.
Barrel: 18½".
Weight: 5 lbs. **Length:** 35" over-all.
Stock: Walnut finished hardwood.
Sights: Blade front, step adj. rear.
Features: Single-shot Martini-type breech block. Hammer must be cocked by hand independent of lever prior to firing. Automatic ejection. Satin black frame finish.
Price: $66.80

TRADEWINDS MODEL 311-A BOLT ACTION RIFLE
Caliber: 22 LR, 5-shot (10-shot mag. avail.).
Barrel: 22½".
Weight: 6 lbs. **Length:** 41¼".
Stock: Walnut, Monte Carlo with hand checkered p.g. and fore-end.
Sights: Ramp front with hood, folding leaf rear, receiver grooved for scope mt.
Features: Sliding safety locks trigger and bolt handle. Imported by Tradewinds.
Price: $185.00

STERLING BACKPACKER RIFLE
Caliber: 22 S, L, LR, single shot.
Barrel: 18".
Weight: 3¼ lbs. **Length:** 34", assembled.
Stock: Plastic stock and fore-end.
Sights: Blade front, rear adj. for e.
Features: Lightweight take-down rifle. Measures 19" when taken down. Snaps together easily. Introduced 1979. From Sterling Arms.
Price: $49.95

WESTERN FIELD 852 BOLT ACTION RIFLE
Caliber: 22 LR; 7-shot clip.
Barrel: 24" round tapered.
Length: 43" over-all. **Weight:** 6½ lbs.
Stock: Walnut-finished hardwood.
Sights: Bead front, rear adj. for e.
Features: Thumb operated safety. Scope not included.
Price: $69.95
Price: Model 840 in 22 WRM (illus.) $79.95

SHOTGUNS—AUTOLOADING

BENELLI AUTOLOADING SHOTGUN
Gauge: 12 ga. (5-shot, 3-shot plug furnished).
Barrel: 26" (Skeet, Imp. Cyl., Mod.); 28" (Spec., Full, Imp. Mod., Mod.). Vent. rib.
Weight: 6¾ lbs.
Stock: European walnut. 14"x1½"x2½". Hand checkered p.g. and fore-end.
Sights: Metal bead front.
Features: Quick interchangeable barrels. Cross-bolt safety. Hand engraved on higher grades. Imported from Italy by Heckler & Koch, Inc.
Price: Standard model $388.00
Price: Engraved $445.00
Price: Slug model $458.00
Price: Extra barrels $187.00

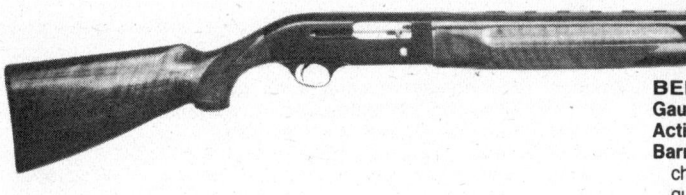

BERETTA A-301 AUTO SHOTGUN
Gauge: 12 or 20
Action: Gas operated.
Barrel: 12 ga.—22" (slug); 26" (Imp. Cyl.); 28" (Mod., Full); 30" (Full, 3" chamber); 20 ga.—28". (Full, Mod.); 26" (Imp. Cyl.). Vent. rib except slug gun.
Weight: 6 lbs., 5 ozs. (20 ga., 28").
Stock: 14⅛"x1⅜"x2⅜", European walnut. Magnum guns have recoil pad.
Features: All gas system parts are of stainless steel. Alloy receiver decorated with scroll pattern engraving. Push button safety in trigger guard Introduced 1977. Imported by The Beretta Arms Co.
Price: 12 or 20, 2¾" $470.00
Price: 12 or 20 ga., 3" Magnum $515.00
Price: Slug gun $470.00
Price: Extra barrels, from $160.00
Price: 12 ga. with four interchangeable choke tubes ... $580.00

Beretta A-301 Skeet and Trap
Same as standard A-301 except: Trap has M.C. stock (14¼"x1⅜"x1 9/16"x1⅝") with recoil pad, gold plated trigger, trap choke 30" bbl. Skeet gun has Skeet choke, gold plated trigger, Skeet stock (14¼"x1⅜"x2⅜"x 2 9/16") and 26" barrel. Introduced 1977. Imported by Beretta Arms Co.
Price: Skeet, 12 or 20 ga. $470.00
Price: Trap, 12 or 20 ga. $485.00
Price: Extra barrels $170.00

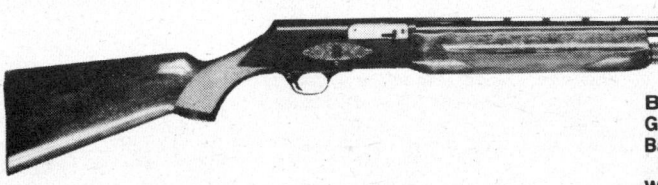

BROWNING B/2000 GAS OPERATED AUTO SHOTGUN
Gauge: 12 or 20 ga.; 5-shot, 4-shot in Magnum.
Barrel: 26", 28" or 30" in 2¾" Field Models, plain or vent. rib; 28", 30" or 32" in 3" Magnum models, vent. rib only.
Weight: 7½ lbs. (26" vent. rib) **Length:** 45⅜" (26" bbl.).
Stock: French walnut, hand checkered, full pistol grip, no recoil pad 14¼"x1⅝"x2½".
Sights: Medium raised bead, German nickel silver.
Features: Internal self-cleaning gas system, soft recoil, speed loading/unloading, extra bbls. interchangeable without factory fitting. No adjustment necessary to gas system for varying loads.
Price: 12 or 20 ga. vent. rib $439.95
Price: Vent. rib, 3" Mag. $439.95
Price: Buck Special $439.95
Price: Buck Special with accessories $457.45
Price: Extra barrels $143.25

Browning B/2000 20 ga. Skeet Model
Similar to 12 ga. target guns except 20 ga. only, has conventional vent. rib with front and center ivory beads; does not have the special high post floating rib. Skeet stock and pad, semi-beavertail fore-end; 2¾" chamber.
Price: $439.95

Browning B/2000 12 ga. Trap and Skeet Models
Similar to field grade B/2000 except has a special high post floating vent. rib mated to a special receiver rib; front and center ivory beads; special Skeet or trap recoil pads fitted. Trap model has Monte Carlo stock (14⅜"x1⅜"x1⅜"x2⅛"); Skeet has Skeet stock (14⅜"x1½"x2"). Checkered French walnut with semi-beavertail fore-end; 2¾" chamber.
Price: With high post vent. rib $474.95

BROWNING AUTO-5 LIGHT 12 and 20
Gauge: 12, 20; 5-shot; 3-shot plug furnished; 2¾" chamber.
Action: Recoil operated autoloader; takedown.
Barrel: 26" (Skeet boring in 12 & 20 ga., Cyl., Imp. Cyl., Mod. in 20 ga.); 28" (Skeet in 12 ga., Mod., Full); 30" (Full in 12 ga.).
Weight: 12 ga. 7¼ lbs., 20 ga. 6⅜ lbs.
Stock: French walnut, hand checkered half-p.g. and fore-end. 14¼" x 1⅝" x 2½".
Features: Receiver hand engraved with scroll designs and border. Double extractors, extra bbls. interchangeable without factory fitting; mag. cut-off; cross-bolt safety.
Price: Vent. rib only $479.95
Price: Extra barrels, vent. rib only $151.50

Browning Auto-5 Light Skeet
Same as Light Standard except: 12 and 20 ga. only, 26" or 28" bbl. (Skeet). With vent. rib. Wgt. 6⅜-7½ lbs. $479.95

SHOTGUNS—AUTOLOADING

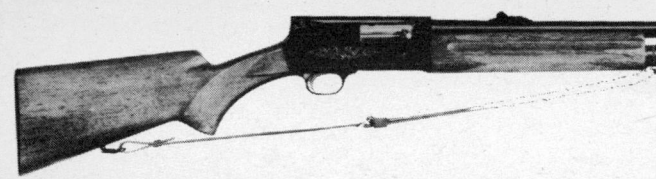

Browning Auto-5 Magnum 12
Same as Std. Auto-5 except: chambered for 3" magnum shells (also handles 2¾" magnum and 2¾" HV loads). 28" Mod., Full; 30" and 32" (Full) bbls. 14"x1⅝"x2½" stock. Recoil pad. Wgt. 8¾ lbs.
Price: Vent. rib only $489.95

Browning Auto-5 Light 12, 20, or 12 Buck Special
Same as A-5 Light model except: 24" bbl. choked for slugs, gold bead front sight on contoured ramp, rear sight adj. for w.&e. Wgt. 12 ga., 7 lbs.; 20 ga., 6 lbs. 2 oz.; 3" Mag. 12, 8¼ lbs. Illus.
Price: $489.95
Price: 12 or 20 ga. Magnum $499.95
All Buck Specials are available with carrying sling, detachable swivels and swivel attachments for $10.00 extra.

Browning Auto-5 Magnum 20
Same as Magnum 12 except barrels 28" Full or Mod., or 26" Full, Mod. or Imp. Cyl. With ventilated rib, 7½ lbs. $489.95

FRANCHI 530 AUTOMATIC TRAP
Gauge: 12 only, 2¾" chamber.
Barrel: 30" (Full or Imp. Mod.). Supplied with three interchangeable choke tubes.
Weight: 8 lbs. 6 ozs.
Stock: Select French walnut. Hand-applied oil finish, hand checkered p.g. and fore-end. Stock is interchangeable and drilled and tapped for recoil reducer. Choice of straight or M.C. stock in three sizes.
Features: Specially tuned gas system. Target grade trigger. Chrome lined bore and chamber. All stocks are cast-off for right-handed shooters—left-hand models available. Has Franchi's "Hi-Loft" vent. rib. Gun has matte blue to reduce light reflection. Comes with a snap-in shell catcher for singles, shell deflector for doubles. Introduced 1978. From Stoeger Industries.
Price: $695.00

FRANCHI MAGNUM AUTO SHOTGUN
Gauge: 12 or 20, 3-inch shells.
Action: Recoil-operated automatic.
Barrel: 32", 12 ga.; 28", 20 ga., both Full.
Weight: 12 ga. 8¼ lbs., 20 ga. 6 lbs.
Stock: Epoxy-finished walnut with recoil pad.
Features: Chrome-lined bbl., easy takedown. Available with ventilated rib barrel. Imported from Italy by Stoeger Industries.
Price: Vent. rib only $349.95

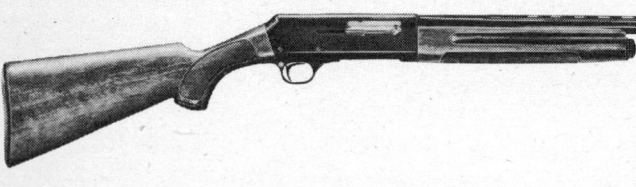

Franchi Slug Gun
Same as Standard automatic except 22" cylinder bored bbl., adj. rear sight, sling swivels.
Price: 12 or 20 ga. $349.95

FRANCHI STANDARD AUTO SHOTGUN
Gauge: 12, 20 or 28, 5-shot. 2¾" or 3" chamber.
Action: Recoil-operated automatic.
Barrel: 24" (Imp. Cyl. or Cyl.); 26" (Imp. Cyl. or Mod.); 28" (Skeet, Mod. or Full); 30", 32". (Full).
Weight: 12 ga. 6¼ lbs., 20 ga. 5 lbs. 2 oz.
Stock: Epoxy-finished walnut.
Features: Chrome-lined bbl., easy takedown, 3-round plug provided. Available with plain round or ventilated rib barrel. Imported from Italy by Stoeger Industries.
Price: Vent. rib 12, 20 .... $334.95
Price: Hunter model (engraved, 12 or 20) $359.95

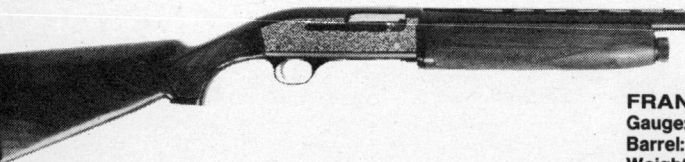

FRANCHI MODEL 500 GAS AUTO
Gauge: 12 only (2¾" chamber); 4-shot magazine, 2-shot plug furnished.
Barrel: 26" (Imp. Cyl., Mod.), 28" (Mod., Imp. Mod., Full).
Weight: About 7 lbs.
Stock: Select walnut, checkered p.g. and fore-end; semi-gloss finish.
Sights: Metal bead front.
Features: Gas operated, fixed barrel. Shell carrier need not be unlocked for loading. Ventilated rib with matted top surface; chrome lined barrel. Deluxe (Model 520) is identical except for full engraving on receiver sides. Imported by Stoeger Industries.
Price: Field Grade $348.95

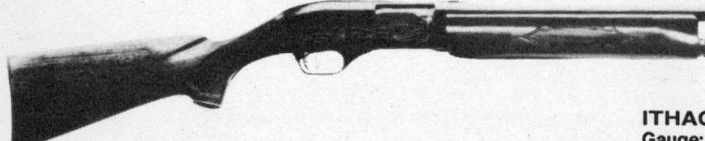

Ithaca Model 51 Featherlight Deluxe Skeet
Same gun as Model 51 Skeet with fancy American walnut stock, 28" or 29" (Skeet) barrel.
Price: $435.00

Ithaca Model 51 Magnum
Same as Standard Model 51 except has 3" chambers.
Price: With vent rib $384.00

ITHACA MODEL 51 FEATHERLIGHT AUTOMATIC
Gauge: 12 or 20 ga., 2¾" chamber.
Action: Gas-operated, rotary bolt has three locking lugs. Takedown. Self-compensating for high or low base loads.
Barrel: Roto-Forged, 30" (Full), 28" (Full, Mod., or Skeet), 26" (Imp. Cyl. or Skeet). Extra barrels available. Raybar front sight. Vent. rib $25.00 extra.
Stock: 14"x1⅝"x2½". Hand checkered walnut, white spacers on p.g. and under recoil pad.
Weight: About 7½ lbs.
Features: Hand fitted, engraved receiver, 3 shot capacity, safety is reversible for left hand shooter.
Price: Standard $319.00
Price: With vent. rib $359.00

SHOTGUNS — AUTOLOADING

Ithaca Model 51 Featherlight Deluxe Trap
Same gun as standard Model 51 with fancy American walnut trap stock, 30" (Full or Imp. Cyl.) or 28" (Full or Imp. Mod.) barrel.
Price: .... $445.00   With Monte Carlo stock $460.00

ITHACA MODEL 51 DEERSLAYER
Gauge: 12 or 20 ga., 2¾" chamber.
Action: Gas-operated, semi-automatic.
Barrel: 24", special bore.
Weight: 7½ lbs. (12 ga.), 7¼ lbs. (20 ga.).
Stock: 14"x1½"x2¼", American walnut. Checkered p.g. and fore-end.
Sights: Raybar front, open rear adj. for w. and e.
Features: Sight base grooved for scope mounts. Easy takedown, reversible safety. Scope optional.
Price: $348.00

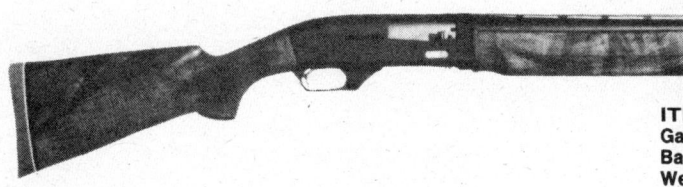

KASSNAR FOX AUTO SHOTGUN
Gauge: 12 only (2¾" or 3").
Barrel: 26" (Imp. Cyl., Mod., Skeet), 28" (Full, Mod.), 30" (Full). Vent rib.
Weight: 7¼ lbs.
Stock: American walnut.
Sights: Metal bead front.
Features: Cross bolt safety, interchangeable barrels. From Kassnar Imports.
Price: $314.95

ITHACA MAG 10 GAS OPERATED SHOTGUN
Gauge: 10, 3½" chamber, 3-shot.
Barrel: 32" only. Full choke.
Weight: 11¼ lbs.
Stock: American walnut, checkered p.g. and fore-end (14⅛"x2⅜"x1½"), p.g. cap, rubber recoil pad.
Sights: White Bradley.
Features: "Countercoil" gas system. Piston, cylinder, bolt, charging lever, action release and carrier made of stainless steel. ⅜" vent. rib. Reversible cross-bolt safety. Low recoil force. Deluxe model has full fancy claro American black walnut.
Price: Standard, plain barrel $485.00
Price: Deluxe, vent. rib $620.00
Price: Standard, vent. rib $530.00
Price: Supreme, vent. rib $725.00
Price: Mag 10 Roadblocker (20" barrel) $497.50

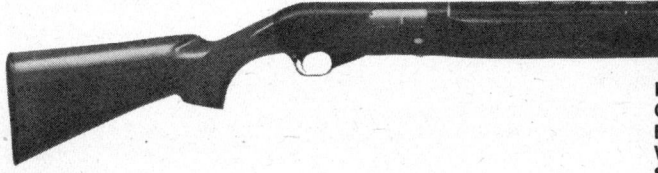

KAWAGUCHIYA K.F.C. M-250 AUTO SHOTGUN
Gauge: 12, 2¾".
Barrel: 26", 28", 30" (Imp. Cyl. Mod., Full).
Weight: 7 lbs. 6 ozs. Length: 48" over-all (28" barrel).
Stock: 14⅛"x1½"x2½". French walnut, checkered p.g. and fore-end.
Features: Gas-operated, ventilated barrel rib. Has only 79 parts. Cross-bolt safety is reversible for left-handed shooters. Introduced 1980. From La Paloma Marketing.
Price: Standard Grade $399.00
Price: Deluxe Grade (silvered, etched receiver) $429.95

MANUFRANCE AUTO SHOTGUN
Gauge: 12 ga., (2¾" or 3"), 3-shot.
Action: Gas operated.
Barrel: 26" (Imp. Cyl.), 28" (Mod.), 30" (Full); vent. rib.
Weight: 6¾ lbs. Length: 48" over-all.
Stock: French walnut, hand checkered p.g. and fore-end.
Features: Magazine cut-off; black matte finish receiver; quick take-down; interchangeable barrels available. Imported by Interarms.
Price: $279.00

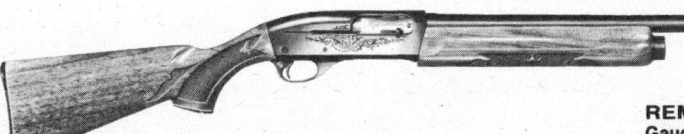

REMINGTON MODEL 1100 AUTO
Gauge: 12, 16 (5-shot); 3-shot plug furnished.
Action: Gas-operated autoloader.
Barrel: 26" (Imp. Cyl.), 28" (Mod., Full), 30" Full in 12 ga. only.
Stock: 14"x1½"x2½" American Walnut, checkered p.g. and fore-end.
Weight: 12 ga. 7½ lbs., 16 ga. 7⅜ lbs.
Features: Quickly interchangeable barrels within gauge. Matted receiver top with scroll work on both sides of receiver. Crossbolt safety.
Price: .... $340.95   With vent. rib $378.95
Price: Left hand model with vent. rib $397.95

SHOTGUNS—AUTOLOADING

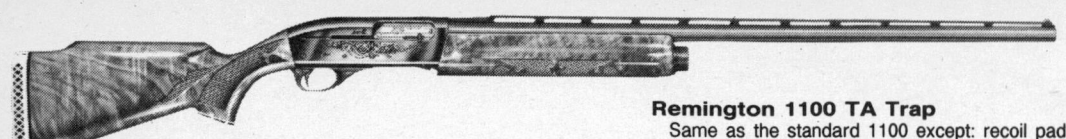

Remington 1100 SA Skeet
Same as the 1100 except: 26" bbl., special Skeet boring, vent. rib (high rib on LT-20), ivory bead front and metal bead middle sights. 14"x1½"x2½" stock. 12, 20, 28, 410 ga. Wgt. 7½ lbs., cut checkering, walnut, new receiver scroll.
Price: $389.95
Price: Left hand model with vent. rib $409.95
Price: 28 & 410 ga., 25" bbl. $394.95
Price: 20 ga. LT-20 Skeet SA $389.95
Price: Tournament Skeet (28, 410) $464.95
Price: Tournament Skeet (12 or 20) $459.95

Remington 1100 Magnum
Same as 1100 except: chambered for 3" magnum loads. Available in 12 ga. (30") or 20 ga. (28") Mod. or Full, 14"x1½"x2½" stock with recoil pad. Wgt. 7¾ lbs.
Price: $376.95
Price: With vent. rib $414.95
Price: Left hand model with vent. rib $433.95

Remington 1100D Tournament Auto
Same as 1100 Standard except: vent. rib, better wood, more extensive engraving $1,400.00

Remington 1100F Premier Auto
Same as 1100D except: select wood, better engraving $2,800.00
With gold inlay $4,200.00

Remington 1100 TA Trap
Same as the standard 1100 except: recoil pad. 14⅜"x1⅜"x1¾" stock. Right- or left-hand models. Wgt. 8¼ lbs. 12 ga. only. 30" (Mod. Trap, Full) vent. rib bbl. Ivory bead front and white metal middle sight.
Price: .... $397.95   With Monte Carlo stock $407.95
Price: 1100TA Trap, left hand $417.95
Price: With Monte Carlo stock $427.95
Price: Tournament Trap $470.95
Price: Tournament Trap with M.C. stock, better grade wood, different checkering, cut checkering $480.95

Remington 1100 Extra bbls.: Plain $85.95 (20, 28 & 410, $89.95). Vent. rib $123.95 (20, 28 & 410, $127.95). Vent. rib Skeet $131.95. Vent. rib Trap $131.95. Deer bbl. $99.95. Available in the same gauges and chokes as shown on guns. **Prices are approximate.**

Remington 1100 Small Gauge
Same as 1100 except: 28 ga. 2¾" (5-shot) or 410, 3" (except Skeet, 2½" 4-shot). 45½" over-all. Available in 25" bbl. (Full, Mod., or Imp. Cyl.) only.
Price: Plain bbl. .... $344.95   With vent. rib $382.95

Remington 1100 LT-20
Basically the same design as Model 1100, but with special weight-saving features that retain strength and dependability of the standard Model 1100.
Barrel: 28" (Full, Mod.), 26" (Imp. Cyl.).
Weight: 6½ lbs.
Price: .... $340.95   With vent. rib $378.95
Price: LT-20 magnum (28" Full) $376.95
Price: With vent. rib $414.95
Price: LT-20 Deer Gun (20" bbl.) $377.95
Price: LT-20 Ltd. has 23" (Mod. or Imp. Cyl.) barrel, 1" shorter stock $378.95

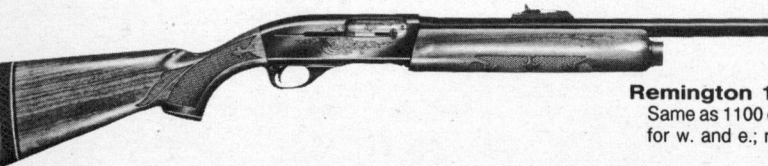

Remington 1100 Deer Gun
Same as 1100 except: 12 ga. only, 22" bbl. (Imp. Cyl.), rifle sights adjustable for w. and e.; recoil pad with white spacer. Weight 7¼ lbs. $377.95

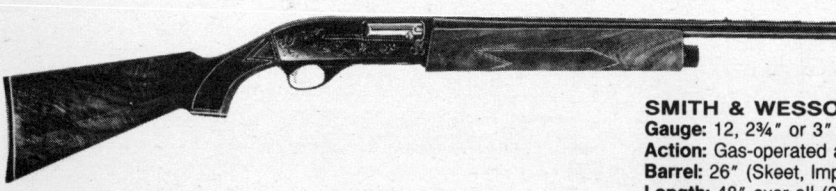

Smith & Wesson Model 1000 20 Gauge & 20 Magnum
Similar to 12 ga. model except slimmed down to weigh only 6½ lbs. Has self-cleaning gas system. Choice of four interchangeable barrels (26", Imp. Cyl. or Skeet, 28" Mod. or Full).
Price: $380.95
Price: Extra barrels $123.85
Price: With 3" chamber, (Mod., Full) $416.95

SMITH & WESSON MODEL 1000 AUTO
Gauge: 12, 2¾" or 3" chamber, 4-shot.
Action: Gas-operated autoloader.
Barrel: 26" (Skeet, Imp. Cyl.), 28" (Mod., Full), 30" (Mod. Full).
Length: 48" over-all. **Weight:** 7½ lbs. (28" bbl.).
Stock: 14"x1½"x2⅜", American walnut.
Features: Interchangeable crossbolt safety, vent. rib with front and middle beads, engraved alloy receiver, pressure compensator and floating piston for light recoil.
Price: $380.95
Price: Extra barrels (as listed above) $123.85
Price: Extra 22" barrel (Cyl. bore) with rifle sights $99.75
Price: With 3" chamber, 30" (Mod., Full) barrel $416.95

Smith & Wesson Model 1000S Super Skeet Shotgun
Similar to Model 1000 except has "recessed-type" Skeet choke with a compensator system to soften recoil and reduce muzzle jump. Stock has right-hand palm swell. Trigger is contoured (rounded) on right side; pull is 2½ to 3 lbs. Vent. rib has double sighting beads with a "Bright Point" flourescent red front bead. Fore-end cap weights (included) of 1 and 2 oz. can be used to change balance. Select-grade walnut with oil finish. Barrel length is 25", weight 8¼ lbs., over-all length 45.7". Stock measures 14"x1½"x2½" with .08" cast-off at butt, .16" at toe.
Price: $650.00
Price: Super Skeet interchangeable barrel $210.00

SHOTGUNS—AUTOLOADING

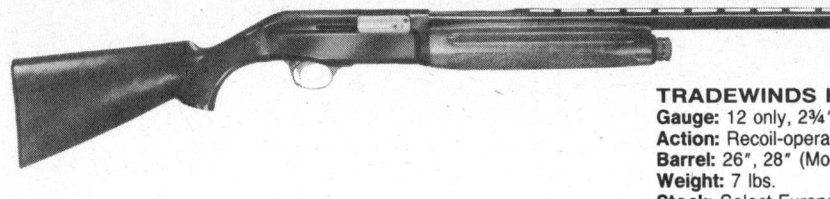

TRADEWINDS H-170 AUTO SHOTGUN
Gauge: 12 only, 2¾" chamber.
Action: Recoil-operated automatic.
Barrel: 26", 28" (Mod.) and 28" (Full), chrome lined.
Weight: 7 lbs.
Stock: Select European walnut stock, p.g. and fore-end hand checkered.
Features: Light alloy receiver, 5-shot tubular magazine, ventilated rib. Imported by Tradewinds.
Price: **$340.00**

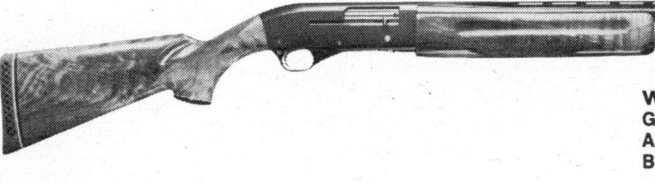

WEATHERBY CENTURION AUTO
Gauge: 12 only, 2¾" chamber.
Action: Gas operated autoloader with "Floating Piston."
Barrel: 26" (Mod., Imp. Cyl, Skeet), 28" (Full, Mod.), 30" (Full, Full Trap, Full 3" Mag.), Vent. Rib.
Weight: About 7½ lbs. **Length:** 48¼" (28").
Stock: Walnut, hand checkered p.g. and fore-end, rubber recoil pad with white line spacer.
Features: Cross bolt safety, fluted bolt, gold plated trigger. Imported by Weatherby.
Price: Field or Skeet grade . **$399.95** Trap grade **$429.95**
Price: Extra interchangeable barrels, from **$149.95**

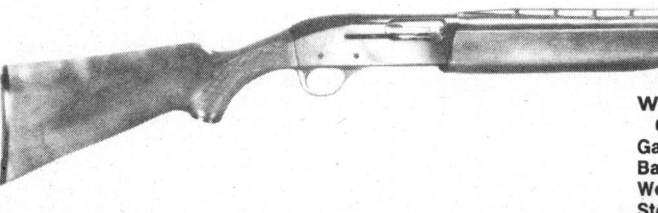

WESTERN FIELD AUTOLOADING SHOTGUN MODEL 650
Gauge: 12 only.
Barrel: 28" (Full, Mod., Imp. Cyl. choke tubes).
Weight: About 7¾ lbs.
Stock: Walnut finished hardwood.
Sights: Metal bead front.
Features: Interchangeable barrel and Accu-Choke tubes; vent. rib; top safety. From Montgomery Ward.
Price: Ward's catalog #10650 .... **$249.99**

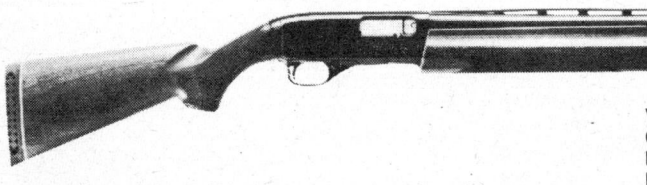

WINCHESTER SUPER-X MODEL 1 XTR AUTO
Gauge: 12, 4-shot.
Barrel: 26" (Imp. Cyl.), 28" (Mod., Full), 30" (Full).
Length: 46" over-all (26" bbl.)
Stock: American walnut with cut-checkered p.g. and fore-end, 14"x1½"x2½" (Field).
Sights: Metal bead front.
Features: Receiver and all metal parts made of machined steel. Straight-line, 3-piece bolt, short-stroke gas system, all steel trigger assembly, steel shell carrier.
Price: Vent. rib **$500.00**
Extra Barrels:
Price: Field, plain, 26", 28", 30" (Full, Mod., Imp. Cyl.) **$93.95**
Price: Field, vent. rib, 26", 28", 30" (Full, Mod., Imp. Cyl.) **$130.95**
Price: Trap or Skeet, 26", 30", (Full, Skeet) **$136.95**

Winchester Super-X Model 1 Trap and Skeet Models
Same as Field model except: Trap has 30" bbl., vent. rib (Full) and regular or Monte Carlo stock. Engraved receiver, red bead front sight, black rubber recoil pad with white spacer—**$576.00** for regular stock, **$589.00** for Monte Carlo. Skeet model has 26" vent. rib barrel (Skeet), otherwise same as trap gun—**$576.00**.

WINCHESTER 1400 AUTOMATIC MARK II
Gauge: 12, and 20 (3-shot).
Action: Gas operated autoloader. Front-locking 4-lug rotating bolt locks in bbl. Alloy receiver. Push button action release.
Barrel: Winchoke 28", Full, Mod. and Imp. Cyl. tubes only. Metal bead front sight. Available only with Winchoke.
Stock: 14"x1½"x2⅜". American walnut, new-design checkered p.g. and fore-end; fluted comb, p.g. cap, recoil pad.
Weight: With 26" bbl., 20 ga. 6½ lbs.; 16, 12 ga. 6¾ lbs.; 46⅝" over-all.
Features: Self-compensating valve adjusts for std. or magnum loads. Bbls. interchangeable without fitting. Crossbolt safety in front of trigger guard.
Price: .... **$275.00** With vent. rib **$298.00**
Price: Extra barrel, field, with Winchoke **$81.95**
Price: As above, field, vent. rib **$102.95**
Price: Deer barrel **$88.95**

Consult our Directory pages for the location of firms mentioned.

SHOTGUNS—AUTOLOADING

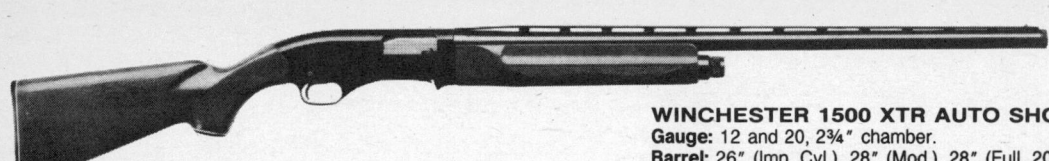

Consult our Directory pages for the location of firms mentioned.

WINCHESTER 1500 XTR AUTO SHOTGUN
Gauge: 12 and 20, 2¾" chamber.
Barrel: 26" (Imp. Cyl.), 28" (Mod.), 28" (Full, 20 ga. only), 30" (Full, 12 ga. only). Plain or vent rib, with or without Winchoke tubes.
Weight: 6½ to 7¼ lbs. **Length:** 46⅝" to 50⅝" over-all.
Stock: American walnut, cut-checkered p.g. and fore-end. Field, vent. rib dimensions are 14"x1½"x2½".
Sights: Metal bead front.
Features: New Winchester XTR fit and finish. Gas-operated auto; self-adjusting system; front locking, rotating bolt. Interchangeable barrels in 3 standard lengths and chokes, or Winchoke system. Engine turned bolt, nickel plated carrier, cross-bolt safety. Introduced 1978.
Price: Plain barrel, 12 or 20 .... $304.00
Price: Vent. rib, 12 or 20 .... $331.00
Price: Plain barrel with Winchoke $319.00
Price: Vent. rib barrel with Winchoke $347.00
Price: Extra barrel, field $84.95
Price: As above, with Winchoke $100.95
Price: Extra barrel, vent. rib $109.95
Price: As above, with Winchoke $125.95

SHOTGUNS—SLIDE ACTION

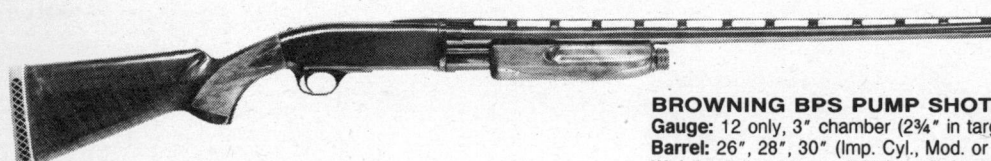

ITHACA MODEL 37 FEATHERLIGHT
Gauge: 12, 20 (5-shot; 3-shot plug furnished).
Action: Slide; takedown; bottom ejection.
Barrel: 26", 28", 30" in 12 ga. 26" or 28" in 20 ga. (Full, Mod. or Imp. Cyl.).
Stock: 14"x1⅝"x2⅝". Checkered walnut capped p.g. stock and fore-end.
Weight: 12 ga. 6½ lbs., 20 ga. 5¾ lbs.
Features: Ithaca Raybar front sight; decorated receiver, crossbolt safety; action release for removing shells.
Price: Standard $255.00
Price: Standard Vent Rib $296.00

ITHACA 37 BASIC FEATHERLITE
Gauge: 12 ga; 2¾" chamber or 3".
Barrel: 26" (Imp. Cyl.), 28" (Mod.) or 30" (Full).
Weight: 6¾ lbs.
Stock: Walnut, uncheckered and finished with tung oil.
Features: All metal surfaces vapor blasted to a non-glare matte finish. Fore-end is the traditional "Ring tail" style. Plain or vent Rib. Introduced 1980.
Price: Plain barrel $242.00
Price: Vent Rib $278.00
Price: Magnum, Full choke $305.00

Ithaca Model 37 Magnum
Same as standard Model 37 except chambered for 3" shells with resulting longer receiver. Stock dimensions are 14"x1⅞"x1½". Grip cap has a Sid Bell-designed flying mallard on it. Has a recoil pad, vent. rib barrel with Raybar front sight. Available in 12 or 20 ga. with 30" (Full) or 28" (Mod.) barrel. Weight about 7¼ lbs. Introduced 1978.
Price: $323.00

BROWNING BPS PUMP SHOTGUN
Gauge: 12 only, 3" chamber (2¾" in target guns). 5-shot magazine.
Barrel: 26", 28", 30" (Imp. Cyl., Mod. or Full).
Weight: 7 lbs. 12 ozs. (28" barrel). **Length:** 48¾" over-all (28" barrel).
Stock: 14¼"x1½"x2½". Select walnut, semi-beavertail fore-end, full p.g. stock.
Features: Bottom feeding and ejection, receiver top safety, high post vent. rib. Double action bars eliminate binding. Vent. rib barrels only. Introduced 1977. From Browning.
Price: Grade I, Hunting $299.95
Price: Grade I, Trap $309.95
Price: Extra Trap barrel .. $104.50   Extra Hunting barrel $99.50
Price: Buck Special (no accessories) $314.95
Price: Buck Special with accessories $332.45

Ithaca Model 37 De Luxe Featherlight
Same as Model 37 except: checked stock with p.g. cap; beavertail fore-end; recoil pad. Wgt. 12 ga. 6¾ lbs.
Price: With vent. rib $305.00

Ithaca Model 37 Deerslayer
Same as Model 37 except: 26" or 20" bbl. designed for rifled slugs; sporting rear sight, Raybar front sight; rear sight ramp grooved for Redfield long eye relief scope mount. 12, or 20 gauge. With checkered stock, beavertail fore-end and recoil pad.
Price: $285.00
Price: As above with special select walnut stock $341.00

Ithaca Model 37 Supreme
Same as Model 37 except: hand checkered beavertail fore-end and p.g. stock, Ithaca recoil pad and vent. rib $450.00
37 Supreme also with Skeet (14"x1½"x2¼") or Trap (14½"x1½"x1⅞") stocks at no extra charge.
Other options available at extra charge.

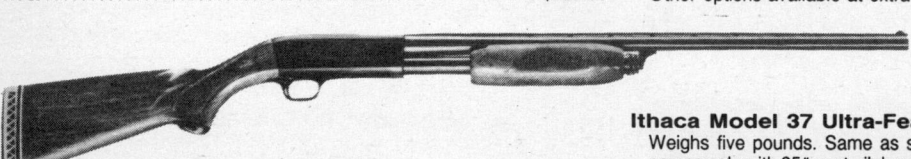

Ithaca Model 37 Ultra-Featherlight
Weighs five pounds. Same as standard Model 37 except in 20 ga. only, comes only with 25" vent. rib barrel choked Full, Mod. or Imp. Cyl. Has recoil pad, gold plated trigger, Sid Bell-designed grip cap. Also available as Ultra-Deerslayer with 20" barrel.
Price: $314.00

SHOTGUNS—SLIDE ACTION

MARLIN 120 MAGNUM PUMP GUN
Gauge: 12 ga. (2¾" or 3" chamber) 5-shot; 3-shot plug furnished.
Action: Hammerless, side ejecting, slide action.
Barrel: 20" slug, 26" (Imp. Cyl.), 28" (Mod.), 30" (Full), with vent. rib or 38" MXR plain.
Length: 50½" over-all (30" bbl.). **Weight:** About 8¼ lbs.
Stock: 14"x1½"x2⅜". Checkered walnut, capped p.g., semi-beavertail checkered fore-end. Mar-Shield® finish.
Features: Interchangeable bbls., slide lock release; large button cross-bolt safety.
Price: **$252.95**
Price: Extra barrels, about **$77.95**

MARLIN GLENFIELD 778 PUMP GUN
Gauge: 12 (2¾" or 3" chamber). 5-shot, 3-shot plug furnished.
Barrel: 20" slug (with sights), 26" (Imp. Cyl.), 28" (Mod.), 30" (Full), all with or without rib; 38" MXR (Full), no rib.
Weight: 7¾ lbs. **Length:** 48½" over-all.
Stock: Walnut-finished hardwood. Semi-beavertail fore-end, vent. recoil pad. Checkered p.g.
Features: Machined steel receiver, double action bars, engine-turned bolt, shell carrier and bolt slide. Interchangeable barrel. Introduced 1978.
Price: Plain barrel **$183.95**
Price: Vent. rib barrel **$208.95**

Mossberg Model 500ELR
Similar to Model 500 except: 410 bore only, 26" bbl. (Full); 2½", 3" shells; holds six 2¾" or five 3" shells. Walnut-finished stock with checkered p.g. and fore-end, fluted comb and recoil pad (14"x1¼"x2½"). Weight about 6 lbs., length over-all 45¾".
Price: With vent. rib barrel **$219.95**

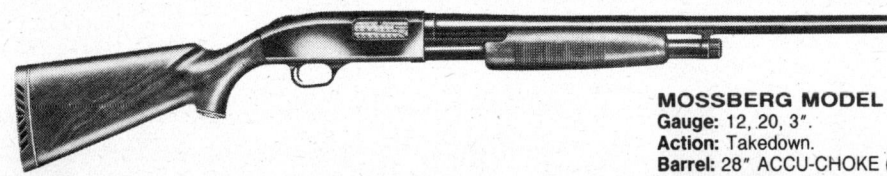

MOSSBERG MODEL 500 ALDR, CLDR
Gauge: 12, 20, 3".
Action: Takedown.
Barrel: 28" ACCU-CHOKE (interchangeable tubes for Imp. Cyl., Mod., Full). Vent. rib only.
Weight: 6¾ lbs. (20-ga.), 7¼ lbs. (12-ga.) **Length:** 48" over-all.
Stock: Walnut-finished hardwood; checkered p.g. and fore-end; recoil pad. (14"x1½"x2½").
Features: Side ejection; top tang safety; trigger disconnector prevents doubles. Easily interchangeable barrels within gauge.
Price: Vent. rib **$229.95**
Price: Extra barrels, from **$72.95**

Mossberg Model 500AHT/AHTD
Same as Model 500 except 12 ga. only with extra-high Simmons Olympic-style free floating rib and built-up Monte Carlo trap-style stock. 30" barrel (Full), 28" ACCU-CHOKE with 3 interchangeable choke tubes (Mod., Imp. Mod., Full).
Price: With 30" barrel, fixed choke **$326.95**
Price: With ACCU-CHOKE barrel, 28" or 30" **$336.95**

Mossberg Model 500ALMR
Similar to Model 500ALDR with vent. rib 30" or 32" barrel. Chambered for 2¾" or 3" shells. Full choke only in 12 ga. Walnut-finish stock, checkered p.g. and fore-end; fluted comb; recoil pad (14"x1½"x2½"). Receiver has pintail and canvasback etched scenes.
Price: **$235.50**

Mossberg Model 500ALS Slugster
Same as standard Model 500 except has Slugster barrel with ramp front sight, open adj. folding-leaf rear, running deer scene etched on receiver. 12 ga.—18½", 24"; 20 ga.—24" bbl.
Price: **$213.95**

REMINGTON 870 WINGMASTER PUMP GUN
Gauge: 12, 16, 20, (5-shot; 3-shot wood plug).
Action: Takedown, slide action.
Barrel: 12, 16, 20, ga., 26" (Imp. Cyl.); 28" (Mod. or Full); 12 ga., 30" (Full).
Stock: 14"x1⅝"x2½". Checkered walnut, p.g.; fluted extension fore-end; fitted rubber recoil pad.
Weight: 7 lbs., 12 ga. (7¾ lbs. with Vari-Weight plug); 6¾ lbs. 16 ga.; 6½ lbs., 20 ga. 48½" over-all (28" bbl.).
Features: Double action bars, crossbolt safety. Receiver machined from solid steel. Hand fitted action.
Price: Plain bbl. .... **$268.95** Vent. rib **$306.95**
Price: Riot gun, 18" or 20" Riot bore, (12 ga. only) **$247.95**
Price: Riot gun, 20" Imp. Cyl., rifle sights **$269.95**
Price: Left hand, vent. rib, 12 and 20 ga. **$324.95**

Remington 870 Magnum
Same as the M870 except 3" chamber, 12 ga. 30" bbl. (Mod. or Full), 20 ga. 28" bbl. (Mod. or Full). Recoil pad installed. Wgt., 12 ga. 8 lbs., 20 ga. 7½ lbs.
Price: Plain bbl. .... **$296.95** Vent. rib bbl. **$334.95**
Price: Left hand model, vent. rib. bbl. **$352.95**

CAUTION: PRICES CHANGE, CHECK AT GUNSHOP.

SHOTGUNS—SLIDE ACTION

Remington 870 SA Skeet
Same as the M870 except: 26" bbl. Skeet bored. Vent. rib with ivory front and white metal middle beads. 14"x1⅝"x2½" stock with rubber recoil pad, 12 or 20 ga. only $311.95
Price: 28 and 410 ga., 25" bbl., no recoil pad $316.95

Remington 870 Extra Barrels
Plain **$73.95**. Vent. rib **$119.95**. Vent. rib Skeet **$118.95**. Vent. rib Trap **$118.95**. 34" Trap **$124.95**. With rifle sights **$91.95**. Available in the same gauges and chokes as shown on guns. **Prices are approximate.**

Remington 870F Premier
Same as M870, except select walnut, better engraving $2,800.00
Price: With gold inlay $4,200.00

Remington 870D Tournament
Same as 870 except: better walnut, hand checkering, Engraved receiver & bbl. Vent. rib. Stock dimensions to order $1,400.00

Remington 870 TB Trap
Same as the M870 except: 12 ga. only, 30" (Mod., Full) vent. rib. bbl., ivory front and white metal middle beads. Special sear, hammer and trigger assy. 14⅜"x1½"x1⅞" stock with recoil pad. Hand fitted action and parts. Wgt. 8 lbs. $353.95
Price: With Monte Carlo stock $363.95
Price: Model 870TA Trap $317.95
Price: TA Trap with Monte Carlo stock $327.95

Remington Model 870 Brushmaster Deluxe
Carbine version of the M870 with 20" bbl. (Imp. Cyl.) for rifled slugs. 40½" over-all, wgt. 6½ lbs. Recoil pad. Adj. rear, ramp front sights. 12 or 20 ga. Deluxe $269.95
Price: 20-ga. Lightweight version $292.95

Remington 870 Small Gauges
Exact copies of the large ga. Model 870, except that guns are offered in 20, 28 and 410 ga. 25" barrel (Full, Mod., Imp. Cyl.).
Plain barrel $271.95
D and F grade prices same as large ga. M870 prices.
Price: With vent. rib barrel $309.95
Price: Lightweight Magnum, 20 ga. plain bbl. (5¾ lbs.) $299.95
Price: Lightweight Magnum, 20 ga., vent. rib bbl. $337.95

Smith & Wesson Model 916T Takedown Shotgun
Same as standard Model 916 except has interchangeable barrel capability. Available in 12 or 20 ga. 26" (Imp. Cyl.), 28" (Mod., Full) 30" (Full). Extra barrels available in 20" (Cyl.) with rifle sights, 26" (Imp. Cyl.), 28" (Full or Mod.), 30" (Full), plain or vent. rib.
Price: 916T, plain barrel $173.50
Price: 916T, vent. rib barrel, recoil pad $206.00
Price: Extra barrel, plain $47.35
Price: Extra barrel, rifle sights $59.50
Price: Extra barrel, vent. rib $87.70

SMITH & WESSON Model 916 Pump Gun
Gauge: 12, 20 (3"), 6-shot (3-shot plug furnished).
Barrel: 20" (Cyl.), 26" (Imp. Cyl.), 28" (Mod., Full or adj. choke) 30" (Full), plain. Vent. rib 26", 28", 30".
Weight: 7¼ lbs. (28" plain bbl.).
Stock: 14"x2½"x1⅝", American walnut, fluted comb, finger-grooved fore-end.
Features: Vent. rib, vent. recoil pad, adj. choke available as options. Satin finish steel receiver with non-glare top.
Price: Plain bbl., no recoil pad $167.50
Price: With vent. rib and recoil pad (illus.) $200.00
Price: With 20" slug barrel RS $192.00
Price: As above with recoil pad $198.50

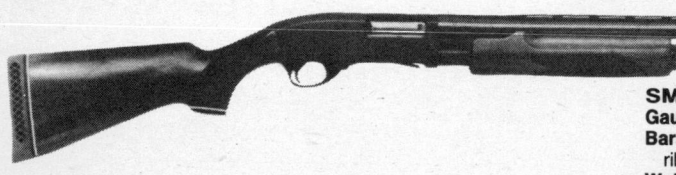

SMITH & WESSON MODEL 1000 PUMP
Gauge: 12, 3" chamber.
Barrel: 22" (Cyl.) with rifle sights, 26" (Imp. Cyl.), 28" (Mod.), 30" (Full), vent. rib or plain.
Weight: About 7½ lbs. **Length:** 48½" over-all (28" bbl.).
Stock: 14"x1⅜"x2¼". American walnut
Features: Dual action bars for smooth functioning. Rubber recoil pad, steel receiver, chrome plated bolt. Cross-bolt safety reversible for left-handed shooters. Introduced 1980.
Price: With vent. rib barrel $316.95
Price: With plain barrel $278.95
Price: Extra vent. rib barrel $111.75
Price: Extra plain barrel $70.00
Price: Slug barrel with rifle sights $87.65

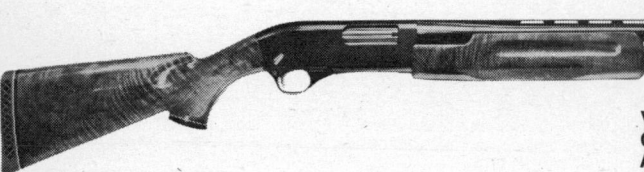

WEATHERBY PATRICIAN PUMP
Gauge: 12 only, 3" chamber.
Action: Short stroke slide action.
Barrel: 26" (Mod., Imp. Cyl, Skeet), 28" (Full, Mod.) 30" (Full, Full Trap, 3" Mag. Full). Vent. Rib.
Weight: About 7½ lbs. **Length:** 48⅛" (28" bbl.)
Stock: Walnut hand checkered p.g. and fore-end, white line spacers at p.g. cap and recoil pad.
Features: Short stroke action, hidden magazine cap, crossbolt safety.
Price: Field or Skeet grade **$379.95**   Trap grade $409.95
Price: Extra interchangeable bbls. $149.95

SHOTGUNS—SLIDE ACTION

WESTERN FIELD 550 PUMP SHOTGUN
Gauge: 12 and 20.
Action: Slide action, takedown; top tang safety.
Barrel: 12 ga. 26" (Variable); 28" (Mod.); 30" (Full); 20 ga. 26" (Variable); 28" (Mod., Full).
Stock: Walnut finished p.g. stock, molded buttplate, serrated fore-end.
Weight: 8½ lbs.
Features: Straight-line feed, interchangeable bbls., trigger disconnector prevents doubling.
Price: **$134.99**
Price: As above, but with variable choke in 12 or 20 ga. **$144.99**
Price: Slug gun with 24 bbl. without choke **$179.99**
Price: Deluxe Vent. rib models available with ACCU-CHOKE **$199.99**
Price: Vent rib models with variable choke **$169.99**

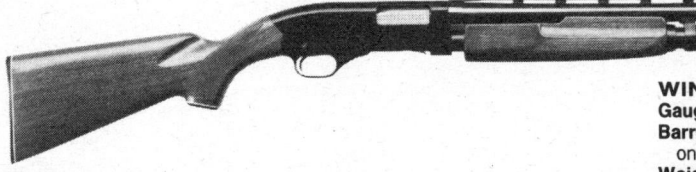

WINCHESTER 1300 XTR PUMP GUN
Gauge: 12 and 20, 3" chamber, 5-shot.
Barrel: 26" (Imp. Cyl.), 28" (Mod.), 28" (Full, 20-ga. only), 30" (Full, 12-ga. only). Plain or vent. rib, with or without Winchoke.
Weight: 6½ to 7¼ lbs. **Length:** 46⅝" to 50⅝" over-all.
Stock: American walnut, cut-checkered p.g. and fore-end. Field, vent. rib dimensions are 14"x1½"x2½".
Sights: Metal bead front.
Features: New Winchester XTR fit and finish. Has twin action bars, cross-bolt safety, Alloy receiver and trigger guard. Front-locking, rotating bolt. Nickel plated carrier, engine-turned bolt. Introduced 1978.
Price: Plain barrel **$242.00**
Price: Vent. rib **$270.00**
Price: Plain barrel with Winchoke **$257.00**
Price: Vent. rib with Winchoke **$285.00**
Price: Extra field barrel **$81.95**
Price: As above with Winchoke **$97.95**
Price: Extra field barrel with vent. rib **$106.95**
Price: As above with Winchoke **$122.95**
Price: Model 1300 Deer Gun **$270.00**
Winchester 1200 Extra Barrels: Field w/o sights, 12, 20 ga. **$73.95**. Field with vent. rib, 12, 20 ga. **$94.95**
Price: Extra plain Field bbl., Winchoke **$78.95**
Price: Extra vent rib bbl., Winchoke **$99.95**

WINCHESTER 1200 FIELD PUMP GUN
Gauge: 12 and 20 (5-shot; 3-shot plug installed).
Action: Slide; front locking 4-lug rotating bolt locks into bbl. Alloy receiver, cross-bolt safety in front of trigger guard. Take-down.
Barrel: 26" (Imp. Cyl.), 28" (Mod., Full) and 30" Full (12 ga. only). Metal bead front sight.
Stock: 14"x1⅜"x2⅜". American walnut with new-design checkered p.g. and fore-end; fluted comb, recoil pad. Steel p.g. cap.
Weight: 12 ga. 6½ lbs. with 26" bbl. 46⅝" over-all.
Price: .... **$214.00**   With vent. rib **$236.00**

SHOTGUNS—OVER-UNDER

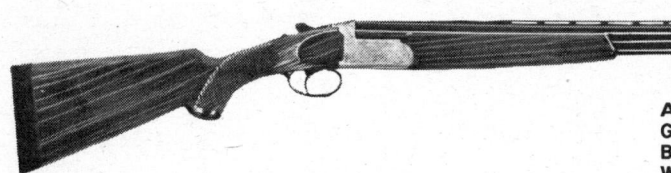

ARMSPORT MODEL 2500 O/U
Gauge: 12 or 20 ga.
Barrel: 26" (Imp. Cyl. & Mod.); 28" (Mod. & Full); vent. rib.
Weight: 8 lbs.
Stock: European walnut, hand checkered p.g. and fore-end.
Features: Single selective trigger, automatic ejectors, engraved receiver. Imported by Armsport.
Price: **$695.00**
Price: With extractors only **$595.00**

ASTRA MODEL 750 O/U SHOT GUN
Gauge: 12 ga., (2¾").
Barrel: 28" (Mod. & Full or Skeet & Skeet), 30" Trap (Mod. & Full)
Weight: 6½ lbs.
Stock: European walnut, hand-checkered p.g. and fore-end.
Features: Single selective trigger, hand-engraved receiver, selective auto ejectors, vent. rib. Introduced 1980. From L. Joseph Rahn, Inc.
Price: **$565.00**
Price: With extractors only **$480.00**
Price: Trap or Skeet (M.C. stock and recoil pad.) **$653.00**

Astra Model 650 O/U Shotgun
Same as Model 750 except has double triggers.
Price: With extractors **$402.00**
Price: With ejectors **$503.00**

BAIKAL MC-5-105 O/U
Gauge: 20 ga., 2¾" chambers.
Barrel: 26" (Imp. Cyl. & Mod., Skeet & Skeet).
Weight: 5¾ lbs.
Stock: Fancy hand checkered walnut. Choice of p.g. or straight stock, with or without cheekpiece. Fore-end permanently attached to barrels.
Features: Fully engraved receiver. Double triggers, extractors. Chrome barrels, chambers and internal parts. Hand-fitted solid rib. Hammer interceptors. Comes with case. Imported by Commercial Trading Imports.
Price: MC-5-105 .... **$1,295.00**
Price: MC-6-12, as above except in 12 gauge **$1,900.00**

SHOTGUNS — OVER-UNDER

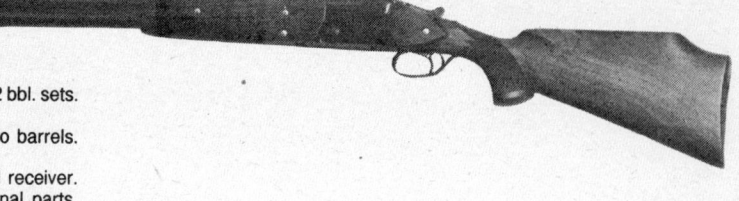

BAIKAL MC-8-0 O/U
Gauge: 12 ga., 2¾" chambers.
Barrel: 26" special parabolic Skeet, 28" (Mod. & Full). Available in 2 bbl. sets.
Weight: 7¾ lbs.
Stock: Fancy walnut. Beavertail fore-end permanently attached to barrels. Hand checkered p.g. and fore-end. Monte Carlo.
Features: Handmade competition shotgun. Blued, hand-engraved receiver. Single trigger, extractors. Chrome barrels, chambers and internal parts. Hand fitted vent. rib. Comes with case. Imported by Commercial Trading Imports.
Price: MC-8-0 Skeet $2,450.00
Price: MC-8-01 Trap $2,450.00

BAIKAL MC-7 O/U
Gauge: 12 or 20 ga., 2¾" chambers.
Barrel: 12 ga. 28" (Mod. & Full), 20 ga. 26" (Imp. Cyl. & Mod.).
Weight: 7 lbs. (12 ga.), 6¾ lbs. (20 ga.)
Stock: Fancy walnut. Hand checkered, with or without p.g. and cheekpiece. Beavertail fore-end.
Features: Fully chiseled and engraved receiver. Chrome barrels, chambers and internal parts. Double trigger, selective ejectors. Solid raised rib. Single selective trigger available. Comes with case. Imported by Commercial Trading Imports.
Price: $2,730.00

BAIKAL MC-109 O/U
Gauge: 12 ga., 2¾" chambers.
Barrel: 28" (Mod. & Full).
Weight: 7¼ lbs.
Stock: Fancy walnut. Choice of p.g. or straight stock, with or without cheekpiece. Beavertail fore-end. Hand carved and checkered to customer's specs.
Features: Handmade sidelock shotgun. Removable sideplates. Chrome barrels, chambers and internal parts. Single selective trigger, selective ejectors, cocking indicators, hammer interceptors. Hand chiseled scenes on receiver to customer specs. Inlays to customer specs. Comes with case. Imported by Commercial Trading Imports.
Price: Special order only $5,035.00

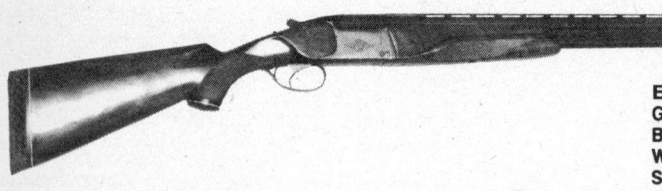

BAIKAL IJ-27E1C O/U
Gauge: 12 ga., 2¾" chambers, 20 ga., 3" chambers.
Barrel: 26" (Skeet & Skeet), 28" (Mod. & Full).
Weight: 7¾ lbs.
Stock: Hand checkered walnut, rubber recoil pad. Ventilated fore-end. White spacers at p.g. and recoil pad.
Features: Single selective trigger. Chrome barrels, chambers and internal parts. Hand fitted vent. rib. Hand engraved receiver. Selective extractors/ejectors. Imported by Commercial Trading Imports.
Price: $429.95
Price: With silver receiver inlays $585.00
Price: Skeet or Trap versions $429.95

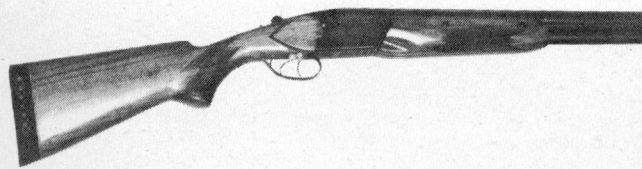

BAIKAL TOZ-34E SOUVENIR O/U
Gauge: 12 or 28 ga., 2¾".
Barrel: 12 ga.—28" (Mod. & Full), 28 ga.—26" (Mod. & Full).
Weight: 12 ga.—7¾ lbs.; 28 ga.—6¾ lbs.
Stock: Hand checkered fancy European walnut. Permanently attached fore-end. Rubber recoil pad.
Features: Double triggers, chrome lined barrels and chambers, cocking indicators. Hand engraved receiver. Hammer interceptors. Extractors only. Silvered, hand-engraved receiver. Imported by Commercial Trading Imports.
Price: $675.00

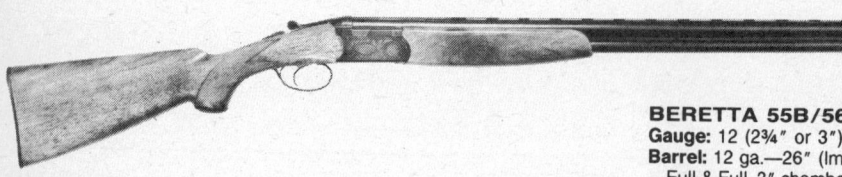

BERETTA 55B/56E O/U SHOTGUNS
Gauge: 12 (2¾" or 3") or 20 (3").
Barrel: 12 ga.—26" (Imp. Cyl. & Mod.); 28" (Mod. & Full); 30" (Mod. & Full, Full & Full, 3" chambers) 20 ga.—26" (Imp. Cyl. & Mod.); 28" (Mod. & Full).
Weight: 5 lbs. 8 ozs. (20 ga.); 7 lbs, 3 ozs. (12 ga.).
Stock: 14⅛"x1⁷⁄₁₆"x2⅜". Hand checkered European walnut. Recoil pad on 12 ga., 3" Mag. guns. P.g. cap standard.
Features: Single selective trigger, plain extractors, automatic safety. Model S55B has light scroll engraving on receiver and selective auto ejectors. Introduced 1977. Imported by Beretta Arms Co.
Price: S56E $688.00
Price: S55B $585.00

Beretta S58 Skeet
Same as S55B/56E guns except stocked to Skeet dimensions; 10mm vent. rib, Boehler steel barrels, light trigger pull. Both models have light scroll engraving on silver-gray receivers. Introduced 1977.
Price: $775.00

SHOTGUNS—OVER-UNDER

Browning Citori O/U Sporter
Similar to standard Citori except; comes with 26" (Mod. & Full, Imp. Cyl. & Mod.) only; straight grip stock with schnabel fore-end; satin oil finish.
Price: Grade I, 12 and 20 .... $614.95
Price: Grade I, 28 and 410 .... $649.95
Price: Grade II, 12 and 20 .... $1,065.00
Price: Grade V, 12 and 20 .... $1,600.00
Price: Grade II, 28 and 410 .... $1,090.00
Price: Grade V, 28 and 410 .... $1,640.00

Browning Citori O/U Trap Models
Similar to standard Citori except: 12 gauge only; 30", 32" (Full & Full, Imp. Mod. & Full, Mod. & Full), 34" single barrel in Combo Set (Full, Imp. Mod., Mod.); Monte Carlo cheekpiece (14⅜"x1⅜"x1⅜"x2"); fitted with trap-style recoil pad; conventional target rib and high post target rib.
Price: Grade I, (high post rib) $689.95
Price: Grade II (high post rib) $1,150.00
Price: Grade V (high post rib) $1,700.00
Price: Grade I Combo (32" O/U & 34" single bbl., high post ribs) incl. luggage case $1,150.00

Browning Citori O/U Skeet Models
Similar to standard Citori except: 26", 28" (Skeet & Skeet) only; stock dimensions of 14⅜"x1½"x2", fitted with Skeet-style recoil pad; conventional target rib and high post target rib.
Price: Grade I, 12 & 20 (high post rib) $674.95
Price: Grade I, 20 ga. (high post rib) $684.95
Price: Grade I, 28 & 410 (high post rib) $719.00
Price: Grade II, all gauges (high post rib) $1,150.00
Price: Grade V, all gauges (high post rib) $1,700.00

BROWNING SUPERPOSED SUPER-LIGHT Presentation Series
Gauge: 12, & 20 2¾" chamber.
Action: Boxlock, top lever, single selective trigger. Bbl. selector combined with manual tang safety.
Barrels: 26½" (Mod. & Full, or Imp. Cyl. & Mod.)
Weight: 6⅜ lbs., average
Stock: Straight grip (14¼" x 1⅝" x 2½") hand checkered (fore-end and grip) select walnut.
Features: The Presentation Series is available in four grades and covers the Superposed line. Basically this gives the buyer a wide choice of engraving styles and designs and mechanical options which would place the gun in a "custom" bracket. Options are too numerous to list here and the reader is urged to obtain a copy of the latest Browning catalog for the complete listing. Series introduced 1977.
Price: From $3,740.00

Browning Presentation Superposed Lightning Trap 12
Same as Browning Lightning Superposed except: semi-beavertail fore-end and ivory sights; stock, 14⅜"x1⁷⁄₁₆"x1⅝". 7¾ lbs. 30" (Full & Full, Full & Imp. Mod. or Full and Mod.)
Price: From $3,750.00

Browning Presentation Superposed All-Gauge Skeet Set
Consists of four matched sets of barrels in 12, 20, 28 and 410 ga. Available in either 26½" or 28" length. Each bbl. set has a ¼" wide vent. rib with two ivory sight beads. Grade 1 receiver is hand engraved and stock and fore-end are checkered. Weight 7 lbs., 10 oz. (26½" bbls.), 7 lbs., 12 oz. (28" bbls.). Presentation 1 **$8,400.00**, Presentation 4 **$14,800.00**.

Browning Presentation Superposed Combinations
Standard and Lightning models are available with these factory fitted extra barrels: 12 and 20 ga., same gauge bbls.; 12 ga., 20 ga. bbls.; 20 ga., extra sets 28 and/or 410 gauge; 28 ga., extra 410 bbls. Extra barrels may be had in Lightning weights with Standard models and vice versa. Prices range from **$5,150.00** (12, 20 ga., one set extra bbls. same gauge) for the Presentation 1 Standard to about **$14,800.00** for the Presentation 4 grade in a 4-barrel matched set (12, 20, 28 and 410 gauges).

Browning Presentation Superposed Lightning Skeet
Same as Standard Superposed except: Special Skeet stock, fore-end; center and front ivory bead sights. Wgt. 6½-7¾ lbs.
Price: All gauges, from $3,750.00

Browning Presentation Superposed Magnum 12
Browning Superposed 3" chambers; 30" (Full and Full or Full and Mod.) barrels, Stock, 14¼"x1⅝"x2½" with factory fitted recoil pad. Weight 8 lbs.
Price: From $3,700.00

Superposed Presentation Broadway Trap 12
Same as Browning Lightning Superposed except: ⅝" wide vent. rib; stock, 14⅜"x1⁷⁄₁₆"x1⅝". 30" or 32" (Imp. Mod., Full; Mod., Full; Full, Full). 8 lbs. with 32" bbls.
Price: From $3,840.00

Browning Presentation Superposed Lightning
7-7¼ lbs. in 12 ga. 6-6¼ lbs. in 20 ga.
Price: From $3,700.00

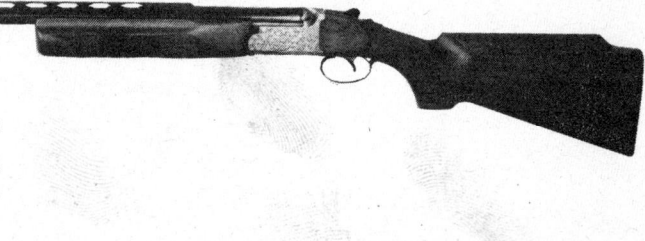

CONTENTO O/U SHOTGUNS
Gauge: 12 (2¾") only.
Action: Boxlock, with Woodward side-lugs and double internal bolts for extra low profile.
Barrel: Field 26", 28"; Skeet 28"; Pigeon 29½"; Trap 32" Trap models have high post ribs with option of screw-in chokes in both O/U and single barrels. All have vent. side ribs.
Weight: 6.7 to 8.2 lbs.
Stock: Hand checkered European walnut with Monte Carlo. 14½"x1⁷⁄₁₆". Recoil pad included for individual fitting.
Features: Single selective trigger, auto ejectors. Extra Lusso model has fancy walnut and extensive Florentine engraving. All models in three grades; Standard, Lusso, and Extra Lusso. Introduced 1978. From Ventura Imports.
Price: MK 2 O/U $940.00
Price: MK 2 O/U and single bbl., screw-in chokes $1,633.00
Price: MK 3 O/U $1,445.00
Price: MK 3 O/U and single bbl., screw-in chokes $2,373.00

SHOTGUNS—OVER-UNDER

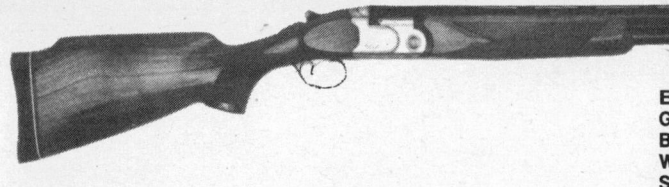

BERETTA SO-3 O/U SHOTGUN
Gauge: 12 ga. (2¾" chambers).
Action: Back-action sidelock.
Barrel: 26", 27", 28", 29" or 30", chokes to customer specs.
Stock: Standard measurements—14⅛"x1⁷⁄₁₆"x2⅜". Straight "English" or p.g.-style. Hand checkered European walnut.
Features: SO-3—"English scroll" floral engraving on action body, sideplates and trigger guard. Stocked in select walnut. SO-3EL—as above, with full engraving coverage. Hand-detachable sideplates. SO-3EELL—as above with deluxe finish and finest full coverage engraving. Internal parts gold plated. Top lever is pierced and carved in relief with gold inlaid crown. Introduced 1977. Imported by Beretta Arms Co.
Price: SO-3 .... $4,680.00
Price: SO-3EL $6,015.00
Price: SO-3EELL $8,050.00

BERETTA SERIES 680 OVER-UNDER
Gauge: 12 (2¾").
Barrel: 29½" (Imp. Mod. & Full, Trap), 28" (Skeet & Skeet).
Weight: About 8 lbs.
Stock: Trap—14⅜"x1¼"x2⅛"; Skeet—14⅜"x1⅜"x2⁷⁄₁₆". European walnut with hand checkering.
Sights: Luminous front sight and center bead.
Features: Trap Monte Carlo stock has deluxe trap recoil pad, Skeet has smooth pad. From Beretta Arms Co.
Price: Skeet or Trap gun $1,340.00
Price: As above with fitted case $1,455.00
Price: M686 Field gun $855.00
Price: M685 Field gun $720.00
Price: M687EL, Field $1,790.00
Price: M680 Single bbl. Trap, 32" or 34" $1,340.00
Price: M680 Combo Trap O/U, with single bbl. $1,850.00

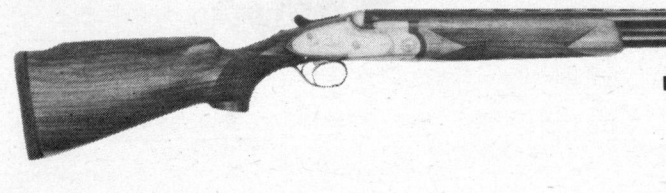

Beretta SO-4 Target Shotguns
Target guns derived from Model SO-3EL. Light engraving coverage. Single trigger. Skeet gun has 28" (Skeet & Skeet) barrels, 10mm rib, p.g. stock (14⅛"x2⁹⁄₁₆"x1⅜"), fluted beavertail fore-end. "Skeet" is inlaid in gold into trigger guard. Weight is about 7 lbs. 10 ozs. Trap guns have 30" (Imp. Mod. & Full or Mod. & Full) barrels, trap stock dimensions, fluted beavertail fore-end. Weight is about 7 lbs. 12 ozs. "Trap" is inlaid in gold into trigger guard. Special dimensions and features, within limits, may be ordered. Introduced 1977. Imported by Beretta Arms Co.
Price: Skeet $5,120.00
Price: Trap $5,120.00

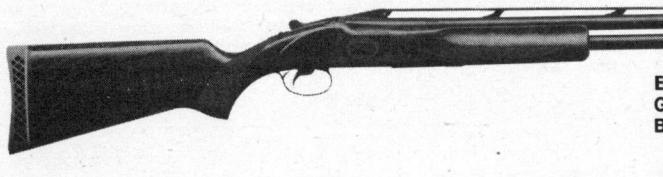

BROWNING ST-100 O/U TRAP GUN
Gauge: 12 ga. only, 2¾".
Barrel: 30" (Full & Full, Imp. Mod. & Full, Mod. & Full). Five-position impact adjustment device allows various points of impact. Floating under barrel expands and contracts during shooting.
Weight: About 8 lbs.
Stock: Select walnut with high gloss finish. Hand checkered p.g. and semi-beavertail fore-end. Measures 14⅜"x1⁷⁄₁₆"x1⅝".
Sights: Front and center ivory beads.
Features: Designed expressly for trap shooting. Has high post, floating Broadway rib; selective auto. ejectors; single selective mechanical trigger with deep contour; top tang manual safety incorporated in barrel selector. Introduced 1979.
Price: $3,250.00

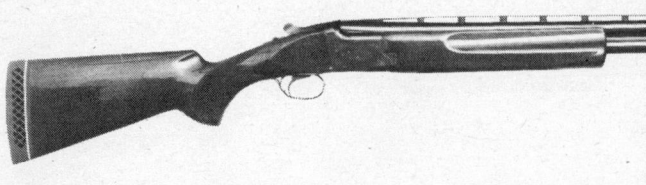

BROWNING CITORI O/U SHOTGUN
Gauge: 12, 20, 28 and 410.
Barrel: 26", 28" (Mod. & Full, Imp. Cyl. & Mod.), in all gauges (30" Mod. & Full, Full & Full) in 12-ga. only.
Weight: 6 lbs. 8 ozs. (26" 410) to 7 lbs. 13 ozs. (30" 12-ga.).
Length: 43" over-all (26" bbl.).
Stock: Dense walnut, hand checkered, full p.g., beavertail fore-end. Field-type recoil pad on 12-ga. models. on 12 ga. field guns and Trap and skeet models.
Sights: Medium raised beads, German nickel silver.
Features: Barrel selector integral with safety, auto ejectors, three-piece takedown.
Price: Grade I, 12 and 20 .... $614.95
Price: Grade I, 28 and 410 .... $649.95
Price: Grade II, 12 and 20 .... $1,065.00
Price: Grade V, 12 and 20 .... $1,600.00
Price: Grade II, 28 and 410 .... $1,090.00
Price: Grade V, 28 and 410 .... $1,640.00

Consult our Directory pages for the location of firms mentioned.

SHOTGUNS—OVER-UNDER

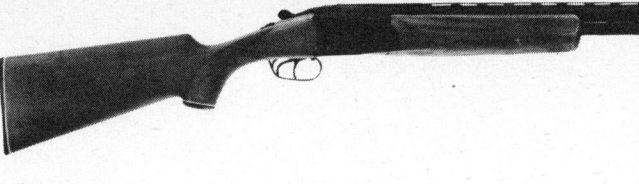

ERA "THE FULL LIMIT" O/U SHOTGUN
Gauge: 12 or 20 ga., 2¾".
Barrel: 28" (Mod. & Full); vent. top and middle ribs.
Weight: 7¾ lbs.
Stock: Walnut-finished hardwood, hand checkered.
Features: Auto. safety; extractors; double triggers; engraved receiver. Imported from Brazil by F.I.E.
Price: $199.95
Price: Trap or Skeet versions $217.95

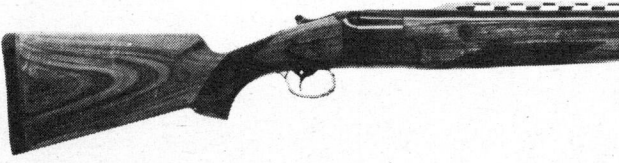

FRANCHI MODEL 2003 TRAP O/U
Gauge: 12 only (2¾" chambers).
Barrel: 30", 32" (Imp. Mod. & Full, Full & Full).
Weight: 8½ lbs.
Stock: 14½"x1⅞"x1½". Fancy French walnut; checkered p.g. and fore-end. Available in Monte Carlo or straight style; interchangeable. Different dimensions avail.
Features: "Ceiling-Swell" trap trigger with barrel selector; separated barrels; steel muzzle collar to maintain alignment; raised, vent. trap rib. Buttstock drilled and tapped for recoil reducer. Comes with hard luggage-type fitted case. From Stoeger Industries.
Price: $1,400.00

Franchi Model 2005/2 Trap Combo
Same as Model 2003/2004 except comes with two barrel sets—one single, one O/U in same lengths and chokes as specified for those models. Also comes with fitted case.
Price: $2,160.00

Franchi Model 2005/3 Trap Combo
Same as Model 2005/2—two barrel sets in 30" or 32" O/U and 32" or 34" single upper—except custom choking is offered.
Price: $2,825.00

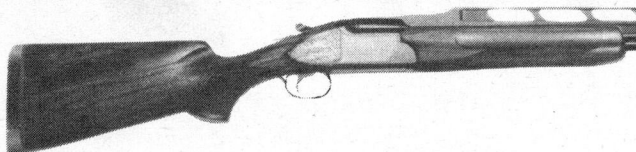

Franchi 3000/2 Trap Undergun Combo
Same as the Model 2005/2 except comes with 30" or 32" O/U and 32" or 34" underbarrel and three interchangeable choke tubes—Full, Imp. Mod. and Mod. Also comes with fitted case.
Price: $2,995.00

GOLDEN EAGLE MODEL 5000 GRADE I O/U
Gauge: 12 ga. (2¾" or 3") or 20 ga. (3").
Action: Boxlock.
Barrel: 26" (Mod. & Imp. Cyl., Skeet & Skeet), 28" (Mod. & Imp. Cyl., Full & Mod., Skeet & Skeet), 30" (Full & Full, Full & Mod., Full & Imp. Mod.), 32" (Full & Full, Full & Imp. Mod., Full & Mod.).
Weight: 6¼-8 lbs.
Stock: 14"x1½"x2½"x⅛" cast-off (Field; 14⅜"x1⅜"x1⅞"x¼" cast-off (Trap); select walnut.
Features: Single selective mechanical trigger; vent. top rib; selective ejectors; non-automatic tang safety/barrel selector; rubber recoil pad. Lifetime warranty to original owner. Imported by Golden Eagle Firearms.
Price: Grade I Field $899.00
Price: Grade I Trap $949.00
Price: Grade I Skeet $999.00

Golden Eagle Model 5000 Grade II O/U
Similar to Grade I except: Field only has gold colored mechanical trigger, others have gold inertia type; vent. side ribs; finer engraving and checkering; Trap model has wider rib; Field has brass beads, Skeet and Trap have ivory. Available in 12, 20, 28 and 410 gauge three barrel sets. 28 and 410 gauges priced slightly higher.
Price: Grade II Field $999.00
Price: Grade II Trap $1,049.00
Price: Grade II Skeet $1,149.00

Golden Eagle Model 5000 Grade III Grandee o/u
12 ga. only, 26" (Skeet & Skeet) or 30" (Full & Imp. Mod.); finer checkering and nearly full coverage receiver engraving; silver finish receiver. Comes with hard luggage-style case.
Price: Grade III Grandee Trap $3,499.00
Price: Grade III Grandee Skeet $3,499.00

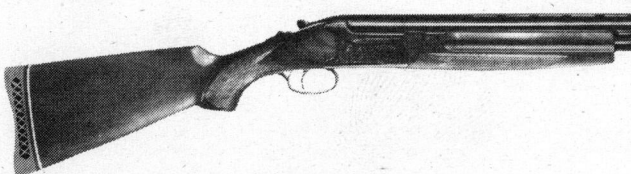

H&R MODEL 1212 "WATERFOWL" O/U
Gauge: 12 ga. only (3" chambers).
Barrel: 30" (Full & Mod.).
Weight: 7½ lbs. **Length:** 46¾" over-all.
Stock: 14⅜"x1½"x2", hand checkered walnut.
Sights: Gold bead front on vent. rib.
Features: Vent. rib; single selective trigger; engraved action; rubber recoil pad. Imported from Spain by Harrington & Richardson.
Price: $489.00

Harrington & Richardson Model 1212 "Field Gun" o/u
Same as "Waterfowl" except has 2¾" chambers, 28" barrel (Imp. Cyl. & Imp. Mod.), no recoil pad.
Price: $475.00

SHOTGUNS—OVER-UNDER

HEYM MODEL 77/55 O/U SHOTGUN
Gauge: Model 77—12 ga. (2¾"), Model 55—16, 20 ga. (2¾" or 3").
Barrel: 28" (Full & Mod.) standard; other lengths and chokes to customer specs.
Weight: 6¾-7½ lbs.
Stock: European walnut, hand-checkered p.g. and fore-end.
Features: Boxlock or full sidelock action; Kersten double cross bolt, double under lugs; cocking indicators. Arabesque or hunting engraving. Options include interchangeable barrels, front trigger that functions as a single non-selective trigger, deluxe engraving and stock carving. Contact Heym for more data.
Price: Model 55F or 77F boxlock $3,085.00
Price: Model 55FSS or 77FSS sidelock $4,227.00
Price: Interchangeable o/u rifle barrels $2,628.00
Price: Interchangeable rifle-shotgun barrels $1,757.00

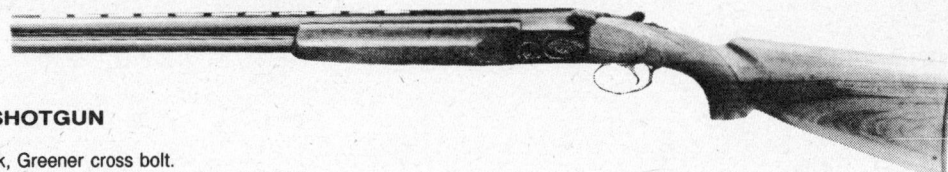

KASSNAR/FIAS SK-1 O/U SHOTGUN
Gauge: 12 or 20 ga. (3" chambers).
Action: Top lever break open, boxlock, Greener cross bolt.
Barrel: 26" (Imp. Cyl. & Mod.), 28" (Mod. & Full), 30" (Mod. & Full), 32" (Full & Full).
Weight: 6-6½ lbs.
Stock: Select European walnut. 14"x2¼"x1¼".
Features: Double triggers and non-automatic extractors. Checkered p.g. and fore-end. Imported by Kassnar Imports.
Price: $399.95

Kassnar/Fias SK-3 O/U Shotgun
Same as SK-1 except has single selective trigger $419.95

Kassnar/Fias SK-4D O/U Shotgun
Same as SK-4 except has deluxe receiver engraving, sideplates, better wood $499.95

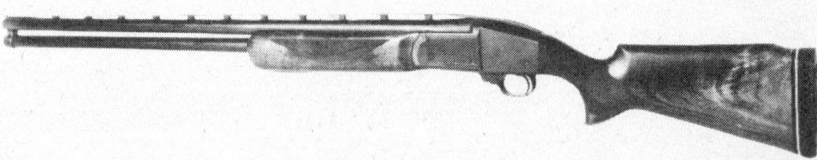

LJUTIC BI GUN O/U SHOTGUN
Gauge: 12 ga only.
Barrel: 28" or 33", choked to customer specs.
Weight: To customers specs.
Stock: To customer specs. Oil finish, hand checkered.
Features: Custom-made gun. Hollow-milled rib, choice of pull or release trigger, pushbutton opener in front of trigger guard. From Ljutic Industries.
Price: .... P.O.R.

Ljutic Four Barrel Skeet Set
Similar to Bi Gun except comes with matched set of four 28" barrels in 12, 20, 28 and 410. Ljutic Paternator chokes and barrel are integral. Stock is to customer specs, of American or French walnut with fancy checkering.
Price: Four barrel set $15,000.00

MERKEL 201E O/U
Gauge: 12, 16, 20, 28, 3" chambers on request.
Action: Kersten double crossbolt.
Barrel: 26" (Mod. & Imp. Cyl., Cyl. & Imp. Cyl)
Weight: 6¾ lbs.
Stock: Walnut with p.g. or English style. 14¼"x1½"x2¼".
Features: Double, single or single selective trigger, cocking indicators. Fine hunting scene engraving. Imported by J. J. Jenkins.
Price: With single selective trigger $3,123.00

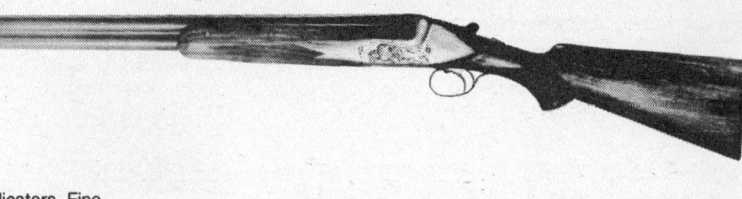

MERKEL MODEL 203E O/U
Gauge: 12, 16, 20, 28, 3" chambers on request.
Action: Merkel H&H hand-detachable side locks with double sears. Double crossbolt breech.
Barrel: 26" (Mod. & Imp. Cyl.).
Weight: 7 lbs.
Stock: Deluxe walnut with p.g. or English style. 14¼"x1½"x2¼".
Features: Double, single or single selective trigger. Cocking indicators. Choice of arabesque or fine hunting scene engraving. Imported by J. J. Jenkins.
Price: With single selective trigger $5,315.95

SHOTGUNS—OVER-UNDER

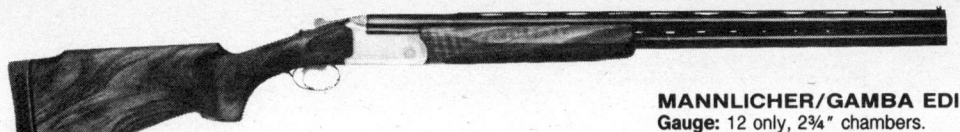

MANNLICHER/GAMBA EDINBURGH O/U SHOTGUNS
Gauge: 12 only, 2¾" chambers.
Barrel: Skeet—26.5" (Skeet); Trap—30", 32" (trap chokes); Mono Trap—32", 34" (trap choke).
Weight: 7¼ to 7¾ lbs.
Stock: Trap—14½"x1½"x2"; Skeet—14"x1¼"x2"xN.A. Select walnut with M.C. trap stock. Hand checkered, rubbed European oil finish. Skeet comes with high gloss lacquer finish and Skeet pad.
Features: Chrome lined barrels, double vent. ribs, shaped single trigger (selective available), auto ejectors, silvered receiver with light border scroll engraving. Made by Renato Gamba, Imported by Steyr Daimler Puch of America.
Price: Trap o-u **$1,699.50**
Price: Skeet o-u **$1,699.50**
Price: Mono Trap **$1,699.50**

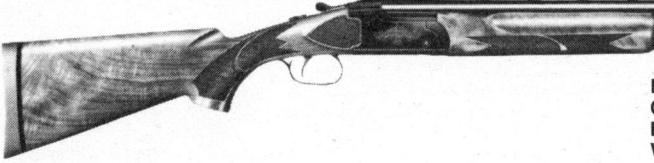

REMINGTON 3200 COMPETITION TRAP
Gauge: 12 ga. (2¾" chambers).
Barrel: 30" (Full & Full, Full & Imp. Mod., Full & Mod.), 32" (Full & Imp. Mod.).
Weight: 8¼ lbs. (30" bbl.). **Length:** 48" over-all (30" bbl.).
Stock: Fancy walnut checkered 20 l.p.i. Full beavertail fore-end. Satin finish. 14⅜"x2"x1½". Optional 1⅜" or 1½" drop on Monte Carlo stocks.
Features: Super-fast lock time, separated barrels, engraved receiver. Combination manual safety and barrel selector on top tang. Single selective trigger. Ivory bead front sight, white-metal middle.
Price: Special Trap **$1,200.00**
Price: Competition Trap with M.C. stock **$1,350.00**
Price: Pigeon (28", Imp. Mod. & Full) **$1,350.00**

Remington 3200 Competition Skeet
Same as Trap except: 26" or 28" (Skeet & Skeet) barrels, stock measures 14"x2⅛"x1½". Over-all length is 43" with 26" barrels, weight is 7¾ lbs.
Price: Skeet **$1,125.00**
Price: Competition Skeet **$1,350.00**
Price: Competition Skeet 4-bbl. set (bbls. for 12, 20, 28 and 410 in luggage case **$3,900.00**

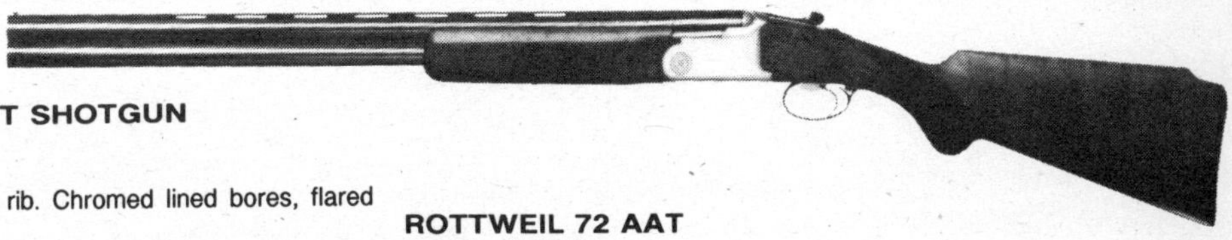

ROTTWEIL OLYMPIA '72 SKEET SHOTGUN
Gauge: 12 ga. only.
Action: Boxlock.
Barrel: 27" (special Skeet choke), vent. rib. Chromed lined bores, flared chokes.
Weight: 7¼ lbs. **Length:** 44½" over-all.
Stock: French walnut, hand checkered, modified beavertail fore-end. Oil finish.
Sights: Metal bead front.
Features: Inertia-type trigger, interchangeable for any system. Frame and lock milled from steel block. Retracting firing pins are spring mounted. All coil springs. Selective single trigger. Action engraved. Extra barrels are available. Introduced 1976. Imported from West Germany by Eastern Sports Int.
Price: **$2,750.00**
Price: Trap model (Montreal) is similar to above except has 30" (Imp. Mod. & Full) bbl., weighs 8 lbs., 48½" over-all **$2,750.00**

ROTTWEIL 72 AAT
Gauge: 12, 2¾".
Barrel: 32" (Imp. Mod. & Full).
Weight: About 8 lbs.
Stock: 14½"x1⅜"x1⅜"x1⅞". Monte Carlo style of selected French walnut with oil finish. Checkered fore-end and p.g.
Features: Has infinitely variable point of impact via special muzzle collar. Extra single lower barrels available—32" (Imp. Mod.) or 34" (Full). Special trigger groups—release/release or release/pull—also available. Introduced 1979. From Eastern Sports International.
Price: With single lower barrel **$2,795.00**
Price: Combo (single and o/u barrels) **$4,495.00**
Price: Interchangeable trap trigger group **$481.25**

ROTTWEIL AMERICAN TRAP COMBO
Gauge: 12 ga. only.
Action: Boxlock.
Barrel: Separated o/u, 32" (Imp. Mod. & Full); single is 34" (Full), both with high vent. rib.
Weight: 8½ lbs. (o/u and single)
Stock: Monte Carlo style, walnut, hand checkered and rubbed. Unfinished stocks available. Double vent. recoil pad. Choice of two dimensions.
Sights: Plastic front in metal sleeve, center bead.
Features: Interchangeable inertia-type trigger groups. Trigger groups available: single selective; double triggers;, release-pull; release-release selective. Receiver milled from block steel. Chokes are hand honed, test fired and reworked for flawless patterns. All coil springs, engraved action. Introduced 1977. Imported from West Germany by Eastern Sports Int'l.
Price: **$3,495.00**
Price: American Trap O/U (as above except only with O/U bbls.) **$2,750.00**
Price: American Skeet O/U **$2,750.00**

ROTTWEIL SUPREME FIELD O/U SHOTGUN
Gauge: 12 only.
Action: Boxlock.
Barrel: 28" (Mod. & Full, Imp. Cyl. & Imp. Mod., Mod. & Full), vent. rib.
Weight: 7¼ lbs. **Length:** 47" over-all.
Stock: Select French walnut, hand checkered and rubbed. Checkered p.g. and fore-end, plastic buttplate. Unfinished stocks available.
Sight: Metal bead front.
Features: Removable single trigger assembly with button selector (same trigger options as on American Trap Combo); retracting spring mounted firing pins; engraved action. Extra barrels available. Imported from West Germany by Eastern Sports Int.
Price: **$2,750.00**
Price: Live Pigeon (28" Mod. & Full) **$2,750.00**

SHOTGUNS—OVER-UNDER

RUGER "RED LABEL" O/U SHOTGUN
Gauge: 20 only, 3" chambers.
Barrel: 26", (Skeet & Skeet, Imp. Cyl. & Mod., Full & Mod.).
Weight: About 7 lbs. **Length:** 43" (26" barrels).
Stock: 14"x1½"x2½". Straight grain American walnut. Checkered p.g. and fore-end, rubber recoil pad.
Features: Initial production guns provided with 26" barrels (28" will be available in 1978). Premium grade 20 gauge models and 12 gauage guns will be offered later. Patented barrel side spacers may be removed if desired. Introduced 1977.
Price: About $675.00

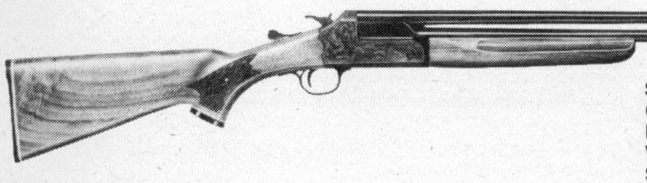

SAVAGE MODEL 242 O/U
Gauge: 410 (3" chambers).
Barrel: 24" (Full & Full).
Weight: 7 lbs. **Length:** 40" over-all
Stock: 14"x1¾"x2¾". Checkered walnut.
Sights: Bead front.
Features: Two-way opening top lever, barrel selector on hammer. Color case-hardened frame, blued barrels. Measures 24" when taken down. Introduced 1977.
Price: $156.20

TIKKA MODEL 77 O/U SHOTGUN
Gauge: 12, 2¾".
Barrel: 27" or 30", (Imp. Cyl., Mod., Imp. Mod., Full).
Weight: About 6¾ lbs.
Stock: Walnut, with Monte Carlo roll-over cheekpiece. Skip-line checkering on p.g. and fore-end.
Features: Ventilated rib is 10mm wide. Ejectors; barrel selector; single trigger. Skeet version available. Introduced 1979. From Ruko Sporting Goods.
Price: About $735.00

Valmet 412KE Target Series
Trap and Skeet versions of 412 gun. Auto. ejectors only; 12 ga., 2¾" chambers, 30" barrels (Imp. & Full.—Trap, Skeet & Skeet—Skeet). Trap stock measures 14³⁄₁₀"x1²⁄₅"x1³⁄₅"x2½"; Skeet stock measures 13⁹⁄₁₀x 1⁴⁄₅"x2⁴⁄₅"x1⁴⁄₅". Trap weight 7⅝ lbs.: Skeet weight 7½ lbs. Non-automatic safety. Introduced 1980. From Valmet.
Price: Trap $579.00
Price: Skeet $574.00

VALMET MODEL 412K OVER-UNDER
Gauge: 12 or 20 ga. (2¾" or 3")
Barrel: 26" (Imp. Cyl. & Mod.), 28" (Mod. & Full), 30" (Mod. & Full); vent. rib.
Weight: About 7½ lbs.
Stock: American walnut. Standard dimensions-13⁹⁄₁₀"x1½"x2²⁄₅". Checkered p.g. and fore-end.
Features: Model 412K is extractor (basic) model. Free interchangeability of barrels, stocks and fore-ends into KE (auto. ejector) model, double rifle model, combination gun, etc. Barrel selector in trigger; auto. top tang safety; barrel cocking indicators. Double triggers optional. Introduced 1980. From Valmet.
Price: Model 412K (extractors) $524.00
Price: Model 412 KE (ejectors) $569.00

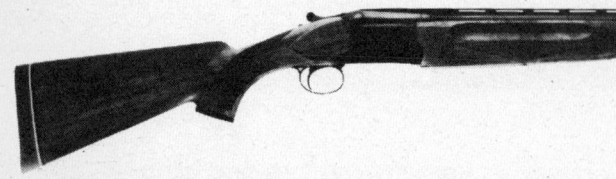

WEATHERBY OLYMPIAN O/U SHOTGUN
Gauge: 12 (2¾"; 3" for 30" barrel only), 20 (3").
Action: Boxlock (simulated side-lock).
Barrel: 12 ga. 30" (Full & Mod.), 28EI (Full & Mod., Mod. & Imp. Cyl., Skeet & Skeet); 20 ga. 28", 26" (Full & Mod., Mod. & Imp. Cyl., Skeet & Skeet).
Weight: 7 lbs., 8 ozs. (12 ga. 26").
Stock: American walnut, checkered p.g. and fore-end. Rubber recoil pad. Dimensions for field and Skeet models, 20 ga. 14"x1½"x2½".
Features: Selective auto ejectors, single selective mechanical trigger. Top tang safety, Greener cross-bolt. Introduced 1978. From Weatherby.
Price: 12 or 20, Field and Skeet $749.95
Price: 12 ga. Trap $829.95

WEATHERBY REGENCY O/U SHOTGUN
Gauge: 12 ga. (2¾" chambers), 20 ga. (3" chambers).
Action: Boxlock (simulated side-lock) top lever break-open. Selective auto ejectors, single selective trigger (selector inside trigger guard).
Barrel: 28" with vent rib and bead front sight, Full & Mod., Mod. & Imp. Cyl. or Skeet & Skeet.
Weight: 12 ga. 7⅜ lbs., 20 ga. 6⅞ lbs.
Stock: American walnut, checkered p.g. and fore-end (14¼"x1½"x2½").
Features: Mechanically operated trigger. Top tang safety, Greener cross-bolt, fully engraved receiver, recoil pad installed.
Price: 12 or 20 ga. Field and Skeet $1,098.95
Price: 12 ga. Trap Model $1,198.95

SHOTGUNS—OVER-UNDER

WINCHESTER XPERT O/U SHOTGUN
Gauge: 12 and 20, 3" chambers.
Barrel: Field: 26" (Imp. Cyl. and Mod.) 28" (Mod. and Full), 30" (Full & Full); Skeet: 2¾" chambers, 27" (Skeet & Skeet); Trap: 12 only, 2¾" chambers, 30" (Full & Full). Vent. rib with metal bead front sight.
Weight: 6½ lbs. **Length:** 42¾" over-all (26" barrels).
Stock: 14"x1½"x2½". Walnut stock and fore-end, high-gloss finish.
Features: Plain blue receiver, no engraving. Single trigger, auto. ejectors, barrel selector safety. Trap gun avail. with either regular or Monte Carlo stock, with rubber recoil pad.
Price: Field (illus.) $726.00
Price: Skeet $748.00
Price: Trap (std. stock) $748.00
Price: Trap (Monte Carlo stock) $764.00

WINCHESTER 101 O/U FIELD GUN
Gauge: 12 and 28, 2¾"; 20 and 410, 3".
Action: Top lever, break open. Manual safety combined with bbl. selector at top of receiver tang.
Barrel: Vent. rib 26" 12, 26½", 20 and 410 (Imp. Cyl., Mod.), 28" (Mod & Full), 30" 12 only (Mod. & Full). Metal bead front sight. Chrome plated chambers and bores.
Stock: 14"x1½"x2½". Checkered walnut p.g. and fore-end; fluted comb.
Weight: 12 ga. 7¾ lbs. Others 6¼ lbs. **Length:** 44¾" over-all (28" bbls.).
Features: Single selective trigger, auto ejectors. Hand engraved receiver.
Price: 12 or 20 ga. $902.00
Price: 101 XTR with Winchoke system, 12 ga. only $977.00

Winchester Model 101 Pigeon Grade
Same as Model 101 Field except has new-design vent. rib with bead front and middle sights, hand-engraved satin finish receiver, knurled, non-slip trigger. Stock and fore-end of fancy French walnut, hand checkered p.g. and fore-end. 12, 20, 28 or 410 ga., 2¾" or 3" chambers. Barrels run from 26" through 32" with a full range of chokes. Weighs 8¼ lbs.
Price: Standard trap stock, with gun case $1,170.00
Price: Monte Carlo stock $1,170.00
Price: Field grade $1,115.00
Price: 28, 410 skeet $1,245.00
Price: 12, 20 ga. Skeet $1,170.00
Price: Three-gauge Skeet set $2,725.00
Price: XTR with Winchoke system $1,190.00

Consult our Directory pages for the location of firms mentioned.

Winchester 101 Magnum Field Gun
Same as 101 Field Gun except: chambers 3" Magnum shells; 12 ga. only 30" (Full & Full or Mod. & Full); hand-engraved receiver, select French walnut stock with fluted comb, hand-checkered pistol grip and beavertail fore-end with recoil pad $913.00

ZOLI SILVER SNIPE O/U SHOTGUN
Gauge: 12, 20 (3" chambers).
Action: Purdey type double boxlock, crossbolt.
Barrel: 26" (I.C.& Mod.), 28" (Mod.&Full), 30", 12 only (Mod.&Full); 26" Skeet (Skeet & Skeet), 30" Trap (Full & Full).
Weight: 6½ lbs. (12 ga.).
Stock: Hand checkered European walnut, p.g. and fore-end.
Features: Auto safety (exc. Trap and Skeet), vent rib, single trigger, chrome bores. Imported from Italy by Galef, Mandall Shooting Supplies.
Price: Field $416.75

Zoli Golden Snipe O/U Shotgun
Same as Silver Snipe except selective auto ejectors.
Price: Field $489.00

A. ZOLI DELFINO S.P. O/U
Gauge: 12 or 20 (3" chambers).
Barrel: 28" (Mod. and Full); vent. rib.
Weight: 5½ lbs.
Stock: Walnut. Hand checkered p.g. and fore-end; cheekpiece.
Features: Color case hardened receiver with light engraving; chrome lined barrels; automatic sliding safety; double triggers; ejectors. From Mandall Shooting Supplies.
Price: $499.50

SHOTGUNS — DOUBLE BARREL

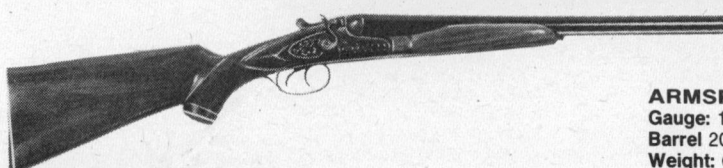

ARMSPORT WESTERN DOUBLE
Gauge: 12 only (3" chambers).
Barrel 20".
Weight: 6½ lbs.
Stock: European walnut, checkered p.g. and beavertail fore-end.
Sights: Metal front bead on matted solid rib.
Features: Exposd hammers. Imported by Armsport.
Price: $500.00

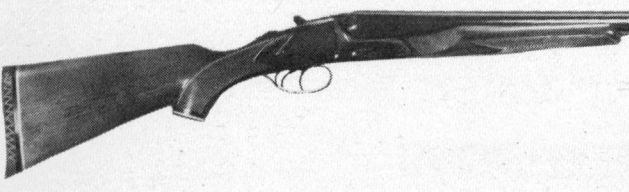

ARMSPORT GOOSEGUN SIDE-BY-SIDE
Gauge: 10 ga. (3½" chambers).
Barrel: 32" (Full & Full). Solid matted rib.
Weight: 11 lbs.
Stock: European walnut, checkered p.g. and fore-end.
Features: Double triggers, vent. rubber recoil pad with white spacer. Imported by Armsport.
Price: $595.00

AYA MODEL XXV BL, SL DOUBLE
Gauge: 12, 16, 20.
Barrel: 25", chokes as specified.
Weight: 5 lbs., 15 oz. to 7lbs., 8oz.
Stock: 14½"x2¼"x1½". European walnut. Straight grip stock with classic pistol grip, checkered butt.
Features: Boxlock (Model BL), sidelock (Model SL). Churchill rib, auto ejectors, double triggers (single available), color case-hardened action (coin-finish available). From Wm. Larkin Moore & Co.
Price: BL, 12 ga. $1,000.00
Price: BL, 20 ga. $1,050.00
Price: SL, 12 ga. $1,600.00
Price: SL, 20 ga. $1,650.00

AYA MODEL 117 DOUBLE BARREL SHOTGUN
Gauge: 12 (2¾"), 20 (3").
Action: Holland & Holland sidelock, Purdey treble bolting.
Barrel: 26" (Imp. Cyl. & Mod.) 28" (Mod. & Full).
Stock: 14½"x2⅜"x1½". Select European walnut, hand checkered p.g. and beavertail fore-end.
Features: Single selective trigger, automatic ejectors, cocking indicators; concave barrel rib; hand-detachable lockplates; hand engraved action. Imported by Interarms.
Price: $1,050.00

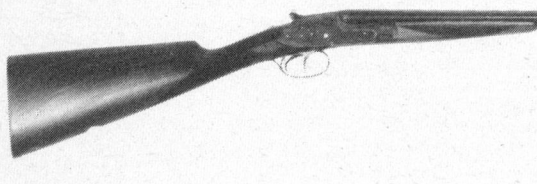

AYA No. 2 SIDE-BY-SIDE
Gauge: 12, 16, 20, 28, 410.
Barrel: 26", 27", 28", choked to customer specs.
Weight: 5 lbs. 15 oz. to 7½ lbs.
Stock: 14½"x2¼"x1½". European walnut. Straight grip stock, checkered butt, classic fore-end. Can be made to custom dimensions.
Features: Sidelock action with auto. ejectors, double triggers standard, single trigger optional. Hand-detachable locks. Color case-hardened action. From Wm. Larkin Moore & Co.
Price: 12, 16, 20 ga., from $1,075.00
Price: 28 ga., from $1,150.00
Price: 410 ga., from $1,200.00

AYA Model 56 Side-by-Side
Similar to the No. 1 except in 12, 16 or 20 ga. only, available with raised, level or vent rib. Does not have hand-detachable locks.
Price: $2,600.00

AYA No. 1 Side-by-Side
Similar to the No. 2 except barrel lengths to customer specifications. Barrels are of chrome-nickel steel.
Price: 12, 16, 20 ga., from $2,450.00
Price: 28 ga., from $2,650.00
Price: 410 ga., from $2,750.00

Consult our Directory pages for the location of firms mentioned.

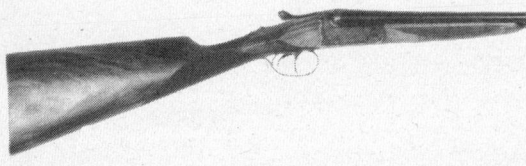

AYA No. 4 SIDE-BY-SIDE
Gauge: 12, 16, 20, 28 & 410.
Barrel: 26", 27", 28" (Imp. Cyl. & Mod. or Mod. & Full).
Weight: 5 lbs. 2oz. to 6½ lbs.
Stock: 14½"x2¼"x1½". European walnut. Straight grip with checkered butt, classic fore-end.
Features: Boxlock action, color case-hardened, automatic ejectors, double triggers (single trigger available). From William Larkin Moore & Co.
Price: 12 ga. $995.00
Price: 20, 28 ga. $1,035.00
Price: 410 ga. $1,095.00

SHOTGUNS—DOUBLE BARREL

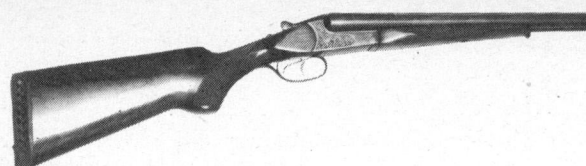

BAIKAL MC-110 SIDE-BY-SIDE
Gauge: 12 or 20 ga., 2¾" chambers.
Barrel: 12 ga. 28" (Mod. & Full), 20 ga. 26" (Imp. Cyl. & Mod).
Weight: 6 lbs. (20 ga.), 6¾ lbs. (12 ga.).
Stock: Fancy walnut. Hand checkered p.g. and fore-end. Choice of full p.g. or straight stock. Semi-beavertail fore-end.
Features: Fully engraved receiver with animal and bird scenes. Engraved trigger guard and tang. Double trigger. Chrome barrels, chambers and internal parts. Raised solid rib. Extractors, hammer interceptors. Auto. safety. Comes with case. Imported by Commercial Trading Imports.
Price: $3,200.00

BAIKAL IJ-58MAE SIDE-BY-SIDE
Gauge: 12 ga., 2¾" chambers, 20 ga., 3" chambers.
Barrel: 26" (Imp. Cyl. & Mod.), 28" (Mod. & Full).
Weight: 6¾ lbs.
Stock: Walnut. Hand checkered p.g. and beavertail fore-end.
Features: Hinged front double trigger. Chrome barrels and chambers. Hammer interceptors. Fore-end center latch. Hand engraved receiver. Selective ejection or extraction. Imported by Commercial Trading Imports.
Price: About $267.95

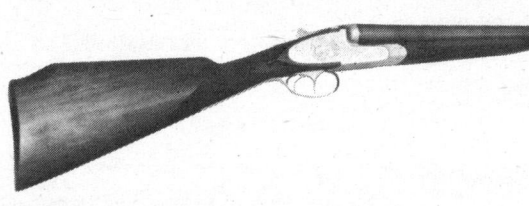

BAIKAL MC-111 SIDE-BY-SIDE
Gauge: 12 ga., 2¾" chambers.
Barrel: To customer's specifications, choice of chokes.
Weight: 7 lbs.
Stock: Fancy walnut. Choice of p.g. or straight stock. Gold and silver inlays in butt. Semi-beavertail fore-end. Monte Carlo. To customer's specifications.
Features: Handmade sidelock shotgun. Removable sideplates. Chrome barrels, chambers and internal parts. Selective ejectors, single selective trigger, hammer interceptors, cocking indicators. Hand chiseled animal and bird scenes on receiver. Comes with case. Imported by Commercial Trading Imports.
Price: Special order only $5,400.00

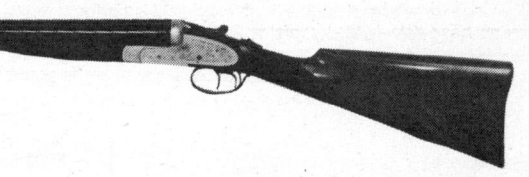

BERNARDELLI XXVSL DOUBLE
Gauge: 12.
Action: Holland & Holland-style sidelock with double sears.
Barrel: Demi-block (chopper lump), 25", choice of choke.
Weight: About 6½ lbs. **Length:** To customer specs.
Stock: Best walnut with dimensions to customer specs.
Features: Firing pins removable from face of standing breech; manual or auto safety; selective auto ejectors; classic or beavertail fore-end. Imported by Knight & Knight.
Price: With fitted luggage case $1,865.00

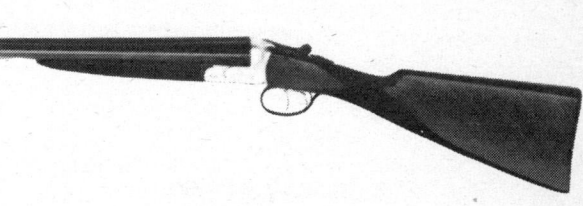

BERETTA M-424 SIDE-BY-SIDE
Gauge: 12 (2¾"), 20 (3").
Action: Beretta patent boxlock; double underlugs and bolts.
Barrel: 12 ga.—26" (Imp. Cyl. & Mod.), 28" (Mod. & Full); 20 ga.—26" (Imp. Cyl. & Mod.), 28" (Mod. & Full).
Weight: 6 lbs. 14 ozs. (20 ga.).
Stock: 14⅛"x1⁹⁄₁₆"x2⁹⁄₁₆". "English" straight-type; hand checkered European walnut.
Features: Coil springs throughout action; double triggers (front is hinged); automatic safety; extractors. Concave matted barrel rib. Introduced 1977. Imported by Beretta Arms Co.
Price: $757.00

Beretta M-426E Side-By-Side
Same as M-424 except action body is engraved; pistol grip stock; a silver pigeon is inlaid into top lever; single selective trigger; selective automatic ejectors. Introduced 1977. Imported by Beretta Arms Co.
Price: $986.00

Consult our Directory pages for the location of firms mentioned.

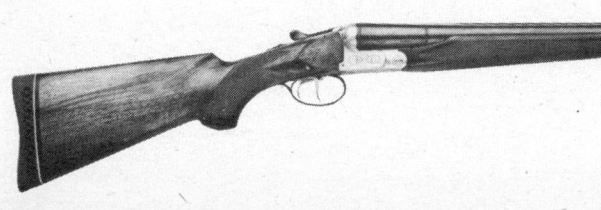

Beretta Model 410 Side-By-Side
Scaled-up version of M426 except in 10 gauge (3½"). Has chrome lined bores, double triggers, 32" barrels (Full & Full), plain extractors, raised matted rib. Receiver has silvered finish with engraving. Weight is about 10 lbs.
Price: $1,135.00

SHOTGUNS—DOUBLE BARREL

BROWNING B-SS
Gauge: 12 (2¾"), 20 (3").
Action: Top lever break-open action, top tang safety, single trigger.
Barrel: 26" (Mod. and Full or Imp. Cyl. and Mod.), 28" (Mod. and Full), 30" (Full & Full or Mod & Full).
Weight: 6¾ lbs. (26" bbl., 20 ga.); 7½ lbs. (30" bbl., 12 ga.).
Stock: 14¼"x1⅝"x2½". French walnut, hand checkered. Full p.g., full beavertail fore-end.
Features: Automatic safety, automatic ejectors. Hand engraved receiver, mechanical single selective trigger with barrel selector in rear of trigger guard.
Price: Grade I, 12 or 20 ga. $464.95
Price: Grade II, 12 or 20 ga. $825.00

Browning BSS Sporter
Similar to standard BSS except has straight-grip stock and full beavertail fore-end with traditional oil finish. Introduced 1977.
Price: Grade I, 12 or 20 ga. $464.95
Price: Grade II, 12 or 20 ga. $825.00

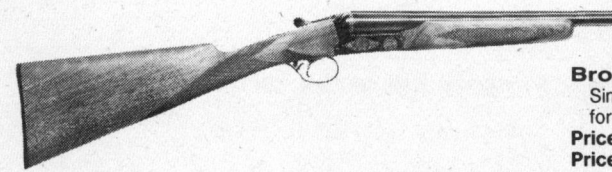

CHAPUIS PROGRESS RBV, R-20 SIDE-BY-SIDE
Gauge: 12 ga. (2¾"), 20 ga. (3").
Barrel: 26½" or 27½" depending on choke (any choke available). Chrome-moly steel with chrome plated bores.
Weight: About 6¼ lbs.
Stock: Select French or American walnut, oil finish. Fine checkering on p.g. and fore-end. Right or left-hand stock available with straight English or p.g. style design. Deluxe wood, grip cap, etc. available as options.
Features: Single barrel joining rib. Auto ejectors are standard. Double triggers. Scroll engraving on frame and sideplates. Extra barrel set available. Introduced 1979. Imported by R. Painter Co.
Price: $1,415.00
Price: Extra barrel set $390.24
Price: Model Progress-RG (boxlock) $832.00
Price: Progress-Hobby (same as RBV/R-20 except profuse engraving, presentation French walnut stock, bbls. browned) .... P.O.R.
Price: Progress-Slug (boxlock-style with right barrel rifled for slugs) $954.00

CRUCELEGUI HERMANOS MODEL 150 DOUBLE
Gauge: 12 or 20 (2¾" chambers).
Action: Greener triple crossbolt.
Barrel: 20", 26" 28", 30", 32" (Cyl. & Cyl., Full & Full, Mod. & Full, Mod. & Imp. Cyl., Imp. Cyl. & Full, Mod. & Mod.).
Weight: 5 to 7¼ lbs.
Stock: Hand checkerd walnut, beavertail fore-end.
Features: Exposed hammers; double triggers; color casehardened receiver; sling swivels; chrome lined bores. From Mandall Shooting Supplies.
Price: $225.00

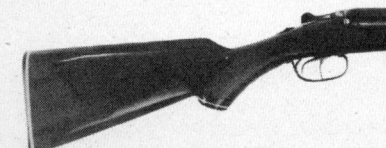

F.I.E. "The Brute" DOUBLE BARREL
Gauge: 12, 20 (2¾" chambers), 410 (3" chambers).
Action: Boxlock.
Barrel: 19"
Weight: 5 lbs. 2 ozs. **Length:** 30" over-all.
Stock: Hand checkered walnut with full beavertail fore-end.
Features: The smallest, lightest double barrel shotgun available. Measures only 30" over-all. Introduced 1979. From F.I.E. Corp.
Price: $174.95

ERA "Bird Hunter" DOUBLE BARREL SHOTGUN
Gauge: 12, 16, 20, (2¾" chambers), 410 (3" chambers).
Action: Boxlock.
Barrel: 12 (30"), 16 ga. 28" (Mod. & Full); 20 ga. 28" (Mod. & Full); 410 ga. 26" (Mod. & Full).
Stock: Hand checkered walnut, beavertail fore-end, white line spacers on p.g. cap and butt plate.
Features: Raised matted rib, double triggers, engraved receiver. Auto. disconnector. Extractors only. Imported from Brazil by F.I.E. Corp.
Price: $136.95
Price: 12, 16 or 20 ga. Riot Model, 18" bbl. $152.95
Price: 12, 16 or 20 ga. Quail Model, 20" bbl. $152.95

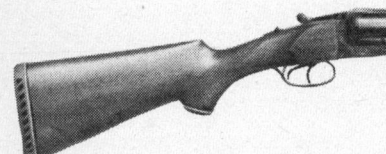

GIB 10 GAUGE MAGNUM SHOTGUN
Gauge: 10 ga. (3½" chambers).
Action: Boxlock.
Barrel: 32" (Full).
Weight: 10 lbs.
Stock: 14½"x1½"x2⅝". European walnut, checkered at p.g. and fore-end.
Features: Double triggers; color hardened action, rest blued. Front and center metal beads on matted rib; ventilated rubber recoil pad. Fore-end release has positive Purdey-type mechanism. Imported by Mandall Shooting Supplies.
Price: $399.50

GALEF'S DOUBLE BARREL SHOTGUN

Gauge: 10 (3½"); 12, 20, 410 (3"); 16, 20 (2¾").
Action: Modified Anson & Deeley boxlock, case hardened.
Barrel: 32" 10, 12 only (Full & Full); 30" 12 only (Mod.& Full); 28" all exc. 410 (Mod.& Full); 26" 12, 20, 28 (I.C.&Mod.); 26" 410 only (Mod.& Full); 22" 12 only (I.C.& I.C.).
Weight: 10½ lbs.(10), 7¾ lbs.(12) to 6 lbs.(410).
Stock: Hand checkered European walnut, p.g., beavertail fore-end, rubber recoil pad. Dimensions vary with gauge.
Features: Auto safety, plain extractors. Imported from Spain by Galef.
Price: 10 ga. .... **$439.00** 12 - 410 .... **$373.80**

GARBI MODEL 60 SIDE-BY-SIDE

Gauge: 12, 16, 20 (2¾" chambers).
Barrel: 26", 28", 30"; choked to customer specs.
Weight: 5½ to 6½ lbs.
Stock: Select walnut. Dimensions to customer specs.
Features: Sidelock action. Scroll engraving on receiver. Hand checkered stock. Double triggers. Extractors. Imported by L. Joseph Rahn, Inc.
Price: **$790.00**
Price: With demi-bloc barrels and ejectors **$1,085.00**

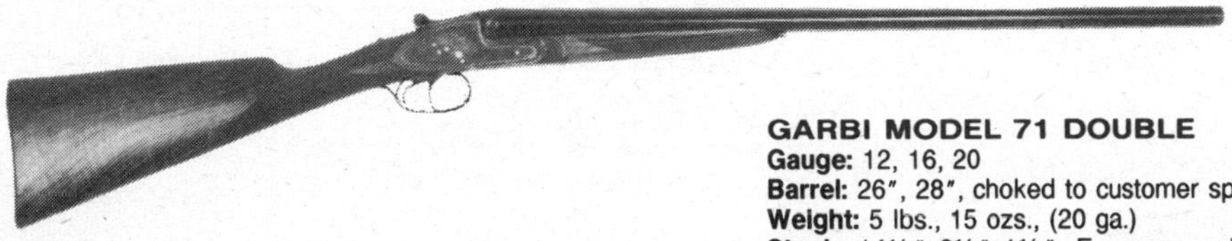

KASSNAR-ZABALA DOUBLE BARREL SHOTGUN

Gauge: 10 (3½"), 12, 20, 410.
Action: Anson & Deeley-type boxlock with double underlocking lugs.
Barrel: 26" (Imp. Cyl. & Mod.), 28", 30" (Mod. & Full), 32" (Full & Full). Raised, matted solid rib.
Weight: About 7 lbs. (12 ga.).
Stock: French walnut with plastic finish. Hand checkered p.g. and beavertail fore-end. 14¼"x1⅝"x2¼".
Features: Hand engraved action, blue finish. Double triggers; front trigger hinged. Metal bead front sight. From Kassnar Imports.
Price: 12, 20 or 410 ga **$350.00**
Price: 10 gauge **$410.00**

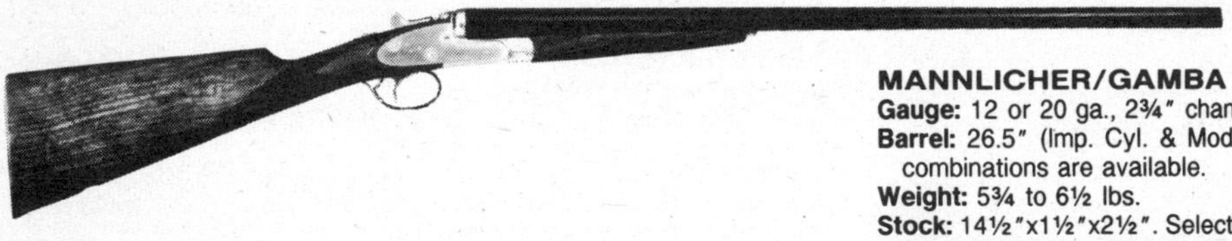

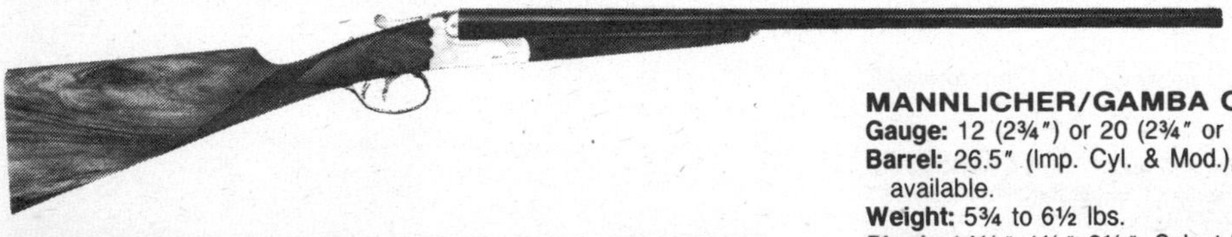

MERCURY MAGNUM DOUBLE BARREL SHOTGUN

Gauge: 10 (3½"), 12 or 20 (3") magnums.
Action: Triple-lock Anson & Deeley type.
Barrel: 28" (Full & Mod.), 12 and 20 ga.; 32" (Full & Full), 10 ga.
Weight: 7¼ lbs. (12 ga.); 6½ lbs. (20 ga.); 10⅛ lbs. (10 ga.). **Length:** 45" (28" bbls.).
Stock: 14" x 1⅝" x 2¼" walnut, checkered p.g. stock and beavertail fore-end, recoil pad.
Features: Double triggers, front hinged, auto safety, extractors; safety gas ports, engraved frame. Imported from Spain by Tradewinds.
Price: (12, 20 ga.) **$295.00**
Price: (10 ga.) **$480.00**

GARBI MODEL 51 SIDE-BY-SIDE

Gauge: 12, 16, 20 (2¾" chambers).
Barrel: 28" (Mod. & Full).
Weight: 5½ to 6½ lbs.
Stock: Walnut, to customer specs.
Features: Boxlock action; hand-engraved receiver; hand-checkered stock and fore-end; double triggers; extractors. Introduced 1980. Imported by L. Joseph Rahn, Inc.
Price: **$490.00**

Garbi Model 62

Similar to Model 60 except choked Mod. & Full, plain receiver with engraved border, demi-bloc barrels, gas exhaust valves, jointed triggers, extractors. Imported by L. Joseph Rahn.
Price: **$790.00**
Price: With ejectors **$1,064.00**

GARBI MODEL 71 DOUBLE

Gauge: 12, 16, 20
Barrel: 26", 28", choked to customer specs.
Weight: 5 lbs., 15 ozs., (20 ga.)
Stock: 14½"x2¼"x1½". European walnut. Straight grip, checkered butt, classic fore-end.
Features: Sidelock action, automatic ejectors, double triggers standard. Color case-hardened action, coin finish optional. Five other models are available. From Wm. Larkin Moore.
Price: Model 71, from **$1,250.00**

MANNLICHER/GAMBA LONDON DOUBLE

Gauge: 12 or 20 ga., 2¾" chambers.
Barrel: 26.5" (Imp. Cyl. & Mod.), 27.5" (Mod. & Full) are standard. Other combinations are available.
Weight: 5¾ to 6½ lbs.
Stock: 14½"x1½"x2½". Select European walnut with finely cut hand checkered straight grip. Checkered butt. Hand rubbed European oil finish.
Features: Sidelock action based on the Holland & Holland system with double safety and three-lug Purdey locking system. Chrome lined barrels, auto ejectors, single or double triggers. Made by Renato Gamba, imported by Steyr Daimler Puch of America.
Price: Double trigger, either gauge, with leather case **$3,130.00**
Price: Single trigger, either gauge, with leather case **$3,280.00**

MANNLICHER/GAMBA OXFORD DOUBLE

Gauge: 12 (2¾") or 20 (2¾" or 3").
Barrel: 26.5" (Imp. Cyl. & Mod.), 27.5" (Mod. & Full). Other combinations available.
Weight: 5¾ to 6½ lbs.
Stock: 14½"x1½"x2½". Select European walnut, hand checkered straight grip. Checkered butt. Hand rubbed European oil finish.
Features: Boxlock action based on the Anson & Deeley system. Auto ejectors, chrome lined barrels. Single or double trigger (double with articulated front trigger). Made by Renato Gamba, imported by Steyr Daimler Puch of America.
Price: Double trigger, either gauge **$1,455.00**
Price: Single trigger, either gauge **$1,575.00**
Price: Optional leather case **$185.00**

SHOTGUNS—DOUBLE BARREL

MERKEL 147E SIDE-BY-SIDE
Gauge: 12, 16, 20, 3" chambers on request.
Action: Anson-Deeley with double hook bolting and Greener breech.
Barrel: 26" (Mod. & Imp. Cyl., Cyl. & Imp. Cyl.).
Weight: 6¼ to 6½ lbs.
Stock: Walnut. English style or p.g., 14¼"x1½"x2¼".
Features: Hunting scene engraving. Double, single or single selective trigger. Imported by J. J. Jenkins.
Price: With double triggers **$1,104.35**
Price: Model 47E (as above except has scroll engraving) **$944.25**

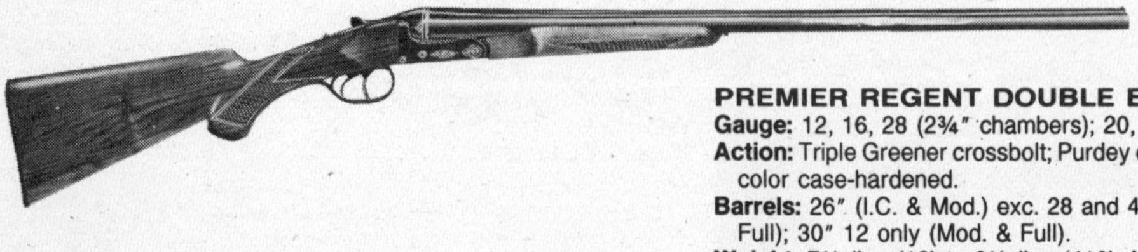

PREMIER MONARCH DOUBLE BARREL SHOTGUN
Gauge: 12, 16 (2¾"), 20 (2¾" or 3").
Action: Triple Greener crossbolt.
Barrel: 26", 12 and 20 (Mod. & Imp. Cyl.), 28", 12, 16, 20 (Mod. & Full).
Weight: About 7 lbs. **Length:** 44½" over-all (28" barrels).
Stock: 14"x1⅝"x2½". Fancy French walnut, checkered p.g. and fore-end.
Sights: Metal bead, front and middle.
Features: Solid tapered rib; double triggers, auto. ejectors and safety, selective extractors; engraved action. Imported from Europe by Premier.
Price: **$449.70**

Premier Presentation Double Barrel Shotgun
Same as Monarch except has gold and silver inlayed hunting scenes. Stock style and measurements to customer specs, as well as gauge, barrel length and choking.
Price: With one set of barrels **$971.60**
Price: Extra barrels **$306.00**

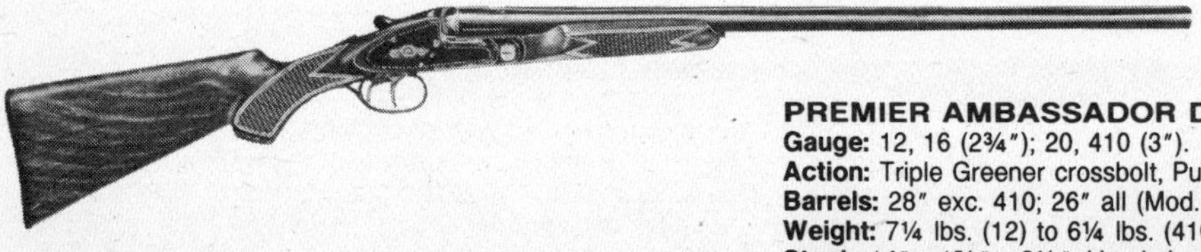

RICHLAND MODEL 200 DOUBLE BARREL SHOTGUN
Gauge: 12, 16, 20, 28 or 410 (12, 16 and 28 have 2¾" chambers, 20 and 410 3").
Barrel: 22" 20 ga. (Imp. Cyl. & Mod.) 26" (Imp. Cyl. & Mod., Mod. & Full 410 ga.), 28" (Mod. & Full).
Weight: 6¼ to 7¼ lbs.
Stock: 14½"x2⅜"x1½". Spanish walnut, checkered p.g. and fore-end; cheekpiece and rubber vent. recoil pad.
Sights: Metal bead front.
Features: Anson & Deely type action with double under-locking lugs; spring loaded firing pins removeable from front of action. Double triggers blue finish with light engraving. Imported by Richland Arms.
Price: **$360.00**

Richland Model 711 Magnum Shotgun
Similar to Model 200 except in 12 ga. (3") or 10 ga. (3½") magnums. Choked Full & Full, 12 ga. has 30" barrels, 10 ga. has 32". Weight is 7¾ lbs. (12), 11 lbs. (10.) Uses Purdey triple lock system, auto. safety with double triggers, raised full-length rib with metal beads at front and center.
Price: 12 ga. Magnum **$400.00**
Price: 10 ga. Magnum **$455.00**

MERKEL 147S SIDE-BY-SIDE
Gauge: 12, 16, 20 ga. with 3" chambers on request.
Action: Sidelock with double hook bolting and Greener breech. Trigger catch bar.
Barrel: 26" (Mod. & Imp. Cyl., Cyl. & Imp. Cyl.).
Weight: 6½ to 6¾ lbs.
Stock: Walnut finish. English style or p.g., 14¼"x1½"x2¼".
Features: 30% faster trigger than conventional lock design. Hunting scene engraving. Highest grade side-by-side Merkel. Double, single or single selective trigger. Imported by J. J. Jenkins.
Price: With double trigger **$2,486.00**

PREMIER REGENT DOUBLE BARREL SHOTGUN
Gauge: 12, 16, 28 (2¾" chambers); 20, 410 (3" chambers).
Action: Triple Greener crossbolt; Purdey optional on 28, 410. Hand-engraved, color case-hardened.
Barrels: 26" (I.C. & Mod.) exc. 28 and 410 only (Mod. & Full); 28" (Mod. & Full); 30" 12 only (Mod. & Full).
Weight: 7¼ lbs. (12) to 6⅛ lbs. (410). **Length:** 42½" (26" bbls.).
Stock: 14" x 1⅝" x 2½". Hand-checkered walnut, p.g. and fore-end. White line spacers at butt and grip cap.
Features: Matted tapered rib, double triggers, auto safety. Extra bbl. sets avail. Imported from Europe by Premier.
Price: **$222.95**
Price: With two sets of barrels, 12 ga. .... **$423.00** 20 ga. **$386.75**
Price: Extra barrels, fitted **$180.00**

Premier Brush King Double Barrel Shotgun
Same as Regent except 12 and 20 ga. only, 22" bbls. (I.C. & Mod.), weight 6¼ lbs. (12), 5¾ lbs. (20). Straight English-style stock and fore-end.
Price: **$241.45**

Premier Magnum Express Double Barrel Shotgun
Similar to Regent except 10 ga. (3½" chambers) 32" or 12 ga. (3" chambers) 30", both Full & Full. Recoil pad, beavertail fore-end.
Price: 12 ga. **$251.00**
Price: 10 ga. **$280.00**

PREMIER AMBASSADOR DOUBLE BARREL SHOTGUN
Gauge: 12, 16 (2¾"); 20, 410 (3").
Action: Triple Greener crossbolt, Purdey avail. on 410; side locks.
Barrels: 28" exc. 410; 26" all (Mod. & Full).
Weight: 7¼ lbs. (12) to 6¼ lbs. (410). **Length:** 44½".
Stock: 14" x 1⅝" x 2½": Hand-checkered walnut, p.g., beavertail fore-end. White line spacers at butt and grip cap.
Features: Cocking indicators, double triggers, auto safety. Hand-engraved, color case-hardened action. Imported from Europe by Premier.
Price: **$306.00**

Premier Continental Double Hammer Shotgun
Same as Ambassador except outside hammers, not avail. in 410.
Price: **$278.15**

Consult our Directory pages for the location of firms mentioned.

CAUTION: PRICES CHANGE. CHECK AT GUNSHOP.

SHOTGUNS — DOUBLE BARREL

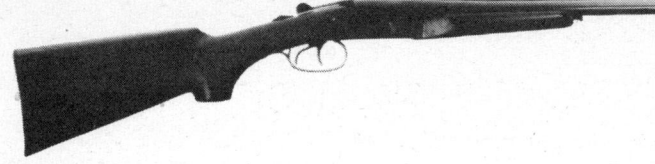

ROSSI "SQUIRE" DOUBLE BARREL
Gauge: 12, 20, 410 (3" chambers).
Barrel: 12 ga.—26" (Imp. Cyl. & Mod.), 28" (Mod. & Full); 20 ga.—28" (Mod. & Full); 410—26" (Full & Full).
Weight: About 7½ lbs.
Stock: Walnut finished hardwood.
Features: Double triggers, raised matted rib, beavertail fore-end. Massive twin underlugs mesh with synchronized sliding bolts. Introduced 1978. Imported by Interarms.
Price: 12 ga., 20 ga. $270.00
Price: 410 .... $285.00

ROSSI OVERLAND DOUBLE BARREL
Gauge: 12, 20, 410 (3" chambers).
Action: Sidelock with external hammers; Greener crossbolt.
Barrel: 12 ga., 20" (Imp. Cyl., Mod.) 28" (Mod. & Full), 20 ga., 20" (Mod., Full), 410 ga., 26" (Full & Full).
Weight: 6½ to 7 lbs.
Stock: Walnut p.g. with beavertail fore-end.
Features: Solid raised matted rib. Exposed hammers. Importerd by Interarms.
Price: 12 or 20 .... $260.00
Price: 410 ga. $270.00

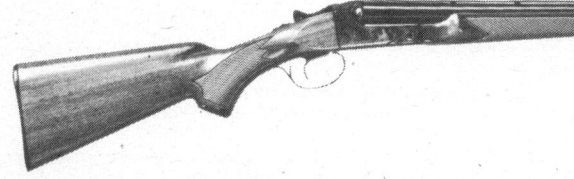

SAVAGE FOX MODEL B-SE DOUBLE
Gauge: 12, 20, 410 (20, 2¾" and 3"; 410, 2½" and 3" shells).
Action: Hammerless, takedown; non-selective single trigger; auto. safety. Automatic ejectors.
Barrel: 12, 20 ga. 26" (Imp. Cyl., Mod.); 12 ga. (Mod., Full); 410, 26" (Full, Full). Vent. rib on all.
Stock: 14"x1½"x2½". Walnut, checkered p.g. and beavertail fore-end.
Weight: 12 ga. 7 lbs., 16 ga. 6¾ lbs., 20 ga. 6½ lbs., 410 ga. 6¼ lbs.
Features: Decorated, case-hardened frame; white bead front and middle sights.
Price: $316.50
Also available with double triggers, case hardened frame, without white line spacers and auto. ejectors as Model B $273.45
Price: Model BE, same as Model B above except has extractors and auto ejectors $316.50

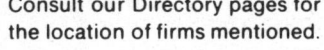

Consult our Directory pages for the location of firms mentioned.

SAVAGE-STEVENS MODEL 311 DOUBLE
Gauge: 12, 16, 20, 410 (12, 20 and 410, 3" chambers).
Action: Top lever, hammerless; double triggers, auto top tang safety.
Barrel: 12, 16, 20 ga. 36" (Imp. Cyl., Mod.); 12 ga. 28" (Mod., Full); 12 ga. 30" (Mod., Full); 410 ga. 26" (Full, Full).
Length: 45¾" over-all. **Weight:** 7-8 lbs. (30" bbl.).
Stock: 14"x1½"x2½". Walnut finish, p.g., fluted comb.
Features: Box type frame, case-hardened finish.
Price: $202.35

VENTURA MODEL 53 DOUBLE
Gauge: 28 (2¾"), 410 (3").
Action: Anson & Deeley boxlock with double underlugs.
Barrel: 25", 26" and 28" with chokes according to gauge and use.
Weight: 5 lbs., 5 oz. (28 ga.); 5 lbs. (410).
Stock: Select European walnut, hand checkered. Straight English or Pistol grip stock with slender beavertail fore-end.
Features: Single selective or double triggers, automatic ejectors, hand-engraved scalloped frame. Introduced 1980. From Ventura Imports.
Price: From $995.00

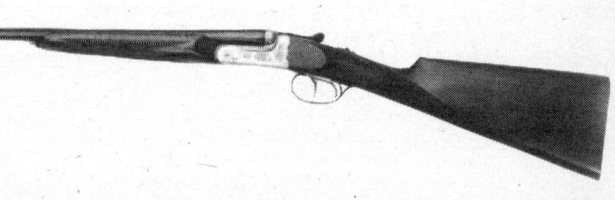

SHOTGUNS — DOUBLE BARREL

VENTURA MODELS 62, 64 & 66 DOUBLES
Gauge: 12 (2¾"), 20 (3").
Action: H&H sidelock with double underbolts. Model 66 with treble bolting and side clips.
Barrel: 25", 26", 28", 30" with chokes according to gauge and use.
Weight: 12 ga. from 6 lbs., 7 ozs; 20 ga. from 5 lbs., 8 ozs.
Stock: Select figured European walnut, hand checkered. Straight English or pistol grip stock with slender beavertail fore-end. Model 66 has fancy walnut.
Features: Single selective or double triggers, automatic ejectors. Model 62 has Purdey style engraving, Model 64 (illus.) and 66 have Florentine. All models have cocking indicators, gas escape valves, intercepting safeties. Introduced 1978. From Ventura Imports.
Price: Model 62, from $1,100.00
Price: Model 64, from $1,200.00
Price: Model 66, from $1,330.00

VENTURA MODEL 51 DOUBLE
Gauge: 12 (2¾").
Action: Anson & Deeley boxlock with double underlugs.
Barrel: 25", (XXV), 26", 28", 30", with chokes according to gauge and use.
Weight: 6 lbs., 10 ozs. (28" bbl.).
Stock: Select European walnut, hand checkered. Straight English or pistol grip stock with slender beavertail fore-end.
Features: Single selective trigger, automatic ejectors. Hand-engraved action. Deluxe model with 25" barrels (XXV) and Churchill rib. Introduced 1978. From Ventura Imports.
Price: $645.00
Price: Model XXV $775.00

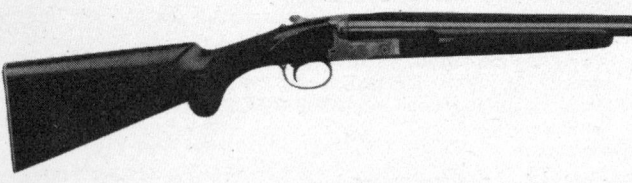

WINCHESTER 21 CUSTOM DOUBLE GUN
12, 16 or 20 ga. Almost any choke or bbl. length combination. Matted rib, 2¾" chambers, rounded frame, stock of AA-grade full fancy American walnut to customer's dimensions; straight or p.g., cheekpiece, Monte Carlo and/or offset; field. Skeet or trap fore-end. Full fancy checkering, engine-turned receiver parts, gold plated trigger and gold oval name plate (optional) with three initials .... **Price on request from factory.**

Winchester 21 Pigeon Grade
Same as Custom grade except: 3" chambers, available in 12 and 20 ga.; matted or vent. rib, leather covered pad (optional), style "A" stock carving and style "6" engraving (see Win. catalog); gold inlaid p.g. cap, gold nameplate or 3 gold initials in guard .... **Price on request from factory.**

WINCHESTER MODEL 23 PIGEON GRADE DOUBLE
Gauge: 12, 3" chambers.
Barrel: 26", 28", 30" (Imp. Cyl. & Mod., Mod. & Full, Full & Full). Vent. rib.
Weight: 7 lbs. **Length:** 46¾" over-all (30" bbls.)
Stock: High grade American walnut, beavertail fore-end. Deep cut checkering, new warm, rich color, high-lustre finish. 14"x1½"x2½".
Features: Mechanical trigger; ventilated tapered rib; selective ejectors. A 20 gauge version will be introduced in 1979 with 26" or 28" (Imp. Cyl. & Mod. or Mod. & Full) barrels, weight of 6½ lbs. Receiver, top lever and trigger guard have silver gray satin finish and fine line scroll engraving. Introduced 1978.
Price: $980.00

Winchester 21 Grand American
Same as Custom and Pigeon grades except: style "B" stock carving, with style "6" engraving, all figures gold inlaid; extra pair of bbls. with beavertail fore-end, engraved and carved to match rest of gun; full leather trunk case or all, with canvas cover .... **Price on request from factory.**

SHOTGUNS — BOLT ACTION

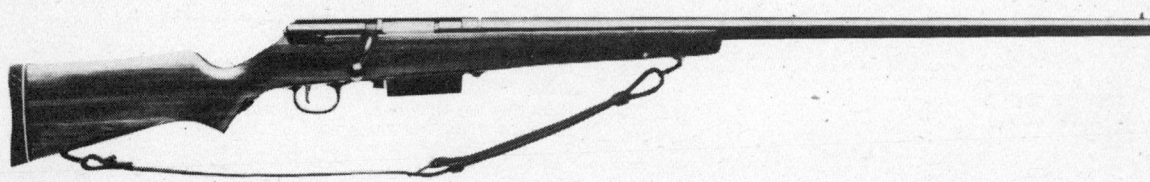

MARLIN MODEL 55 GOOSE GUN BOLT ACTION
Gauge: 12 only, (3" mag. or 2¾").
Action: Bolt action, thumb safety, detachable 2-shot clip. Red cocking indicator.
Barrel: 36", Full choke.
Weight: 8 lbs., 57" over-all.
Stock: Walnut, p.g., ventilated recoil pad, leather strap & swivels. Mar-Shield® finish.
Features: Tapped for receiver sights. Swivels and leather carrying strap. Gold-plated trigger. Brass bead front sight, U-groove rear sight.
Price: $115.95

MARLIN SUPERGOOSE 10 M5510
Gauge: 10, 3½" Magnum or 2⅞" regular, 2-shot clip.
Barrel: 34" (Full), bead front sight, U-groove rear sight.
Weight: About 10½ lbs. **Length:** 55½" over-all.
Stock: Extra long American black walnut with p.g., Pachmayr vent. pad., white butt spacer.
Features: Bolt action, removable 2-shot clip magazine. Gold plated trigger, positive thumb safety, red cocking indicator. Comes with quick-detachable swivels and leather carrying strap.
Price: $206.95

SHOTGUNS—BOLT ACTION

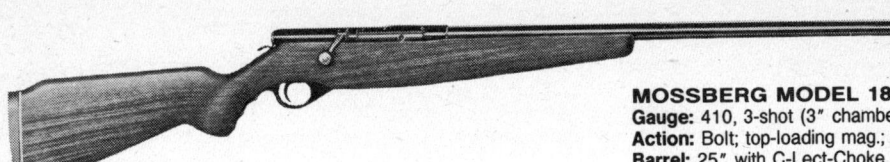

MOSSBERG MODEL 183K BOLT ACTION
Gauge: 410, 3-shot (3" chamber).
Action: Bolt; top-loading mag.; thumb safety.
Barrel: 25" with C-Lect-Choke.
Weight: 5¾ lbs. **Length:** 45¼" over-all.
Stock: Walnut finish, p.g., Monte Carlo comb., rubber recoil pad w/spacer.
Features: Moulded trigger guard with finger grooves, gold bead front sight.
Price: $96.50

MOSSBERG MODEL 395K BOLT ACTION
Gauge: 12, 3-shot (3" chamber).
Action: Bolt; takedown; detachable clip.
Barrel: 26" with C-Lect-Choke.
Weight: 7½ lbs. **Length:** 45¾" over-all.
Stock: Walnut finish, p.g. Monte Carlo comb; recoil pad.
Features: Streamlined action; top safety; grooved rear sight.
Price: $111.50
  Also available in 20 ga. 3" chamber 28" bbl. 6¼ lbs., as M385K $104.95

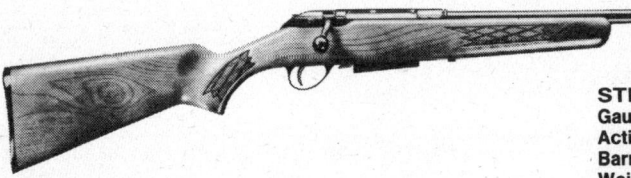

STEVENS SUPER VALUE 58 BOLT ACTION SHOTGUN
Gauge: 410 ga. (2½" and 3" chambers), 3-shot clip.
Action: Self-cocking bolt; double extractors; thumb safety.
Barrel: 24", Full choke.
Weight: 5½ lbs. **Length:** 43" over-all.
Stock: Walnut finish, checkered fore-end and p.g., recoil pad.
Features: Crisp trigger pull, Electro-Cote stock finish.
Price: .... N.A.

WESTERN FIELD BOLT ACTION SHOTGUN
Gauge: 12, 20 or 410 (3" chamber).
Action: Self cocking, bolt action. Thumb safety. 3-shot magazine.
Barrel: 24" (Full) 410, 26" (20 ga.), 28" (12 ga.).
Weight: 5½ lbs. **Length:** 44½" over-all (410 ga.).
Stock: Hardwood, Monte Carlo design.
Features: Top safety, grooved rear sight.
Price: 410 ga. $82.99
Price: 20 ga. $82.99
Price: 12 ga. $92.99

SHOTGUNS—SINGLE BARREL

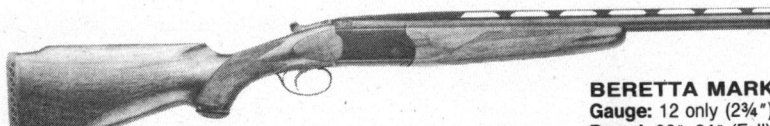

BERETTA MARK II SINGLE BARREL
Gauge: 12 only (2¾").
Barrel: 32", 34" (Full).
Weight: About 8 lbs.
Stock: 14⅜"x1⅜"x1⅝". European walnut, checkered p.g. and fore-end.
Features: Action, barrel and stock derive from S58 over-under. Trap rib, two sight beads, chrome lined bores. Ventilated recoil pad. From Beretta Arms Co.
Price: $530.00

BAIKAL IJ-18E SINGLE BARREL
Gauge: 12 or 20 ga., 2¾" chambers; 410 ga., 3" chamber.
Barrel: 12 ga. 28" (Mod.), 30" (Full), 20 ga. 26" (Mod.), 410 ga. 26" (Full).
Weight: 5¾ lbs.
Stock: Walnut-finished hardwood. Hand checkered p.g. White spacers on buttplate.
Features: Chrome barrel and chamber. Cross-bolt safety in trigger guard. Cocking indicator. Selective ejector-extractor. Imported by Commercial Trading Imports.
Price: $73.50

CAUTION: PRICES CHANGE. CHECK AT GUNSHOP.

SHOTGUNS—SINGLE BARREL

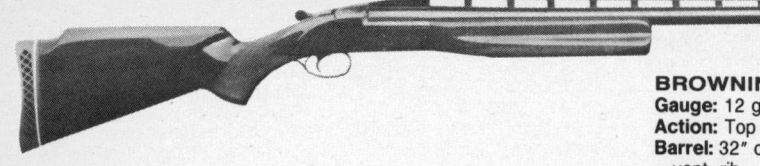

BROWNING BT-99 COMPETITION TRAP SPECIAL
Gauge: 12 gauge only (2¾").
Action: Top lever break-open, hammerless.
Barrel: 32" or 34" (Mod., Imp. Mod. or Full) with ¹¹⁄₃₂" wide high post floating vent. rib.
Weight: 8 lbs. (32" bbl.).
Stock: French walnut; hand checkered, full pistol grip, full beavertail fore-end; recoil pad. Trap dimensions with M.C. 14⅜"x1⅜"x1⅜"x2".
Sights: Ivory front and middle beads.
Features: Gold plated trigger with 3½-lb. pull, deluxe trap-style recoil pad, auto ejector, no safety. Also available in engraved Pigeon Grade.
Price: Grade I Competition $599.95
Price: Grade I Competition with extra bbl. $850.00
Price: Pigeon Grade Competition $1,350.00

CBC "THE GAMEGETTER" DELUXE SINGLE BARREL
Gauge: 12, 20 (2¾"), 410 (3").
Action: Button-break on trigger guard.
Barrel: 12 & 20 ga. 28" (Full); 410 ga. 26" (Full).
Weight: 6½ lbs.
Stock: Walnut finished hardwood, full beavertail fore-end.
Sights: Metal bead front.
Features: Exposed hammer. Automatic ejector. Imported from Brazil by F.I.E. Corp.
Price: $51.95
Price: 20 and 410, Youth Model $54.95
Price: Combo rifle-shotgun (20 ga. or 30-30 interchangeable bbls.) $86.95

ERA "THE S.O.B." SINGLE BARREL SHOTGUN
Shortened version of "The Gamegetter" with 18" barrel, cut-off buttstock. Weighs 4½ lbs. Introduced 1979. From F.I.E. Corp.
Price: $74.95

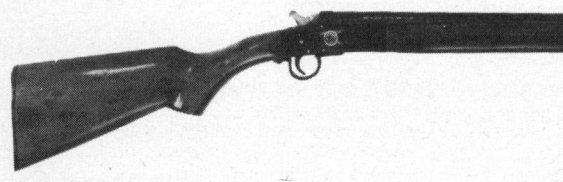

ERA "THE WINNER" SINGLE BARREL SHOTGUN
Gauge: 12, 16, 20 (2¾"), 410 (3").
Barrel: 12 ga. 30" & 20 ga. 28" (Full); 410 ga. (Full).
Weight: 6½ lbs.
Stock: Walnut stained hardwood, beavertail fore-end.
Sights: Metal bead front.
Features: Trigger guard is pulled to open action. Exposed hammer, auto extractor. Imported from Brazil by F.I.E. Corp.
Price: $48.95
Price: 20 and 410 ga. Youth Model $51.95

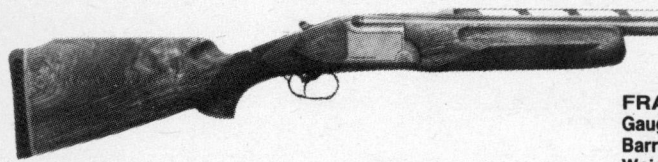

FRANCHI MODEL 2004 SINGLE BARREL TRAP
Gauge: 12 only (2¾" chamber).
Barrel: 32" or 34" (Imp. Mod. or Full).
Weight: About 8 lbs.
Stock: 14½"x1⅞"x1½". Fancy French walnut; checkered p.g. and fore-end. Available in Monte Carlo or straight style (interchangeble). Different dimensions avail.
Features: "Ceiling-Sell" trap trigger; raised competition, ventilated, trap rib. Buttstock drilled and tapped for recoil reducer. Comes with fitted luggage-type hard case. From Stoeger Industries.
Price: $1,400.00

GALEF COMPANION SINGLE BARREL SHOTGUN
Gauge: 12, 20, 410 (3"); 16, 28 (2¾").
Action: Folding boxlock.
Barrel: 28" exc. 12 (30") and 410 (26"), all Full.
Weight: 5½ lbs. (12) to 4½ lbs. (410).
Stock: 14"x1½"x2⅝" hand checkered walnut, p.g.
Features: Non-auto safety, folds. Vent. rib $5.00 additional. Imported from Italy by Galef.
Price: Plain bbl. .... $138.00   Vent. rib $152.00

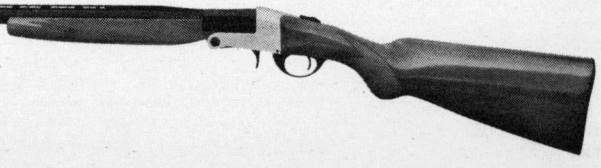

SHOTGUNS—SINGLE BARREL

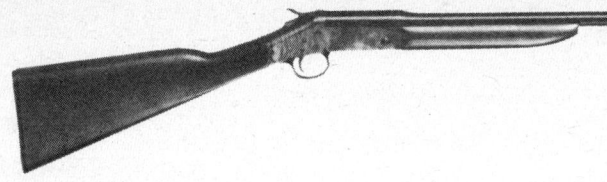

H & R Model 088
Same features as Model 058 except has semi-pistol grip stock. Available in most popular gauge and choke combinations, including 12 ga. with 30" or 32" (Full) barrel. Junior model also available (does not have recoil pad).
Price: **$68.75**

H & R Model 176 Magnums
Same as Model 058 except in 10 gauge (3½" chamber) and 12 gauge (3" chamber) with 36" (Full) barrels. Also available with 32" (Full) barrel in 10, 12, 16 (2¾" chamber) and 20 (3" chamber) gauges. All barrels specially designed for steel shot use. Special long fore-end and recoil pad.
Price: From **$84.50**

H & R TOPPER MODELS 058 and 098
Gauge: 12, 20 and 410. (2¾" or 3" chamber), 16, 28 (2¾" only).
Action: Takedown. Side lever opening. External hammer, auto ejection. Case hardened frame.
Barrel: 12 ga., 28", 30"; 20 and 410 ga., 28". (Full choke). 12, 16, 20 ga. available 28" (Mod.), 28 and 410 ga., 26" (Mod., Full).
Stock: Walnut finished hardwood; p.g., (14"x1¾"x2½").
Weight: 5 to 6½ lbs., according to gauge and bbl. length.
Features: Self-adj. bbl. lock; coil springs throughout.
Price: M58 .... **$79.50**
Model 98, Topper Deluxe Nickel frame, ebony finished stock. 12, 20 and 410 ga., 26" barrel **$79.50**

H & R Topper Jr. Model 490
Like M058 except ideally proportioned stock for the smaller shooter. Can be cheaply changed to full size. 20 ga. (Mod.), 28 ga. (Mod.) or 410 (Full) 26" bbl. Weight 5 lbs., 40½" over-all **$79.50**

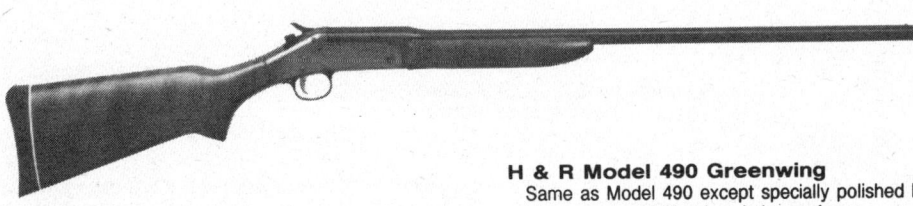

H & R Topper Buck Model 162
Same as M58 except 12 or 20 ga. 24" cyl. bored bbl., adj. folding leaf rear sight, blade front, 5½ lbs.; over-all 40". Cross bolt safety: push-button action release **$89.50**

H & R Model 490 Greenwing
Same as Model 490 except specially polished blue finish with gold-finish trigger and gold-filled inscription on frame.
Price: **$89.50**

ITHACA 5E GRADE SINGLE BARREL TRAP GUN
Gauge: 12 only.
Action: Top lever break open hammerless, dual locking lugs.
Barrel: 30" or 32", rampless vent. rib.
Stock: (14½"x1½"x1⅞"). Select walnut, checkered p.g. and beavertail fore-end, p.g. cap, recoil pad, Monte Carlo comb, cheekpiece, Cast-on, cast-off or extreme deviation from standard stock dimensions $100 extra. Reasonable deviation allowed without extra charge.
Features: Frame, top lever and trigger guard extensively engraved and gold inlaid. Gold name plate in stock.
Price: Custom made **$5,500.00**
Price: $7,500 Grade **$7,500.00**

> Consult our Directory pages for the location of firms mentioned.

LJUTIC MONO GUN SINGLE BARREL
Gauge: 12 ga. only.
Barrel: 34", choked to customer specs; hollow-milled rib, 35½" sight plane.
Weight: Approx. 9 lbs.
Stock: To customer specs. Oil finish, hand checkered.
Features: Pull or release trigger; removeable trigger guard contains trigger and hammer mechanism; Ljutic pushbutton opener on front of trigger guard. From Ljutic Industries.
Price: **$3,795.00**
Price: With Olympic Rib, custom 32" barrel, 2 screw-in chokes .. **$3,995.00**

Ljutic Adjustable Barrel Mono Gun
Similar to standard Mono except has micrometer-adjustable choke (allows shooter to adj. the pattern from flat to an elevation of 4 feet), choice of Olympic, step-style or standard rib. Custom stock measurements, fancy wood, etc. **$3,995.00**

SHOTGUNS— SINGLE BARREL

MONTE CARLO SINGLE BARREL SHOTGUN
Gauge: 12 (2¾" chamber).
Action: Monte Carlo, bottom release.
Barrel: 32" (Trap).
Weight: 8¼ lbs.
Stock: 14½"x1⅛"x1⅝" hand checkered walnut, p.g., beavertail fore-end, recoil pad.
Features: Auto ejector, slide safety, gold plated trigger. Imported from Italy by Galef.
Price: $317.00

ROTTWEIL AMERICAN TRAP SINGLE
Gauge: 12 ga. only.
Action: Boxlock.
Barrel: 34" (Full); vent. rib. Chrome bore (except choke).
Weight: 8½ lbs.
Stock: Monte Carlo of select French walnut. Satin oil finish. Hand-checkered p.g. and fore-end. Two lengths available: 14¾"x1⅜"x1⅜"x1⅞" or 14½"x1⅜"x1⅜"x1⅞".
Sights: Plastic front in metal sleeve, center bead.
Features: Interchangeable trigger groups—special single convertible for O/U barrel use, or release-release single selective. Milled receiver. Choke is hand honed. All coil springs, engraved action. Introduced 1978. Imported by Eastern Sports Int.
Price: $2,750.00

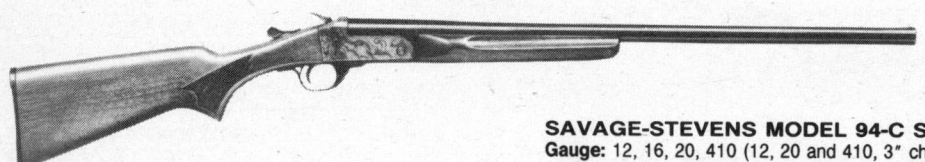

Stevens M94-Y Youth's Gun
Same as Model 94-C except: 26" bbl., 20 ga. Mod. or 410 Full, 12½" stock with recoil pad. Wgt. about 5½ lbs. 40½" over-all. $82.50

SAVAGE-STEVENS MODEL 94-C Single Barrel Gun
Gauge: 12, 16, 20, 410 (12, 20 and 410, 3" chambers).
Action: Top lever break open; hammer; auto. ejector.
Barrel: 12 ga. 28", 30", 32", 36"; 16, 20 ga. 28"; 410 ga. 26". Full choke only.
Weight: About 6 lbs. **Length:** 42" over-all (26" bbl.).
Stock: 14"x1½"x2½". Walnut finish, checkered p.g. and fore-end.
Features: Color case-hardened frame, low rebounding hammer.
Price: 26" to 32" bbls. ...... $72.90 36" bbl. $75.80

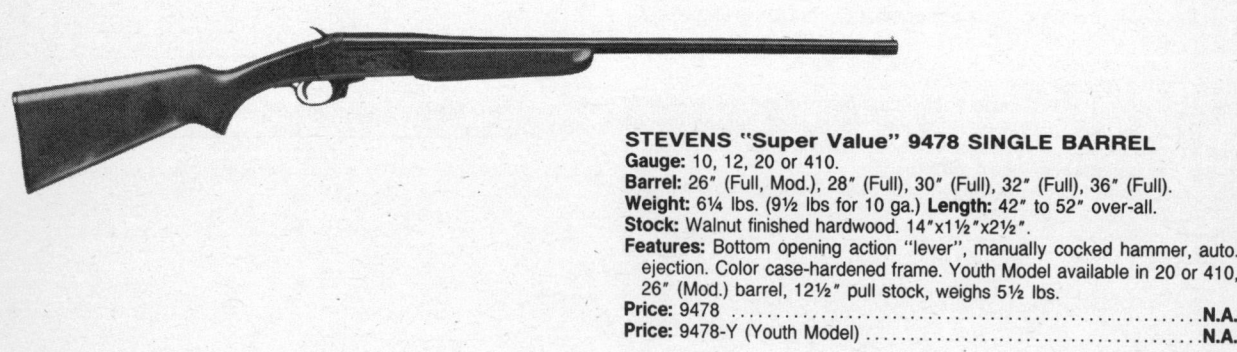

STEVENS "Super Value" 9478 SINGLE BARREL
Gauge: 10, 12, 20 or 410.
Barrel: 26" (Full, Mod.), 28" (Full), 30" (Full), 32" (Full), 36" (Full).
Weight: 6¼ lbs. (9½ lbs for 10 ga.) **Length:** 42" to 52" over-all.
Stock: Walnut finished hardwood. 14"x1½"x2½".
Features: Bottom opening action "lever", manually cocked hammer, auto. ejection. Color case-hardened frame. Youth Model available in 20 or 410, 26" (Mod.) barrel, 12½" pull stock, weighs 5½ lbs.
Price: 9478 .... N.A.
Price: 9478-Y (Youth Model) .... N.A.

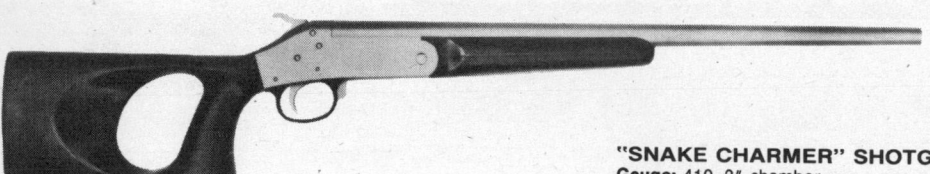

"SNAKE CHARMER" SHOTGUN
Gauge: 410, 3" chamber.
Barrel: 18⅛" (Cyl.)
Weight: 3½ lbs. **Length:** 28⅛" over-all.
Stock: Moulded plastic, thumbhole type.
Sights: None.
Features: Measures 19" when taken apart. All stainless steel construction. Storage compartment in buttstock holds four spare rounds of 410. Introduced 1978. From H. Koon, Inc.
Price: $99.95
Price: Vinyl carrying case $6.95

BLACK POWDER GUNS

The following pages catalog the black powder arms currently available to U.S. shooters. These range from quite precise replicas of historically significant arms to totally new designs created expressly to give the black powder shooter the benefits of modern technology.

Most of the replicas are imported, and many are available from more than one source. Thus examples of a given model such as the 1860 Army revolver or Zouave rifle purchased from different importers may vary in price, finish and fitting. Most of them bear proof marks, indicating that they have been test fired in the proof house of their country of origin.

A list of the importers and the retail price range are included with the description for each model. Many local dealers handle more than one importer's products, giving the prospective buyer an opportunity to make his own judgment in selecting a black powder gun. Most importers have catalogs available free or at nominal cost, and some are well worth having for the useful information on black powder shooting they provide in addition to their detailed descriptions and specifications of the guns.

A number of special accessories are also available for the black powder shooter. These include replica powder flasks, bullet moulds, cappers and tools, as well as more modern devices to facilitate black powder cleaning and maintenance. Ornate presentation cases and even detachable shoulder stocks are also available for some black powder pistols from their importers. Again, dealers or the importers will have catalogs.

The black powder guns are arranged in four sections: Single Shot Pistols, Revolvers, Muskets & Rifles, and Shotguns. The guns within each section are arranged by date of the original, with the oldest first. Thus the 1847 Walker replica leads off the revolver section, and flintlocks precede percussion arms in the other sections.

BLACK POWDER SINGLE SHOT PISTOLS—FLINT & PERCUSSION

CHARLEVILLE FLINTLOCK PISTOL
Caliber: 69.
Barrel: 7½".
Weight: 48 ozs. **Length:** 13½" ovr-all.
Stock: Walnut.
Sights: None.
Features: Brass frame, polished steel barrel, brass buttcap and backstrap. Replica of original 1777 pistol. Imported by Navy Arms Co.
Price: $125.00

NAVY ARMS WHEELLOCK PISTOL
Caliber: 45.
Barrel: 17".
Weight: 4½ lbs. **Length:** 25" over-all.
Stock: Walnut.
Sights: None.
Features: Authentic reproduction of an early wheellock pistol. Also available in carbine form with 27" barrel, 45-cal., over-all length of 39" and weighs 6 lbs. Imported by Navy Arms.
Price: Pistol. $195.00
Price: Pistol kit $150.00
Price: Carbine $225.00

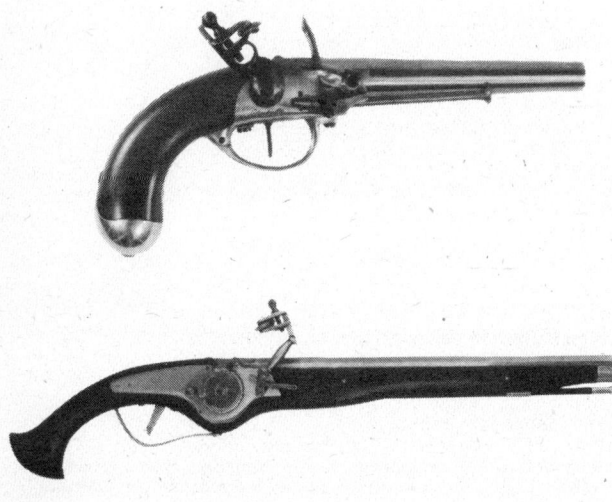

BLACK WATCH SCOTCH PISTOL
Caliber: 58.
Barrel: 7".
Weight: 1½ lbs. **Length:** 12" over-all.
Stock: Brass.
Sights: None.
Features: Faithful reproduction of this military flintlock. From Dixie, Hopkins & Allen, Navy Arms.
Price: .... $99.95 to $125.00

TOWER FLINTLOCK PISTOL
Caliber: 45, 69.
Barrel: 8¼".
Weight: 40 oz. **Length:** 14" over-all.
Stock: Walnut.
Sights: Fixed.
Features: Engraved lock, brass furniture. Specifications, including caliber, weight and length may vary with importers. Available as flint or percussion. Imported by F.I.E., CVA (only percussion in finished form.)
Price: $59.95
Price: Kit form, flintlock (CVA) $46.95
Price: Kit form, percussion (CVA) $51.95

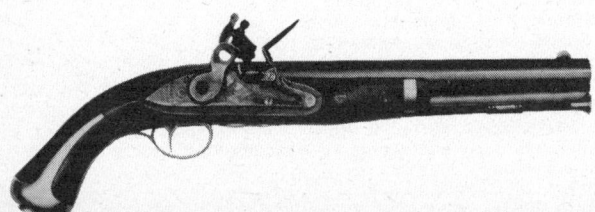

HARPER'S FERRY 1806 PISTOL
Caliber: 54.
Barrel: 10".
Weight: 40 oz. **Length:** 16" over-all.
Stock: Walnut.
Sights: Fixed.
Features: Case hardened lock, brass mounted browned bbl. Replica of the first U.S. Gov't.-made flintlock pistol. Imported by Navy Arms, Hawes.
Price: .... $95.00 to $125.00

CAUTION: PRICES CHANGE. CHECK AT GUNSHOP.

BLACK POWDER SINGLE SHOT PISTOLS—FLINT & PERCUSSION

KENTUCKY FLINTLOCK PISTOL
Caliber: 44, 45.
Barrel: 10⅛".
Weight: 32 oz. **Length:** 15½" over-all.
Stock: Walnut.
Sights: Fixed.
Features: Case hardened lock, blued bbl.; available also as brass bbl. flint Model 1821 ($110.00, Navy). Imported by Navy Arms, The Armoury, Century, F.I.E., Dixie (made in Belgium, has brass buttcap, illus.), CVA (kit only), Hawes, Kassnar, Hopkins & Allen.
Price: .... $40.95 to $142.00
Price: In kit form, from $112.00
Price: Brass barrel (Navy Arms) $110.00

Kentucky Percussion Pistol
Similar to flint version but percussion lock. Imported by The Armoury, Navy Arms, F.I.E., Hawes, CVA, Dixie, Century, Markwell, Armsport, Sile, Hopkins & Allen.
Price: .... $26.95 to $91.80
Price: Brass barrel $132.00
Price: In kit form .... $35.95 to $102.00

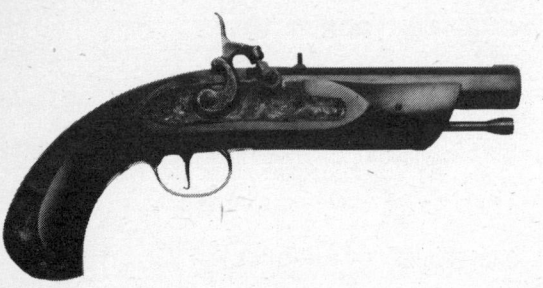

CVA COLONIAL PISTOL
Caliber: 45 (.451" bore).
Barrel: 6¾", octagonal, rifled.
Length: 12¾" over-all.
Stock: Selected hardwood.
Features: Case hardened lock, brass furniture, fixed sights. Available in either flint or percussion. Imported by CVA.
Price: Percussion $56.95
Also available in kit form, either flint or percussion. Stock 95% inletted.
Price: Flint $41.45
Price: Percussion $34.95

CVA PERCUSSION MOUNTAIN PISTOL
Caliber: 45 or 50 cal.
Barrel: 9", octagon. 15/16" across flats.
Weight: 43 oz. **Length:** 15" over-all.
Stock: American maple.
Sights: German silver blade front, fixed primitive rear.
Features: Engraved percussion-style lock. Adjustable sear engagement. Fly and bridle. Hooked breech. Browned steel on finished pistol. German silver wedge plates. Stainless steel nipples. Hardwood ramrod. Belt hook. Introduced 1978. From CVA.
Price: $103.45
Price: Kit form $79.95

KENTUCKY BELT PERCUSSION PISTOL
Caliber: 45.
Barrel: 7", rifled.
Weight: 29 oz. **Length:** 12" over-all.
Stock: Walnut.
Sights: Fixed.
Features: Engraved lock, brass furniture, steel ramrod. Available as flint or percussion. Imported by Hawes.
Price: $68.95
Price: Kit form $44.95

DIXIE OVERCOAT PISTOL
Caliber: 39.
Barrel: 4", smoothbore.
Weight: 13 oz. **Length:** 8" over-all.
Stock: Walnut-finished hardwood. Checkered p.g.
Sights: Fixed.
Features: Shoots .380" balls. Breech plug and engraved lock are burnished steel finish; barrel and trigger guard blued.
Price: Plain model $26.95
Price: Engraved model $34.50

DIXIE LINCOLN DERRINGER
Caliber: 41.
Barrel: 2", 8 lands, 8 grooves.
Weight: 7 oz. **Length:** 5½" over-all.
Stock: Walnut finish, checkered.
Sights: Fixed.
Features: Authentic copy of the "Lincoln Derringer." Shoots .400" patched ball. German silver furniture includes trigger guard with pineapple finial, wedge plates, nose, wrist, side and teardrop inlays. All furniture, lockplate, hammer, and breech plug engraved. Imported from Italy by Dixie Gun Works.
Price: With wooden case $144.95
Price: Kit (Not engraved) $54.95

BLACK POWDER SINGLE SHOT PISTOLS—FLINT & PERCUSSION

PHILADELPHIA DERRINGER PERCUSSION PISTOL
Caliber: 41, 45.
Barrel: 3⅛".
Weight: 14 oz. **Length:** 7" over-all.
Stock: Walnut, checkered grip.
Sights: Fixed.
Features: Engraved wedge holder and bbl. Also available in flintlock version (Armoury, $29.95). Imported by Sile (45-cal. only), Hawes, CVA. Hopkins & Allen.
Price: .... $18.37 to $107.50
Price: Kit form (CVA) $31.95

DIXIE BRASS FRAME DERRINGER
Caliber: 41.
Barrel: 2½".
Weight: 7 oz. **Length:** 5½" over-all.
Stock: Walnut.
Features: Brass frame, color case hardened hammer and trigger. Shoots .395" round ball. Engraved model available. From Dixie Gun Works.
Price: Plain model $39.50
Price: Engraved model $49.95

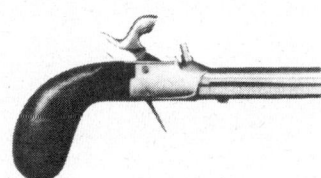

Richland "Mississippi Derringer"
Similar to Dixie Brass Frame Derringer except over-all length is 5⅜". Comes complete or as kit.
Price: Complete $29.95
Price: Kit form $23.95

CLASSIC ARMS ELGIN CUTLASS PISTOL
Caliber: 44 (.440").
Barrel: 4¼".
Weight: 21 oz. **Length:** 12" over-all.
Stock: Walnut.
Sights: None.
Features: Replica of the pistol used by the U.S. Navy as a boarding weapon. Smoothbore barrel. Available as a kit or finished. From Classic Arms Ltd.
Price: Kit $69.95
Price: Finished $89.95

> Consult our Directory pages for the location of firms mentioned.

BUCCANEER DOUBLE BARREL PISTOL
Caliber: 36, 44 or 45 (Hawes).
Barrel: 9½".
Weight: 40 oz. **Length:** 15½" over-all.
Stock: Walnut, one piece.
Sights: Fixed.
Features: Case hardened and engraved lockplate, solid brass fittings. Percussion or flintlock. Imported by Hawes Firearms, The Armoury (44-cal. only). Available as the "Corsair" from Armsport (44 cal. only).
Price: Complete .... $73.95 to $109.95
Price: Kit form .... $61.95 to $65.95
Price: Corsair, complete .... $99.50 Kit $86.00

DIXIE PHILADELPHIA DERRINGER
Caliber: 41.
Barrel: 3½", octagon.
Weight: 8 oz. **Length:** 5½" over-all.
Stock: Walnut, checkered p.g.
Sights: Fixed.
Features: Barrel and lock are blued; brass furniture. From Dixie Gun Works.
Price: $39.95

Armsport New Orleans Derringer
Similar to Dixie Brass Frame Derringer shown nearby. Available either complete or in kit form. From Armsport.
Price: Complete $45.00
Price: Kit form $32.50

T.G.A. LIEGE DERRINGER
Caliber: 451".
Barrel: 2⅜".
Weight: 7 oz. **Length:** 6½" over-all.
Stock: Walnut.
Sights: None.
Features: Removable round, rifled barrel. All metal parts case-hardened. Folding trigger. Introduced 1980. From Trail Guns Armory.
Price: $55.00

BOUNTY HUNTER PERCUSSION PISTOL
Caliber: 44.
Barrel: 17".
Weight: 3½ lbs. **Length:** 22" over-all.
Stock: Oil stained walnut.
Sights: Fixed.
Features: A Kentucky-style pistol with long barrel. Polish brass furniture, blued barrel, color case hardened lock. Kit or complete. From Hopkins & Allen.
Price: $86.95

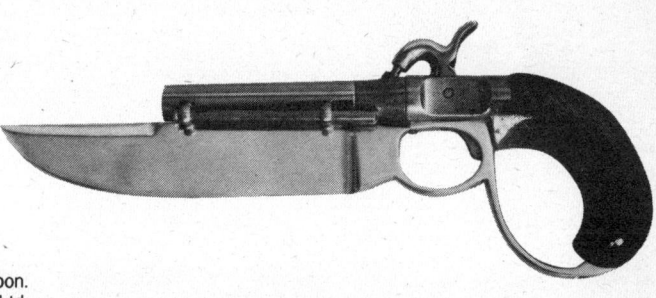

HOPKINS & ALLEN BOOT PISTOL
Caliber: 36 or 45.
Barrel: 6".
Weight: 42 oz. **Length:** 13" over-all.
Stock: Walnut.
Sights: Silver blade front; rear adj. for e.
Features: Under-hammer design. From Hopkins & Allen.
Price: $69.95

BLACK POWDER SINGLE SHOT PISTOLS—FLINT & PERCUSSION

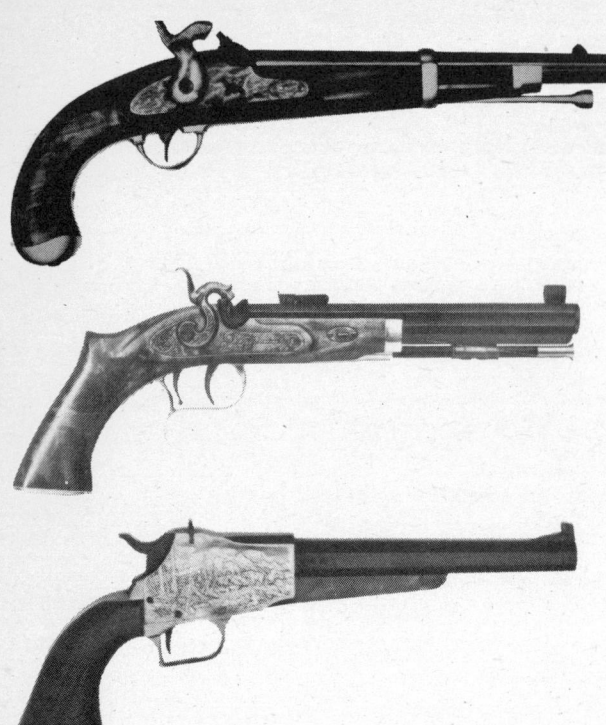

HARPER'S FERRY MODEL 1855 PERCUSSION PISTOL
Caliber: 58.
Barrel: 11¾", rifled.
Weight: 56 oz. **Length:** 18" over-all.
Stock: Walnut.
Sights: Fixed.
Features: Case hardened lock and hammer; brass furniture; blued bbl. Shoulder stock available, priced at $35.00. Imported by Navy Arms.
Price: $150.00
Price: With detachable shoulder stock $190.00

THOMPSON/CENTER PATRIOT PERCUSSION PISTOL
Caliber: 45.
Barrel: 9¼".
Weight: 36 oz. **Length:** 16" over-all.
Stock: Walnut.
Sights: Patridge-type. Rear adj. for w. and e.
Features: Hook breech system; double set triggers; coil mainspring. From Thompson/Center Arms.
Price: $155.00

TROPHY WINNER PERCUSSION TARGET PISTOL
Caliber: 44.
Barrel: 10" octagonal.
Weight: 42 oz.
Stocks: Walnut.
Sights: Bead front, rear adj. for w. and e.
Features: Engraved scenes on frame sides; brass backstrap and trigger guard; case hardened frame and hammer. Imported by Dixie.
Price: $79.95
Price: Optional 28-ga. shotgun barrel, 10" long $12.95

BLACK POWDER REVOLVERS

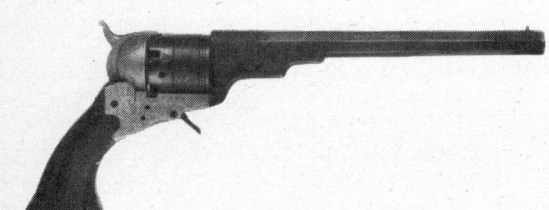

NAVY ARMS COLT PATTERSON
Caliber: 36, 6-shot.
Barrel: 9".
Weight: 2½ lbs. **Length:** 14" over-all.
Stocks: Walnut.
Sights: Fixed.
Features: Made in a limited edition of 500 standard guns and 50 engraved models. Imported by Navy Arms.
Price: Standard $195.00
Price: Engraved $500.00

COLT 1847 WALKER PERCUSSION REVOLVER
Caliber: 44.
Barrel: 9", 7 groove, RH twist.
Weight: 73 oz.
Stocks: One-piece walnut.
Sights: German silver front sight, hammer notch rear.
Features: Made in U.S. by Colt. Faithful reproduction of the original gun, including markings. Color cased frame, hammer, loading lever and plunger. Blue steel backstrap, brass square-back trigger guard. Blued barrel, cylinder, trigger and wedge. Accessories available. Re-introduced 1979.
Price: $446.95

WALKER 1847 PERCUSSION REVOLVER
Caliber: 44, 6-shot.
Barrel: 9".
Weight: 72 oz. **Length:** 15½" over-all.
Stocks: Walnut.
Sights: Fixed.
Features: Case hardened frame, loading lever and hammer; iron backstrap; brass trigger guard; engraved cylinder. Imported by Sile, Navy Arms.
Price: .... $125.00 to $150.65

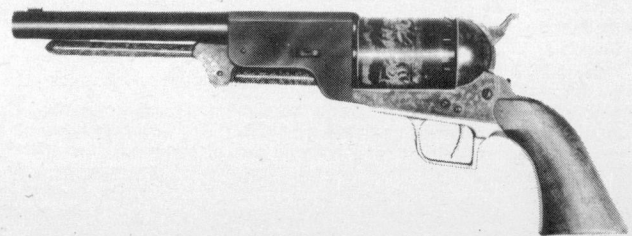

BLACK POWDER REVOLVERS

COLT 1st MODEL DRAGOON
Caliber: 44.
Barrel: 7½", part round, part octagon.
Weight: 66 oz.
Stocks: One piece walnut.
Sights: German silver blade front, hammer notch rear.
Features: First model has oval bolt cuts in cylinder, square-back flared trigger guard, V-type mainspring, short trigger. Ranger and Indian scene on cylinder. Color cased frame, loading lever, plunger and hammer; blue barrel, cylinder, trigger and wedge. Polished brass backstrap and trigger guard. Re-introduced in 1979. From Colt.
Price: $356.95

Colt 2nd Model Dragoon Revolver
Similar to the 1st Model except this model is distinguished by its rectangular bolt cuts in the cylinder, straight square-back trigger guard, short trigger and flat mainspring with roller in hammer.
Price: $356.95

COLT BABY DRAGOON REVOLVER
Caliber: 31.
Barrel: 4", 7 groove, RH twist.
Weight: About 21 oz.
Stocks: Varnished walnut.
Sights: Brass pin front, hammer notch rear.
Features: Unfluted cylinder with Ranger and Indian scene; cupped cylinder pin; no grease grooves; one safety pin on cylinder and slot in hammer face; straight (flat) mainspring. Silver backstrap and trigger guard. Re-introduced in 1979. From Colt.
Price: $322.50

Colt 3rd Model Dragoon Revolver
Similar to the 1st Model except has oval trigger guard, long trigger, flat mainspring and rectangular bolt cuts.
Price: $356.95

SECOND MODEL DRAGOON 1848 REVOLVER
Caliber: 44, 6-shot.
Barrel: 7½".
Weight: 64 oz. **Length:** 14" over-all.
Stocks: One piece walnut.
Sights: Fixed.
Features: Case hardened frame, loading lever and hammer; engraved cylinder scene; safety notches on hammer, safety pin in cylinder. Imported by Sile, Dixie and Navy Arms. First and Third Models also available.
Price: .... $137.50 to $150.65
Price: Third Model $150.65

BABY DRAGOON 1848 PERCUSSION REVOLVER
Caliber: 31, 5-shot.
Barrel: 4", 5", 6".
Weight: 24 oz. (6" bbl.). **Length:** 10½" (6" bbl.).
Stocks: Walnut.
Sights: Fixed.
Features: Case hardened frame; safety notches on hammer and safety pin in cylinder; engraved cylinder scene; octagonal bbl. Imported by Sile, F.I.E., Hawes.
Price: .... $54.95 to $88.00
Price: Kit form (F.I.E. Corp.) $52.50
Price: Fully engraved (F.I.E. Corp.) $60.95

Consult our Directory pages for the location of firms mentioned.

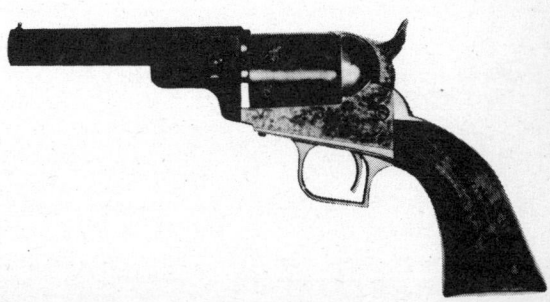

1850 WELLS FARGO PERCUSSION REVOLVER
Caliber: 31, 5-shot.
Barrel: 3", 4", 5", 6".
Weight: 22 oz.
Stocks: Walnut.
Sights: Fixed.
Features: No loading lever; square-back trigger guard; case hardened frame and hammer; engraved cylinder; brass trigger guard and back-strap. Imported by Hawes.
Price: $95.00
Price: Kit form $91.95

CAUTION: PRICES CHANGE. CHECK AT GUNSHOP.

BLACK POWDER REVOLVERS

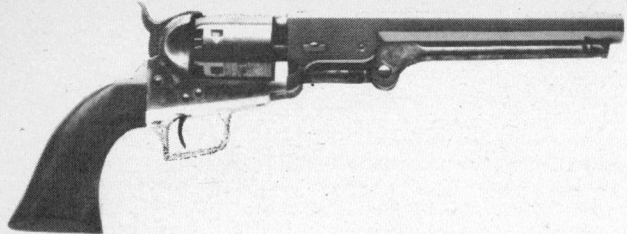

Colt 1861 Navy Percussion Revolver
Similar to 1851 Navy except has round 7½" barrel, rounded trigger guard, German silver blade front sight, "creeping" loading lever.
Price: **$333.95**

COLT 1851 NAVY PERCUSSION REVOLVER
Caliber: 36.
Barrel: 7½", octagonal, 7 groove, LH twist.
Weight: 42 oz.
Stocks: One-piece varnished walnut.
Sights: Brass pin front, hammer notch rear.
Features: Made in U.S. by Colt. Faithful reproduction of the original gun. Color cased frame, loading lever, plunger, hammer and latch. Blue cylinder, trigger, barrel, screws, wedge. Silver plated brass backstrap and square-back trigger guard. Accessories available. Re-introduced in 1979.
Price: **$333.95**

Lyman 1851 Squareback Navy 36
Same as standard Colt model except 36 cal. only, has square-back trigger guard, nickel plated backstrap, color case hardened frame **$149.95**
Price: Kit form **$109.95**

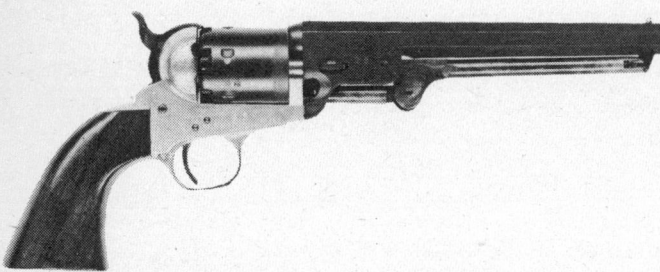

1851 NAVY-SHERIFF
Same as 1851 Sheriff model except: 4" barrel, fluted cylinder, belt ring in butt. Imported by Navy Arms, Hawes, Richland, Armoury, Euroarms of America.
Price: .... **$50.00 to $114.95**
Price: Kit form (Hawes) **$44.95**

NAVY MODEL 1851 PERCUSSION REVOLVER
Caliber: 36 or 44, 6-shot.
Barrel: 7½".
Weight: 42 oz. **Length:** 13" over-all.
Stocks: Walnut finish.
Sights: Fixed.
Features: Brass backstrap and trigger guard; some have engraved cylinder with navy battle scene; case hardened frame, hammer, loading lever. Imported by Shore, (36 cal. only), The Armoury, Navy Arms, Hawes, Valor, Century, F.I.E., Dixie, (illus.) Richland, Euroarms of America, Kassnar, Sile, Armsport, Hopkins & Allen.
Price: Brass frame .... **$31.50 to $108.95**
Price: Steel frame .... **$40.95 to $110.00**
Price: Kit form .... **$30.95 to $66.50**
Price: Engraved model (F.I.E., Dixie) .... **$51.50 to $52.95**
Price: Also as "Hartford Pistol," Kit (Richland) .. **$59.95** Complete . **$79.95**
Price: Also as "Hartford Dragoon Buntline" (Hopkins & Allen) **$166.95**

ARMY 1851 PERCUSSION REVOLVER
Caliber: 44, 6-shot.
Barrel: 7½".
Weight: 45 oz. **Length:** 13" over-all.
Stocks: Walnut finish.
Sights: Fixed.
Features: 44 caliber version of the 1851 Navy. Imported by Sile, Valor, The Armoury, Richland.
Price: .... **$33.50 to $138.00**

1851 SHERIFF MODEL PERCUSSION REVOLVER
Caliber: 36, 44, 6-shot.
Barrel: 5".
Weight: 40 oz. **Length:** 10½" over-all.
Stocks: Walnut.
Sights: Fixed.
Features: Brass back strap and trigger guard; engraved navy scene; case hardened frame, hammer, loading lever. Available with brass frame from some importers at slightly lower prices. Imported by Sile, The Armoury, Navy Arms, Hawes, Richland.
Price: Steel frame .... **$41.95 to $110.00**
Price: Brass frame .... **$34.95 to $102.00**
Price: Kit, brass or steel frame (Hawes, Sile) .... **$66.15 to $87.40**

NEW MODEL 1858 ARMY PERCUSSION REVOLVER
Caliber: 36 or 44, 6-shot.
Barrel: 6½" or 8".
Weight: 40 oz. **Length:** 13½" over-all.
Stocks: Walnut.
Sights: Fixed.
Features: Replica of Remington Model 1858. Also available from some importers as Army Model Belt Revolver in 36 cal., shortened and lightened version of the 44. Target Model (Hawes, Iver Johnson, Navy) has fully adj. target rear sight, target front, 36 or 44 ($74.95-$152.45). Imported by Navy Arms, Century, F.I.E., Hawes, Valor, Iver Johnson, The Armoury, Shore (44 cal., 8" bbl. only), Richland, Euroarms of America (engraved and plain), Armsport, Hopkins & Allen, Sile, Kassnar.
Price: .... **$49.95 to $128.95**
Price: Kit form .... **$66.95 to $106.95**
Price: Nickel finish (Navy Arms) **$125.00**
Price: Stainless steel (Euroarms, Navy Arms, Sile) .... **$140.00 to $175.90**
Price: Target model (Hawes, Sile, Euroarms, H & A) ... **$95.95 to $149.95**

LYMAN 44 NEW MODEL ARMY REVOLVER
Caliber: 44, 6-shot.
Barrel: 8".
Weight: 40 oz. **Length:** 13½" over-all.
Stock: Walnut.
Sights: Fixed.
Features: Replica of 1858 Remington. Brass trigger guard and backstrap, case hardened hammer and trigger. Solid frame with top strap. Heavy duty nipples. From Lyman Products.
Price: **$155.95**
Price: Kit form **$119.95**

COLT 1860 ARMY PERCUSSION REVOLVER
Caliber: 44.
Barrel: 8", 7 grooves, LH twist.
Weight: 42 oz.
Stocks: One-piece walnut.
Sights: German silver front sight, hammer notch rear.
Features: Made in U.S. by Colt. Steel backstrap cut for shoulder stock; brass trigger guard. Cylinder has Navy scene. Color case hardened frame, hammer, loading lever. Basically a continuation of production with all original markings, etc. Original-type accessories available. Re-introduced 1979.
Price: **$342.50**

BLACK POWDER REVOLVERS

1860 ARMY PERCUSSION REVOLVER
Caliber: 44, 6-shot.
Barrel: 8".
Weight: 40 oz. **Length:** 13⅝" over-all.
Stocks: Walnut.
Sights: Fixed.
Features: Engraved navy scene on cylinder; brass trigger guard; case hardened frame, loading lever and hammer. Some importers supply pistol cut for detachable shoulder stock, have accessory stock available. Imported by Navy Arms, Shore, The Armoury, Dixie (half-fluted cylinder, not roll engraved), Lyman, Iver Johnson, Richland, Euroarms of America (engraved model), Armsport, Sile, Hawes.
Price: .... $44.95 to $162.00
1861 Navy: Same as Army except 36 cal., 7½" bbl., wt. 41 oz., cut for stock; round cylinder (fluted avail.), from Navy/Replica $110.00
Price: Kit (Lyman) $119.95

Colt 1862 Pocket Police Revolver
Similar to 1862 Pocket Navy except has 5½" round barrel, fluted cylinder, different markings and loading lever. Faithful reproduction of the original gun.
Price: $313.50

Consult our Directory pages for the location of firms mentioned.

1861 NAVY MODEL REVOLVER
Caliber: 36, 6-shot.
Barrel: 7½".
Weight: 2½ lbs. **Length:** 13" over-all.
Stocks: One piece smooth walnut.
Sights: Fixed.
Features: Shoots .380" ball. Case-hardened frame, loading lever and hammer. Cut for shoulder stock. Non-fluted cylinder. From Navy Arms, Iver Johnson, Euroarms of America.
Price: .... $100.00 to $110.00
Price: With full fluted cyl. .... $100.00 to $104.95

COLT 1862 POCKET NAVY PERCUSSION REVOLVER
Caliber: 36.
Barrel: 5½", octagonal, 7 groove, LH twist.
Weight: 27 oz.
Stocks: One piece varnished walnut.
Sights: Brass pin front, hammer notch rear.
Features: Made in U.S. by Colt. Rebated cylinder, hinged loading lever, silver plated backstrap and trigger guard, color cased frame, hammer, loading lever, plunger and latch, rest blued. Has original-type markings. Re-introduced 1979.
Price: $313.50

1862 POLICE MODEL PERCUSSION REVOLVER
Caliber: 36, 5-shot.
Barrel: 4½", 5½", 6½".
Weight: 26 oz. **Length:** 12" (6½" bbl.).
Stocks: Walnut.
Sights: Fixed.
Features: Half-fluted and rebated cylinder; case hardened frame, loading lever and hammer; brass trigger guard and back strap. Imported by Sile, Navy Arms, Euroarms of America.
Price: $125.00
Price: Cased with accessories $140.00

1853 POCKET NAVY MODEL REVOLVER
Caliber: 36, 6-shot.
Barrel: 4½", 5½", 6½".
Weight: 26 oz. **Length:** 12" over-all (6½" bbl.).
Stocks: Smooth walnut.
Sights: Fixed.
Features: Shortened version of std. Navy model. Case hardened frame, hammer and loading lever; brass backstrap and trigger guard. Imported by Navy Arms.
Price: $125.00

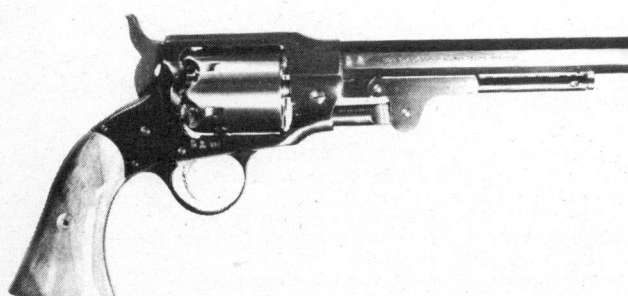

ROGERS & SPENCER PERCUSSION REVOLVER
Caliber: 44.
Barrel: 7½".
Weight: 47 oz. **Length:** 13¾" over-all.
Stocks: Walnut.
Sights: Cone front, integral groove in frame for rear.
Features: Accurate reproduction of a Civil War design. Solid frame; extra large nipple cut-out on rear of cylinder; loading lever and cylinder easily removed for cleaning. Comes with six spare nipples and wrench/screwdriver. From Euroarms of America, Navy Arms, Dixie.
Price: About $120.00
Price: Nickel plated $120.00
Price: Kit version $95.00
Price: Target version (Dixie) $160.00

BLACK POWDER REVOLVERS

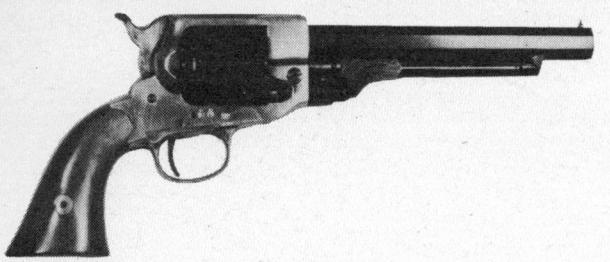

SPILLER & BURR REVOLVER
Caliber: 36.
Barrel: 7", octagon.
Weight: 2½ lbs. **Length:** 12½" over-all.
Stocks: Two-piece walnut.
Sights: Fixed.
Features: Reproduction of the C.S.A. revolver. Brass frame and trigger guard. Also available as a kit. From Dixie, Navy Arms, Richland, Armsport.
Price: .... $69.95 to $100.00
Price: Kit form .... $39.95 to $65.00

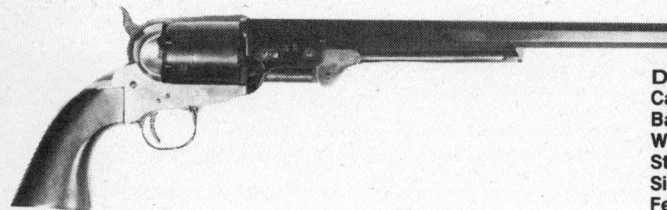

DIXIE "WYATT EARP" REVOLVER
Caliber: 44.
Barrel: 12" octagon.
Weight: 46 oz. **Length:** 18" over-all.
Stock: Two piece walnut.
Sights: Fixed.
Features: Highly polished brass frame, backstrap and trigger guard; blued barrel and cylinder; case hardened hammer, trigger and loading lever. Navy-size shoulder stock ($40.00) will fit with minor fitting. From Dixie Gun Works.
Price: $79.50

GRISWOLD & GUNNISON PERCUSSION REVOLVER
Caliber: 36, 44, 6-shot.
Barrel: 7½".
Weight: 44 oz. (36 cal.). **Length:** 13" over-all.
Stocks: Walnut.
Sights: Fixed.
Features: Replica of famous Confederate pistol. Brass frame, backstrap and trigger guard; case hardened loading lever; rebated cylinder (44 cal. only). Imported by Navy Arms.
Price: $74.95
Price: As above from Sile (1851 Confederate) $75.90

RICHLAND 44 BALLISTER REVOLVER
Caliber: 44, 6-shot.
Barrel: 12".
Weight: 2¾ lbs.
Stocks: Two-piece walnut.
Sights: Fixed.
Features: Barrel and cylinder blued, frame and trigger guard are brass; hammer and loading lever are color case hardened. From Richland Arms.
Price: $78.00

RUGER 44 OLD ARMY PERCUSSION REVOLVER
Caliber: 44, 6-shot. Uses .457" dia. lead bullets.
Barrel: 7½" (6-groove, 16" twist).
Weight: 46 oz. **Length:** 13½" over-all.
Stocks: Smooth walnut.
Sights: Ramp front, rear adj. for w. and e.
Features: Stainless steel standard size nipples, chrome-moly steel cylinder and frame, same lockwork as in original Super Blackhawk. Also available in stainless steel in very limited quantities. Made in USA. From Sturm, Ruger & Co.
Price: Stainless steel $225.00
Price: Blued steel $172.50

BLACK POWDER MUSKETS & RIFLES

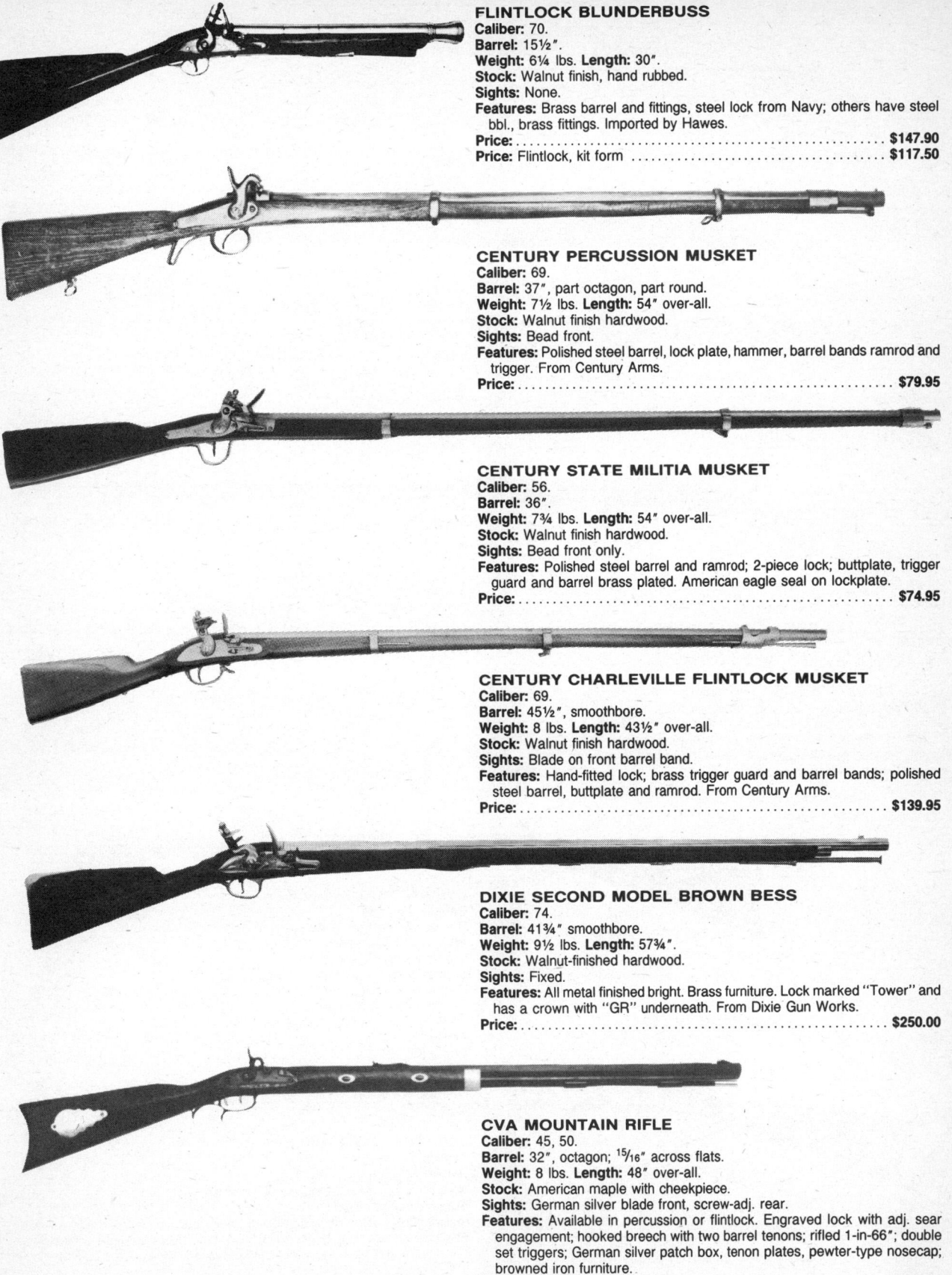

FLINTLOCK BLUNDERBUSS
Caliber: 70.
Barrel: 15½".
Weight: 6¼ lbs. **Length:** 30".
Stock: Walnut finish, hand rubbed.
Sights: None.
Features: Brass barrel and fittings, steel lock from Navy; others have steel bbl., brass fittings. Imported by Hawes.
Price: $147.90
Price: Flintlock, kit form $117.50

CENTURY PERCUSSION MUSKET
Caliber: 69.
Barrel: 37", part octagon, part round.
Weight: 7½ lbs. **Length:** 54" over-all.
Stock: Walnut finish hardwood.
Sights: Bead front.
Features: Polished steel barrel, lock plate, hammer, barrel bands ramrod and trigger. From Century Arms.
Price: $79.95

CENTURY STATE MILITIA MUSKET
Caliber: 56.
Barrel: 36".
Weight: 7¾ lbs. **Length:** 54" over-all.
Stock: Walnut finish hardwood.
Sights: Bead front only.
Features: Polished steel barrel and ramrod; 2-piece lock; buttplate, trigger guard and barrel brass plated. American eagle seal on lockplate.
Price: $74.95

CENTURY CHARLEVILLE FLINTLOCK MUSKET
Caliber: 69.
Barrel: 45½", smoothbore.
Weight: 8 lbs. **Length:** 43½" over-all.
Stock: Walnut finish hardwood.
Sights: Blade on front barrel band.
Features: Hand-fitted lock; brass trigger guard and barrel bands; polished steel barrel, buttplate and ramrod. From Century Arms.
Price: $139.95

DIXIE SECOND MODEL BROWN BESS
Caliber: 74.
Barrel: 41¾" smoothbore.
Weight: 9½ lbs. **Length:** 57¾".
Stock: Walnut-finished hardwood.
Sights: Fixed.
Features: All metal finished bright. Brass furniture. Lock marked "Tower" and has a crown with "GR" underneath. From Dixie Gun Works.
Price: $250.00

CVA MOUNTAIN RIFLE
Caliber: 45, 50.
Barrel: 32", octagon; 15/16" across flats.
Weight: 8 lbs. **Length:** 48" over-all.
Stock: American maple with cheekpiece.
Sights: German silver blade front, screw-adj. rear.
Features: Available in percussion or flintlock. Engraved lock with adj. sear engagement; hooked breech with two barrel tenons; rifled 1-in-66"; double set triggers; German silver patch box, tenon plates, pewter-type nosecap; browned iron furniture.
Price: Either caliber, kit, percussion $156.95
Price: Kit, flintlock $169.95
Price: Finished rifle, percussion $234.95
Price: Finished rifle, flintlock $249.95

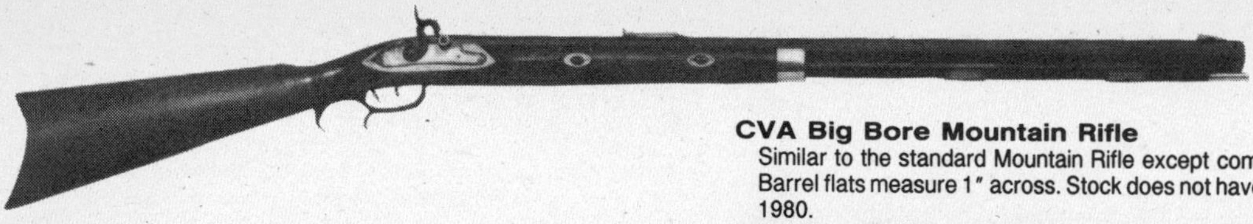

BLACK POWDER MUSKETS & RIFLES

CVA Big Bore Mountain Rifle
Similar to the standard Mountain Rifle except comes in 54 or 58 cal. only. Barrel flats measure 1" across. Stock does not have a patch box. Introduced 1980.
Price: 54 or 58 cal., complete rifle **$244.95**
Price: 54 or 58 cal., kit **$164.95**
Price: 54 cal. flintlock, kit only **$174.95**

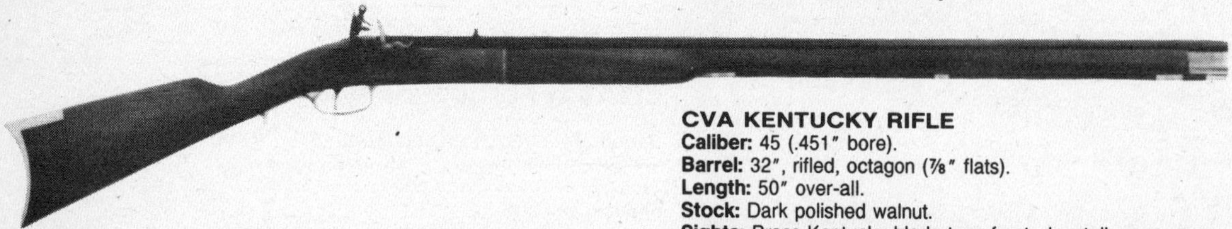

CVA KENTUCKY RIFLE
Caliber: 45 (.451" bore).
Barrel: 32", rifled, octagon (⅞" flats).
Length: 50" over-all.
Stock: Dark polished walnut.
Sights: Brass Kentucky blade type front, dovetail open rear.
Features: Available in either flint or percussion. Stainless steel nipple included. Imported by CVA.
Price: Percussion **$149.95**
Price: Flint **$157.95**
Price: Percussion Kit **$89.95**
Price: Flint Kit **$99.95**

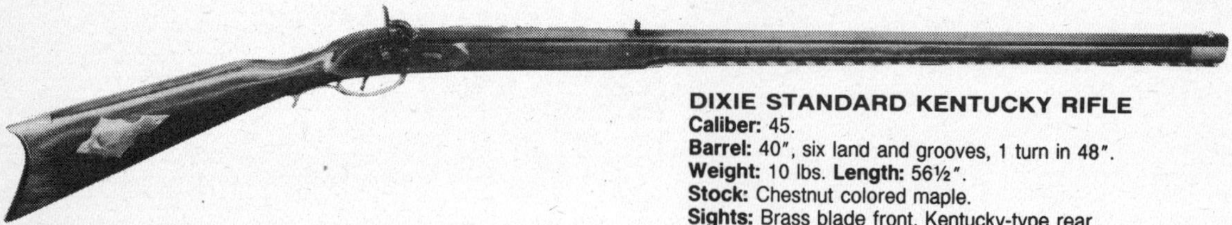

DIXIE STANDARD KENTUCKY RIFLE
Caliber: 45.
Barrel: 40", six land and grooves, 1 turn in 48".
Weight: 10 lbs. **Length:** 56½".
Stock: Chestnut colored maple.
Sights: Brass blade front, Kentucky-type rear.
Features: Trigger guard, buttplate, patchbox and thimbles are brass. Color case hardened lock. From Dixie Gun Works.
Price: Percussion **$260.00**

DIXIE TENNESSEE MOUNTAIN RIFLE
Caliber: 50.
Barrel: 41½", 6-groove rifling, brown finish.
Length: 56" over-all.
Stock: Walnut, oil finish; Kentucky-style.
Sights: Silver blade front, open buckhorn rear.
Features: Re-creation of the original mountain rifles. Early Schultz lock interchangeable flint or percussion with vent plug or drum and nipple. Tumbler has fly. Double-set triggers. All metal parts browned. From Dixie.
Price: Flint and Percussion, finished rifle **$225.00**
Price: Kit **$175.00**

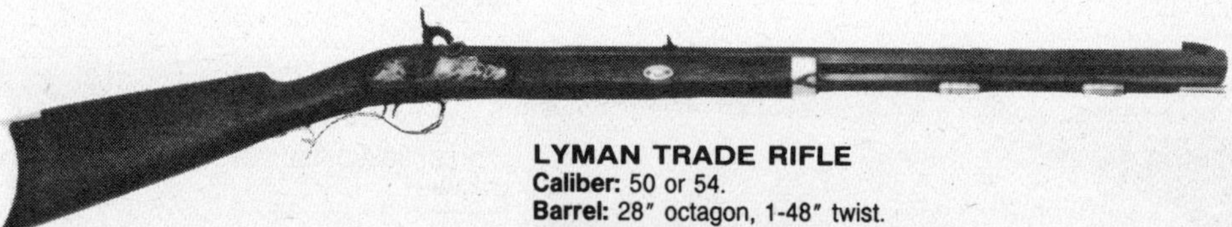

LYMAN TRADE RIFLE
Caliber: 50 or 54.
Barrel: 28" octagon, 1-48" twist.
Weight: 8¾ lbs. **Length:** 45" over-all.
Stock: European walnut.
Sights: Blade front, open rear adj. for w.
Features: Polished brass furniture with blue steel parts. Hook breech, single trigger, coil spring percussion lock. Steel barrel rib and ramrod ferrules. Percussion only. Introduced 1979. From Lyman.
Price: **$224.95**
Price: Kit **$179.95**

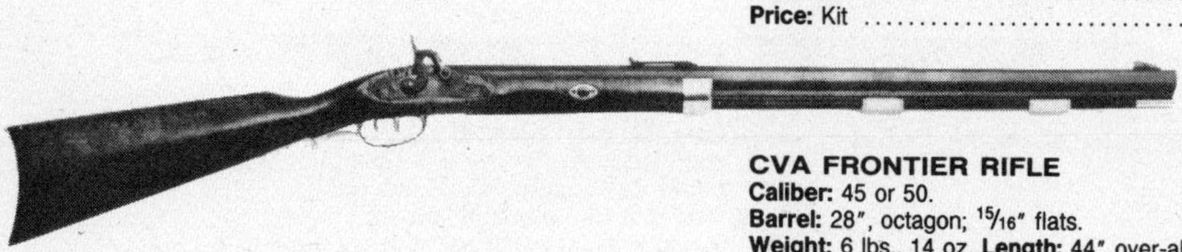

CVA FRONTIER RIFLE
Caliber: 45 or 50.
Barrel: 28", octagon; ¹⁵⁄₁₆" flats.
Weight: 6 lbs., 14 oz. **Length:** 44" over-all.
Stock: American hardwood.
Sights: Brass blade front, screw-adj. open rear.
Features: Available in flint or percussion. Solid brass nosecap, trigger guard, buttplate, thimbles and wedge plates; blued barrel; color case-hardened lock and hammer. Double set triggers, patented breech plug/bolster, V-type mainspring. Hooked breech. Introduced 1980.
Price: 45 or 50 cal., percussion, complete rifle **$179.95**
Price: 45 or 50 cal., percussion, kit **$139.95**
Price: 50 cal. flint, kit only **$149.95**

Consult our Directory pages for the location of firms mentioned.

CAUTION: PRICES CHANGE. CHECK AT GUNSHOP.

BLACK POWDER MUSKETS & RIFLES

HOPKINS & ALLEN MINUTEMAN RIFLE
Caliber: 36, 45, 50.
Barrel: 39", 15/16" octagon.
Weight: 9½ lbs.
Stock: One piece, American maple.
Sights: Silver blade front, notched Kentucky rear.
Features: Cut-rifled barrel, percussion lock with fly. Authentic Pennsylvania Bedford styling. Available as kit or assembled. Made in U.S.A. Available in flint or percussion lock.
Price: Flint, complete $289.95
Price: Percussion, complete $274.95

Hopkins & Allen Model 7000 Short Rifle
Same as H&A Minuteman except has 2-piece beech stock without patchbox. Converts easily from flint to percussion. Has 34" barrel, 15/16" diameter. Made in U.S. by H.&A. Kit or finished.
Price: Complete $131.95
Price: Kit $99.95

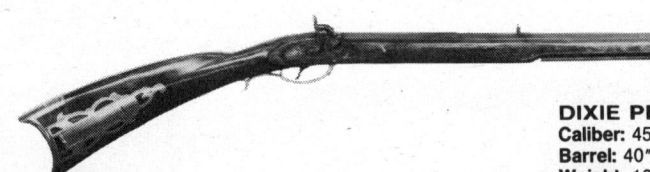

DIXIE PENNSYLVANIA PERCUSSION RIFLE
Caliber: 45.
Barrel: 40", octagon.
Weight: 10 lbs. **Length:** 55".
Stock: Maple, Roman nose comb.
Sights: Fixed, Kentucky open-type.
Features: Brass patchbox, wide buttplate, color case hardened lock, blue barrel. From Dixie Gun Works.
Price: Percussion $297.50

PENNSYLVANIA HALF-STOCK PLAINS RIFLE
Caliber: 45 or 50.
Barrel: 32", rifled, 15/16" dia.
Weight: 8½ lbs.
Stock: Walnut.
Sights: Fixed.
Features: Available in flint or percussion. Blued lock and barrel, brass furniture. Offered complete or in kit form. From Hopkins & Allen, The Armory.
Price: Flint $279.95
Price: Percussion $267.95

HOPKINS & ALLEN DELUXE BUGGY RIFLE
Caliber: 36 or 45.
Barrel: 20", octagonal.
Weight: 6½ lbs. **Length:** 37" over-all.
Stock: American walnut.
Features: A shortened version of the under-hammer Heritage rifle. Blued barrel and receiver, black plastic buttplate.
Price: $199.95

KENTUCKY FLINTLOCK RIFLE
Caliber: 44 or 45.
Barrel: 35".
Weight: 7 lbs. **Length:** 50" over-all.
Stock: Walnut stained, brass fittings.
Sights: Fixed.
Features: Available in Carbine model also, 28" bbl. Some variations in detail, finish. Kits also available from some importers. Imported by Navy Arms, The Armoury, Century, Challenger, F.I.E., Hawes, Kassnar, CVA, Armsport, Hopkins & Allen, Sile, Shore (45-cal. only).
Price: .... $59.95 to $200.00
Price: Kit form (CVA, Numrich, Hawes, F.I.E., Sile) ..... $72.95 to $171.50
Price: Deluxe model, flint or percussion (Navy Arms, Sile), about . $375.00

Kentucky Percussion Rifle
Similar to flintlock except percussion lock. Finish and features vary with importer. Imported by Navy Arms, F.I.E. Corp., The Armoury, Challenger, Dixie, CVA, Valor, Hawes, Kassnar, Armsport (rifle-shotgun combo), Shore, Sile.
Price: .... $54.95 to $229.95
Price: Kit form (F.I.E., Sile) $151.80
Price: Armsport combo $210.00

DIXIE PLAINSMAN RIFLE
Caliber: 45 or 50.
Barrel: 32", octagon.
Weight: 8 lbs. **Length:** 47½".
Stock: Cherry wood.
Sights: Brass blade front, buckhorn rear.
Features: Bolster-type breech plug with blow-out screw, brass stock furniture.
Price: $205.00

KENTUCKIAN RIFLE & CARBINE
Caliber: 44.
Barrel: 35" (Rifle), 27½" (Carbine).
Weight: 7 lbs. (Rifle), 5½ lbs. (Carbine). **Length:** 51" (Rifle) over-all, carbine 43".
Stock: Walnut stain.
Sights: Brass blade front, steel V-Ramp rear.
Features: Octagon bbl., case hardened and engraved lock plate. Brass furniture. Imported by Dixie, Euroarms of America.
Price: Rifle or carbine, flint or percussion .... $135.00 to $145.00

DIXIE FLINT SWIVEL BREECH RIFLE
Caliber: 45.
Barrel: 32", octagon.
Weight: 11½ lbs. **Length:** 48½" over-all.
Stock: Curly maple.
Sights: Fixed.
Features: Wood panelled barrels rotate for second shot. Single trigger. Brass furniture. From Dixie Gun Works.
Price: Flintlock $540.00
Price: Percussion $415.00

CAUTION: PRICES CHANGE. CHECK AT GUNSHOP.

BLACK POWDER MUSKETS & RIFLES

YORK COUNTY RIFLE
Caliber: 45.
Barrel: 36", rifled, 7/8" octagon, blue.
Weight: 7½ lbs. **Length:** 51½" over-all.
Stock: Maple, one piece.
Sights: Blade front, V-notch rear, brass.
Features: Adjustable double-set triggers. Brass trigger guard, patchbox, buttplate, nosecap and sideplate. Case-hardened lockplate. From Dixie Gun Works.
Price: Percussion $152.95
Price: Flint $162.95

MOWREY GEORGIA TREE GUN
Caliber: 54, 58.
Barrel: 22".
Weight: 7¼ lbs. **Length:** 38" over-all.
Stock: Walnut.
Sights: Blade front, step adj. rear.
Features: Shortened version of Allen & Thurber Special rifle especially suited for tree stand shooting. Made by Mowrey, available from Interarms.
Price: Complete gun $239.00

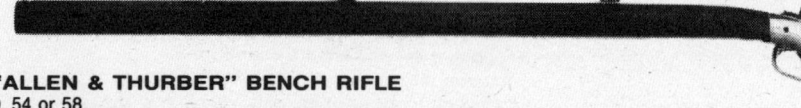

MOWREY "ALLEN & THURBER" BENCH RIFLE
Caliber: 45, 50, 54 or 58.
Barrel: 36" over-all with false muzzle. 1½" octagon.
Weight: 24½ lbs. **Length:** 54" over-all.
Stock: Cherry wood with large cheekpiece, Schalk-type brass buttplate. Finished with 10 coats of hand-rubbed oil.
Sights: Available with target peep or non-magnifying tube sight.
Features: Polished solid brass furniture, browned iron. Introduced 1977. From Mowrey Gun Works.
Price: With peep sight $415.00
Price: With tube sight $498.50

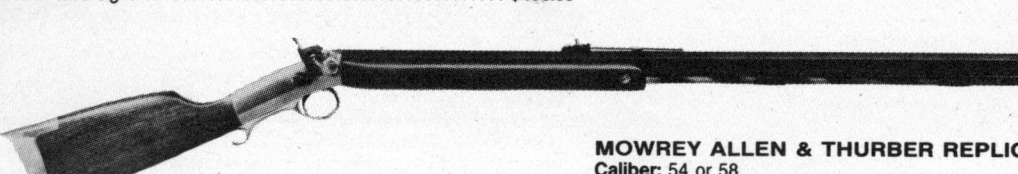

MOWREY ALLEN & THURBER REPLICA
Caliber: 54 or 58.
Barrel: 32", 8-groove rifling, octagon.
Weight: 10¼ lbs. **Length:** 48" over-all.
Stock: Walnut with curved brass buttplate.
Sights: Open, adj. for w. & e.
Features: Polished brass furniture, brass fore-end, ramrod. Made by Mowrey, available from Interarms.
Price: Complete $229.00

MOWREY HAWK
Caliber: 45, 50, 54 or 58.
Barrel: 32".
Weight: 9½ lbs. **Length:** 49" over-all.
Stock: Walnut, sporter-type with cheek-piece, walnut fore-end.
Sights: Open, fully adj. for w. and e.
Features: Hawkins-type buttplate and action housing of brass. Adj. trigger. Made by Mowrey, available from Interarms.
Price: Complete $249.00

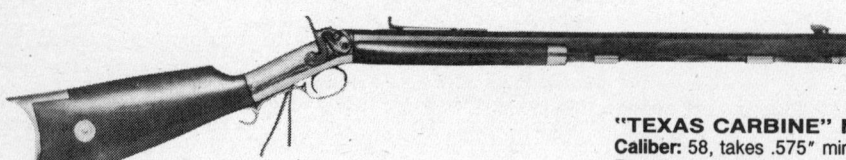

"TEXAS CARBINE" Model 1 of 1000
Caliber: 58, takes .575" mini-ball or round ball.
Barrel: 24" octagon, 4-groove.
Weight: 8 lbs. **Length:** 39" over-all.
Stock: Walnut stock and fore-end, brass fore-end cap.
Sights: Adjustable front and rear.
Features: Model "1 of 1000". Saddle ring with leather thong and Texas seal imbedded in stock. Distributed by Trail Guns Armory.
Price: $250.00

RICHLAND MICHIGAN RIFLE
Caliber: 45, 50.
Barrel: 26" octagon, 7/8" flats.
Weight: 5¾ lbs. **Length:** 41⅜" over-all.
Stock: Hand finished maple.
Sights: Blade front, open fixed rear drift adj. for w.
Features: Color case hardened lock plate; brass patch box, buttplate, trigger guard, fore-end tip and sights; adjustable double set triggers. From Richland Arms.
Price: Percussion $186.00
Price: Flintlock $200.00
Price: Kit form, percussion $144.00
Price: Kit form, flintlock $154.00

THOMPSON/CENTER HAWKEN RIFLE
Caliber: 45, 50 or 54.
Barrel: 28" octagon, hooked breech.
Stock: American walnut.
Sights: Blade front, rear adj. for w. & e.
Features: Solid brass furniture, double set triggers, button rifled barrel, coil-type main spring. From Thompson/Center Arms.
Price: Percussion Model (45, 50 or 54 cal.) $245.00
Price: Flintlock model (45 or 50 cal. only) $255.00

BLACK POWDER MUSKETS & RIFLES

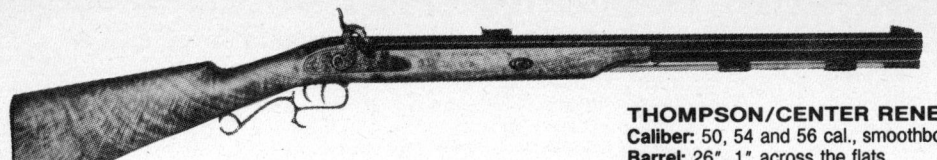

THOMPSON/CENTER RENEGADE RIFLE
Caliber: 50, 54 and 56 cal., smoothbore.
Barrel: 26", 1" across the flats.
Weight: 8 lbs.
Stock: American walnut.
Sights: Open hunting (Patridge) style, fully adjustable for w. and e.
Features: Coil spring lock, double set triggers, blued steel trim.
Price: Percussion model $185.00
Price: With accessory pack (includes 20 maxi-balls, maxi-lube, adjustable powder measure, bullet starter, nipple and nipple wrench) $204.50
Price: Flintlock model, 50 and 54 cal. only $190.00

THOMPSON/CENTER SENECA RIFLE
Caliber: 36, 45.
Barrel: 27".
Weight: 6½ lbs.
Stock: American walnut.
Sights: Open hunting style, square notch rear fully adj. for w. and e.
Features: Coil spring lock, octagon bbl. measures $13/16$" across flats, brass stock furniture.
Price: Rifle $245.00
Price: Rifle with accessory kit (includes jar of Maxi-Lub, box of 20 cast Maxi-Balls, powder measure, short starter, extra nipple & nipple wrench) $264.50

BUFFALO HUNTER PERCUSSION RIFLE
Caliber: 58.
Barrel: 25½".
Weight: 8 lbs. **Length:** 41½" over-all.
Stock: Walnut finished, hand checkered, brass furniture.
Sights: Fixed.
Features: Designed for primitive weapons hunting. 20 ga. shotgun bbl. also available $45.00. Imported by Navy Arms, Dixie.
Price: $200.00

SILE HAWKEN HUNTER CARBINE
Caliber: 45, 50, 54.
Barrel: 22", full octagon with hooked breech and hard chrome smooth bore.
Weight: 7 lbs. **Length:** 38" over-all.
Stock: Walnut with checkered p.g. and fore-end, rubber recoil pad.
Sights: Blade front, fully adjustable open rear.
Features: Black oxidized brass hardware, engraved case hardened lock plate, sear fly and coil spring mechanism. Stainless steel nipple. Adjustable double set triggers. From Sile Dist.
Price: Percussion $217.30
Price: Flintlock $227.10
Price: Hawken Super Deluxe Rifle $217.30

ARMOURY R140 HAWKIN RIFLE
Caliber: 45, 50 or 54.
Barrel: 29".
Weight: 8¾" to 9 lbs. **Length:** 45¾" over-all.
Stock: Walnut, with cheekpiece.
Sights: Dovetail front, fully adjustable rear.
Features: Octagon barrel measures ⅜" across flats; removable breech plug; double set triggers; blued barrel, brass stock fittings, color case hardened percussion lock. From Armsport and The Armoury.
Price: .... $175.00 to $282.00
Price: Kit (Armsport) $157.50

HAWKEN RIFLE
Caliber: 45, 50, 54 or 58.
Barrel: 28", blued, 6-groove rifling.
Weight: 8¾ lbs. **Length:** 44" over-all.
Stock: Walnut finish.
Sights: Blade front, fully adj. rear.
Features: Coil mainspring, double set triggers, polished brass furniture. Also available with chrome plated bore or in flintlock model. Introduced 1977. From Kassnar, Sile, Hawes, Dixie (45 or 50 only, walnut stock), Armsport, Shore (50-cal. only).
Price: .... $175.00 to $229.95
Price: Hard chrome bore, Sile, about $238.95

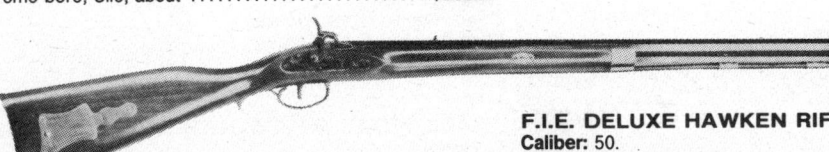

F.I.E. DELUXE HAWKEN RIFLE
Caliber: 50.
Barrel: 28".
Weight: 7 lbs. **Length:** 43½" over-all.
Stock: Dark polished walnut.
Sights: Blade front, open read adj. for w.
Features: Brass patchbox, trigger guard, buttplate and furniture; color case hardened lock, rest blued. From F.I.E. Corp.
Price: $156.95
Price: Kit form $131.95
Price: Finished flintlock model $166.95

CAUTION: PRICES CHANGE. CHECK AT GUNSHOP.

BLACK POWDER MUSKETS & RIFLES

ITHACA-NAVY HAWKEN RIFLE
Caliber: 50.
Barrel: 32" octagonal, 1-inch dia.
Weight: About 9 lbs.
Stock: Black walnut.
Sights: Blade front, rear adj. for w.
Features: Completely made in U.S. Hooked breech, 1⅞" throw percussion lock. Attached twin thimbles and under-rib. German silver barrel key inlays, Hawken-style toe and buttplates, lock bolt inlays, barrel wedges, entry thimble, trigger guard, ramrod and cleaning jag, nipple and nipple wrench. American made. Introduced 1977. From Navy Arms.
Price: Complete, percussion $395.00
Price: Kit, percussion $275.00
Price: Complete, flint $425.00
Price: Kit, flint $300.00

Armsport Hawken Rifle-Shotgun Combo
Similar to Hawken above except 50-cal. only, with 20 gauge shotgun barrel. From Armsport.
Price: $250.00

NUMRICH HALF-STOCK PLAINS RIFLE
Caliber: 31, 36, 45 or 50.
Barrel: 32".
Weight: 10 lbs.
Stock: Maple.
Sights: Blade front, fixed near.
Features: Hand-rubbed stock. Available with rifled or smooth bore. Brass stock furniture. From Numrich Arms.
Price: $174.00

RICHLAND PERCUSSION WESSON RIFLE
Caliber: 50.
Barrel: 28", 1⅛" octagon.
Length: 45" over-all.
Stock: Walnut.
Sights: Blade front, rear adj. for e.
Features: Adjustable double set triggers, color case hardened frame. Introduced 1977. From Richland Arms.
Price: With false muzzle $295.00
Price: Engraved version $412.00

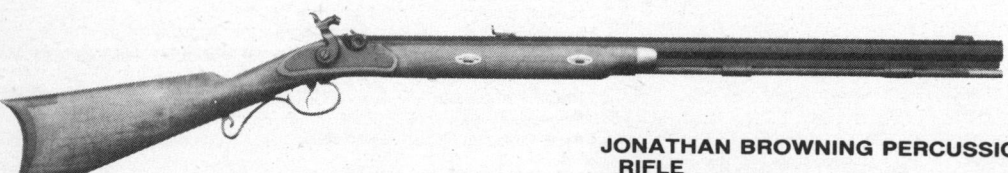

Consult our Directory pages for the location of firms mentioned.

JONATHAN BROWNING PERCUSSION MOUNTAIN RIFLE
Caliber: 45, 50 or 54.
Barrel: 30", 1" across flats.
Stock: Traditional half-stock with semi-cheekpiece.
Sights: Blade front, Buckhorn rear screw-adj. for e.
Features: Single set trigger; hooked breech. 45-cal. rifled 1 in 56", 50-cal. rifled 1 in 62", 54-cal. rifled 1 in 66" twist. Offered in choice of browned steel or brass finish on buttplate, trigger guard and complimentary furniture. Hickory ramrod with brass ends. Spare nipple and cleaning jag included. Introduced 1977. From Browning.
Price: Brass or browned furniture, 45, 50 or 54 cal. $399.95

HAWKEN HURRICANE & HUNTER
Caliber: 45 or 50.
Barrel: 28", octagon.
Weight: 6 lbs. **Length:** 44¾" over-all.
Stock: American walnut.
Sights: Blade front, open fixed rear.
Features: American made. Curved buttplate, brass stock furniture. From Navy Arms.
Price: 45 or 50 cal. $195.00
Price: Hawken Hunter (58 cal.) $195.00
Price: Hawken kit $149.95

PARKER-HALE ENFIELD 1853 MUSKET
Caliber: .577".
Barrel: 39", 3-groove cold-forged rifling.
Weight: About 9 lbs. **Length:** 55" over-all.
Stock: Seasoned walnut.
Sights: Fixed front, rear step adj. for elevation.
Features: Three band musket made to original specs from original gauges. Solid brass stock furniture, color hardened lock plate, hammer; blued barrel, trigger. Imported from England by Navy Arms.
Price: $400.00

London Armory Co. 3-Band Musket
Re-creation of the famed London Armory Company Pattern 1853 Enfield Musket. One-piece walnut stock, brass buttplate, trigger guard and nosecap. Lockplate marked "1862 L.A. Co." and with a British crown. Blued Baddeley barrel bands. From Dixie, Euroarms of America.
Price: $200.00
Price: 2-Band rifle $200.00

PARKER-HALE WHITWORTH MILITARY TARGET RIFLE
Caliber: 45.
Barrel: 36".
Weight: 9¼ lbs. **Length:** 52½" over-all.
Stock: Walnut. Checkered at wrist and fore-end.
Sights: Hooded post front, open step-adjustable rear.
Features: Faithful reproduction of the Whitworth rifle, only bored for 45-cal. Trigger has a detented lock, capable of being adjusted very finely without risk of the sear nose catching on the half-cock bent and damaging both parts. Introduced 1978. Imported from England by Navy Arms.
Price: $575.00

BLACK POWDER MUSKETS & RIFLES

PARKER-HALE ENFIELD 1861 CARBINE
Caliber: 577.
Barrel: 24″.
Weight: 7½ lbs. **Length:** 40¼″ over-all.
Stock: Walnut.
Sights: Fixed front, adj. rear.
Features: Percussion muzzle loader, made to original 1861 English patterns. Imported from England by Navy Arms.
Price: $300.00

PARKER-HALE ENFIELD PATTERN 1858 NAVAL RIFLE
Caliber: .577″.
Barrel: 33″.
Weight: 8½ lbs. **Length:** 48½″ over-all.
Stock: European walnut.
Sights: Blade front, step adj. rear.
Features: Two-band Enfield percussion rifle with heavy barrel. 5-groove progressive depth rifling, solid brass furniture. All parts made exactly to original patterns. Imported from England by Navy Arms.
Price: $370.00

ERMA-EXCAM GALLAGER CARBINE
Caliber: .54 (.540″ ball).
Barrel: 22⅓″.
Weight: 7¼ lbs. **Length:** 39″ over-all.
Stock: European walnut.
Sights: Post front, rear adjustable for w. & e.
Features: Faithful reproduction of the 1860 breech-loading carbine. Made in West Germany. Imported by Excam. Introduced 1978.
Price: $319.00

GALLAGER 1860 CARBINE
Caliber: .54″.
Barrel: 22½″, 16-groove rifling.
Weight: 7¼ lbs. **Length:** 39″ over-all.
Stock: Beechwood.
Sights: Fixed front, adj. V-notch Buckhorn rear.
Features: Reproduction of the breech-loading Civil War percussion carbine; loads using a brass cartridge. Comes with cleaning rod and attachments, spare nipple, one cartridge, nipple wrench. Imported by Jana.
Price: $199.95
Price: Extra cartridges, each $1.30

F.I.E. PERCUSSION BERDAN RIFLE
Caliber: 45.
Barrel: 25″, rifled, octagon.
Weight: 7 lbs. **Length:** 42¾″ over-all.
Stock: Walnut-finished hardwood.
Sights: Brass blade front, adj. open rear.
Features: Double-set triggers; brass trigger guard, patch box and buttplate. From F.I.E. Corp.
Price: $87.95

DIXIE ENFIELD MUSKETOON
Caliber: 58 (.577″).
Barrel: 24″, 6 lands, 6 grooves.
Weight: 7 lbs. **Length:** 41″ over-all.
Stock: Walnut with brass fittings.
Sights: Original style fixed front, adjustable rear.
Features: Uses standard .575″ Minie ball or .570″ round ball. Made in Italy. From Dixie Gun Works and the Armoury.
Price: .... $179.95 to $186.00

U.S. M-1862 REMINGTON CONTRACT RIFLE
Caliber: 58.
Barrel: 33″.
Weight: 9½ lbs. **Length:** 48½″ over-all.
Stock: Walnut, brass furniture.
Sights: Blade front, folding 3-leaf rear.
Features: Re-creation of the 1862 military rifle. Each rifle furnished with two stainless steel nipples. From Dixie, Euroarms of America.
Price: About $200.00

COOK & BROTHER CONFEDERATE CARBINE
Caliber: 58.
Barrel: 24″.
Weight: 7½ lbs. **Length:** 40½″ over-all.
Stock: Select walnut.
Features: Re-creation of the 1861 New Orleans-made artillery carbine. Color case-hardened lock, browned barrel. Buttplate, trigger guard, barrel bands, sling swivels and nosecap of polished brass. From Euroarms of America.
Price: $190.00

CAUTION: PRICES CHANGE. CHECK AT GUNSHOP.

BLACK POWDER MUSKETS & RIFLES

Shiloh New Model 1863 Sharps Carbine
Shortened, carbine version of the 1863 rifle. Caliber 54. Has 22" barrel, black walnut stock without patch box, single barrel band. Weighs 8lbs., 12 ozs., over-all length is 39⅛". Made in U.S. by Shiloh Rifle Co. Available from C. Sharps Arms Co.
Price: **$399.00**

SHILOH NEW MODEL 1863 SHARPS RIFLE
Caliber: 54.
Barrel: 30", 1-in 48".
Weight: 8¾ lbs. **Length:** 47" over-all.
Stock: Black walnut, oil finish.
Sights: Blade front, rear leaf adj. for e.
Features: Duplicate of original percussion rifle. Receiver sideplate, hammer, buttplate, patch box color hardened; barrel is blue-black. Twelve different models of the Sharps now available in many original chamberings. Made in U.S. by Shiloh Rifle Co. Available from C. Sharps Arms Co.
Price: **$499.00**

SHILOH SHARPS 1874 MILITARY RIFLE
Caliber: 45-70, 50-70.
Barrel: 30", Round.
Weight: 8¾ lbs.
Stock: American walnut.
Sights: Blade front, Lawrence-style open rear.
Features: Military-style fore-end with three barrel bands and 1¼" sling swivels. Color case-hardened receiver, buttplate and barrel bands, blued barrel. Recreation of the original Sharps rifles. Five other models in many original chamberings available. From C. Sharps Arms Co.
Price: 1874 Military Rifle **$499.00**
Price: 1874 Carbine **$399.00**
Price: 1874 Business Rifle **$490.00**
Price: 1874 Sporting Rifle No. 2 .... **$549.00**
Price: 1874 Sporting Rifle No. 3 .... **$524.00**
Price: 1874 Long Range Express Sporting Rifle ... **$680.00**

Consult our Directory pages for the location of firms mentioned.

SILE SHARPS MILITARY CARBINE
Caliber: 54 Sharps.
Barrel: 22", round, polished blue.
Weight: 7¾ lbs. **Length:** 39" over-all.
Stock: Walnut.
Sights: Blade front, rear adj. for w. and e.
Features: Faithful reproduction of the original 1863 carbine. Receiver, sideplate, hammer and buttplate are color case hardened. Rifle model has 28" barrel, checkered p.g. and fore-end. Six different models of the Sharps are now available. Introduced 1977. From Sile Distributors, Shore.
Price: Carbine, about **$283.95**
Price: Rifle, about **$300.00**

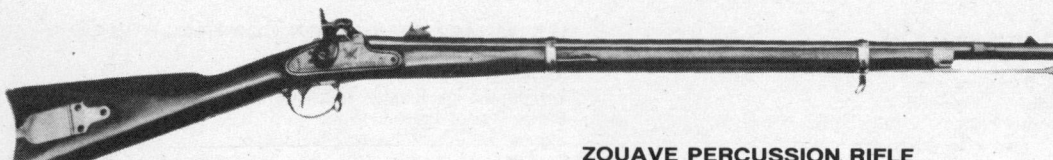

ZOUAVE PERCUSSION RIFLE
Caliber: 58, 59.
Barrel: 32½".
Weight: 9½ lbs. **Length:** 48½" over-all.
Stock: Walnut finish, brass patch box and buttplate.
Sights: Fixed front, rear adj. for e.
Features: Some small details may vary with importers. Also available from Navy Arms as carbine, with 22" bbl. Extra 20 ga. shotgun bbl. $45.00. Imported by Navy Arms, Shore (58-cal. only), F.I.E., Dixie, Hawes, Kassnar.
Price: .... **$87.95 to $200.00**
Price: Kit form (Hawes) **$114.95**

LYMAN HAWKEN PLAINS RIFLE
Caliber: 50.
Barrel: 28", 1-48" twist.
Weight: 8¾ lbs. **Length:** 45" over-all.
Stock: European walnut.
Sights: Blade front, fully adj. rear.
Features: Double set trigger, hooked breech system, brass stock furniture, patch box. Imported from Italy by Lyman.
Price: Percussion **$237.95**
Price: Kit, percussion **$189.95**

Mississippi Model 1841 Percussion Rifle
Similar to Zouave Rifle but patterned after U.S. Model 1841. Imported by Navy Arms, Dixie.
Price: **$200.00**

BLACK POWDER MUSKETS & RIFLES

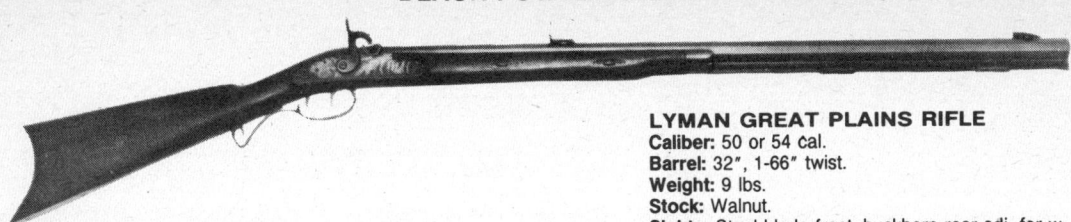

LYMAN GREAT PLAINS RIFLE
Caliber: 50 or 54 cal.
Barrel: 32", 1-66" twist.
Weight: 9 lbs.
Stock: Walnut.
Sights: Steel blade front, buckhorn rear adj. for w. & e.
Features: Browned steel furniture. Coil sring lock, Hawken-style trigger guard and double set triggers. Round thimbles recessed and sweated into rib. Steel wedge plates and toe plates. Introduced 1980. From Lyman.
Price: Percussion $289.95
Price: Flintlock $324.95
Price: Percussion Kit $224.95

REVOLVING PERCUSSION CARBINE
Caliber: 44, 6-shot.
Barrel: 18", 20".
Weight: 5 lbs. **Length:** 38" over-all.
Stock: Walnut, brass buttplate.
Sights: Blade front adj. for w., buckhorn rear adj. for e.
Features: Action based on 1858 Remington revolver. Brass trigger guard. Imported by Navy/Replica.
Price: $185.00

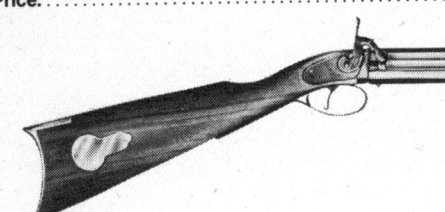

HOPKINS & ALLEN O/U PERCUSSION RIFLE
Caliber: 45.
Barrel: 28".
Weight: 8½ lbs. **Length:** 43" over-all.
Stock: Walnut.
Sights: Fixed.
Features: Barrels rotate for second shot. Each barrel has a set of sights. From Hopkins & Allen.
Price: $199.95

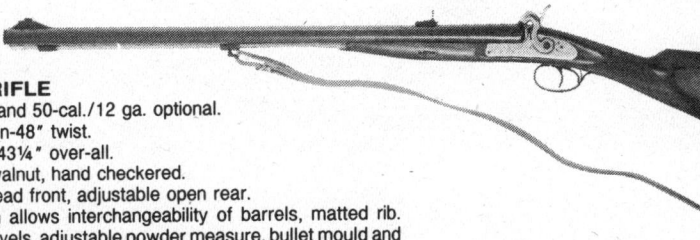

KODIAK DOUBLE RIFLE
Caliber: 58 (std.), 50 cal. and 50-cal./12 ga. optional.
Barrel: 28", 5 grooves, 1-in-48" twist.
Weight: 9½ lbs. **Length:** 43¼" over-all.
Stock: Czechoslovakian walnut, hand checkered.
Sights: Adjustable gold bead front, adjustable open rear.
Features: Hooked breech allows interchangeability of barrels, matted rib. Comes with sling and swivels, adjustable powder measure, bullet mould and bullet starter. Engraved lock plates, top tang and trigger guard. Locks and top tang polished, rest browned. From Trail Guns Armory, Inc.
Price: 58 cal. SxS $495.00
Price: 50 cal. SxS $495.00
Price: 50 cal. x 12 ga., 58x12 .... $495.00
Price: Spare barrels, 58 cal. SxS, 50 cal. SxS $267.50
Price: Spare barrels, 50 cal. x 12 ga., 58x12 .... $267.50
Price: Spare barrels, 12 ga. x 12 ga. $160.00

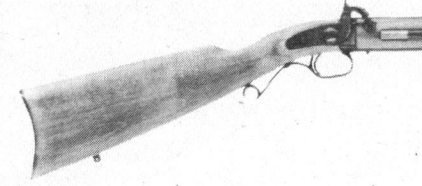

LOVEN MODEL 10 SWIVEL BREECH RIFLE/CARBINE
Caliber: 45.
Barrel: 22" or 28", octagon.
Weight: 7¾ to 8½ lbs. **Length:** 37½" over-all (22" bbl.)
Stock: Maple with matching barrel panels.
Sights: Open, fixed; one set for each barrel.
Features: Barrels are easily removed and interchangeable, and rotate for a quick second shot. Positive barrel indexing system. Maple ramrod accepts standard threaded accessories. Metal parts are blued. Percussion only. Introduced 1979. Made in U.S. by Loven Firearms.
Price: Either barrel length $287.70

Loven Model 13 Swivel Breech Rifle/Carbine
Same as Model 13 except available in 45, 50 or 54 caliber. Octagon barrel measures 15/16" across flats. Stock and barrel panels of select walnut, brass furniture. 22" or 28" barrel. Weight 8¾ to 12½ lbs. Percussion only.
Price: Either barrel length $327.70

FRAZIER MATCHMATE PERCUSSION RIFLES
Caliber: 32, 36, 40, 45, 50 or 54.
Barrel: 26" to 38". Douglas Premium M/L. Octagon. Choice of diam.—13/16", 7/8", 15/16", 1" or 1⅛".
Weight: 8 lbs. and up. Varies with size and wood. **Length:** 52½" over-all (32" bbl.)
Stock: Laminated of 5 layers of imported exotic high figure hardwoods. Thumbhole p.g., cheekpiece in line with bore. Satin finish. Adj. hooked buttplate.
Sights: Redfield Olympic front on detachable base (insert set included), Redfield #75 micro peep rear.
Features: A unique rifle designed for competition shooting. Underhammer action with Anschutz-Mauser set triggers. Comes with set of 8 weights to control balance, Lyman mould, short starter and rod. Adj. coil mainspring; stainless steel flashguard around nipple. Action housed in breech but removes easily for cleaning. Write for full specifics. From Frazier Matchmate Inc.
Price: Standard Offhand Rifle (illus.), from $800.00
Price: Custom Offhand Rifle, from $900.00
Price: "National Unilimited" bench rest rifle, from $750.00

Consult our Directory pages for the location of firms mentioned.

BLACK POWDER MUSKETS & RIFLES

Loven Model 16 Swivel Breech Rifle/Carbine
Same as Model 13 except availble in 45, 50 or 54 caliber. Stock and full-length barrel panels of curly or birdseye maple. Color case-hardened lock and furniture. Percussion only.
Price: $457.70

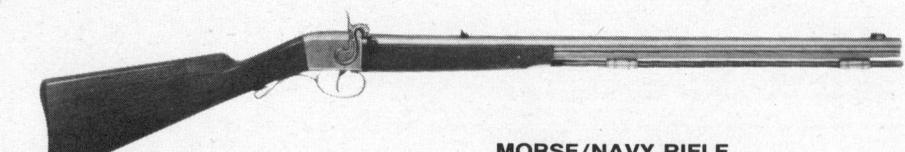

MORSE/NAVY RIFLE
Caliber: 45, 50 or 58.
Barrel: 26", octagonal.
Weight: 6 lbs. (45 cal.). **Length:** 41½" over-all.
Stock: American walnut, full p.g.
Sights: Blade front, open fixed rear.
Features: Brass action, trigger guard, ramrod pipes. From Navy Arms.
Price: $149.95

YORKSHIRE RIFLE
Caliber: 45.
Barrel: 36", rifled, ⅞" octagon.
Weight: 7½ lbs. **Length:** 51¾" over-all.
Stock: Select maple.
Sights: Blade front, open U-notch rear.
Features: Adj. double set triggers. Brass front and rear sights, trigger guard, patch box, buttplate and fore-end. Case hardened lock plate. From Richland.
Price: Percussion .... $144.00 to $150.00
Price: Flintlock .... $153.00 to $159.95

BLACK POWDER SHOTGUNS

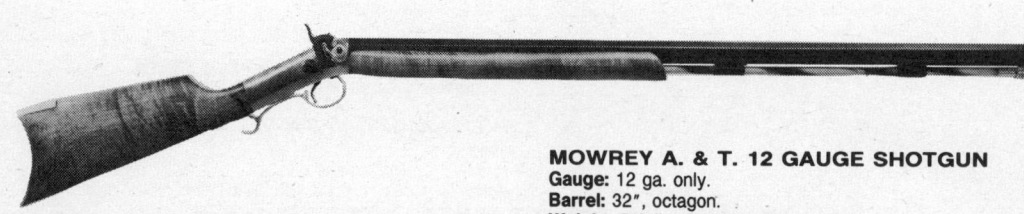

SINGLE BARREL PERCUSSION SHOTGUN
Gauge: 12, 20, 28.
Barrel: 28".
Weight: 4½ lbs. **Length:** 43" over-all.
Stock: Walnut finish, choice of half or full stock.
Features: Finish and features vary with importer. Imported by Dixie.
Price: .... $32.95 to $59.95

CENTURY SINGLE BARREL PERCUSSION SHOTGUN
Gauge: 28.
Barrel: 31" (Cyl.), part octagon.
Weight: 4¼ lbs. **Length:** 48½" over-all.
Stock: Walnut finish hardwood; checkered at small of butt.
Sights: Bead front only.
Features: Suitable for ball or shot; blue barrel; lock, buttplate, trigger guard, breech and patch box are case hardened; steel ramrod. From Century Arms.
Price: $32.95

MOWREY A. & T. 12 GAUGE SHOTGUN
Gauge: 12 ga. only.
Barrel: 32", octagon.
Weight: 7½ lbs. **Length:** 48" over-all.
Stock: Maple, oil finish, brass furniture.
Sights: Bead front.
Features: Available in percussion only. Uses standard 12 ga. wadding. Made by Mowrey.
Price: Complete $229.00
Price: Kit form $154.00

SILE DELUXE DOUBLE BARREL SHOTGUN
Gauge: 12.
Barrel: 28" (Cyl. & Cyl.); hooked breech, hard chrome lining.
Weight: 6 lbs. **Length:** 44½" over-all.
Stock: Walnut, with checkered grip.
Features: Engraved, polished blue and color case-hardened hardware, locks are color case-hardened and engraved. Steel buttplate; brass bead front sight. From sile.
Price: Percussion only $244.40
Price: Confederate Cavalry Model (shortened version of above model with 14" bbl. 30½" o.a.l.) $244.40

BLACK POWDER SHOTGUNS

TRAIL GUNS KODIAK 10 GAUGE DOUBLE
Gauge: 10.
Barrel: 30¾" (Cyl. bore).
Weight: About 9 lbs. **Length:** 47⅛" over-all.
Stock: Walnut, with cheek rest. Checkered wrist and fore-end.
Features: Chrome plated bores; engraved lockplates; brass bead front and middle sights; sling swivels. Introduced 1980. From Trail Guns Armory.
Price: $379.95

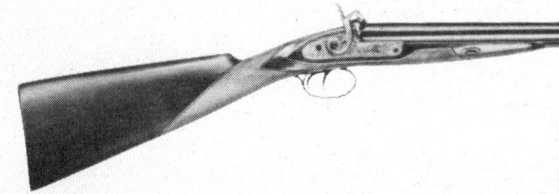

NAVY CLASSIC DOUBLE BARREL SHOTGUN
Gauge: 12.
Barrel: 28".
Weight: 7 lbs., 12 ozs. **Length:** 45" over-all.
Stock: Walnut.
Features: Color case-hardened lock plates and hammers; hand checkered stock. Imported by Navy Arms.
Price: $275.00

CENTURY "KENTUCKY" TYPE SHOTGUN
Gauge: 24.
Barrel: 29" (Cyl.).
Weight: 4¼ lbs. **Length:** 44" over-all.
Stock: European walnut, checkered at wrist.
Sights: Bead front only.
Features: English style stock, inletted patch box; steel ramrod. From Century Arms.
Price: Flintlock, full stock $29.95
Price: Flintlock, sporter $29.95

EOA MAGNUM CAPE GUN
Gauge: 12.
Barrel: 32", open choked.
Weight: 7½ lbs. **Length:** 47½" over-all.
Stock: European walnut, oil finished.
Features: Classic English-styled single barrel shotgun. Barrel, underrib, thimbles, nosecap, trigger guard and buttplate blued. Lock left in the white with scroll engraving. From Euroarms of America.
Price: $200.00

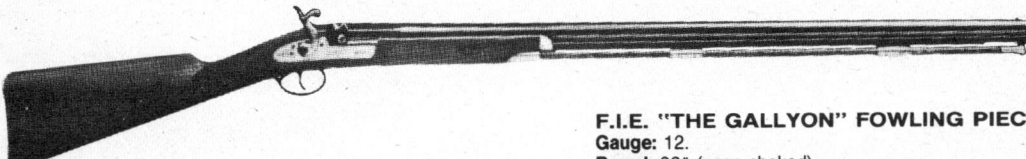

F.I.E. "THE GALLYON" FOWLING PIECE
Gauge: 12.
Barrel: 32" (open choked).
Weight: 7½ lbs.
Stock: European walnut, English style. Hand checkered, satin oil finish.
Sights: Bead front.
Features: Faithful reproduction of an old English fowling piece. Fine scroll engraving on lock, barrel and trigger guard. Steel buttplate. Introduced 1979. From F.I.E. Corp.
Price: $169.95

MORSE/NAVY SINGLE BARREL SHOTGUN
Gauge: 12 ga.
Barrel: 26".
Weight: 5 lbs. **Length:** 41½" over-all.
Stock: American walnut, full p.g.
Sights: Front bead.
Features: Brass receiver, black buttplate. From Navy Arms.
Price: $149.95

DOUBLE BARREL PERCUSSION SHOTGUN
Gauge: 12.
Barrel: 30" (I.C.& Mod.).
Weight: 6¼ lbs. **Length:** 45" over-all.
Stock: Hand checkered walnut, 14" pull.
Features: Double triggers, light hand engraving. Details vary with importer. Imported by Navy Arms, The Armoury, Dixie, Euroarms of America, Hopkins & Allen.
Price: Upland .... $125.00 to $200.00
Price: Model 300 Mag. (Navy) $275.00

> Consult our Directory pages for the location of firms mentioned.

AIR GUNS—HANDGUNS

Guns in this section are powered by: A) disposable CO^2 cylinders, B) hand-pumped compressed air released by trigger action, C) air compressed by a spring-powered piston released by trigger action. Calibers are generally 177 (BB or pellet) and 22 (ball or pellet); a few guns are made in 20 or 25 caliber. Pellet guns are usually rifled, those made for BB's only are smoothbore.

BSA SCORPION AIR PISTOL
Caliber: 177 or 22.
Barrel: 7⅞", rifled.
Weight: 3.6 lbs. **Length:** 15¾" over-all.
Power: Spring-air, barrel cocking.
Stock: Moulded black plastic contoured with thumbrest.
Sights: Interchangeable bead or blade front with hood, open rear adjustable for w. & e.
Features: Muzzle velocity of 510 fps (177) and 380 fps (22). Comes with pellets, oil, targets and steel target holder. Scope and mount optional. Introduced 1980. From Precision Sports.
Price: 177 or 22 cal. $99.95
Price: 1.5x15 scope and mount $34.95

BEEMAN'S 800 TARGET/SPORT PISTOL
Caliber: 177, single shot.
Barrel: 7", rifled steel.
Weight: 3.2 lbs. **Length:** 16" over-all.
Power: Spring, barrel cocking.
Stocks: Checkered, wood-grained synthetic.
Sights: Hooded front with interchangeable inserts, micro click rear with 4 rotating notches.
Features: Velocity 420 fps MV. Advanced recoilless action. Shoulder stock and scope mount available. Imported by Beeman's.
Price: Right hand $168.50
Price: Left hand $171.00

BEEMAN/WEBLEY "TEMPEST" AIR PISTOL
Caliber: 177 or 22, single shot.
Barrel: 6.75", rifled ordnance steel.
Weight: 32 oz. **Length:** 9" over-all.
Stocks: Checkered black epoxy with thumbrest.
Sights: Post front; rear has sliding leaf rear adjustable for w. and e.
Features: Adjustable trigger pull, manual safety. Velocity 530 fps (177 cal.). Steel piston in steel liner for maximum performance and durability. Shoulder stock available. Introduced 1979. Imported by Beeman's.
Price: $89.95

BEEMAN'S 900 MATCH PISTOL
Caliber: 177, single shot.
Weight: 3.3 lbs. **Length:** 16.5" over-all.
Power: Barrel cocking spring.
Stocks: Walnut with adjustable palm rest and sliding support plate.
Sights: Adj. post front from 2.5mm to 4.0mm width; adj. rear with interchangeable notches.
Features: Recoilless action; trigger adj. for length of pull, area of contact, travel length, pre-travel weight, pressure point and weight; auto. cocking safety trigger stop; rear sight has three positions; new removeable barrel weights. Shoulder stock and scope/mount available. Imported by Beeman's.
Price: With case, right hand $399.95
Price: With case, left hand $369.95
Price: Without case, right hand $429.95
Price: Without case, left hand $399.95

BEEMAN'S 700 TARGET/SPORT PISTOL
Caliber: 177, single shot.
Barrel: 7", rifled steel.
Weight: 3.1 lbs. **Length:** 16" over-all.
Power: Spring, barrel cocking.
Stocks: Checkered, wood-grained synthetic.
Sights: Hooded fixed front, micro-click rear with 4 rotating notches.
Features: Adjustable double-pull trigger. Auto. safety. Scope mount available. Velocity 420 fps MV. Shoulder stock and scope available. Imported by Beeman's.
Price: Right hand $110.00
Price: Left hand $112.50

BEEMAN/WEBLEY "HURRICANE" PISTOL
Caliber: 177 or 22.
Barrel: 8", rifled.
Weight: 2.4 lbs. **Length:** 16 9/16" over-all.
Power: Spring.
Stocks: Thumbrest, checkered.
Sights: Hooded front, micro-click rear adj. for w. and e.
Features: Velocity of 530 fps (177-cal.). Single stroke cocking, adjustable trigger pull, manual safety. Scope base included; 1.5x scope $39.95 extra. Shoulder stock available. Introduced 1977. Imported by Beeman's.
Price: $99.95

AIR GUNS—HANDGUNS

BEEMAN/WISCHO S-20 STANDARD
Caliber: 177.
Barrel: 7".
Weight: 2 lbs., 2 oz.
Power: Spring piston.
Stock: Walnut.
Sights: Hooded front, open rear adj. for elevation.
Features: Stock suitable for right or left-handed shooters; 24 oz. trigger pull. Introduced 1980. Imported by Beeman's.
Price: **$100.00**

BEEMAN/FEINWERKBAU MODEL 80 MATCH PISTOL
Caliber: 177, single shot.
Barrel: 7.5".
Weight: 2.8 to 3.2 lbs. (varies with weight selection). **Length:** 16.4" over-all.
Power: Spring piston, single-stroke sidelever cocking.
Stocks: Stippled walnut with adjustable palm shelf.
Sights: Interchangeable-blade front, rear notch micro. adj. for w. and e.
Features: Two-stage trigger adjustable for finger length. Recoilless operation. Interchangeable weights attach to frame, not barrel. Weights may be arranged to suit balance preference. Cocking effort 16 lbs. Muzzle velocity 475-525 fps. Introduced 1978. Imported by Beeman's.
Price: Right-hand **$595.00**
Price: Left-hand **$620.00**

BENJAMIN SUPER S. S. TARGET PISTOL SERIES 130
Caliber: BB, 22 and 177; single shot.
Barrel: 8"; BB smoothbore; 22 and 177, rifled.
Length: 11". **Weight:** 2 lbs.
Power: Hand pumped.
Features: Bolt action; fingertip safety; adj. power.
Price: M130, BB **$50.70**
Price: M132, 22 .... **$50.70**
Price: M137, 177 .... **$50.70**

BEEMAN MODEL 850 AIR PISTOL
Caliber: 177, single shot.
Barrel: 7", rifled steel.
Weight: 3.2 lbs. **Length:** 16" over-all.
Power: Spring, barrel cocking.
Stocks: Checkered, wood-grained synthetic.
Sights: Infinite width rotating post front 2.5 to 4mm, micro click rear with 4 rotating notches.
Features: Velocity 420 fps. Advanced recoilless action. Rotating barrel housing for easier cocking. Optional muzzle weight available. Chocie of right- or left-hand grips; can be ambidextrous. Scope mount and shoulder stock available. Introduced 1979. Imported by Beeman's.
Price: Right-hand **$195.00**
Price: Left-hand **$197.50**

CROSMAN 454 BB PISTOL
Caliber: BB, 16-shot.
Length: 11" over-all. **Weight:** 30 oz.
Power: Standard CO_2.
Stocks: Contoured with thumbrest.
Sights: Patridge-type front, fully adj. rear.
Features: Gives about 80 shots per powerlet, slide-action safety, steel barrel, die-cast receiver. Lanyard ring for easy piercing of CO_2 cylinder.
Price: About **$27.99**

Consult our Directory pages for the location of firms mentioned.

Crossman Model 1600 Air Pistol
Same specifications as Model 454 except has fixed sights, black plastic grips, no lanyard ring.
Price: About **$23.00**

CROSMAN PEACEMAKER "44"
Caliber: 177, 6 shot.
Barrel: 4¾", button rifled.
Length: 10⅜". **Weight:** 34 oz.
Power: Crosman CO_2 Powerlet
Features: Revolving cylinder, walnut finished grips. Positive valve design. Single-action.
Price: About **$21.99**

CROSMAN MODEL 1322 AIR PISTOL
Caliber: 22, single shot.
Barrel: 8", button rifled.
Length: 11¾". **Weight:** 37 oz.
Power: Hand pumped.
Sights: Blade front, rear adj. for w. and e.
Features: Moulded plastic grip, hand size pump forearm. Cross bolt safety. Also available in 177 Cal. as **Model 1377**.
Price: About **$36.99**

CAUTION: PRICES CHANGE. CHECK AT GUNSHOP.

AIR GUNS—HANDGUNS

CROSMAN 38T TARGET REVOLVER
Caliber: 177, 6-shot.
Barrel: 6", rifled.
Length: 11". **Weight:** 43 oz.
Power: CO_2 Powerlet cylinder.
Features: Double action, revolving cylinder. Adj. rear sight.
Price: About $37.99

Crosman 38C Combat Revolver
Same as 38 Target except 3½" BBL., 38 oz., about $37.99

CROSMAN MARK I TARGET PISTOL
Caliber: 22, single shot.
Barrel: 7¼", button rifled.
Length: 11". **Weight:** 42 oz.
Power: Crosman Powerlet CO_2 cylinder.
Features: New system provides same shot-to-shot velocity, adj. from 300- to 400 fps. Checkered thumbrest grips, right or left. Patridge front sight, rear adj. for w. & e. Adj. trigger.
Price: About $43.00

Crosman Mark II Target Pistol
Same as Mark I except 177 cal., about $43.00

DAISY 179 SIX GUN
Caliber: BB, 12-shot.
Barrel: Steel lined, smoothbore.
Length: 11½". **Weight:** NA
Power: Spring.
Features: Forced feed from under-barrel magazine. Single action, molded wood grained grips.
Price: About $14.00

DAISY MODEL 188 BB/PELLET PISTOL
Caliber: 177.
Barrel: 9.9".
Weight: 1.67 lbs. **Length:** 12" over-all.
Stocks: Die-cast metal; checkered with thumbrest.
Sights: Blade and ramp front, notched rear.
Features: Single shot for pellets, 24-shot for BBs. Spring action with under-barrel cocking lever. Grip and receiver of die-cast metal. Introduced 1979.
Price: About $14.00

FEINWERKBAU FWB-65 MKI AIR PISTOL
Caliber: 177.
Barrel: 7½"; fixed bbl. wgt. avail.
Length: 14½" over-all. **Weight:** 42 oz.
Power: Spring, sidelever cocking.
Stocks: Walnut, stippled thumbrest.
Sights: Front, interchangeable post element system, open rear, click adj. for w. & e. and for sighting notch width. Scope mount avail.
Features: Cocking effort 9 lbs. 2-stage trigger, 4 adjustments. Quiet firing, 525 fps. Programs instantly for recoil or recoilless operation. Permanently lubricated. Steel piston ring. Special switch converts trigger from 17.6 oz. pull to 42 oz. let-off. Available from Air Rifle Hdq., Beeman's.
Price: Right-hand .... $485.00 to $608.50
Price: Left-hand $499.50

Feinwerkbau Model 65 International Match Pistol
Same as FWB 65 MKI pistol except: new adj. wood grips to meet international regulations, optional 3 oz. barrel sleeve weight. Available from Air Rifle Hdqtrs., Beeman's.
Price: Right-hand $545.00
Price: Left-hand $568.50

HAMMERLI "MASTER" CO_2 TARGET PISTOL
Caliber: 177 waisted pellets.
Barrel: 6.4", 12-groove.
Length: 16". **Weight:** 38.4 oz.
Power: 12 gram cylinder.
Stocks: Plastic with thumbrest and checkering.
Sights: Ramp front, micro rear, click adj. Adj. sight radius from 11.1" to 13.0".
Features: Single shot, manual loading. Residual gas vented automatically. 5-way adj. trigger. Available from Mandall Shooting Supplies.
Price: $350.00

AIR GUNS—HANDGUNS

HEALTHWAYS TOPSCORE 9100 AIR PISTOL
Caliber: 177, BB, 50-shot magazine.
Barrel: 6½".
Weight: 28 oz.
Power: Spring.
Stocks: Checkered, integral with frame.
Sights: Open, fixed.
Features: Quick, top-load magazine mass loads 50 BBs at a time. Cock by releasing a locking lever on left side of frame and lifting barrel.
Price: $22.95

HEALTHWAYS 9401 CO_2 AUTOMATIC PISTOL
Caliber: BB, 100-shot repeater.
Barrel: 5⅞", smooth.
Length: 9½". **Weight:** 28 oz.
Stocks: Simulated walnut with thumbrest.
Power: 8.5 or 12.5 gram CO_2 cylinders.
Features: 3 position power switch. Auto. ammunition feed. Positive safety.
Price: $32.95

MARKSMAN #1010 REPEATER PISTOL
Caliber: 177, 20-shot repeater.
Barrel: 2½", smoothbore.
Length: 8¼". **Weight:** 24 oz.
Power: Spring.
Features: Thumb safety. Uses BBs, darts or pellets. Repeats with BBs only.
Price: Black finish $14.95

PRECISE/RO-72 BULLSEYE AIR PISTOL
Caliber: 177, single shot.
Barrel: 7¼", rifled.
Weight: 35 oz.
Power: Spring air, barrel cocking.
Stock: Molded plastic with thumbrest.
Sights: Hooded front, micro. adj. open rear for w. and e.
Features: Four interchangeable front sights—triangle, bead, narrow post, wide post. Rear sight rotates to give four distinct sight pictures. Muzzle velocity 325 fps. Precise, importer.
Price: $35.00

POWER LINE 717/722 PELLET PISTOLS
Caliber: 177 (Model 717), 22 (Model 722), single shot.
Barrel: 9.61".
Weight: 48 oz. **Length:** 13½" over-all.
Stocks: Molded wood-grain plastic, with thumbrest.
Sights: Blade and ramp front, micro. adjustable notch rear.
Features: Single pump pneumatic pistol. Rifled brass barrel. Cross-bolt trigger block. Muzzle velocity 360 fps (177 cal.), 290 fps (22 cal.). From Daisy. Introduced 1979.
Price: Either model, about $43.00

POWER LINE CO_2 1200 CUSTOM TARGET PISTOL
Caliber: BB, 177
Barrel: 10½", smooth
Weight: 30 oz. **Length:** 11¼" over-all.
Power: Daisy CO_2 cylinder.
Stocks: Contoured, checkered moulded wood-grain plastic.
Sights: Blade ramp front, fully adj. square notch rear.
Features: 60-shot BB reservoir, gravity feed. Cross bolt safety. Velocity of 420-450 fps for more than 100 shots.
Price: About $30.00

CAUTION: PRICES CHANGE. CHECK AT GUNSHOP.

AIR GUNS—HANDGUNS

SHERIDAN MODEL EB CO_2 PISTOL
Caliber: 20 (5mm).
Barrel: 6½", rifled, rust proof.
Weight: 27 ozs. **Length:** 9" over-all.
Power: 12 gram CO_2 cylinder.
Stocks: Checkered simulated walnut. Left- or right-handed.
Sights: Blade front, fully adjustable rear.
Features: Turn-bolt single-shot action. Gives about 40 shots at 400 fps per CO_2 cylinder.
Price: $47.50

SMITH & WESSON MODELS 78G & 79G
Caliber: 22 cal. pellet (78G), 177 cal. pellet (79G), single-shot.
Barrel: 8½", rifled steel.
Weight: 42 oz.
Power: 12.5 gram CO_2 cartridge.
Stocks: Simulated walnut, checkered. Thumbrest. Left or right hand.
Sights: Patridge front, fully adj. rear with micro. click windage adjustment.
Features: Pull-bolt action, crossbolt safety. High-low power adjustment. Gun blue finish.
Price: $53.45

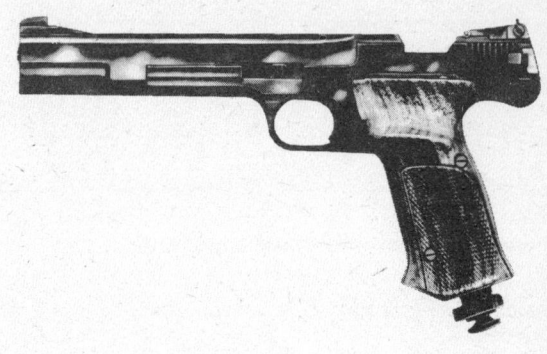

WALTHER MODEL LP-3
Caliber: 177, single shot.
Barrel: 9⅜", rifled.
Length: 13³⁄₁₆". **Weight:** 45½ oz.
Power: Compressed air, lever cocking.
Features: Recoiless operation, cocking in grip frame. Micro-click rear sight, adj. for w. & e., 4-way adj. trigger. Plastic thumbrest grips. Imported by Interarms.
Price: $430.00

Walther Model LP-3 Match Pistol
Same specifications as LP-3 except for grips, frame shape and weight. Has adjustable walnut grips to meet international shooting regulations. Imported by Interarms.
Price: $540.00

WALTHER MODEL LP-53 PISTOL
Caliber: 177, single shot.
Barrel: 9⅜".
Length: 12⅜" over-all. **Weight:** 40.5 oz.
Power: Spring air.
Features: Micrometer rear sight. Interchangeable rear sight blades. Target grips. Bbl. weight available at extra cost. Interarms, Alexandria, Va.
Price: $250.00

> Consult our Directory pages for the location of firms mentioned.

WEIHRAUCH HW-70 AIR PISTOL
Caliber: 177, single shot.
Barrel: 6¼", rifled.
Length: 12¾" over-all. **Weight:** 38 oz.
Sights: Hooded post front, square notch rear adj. for w. and e.
Power: Spring, barrel cocking.
Features: Adj. trigger. 24-lb. cocking effort, 410 f.p.s. M.V.; automatic barrel safety. Available from Air Rifle HQ, Beeman's.
Price: $94.50

WISCHO BSF S-20 CUSTOM MATCH PISTOL
Caliber: 177, single shot.
Barrel: 7" rifled.
Length: 15.8" over-all. **Weight:** 45 oz.
Stocks: Walnut with thumbrest.
Sights: Bead front, rear adj. for e.
Power: Spring, barrel cocking.
Features: Cocking effort of 17 lbs.; M.V. 450 f.p.s.; adj. trigger. Optional scope and mount available. Detachable aluminum stock. Available from Beemans. Air Rifle HQ.
Price: $112.50

AIR GUNS—LONG GUNS

A.R.H./FEINWERKBAU F-124 SCX RIFLE
Caliber: 177.
Barrel: 18¼", rifled, hinged-type.
Weight: 8 lbs. 14 ozs. **Length:** 43½" over-all.
Power: Spring air, single stroke barrel cocking.
Stock: Walnut-finished hardwood.
Sights: 3x-7x ⅞"-tube wide field scope furnished.
Features: Equipped with 1" sling, detachable swivels, filler screws, and internal accurization for optimum velocity and accuracy. From Air Rifle Headquarters.
Price: **$398.50**

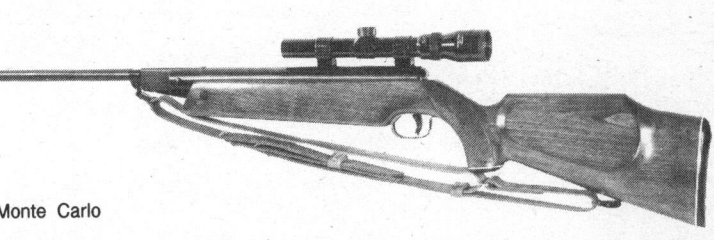

A.R.H./WEIRAUCH HW 35 DX
Caliber: 177.
Barrel: 19¼", rifled, hinged-type.
Weight: 9 lbs., 4 ozs. **Length:** 44½" over-all.
Power: Spring air, single stroke barrel cocking.
Stock: Walnut with Monte Carlo cheekpiece, hand-cut checkering, beavertail fore-end and rubber buttplate.
Sights: 2x-6x 1"-tube wide field scope included.
Features: Comes with 1" sling, detachable swivels, filler screws, trigger shoe, automatic safety. Accurized internally for optimum performance. From Air Rifle Headquarters.
Price: **$498.50**

A.R.H./FEINWERKBAU F-12 CX
Caliber: 177.
Barrel: 18¼", rifled.
Weight: 8 lbs., 14 ozs. **Length:** 43½" over-all.
Power: Spring air, single stroke barrel cocking.
Stock: Walnut-finished hardwood, hand-cut checkered p.g., Monte Carlo cheekpiece.
Sights: 2x-6x 1"-tube wide field scope included.
Features: Comes with 1" sling, detachable swivels, filler screws, trigger shoe. Internally accurized for optimum performance. From Air Rifle Headquarters.
Price: **$518.50**

A.R.H./WISCHO MODEL 70 DX
Caliber: 177.
Barrel: 19", rifled, hinged-type.
Weight: 7 lbs., 10 ozs. **Length:** 44" over-all.
Power: Spring air, single stroke barrel cocking.
Stock: Walnut-finished hardwood with cheekpiece, checkered p.g. and fore-end and rubber buttplate.
Sights: 2x-6x 1"-tube wide field scope included.
Features: Comes with 1" sling, detachable swivels, filler screws, trigger shoe, and total internal accurization for optimum performance. From Air Rifle Headquarters.
Price: **$478.50**

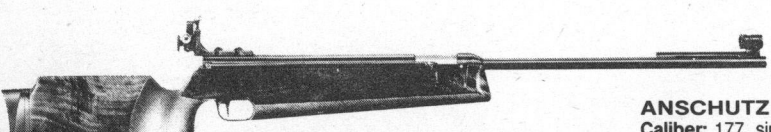

ANSCHUTZ 250 TARGET RIFLE
Caliber: 177, single shot.
Barrel: 18½", rifled, one piece with receiver.
Length: 45". **Weight:** 11 lbs. with sights.
Power: Spring, side-lever cocking, 17 lb. pull.
Features: Recoilless operation. Two-stage adj. trigger. Checkered walnut p.g. stock with Monte Carlo comb & cheekpiece; adj. buttplate; accessory rail. Available from Air Rifle Hdqtrs., Beeman's.
Price: **$598.50**

AIR GUNS—LONG GUNS

BSA BUCCANEER AIR RIFLE
Caliber: 177 or 22.
Barrel: 18.5", rifled.
Weight: 6 lb. **Length:** 35.5" over-all.
Power: Spring-air, barrel cocking.
Stock: High impact polyurethane, thumbhole design.
Sights: Interchangeable bead or blade front, aperture rear adjustable for windage and elevation.
Features: Adjustable trigger; non-automatic safety; checkered p.g. and fore-end. Comes with targets and steel target holder, oil, pellets. Scope and mounts optional. Introduced 1980. From Precision Sports.
Price: 177 or 22 cal. $124.95
Price: 5x15 scope and mount $34.95

BSA AIRSPORTER-S AIR RIFLE
Caliber: 177 or 22.
Barrel: 19.5", rifled.
Weight: 8 lbs. **Length:** 44.7" over-all.
Power: Spring air, underlever action.
Stock: Oil-finished walnut, high comb Monte Carlo checkpiece.
Sights: Ramp front with interchangeable bead and blade, adjustable for height; tangent-type rear adj. for w. & e.
Features: Muzzle velocity of 825 fps (177) and 635 fps (22). Fully adj. trigger. Cylinder is a large diameter, one-piece impact extrusion. Scope and mount optional. Introduced 1980. From Precision Sports.
Price: 177 or 22 cal. $249.95
Price: 4x20 scope and mount $34.95

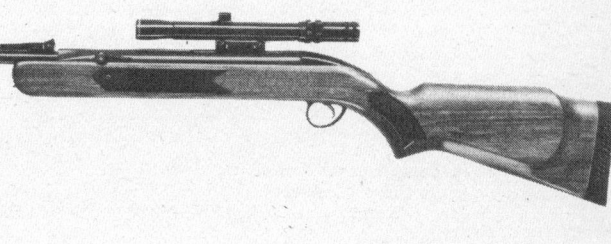

BSA MERCURY AIR RIFLE
Caliber: 177 or 22.
Barrel: 18.5", rifled.
Weight: 7 lbs. **Length:** 43.5" over-all.
Power: Spring-air, barrel cocking.
Stock: European hardwood. Monte Carlo checkpiece, ventilated butt pad.
Sights: Adjustable bead/blade front, tangent rear adj. for w. & e.
Features: Muzzle velocity of 700 fps (177) and 550 fps (22). Reversible. "V" and "U" notch rear sight blade. Single stage match-type trigger, adj. for weight of pull and sear engagement. Scope and mount optional. Introduced 1980. From Precision Sports.
Price: 177 or 22 cal. $164.95
Price: 4x20 scope and mount $34.95

BSA METEOR/METEOR SUPER AIR RIFLES
Caliber: 177 or 22.
Barrel: 18.5", rifled.
Weight: 6 lbs. **Length:** 42" over-all.
Power: Spring-air, barrel cocking.
Stock: European hardwood.
Sights: Adj. bead/blade front, adj. tangent rear with reversible "U" and "V" notch blade.
Features: Muzzle velocity of 650 fps (177) and 500 fps (22). Aperture rear sight element supplied. Cylinder is dovetailed for scope mounting. Adjustable trigger mechanism. Meteor Super has M.C. checkpiece, vent. rubber recoil pad. Introduced 1980. From Precision Sports.
Price: Meteor $99.95
Price: Meteor Super $114.95

BEEMAN/FEINWERKBAU 127 SPORTER
Caliber: 22.
Barrel: 18.3".
Weight: 6.8 lbs. **Length:** 43½" over-all.
Power: Spring piston air; single stroke barrel cocking.
Stock: Walnut finished hardwood.
Sights: Tunnel front; click-adj. rear for w., slide-adj. for e.
Features: Velocity 620-680 fps, cocking effort of 18 lbs. Auto. safety, adj. trigger. Standard model has no checkering, cheekpiece, or swivels. Deluxe has hand-checkered p.g. and fore-end, high comb cheekpiece, ⅞" sling swivels and buttplate with white spacer. Imported by Beeman's.
Price: Standard model $209.50
Price: Deluxe model $249.95
Price: Custom model (special order) $392.50

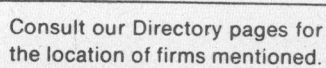

Consult our Directory pages for the location of firms mentioned.

AIR GUNS—LONG GUNS

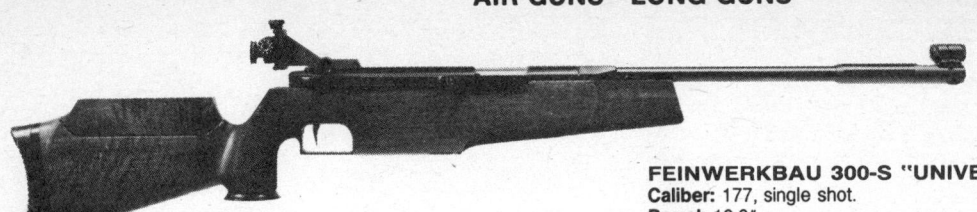

FEINWERKBAU 300-S "UNIVERSAL" MATCH
Caliber: 177, single shot.
Barrel: 19.9".
Weight: 10.2 lbs. (without barrel sleeve). **Length:** 43.3" over-all.
Power: Spring piston, single stroke sidelever.
Stock: Walnut, stippled p.g. and fore-end. Detachable cheekpieces (one std., high for scope use). Adjustable buttplate, accessory rail. Buttplate and grip cap spacers included.
Sights: Two globe fronts with interchangeable inserts. Rear is match aperture with rubber eyecup and sight viser.
Features: Recoilless, vibration free. Grooved for scope mounts. Steel piston ring. Cocking effort about 9½ lbs. Barrel sleeve optional. Left-hand model available. Introduced 1978. Imported by Air Rifle Headquarters, Beeman's.
Price: Right-hand . . . . . $760.00 to $824.50 **Price:** Left-hand $820.00

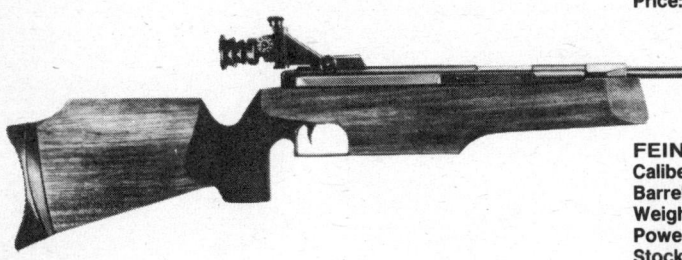

FEINWERKBAU 300-S "Junior" MATCH
Caliber: 177, single shot.
Barrel: 17⅛".
Weight: 8.8 lbs. **Length:** 40" over-all.
Power: Spring piston, single stroke sidelever cocking.
Stock: Walnut. Stippled grip, adjustable buttplate. Scaled-down for youthful or slightly built shooters.
Sights: Globe front with interchangeable inserts, micro. adjustable rear.
Features: Adjustable trigger, recoilless operation. Left-hand model available on special order. Introduced 1978. Imported by Air Rifle Headquarters, Beeman's.
Price: Right-hand . . . . . $598.50 to $648.50 **Price:** Left-hand $655.00

BEEMAN/WEBLEY OSPREY AIR RIFLE
Caliber: 177 or 22.
Barrel: 18½".
Weight: 7¾ lbs. **Length:** 43¼" over-all.
Power: Spring piston air; one stroke side-lever.
Stock: Walnut; sculptured cheekpiece, Monte Carlo comb, rubber buttplate.
Sights: Hooded front, micro. click rear adj. for w. & e. Receiver grooved for aperture sight or scope.
Features: Manual safety plus cocking lever safety to prevent accidental closing. Steel automotive-type piston rings. Velocity 700 fps (177), 550 fps (22). Trigger is adjustable from 3 to 8 lbs. Imported by Beeman's Precision Airguns.
Price: $229.95

BEEMAN/WEIRAUCH HW60 SMALL BORE RIFLE
Caliber: 22 LR.
Barrel: 26.8".
Weight: 10.8 lbs. **Length:** 45.7".
Stock: Walnut, with adj. buttplate.
Sights: Hooded ramp front with inserts, match aperture rear.
Features: Single shot. Adj. match trigger with push-button safety. Stippled fore-end and pistol grip. Rail with adj. swivel. Left-hand version available. Introduced 1980. Imported by Beeman's.
Price: $495.00

BEEMAN'S Model 100 TARGET RIFLE
Caliber: 177, single shot.
Barrel: 18.7", rifled.
Weight: 6 lbs. **Length:** 42" over-all.
Power: Spring, barrel cocking.
Sights: Hooded front, 4-notch rotating rear micro. adj. for w. & e.
Features: Velocity 660 fps MV. Grooved for scope or peep sights; 17 lbs. single stroke cocking; adjustable trigger. Imported by Beeman's.
Price: $149.95

BEEMAN MODEL 250 AIR RIFLE
Caliber: 177 and 22.
Barrel: 20.4".
Weight: 7.7 lbs.
Power: Spring piston.
Sights: Globe front with inserts; micrometer rear.
Features: Velocity of 800-830 fps (177-cal.). Grooved for scope mounts. Automatic safety. Adjustable trigger. Introduced 1980. Imported by Beeman.
Price: $210.00

BEEMAN/WEBLEY VULCAN AIR RIFLE
Caliber: 177 or 22.
Barrel: 17⅛", rifled steel.
Weight: 6.8 lbs. **Length:** 41" over-all.
Power: Spring piston air, barrel cocking.
Stock: Beech with cheekpiece and rubber buttplate.
Sights: Hooded front; micro click rear adj. for w. & e.
Features: Receiver grooved for scope mounting. Manual safety. Trigger adjustable down to about 2 lbs. Velocity 750 fps (177), 600 fps (22). Imported by Beeman's.
Price: $149.95

CAUTION: PRICES CHANGE. CHECK AT GUNSHOP.

AIR GUNS—LONG GUNS

BEEMAN'S Model 200 SPORTER RIFLE
Caliber: 177, single shot.
Barrel: 19", rifled steel.
Weight: 7.1 lbs. **Length:** 44.3" over-all.
Power: Spring, barrel cocking.
Stock: Adult-size walnut finished, soft rubber buttplate.
Sights: Hooded front with removable insert, steel rear adj. for w. & e.
Features: Scope and aperature sight ramp; adj. 2-stage trigger. Imported by Beeman's.
Price: **$196.50**

BEEMAN MODEL 400 RECOILLESS MATCH RIFLE
Caliber: 177, single shot.
Barrel: 18.9".
Weight: 10.7 lbs. **Length:** 44½" over-all.
Power: Spring-piston, single-stroke side lever cocking.
Stock: European walnut with full length fore-end accessory rail, curved adjustable rubber buttplate, stippled grip.
Sights: Globe front with adjustable aperture and optional standard inserts; rear aperture sight with micrometer adjustments for w. and e.
Features: Double-acting 2-piston recoilless action—receiver does not move. Cocking effort 9 lbs. Fully adjustable trigger including length of pull and lateral angle. Left-hand version with left-hand lever available. Detachable muzzle weight. Front aperture is unique neoprene O-ring with knurled ring to vary size. Non-reflective finish. Left-hand version has reversed cocking lever. Imported by Beeman's.
Price: **$555.00**
Price: Left-hand model **$598.50**

BSF 55, S-60, S-70 RIFLES

Model:	Wischo 55S	S-60 (illus.)	B55 Deluxe
Caliber:	177 or 22	177 or 22	177
Barrel:	16"	19"	19"
Rifled:	Yes	Yes	Yes
Length:	40½"	43½"	43¾"
Weight:	6¼ lbs.	6½ lbs.	6½ lbs.
MV:	763, 580	763, 580	763
Sights:	Elev. only	w. & e.	w. & e.
Price:	$175.00 to $214.50	$124.95 to $145.00	$190.00 to $258.50

Features: Spring piston powered, barrel cocking. Blued metal. Adj. 2-stage triggers. Beech stocks on 55S and S-60, have checkered p.g. S-70 mechanically identical to S-60. Beech, checkered p.g. and fore-end. Raised cheek pad, curved rubber buttplate. Available from A.R.H., Beeman's (Wischo 55S only) and Fanta.

WISCHO 70 SPORTING RIFLE
Caliber: 177 or 22, single shot.
Barrel: 16¼", rifled.
Length: 41". **Weight:** 6¼ lbs.
Power: Spring (barrel cocking).
Features: High velocity (750 fps in 177) and accuracy combined with rapid loading, can be reloaded in 5 seconds. Stock is walnut finished with checkered p.g. and buttplate. Open rear, bead front sights; receiver grooved for scope mounting. Trigger is adjustable. Air Rifle Headquarters, importer.
Price: **$258.50**

BENJAMIN SERIES 3100 SUPER REPEATER RIFLES
Caliber: BB, 100-shot; 22, 85-shot.
Barrel: 23", rifled or smoothbore.
Length: 35". **Weight:** 6¼ lbs.
Power: Hand pumped.
Features: Bolt action. Piggy back full view magazine. Bar V adj. rear sight. Walnut stock and pump handle.
Price: M3100, BB .... **$62.45** M3120, 22 rifled **$62.45**

CROSMAN MODEL 73 SADDLE PAL CO^2
Caliber: 177 pellets or BBs, 16-shot magazine.
Barrel: 18", steel.
Weight: 3¼ lbs. **Length:** 34¾" over-all.
Stock: Simulated wood.
Sights: Ramp front, rear adj. for e.
Features: Positive lever safety. Velocity is 425 fps (pellets), 440 fps (BBs). 100 shots per CO_2 cartridge.
Price: About **$24.00**

BENJAMIN SERIES 340 AIR RIFLE
Caliber: 22 and 177 pellets or BB; single shot.
Barrel: 23", rifled and smoothbore.
Length: 35". **Weight:** 6 lbs.
Power: Hand pumped.
Features: Bolt action, walnut Monte Carlo stock and pump handle. Ramp-type front sight, adj. stepped leaf type rear. Push-pull safety.
Price: M340, BB **$62.45**
Price: M342, 22 .... **$62.45** M347, 177 .... **$62.45**

AIR GUNS – LONG GUNS

CROSMAN MODEL 2200 MAGNUM AIR RIFLE
Caliber: 22, single-shot.
Barrel: 19", rifled steel.
Weight: 4 lbs., 13 ozs. **Length:** 39¾" over-all.
Stock: Full-size, wood-grained plastic with checkered p.g. and fore-end.
Sights: Ramp front, open step-adjustable rear.
Features: Variable pump power—3 pumps give 395 fps, 6 pumps 530 fps, 10 pumps 620 fps (average). Full-size adult air rifle. Has white line spacers at pistol grip and buttplate, nickel plated receiver. Introduced 1978.
Price: About $46.99

CROSMAN MODEL 788 BB SCOUT RIFLE
Caliber: 177, BB.
Barrel: 14", steel.
Weight: 2 lbs. 3 ozs. **Length:** 31" over-all.
Stock: Wood-grained ABS plastic.
Sights: Blade on ramp front, open adj. rear.
Features: Variable pump power—3 pumps give MV of 330 fps, 6 pumps 437 fps, 10 pumps 470 fps (BBs, average). Steel barrel, cross-bolt safety. Introduced 1978.
Price: About $21.00

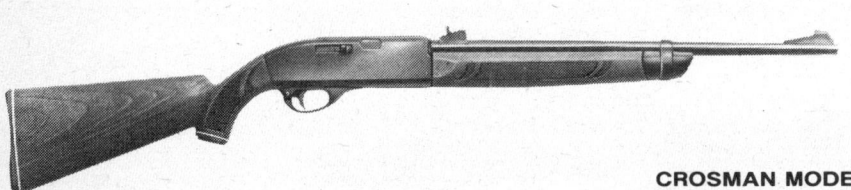

CROSMAN AMERICAN CLASSIC 766 AIR RIFLE
Caliber: 177 pellets or BBs, 15-shot magazine.
Barrel: 19" rifled.
Weight: About 5 lbs. **Length:** 39½" over-all.
Power: Pump-up, pneumatic.
Stock: Wood-grained checkered ABS plastic.
Features: Three pumps gives about 450 fps, 10 pumps about 700 fps. Cross-bolt safety; concealed reservoir holds over 180 BBs.
Price: About $43.99

CROSMAN MODEL 760 POWERMASTER
Caliber: BB, 180 shot.
Barrel: 19½", rifled steel.
Length: 35". **Weight:** 4⅛ lbs.
Power: Pneumatic, hand pump.
Features: Short stroke, power determined by number of strokes. Walnut finished plastic checkered stock and fore-end. Post front sight and adjustable rear sight. Cross-bolt safety. Scope and mount optional.
Price: About $36.00

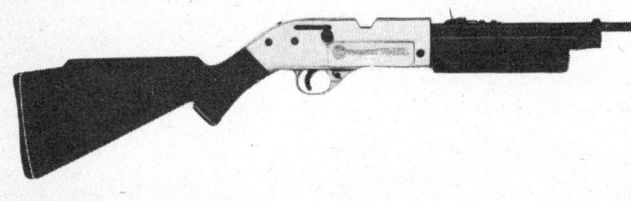

CROSMAN 760XL PUMP RIFLE
Caliber: BB, 180-shot or 177 cal. pellet (single-shot).
Barrel: 19", button rifled.
Length: 36" over-all. **Weight:** 4¾ lbs.
Power: Hand pumped.
Stock: Full-size, wood-grained plastic with Monte Carlo.
Sights: Hooded front, step adj. rear for w. & e.
Features: Receiver grooved for scope mounting, brass plated receiver, cross-bolt safety.
Price: About $39.99

DAISY RIFLES

Model:	95	111	105
Caliber:	BB	BB	BB
Barrel:	18"	18"	13½"
Length:	35"	35"	30½
Power:	Spring	Spring	Spring
Capacity:	700	700	450
Price: About	$23.00	$19.00	$15.00

Features: 95 stock is wood, fore-end plastic; 105 and 111 have plastic stocks.

DAISY 1894 SPITTIN' IMAGE CARBINE
Caliber: BB, 40-shot.
Barrel: 17½", smoothbore.
Length: 38⅜".
Power: Spring.
Features: Cocks halfway on forward stroke of lever, halfway on return.
Price: About $32.00

DAISY MODEL 840
Caliber: 177 pellet (single-shot) or BB (350-shot).
Barrel: 19", smoothbore, steel.
Weight: 3¼ lbs. **Length:** 37⅛" over-all.
Stock: Moulded wood-grain stock and fore-end.
Sights: Ramp front, open, adj. rear.
Features: Single pump pneumatic rifle. Muzzle velocity 325 fps (BB), 300 fps (pellet). Steel buttplate; straight pull bolt action; cross-bolt safety. Fore-end forms pump lever. Introduced 1978.
Price: About $23.00

Daisy Model 845 Target Gun
Special target version of the Model 840. Same as the 840 except comes with globe front sight and No. 5845 Daisy Receiver Sight.
Price: About $26.00

CAUTION: PRICES CHANGE. CHECK AT GUNSHOP.

AIR GUNS—LONG GUNS

DAISY 499 MATCH TARGET
Caliber: BB, single shot.
Barrel: 18", smoothbore.
Weight: About 4 lbs. **Length:** 36¼" over-all.
Stock: Stained harwood, Monte Carlo-style. Fore-end has provision for adding extra weight.
Sights: Globe front, peep rear (Daisy No. 5845, fully adj.)
Features: Official model of the NRA-sanctioned Daisy/U.S. Jaycees Shooting Education Program. Introduced 1980.
Price: About $34.00

POWER LINE 880 PUMP-UP AIR GUN
Caliber: 177 pellets, BB.
Barrel: Smooth bore, steel.
Length: 37¾" over-all. **Weight:** 6 lbs.
Power: Spring air.
Stock: Wood grain moulded plastic.
Sights: Ramp front, open rear adj. for e.
Features: Crafted by Daisy. Variable power (velocity and range) increase with pump strokes. 10 strokes for maximum power. 100-shot BB magazine. Cross-bolt trigger safety. Positive cocking valve.
Price: About $38.00

POWER LINE 881 PUMP-UP AIR GUN
Caliber: 177 pellets, BB.
Barrel: Decagon rifled.
Length: 37¾" over-all. **Weight:** 6 lbs.
Power: Spring air.
Stock: Wood grain moulded plastic with Monte Carlo cheekpiece.
Sights: Ramp front, step-adj. rear for e.
Features: Crafted by Daisy. Accurized version of Model 880. Checkered fore-end and p.g.
Price: About $43.00

POWER LINE MODEL 917/922
Caliber: 177 or 22 pellets, 5-shot clip.
Barrel: 20.8". Decagon rifled brass barrel.
Weight: 5 lbs. **Length:** 37¾" over-all.
Stock: Molded wood-grained plastic with checkered p.g. and fore-end.
Sights: Ramp front, full adj. open rear.
Features: Muzzle velocity from 285 fps (two pumps) to 555 fps. (ten pumps). Straight pull bolt action. Separate buttplate and grip cap with white spacers. Introduced 1978.
Price: About $47.00

Power Line 977 Target Rifle
Similar to Model 917/922 except has engraved black finish receiver; hooded front sight with aperture inserts, fully adj. precision rear with micrometer calibrations. Has 5-shot clip, molded Monte Carlo stock.
Price: About $57.00

DAISY 1938 RED RYDER COMMEMORATIVE BB CARBINE
Caliber: BB, 650-shot repeating action.
Barrel: Sturdy steel, under-barrel loading port.
Length: 35" over-all. **Weight:** 3½ lbs.
Stock: Wood stock burned with Red Ryder lariat signature.
Sights: Post front, adjustable V-slot rear.
Features: Wood fore-end. Saddle ring with leather thong. Lever cocking. Gravity feed. Controlled velocity. Commemorates one of Daisy's most popular guns, the Red Ryder of the 1940s and 1950s.
Price: About $28.00

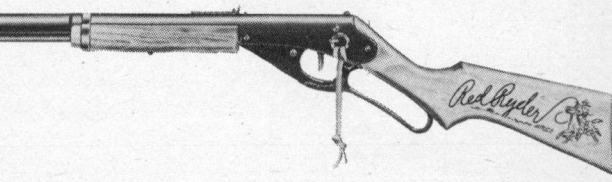

PRECISE MINUTEMAN MK.II REPEATER AIR RIFLE
Caliber: 177, 25-shot.
Barrel: 17½", 12 groove rifling.
Length: 37½". **Weight:** 6½ lbs.
Power: Spring, barrel cocking.
Features: M.V. 675 fps. Micro, adj. target sights, adj. trigger; target type recoil pad, M.C. comb and cheekpiece. Precise, importer.
Price: $125.00

Precise Minuteman Pistol Grip Rifle
Same as repeater version except: available in either 177 or 22 cal.; receiver grooved for scope mounting.
Price: $98.00

AIR GUNS—LONG GUNS

PRECISE MINUTEMAN MKI REPEATER AIR RIFLE
Caliber: 177.
Barrel: 17¼", 12-groove rifling.
Length: 41" over-all. **Weight:** 5¼ lbs.
Power: Spring, barrel cocking.
Stock: Walnut finish.
Sights: Hooded front, micro. adj. rear.
Features: 25-shot automatic pellet feed, m.v. 625 fps. Precise, importer.
Price: **$100.00**

FEINWERKBAU 300-S SERIES MATCH RIFLE
Caliber: 177.
Barrel: 19.9", fixed solid with receiver.
Length: 42.8" over-all. **Weight:** Approx. 10 lbs. with optional bbl. sleeve.
Power: Single stroke sidelever, spring piston.
Stock: Match model—walnut, deep fore-end, adj. buttplate.
Sights: Globe front with interchangeable inserts. Click micro. adj. match aperture rear.
Features: Recoilless, vibration free. Grooved for scope mounts. Permanent lubrication, steel piston ring. Cocking effort 9 lbs. Optional 10 oz. bbl. sleeve. Available from A.R.H., Beeman's.
Price: Right hand .... **$675.00 to $698.50**
Price: Left hand .... **$728.50 to $768.50**

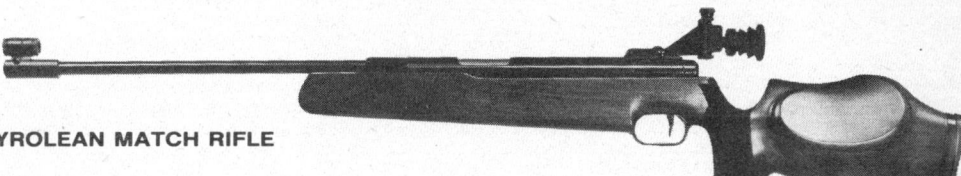

FEINWERKBAU 300-S TYROLEAN MATCH RIFLE
Caliber: 177, single shot.
Barrel: 19.9".
Length: 42.8" over-all. **Weight:** 9.5 lbs.
Power: Spring air, sidelever.
Stock: Walnut. High Tyrolean cheekpiece, medium weight fore-end.
Sights: Globe front with inserts, micro. adj. rear aperture.
Features: Barrel and receiver recoil together to eliminate felt recoil. 4-way adj. trigger. Muzzle velocity 640 fps. Optional 10 oz. bbl. sleeve. Left-hand model available. Available from A.R.H.
Price: **$768.50**

FEINWERKBAU F300S RUNNING BOAR (RT)
Caliber: 177.
Barrel: 19.9", rifled.
Weight: 10.9 lbs., 4 ozs. **Length:** 43" over-all.
Power: Single stroke sidelever, spring piston.
Stock: Walnut with adjustable buttplate, grip cap and comb. Designed for fixed and moving target use.
Sights: None furnished; scope optional.
Features: Recoilless, vibration free. Permanent lubrication and seals. Barrel stabilizer weight included. Crisp single-stage trigger. Available from Air Rifle Headquarters and Beeman's (special order only).
Price: **$678.50**

FEINWERKBAU 124 SPORTER
Caliber: 177.
Barrel: 18.3".
Length: 43.5" over-all. **Weight:** 6.8 lbs.
Power: Spring air; single stroke barrel cocking.
Stock: Walnut finished hardwood.
Sights: Tunnel front, fully adj. open rear.
Features: Velocity over 800 fps. Cocking effort 19 lbs. Automatic safety, adj. trigger. Standard model has no checkering or cheekpiece. Deluxe has checkered p.g. and fore-end, high comb cheekpiece, sling swivels and rubber buttplate with white line spacer. Grooved for peep sight or scope mount. Available from A.R.H. and Beeman's.
Price: Standard model .... **$209.50 to $238.50**
Price: Deluxe model .... **$249.95 to $278.50**
Price: Deluxe left-hand .... **$269.95 to $298.50**

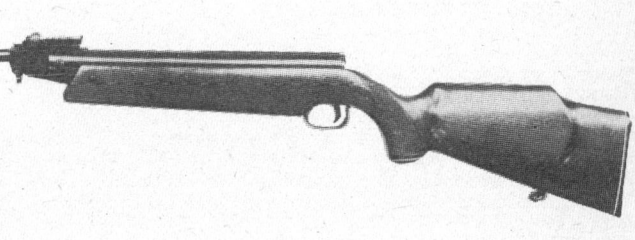

CAUTION: PRICES CHANGE. CHECK AT GUNSHOP.

AIR GUNS—LONG GUNS

Beeman/Feinwerkbau 124 Custom Sporter
Same as Deluxe 124 except assembled in U.S. with select American walnut stock with cheekpiece, rosewood p.g. cap, white line spacers, rubber buttplate, oil finish. Velocity approx. 820 fps, cocking effort 16-18 lbs., q.d. swivels. Accurized version of 124. Options include trigger shoe and cast, checkered trigger guard, front sight with interchangeable inserts. Imported and assembled by Beeman's $535.00

HS 828 (ORIGINAL 45) CX AIR RIFLE
Caliber: 177, single shot.
Barrel: 20½".
Weight: 8¼ lbs. **Length:** 45½" over-all.
Power: Barrel cocking, spring-type.
Stock: Walnut finished hardwood.
Sights: Tasco 6IIV-FM 2x-6x scope
Features: Velocity of 830-842 fps. Manual safety. Cocking effort of 34 lbs. Comes with open sights. Introduced 1980. Imported by Air Rifle Headquarter.
Price: $298.50

MARKSMAN 740 AIR RIFLE
Caliber: 177, 100-shot.
Barrel: 15-½", smoothbore.
Length: 36½". **Weight:** 4 lbs., 2 oz.
Power: Spring, barrel cocking.
Stock: Moulded high-impact ABS plastic.
Sights: Ramp front, open rear adj. for e.
Features: Automatic safety; fixed front, adj. rear sights; shoots 177 cal. BB's pellets and darts. Velocity about 450 fps.
Price: $29.50

NORICA 80-G TARGET RIFLE
Caliber: 177, single shot.
Barrel: 18".
Weight: 6 lbs., 14 ozs. **Length:** 43" over-all.
Power: Barrel cocking, spring type.
Stock: Walnut stained beechwood
Sights: Globe front with interchangeable inserts; rear is adj. for w. and e. and has interchangeable inserts.
Features: Two-stage trigger with provision for adjustments. Stock has hefty pistol grip with black cap, buttplate and beavertail fore-end. Cocking effort is 20 lbs. Imported from Spain by Air Rifle Headquarters. Introduced 1980.
Price: $168.50

NORICA MODEL 73
Caliber: 177, single shot.
Barrel: 17¾".
Weight: 6½ lbs. **Length:** 41½" over-all.
Power: Barrel cocking, spring type.
Stock: Walnut-finished hardwood
Sights: Globe front with interchangeable inserts, open rear adj. for w. and e.
Features: Two-stage trigger with 3 lb. pull. Cocking effort of 18 lbs. Velocity of 637 fps. Rear cylinder is dovetailed for scope mounts. Introduced 1980. Imported from Spain by Air Rifle Headquarters.
Price: $118.50

PRECISE MINUTEMAN TOURNAMENT AIR RIFLE
Caliber: 177, 22, single shot.
Barrel: 18". 12-groove rifling.
Length: 43" over-all. **Weight:** 6¾ lbs.
Power: Spring, barrel cocking.
Features: Muzzle velocty of 670 fps. Micro. adj. rear sight, hooded front. Walnut finish stock; Monte Carlo comb with cheek piece, recoil pad. Receiver grooved for scope mounting. Precise, importer.
Price: $90.00

Precise Minuteman Carbine
Same as Tournament model except has plain stock without Monte Carlo comb, cheekpiece; over-all length 41", weight 5¼ lbs., M.V. 625 fps. $75.00

SIG-HAMMERLI MODELS 401 & 403 AIR RIFLE
Caliber: 177, single shot.
Weight: 7.8 lbs. **Length:** 44" over-all.
Power: Spring air, sidelever cocking.
Stock: Beechwood.
Sights: Globe front accepts interchangeable inserts; fully adj. open rear (Model 401) or match aperture rear (Model 403).
Features: Sidelever cocking effort of 20 lbs. Automatic safety. Model 403 has a 2-lb. barrel sleeve and adj. buttplate. Fully adj. trigger. Introduced 1980. Imported by Great Lakes Airguns.
Price: Model 401 .... $136.04
Price: Model 403 (shown) $239.95

SHERIDAN CO^2 AIR RIFLES
Caliber: 5mm (20 cal.), single shot.
Barrel: 18½", rifled.
Weight: 6 lbs. **Length:** 37" over-all.
Stock: Walnut sporter.
Power: Standard 12.5 gram CO^2 cylinder.
Sights: Open, adj. for w. and e. Optional Sheridan Williams 5D-SH receiver sight or Weaver D4 scope.
Features: Bolt action single shot, CO^2 powered. Velocity approx. 514 fps., manual thumb safety. Blue or Silver finish. Left-hand models avail. at same prices.
Price: CO^2 Blue Streak $79.95
Price: CO^2 Silver Streak $82.95
Price: CO^2 Blue Streak with receiver sight $92.95
Price: CO^2 Blue Streak with Weaver D4 scope $111.50

SIG-HAMMERLI MILITARY LOOK 420
Caliber: 177 or 22, single shot.
Barrel: 19" rifled.
Weight: About 7 lbs. **Length:** 44¼" over-all.
Stock: Synthetic stock and handguard.
Sights: Open, fully adj.
Features: Side lever cocking; adjustable trigger; rifled steel barrel. Introduced 1977. Imported by Mandall Shooting Supplies, Fanta.
Price: .... $178.00 to $199.50

Consult our Directory pages for the location of firms mentioned.

AIR GUNS—LONG GUNS

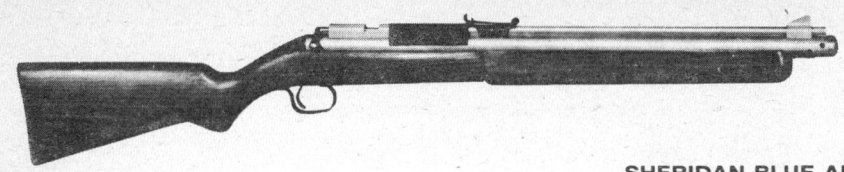

WALTHER LGV SPECIAL
Caliber: 177, single shot.
Barrel: 16", rifled.
Length: 41⅜". **Weight:** 10¼ lbs.
Power: Spring air (barrel cocking).
Features: Micro. click adj. aperture receiver sight; Adj. trigger. Walnut match stock, adj. buttplate. Double piston provides vibration-free shooting. Easily operated bbl. latch. Removable heavy bbl. sleeve. 5-way adj. trigger. Imported by Interarms.
Price: $600.00

WALTHER LGR RIFLE
Caliber: 177, single-shot.
Barrel: 19½", rifled.
Length: 44¼" over-all. **Weight:** 10.2 lbs.
Power: Side lever cocking, compressed air.
Stock: French walnut.
Sights: Replaceable insert hooded front, Walther micro. adjustable rear.
Features: Recoilless operation. Trigger adj. for weight, pull and position. High comb stock with broad stippled fore-end and p.g. Imported by Interarms.
Price: $725.00

SHERIDAN BLUE AND SILVER STREAK RIFLES
Caliber: 5mm (20 cal.), single shot.
Barrel: 18½", rifled.
Length: 37". **Weight:** 5 lbs.
Power: Hand pumped (swinging fore-end).
Features: Rustproof barrel and piston tube. Takedown. Thumb safety. Mannlicher type walnut stock. Left-hand models same price.
Price: Blue Streak .... $79.95 Silver Streak $82.95
Sheridan accessories: Intermount, a base for ⅜" Tip-Off scope mounts, **$9.95**; Sheridan-Williams 5DSH receiver sight, **$9.75** Sheridan Pelletrap, **$14.95**; Sheridan 5mm pellets, **$4.50** for 500. Weaver 4 x scope and Intermount installed **$29.90 (extra).**

Walther LGR Match Air Rifle
Same basic specifications as standard LGR except has a high comb stock, sights are mounted on riser blocks. Introduced 1977.
Price: $800.00

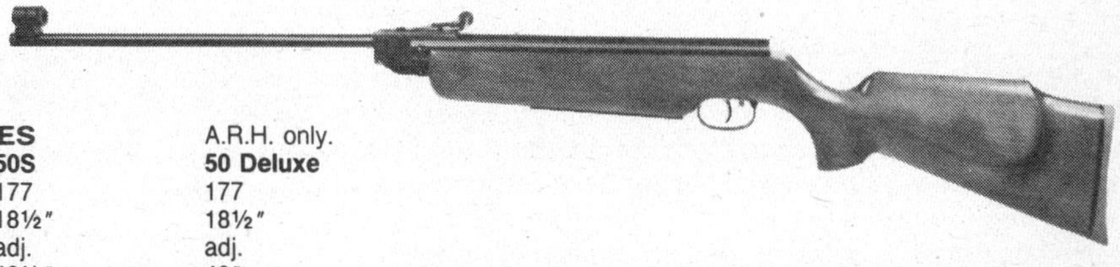

WEIHRAUCH 30 & 50 SERIES RIFLES

Model:	30S	30M-II	50S	A.R.H. only. 50 Deluxe
Caliber:	177	177	177	177
Barrel:	17"	17"	18½"	18½"
Trigger:	adj.	adj.	adj.	adj.
Length:	40"	40"	43½"	43"
Wgt., lbs.:	5½	5½	7	7
Price:	$139.95	$128.50	$150.00	$218.50

Features: All are rifled and spring-operated by single stroke cocking. Post and ramp front sights (50M has globe front with 4 inserts). Open click rear sights, adj. for w. & e. Walnut finished stocks. 30M-II and 50 Deluxe have cheekpiece, wide fore-end, M.C. comb, ⅞" sling swivels. MV of all 660-705 fps. Available from Air Rifle Hdqtrs., Beeman's, Fanta.

WEIHRAUCH 55 TARGET RIFLES

Model:	55SM	55MM	55T
Caliber:	177	177	177
Barrel:	18½"	18½"	18½"
Length:	43½"	43½"	43½"
Wgt. lbs.:	7.8	7.8	7.8

Rear sight: All aperture
Front sight: All with globe and 4 interchangeable inserts.
Power: All springs (barrel cocking). 660-700 fps.
Price: $298.50 $398.50 $399.50
Features: Trigger fully adj. and removable. Micrometer rear sight adj. for w. and e. on all. P.g. high comb stock with beavertail fore-end, walnut finish stock on 55SM. Walnut stock on 55MM, (illus.) Tyrolean stock on 55T. Available from Air Rifle Hdqtrs., Beeman's, Fanta.

> Consult our Directory pages for the location of firms mentioned.

WEIHRAUCH 35 SPORTER RIFLES

Model:	35/S	35L	35EB	35TH
Caliber:	177	177	177 or 22	177
Barrel:	19½"	19½"	19½"	19½"
Length:	45½"	43½"	45½"	44½"
Wgt. lbs.:	7.9	8	8	8.6
Rear sight:	open	open	Open	Open
Front sight:	All with globe and 5 interchangeable inserts.			
Power:	All spring (barrel cocking).			
Price:	$214.50	$234.95	$259.95	$240.00

Features: Trigger fully adj. and removable. Manual safety. Open rear sight click adj. for w. and e. P.g. high comb stock with beavertail fore-end, walnut finish, except 35E has checkered walnut with standard cheekpiece. 35L has Bavarian cheekpiece stock. Model 35EB with American-styled stock with cheekpiece, white spacers and sling swivels. Model 35TH (Beeman's only) has thumbhole stock. Beeman's does not have Model 35/S. Available from Air Rifle Hdqtrs., Beeman's, Fanta.

Chokes & Brakes

Choke-Matic
Cutts Compensator

The Cutts Compensator is one of the oldest variable choke devices available. Manufactured by Lyman Gunsight Corporation, it is available with either a steel or aluminum body. A series of vents allows gas to escape upward and downward, reducing recoil without directing muzzle blast toward nearby shooters. For the 12-ga. Comp body, six fixed-choke tubes are available: the Spreader—popular with Skeet shooters; Improved Cylinder; Modified; Full; Superfull, and Magnum Full. Full,

Modified and Spreader tubes are available for 12, or 20, and an Adjustable Tube, giving Full through Improved Cylinder chokes, is offered in 12, or 20 gauges. Cutts Compensator, complete with wrench, adaptor and any single tube $54.95; with adjustable tube $69.95. All single choke tubes $14.95 each. No factory installation is available and stock is limited on gauges.

Dahl Muzzle Blast Controller

Only 1⅞" long by ¾" in diameter, this device is claimed to reduce recoil up to 30%. An outer sleeve, threaded onto the gun muzzle, is threaded on the inside to accept a machined plug which is bored through for bullet passage. Gas behind the bullet is bled off through slots in the plug, swirled through a number of tiny passages while contained by the sleeve, and then vented upward, this final action offsetting muzzle jump without discomfort to the shooter or bystanders. Price is $40.00, installed.

Emsco Choke

E. M. Schacht of Waseca, Minn., offers the Emsco, a small diameter choke which features a precision curve rather than a taper behind the 1½" choking area. 9 settings are available in this 5 oz. attachment. Its removable recoil sleeve can be furnished in dural if desired. Choice of three sight heights. For 12, 16 or 20 gauge. Price installed, $22.95. Not installed, $17.50.

Jet-Away Choke

Arms Ingenuity Corp., makers of the Jet-Away, say that this device controls patterns through partial venting of the powder gases which normally enlarge patterns. The Jet-Away has a series of three slots in the top of the tube and a sliding control sleeve. When the sleeve is in its rearward position, all slots are uncovered, the maximum of gas is vented and patterns are densest. To obtain more open patterns, the sleeve is moved to cover one or more slots. In 12, 16 or 20 gauge only, the Jet-Away is made of aluminum, weighs 3 ozs. $35.00 installed.

Lyman CHOKE

The Lyman CHOKE is similar to the Cutts Comp in that it comes with fixed-choke tubes or an adjustable tube, with or without recoil chamber. The adjustable tube version sells for $32.00 with recoil chamber, $27.00 without, in 12 or 20 gauge. Lyman also offers a Single-Choke Adaptor at $5.00. This device may be used with or without a recoil-reduction chamber; cost of the latter is $5.00 extra. Available in 12 or 20 gauge only, no factory installation offered.

Mag-Na-Port

EDM is the process to "install" this muzzle venting process on any firearm except those having shrouded barrels. EDM is a metal-erosion technique using carbon electrodes that control the area to be processed. The Mag-Na-Port venting process utilizes small trapezoidal openings that go into and through the barrel that direct powder gases upward and outward to reduce recoil.

The resultant opening made by the EDM process is smoothly and cleanly made, with no burring in or out. No effect is had on bluing or nickeling outside the Mag-Na-Port area so no refinishing is needed. Cost for the Mag-Na-Port treatment is $45.00 for handguns, $60.00 for rifles, plus transportation both ways, and $1.50 for handling.

Poly-Choke

The Poly-Choke Co. manufacturers of the original adjustable shotgun choke now offers two models, the Deluxe Ventilated and the Deluxe Standard. Each provides 9 choke settings including Xtra-Full and Slug. The Ventilated model which will reduce approximately 20% of a shotguns recoil, is priced at $39.95. The Standard model is $37.95.

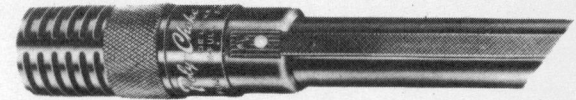

The Poly-Choke Co. is in its 50th year. Millions of Poly-Chokes are in use throughout the world. The Company also manufactures Ventilated Ribs for shotguns and handguns.

Pro-Port

A compound ellipsoid muzzle venting process similar to Mag-na-porting, only exclusively applied to shotguns. Like Mag-na-porting, this system reduces felt recoil, muzzle jump, and shooter fatigue. Very helpful for doubles shooters. Pro-Port is a patented process and installation is available in both the U.S. and Canada. Cost for the Pro-Port process is $110.00 for over-unders (both barrels); $80.00 for only the bottom barrel; $80.00 for side-by-sides; and $65.00 for single barrel shotguns. Prices do not include shipping and handling.

Micrometer Receiver Sights

LYMAN No. 57
¼-min. clicks. Target or Stayset knobs. Quick release slide, adjustable zero scales. Made for almost all modern rifles. Price $34.95

LYMAN No. 66
Fits close to the rear of flat-sided receivers, furnished with target or Stayset knobs. Quick release slide, ¼-min. adj. For most lever or slide action or flat-sided automatic rifles. Price $34.95

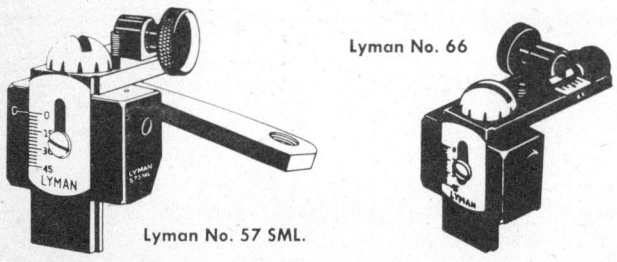

REDFIELD "PALMA" TARGET SIGHT
Windage and elevation adjustments are ¼-MOA and can be adjusted for "hard" or "soft" feel. Repeatability error limited to .001" per click. Windage latitude 36 MOA, elevation 60 MOA. Mounting arm has three positions, providing ample positioning latitude for other sighting aids such as variable diopter correction, adjustable filters. An insert in the sighting disc block accepts either the standard American sighting disc thread or the European 9.5mm × 1 metric thread. Elevation staff and the sighting disc block have dovetail construction for precise travel. Price $160.70

WILLIAMS FP
Internal click adjustments. Positive locks. For virtually all rifles, T/C Contender, plus Win., Rem. and Ithaca shotguns. Price $25.00
With Twilight Aperture $25.75
With Target Knobs $29.70
With Target Knobs & Twilight Aperture $30.45
With Square Notched Blade $26.30
With Target Knobs & Square Notched Blade $31.00

B-SQUARE SMLE (LEE-ENFIELD)
For No. 4 and Jungle carbine. No drilling or tapping required. ³⁄₃₂" disc furnished. Price $5.95

BUEHLER
"Little Blue Peep" auxiliary rear sight used with Buehler scope mounts. Price $3.35

FREELAND TUBE SIGHT
Uses Unertl 1" micrometer mounts. For 22-cal. target rifles, inc. 52 Win., 37, 40X Rem. and BSA Martini. Price, less peep $90.00

WILLIAMS 5-D SIGHT
Low cost sight for shotguns, 22's and the more popular big game rifles. Adjustment for w. and e. Fits most guns without drilling or tapping. Also for Br. SMLE. Price $14.15
With Twilight Aperture $14.90
Extra Shotgun Aperture $3.75

WILLIAMS GUIDE
Receiver sight for .30 M1 Car., M1903A3 Springfield, Savage 24's, Savage-Anschutz rifles and Wby. XXII. Utilizes military dovetail; no drilling. Double-dovetail W. adj., sliding dovetail adj. for E. Price $13.55
With Twilight Aperture $14.30
With Open Sight Blade $12.50

Sporting Leaf and Tang Sights

BURRIS FOLDING LEAF
Two-way leaf rear sight with dovetail. Hefty spring holds sight in upright position. One height—.350" to .475" (Model FLL.) Price $7.95

BURRIS SPORTING REAR SIGHT
Made of spring steel, supplied with multi-step elevator for coarse adjustments and notch plate with lock screw for finer adjustments. Price .. $9.95

LYMAN No. 16
Middle sight for barrel dovetail slot mounting. Folds flat when scope or peep sight is used. Sight notch plate adjustable for e. White triangle for quick aiming. 3 heights; A—.400" to .500", B—.345" to .445", C—.500" to .600". Price $7.50

MARBLE FALSE BASE
New screw-on base for most rifles replaces factory base. ⅜" dovetail slot permits installation of any Marble rear sight. Can be had in sweat-on models also. Price $3.60

MARBLE CONTOUR RAMP
For late model Rem. 725, 740, 760, 742 rear sight mounting. ⁹⁄₁₆" between mounting screws. Price $8.00

MARBLE FOLDING LEAF
Flat-top or semi-buckhorn style. Folds down when scope or peep sights are used. Reversible plate gives choice of "U" or "V" notch. Adjustable for elevation. Price $7.20
Also available with both w. and e. adjustment $8.40

MARBLE SPORTING REAR
With white enamel diamond, gives choice of two "U" and two "V" notches of different sizes. Adjustment in height by means of double step elevator and sliding notch piece. For all rifles; screw or dovetail installation. Price $7.40—$8.40

MARBLE SPORTING REAR
Single step elevator. "U" notch with white triangle aiming aid. Lower priced version of double step model. Price $5.00

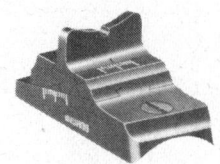

WILLIAMS DOVETAIL OPEN SIGHT
Open rear sight with w. and e. adjustment. Furnished with "U" notch or choice of blades. Slips into dovetail and locks with gib lock. Heights from .281" to .531". Price with blade $7.80
Less Blade $5.10
Extra Blades $2.70

WILLIAMS GUIDE OPEN SIGHT
Open rear sight with w. and e. adjustment. Bases to fit most military and commercial barrels. Choice of square "U" or "V" notch blade, ³⁄₁₆", ¼", ⁵⁄₁₆", or ⅜" high $9.40
Extra blades, each $2.70
Price, less blade $6.70

FREELAND SUPERIOR
Furnished with six 1" plastic apertures. Available in 4½"-6½" lengths. Made for any target rifle. Price with base $29.00
Price with 6 metal insert apertures $31.00
Price, front base $6.40

Front Sights

BURRIS FRONT SIGHTS
Two styles: Patridge, gold bead. Widths are .250", .340", .500" and Mauser .310"..from **$4.50 to $5.00**

LYMAN BLADE & DOVETAIL SIGHTS
Made with gold or ivory beads 1/16" to 3/32" wide and in varying heights for most military and commercial rifles. Price **$6.50**

MARBLE STANDARD
Ivory, red, or gold bead. For all American made rifles. 1/16" wide bead with semi-flat face which does not reflect light. Specify type of rifle when ordering. Price **$4.25**

MARBLE-SHEARD "GOLD"
Shows up well even in darkest timber. Shows same color on different colored objects; sturdily built. Medium bead. Various models for different makes of rifles so specify type of rifle when ordering. Price **$5.25**

MARBLE CONTOURED
Same contour and shape as Marble-Sheard but uses standard 1/16" or 3/32" bead, ivory, red or gold. Specify rifle type **$4.80**

WILLIAMS GUIDE BEAD SIGHT
Fits all shotguns. 1/8" ivory, red or gold bead. Screws into existing sight hole. Various thread sizes and shank lengths **$2.85**
Cultured Pearl Guide Bead **$6.00**

Globe Target Front Sights

FREELAND TWIN SET
Two Freeland Superior or Junior Globe Front Sights, long or short, allow switching from 50 yd. to 100 yd. ranges and back again without changing rear sight adjustment. Sight adjustment compensation is built into the set; just interchange and you're "on" at either range. Set includes 6 plastic apertures.
Twin set (long or short) **$45.00**
Price with 6 metal apertures **$49.00**

FREELAND MILITARY
Short model for use with high-powered rifles where sight must not extend beyond muzzle. Screw-on base; six plastic apertures. Price **$29.00**
Price with 6 metal apertures **$31.00**
Price, front base **$6.40**

LYMAN No. 17A
7 interchangeable inserts which include 4 apertures, one transparent amber and two posts .50" and .100" in width. Price **$13.95**

REDFIELD Nos. 63 and 64
For rifles specially stocked for scopes where metallic sights must be same height as scopes. Instantly detachable to permit use of scope. Two styles and heights of bases. Interchangeable inserts. No. 64 is 1/4" higher. With base, Price **$18.30**

REDFIELD No. 65
1" long, 5/8" diameter. Standard dovetail base with 7 aperture or post inserts which are not reversible. For any rifle having standard barrel slot. 13/32" height from bottom of base to center of aperture. No. 65NB same as above with narrow base for Win. 64 N.R.A., 70, and Savage 40, 45, and 99 with ramp front sight base. Price **$19.90**

REDFIELD No. 66
Replaces entire removable front sight stud, locked in place by screw in front of barrel band. 3/4" from bottom of base to center of aperture. For Spgfld. 1903. Price **$19.90**

REDFIELD No. 68
For Win. 52, heavy barrel, Sav. 19 and 33, and other rifles requiring high front sight. 17/32" from bottom of base to center of aperture. Standard dovetail size only. Price **$19.90**

REDFIELD OLYMPIC FRONT
Detachable. 10 inserts—5 steel, sizes .090", .110", .120", .140", .150"; one post insert, size .100"; four celluloid, sizes .090", .110", .120", .140". Celluloid inserts in clear, green, or amber, with or without cross hairs. For practically all rifles and with any type rear sight. Fits all standard Redfield, Lyman, or Fecker scope blocks. With base, Price **$31.90**

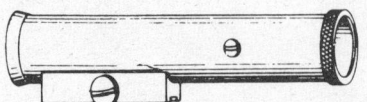

REDFIELD INTERNATIONAL SMALLBORE FRONT
Similar to Olympic. Drop-in insertion of eared inserts. Outer sleeve prevents light leakage. Comes complete with 6 clear inserts and 6 skeleton inserts **$37.90**

REDFIELD INTERNATIONAL MILITARY BIG BORE
Same as International Match except tube only 2 1/4" long. For 30 cal. use. Price **$37.90**

Ramp Sights

LYMAN SCREW-ON RAMP AND SIGHT
Used with 8 40 screws but may also be brazed on. Heights from .10" to .350". Price with sight .... **$11.90** Price: Ramp without sight **$8.95**

MARBLE FRONT RAMPS
Available in either screw-on or sweat-on style. 5 heights; 3/16", 5/16", 3/8", 7/16", 9/16". Standard 3/8" dovetail slot. Price **$7.50**
Hoods for above ramps **$1.65**

WILLIAMS SHORTY RAMP
Companion to "Streamlined" ramp, about 1/2" shorter. Screw-on or sweat-on. It is furnished in 1/8", 3/16", 9/32", and 3/8" heights without hood only. Price **$6.70**

WILLIAMS STREAMLINED RAMP
Hooded style in screw-on or sweat-on models. Furnished in 9/16", 7/16", 3/8", 5/16", 3/16" heights. Price with hood **$10.55**
Price without hood **$8.75**

Handgun Sights

BO-MAR DE LUXE
Gives 3/8" w. and e. adjustment at 50 yards on Colt Gov't 45, sight radius under 7". For GM and Commander models only. Uses existing dovetail slot. Has shield-type rear blade. Price **$38.00**

BO-MAR LOW PROFILE RIB
Streamlined rib with front and rear sights; 7 1/8" sight radius. Brings sight line closer to the bore than standard or extended sight and ramp. Weighs 4 oz. Made for Ruger Mark I Bull Barrel, Colt Gov't 45, Super 38, and Gold Cup 45 and 38. Price **$50.00**
With extended sight and ramp, 8 1/8" radius, 5 3/4 oz. Price **$57.00**
Rib & tuner—inserted in Low Profile Rib—accuracy tuner. Adjustable for barrel positioning. Price **$59.00**

BO-MAR COMBAT RIB
For S&W Model 19 revolver with 4" barrel. Sight radius 5¾"; weight 5½ oz. Price **$50.00**

BO-MAR FAST DRAW RIB
Streamlined full length rib with integral Bo-Mar micrometer sight and serrated fast draw sight. For Browning 9mm, S&W 39, Colt Commander 45, Super Auto and 9mm. Price **$50.00**

BO-MAR WINGED RIB
For S&W 4" and 6" length barrels—K-38 M10, HB 14 and 19. Weight for the 6" model is about 7¼ ozs. Price **$58.00**

BO-MAR COVER-UP RIB
Adj. rear sight, winged front guards. Fits right over revolver's original front sight. For S&W 4" M-10HB, M-13, M-58, M-64 & 65. Ruger 4" models SDA-34, SDA-84, SS-34, SS-84, GF-34, GF-84. Price **$56.00**

MICRO
Click adjustable w. and e. rear with plain or undercut front sight in ⅛" widths. Standard model available for 45, Super 38 or Commander autos. Low model for above pistols plus Colt Service Ace. Also for Ruger with 4¾" or 6" barrel. Price for sets **$28.50**
Price with ramp front sight **$35.00**
Adjustable rear sight only **$24.00**
Front ramp only, with blade **$14.00**

MICRO
All-steel replacement for Ruger single-action and double-action revolvers. Two styles: MR-44 for square front end of sight leaf **$18.00**

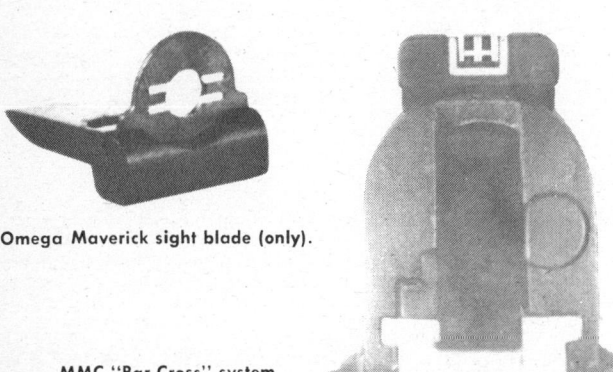

Omega Maverick sight blade (only).

MMC "Bar Cross" system.

MMC "BAR CROSS" SIGHT SYSTEM
Provides a quick, clear sight picture in a variety of lighting conditions. Black oxide finish is non-reflective. Front sight has a horizontal white bar with vertical white bar, gives illusion of cross hair in poor light. Fixed rear comes with or without white outline. Various front blades available.
White outline rear sight **$14.55**
Plain rear **$11.40**
Ramp Bar Cross front **$10.45**

MMC COMBAT DESIGN
Available specifically for Colt M1911 and descendants, High Standard autos, Ruger standard autos. Adaptable to other pistols. Some gunsmithing required. Not necessary to replace front sight.
Price, less leaf **$22.00**
Plain leaf **$6.55**
White outline leaf **$9.60**
Extra for satin nickel finish (base only) **$7.60**

MMC NO. 5
Fully adjustable and replaces the factory sight for S&W M39 and M59. Supplied assembled. ⅛" wide notch, white outline or plain. Not necessary to replace front sight.
Complete, plain **$51.75**
White outline **$54.65**
Extra for satin nickel finish (base only) **$7.60**

OMEGA OUTLINE SIGHT BLADES
Replacement rear sight blades for Colt and Ruger single action guns and the Interarms Virginian Dragoon. Standard Outline available in gold or white notch outline on blue metal.
Price **$5.95**

OMEGA MAVERICK SIGHT BLADES
Replacement "peep-sight" blades for Colt, Ruger SAs, Virginian Dragoon. Three models available—No. 1, Plain, No. 2, Single Bar, No. 3 Double Bar Rangefinder.
Price, each **$6.95**

Sight Attachments

FREELAND LENS ADAPTER
Fits 1⅛" O.D. prescription ground lens to all standard tube and receiver sights for shooting without glasses. Price without lens **$40.50**
Price: Clear lens ground to prescription **$20.00**
Price: Yellow or green prescription lens **$20.00**

MERIT ADAPTER FOR GLOBE FRONT SIGHTS
An Iris Shutter Disc with a special adapter for mounting in Lyman or Redfield globe front sights. Price **$38.00**

MERIT IRIS SHUTTER DISC
Eleven clicks gives 12 different apertures. No. 3 and Master, primarily target types, .022" to .125"; No. 4, ½" dia. hunting type, .025" to .155". Available for all popular sights. The Master Disc, with flexible rubber light shield, is particularly adapted to extension, scope height, and tang sights. All Merit Deluxe models have internal click springs; are hand fitted to minimum tolerance.
Std. Master .... **$41.25** Master Deluxe **$51.25**

MERIT LENS DISC
Similar to Merit Iris Shutter (Model 3 or Master) but incorporates provision for mounting prescription lens integrally. Lens may be obtained locally, or prescription sent to Merit. Sight disc is ⁷⁄₁₆" wide (Mod. 3), or ¾" wide (Master). Lens, ground to prescription, **$19.00** Standard tints, **$23.50**. Model 3 Deluxe. Price **$52.50**
Master Deluxe **$61.25**

MERIT OPTICAL ATTACHMENT
For revolver and pistol shooters. Instantly attached by rubber suction cup to regular or shooting glasses. Any aperture .020" to .156". Price, Deluxe (swings aside) **$44.00**

REDFIELD SURE-X SIGHTING DISC
Eight hole selective aperture. Fits any Redfield target sight. Each click changes aperture .004". Price **$16.90**

REDFIELD SIGHTING DISCS
Fit all Redfield receiver sights. .046" to .093" aperture. ⅜", ½" and ⅞" O.D. Price, each **$3.30**

WILLIAMS APERTURES
Standard thread, fits most sights. Regular series ⅜" to ½" O.D., .050" to .125" hole. "Twilight" series has white reflector ring. .093" to .125" inner hole. Price, regular series ... **$2.00**. Twilight series **$2.75**
New wide open ⁵⁄₁₆" aperture for shotguns fits 5-D and Foolproof sights. Price **$3.75**

Shotgun Sights

ACCURA-SITE
For shooting shotgun slugs. Three models to fit most shotguns—"A" for vent. rib barrels, "B" for solid ribs, "C" for plain barrels. Rear sight has windage and elevation provisions. Easily removed and replaced. Includes front and rear sights.
Price: .... **$14.95 to $18.95**

FOR DOUBLE BARREL SHOTGUNS (PRESS FIT)
Marble 214—Ivory front bead, ¹¹⁄₆₄" ... **$2.40**; 215—same with .080" rear bead and reamers ... **$8.15.** Marble 220—Bi-color (gold and ivory) front bead, ¹¹⁄₆₄" and .080 rear bead, with reamers ... **$9.25;** Marble 221—front bead only ... **$3.50.** Marble 223—Ivory rear .080 ... **$2.20.** Marble 224—Front sight reamer for 214-221 beads ... **$2.25;** Marble 226—Rear sight reamer for 223 .... **$1.75**

FOR SINGLE OR DB SHOTGUNS (SCREW-ON FIT)
Marble 217—Ivory front bead ¹¹⁄₆₄" ... **$2.65;** Marble 216 **$5.50** Marble 218—Bi-color front, ¹¹⁄₆₄" ... **$3.85;** Marble 219 ... **$6.70** Marble 223T—Ivory rear .080 .... **$3.65**
Marble Bradley type sights 223BT—⅛", ⁵⁄₆₄" and ¹¹⁄₆₄" long. Gold, Ivory or Red bead **$2.50**

SLUG SITE
A combination V-notch rear and bead front sight made of adhesive-backed formed metal approx. 7" over-all. May be mounted, removed and re-mounted as necessary, using new adhesive from the pack supplied **$10.00**

WILLIAMS SHOTGUN RAMP
Designed to elevate the front bead for slug shooting or for guns that shoot high. Diameters to fit most 12, 16, 20 ga. guns. Fastens by screw-clamp, no drilling required. Price, with Williams gold bead **$6.45**
Price, without bead **$4.75**
Price, with Guide Bead **$7.60**

CAUTION: PRICES CHANGE. CHECK AT GUNSHOP.

SCOPES & MOUNTS
HUNTING, TARGET ■ & VARMINT ■ SCOPES

Maker and Model	Magn.	Field at 100 Yds. (feet)	Relative Brightness	Eye Relief (in.)	Length (in.)	Tube Diam. (in.)	W&E Adjustments	Weight (ozs.)	Other Data	Price
American Import Co.										
Dickson 200	4	19	13.7	3.5	11.5	¾	Int.	6	Complete with mount for 22-cal. RF rifles.	$ 9.95
Dickson 218	2½	32	164	3.7	12	1	Int.	9.3		36.95
Dickson 220	4	29	64	3.6	12	1	Int.	9.1	Standard crosshair reticle, coated lenses.	34.95
Dickson 226	6	20	44.7	3.7	13	1	Int.	10	Anodized finish.	41.50
Dickson 228	4	37	64	3.3	12	1	Int.	10.5	Wide angle.	44.95
Dickson 230	4	37	100	3.8	12.4	1	Int.	12	Wide angle.	52.95
Dickson 233	4	42	64	3	9.6	1	Int.	14.5	Post and crosshair, 3 post, tapered post,	66.95
Dickson 240	3-9	37-12.3	112-13	3	12.8	1	Int.	13.8	crosshair and 4-post crosshair all avail. as	52.95
Dickson 242	3-9	37-12.3	177-19.4	3	12.8	1	Int.	15.2	options.	55.95
Burris										
4x Fullfield	3.8	37	49	3¼	11¼	1	Int.	11	3" dot $10.00 extra.	129.95
2x-7x Fullfield HiLume	2.5-6.8	50-19	81-22	3¼	11⅞	1	Int.	14	1"-3" dot $10.00 extra.	175.95
3x-9x Fullfield HiLume	3.3-8.6	40-15	72-17.6	3¼	12¾	1	Int.	15	1"-3" dot $10.00 extra.	189.95
2¾ Fullfield	2.7	53	49	3¼	10½	1	Int.	9		116.95
6x Fullfield	5.8	24	36	3¼	13	1	Int.	12		139.95
1¾-5x Fullfield HiLume	2.5-6.8	70-27	121-25	3¼	10¾	1	Int.	13		159.95
4x-12x Fullfield	4.4-11.8	28-10½	—	3-3¼	15	1	Int.	18	Dot reticle $10 extra. Target knobs $15 extra.	231.95
6x-18x Fullfield	6.5-17.6	17-7.5	—	3-3¾	15.8	1	Int.	18.5	½-minute dot $10 extra. LER= Long Eye Re-	$235.95
10x Fullfield	9.8	12½	—	3¼	15	1	Int.	15	lief. Ideal for forward mounting or on hand-	183.95
12x Fullfield	11.8	11	—	3¼	15	1	Int.	15	guns. Plex or cross hair only. Target knobs	190.95
2x LER	1.7	21	—	10-24	8¾	1	Int.	6.8	($15 extra) available for 3x. Matte "Safari"	95.85
3x LER	2.7	17	—	10-20	8⅞	1	Int.	6.8	finish avail. on 4x, 6x, 2-7x, 3-9x with Plex	102.95
2x-7x Mini	2.5-6.9	32-14	—	3¾	9⅜	1	Int.	10.5	reticle, $10 extra.	141.95
4x Mini	3.6	24	—	3¾	8¼	1	Int.	7.8		98.95
6x Mini	5.5	17	—	3¾	9	1	Int.	7.8		106.95
8x Mini	7.6	13	—	3¾	9⅞	1	Int.	8.9		111.95
3x-9x Mini	3.6-8.8	25-11	—	3¾	9⅞	1	Int.	11.5		147.95
Bushnell										
Scope Chief VI	4	29	96	3½	12	1	Int.	9.3	All ScopeChief, Banner and Custom models	104.95
ScopeChief VI	3-9	35-12.6	267-30	3½-3⅓	12.6	1	Int.	14.3	come with Multi-X reticle, with or without	169.95
ScopeChief VI	2½-8	45-14	247-96	3.7-3.3	11.2	1	Int.	12.1	BDC (bullet drop compensator) that elimi-	144.95
ScopeChief VI	1½-4½	73.7-24.5	267.30	3.5-3.5	9.6	1	Int.	9.5	nates hold-over. Prismatic Rangefinder (PRF)	139.95
Custom 22	4	28.4	—	2½	10⁵⁄₁₆	⅞	Int.	5¼	on some models. Contact Bushnell for data	31.95
Custom 22	3-7	29-13.6	28-5	2¼-2½	10	⅞	Int.	6½	on full line. Price includes BDC—deduct $5 if	37.95
Banner	2½	45	96	3½	10.9	1	Int.	8	not wanted. Add $30.00 for PRF.	74.95
Banner 32mm	4	29	96	3½	12	1	Int.	10	BDC feature available in all Banner models,	89.95
Banner 40mm	4	37⅓	150	3	12⅓	1	Int.	12	except 2.5x.	119.95
Banner	6	19½	42	3	13½	1	Int.	10½	Wide angle.	99.95
Banner 22	4	27.5	37.5	3	11⅝	1	Int.	8	Complete with mount rings.	42.95
Banner Silhouette	10	12	24	3	14½	1	Int.	14.6	Equipped with Wind Drift Compensator and	159.95
Banner	10	12	24	3	14½	1	Int.	14.6	Parallax-free Adjustment.	129.95
Banner	1½-4	63-28	294-41	3½	10½	1	Int.	10.3	Parallax focus adjustment.	117.95
Banner	1¾-4½	71-27	216-33	3	10.2	1	Int.	11½	Wide angle.	132.95
Banner 32mm	3-9	39-13	171-19	3½	11.5	1	Int.	11		127.95
Banner 38mm	3-9	43-14.6	241-26½	3	12	1	Int.	14	Wide angle.	154.95
Banner 40mm	3-9	35-12.6	267-30	3½	13	1	Int.	13		169.95
Banner	4-12	29-10	150-17	3.2	13½	1	Int.	15½	Parallax focus adjustment.	149.95
Magnum Phantom	1.3	17	441	7-21	7.8	¹⁵⁄₁₆	Int.	5½	Phantoms intended for handgun use.	59.95
Magnum Phantom	2½	9	100	8-21	9.7	¹⁵⁄₁₆	Int.	6½	Mount separate.	62.95
Davis Optical										
Spot Shot 1½"	10,12 15,20 25,30	10-4	—	2	25	.75	Ext.	—	Focus by moving non-rotating obj. lens unit. Ext. mounts included. Recoil spring $3.50 extra.	107.25
Spot Shot 1¼"	10,12, 15,20	10-6	—	2	25	.75	Ext.	—		83.50
Hutson										
■ Handgunner	1	9	—	25	5¼	—	Ext.	5	CH ⅞" obj. lens. Adj. in mount. $16.95	45.00
	1.7	4.5	—	25	5½	—	Ext.	5		49.50
Jana										
Economy 4x	4	28	—	3.5	11¾	1	Int.	9.5		27.50
Standard 4x	4	28	—	3.5	11¾	1	Int.	9.5	All models equipped with DX reticle except	32.00
Deluxe 4x	4	26	—	3.5	13	1	Int.	12	for economy 4X & 4X .22 Scopes. Parker	53.00
Standard 3x9	3-9	35-14	—	3.2	12	1	Int.	11.5	Hale models are wide-angle style.	34.50
Deluxe 3x9	3-9	35-14	—	3.5	12½	1	Int.	13		57.75
22 Economy 4x	4	19	—	2.75	11½	¾	Int.	7		10.00
22 Deluxe 4x	4	23	—	2.3	12	⅞	Int.	8		17.25
22 Deluxe 3x7	3-7	28-12	—	3	12	⅞	Int.	9		30.50
Parker-Hale 4x	4	36	—	3	11⅞	1	Int.	12		66.00
Parker-Hale 3x9	3-9	43.5-16.5	—	3.6	12½	1	Int.	12.5		96.00
Jason										
860	4	29	64	3	11.8	1	Int.	9.2		39.00
861	3-9	35-13	112-12	3	12.7	1	Int.	10.9		57.00
862	4	19	14	2	11	¾	Int.	5.5	Constantly centered reticles, ballbearing	12.50
864	6	19	28	3	11.8	1	Int.	12.2	click stops, nitrogen filled tubes, coated	41.00
865	3-9	35-13	177-19	3	13	1	Int.	12.2	lenses. 4-Post crosshair about $3.50 extra on	60.00
869	4	19	25	2	11.4	¾	Int.	6	models 860, 861, 864, 865, 873, 875, 877, 878.	16.00

HUNTING, TARGET■ & VARMINT ■ SCOPES

Maker and Model	Magn.	Field at 100 Yds. (feet)	Relative Bright-ness	Eye Relief (in.)	Length (in.)	Tube Diam. (in.)	W&E Adjust-ments	Weight (ozs.)	Other Data	Price
Jason (continued)										
873	4	29	100	3	12.7	1	Int.	11.1		$ 46.00
875	3-9	35-13	177-19	3	13	1	Int.	12.2		61.00
877	4	37	100	3	11.6	1	Int.	11.6		56.00
878	3-9	42.5-13.6	112-12	2.7	12.7	1	Int.	12.7		66.00
Kahles										
Helia Super 2/S	2.5	57.2	64	3.15	9.6	1" or 26mm	Int.	11.3	L Model (Alloy) weights 10.5 oz.	252.00
Helia Super 4/S	4	32.9	60	3.15	11	1" or 26mm	Int.	12.9	L Model — 11 oz.	289.00
Helia Super 6/S	6	22.5	49	3.15	12.2	1" or 26mm	Int.	15.7	L Model — 12.9 oz.	314.00
Helia Super 8/S	8	17.4	49	3.15	14	1" or 26mm	Int.	20.6	L Model — 17.8 oz.	349.00
Helia Super 15/S	1.5-4.5	89.6-30	176-19.6	3.15	10	1" or 26mm	Int.	12.2	L Model — 10 oz.	336.00
Helia Super 27/S	2.3-7	45.7-21	182-19.5	3.15	11.4	1" or 26mm	Int.	13.3	L Model — 10 oz.	460.00
Helia Super 39/S	3-9	36.5-16.4	196-22	3.15	12.6	1" or 26mm	Int.	16.2	L Model — 12.25 oz.	489.00
ZF 69	6	22.5	49	3.15	12.2	26mm	Int.	16.8	Alloy only. All models except ZF69 available in alloy or steel tube. Imported by DelSports, Inc.	524.00
Kassnar										
2x-7x Wide Angle	2-7	49-19	258-21	3-2.7	11	1	Int.	12.8		94.95
3x-9x Wide Angle	3-9	42-15	112-13	3-2.7	12.2	1	Int.	13	Also in 3x-9x40—$109.95	99.95
4x32 Wide Angle	4	36	64	3.5	12	1	Int.	9.2	Also in 4x40—$79.95	69.95
6x40 Wide Angle	6	24	44	3	12.8	1	Int.	12	Other models avail., including ¾" and ⅞"	84.95
1.5x-4x Std.	1.5-4	52-27	177-25	4.4-3	10	1	Int.	9.5	tubes for 22-cal. rifles. Contact Kassnar for	79.95
2x-7x Std.	2-7	42-16	256-21	3.1-3	11	1	Int.	12.5	details.	84.95
3x-9x Std.	3-9	36-13	112-13	3.1-3	12.2	1	Int.	13.5	Also in 3x-9x40—$89.95	87.95
4x-12x40 Std.	4-12	27-9.6	100-11	3-2.7	13.5	1	Int.	16		159.95
2.5x32 Std.	2.5	36	164	3.6	12	1	Int.	9.3		64.95
Leupold										
M8-2xEER	1.8	22	—	10-24	8.1	1	Int.	6.8	Extended Eye Relief of from 10" to 24" for	124.50
M8-4x EER	3.5	7.7	—	10-24	8.4	1	Int.	7.6	top ejecting arms, muzzleloaders. 50-ft. Focus	151.50
2.5 Compact	2.3	42	—	4.3	8.5	1	Int.	7.4	Adapter for indoor target ranges, $29.50.	132.50
4x Compact	3.6	26.5	—	4.1	10.3	1	Int.	8.5		151.50
M8	3	43	45	3.85	10.13	1	Int.	8.25	Constantly centered reticles; in addition to	141.50
M8	4	30	50	3.85	11.50	1	Int.	9.00	the crosshair reticle, the post, tapered (CPC), post and duplex, and duplex reticles are op-	151.50
M8	6	18	—	3.85	11.7	1	Int.	10.3	tional at no extra cost. Dot reticle $14 extra.	160.50
M8 Adj. Obj.	8	14	32	3.60	12.60	1	Int.	12.75	2x suitable for handgun and Win. 94.	215.50
M8 Adj. Obj.	10	10	16	3½	13	1	Int.	13¾	Also in 10x Silhouette—$217.50	215.50
M8 Adj. Obj.	12	9	11	3½	14½	1	Int.	14		218.50
M8 Adj. Obj.	24	4½	—	3½	15¼	1	Int.	15½	Mounts solidly on action. ¼ MOA clicks.	304.50
Vari-X II	1-4	70-28	—	4¼-3½	9½	1	Int.	9½	Crosshair or dot.	185.50
Vari-X II	2-7	42-18	144-17	3.7-4.12	11.00	1	Int.	10.75		202.50
Vari-X II	3-9	30.5-13	208-23	3.5-4.12	12.60	1	Int.	13.75	With adj. obj.—$244.50	217.50
Vari-X III	1½-5	64-23	—	4½-3½	9¾	1	Int.	9¾		220.50
Vari-X III	2½-8	36-12½	—	4¼-3½	11¾	1	Int.	11½		248.50
Vari-X III	3½-10	29½-10½	—	4-3½	12¾	1	Int.	12¾	With adj. obj.—$258.50	249.50
Lyman										
Lyman 4x	4	30	—	3¼	12	1	Int.	10	Choice of standard CH, tapered post, or tapered post and CH reticles. All-weather reticle caps. All Lyman scopes have new Perma-Center reticle which remains in optical center regardless of changes in W&E. Adj. for parallax.	139.95
Variable	1¾-5	47-18	—	3	12¼	1	Int.	12¼		149.95
■ 20x LWBR	20	5.5	—	2¼	17⅛	1	Int.	15¼	⅛ or ¼ MOA clicks.	309.95
■ All-American	3-9	39-13	—	3¾-3¼	10½	1	Int.	14	Non-rotating objective lens focusing. ¼ MOA	169.95
2x-7x Var.	1.9-6.8	49-19	—	3¼	11⅝	1	Int.	10½	click adjustments. Sunshade, $4.95 extra.	159.95
25x LWBR	25	4.8	—	3	17	1	Int.	19	Wood cases, $29.95 extra. 5 different dot reticles, $12.50 extra.	339.95
Metallic Silhouette 6x-SL	6.2	20	—	3¼	13⅞	1	Int.	14¼	Standard crosswire, 4 Center-Range reticles.	209.95
Metallic Silhouette 8x-SL	8.1	14	—	3¼	14⅝	1	Int.	15¼	Std. Fine, Extra Fine, 1 Min. Dot. ½-Min. Dot, ¼-Min. Dot reticles. External adjustment	219.95
Metallic Silhouette 10x-SL	10	12	—	3¼	15⅜	1	Int.	15¼	knobs; hand lapped zero repeat w. and e. systems. Choice of 9 reticles.	229.95
Precise										
20112	4-12	28-9	100-10.8	3.1-2.9	14.2	1	Int.	16	Parallax correction adj. from 25 yds. to infinity.	100.00
20241	4	23	13¾	3¾	10¾	¾	Int.	6.0	22 Scope with crosshair.	11.95
20244	4	29	64	3½	12	1	Int.	9.1	Luma-Glo crosshair.	39.95
20245	4	29	64	3½	12	1	Int.	9.1	Luma-Glo Post.	42.00
20251	3-9	35¾-12¾	112¼-12½	3	12¾	1	Int.	13.8	Luma-Glo crosshair.	58.00
20462	4	29	64	3½	12	1	Int.	9.1	Waterproof, Duplex Luma-Glo crosshair.	47.00
20463	3-9	35¾-12¾	176¾-19½	3	12¾	1	Int.	15.2	Amber-Glo Filter, Rubber Ring of Safety in-	70.00
20467	3-9	35¾-12¾	112½-12½	3	12¾	1	Int.	13.8	cluded.	68.00
20562	4	37.3	64	3¼	11¾	1	Int.	10.5	Waterproof, Duplex Luma-Glo crosshair,	58.00
20563	3-9	42½-13½	176¾-19½	3-2½	12¾	1	Int.	14.1	Wideview. Amber-Glo Filter, Rubber Ring of	80.00
20567	3-9	42½-13½	112½-12½	3-2½	12¾	1	Int.	13.4	Safety included.	78.00

HUNTING, TARGET ■ & VARMINT ■ SCOPES

Maker and Model	Magn.	Field at 100 Yds. (feet)	Relative Bright-ness	Eye Relief (in.)	Length (in.)	Tube Diam. (in.)	W&E Adjust-ments	Weight (ozs.)	Other Data	Price
Redfield										
Traditional 4x¾"	4	24½	27	3½	9⅜	.75	Int.	—		$ 71.35
Traditional 2½x	2½	43	64	3½	10¼	1	Int.	8½		107.05
Traditional 4x	4	28½	56	3½	11⅜	1	Int.	9¾		121.35
Traditional 6x	6	19	—	3½	12½	1	Int.	11½		139.20
Traditional 3x-9x* Royal	3-9	34-11	—	3½-4¼	12½	1	Int.	13		212.35
Traditional 2x-7x*	2-7	42-14	207-23	3½	11¼	1	Int.	12		162.45
Traditional 3x-9x*	3-9	34-11	163-18	3½	12½	1	Int.	13	*Accu-Trac feature avail. on these scopes. Traditionals have round lenses. 4-Plex reticle is standard.	192.80
Traditional 8xMS	8	16.6	—	3-3¾	14⅛	1	Int.	17 1/5		217.80
Traditional 10xMS	10	12.6	—	3-3¾	14⅛	1	Int.	17½		232.10
Traditional 12xMS	12.4	8.1	—	3-3¾	14⅛	1	Int.	17.5		248.15
Pistol Scopes 1½xMP	1.5	14	—	19-32	9 13/16	1	Int.	10.5	"Magnum Proof." Specially designed for magnum and auto pistols. Uses "Double Dovetail" mounts.	117.80
2½xMP	2.5	9	—	14-24	9 13/16	1	Int.	10.5		124.95
4xMP	3.6	9	—	12-22	9 11/16	1	Int.	11.1		141.00
Traditional 4x-12x*	4-12	26-9	112-14	3½	13⅞	1	Int.	14	*Accu-Trac feature avail. on these scopes.	249.95
Traditional 6x-18x*	6-18	18-6	50-6	3½	13 15/16	1	Int.	18		276.75
Low Profile Scopes Widefield 2¾xLP	2¾	55½	69	3½	10½	1	Int.	8		139.20
Widefield 4xLP	3.6	37½	84	3½	11½	1	Int.	10		157.10
Widefield 6x	6	24	—	3½	12¾	1	Int.	11		171.35
Widefield 1¾x5xLP	1¾-5	70-27	136-21	3½	10¾	1	Int.	11½		187.45
Widefield 2x7xLP*	2-7	49-19	144-21	3½	11¾	1	Int.	13		205.30
Widefield 3x-9xLP*	3-9	39-15	112-18	3½	12½	1	Int.	14		241.00
3200 Target	16, 20, 24	6½, 5¼, 4, 3¾	9, 6, 3¼, 2¼	2½	23¼	1	Int.	21	Mounts solidly. 20x—$317.80, 24x—$328.55	308.95
6400 Target	16, 20, 24	6½, 5, 4½	5¾, 3½, 2½	3	17	1	Int.	18	Mounts on receiver. CH or dot. 20x—$285.65, 24x—$294.60	276.75
Sanders										
Bisley 2½x20	2½	42	64	3	10¾	1	Int.	8¼	Alum. alloy tubes, ¼" adj. coated lenses.	48.50
Bisley 4x33	4	28	64	3	12	1	Int.	9	Five other scopes are offered; 6x45 at $68.50, 8x45 at $70.50, 2½x7x at $69.50, 3-9x33 at $72.50 and 3-9x40 at $78.50. Rubber lens covers (clear plastic) are $3.50. Write to Sanders for details.	52.50
Bisley 6x40	6	19	45	3	12½	1	Int.	9½		56.50
Bisley 8x40	8	18	25	3¼	12½	1	Int.	9½		62.50
Bisley 10x40	10	12½	16	2½	12½	1	Int.	10¼		64.50
Bisley 5-13x40	5-13	29-10	64-9	3	14	1	Int.	14	Choice of reticles in CH, PCH, 3-post.	86.50
Southern Precision										
556	3-7	24.5-11.5	43.5-8.1	2 .4	12	⅞	Int.	10.3		24.95
558	4	15.7	13.7	3.7	10.7	¾	Int.	6.1		8.95
564CW	4	30	64	3.7	12	1	Int.	9.1		29.95
567DW	6	23.5	44.7	3.1	12.5	1	Int.	10		37.95
576CW	3-9	35.8-12.7	112.4-13	3.1-2.9	12.8	1	Int.	13.8		45.00
579DWE	4-12	43-16	100-11.1	3.1-2.5	14.3	1	Int.	16		69.50
Swarovski										
Habicht 1.5x20 DV SD 1A	1.5	69	—	3⅛	10	26mm	Int.	11.9	All models steel except LD model light alloy. Double adj. All weather scopes. 4x & 6x Scopes fitted with centered reticles—4 different designs. 5 Year warranty. Spirit Level. $66. IMPORTER: Strieter Corp.	435.00
Habicht 4x32 DV SD 1A	4	30	—	3⅛	11	26mm	Int.	13.3		455.00
Habicht 4x32 DV LD 1A	4	30	—	3⅛	11	26mm	Int.	11.9		455.00
NOVA 4x32 DV SD 1A	4	30	—	3⅛	11	26mm	Int.	13.3		475.00
Habicht 6x42 DV SD 1A	6	20	—	3¼	11	26mm	Int.	15.4		570.00
NOVA 6x42 DV SD 1A	6	20	—	3¼	12	26mm	Int.	15.4		590.00
Swift										
Mark I 4x15	4	23	—	2	11	.75	Int.	6¾		20.00
Mark I 4x32	4	29	—	3½	12	1	Int.	9	All swift Mark I scopes, with the exception of the 4x15m have Quadraplex reticles and are fog-proof and waterproof. The 4x15 has cross-hair reticle and is non-waterproof.	62.00
Mark I 4x32 WA	4	37	—	3½	11¾	1	Int.	10½		70.00
Mark I 4x40 WA	4	35½	—	3¾	12¼	1	Int.	12		80.00
Mark I 3-9x32	3-9	35¾-12¾	—	3	12¾	1	Int.	13¾		81.25
Mark 1 3-9x40 WA	3-9	42½-13½	—	2¾	12¾	1	Int.	14		94.00
Mark I 6x40	6	18	—	3¾	13	1	Int.	10		72.50
Mark I 1½-4½x32	1½-4½	55-22	—	3½	12	1	Int.	13		87.50
Tasco										
611V Wide Angle	2-6	66-25	100-16	2¾	10	1	Int.	9.5	Lens covers furnished. Constantly centered reticles. Write the importer, Tasco, for data on complete line.	114.95
627W	3-9	35-14	177-19	3½	12⅛	1	Int.	13		99.95
628V Wide Angle	3-9	43.5-15	177-19	3½	12	1	Int.	12¼	Brass tube for Hawkins, Plains, Pa.	149.95
1860 Tube Sight	4	12½	14	3	32½	¾	Ext.	25	½-stock, FIE, Zouave and Ky.	124.95
1903 Tube Sight	4	14	14	3¾	18½	¾	Ext.	17½	Brass tube. For Savage #72 and Gallagher.	104.95
United										
Golden Hawk	4	30	64	—	11⅞	—	Int.	9½		77.50
Golden Grizzly	6	18½	44	—	11⅞	1	Int.	11		105.00
Golden Falcon	4-9	29½-14	100-20	—	13½	1	Int.	12¾	Anodized tubes, nitrogen filled. Write United for data on complete line.	111.50
Golden Plainsman	3-12	33-12½	169-11	—	13½	1	Int.	12¾		110.00
Unertl										
■ 1" Target	6, 8, 10	16-10	17.6-6.25	2	21½	.75	Ext.	21		139.00
■ 1¼" Target	8,10,12,14	12-6	15.2-5	2	25	.75	Ext.	25	Dural ¼ MOA click mounts. Hard coated lenses. Non-rotating objective lens focusing.	183.00
■ 1½" Target	8,10,12,14, 16,18,20,24	11.5-3.2	—	2¼	25½	.75	Ext.	31		208.00
■ 2" Target	8,10,12, 14,16,18, 24,30,36	—	22.6-2.5	2¼	26¼	1	Ext.	44	¼ MOA click mounts.	281.00
■ Varmint, 1¼"	6,8,10,12	14.1-7	28.7-1	2½	19½	.875	Ext.	26	With target mounts.	184.00
■ Ultra Varmint, 2"	8,10 12,15	12.6-7	39.7-11	2½	24	1	Ext.	34	With calibrated head.	263.00
■ Small Game	4, 6	25-17	19.4-8.4	2¼	18	.75	Ext.	16	Same as 1" Target but without objective lens focusing.	105.00

(continued)

CAUTION: PRICES CHANGE. CHECK AT GUNSHOP.

HUNTING, TARGET ■ & VARMINT ■ SCOPES

Maker and Model	Magn.	Field at 100 Yds. (feet)	Relative Bright-ness	Eye Relief (in.)	Length (in.)	Tube Diam. (in.)	W&E Adjust-ments	Weight (ozs.)	Other Data	Price
Unertl (continued)										
■ Vulture	8 10	11.2 10.9	29 18½	3-4 —	15⅝ 16⅛	1	E or I	15½	Price with ¼ MOA click mounts.	$202.00
■ Programmer 200	8,10,12, 14,16,18, 20,24,30,36	11.3-4	39-1.9	—	26½	1	Ext.	45	With new Posa mounts. Range focus unit near rear of tube. Price is with Posa mounts. Magnum clamp. With standard mounts and clamp ring $188.	349.00
■ BV-20	20	8	4.4	4.4	17⅞	1	Ext.	21¼		242.00
Universal										
UE-4	4	29	64	3½	12	1	Int.	9.1		28.95
UK-4*	3-9	36-13	112-13	3	12.8	1	Int.	13.8		43.95
UK*	3-9	36-13	112-13	3	12.8	1	Int.	13.8		42.95
UL-4	3-9	36-13	177-19	3	12.8	1	Int.	15.2	*All scopes have alloy tubes, constantly cen-	46.95
UE40-4	4	29	100	3½	12½	1	Int.	10	tered reticles, coated lenses. Asterisk denotes	30.95
UD	4	23	25	2	12	⅞	Int.	12	quadraplex reticle is avail., otherwise standard	21.95
UA	4	16	14	4	10.8	¾	Int.	10.8	crosshair is offered. Write to Universal Sport-	9.95
UEW-4 Wide Angle*	4	35	64	3¼	12¼	1	Int.	12	ing Goods for details.	28.95
Weatherby										
Mark XXII	4	25	50	2½-3½	11¾	⅞	Int.	9¼	Focuses in top turret.	57.95
Premier Standard	2¾	45	212	3½	11¾	1	Int.	12¼		126.95
Premier Standard	4	31	100	3½	12¾	1	Int.	12¼	Centered, non-magnifying reticles. Binocular	137.95
Premier Standard	3-9	43½-14½	177-19	3	12	1	Int.	14¾	focusing. Lumi-Plex $10 extra.	142.95
Premier Wide Angle	4	35¾	100	3	11¾	1	Int.	14		159.95
Premier Wide Angle	43½-14¾	177-19	3	12	1	Int.	14¾			169.95
Weaver										
K1.5	1½	55	—	5¼	9⅜	1	Int.	9¾	Avail. with mount for Rem. 1100 or 870, Dual-X	82.00
K2.5	2.6	38	—	4½	10⅜	1	Int.	10¼	reticle. K1.5—$108.50, K2.5—$108.50.	82.00
K3	3.2	34	—	4	10⅝	1	Int.	10¼		88.50
K4	4.1	27	—	4	11¾	1	Int.	12	Steel-Lite II (lighter weight, glossy finish) in K,	95.50
K6	5.9	19	—	3⅞	13½	1	Int.	13½	V and Wider View scopes.	115.00
K8	7.7	15	—	3½	15	1	Int.	15½	Crosshair and Dual-X reticle optional on all K	131.50
K10F	10	12	—	3½	15¾	1	Int.	16¼	and V scopes (except no RF in K1.5, K2.5, K3	137.00
K12F	11.6	10	—	3½	16	1	Int.	16½	and K3W; no post in K8, 10, 12; no post or RF	150.50
K3-W	2.9	48	—	3½	11	1	Int.	11	in T models). Dot, post and RF $15.00 extra in	118.00
K4-W	3.7	38	—	3⅝	11 13/16	1	Int.	13	K and V models only. Objective lens on K10F,	124.00
K6-W	6	24	—	3½	13¼	1	Int.	14½	K12F, V9F, V12F and V9WF focuses for range.	144.50
									Dot and fine crosshair $15.00 extra in T models.	
M39V	3-9	32-11	—	5-3¾	13¼	1	Int.	11¾	¼" Graduated adjustments Dual-X reticle only.	81.00
M1	4	26	—	4	11⅝	1	Int.	9½	¼" Graduated adjustments Dual-X reticle only.	57.00
M1-SF-TO	4	26	—	4	11⅝	1	Int.	9½	Special short focused at 40 yds. for rimfire rifles.	57.00
M34W	4	27	—	2	11⅞	.750	Int.	5½	Crosshair reticle only.	17.15
M34	4	25	—	2	11⅝	.750	Int.	5½	Crosshair reticle only.	13.25
V4.5-W	1.6-4.2	74-27	—	4¼-3¾	10⅜	1	Int.	14¼		152.00
V7-W	2.6-6.9	43-17	—	3⅝-3¾	12⅜	1	Int.	15¼	Micro-Trac standard on all K and V models.	165.00
V9F	3.3-8.8	31-12	—	3¾	14	1	Int.	17½	¼" Graduated adjustments.	151.50
V9-W	3.3-9	35-13	—	3⅝	14⅛	1	Int.	18¼		169.50
V9-WF	3.3-9	35-13	—	3⅝	14	1	Int.	18¼	¼-minute adj.	180.00
V4.5	1.6-4.3	63-24	—	4⅜-3⅞	10⅜	1	Int.	13½		122.00
V7	2.5-6.7	40-15	—	4-3⅞	12⅜	1	Int.	14½		135.00
V9	3.3-8.8	31-12	—	3¾	14⅛	1	Int.	17½		139.00
V12F	4.4-11.8	23-9	—	3⅞-4¼	14	1	Int.	17½		161.50
T6	6	19	—	3½	14¼	1	Int.	17¾		200.00
T10	10	11	—	3½	15	1	Int.	18		213.50
T16	16	7	—	3⅝	15¾	1	Int.	18¾		225.00
T20	20	4.8	—	3¾	18½	1	Int.	20	¼-minute adj.	253.50
T25	25	4.2	—	3¾	19⅛	1	Int.	20		266.50
T-30	30	3.3	—	3½	19⅜	1	Int.	21	¼" click stops. Crosshair and Dual-X standard on T models.	295.00
V22	3-5.8	31-16	—	1⅝-2¼	12⅜	.875	Int.	7¾	$2.50 extra for Dual-X on V22 $3 extra for Dual	32.00
D4	4.2	29	—	2¼	11⅞	.875	Int.	6½	X reticle on D4, D6. D model prices include N	24.00
D6	6.2	20	—	2¼	12 5/16	.875	Int.	6¾	or Tip-Off mount.	26.50
Qwik-Point	1	—	—	6	—	—	Int.	8	Projects red dot aiming point.	62.50
Williams										
Twilight Crosshair	2½	32	64	3¾	11¼	1	Int.	8½	TNT models.	76.50
Twilight Crosshair	4	29	64	3½	11¾	1	Int.	9½		82.00
Twilight Crosshair	2-6	45-17	256-28	3	11½	1	Int.	11½		110.75
Twilight Crosshair	3-9	36-13	161-18	3	12¾	1	Int.	13½		116.35

■ Signifies target and/or varmint scope.

Hunting scopes in general are furnished with a choice of reticle—crosshairs, post with crosshairs, tapered or blunt post, or dot crosshairs, etc.

The great majority of target and varmint scopes have medium or fine crosshairs but post or dot reticles may be ordered.

W—Windage E—Elevation MOA—Minute of angle or 1" (approx.) at 100 yards, etc.

The latest addition to the family of Weaver T Model scopes is the T30. The new 30x is designed specifically for the experienced benchrest competitor. Eye relief is 3¾".

TELESCOPE MOUNTS

Maker, Model, Type	Adjust.	Scopes	Suitable for	Price
B-Square				
Dovetail Rings	No	1" scopes	All dovetail receivers such as Nylon 66. No drilling or tapping.	$14.95
M-94 Mono-Mount	No	1", long eye relief such as Leupold M8-2X. Mounts ahead of action.	M-94 Winchester No drilling or tapping.	19.95
M-94 Side Mount	W&E	All 1" scopes.	M-94 Winchester. No drilling or tapping.	24.95
AR-15 Base	No	Use any Weaver-type ring (not included)	Colt AR-15 rifle. No drilling or tapping.	19.95
AR-15 Mount	W&E	All 1" scopes.	Colt AR-15 rifles. No drilling or tapping.	24.95
Mini-14 Mount	W&E	All 1" scopes.	Ruger Mini-14 (Mounts on top of receiver. Gunsmith Drill Jig available for guns not drilled $34.95)	24.95
One-piece Base Mounts	No	1" scopes	Most popular rifles.	19.95
LWS, LWB	W&E	1" scopes	All popular rifles.	24.95
Remington Models	No	1" scopes	Remington 600, 700, 788 and 1100 models	19.95
Ruger Blackhawk	No	1" scopes	Ruger Blackhawk revolver (has bolted rings).	31.95
T-C Contender	No	1" scopes	T-C Contender, all calibers. Heavy Recoil Model	31.95
Buehler				
One Piece (T)	W only	1" split rings, 3 heights 1" split rings, 3 heights 26mm, 26½mm, 28mm	Most popular models. Fully engraved. Special.	Complete 45.00 Rings only—63.50 Rings only—33.00
One Piece Micro Dial	W&E	1" split rings, 3 heights	Most popular models.	Complete 55.75
Two Piece (T)	W only	1" split rings, 3 heights	Most popular models incl. Wea. Silhouette	Complete 45.00
One Piece Pistol (T)	W only	1" split rings, 3 heights	14 models.	Complete 45.00
Burris				
Supreme One Piece (T)	W only	1" split rings, 3 heights	Most popular rifles.	22.95
Trumont Two Piece (T)	W only	1" split rings, 3 heights	Universal, rings, mounts fit Burris Universal, Redfield, Leupold and Browning bases, Comparable prices.	1 piece base—15.00 2 piece base—12.50
Browning Auto Mount	No	¾", 1" split rings	Browning Standard 22 Auto rifle.	10.95
Sight-Thru Mount	No	1" split rings	Most popular rifles.	16.95
Rings Mounts	No	¾", 1" split rings	Grooved receivers.	¾" rings—10.95 1" rings—10.95
L.E.R. Mount Bases	No	1" split rings	Universal dovetail; accept Burris, Universal, Redfield, Leupold rings. For Dan Wesson, S&W, Virginian, Ruger Blackhawk, Contender, Win. 94	12.50
Extension Rings	No	1" scopes	Medium standard front, extension rear, per pair Low standard front, extension rear, per pair	26.95 26.95
Bushnell				
Detachtable (T) mounts only	W only	1" split rings, uses Weaver bases.	Most popular rifles. Includes windage adj.	Rings—12.50
22 mount	No	1" only		Rings— 5.95
All Purpose	No	Phantom	V-block bottoms lock to chrome-moly studs seated into two 6-48 holes. Rem. XP-100.	11.95
Rigid	No	Phantom	Heavy loads in Colt, S&W, Ruger revolvers, Ruger Hawkeye.	12.95
94 Win.	No	Phantom	M94 Win., center dovetail.	15.95
Clearview				
Universal Rings (T)	No	1" split rings	All popular rifles including Sav. 99. Uses Weaver Bases.	16.95
Mod 101, & 336	No	1" split rings	Rings have wide oval effect for use of open sights.	15.95
Model 104	No	1" split rings	For 22 rimfire rifles, with grooved receivers or bases.	9.95
SM-94	No	1" split rings	Remington 14, 141, Sears 54, 100, Win. 94, 94-375.	20.95
Conetrol				
One Piece (T)	W only	1", 26mm, 26.5mm solid or split rings, 3 heights	All popular rifles, including metric-drilled foreign guns.	Huntur—36.96-39.95 Bases only—19.98 Solid Rings, ea.— 8.49
Two Piece (T)	W only	Same.	All rifles which will take conventional top mount low over receiver.	Split Rings, ea.— 9.99
One Piece (S)	W only	Same.	Win. 94, Krag, older split-bridge Mannlicher Schoenauer, Ruger Mini-14, M-1 Garand, SMLE No. 1, etc.	Gunnur—45.93-49.95 Bases only—24.99 Solid Rings, ea.—10.47 Split Rings, ea.—12.48
'DapTar' Bases (T) Pistol Bases (T)	W only	Same.	All popular guns with integral mounting provision.	Custum—54.93-59.91 Bases only—29.97 Solid Rings, ea.—12.48 Split Rings, ea.—14.97
Pistol Bases (T)	W only	1" scopes	Rem. XP-100, T/C Contender, Colt SAA, Ruger 22 Auto	
Pistol Bases, 3-ring (T)	W only	1" scopes	Rem. XP-100, T/C Contender, Colt SAA. Add cost of 3rd ring.	
EAW				
Pivot Mount	W&E	1" or 26mm	Most popular magazine rifles	125.00-135.00
Griffin & Howe				
Standard Double Lever (S).	No	1" or 26mm split rings.	All popular models (Garand $100; Win. 94 $100). All rings $45.	100.00
Holden				
Ironsighter Center Fire	No	1" Split rings	Most popular rifles including Ruger Mini-14, H&R M700, Win. 94BB and muzzle loaders. Rings have oval holes to permit use of ironsights.	15.95
Ironsighter 22 cal. rimfire Model #500 Model #600	No No	1" Split rings ⅞" Split rings also fits ¾".	For 1" dia. scopes For ¾" or ⅞" dia. scopes	8.49 8.49

(Continued)

Telescope Mounts—continued

TELESCOPE MOUNTS

Maker, Model, Type	Adjust.	Scopes	Suitable for	Price
Holden (continued)				
Ironsighter Handguns	No	1" Split rings	For 1" dia. extended eye relief scopes	$17.95
Holden "Straight Shooter" Bullet Drop Compensating Scope Mount	Yes	1" Split rings	Fits Redfield and Weaver bases.	39.95
Jaeger				
QD, with windage (S)	W only	1", 3 heights.	All popular models.	$88.00
Jaguar				
QD Dovetail (T)	No	1", 26mm and 26½mm rings.	For BSA Monarch rifle (Galef, importer).	23.30
Kesselring				
Standard QD (T)	W only	¾", ⅞", 1", 26mm split rings.	All popular rifles, one or two piece bases.	29.95
See-Em-Under (T)	W only	Same.	Rem. 760, 740, Win. 100, 88, Marlin 336	35.00
Dovetail (T)	W only	1", 26mm.	Steyr 22, Sako, BRNO, Krico	35.00
Kris Mounts				
Side-Saddle	No	1", 26mm split rings.	One-piece mount for Win. 94	10.98
Two Piece (T)	No	1", 26mm split rings.	Most popular rifles and Ruger	7.98
One Piece (T)	No	1", 26mm split rings.	Blackhawk revolver. Mounts have oval hole to permit use of iron sights.	10.98
Kwik-site (T)	No	1" split rings.	Wider-View, $15.75. Mounts scope high to permit iron sight use. Offset base for 94 Win.	14.75 19.95
Leupold				
STD (T)	W only	1" only, 3 heights. Interchange with Redfield Jr. and Sr. components.	Most popular rifles.	Rings—23.90 Base—15.90
45 ACP "Gold Cup" Mount	No	1" split rings.	For M8-2x or 4x EER mounting on a Colt Gold Cup N.M. 45.	31.50
Marlin				
One Piece QD (T)	No	1" split rings.	Most Marlin and Glenfield lever actions.	7.95
Numrich				
Side Mount	No	1" split rings.,	M-1 carbine.	7.95
Pachmayr				
Lo-Swing (S)	Yes	¾", ⅞", 1", 26mm solid or split loops.	All popular rifles, including Ruger Mini-14, Browning BBR. Scope swings aside for instant use of iron sights.	30.00
Lo-Swing (T)	Yes	¾", ⅞", 1", 26mm split rings.	Adjustable base. Win. 70, 88; Rem. 721, 722, 725, 740, 760; Mar. 336; Sav. 99. New model for Colt Sauer.	35.00
Parker-Hale				
Roll-Off	No	1" and 26mm.	Most popular rifles.	15.55
Precise				
40421 (rings only)	No	1" tube; not over 32mm obj.	Fit Weaver bases.	7.50
40422 (rings only)	No	1" tube; 40mm obj. scopes.		7.50
Redfield				
JR-SR (T)	W only	¾", 1", 26mm.	Low, med. & high, split rings. Reversible extension front rings for 1". 2-piece bases for Mannlicher-Schoenauer and Sako. Colt Sauer bases $27.90.	Rings—23.90 Bases—15.90-25.90 Rings—43.10
Ring (T)	No	¾" and 1".	Split rings for grooved 22's. See-thru mounts $21.90.	17.90
Double Dovetail MP	No	1", split rings.	Used with MP scopes for: S&W K or N frame, XP-100, Colt J or I frame, T/C Contender, Colt autos, black powder rifles.	44.00
S&K				
Insta-Mount (T) base only	No	Most take S&K or Weaver rings.	M1903, A3, M1 Carbine, Lee Enfield #3, #4, #5, P14, M1917, M98 Mauser, FN Auto, AR-15, AR-180, M-14, M-1. Bases—M94, 64.	11.00-20.00 10.00
Conventional rings and bases	No	1" split rings.	Most popular rifles. For "see through underneath" risers, add $4.15.	24.20
Sako				
QD Dovetail	W only	1" only.	Sako, or any rifle using Sako action. 3 heights available. Stoeger, importer.	39.95
Savage				
No. 40 (S)	No	1"	For Savage 340, 840 Springfield.	5.10
No. 70	No	1"	For Savage 170, 170-C rifles.	5.10
B-5	No	1"	For 24V, 222 or 30-30.	15.75
Tasco				
790 and 792 series	Yes	1" split rings, regular or high.	Many popular rifles.	9.95
794	No	Split rings.	For 22s with grooved receivers.	9.95
795 Quick Peep	No	1" only.	Most popular rifles.	11.95
800LSeries (with base)	No	1" only	Most popular rifles.	13.95
Unertl				
Posa (T)	Yes	¾", ⅞", 1" scopes.	Unertl target or varmint scope.	Per set 47.00
¼ Click (T)	Yes	¾", 1" target scopes.	Any with regular dovetail scope bases.	Per set 41.00
Weaver				
Detachable Mount (T & S)	No	¾", ⅞", 1", 26mm.	Nearly all modern rifles. Extension rings, 1" $17.75.	15.50
Type N (S)	No	⅞" scopes only.	Same. High or low style mounts.	8.20
Pivot Mount (T)	No	1"	Most modern big bore rifles.	19.20
Tip-Off (T)	No	¾", ⅞".	22s with grooved receivers.	8.20
Tip-Off (T)	No	1", two-piece	Same. Adapter for Lee Enfield—$7.50.	15.50
See-Thru Mount	No	1" split rings and ⅞"-tip-off. Fits all top mounts.	⅞"—$10.50 1" See-Thru extension—$17.75.	15.50
Williams				
Offset (S)	No	¾", ⅞", 1" 26mm solid, split or extension rings.	Most rifles. Br. S.M.L.E. (round rec.) $3.85 extra.	31.85
QC (T)	No	Same.	Same.	26.20
QC (S)	No	Same.	Most rifles.	26.20
Low Sight-Thru	No	1", ⅞", sleeves $1.80	Most rifles.	15.70
Sight-Thru	No	1", ⅞", sleeves $1.80	Many modern rifles.	15.70
Streamline	No	1" (bases form rings)	Most popular rifles.	15.00

(S)—Side Mount   (T)—Top Mount   22mm=.866"   25.4mm=1"   26mm=1.024"   26.5mm=1.045"   30mm=1.181"

CAUTION: PRICES CHANGE. CHECK AT GUNSHOP.

SPOTTING SCOPES

BAUSCH & LOMB DISCOVERER—15X to 60X zoom, 60mm objective. Constant focus throughout range. Field at 1000 yds. 40 ft. (60X), 156 ft. (15X). Comes with lens caps. Length 17½", wgt. 48½ oz. **$375.00**
BUSHNELL SPACEMASTER®—60mm objective. Field at 1000 yds., 158' to 37'. Relative brightness, 5.76. Wgt., 36 oz. Length closed, 11⅝". Prism focusing, without eyepiece **$198.00**
    15X, 20X, 25X, 40X and 60X eyepieces, each **$37.00**
    22X wide angle eyepiece **$42.00**
BUSHNELL SPACEMASTER 45°—Same as above except: Wgt., 43 oz., length closed 13". Eyepiece at 45°, without eyepiece.
    Price: **$253.00**

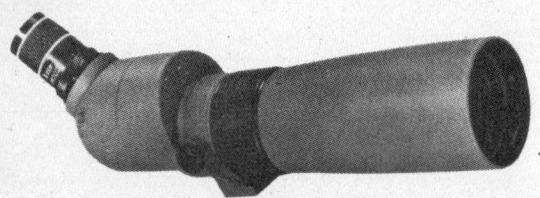

Bushnell 45° Spacemaster 60mm scope.

BUSHNELL ZOOM SPACEMASTER—20X-45X zoom. 60mm objective. Field at 1000 yards 120'-72'. Relative brightness 9-1.7. Wgt. 36 oz., length 11⅝"
    Price: **$295.00**
BUSHNELL SENTRY®—50mm objective. Field at 1000 yards 120'-45'. Relative brightness 6.25. Wgt., 25½ oz., length 12⅝", without eyepiece.
    Price: **$107.00**
    20X, 32X and 48X eyepieces, each **$32.00**
BUSHNELL ZOOM SPOTTER—40mm objective. 9X-30X var. power.
    Price: **$84.50**
BUSHNELL COMPETITOR—40mm objective. Prismatic. Field at 1000 yards 140'. Minimum focus 33'. Length 12½", weight 18½ oz. .. **$79.50**
BUSHNELL TROPHY—16X 36X zoom. Rubber armored, prismatic. 50mm objective. Field at 1000 yards 131' to 90'. Minimum focus 20'. Length with caps 13⅝", weight 38 oz. **$236.00** With interchangeable eyepieces—20x, 32x, 48x **$179.00**
BUSHNELL—10x30mm hand telescope. Field 183 ft. at 1000 yards. Weight 11 ozs.; 10" long. Tripod mount **$24.95**
DICKSON 270—20x to 60x variable, 60mm objective, achromatic coated objective lens, complete with metal table tripod with 5' vertical and horizontal adjustments. Turret type, 20x, 30x, 40x 60x.
    Price **$239.95**
DICKSON 274A—20x to 60x variable zoom. 60mm achromatic coated objective lens, complete with adjustable metal table tripod.
    Price **$110.00**
DICKSON 274B—As above but with addition of 4×16 Finder Scope.
    Price **$121.95**
HUTSON CHROMATAR 60—63.4mm objective. 22.5X eyepiece at 45°. Wgt. 24 oz. 8" over-all. 10½ foot field at 100 yards. **$119.00**
    15X or 45X eyepieces, each **$22.00**
HY-SCORE MODEL 460—60mm objective. 20X eyepiece included. Field at 100 yds. 15.8 to 3.2 ft. Length closed 11". Wgt., 35 oz. **$199.95**
    Zoom—20X to 45X **$249.95**
SOUTHERN PRECISION MODEL 550—60mm objective and 5 eyepieces from 15X to 60X; folding tripod. 14¾", Wgt., 4¼ lbs. **$129.50**
SOUTHERN PRECISION ZOOM MODEL 543—60mm objective, 15X to 50X; folding tripod. 18", wgt. 4½ lbs. with tripod (included) **$119.95**
SOUTHERN PRECISION MODEL 552—80mm objective, 20X. Folding tripod. 13", wgt. 3 lbs. **$117.50**
SWAROVSKI HABICHT 30x75 IRALIN TELESCOPE—75mm objective, 30X. Field at 1,000 yds. 90ft. Minimum, focusing distance 90 ft. Length: closed 13 in., extended 20½". Weight: 47 oz. Precise recognition of smallest details even at dusk. Leather or rubber covered.
    Price: **$885.00**
Same as above with short range supplement. Minimum focusing distance 24 to 30 ft.
    Price: **$920.00**
SWIFT TELEMASTER M841—60mm objective. 15X to 60X variable power. Field at 1000 yards 160 feet (15X) to 40 feet (60X). Wgt. 3.4 lbs. 17.6" over-all.
    Price: **$385.00**
    Tripod for above **$76.50**
    Photo adapter **$17.50**
    Case for above **$56.50**
SWIFT TELEMASTER JR. M842—25-50mm zoom spotting scope. Smaller version of M841 with same features. 14.9" over-all, wgt. 2.2 lbs. **$255.00**
SWIFT M843 45° SPOTTING SCOPE—60mm objective. 30X, 40X, 60X eyepieces available. Eyepiece is tilted for easy viewing. 13½" o.a., 1.68 lbs.
    Price: **$210.00**
SWIFT M844 PRISMATIC SPOTTING SCOPE, MK. II—60mm objective. Comes with 20X eyepiece; 15X, 30X, 40X, 50X, 60X available. Built-in sunshade. Field at 1000 yds. with 20X, 120 ft. Length 13.7", wgt. 2.1 lbs.
    Price: **$245.00**
SWIFT M700 SCOUT—9X-30X, 30mm spotting scope. Length 15½", weighs 2.1 lbs. Field of 204 ft. (9X), 60 ft. (30X).
    Price: **$89.95**
TASCO 18T ZOOM—60mm objective. 20X to 60X variable power. Field at 100 yards 9 feet (20X) to 3 feet (60X). Wgt. 4 lbs. 16" overall .. **$199.95**
TASCO 28T ANGLEVIEW—60mm objective. 25X, resolves to 2 sec. at 100 yds. Rapid focus knob. Table top tripod with adj. elevation leg. Camera tripod adapter, extending sun shade. Wgt., 6 lbs., length 16½". Complete with lens covers **$399.95**
TASCO 8T SPOTTING 60—60mm objective, 4 par-focal, variable power eye-lenses 15X, 30X, 40X and 60X. Resolves 2.8 sec. at 100 yds. Wgt., 4 lbs., length 16½" **$299.95**
UNERTL "FORTY-FIVE" SCOPE—20X (single power only, no interchangeable eyepieces). 54mm objective. Field of view at 100 yds. 10'10". Eye relief 1.074". Has 45° angular eyepiece. Weight about 2 lbs. Over-all length 15¾". From **$195.00**
UNERTL RIGHT ANGLE—63.5mm objective. 24X. Field at 100 yds., 7 ft. Relative brightness, 6.96. Eye relief, ½". Wgt., 41 oz. Length closed, 19". Push-pull and screw-focus eyepiece. 16X and 32X eyepieces $18 each.
    Price: **$219.00**
UNERTL STRAIGHT PRISMATIC—Same as Unertl Right Angle except: straight eyepiece and wgt. of 40 oz. **$185.00**
UNERTL 20X STRAIGHT PRISMATIC—54mm objective. 20X. Field at 100 yds., 8.5 ft. Relative brightness, 6.1. Eye relief, ½". Wgt., 36 oz. Length closed, 13½". Complete with lens covers **$155.00**
UNERTL TEAM SCOPE—100mm objective. 15X, 24X. 32X eyepieces. Field at 100 yds. 13 to 7.5 ft. Relative brightness, 39.06 to 9.79. Eye relief, 2" to 1½". Weight, 13 lbs. 29⅞" overall. Metal tripod, yoke and wood carrying case furnished (total weight, 80 lbs.) **$734.00**
WEATHERBY—60mm objective, 20X-45X zoom **$305.95**
    Tripod for above **$65.95**

SCOPE ATTACHMENTS

BUTLER CREEK LENS COVERS—Waterproof, dustproof. Springs open at a touch. Work in all weather. Sizes to fit all scopes. Per pair **$9.95**
DAVIS TARGETEER—Objective lens/tube units that attach to front of low power scopes, increase magnification to 8X. 1¼" lens, **$27.50**, 1½" lens **$32.50**
HERMANN LONGHORN DUST CAPS—All leather. Connected leather straps, hand made, natural color. For all popular scopes. **$6.50**
LEE TACKHOLE DOTS—Various size dots for most scopes. Price **$15.00**—**$22.50**
W. H. SIEBERT—Converts Lyman, Leupold, Unertl and Weaver K model varmint scopes to 15X-36X **$40.00**
STORM KING LENS CAPS—A hinged glass-and-rubber protector set (2), made in various sizes for all scopes. May be unhinged or sighted through. Anderson Mfg. Co. Per pair **$5.45**
    Price: with Haze Cutter **$6.55**
SUPREME LENS COVERS—Hinged protectors for most scope models, front and rear lenses shielded. Butler Creek Corp. Per pair, postpaid. **$7.95**

SPOTTING SCOPE STANDS

FREELAND ALL ANGLE—Tripod adjustable for elevation. Left or right side mount with worm drive clamp. Folding legs. Clamps available for any scope tube size. Gray crinkle finish. Price **$37.70**
    Also 12" 18", 24" extensions **$7.00, $9.35, $10.80**
FREELAND OLYMPIC—Bipod adjustable for elevation. All angle mount with padded worm drive clamp. Folding legs. Clamps available for any scope tube size. Gray crinkle finish. Price...................... **$44.00**
    Also 12", 18", 24" extensions **$7.00, $9.35, $10.80**
    Zoom head for tripod or bipod **$20.50**
FREELAND REGAL BIPOD—Choice of saddle or zoom head. All adjustment knobs are oversize for easy adjusting. Large "ball" carrying knob. Gray finish. **$45.00**
    Above with stability weight **$62.60**
    12", 18", 24" extensions **$7.00, $9.35, $10.80**
FREELAND GALLERY SPECIAL BIPOD—For all shooting positions. Zoom or saddle head. Adjustable for elevation. Comes with bipod base, gallery special head assembly and 12" extension. Gray finish, saddle head. **$42.00**
    As above with 18" extension **$43.20**
    Gallery Tripod (includes base, saddle head assembly and 12" extension) **$42.00**
    Zoom Gallery Bipod **$43.00**
    Zoom Gallery Tripod **$42.00**

ARMS ASSOCIATIONS IN AMERICA AND ABROAD

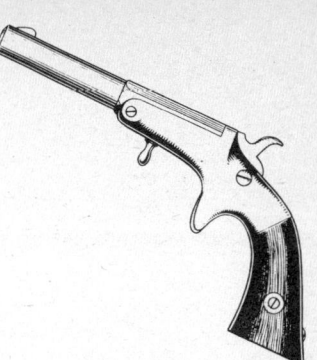

UNITED STATES

ALABAMA
Alabama Gun Collectors Assn.
Dick Boyd, P.O. Box 5548, Tuscaloosa, AL 35405

ALASKA
Alaska Gun Collectors Assn.
Gene Coppedge, P.O. Box 4-1898, Anchorage, AK 99509

ARIZONA
Arizona Gun Collectors Assn., Inc.
Miles S. Vaughn, Secy., P.O. Box 1129, Tucson, AZ 85702

CALIFORNIA
Burbank Rifle & Revolver Club, Inc.
P.O. Box 6765, Burbank, CA 91510
Calif. Hunters & Gun Owners Assoc.
V. H. Wacker, 2309 Cipriani Blvd., Belmont, CA 94002
Greater Calif. Arms & Collectors Assn.
Donald L. Bullock, 8291 Carburton St., Long Beach, CA 90808
Los Angeles Gun & Ctg. Collectors Assn.
F. H. Ruffra, 20810 Amie Ave., Torrance, CA 90503

COLORADO
Pikes Peak Gun Collectors Guild
Charles Cell, 406 E. Uintah St., Colorado Springs, CO 80903

CONNECTICUT
Antique Arms Coll. Assn. of Conn.
T. N. Reiley, 17 Philip Rd., Manchester, CT 06040
Ye Conn. Gun Guild, Inc.
Robert L. Harris, P.O. Box 8, Cornwall Bridge, CT 06754

DELAWARE
Delaware Antique Arms Collectors
C. Landis, 2408 Duncan Rd., Wilmington, DE 19808

GEORGIA
Georgia Arms Collectors
Cecil W. Anderson, P.O. Box 218, Conley, GA 30027

HAWAII
Hawaii Historic Arms Assn.
Roy D. Warren, P.O. Box 1733, Honolulu, HI 96806

IDAHO
Idaho State Rifle and Pistol Assn.
Tom Price, 3631 Pineridge Dr., Coeur d'Alene, ID 83814

ILLINOIS
Central Illinois Gun Collectors Assn., Inc.
Joe Richardson, R.R. 3, Jacksonville, IL 62650
Fox Valley Arms Fellowship, Inc.
P.O. Box 301, Palatine, IL 60067
Illinois Deer Hunters Assn.
Terry Jenkins, 5002 Stewart Dr., Decatur, IL 62521
Illinois State Rifle Assn.
224 S. Michigan Ave., Room 200, Chicago, IL 60604
Illinois Gun Collectors Assn.
P.O. Box 1694, Kankakee, IL 60901
Little Fort Gun Collectors Assn.
Ernie Robinson, P.O. Box 194, Gurnee, IL 60031
Mississippi Valley Gun & Cartridge Coll. Assn.
Harold S. Parsons, R.R. No. 2, Alexis, IL 61412
Sauk Trail Gun Collectors
Gordell Matson, P.O. Box 645, Milan, IL 61264
Wabash Valley Gun Collectors Assn., Inc.
Mrs. Betty Baer, 1659 N. Franklin St., Danville, IL 61832

INDIANA
Indiana Sportsmen's Council—Legislative
Maurice Latimer, P.O. Box 93, Bloomington, IN 47401
Indiana State Rifle & Pistol Assn.
Thos. Glancy, P.O. Box 552, Chesterton, IN 46304
Southern Indiana Gun Collectors Assn., Inc.
Harold M. McClary, 509 N. 3rd St., Boonville, IN 47601

IOWA
Central States Gun Collectors Assn.
Avery Giles, 1104 S. 1st Ave., Marshtown, IA 50158

KANSAS
Four State Collectors Assn.
M. G. Wilkinson, 915 E. 10th, Pittsburg, KS 66762
Kansas Cartridge Coll. Assn.
Bob Linder, Box 84, Plainville, KS 67663
Missouri Valley Arms Collectors Assn.
Chas. F. Samuel, Jr., Box 8204, Shawnee Mission, KS 66208

KENTUCKY
Kentuckiana Arms Coll. Assn.
Tony Wilson, Pres., Box 1776, Louisville, KY 40201
Kentucky Gun Collectors Assn., Inc.
J. A. Smith, Box 64, Owensboro, KY 42301

LOUISIANA
Bayou Gun Club
David J. Seibert, Jr., 2820 Ramsey Dr., New Orleans, LA 70114
Ft. Miro Muzzleloaders
Sandra Rushing, P.O. Box 256, Main St., Grayson, LA 71435.

MARYLAND
Baltimore Antique Arms Assn.
Stanley I. Kellert, R.D. 1, Box 256, Lutherville, MD 21093

MASSACHUSETTS
Bay Colony Weapons Collectors Inc.
Ronald B. Santurjian, 47 Homer Rd., Belmont, MA 02178
Massachusetts Arms Collectors
John J. Callan, Jr., P.O. Box 1001, Worcester, MA 01613

MICHIGAN
Royal Oak Historical Arms Collectors, Inc.
Dee Hamal, P.O. Box 202, Royal Oak, MI 48067

MINNESOTA
Minnesota Weapons Coll. Assn., Inc.
Box 662, Hopkins, MN 55343

MISSISSIPPI
Mississippi Gun Collectors Assn.
Mrs. Jack E. Swinney, P.O. Box 1332, Hattiesburg, MS 39401

MISSOURI
Edwardsville, Ill. Gun Collectors
A. W. Stephensmeier, 1055 Warson Woods Dr., St. Louis, MO 63122
Mineral Belt Gun Coll. Assn.
D. F. Saunders, 1110 Cleveland Ave., Monett, MO 65708

MONTANA
Montana Arms Collectors Assn.
Lewis E. Yearout, 308 Riverview Dr. East, Great Falls, MT 59404
The Winchester Arms Coll. Assn.
Lewis E. Yearout, 308 Riverview Dr. East, Great Falls, MT 59404

NEBRASKA
Nebraska Gun & Cartridge Collectors
E. M. Zalud, 710 West 6th St., North Platte, NB 69101

NEW HAMPSHIRE
New Hampshire Arms Collectors Inc.
Frank H. Galeucia, Rte. 28, Box 44, Windham, NH 03087

NEW JERSEY
Englishtown Benchrest Shooters Assn.
Tony Hidalgo, 6 Capp St., Carteret, NJ 07008
Experimental Ballistics Associates
Ed Yard, 110 Kensington, Trenton, NJ 08618
Jersey Shore Antique Arms Collectors
Joe Sisia, P.O. Box 100, Bayville, NJ 08721
New Jersey Arms Collectors Club, Inc.
Angus Laidlaw, 230 Valley Rd., Montclair, NJ 07042

NEW MEXICO
New Mexico Gun Collectors Assn.
Jack Daniels, 3107 Central Ave., NE, Albuquerque, NM 87111

NEW YORK
Hudson-Mohawk Arms Collectors Assn., Inc.
Bennie S. Pisarz, 6 Lamberson St., Dolgeville, NY 13329
Iroquois Arms Collectors Assn.
Dennis Freeman, 12144 McNeeley Rd., Akron, NY 14001
Mid-State Arms Coll. & Shooters Club
Jack Ackerman, 24 S. Mountain Terr., Binghamton, NY 13903
Westchester Arms Collectors Club, Inc.
F. E. Falkenbury, Secy., 79 Hillcrest Rd., Hartsdale, NY 10530

NORTH CAROLINA
Carolina Gun Collectors Assn.
David Blalock, Jr., Rt. 1, Linden, NC 28356

OHIO
Central Ohio Gun and Indian Relic Coll. Assn.
Coyt Stookey, 134 E. Ohio Ave., Washington C.H., OH 43160
Maumee Valley Gun Collectors Assn.
A. Kowalka, 3203 Woodville Rd., Northwood, OH 43619
National Bench Rest Shooters Assn., Inc.
Bernice McMullen, 607 W. Line St., Minerva, OH 44657
Ohio Gun Collectors, Assn., Inc.
P.O. Box 300, Mount Gilead, OH 43338
The Stark Gun Collectors, Inc.
Russ McNary, 147 Miles Ave., N.W., Canton, OH 44708

OKLAHOMA
Indian Territory Gun Collectors Assn.
P.O. Box 4491, Tulsa, OK 74104

OREGON
Oregon Cartridge Coll. Assn.
Richard King, 3228 N.W. 60th, Corvallis, OR 97330
Oregon Arms Coll. Assn., Inc.
Ted Dowd, P.O. Box 25103, Portland, OR 97225

PENNSYLVANIA
Presque Isle Gun Coll. Assn.
James Welch, 156 E. 37 St., Erie, PA 16506

SOUTH CAROLINA
Belton Gun Club Inc.
J. K. Phillips, Route 1, Belton SC 29627
South Carolina Arms Coll. Assn.
J. W. McNelley, 3215 Lincoln St., Columbia, SC 29201

SOUTH DAKOTA
Dakota Territory Gun Coll. Assn., Inc.
Curt Carter, Castlewood, SD 57223

TENNESSEE
Memphis Antique Weapons Assn.
Nelson T. Powers, 4672 Barfield Rd., TN 38117
Smoky Mountain Gun Coll. Assn., Inc.
M. C. Wiest, P.O. Box 8880, Knoxville, TN 37916
Tennessee Gun Collectors Assn., Inc.
M. H. Parks, 3556 Pleasant Valley Rd., Nashville, TN 37204

TEXAS
Houston Gun Collectors Assn.
P.O. Box 37369, Houston, TX 77036
Texas State Rifle Assn.
Lafe R. Pfeifer, P.O. Drawer 340809, Dallas TX 75234

UTAH
Utah Gun Collectors Assn.
S. Gerald Keogh, 875 20th St., Ogden, UT 84401

VIRGINIA
Virginia Arms Collectors & Assn.
Clinton E. Jones, P.O. Box 333, Mechanicsville, VA 23111

WASHINGTON
Washington Arms Collectors, Inc.
J. Dennis Cook, P.O. Box 7335, Tacoma, WA 98407

WISCONSIN
Great Lakes Arms Coll. Assn., Inc.
E. Warnke, 1811 N. 73rd St. Wauwatosa, WI 53213
Wisconsin Gun Collectors Assn., Inc.
Rob. Zellmer, P.O. Box 181, Sussex, WI 53089

WYOMING
Wyoming Gun Collectors
Bob Funk, Box 1805, Riverton, WY 82501

NATIONAL ORGANIZATIONS
Amateur Trap Shooting Assn.
P.O. Box 458, Vandalia, OH 45377
The American Air Gun Assn. Inc.
P.O. Box 226, Depew, NY 14043
American Association of Shotgunning
P.O. Box 2405, Reno, NV 89505
American Defense Preparedness Assn.
Rosslyn Center, 1700 N. Moore St., Suite 900, Arlington, VA 22209
The American Pistol Institute
Jeff Cooper, P.O. Box 401, Paulden, AZ 86334
American Police Pistol & Rifle Assn.
1100 N.E. 125th St., No. Miami, FL 33161
American Single Shot Rifle Assn.
L. B. Thompson, 987 Jefferson Ave., Salem, OH 44460
American Society of Arms Collectors, Inc.
Robt. F. Rubendunst, 6550 Baywood Lane, Cincinnati, OH 45224
Armor & Arms Club
J. K. Watson, Jr., 25 Broadway, New York, NY 10004
Association of Firearm and Toolmark Examiners
Eugenia A. Bell, Secy., 785 Esterel Dr., La Jolla, CA 92037
Boone & Crockett Club
424 N. Washington St., Alexandria, VA 22314
Cast Bullet Assn., Inc.
Sidney F. Musselman, 5522 Trent St., Chevy Chase, MD 20015
Citizens Committee for the Right to Keep and Bear Arms
Natl. Hq.: Bellefield Office Park, 1601 114, S.E., Suite 151, Bellevue, WA 98004
Deer Unlimited of America, Inc.
P.O. Box 509, Clemson, SC 29631
Ducks Unlimited, Inc.
P.O. Box 66300, Chicago, IL 60666
Experimental Ballistics Assoc.
Ed Yard, 110 Kensington, Trenton, NJ 08618
International Benchrest Shooters
Evelyn Richards, 411 N. Wilbur Ave, Sayre, PA 18840
International Cartridge Coll. Assn., Inc.
Ellie Dodd, 1912 Sandra Ave., Metairie, LA 70003
International Handgun Metallic Silhouette Assoc.
Box 1609, Idaho Falls, ID 83401
Miniature Arms Collectors/Makers Society Ltd.
Joseph J. Macewicz, 104 White Sand Lane, Racine, WI 53402
National Assn. of Federally Licd. Firearms Dealers
Andrew Molchan, 7001 N. Clark St., Chicago, IL 60626

National Automatic Pistol Collectors Assn.
Tom Knox, P.O. Box 15738, Tower Grove Station, St. Louis, MO 63163
National Bench Rest Shooters Assn., Inc.
Stella Buchtel, 5735 Sherwood Forest Dr., Akron, OH 44139
National Deer Hunter Assn.
1415 Fifth St. So., Hopkins, MN 55343
National Muzzle Loading Rifle Assn.
Box 67, Friendship, IN 47021
National Police Officers Assn. of America
609 West Main St., Louisville, KY 40202
National Reloading Mfrs. Assn., Inc.
1221 S.W. Yamhill St., Portland, OR 97205
National Rifle Assn.
1600 Rhode Island Ave., N.W., Washington, DC 20036
National Shooting Sports Fdtn., Inc.
Arnold H. Rohlfing, Exec. Director, 1075 Post Rd., Riverside, CT 06878
National Skeet Shooting Assn.
Ann Myers, P.O. Box 28188, San Antonio, TX 78228
National Wild Turkey Federation, Inc.
P.O. Box 530, Edgefield, SC 29824
North American Edged Weapon Collectors Assn.
John Cox, 2224 Wyandoge Dr., Oakville, Ont. L6L 2T5, Canada
North-South Skirmish Assn., Inc.
John L. Rawls, Route 1, Box 226A, Bentonville, VA 22610
Ruger Collector's Assn., Inc.
Col. L. O. Friesz, P.O. Box 290, Southport, CT 06490
Second Amendment Foundation
Bellefield Office Park, 1601—114th S.E., Suite 157, Bellevue, WA 98004
Sporting Arms and Ammunition Mfrs. Inst., Inc.
420 Lexington Ave., New York, NY 10017
U.S. Revolver Assn.
Stanley A. Sprague, 59 Alvin St., Springfield, MA 01104
Winchester Arms Collectors Assoc.
Lewis E. Yearout, 308 Riverview Dr.,E, Great Falls, MT 59404

AUSTRALIA
Sporting Shooters' Assn. of Australia Inc.
Mrs. A. Brummell, P.O. Box 154, Punchbowl 2196, New South Wales, Australia

CANADA
ALBERTA
Canadian Historical Arms Society
P.O. Box 901, Edmonton, Alb., Canada T5J 2L8

NEW BRUNSWICK
Canadian Black Powder Federation
Mrs. Shirley Stuart, 1359 McLaughlin Rd., R.R. #4, Moncton, N.B., Can. E1C 8J8

ONTARIO
Oshawa Antique Gun Coll. Inc.
William A. Vaughan, Box 544, Whitby, Ont. L1N 5V3, Canada

QUEBEC
Lower Canada Arms Collectors Assn., Inc.
Jon Kirton, P.O. Box 564, Stock Exchange Tower, 800 Place Victoria, Montreal, Quebec, Can. H4Z 1S8

EUROPE
ENGLAND
Arms and Armour Society of London
Joseph G. Rosa, 17 Woodville Gardens, Ruislip, Middlesex HA4 7NB
British Cartridge Collectors Club
Peter F. McGowan, 15 Sandhurst Dr., Ruddington, Nottingham
Historical Breechloading Smallarms Assn.
D. J. Penn, M.A., Imperial War Museum, Lambeth Rd., London SE1 6HZ, England. Journal is $8 a yr.
Muzzle Loaders' Assn. of Great Britain
Membership Records, 12 Frances Rd., Baginton, Coventry, England
National Rifle Assn. (British)
Bisley Camp, Brookwood, Woking, Surrey, GU24 OPB, England

GERMANY (WEST)
Deutscher Schutzenbund
Lahnstrasse, 6200 Wiesbaden-Klarenthal, West Germany

NEW ZEALAND
New Zealand Deerstalkers Assn.
J. M. Murphy, P.O. Box 6514, Wellington, New Zealand

SOUTH AFRICA
Historical Firearms Soc. of South Africa
P.O. Box 145, 7725 Newlands, Republic of South Africa
South African Reloaders Assn.
Box 27128, Sunnyside, Pretoria 0132, South Africa

PERIODICAL PUBLICATIONS

Air Gun Magazine
P.O. Box 961, Macedon, NY 14502.
Airgun World
10 Sheet St., Windsor, Berks., SL4 1BG, England. $20 for 12 issues. Monthly magazine catering exclusively to the airgun enthusiast.
Alaska Magazine
Alaska Northwest Pub. Co., Box 4-EEE, Anchorage, AK 99509. $15.00 yr. Hunting and fishing articles.
The American Blade*
Beinfeld Publishing, Inc., 12767 Saticoy St., No. Hollywood, CA 91605. $9.00 yr. Add $6 f. foreign subscription. A magazine for all enthusiasts of the edged blade.
American Field†
222 W. Adams St., Chicago, IL. 60606. $12.00 yr. Field dogs and trials, occasional gun and hunting articles.
American Firearms Industry
Nat'l. Assn. of Federally Licensed Firearms Dealers, 7001 No. Clark St., Chicago, IL 60626. $15 yr. For firearms dealers & distributors.
The American Handgunner
591 Camino de la Reina, San Diego, CA 92108. $9.95 yr. Articles for handgun enthusiasts, collectors and hunters.
The American Hunter (M)
Natl. Rifle Assn., 1600 Rhode Island Ave. N.W., Washington, DC 20036. $15.00 yr. Wide scope of hunting articles.
The American Rifleman (M)
National Rifle Assn., 1600 Rhode Island Ave., N.W., Wash. DC 20036. $15.00 yr. Firearms articles of all kinds.
The American Shotgunner
P.O. Box 3351, Reno, NV 89505. $15.00 yr. Official publ. of the American Assn. of Shotgunning. Industrial shooting, reloading, used gun classifieds. Membership and benefits w. yrly. subscr.
The American West*
Amer. West Publ. Co., 20380 Town Center Lane, Suite 160, Cupertino, CA 95014. $15.00 yr.
Arms Gazette
Beinfeld Publ., Inc., 12767 Saticoy St., No. Hollywood, CA 91605. $15.00 yr.; add $5 foreign subscr. Excellent brief articles for the collector of antique and modern firearms.
Australian Shooters' Journal
P. O. Box 1064, G.P.O. Adelaide, SA 5001, Australia. $20.00 yr. locally; $25.00 yr. overseas. Hunting and shooting articles.
Black Powder Times
P.O. Box 842, Mount Vernon, WA 98273. $8.00 for 12 issues.
The Buckskin Report
P. O. 885, Big Timber, MT 59011. $15.00 yr. Articles for the blackpowder shooter.
Canada GunSport
P.O. Box 201, Willowdale, Ont., Canada M2N 2S9. $9.95 yr. Articles on guns, hunting, shooting, plus gun ads of all kinds.
Canadian Journal of Arms Collecting (Q)
Museums Restoration Service P.O. Drawer 390, Bloomfield, Ont., Canada KOK IGO. $7.50 yr.
Deer Unlimited*
P.O. Box 509, Clemson, SC 29631. $12.00 yr.
Deutsches Waffen Journal
Journal-Verlag Schwend GmbH, Postfach 100340, D7170 Schwabisch Hall, Germany. DM48.00 yr. plus DM10.80 postage. Antique and modern arms. German text.
Ducks Unlimited, Inc. (M)
P.O. Box 66300, Chicago, IL 60666.
Enforcement Journal (Q)
Frank J. Schira, editor, Natl. Police Officers Assn., 609 West Main St., Louisville, KY 40202 $6.00 yr.
The Field†
The Harmsworth Press Ltd., Carmelite House, London E.C.4 England. $56.00 yr. Hunting and shooting articles, and all country sports.
Field & Stream
CBS Publications, 1515 Broadway, New York, N.Y. 10036. $9.94 yr. Articles on firearms plus hunting and fishing.
Fur-Fish-Game
A. R. Harding Pub. Co., 2878 E. Main St., Columbus, OH 43209. $7.00 yr. "Gun Rack" column by Don Zutz.
Gray's Sporting Journal*
Gray's Sporting Journal Co., 1330 Beacon St., Brookline, MA 02146 $19.50 f. 7 Issues. Hunting and fishing journals.
The Gun Report
World Wide Gun Report, Inc., Box 111, Aledo, IL 61231. $15.00 yr. For the gun collector.
The Gunrunner
Div. of Kexco Publ. Co. Ltd., Box 565, Lethbridge, Alb., Canada T1J 3Z4. $6.00 yr Newspaper, listing everything from antiques to artillery.
Gun Week
Hawkeye Publishing, Inc., P. O. Box 411, Station C, Buffalo NY 14209. $12.00 yr. U.S. and possessions; $16.00 yr. other countries. Tabloid paper on guns, hunting, shooting.
Gun World
Gallant Publishing Co., 34249 Camino Capistrano, Capistrano Beach, CA 92624. $9.00 yr. For the hunting, reloading and shooting enthusiast.
Guns & Ammo
Petersen Pub. Co., 8490 Sunset Blvd., Los Angeles, CA 90069. $10.95 yr. Guns, shooting, and technical articles.
Guns
Guns Magazine, 591 Camino de la Reina, San Diego, CA 92108. $11.95 yr. Articles for gun collectors, hunters and shooters.
Guns Review
Ravenhill Pub. Co. Ltd., Standard House, Bonhill St., London E.C. 2A 4DA, England. $23.30 USA & Canada yr. For collectors and shooters.
Handloader*
Wolfe Pub. Co. Inc., Box 3030, Prescott, AZ 86302 $10.00 yr. The journal of ammunition reloading.
International Shooting Sport*
Union Internationale de Tir, Bavariaring 21, D-8000 Munich 2, Germany. (Deutsche Mark) DM27.00 yr., p.p. For the International target shooter.
The Journal of the Arms & Armour Society (M)
Joseph G. Rosa (Secy.), 17 Woodville Gardens, Ruislip, Middlesex HA4 7NB, England. $16.00 yr. Articles for the historian and collector.
Journal of the Historical Breechloading Smallarms Assn.
Publ. annually, Imperial War Museum, Lambeth Road, London SE1 6HZ, England. $8 yr. Articles for the collector plus mailings of lecture transcripts, short articles on specific arms, reprints, etc.
Knife World
Knife World Publications, P.O. Box 3395, Knoxville, TN 37917. $8.00 yr., $14.00 2 yrs. The monthly publication f. knife enthusiasts and collectors.
Law and Order
Law and Order Magazine, 5526 N. Elston Ave., Chicago, IL 60630 $11.00 yr. Articles on weapons for law enforcement, etc.
The Lookout(M)
Canadian Black Powder Federation Newsletter, 2188 W. 46th Ave., Vancouver, B.C. V6M 2L1, Canada; $10.00 f. 6 issues.
Man At Arms*
222 West Exchange St., Providence, RI 02903. $15.00 yr. The magazine of arms collecting-investing.
Muzzle Blasts (M)
National Muzzle Loading Rifle Assn. P.O. Box 67, Friendship, IN 47021. $14.00 yr. For the black powder shooter.
The Muzzleloader Magazine*
Rebel Publishing Co., Inc., Route 5, Box 347-M, Texarkana, TX 75503. $7.50 yr. The publication for black powder shooters.
National Defense (M)*
American Defense Preparedness Assn., Rosslyn Center, Suite 900, 1700 North Moore St., Arlington, VA 22209. $22.50 yr. Articles on military-related topics, including weapons, materials technology, management and policy.
National Rifle Assn. Journal (British) (Q)
Natl. Rifle Assn. (BR.), Bisley Camp, Brookwood, Woking, Surrey, England. GU24 OPB. $12.00 inc. air postage.
National Wildlife*
Natl. Wildlife Fed., 1412 16th St. N.W., Washington, DC 20036. $9.50 yr. (6 issues); *International Wildlife*, 6 issues, $9.50 yr. Both, $14.50 yr., plus membership benefits.
New Zealand Wildlife (Q)
New Zealand Deerstalkers Assoc. Inc., P.O. Box 6514, Wellington, N.Z. $3.00 U.S. and Canada, elsewhere on application. Hunting and shooting articles.
Northwestern Sportsman
Box 1208, Big Timber, MT 59011. $10.00 yr.
Outdoor Life
Times Mirror Magazines, Inc., 380 Madison Ave., New York, NY 10017. $11.94 yr. Shooting columns by Jim Carmichel, and others.
Point Blank
Citizens Committee for the Right to Keep and Bear Arms (sent to contributors) 1601 114th S.E., Suite 151, Bellevue, WA 98004
Police Command (M)
1100 NE 125th St., N. Miami, FL 33161
The Police Marksman*
217 S. Court St., Montgomery, AL 36104. $15.00 yr.
Police Times (M)
1100 N.E. 125th St., No. Miami, Fla. 33161.
Popular Mechanics
Hearst Corp., 224 W. 57th St., New York, NY 10019. $8.97 yr., $14.97 Canada and foreign. Hunting, shooting and camping articles.
Precision Shooting
Precision Shooting, Inc., Box 6, Athens, PA 18810. $9.00 yr. Journal of the International Benchrest Shooters and target shooting in general.
Rifle*
Wolfe Publishing Co. Inc., Box 3030, Prescott, AZ 86302. $10.00 yr. Journal of the NBRSA. The magazine for shooters.
Saga
Gambi Publ., 333 Johnson Ave., Brooklyn, N.Y. 11206. $12.00 yr. U.S.
Second Amendment Reporter
Second Amendment Fdn., Bellefield Off. Pk., 1601—114th St. SE, Suite 157, Bellevue, WA 98004. $15.00 yr. (non-contributors).
The Shooting Industry
Publisher's Dev. Corp., 591 Camino de la Reina, Suite 200, San Diego, CA 92108. $25.00 yr. To the trade $12.50.
Shooting Magazine
10 Sheet St., Windsor, Berksh., SL4 1BG England. $20.00 for 12 issues. Monthly journal catering mainly to claypigeon shooters.
The Shooting Times & Country Magazine (England) †
10 Sheet St., Windsor, Berkshire SL4 1BG, England. $49.40 yr. (52 issues). Game shooting, wild fowling, hunting, game fishing and firearms articles.
Shooting Times
PJS Publications, News Plaza, P.O. Box 1790, Peoria, IL 61656. $11.95 yr. Guns, shooting, reloading; articles on every gun activity.

Shooter's Journal*
TRM Publications, Inc., 2145 W. LaPalma, Anaheim, CA 92801. $4.50 yr.

The Shotgun News‡
Snell Publishing Co., Box 669, Hastings, NB 68901. $7.50 yr. Sample copy $2.00. Gun ads of all kinds.

Shotgun West
2052 Broadway, Santa Monica, CA 90404. $8.50 yr. Trap, Skeet and international shooting, scores, articles, schedules.

The Sixgunner (M)
Handgun Hunters International, P. O. Box 357 MAG, Bloomingdale, OH 43910

The Skeet Shooting Review
National Skeet Shooting Assn., P.O. Box 28188, San Antonio, TX 78228. $12.00 yr. (Assn. membership of $15.00 includes mag.) Scores, averages, skeet and hunting articles.

Sporting Goods Business
Gralla Publications, 1515 Broadway, New York, NY 10036. Trade journal.

The Sporting Goods Dealer
1212 No. Lindbergh Blvd., St. Louis, Mo. 63166. $9.00 yr. The sporting goods trade journal.

Sporting Gun
Bretton Court, Bretton, Peterborough PE3 8DZ, England. $18.00 (airmail $45.00) yr. For the game and clay enthusiasts.

Sports Afield
The Hearst Corp., 250 W. 55th St., New York, N.Y. 10019. $15.00 yr. Grits Gresham on firearms, ammunition and hunting.

Sports Merchandiser
A W.R.C. Smith Publication, 1760 Peachtree Rd. NW, Atlanta, GA 30357. Trade Journal.

TACARMI
Via Volta 60, 20090 Cusago (Milan), Italy. $37.20 yr. Antique and modern guns. (Italian text.)

Trap & Field
1100 Waterway Blvd., Indianapolis, IN 46202. $14.00 yr. Official publ. Amateur Trapshooting Assn. Scores, averages, trapshooting articles.

Turkey Call* (M)
Natl. Wild Turkey Federation, Inc., P.O. Box 467, Edgefield, SC 29824. $12.00 w. membership.

The U.S. Handgunner (M)
U.S. Revolver Assn., 59 Alvin St., Springfield, MA 01104. $5.00 yr. General handgun and competition articles.

Waterfowler's World*
P.O. Box 38306, Germantown, TN 38138. $10.00 yr.

Wisconsin Sportsman*
Wisconsin Sportsman, Inc., P.O. Box 2266, Oshkosh, WI 54903. $7.50.

* Published bi-monthly † Published weekly ‡ Published twice per month. All others are published monthly.
M Membership requirements; write for details. Q Published Quarterly.

Shooting Sports Booklets & Pamphlets

Basic Pistol Marksmanship—Textbook for basic pistol courses. 25¢[2]

Basic Rifle Marksmanship—Textbook for basic rifle courses. 25¢ ea.[2]

The Elk—125-page report on the hunting and management of this game animal, more properly called *wapiti*. Extensive biblio. $1.00.[4]

Free Films—Brochure listing outdoor movies available to sportsmen's clubs. Free.[1]

The Gun Law Problem—Information about firearms Legislation. Free.[2]

How to be a Crack Shot—A 14-page booklet detailing everything necessary to becoming an outstanding shot. Free.[3]

Fundamentals of Claybird Shooting—A 39-page booklet explaining the basics of Skeet and trap in non-technical terms. Many diagrams. Free.[4]

Hunter Safety Instructor's Guide—How to conduct an NRA Hunter Safety Course. 25¢ ea.[2]

Hunting and Shooting Sportsmanship—A 4-page brochure defining the "true sportsman" and giving information on the outdoor field. 10¢[1]

Junior Rifle Handbook—Information about the NRA junior program with short instruction course. (25 copies issued to each new affiliated junior club without charge.) 25¢ ea.[2]

NRA Hunter Safety Handbook—Textbook for students. 10¢ ea.[2]

Game, Gunners and Biology—A thumbnail history of American wildlife conservation. 50¢ ea.[4]

Trap or Skeet Fundamentals—Handbooks explaining fundamentals of these two sports, complete with explicit diagrams to start beginners off right. Free.[3]

25 Foot Shooting Program—Complete information on a short range shooting program with CO_2 and pneumatic rifles and pistols. 35¢[2]

When Your Youngster Wants a Gun—Straightforward answers to the 15 questions most frequently asked by parents. 8 pp. 25¢ ea.[1]

The Cottontail Rabbit—56-page rundown on America's most popular hunting target. Where to find him, how to hunt him, how to help him. Bibliography included. $1.00 ea.[4]

For the Young Hunter—A 32-page booklet giving fundamental information on the sport. Single copies free, 15¢ each in bulk.[4]

Gray and Fox Squirrels—112-page paperbound illustrated book giving full rundown on the squirrel families named. Extensive bibliography. $1.00 ea.[4]

The Mallard—80-page semi-technical report on this popular duck. Life cycle, laws and management, hunting—even politics as they affect this bird—are covered. Bibliography. $1.00 ea.[4]

NRA Federal Firearms Laws—A 28-page booklet digesting the several U.S. gun laws affecting the citizen today. Free to NRA members.[2]

NRA Firearms & Ammunition Fact Book—352-page book of questions and answers, ballistic charts and tables, descriptions of firearms and ammunition. NRA, Washington, D.C., 1964. $2.00 ea. ($1.75 to NRA members).

NRA Firearms Assembly Handbook, Volumes I and II—Articles describing the assembly and disassembly of various arms. Vol. I. 160 pp., covers 77 guns, Vol. II, 176 pp., 87 guns. Illustrated with exploded-view and supplementary drawings. NRA, Washington, D.C., 1960 and 1964. $3.50 ea. ($2.50 to NRA members).

NRA Firearms Handling Handbook—21 major articles on the proper useage of most types of small arms available to civilians. Illus. NRA, Washington, D.C., 1962, 80 pp. $2.75 ($1.75 to NRA members).

NRA Gun Collectors Handbook—20 feature articles on all phases of gun collecting, plus a listing of all important museums. NRA, Washington, D.C., 1959. 48 pp., illus. $2.50 ($1.50 to NRA members).

NRA Handloader's Guide—Enlarged & Revised. A successor to the *NRA Illustrated Reloading Handbook,* this excellent new work covers all aspects of metallic-case and shotshell reloading. Washington, D.C., 1969, fully illus. $5.00 (NRA members, $4.00).

NRA Hunters Handbook—51 major pieces, 18 shorter ones. NRA, Washington, D.C., 1960. 72 pp., illus. $3.00 ($2.00 to NRA members).

NRA Illustrated International Shooting Handbook—18 major articles detailing shooting under ISU rules, training methods, etc. NRA, Washington, D.C., 1964. $2.50 ea. ($1.50 to NRA members).

NRA Illustrated Shotgun Handbook—50 articles covering every phase of smoothbore shooting, including exploded views of many shotguns. NRA, Washington, D.C., 1964. 128 pp. $3.00 ea. ($2.00 to NRA members).

NRA Questions and Answers Handbook—150 queries and replies on guns and shooting. NRA, Washington, D.C., 1959. 46 pp. with index, illus. $2.50 ($1.50 to NRA members).

NRA Shooters Guide—40 articles of high interest to shooters of all kinds. Over 340 illus. NRA, Washington, D.C., 1959. 72 pp, $3.00 ($2.00 to NRA members).

NRA Shooting Handbook—83 major articles plus 35 shorts on every phase of shooting. NRA, Washington, D.C., 1961. 224 pp., illus. $4.50 ($3.50 to NRA members).

Principles of Game Management—A 25-page booklet surveying in popular manner such subjects as hunting regulations, predator control, game refuges and habitat restoration. Single copies free, 15¢ each in bulk.[4]

The Ring-Necked Pheasant—Popular distillation of much of the technical literature on the "ringneck." 104-page paperbound book, appropriately illustrated. Bibliography included. $1.00 ea.[4]

Ruffed Grouse, by John Madson—108-page booklet on the life history, management and hunting of *Bonasa umbellus* in its numerous variations. Extensive biblio. $1.00.[4]

Firearms Prohibition—A logical examination of the arguments used to justify confiscation and the reasons why it won't control crime. 25¢ ea.[1]

Fact Pack II—Authoritative and complete study on gun use and ownership. This is a valuable 102-page reference. $2.00 ea.[1]

---

[1] National Shooting Sports Foundation, Inc. 1075 Post Road, Riverside, Conn. 06878

[2] National Rifle Association of America, 1600 Rhode Island Ave., Washington, D.C. 20036

[3] Remington Arms Company, Dept. C.—Bridgeport, Conn. 06602

[4] Olin Mathieson Conservation Dept., East Alton, Ill. 62024

[5] Winchester-Western, Shotgun Shooting Promotion, 275 Winchester Ave., New Haven, CT 06504

The Arms Library for
COLLECTOR · HUNTER · SHOOTER · OUTDOORSMAN

A selection of books—old, new and forthcoming—for everyone in the arms field, with a brief description by... JOE RILING

ballistics and handloading

ABC's of Reloading, 2nd Edition, by Dean A. Grennell, DBI Books, Inc., Northfield, IL, 1980. 288 pp., illus. Paper covers. $8.95.
A natural, logical, thorough set of directions on how to prepare shotgun shells, rifle and pistol cases prior to reloading.
American Ammunition and Ballistics, by Edward A. Matunas, Winchester Press, New York, NY, 1979. 288 pp., illus. $12.50.
A complete reference book covering all presently manufactured and much discontinued American rimfire, centerfire, and shotshell ammunition.
Ballistic Science for the Law Enforcement Officer, by Charles G. Wilber, Ph.D., Charles C. Thomas, Springfield, IL, 1977. 309 pp., illus. $23.00.
A scientific study of the ballistics of civilian firearms.
Ballistics & the Muzzle Loading Rifle, by Wm. C. Herring, Nat'l. Muzzle Loading Rifle Assn., Friendship, IN, 1974. 111 pp., illus. Paper covers. $5.95.
A manual of black powder reloading and ballistic data.
Ballistics in the Seventeenth Century, by A. R. Hall. 1st J. & J. Harper ed. 1969 [from the Cambridge University Press ed. of 1952]. 186 pp., illus., with tables and diagrams. $13.50.
A profound work for advanced scholars, this is a study in the relations of science and war, with reference principally to England.
The Bullet Swage Manual, by Ted Smith, Corbin Manufacturing & Supply, Inc., Phoenix, OR, limited second edition, 1976. 43 pp., illus. Paper covers. $3.50.
A good first swaging book, written by a master die-maker.
Cartridges of the World 4th Edition, by Frank C. Barnes, DBI Books, Northfield, IL, 352 pp., illus. Paper covers. $9.95.
Gives the history, dimensions, performance and physical characteristics for more than 1,000 different cartridges.
Cast Bullets, by Col. E. H. Harrison, A publication of the National Rifle Association of America, Washington, DC, 1979. 144 pp., illus. Paper covers. $9.00.
An authoritative guide to bullet casting techniques and ballistics.
The Complete Book of Practical Handloading, by John Wooters, Winchester Press, NY, 1976. 320 pp., illus. $12.50
An up-to-the-minute guide for the rifleman and shotgunner.
Computer for Handloaders, by Homer Powley. A slide rule plus 12 page instruction book for use in finding charge, most efficient powder and velocity for any modern centerfire rifle. $5.50
The Corbin Handbook & Catalog of Bullet Swaging No. III, compiled by Dave Corbin, Corbin Manufacturing & Supply, Inc., Phoenix, OR, 1977. 73 pp., illus. Paper covers. $2.50.
Information on Corbin products including reloading press dies, accessories, chemicals and the Mity Mite System of hand swaging.
Corbin Technical Bulletins, Volume I, compiled by Dave Corbin, Corbin Manufacturing & Supply Inc., Phoenix, OR, 1977. 66 pp., illus. Paper covers. $5.00.
Answers in depth the specific questions dealers and handloaders have about bullet swaging, plus new techniques.
A Digest of Cartridges for Small Arms Patented in the United States, England and France, by W. A. Bartlett and D. B. Gallatin, Museum Restoration Service, Ontario, Canada, 1977. 52 pp., illus. Paper covers. $4.95.
A facsimile reprint of the very scarce 1878 edition. A classic publication for the cartridge collector.
Discover Swaging, by Dave Corbin, Stackpole Books, Harrisburg, PA, 1979. 288 pp., illus. $14.95.
Improve the power and field accuracy of your firearms with the first complete guide to the art and science of custom bullet making.
Firearms Identification, by Dr. J. H. Mathews, Charles C. Thomas, Springfield, IL, 1973 3 vol. set. A massive, carefully researched, authoritative work published as:
Vol. I. **The Laboratory Examination of Small Arms....** 400 pp., illus. $51.50.
Vol. II. **Original Photographs and Other Illustrations of Handguns.** 492 pp., illus. $51.50.
Vol. III. **Data on Rifling Characteristics of Handguns and Rifles.** 730 pp., illus. $80.00.
Firearms Investigation, Identification and Evidence, by J. S. Hatcher, Frank J. Jury and Jac Weller. Stackpole Books, Harrisburg, PA, 1977. 536 pp. illus. $22.50.
Reprint of the 1957 printing of this classic book on forensic ballistics. Indispensable for those interested in firearms identification and criminology.
Game Loads and Practical Ballistics For The American Hunter, by Bob Hagel, Alfred A. Knopf, NY, NY, 1978. 315 pp., illus., hardbound. $12.95.
Everything a hunter needs to know about ballistics and performance of commercial hunting loads.
Handbook for Shooters and Reloaders, by P. O. Ackley, Salt Lake City, UT, 1970. Vol. I, 567 pp., illus. $9.75. Vol. II, a new printing with specific new material. 495 pp., illus. $9.75. Both volumes. Paper covers $19.50.

Handloader's Digest, 8th Edition, edited by John T. Amber, DBI Books Inc., Northfield, IL, 1978. 288 pp., illus. Paper covers. $7.95.
This completely new edition contains the latest data on ballistics, maximum loads, new tools, equipment, etc., plus a fully illus. catalog section, current prices and specifications.
Handloader's Digest Bullet and Powder Update, edited by Ken Warner, DBI Books, Inc., Northfield, IL, 1980. 128 pp., illus. Paper covers. $4.95.
An update on the last ed. of "Handloader's Digest" the 8th edition. Included is a round-up piece on new bullets, another on new primers and powders plus five shooters' reports on the various types of bullets.
Handloading for Handgunners, by Geo. C. Nonte, DBI Books, Inc., Northfield, IL, 1978. 288 pp., illus. Paper covers. $7.95.
An expert tells the ins and outs of this specialized facet of reloading.
Handloading for Hunters, by Don Zutz, Winchester Press, NY, 1977. 288 pp., illus. $12.50.
Precise mixes and loads for different types of game and for various hunting situations with rifle and shotgun.
Hazards and Problems of Handloading, by Fred Tucker, Fred Tucker, Moore, OK, 1963. 70 pp., illus., paper covers. $3.50.
Covers features of handloading which are not always mentioned in standard manuals.
Hodgdon "New" Data Manual No. 23, Hodgdon Powder Co., Shawnee Mission, KS, 1977. 192 pp., illus. $4.95.
New data on Pyrodex and black powder. New section on how to reload for beginners. Information on rifle, pistol, shotgun and lead bullet loads.
The Home Guide to Cartridge Conversions, by Maj. George C. Nonte, Jr., The Gun Room Press, Highland Park, NJ, 1976. 404 pp., illus. $12.95
Revised and updated version of Nonte's definitive work on the alteration of cartridge cases for use in guns for which they were not intended.
Hornady Handbook of Cartridge Reloading, Rifle-Pistol, Vol. 2, by J. W. Hornady, Hornady Mfg. Co., Inc., Grand Island, NB, 1973. 512 pp., illus. $5.95.
A comprehensive guide to handloading and shooting; nearly 100 rifle/pistol cartridge combinations. Thousands of loads.
Lyman Black Powder Handbook, ed. by C. Kenneth Ramage, Lyman Products for Shooters, Middlefield, CT, 1975. 239 pp., illus. Paper covers. $6.95.
The most comprehensive load information ever published for the modern black powder shooter.
Lyman Cast Bullet Handbook. Lyman Gunsight Corp., Middlefield, CT, 1973. 260 pp., illus. Paper covers. $6.95
A long-awaited and fine reference for handloaders.
Lyman Handbook No. 45. Lyman Gunsight Corp., Middlefield, CT, 1967. $5.95.
Latest edition of a favorite reference for ammunition handloaders, whether novice or veteran.
Lyman Pistol & Revolver Handbook, edited by C. Kenneth Ramage, Lyman Publications, Middlefield, CT, 1978. 280 pp., illus. Paper covers. $6.95.
An extensive reference of load and trajectory data for the handgun.
Lyman Shotshell Handbook 2nd ed., edited by C. Kenneth Ramage, Lyman Gunsight Corp., Middlefield, CT, 1976. 288 pp., illus., paper covers. $6.95.
Devoted exclusively to shotshell reloading, this book considers: gauge, shell length, brand, case, loads, buckshot, etc. plus an excellent reference section. Some color illus.
Make Muzzle Loader Accessories, by R. H. McCrory, R. H. McCrory, Publ., 1971, 46 pp. Paper $2.50
A revised 2nd ed. covering over 20 items from powderhorns to useful tools. Well illus.
Metallic Reloading Basics, edited by C. Kenneth Ramage, Lyman Publications, Middlefield, CT, 1976. 60 pp., illus. Paper covers. $1.95.
Provides the beginner with loading data on popular bullet weights within the most popular calibers.
Modern Handloading, by Maj. Geo. C. Nonte. Winchester Press, NY, 1972. 416 pp., illus. $10.00.
Covers all aspects of metallic and shotshell ammunition loading, plus more loads than any book in print; state and Federal laws, reloading tools, glossary.
Nosler Reloading Manual Number One, compiled and edited by Bob Nosler, Nosler Bullets, Inc., Bend, OR, 1976. 234 pp., illus. $5.95.
Provides thorough coverage of powder data, specifically tailored to the well-known Nosler partition and solid base bullet designs in all weights and calibers.
Pet Loads, by Ken Waters, Wolfe Publ. Co., Inc., Prescott, AZ, 1979. Unpaginated. In looseleaf form. $29.50.
A collection of the last 13 years' articles on more than 70 metallic cartridges. Most calibers featured with updated material.
Pocket Manual for Shooters and Reloaders, by P. O. Ackley. publ. by author, Salt Lake City, UT, 1964. 176 pp., illus., spiral bound. $4.95.
Good coverage on standard and wildcat cartridges and related firearms in popular calibers.
The PSI Calculator, a slide rule designed by Homer Powley to add maximum chamber pressure to the velocity and powder charge computed. $5.00.
Reloader's Guide, by R. A. Steindler, Stoeger Publ. Co., Hackensack, NJ, 1975. 223 pp., illus. Paper covers. $6.95
Complete, fully illustrated step-by-step guide to handloading ammunition.

Sierra Bullets Reloading Manual, Second Edition, by Robert Hayden et al, The Leisure Group, Inc., Santa Fe Springs, CA, 1978. 700 pp., illus. Looseleaf binder. $11.95.
Includes all material in the original manual and its supplement updated, plus a new section on loads for competitive shooting.
Small Arms Ammunition Identification Guide. Anubus Press, Houston, TX, 1971. 151 pp., illus. Paper, $6.00.
A reprint of the guide originally published as FSTC-CW-07-02-66, revised.
Small-Caliber Ammunition Identification Guide Volume I: Small Arms Cartridges up to 15mm, by R. T. Huntington, Military Arms Research Service, San Jose, CA, 1978. 204 pp., illus. Paper covers. $9.95.
Covers center-fire military cartridges from 25 ACP to 15mm Besa. Historical employment, weapons used, and a comprehensive section on headstamps.
Small-Caliber Ammunition Identification Guide Volume II: Small Arms Cartridges 20mm to 40mm, by R. T. Huntington, Military Arms Research Service, San Jose, CA, 1978. 165 pp., illus. Paper covers. $9.95.
Identifies the large infantry and aircraft cartridges giving full coverage to Soviet and East Bloc ammunition.
Speer Reloading Manual Number 10, Omark Industries, Inc., Lewiston, ID, 1979. 560 pp., illus. Paper covers. $8.50.
Expanded version with facts, charts, photos, tables, loads and tips.
The .30-'06, by W. L. Godfrey, Elk Mountain Shooters Supply, Inc., Pasco, WA, 1975. 425 pp., illus. Spiral bound. $10.00
A valuable source book for the advanced handloader.
.243 & 6mm, by W. L. Godfrey, Elk Mountain Shooters Supply, Pasco, WA, 1978. 315 pp. Charts and graphs. Spiral bound. $10.
Fills the gap between the technical and popular literature, usable by the beginner.
Why Not Load Your Own? by Col. T. Whelen. A. S. Barnes, New York, 1957, 4th ed., rev. 237 pp., illus, $7.95.
A basic reference on handloading, describing each step, materials and equipment. Loads for popular cartridges are given.
Yours Truly, Harvey Donaldson, by Harvey Donaldson, Wolfe Publ. Co., Inc., Prescott, AZ, 1980. 288 pp., illus. $19.50.
Reprint of the famous columns by Harvey Donaldson which appeared in "Handloader" from May 1966 through December 1972.

COLLECTORS

Accoutrement Plates, North and South, 1861-1865, by Wm. G. Gavin. Geo. Shumway, York, PA, 1975. 236 pp., 220 illus. Paper $14.00, Cloth $20.00.
The 1st detailed study of Civil War belt buckles and cartridge box insignia. Dimensions, materials, details of manufacture, relative and dollar values given.
Adams Revolvers 1851-1891, by W.H.J. Chamberlain and A.W.F. Taylerson, Herbert Jenkins, London, England, 1977. 256 pp., illus. $31.50.
Full story of the design, evolution and manufacture of the weapons produced by the chief rival of Sam Colt.
The Age of Firearms, by Robert Held. Digest Books, Inc., Northfield, IL, 1970. New, fully rev. and corrected ed., paper covers. 192 pp., fully illus. $4.95.
A popular review of firearms since 1475 with accent on their effects on social conditions, and the craft of making functional/artistic arms.
Air Guns, by Eldon G. Wolff. Milwaukee Public Museum, Milwaukee, WI, 1958. 198 pp., illus. Paper, $6.00.
A scholarly and comprehensive treatise, excellent for student and collectors' use, of air gun history. Every form of arm is described, and a list of 350 makers is included.
American Boys' Rifles 1890-1945, by Jim Perkins, RTP Publishers, Pittsburg, PA, 1976. 245 pp., illus. $17.50.
The history and products of the arms companies who made rifles for the American boy, 1890-1945.
American, British & Continental Pepperbox Firearms, by Jack Dunlap. H. J. Dunlap, Los Altos, CA, 1964. 279 pp., 665 illus. $17.95.
Comprehensive history of production pepperpots from early 18th cent. through the cartridge pepperbox. Variations are covered, with much data of value to the collector.
The American Cartridge, by Charles R. Suydam, Borden Publ. Co., Alhambra, CA, rev. ed., 1973. 184 pp., illus. $8.50.
An illus. study of the rimfire cartridge in the U.S.
American Engraved Powder Horns, by Stephen V. Grancsay. Originally published by The Metropolitan Museum of Art, at NYC, 1945. The 1st reprint publ. by Ray Riling Arms Books Co., Phila., PA, 1976. 96 pp. plus 47 full-page plates. $22.50.
A study based on the J. H. Grenville Gilbert collection of historic, rare and beautiful powder horns. A scholarly work by an eminent authority. Long out of print and offered now in a limited edition of 1000 copies.
American Engraved Powder Horns: The Golden Age 1755-1783, by John S. duMont, Phoenix Publications, Canaan, NH, 1978. 120 pp., illus. Limited, signed and numbered edition. $29.50.
Illustrates and describes many rare and hitherto unknown examples owned by famous collectors and museums.
American Handgun Patents 1802-1924, by Jos. Macewicz, Museum Restoration Service, Ontario, Canada, 1978. 44 pp., illus. Paper covers. $4.95.
A must for the serious handgun collector.
The American Percussion Revolver, by F. M. Sellers and Sam E. Smith. Museum Restoration Service, Ottawa, Canada, 1970. 200 pp., illus. $15.00.
All inclusive from 1826 to 1870. Over 200 illus., with profuse coverage on lesser-known arms.
American Pistol and Revolver Patents 1800 to 1925, compiled by Jos. J. Macewicz, Museum Restoration Service, Ottawa, Canada, 1977. 52 pp., illus. Paper covers. $4.95.
A chronological listing of patents issued in the U.S.A. from 1800 to 1925. Cross indexed by inventor.
American Sporting Arms of the 18th & 19th Century, compiled by Herbert G. Houze, Chicago Historical Society, Chicago, IL, 1975. 32 pp., illus. Paper covers. $3.75
A catalog of the Chicago Historical Society collection of antique sporting and martial firearms.
Antique European and American Firearms in the Hermitage Museum, by L. Tarassuk. Arco Pub. Co., NY, 1972. 224 pp., 130 pp. of illus., 54 pp. in full color. $20.00.
Selected from the museum's 2500 firearms dating from the 15th to 19th centuries, including the magnificently decorated Colt rifle and pistols presented by Samuel Colt to Tzars Nicholas 1st and Alexander II.
Antique Firearms, by Frederick Wilkinson, Presidio Press, San Rafael, CA, 1977. 276 pp., illus. $14.95.
Traces the history of firearms from their introduction to 14th century Europe through to the appearance of the modern repeating rifle.
Antique Guns in Color 1250-1865, by Robert Wilkinson-Latham, Blanford Press, London, England, 1978. 211 pp., illus. $11.95.
Layman and collector will find this a fascinating survey of firearms. Illustrated in color.
Antique Guns from the Stagecoach Collection, by Hank Bowman, Arco Publ. Co., New York, NY, 1969. 112 pp., illus. $3.50.
Covers many collector rarities, fine cased weapons and one-of-a-kind specimens.
Antique Pistol Collecting 1400-1860, by Jame Frith and Ronald Andrews, The Holland Press, London, England, 1978. 122 pp., illus. $45.
A brief resume of the evolution of pistols (mainly English) to the close of the percussion revolver era.
Arms and Armor Annual, Volume I, edited by Robert Held, Digest Books, Inc., Northfield, IL, 1973. 320 pp., illus., paper covers. $9.95.
Thirty outstanding articles by the leading arms and armor historians of the world.
Arms and Equipment of the Civil War, by Jack Coggins, Doubleday & Co., Inc, NY, 1962. 160 pp., $12.00.
Tools of war of the blue and the grey. Infantry, cavalry, artillery, and navy: guide to equipment, clothing, organization, and weapons. Over 500 illus.
Arms Makers of Maryland, by Daniel D. Hartzler, George Shumway, York, PA, 1975. 200 pp., illus. $35.00.
A thorough study of the gunsmiths of Maryland who worked during the late 18th and early 19th centuries.
Arms Through the Ages, by William Reid, Harper & Row, NY, 1976. 288 pp., illus. $35.
A handsome volume enchanced in impressive style with nearly 800 specially drawn color and black-and-white drawings.
Arms of the World—1911, ed. by Joseph J. Schroeder, Jr., Digest Books, Inc., Northfield, IL, 1972, 420 pp., profusely illus. $5.95.
Reprint of the Adolph Frank ALFA 21 catalog of 1911 in 4 languages—English, German, French, Spanish.
Armsmear, ed. by Henry Barnard, Beinfeld Publ., Inc., North Hollywood, CA, 1976. 399 pp., illus. $24.95.
A reprint of the memorial to Samuel Colt and his work, including 100 pp. on Colt revolvers and the armory. Limited, numbered edition.
Artillery Through the Ages, by A. Manucy, Normount Armament Co., Wickenburg, AZ, 1971. 92 pp., illus. Paper, $2.50
A short history of cannon, emphasizing types used in America.
Australian Service Longarms, by Ian D. Skennerton, I. D. Skennerton, Margate, Australia, 1975. 213 pp., illus. $23.50.
A study of the firearms used in Australian service, from the first landing there (1788) to the present day.
Ballard Rifles in the H. J. Nunnemacher Coll., by Eldon G. Wolff. Milwaukee Public Museum, Milwaukee, Wisc., 2nd ed. 1961. Paper, 77 p. plus 4 pp. of charts and 27 plates. $3.50.
A thoroughly authoritative work on all phases of the famous rifles, their parts, patent and manufacturing history.
Basic Documents on U.S. Marital Arms, commentary by Col. B. R. Lewis, reissue by Ray Riling, Phila., Pa., 1956 and 1960.
Rifle Musket Model 1855. The first issue rifle of musket caliber, a muzzle loader equipped with the Maynard Primer, 32 pp. $2.50.
Rifle Musket Model 1863. The Typical Union muzzle-loader of the Civil War, 26 pp. $1.75.
Breech-Loading Rifle Musket Model 1866. The first of our 50 caliber breechloading rifles, 12 pp. $1.75.
Remington Navy Rifle Model 1870. A commercial type breech-loader made at Springfield, 16 pp. $1.75.
Lee Straight Pull Navy Rifle Model 1895. A magazine cartridge arm of 6mm caliber. 23 pp. $3.00.
Breech-Loading Rifle Musket Model 1868. The first 50-70 designed as such. 20 pp. $1.75.
Peabody Breech-Loading Arms (five models)—27 pp. $2.75.
Ward-Burton Rifle Musket 1871—16 pp. $2.50.
Springfield Rifle, Carbine & Army Revolvers (cal. 45) model 1873 including Colt and Smith & Wesson hand arms. 52 pp. $3.00.
U.S. Magazine Rifle and Carbine (cal. 30) Model 1892 (the Krag Rifle) 36 pp. $3.00.
Basic Manual of Military Small Arms, by W. H. B. Smith, Stackpole Books, Harrisburg, PA, 1979. 213 pp., illus. $20.00.
Facsimile edition of the original 1943 edition. A detailed description of the maintenance and use of hundreds of WW II weapons, some still in use today.
The Bedford County Rifle and its Makers, by Calvin Hetrick, George Shumway, York, PA, 1973. 39 pp., illus., paper covers. $5.00.
Reprint of Hetrick's study of the graceful and distinctive muzzle-loading rifles made in Bedford County, PA.
The Boxer Cartridge in the British Service, by B. A. Temple, B. A. Temple, Burbank, Australia, 1977. 250 pp., illus. $30.
This work relates the history of the Boxer Cartridge as used by Britain and her colonies from 1866 to the 1930s.
The Breech-Loader in the Service, 1816-1917, by Claud E. Fuller, N. Flayderman, New Milford, Conn., 1965. 381 pp., illus. $14.50.
Revised ed. of a 1933 historical reference on U.S. standard and experimental military shoulder arms. Much patent data, drawings, and photographs of the arms.
A voluminous work that covers handloading—and other things—in great detail. Replete with data for all cartridge forms.
A Brief History of Bullet Moulds, by Codman Parkerson, Pioneer Press, Union City, TN, 1975. 31 pp., illus. Paper covers. $1.75. Thoroughly examines the evolution of bullet moulds from their earliest forms to today's advanced types.
British and American Flintlocks, by Fred. Wilkinson. Country Life Books, London, 1971. 64 pp., illus. $2.95.
Historical and technical aspects of flintlock firearms, in military and civilian use.
The British Duelling Pistol, by John A. Atkinson, Museum Restoration Service, Bloomfield, Canada, 1978. 108 pp., illus. $15.
Enables firearms enthusiasts to trace the origin and development of the English duelling pistol.
British Military Longarms 1815-1865, by D. W. Bailey. Stackpole Books, Harrisburg, PA, 1972. 79 pp., illus. $5.95.
Concise account, covering muskets, carbines, rifles and their markings.
F. N. Browning Light Semi-Automatic Rifle, Caliber .308, Browning Arms Co., 1979. 130 pp., illus. Paper covers. $7.50.
Manual for the Browning Arms semi-auto rifle for military target shooting and sporting purposes.

California Gunsmiths 1846-1900, by Lawrence P. Sheldon, Far Far West Publ., Fair Oaks, CA, 1977. 289 pp., illus. $29.65.

A study of early California gunsmiths and the firearms they made.

Cartology Savalog, by Gerald Bernstein, Gerald Bernstein, St. Louis, MO, 1976. 177 pp., illus. Paper covers. $8.95.

An infinite variations catalog of small arms ammunition stamps.

Cartridge Headstamp Guide, by H. P. White and B. D. Munhall. H. P. White Laboratory, Bel Air, MD, 1978. 263 pp., illus. $25.75.

An important reference on headstamping of small arms ammo, by manufacturers in many countries. Clear illus. of 1936 headstamps of every type.

Cartridges for Collectors, by Fred A. Datig. Borden Publishing Co., Alhambra, Calif, Vol. I (Centerfire), 1958; Vol. II (Rimfire and Misc.) Types, 1963; Vol. III (Additional Rimfire, Centerfire, and Plastic,) 1967. Each of the three volumes 176 pp., well illus. and each priced at $7.50.

Vol. III supplements the first two books and presents 300 additional specimens. All illus. are shown in full-scale line drawings.

Cast Iron Toy Pistols 1870-1940, by Charles W. Best, Rocky Mountain Arms & Antiques, Englewood, CO, 1973. 217 pp., illus. $15.00.

Provides photographs and descriptions of most of the iron toy pistols made, plus values and rarity guides.

A Century of Guns and Shooting, by H. J. Blanch, EP Publ., Ltd., London, England, 1976. 153. pp., illus. $12.00.

A reprint of the scarce 1909 London edition. A sketch of the leading types of sporting and military small arms, with over 150 illustrations of guns and rifles.

Civil War Carbines, by A. F. Lustyik. World Wide Gun Report, Inc., Aledo, ILL, 1962. 63 pp., illus. paper covers, $2.00.

Accurate, interesting summary of most carbines of the Civil War period, in booklet form, with numerous good illus.

Civil War Collector's Encyclopedia, Volume II, by Francis R. Lord, Lord American Research, Inc. West Columbia, SC, 1976. 224 pp., illus. $19.50.

A companion to Volume I. Over 300 illustrations. Covers insignia, guns, bayonets, swords, etc.

Civil War Guns, by William B. Edwards, Castle Books, NY, 1976. 438 pp., illus. $10.00

Describes and records the exciting and sometimes romantic history of forging weapons for war and heroism of the men who used them.

Civil War Weapons, by C. B. Colby, Coward, McCann & Geoghegan, NY, 1962. 48 pp., illus. $4.95.

Small arms and artillery of the Blue and Gray.

J. P. Clabrough & Bros.—Gunmakers, by Lawrence P. Shelton, Far Far West Publishers, Fair Oaks, CA, 1978. 119 pp., illus. Paper covers. $11.50.

History of the company plus a facsimile reprint of the 1892-93 Clabrough, Golcher & Co. catalog, and excerpts from four other catalogs of concerns who carried Clabrough guns.

The Collecting of Guns, ed. by Jas. E. Serven. Stackpole Books, Harrisburg, PA, 1964. 272 pp., illus. $5.95.

A new and massive compendium of gun lore for serious collectors by recognized experts. Separate chapters cover major categories and aspects of collecting. Over 600 firearms illus. Handsomely designed, deluxe binding in slip case.

A Collection of Pistol Points, by Gerry Ford, Ford Graphics, London, England, ca. 1977. 56 pp., illus. Paper covers. $2.95.

A handy reference of twenty-three articles from the pages of the British publication "Guns Review" on antique arms.

The Collector's Handbook of U.S. Cartridge Revolvers, 1856 to 1899, by W. Barlow Fors, Adams Press, Chicago, IL, 1973. 96 pp., illus. $6.00.

Concise coverage of brand names, patent listings, makers' history, and essentials of collecting.

The Collector's Illustrated Guide to Firearms, by Martin Miller, Barrie & Jenkins, London England, 1978. 304 pp., illus. $24.95.

Covers early weapons, matchlocks, snaphaunces, wheellocks, flintlocks, percussion, air weapons and accessories. Profusely illustrated.

Colonel Colt, London, by Joseph G. Rosa, Fortress Publ., Inc., Stoney Creek, Ontario, Can., 1976. 208 pp., illus. $26.50.

The history of Colt's London firearms 1851-1857. Details the arms produced in the London armoury.

Colt 1896 English Price List, a reprint by Americana Archives, Topsfield, MA, 1976. 16 pp., illus. Paper covers. $3.00.

Illustrates and prices (in English currency) the full Colt line of the period.

Colt Firearms Catalog, 1934, a reprint by Americana Archives, Topsfield, MA, 1976. 40 pp., illus. Paper covers. $4.00.

28 Colt revolvers and automatic pistols are described and illustrated.

Colt Firearms from 1836, by James E. Serven, new 8th edition, Stackpole Books, Harrisburg, PA, 1979. 398 pp., illus. $22.95.

Excellent survey of the Colt company and its products. Updated with new SAA production chart and commemorative list.

The Colt Heritage, by R. L. Wilson, Simon & Schuster, 1979. 358 pp., illus. $39.95.

The official history of Colt firearms 1836 to the present.

Colt Peacemaker Dictionary & Encyclopedia Illustrated, by Keith A. Cochran, Colt Collectors Press, Rapid City, SD, 1976. 300 pp., illus. Paper covers, $12.95. Cloth, $15.95.

Over 1300 entries pertaining to everything there is to know about the Colt Peacemaker.

Colt Pistols, by R. L. Wilson and R. E. Hable, Taylor Publ. Co, Dallas, TX, 1977. 400 pp., illus. $100.00.

A non-technical book presenting a superb collection of Colt handguns in color.

Colt Tips, by E. Dixon Larson. Pioneer Press, Union City, TN, 1972. 140 pp., illus. Paper covers. $3.95.

Comprehensive, discriminating facts about Colt models from 1836 to 1898.

Colt's SAA Post War Models, by George Garton, Beinfield Publishing, Inc., No. Hollywood, CA, 1978. 176 pp. illus. $17.95.

Complete story on these arms including charts, tables and production information.

Colt's Variations of the Old Model Pocket Pistol, 1848 to 1872, by P. L. Shumaker. Borden Publishing Co., Alhambra, CA 1966, a reprint of the 1957 edition. 150 pp., illus. $6.00.

A useful tool for the Colt specialist and a welcome return of a popular source of information that had been long out-of-print.

Confederate Longarms and Pistols, "A Pictorial Study", by Richard Taylor Hill and Edward W. Anthony, Taylor Publishing Co., Dallas, TX, 1978. $29.95.

A reference work identifying over 175 Confederate arms through detailed photography, and a listing of information.

Custer Battle Guns, by John S. du Mont, The Gunroom Press, Highland Park, NJ, 1977. 113 pp., illus. $10.00.

Complete story of the guns at the Little Big Horn.

Deanes' Manual of the History and Science of Fire-arms, by J. Deane. Standard Publications, Huntington, WV, 1946 facsimile reprint of the rare English original of 1858. 291 pp., three folding plates. $6.00.

A history of firearms, plus design and manufacture of military and sporting arms.

Description of the Bergman Pistol (selfloader) with Explanation of the New Breech-Closure System for Firearms, A facsimile reprint by Handgun Press, Chicago, IL, 1979. 13 pp. plus folding chart. Paper covers. $4.00.

A facsimile reprint of the 1896 Bergman pistol manual.

A Digest of Cartridges for Small Arms Patented in the United States, England and France, by W. A. Bartlett and D. B. Gallatin, Museum Restoration Service, Ottawa, Canada, 1977. 52 pp., illus. Paper covers. $4.95.

Reprint of the very scarce 1878 edition. A classic publication for the cartridge collector.

Digest of Patents Relating to Breech-Loading and Magazine Small Arms (1836-1873), by V. D. Stockbridge, WA, 1874. Reprinted 1963 by E. N. Flayderman, Greenwich, Conn. $12.50.

An exhaustive compendium of patent documents on firearms, indexed and classified by breech mechanism types, valuable reference for students and collectors.

Dutch Firearms, by Arne Hoff, ed. by Walter A. Stryker, Philip Wilson Publishers Ltd., Sotheby Parke Bernet Publications, London, England, 1978. 264 pp., illus. $85.00.

An important and essential work of reference for all museums and private collectors.

Dutch Muskets & Pistols, by J. B. Kist, J. P. Puype, and W. Van Der Mark, George Shumway, York, PA, 1974. 176 pp., illus. $25.00.

An illus. history of 17th Century gunmaking in the Low Countries.

The Samuel E. Dyke Collection of Kentucky Pistols, by Frank Klay, The Gun Room Press, Highland Park, NJ, 1974. 30 pp., illus. Paper covers. $1.75.

Reprint of a study of Kentucky pistols in the collection of the dean of Kentucky pistol collectors.

Early Indian Trade Guns—1625 to 1775, by T. M. Hamilton. Museum of the Great Plains, Lawton, Okla. 1969. 34 pp., well illus., paper covers. $3.50.

Detailed descriptions of subject arms, compiled from early records and from the study of remnants found in Indian country.

Early Loading Tools and Bullet Molds, by R. H. Chamberlain. The Farm Tribune, Porterville, GA, 1971. 75 pp., illus. Paper covers, $5.00.

An excellent aid to collectors.

1888 Colt Catalog, a facsimile reprint by Bob Deter, Anderson, SC, 1978. 35 pp., illus. Paper covers. $4.50.

Reprint of Colt's catalog of military and sporting firearms fully illustrating the pistols, rifles and shotguns of the era.

English Gunmakers, by DeWitt Bailey and Douglas A. Nie, Arms & Armour Press, London, England, 1978. 128 pp., illus. $15.

The Birmingham and Provincial gun trade in the 18th and 19th century.

English Pistols & Revolvers, by J. N. George. Arco Publ. Co., Inc., N.Y.C., 1962, 256 pp., 28 plates, $19.50.

The 2nd reprinting of a notable work first publ. in 1938. Treats of the historical development and design of English hand firearms from the 17th cent. to the present. A much better book than the former reprint, particularly as to clarity of the tipped-in plates.

Engraved Powder Horns of the French and Indian War and Revolutionary War Era, by Nathan L. Swayze, Gun Hill Publishing Co., Yazoo City, MS, 1978. 235 pp., illus. $25.

Describes and pictures a large and varied selection of engraved powder horns. Includes color section, drawings of engraved horns, etc.

Ethan Allen, Gunmaker, by Harold R. Mouillesseaux, Museum Rest. Serv., Ottawa, Ont., Can., 1973. 170 pp., illus. $19.95.

A complete history of Ethan Allen, his arms and his companies.

Famous Guns from the Smithsonian Collection, by H. W. Bowman. Arco Publ. Co., Inc., NY, 1967. 112 pp., illus. $3.50.

The finest of the "Famous Guns" series.

Famous Guns from the Winchester Collection, by H. W. Bowman. Arco Publ. Co., NYC, 1958 and later. 144 pp., illus. $3.50.

The gems of the hand and shoulder arms in the great collection at New Haven, CT.

Famous Pistols and Hand Guns, edited by A. J. R. Cormack, Profile Publications, Berkshire, England, 1977. 160 pp., illus. $5.98.

World famous pistols and hand guns are described in detail with hundreds of illustrations.

Fifteen Years in the Hawken Lode, by John D. Baird, The Gun Room Press, Highland Park, NJ, 1976. 120 pp., illus. $12.95.

A collection of thoughts and observations gained from many years of intensive study of the guns from the shop of the Hawken brothers.

'51 Colt Navies, by N. L. Swayze. Gun Hill Publ. Co., Yazoo City, MS, 1967. 243 pp., well illus. $15.00.

The first major effort devoting its entire space to the 1851 Colt Navy revolver. There are 198 photos of models, sub-models, variations, parts, markings, documentary material, etc. Fully indexed.

Fine Arms from Tula, compiled by Valentin Mavrodin, Harry N. Abrams, Inc. N.Y., NY, 1977. 14 pp. of text plus 137 full color plates. $25.

The fine arms wrought by the artisans of Tula in the 18th and 19th century, now in the Hermitage Museum.

Firearms of the Confederacy, by Claud R. Fuller & Richard D. Steuart, Quarterman Publ., Inc., Lawrence, MA, 1977. 333 pp., illus. $25.00.

The shoulder arms, pistols and revolvers of the Confederate soldier, including the regular United States Models, the imported arms and those manufactured within the Confederacy.

Firearms on the Frontier: Guns at Fort Michilimackinac 1715-1781, by T. M. Hamilton, Report No. 5 in the Reports in Mackinac History and Archaeology Series, Mackinac Island State Park Commission, Lansing, MI, 1976. 39 pp., illus. Paper covers. $3.00.

Report on the gun parts and related material recovered in the excavation of Fort Michilimackinac.

Flayderman's Guide to Antique American Firearms . . . and Their Values, 2nd Edition, by Norm Flayderman, DBI Books, Inc., Northfield, IL, 1980. 608 pp., illus. Paper covers. $15.95.

All values in this new second edition have been completely brought up-to-date and a number of guns not covered in the first edition have been included.

Flintlock Guns and Rifles, by F. Wilkinson, Stackpole Books, Harrisburg, PA, 1971. 80 pp., $4.95.

Illus. reference guide for 1650-1850 period showing makers, mechanisms and users.

The Flintlock, Its Origin and Development, by Torsten Lenk; J. T. Hayward, Editor, Holland Press, London, 1964. 192 pp., 134 illus. $30.00.

First English-text version of the 1939 Swedish work termed "the most important book on the subject." Original illus. are reproduced, and a new index and bibliography complete this valuable book.

Flintlock Pistols, by F. Wilkinson, Fortress Publ., Inc., Stoney Creek, Ontario, Can., 1977. 76 pp., illus. Paper covers. $3.95.

An illustrated reference guide to flintlock pistols from the 17th to the 19th centuries.

Forsyth & Co.—Patent Gunmakers, by W. Keith Neal and D. H. L. Back. G. Bell & Sons, London, 1st ed., 1969, 280 pp., well illus. $20.

An excellent study of the invention and development of the percussion system by the Rev. Alexander Forsyth in the early 19th century. All Forsyth types are covered, plus a diary of events from 1768 to 1852.

.45-70 Rifles, by J. Behn, Rutgers Book Center, Highland Park, NJ, 1972. New ed., 150 pp., illus. $5.95.

Covers the official U.S. Army small arms cartridge and the weapons for its use.

The 45/70 Trapdoor Springfield Dixie Collection, compiled by Walter Crutcher and Paul Oglesby, Pioneer Press, Union City, TN, 1975. 600 pp., illus. Paper covers. $9.95.

An illustrated listing of the 45-70 Springfields in the Dixie Gun Works Collection. Little known details and technical information is given, plus current values.

Four Centuries of Liège Gunmaking, by Claude Gaier, English translation by F. J. Norris, Sotheby/Parke Bernet, London, England, 1976. 287 pp., illus. $90.00.

An essential reference work for all serious students of firearms, for specialist collectors and for everyone interested in gunmaking, engraving and the evolution of guns.

French Pistols and Sporting Guns, by A. N. Kennard. Transatlantic Arts, Inc., Levittown, NY, 1972. 63 pp., illus. $3.95.

Traces the technical evolution of French pistols and sporting guns from matchlock to breechloader.

French Military Weapons, 1717-1938, by James E. Hicks. N. Flayderman & Co., New Milford, CT, 1964. 281 pp., profusely illus. $9.50.

A valuable reference work, first publ. 1938 as *Notes on French Ordnance*, this rev. ed. covers hand, shoulder, and edged weapons, ammunition and artillery, with history of various systems.

Georgian Pistols: The Art and Craft of the Flintlock Pistol, 1715-1840, by Norman Dixon, George Shumway Publisher, York, PA, 1971. 184 pp. illus. $20.00.

The art of the Georgian gunmaker, describing the evolution of the holster and duelling pistols, with certain changes in style of the turn-off pistol.

German Mauser Rifle—Model of 1898, by J. E. Coombes and J. L. Aney. A reprint in paper covers by Francis Bannerman Sons, New York, NY, of their 1921 publication. 20 pp., well illus. $2.50.

Data on the subject weapon and its W. W. I development. Bayonets and ammunition are also described and illus.

German Pistols and Holsters 1934-1945, by Maj. Robert D. Wittington III, The Gun Room Press, Highland Park, NJ, 1976. 224 pp., illus. $15.

A manual for collectors on subject items issued to military, police and NSDAP. Covers all models of various designs, including those of foreign manufacture.

The German Rifle, by John Walter, Fortress Publ. Inc., Ontario, Canada, 1979. 160 pp., illus. $14.95.

A comprehensive illustrated history of the standard designs, 1877-1945.

German Small Arms, by A. J. R. Cormack, Exeter Books, New York, NY, 1979. 160 pp., illus. $6.98.

A history of the pre-war build up of German weapon production. All basic infantry weapons are covered in detail.

A Glossary of the Construction, Decoration and Use of Arms and Armor in all Countries and in all Times, by Geo. C. Stone, Jack Brussel, NY, 2nd reprint, 1966, 694 pp., illus. $10.98.

The outstanding work on its subject, authoritative and accurate in detail. The major portion is on oriental arms.

Great British Gunmakers 1740-1790, by W. Keith Neal & D. H. L. Back, Sotheby Parke Bernet Publications, Los Angeles, CA, 1975. 196 pp., illus. $80.00.

The history of John Twigg and the Packington Guns.

The Great Guns, by H. L. Peterson and Robt. Elman. Grosset & Dunlap, NY, 1972. $8.98.

Basic and general history with 70 full color illustrations and 140 photos of some of the finest guns from American collections. A well written text.

Great Sporting Posters of the Golden Age, by Sid Latham, Stackpole Books, Harrisburg, PA, 1978. 48 pp., illus. $9.95.

Over 20 nostalgic full-color reproductions of early 20th century calendars, posters, and other advertisements from sporting goods and firearms manufacturers.

The Gun, by Christopher Roads, Methuen Publishers, Ontario, Canada, 1978. 144 pp., illus. $12.50.

Covers the development of the gun from the invention of gunpowder to the highly sophisticated weapons being developed today.

Gun Collector's Digest, Volume II, edited by Joseph J. Schroeder, Jr. DBI Books, Inc., Northfield, IL, 1976, 288 pp., illus. Paper covers $7.95.

Comprehensive coverage on guns, gun shows, bayonets, commemoratives, security, gun laws, current Treasury regulations. Includes updated collectors bibliography and gun show directory.

The Gun Collector's Fact Book, by Louis W. Steinwedel, Arco Publ. Co., NY, 1975. 256 pp., illus. Paper covers. $5.95; Cloth, $10.00.

An illus. introduction to "the gentle art of gun collecting"—where and how to buy antique guns, points that affect their value, and hints on restoration.

The Gun Collector's Handbook of Values 1980-1981, by C. E. Chapel, Coward, McCann & Geoghegan, Inc., New York, NY, 1980. 462 pp., illus. $16.95.

Thirteenth rev. ed. of the best-known price reference for collectors.

Gun Digest Book of Modern Gun Values, 2nd. Ed., by Jack Lewis, DBI Books, Inc., Northfield, IL, 1978. 288 pp., illus. $7.95.

Revised and updated prices give latest values. Invaluable guide for buying, selling, trading or identifying guns—handguns, rifles and shotguns are covered in separate sections. Feature articles relate to collecting and values.

Gunfighter Colts & Rigs, by Fred Warner, Colt Collector Press, Rapid City SD 1977. 100 pp., illus. Paper covers. $5.

The fast-draw rigs of the famous Western gunfighters.

Gunmakers of Indiana, by A. W. Lindert. Publ. by the author, Homewood, IL, 1968, 3rd ed. 284 pp., illus. Large format. $15.00.

An extensive and historical treatment, illus. with old photographs and drawings.

Gunmarks, by David Byron, Crown Publishers, Inc., New York, NY, 1979. 185 pp., illus. $10.00.

Tradenames, codemarks, and proofs from 1870 to the present.

Gun Traders Guide, 8th Edition, by Paul Wahl, Stoeger Publ. Co., S. Hackensack, NJ, 1978. 256 pp., illus. Paper covers. $7.95.

A fully illustrated and authoritative guide to identification of modern firearms with current market values.

Guns & Other Arms, edited by William Guthman, Mayflower-Main Street Press, New York, NY, 1980. 350 pp. illus. $7.95.

An anthology of articles from "Antiques Magazine" that comprise a 400-year history of arms in America.

Guns of the World, edited by Hans Tanner, Bonanza Books, NY, 1977. 400 pp., illus. $5.98.

The complete collector's and trader's guide.

The Gunsmiths of Canada, by S. James Gooding, Museum Rest. Serv., Ottawa, Ont., Can., 1974. 32 pp., illus. Paper covers. $2.00.

Names, dates and locations for over 800 gunsmiths, plus bibliography.

Gunsmiths of Ohio—18th & 19th Centuries: Vol. I, Biographical Data, by Donald A. Hutslar, George Shumway, York, PA, 1973. 444 pp., illus. $35.00.

An important source book, full of information about the old-time gunsmiths of Ohio.

Hall's Breechloaders, by R. T. Huntington, Geo. Shumway, Publ. 1972. 369 pp., illus. Paper, $18.00.

Definitive treatise on John H. Hall and his inspectors. Shows all known models of the Hall rifle, appurtenances and pistol.

Handbook of Identification Marks on Canadian Arms, by R. Barrie Manarey, Century Press, Alberta, Can., 1973. 82 pp., illus. Paper covers. $6.00.

Lists over 1000 translations of codes and initials which appear on Canadian arms.

The Hawken Rifle: Its Place in History, by Charles E. Hanson, Jr., The Fur Press, Chadron, NB, 1979. 104 pp., illus. Paper covers. $6.00.

A fascinating and factual story of weapons on the American frontier, 1810 to 1850.

Hawken Rifles, The Mountain Man's Choice, by John D. Baird, The Gun Room Press, Highland Park, NJ, 1976. 95 pp., illus. $12.95.

Covers the rifles developed for the Western fur trade. Numerous specimens are described and shown in photographs.

Historical Hartford Hardware, by William W. Dalrymple, Colt Collector Press, Rapid City, SD, 1976. 42 pp., illus. Paper covers. $5.00.

Historically associated Colt revolvers.

A History of the Colt Revolver, by Charles T. Haven and Frank A. Belden, Outlet Books, New York, NY, 1978. 711 pp., illus. $10.95.

A giant of a book packed with information and pictures about the most cherished American revolver.

A History of Firearms, by H. L. Peterson. Chas. Scribner's Sons, N.Y.C., 1961. 57 pp., profusely illus. $5.95.

From the origin of firearms through each ignition form and improvement to the M-14. Drawings by Daniel D. Feaser.

History of Modern U.S. Military Small Arms Ammunition, Vol. 2, 1940-1945, By F. W. Hackley, W. M. Woodin and E. L. Scranton, The Gun Room Press, Highland Park, NJ, 1976. 300 pp., illus. $25.00.

A unique book covering the entire field of small arms ammunition developed during the critical World War II years.

History of Smith & Wesson, by Roy G. Jinks, Beinfeld Publ., Inc., No. Hollywood, CA, 1977. 290 pp., illus. $15.95.

A record of 125 years of progress and excellence in producing fine products.

The History of Weapons of the American Revolution, by George C. Neuman, Outlet Books, NY, 1976. 373 pp., illus. $6.98.

A new printing of this important and timely work. Traces the history of Revolutionary War weapons of all types.

The History of Winchester Firearms 1866-1975, 4th ed., ed. by George R. Watrous, James C. Rikhoff and Thomas H. Hall, Winchester Press, NY, 1975. 229 pp., illus. $15.00 in slipcase.

A comprehensive record of each model and the part it played in the establishment of Winchester's reputation for arms of the highest quality.

Holland & Holland Gun & Rifle Makers, a facsimile reprint of the 1924 catalog of Holland & Holland, Ltd., by Empire Press, Santa Fe, NM, 1978. 32 pp., illus. Paper. $7.50.

A fine reproduction of one of this firm's early catalogs.

Hopkins & Allen Gun Guide and Catalog (ca. 1913). Wagle Publ., Lake Wales, FA, 1972. 32 pp., illus. Paper covers. $5.00.

Facsimile of the original catalog. Shows the firms rifles, shotguns and pistols, and includes prices. Full color cover painting by Dan Smith.

Identifying Old U.S. Muskets, Rifles & Carbines, by Col. A. Gluckman. Stackpole Books, Harrisburg, PA, 1973. 487 pp., illus. $3.98.

Collector's guide to U.S. long arms, first publ. 1959. Numerous models of each type are described and shown, with histories of their makers.

Illustrated British Firearms Patents 1714-1853, comp. and ed. by Stephen V. Grancsay and Merrill Lindsay. Winchester Press. NY, 1969. Unpaginated. $20.00.

Facsimile of patent documents with a bibliography. Limited, numbered ed. of 1000, bound in ¾ leather and marbled boards.

Illustrated Encyclopedia of Modern Small Arms of the World, by Major F. Myatt, Outlet Publishers, New York, NY, 1978. 260 pp., illus. with over 200 full color photos. $12.98.

Comprehensive color directory of the most important small arms developed and used in the 20th century.

The Illustrated Encyclopedia of 19th Century Firearms, by Major F. Myatt, Cresent Books, New York, NY, 1979. 216 pp., illus. $12.98.

An illustrated history of the development of the world's military firearms during the 19th century.

An Illustrated History of Guns and Small Arms, by Joseph G. Rosa and Robin May, Castle Books, Secaucus, NJ, 1976. 96 pp., 135 color photographs. $7.98.

The story of the gun in all its forms from the invention of gunpowder to the rapid fire arms of today, and from tiny hand guns to machine guns.

The Kentucky Rifle, by Merrill Lindsay. Arma Press, NY/The Historical Society of York County, York, PA, 1972. 100 pp., 81 large colored illustrations. $15.

Presents in precise detail and exact color 77 of the finest Kentucky rifles ever assembled in one place. Also describes the conditions which led to the development of this uniquely American arm.

Kentucky Rifle Patchboxes & Barrel Marks, by Roy F. Chandler, Valley View Offset, Duncannon, PA, 1971. 400 pp., $20.00.

Reference work illustrating hundreds of patchboxes, together with the mark or signature of the maker.

Kentucky Rifles and Pistols 1756-1850, compiled by members of the Kentucky Rifle Association, Wash., DC, Golden Age Arms Co., Delaware, OH, 1976. 275 pp., illus. $22.50

Profusely illustrated with more than 300 examples of rifles and pistols never before published.

The Krag Rifle Story, by Franklin B. Mallory and Ludwig Olson, Springfield Research Service, Silver Spring, MD, 1979. 224 pp., illus. $20.00.

Covers both U.S. and European Krags. Gives a detailed description of U.S. Krag rifles and carbines and extensive data on sights, bayonets, serial numbers, etc.

Krag Rifles, by William S. Brophy, Beinfeld Pub. Inc., No. Hollywood, CA, 1980. 200 pp., illus. $24.95.

The first comprehensive work detailing the evolution and various models, both military and civilian.

Lancaster's, The Gun House, facsimile reprint of the 1924 catalog of Charles Lancaster & Co. Ltd., by Empire Press, Santa Fe, NM, 1978. 48 pp., illus. Paper covers. $12.50.

A fine reproduction of a famous English gun manufacturers catalog.

The Lee: British Service Rifle from 1880 to 1960, by Robert J. Dynes, Museum Restoration Service, Bloomfield, Ontario, Canada, 1978. 24 pp., illus. Paper covers. $2.50.

Description of the development and evolution of the arm which was used for more than 60 years over more than half of the world.

Lever Action Magazine Rifles Derived from the Patents of Andrew Burgess, by Samuel L. Maxwell Sr., Samuel L. Maxwell, Bellevue, WA, 1976. 368 pp., illus. $29.95.

The complete story of a group of lever action magazine rifles collectively referred to as the Burgess/Morse, the Kennedy or the Whitney.

The Lewis Gun, by J. David Truby, Paladin Press, Boulder, CO, 1976. 203 pp., illus. $25.

A pictorial history of this famous gun.

The Lifesaving Guns of David Lyle, by J. P. Barnett, South Bend Replicas, Inc., South Bend, IN, 1976. 105 pp., illus. Paper covers. $6.95.

For students of firearms and maritime history; a useful and important corpus of information not available anywhere else.

J. P. Lovell Arms Co. 1890 Catalog of Guns and Hunting Supplies, The American Historical Catalog Collection, The Pyne Press, Princeton, NJ, 1971. 88 pp., illus. Stiff paper covers. $3.50.

Facsimile of the original catalog. Illus. with pictures of shotguns, rifles, pistols, revolvers, sights, and other firearms accessories.

Luger: An Illustrated History of the Handguns of Hugo Borchardt and Georg Luger, 1875-1975, by John Walter, Fortress Publ., Inc., Stoney Creek, Ontario, Can., 1977. 256 pp., illus. $27.50.

A full and comprehensive coverage of the world's most famous pistol.

Luger Tips, by Michael Reese II, Pioneer Press, Union City, TN, 1976. 96 pp., illus. Paper covers. $7.50

A compilation of the author's articles on the Luger which appeared in *Guns and Ammo* magazine.

The Lyle Official Arms and Armour Review 1979, compiled by Margaret Anderson, Lyle Publications, Selkirkshire, Scotland, 1978. 382 pp., illus. $14.95.

Compiled prices on edged weapons, firearms and militaria from the auctions by Wallis & Wallis. Prices in English pounds and U.S. dollars.

Maine Made Guns and Their Makers, by Dwight B. Demeritt, Main State Museum, Hallowell, ME, 1973. 209 pp., illus. $22.00.

A fine reference work on Maine gunsmiths.

Manhattan Firearms, by Waldo E. Nutter, Stackpole Books, Harrisburg, PA, 1958. 250 pp., illus., in halftone. $10.00.

Complete history of the Manhattan Firearms Mfg. Co., and its products. Excellent specialized reference.

Manual of Pistol and Revolver Cartridges Volume I, Centerfire Metric Calibers, by Hans A. Erlmeier and Jakob H. Brandt, Journal-Verlag, Weisbaden, Germany, second edition, 1978. 271 pp., illus. $9.95.

A reference work in both German and English text which lists cartridges both by caliber and alphabetically. Contains accurate scale photographs for cartridge identification.

Manual of Rifling and Rifle Sights, by Lt.-Col. Viscount Bury, M.P., Ray Riling Arms Books Co., Phila., PA, 1971. 47 pp., Paper, $3.50.

Reprint of 1864 London edition done for the British National Rifle Ass'n. 141 illus., plus 3 folding plates.

Mauser Bolt Rifles, by Ludwig Olson, F. Brownell & Son, Inc., Montezuma, IA, 1976. 364 pp., illus. $24.95.

The most complete, detailed, authoritative and comprehensive work ever done on Mauser bolt rifles.

Military Arms of Canada, by Upper Canada Hist. Arms Soc. Museum Restoration Serv., West Hill, Ont., 1963. 43 pp., illus. $2.50.

Booklet cont. 6 authoritative articles on the principal models of Canadian mil. small arms. Gives characteristics of each, makers, quantities produced.

Military Breech-Loading Rifles, by V. D. Majendie and C. O. Browne, Fortress Publ., Inc., Stoney Creek, Ontario, Can., 1973. 129 pp. plus index, illus. $8.50.

A new ed. of the 1870 work dealing with the Snider, the Martini-Henry and Boxer ammunition.

Military Rifles of Japan, 1897-1945, by Fred L. Honeycutt, Jr. and F. Patt Anthony, published by the authors, Lake Park, FL, 1977. 212 pp., illus. $19.

A definitive work giving descriptions and serial number ranges of over 100 rifle variations.

Military Small Arms of the 20th Century, by Ian V. Hogg and John Weeks, Fortress Publ., Inc., Stoney Creek, Ontario, Can., 1977. 284 pp., illus. $24.95.

A new and enlarged edition covering small-caliber firearms from 1900 to 1977. Over 600 illustrations.

Miniature Arms, by Merrill Lindsay. Winchester Press, New York, NY, 1970. 111 pp., illus. $5.95.

A concise study of small-scale replicas of firearms and other weapons of collector interest. Fine color photographs.

Modern Guns, Identification and Values, 2nd Revised Edition, by Russell Quertermous and Steve Quertermous, Collectors Books, Paducah, KY, 1980. 415 pp., illus. Paper covers. $11.95.

A descriptive, handy, and illustrated reference of realistic gun values.

Modern Small Arms, by Major Frederick Myatt, Cresent Books, New York, NY, 1978. 240 pp., illus. $12.98.

An illustrated encyclopedia of famous military firearms from 1873 to the present day.

M1 Carbine, Design, Development and Production, by Larry Ruth, Desert Publications, Cornville, AZ. 300 pp., illus. Paper covers $14.95.

The complete history of one of the world's most famous and largest produced firearms.

More Single Shot Rifles, by James C. Grant, The Gun Room Press, Highland Park, NJ, 1976. 324 pp., illus. $12.50

Details the guns made by Frank Wesson, Milt Farrow, Holden, Borchardt, Stevens, Remington, Winchester, Ballard and Peabody-Martini.

The Muzzle-Loading Cap Lock Rifle, by Ned H. Roberts, George Shumway Publisher, York, PA and Track of the Wolf Co., Osseo, MN, 1978. 308 pp., illus. $24.50.

Reprint of the revised and enlarged privately printed edition of this general survey of its subject and of the makers of the rifles.

The NRA Collector's Series, Digest Books, Inc., Northfield, IL, 1971, 84 pp. paper covers $2.95.

Reprint of the three predecessors of *American Rifleman* magazine and the first edition of *American Rifleman.*

The NRA Gun Collectors Guide, by staff members of NRA. National Rifle Assn., Washington, D.C., 1972. 256 pp., well illus. $4.50.

A wealth of information on collecting and collectors arms, with 64 major and 41 short articles, selected from the last 18 years of "The American Rifleman."

The New England Gun, by Merrill Lindsay, David McKay Co., NY, 1976. 155 pp., illus. Paper covers, $12.50. Cloth, $20.00

A study of more than 250 New England guns, powder horns, swords, and polearms in an exhibition by the New Haven Colony Historical Society.

Simeon North: First Official Pistol Maker of the United States, by S. North and R. North, Rutgers Book Center, Highland Park, NJ, 1972. 207 pp., illus. $7.95.

Exact reprint of the original. Includes chapters on New England pioneer manufacturers and on various arms.

The Northwest Gun, by Charles E. Hanson, Jr., Nebraska State Historical Society, Lincoln, NB, 1976. 85 pp., illus., paper covers. $6.

Number 2 in the Society's "Publications in Anthropology." Historical survey of rifles which figured in the fur trade and settlement of the Northwest.

Notes on U.S. Ordnance, vol. II, 1776-1941, by James E. Hicks. Modern Books & Crafts, Greens Farms, Conn., 1971. 252 pp., illus. $8.00.

Updated version of a standard work on development of military weapons used by U.S. forces, from handguns to coast artillery and aerial bombs. This is not to be confused with Hicks 1940 United States Ordnance, referring mainly to Ordnance correspondence as Vol. II.

One Hundred Great Guns, by Merrill Lindsay, Walker & Co., NY, 1967. $35.00.

Here, in more than 200 superb full-color plates, is the flower of the gunmaker's art, perhaps the most famous and important of the world's firearms.

An Outline of the History and Development of Hand Firearms, from the Earliest Period to About the End of the Fifteenth Century, by R. C. Clephan [Original ed., 1906]. A reprint in 1946 by Standard Publications, Inc., Huntington, W.Va. 60 pp., illus. $4.00.

A worthy facsimile of a very scarce, concise and scholarly work.

Patterson Colt Pistol Variations, by R. L. Wilson and R. Phillips, Jackson Arms Co., Dallas, TX, 1979. 250 pp., illus. $35.00.

A tremendous book about the different models and barrel lengths in the Paterson Colt story.

Peacemaker Evolutions & Variations, by Keith A. Cochran, Colt Collectors Press, Rapid City, SD, 1975. 47 pp., illus. Paper covers. $5.00.

Corrects many inaccuracies found in other books on the Peacemaker and gives much new information regarding this famous arm.

Pennsylvania Longrifles of Note, by George Shumway, George Shumway, Publisher, York, PA, 1977. 63 pp., illus. Paper covers. $6.50.

Illustrates and describes samples of guns from a number of Pennsylvania rifle-making schools.

Percussion Guns & Rifles, by D. W. Bailey. Stackpole Books, Harrisburg, PA, 1972. 79 pp., illus. $5.95.

A guide to the muzzle-loading percussion guns and rifles of the 19th century.

The Plains Rifle, by Charles E. Hanson, Jr., The Gun Room Press, Highland Park, NJ, 1977. 171 pp., illus. $11.95.

Historical survey of popular civilian arms used on the American frontiers, their makers, and their owners.

Plates & Buckles of the American Military 1795-1874, by Sydney C. Kerksis, The Gilgal Press, Kenesaw, GA, 1974. 567 pp., illus. $27.50.

Covers some 448 different belt and accoutrement plates from the postrevolution period to the "Hagner" plate of 1874.

The Post-War Colt Single-Action Revolvers, by Don Wilkerson, The Single Action Shop, Apple Valley, MN, 1978. 152 pp., illus. $17.95.

Detailed descriptions of 37 variations, plus information on engraved and special models.

Price List of the U.S. Cartridge Company's Ammunition, A 1969 reprint of the 1891 original, publ. by J. C. Tillinghast, Marlow, N.H. 29 pp., illus., paper covers. $2.50.

Displays many of the now hard-to-find cartridges.

Providence Tool Co. Military Arms, by Edward A. Hull, Edward A. Hull, Valparaiso, FL, 1978. 76 pp., illus. Paper covers. $6.95.

A comprehensive account of the company's muskets, Peabody and Martini rifles, and Roberts and Peabody conversion muskets, as well as edged weapons.

Purdey Guns & Rifles, facsimile reprint of the 1931 James Purdey & Sons Ltd. catalog, by Empire Press, Santa Fe, NM, 1978. 27 pp., illus. Paper covers. $7.50

Fine reproduction of one of the most famous of English gun manufacturers catalogs.

The Rappahannock Forge, by Nathan L. Swayze, The American Society of Arms Collectors, Gun Room Press, Highland Park, NJ, 1976. 40 pp., illus. Paper covers. $2.

The first in-depth research done on surviving Rapa Forge firearms as well as being an authoritative history of James Hunter.

Rare Selections from Old Gun Catalogs 1888-1919, edited by Joseph J. Schroeder, DBI Books, Inc., Northfield, IL, 1978. 96 pp., illus. Paper covers. $4.95.

Selections from rare old gun catalogs.

The Rare and Valuable Antique Arms, by James E. Serven, Pioneer Press, Union City, TN, 1976. 106 pp., illus. Paper covers. $4.95.

A guide to the collector in deciding which direction his collecting should go, investment value, historic interest, mechanical ingenuity, high art or personal preference.

Red Coat and Brown Bess, by Anthony D. Darling. Museum Restoration Service, Ottawa, Ontario, Can., 1970. Paper covers, 63 pp., very well illus., in line and halftone. $3.00.

An unusually excellent treatise on the British Army in 1774-1775. Includes detailed text and illus. of various models of the "Brown Bess," plus "Records of the Battles, Sieges and Skirmishes of the American Revolution."

Remington Arms in American History, by A. Hatch, Rinehart & Co., NY, 1956. 359 pp., illus. $6.50.

Collector's guide with appendix of all Remington arms, ballistics tables, etc.

Remington Catalog (Price List) of 1885, a reprint in facsimile, by The Rocky Mountain Investment and Antique Co., Cheyenne, WY, 1969. 48 pp., well illus., paper covers. $3.00.

All rifles, handguns, cane gun, sights, cartridges, shotguns, accessories etc. A priced catalog.

E. Remington & Sons, Reduced Price List for 1877, reprinted by Pioneer Press, Union City, TN, 1977. 42 pp., illus. Paper covers. $1.95.

A facsimile reprint showing all models of rifles, shotguns, pistols, etc. manufactured during this period by this firm.

Remington Rolling Block Firearms, by Konrad F. Schreier, Jr., Pioneer Press, Union City, TN, 1977. 65 pp., illus. Paper covers. $5.00.
A collectors listing of the famous rolling block action arms made by E. Remington & Sons.
Remington Tips, By E. Dixon Larson, Pioneer Press, Union City, TN, 1975. 99 pp., illus. Paper covers. $4.95.
Tips for collectors of Remington Handguns. Covers percussion, conversions, early cartridge models, etc.
The Revolver, Its Description, Management, and Use, by P. E. Dove. Arms and Armour Press, London, 1968. 57 pp., 6 engravings, stiff paper wrappers. $3.75.
A facsimile reprint of a rare classic, dealing principally with the Adams revolver compared to the qualities of the Colt.
Rifled Infantry Arms, by J. Schon; trans. by Capt. J. Gorgas, USA. Dresden, 1855; facsimile reprint by W. E. Meuse, Schuylersville, NY, 1965. 54 pp., illus. $2.50.
Reprint of classic essay on European military small arms of the mid-19th century. Paper covers.
1901 John Rigby & Co. Catalog, a facsimile reprint by Empire Press, Santa Fe, NM, 1980. 15 pp., illus. Paper covers. $5.00.
A facsimile reprint of this famous British gunmaker's 1901 catalog.
1932 Rigby Double Rifles, a facsimile reprint by Empire Press, Santa Fe, NM, 1980. 15 pp., illus. Paper covers. $7.50.
A facsimile reprint of the 1932 catalog of John Rigby & Co., London.
Ruger Automatic Pistols and Single Action Revolvers With Check List, by Hugo A. Lueders, Houston, TX, 1978. 56 pp., illus. Paper covers. $6.
A useful tool for the tyro collector in the Ruger field to identify the major variations.
Ruger Rimfire Revolvers 1953-1973, by J. C. Munnell, J. C. Munnell, McKeesport, PA, 1978. 48 pp., illus. Paper covers. $5.95.
A definitive work on the most neglected facet of Ruger collecting.
The 'Russian' Colts, sponsored by the Colt Historical Foundation, Beinfeld Publ., Inc., No. Hollywood, CA, 1979. 31 pp., illus. Paper covers. $3.95.
Published on the occasion of a loan exhibition of the presentation Russian Colt revolvers by The State Hermitage Museum, Leningrad to The Metropolitan Museum of Art, N.Y.
Samuel Colt's New Model Pocket Pistols; The Story of the 1855 Root Model Revolver, by S. Gerald Keogh, S. G. Keogh, Ogden, UT, 1974. 31 pp., illus., paper covers. $3.50; hardbound $8.50.
Collector's reference on various types of the titled arms, with descriptions, illustrations, and historical data.
Savage Arms Co. 1900 Catalog, a facsimile reprint by Sand Pond Gun Shop, Marlow, NH, 1978. 55 pp., illus. Paper covers. $5.
Shows all grades of engraving for the Model 99 Savage, sporting and military rifles, cartridges, sights, and the Savage "Ideal" reloading tools.
Savage Automatic Pistols, by James R. Carr. Publ. by the author, St. Charles, Ill., 1967. A reprint. 129 pp., illus. with numerous photos. $6.50.
Collector's guide to Savage pistols, models 1907-1922, with features, production data, and pictures of each. A reprint of the circa 1912 Savage promotional and instructive booklet titled *It Banishes Fear* is recommended to accompany the above. Paper wrappers, 32 pp. $1.50.
Scottish Arms Makers, by C. E. Whitelaw, ed. by Sarah Barter, Fortress Publ., Inc., Stoney Creek, Ontario, Can., 1977. 338 pp. illus. $29.95.
A bibliographical dictionary of firearms makers, edged weapons and armor working in Scotland from the 14th century to 1870.
Sharps Firearms, by Frank Sellers, Beinfeld Publ., Inc., No. Hollywood, CA, 1977. Large format with over 500 photographs. $34.95.
The first complete review of the famous Sharps Firearms Co. and a detailed examination of every product made by them.
The following four items were published by the Americana Archives Publ. Co., Topsfield, MA.
Sharps Rifle: The Gun That Shaped American Destiny, by Martin Rywell, Pioneer Press, Union City, TN, 1977. 156 pp., illus. Paper covers. $2.95.
The role of Sharps guns in American history.
Sharps' Rifle Manufacturing Company Catalog, 1859, a facsimile reprint. 1976. 16 pp., illus. Paper covers. $3.
Shows the carbine and rifle, the forms for shot and powder tubes, plus cleaning directions.
Sharps' Rifle Manufacturing Company Catalog, 1864, a facsmilie reprint. 1976. 16 pp., illus. Paper covers. $3.
Illustrates the carbine, sporting rifle and army rifle with bayonet. Complete instructions on use, preparing charges and a manual of arms.
Sharps' Rifle Manufacturing Company Catalog, 1874, a facsimile reprint. 1976. 32 pp., illus. Paper covers. $3.
Six different rifles are illustrated, including the famous Creedmoor.
Shotgun Shells: Identification, Manufacturers and Checklist for Collectors, by F. H. Steward. B. and P. Associates, St. Louis, Mo., 1969. 101 pp., illus., paper covers. $10.00.
Historical data for the collector.
Small Arms, by Frederick Wilkinson, Hawthorne Books, Inc., New York, 1966. 256 pp., illus. $4.95.
A history of small firearms, techniques of the gunsmith, equipment used by combatants, sportsmen and hunters.
Small Arms of the Sea Services, by Robt. H. Rankin. N. Flayderman & Co., New Milford, CT, 1972. 227 pp., illus. $14.50.
Encyclopedic reference to small arms of the U.S. Navy, Marines and Coast Guard. Covers edged weapons, handguns, long arms and others, from the beginnings.
Smith and Wesson 1857-1945, by Robert J. Neal and Roy J. Jenks. A. S. Barnes and Co., Inc., NYC, 1975. 500 pp., illus. with over 300 photos and 90 radiographs. $25.00.
A long-needed book, especially for knowledgeable enthusiasts and collectors. Covers an investigation of the series of handguns produced by the Smith and Wesson Company.
Southern Derringers of the Mississippi Valley, by Turner Kirkland. Pioneer Press, Tenn., 1971. 80 pp., illus., paper covers. $2.00.
A guide for the collector, and a much-needed study.
Spanish Military Weapons in Colonial America, 1700-1821, by S. B. Brinckerhoff & P. A. Chamberlain. Stackpole Books, Harrisburg, PA, 1972. 160 pp., illus. $14.95.
Spanish arms and armaments described and illustrated in 274 photographic plates. Includes firearms, accoutrements, swords, polearms and cannon.
Sporting Posters of the Golden Age, by Sid Latham, Stackpole Books, Harrisburg, PA, 1978. 48 pp., twenty four reproductions of rare sporting prints. Paper covers. $8.95.
Full-color scenes, removable for framing, depicting the finest moments afield by the best sporting artists of the century.
The Standard Directory of Proof-Marks, ed. by R. A. Steindler, The John Olson Company, Paramus, NJ, 1976. 144 pp., illus. Paper covers. $5.95.
A comprehensive directory of the proof-marks of the world.
"Standard" Self-Cocking Pistol, A facsimile reprint by Handgun Press, Chicago, IL, 1979. 16 pp. illus. Paper covers. $4.00.
A facsimile reprint of the 1898 Schwarzlose pistol manual.
Starr Arms Co., 1864 Catalog, a reprint. 1976. 22 pp., illus. Paper covers. $3.
Contains operating and disassembly instructions, trial results and military testimonials.
Stevens Pistols and Pocket Rifles, by K. L. Cope, Museum Restoration Service, Ottawa, Can., 1971. 104 pp. $8.50.
All are shown, identified, detailed, variations, listings of dates, etc.
The Story of Allen & Wheelock Firearms, by H. H. Thomas, C. J. Krehbiel Co., Cincinnati, OH, 1965. 125 pp., illus. $10.95.
A comprehensive study of the firearms made by the firm of Allen & Wheelock.
The Story of Firearms Ignition, by Edsall James, Pioneer Press, Union City, TN, 1975. 22 pp., illus. Paper covers. $3.50
Mechanical design and the firing contrivances for guns from early matchlocks to modern cartridge arms.
A Study of the Colt Single Action Army Revolver, by R. Graham, J. A. Kopec, and C. K. Moore, publ. by the authors, La Puente, CA, 1975. Over 500 pp., illus. $39.95.
A definitive work on the famous Colt Single Action revolver. Contains many new facts never before published.

Summary of D.C.M. Rifle Sales 1922-1942, compiled by Springfield Research Service, Silver Spring, MD, 1976. 80 pp. Paper covers. $4.
A compilation of individual serial numbers of rifles sold by the Ordnance Department between 1922 and 1942.
Swiss Handguns, by Fritz Hausler, publ. by the author, Frauenfeld, Switzerland, 1975. 140 pp., illus. $18.95.
Helvetian pistols and revolvers from 1817 to the present day in text and illustrations.
The 36 Calibers of the Colt Single Action Army, by David M. Brown. Publ. by the author at Albuquerque, NM, new reprint 1971. 222 pp., well-illus. $15.00.
Edited by Bev Mann of *Guns Magazine*. This is an unusual approach to the many details of the Colt S.A. Army revolver. Halftone and line drawings of the same models make this of especial interest.

Thompson Guns: 1929 Commercial Price List and Catalog, published by Auto-Ordnance Corp., Ray Riling Arms Books Co., Phila., PA, 1976. A facsimile reprint. 18 pp., illus., paper covers. $5.
A limited, numbered reprint of the scarce 1929 Catalog on the Thompson Submachine Gun.
Those Other Colts, or Colt Conversions, by Albert Watson III, Colt Collector Press, Rapid City, SD, 1975. 32 pp., illus. Paper covers. $5.00.
Factory alterations to Colt holster pistols from the percussion cap to self-contained cartridge models.
Thoughts on the American Flintlock Pistol, by Samuel E. Dyke, George Shumway, York, PA, 1974. 61 pp., illus. Paper covers. $5.00.
Reprint of the "Kentucky Pistol" section from Dillin's book "The Kentucky Rifle."
Thoughts on the Kentucky Rifle in its Golden Age, by Joe Kindig, Jr. George Shumway, York, PA, 1975. A facsimile reprint of the 1960 original. 561 pp., replete with fine arms and data on many makers. $49.50.
Covers mainly the arms and their makers in the Lancaster area of Pennsylvania. An authoritative work.
The Trapdoor Springfield, by M. D. Waite and B. D. Ernst, Beinfeld Publ. Co., Inc., No. Hollywood, CA, 1979. 250 pp., illus. $19.95.
The first comprehensive book on the famous standard military rifle of the 1873-92 period.

A Treatise on the Snider: the British Soldier's Firearm 1866-c. 1880, by Ian D. Skennerton, Ian D. Skennerton, Queensland, Australia, 1977. 181 pp., illus. $23.50.
Development, manufacture and issue of the Snider rifles and carbines for that period.
200 Years of American Firearms, by James E. Serven, DBI Books, Inc., Northfield, IL, 1975. 224 pp., illus. Paper covers. $7.95.
Covers the evolution of firearms in America from those carried by Spanish explorers to the M-16 rifle.
Underhammer Guns, by H. C. Logan. Stackpole Books, Harrisburg, PA, 1964. 250 pp. illus. $10.00.
A full account of an unusual form of firearm dating back to flintlock days. Both American and foreign specimens are included.
U.S. Army Weapons 1784-1791, by Wm. H. Guthman, The American Soc. of Arms Coll., 1975. 94 pp., illus. Paper covers. $6.50.
A detailed study of the surplus weapons and accoutrements stored in Federal arsenals after the Revolutionary War.
U.S. Cartridge Co. Collection of Firearms, We, Inc., Old Greenwich, CT., 1970. 142 pp., illus. $6.00.
Describes each arm in detail as to manufacture, action, period of use, function, markings, patents, makers, etc.
U.S. Cartridges and Their Handguns, by Charles R. Suydam, Beinfeld Publ., Inc., No. Hollywood, CA, 1977. 200 pp., illus. Paper covers. $9.95.
The first book ever showing which gun used what cartridge. A must for the gun and cartridge collector.
U.S. Firearms: The First Century, 1776-1875, by D. F. Butler. Winchester Press, NY, 1971. 320 pp., illus. $15.00.
A rich mine of carefully researched information and data on American firearms of this period. Illustrated with photos, schematics and historical documents.
U.S. Martial and Semi-Martial Single-Shot Pistols, by C. E. Chapel, Coward-McCann Inc., NYC, 1962. 352 pp., over 150 illus. $10.00.
Describes in detail all single shot martial pistols used by the US armed forces and by military units of the states. A definitive guide.
U.S. Military Firearms, 1776-1956, by Maj. Jas. E. Hicks. J. E. Hicks & Son. La Canada, Calif., 216 pp., incl. 88 pages of fine plates. $12.50.
Covering 180 years of America's hand and shoulder weapons. The most authoritative book on this subject. Packed with official data.
U.S. Military Small Arms 1816-1865, by R. M. Reilly. The Eagle Press, Inc., Baton Rouge, La., 1970. 275 pp., illus. $22.50.
Describes and superbly illustrates every known type of primary and secondary martial firearm of the period 1816-1865. Limited, numbered ed.
The Virginia Manufactory of Arms, by Giles Cromwell, University Press of Virginia, Charlottesville, VA, 1975. 205 pp., illus. $25.00.
The only complete history of the Virginia Manufactory of Arms which produced muskets, pistols, swords, and cannon for the state's militia from 1802 through 1821.
Volcanic Firearms—and Their Successors, by Edsall James, Pioneer Press, Union City, TN, 1976. 30 pp., illus. Paper covers. $2.50.
The story of those rare Volcanic guns, and the repeaters that were developed later as a result of the Volcanics.
Walther Models PP and PPK, 1929-1945, by James L. Rankin, assisted by Gary Green, James L. Rankin, Coral Gables, FL, 1974. 142 pp., illus. $14.00.
Complete coverage on the subject as to finish, proof marks and Nazi Party inscriptions.

Walther Volume II, Engraved, Presentation and Standard Models, by James L. Rankin, J. L. Rankin, Coral Galbes, FL 1977. 112 pp., illus. $17.50.
The new Walther book on embellished versions and standard models. Has 88 photographs, including many color plates.

Weapons & Equipment of the Victorian Soldier, by Donald Featherstone, Blandford Press, Dorset, England, 1978. 130 pp., illus. $14.95.
Describes the arms, equipment, drill and battle and march formations for infantry and cavalry during the long reign of Queen Victoria.

Westley Richards Gun & Rifle Makers to H. M. King George V, List E, facsimile reprint of the 1920 catalog of Westley Richards & Co., Ltd., by Empire Press, Santa Fe, NM, 1978. 36 pp., illus. Paper covers. $10.
A fine reproduction of this famous English gun manufacturers catalog.

Westley Richards Modern Sporting Rifles and Cartridges 1932, a facsimile reprint by Empire Press, Santa Fe, NM, 1980. 60 pp., illus. Paper covers. $12.50.
A facsimile reprint of this famous British gunmakers 1932 catalog.

The Whitney Firearms, by Claud Fuller. Standard Publications, Huntington, W. Va., 1946. 334 pp., many plates and drawings. $25.00.
An authoritative history of all Whitney arms and their maker. Highly recommended. An exclusive with Ray Riling Arms Books Co.

The William M. Locke Collection, compiled by Robert B. Berryman, et al, The Antique Armory, Inc., East Point, GA, 1973. 541 pp., illus. $40.00.
A magnificently produced book illustrated with hundreds of photographs of guns from one of the finest collection of American firearms ever assembled.

Winchester Catalog of 1891, a facsimile reprint by the Rocky Mountain Investment and Antique Co., Cheyenne, WY, 1973. 84 pp., well illus., paper covers. $5.00.
All rifles, shotguns, reloading tools and ammunition of the time. A priced catalog.

Winchester—The Gun That Won the West, by H. F. Williamson. Combat Forces Press, Washington, D.C., 1952. Later eds. by Barnes, NY 494 pp., profusely illus., paper covers. $9.95.
A scholarly and essential economic history of an honored arms company, but the early and modern arms introduced will satisfy all but the exacting collector.

The Winchester Book, by Geo. Madis. Art & Reference House, Lancaster, Texas. New revised 4th edition, 1978. 542 pp., illus. $35.00.
First release of 1,000 autographed deluxe copies at this special price.

Winchester Repeating Firearms Co. Catalog 1875, facsimile reprint by King & Co., Peoria, IL, 1978. 64 pp., illus. Paper covers. $5.
Exhibiting repeating firearms, rifled muskets, carbines, hunting and target rifles and metallic cartridges manufactured by Winchester Repeating Arms Co.

Winchester Repeating Arms Co. Catalog, February, 1893, facsimile reprint by King & Co., Peoria, IL, 1978. 84 pp., illus. Paper covers. $4.50.
Exhibiting repeating firearms, single shot rifles, rifled muskets, carbines, repeating shotguns, Hotchkiss magazine firearms for military and sporting use.

Winchester Repeating Arms Co. Catalogue No. 58, December, 1896, a facsimile reprint by Empire Press, Santa Fe, NM, 1980. 130 pp., illus. Paper covers. $7.50.
A facsimile reprint of Winchester's 1896 catalog exhibiting repeating rifles, carbines and muskets, etc.

Winchester Repeating Arms Co. Catalog, October, 1897, Highly Finished Arms, a facsimile reprint by Rocky Mountain Investment and Antique Co., Cheyenne, WY, 1970. 28 pp., illus. Paper covers. $7.50.
A facsimile reprint of Winchester's catalog showing artistically ornamented arms.

Winchester Sales Manual 1938, a facsimile reprint by Empire Press, Santa Fe, NM, 1980. 66 pp., illus. Paper covers. $10.00.
A facsimile reprint of the manual given to the sales personel to familiarize them with the company history and products.

James Woodward & Sons Catalog, 1925, a facsimile reprint by Empire Press, Santa Fe, NM, 1979. 20 pp., illus. $7.50.
A facsimile reprint of this famous British gunmaker's 1925 catalog showing complete line of shotguns and rifles.

World of Lugers: Proof Marks, Vol. I, by Sam Costanzo, Sam Costanzo, Mayfield Heights, OH, 1977. 432 pp., illus. $17.95.
Complete listing of different variations of proof marks on the Luger. A limited, signed edition.

World of Lugers: Volume I, Serial Numbers of Lugers Issued to German Agents in the U.S. 1913-16, by Sam Costanzo, Sam Costanzo, Wickliffe, OH, 1975. 79 pp., illus. Paper covers. $5.50.
The Lugers issued by Hans Tauscher to German espionage agents in the United States and Canada during the period 1913-1916. Also included is Government correspondence used as evidence in the Hans Tauscher court trial.

Wyatt Earp & the "Buntline Special" Myth, by William B. Shillingberg, Blaine Publ. Co., Tucson, AZ, 1976. 64 pp., illus. Paper covers. $3.95.
Much unpublished material on Earp, including the association with his later "biographer" Stuart N. Lake—himself the inventor of the Buntline presentation legend.

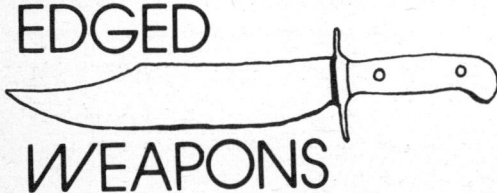

EDGED WEAPONS

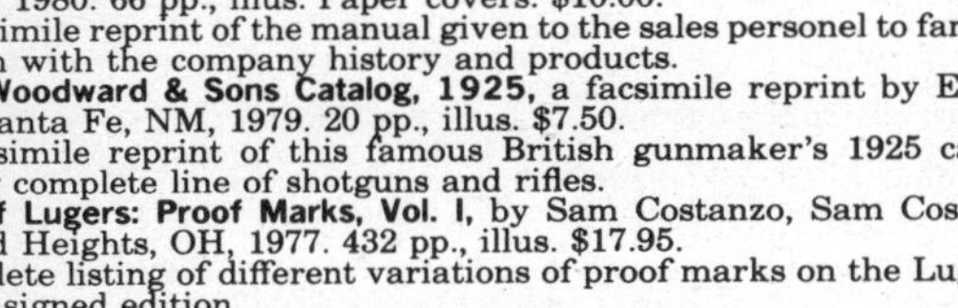

The Robert Abels Collection of Bowie Type Knives of American Interest, by Robert Abels, Robert Abels, Hopewell Junction, NY, 1974. 20 pp., illus. Paper covers. $1.95.
A selection of American Bowie-type knives from the collection of Robert Abels.

Allied Bayonets of World War 2, by J. Anthony Carter, Arco Publ., Co., NY, 1969. 80 pp., illus. $3.50.
Illustrates and describes all bayonets issued to the Allied armed forces between 1939 and 1946.

American Axes, by Henry Kauffman, The Stephen Greene Press, Brattleboro, VT, 1972. 200 pp., illus. $12.50.
A definitive work on the subject. Contains a roster of American axe makers, glossary and notes on the care and use of axes.

The American Bayonet 1176-1964, by Albert N. Hardin, Jr., Albert N. Hardin, Jr., Pennsauken, NJ, 1977. 234 pp., illus. $24.50.
Describes and illustrates over two hundred separate and distinct types of American bayonets from Colonial times to the present day.

American Handmade Knives of Today, by B. R. Hughes, Pioneer Press, Union City, TN, 1972. 56 pp., illus. Paper covers. $2.95.
A basic primer for novices who are just beginning to take an interest in handmade cutlery.

American Indian Tomahawks, by Harold L. Peterson, Museum of the American Indian, Heye Foundation, NY, 1965. 142 pp., illus. $10.00.
A brief description of various types and their makers.

American Knives: The First History and Collector's Guide, by Harold L. Peterson, Charles Scribner's Sons, NY, 1958. 178 pp., illus Paper covers. $4.95.
A landmark work and a book that will whet the appetite of knife collectors everywhere.

American Polearms 1526-1865, by Rodney Hilton Brown, N. Flayderman & Co., New Milford, CT, 1967. 198 pp., illus. $14.50.
The lance, halbred, spontoon, pike and naval boarding weapons used in the American military forces through the Civil War.

American Socket Bayonets 1717-1873, by Donald B. Webster, Jr., Museum Restoration Service, Ontario, Canada, 1964. 47 pp., illus. Paper covers. $2.50.
Helps identify the many variations of the triangular and angular bayonets used by the U.S. Army.

The American Sword, 1775-1945, by Harold L. Peterson, Ray Riling Arms Books, Co., Phila., PA, 1980. 286 pp. plus 60 pp. of illus. $22.50.
1977 reprint of a survey of swords worn by U.S. uniformed forces, plus the rare "American Silver Mounted Swords, (1700-1815)."

The Art of Blacksmithing, by Alex W. Bealer, Funk & Wagnalls, New York, NY, revised edition, 1976. 438 pp., illus. $16.95.
Required reading for anyone who makes knives or is seriously interested in the history of cutlery.

The Arts of the Japanese Sword, by B. W. Robinson, Faber and Faber, London, England, 1978. 218 pp., illus. $33.00.
Detailed information on making blades, chief schools of Japanese swordsmiths, care, cleaning and marks.

Australian Service Bayonets, by Ian D. Skennerton, Ian D. Skennerton, Margate, Australia, 1976. 134 pp., illus. $23.50.
Australian bayonets their production, proof and issue markings, experimental models, etc.

Basic Manual of Knife Fighting, by William L. Cassidy, Paladin Press, Boulder, CO, 1978. 41 pp., illus. Paper covers. $4.
A manual presenting the best techniques developed by the experts from 1930 to date.

The Bayonet, by Anthony Carter and John Walter, Charles Scribner's Sons, NY, 1974. 124 pp., illus, $11.50.
A history of knife and sword bayonets 1850-1970.

Bayonet Fighting, by U.S. Dept. of the Army, reprinted by Normount Technical Publ., Wickenburg, AZ, 1973. 76 pp., illus. Paper covers. $1.50.
A facsimile reprint of FM23-25.

Bayonets Illustrated, by Bert Walsh, A Bashall Caves Publ., Dublin, Ireland, 1970. 49 pp., illus. $6.50.
162 detailed line drawings of bayonets from many countries and periods.

Bayonets of the World, Volume I, by Paul Kiesling, Military Collectors Service, Kedichem, Holland, 1973. 278 plates. $19.95.
Covers bayonets up to 515mm in length, includes scabbards, sockets, etc.

Bayonets of the World, Volume 2, by Paul Kiesling, Military Collectors Service, Kedichem, Holland, 1974. 131 pp., illus. $19.95.
Covers bayonets of all types and all countries. Arranged in size starting with 515mm and larger.

Bayonets of the World, Volume 3, by Paul Kiesling, Military Collectors Service, Kedichem, Holland, 1975. 130 pp., illus. $19.95.
Part 3 of this fine series on bayonets of all countries. Includes a cross index reference for all three volumes.

Bayonets of the World, Volume 4, by Paul Kiesling, Military Collectors Service, Kedichem, Holland, 1977. 190 pp., illus. $24.00.
The final volume in this monumental work on bayonets.

The Best of Knife World, Volume I, edited by Knife World Publ., Knoxville, TN, 1980. 92 pp., illus. Paper covers. $3.95.
A collection of articles about knives. Reprinted from monthly issues of Knife World.

Blacksmithing for the Home Craftsman, by Joe Pehoski, Joe Pehoski, Washington, TX, 1973. 44 pp., illus. Paper covers. $2.50.
This informative book is chock-full of drawings and explains how to make your own forge.

Blades and Barrels, by H. Gordon Frost, Wallon Press, El Paso, TX, 1972. 298 pp., illus. $16.95.
The first full scale study about man's attempts to combine an edged weapon with a firearm.

Bowie Knives, by Robert Abels, Robert Abels, NY, 1960. 48 pp., illus. Paper covers. $3.00.
A booklet showing knives, tomahawks, related trade cards and advertisements.

British Cut and Thrust Weapons, by John Wilkinson Latham, Charles E. Tuttle Co., VT, 1971. 112 pp., illus. $7.50.
Well illustrated study tracing the development of edged weapons and their adoption by the British armed forces.

British Military Swords from 1800 to the Present Day, by John Wilkinson Latham, Crown Publ., Inc. NY, 1966. 79 pp., illus. $3.95.
Survey of British swords used by various branches of the army with data on their manufacture, specifications and procurement.

The Collector's Pictorial Book of Bayonets, by Frederick J. Stephens, Hippocrene Books, Edison, NJ, 1977. 127 pp., illus. Paper covers. $3.95.
A photo reference to bayonets of over 20 countries with information pertaining to each.

The Complete Book of Knife Fighting, by William L. Cassidy, Paladin Press, Boulder, CO, 1975. 119 pp., illus. $10.95.
Most complete book of knife fighting technique and history with every facet covered.

Custom Knife . . . II, by John Davis Bates, Jr., and James Henry Schippers, Jr., Custom Knife Press, Memphis, TN, 1974. 112 pp., illus. $20.00.
The book of pocket knives and folding hunters. A guide to the 20th century makers' art.

The Cutlery Story: From Stone Age to Steel Age, by Lewis D. Bement, Custom Cutlery Co., Dalton, GA, 1972. 36 pp., illus. Paper covers. $3.50.
A classic booklet about the history, romance, and manufacture of cutlery from the earliest times to modern methods of manufacture.

A Directory of Sheffield: Including the Manufacturers of the Adjacent Villages, a facsimile reprint of the 1707 London edition, Da Capo Press, Inc., NY, 1969. Illus. $11.50.
With the several marks of the cutlers, scissor and edge-tool makers.

Edge of the Anvil, by Jack Andrews, Rodale Press, Emmaus, PA, 1978. 224 pp., illus. $9.95.
A basic blacksmith book.
Edged Weapons of the American Revolution 1775-1783, by Geo. C. Neumann, American Defense Preparedness Assoc., Wash., DC, 1975. 16 pp., illus. Paper covers. $2.00.
A monograph outlining the various types of swords, bayonets, knives and other edged weapons used by the Continental forces.
Edged Weapons, a Collectors Guide, by Frederick J. Stephens, Spur Books, London, England, 1978. 160 pp., illus. $14.95.
A comprehensive survey of the entire field of these weapons from all parts of the world.
An Encyclopedia of Knives, by Norman M. Strung, J. B. Lippincott Co., Phila., PA, 1977. 219 pp., illus. $12.50.
An illustrated consumer's guide to buying, using, sharpening, and caring for all over-the-counter knives.
European Edged Weapons, by Terrence Wise, Almark Publ. Co., Ltd., London, England, 1974. 96 pp., illus. Paper covers. $4.95; Cloth. $7.25.
The development of swords, axes, bayonets and other edged weapons in Europe.
European Swords and Daggers in the Tower of London, by Arthur Richard Dufty, Her Majesty's Stationery Office, London, England, 1974. 157 pp., illus. $19.95.
An illustrated and descriptive guide to the swords and daggers in the Tower of London Armouries collections.
The Fighting Knife, by W. D. Randall, Jr. and Col. Rex Applegate, W. D. Randall, Orlando, FL, 1975. 60 pp., illus. Paper covers. $2.75.
Manual for the use of Randall-made fighting knives and similar types.
For Knife Lovers Only, by Harry K. McEvoy, Knife World Publ., Knoxville, TN, 1979. 67 pp., illus. Paper covers. $4.95.
A fascinating and unusual approach to the story of knives.
The German Bayonet, by John Walter, Arms and Armour Press, London, England, 1976. 128 pp., illus. $12.50.
A comprehensive illustrated history of regulation patterns, 1871-1945.
German Ersatz Bayonets, by Anthony Carter, The Lyon Press, East Sussex, England, 1976. 64 pp., illus. $12.95.
A concise illustrated history of the emergency all-metal designs, 1914-18.
A Guide to Handmade Knives, edited by Mel Tappan, The Janus Press, Inc., Los Angeles, CA, 1977. Paper covers. $9.50; Deluxe hardbound. $19.50.
The official directory of the Knifemakers Guild.
Gun Digest Book of Folding Knives, by Jack Lewis and B. R. Hughes, DBI Books, Inc. Northfield, IL, 1977. 288 pp., illus. Paper covers. $7.95.
A cut above any other volume published on pocket or folding knives.
The Gun Digest Book of Knives, by B. R. Hughes and Jack Lewis, DBI Books, Inc., Northfield, IL, 1973. 228 pp., illus. Paper covers. $6.95.
How to collect, buy and care for knives.
The History of the John Russell Cutlery Company, 1833-1936, by Robert L. Merriam et al, The Bete Press, Greenfield, MA, 1976. 120 pp., illus. $12.95.
A complete history of the people, places and events behind legendary American knives such as the Barlow, Green River Knife, Dadley and others.
The House of Wostenholm 1745-1945, by Harold Bexfield, George Wostenholm & Son, Ltd., Sheffield, England, 1945. 40 pp., illus. $9.95.
A short history of Sheffield cutlery and the House of Wostenholm.
How to Make Knives, by Richard W. Barney & Robert W. Loveless, Beinfield Publ., Inc., No. Hollywood, CA, 1977. 178 pp., illus. Paper covers. $9.95; Deluxe hardbound. $15.95.
A book filled with drawings, illustrations, diagrams, and 500 how-to-do-it photos.
The Indian Sword, by P. S. Rawson, Arco Pub. Co., Inc., NY, 1968. 108 pp., illus. $8.50.
The various types of Indian swords are accurately classified and the techniques and local styles of decoration are identified.
Introduction to Japanese Swords, by William M. Hawley, William M. Hawley, Hollywood, CA, 1973. 20 pp., illus. Paper covers. $3.50.
Clear concise details of construction that made Japanese swords the world's finest edged weapons.
The I*XL Cutlery, reprinted by Americana/Reed, Louisville, KY, 1975. 53 pp., illus. Paper covers. $5.00.
A facsimile reprint of the first catalog issued by the firm of George Wostenholm & Son Ltd. in 1885.
Ka-Bar Dependable Pocket Knives, reprinted by Ka-Bar Knives, Olean, NY, 1976. Unpaginated. Paper covers. $3.50.
A facsimile reprint of the 1925 Union Cutlery Co. catalog with many illustrations of old Ka-Bar knives.
Kentucky Knife-Traders Manual No. 5, by R. B. Ritchie, Hindman, KY, 1975. 103 pp., illus. Paper covers. $6.50.
A listing of pocketknives and razor values.
Knife Album, by Col. Robert Mayes, Col. Robert Mayes, Middlesboro, KY, 1975. 554 pp., illus. $14.95.
Information pertaining to knives by the prominent makers.
The Knife Album Price Guide 1976 Edition, by Robert Mayes, Robert Mayes, Middlesboro, KY, 1976. 174 pp. Paper covers. $6.00.
The only book on identification and accurate pricing.
Knife Digest, First Annual Edition, edited by William L. Cassidy, Knife Digest Publ. Co., Berkeley, CA, 1974. 285 pp., illus. Paper covers. $5.95.
The first annual publication ever produced for the knife and edged weapon enthusiast and collector.
Knife Digest, Second Annual Edition, edited by William L. Cassidy, Knife Digest Publ. Co., Berkeley, CA, 1976. 178 pp., illus. Paper covers. $7.95; Cloth. $15.00.
The second annual edition of the internationally known book on blades.
Knife Throwing, Sport ... Survival ... Defense, by Blackie Collins, Knife World Publ., Knoxville, TN, 1979. 31 pp., illus. Paper covers. $3.00.
How to select a knife, how to make targets, how to determine range and how to survive with a knife.
Knife Throwing a Practical Guide, by Harry K. McEvoy, Charles E. Tuttle Co., Rutland, VT, 1973. 108 pp., illus. Paper covers. $3.95.
If you want to learn to throw a knife this is the "bible."
Knife Throwing in the Professional Style, by Harry K. McEvoy, The Tru-Bal Co., Grand Rapids, MI, 1969. 24 pp., illus. Paper covers. $1.95.
A brief handbook on the professional aspects of knife throwing.
Knifecraft: A Comprehensive Step-by-Step Guide to the Art of Knifemaking, by Sid Latham, Stackpole Books, Harrisburg, PA, 1978. 224 pp., illus. $16.95.
An exhaustive volume taking both amateur and accomplished knifecrafter through all the steps in creating a knife.
Knifemakers of Old San Francisco, by Bernard R. Levine, Badger Books, San Francisco, CA, 1978. 240 pp., illus. $12.95.
The story about the knifemakers of San Francisco, the leading cutlers of the old West.

The Knife Makers Who Went West, by Harvey Platts, Longspeak Press, Longmont, CO, 1978. 200 pp., illus. $19.95.
Factual story of an important segment of the American cutlery industry. Primarily about Western knives and the Platts knife makers.
Knives and Knifemakers, by Sid Latham, Winchester Press, NY, 1973. 152 pp., illus. $15.00.
Lists makers and suppliers of knife-making material and equipment.
Light But Efficient, by Albert N. Hardin, Jr. and Robert W. Hedden, Albert N. Hardin, Jr., Pennsauken, NJ, 1973. 103 pp., illus. $7.95.
A study of the M1880 Hunting and M1890 intrenching knives and scabbards.
Marble Knives and Axes, by Konrad F. Schreir, Jr., Beinfeld Publ., Inc., No. Hollywood, CA, 1978. 80 pp., illus. Paper covers. $5.95.
The first work ever on the knives and axes made by this famous old, still-in-business, manufacturer.
The Modern Blacksmith, by Alexander G. Weygers, Van Nostrand Reinhold Co., NY, 1977. 96 pp., illus. $8.95.
Shows how to forge objects out of steel. Use of basic techniques and tools.
"Napanoch" a "White Man's" Knife with a "Red Man's" Name, by Rhett C. Stidham, Rhet C. Stidham, Belpre, OH 1976. 27 pp., illus. Paper covers. $5.00.
The history of the early 1900's Napanoch Knife Works, plus illustrations of the knives made by them.
Nathan Starr Arms Maker 1776-1845, by James E. Hicks, The Restoration Press, Phoenix, AZ, 1976. 166 pp., illus. $12.95.
Survey of the work of Nathan Starr of Middletown, CT, in producing edged weapons and pole arms for the U.S., 1799-1840, also some firearms.
Naval Swords, by P. G. W. Annis, Stackpole Books, Harrisburg, PA, 1970. 80 pp., illus. $5.50.
British and American naval edged weapons 1660-1815.
Naval Swords and Firearms, by Cmdr. W. E. May, R. N. and A. N. Kennard, Pendragon House, Palo Alto. CA, 1978. 22 pp., illus. Paper covers. $3.00.
British naval swords, dirks, pikes, etc. With an explanatory text.
Official Guide to Pocket Knives, by James F. Parker and J. Bruce Voyles, House of Collectibles, Florence, AL, 1976. 460 pp., illus. Paper covers. $5.95.
Price guide for buying and selling. Featuring Case, Winchester, Cattaraugus, Remington, Russell, and many more.
A Photographic Supplement of Confederate Swords with Addendum, by William A. Albaugh III, Moss Publications, Orange, VA, 1979. 259 pp., illus. $20.00.
A new updated edition of the classic work on Confederate edged weapons.
Pictorial Price Guide Romance of Collecting Case Knives, by Mrs. Dewey P. Ferguson, Fairborn, OH, 1978. 208 pp., illus. Paper covers. $8.00.
The largest work on the subject yet written, and enthusiastically recommended by the Case factory.
Pocket Knife Book 1 & 2—Price Guide, by Roy Ehrhardt, Heart of America Press, Kansas City, MO, 1974. 96 pp., illus. Spiral bound stiff paper covers. $6.95.
Reprints from the pocket knife sections of early manufacturers and sporting goods catalogs.
Pocket Knife Book 3—Price Guide, by Roy and Larry Ehrhardt, Heart of America Press, Kansas City, MO, 1974. Spiral bound stiff paper covers. $6.95.
Compiled from sections of various product sales catalogs of both Winchester and Marble Co. dating from the '20s and '30s.
The Pocketknife Collector's Friend, by D. Hanby, Hanby Enterprises, Morgan City, AL, 1973. 12 pp. Paper covers. $3.50.
An alphabetical listing of makers with their locations and prices of their products in mint and used condition.
The Pocketknife Manual, by Blackie Collins, Blackie Collins, Rock Hill, SC, 1976. 102 pp., illus. Paper covers. $5.50.
Building, repairing and refinishing pocketknives.
Practical Blacksmithing, edited by J. Richardson, Outlet Books, NY, 1978. 4 volumes in one, illus. $7.98.
A reprint of the extremely rare, bible of the blacksmith. Covers every aspect of working with iron and steel, from ancient uses to modern.
The Practical Book of Knives, by Ken Warner, Winchester Press, New York, NY, 1976. 224 pp., illus. $10.00.
All about knives for sport and utility.
Presenting America's Aristocracy of Fine Cutlery, reprinted by American Reprints, St. Louis, MO, n.d. 40 pp., illus. Paper covers. $3.50.
Reprint of a W. R. Case & Sons pocket knife catalog.
Price Guide to Romance of Knife Collecting, 1978 Edition, by Mrs. Dewey P. Ferguson, Fairborn, OH, 1978. 136 pp. Paper covers. $6.00.
The official guide to prices of Case knives.
A Primer of German Military Knives of the Two World Wars, by Gordon A. Hughes, Gordon A. Hughes, Sussex, England, 1976. 20 pp., illus. Paper covers. $4.00.
Detailed line drawings of some 40 trench combat knives of Imperial and Nazi Germany together with sheath variations.
A Primer of Military Knives: European & American, Combat, Trench & Utility Knives, by Gordon Hughes and Barry Jenkins, Brighton, England, 1973. 24 pp., illus. Paper covers. $5.00.
A primer of the knives used in the First and Second World Wars, with line drawings of the weapons and descriptive text.
A Primer of World Bayonets, by John Walter and Gordon Hughes, Brighton, England, 1969. In two volumes. Vol. I, 26 pp.; Vol. 2, 23 pp., illus. Paper covers. $6.50.
Vol. I, common knife and sabre bayonets. Vol. 2, further knife, sabre and socket bayonets.
The Rapier and Small-Sword 1460-1820, by A. V. B. Norman, Arms and Armour Press, London, Eng., 1980. 416 pp., illus. $95.00.
The story of the evolution of the rapier and its successor, the smallsword, by one of the world's great experts on edged weapons.
Rapiers, by Eric Valentine, Stackpole Books, Harrisburg, PA, 1968. 76 pp., illus. $5.50.
A desirable monograph, first on its subject to be published in English.
Regulation Military Swords, by J. Wilkinson-Latham, Star Products, London, England, 1970. 32 pp., illus. Paper covers. $4.95.
A detailed comparison of the military swords used by Great Britain, the United States, France, Germany, Austria, Sweden and Russia.
Remington Cutlery, reprinted by American Reprints, St. Louis, MO, 1969. Unpaginated, illus. Paper covers. $2.50.
A facsimile reprint of a 1936 pocket knife catalog issued by Remington Arms Co.
Rice's Trowel Bayonet, reprinted by Ray Riling Arms Books, Co., Phila., PA, 1968. 8 pp., illus. Paper covers. $3.00.
A facsimile reprint of a rare circular originally published by the U.S. Government in 1875 for the information of U.S. Troops.

Romance of Collecting Cattaraugus, Robeson, Russell, and Queen, by Mrs. Dewey P. Ferguson, Fairborn, OH, 1978. 220 pp., illus. Paper covers. $10.00.
Pictorial price guide. All companies listed with a history of their founding.

Romance of Knife Collecting, by Dewey P. Ferguson, Dewey P. Ferguson, Fairborn, OH, 4th ed., 1978. 176 pp., illus. Paper covers. $5.00.
A "must-have" by the modern master of pocketknife history.

Russell Green River Works Cutlery, reprinted by Dewey P. Ferguson, Fairborn, OH, 1970. 49 pp., illus. Paper covers. $5.00.
Facsimile reprint of an early pocketknife catalog with a modern pricing guide added.

Russian Military Swords 1801-1917, by E. Mollo, Historical Research Unit, London, England, 1973. 56 pp., illus. Paper covers $13.50.
First book in English to examine and classify the various swords used by the Russian Army from Alexander I to the Revolution.

The Samurai Sword, by John M. Yumoto, Charles E. Tuttle Co., Rutland, VT, 1958. 191 pp., illus. $9.95.
A must for anyone interested in Japanese blades, and the first book on this subject written in English.

Schrade Pocket Knives and Price Guide, Catalog 'E' and Supplements, reprinted by A. G. Russell Knife Collectors Club, A. G. Russell, Springdale, AR, 1971. 123 pp., illus. Paper covers. $5.00.
Hundreds of illustrations of Schrade pocket knives with their values.

Scottish Swords from the Battlefield at Culloden, by Lord Archibald Campbell, The Mowbray Co., Providence, RI, 1973. 63 pp., illus. $5.00.
A modern reprint of an exceedingly rare 1894 privately printed edition.

Scottish Swords and Dirks, by John Wallace, Stackpole Books, Harrisburg, PA 1970. 80 pp., illus. $5.50.
An illustrated reference guide to Scottish edged weapons.

Secrets of Modern Knife Fighting, by David E. Steele, Phoenix Press, Arvada, CO, 1974. 149 pp., illus. Paper covers. $9.95; Cloth. $15.00.
Details every facet of employing the knife in combat, including underwater fighting.

The Sheffield Bowie & Pocket-Knife Makers 1825-1925, by Richard Washer, T. A. Vinall, Nottingham, England, 1974. 144 pp., illus. $14.50.
Alphabetical listing of all known makers with their various identification marks and their periods of manufacture.

E. C. Simmons "Keen Kutter" Cutlery and Tools, reprinted by American Reprints Co., St. Louis, MO, 1970. 56 pp., illus. Paper covers. $3.50.
A facsimile reprint of a 1930 E. C. Simmons catalog.

Step-by-Step Knifemaking, by Davis Boye, Rodale Press, Emmous, PA, 1978. 288 pp., illus. $10.95.
Gives the fundamentals of knifemaking and shows how to make knives either as a hobby or as a business.

The Sword and Bayonet Makers of Imperial Germany 1871-1918, by John Walter, Fortress Publ., Inc., Stoney Creek, Ontario, Can., 1973. 120 pp., illus. $6.50.
Here for the first time is a comprehensive reference to the edged weapons producers of swords, sidearms, bayonets of Imperial Germany.

The Sword and Firearms Collection of the Society of the Cinncinnati, by John Brewer Brown, The Society of the Cinncinnati, Wash., DC, limited, numbered edition, 1965. 120 pp., illus. $10.00.
With biographical sketches of the original owners.

Sword, Lance and Bayonet, by Charles ffoulkes and E. C. Hopkinson, Arco Pub. Co., Inc., NY, 1967. 147 pp., illus. $7.50.
A facsimile of the first attempt at a consecutive account of the arms, both general and official use, since the discarding or armor.

Swords of the British Army, by Brian Robson, Fortress Publ., Inc., Ontario, Can., 1975. 208 pp., illus. $22.50.
The regulations, patterns, 1788-1914.

Swords and Daggers, by Eduard Wagner, Hamlyn, London, 1975. 253 pp., illus. $4.95.
Traces all types of European cut-and-thrust weapons from ancient times through their development to the twentieth century.

Swords and Other Edged Weapons, by Robert Wilkinson-Latham, Arco Publishing Co., New York, NY, 1978. 227 pp., illus. $8.95.
Traces the history of the "Queen of Weapons" from its earliest forms in the stone age to the military swords of the Twentieth century.

Swords for Sea Service, by Cmdr. W. E. May & P. G. W. Annis, Her Majesty's Stationery Office, London, England, 1970. A 2 volume set, 256; 398 pp., illus. $35.
A study based on the sword collection, which includes dirks and cutlasses, in the National Maritime Museum at Greenwich.

Tomahawks Illustrated, by Robert Kuck, Robert Kuck, New Knoxville, OH, 1977. 112 pp., illus. Paper covers. $8.50.
A pictorial record to provide a reference in selecting and evaluating tomahawks.

U.S. Military Knives, Bayonets and Machetes, Book III, by M. H. Cole, M. H. Cole, Birmingham, AL, 1979. 219 pp., illus. $23.00.
The most complete text ever written on U.S. military knives, bayonets, machetes and bolo's.

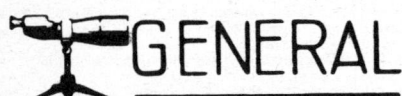

GENERAL

A.B.C. of Snap Shooting, by Horace Fletcher, Americana Archives Publ. Co., Topsfield, MA., 1971. 48 pp., illus. Paper, $4.00.
Authentic reproduction of a rare 1881 original.

Air Gun Batteries, by E. G. Wolff. Public Museum, Milwaukee, Wisc., 1964. 28 pp., illus., paperbound. $1.50.
Study of discharge mechanisms on reservoir air guns.

Air Gun Digest, by Robert Beeman & Jack Lewis, DBI Books, Inc., Northfield, IL, 1977. 224 pp., illus. Paper covers. $6.95.
Traces the first air, spring air, CO_2 and other types from prototype to current models.

The Album of Gunfighters, by J. Marvin Hunter and Noah H. Rose, Warren Hunter, Helotes, Texas, 1965. 4th printing. 236 pp., wonderfully illus., with spectacular oldtime photos. $30.
For the serious gunfighter fan there is nothing to equal this factual record of the men-behind-the-star and the human targets that they faced.

To All Sportsmen; and Particularly to Farmers and Gamekeepers, by Col. Geo. Hanger, Richmond Publ. Co., Richmond, England, 1971. 226 pp. $12.50.
Reprint of an 1814 work on hunting, guns, horses, veterinary techniques, etc.

Allied Pistols, Rifles and Grenades, by Peter Chamberlain and Terry Gander, Arco Publ. Co., NY, 1977. 64 pp., illus. Paper covers. $4.95.
Describes and illustrates the subject items used by the Allied forces in WW II.

American Artillery in the Mexican War 1846-47, by Lester R. Dillon, Jr., Presidial Press, Austin, TX, 1975. 120 pp., illus. $7.95.
An in depth critical analysis of the crucial role played by artillery in the United States' victory in the Mexican War.

The American B.B. Gun, by A. T. Dunathan, A. S. Barnes, S. Brunswick, NJ, 1971. 154 pp., illus. $10.00.
Identification reference and a price guide for B.B. guns, plus a brief history and advertising plates.

American Game Birds of Field and Forest, by F. C. Edminster, Book Sales, NY, 1972 490 pp. 99 plates. $6.95.
18 species; their origin, history, range, food, diseases, etc.

Americans and their Guns, compiled by Jas. B. Trefethen, ed. by Jas. E. Serven, Stackpole Books, Harrisburg, PA, 1967. 320 pp., illus. $9.95.
The National Rifle Association of America story through nearly a century of service to the nation. More than a history—a chronical of help to novice and expert in the safe and proper use of firearms for defense and recreation, as well as a guide for the collector of arms.

Anti-Aircraft Guns, by Peter Chamberlain and Terry Gander, Arco Publ. Co., NY, 1976. 64 pp., illus. Paper covers. $4.95.
Surface-to-air guns of all the major combatants, together with their components and complete listing of main data points.

Anti-Tank Weapons, by Peter Chamberlain and Terry Gander, Arco publ. Co., NY, 1974. 64 pp., illus. Paper covers. $4.95.
Covers anti-tank guns, rifles, mines and grenades, plus such recoilless weapons as the bazooka and the German Panzerfaust.

Archer's Digest, 2nd ed., ed. by Jack Lewis, DBI Books, Inc., Northfield, IL, 1977. 288 pp., illus. Paper covers. $7.95.
The latest technical data on compound bows plus essential chapters on equipment selection, tactics for bowhunting and fishing.

Archery: Its Theory and Practice, by H. A. Ford. Geo. Shumway, York, PA, 1971. 128 pp., illus. $10.00.
Reprint of the scarce 1856 ed.

Arco Gun Book, ed. by Larry Koller. Arco Publ. Co. Inc., NYC, 1962 397 pp., illus. $7.95.
A concise encyclopedia for arms collectors, shooters and hunters.

Armoured Forces, by R. M. Ogorkiewicz. Arco Pub. Co., NY, 1970. 475 pp., illus. Paper covers, $7.95.
A history of the armored forces and their vehicles.

Arms for Texas, by Michael J. Koury. The Old Army Press, Fort Collins, CO, 1973. 94 pp., illus. $7.50.
A study of the Republic of Texas guns.

Arms of the World: The 1911 Alfa Catalogue. Edited by Joseph J. Schroeder, Jr. Digest Books, Northfield, IL, 420 pg., Paper, $5.95.
Reprint in 4 languages of thousands of guns, cartridges, swords, helmets, tools, etc. Profusely illus., and priced the 1911 way.

The Art of Archerie, by Gervase Markham. A reprint of the 1634 original, publ. in London. Geo. Shumway, York, PA, 1968. 172 pp. $15.00.
This classic treatise, written to keep alive the art of archery in warfare, treats with the making of longbows and their use. A scholarly introduction to the new issue by S. V. Grancsay adds an enlightening historical perception.

The Art of Survival, by C. Troebst. Doubleday & Co., Garden City, NY. 1965. 312 pp. illus. $6.95. Paper covers. $3.50.
Narratives of devices of survival in difficult terrain or circumstances and evaluation of rescue and life-saving procedures.

Artillery, by O. F. G. Hogg, Archon Books, Hamden, CT. 1970. 330 pp., illus. $17.50.
Artillery, its origin, heyday, and decline.

Author and Subject Index to the American Rifleman Magazine 1971-1975, by W. R. Burrell, Galesburg, MI, 1973-75. 64 pp., Paper covers. $6.50.
Alphabetical listing by author, title and subject of this famous arms publication.

Automatic & Concealable Firearms Design Book Volume I, an anonymous work, Paladin Press, Boulder, CO, 1979. 32 pp., illus. Paper covers. $12.00.
Plans for ten weapons are presented, seven of which are totally improvised.

Automatic and Concealable Firearms Design Book, Volume II, an anonymous work, Paladin Press, Boulder, CO, 1980. 66 pp., illus. Paper covers. $12.00.
Firearms designed and hand-built by rural gunsmiths in the Phillipines from the end of WW II to the 1960's.

Axis Pistols, Rifles and Grenades, by Peter Chamberlain and Terry Gander, Arco Publ. Co., NY, 1977. 64 pp., illus. Paper covers. $4.95.
Photographs and descriptions of those arms used by the axis powers during WW II.

Baron von Steuben and his Regulations, by Joseph R. Riling, Ray Riling Arms Books Co., Philadelphia, Penna., 1966. 207 pp., illus. $20.00.
A documented book on this great American Major General and the creation by him of the first official "Regulations." Includes the complete facsimile of these regulations.

Beginner's Guide to Guns and Shooting, by Clair F. Rees, DBI Books, Inc., Northfield, IL, 1978. 224 pp., illus. Paper covers. $6.95.
Indispensible to the beginner, and an enlightening review for the seasoned sportsman.

Black Powder Gun Digest, 2nd ed., by Jack Lewis and Robert Springer, DBI Books, Inc., Northfield, IL, 1977. 288 pp., illus. Paper covers. $7.95.
A most comprehensive, authoritative book on black powder rifles, handguns, scatterguns and accessories.

Black Powder Guide 2nd ed., by George C. Nonte, Jr., Stoeger Publ. Co., So. Hackensack, NJ, 1976. 254 pp., illus. Paper covers. $6.95.
A complete guide to muzzle-loading rifles, pistols and shotguns—flintlock and percussion.

Black Powder Snapshots, by Herb Sherlock. Standard Publications. Huntington, W. VA, 50 pp., illus. $10.00.
Deluxe large volume containing 23 major Sherlock drawings and 95 punchy, marginal sketches.

The Book of the American Woodcock, by Wm. G. Sheldon, Ph.D. University of Mass. Press, Amherst, 1967. 227 pp., bibliography, appendices and index. $10.00

Brassey's Infantry Weapons of the World, 2nd Edition, edited by J. I. H. Owen, Brassey's Publishers Ltd., London, England, 1979. 480 pp., illus. $55.00.
Infantry weapons, including infantry support vehicles, and combat aids in current use by the regular and reserve forces of all nations.

Brassey's Infantry Weapons of the World 1950-1975, edited by Maj. Gen. J. I. H. Owen, Bonanza Books, NY, 1977. 323 pp., illus. $7.98.
Infantry weapons and combat aids in current use by the regular and reserve forces of all nations.

Brassey's NATO Infantry and Its Weapons, ed. by J. I. H. Owen, Westview Press, Boulder, CO, 1976. 194 pp., illus. $14.50.
Man-portable weapons and equipment in service with the regular and reserve forces.

Brassey's Warsaw Pact Infantry and Its Weapons, edited by J. I. H. Owen, Brassey's Publishers Ltd., London, England, 1976. 112 pp., illus. $11.95.
Man-portable weapons and equipment in service with the regular and reserve forces of the Warsaw Pact Nations.

The British Code of Duel, Richmond Publ. Co., Richmond, England, 1971. 144 pp. Reprint of the 1824 ed. Reference on the laws of honour and the character of gentlemen. Together with **The Art of Duelling,** same publ., 1971. 70 pp. Reprint of the 1836 London ed. Both books $11.50.
Information useful to young Continental tourists.

Carbine; The Story of David Marshall "Carbine" Williams, by Ross E. Beard, Jr., The Sandlapper Store, Inc., Lexington, SC, 1977. 315 pp., illus. Deluxe limited edition, numbered and signed by the author and "Carbine." $25.
The story of the man who invented the M1 Carbine and holds 52 other firearms patents.

Carbine Handbook, by Paul Wahl. Arco Publ. Co., N.Y.C., 1964. 80 pp., illus. $6.00. Paperbound, $4.95.
A manual and guide to the U.S. Carbine, cal. .30, M1, with data on its history, operation, repair, ammunition, and shooting.

The Code of Honor; or Rules for the Government of Principals and Seconds in Duelling, by John Lyde Wilson, Ray Riling Arms Books Co., Phila., PA, 1971. 48 pp. Paper, $3.50.
Reprint of the rare 1858 edition.

Colonial Riflemen in the American Revolution, by Joe D. Huddleston, George Shumway Publisher, York, PA, 1978. 70 pp., illus. $18.00.
This study traces the use of the longrifle in the Revolution for the purpose of evaluating what effects it had on the outcome.

The Complete Black Powder Handbook, by Sam Fadala, DBI Books, Inc., Northfield, IL, 1979. 288 pp., illus. Paper covers. $7.95.
Everything you want to know about black powder firearms and their shooting.

The Complete Book of Trapping, by George Clawson, Winchester Press, NY, 1977. 256 pp., illus. $8.95.
All about fur trapping—from the earliest days to today's humane and profitable methods of harvesting pelts.

The Complete Book of Trick and Fancy Shooting, by Ernie Lind, Winchester Press, NY, 1972. 159 pp., illus. $6.95.
Step-by-step instructions for acquiring the whole range of shooting skills with rifle, pistol and shotgun; includes practical hints on developing your own shooting act.

The Complete Cannoneer, by M. C. Switlik, Ray Russell Books, Rochester, MI, 1979. 174 pp., illus. $10.00.
Observations on muzzle loading cannon, plus a reprinting of the Regulations on artillery drill for 1861.

The Complete Illustrated Encyclopedia of the World's Firearms, by Ian V. Hogg, A & W Publishers, New York NY, 1978, 328 pp., illus. $24.95.
Military and civilian firearms from the beginnings to the present day... An A-Z directory of makes and makers from 1830.

The Complete Machine-Gun 1885 to the Present, by Ian V. Hogg and John Batchelor, Exeter Books, New York, NY, 1979. 128 pp., illus. $7.98.
Traces the history of the machine-gun and describes the various principles on which the guns operate and assesses the qualities of the individual weapons.

Confederate Cannon Foundries, by Larry Daniel and Riley Gunter, Pioneer Press, Union City, TN, 1977. 114 pp., illus. $12.95.
Covers every known foundry in the South in detail, and is very well illustrated.

Conquering the Frontiers, by James E. Serven, The Foundation Press, Tucson, AZ, 1974. 256 pp., illus. $19.95.
Stories of American pioneers and the guns which helped them establish a new life.

Coping with Camp Cooking, by M. W. Stephens and G. S. Wells. Stackpole Books, Harrisburg, PA 1966. 94 pp., illus., decorated boards. $2.95.
Hints and recipes selected from the editors' writings appearing in Camping Guide Magazine.

Dead Aim, by Lee Echols, Acme Printing Co., San Diego, CA, a reprint, 1972. 116 pp., illus. $6.00.
Nostalgic antics of hell-raising pistol shooters of the 1930s.

The Decorated Gun, by Carson Ritchie, A. S. Barnes & Co., New York, NY, 1980. 160 pp., illus. $15.00.
An extensively researched book on the sometimes elaborately decorated cannons of the 16th century.

The Deer of North America, by Leonard Lee Rue, Outdoor Life-Crown Publishers, New York, NY, 1979. 463 pp., illus. $12.95.
An illustrated guide to their lives, their world, their relations with man.

Description of U.S. Military Rifle Sights, by Edw. A. Tolosky, E. A. Tolosky, Publ., 1971. 117 pp. Paper, $8.50.
Covers period from 1861 to 1940. New and excellent work for collectors and fans of the U.S. Military. Definitive text, full-size line drawings.

The Diary of Colonel Peter Hawker, by Col. P. Hawker, Richmond Publ. Co., Richmond, England. 1971. 759 pp., illus. $21.95.
Reprint of the 1893 ed. covers shooting in every way and how to outwit your opponent!

Dictionary of Weapons & Military Terms, by John Quick, McGraw-Hill, NY, 1973. 515 pp., illus. $25.00.
Describes the principal weapons and weapon systems from ancient times to present day.

Eli Whitney and the Whitney Armory, by Merrill Lindsay, Arma Press, North Branford, CT, 1979. 95 pp., illus. Paper covers. $4.95. Cloth. $9.95.
History of the Whitney Armory 1767-1862, with notes on how to identify Whitney flintlocks.

The Encyclopedia of Infantry Weapons of World War II, by Ian V. Hogg, Harper & Row, New York, NY, 1977. 192 pp., illus. $15.95.
A fully comprehensive and illustrated reference work including every major type of weapon used by every army in the world during World War II.

Encyclopedia of Modern Firearms, Vol. 1, compiled and publ. by Bob Brownell, Montezuma, IA, 1959. 1057 pp. plus index, illus. $36.25. Dist. by Bob Brownell, Montezuma, IA 50171.
Massive accumulation of basic information of nearly all modern arms pertaining to "parts and assembly." Replete with arms photographs, exploded drawings, manufacturers' lists of parts, etc.

The Experts Book of the Shooting Sports, ed. by D. E. Petzal. Simon and Schuster, NY, 1972. 320 pp., illus. $9.95.
America's foremost shooting and hunting experts disclose the secrets of their specialties.

Famous Guns that Won the West, by James Wycoff, Arco Publ., Inc., NY, 1975. 112 pp., illus. Paper covers. $2.
A story about the pioneer guns that won the West and which made the West famous at the same time.

Firearms Control, by Colin Greenwood, Routledge & Kegan Paul, London (England), 1972. 274 pp. $13.50.
A study of armed crime and firearms control in England and Wales.

The Firearms Dictionary, by R. A. Steindler, Paladin Press, Boulder, CO, 1976. 288 pp., illus. Paper covers, $6.95. Cloth, $12.50.
The basic illustrated reference encyclopedia of gun language. Defines over 1800 English and foreign terms relating to firearms, ammunition, accessories and gun repairing techniques.

Firearms Encyclopedia, by George C. Nonte, Jr., Outdoor Life/Harper & Row, NY, 1973. 341 pp., illus. $17.95.
A to Zed coverage of gun and shooting terms, plus a complete appendix of useful information and an index.

Firearm Silencers, by D. B. McLean. Anubus Press, Houston, TX, 1968. 123 pp., illus., paperbound. $7.95.
The history, design, and development of silencers for U.S. military firearms.

Firearms, Traps & Tools of the Mountain Men, by Carl P. Russell. A. A. Knopf, NY, 1967. 448 pp., illus. in line drawings. Paper covers. $6.95.
Detailed survey of fur traders' equipment in the early days of the west.

Game and Bird Calling by A. C. Becker, Jr., A. S. Barnes and Co., NY, 1972. 147 pp., illus. $4.95.
Discusses various types of calls and techniques used by hunters—tyros and professionals.

Game and Fish Cookbook, by H. and J. Barnett. Grossman Publ., New York, NY 1968. 162 pp., illus. $7.95.
Special culinary attention to fish and game, with interesting and different touches.

Game in the Kitchen, by B. Flood and W. C. Roux (eds.). Barre Publ., Barre, MA 1st ed., 1968, 234 pp., illus. $7.50.
A fish and game cookbook, with menus and information on preservation, cooking and serving.

German Infantry Weapons of World War II, by A. J. Barker. Arco Publ. Co., New York, NY 1969, 76 pp., illus. $5.00.
Historical and statistical data on all types of the subject weapons, ammunition, etc.

Giving up the Gun; Japan's Reversion to the Sword 1543-1879, by Noel Perrin, David R. Godine Publishers, Boston, MA, 1978. 112 pp., illus. $8.95.
A technically sophisticated civilization who voluntarily decided to revert to an earlier, less advanced military weapon.

Grandi Incisioni Su Armi D'Oggi, by Mario Abbiatico, Gianoberto Lupi, and Franco Vacarri, Editoriale Olimpia, Brescia, Italy, 1977. 290 pp., illus. $35.00.
The work of forty Italian engravers is represented in this magnificent work on great gun engraving of today. **Italian text.**

Guide to United States Machine Guns, by K. F. Schreier, Jr., Normount Armament Co., Wickenburg, AZ, 1971. 178 pp., illus. Paper, $4.95.
All machine guns procured by the U.S. Armed Forces and some of an experimental nature.

Gun Carriages: An Aide Memoire to the Military Sciences, 1846, by R. J. Nelson. Museum Restoration Service, Ottawa, Canada, 1972. 64 pp. Paper covers. $3.00.
Originally prepared in 1846 as a manual for the officers of the British Army. Illus. with detailed scaled drawings, plus tables of dimensions and weights.

Gun Control, by Robert J. Kukla, Stackpole Books, Harrisburg, PA, 1973. 448 pp., illus. Paper cover $4.95.
A written record of the efforts to eliminate the private possession of firearms in America.

Gun Digest Book of Metallic Silhouette Shooting, by Elgin Gates, DBI Books, Inc., Northfield, IL, 1979. 256 pp., illus. Paper Covers. $6.95.
Examines all aspects of this fast growing sport including history, rules and meets.

The Gun Digest, 1981, 35th Edition, edited by Ken Warner, DBI Books, Inc., Northfield, IL, 1980. 448 pp., illus. Paper covers. $9.95.
The world's greatest gun book in its 35th annual edition.

Gun Digest Book of Gun Accessories, by Joseph Schroeder and the editors of Gun Digest, DBI Books, Inc., Northfield, IL, 1980. 288 pp., illus. Paper covers. $8.95.
The first single source reference for gun related items ever published.

Gun Digest Book of Modern Gun Values, 2nd ed., by Jack Lewis, DBI Books, Inc., Northfield, IL, 1978. 288 pp., illus. $7.95.
Invaluable guide for buying, selling, trading or identifying guns—handguns, rifles and shotguns are covered in separate sections. Feature articles relate to collecting and values.

Gun Digest Book of Exploded Firearms Drawings 2nd Edition, edited by Harold A. Murtz, DBI Books, Inc., Northfield, IL, 1978. 320 pp., illus. Paper covers. $7.95.
Hundreds of exploded drawings of modern and collector's firearms.

Gun Digest Treasury, 5th Edition, edited by John T. Amber, DBI Books, Inc., Northfield, IL, 1977. 288 pp., illus. Paper covers. $7.95.
The best articles from the first 30 years of Gun Digest.

Gundogs, Their Care and Training, by M. Brander. A. & C. Black, London, Eng., 1969. 97 pp., illus. $4.95.

Gun Fun with Safety, by G. E. Damon. Standard Publications, Huntington, W. VA, 1947. 206 pp., well illus. $6.00.
A long out-of-print work that is still much sought. A fine general coverage of arms and ammunition, old and new, with chapters on shooting, targets, etc., with safety always upper-most.

Gun Talk, edited by Dave Moreton. Winchester Press, NY, 1973. 256 pp., illus. $9.95.
A treasury of original writing by the top gun writers and editors in America. Practical advice about every aspect of the shooting sports.

The Gun That Made the Twenties Roar, by Wm. J. Helmer, rev. and enlarged by George C. Nonte, Jr., The Gun Room Press, Highland Park, NJ, 1977. Over 300 pp., illus. $16.95.
Historical account of John T. Thompson and his invention, the infamous "Tommy Gun."

The Gunfighter, Man or Myth? by Joseph G. Rosa, Oklahoma Press, Norman, OK, 1969. 229 pp., illus., (including weapons). $9.95.
A well-documented work on gunfights and gunfighters of the West and elsewhere. Great treat for all gunfighter buffs.

The Gunfighters, by Dale T. Schoenberger, The Caxton Printers, Ltd., Caldwell, ID, 1971. 207 pp., illus. $12.95.
Startling expose of our foremost Western folk heroes.

Guns, by Dudley Pope. Delacorte Press, N.Y.C., 1965. 256 pp., illus. $9.98.
Concise history of firearms, stressing early museum-quality weapons. Includes small arms as well as artillery, naval, and airborne types. Fine photographs, many in color.

Guns and Ammo 1980 Annual, ed. by Ralph C. Glaze, Petersen Publ. Co., Los Angeles, CA, 1979. 320 pp., illus. Paper covers. $6.95.
Annual catalog of sporting firearms and accessories, with numerous articles for the gun enthusiast.

Guns & Ammo Guide to Guns for Home Defense, by Elmer Keith, et al, Petersen Publ. Co., Los Angeles, CA, 1975. 176 pp., illus. Paper covers. $3.95.
How to select a gun for home defense, and learning how to use it.
Guns and How They Work, by Ian V. Hogg, Everest House, New York, NY, 1979. 185 pp., illus. $16.95.
Acomprehensive guide to hand guns, from muzzle loaders to automatics, and how their mechanisms operate.
Guns Illustrated 1981, 13th Edition, edited by Harold A. Murtz, DBI Books, Inc., Northfield, IL, 1980. 288 pp., illus. Paper covers. $7.95.
Technical articles for gun enthusiasts plus a complete illustrated catalog of all current guns, ammunition and accessories including specifications and prices.
Guns; An Illustrated History of Artillery, ed. by Jos. Jobe, New York Graphic Society, Greenwich, CT, 1971. 216 pp., illus. $17.98.
Traces the history and technology of artillery from its beginnings in the 14th century to its 20th century demise in the face of aerial bombs and guided missiles.
The Guns of Harpers Ferry, by S. E. Brown Jr. Virginia Book Co., Berryville, VA, 1968. 157 pp., illus. $20.00.
Catalog of all known firearms produced at the U.S. armory at Harpers Ferry, 1798-1861, with descriptions, illustrations and a history of the operations there.
The Gunsmith in Colonial Virginia, by Harold B. Gill, Jr., University Press of Virginia, Charlottesville, VA, 1975. 200 pp., illus. Paper covers, $7.50; Cloth, $10.00.
The role of the gunsmith in colonial Virginia from the first landing at Jamestown through the Revolution is examined, with special attention to those who lived and worked in Williamsburg.
Handbook for Hythe, by H. Busk, Richmond Pub. Co., Richmond, England, 1971. 194 pp., illus. $12.50.
Reprint of the 1860 ed. explaining laws of projectiles with an introduction to the system of musketry.
Handbook of Self-Defense for Law Enforcement Officers, by John Martone. Arco Publ. Co., New York, NY, 1968. 1st ed., 4th printing, 111 pp., $4.00.
A clearly-illustrated manual on offensive and defensive techniques recommended for the use of policemen.
The Handy Sportsman, by Loring D. Wilson, Winchester Press, NY, 1976. 256 pp., illus. $10.95.
29 inexpensive, easy-to-build sporting accessories for the hunter and fisherman.
Hatcher's Notebook, by Maj. Gen. J. S. Hatcher. Stackpole Books, Harrisburg, Pa., 1952. 2nd ed. with four new chapters, 1957. 629 pp., illus. $13.95.
A dependable source of information for gunsmiths, ballisticians, historians, hunters, and collectors.
Hibbard, Spencer, Bartlett & Co. Catalog. American Reprints, St. Louis, MO, 1969. 92 pp., illus. Paper, $5.00.
Reprint of 1884 catalog on guns, rifles, revolvers, ammo, powder flasks, etc. Descriptions and contemporary prices.
A History of Artillery, by Col. H. C. B. Rogers, The Citadel Press, Secaucus, NJ. 1975. 230 pp., illus. $7.95.
Traces the entire history of artillery, its use in sieges, in the field and at sea.
A History of Firearms, by Major Hugh B. C. Pollard, Burt Franklin, NY, a facsimile ed. with a new introduction by Joseph R. Riling, 1973. 320 pp., illus. $25.50.
An excellent survey of the development of hand firearms. Lists over 2,000 American and foreign gunmakers.
A History of Marksmanship, by Charles Chenevix Trench, Follett Publ. Co., Chicago, IL, 1972. 319 pp., illus. $12.95.
A complete and wide-ranging survey of the marksman and his weapons, in peace and in war.
Home Book of Taxidermy and Tanning, by G. J. Grantz, Stackpole Books, Harrisburg, PA, 1969, 160 pp., illus. $7.95.
Amateur's primer on mounting fish, birds, animals, and trophies.
Home Guide to Muzzle Loaders, by Geo. C. Nonte, Jr., Stackpole Books, Harrisburg, PA, 1974. 219 pp., illus. $6.95.
From the basics of muzzle loading, its ammo, to the differences between the modern and replica muzzle loader, plus how-to-make one.
How to Build Your Home in the Woods, by Bradford Angier, Stackpole Books, Harrisburg, PA, 1967, 310 pp., illus. $8.95.
Detailed instructions on building cabins, shelters, etc., with natural materials. How to obtain food from nature, and how to live in the wilderness in comfort.
How to Cook His Goose (and other wild game), by Karen Green and Betty Black, Winchester Press, NY, 1973. 198 pp. Paper covers, $3.95; cloth, $6.95.
An informative and delightful guide to preparing and cooking game of all types.
How Terrorists Kill, by J. David Truby, Paladin Press, Boulder, CO, 1978. 87 pp., illus. Paper covers. $6.
The complete terrorist arsenal.
The Identification and Registration of Firearms, by Vaclav "Jack" Krcma, C. C. Thomas, Springfield, IL, 1971. 173 pp., illus. $17.50.
Analysis of problems and improved techniques of recording firearms data accurately.
The Illustrated Book of Guns and Rifles, edited by Frederick Wilkinson, Hamlyn Publishing Group Ltd., London, England, 1979. 191 pp., illus. $10.98.
A wide-ranging and fascinating study of the longarm weapons of the soldier and sportsman.
The Illustrated Book of Pistols, edited by Frederick Wilkinson, Hamlyn Publishing Group Ltd., London, England, 1979. 191 pp., illus. $10.98.
A description of the pistol's evolution and use both in peace and war.
Instructions to Young Sportsmen: Guns and Shooting, by Col. P. Hawker, Richmond Publ. Co., Richmond, England, 1971. 507 pp., illus. $19.95.
Reprint of the 1833 British work on guns, shooting and killing game.
The International Arms Review 2, ed. by John Olson, Jolex, Inc., Oakland, NJ, 1979. 299 pp., illus. Paper covers. $6.95.
Interesting reading for those interested in weaponry, whether he be student, or collector, or someone whose occupation is largely based on the use of firearms.
Kill or Get Killed, by Col. Rex Applegate, new rev. and enlarged ed., Paladin Press, Boulder, CO, 1976. 421 pp., illus. $15.95.
For police and military forces. Last word on mob control.
Kuhlhoff on Guns, by Pete Kuhlhoff, Winchester Press, NY, 1970. 180 pp., illus. $5.95.
A selection of firearms articles by the late Gun Editor of *Argosy* Magazine.
Law Enforcement Bible, ed. by Robert A. Scanlon, Stoeger Publishing Co., South Hackensack, NJ, 1978. 480 pp., illus. Paper covers. $7.95.
The world's standard law enforcement reference book. Much on combat shooting and combat speed reloading.
Law Enforcement Handgun Digest, 3rd Edition, by Jack Lewis, DBI Books, Inc., Northfield, IL, 1980. 288 pp., illus. Paper covers. $8.95.
Covers such subjects as the philosophy of a firefight, SWAT, weapons, training, combat shooting, etc.
Limited War Sniping, by Pete Senich, Paladin Press, Boulder, CO, 1978. 150 pp., illus. $15.95.
The most complete pictorial history of modern war sniping ever compiled.
Lyman Muzzleloaders' Handbook, first ed., edited by C. Kenneth Ramage, Lyman Publ., Middlefield, CT, 1976. 248 pp., illus. Paper covers. $6.95.
A complete black powder catalog of all such rifles, pistols, shotguns, kits and accessories available today.

Marksmanship: Secrets of High Scoring from a World Champ, by Gary L. Anderson. Simon & Schuster, NY, 1972. 79 pp. $5.95.
Illus. step-by-step guide to target shooting. Covers equipment, ammunition, breath control, arm position, etc.
Marlin Catalog of 1897. A reprint in facsimile by the Rocky Mountain Investment and Antique Co.; Cheyenne, WY, 1969. 192 pp. Well illus., paper covers, $5.00.
All models are covered, cartridges, sights, engraving, accessories, reloading tools, etc.
Marlin Catalog, 1905, Rocky Mountain Investment and Antique Co.; Cheyenne, WY, 1971. 128 pp. Paper, $5.00.
Reprint. Rifles, shotguns, pistols, tools, cartridge information, factory engraving and carving illustrated and described.
Medicolegal Investigation of Gunshot Wounds, by Abdullah Fatteh, J. B. Lippincott Co., Phila., PA, 1977. 272 pp., illus. $22.50.
A much-needed work, clearly written and easily understood, dealing with all aspects of medicolegal investigation of gunshot wounds and deaths.
Mexican Military Arms, The Cartridge Period, by James B. Hughes, Jr. Deep River Armory, Inc., Houston, TX, 1967. 135 pp., photos and line drawings. $4.50.
An interesting and useful work, in imprinted wrappers, covering the period from 1866 to 1967.
Modern Firearms, by Yves Cadiou and Alphonse Richard, William Morrow and Co., Inc., NY, 1977. 224 pp., illus. $19.95.
This excellently illustrated volume on the development of firearms concentrates on the evolution of modern handguns and rifles.
Naval Gun, by Ian Hogg and John Batchelor, Blandford Press, Dorset, England, 1978. 144 pp., illus. $24.95.
Traces history and development of the naval gun from the earliest days of the invention of gunpowder; from the 2-inch bore to the massive quadruple-mounted, 18-inch weapons of WW II.
The 1951 Gun Digest Commemorative 5th Edition, edited by John T. Amber, DBI Books, Inc., Northfield, IL, 1977. 224 pp., illus. Paper covers. $6.95.
A reprint of the classic 5th edition, the first edition edited by John T. Amber.
No Second Place Winner, by Wm. H. Jordan, publ. by the author, Shreveport, LA (Box 4072), 1962. 114 pp., illus. $7.50.
Guns and gear of the peace officer, ably discussed by a U.S. Border Patrolman for over 30 years, and a first-class shooter with handgun, rifle, etc.
North American Ducks, Geese, and Swans, by Donald S. Heintzelman, Winchester Press, NY, 1978. 224 pp., illus. $15.00.
An illustrated guide to all the species that inhabit or regularly visit North America.
North American FALS; Nato's Search for a Standard Rifle, by R. Blake Stevens, Collector Grade Publications, Dallas, TX, 1979. 220 pp., illus. $20.00.
The history and development of the FAL in North America from 1950 to 1976.
Olympic Shooting, by Colonel Jim Crossman, NRA, Washington, DC, 1978. 136 pp., illus. $12.95.
The complete, authoritative history of U.S. participation in the Olympic shooting events from 1896 until the present.
Outdoor Life Gun Data Book, by F. Philip Rice, Harper & Row Publ., Inc., NY, 1975. 480 pp., illus. $11.95.
Packed with formulas, data, and tips essential to the modern hunter, target shooter, gun collector, and all others interested in guns.
Outdoor Tips, by L. W. Johnson, Robt. Elman & Jerry Gibbs. Benjamin Co., NY, 1972. 190 pp., illus. Paper covers. $2.95.
Authoritative chapters on American hunting, fishing, camping, other outdoor activities.
The Practical Book of Guns, by Ken Warner, Winchester Press, New York, NY, 1978. 261 pp., illus. $10.95.
A book that delves into the important things about firearms and their use.
Principles of Small Arms, by Major A. J. Barker, Paladin Press, Boulder, CO, 1977. 82 pp., illus. Paper covers. $4.00.
Covers stopping power of small arms bullets, construction and operation of automatic weapons; characteristics of pistols, rifles, and barrel, sights, ammunition design and development problems.
E. C. Prudhomme, Master Gun Engraver, A Retrospective Exhibition: 1946-1973, intro. by John T. Amber, The R. W. Norton Art Gallery, Shreveport, LA, 1973. 32 pp., illus., paper covers. $3.50.
Examples of master gun engraving by Jack Prudhomme.
The Quiet Killers II: Silencer Update, by J. David Truby, Paladin Press, Boulder, CO, 1979. 92 pp., illus. Paper covers. $6.00.
A unique and up-to-date addition to your silencer bookshelf.
Redbook of Used Gun Values, rev. 1979 ed., Publishers Dev. Corp., Skokie, IL, 1979. 130 pp. Paper covers. $3.95.
Today's values for commercial firearms, listed by manufacturer.
Remington Arms Revised Price-List, 1902. Arthur McKee, Northport, NY, n.d. 64 pp. Paper covers. $4.00.
Reprint, fully illustrated.
Remington Firearms, 1906 Catalog, Arthur McKee, Northport, NY, n.d., 48 pp., illus. Paper covers. $4.00.
Reprint. Guns, parts, ammo., prices, etc.
The Reverend Alexander John Forsyth, 1768-1843, by John Reid, Fortress Publ., Inc., Stoney Creek, Ontario, Can., 1976. 38 pp., illus. $2.75.
A reprint of 19th Century book about the life of this inventor.
Sam Colt: Genius, by Robt. F. Hudson, American Archives Publ. Co., Topsfield, MA, 1971. 160 pp., illus. Plastic spiral bound. $6.50.
Historical review of Colt's inventions, including facsimiles of patent papers and other Colt information.
Scloppetaria, by Capt. H. Beaufroy, Richmond Publ. Co., Richmond, England, 1971. 251 pp. $14.00.
Reprint of the 1808 edition written under the pseudonym "A Corporal of Rilfemen". Covers rifles and rifle shooting, the first such work in English.

Shoot Out, by Tony Lesce, Desert Publications, Cornville, AZ, 1979. 81 pp., illus. Paper covers. $4.95.
A book which separates fact from fiction on the subject of combat and defensive shooting.
Shooter's Bible No.72, 1981 Edition, ed. by R. F. Scott, Stoeger Publ. Co., So. Hackensack, NJ, 1980. 575 pp., illus. Paper covers. $8.95.
Annually published guide to firearms, ammunition and accessories.
The Shooter's Guide: or Complete Sportsman's Companion, by B. Thomas, Richmond Publ. Co., Richmond, England, 1971. 264 pp., illus. $13.50.
Reprint of an 1816 British handbook on hunting small game, game laws, dogs, guns and ammunition.
The Shooter's Workbench, by John A. Mosher, Winchester Press, NY, 1977. 256 pp., illus. $10.95.
Accessories the shooting sportsman can build for the range, for the shop, for transport and the field, and for the handloading bench.
Shooting the Muzzle-Loaders, ed. by R. A. Steindler, J. Philip O'Hara, Inc., Chicago, IL, 1975. 224 pp., illus. Paper covers. $6.95.
A complete treatise on the muzzle-loader written by experts. Covers rifle, shotgun and pistol.
Small Arms of the World, 11th Edition, a complete revision of W. H. B. Smith's firearms classic by Edward Clinton Ezell, Stackpole Books, Harrisburg, PA, 1977. 667 pp., illus. $25.00.
A complete revision of this firearms classic now brings all arms enthusiasts up to date on global weapons production and use.
Sniping, by Ion L. Idreiess, Paladin Press, Boulder, CO, 1978. 120 pp., illus. Paper covers. $4.
Details the lonely, dangerous life of the bush sniper, and the techniques that bring him back alive.
Sporting Arms of the World, by Ray Bearse, Outdoor Life/Harper & Row, N.Y., 1977. 500 pp., illus. $15.95.
A mammoth, up-to-the-minute guide to the sporting world's favorite rifles, shotguns, handguns.
The Sportsman's Eye, by James Gregg, Winchester Press, NY, 1971. 210 pp., illus. $6.95.
How to make better use of your eyes in the outdoors.
The Story of the Guns, by Emerson Tennent. Richmond Publ. Co., Surrey, Eng., 1972. 364 pp. $11.50.
Reprint of the original 1864 London ed. Part I—The Rifled Musket, Part 2—Rifled Ordnance, Part 3—The Iron Navy.
The Survival Handbook, by W. K. Merrill. Winchester Press, NY, 1972. 320 pp., illus. $6.95.
How to stay out of trouble in all kinds of terrain and weather. Detailed advice on shelter, food and first aid for those caught unexpectedly in disaster situations.
Survival Guns, by Mel Tappan, The Janus Press, Inc., Los Angeles, CA, 1976. 458 pp., illus. Paper covers. $9.50.
A guide to the selection, modification and use of firearms and related devices for defense, food gathering, etc. under conditions of long term survival.
The S.W.A.T. Team Manual, by Capt. Robert Cappel, Paladin Press, Boulder, CO, 1979. 150 pp., illus. Paper covers. $10.00.
Covers theories, tactics, and training techniques as practiced by a first-rate SWAT team.
Technical Dictionary for Weapon Enthusiasts, Shooters and Hunters, by Gustav Sybertz. Publ. by J. Neumann-Neudamm, 3508 Melsungen, W. Germany, 1969, 164 pp., semi-soft covers. $12.50.
A German-English and English-German dictionary for the sportsman. An excellent handy work.
Training Your Own Bird Dog, by Henry P. Davis, G. P. Putnam's Sons, New York, NY. New rev. ed., 1969, 168 pp., plus 10 pp. of field trial records. Illus. with photographs. $6.95.
The reappearance of a popular and practical book for the beginner starting his first bird dog—by an internationally recognized authority.
Treasure Hunter's Digest, by Jack Lewis, DBI Books, Inc., Northfield, IL, 1975. 288 pp., illus. $7.95.
Tells where to go, how to find it, etc. with articles on techniques, legendary treasures and laws.
Treatise on Military Small Arms and Ammunition 1888, compiled by Col. J. Bond, R. A. Arms and Armour Press, London, Eng., 1971. 142 pp., illus. $12.50.
Facsimile of the original compiled in 1888 at the School of Musketry, Hythe, and accepted by the British Army as a definitive textbook.
Triggernometry, by Eugene Cunningham. Caxton Printers Lt., Caldwell, ID, 1970. 441 pp., illus. $9.95.
A classic study of famous outlaws and lawmen of the West—their stature as human beings, their exploits and skills in handling firearms. A reprint.
The True Book About Firearms, by R. H. Walton, Frederick Muller, Ltd., London, 1965. 143 pp., illus. $4.00.
How modern weapons work, are used and their effect on history.
Uniforms & Weapons of the Zulu War, by Christopher Wilkinson-Latham, Hippocrene Books, New York, NY, 1979. 96 pp., illus. $12.50.
The author analyzes in great detail the uniforms and weapons used by the British Army and the Colonial forces during the Zulu War.
Weapons: A Pictorial History, by Edwin Tunis, World Publ. Co., NY, 1972. 151 pp., illus. $3.95.
Arms through the ages—from the first stone thrown by prehistoric man to the super bombs and atomic weapons of our own day.
Weapons of the American Revolution, and Accoutrements, by Warren Moore. A & W Books, NY, 1974. 225 pp., fine illus. $15.
Revolutionary era shoulder arms, pistols, edged weapons, and equipment are described and shown in fine drawings and photographs, some in color.
The Webley-Fosbery Automatic Revolver. A reprint of the original undated booklet pupl. by the British makers. Deep River Armory, Houston, TX, 1968. 16 pp., illus., paper. $3.00.
An instruction manual, parts list and sales brochure on this scarce military handgun.
Wild Game Cookbook, by L. E. Johnson. Benjamin Co., NYC, 1968. 160 pp. $2.95.
Recipes, sauces, and cooking hints for preparation of all types of game birds and animals.
The Wilderness Route Finder, by C. Rutstrum, Macmillan Co., NY, 1970. 214 pp. Paper covers $1.95.
Complete guide to finding your way in the wilderness.
The Wildfowler's World, by Hanson Carroll and Nelson Bryant, Winchester Press, NY, 1973. 160 pp., illus. $12.95.
More than 100 breathtaking photographs, many in color, are included.
Wildlife Illustrated, by Ray Ovington, Digest Books, Inc., Northfield, IL. 1974. 8½"x11", 288 pp. Profusely illus. paperbound. $6.95.
Over 200 descriptions and sketches of North American game birds, animals and fishes. Covers lowland and upland game birds, small and large game animals, fresh- and saltwater fish with descriptions, habitat, and traits.
Wildwood Wisdom, by Ellsworth Jaeger. The Macmillan Company, New York, NY, 1964. 491 pp. well-illus. by author. $9.95.
An authoritative work, through many editions; about all there is to know about every detail for the outdoorsman.
Williams Blue Book of Gun Dealings 1977-78, publ. by Williams Gun Sight Co., Davison, MI, 1977. 111 pp., illus. Paper covers. $3.95.
Enlarged ed. of the modern guide to gun values.
World War II Small Arms, by John Weeks, Galahad Books, New York, NY, 1979. 144 pp., illus. $7.98.
The weapons of each of the major combatant nations: their production, history, design, technical features, and use in action.
The World of the White-Tailed Deer, by L. L. Rue III. J. B. Lippincott Co., Phila., 1967. A reprint. 137 pp., fine photos. $8.95.
An eminent naturalist-writer's account of the year-round activities of the white-tailed deer.
The World of the Wild Turkey, by J. C. Lewis. J. B. Lippincott Co., Phila., PA, 1973. 158 pp., illus. $8.95.
The author takes the reader into the wilderness world of the turkey's 6 surviving subspecies.
The World's Great Guns, by Frederick Wilkinson, The Hamlyn Publishing Group Ltd., London, England, 1977. 256 pp., illus. $9.95.
Story of the guns that have helped shape the course of history. Lavishly illustrated.
Your First Gun, by Roderick Willet, Seeley, Service & Co., London, England, 1975. 88 pp., illus. $7.50.
A useful handbook for those about to start shooting, young or old.
The World's Submachine Guns, Volume I, by Thomas B. Nelson, TBN Enterprises, Alexandria, VA, 1979. 747 pp., illus. $24.95.
Covers developments on submachine guns from 1915 to 1963.
The World's Machine Pistols & Submachine Guns, Volume IIa, by Thomas B. Nelson and Daniel D. Musgrave, TBN Enterprises, Alexandria, VA, 1980. 680 pp., illus. $24.95.
Covers developments in machine pistols and submachine guns from 1964-1980.

Gunsmithing

The Art of Engraving, by James B. Meek, F. Brownell & Son, Montezuma, IA, 1973. 196 pp., illus. $19.95.
A complete, authoritative, imaginative and detailed study in training for gun engraving. The first book of its kind—and a great one.
Artistry in Arms. The R. W. Norton Gallery, Shreveport, LA., 1970. 42 pp., illus. Paper, $3.50.
The art of gunsmithing and engraving.
Black Powder Gunsmithing, by Ralph T. Walker, DBI Books, Inc., Northfield, IL, 1978. 288 pp., illus. Paper covers. $7.95.
An overview of the entire subject from replica building to the advanced, intricate art of restoration.
Building the Kentucky Pistol, by James R. Johnston, Golden Age Arms Co., Worthington, OH, 1974. 36 pp., illus. Paper covers. $4.00.
A step-by-step guide for building the Kentucky pistol. Illus. with full page line drawings.
Building the Kentucky Rifle, by J. R. Johnston. Golden Age Arms Co., Worthington, OH, 1972. 44 pp., illus. Paper covers. $5.
How to go about it, with text and drawings.
Checkering and Carving of Gun Stocks, by Monte Kennedy. Stackpole Books, Harrisburg, PA, 1962. 175 pp., illus. $15.95.
Rev., enlarged clothbound ed. of a much sought-after, dependable work.
The Complete Rehabilitation of the Flintlock Rifle and Other Works, by T. B. Tryon. Limbo Library, Taos, NM, 1972. 112 pp., illus. Paper covers. $6.95.
A series of articles which first appeared in various issues of the *American Rifleman* in the 1930s.
Contemporary American Stockmakers, by Ron Toews, Dove Press, Enid, OK, 1979. 215 pp., illus. $75.00.
A limited edition, signed and numbered, illustrating and describing the work of some of America's top stockmakers.
Do-It-Yourself Gunsmithing, by Jim Carmichel, Outdoor Life-Harper & Row, New York, NY, 1977. 371 pp., illus. $13.95.
The author proves that home gunsmithing is relatively easy and highly satisfying.
Firearms Blueing and Browning, by R. H. Angier. Stackpole Books, Harrisburg, PA, 151 pp., illus. $9.95.
A useful, concise text on chemical coloring methods for the gunsmith and mechanic.
Gun Care and Repair, by Monte Burch, Winchester Press, NY, 1978. 256 pp., illus. $10.95.
Everything the gun owner needs to know about home gunsmithing and firearms maintenance.
Gun Digest Book of Firearms Assembly/Disassembly Part I: Automatic Pistols, by J. B. Wood, DBI Books, Inc., Northfield, IL, 1979. 320 pp., illus. Paper covers. $8.95.
A thoroughly professional presentation on the art of pistol disassembly and reassembly. Covers most modern guns, popular older models, and some of the most complex pistols ever produced.
Gun Digest Book of Firearms Assembly/Disassembly Part II: Revolvers, by J. B. Wood, DBI Books, Inc., Northfield, IL, 1979. 320 pp., illus. Paper covers. $8.95.
How to properly dismantle and reassemble both the revolvers of today and of the past.
The Gun Digest Book of Firearms Assembly/Disassembly Part III: Rimfire Rifles, by J. B. Wood, DBI Books, Inc., Northfield, IL, 1980. 288 pp., illus. Paper covers. $8.95.
A most comprehensive, uniform, and professional presentation available for disassembling and reassembling most rimfire rifles.
The Gun Digest Book of Firearms Assembly/Disassembly Part IV: Centerfire Rifles, by J. B. Wood, DBI Books, Inc., Northfield, IL, 1980. 288 pp., illus. Paper covers. $8.95.
A professional presentation on the assembly and reassembly of centerfire rifles.
The Gun Digest Book of Pistolsmithing, by Jack Mitchell, DBI Books, Inc., Northfield, IL, 1980. 288 pp., illus. Paper covers. $8.95.
An experts guide to the operation of each of the handgun actions with all the major functions of pistolsmithing explained.
Gun Owner's Book of Care, Repair & Improvement, by Roy Dunlap, Outdoor Life-Harper & Row, NY, 1974. 336 pp., illus. $12.95.
A basic guide to repair and maintenance of guns, written for the average firearms owner.

Gunsmith Kinks, by F. R. (Bob) Brownell. F. Brownell & Son., Montezuma, I. 1st ed., 1969. 496 pp., well illus. $9.95.
A widely useful accumulation of shop kinks, short cuts, techniques and pertinent comments by practicing gunsmiths from all over the world.

The Gunsmith's Manual, by J. Stelle and W. Harrison, Rutgers Book Center, Highland Park, NJ, 1972. 376 pp., illus. $9.95.
Exact reprint of the original. For the American gunsmith in all branches of the trade.

Gunsmithing, by Roy F. Dunlap. Stackpole Books, Harrisburg, PA, 714 pp., illus. $16.95.
Comprehensive work on conventional techniques, incl. recent advances in the field. Valuable to rifle owners, shooters, and practicing gunsmiths.

Gunsmiths and Gunmakers of Vermont, by Warren R. Horn, The Horn Co., Burlington, VT, 1976. 76 pp., illus. Paper covers. $5.00.
A checklist for collectors, of over 200 craftsmen who lived and worked in Vermont up to and including 1900.

Hand Forging the Muzzle Loading Gun Lock, by "Pryor Mt." Bill Newton, Bill Newton, Deaver, WY, 1978. 38 pp., illus. Paper covers. $6.95.
A brief history of the gun lock with directions for forging your own.

Hobby Gunsmithing, by Ralph Walker, Digest Books, Inc., Northfield, IL, 1972, 320 pp., illus. Paper, $6.95.
Kitchen table gunsmithing for the budding hobbyist.

Home Gun Care & Repair, by P. O. Ackley. Stackpole Books, Harrisburg, PA, 1969. 191 pp., illus. Paper covers. $4.95.
Basic reference for safe tinkering, fixing, and converting rifles, shotguns, handguns.

Home Gunsmithing Digest, 2nd ed., by Robt. Steindler, DBI Books, Inc., Northfield, IL, 1978, 288 pp., very well illus. within stiff decorated paper covers. $7.95.
An unusually beneficial assist for gun owners doing their own repairs, maintenance, etc. Many chapters on tools, techniques and theories.

HOW . . . by L. Cowher, W. Hunley, and L. Johnston. NMLR Assn., IN, 1961. 107 pp., illus. Paper covers. $3.95.
This 1961 rev. ed., enlarged by 3 chapters and additional illustrations, covers the building of a muzzle-loading rifle, target pistol, and powder horn, and tells how to make gunflints.

"How to Build Your Own Wheellock Rifle or Pistol", by Georg Lauber, The John Olson Co., Paramus, NJ, 1976. Paper covers. $6.95.
Complete instructions on building these arms.

"How to Build Your Own Flintlock Rifle or Pistol", by Georg Lauber, The John Olson Co., Paramus, NJ, 1976. Paper covers. $6.95.
The second in Mr. Lauber's three-volume series on the art and science of building muzzle-loading black powder firearms.

"How to Build Your Own Percussion Rifle or Pistol", by Georg Lauber, The John Olson Co., Paramus, NJ, 1976. Paper covers, $6.95.
The third and final volume of Lauber's set of books on the building of muzzle-loaders.

Lock, Stock and Barrel, by R. H. McCrory. Publ. by author at Bellmore, NY, 1966. Paper covers, 122 pp., illus. $5.00.
A handy and useful work for the collector or the professional with many helpful procedures shown and described on antique gun repair.

The Modern Kentucky Rifle, How to Build Your Own, by R. H. McCrory. McCrory, Wantagh, NY, 1961. 68 pp., illus., paper bound. $5.00.
A workshop manual on how to fabricate a flintlock rifle. Also some information on pistols and percussion locks.

The NRA Firearms Assembly Guidebook to Shoulder Arms. National Rifle Assn., Wash., D.C., 1973. 203 pp. Paper covers. $4.
Text and illus. explaining the takedown of 96 rifles and shotguns, domestic and foreign.

The NRA Firearms Assembly Guidebook to Handguns. National Rifle Assn., Wash., D.C., 1973, 206 pp. Paper covers. $4.
Illus. articles on the takedown of 101 pistol and revolver models.

The NRA Gunsmithing Guide, National Rifle Association, Wash., DC, 1971. 336 pp., illus. Paper. $5.50.
Information of the past 15 years from the "American Rifleman," ranging from 03A3 Springfields to Model 92 Winchesters.

Pistolsmithing, by George C. Nonte, Jr., Stackpole Books, Harrisburg, PA, 1974. 560 pp., illus. $17.95.
A single source reference to handgun maintainence, repair, and modification at home, unequaled in value.

Professional Gunsmithing, by W. J. Howe, Stackpole Books, Harrisburg, PA, 1968 reprinting. 526 pp., illus. $17.95.
Textbook on repair and alteration of firearms, with detailed notes on equipment and commercial gunshop operation.

Recreating the American Rifle, by Wm. Buchel & Geo. Shumway, George Shumway, York, PA, 1973. 194 pp. illus. Paper $10.00.
A new edition with additional illustrations showing the workmanship of today's skilled rifle-makers.

Respectfully Yours H. M. Pope, compiled and edited by G. O. Kelver, Brighton, CO, 1976. 266 pp., illus. $16.50.
A compilation of letters from the files of the famous barrelmaker, Harry M. Pope.

The Trade Gun Sketchbook, by Charles E. Hanson, The Fur Press, Chadron, NB, 1979. 48 pp., illus. Paper covers. $4.00.
Complete full-size plans to build seven different trade guns from the Revolution to the Indian Wars and a two-thirds size for your son.

The Trade Rifle Sketchbook, by Charles E. Hanson, The Fur Press, Chadron, NB, 1979. 48 pp., illus. Paper covers. $4.00.
Includes full scale plans for ten rifles made for Indian and mountain men; from 1790 to 1860, plus plans for building three pistols.

Troubleshooting Your Handgun, by J. B. Wood, DBI Books, Inc., Northfield, IL, 1978. 192 pp., illus. Paper covers. $5.95.
A masterful guide on how to avoid trouble and how to operate guns with care.

Troubleshooting Your Rifle and Shotgun, by J. B. Wood, DBI Books, Inc., Northfield, IL, 1978. 192 pp., illus. Paper covers. $5.95.
A gunsmiths advice on how to keep your long guns shooting.

handguns

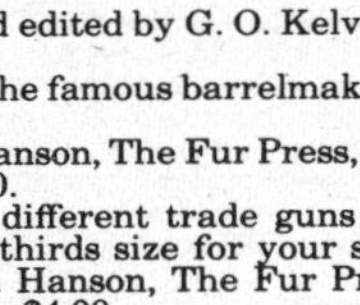

American Pistol and Revolver Design and Performance, by L. R. Wallack, Winchester Press, NY, 1978. 224 pp., illus. $13.95.
How different types and models of pistols and revolvers work, from trigger pull to bullet impact.

Automatic Firearm Pistols, by Elmer Swanson, Wesmore Book Co., Weehawken, NJ. 1st (and only) ed. 1955, 210 pp., well illus. $20.00.
A veritable catalog exclusively on automatic handguns for collectors, with many line drawings and descriptions, plus then-market market values of each.

Blue Steel and Gun Leather, by John Bianchi, Beinfeld Publishing, Inc., No. Hollywood, CA, 1978. 200 pp., illus. $9.95.
A complete and comprehensive review of holster uses plus an examination of available products on today's market.

Book of Pistols & Revolvers, by W. H. B. Smith. Stackpole Books, Harrisburg, PA, 1968. 758 pp., profusely illus. $7.98.
Rev. and enlarged, this encyclopedic reference, first publ. in 1946, continues to be the best on its subject.

Browning Hi-Power Pistols. Anubus Press, Houston, TX, 1968. 48 pp., illus., paperbound. $3.00.
A handbook on all models of Browning Hi-Power Pistols, covering their use, maintenance and repair.

Colt Automatic Pistols, by Donald B. Bady, Borden Publ. Co., Alhambra, CA, 1974. 368 pp., illus. $15.
The rev. and enlarged ed. of a key work on a fascinating subject. Complete information on every automatic marked with Colt's name.

The Colt .45 Auto Pistol, compiled from U. S. War Dept. Techinical Manuals, and reprinted by Desert Publications, Cornville, AZ, 1978. 80 pp., illus. Paper covers. $4.95.
Covers every facet of this famous pistol from mechanical training, manual of arms, disassembly, repair and replacement of parts.

Combat Handgun Shooting, by James D. Mason, Charles C. Thomas, Springfield, IL, 1976. 256 pp., illus. $27.50.
Discusses in detail the human as well as the mechanical aspects of shooting.

Combat Handguns, edited by Edward C. Ezell, Stackpole Books, Harrisburg, PA, 1980. 288 pp., illus. $17.95.
George Nonte's last great work, edited by Edward C. Ezell. A comprehensive reference volume offering full coverage of automatic handguns vs. revolvers, custom handguns, combat autoloaders and revolvers—domestic and foreign, and combat testing.

Combat Shooting for Police, by Paul B. Weston. Charles C. Thomas, Springfield, IL, 1967. A reprint. 194 pp., illus. $13.95.
First publ. in 1960 this popular self-teaching manual gives basic concepts of defensive fire in every position.

The Complete Handgun 1300 to the Present, by Ian V. Hogg and John Batchelor, Exeter Books, New York, NY, 1979. 128 pp., illus. $7.98.
The full story of the development of the handgun from its earliest crude form.

Defensive Handgun Effectiveness, by Carroll E. Peters, Carroll E. Peters, Manchester, TN, 1977. 198 pp., charts and graphs. $10.00.
A systematic approach to the design, evaluation and selection of ammunition for the defensive handgun.

Famous Automatic Pistols and Revolvers Volume 2, ed. by John Olson, Jolex, Inc., Oakland, NJ, 1979. 270 pp., illus. Paper covers. $6.95.
A fully illustrated guide to thirty-seven models of automatic pistols. Contains instructions for disassembly and assembly and exploded views of most arms.

Flattops & Super Blackhawks, by H. W. Ross, Jr., H. W. Ross, Jr., Bridgeville, PA, 1979. 93 pp., illus. Paper covers. $9.75.
An expanded version of the authors book "Ruger Blackhawks" with an extra chapter on Super Blackhawks and the Mag-Na-Ports with serial numbers and approximate production dates.

German Pistols and Revolvers 1871-1945, by Ian V. Hogg, A. & W. Books, NY, 1975. 160 pp., illus. $20.00.
Over 160 photos and drawings showing each gun, plus exploded views, markings, firms, patents, mfg. codes, etc.

Guns Annual Book of Handguns, ed. by Jerome Rakusan, Publishers' Dev. Corp., Skokie, IL, 1974. 98 pp., illus., paper covers. $3.95.
Complete catalog listing all latest models and articles dealing with handguns.

A Handbook on the Primary Identification of Revolvers & Semi-automatic Pistols, by John T. Millard, Charles C. Thomas, Springfield, IL, 1974. 156 pp., illus. $12.50.
A practical outline on the simple, basic phases of primary firearm identification with particular reference to revolvers and semi-automatic pistols.

The Handgun, by Geoffrey Boothroyd, Outlet Publ. Co., NY, 1978. 564 pp., illus. $10.98.
A comprehensive and detailed study of the handgun, from the earliest types to the revolvers and automatics of today.

Handgun Competition, by Maj. Geo. C. Nonte, Jr., Winchester Press, NY, 1978. 288 pp., illus. $12.95.
A comprehensive source-book covering all aspects of modern competitive pistol and revolver shooting.

Handguns Americana, by De Witt Sell. Borden Publ. Co., Alhambra, CA, 1972. 160 pp., illus. $8.50.
The pageantry of American enterprise in providing handguns suitable for both civilian needs and military purposes.

High Standard Automatic Pistols 1932-1950, by Charles E. Petty, American Ordnance Publ., Charlotte, NC, 1976. 124 pp., illus. $12.95.
A definitive source of information for the collector of High Standard pistols.

Home Gunsmithing the Colt Single Action Revolvers, by Loren W. Smith, Ray Riling Arms Books Co., Phila., PA, 1971. 119 pp., illus. $7.95.
Detailed, information on the operation and servicing of this famous and historic handgun.

The Inglis-Browing Hi-Power Pistol, by R. Blake Stevens, Museum Rest. Serv., Ottawa, Can., 1974. 28 pp., illus. Paper covers. $2.00.
The history of this scarce gun and its variations.

Japanese Hand Guns, by F. E. Leithe, Borden Publ. Co., Alhambra, CA, 1968. Unpaginated, well illus. $9.95.
Identification guide, covering models produced since the late 19th century. Brief text material gives history, descriptions, and markings.

Jeff Cooper on Handguns, by Jeff Cooper, Petersen Publishing Co., Los Angeles, CA, 1979. 96 pp., illus. Paper covers. $2.50.
An expert's guide to handgunning. Technical tips on actions, sights, loads, grips, and holsters.

Know Your 45 Auto Pistols—Models 1911 & A1, by E. J. Hoffschmidt, Blacksmith Corp., Stamford, CT, 1974. 58 pp., illus. Paper covers. $4.95.
A concise history of the gun with a wide variety of types and copies illus.

Know Your Walther P.38 Pistols, by E. J. Hoffschmidt, Blacksmith Corp., Stamford, CT, 1974. 77 pp., illus. Paper covers. $4.95.
Covers the Walther models, Armee, M.P., H.P., P-38—history and variations.

Know Your Walther P.P. & P.P.K. Pistols, by E. J. Hoffschmidt, Blacksmith Corp., Stamford, CT, 1975. 87 pp., illus. Paper covers. $4.95.
A concise history of the guns with a guide to the variety and types.

Law Enforcement Handgun Digest, Third Edition, by Dean A. Grennell, DBI Books, Inc., Northfield, IL, 1980. 320 pp., illus. Paper covers. $8.95.
The most comprehensive and up-to-date guide to arms and equipment for law enforcement.

The Luger Pistol (Pistole Parabellum), by F. A. Datig. Borden Publ. Co., Alhambra, CA, 1962. 328 pp., well illus. $9.50.
An enlarged, rev. ed. of an important reference on the arm, its history and development from 1893 to 1945.

Luger Variations, by Harry E. Jones, Harry E. Jones, Torrance, CA, 1975. 328 pp., 160 full page illus., many in color. $22.50.
A rev. ed. of the book known as "The Luger Collector's Bible."

Lugers at Random, by Charles Kenyon, Jr. Handgun Press, Chicago, IL. 1st ed., 1970. 416 pp., profusely illus. $20.00.
An impressive large side-opening book carrying throughout alternate facing-pages of descriptive text and clear photographs. A new boon to the Luger collector and/or shooter.

Lugers Unlimited, by F. G. Tilton, World-Wide Gun Reports, Inc., Aledo, IL, 1965. 49 pp., illus. Paper covers $2.00.
An excellent monograph about one of the most controversial pistols since the invention of hand firearms.

Mauser Pocket Pistols 1910-1946, by Roy G. Pender, Collectors Press, Houston, TX, 1971. 307 pp., $14.50.
Comprehensive work covering over 100 variations, including factory boxes and manuals. Over 300 photos. Limited, numbered ed.

The Mauser Self-Loading Pistol, by Belford & Dunlap. Borden Publ. Co., Alhambra, CA. Over 200 pp., 300 illus., large format. $12.50.
The long-awaited book on the "Broom Handles," covering their inception in 1894 to the end of production. Complete and in detail: pocket pistols, Chinese and Spanish copies, etc.

Ed McGiverns' Book of Fast & Fancy Revolver Shooting, by Ed McGivern, Anniversary ed., Follett Publ. Co., Chicago, IL, 1975. 484 pp., illus. $15.00.
A facsimile of the much-sought-after classic by the dean of revolver shooters.

The Military Four, by Claude V. Holland. C. V. Holland, Bonita Springs, FL, 1972. 64 pp., illus. Paper covers. $3.50.
Technical data, photographs and history of the Luger, Colt, P-38 and Mauser broomhandle pistols.

Military Pistols and Revolvers, by I. V. Hogg. Arco Pub. Co., NY, 1970. 80 pp., illus. $3.50.
The handguns of the two World Wars shown in halftone illus., with brief historical and descriptive text.

The Modern Handgun, by Robert Hertzberg, A&W Books, NY, 1974. 112 pp., well illus. $3.50.
Pistols and revolvers of all types are traced from their beginnings. Data on modern marksmanship included.

The Official U.S. Army Pistol Marksmanship Guide, first authorized repro. of original U.S. Army work. J&A Publ., NY, 1972. 144 pp., illus. Paper covers. $6.50.
Every detail from sight alignment to International Pistol programs—technical and fundamental for championship shooting in easy-to-read illus. form.

The Original Mauser Automatic Pistol, Model 1930, a reprint by Harold C. Bruffett, Croswell, MI, 1973. 32 pp., illus., paper covers. $2.50.
Facsimile of the 1931 English-text export catalog on the "Broom Handle Mauser."

The "Parabellum" Automatic Pistol, Stoeger Publ. Co., S. Hackensack, NJ, 49 pp. plus three fold out tables. $2.00.
An exact reproduction of the instruction book issued in English by the original Luger manufacturer "Deutsche Waffen and Munitionsfabriken, Berlin."

The Pistol Guide, by George C. Nonte, Stoeger Publ. Co., So. Hackensack, NJ, 1980. 256 pp., illus. Paper covers. $7.95.
A unique and detailed examination of a very specialized type of gun: the autoloading pistol.

Pistol and Revolver Digest 2nd Edition, ed. by Dean A. Grennell & Jack Lewis, DBI Books, Inc., Northfield, IL, 1979. 288 pp., illus. Paper covers. $7.95.
Articles on reloading, maintenance and repairs, handguns for silhouette shooting, handgunning for big game, new developments in handguns and handgun ammo, etc.

Pistol & Revolver Guide, 3rd Ed., by George C. Nonte, Follett Publ. Co., Chicago, IL, 1975. 224 pp., illus. Paper covers. $6.95.
A new and up-dated ed. of the standard reference work on military and sporting handguns.

Pistol Shooting as a Sport, by Hans Standl, Crown Publ., Inc., NY, 1976. 117 pp., illus. $5.95.
A guide to expert target shooting with special emphasis on Olympic requirements.

Pistols: A Modern Encyclopedia, by Henry M. Stebbins, Castle Books, NY, 1976. 380 pp., illus. $5.98.
Comprehensive coverage of handguns for every purpose, with material on selection, ammunition and marksmanship.

Pistols of the World, by Ian V. Hogg and John Weeks, Arms and Armour Press, London, England, 1978. 304 pp., illus. $24.95.
A comprehensive illustrated encyclopedia of the world's pistols and revolvers from 1870 to the present day.

Quick or Dead, by William L. Cassidy, Paladin Press, Boulder, CO, 1978. 178 pp., illus. $10.95.
Close-quarter combat firing, with particular reference to prominent twentieth-century British and American methods of instruction.

Report of Board on Tests of Revolvers and Automatic Pistols. From The *Annual Report* of the Chief of Ordnance, 1907. Reprinted by J. C. Tillinghast, Marlow, NH, 1969. 34 pp., 7 plates, paper covers. $5.00.
A comparison of handguns, including Luger, Savage, Colt, Webley-Fosbery and other makes.

Shooting to Live with the One-Hand Gun, by Wm. E. Fairbairn and Eric A. Sykes, Paladin Press, Boulder, CO, 1974. 96 pp., illus. Paper covers. $5.95.
Facsimile of the 1942 instruction manual on the use of the pistol for defense in police work.

System Mauser, a Pictorial History of the Model 1896 Self-Loading Pistol, by J. W. Breathed, Jr., and J. J. Schroeder, Jr. Handgun Press, Chicago, IL, 1967. 273 pp., well illus. 1st limited ed. hardbound. $17.50.

10 Shots Quick, by Daniel K. Stern. Globe Printing Co., San Jose, CA, 1967. 153 pp., photos. $8.50.
History of Savage-made automatic pistols, models of 1903-1917, with descriptive data for shooters and collectors.

Textbook of Automatic Pistols, by R. K. Wilson and Ian V. Hogg, Stackpole Books, Harrisburg, PA, 1975. 416 pp., illus. $24.95.
Complete history of automatic hand-held weaponry, from the origins in the 19th century to now.

U.S. Test Trials 1900 Luger, by Michael Reese II, Pioneer Press, Union City, TN, 1976. 130 pp., illus. Paper covers. $4.95.
Revised edition containing much additional material on the notable American Eagle test pieces. Rare illustrations.

The Walther P-38 Pistol, by Maj. Geo. C. Nonte, Paladin Press, Boulder, CO, 1975. 90 pp., illus. Paper covers. $5.00.
Covers all facets of the gun—development, history, variations, technical data, practical use, rebuilding, repair and conversion.

The Walther Pistols 1930-1945, by Warren H. Buxton, Warren H. Buxton, Los Alamos, NM, 1978. 350 pp., illus. $29.95.
Volume I of a projected 4 volume series "The P.38 Pistol." The histories, evolutions, and variations of the Walther P.38 and its predecessors.

hunting

The ABC of Shooting, ed. by Colin Willock, Andre Deutsch, Ltd., London, England, 1975. 351 pp., illus. $14.95.
A complete shotgun guide to game and rough shooting, wild fowling, pigeon shooting, deer stalking and clay pigeon shooting.

African Hunter, by James Mellon et al, Harcourt Brace Jovanovich, NY, 1975. 522 pp., illus. $39.95.
Hunting Africa's wild animals by a famous hunter and others. Trophies, weapons, best time to hunt and where.

African Rifles & Cartridges, by John Taylor, The Gun Room Press, Highland Park, NJ, 1977. 431 pp., illus. $16.95.
Experiences and opinions of a professional ivory hunter in Africa describing his knowledge of numerous arms and cartridges for big game. A reprint.

Alaskan Hunter, by Roy F. Chandler, Roy F. Chandler, Nokomis, FL, 1977. 281 pp., illus. $16.00.
Vividly told experiences, informative and entrancing.

All About Deer in America, ed. by Robert Elman, Winchester Press, NY, 1976. 256 pp., illus. $10.
Twenty of America's great hunters share the secrets of their hunting success.

All-Season Hunting, by Bob Gilsvik, Winchester Press, NY, 1976. 256 pp., illus. $9.95.
A guide to early-season, late-season and winter hunting in America.

All About Rifle Hunting and Shooting in America, by Steve Ferber, Winchester Press, NY, 1977. 263 pp., illus. $10.00.
Everything the rifle shooter would want to know from shooting the old muzzleloader to the newest cartridge guns.

All About Small-Game Hunting in America, ed. by Russell Tinsley, Winchester Press, NY, 1976. 308 pp., illus. $10.00.
Collected advice by the finest small-game experts in the country.

All About Wildfowling in America, by Jerome Knap, Winchester Press, NY, 1977. 256 pp., illus. $10.00.
More than a dozen top writers provide new and controversial ideas on how-to and where-to hunt wildfowl successfully.

The Art of Hunting Big Game in North America, by Jack O'Connor, Random House, NY, 1978. 418 pp., illus. $13.95.
A new revised and updated edition on technique, planning, skill, outfitting, etc.

Art of Successful Deer Hunting, by F. E. Sell, Stackpole Books, Harrisburg, PA, 1971. 192 pp., paper, $3.95.
Illus. re-issue of "The Deer Hunter's Guide." Western hunting lore for rifle and bow-hunter.

The Best of Nash Buckingham, by Nash Buckingham, selected, edited and annotated by George Bird Evans. Winchester Press, NY, 1973. 320 pp. $10.95.
Thirty pieces that represent the very cream of Nash's output on his whole range of outdoor interests—upland shooting, duck hunting, even fishing.

The Big Game Animals of North America, by Jack O'Connor, Outdoor Life, NY, 1977, updated and revised edition. 238 pp., illus. $14.95.
A classic work on North American big game.

Big Game Hunter's Digest, by Tom Brakefield, DBI Books, Inc., Northfield, IL, 1977. 288 pp., illus. Paper covers. $7.95.
A truly complete reference to North American big game hunting.

Big Game Hunting Around the World, by Bert Klineburger and Vernon W. Hurst, Exposition Press, Jericho, NY, 1969. 376 pp., illus. $15.00.
The first book that takes you on a safari all over the world.

Big Game Hunting in North America, by Dave Petzal, Simon & Schuster, NY, 1977. 223 pp., illus. $10.95.
Expert advice on hunting America's top trophy game, such as antelope, bear, goat, caribou, elk, etc.

Big Game Hunting in the West, by Mike Cramond. Mitchell Press, Vancouver, B.C., Can., 1965. 164 pp., illus. $5.95.
Accounts of hunting many species of big game and predators are given plus a section on rifles, equipment, and useful tips for the field.

The Big Shots; Edwardian Shooting Parties, by Jonathan Garnier Ruffer, Debrett's Peerage Ltd, London, England, 1978. 300 pp., illus. $17.95.
Reveals the secrets behind the Imperial, Royal and Nobel shooting parties that have been an integral part of upper class English life for so long.

Bird Hunting Know-How, by D. M. Duffey. Van Nostrand, Princeton, NJ, 1968. 192 pp., illus. $5.95.
Game-getting techniques and sound advice on all aspects of upland bird hunting, plus data on guns and loads.

Black Powder Hunting, by Sam Fadala, Stackpole Books, Harrisburg, PA, 1978. 192 pp., illus. $10.95.
The author demonstrates successful hunting methods using percussion firearms for both small and big game.

Bobwhite Quail Hunting, by Charley Dickey, printed for Stoeger Publ. Co., So. Hackensack, NJ, 1974. 112 pp., illus., paper covers. $2.95.
Habits and habitats, techniques, gear, guns and dogs.

The Bobwhite Quail, its Life and Management, by Walter Rosene. Rutgers University Press, New Brunswick, NJ. 1st ed., 1969. 418 pp., photographs, maps and color plates. $27.50.
An exhaustive study of an important species which has diminished under the impact of changing agricultural and forestry practices.

A Boy and His Gun, by Edward C. Janes. A. S. Barnes & Co., New York, NY. 207 pp., illus., $5.00.
Introduction to rifles, shooting and hunting techniques for young shooters with practical hints on game shooting with rifle or shotgun.

Complete Book of Bow and Arrow, by G. H. Gillelan, Stackpole Books, Harrisburg, PA, 1971. 320 pp., illus. $9.95.
Encyclopedic reference on archery, gear, rules, skill, etc.

The Complete Book of Deer Hunting, by Byron W. Dalrymple, Winchester Press, NY, 1973. 247 pp., illus. $8.95.
Practical "how-to" information. Covers the 20 odd North-American subspecies of deer.

Complete Book of Hunting, by Clyde Ormond. Harper & Bros., NYC, 1962. 467 pp., well-illus. $11.95.
Part I is on game animals, Part II is on birds. Guns and ammunition, game, habitats, clothing, equipment, etc. hunters' tips are discussed.
The Complete Book of the Wild Turkey, by Roger M. Latham, Stackpole Books, Harrisburg, PA, 1978. 228 pp., illus. $8.95.
A new revised edition of the classic on American wild turkey hunting.
The Complete Guide to Bird Dog Training, by John R. Falk, Winchester Press, NY, 1976. 256 pp., illus. $10.00.
How to choose, raise, train, and care for a bird dog.
Complete Guide to Hunting Across North America, by Byron Dalrymple. Outdoor Life, Harper & Row, NY, 1970. 848 pp., illus. with photos and 50 maps. $10.00.
A large reference work on hunting conditions, locating game, clothing, techniques, transportation, equipment for every region, etc.
The Complete Hunter's Catalog, by Norman Strung, J. B. Lippincott Co., Phila., PA, 1978. 438 pp., illus. $14.95.
Where and how to find the best buy on equipment for shooting sports, hunting, big game, waterfowl, archery and much more.
The Complete Wildfowler, by Grits Gresham, Winchester Press, NY, 1976. 304 pp., illus. $8.95.
A graduate course in wildfowling, this is a down-to-earth, step-by-step education in everything one needs to know on the subject.
Crow Shooting Secrets, by Dick Mermon. Winchester Press, New York, 1970. 149 pp., illus. $5.95.
An expert shares his secrets and touches all the bases.
Death in the Long Grass, by Peter Hathaway Capstick, St. Martin's Press, New York, NY, 1977. 297 pp., illus. $10.
A big game hunter's adventures in the African bush.
Deer Hunting, by R. Smith, Stackpole Books, Harrisburg, PA, 1978. 224 pp., illus. $9.95.
A professional guide leads the hunt for North America's most popular big game animal.
Deer Hunting Across North America, ed. by Nick Sisley, Freshet Press, Rockville Centre, NY, 1976. 200 pp., illus. $12.95.
Covers the physical characteristics and habits of all the North American deer species, tips, guns and cartridges to use, methods of hunting, etc.
Deer Hunting; Tactics and Guns for Hunting All North American Game, by Norman Sprung, J. B. Lippincott Co., Phila., PA, 1973. 237 pp., illus. $7.95.
A comprehensive guide to deer hunting, focusing on whitetailed and mule deer.
The Dove Shooter's Handbook, by Dan M. Russell, Winchester Press, NY, 1974. 256 pp., illus. $6.95.
A complete guide to America's top game bird—natural history, hunting methods, equipment, conservation and future prospects.
Dove Hunting, by Charley Dickey, Galahad Books, NY, 1976. 112 pp., illus. $3.98.
This indispensable guide for hunters deals with equipment, techniques, types of dove shooting, hunting dogs, etc.
Drummer in the Woods, by Burton L. Spiller, Stackpole Books, Harrisburg, PA, 1980. 240 pp., illus. $12.95.
Twenty-one wonderful stories on grouse shooting by "the Poet Laureate of Grouse."
The Duck Hunter's Handbook, by Bob Hinman, Winchester Press, NY, 1974. 252 pp., illus. $8.95.
Down-to-earth, practical advice on bagging ducks and geese.
Ducks of the Mississippi Flyway, ed. by John McKane. North Star Press, St. Cloud, MN, 1969. 54 pp., illus. Paper covers, $2.98.
A duck hunter's reference. Full color paintings of some 30 species, plus descriptive text.
The Education of a Turkey Hunter, by Wm. F. Hanenkrat, Winchester Press, NY, 1974. 216 pp., illus. $8.95.
A complete course on how to hunt turkeys.
Elephant, by D. E. Blunt, Neville Spearman, London, 1971. 260 pp., illus. $22.50.
Reprint of a rare book, a hunter's account of the ways of an elephant.
Expert Advice on Gun Dog Training, ed. by David M. Duffey, Winchester Press, NY, 1977. 256 pp., illus. $10.
Eleven top pros talk shop, revealing the techniques and philosophies that account for their consistent success.
Fur Trapping, by Bill Musgrove and Gerry Blair, Winchester Press, New York, NY, 1979. 320 pp., illus. $10.
Two professional trappers explain how to harvest furbearers to obtain top prices for their pelts.
A Gallery of Waterfowl and Upland Birds, by Gene Hill, with illustrations by David Maass, Pedersen Prints, Los Angeles, CA, 1978. 132 pp., illus. $39.95. Deluxe bound, signed edition, in slipcase. $250.
Gene Hill at his best. Liberally illustrated with fifty-one full-color reproductions of David Maass' finest paintings.
Game Bird Hunting in the West, by Mike Cramond. Mitchell Press, Vancouver, B.C., Can., 1967. 246 pp., illus. $5.95.
Identification and hunting methods for each species of waterfowl and upland game birds, plus a section on shotgun types, equipment, and related subjects for the hunter.
Game and the Gunner, by Pierre Pulling, Winchester Press, NY, 1973. 233 pp., illus. $8.95.
Observations on same conservation and sport hunting.
Getting the Most out of Modern Waterfowling, by John O. Cartier, St. Martin's Press, NY, 1974. 396 pp., illus. $10.95.
The most comprehensive, up-to-date book on waterfowling imaginable.
Good Hunting, by Jas L. Clark, Univ. of Oklahoma Press, Norman, Okla., 1966. 242 pp., illus. $7.95.
Fifty years of collecting and preparing habitat groups for the American Museum.
The Great Arc of the Wild Sheep, by J. L. Clark, Univ. of Oklahoma Press, Norman, Okla., 1978. 247 pp., illus. Paper covers. $8.95.
Every classified variety of wild sheep is discussed, as found in North America, Asia & Europe. Numerous hunting stories by experts are included.
Great Game Animals of the World, by Russell B. Aitken. Winchester Press, NY, 1969. 192 pp. profusely ills. in monochrome and color. $22.50.
Accounts of man's pursuit of big game in all parts of the world, told in many fine pictures.
Green Hills of Africa, by Ernest Hemingway. Charles Scribner's Sons, NY, 1963. 285 pp. illus. Paper covers, $4.95.
A famous narrative of African big-game hunting, first published in 1935.
Grizzly Country, by Andy Russell. A. A. Knopf, NYC, 1973, 302 pp., illus. $8.95.
Many-sided view of the grizzly bear and his world, by a noted guide, hunter and naturalist.
Grouse and Woodcock, An Upland Hunter's Book, by Nick Sisley, Stackpole Books, Harrisburg, PA, 1980. 192 pp., illus. $11.95.
Latest field techniques for effective grouse and woodcock hunting.
Gun Dog, by Richard A. Wolters, E. P. Dutton, New York, NY, 1969. 1st ed., 11th Printing. 150 pp., well illus. $5.95.
A popular manual for upland bird shooters who want to train their dogs to perfection in minimum time.
Gundog Training, by Keith Erlandson, Arco Pub., Inc., New York, NY, 1978. 192 pp., illus. $11.95.
The first book on gundog training written by a practicing professional. The author has been a gamekeeper and gundog trainer for twenty-six years.
Gunning For Upland Birds and Wildlife, by Shirley E. Woods, Jr., Winchester Press, NY, 1976. 208 pp., illus. $10.00.
Practical field tested tips and techniques on two of America's most popular outdoor sports.
Handgun Hunting, by Maj. George C. Nonte, Jr. and Lee E. Jurras, Winchester Press, NY, 1975. 245 pp., illus. $8.95.
A book with emphasis on the hunting of readily available game in the U.S. with the handgun.
Hard Hunting, by Patrick Shaughnessy and Diane Swingle, Winchester Press, New York, NY, 1978, $9.95.
A couple explores a no-frills, low-cost, highly successful, adventurous approach to wilderness hunting.
"Hell, I Was There!", by Elmer Keith, Petersen Publishing Co., Los Angeles, CA, 1979. 308 pp., illus. $19.50.
Adventures of a Montana cowboy who gained world fame as a big game hunter.

Horned Death, by John F. Burger. Standard Publications, Huntington, WV, 1947. 340 pp., illus. $15.00.
Hunting the African cape buffalo.
Horns in the High Country, by Andy Russell, Alfred A. Knopf, NY, 1973. 259 pp., illus. $8.95.
A many-sided view of wild sheep and the natural world in which they live.
How to Hunt, by Dave Bowring, Winchester Press, NY, 1978. 256 pp., illus. $10.95.
A basic guide to hunting big game, small game, upland birds, and waterfowl.
How to Hunt Whitetail Deer, L. A. Anderson. Funk & Wagnalls, NYC, 1968. 116 pp., illus. $5.95.
Useful reference for deer hunters, both novice and experienced, giving basic information and valuable pointers.

How to Measure and Score Big-Game Trophies, by Grancel Fitz, revised edition, David McKay Co., Inc., New York, NY, 1977. 128 pp., illus. $12.50.
The official scoring method used by Boone and Crockett Club and Pope and Young Club. Plus every official scoring chart for all 26 species.
Hunt Close!, by Jerome B. Robinson, Winchester Press, NY, 1978. 224 pp., illus. $10.00.
A realistic guide to training close-working dogs for today's tight cover conditions.
Hunter's Digest, edited by Erwin A. Bauer. Digest Books, Inc., Northfield, IL, 1973. 320 pp., illus. Paper covers. $6.95.
The best ways, times and places to hunt the most popular species of large and small game animals in North America.
The Hunter's Field Guide to Game Birds & Animals of North America, by Robt. Elman, Alfred A. Knopf, NY, 1974. 655 pp. Over 357 illus., including 116 in full color. $12.50.
A comprehensive book on strategy and facts on over 100 game animals, upland birds and waterfowl in North America.
A Hunter's Fireside Book, by Gene Hill Winchester Press, NY, 1972. 192 pp., illus. $7.95
An outdoor book that will appeal to every person who spends time in the field—or who wishes he could.
The Hunter's Game Cookbook, by Jacqueline E. Knight, Winchester Press, NY, 1978. 320 pp., illus. $10.95.
Everything you need to know about the preparation of game from the field to the table.

Hunting the American Wild Turkey, by Dave Harbour, Stackpole Books, Harrisburg, PA, 1975. 256 pp., illus. $9.95.
The techniques and tactics of hunting North America's largest, and most popular, woodland game bird.
Hunting America's Game Animals and Birds, by Robert Elman and George Peper, Winchester Press, NY, 1975. 368 pp., illus. $12.95.
A how-to, where-to, when-to guide—by 40 top experts—covering the continent's big, small, upland game and waterfowl.
Hunting Big Game, by Jack O'Connor, Petersen Publishing Co., Los Angeles, CA, 1979. 96 pp., illus. Paper covers. $3.50.
A guide to hunting big game in North America from the pages of Petersen's "Hunting" magazine.
Hunting Big-Game Trophies; A North America Guide, by Tom Brakefield, E. P. Dutton & Co., Inc., NY, 1976. 446 pp., illus. $10.95.
Where to go, when to go, camp savvy, animal lore, the hunt, etc.
Hunting Dog Know-How, by D. M. Duffey, Van Nostrand, Princeton, NJ, 1965. 177 pp., illus. $6.95.
Covers selection, breeds, and training of hunting dogs, problems in hunting and field trials.
Hunting for all Seasons, by Alex Kay, A & W Books, NY, 1976. 159 pp., illus. $5.95.
The complete how-to handbook on when and where to bag your quarry, how much gun to use on what game.
Hunting Moments of Truth, by Eric Peper and Jim Rikhoff, Winchester Press, NY, 1973. 208 pp., illus. $8.95.
The world's most experienced hunters recount 22 most memorable occasions.

Hunting with Bow and Arrow, by George Laycock and Erwin Bauer. Arco Publ. Co., Inc., NYC, 1966. $3.95.
A practical guide to archery as a present-day sport. Mentions equipment needed and how to select it. Illus. instructions on how to shoot with ease and accuracy.
Hunting Trophy Deer, by John Wootters, Winchester Press, NY, 1977. 288 pp., illus. $13.95.
One of America's most experienced and respected hunting writers provides all the specialized advice you need to succeed at bagging trophy deer.
Hunting Upland Birds, by Chas. F. Waterman. Winchester Press, NY, 1972. 320 pp., illus. $8.95.
Excellent treatment of game habits and habitat, hunting methods, and management techniques for each of the 18 major North American gamebird species.
Hunting the Uplands with Rifle and Shotgun, by Luther A. Anderson, Winchester Press, NY, 1977. 224 pp., illus. $10.
Solid, practical know-how to help make hunting deer and every major species of upland game bird easier and more satisfying.

Hunting Whitetail Deer, by Robert E. Donovan, Winchester Press, NY, 1978. 256 pp., illus. $12.50.

For beginners and experts alike, this book is the key to successful whitetail hunting.

Hunting the Woodlands for Small and Big Game, by Luther A. Anderson, A. S. Barnes & Co., New York, NY, 1980. 256 pp., illus. $12.00.

A comprehensive guide to hunting in the United States. Chapters on firearms, game itself, marksmanship, clothing and equipment.

In Search of the Wild Turkey, by Bob Gooch, Greatlakes Living Press, Ltd., Waukegan, IL, 1978. 182 pp., illus. $9.95.

A state-by-state guide to wild turkey hot spots, with tips on gear and methods for bagging your bird.

Jim Corbett's India, ed. by R. E. Hawkins, Oxford University Press, London, England, 1978. 250 pp., illus. $11.95.

A selection of Jim Corbett's writings from 1907 to 1939 taken from his books on hunting and his expeditions.

The Market Hunter, by David and Jim Kimball, Dillon Press Inc., Minneapolis, MN, 1968. 132 pp., illus. $5.95.

The market hunter, one of the "missing chapters" in American history, is brought to life in this book.

In a simple and entertaining manner the author explains how to live

Modern ABC's of Bird Hunting, by Dave Harbour, Stackpole Books, Harrisburg, PA, 1966. 192 pp., illus. $4.95.

From city's edge to wilderness this gives the occasional hunter the quickest way on how to increase his bag. Covers all game birds of the U.S. and Canada.

Modern Hunting with Indian Secrets, by Allan A. Macfarlan. Stackpole Books, Harrisburg, PA, 1971. 222 pp., $6.50.

How to acquire the new-old skills of the Redman, how to apply them to modern hunting.

Modern Turkey Hunting, by James F. Brady, Crown Publ., N.Y.C., NY, 1973. 160 pp., illus. $6.95.

A thorough guide to the habits, habitat, and methods of hunting America's largest game bird.

More Grouse Feathers, by Burton L. Spiller. Crown Publ., NY, 1972. 238 pp., illus. $7.50.

Facsimile of the original Derrydale Press issue of 1938. Guns and dogs, the habits and shooting of grouse, woodcook, ducks, etc. Illus. by Lynn Bogue Hunt.

Moss, Mallards & Mules and other Hunting and Fishing Stories, by Robert Brister, Winchester Press, NY, 1973. 216 pp., illus. $8.95.

A collection of 27 short stories on hunting and fishing.

Mostly Tailfeathers, by Gene Hill, Winchester Press, NY, 1975. 192 pp., illus. $8.95.

An interesting, general book about bird hunting with some stories on fishing.

North American Big Game, ed. by Wm. H. Nesbitt and Jack S. Parker, The Boone and Crockett Club and the National Rifle Association of America, Wash., DC, 7th ed., 1977. 367 pp., illus. $25.00.

The official records book for outstanding native North American big game trophies.

North American Big Game Hunting, by Byron W. Dalrymple, Winchester Press, NY, 1974. 383 pp., illus. $10.00.

A comprehensive, practical guide, with individual chapters devoted to all native species.

The North American Waterfowler, by Paul S. Bernsen. Superior Publ. Co., Seattle, WA, 1972. 206 pp. Paper covers, $4.95.

The complete inside and outside story of duck and goose shooting. Big and colorful, illus. by Les Kouba.

1001 Hunting Tips, by Robert Elman, Winchester Press, N.Y., NY, 1978. 256 pp., illus. $15.95.

A post-graduate course in big-game hunting, small-game hunting, wildfowling, and hunting upland birds.

The Old Man's Boy Grows Older, by Robert Ruark, Holt, Rinehart and Winston, New York, NY, 1961. 302 pp., illus. $25.00.

A classic by a big-game hunter and world traveler.

One Man's Wilderness, by Warren Page, Holt, Rinehart and Winston, NY, 1973. 256 pp., illus. $8.95.

A world-known writer and veteran sportsman recounts the joys of a lifetime of global hunting.

Outdoor Life's Deer Hunting Book, by Jack O'Connor, et al, Harper & Row Publ., Inc., NY, 1975. 224 pp., illus. $7.95.

A major new work on deer hunting. Covers every aspect of the sport.

The Outlaw Gunner, by Harry M. Walsh, Tidewater Publishers, Cambridge, MD, 1973. 178 pp., illus. $8.50.

A colorful story of market gunning in both its legal and illegal phases.

Paw Prints; How to Identify Rare and Common Mammals by Their Tracks. O. C. Lempfert, NY, 1972. 71 pp., illus. with actual size prints. $7.50.

An authoritive manual for hunters and outdoorsmen.

The Practical Hunter's Dog Book, by John R. Falk, Winchester Press, NY, 1971. 314 pp., illus. $8.95.

Helps to choose, train and enjoy your gun dog.

The Practical Hunter's Handbook, by Anthony J. Acerrano, Winchester Press, New York, NY, 1978. 224 pp., illus. $10.

How the time-pressed hunter can take advantage of every edge his hunting situation affords him.

Practical Pointer Training, by Sherman Webb, Winchester Press, NY 1976. 192 pp., illus. $6.95.

A good bird dog training book that fills the bill.

The Puma, Mysterious American Cat, by S. P. Young and E. A. Goldman, Dover Publ., NY, 1964, 358 pp., illus. Paper covers $3.50.

A two-part work: the first on the history, economic status and control: the second on classifications of the races of the puma.

Ranch Life and the Hunting Trail, by Theodore Roosevelt, Readex Microprint Corp., Dearborn, MI. 1966. 186 pp., With drawings by Frederic Remington. $10.

A facsimile reprint of the original 1899 Century Co. edition. One of the most fascinating books of the West of that day.

Ringneck! Pheasants & Pheasant Hunting, by Ted Janes, Crown Publ., NY, 1975. 120 pp., illus. $8.95.

A thorough study of one of our more popular game birds.

Rowland Ward's Records of Big Game, 17th ed., comp. by G. A. Best, Rowland Ward Pub., Ltd., 1976. 438 pp., illus. $65.

New edition of the authoritive record of big game kills in Africa, by species.

Safari, by Elmer Keith. Safari Publ., La Jolla, CA, 1968. 166 pp., illus. $15.00.

Guide to big game hunting in Africa, with anecdote and expert advice on hunting many species of game. Information on guns, ammunition, equipment, and planning the safari is included. Fine photographs.

Safe Hunting, by Dick Pryce, Winchester Press, NY, 1974. 178 pp., illus. $7.95.

An introduction to hunting, guns, and gun safety.

Selected American Game Birds, by David Hagerbaumer and Sam Lehman, The Caxton Printers, Ltd., Caldwell, ID, 1972. The entire text of this book is executed in decorated calligraphy. $30.00.

Twenty-six of David Hagerbaumer's exquisite original watercolors, representing 29 bird species. A must for every book collector and art lover.

Sheep & Sheep Hunting, by Jack O'Connor, Winchester Press, NY, 1974. 308 pp., illus. $10.95.

Authentic detail about all varieties of wild sheep and how to hunt for them.

Shooting Game, by Michael Kemp, A & C Black, London, England, 1972. 176 pp., illus. $8.95.

A step-by-step course to successful and enjoyable shooting.

Shooting Pictures, by A. B. Frost, with 24 pp. of text by Chas. D. Lanier. Winchester Press, NY, 1972. 12 color plates. Enclosed in a board portfolio. Ed. limited to 750 numbered copies. $75.

Frost's twelve superb 12" by 16" pictures have often been called the finest sporting prints published in the U.S. A facsimile of the 1895-6 edition printed on fine paper with superb color fidelity.

Shots at Mule Deer, by Rollo S. Robinson, Winchester Press, New York, NY, 1970. 209 pp., illus. $15.

Description, strategies for bagging it, the correct rifle and cartridge to use.

Small Game Hunting, by Tom Brakefield, J. B. Lippincott Co., Phila., PA, 1978. 244 pp., illus. $10.

Describes where, when, and how to hunt all major small game species from coast to coast.

The Sportsman's Companion, by Lee Wulff. Harper & Row, N.Y.C., 1968. 413 pp., illus. $11.95.

Compendium of writings by various experts on hunting and fishing for American game. A useful reference for the outdoorsman.

Sportman's Guide to Game Animals, by Leonard Lee Rue III. Harper & Row [Outdoor Life Books], New York, NY, 1st ed., 2nd printing, 1969. 635 pp., illus. with photographs and maps. $8.95.

Exhaustive and capable coverage of the behavior and habits of all North American game animals.

Squirrels and Squirrel Hunting, by Bob Gooch. Tidewater Publ., Cambridge, MD, 1973. 148 pp., illus. $6.

A complete book for the squirrel hunter, beginner or old hand. Details methods of hunting, squirrel habitat, management, proper clothing, care of the kill, cleaning and cooking.

The Standard Book of Hunting and Shooting, R. B. Stringfellow, ed. 1st ed., in 1950 by the Greystone Press, New York, NY, 564 pp., very well illus. $10.00.

An excellent anthology on hunting in America, giving meaningful information on all major species and on all types of guns, sights, ammunition, etc. An abridgement of the larger Hunters Encyclopedia.

Successful Waterfowling, by Zack Taylor, Crown Publ., NY, 1974. 276 pp., illus. $8.95.

The definitive guide to new ways of hunting ducks and geese.

Timberdoodle, by Frank Woolner, Crown Publ., Inc., NY, 1974. 168 pp., illus. $7.95.

A thorough, practical guide to the American woodcock and to woodcock hunting.

Topflight; A Speed Index to Waterfowl, by J. A. Ruthven & Wm. Zimmerman, Moebius Prtg. Co., Milwaukee, WI, 1968. 112 pp. $7.50.

Rapid reference for specie identification. Marginal color band of book directs reader to proper section. 263 full color illustrations of body and feather configurations.

Travel & Adventure in Southeast Africa, by F. C. Selous. A & F Press, N.Y.C., 1967. 522 pp., illus. $27.50.

New edition of a famous African hunting book, first published in 1893.

Trouble With Bird Dogs ... and What to do About Them, by George Bird Evans, Winchester Press, NY, 1976. 288 pp., illus. $10.00.

How to custom-train your dog for specific kinds of hunting.

Turkey Hunter's Guide, by Byron W. Dalrymple, et al, a publication of The National Rifle Association, Washington, DC, 1979. 96 pp., illus. Paper covers. $4.95.

Expert advice on turkey hunting hotspots, guns, guides, and calls.

Upland Bird & Waterfowl Hunting, ed. by Dave Petzal, Simon & Schuster, NY, 1976. 315 pp., illus. $9.95.

A collection of stories by an outstanding panel of knowledgeable experts on the subject.

The Upland Game Hunter's Bible, by Dan Holland. Doubleday, N.Y.C., 1961. 192 pp., illus. paper covers. $2.50.

Hunter's manual on the principal species of American upland game birds and how to hunt them.

Varmint Hunter's Digest, by Jim Dougherty, DBI Books, Inc., Northfield, IL, 1977. 256 pp., illus. Paper covers. $6.95.

The how-to book for varminters.

Water Dog, by R. A. Wolters, E. P. Dutton & Co., NY, 1964. 179 pp., illus. $5.95.

Rapid training manual for working retrievers.

Waterfowl in the Marshes, by A. C. Becker Jr. A. S. Barnes and Co., New York, NY, 1969. 155 pp., photographs. $9.95.

A highly informative and practical guide to waterfowl hunting in America.

The Whitetail Deer Hunter's Handbook, by John Weiss, Winchester Press, New York, NY, 1979. 256 pp., illus. $10.95.

Wherever you live, whatever your level of experience, this brand-new handbook will make you a better deer hunter.

Whitetail: Fundamentals and Fine Points for the Hunter, by George Mattis, World Publ. Co. New York, NY, 1976. 273 pp., illus. $9.95.

A manual of shooting and trailing and an education in the private world of the deer.

Wild Fowl Decoys, by Joel Barber. Dover Publ., N.Y.C., 1954. 156 pp., 134 illus., paperbound. $5.00.

A fine work on making, painting, care and use of decoys in hunting, recently reprinted. Full data on design and construction.

The Wild Sheep in Modern North America, a Boone & Crockett Club Book, Book & Crockett Club, Alexandria, VA, 1976. 302 pp., illus. Paper covers. $10.00.

The most comprehensive data on the past, present and future of these unique game animals.

The Wind on Your Cheek, by William J. Schaldach, Freshet Press, Rockville, NY, 1976. 157 pp., illus. $10.95.

Memories of the days spent upland shooting and trout fishing for almost 60 years.

The Wings of Dawn, by George Reiger, Stein and Day, New York, NY, 1980. 320 pp., illus. $29.95.

The complete book of North American waterfowling.

The Young Shot, by Noel M. Sedgwick, A. & C. Black, London, Eng., 1976. 240 pp., illus. $8.95.

A revised and re-illustrated edition of Sedgwick's original work plus a preface and appendix dealing with changes in law since the first ed.

RIFLES

The Accurate Rifle, by Warren Page. Winchester Press, NY, 1973. 256 pp., illus. $8.95.
A masterly discussion. A must for the competitive shooter hoping to win, and highly useful to the practical hunter.
American Rifle Design and Performance, by L. R. Wallack, Winchester Press, NY, 1977. 288 pp., illus. $12.95.
An authoritative, comprehensive guide to how and why every kind of sporting rifle works.
The Bolt Action: A Design Analysis, by Stuart Otteson, Winchester Press, NY, 1976. 320 pp., illus. $12.95.
Precise and in-depth descriptions, illustrations, and comparisons of 16 bolt actions. A new approach.
Bolt Action Rifles, by Frank de Haas, ed. by John T. Amber, Editor of Gun Digest. DBI Books, Inc., Northfield, IL, 1971. 320 pp., illus. Paper, $7.95.
The definitive work, covering every major design since the Mauser of 1871.
The Book of the Garand, by Maj.-Gen. J. S. Hatcher, The Gun Room Press, Highland Park, NJ, 1977. 292 pp., illus. $11.95.
A new printing of the standard reference work on the U.S. Army M1 rifle.
The Book of Rifles, by W. H. B. Smith. Stackpole Books, Harrisburg, PA, 1963 (3rd ed.). 656 pp., profusely illus. $6.98.
An encyclopedic reference work on shoulder arms, recently up-dated. Includes rifles of all types, arranged by country of origin.
Browning Automatic Rifles, Normount Armament Co., Wickenburg, AZ, 81 pp., illus. Paper, $3.00.
Reprint of Ordnance Manual TM 9-1211, on all types of caliber 30's.
Carbines Cal. .30 M1, M1A1, M2 and M3, by D. B. McLean. Normount Armament Co., Wickenburg, AZ, 1964. 221 pp., well illus., paperbound. $6.95.
U.S. field manual reprints on these weapons, edited and reorganized.
Competitive Rifle Shooting, by James Sweet, Fortress Publ., Stoney Creek, Ontario, Canada, 1978. 120 pp., illus. Stiff card covers. $6.95.
The accepted textbook on target shooting and bedding of target rifles.
The Deer Rifle, by L. R. Wallack, Winchester Press, New York, NY, 1978. 256 pp., illus. $10.95.
Everything the deer hunter needs to know to select and use the arms and ammunition appropriate to his needs.
Description and Instructions for the Management of the Gallery-Practice Rifle Caliber .22—Model of 1903. Inco., 1972. 12 pp., 1 plate. Paper, $2.50.
Reprint of 1907 War Dept. pamphlet No. 1925.
Description of Telescopic Musket Sights, Inco, 1972. 10 pp., 4 plates. Paper, $2.50.
Reprint of 1917 War Dept. pamphlet No. 1957, first publ. in 1908.
The First Winchester, by John E. Parsons. Winchester Press, New York, NY, 1977. 207 pp., well illus., $14.95.
This new printing of *The Story of the 1866 Repeating Rifle* (1st publ. 1955) is revised, and additional illustrations included.
A Forgotten Heritage; The Story of a People and the Early American Rifle, by Harry P. Davis, The Gun Room Press, Highland Park, NJ, 1976. 199 pp., illus. $9.95.
Reprint of a very scarce history, originally published in 1941, the Kentucky rifle and the people who used it.
Garand Rifles M1, M1C, M1D, by Donald B. McLean. Normount Armament Co., Wickenburg, AZ, 1968. Over 160 pp., 175 illus., paper wrappers. $6.95.
Covers all facets of the arm: battlefield use, disassembly and maintenance, all details to complete lock-stock-and-barrel repair, plus variations, grenades, ammo., and accessories; plus a section on 7.62mm NATO conventions.
The Golden Age of Single-Shot Rifles, by Edsall James, Pioneer Press, Union City, TN, 1975. 33 pp., illus. Paper covers. $2.75.
A detailed look at all of the fine, high quality sporting single-shot rifles that were once the favorite of target shooters.
The Gun Digest Book of the .22 Rimfire, by John Lachuk, DBI Books, Northfield, IL, 1978. 224 pp., illus. Paper covers. $6.95.
Everything you want to know about the .22 rimfire and the arms that use it.
Guns Annual Book of Rifles, ed. by Jerome Rakusan, Publishers Development Corp., Skokie, IL, 1974. 102 pp., illus., paper covers. $3.95.
Complete catalog listing plus feature articles on benchrest rifles, reloading, etc.
How to Select and Use Your Big Game Rifle, by Henry M. Stebbins, Combat Forces Press, Washington, 1952. 237 pp., illus. $6.50.
Concise valuable data on rifles, old and new—slide action, lever, semi automatic, and single shot models are covered.
The Hunting Rifle, by Jack O'Connor. Winchester Press, NY, 1970. 352 pp., illus. $8.95.
An analysis, with wit and wisdom, of contemporary rifles, cartridges, accessories and hunting techniques.
The Improved American Rifle, by John R. Chapman, Beinfeld Publ., Inc., No. Hollywood, CA, 1976. 160 pp., illus. $5.95.
A facsimile reprint of the scarce 1848 edition, the earliest book on precision rifle shooting.
John Olson's Book of the Rifle, by John Olson, J. Philip O'Hara, Inc., Chicago, IL, 1974. 256 pp., illus. Paper covers. $6.95.
Rifle data "A to Z"—barrels, actions, stocks, calibers, cartidges, ballistics, scopes, mounts, metallic sights, handloading, gunsmithing, muzzle-loading.
Know Your M1 Garand, by E. J. Hoffschmidt, Blacksmith Corp., Stamford, CT, 1975. 84 pp., illus. Paper Covers. $4.95.
Facts about America's most famous infantry weapon. Covers test and experimental models, Japanese and Italian copies, National Match models.
Maynard Catalog of 1880, a reprint in facsimile by the Rocky Mountain Investment and Antique Co.; Cheyenne, WY, 1969. 32 pp., illus., paper covers. $3.00.
All models, sights, cartridges, targets etc.
The Model 70 Winchester 1937-1964, by Dean H. Whitaker, Taylor Publishing Co., Dallas, TX, 1978. 210 pp., illus. $24.95.
An authoritative reference book on this model. Gives production history, changes, dimensions, specifications on special-order guns, etc.
The M-14 Rifle, facsimile reprint of FM 23-8, Desert Publications, Cornville, AZ. 50 pp., illus. Paper. $4.95.
In this well illustrated and informative reprint, the M-14 and M-14E2 are covered thoroughly.
The Modern Rifle, by Jim Carmichel, Winchester Press, NY, 1975. 320 pp., illus. $12.95.
The most comprehensive, thorough, up-to-date book ever published on today's rifled sporting arms.
100 Years of Shooters and Gunmakers of Single Shot Rifles, by Gerald O. Kelver, Brighton, CO, 1975. 212 pp., illus. Paper covers $7.50.
The Schuetzen rifle, targets and shooters, primers, match rifles, original loadings and much more. With chapters on famous gunsmiths like Harry Pope, Morgan L. Rood and others.
The '03 Springfields, by Clark S. Campbell, Ray Riling Arms Books Co., Phila., PA, 1978. 320 pp., illus. $20.
The most authoritative and definitive work on this famous U.S. rifle, the 1903 Springfield and its 30-06 cartridge.
The Pennsylvania Rifle, by Samuel E. Dyke, Sutter House, Lititz, PA, 1975. 61 pp., illus. Paper covers. $3.00.
History and development, from the hunting rifle of the Germans who settled the area. Contains a full listing of all known Lancaster, PA gunsmiths from 1729 through 1815.
Pictorial History of the Rifle, By G. W. P. Swenson. Ian Allan Ltd., Shepperton, Surrey, England, 1971. 184 pp., illus. $9.50.
Essentially a picture book, with over 200 rifle illustrations. The text furnishes a concise history of the rifle and its development.
Position Rifle Shooting, by Bill Pullum and F. T. Hanenkrat. Winchester Press, NY, 1973. 256 pp., illus. $10.00.
The single most complete statement of rifle shooting principles and techniques, and the means of learning, teaching and using them, ever to appear in print.
The Revolving Rifles, by Edsall James, Pioneer Press, Union City, TN, 1975. 23 pp., illus. Paper covers. $2.50.
Valuable information on revolving cylinder rifles, from the earliest matchlock forms to the latest models of Colt and Remington.
The Rifle Book, by Jack O'Connor, Random House, NY, 1978. 337 pp., illus. $13.95.
The complete book of small game, varmint and big game rifles.
Rifle Guide, by Robert A. Steindler, Stoeger Publishing Co., South Hackensack, NJ, 1978. 304 pp., illus. Paper covers. $7.95.
Complete, fully illustrated guide to selecting, shooting, caring for, and collecting rifles of all types.
The Rifle: and How to Use it, by H. Busk, Richmond Publ. Co., Richmond, England, 1971. 225 pp., illus. $9.00.
Reprint of the 1859 ed. Covers mid-19th century military rifles.
Rifles AR15, M16, and M16A1, 5.56 mm, by D. B. McLean. Normount Armament Co., Wickenburg, AZ, 1968. Unpaginated, illus., paper covers. $6.95.
Descriptions, specifications and operation of subject models are set forth in text and picture.
Schuetzen Rifles, History and Loading, by Gerald O. Kelver, Gerald O. Kelver, Publisher, Brighton, CO, 1972. Illus. $7.50.
Reference work on these rifles, their bullets, loading, telescopic sights, accuracy, etc. A limited, numbered ed.
Shooting the Percussion Rifle, by R. O. Ackerman. Publ. by the author, Albuquerque, N.M., 1966. 19 pp., illus. in line by the author. Paper wrappers, $1.50.
This well prepared work is Book No. 2 of a projected series. This one gives basic information on the use of the muzzle-loading rifle.
Single Shot Rifles and Actions, by Frank de Haas, ed. by John T. Amber, DBI Books, Northfield, IL, 1969. 352 pp., illus. $8.95.
The definitive book on over 60 single shot rifles and actions. Covers history, parts photos, design and construction, etc.
Sir Charles Ross and His Rifle, by Robt. Phillips and J. J. Knap, Museum Restoration Service, Ottawa, Canada., 1969. 32 pp., illus. Paper covers. $2.00.
The story of the man who invented the "Ross Model 1897 Magazine Sporting Rifle," the 1900 under the name of Bennett, and many others.
Small-Bore Target Shooting, by W. H. Fuller, 3rd edition, revised by A. J. Palmer, Barrie & Jenkins, London, England, 1978. 240 pp., illus. $11.95.
Includes an appendix on air rifle shooting, which may become an Olympic Games event in 1980. The complete treatise on the sport of 22 and 177 in competition rifle shooting.
Sniper Rifles of Two World Wars, by W. H. Tantum IV. Museum Restoration Service, Ottawa, Can., 1967. 32 pp., illus. $2.00.
Monograph on high-accuracy rifles used by troops in world wars I and II and in Korea. Paper wrappers.
The Sporting Rifle and its Projectiles, by Lieut. James Forsyth, The Buckskin Press, Big Timber, MT, 1978. 132 pp., illus. $9.50.
Facsimile reprint of the 1863 edition, one of the most authoritative books ever written on the muzzle-loading round ball sporting rifle.
Target Rifle Shooting, by E. G. B. Reynolds & Robin Fulton. Barrie & Jenkins, London, Eng., 1972. 200 pp., illus. $11.95.
For the novice and intermediate shooter who wants to learn the basics needed to become a rifle marksman.
The .22 Rifle, by Dave Petzal. Winchester Press, NY, 1972. 244 pp., illus. $6.95.
All about the mechanics of the .22 rifle. How to choose the right one, how to choose a place to shoot, what makes a good shot, the basics of small-game hunting.
Winchester '73 & '76, the First Repeating Center-Fire Rifles, by D. F. Butler. Winchester Press, New York, NY, 1st ed., 1970. 95 pp., well and tastefully illus. in line, halftones and photos. Color frontispiece. $7.95.
A complete history of the subject arms and their then-new ammunition, plus details of their use on America's western frontiers.

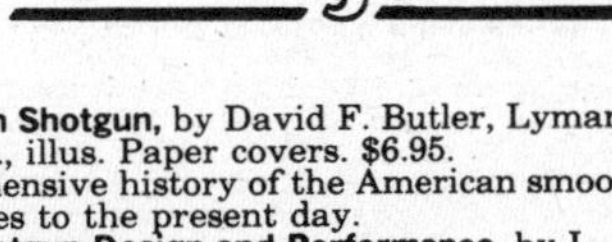

shotguns

The American Shotgun, by David F. Butler, Lyman Publ., Middlefield, CT, 1973. 256 pp., illus. Paper covers. $6.95.
A comprehensive history of the American smoothbore's evolution from Colonial times to the present day.
American Shotgun Design and Performance, by L. R. Wallack, Winchester Press, NY, 1977. 184 pp., illus. $13.95.
An expert lucidly recounts the history and development of American shotguns and explains how they work.
The Art of Wing Shooting, by William Bruce Leffingwell, The Abercrombie & Fitch Library, Arno Press, NY, 1967. 190 pp., illus. $15.
A facsimile reprint first published in 1894. Still regarded by experts as one of the few truly outstanding books in its field.

1909 Baker Gun Catalog, reprinted by Ronald Frodelius, Fayetteville, NY, 1976. 20 pp., illus. Paper covers. $2.95.
A facsimile reprint of a scarce old Baker Arms Co. catalog.
Boss & Co., Guns, Catalog, 1910, a facsimile reprint by Empire Press, Santa Fe, NM, 1980. 7 pp., illus. Paper covers. $5.00.
A facsimile reprint of this famous British gunmakers 1910 catalog, showing their line of fine shotguns.
The British Shotgun Vol. I, 1850-1870, by I. M. Crudgington and D. J. Baker, Barrie & Jenkins, London, England, 1979. 192 pp., illus. $25.
An attempt to trace, as accurately as is now possible, the evolution of the shotgun during its formative years in Great Britain.
The Browning Superposed, a facsimile reprint by Empire Press, Santa Fe, NM, 1980. 32 pp., illus Paper covers. $6.00.
A facsimile reprint of the 1931 catalog of Browning Arms Co. concerning their superposed models.
E. J. Churchill, Ltd., Catalog 1922, Some Notes on Churchill Best Guns, a facsimile reprint by Empire Press, Santa Fe, NM, 1979. 32 pp., illus. Paper covers. $10.00.
A facsimile reprint of this famous British gunmaker's catalog for 1922, showing their line of deluxe shotguns.
Churchill's Game Shooting, ed. by Macdonald Hastings, Michael Joseph, London, England, 1978. 250 pp., illus. $27.50.
A textbook on the successful use of the modern shotgun.
Clay Pigeon Marksmanship, by Percy Stanbury and G. L. Carlisle. Herbert Jenkins, London, 1964. 216 pp., illus. $11.95.
Handbook on learning the skills, with data on guns & equipment and competition shooting at all types of clay targets; by two eminent British writers.
The Complete Book of Clay Target Games, by Edward C. Migdalski, Winchester Press, New York, NY, 1978. 258 pp., illus. $12.95
Discusses the wide variety of informal shooting games that have developed to amuse, intrigue, and frustrate shotgunners.
The Double Shotgun, by Don Zutz, Winchester Press, New York, NY, 1978. 288 pp., illus. $12.50.
The history and development of the most classic of all sporting arms.
The Fowler in Ireland. by Sir Ralph Payne-Gallwey, Richmond Publ. Co., Richmond, England, 1971. 503 pp., illus. $17.50.
Reprint of the 1882 work on wildfowling and wildlife in Ireland.
The Golden Age of Shotgunning, by Bob Hinman, Winchester Press, NY, 1971. 175 pp., illus. $8.95.
The story of American shotgun and wingshooting from 1870 to 1900.
Gough Thomas's Gun Book, by G. T. Garwood. A. & C. Black, London, England, 1969. 160 pp., illus. $15.00.
Excerpts of articles on the shotgun published in *Shooting Times*, by a noted British authority. Wide-ranging survey of every aspect on the shotgun, its use, behavior, care, and lore.
Gunning the Chesapeake, by Roy E. Walsh, Tidewater Publishers, Cambridge, MD, 1971. 117 pp., illus. $7.00.
Duck and goose shooting on the Eastern Shore.
High Pheasants, by Sir Ralph Payne-Gallwey, Richmond Publ. Co., Richmond, England, 1970. 79 pp. $11.50.
The first and last word on its subject.
History and Catalog of Holland & Holland Ltd., distributed by Service Armament Co., Ridgefield, NJ, 1977. 144 pp., illus. Paper covers. $24.95.
A folio containing a reprint of the Holland & Holland 72 page catalog of 1912, together with a 72-page book describing the Holland & Holland gun collection and the history of this famous firm of gunmakers.
How to be a Winner Shooting Skeet & Trap, by Tom Morton, Tom Morton, Knoxville, MD, 1974. 144 pp., illus. Paper covers. $8.95.
The author explains why championship shooting is more than a physical process.
John Olson's Book of the Shotgun, by John Olson, J. Philip O'Hara, Inc., Chicago, IL, 1975. 256 pp., illus. Paper covers. $6.95; cloth, $10.95.
Covers all phases, from design and manufacture to field use and performance.
The Mysteries of Shotgun Patterns, by Geo. G. Oberfell and Chas. E. Thompson, Oklahoma State University Press, Stillwater, OK, Xerox edition, 1978. 328 pp. Paper covers. $20.00.
Shotgun ballistics for the hunter in non-technical language, with information on improving effectiveness in the field.
New England Grouse Shooting, by W. H. Foster, Chas. Scribner's, NY, 193 pp., illus. $25.00.
Many interesting and helpful points on how to hunt grouse.
The New Wildfowler in the 1970's by N. M. Sedgwick, et al. Barrie & Jenkins, London, Eng., 1970. 375 pp., illus. $11.50.
A compendium of articles on wildfowling, hunting practices and conservation. An updated reprint.
Parker Brother Gun Catalog, 1869. B. Palmer, Tyler, TX, 1972. 14 pp., illus. Paper covers. $4.
Facsimile of Charles Parker's first issued catalog on "Parker Breech-Loading Shot Guns."
Parker Guns Catalog 1930, a reprint, by Empire Press, Santa Fe, NM, 1979. 32 pp., illus. Paper covers. $6.50.
Facsimile reprint showing all models, including the Parker single barrel trap gun.
The Parker Gun, by Larry L. Baer, Beinfeld Publ., Inc., No. Hollywood, CA, 1980. 240 pp., illus. $24.95.
Originally published as two separate volumes. This is the only comprehensive work on the subject of America's most famous shotgun. Included are new material and new photographs.
Pigeon Shooting, by Archie Coates, Andre Deutsch Ltd., London, England, 1975. 142 pp., illus. $10.95.
Helpful and practical advice on every facet of the sport.
The Police Shotgun Manual, by Robert H. Robinson, Charles C. Thomas, Springfield, IL 1973. 153 pp., illus. $12.50.
A complete study and analysis of the most versatile and effective weapon in the police arsenal.
The Practical Wildfowler, by John Marchington, Adam and Charles Black, London, England, 1977. 143 pp., illus. $14.95.
Advice to the novice wildfowler on both the practical and ethical aspects of the sport.
Rough Shooting, by G. A. Gratten & R. Willett. Faber & Faber, London, Eng., 1968. 242 pp., illus. $14.95.
The art of shooting, dogs and their training, games, rearing and their diseases, proof marks, etc.
Score Better at Skeet, by Fred Missildine, with Nick Karas. Winchester Press, NY, 1972. 160 pp., illus. $5.95. In paper covers, $2.95.
The long-awaited companion volume to *Score Better at Trap.*
Score Better at Trap, by Fred Missildine. Winchester Press, NY, 1971. 192 pp., illus. $5.95. In paper covers, $2.95.
Step-by-step instructions, fully illustrated, on mastering the game by one of the world's leading coaches.

Score Better at Trap and Skeet, by Fred Missildine, with Nick Karas, Winchester Press, NY, 1978. 352 pp., illus. $10.95.
It's like having personal trap and Skeet lessons from Fred Missildine himself.
75 Years with the Shotgun, by C. T. (Buck) Buckman, Valley Publ., Fresno, CA, 1974. 141 pp., illus. $7.50.
An expert hunter and trapshooter shares experiences of a lifetime.
A Shoot of Your Own, by Michael Kemp, A & C Black, London, England, 1978. 182 pp., illus. $17.50.
The amateur gamekeeper at work. Inducing birds to settle, rearing pheasants, organizing shooting, etc.
Shooting—Why We Miss, by Macdonald Hastings, David McKay Co., Inc., New York, NY, 1977. 78 pp., illus. $6.95.
Questions and answers on the successful use of the shotgun.
The Shotgun Book, by Jack O'Connor, Alfred A. Knopf, New York, NY, 1978. 341 pp., illus. $15.
An indispensable book for every shotgunner containing up-to-the-minute authoritative information on every phase of the shotgun.
Shotgun Digest, by Robert Stack, Digest Books, Inc., Northfield, IL. 1974. 8½"x11", 288 pp. Profusely illus. Paperbound. $6.95.
Movie star Robert Stack is a National Skeet Shooting Hall of Famer and an outstanding shotgunner. He covers all aspects of shotguns and shotgun shooting.
The Shotgun in Combat, by Tony Lesce, Desert Publications, Cornville, AZ, 1979. 148 pp., illus. Paper covers. $4.95.
A history of the shotgun and its use in combat.
Shotgun and Shooter, by Percy Stanbury and G. L. Carlisle, 2nd edition, Barrie & Jenkins, London, England, 1978. 224 pp., illus. $11.95.
Guns, gamekeepers, rough shooting, wildfowling, field trials and decoys.
Shotgun Marksmanship, by Percy Stanbury & G. L. Carlisle, 3rd edition, Barrie & Jenkins, London, England, 1978. 224 pp., illus. $11.95.
This book teaches, through words and photographs, how to become a first-class shot, whether the interest lies in shooting game or in competitive shooting.
Shotgun Shooting Facts, by Gough Thomas, Winchester Press, New York, NY, 1979. 304 pp., illus. $10.
One of the most thoughtful, most provocative books about shotguns and shotgun shooting ever written.
The Shotgunner's Bible, by George Laycock. Doubleday & Co., Garden City, NY, 1969. 173 pp., illus., paper covers. $2.50.
Coverage of shotguns, ammunition, marksmanship, hunting of various types of game, care and safety, etc.
Shotgunner's Guide, by Monte Burch, Winchester Press, New York, NY, 1980. 208 pp., illus. $10.50.
A basic book for the young and old who wants to try shotgunning or who wants to improve his skill.
Shotgunning: The Art and the Science, by Bob Brister, Winchester Press, NY, 1976. 321 pp., illus. $12.95.
Hundreds of specific tips and truly novel techniques to improve the field and target shooting of every shotgunner.
Shotguns & Cartridges, by Gough Thomas. A. & C. Black, London, Eng., 1975. 254 pp., illus. $15.00.
A thoroughly revised and updated book on the understanding of modern guns and cartridges for clay pigeon and game shooting.
Shotguns and Shooting, by A. J. Barker, Paladin Press, Boulder, CO., 1973. 84 pp., illus., paper covers. $4.00, cloth $6.50.
All about shotguns and their use in shooting and hunting.
Shotguns & Shooting, by E. S. McCawley, Jr., Van Nostrand Reinhold Co., NY, 1965. 146 pp. illus. Paper covers. $4.95.
Covers the history and development, types of shotguns and ammunition, shotgun shooting, etc.
Skeet Shooting with D. Lee Braun, Robt. Campbell, ed. Grosset & Dunlap, NY, 1967. 160 pp., illus. Paper covers $3.95.
Thorough instructions on the fine points of Skeet shooting.
L. C. Smith Shotguns, Wm. S. Brophy, Beinfeld Publ., Inc., No. Hollywood, CA, 2nd ed., 1979. 200 pp., illus. $24.95.
The first work ever on this important American gun company. The original factory records form an authenticating basis for this comprehensive study.
Successful Shotgun Shooting, by A. A. Montague. Winchester Press, NY, 1970. 160 pp., illus. $6.95.
The work of a superb shot and a great teacher; even the experts can read with profit.
Trapshooting with D. Lee Braun and the Remington Pros., ed. by R. Campbell. Remington Arms Co., Bridgeport, CT, 1969. 157 pp., well illus., Paper covers. $3.95.
America's masters of the scattergun give the secrets of professional marksmanship.
Westley Richards Shotguns, 1932, facsimile reprint by Empire Press, Santa Fe, NM, 1980. 50 pp., illus. Paper covers. $15.00.
A facsimile reprint of this great gunmakers 1932 catalog.
Wing & Shot, by R. G. Wehle, Country Press, Scottsville, NY, 1967. 190 pp., illus. $12.
Step-by-step account on how to train a fine shooting dog.
The World's Fighting Shotguns, by Thomas F. Swearengen, T. B. N. Enterprises, Alexandria, VA, 1979. 500 pp., illus. $24.95.
The complete military and police reference work from the shotgun's inception to date, with up-to-date developments.
You and the Target, by Kay Ohye, Kay Ohye Enterprises, No. Brunswick, NJ, 1978. 83 pp., illus. Paper covers. $9.95.
All new trapshooting handbook to better scores.

IMPORTANT NOTICE TO BOOK BUYERS

Books listed above may be bought from Ray Riling Arms Books Co., 114 Greenwood Ave., Box 135, Wyncote, PA 19095, phone 215/886-5303. Joe Riling, the proprietor, is the researcher and compiler of "The Arms Library" and a seller of gun books for over 30 years.

The Riling stock includes the books classic and modern, many hard-to-find items, and many not obtainable elsewhere. The above pages list a portion of the current stock. They offer prompt, complete service, with delayed shipments occurring only on out-of-print or out-of-stock books.

NOTICE FOR ALL CUSTOMERS: Remittance in U.S. funds must accompany all orders. For U.S. add 75¢ per book with a minimum of $1.00 per order for postage and insurance. For UPS add 50% to mailing costs.

All foreign countries add 85¢ per book for postage and handling, plus $3. per 10-lb. package or under for safe delivery by registered mail. Parcels not registered are sent at the "buyers risk."

Payments in excess of order or for "Backorders" are credited or fully refunded at request. Books "As-Ordered" are not returnable except by permission and a handling charge on these of $1.00 per book is deducted from refund or credit. Only Pennsylvania customers must include current sales tax.

Full variety of arms books are also available from Fairfield Book Co., Inc. P.O. Box 289, Brookfield Center, CT 06805, Rutgers Book Center, 127 Raritan Ave., Highland Park, NJ 08904.

Directory of the Arms Trade

AMMUNITION (Commercial)

Alcan Shells, (See: Smith & Wesson Ammunition Co.)
Bingham Ltd., 1775-C Wilwat Dr., Norcross, GA 30093
Cascade Cartridge Inc., (See Omark)
DWM (see RWS)
Dynamit Nobel of America, Inc., 105 Stonehurst Court, Northvale, NJ 07647/201-767-1660 (RWS)
Federal Cartridge Co., 2700 Foshay Tower, Minneapolis, MN 55402
Frontier Cartridge Division-Hornady Mfg. Co., Box 1848, Grand Island, NE 68801/308-382-1390
H&H Cartridge Corp., County Road 200 W., Box 104, Greensburg, IN 47240 (Super Vel)
Midway Arms, Inc., R. R. #5, Columbia, MO 65201
Omark-CCI, Inc., Box 856, Lewiston, Ida. 83501
Precision Prods. of Wash., Inc., N. 311 Walnut Rd., Spokane, WA 99206 (Exammo)
RWS (see Dynamit Nobel of America)
Remington Arms Co., Bridgeport, Conn. 06602
Service Armament, 689 Bergen Blvd., Ridgefield, N.J. 07657
Smith & Wesson Ammunition Co., 2399 Forman Rd., Rock Creek, OH 44084
Super Vel (see H&H Cartridge Corp.)
Velet Cartridge Co., N. 6809 Lincoln, Spokane, WA 99208
Weatherby's, 2781 E. Firestone Blvd., South Gate, Calif. 90280
Winchester-Western, East Alton, Ill. 62024

AMMUNITION (Custom)

American Pistol Bullet, 133 Blue Bell Rd., Greensbore, NC 27406/919-272-6151
Bill Ballard, 830 Miles Ave., Billings, MT 59101 (ctlg. 50¢)
Ballistek, Weapons Systems Div., Box 11537, Tucson, AZ 85734/602-294-1991
Beal's Bullets, 170 W. Marshall Rd., Lansdowne, PA 19050 (Auto Mag Specialists)
Bell's Gun & Sport Shop, 3309-19 Mannheim Rd., Franklin Park, IL 60131
Brass Extrusion Labs. Ltd., 800 W. Maple Lane, Bensenville, IL 60106
C. W. Cartridge Co., 71 Hackensack St., Wood-Ridge, NJ 07075
Russell Campbell, 219 Leisure Dr., San Antonio, Tex. 78201
Collectors Shotshell Arsenal, E. Tichy, 365 So. Moore, Lakewood, CO 80226
Crown City Arms, P.O. Box 1126, Cortland, NY 13045
Cumberland Arms, Rt. 1, Shafer Rd., Blantons Chapel, Manchester, TN 37355
E. W. Ellis Sport Shop, RFD 1, Box 315, Corinth, NY 12822
Ellwood Epps Northern Ltd., 210 Worthington St. W., North Bay, Ont. P1B 3B4, Canada
Ramon B. Gonzalez, P.O. Box 370, Monticello, NY 12701
Gussert Bullet & Cartridge Co., Inc., P.O. Box 3945, Green Bay, WI 54303
J-4, Inc., 1700 Via Burton, Anaheim, CA 92806 (custom bullets)
Jensen's Custom Ammunition, 5146 E. Pima, Tucson, AZ 85716
R. H. Keeler, 817 "N" St., Port Angeles, WA 98362/206-457-4702
KTW Inc., 710 Foster Park Rd., Lorain, OH 44053 (bullets)
Dean Lincoln, P.O. Box 1886, Farmington, NM 87401
Lomont Precision Bullets, 4421 S. Wayne Ave., Ft. Wayne, IN 46807/219-694-6792 (custom cast bullets only)
Mansfield Gunshop, Box 83, New Boston, N.H. 03070
Numrich Arms Corp., 203 Broadway, W. Hurley, N.Y. 12491
Robert Pomeroy, Morison Ave., Corinth, ME 04427 (custom shells)
Precision Ammunition & Reloading, 122 Hildenboro Square, Agincourt, Ont. M1W 1Y3, Canada
Precision Prods. of Wash., Inc., N. 311 Walnut Rd., Spokane, WA 99206 (Exammo)
Anthony F. Sailer-Ammunition, 707 W. Third St., P.O. Box L, Owen, WI 54460
Sanders Cust. Gun Serv., 2358 Tyler Lane, Louisville, Ky. 40205
Geo. Spence, 202 Main St., Steele, MO 63877/314-695-4926 (box-primed cartridges)
The 3-D Company, Box 142, Doniphan, NB 68832 (reloaded police ammo)

AMMUNITION (Foreign)

K. J. David & Company, P.O. Box 12595, Lake Park, FL 33043
Dynamit Nobel of America, Inc., 105 Stonehurst Court, Northvale, NJ 07647/201-767-1660 (RWS, Geco, Rottweil)
Guilio Fiocchi S.p.A., 22053 Lecco-Belledo, Italy
Hirtenberger Patronen-, Zündhütchen- & Metallwarenfabrik. A.G., Leobersdorfer Str. 33, A2552 Hirtenberg, Austria
Hy-Score Arms Co., 200 Tillary, Brooklyn, N.Y. 11201
Paul Jaeger Inc., 211 Leedom St., Jenkintown, Pa. 19046
S. E. Laszlo, 200 Tillary, Brooklyn, N.Y. 11201
NORMA-Precision, 798 Cascadilla St., Ithaca, NY 14850
RWS (Rheinische-Westfälische Sprengstoff) see: Dynamit Nobel of America

AMMUNITION COMPONENTS—BULLETS, POWDER, PRIMERS

The Alberts Corp., P.O. Box 157, Franklin Lakes, NJ 07417/201-337-5848 (Taurus bull.)
Alcan, (see: Smith & Wesson Ammunition Co.)
Ammo-O-Mart, P.O. Box 543, Renfrew, Ont., Canada K7V-4B1 (Curry bullets)
Austin Powder Co. (see Red Diamond Dist. Co.)
Ballistic Prods., Inc. 17510 19th Ave. No., Wayzata, MN 55391
Ballistic Research Inc., 935 E. Meadow Dr., Palo Alto, CA 94303 (BRI slug)
Barnes Bullets, P.O. Box 215, American Fork, UT 84003
B.E.L.L., Bell's Gun & Sport Shop, 3309-19 Mannheim Rd., Franklin Pk., IL 60131
Bitterroot Bullet Co., Box 412, Lewiston, ID. 83501. 35¢ (coin or stamps) and #10 SASE for lit.
Brass Extrusion Laboratories, Ltd., 800 W. Maple Lane, Bensenville, IL 60106
Centrix, 2116 N. 10th Ave., Tucson, Ariz
Kenneth E. Clark, 18738 Highway 99, Madera, CA 93637 (Bullets)
Division Lead, 7742 W. 61 Pl., Summit, Ill. 60502
DuPont, Explosives Dept., Wilmington, Del. 19898
Dynamit Nobel of America, Inc., 105 Stonehurst Court, Northvale, NJ 07647/201-767-1660 (RWS percussion caps)
Elk Mountain Shooters Supply Inc., 1719 Marie, Pasco, WA 99301 (Alaskan bullets)
Farmer Bros., 1102 Washington St., Eldora, IA 50627 (Lage wad)
Federal Cartridge Co., 2700 Foshay Tower, Minneapolis, MN 55402 (nickel cases)
Forty Five Ranch Enterprises, 119 S. Main, Miami, Okla. 74354
Godfrey Reloading Supply, Hi-Way 67-111, Brighton, IL 62012 (cast bullets)
Lynn Godfrey, see: Elk Mtn. Shooters Supply
Green Bay Bullets, 233 No. Ashland, Green Bay, Wis. 54303 (lead)
Gussert Bullet & Cartridge Co., Inc., P.O. Box 3945, Green Bay, WI 54303
Hardin Specialty Distr., P.O. Box 338, Radcliff, KY 40160 (empty, primed cases)
Hercules Powder Co., 910 Market St., Wilmington, Del. 19899
Herter's Inc., Waseca, Minn. 56093
Hodgdon Powder Co. Inc., 7710 W. 50th Hwy., Shawnee Mission, KS 66202
Hornady Mfg. Co., Box 1848, Grand Island, Neb. 68801
N. E. House Co., 195 West High St., E. Hampton, CT 06424/203-267-2133 (zinc bases only)
J-4, Inc., 1700 Via Burton, Anaheim, CA 92806 (custom bullets)
Jaro Bullets, P.O. Box 6125, Pasadena, TX 77501
Keel Co., Bullet Metal Div., 327 East "B" St., Wilmington, CA 90744/213-834-2555 (bullet lead)
L. L. F. Die Shop, 1281 Highway 99 North, Eugene, Ore. 97402
Lage Uniwad Co., 1102 Washington St., Eldora, IA 50627
Ljutic Ind., Inc., Box 2117, Yakima, WA 98902 (Mono-wads)
Lomont Precision Bullets, 4421 S. Wayne Ave., Ft. Wayne, IN 46807/219-694-6792 (custom cast bullets)
Lyman Products Corp., Rte. 147, Middlefield, CT 06455
Michael's Antiques, Box 233, Copiague, L.I., NY 11726 (Balle Blondeau)
Miller Trading Co., 20 S. Front St., Wilmington, N.C. 28401
Norma-Precision, 798 Cascadilla St., Ithaca, NY 14850
Nosler Bullets, P.O. Box 688, Beaverton, OR 97005
Robert Pomeroy, Morison Ave., East Corinth, ME 04427
Red Diamond Distributing Co., 1304 Snowdon Dr., Knoxville, TN 37912 (black powder)
Remington-Peters, Bridgeport, Conn. 06602
Sanderson's, 724 W. Edgewater, Portage, Wis. 53901 (cork wad)
Sierra Bullets Inc., 10532 Painter Ave., Santa Fe Springs, CA 90670
Smith & Wesson Ammunition Co., 2399 Forman Rd., Rock Creek, OH 44084
Speer Products Inc., Box 896, Lewiston, Ida. 83501
C. H. Stocking, Rte. 3, Box 195, Hutchinson, Minn. 55350 (17 cal. bullet jackets)
Taurus Bullets, Alberts Corp., P.O. Box 157, Franklin Lakes, NJ 07417/201-337-5848
Taylor Bullets, P.O. Box 21254, San Antonio, TX 78221 (cast)
United Cartridge Co., P.O. Box 604, Valley Industrial Park, Casa Grande, AR 85222/602-836-2510 (P.C. wads)
Vitt & Boos, c/o Mrs. Geo. N. Vitt, P.O. Box 148, Wiscasset, ME 04578 (shotgun slugs)
Winchester-Western, 275 Winchester Ave., New Haven, CT 06504
Wood Die Shop, Box 386, Florence, OR 97439 (17 cal.)
Xelex Ltd., P.O. Box 543, Renfrow, Ont. K7V 4B1, Canada (powder, Curry bullets)
Zero Bullet Co., P.O. Box 1188, Cullman, AL 35055

ANTIQUE ARMS DEALERS

Robert Abels, 2881 N.E. 33 Ct., Ft. Lauderdale, FL 33306/305-564-6985 (Catalog $1.00)
Angcep, (The Gun Shop & Anglers Mail), 6497 Pearl Rd., Cleveland, OH 44130/216-884-7476

Beeman Precision Airguns, Inc., 47 Paul Dr., San Rafael, CA 94903/415-472-7121 (airguns only)
Wm. Boggs, 1243 Grandview Ave., Columbus, Ohio 43212
Ed's Gun House, Lone Pine Trading Post, Highways 61 and 248, Minnesota City, MN 55959/507-689-2922
Ellwood Epps Northern Ltd., 210 Worthington St. W., North Bay, Ont. PIB 3B4, Canada
N. Flayderman & Co., Squash Hollow, New Milford, Conn. 06776
Fulmer's Antique Firearms, Chet Fulmer, P.O. Box 792, Detroit Lakes, MN 56501/218-847-7712
Garcia National Gun Traders, Inc., 225 S.W. 22nd Ave., Miami, Fla. 33135
Herb Glass, Bullville, NY 10915/914-361-3021
Goergen's Gun Shop, Rte. 2, Box 182BB, Austin, MN 55912/507-433-9280
Goodman's for Guns, 1002 Olive St., St. Louis, MO 63101
Griffin's Guns & Antiques, R.R. 4, Peterborough, Ont., Canada K9J 6X5/705-748-3220
Hansen & Company, 244 Old Post Rd., Southport, CT 06490
Holbrook Arms Museum, 12953 Biscayne Blvd., N. Miami, Fla. 33161
Lew Horton Sports Shop, Inc., 450 Waverly St., Framingham, MA 01701
Jackson Arms, 6209 Hillcrest Ave., Dallas, Tex. 75205
Jerry's Gun Shop, 9220 Ogden Ave., Brookfield, Ill. 60513
Lever Arms Serv. Ltd., 771 Dunsmuir St., Vancouver, B.C., Canada V6C 1M9
Charles W. Moore, R.D. 2, Box 276, Schenevus, NY 12155
Museum of Historical Arms, 1038 Alton Rd., Miami Beach, FL 33139 (ctlg. $3)
New Orleans Arms Co., Inc., P.O. Box 26087, New Orleans, LA 70186
O.K. Hardware, Westgate Shopping Center, Great Falls, MT 59404
Old West Gun Room, 3509 Carlson Blvd., El Cerrito, Cal. 94530 (write for list)
Pioneer Guns, 5228 Montgomery, (Cincinnati) Norwood, OH 45212
Pony Express Sport Shop, Inc., 17460 Ventura Blvd., Encino, CA 91316
Martin B. Retting Inc., 11029 Washington, Culver City, Calif. 90230
Ridge Guncraft, Inc., 125 E. Tyrone Rd., Oak Ridge, TN 37830/615-483-4024
S.G. Intl., P.O. Box 702, Hermosa Beach, CA. 90254
San Francisco Gun Exch., 124 Second St., San Francisco, Calif. 94105
Santa Ana Gunroom, P.O. Box 1777, Santa Ana, Calif. 92701
Ward & Van Valkenburg, 114-32nd Ave. N., Fargo, ND 58102
M. C. Wiest, 125 E. Tyrone Rd., Oak Ridge, TN 37830/615-483-4024
J. David Yale, Ltd., 2618 Conowingo Rd., Bel Air, MD 21014/301-838-9479
Lewis Yearout, 308 Riverview Dr. E., Great Falls, MT 59404

BOOKS (ARMS), Publishers and Dealers

Arms & Armour Press, 2-6 Hampstead High Street, London NW3 1PR, England
Beinfeld Publishing, Inc., 12767 Saticoy St., No. Hollywood, CA 91605/213-982-3700
Blacktail Mountain Books, 42 First Ave. West, Kalispell, MT 59901/406-257-5573
DBI Books, Inc., One Northfield Plaza, Northfield, IL 60093/312-441-7010
EPCO Publ. Co., 75-24 64 St., Glendale, NY 11227
Empire Press, P.O. Box 2902, Santa Fe, NM 87501
Fairfield Book Co., Inc., P.O. Box 289, Brookfield Center, CT 06805/800-243-1318
Follett Publishing Co., 1010 W. Washington Blvd., Chicago, IL 60607
Fortress Publications Inc., P.O. Box 241, Stoney Creek, Ont. L8G 3X9, Canada
Guncraft Books, Div. of Ridge Guncraft, Inc., 125 E. Tyrone Rd., Oak Ridge, TN 37830/615-483-4024
Handgun Press, 5832 S. Green, Chicago, IL 60621
Jackson Arms, 6209 Hillcrest Ave., Dallas, TX 75205
Lyman, Route 147, Middlefield, CT 06455
John Olson Co., 294 W. Oakland Ave., Oakland, NJ 07436
Ridge Guncraft Inc., M. C. Wiest, 234 N. Tulane Ave., Oak Ridge, TN 37830
Ray Riling Arms Books Co., 6844 Gorsten St., Philadelphia, PA 19119
Rutgers Book Center, Mark Aziz, 127 Raritan Ave., Highland Park, NJ 08904
Stackpole Books, Cameron & Kelker Sts., Telegraph Press Bldg., Harrisburg, PA 17105
Stoeger Publishing Co., 55 Ruta Court, South Hackensack, NJ 07606
James C. Tillinghast, Box 568, Marlow, NH 03456
Ken Trotman, 2-6 Hampstead High St., London, NW3 1PR, England

BULLET & CASE LUBRICANTS

Birchwood-Casey Co., Inc., 7900 Fuller Rd., Eden Prairie, Minn. 55343 (Anderol)
Chopie Mfg. Inc., 531 Copeland, La Crosse, Wis. 54601 (Black-Solve)
Cooper-Woodward, Box 972, Riverside, Cal. 92502 (Perfect Lube)
D. R. Corbin Mfg. & Supply Inc., P.O. Box 758, Phoenix, OR 97535
Green Bay Bullets, 233 N. Ashland, Green Bay, Wis. 54303 (EZE-Size case lube)
Gussert Bullet & Cartridge Co., Inc., P.O. Box 3945, Green Bay, WI 54203 (Super Lube)
Herter's, Inc., Hiway 13 South, Waseca, MN 56903/507-835-4011 (Perfect Lubricant)
IPCO (Industrial Products Co.), Box 14, Bedford, MA 01730
Javelina Products, Box 337, San Bernardino, CA 92402/714-882-5847 (Alox beeswax)
Jet-Aer Corp., 100 Sixth Ave., Paterson, N.J. 07524
LeClear Industries, P.O. Box 484, Royal Oak, MI 48068
Lenz Prod. Co., Box 1226, Sta. C, Canton, O. 44708 (Clenzoil)
Lyman Products Corp., Rte. 147, Middlefield, CT 06455 (Size-Ezy)
Marmel Prods., P.O. Box 97, Utica, MI 48087 (Marvelube, Marvelux)
Micro Shooter's Supply, Box 213, Las Cruces, N. Mex. 88001 (Micro-Lube)
Mirror Lube, P.O. Box 693, San Juan Capistrano, CA 92675
M&N Bullet Lube, Box 495, Jefferson St., Madras, OR 97741
Pacific Tool Co., P.O. Box 2048, Ordnance Plant Rd., Grand Island, NE 68801/308-384-2308
Phelps Rel. Inc., Box 4004, E. Orange, N.J. 07019
Precision Ammunition & Rel., 122 Hildenboro Square, Agincourt, Ont. M1W 1Y3, Canada
RCBS, Inc., Box 1919, Oroville, Calif. 95965
SAECO Rel. Inc., P.O. Box 778, Carpinteria, CA 93103
Shooters Accessory Supply (SAS), see D. R. Corbin
Tamarack Prods., Inc., Box 224, Barrington, IL 60010 (Bullet lube)
Testing Systems, Inc., 220 Pegasus Ave., Northvale, NJ 07647/201-767-7300

BULLET SWAGE DIES AND TOOLS

Belmont Products, Rte. #1, Friendsville, TN 37737
C-H Tool & Die Corp., P.O. Box L, Owen, WI 54460
Lester Coats, 416 Simpson St., North Bend, OR 97459 (lead wire cutter)
D. R. Corbin Mfg. & Supply Inc., P.O. Box 758, Phoenix, OR 97535
Herter's Inc., Hiway 13 South, Waseca, MN 56093/507-835-4011
Hollywood, Whitney Sales Inc., P.O. Box 875, Reseda, CA 91335
Huntington's Die Specialties, P.O. Box 991, Oroville, CA 95965
Independent Machine & Gun Shop, 1416 N. Hayes, Pocatello, ID 83201 (TNT bullet dies)
L.L.F. Die Shop, 1281 Highway 99 North, Eugene, OR 97402
Rorschach Precision Products, P.O. Box 1613, Irving, TX 75060
SAS Dies, see: D. R. Corbin
Robert B. Simonson, Rte. 2, 2129 Vanderbilt Rd., Kalamazoo, MI 49002
Sport Flite Mfg., Inc., 2520 Industrial Row, Troy, MI 48084/313-280-0648
TNT (see Ind. Mach. & Gun Shop)

CARTRIDGES FOR COLLECTORS

AD Hominem, R.R. 3, Orillia, Ont., Canada L3V 6H3
Antique Arsenal, 365 S. Moore, Lakewood, CO 80226
Cameron's, 16690 W. 11th Ave., Golden, Colo. 80401
Centrefire Sports Dunedin, P.O. Box 1293, 41 Dowling St., Dunedin, New Zealand
Chas. E. Duffy, Williams Lane, West Hurley, N.Y. 12419
Tom M. Dunn, 1342 So. Poplar, Casper, Wyo. 82601
Ellwood Epps (Orillia) Ltd., Hwy. 11 North, Orillia, Ont. L3V 6H3, Canada/705-689-5333
Idaho Ammunition Service, 410 21st Ave., Lewiston, ID 83501
San Francisco Gun Exchange, 124 Second St., San Francisco, CA 94105
Perry Spangler, 519 So. Lynch, Flint, Mich. 48503 (list 50¢)
Ernest Tichy, 365 So. Moore, Lakewood, CO 80226
James C. Tillinghast, Box 568, Marlow, N.H. 03456 (list 50¢)
Lewis Yearout, 308 Riverview Dr. E., Great Falls, MT 59404

CASES, CABINETS AND RACKS—GUN

Action Co., P.O. Box 528, McKinney, TX 75069
Alco Carrying Cases, 601 W. 26th St., New York, N.Y. 10001
Allen Co., Inc., 640 Compton St., Broomfield, CO 80020/303-469-1857
Art Jewel Enterprises, Box 819, Berkeley, IL 60163
Morton Booth Co., Box 123, Joplin, Mo. 64801
Boyt Co., Div. of Welsh Sportg. Gds., Box 1108, Iowa Falls, Ia. 50126
Brenik, Inc., 925 W. Chicago Ave., Chicago, IL 60622
Browning, Rt. 4, Box 624-B, Arnold, MO 63010
Cap-Lex Gun Cases, Capitol Plastics of Ohio, Inc., 333 Van Camp Rd., Bowling Green, OH 43402
Dara-Nes Inc., P.O. Box 119, East Hampton, CT 06424/203-267-4175 (firearms security chests)
East-Tenn Mills, Inc., 2300 Buffalo Rd., Johnson City, TN 37601 (gun socks)
Ellwood Epps (Orillia) Ltd., R.R. 3, Hwy. 11 North, Orillia, Ont. L3V 6H3, Canada/705-689-5333 (custom gun cases)
Norbert Ertel, Box 1150, Des Plaines, IL 60018 (cust. gun cases)
Flambeau Plastics Corp., 801 Lynn, Baraboo, Wis. 53913
Gun-Ho Case Mfg. Co., 110 East 10 St., St. Paul, Minn. 55101
Harbor House Gun Cabinets, 12508 Center St., South Gate, CA 90280
B. E. Hodgdon, Inc., 7710 W. 50 Hiway, Shawnee-Mission, Kans. 66202
Marvin Huey Gun Cases, Box 98, Reed's Spring, MO 65737/417-538-4233 (handbuilt leath. cases)
Ithaca Gun Co., Terrace Hill, Ithaca, N.Y. 14850
Jumbo Sports Prods., P.O. Box 280-Airport Rd., Frederick, MD 21701
Kalispel Metal Prods. (KMP), Box 267, Cusick, WA 99119 (aluminum boxes)
Kolpin Mfg., Inc., Box 231, Berlin, WI 54923/414-361-0400
Marble Arms Corp., 420 Industrial Park, Gladstone, Mich. 49837
Bill McGuire, 1600 No. Eastmont Ave., East Wenatchee, WA 98801 (custom cases)
W. A. Miller Co., Inc. (Wamco), Mingo Loop, Oguossoc, ME 04964 (wooden handgun cases)
National Sports Div., Medalist Ind., 19 E. McWilliams St., Fond du Lac, WI 54935
Nortex Co., 2821 Main St., Dallas, Tex. 75226 (automobile gun rack)
North American Case, Inc., Industrial Park Rd., Johnstown, PA 15904/814-266-8941

North Star Devices, Inc., P.O. Box 2095, North St., Paul, MN 55109 (Gun-Slinger portable rack)
Paul-Reed, Inc., P.O. Box 227, Charlevoix, Mich. 49720
Penguin Industries, Inc., Airport Industrial Mall, Coatesville, PA 19320/215-384-6000
Precise, 3 Chestnut, Suffern, NY 10901
Protecto Plastics, Inc., 201 Alpha Rd., Wind Gap, Pa. 18091 (carrying cases)
Provo Steel & Supply Co., P.O. Box 977, Provo, UT 84601 (steel gun cases)
Richland Arms Co., 321 W. Adrian, Blissfield, Mich. 49228
Saf-T-Case Mfg. Co., P.O. Box 5472, Irving, TX 75062
San Angelo Co. Inc., Box 984, San Angelo, TX 76901
Buddy Schoellkopf, 4949 Joseph Hardin Dr., Dallas, TX 75236
Se-Cur-All Cabinet Co., K-Prods., P.O. Box 2052, Michigan City, IN 46360/219-872-7957
Security Gun Chest, see: Tread Corp.
Sile Distr., 7 Centre Market Pl., New York, N.Y. 10013 (leg o'mutton case)
Stearns Mfg. Co., P.O. Box 1498, St. Cloud, MN 56301
Straight Shooter Gun Cases, P.O. Box 10, Teaneck, NJ 07666
Stowline Inc., 811 So. 1st, Kent, WA 98031
Tread Corp., P.O. Box 13207, 1734 Granby St. N.E., Roanoke, VA 24012 (security gun chest)
Trik Truk, P.O. Box 3760, Kent, WA 98301 (P.U. truck cases)
Vanguard Prods. Corp., 545 Cedar Lane, Box #10, Teaneck, NJ 07666 (Straight Shooter gun cases)
Weather Shield Sports Equipm. Inc., Rte. #3, Petoskey Rd., Charlevoix, MI 49720
Woodstream Corp., Box 327, Lititz, Pa. 17543
Yield House, Inc., RFD, No. Conway, N.H. 03860

CHOKE DEVICES & RECOIL ABSORBERS

Arms Ingenuity Co., Box 1; 51 Canal St., Weatogue, CT 06089/203-658-5624 (Jet-Away)
C&H Research, 115 Sunnyside Dr., Lewis, KS 67552/316-324-5445 (Mercury recoil suppressor)
Dahl's Gun Shop, 6947 King Ave., Route 4, Billings, MT 59102
Diverter Arms, Inc., P.O. Box 22084, Houston, TX 77027 (shotgun diverter)
Edwards Recoil Reducer, 269 Herbert St., Alton, Ill. 62002
Emsco Variable Shotgun Chokes, 101 Second Ave., S.E., Waseca, MN 56093/507-835-1481
Herter's Inc., Waseca, Minn. 56093. (Vari-Choke)
J & K Enterprises, Rte. 1, B.O.B. 202-A, Scappoose, OR 97056 (Mercury recoil absorbers)
Lyman Products Corp., Rte. 147, Middlefield, CT 06455 (Cutts Comp.)
Mag-Na-Port Arms, Inc., 30016 S. River Rd., Mt. Clemens, MI 48043 (muzzle-brake system)
Mag-Na-Port of Canada, 1861 Burrows Ave., Winnipeg, Manitoba R2X 2V6, Canada
Poly-Choke Co., Inc., Box 296, Hartford, Conn. 06101
Pro-Port Canada, 1861 Burrows Ave., Winnipeg, Manitoba R2X 2V6, Canada
Pro-Port U.S.A., 30016 South River Rd., Mt. Clemens, MI 48045/313-469-7323

CHRONOGRAPHS AND PRESSURE TOOLS

B-Square Co., Box 11281, Ft. Worth, Tex. 76110
Custom Chronograph Co., Rt. 1, Box 193A, Tonasket, WA 98855/508-486-4379
Diverter Arms, Inc., P.O. Box 22084, Houston, TX 77027 (press. tool)
Herter's, Waseca, Minn. 56093
Oehler Research, P.O. Box 9135, Austin, Tex. 78756
Sundtek Co., P.O. Box 744, Springfield, Ore. 97477
Telepacific Electronics Co., Inc., P.O. Box 2210, Escondido, CA 92025
Tepeco, P.O. Box 502, Moss Point, MS 601-475-7645 (Tepeco Speed-Meter)
Vibra-Tek, 2807 N. Prospect St., Colorado Springs, CO 80907 (Kronoscope)
M. York, 5508 Griffith Rd., Gaithersburg, MD 20760 (press. tool)

CLEANING & REFINISHING SUPPLIES

A 'n A Co., Box 571, King of Prussia, PA 19406 (Valet shotgun cleaner)
Armite Labs., 1845 Randolph St., Los Angeles, CA 90001 (pen oiler)
Armoloy Co. of Ft. Worth, 204 E. Daggett St., Ft. Worth, TX 76104
Birchwood-Casey, 7900 Fuller Rd., Eden Prairie, MN 55344/612-927-1733
Bisonite Co., Inc., P.O. Box 84, Kenmore Station, Buffalo, NY 14217
Blue and Gray Prods., Inc., 817 E. Main St., Bradford, PA 16701
Jim Brobst, 299 Poplar St., Hamburg, Pa. 19526 (J-B Compound)
GB Prods. Dept., H & R, Inc., Industrial Rowe, Gardner, MA 01440
Browning Arms, Rt. 4, Box 624-B, Arnold, Mo. 63010
J. M. Bucheimer Co., P.O. Box 280, Airport Rd., Frederick, MD 21701/301-662-5101
Burnishine Prod. Co., 8140 N. Ridgeway, Skokie, Ill. 60076 (Stock Glaze)
Caddie Products Corp., Div. of Jet-Aer, Paterson, NJ 07524 (the Cloth)
Chem-Pak Inc., Winchester, VA 22601 (Gun-Savr. protect. & lubricant)
Chopie Mfg. Inc., 531 Copeland, La Crosse, Wis. 54601 (Black-Solve)
Clenzoil Co., Box 1226, Sta. C, Canton, O. 44708
Clover Mfg. Co., 139 Woodward Ave., Norwalk, CT 06856 (Clover compound)
Dri-Slide, Inc., Industrial Park, 1210 Locust St., Fremont, MI 49412
Durango U.S.A., P.O. Box 1029, Durango, CO 81301 (cleaning rods)
Forty-Five Ranch Enterpr., 119 S. Main St., Miami, Okla. 74354
Gun-All Products, Box 244, Dowagiac, Mich. 49047
Frank C. Hoppe Div., Penguin Ind., Inc., Airport Industrial Mall, Coatesville, PA 19320/215-384-6000
J & G Rifle Ranch, Box S 80, Turner, MT 59542
Jet-Aer Corp., 100 Sixth Ave., Paterson, N.J. 07524 (blues & oils)
Kellog's Professional Prods., Inc., P.O. Box 1201, Sandusky, OH 44870
K.W. Kleinendorst, 48 Taylortown Rd., Montville, N.J. 07045 (rifle clg. cables)
LPS Res. Labs. Inc., 2050 Cotner Ave., Los Angeles, Calif. 90025
LEM Gun Spec., Box 31, College Park, Ga 30337 (Lewis Lead Remover)
Liquid Wrench, Box 10628, Charlotte, N.C. 28201 (pen. oil)
Lynx Line Gun Prods. Div., Protective Coatings, Inc., 20626 Fenkell Ave., Detroit, MI 48223
Marble Arms Co., 420 Industrial Pk., Gladstone, Mich. 49837
Micro Sight Co., 242 Harbor Blvd., Belmont, Ca. 94002 (bedding)
Mirror-Lube, P.O. Box 693, San Juan Capistrano, CA 92675
New Method Mfg. Co., Box 175, Bradford, Pa. 16701 (gun blue)
Northern Instruments, Inc., 6680 North Highway 49, Lino Lake, MN 55014 (Stor-Safe rust preventer)
Numrich Arms Co., West Hurley, N.Y. 12491 (44-40 gun blue)
Old World Oil Products, 3827 Queen Ave. No., Minneapolis, MN 55412
Original Mink Oil, Inc., P.O. Box 20191, 10652 N.E. Holman, Portland, OR 97220/503-255-2814
Outers Laboratories, Route 2, Onalaska, WI 54650/608-783-1515 (Gun-slick kits)
Radiator Spec. Co., 1400 Independence Blvd., Charlotte, N.C. 28201 (liquid wrench)
Reardon Prod., 103 W. Market St., Morrison, IL 61270 (Dry-Lube)
Rice Gun Coatings, 1521-43rd St., West Palm Beach, FL 33407
Rig Products Co., Div. of Mitann, Inc., 21320 Deering Ct., Canoga Park, CA 91304/213-883-4700
Rusteprufe Labs., Sparta, WI 54656
San/Bar Corp., Chemicals Div., P.O. Box 11787, 17422 Pullman St., Santa Ana, CA 92711 (Break-Free)
Saunders Sptg. Gds., 338 Somerset, No. Plainfield, NJ 07060 (Sav-Bore)
Schultea's Gun String, 67 Burress, Houston, TX 77022 (pocket-size rifle cleaning kit)
Service Armament, 689 Bergen Blvd., Ridgefield, N. J. 07657 (Parker-Hale)
Silicote Corp., Box 359, Oshkosh, Wis. 54901 (Silicone cloths)
Silver Dollar Guns, P.O. Box 475, 10 Frances St., Franklin, NH 03235 (Silicone oil)
Sportsmen's Labs., Inc., Box 732, Anoka, Minn. 55303 (Gun Life lube)
Taylor & Robbins, Box 164, Rixford, Pa. 16745 (Throat Saver)
Testing Systems, Inc., 220 Pegasus Ave., Northvale, NJ 07647/201-767-7300 (gun lube)
Texas Platers Supply Co., 2453 W. Five Mile Parkway, Dallas, TX 75233 (plating kit)
Totally Dependable Prods., Inc., P.O. Box 277, Zieglerville, PA 19492
C. S. Van Gorden, 120 Tenth Ave., Eau Claire, Wis. 54701 (Instant Blue)
WD-40 Co., 1061 Cudahy Pl., San Diego, CA 92110
West Coast Secoa, 3915 U S Hwy. 98S, Lakeland, FL 33801 (Teflon coatings)
Williams Gun Sight, 7389 Lapeer Rd., Davison, Mich. 48423 (finish kit)
Winslow Arms Inc., P.O. Box 783, Camden, SC 29020 (refinishing kit)
Wisconsin Platers Supply Co., see: Texas Platers Supply Co.
Woodstream Corp., P.O. Box 327, Lititz, Pa. 17543 (Mask)
Zip Aerosol Prods., 21320 Deering Court, Canoga Park, CA 91304

CUSTOM GUNSMITHS

Walter Abe, Abe's Gun Shop, 5120¾ Huntington Dr., Los Angeles, CA 90032/213-227-4870
Ahlman Cust. Gun Shop, R.R. 1, Box 20, Morristown, Minn. 55052
Don Allen, Rte. 1, Timberland, Northfield, MN 55057
Amrine's Gun Shop, 937 Luna Ave., Ojai, CA 93023
Anderson's Guns, Jim Jares, 706 S. 23rd St., Laramie, WY 82070
Antique Arms, D. F. Saunders, 1110 Cleveland Ave., Monett, MO 65708 (Hawken copies)
R. J. Anton, 874 Olympic Dr., Waterloo, IA 50701
Armas Erbi, S.C.I., Box 45, Elgoibar, Spain
John A. Armbrust, 313 E. 11th St., Mishawaka, IN 46544
Atkinson Gun Co., P.O. Box 512, Prescott, AZ 86301
E. von Atzigen, The Custom Shop, 890 Cochrane Crescent, Peterborough, Ont., K9H 5N3 Canada/705-742-6693
Richard W. Baber, 28 Dudley Ave., Colorado Springs, CO 80909
Bacon Creek Gun Shop, Cumberland Falls Rd., Corbin, Ky. 40701
Bain and Davis Sptg. Gds., 599 W. Las Tunas Dr., San Gabriel, Calif. 41776
Stan Baker, 5303 Roosevelt Way NE, Seattle, WA 98105 (shotgun specialist)
Joe J. Balickie, Rte. 2, Box 56-G, Apex, NC 27502
Wm. G. Bankard, 4211 Thorncliff Rd., Baltimore, MD 21236 (Kentuckys)
Barta's, Rte. 1, Box 129-A, Cato, Wis. 54206
Roy L. Bauer, c/o C-D Miller Guns, St. Onge, SD 57779
Bell's Gun & Sport Shop, David Norin, 3319 Mannheim Rd., Franklin Park, IL 60131 (handguns)
Bennett Gun Works, 561 Delaware Ave., Delmar, N.Y. 12054
Irvin L. Benson, Saganaga Lake, Pine Island Camp, Ontario, Canada (via Grand Marais, MN 55604)
Gordon Bess, 708 River St., Canon City, Colo. 81212
Bruce Betts Gunsmith Co., 100 W. Highway 72, Rolla, MO 65401
Al Biesen, W. 2039 Sinto Ave., Spokane, WA 99201
Roger Biesen, W. 2039 Sinto Ave., Spokane, WA 99201

John Bivins, Jr., 200 Wicklow Rd., Winston-Salem, NC 27106
Boone Mountain Trading Post, 118 Sunrise Rd., Saint Marys, PA 15857/814-834-4879
Victor Bortugno, Atlantic & Pacific Arms Co., 4859 Virginia Beach Blvd., Virginia Beach, VA 23462
Art Bourne, see: Guncraft
Breckheimers, Rte. 69-A, Parish, NY 13131
John P. Brown, Jr., Brown's Gun Shop, 3107 Elinore Ave., Rockford, IL 61103/815-962-1236
L. H. Brown, Brown's Rifle Ranch, 1820 Airport Rd., Kalispell, MT 59901
Lenard M. Brownell, Box 25, Wyarno, WY 82845 (Custom rifles)
E. J. Bryant, 3154 Glen St., Eureka, CA 95501
David Budin, Main St., Margaretville, NY 12455
George Bunch, 7735 Garrison Rd., Hyattsville, Md. 20784
Samuel W. Burgess, 25 Squam Rd., Rockport, MA 01966 (bluing repairs)
Leo Bustani, P.O. Box 8125, W. Palm Beach, Fla. 33407
Cache La Poudre Rifleworks, 168 No. College Ave., Ft. Collins, CO 80524/303-482-6913/303-482-6913 (cust. ML)
Cameron's Guns, 16690 W. 11th Ave., Golden, CO 80401
Lou Camilli, 4700 Oahu Dr. N.E., 4700 Oahu Dr. N.E., Albuquerque, NM 87111/505-293-5259 (ML)
Carter Gun Works, 2211 Jefferson Pk. Ave., Charlottesville, VA 22903
Ralph L. Carter, Carter's Gun Shop, 225 G St., Penrose, CO 81240/303-372-6240
R. MacDonald Champlin, P.O. Box 74, Wentworth, NH 03282 (ML rifles and pistols)
Mark Chanlynn, Bighorn Trading Co., 1704-14th St., Boulder, CO 80302
N. C. Christakos, 2842 N. Austin, Chicago, IL 60634
Jim Clark, Custom Gun Shop, 5367 S. 1950 West, Roy, UT 84067
Classic Arms Corp., P.O. Box 8, Palo Alto, CA 94302/415-321-7243
Kenneth E. Clark, 18738 Highway 99, Madera, Calif. 93637
Richard G. Cole, Box 159, Saegertown, PA 16433
John Corry, P.O. Box 109, Deerfield, IL 60015/312-541-6250 (U.S. agent for Frank E. Malin & Son)
The Country Gun Shoppe Ltd., 251 N. Front St., Monument, CO 80132
Crest Carving Co., 14849 Dillow St., Westminster, Ca. 92683
Crocker, 1510 - 42nd St., Los Alamos, NM 87544 (rifles)
Philip R. Crouthamel, 513 E. Baltimore, E. Lansdowne, PA 19050
Jim Cuthbert, 715 S. 5th St., Coos Bay, Ore. 97420
Dahl's Custom Stocks, Rt. 4, Box 187, Schofield Rd., Lake Geneva, WI 53147
Dahl's Gunshop, 6947 King Ave., Billings, MT 59102
Homer L. Dangler, Box 254, Addison, MI 49220 (Kentucky rifles)
Davis Gun Shop, 7213 Lee Highway, Falls Church, VA 22046
Dee Davis, 5658 So. Mayfield, Chicago, Ill. 60638
Jack Dever, 8520 N.W. 90, Okla. City, OK 73132
R. H. Devereaux, 475 Trucky St., St. Igance, MI 49781
Dominic DiStefano, 4303 Friar Lane, Colorado Springs, CO 80907
Bill Dowtin, P.O. Box 72, Celina, TX 75009
Drumbore Gun Shop, 119 Center St., Lehigton, PA 18235
Charles Duffy, Williams Lane, W. Hurley, N.Y. 12491
David R. Dunlop, Rte. 1, Box 199, Rolla, ND 58367
D. W. Firearms, D. Wayne Schlumbaum, 1821 - 200th S.W., Alderwood Manor, WA 98036
John H. Eaton, 8516 James St., Upper Marlboro, MD 20870
Bob Emmons, 238 Robson Rd., Grafton, OH 44044
Bill English, 4411 S. W. 100th, Seattle, Wash. 98146
Ken Eyster, Heritage Gunsmiths Inc., 6441 Bishop Rd., Centerburg, OH 43011/614-625-6131
N. B. Fashingbauer, P.O. Box 366, Lac Du Flambeau, WI 54538/715-588-7116
Ted Fellowes, Beaver Lodge, 9245-16th Ave., S.W., Seattle, WA 98106/206-763-1698 (muzzleloaders)
H. J. and L. A. Finn, 12565 Gratiot Ave., Detroit, MI 48205
Jack First Distributors Inc., 44633 Sierra Highway, Lancaster, CA 93534/805-942-2016
Marshall F. Fish, Rt. 22 North, Westport, NY 12993
Jerry Fisher, 1244—4th Ave. West, Kalispell, Mont. 59901
Flynn's Cust. Guns, P.O. Box 7461, Alexandria, LA 71306/318-445-7130
Larry L. Forster, Box 212, Gwinner, ND 58040
Clark K. Frazier/Matchmate, RFD 1, Rawson, OH 45881
Jay Frazier, Box 8644, Bird Creek, AK 99540
Freeland's Scope Stands, 3737—14th Ave., Rock Island, Ill. 61201
Fredrick Gun Shop, 10 Elson Drive, Riverside, R.I. 02915
R. L. Freshour, P.O. Box 2837, Texas City, TX 77590
Frontier Arms, Inc., 420 E. Riding Club Rd., Cheyenne, Wyo. 82001
Frontier Shop & Gallery, The Depot, Main St., Riverton, WY 82501/307-856-4498
Fuller Gunshop, Cooper Landing, Alas. 99572
Garcia Natl. Gun Traders, Inc., 225 S.W. 22nd Ave., Miami, Fla. 33135
Gentry's Bluing and Gun Shop, 314 N. Hoffman St., Belgrade, MT 59714/406-388-4806
Ed Gillman, R.R. 6, Box 195, Hanover, PA 17331
Dale Goens, Box 224, Cedar Crest, NM 87008
A. R. Goode, 12845 Catoctin Furnace Rd. Thurmont, MD 21788/301-271-2228
Gordie's Gun Shop, Gordon Mulholland, 1401 Fulton St., Streator, IL 61364/815-672-7202
Charles E. Grace, 10144 Elk Lake Rd., Williamsburg, MI 49690
Roger M. Green, Box 984, Glenrock, WY 82637/307-436-9804
Griffin & Howe, 589 Broadway, New York, N.Y. 10012
H. L. "Pete" Grisel, 61912 Skyline View Dr., Bend, OR 97701/503-389-2649 (rifles)
Gun City, 504 Main Ave., Bismarck, ND 58501
Guncraft (Kamloops) Ltd., 127 Victoria St., Kamloops, B.C. V2C 1Z4, Canada/604-374-2151
Guncraft (Kelowna) Ltd., 1771 Harvey Ave., Kelowna, B.C. V1Y 6G4, Canada
The Gunshop, R. D. Wallace, 320 Overland Rd., Prescott, AZ 86301
H & R Custom Gun Serv., 68 Passaic Dr., Hewitt, N.J. 07421
Paul Haberly, 2364 N. Neva, Chicago, IL 60635
Martin Hagn, Herzogstandweg 41, 8113 Kochel a. See, W. Germany (s.s. actions & rifles)
Chas. E. Hammans, Box 788, Stuttgart, AR 72160
Harkrader's Cust. Gun Shop, 825 Radford St., Christiansburg, VA 24073
Harp's Gun Repair Shop, 3349 Pio-Nono Circle, Macon, GA 31206 (cust. rifles)
Rob't W. Hart & Son Inc., 401 Montgomery St., Nescopeck, PA 18635 (actions, stocks)
Hal Hartley, 147 Blairs Fork Rd., Lenoir, NC 28645
Hartmann & Weiss KG, Rahlstedter Str. 139, 2000 Hamburg 73, W. Germany
Hubert J. Hecht, 55 Rose Mead Circle, Sacramento, CA 95831
Edw. O. Hefti, 300 Fairview, College Sta., Tex. 77840
Iver Henriksen, 1211 So. 2nd St. W., Missoula, MT 59801
Wm. Hobaugh, Box M, Philipsburg, MT 59858
Hodgson, Joseph & Assoc., 1800 Commerce St. 7S, Boulder, CO 80301
Richard Hodgson, 5589 Arapahoe, Unit 104, Boulder, CO 80301
Hoenig Rodman, 6521 Morton Dr., Boise, ID 83705/208-375-1116
Dick Holland, 422 N.E. 6th St., Newport, OR 97365/503-265-7556
Hollingsworth's Guns, Route 1, Box 55B, Alvaton, KY 42122/502-842-3580
Hollis Gun Shop, 917 Rex St., Carlsbad, NM 88220
Bill Holmes, Rt. 2, Box 242, Fayetteville, AR 72701/501-521-8958
Douglas Hough, 3626 W. 4th Ave., Vancouver, B.C. V6R 1P1, Canada
Huntington's, P.O. Box 991, Oroville, CA 95965
Hyper-Single Precision SS Rifles, 520 E. Beaver, Jenks, OK 74037
Independent Machine & Gun Shop, 1416 N. Hayes, Pocatello, Ida. 83201
Jackson's, Box 416, Selman City, TX 75689
Paul Jaeger, 211 Leedom St., P.O. Box 67, Jenkintown, PA 19046
J. J. Jenkins Ent. Inc., 375 Pine Ave. No. 25, Goleta, CA 93017/805-967-1366
Jerry's Gun Shop, 9220 Ogden Ave., Brookfield, Ill. 60513
Bruce Jones, 389 Calla Ave., Imperial Beach, CA 92032
Joseph & Associates, 4810 Riverbend Rd., Boulder, CO 80301/303-332-6720
Jos. Jurjevic, Gunshop, 605 Main St., Marble Falls, TX 78654
John Kaufield Small Arms Eng. Co., 7698 Garden Prairie Rd., Garden Prairie, IL 61038 (restorations)
Ken's Gun Specialties, K. Hunnell, Lakeview, AR 72642/501-431-5606
Kennedy Gun Shop, Rte. 12, Box 21, Clarksville, TN 37040/615-647-6043
Monte Kennedy, P.O. Box 214, Kalispell, MT 59901
Kennon's Custom Rifles, 5408 Biffle, Stone Mtn., GA 30083/404-469-9339
Stanley Kenvin, 5 Lakeville Lane, Plainview, NY 11803/516-931-0321
Kesselring Gun Shop, 400 Pacific Hiway No., Burlington, WA 98233/206-724-3113
Don Klein Custom Guns, Box 277, Camp Douglas, WI 54618
K. W. Kleinendorst, 48 Taylortown Rd., Montville, NJ 07045
J. Korzinek, RD #2, Box 73, Canton, PA 17724/717-673-8512 (riflesmith)
L&W Casting Co., 5014 Freeman Rd. E., Puyallup, WA 98371
Sam Lair, 520 E. Beaver, Jenks, OK 74037
Maynard Lambert, Kamas, UT 84036
LanDav Custom Guns, 7213 Lee Highway, Falls Church, VA 22046
Harry Lawson Co., 3328 N. Richey Blvd., Tucson, Ariz. 85716
John G. Lawson, 1802 E. Columbia, Tacoma, Wa. 98404
Gene Lechner, 636 Jane N.E., Albuquerque, NM 87123
LeDel, Inc., Main and Commerce Sts., Cheswold, Del. 19936
Mark Lee, c/o Don Allen, Inc., RR 1, Timberlane, Northfield, MN 55057/507-645-9216
Bill Leeper, see: Guncraft
Art LeFeuvre, 1003 Hazel Ave., Deerfield, Ill. 60015
LeFever Arms Co., R.D. 1, Lee Center-Stokes Rd., Lee Center, NY 13363/315-337-6722
Lenz Firearms Co., 1480 Elkay Dr., Eugene, OR 97404
Al Lind, 7821—76th Ave. S.W., Tacoma, WA 98498
Max J. Lindauer, R.R. 2, Box 27, Washington, MO 63090
Robt. L. Lindsay, J & B Enterprises, 9416 Emory Grove Rd., Gaithersburg, MD 20760/301-948-2941 (services only)
Ljutic Ind., Box 2117, Yakima, WA 98902 (Mono-Wads)
Llanerch Gun Shop, 2800 Township Line, Upper Darby, PA 19082/215-789-5462
Jim Lofland, 2275 Larkin Rd., Boothwyn, PA 19061 (SS rifles)
London Guns, 1528—20th St., Santa Monica, CA 90404
Frank E. Malin & Son (see: John Corry)
Monte Mandarino, c/o Bivins, 200 Wicklow Rd., Winston Salem, NC 27106 (Penn. rifles)
McCann's Muzzle-Gun Works, 200 Federal City Rd., Pennington, NJ 08354/609-737-1070 (ML)
McCormick's Gun Bluing Service, 609 N.E. 104th Ave., Vancouver, WA 98664
Bill McGuire, 1600 N. Eastmont Ave., East Wenatchee, WA 98801
R. J. Maberry, 511 So. K, Midland, Tex. 79701
Harold E. MacFarland, Route #4, Box 1249 Cottonwood, AZ 86326/602-634-5320
Monte Mandarino, Box 62087, New Orleans, LA 70186 (Penn. rifles)
Marcos Gunsmithing, 438 Main St., Paterson, NJ 07501
Dale Marfell, 107 N. State St., Litchfield, IL 62056
Marquart Precision Co., Box 1740, Prescott, AZ 86301
Marsh Al's, Rt. #3, Box 729, Preston, ID 83263
E. H. Martin's Gun Shop, 937 S. Sheridan Blvd., Lakewood, CO 80226
Mashburn Arms Co., 1218 N. Pennsylvania, Oklahoma City, OK 73107
Seely Masker, Custom Rifles, 261 Washington Ave., Pleasantville, NY 10570

Geo. E. Mathews & Son Inc., 10224 S. Paramount Blvd., Downey, CA 90241
Maurer Arms, 2366 Frederick Dr., Cuyahoga Falls, Ohio 44221 (muzzleloaders)
John E. Maxson, Box 332, Dumas, TX 79029/806-935-5990 (high grade rifles)
Eric Meitzner, c/o Don Allen, Inc., Rt. 1, Timberlane, Northfield, MN 55057/507-645-9216
Miller Custom Rifles, 655 Dutton Ave., San Leandro, CA 94577
Miller Gun Works, P.O. Box 7326, Tamuning, Guam 96911
C.D. Miller Guns, Purl St., St. Onge, SD 57779
David Miller Co., 3131 E. Greenlee Rd., Tucson, AZ 85716/602-326-3117 (classic rifles)
Earl Milliron, 1249 N.E. 166th Ave., Portland, Ore. 97230
Wm. Larkin Moore Co., 31360 Via Colinas, Suite 109, Westlake Village, CA 91360/213-889-4160
Larry Mrock, R.F.D. 3, Woodhill-Hooksett Rd., Bow, NH 03301/603-224-4096 (broch. $3)
Clayton N. Nelson, R.R. #3, Box 119, Enid, OK 73701
Newman Gunshop, 119 Miller Rd., Agency, Ia. 52530
William J. Nittler, 290 More Drive, Boulder Creek, CA 95006 (shotgun repairs)
Jim Norman, Jim's Gunstocks, 11230 Calenda Rd., San Diego, CA 92127/714-487-4173
Nu-Line Guns, Inc., 1053 Caulkshill Rd., Harvester, MO 63303/314-441-4500
O'Brien Rifle Co., 324 Tropicana No. 128, Las Vegas, Nev. 89109
Warren E. Offenberger, Star Route, Reno, Oh 45773 (ML)
Vic Olson, 5002 Countryside Dr., Imperial, MO 63052/314-296-8086
Pachmayr Gun Works, 1220 S. Grand Ave., Los Angeles, Calif. 90015
Charles J. Parkinson, 116 Wharncliffe Rd. So., London, Ont., Canada N6J2K3
Byrd Pearson, 191 No. 2050 W., Provo, UT 84601
John Pell, 410 College Ave., Trinidad, CO 81082
C. R. Pedersen & Son, Ludington, Mich. 49431
Al Petersen, Box 8, Riverhurst, Sask., Canada S0H3P0
A. W. Peterson Gun Shop, 1693 Old Hwy. 441, Mt. Dora, FL 32757 (ML rifles, also)
Phillip Pilkington, P.O. Box 2284, University Station, Enid, OK 73701
Ready Eddie's Gun Shop, 501 Van Spanje Ave., Michigan City, IN 46360
R. Neal Rice, 5152 Newton, Denver, CO 80221
Ridge Guncraft, Inc., 125 E. Tyrone Rd., Oak Ridge, Tenn. 37830/615-483-4024
Rifle Ranch, Jim Wilkinson, Rte. 5, Prescott, AZ 86301
Rifle Shop, Box M, Philipsburg, MT 59858
Wm. A. Roberts II, Rte. 4, Box 34, Athens, AL 35611 (ML)
W. Rodman, 6521 Morton Dr., Boise, ID 83705
Carl Roth, 4728 Pineridge Ave., Cheyenne, WY 82001 (rust bluing)
Royal Arms, Inc., 10064 Bert Acosta, Santee, Calif. 92071
Murray F. Ruffino, Rt. 2, Milford, ME 04461
Rush's Old Colonial Forge, 106 Wiltshire Rd., Baltimore, MD 21221 (Ky.-Pa. rifles)
Russell's Rifle Shop, Route 5, Box 92, Georgetown, TX 78626/512-778-5338 (gunsmith services)
Lewis B. Sanchez, Cumberland Knife & Gun Works, 5661 Bragg Blvd., Fayetteville, NC 28303
Sanders Custom Gun Serv., 2358 Tyler Lane, Louisville, Ky. 40205
Sandy's Custom Gunshop, Rte. #1, Rockport, Ill. 62370
Saratoga Arms Co., R.D. 3, Box 387, Pottstown, Pa. 19464
Roy V. Schaefer, 965 W. Hilliard Lane, Eugene, OR 97404
N.H. Schiffman Cust. Gun Serv., 963 Malibu, Pocatello, ID 83201
SGW, Inc. (formerly Schuetzen Gun Works), 624 Old Pacific Hwy. S.E., Olympia, WA 98503/206-456-3471
Schumaker's Gun Shop, Rte. 4, Box 500, Colville, WA 99114/509-684-4848
Schwartz Custom Guns, 9621 Coleman Rd., Haslett, Mich. 48840
Schwarz's Gun Shop, 41-15th St., Wellsburg, W. Va. 26070
Shaw's, Rt. 2, Box 407-L, Escondido, CA 92025/714-728-7070
Shell Shack, 113 E. Main, Laurel, MT 59044
George H. Sheldon, P.O. Box 489, Franklin, NH 03235 (45 autos & M-1 carbines only)
Lynn Shelton Custom rifles, P.O. Box 681, Elk City, OK 73644
Shilen Rifles, Inc., 205 Metropark Blvd., Ennis, TX 75119
Harold H. Shockley, 204 E. Farmington Rd., Hanna City, IL 61536 (hot bluing & plating)
Shootin' Shop, Inc., 1169 Harlow Rd., Springfield, OR 97477/503-747-0175
Walter Shultz, 1752 N. Pleasantview Rd., Pottstown, PA 19464
Silver Dollar Guns, P.O. Box 475, 10 Frances St., Franklin, NH 03235 (45 autos & M-1 carbines only)
Simmons Gun Spec., 700 Rogers Rd., Olathe, Kans. 66061
Simms Hardward Co., 2801 J St., Sacramento, Calif. 95816
Skinner's Gun Shop, Box 30, Juneau, Alaska 98801
Markus Skosples, c/o Ziffren Sptg. Gds., 124 E. Third St., Davenport, IA 52801
Jerome F. Slezak, 1290 Marlowe, Lakewood (Cleveland), OH 44107
Small Arms Eng., 7698 Garden Prairie Rd., Garden Prairie, IL 61038 (restorations)
John Smith, 912 Lincoln, Carpentersville, Ill. 60110
Snapp's Gunshop, 6911 E. Washington Rd., Clare, Mich. 48617
Southern Blueing, 6027-B N.W. 31st Ave., Ft. Lauderdale, FL 33309 (blueing)
Southern Penna. Sporting Goods Center, R.D. No. 1, Spring Grove, PA 17362/717-225-5908
Fred D. Speiser, 2229 Dearborn, Missoula, MT 59801
Sport Service Center, 2364 N. Neva, Chicago, IL 60635
Sportsman's Bailiwick, 5306 Broadway, San Antonio, TX 78209

Sportsmens Equip. Co., 915 W. Washington, San Diego, Calif. 92103
Sportsmen's Exchange & Western Gun Traders, Inc., P.O. Box 111, 560 S. "C" St., Oxnard, CA 93030/805-483-1917
George B. Spring, RFD #4, Rt. 82, Salem, CT 06415/203-859-0561
Jess L. Stark, 12051 Stroud, Houston, TX 77072
Ken Starnes, Rt. 1, Box 89-C, Scorggins, TX 75480/214-365-2566
Keith Stegall, Box 696, Gunnison, Colo. 81230
Victor W. Strawbridge, 6 Pineview Dr., Dover Point, Dover, NH 03820 (antique arms restoring)
W. C. Strutz, Rte. 1, "Woodland", Eagle River, WI 54521
Suter's House of Guns, 332 N. Tejon, Colorado Springs, Colo. 80902
Swanson Custom Firearms, 1051 Broadway, Denver, Colo. 80203
A. D. Swenson's 45 Shop, P.O. Box 606, Fallbrook, CA 92028
T-P Shop, 212 E. Houghton, West Branch, Mich. 48661
Talmage Ent., 43197 E. Whittier, Hemet, CA 92343
Taylor & Robbins, Box 164, Rixford, Pa. 16745
Gordon Tibbitts, 1378 Lakewood Circle, Salt Lake City, UT 84117
Daniel Titus, 119 Morlyn Ave., Bryn Mawr, PA 19010
Tom's Gunshop, 4435 Central, Hot Springs, AR 71901
Trinko's Gun Serv., 1406 E. Main, Watertown, Wis. 53094
Herb. G. Troester's Accurizing Serv., 2292 W. 1000 North, Vernal, UT 84078/801-789-2158
Dennis A. "Doc" Ulrich, 2511 S. 57th Ave., Cicero, IL 60650
Brent Umberger, Sportsman's Haven, R.R. 4, Cambridge, OH 43725
Upper Missouri Trading Co., Inc., Box 181, Crofton, MO 68730
Chas. VanDyke, 201 Gatewood Cir. W., Burleson, TX 76028/817-295-7373 (shotgun & recoil pad specialist)
Milton Van Epps, Rt. 69-A, Parish, NY 13131
VanHorn, 5124 Huntington Dr., Los Angeles, CA 90032
J. W. Van Patten, Box 145, Foster Hill, Milford, Pa. 18337
Vic's Gun Refinishing, 6 Pineview Dr., Dover, NH 03820 (antique arms restorations)
Walker Arms Co., R. 2, Box 73, Selma, AL 36701
Walker Arms Co., 127 N. Main St., Joplin, MO 64801
R. D. Wallace, 320 Overland Rd., Prescott, AZ 86301
R. A. Wardrop, Box 245, 409 E. Marble St., Mechanicsburg, PA 17055
Weatherby's, 2781 Firestone Blvd., South Gate, Calif. 90280
Jerry Wetherbee, 63470 Hamehook Rd., Bend, OR 97701/503-389-6080 (ML)
Cecil Weems,, Box 657, Mineral Wells, TX 76067
Wells Sport Store, 110 N. Summit St., Prescott, Ariz. 86301
R. A. Wells, 3452 N. 1st, Racine, Wis. 53402
Robert G. West, 27211 Huey Lane, Eugene, OR 97402/503-689-6610
Western Gunstocks Mfg. Co., 550 Valencia School Rd., Aptos, CA 95003
Duane Wiebe, P.O. Box 497 Lotus, CA 95651/916-626-6240
M. Wiest & Son, 125 E. Tyrone Rd., Oak Ridge, TN 37830/615-483-4024
W. C. Wilber, 400 Lucerne Dr., Spartanburg, SC 29302
Williams Gun Sight Co., 7389 Lapeer Rd., Davison, Mich. 48423
Bob Williams, P.O. Box 143, Boonsboro, MD 21713
Williamson-Pate Gunsmith Service, 117 W. Pipeline, Hurst, TX 76053/817-268-2887
Wilson Gun Store Inc., R.D. 1, Rte. 225, Dauphin, Pa. 17018
Thomas E. Wilson, 644 Spruce St., Boulder, CO 80302 (restorations)
Robert M. Winter, Box 484, Menno, SD 57045
Lester Womack, Box 17210, Tucson, AZ 85731/602-298-2036
Stan Wright, Billings Gunsmiths Inc., 421 St. Johns Ave., Billings, MT 59101/406-245-3337
J. David Yale, Ltd., 2618 Conowingo Rd., Bel Air, MD 21014/301-838-9479 (ML work)
Mike Yee, 4700-46th Ave. S.W., Seattle, WA 98116
York County Gun Works, RR 4, Tottenham, Ont., L0G 1W0 Canada (muzzleloaders)
Russ Zeeryp, 1601 Foard Dr., Lynn Ross Manor, Morristown, TN 37814
John G. Zimmerman, 60273 N.W. 31st Ave., Ft. Lauderdale, FL 33309

CUSTOM METALSMITHS

Ted Blackburn, 85 E. 700 South, Springfield, UT 84663 (precision metalwork)
Tom Burgess, 180 McMannamy Draw, Kalispell, MT 59901
Dave Cook, Dave's Gun Shop, 720 Hancock Ave., Hancock, MI 49930
Homer Culver, 1219 N. Stuart, Arlington, VA 22201
John H. Eaton, 8516 James St., Upper Marlboro, MD 20870
Geo. M. Fullmer, 2499 Mavis St., Oakland, CA 94601/415-533-4193 (precise chambering—300 cals.)
Harkrader's Custom Gun Shop, 825 Radford St., Christiansburg, VA 24073
Huntington's, P.O. Box 991, Oroville, CA 95965
Ken Jantz, Rt. 1, Sulphur, OK 73086/405-622-3790
Terry K. Kopp, Highway 13, Lexington, MO 64067/816-259-2083
R. H. Lampert, Rt. 1, Box 61, Guthrie, MN 56451
Mark Lee, c/o Don Allen, Inc., R.R. 1, Timberlane, Northfield, MN 55057
Paul's Precision Gunworks, 420 Eldon, Corpus Christi, TX 78412
Dave Talley, 124 Whitehaven Dr., Greenville, SC 29611/803-246-4648
John Vest, 6715 Shasta Way, Klamath Falls, OR 97601/503-884-5585
Herman Waldron, Box 475, Pomeroy, WA 99347
Edward S. Welty, R.D. 2, Box 25, Cheswick, PA 15024
Dick Willis, 141 Shady Creek Rd., Rochester, NY 14623

DECOYS

Carry-Lite, Inc., 5203 W. Clinton Ave., Milwaukee, WI 53223
Custom Purveyors, P.O. Box 886, Fort Lee, NJ 07024
Deeks, Inc., P.O. Box 2309, Salt Lake City, UT 84114
G & H Decoy Mfg. Co., P.O. Box 937, Henryetta, OK 74437
Sports Haven Inc., P.O. Box 88231, Seattle, WA 98188

Tuff-Lite Decoy Co., P.O. Box 1232-Gimlet Hangar, Ketchum, ID 83340
Tex Wirtz Ent., Inc., 1925 Hubbard St., Chicago, IL 60622
Woodstream Corp., P.O. Box 327, Lititz, PA 17543

ENGRAVERS, ENGRAVING TOOLS

John J. Adams, 47 Brown Ave., Mansfield, MA 02048/617-339-4613
Aurum Etchings, P.O. Box 401059, Garland, TX 75040 (acid engraving)
Joseph C. Bayer, 439 Sunset Ave., Sunset Hill Griggstown, RD 1, Princeton, NJ 08540/201-359-7283
Sid Bell Originals, R.D. 2, Tully, NY 13159
Weldon Bledsoe, 6812 Park Place Dr., Fort Worth, Tex. 76118
Carl Bleile, Box 11285, Cincinnati, OH 45211/513-662-0802
Roger C. Bleile, Box 5112, Cincinnati, OH 45205/513-251-0249
Erich Boessler, Am Vogeltal 3, 8732 Münnerstadt, W. Germany
Henry "Hank" Bonham, 218 Franklin Ave., Seaside Heights, NJ 08751
Bryan Bridges, 6350 E. Paseo San Andres, Tucson, AZ 85710
Burgess Vibrocrafters (BVI), Rt. 83, Grayslake, Ill. 60030
Winston Churchill, Twenty Mile Stream Rd., RFD Box 29B, Proctorsville, VT 05153/802-226-7772
Crocker Engraving, 1510 - 42nd St., Los Alamos, NM 87544
Art A. Darakis, RD #2, Box 165D, Fredericksburg, OH 44627/216-695-4271
Tim Davis, 230 S. Main St., Eldorado, OH 45321
James R. DeMunck, 3012 English Rd., Rochester, NY 14616
Gerald R. Desquesnes, 4890 Pompana Rd., Venice, FL 33595/813-484-5391
Howard M. Dove, 402 Roanoke St., Blacksburg, VA 24060
Ernest Dumoulin-Deleye, 8 rue Florent Boclinville, 4410 Herstal (Vottem), Belgium
Bill Dyer, P.O. Box 75255, Oklahoma City, Okla. 73107
Wilton L. English, 12009-B Barksdale Dr., Omaha, NB 68123
Ken Eyster, Heritage Gunsmiths Inc., 6441 Bishop Rd., Centerburg, OH 43011/614-625-6131
John Fanzoi, P.O. Box 25, Ferlach, Austria 9170
Jacqueline Favre, 3111 So-Valley View Blvd., Suite B-214, Las Vegas, NV 89102
Armi FERLIB, 46 Via Costa, 25063 Gardone V.T. (Brescia), Italy
Lynn Fliger, 5036 Hughes Ave. NE, Fridley, MN 55421
Heinrich H. Frank, 210 Meadow Rd., Whitefish, MT 59937/406-862-2681
Leonard Francolini, P.O. Box 32, West Granby, CT 06090/203-653-2336
J. R. French, 2633 Quail Valley, Irving TX 75060
GRS Corp., P.O. Box 1153, Emporia, KS 66801/316-343-1084 (Gravermeister tool)
Ed F. Giles, 204 Tremont St., Rehoboth, MA 02769
Donald Glaser, 1520 West St., Emporia, Kans. 66801
Eric Gold, Box 1904, Flagstaff, AZ 86002
Daniel Goodwin, P.O. Box 66, Kalispell, MT 59901
Howard V. Grant, P.O. Box 396, Lac Du Flambeau, WI 54538
John Gray, 3923 Richard Dr. NE, Cedar Rapids, IA 52402
Griffin & Howe, 589 Broadway, N.Y., N.Y. 10012
F. R. Gurney Engraving Method Ltd., #2301, 9925 Jasper Ave., Edmonton, Alberta, Can. T5J 2X4/403-426-7474
Neil Hartliep, Box 733, Fairmont, Minn. 56031
Frank E. Hendricks, Inc., Rt. 2, Box 189J, San Antonio, TX 78229
Heidemarie Hiptmayer, Guncraft (Kelowna) Ltd., 1771 Harvey Ave., Kelowna, BC V1Y 6G4 Canada/604-860-8977
Steve Huff, P.O. Box 8663, Missoula, MT 59807/406-721-1740
Ralph W. Ingle, #4 Missing Link, Rossville, GA 30741
Paul Jaeger, 211 Leedom, Jenkintown, Pa. 19046
Bill Johns, 2217 No. 10th, McAllen, TX 78501
T. J. Kaye, 4745 Dellwood, Beaumont, TX 77706
Lance Kelly, 4226 Lamar St., Decatur, GA 30035
Jim Kelso, P.O. Box 518, Preston, WA 98050
Kleinguenther's, P.O. Box 1261, Seguin, TX 78155
E. J. Koevenig, Engraving Service, Keystone, SD 57751
John Kudlas, 622-14th St. S.E., Rochester, MN 55901/507-288-5579
Ben Lane, Jr., 2118 Lipscomb Dr., Amarillo, TX 79109
Beth Lane, 201 S. Main St., Pontiac, IL 61764
Herb Larsen, 2021 Guilford Dr., Abbotsford, B.C. V2S 5K5, Canada
W. Neal Lewis, Rt. 8, Box 5-B, Bowers Rd., Newnan, GA 30263/404-251-3045
Frank Lindsay, 1326 Tenth Ave., Holdrege, NB 68949
London Guns, 1528-20th St., Santa Monica, CA 90404
Ed. J. Machu, Jr., Sportsman's Bailiwick, 5306 Broadway, San Antonio, TX 78209
Lynton S.M. McKenzie, 5589 Arapahoe, Unit 104, Boulder, CO 80301
Wm. H. Mains, 3111 So. Valley View Blvd., Suite B-214, Las Vegas, NV 89102
Robert E. Maki, 814 Revere Rd., Glenview, IL 60025/312-724-8238
Rudy Marek, Rt. 1, Box 1A, Banks, Ore. 97106
Franz Marktl, P.O. Box 716, Kalispell, MT 59901
S. A. Miller, Miller Gun Works, P.O. Box 7326, Tamuning, Guam 96911
Frank Mittermeier, 3577 E. Tremont Ave., New York, N.Y. 10465
NgraveR Co., 879 Raymond Hill Rd., Oakdale, CT 06370 (engr. tool)
New Orleans Jewelers Supply, 206 Chartres St., New Orleans, LA 70130
Hans Obiltschnig, 12. November St. 7, 9170 Ferlach, Austria
Warren E. Offenberger, Star Route, Reno, OH 45773
Oker's Engraving, 280 Illinois St., Crystal Lake, IL 60014
Gale Overbey, 612 Azalea Ave., Richmond, VA 23227
Pachmayr Gun Works, Inc., 1220 S. Grand Ave., Los Angeles, CA 90015/213-748-7271
Marcello Pedini, 470 Deer Park Ave., Dix Hills, NY 11746
Barbara Pierce, 248 E. Ridgeway, Hermiston, OR 97838/503-567-1661
Arthur Pitetti, Hawk Hollow Rd., Denver, NY 12421
Jeremy W. Potts, 912 Poplar St., Denver, CO 80220/303-355-5462
Wayne E. Potts, 912 Poplar St., Denver, CO 80220/303-355-5462
E. C. Prudhomme, 513 Ricou-Brewster Bldg., Shreveport, LA 71101
Martin Rabeno, Spook Hollow Trading Co., Box 37F, RD #1, Ellenville, NY 12428/914-647-4567
Wayne Reno, c/o Blackhawk Mtn., 1337 Delmar Parkway, Aurora, CO 80010
John and Hans Rohner, Sunshine Canyon, Boulder, Colo. 80302
Joe Rundell, 6198 Frances Rd., Clio, MI 48420/313-687-0559
Robert P. Runge, 94 Grove St., Ilion, N.Y. 13357
A. E. Scott, 609 E. Jackson, Pasadena, TX 77506
Shaw-Leibowitz, Rt. 1, Box 421, New Cumberland, W.Va. 26047 (etchers)
George Sherwood, Box 735, Winchester, OR 97495/503-672-3159
Ben Shostle, The Gun Room, 1201 Burlington Dr., Muncie, IN 47302
Ron Skaggs, 508 W. Central, Princeton, IL 61536
Russell J. Smith, 231 Springdale Rd., Westfield, Mass. 01085
George B. Spring, RFD #4, Rte. 82, Salem, CT 06415/203-859-0561
Robt. Swartley, 2800 Pine St., Napa, Calif. 94559
George W. Thiewes, 1846 Allen Lane, St. Charles, IL 60174/312-584-1383
Anthony Tuscano, 1473 Felton Rd., South Euclid, OH 44121
Robert Valade, Rte. 1, Box 30-A, Cove, OR 97824
John Vest, 6715 Shasta Way, Klamath Falls, OR 97601
Ray Viramontez, 4348 Newberry Ct., Dayton, OH 45432
Louis Vrancken, 30-rue sur le bois, 4531 Argenteau (Liege), Belgium
Vernon G. Wagoner, 12271 N. Chama Dr., Fountain Hills, AZ 85268/602-837-1789
Terry Wallace, 385 San Marino, Vallejo, CA 94590
Floyd E. Warren, 1273 St. Rt. 305 N.E. Rt. #3, Cortland, OH 44410
John E. Warren, P.O. Box 72, Eastham, Mass. 02642
Rachel Wells, 110 N. Summit St., Prescott, AZ 86301
Sam Welch, Box 2152, Kodiak, AK 99615
Mel Wood, 3901 Crestmont Dr., Santa Maria, CA 93454
Dwain Wright, 67168 Central, Bend, OR 97701/503-389-5558 (ctlg. $3)

GAME CALLS

Black Duck, 1737 Davis, Whiting, Ind. 46394
Burnham Bros., Box 669, 912 Main St., Marble Falls, TX 78654/512-693-3112
Faulk's, 616 18th St., Lake Charles, La. 70601
Lohman Mfg. Co., P.O. Box 220, Neosho, MO 64850/417-451-4438
Mallardtone Game Calls, 2901 16th St., Moline, IL 61265
Phil. S. Olt Co., Box 550, Pekin, Ill. 61554
Penn's Woods Products, Inc., 19 W. Pittsburgh St., Delmont, Pa. 15626
Scotch Game Call Co., Inc., 60 Main St., Oakfield, NY 14125
Johnny Stewart Wildlife Calls, Box 7954, Waco, Tex. 76710
Sure-Shot Game Calls, Inc., P.O. Box 816, Groves, TX 77619
Thomas Game Calls, P.O. Box 336, Winnsboro, TX 75494
Weems Wild Calls, 500 S. 7th, Fort Smith, AR 72901
Tex Wirtz Ent., Inc., 1925 W. Hubbard St., Chicago, Ill. 60622

GUNMAKERS, FERLACH, AUSTRIA

Ludwig Borovnik, Dollichgasse 14, A-9170
Johann Fanzoj, Griesgasse 1, A-9170
Wilfried Glanznig, Werkstr. 9, A-9170
Josef Hambrusch, Gartengasse 2, A-9170
Karl Hauptmann, Bahnhofstr. 5, A-9170
Gottfried Juch, Pfarrhofgasse 2, A-9170
Josef Just, Hauptplatz 18, A-9170
Jakob Koschat, 12.-November-Str. 2, A-9170
Johann Michelitsch, 12.-November-Str. 2, A-9170
Josef Orasche, Lastenstr. 5, A-9170
Komm.-Rat A. Sch. Outschar, Josef-Orgis-Gasse 23, A-9170
Valentin Rosenzopf's Erbe, Griesgasse 2, A-9170
Helmut Scheiring-Düsel, 10.-Oktober-Str. 8, A-9170
R. Franz Schmid, Freibacherstr. 10, A-9170
Anton Sodia, Uterferlach 39, A-9170
Vinzenz Urbas, Neubaugasse 6, A-9170
Benedikt Winkler, Postgasse 1, A-9170
Josef Winkler, Neubaugasse 1, A-9170

GUN PARTS, U. S. AND FOREIGN

Badger Shooter's Supply, Box 397, Owen, WI 54460
Behlert Custom Guns, Inc., 725 Lehigh Ave., Union, NJ 07083 (handgun parts)
Philip R. Crouthamel, 513 E. Baltimore, E. Lansdowne, Pa. 19050
Charles E. Duffy, Williams Lane, West Hurley, N.Y. 12491
Federal Ordnance Inc., 9649 Alpaca St., So. El Monte, CA 91733/213-283-3880
Jack First Distributors Inc., 44633 Sierra Highway, Lancaster, CA 93534/805-942-2016
Gun-Tec, P.O. Box 8125, W. Palm Beach, FL 33407 (Win. mag. tubing; Win. 92 conversion parts)
Hunter's Haven, Zero Prince St., Alexandria, Va. 22314
Walter H. Lodewick, 2816 N.E. Halsey, Portland, OR 97232
Marsh Al's, Rte. #3, Box 729, Preston, ID 83263 (Contender rifle)
Numrich Arms Co., West Hurley, N.Y. 12491
Pacific Intl. Merch. Corp., 2215 "J" St., Sacramento, CA 95816 (Vega 45 Colt mag.)
Potomac Arms Corp. (see Hunter's Haven)
Martin B. Retting, Inc., 11029 Washington, Culver City, Cal. 90230
Sarco, Inc., 323 Union St., Stirling, NJ 07980
Sherwood Intl. Export Corp., 18714 Parthenia St., Northridge, CA 91324

Simms, 2801 J St., Sacramento, CA 95816
Clifford L. Smires, R.D., Box 39, Columbus, NJ 08022 (Mauser rifles)
Springfield Sporters Inc., R.D. 1, Penn Run, PA 15765/412-254-2626
N. F. Strebe Gunworks, 4926 Marlboro Pike, S.E., Washington, D.C. 20027
Triple-K Mfg. Co., 568-6th Ave., San Diego, CA 92101 (magazines, gun parts)

GUNS (Foreign)

Abercrombie & Fitch, 2302 Maxwell Lane, Houston, TX 77023 (Ferlib)
Alpha Arms, Inc., 1602 Stemmons, Suite "D," Carrollton, TX 75006/214-245-3115
American Arms International P.O. Box 11717, Salt Lake City, UT 84147/531-0180
Action Arms, 4567 Bermuda, Philadelphia, PA 19124/215-744-3400
AYA (Aguirre y Aranzabal) see: IGI Domino or Wm. L. Moore (Spanish shotguns)
Pedro Arrizabalaga, Eibar, Spain
Armoury Inc., Rte. 202, New Preston, CT 06777
Armsport, Inc., 3590 N.W. 49th St., Miami, FL 33142/305-592-7850
Beeman's Precision Airguns, Inc., 47 Paul Dr., San Rafael, CA 94903/415-472-7121 (FWB, Weihrauch firearms)
Benelli Armi, S.p.A., via della Stazione 50, 61029 Urbino, Italy
Beretta Arms Co., Inc., P.O. Box 697, Ridgefield, CT 06877
Blaser/Vinzenz Huber GmbH, P.O. Box 2245, D-7900 Ulm, W. Germany
Britarms, Ltd., Unit 1, Raban's Close, Raban's Lane Industrial Estate, Aylesbury, Bucks., England
Bretton, 21 Rue Clement Forissier, 42-St. Etienne, France
Browning (Gen. Offices), Rt. 1, Morgan, UT 84050/801-876-2711
Browning, (parts & service), Rt. 4, Box 624-B, Arnold, MO. 63010/314-287-6800
Carlo Casartelli, 25062 Concesio (Brescia), Italy
Century Arms Co., 3-5 Federal St., St. Albans, Vt. 05478
Champlin Firearms, Inc., Box 3191, Enid, OK 73701
Ets. Chapuis, 42380 St. Bonnet-le-Chateau, France (see R. Painter)
Commercial Trading Imports, Inc., 2125 Center Ave., Suite 201, Fort Lee, NJ 07024/201-461-8833 (Russian shotguns)
Connecticut Valley Arms Co., Saybrook Rd., Haddam, CT 06438 (CVA)
Walter Craig, Inc., Box 927-A Selma, AL 36701
Creighton & Warren, P.O. Box 15723, Nashville, TN 37215 (Krieghoff combination guns)
Morton Cundy & Son, Ltd., P.O. Box 315, Lakeside, MT 59922
Charles Daly (see: Outdoor Sports HQ.)
Davis Gun Shop, 7213 Lee Highway, Falls Church, VA 22046 (Fanzoj, Ferlach; Spanish guns)
Dikar s. Coop. (see: Connecticut Valley Arms Co.)
Dixie Gun Works, Inc., Hwy 51, South, Union City, TN 38261/901-885-0561 ("Kentucky" rifles)
Dynamit Nobel of America, Inc., 105 Stonehurst Court, Northvale, NJ 07647/201-767-1660 (Rottweil)
Ernest Dumoulin-Deleye, 8 rue Florent Boclinville, 4410 Herstal (Vottem), Belgium
Peter Dyson Ltd., 29-31 Church St., Honley, Huddersfield, Yorkshire HD7 2AH, England (accessories f. antique gun collectors)
Excam Inc., 4480 E. 11 Ave., P.O. Box 3483, Hialeah, FL 33013
Armi Fabbri, Casella 206, Brescia, Italy 25100
Famars, Abbiatico & Salvinelli, Via Cinelli 29, Gardone V.T. (Brescia), Italy 25063
J. Fanzoj, P.O. Box 25, Ferlach, Austria 9170
F.E.T.E. Corporation, 2867 W. 7th St., Los Angeles, CA 90005 (A. Zoli guns)
Armi FERLIB, 46 Via Costa, 25063 Gardone V.T. (Brescia), Italy
Ferlach (Austria) of North America, P.O. Box 430435, S. Miami, FL 33143
Firearms Center Inc. (FCI), 308 Leisure Lane, Victoria, TX 77901
Firearms Imp. & Exp. Corp., 4530 NW 135th St., Opa-Locka, FL 33054/305-685-5966
Flaig's Lodge, Millvale, Pa. 15209
Auguste Francotte & Cie, S.A., 61 Mont St. Martin, 4000 Liege, Belgium
Freeland's Scope Stands, Inc., 3737 14th Ave., Rock Island, Ill. 61201
J. L. Galef & Son, Inc., 85 Chambers, New York, N.Y. 10007
Renato Gamba, Fabbrica d'Armi, via Petrarca, 25060 Ponte Zanano di Sarezzo (Brescia), Italy
Armas Garbi, Urki #12, Eibar (Guipuzcoa) Spain (shotguns, see W. L. Moore)
Gastinne Renette, 39 Ave. F.D. Roosevelt, 75008 Paris, France
Golden Eagle Firearms, 5803 Sovereign, Suite 206, Houston, TX 77036
Georges Granger, 66 Cours Fauriel, 42 St. Etienne, France
Hawes National Corp., 15424 Cabrito Rd., Van Nuys, CA 91406
Healthways, Box 45055, Los Angeles, Calif. 90061
Gil Hebard Guns, Box 1, Knoxville, IL 61448 (Hammerli)
Heckler & Koch Inc., 933 N. Kenmore St., Suite 218, Arlington, VA 22201
A. D. Heller, Inc., Box 56, 2322 Grand Ave., Baldwin, NY 11510
Herter's, Waseca, Minn. 56093
Heym, Friedr. Wilh., Box 861, Bolton, Ont. L0P 1A0, Canada
Hunting World, 16 E. 53d St., New York, NY 10022
IGI Domino Corp., 200 Madison Ave., New York, NY 10016/212-889-4889 (AYA, Breda)
Incor, Inc., P.O. Box 132, Addison, TX 75001/214-386-7000
Interarmco, see: Interarms (Walther)
Interarms Ltd., 10 Prince St., Alexandria, Va. 22313 (Mauser, Valmet M-62/S)
International Distr., Inc., 7290 S.W. 42nd St., Miami, FL 33155 (Taurus rev.)
Italguns, Via Voltabo, 20090 Cusago (Milano) Italy
Ithaca Gun Co., Terrace Hill, Ithaca, NY 14850

Paul Jaeger Inc., 211 Leedom St., Jenkintown, Pa. 19046
Jana Intl. Co., Box 1107, Denver, Colo. 80201 (Parker-Hale)
J. J. Jenkins Enterprises, Inc., 375 Pine Ave. No. 25, Goleta, CA 93017/805-967-1366 (Gebrüder Merkel)
Kassnar Imports, 5480 Linglestown Rd., Harrisburg, PA 17110
Kimel Industries, P.O. Box 335, Matthews, NC 28105
Kleinguenther's, P.O. Box 1261, Seguin, TX 78155
Knight & Knight, 5930 S.W. 48 St., Miami, FL 33155 (made-to-order only)
Dr. Kortz Elko, 28 rue Ecole Moderne, 7400 Soignes, Belgium
L. A. Distributors, 4 Centre Market Pl., New York, N.Y. 10013
La Paloma Marketing, 4500 E. Speedway Blvd., Suite 93, Tucson, AZ 85712/602-881-4750 (K.F.C. shotguns)
S. E. Laszlo, 200 Tillary St., Brooklyn, N.Y. 11201
Lever Arms Serv. Ltd., 771 Dunsmuir, Vancouver, B.C., Canada V6C 1M9
Liberty Arms Organization, Box 306, Montrose, Calif. 91020
McQueen Sales Co. Ltd., 1760 W. 3rd Ave., Vancouver, B.C., Canada V6J 1K5
Mandall Shtg. Suppl. Corp., 3616 N. Scottsdale Rd., Scottsdale, AZ 85251/602-945-2553
Mannlicher Div., Steyr Daimler Puch of Amer., 85 Metro Way, Secaucus, NJ 07094
Manu-Arm, St. Etienne, France
Manufrance, 100-Cours Fauriel, 42 St. Etienne, France
Mendi s. coop. (see: Connecticut Valley Arms Co.)
Merkuria, P.O. Box 18, 17005 Prague, Czechoslovakia (BRNO)
Mitchell Arms Corp., 116 East 16th St., Costa Mesa, CA 92627/714-548-7701 (Uberti pistols)
Wm. Larkin Moore, 31360 Via Colinas, Suite 109, Westlake Village, CA 91360/213-889-4160 (AYA, Garbi, Ferlib, Piotti, Lightwood)
Navy Arms Co., 689 Bergen Blvd., Ridgefield, N.J. 07657
Outdoor Sports Headquarters, Inc., 2290 Arbor Blvd., Dayton, OH 45439/513-294-2811 (Charles Daly shotguns)
P.M. Air Services, Inc., P.O. Box 1573, Costa Mesa, CA 92626
Pachmayr Gun Works, 1220 S. Grand Ave., Los Angeles, CA 90015
Pacific Intl. Merch. Corp., 2215 "J" St., Sacramento, CA 95816
Rob. Painter, 2901 Oakhurst Ave., Austin, TX 78703 (Chapuis)
Parker-Hale, Bisleyworks, Golden Hillock Rd., Sparbrook, Birmingham B11 2PZ, England
Ed Paul Sptg. Goods, 172 Flatbush Ave., Brooklyn, N.Y. 11217 (Premier)
Picard-Fayolle, 42-rue du Vernay, 42100 Saint Etienne, France
Pragotrade, a Div. of Molokov Canada, Inc., 307 Humberline Dr., Rexdale, Ont. M9W 5V1, Canada/416-675-1322
Precise, 3 Chestnut, Suffern, NY 10901
Precision Sports, 798 Cascadilla St., Ithaca, NY 14850/607-273-2993
Premier Shotguns, 172 Flatbush Ave., Brooklyn N.Y. 11217
Leonard Puccinelli Co., 11 Belle Ave., San Anselmo, CA 94960/415-456-1666 (I.A.B., Rizzini shotguns of Italy)
RG Industries, Inc., 2485 N.W. 20th St., Miami, FL 33142 (Erma)
L. Joseph Rahn, Inc., First Natl. Bldg., Room 502, 201 S. Main St., Ann Arbor, MI 48104 (Garbi, Astra shotguns)
Ravizza Caccia Pesca Sport, s.p.a., Via Volta 60, 20090 Cusago, Italy
Richland Arms Co., 321 W. Adrian St., Blissfield, Mich. 49228
F.lli Rizzini, 25060 Magno di Gardone V.T., (Bs.) Italy
Rottweil, see: Dynamit Nobel of America
Ruko Sporting Goods Inc., 195 Sugg Rd., Buffalo, NY 14225 (Tikka)
SKB Sports Inc., 190 Shepard, Wheeling, IL 60090
Sanderson's, 724 W. Edgewater, Portage, Wis. 53901
Victor Sarasqueta, S.A., P.O. Box 25, 3 Victor Sarasqueta St., Eibar, Spain
Sarco, Inc., 323 Union St., Stirling, NJ 07980/201-647-3800
Savage Arms Corp., Westfield, Mass. 01085 (Anschutz)
W. C. Scott & Co. (British shotguns), see: Griffin & Howe
Security Arms Co., See: Heckler & Koch
Service Armament, 689 Bergen Blvd., Ridgefield, N.J. 07657 (Greener Harpoon Gun)
Sherwood Intl. Export Corp., 18714 Parthenia St., Northridge, CA 91324
Shore Galleries, Inc., 3318 W. Devon Ave., Chicago, IL 60645
Shotguns of Ulm, 7 Forest Glen, Highland Park, NJ 08904/201-297-0573
Sile Distributors, 7 Centre Market Pl., New York, 10013
Simmons Spec., Inc., 700 Rogers Rd., Olathe, Kans. 66061
Sloan's Sprtg. Goods, Inc., 10 South St., Ridgefield, CT 06877
Franz Sodia Jagdgewehrfabrik, Schulhausgasse 14, 9170 Ferlach, (Kärnten) Austria
Solersport, 23629 7th Ave. West, Bothell, WA 98011 (Unique)
Steyr-Daimler-Puch of America, Inc., see: Mannlicher
Stoeger Industries, 55 Ruta Ct., S. Hackensack, NJ 07606/201-440-2700
Tradewinds, Inc., P.O. Box 1191, Tacoma, Wash. 98401
Uberti, Aldo & Co., Via G. Carducci 41 or 39, Ponte Zanano (Brescia) Italy
Ignacio Ugartechea, Apartado 21, Eibar, Spain
Valmet Sporting Arms Div., 7 Westchester Plaza, Elmsford, NY 10523/914-347-4440
Valor Imp. Corp., 5555 N.W. 36th Ave., Miami, FL 33142
Valtra Inc., One Rockefeller Plaza, Suite 1715, New York, NY 10020/212-765-4660 (Valmet)
Ventura Imports, P.O. Box 2782, Seal Beach, CA 90740 (European shotguns)
Verney-Carron, B.P. 88, 17 Cours Fauriel, 42010 St. Etienne Cedex, France
Waffen-Frankonia, Box 6780, 87 Wurzburg 1, W. Germany
Weatherby's, 2781 Firestone Blvd., So. Gate, Calif. 90280 (Sauer)
Fabio Zanotti di Stefano, Via XXV Aprile 1, 25063 Gardone V.T. (Brescia) Italy
Zavodi Crvena Zastava, 29 Novembra St., No. 12, Belgrade, Yugosl.
Antonio Zoli & Co., 39 Via Zanardelli, 25063 Gardone V.T., Brescia, Italy

GUNS & GUN PARTS, REPLICA AND ANTIQUE

Antique Gun Parts, Inc., 1118 S. Braddock Ave., Pittsburgh, PA 15218 (ML)

Armoury Inc., Rte. 202, New Preston, CT 06777
Artistic Arms, Inc., Box 23, Hoagland, IN 46745 (Sharps-Borchardt replica)
Bob's Place, Box 283J, Clinton, IA 52732 (obsolete Winchester parts only)
Carter Gun Works, 2211 Jefferson Pk. Ave., Charlottesville, Va. 22903
Darr Tool Co., P.O. Box 778, Carpinteria, CA 93013 (S.S. items)
Dixie Gun Works, Inc., Hwy 51, South, Union City, TN 38261/901-885-0561
Federal Ordnance Inc., 9649 Alpaca St., So. El Monte, CA 91733/213-283-3880
Fred Goodwin, Sherman Mills, ME 04776 (antique guns & parts)
Log Cabin Sport Shop, 8010 Lafayette Rd., Lodi, OH 44254/216-948-1082 (ctlg. $3)
Edw. E. Lucas, 32 Garfield Ave., East Brunswick, NY 08816 (45/70 Springfield parts)
Lyman Products Corp., Middlefield, CT 06455
Tommy Munsch Gunsmithing, Rt. 2, Box 248, Little Falls, MN 56345 (parts list $1; oth. inq. SASE)
Numrich Arms Co., West Hurley, N.Y. 12491
Replica Models, Inc., 610 Franklin St., Alexandria, VA 22314
S&S Firearms, 88-21 Aubrey Ave., Glendale, N.Y. 11227
Sarco, Inc., 323 Union St., Stirling, NJ 07980/201-647-3800
C. H. Stoppler, 1426 Walton Ave., New York, NY 10452 (miniature guns)
Upper Missouri Trading Co., 3rd & Harold Sts., Crofton, NB 68730
C. H. Weisz, Box 311, Arlington, VA 22210
W. H. Wescombe, P.O. Box 488, Glencoe, CA 95232 (Rem. R.B. parts)

GUNS (Pellet)

Air Rifle Hq., 247 Court St., Grantsville, W. Va. 26147
Beeman's Precision Airguns, 47 Paul Dr., San Rafael, CA 94903/415-472-7121
Benjamin Air Rifle Co., 1525 So. 8th St., Louis, Mo. 63104
Crosman Airguns, 980 Turk Hill Rd., Fairport, NY 14450/716-223-6000
Daisy Mfg. Co., Rogers, Ark. 72756 (also Feinwerkbau)
K. J. David & Co., P.O. Box 12595, Lake Park, FL 33403/305-844-5124
Fanta Air Rifles, Box 8122, La Crescenta, Calif. 91214
J. L. Galef & Son, Inc., 85 Chambers St., New York, N.Y. 10007 (B.S.A.)
Great Lakes Airguns, S6175 So. Park Ave., Hamburg, NY 14075
Harrington & Richardson Arms Co., Industrial Rowe, Gardner, MA 01440 (Webley)
Healthways, Box 45055, Los Angeles, Calif. 90061
Gil Hebard Guns, Box 1, Knoxville, Ill. 61448
Hy-Score Arms Co., 200 Tillary St., Brooklyn, N.Y. 11201
Interarms, 10 Prince, Alexandria, Va. 22313 (Walther)
Paul Jaeger, Inc., 211 Leedom St., Jenkintown, PA 19046
LARC International, P.O. Box 34007, Coral Gables, FL 33134
Marksman Products, P.O. Box 2983, Torrance, CA 90509
Power Line (see: Daisy Mfg. Co.)
Precise, 3 Chestnut, Suffern, NY 10901
Precision Sports, 798 Cascadilla St., Ithaca, NY 14850/607-273-2993 (B.S.A.)
Service Armament, 689 Bergen Blvd., Ridgefield, N.J. 07657 (Webley)
Sheridan Products, Inc., 3205 Sheridan, Racine, Wis. 53403
Smith & Wesson, 2100 Roosevelt Ave., Springfield, MA 01104

GUNS, SURPLUS—PARTS AND AMMUNITION

Century Arms, Inc., 3-5 Federal St., St. Albans, Vt. 05478
Walter Craig, Inc., Box 927-A, Selma, AL 36701
Eastern Firearms Co., 790 S. Arroyo Pkwy., Pasadena, Calif. 91105
Garcia National Gun Traders, 225 S.W. 22nd, Miami, Fla. 33135
Hunter's Lodge, 200 S. Union, Alexandria, Va. 22313
Lever Arms Serv. Ltd., 771 Dunsmuir St., Vancouver, B.C., Canada V6C IM9
Mars Equipment Corp., 3318 W. Devon, Chicago, Ill. 60645
Pacific Intl. Merch. Corp., 2215 "J" St., Sacramento, CA 95816
Plainfield Ordnance Co., Box 447, Dunellen, N.J. 08812
Sarco, Inc., 323 Union St., Stirling, NJ 07980/201-647-3800
Service Armament Co., 689 Bergen Blvd., Ridgefield, N.J. 07657
Sherwood Intl. Export Corp., 18714 Parthenia St., Northridge, CA 91324
Springfield Sporters Inc., R.D. 1, Penn Run, PA 15765/412-254-2626

GUNS, U.S.-made

A.I.G. Corp., 7 Grasso Ave., North Haven, CT 06473
AMT (Arcadia Machine & Tool), 11666 McBean Dr., El Monte, CA 91732
A. R. Sales Co., 9624 Alpaca St., South El Monte, CA 91733 (Mark IV sporter)
Accuracy Systems, Inc., 2105 S. Hardy Dr., Tempe, AZ 85282
American Arms & Ammunition Co., 1015 N.W. 72nd St., Miami, FL 33150 (Budischowski)
ArmaLite, 118 E. 16th St., Costa Mesa, Calif. 92627
Artistic Arms, Inc., Box 23, Hoagland, IN 46745 (Sharps-Borchardt)
Auto-Ordnance Corp., Box ZG, West Hurley, NY 12491
Bauer Firearms, 34750 Klein Ave., Fraser, MI 48026
Bortmess Gun Co., Inc., RD #2, Box 3, Scenery Hill, PA 15360/412-945-5175
Brown Precision Co., P.O. Box 270W; 7786 Molinos Ave. Los Molinos, CA 96055/916-384-2506 (High Country rifle)
Browning (Gen. Offices), Rt. 1, Morgan, UT 84050/801-876-2711
Browning (Parts & Service), Rt. 4, Box 624-B, Arnold, MO 63010/314-287-6800
Challanger Mfg. Corp., 118 Pearl St., Mt. Vernon, NY 10550 (Hopkins & Allen)

Champlin Firearms, Inc., Box 3191, Enid, Okla. 73701
Charter Arms Corp., 430 Sniffens Ln., Stratford, CT 06497
Classic Arms Ltd., 20 Wilbraham St., Palmer, MA 01069/413-596-9691 (BP guns)
Colt, 150 Huyshope Ave., Hartford, CT 06102
Commando Arms, Inc., Box 10214, Knoxville, Tenn. 37919
Coonan Arms, Inc., 570 S. Fairview, St. Paul, MN 55116/612-699-5639 (357 Mag. Autom.)
Crown City Arms, P.O. Box 1126, Cortland, NY 13045 (45 auto handgun)
Cumberland Arms, Rt. 1, Shafer Rd., Blanton Chapel, Manchester, TN 37355
Day Arms Corp., 2412 S.W. Loop 410, San Antonio, TX 78227
Leonard Day & Co., 316 Burts Pits Rd., Northampton, MA 01060 (ML)
Detonics 45 Associates, 2500 Seattle Tower, Seattle, WA 98101 (auto pistol)
DuBiel Arms Co., 1724 Baker Rd., Sherman, TX 75090/214-893-7313
EE-DA-How Long Rifles, Inc., 3318 Camrose Lane, Boise, ID 83705
EMF Co. Inc., Box 1248, Studio City, CA 91604 (T.D.A. rev.)
FTL Marketing Corp., 12521-3 Oxnard St., No. Hollywood, CA 91601/213-985-2939
Falling Block Works, P.O. Box 22, Troy, MI 48084
Firearms Imp. & Exp. Corp., 4530 NW 135th St., Opa-Locka, FL 33054/305-685-5966 (FIE)
Freedom Arms Co., Freedom, WY 83120 (mini revolver, Casull rev.)
Freshour Mfg. Co., 1914 - 15th Ave. N., Texas City, TX 77590 (Ranger rifle)
Golden Age Arms Co., 14 W. Winter St., Delaware, OH 43015
Gwinn Firearms, #19 Freedom Industrial Park, Bangor, ME 04401/207-848-3333
Harrington & Richardson, Industrial Rowe, Gardner, MA 01440
Hatfield's, 2028 Frederick Ave., St. Joseph, MO 64501 (squirrel rifle)
A. D. Heller, Inc., Box 268, Grand Ave., Baldwin, NY 11510
High Standard Sporting Firearms, 31 Prestige Park Circle, East Hartford, CT 06108
Holmes Firearms Corp., Rte. 6, Box 242, Fayetteville, AR 72701
Hopkins & Allen Arms, #1 Melnick Rd., Monsey, NY 10952
Hyper-Single Precision SS Rifles, 520 E. Beaver, Jenks, OK 74037
Ithaca Gun Co., Ithaca, N.Y. 14850
Iver Johnson Arms Inc., P.O. Box 251, Middlesex, NJ 08846
J & R carbine, (see: PJK Inc.)
Paul Jaeger, Inc., 211 Leedom St., Jenkintown, PA 19046
Kimber of Oregon, Inc., 9039 S.E. Jannsen Rd., Clackamas, OR 97015/503-656-1704
H. Koon, Inc., 1602 Stemmons, Suite D, Carrollton, TX 75006
L.E.S., 2301 Davis St., North Chicago, IL 60064/312-473-9484
Ljutic Ind., Inc., P.O. Box 2117, Yakima, WA 98902 (Mono-Gun)
Ljutic Intl., 101 Carmel Dr., Suite 120, Carmel, IN 46032/317-848-5051
M & N Distributors, 3040 Lomita Blvd., Torrance, CA 90505/213-530-9000 (Budischowsky)
Marlin Firearms Co., 100 Kenna Dr., New Haven, Conn. 06473
Merrill Co. Inc., 704 E. Commonwealth, Fullerton, CA 92631/714-879-8922
O. F. Mossberg & Sons, Inc., 7 Grasso St., No. Haven, Conn. 06473
Mowrey Gun Works, Box 28, Iowa Park TX 76367
Navy Arms Co., 689 Bergen Blvd., Ridgefield, N.J. 07657
North Star Arms, R.2, Box 74A, Ortonville, MN 56278 (The Plainsman)
Numrich Arms Corp., W. Hurley, N.Y. 12491
PJK, Inc., 1527 Royal Oak Dr., Bradbury, Ca 91010 (J&R Carbine)
Plainfield Machine Co., Inc., Box 447, Dunellen, N.J. 08812
Plainfield Inc., 292 Vail Ave., Piscataway, NJ 08854
R G Industries, 2485 N.W. 20th SE., Miami, FL 33142
Raven Arms, 1300 Bixby Dr., Industry, CA 91745
Remington Arms Co., Bridgeport, Conn. 06602
Ruger (see Sturm, Ruger & Co.)
Savage Arms Corp., Westfield, Mass. 01085
Sears, Roebuck & Co., 825 S. St. Louis, Chicago, Ill. 60607
Semmerling Corp., P.O. Box 400, Newton, MA 02160
Sharon Rifle Barrel Co., P.O. Box 1197, Kalispell, MT 59901
Sharps Rifle Co., 3428 Shakertown Rd., Dayton, OH 45430
Shiloh Products, 37 Potter St., Farmingdale, NY 11735 (Sharps)
Smith & Wesson, Inc., 2100 Roosevelt Ave., Springfield, MA 01101
Sporting Arms, Inc., 9643 Alpaca St., So. El Monte, CA 91733 (M-1 carbine)
Springfield Armory, 111 E. Exchange St., Geneseo, IL 61254
Sterling Arms Corp., 211 Grand St., Lockport, NY 14094/716-434-6631
Sturm, Ruger & Co., Southport, Conn. 06490
Thompson-Center Arms, Box 2405, Rochester, N.H. 03867
Trail Guns Armory, 1634 E. Main St., League City, TX 77573 (muzzleloaders)
United Sporting Arms, Inc., 35 Gilpin Ave., Hauppauge, L.I., NY 11787
United States Arms Corp., Doctors Path and Middle Road, Riverhead, NY 11901 (Abilene SA rev.)
Universal Firearms, 3740 E. 10th Ct., Hialeah, FL 33013
Ward's, 619 W. Chicago, Chicago, Ill. 60607 (Western Field brand)
Weatherby's, 2781 E. Firestone Blvd., South Gate, Calif. 90280
Dan Wesson Arms, 293 So. Main St., Monson, Mass. 01057
Wichita Eng. & Supply, Inc., P.O. Box 11371, Wichita, KS 67202
Wildey Firearms Co., Inc., P.O. Box 4264, New Windsor, NY 12250/203-272-7215
Wilkinson Arms, 803 N. Glendora Ave, Covina, CA 91724 (Diane 25 ACP auto pistol)
Winchester Repeating Arms Co., New Haven, Conn. 06504
Winslow Arms Co., Inc., P.O. Box 783, Camden, SC 29020

GUNSMITHS, CUSTOM (see Custom Gunsmiths)

GUNSMITHS, HANDGUN (see Pistolsmiths)

GUNSMITH SCHOOLS

Colorado School of Trades, 1545 Hoyt, Lakewood, CO 80215
Lassen Community College, P.O. Box 3000, Susanville, CA 96130
Modern Gun Repair School Inc., 4225 N. Brown Ave., Scottsdale, AZ 85252
Montgomery Technical Institute, P.O. Drawer 487, Troy, NC 27371
Murray State College, Tishomingo, OK 73460
North American School of Firearms, 4401 Birch St., Newport Beach, CA 92663 (correspondence)
Oregon Institute of Technology, Small Arms Dept., Klamath Falls, OR 97601
Penn. Gunsmith School, 812 Ohio River Blvd., Avalon, Pittsburgh, Pa. 15202
Police Sciences Institute, 4401 Birch St., Newport Beach, CA 92660/714-546-7360 (General Law Enforcement Course)
Trinidad State Junior College, Trinidad, Colo. 81082
Yavapai College, 1100 East Sheldon St., Prescott, AZ 86301/602-445-7300

GUNSMITH SUPPLIES, TOOLS, SERVICES

Albright Prod. Co., P.O. Box 1144, Portola, CA 96122 (trap buttplates)
Alley Supply Co., Carson Valley Industrial Park, Gardnerville, NV 89410
Ametek, Hunter Spring Div., One Spring Ave., Hatfield, PA 19440/215-822-2971 (trigger gauge)
Anderson Mfg. Co., P.O. Box 3120, Yakima WA 98903 (tang safe)
Armite Labs., 1845 Randolph St., Los Angeles, Cal. 90001 (pen oiler)
B-Square Co., Box 11281, Ft. Worth, Tex. 76110
Jim Baiar, 490 Halfmoon Rd., Columbia Falls, MT 59912 (hex screws)
Behlert Custom Guns, Inc., 725 Lehigh Ave., Union, NJ 07083
Al Biesen, W. 2039 Sinto Ave., Spokane, WA 99201 (grip caps, buttplates)
Bonanza Sports Mfg. Co., 412 Western Ave., Faribault, Minn. 55021
Brookstone Co., 125 Vose Farm Rd., Peterborough, NH 03458
Bob Brownell's, Main & Third, Montezuma, Ia. 50171
Lenard M. Brownell, Box 25, Wyarno, WY 82845/307-737-2468 (cust. grip caps, bolt handle, etc.)
W. E. Brownell, 1852 Alessandro Trail, Vista, Calif. 92083 (checkering tools)
Maynard P. Buehler, Inc., 17 Orinda Hwy., Orinda, Calif. 94563 (Rocol lube)
Burgess Vibrocrafters, Inc. (BVI), Rte. 83, Grayslake, Ill. 60030
M. H. Canjar, 500 E. 45th, Denver, Colo. 80216 (triggers, etc.)
Chapman Mfg. Co., Rte. 17 at Saw Mill Rd., Durham, CT 06422
Chase Chemical Corp., 3527 Smallman St., Pittsburgh, PA 15201 (Chubb Multigauge)
Chubb (see Chase Chem. Co.)
Chicago Wheel & Mfg. Co., 1101 W. Monroe St., Chicago, Ill. 60607 (Handee grinders)
Christy Gun Works, 875-57th St., Sacramento, Calif. 95819
Clover Mfg. Co., 139 Woodward Ave., Norwalk, CT 06856 (Clover compound)
Clymer Mfg. Co., 14241 W. 11 Mile Rd., Oak Park, Mich. 48237 (reamers)
Colbert Industries, 10107 Adella, South Gate, Calif. 90280 (Panavise)
A. Constantine & Son, Inc., 2050 Eastchester Rd., Bronx, N.Y. 10461 (wood)
Dave Cook, 720 Hancock Ave., Hancock, MI 49930 (metalsmithing only)
Cougar & Hunter, G 6398 W. Pierson Rd., Flushing, Mich. 48433 (scope jigs)
Alvin L. Davidson Prods. f. Shooters, 1215 Branson, Las Cruces, NM 88001 (action sleeves)
Dayton-Traister Co., 9322 - 900th West, P.O. Box 593, Oak Harbor, WA 98277 (triggers)
Delta Arm Sporting Goods, Highway 82 West, Indianola, MS 38751/601-887-5566 (Lightwood/England)
Dem-Bart Checkering Tools, Inc., 6807 Hiway #2, Snohomish, WA 98290/206-568-7536
Dremel Mfg. Co., 4915-21st St., Racine, WI 53406 (grinders)
Chas. E. Duffy, Williams Lane, West Hurley, N.Y. 12491
Peter Dyson Ltd., 29-31 Church St., Honley, Huddersfield, Yorksh. HD7 2AH, England (accessories f. antique gun coll.)
E-Z Tool Co., P.O. Box 3186, 25 N.W. 44th Ave., Des Moines, Ia. 50313 (lathe taper attachment)
Edmund Scientific Co., 101 E. Glouster Pike, Barrington, N.J. 08007
F. K. Elliott, Box 785, Ramona, Calif. 92065 (reamers)
Emco-Lux, 2050 Fairwood Ave.; P.O. Box 07861 Columbus, OH 43207/614-445-8328
Forster Products, Inc., 82 E. Lanark Ave., Lanark, IL 61046/815-493-6360
Keith Francis Inc., 1020 W. Catching Slough Rd., Coos Bay, OR 97420/503-269-2021 (reamers)
G. R. S. Corp., P.O. Box 1153, Emporia, KS 66801/316-343-1084 (Gravermeister)
Gager Gage and Tool Co., 27509 Industrial Blvd., Hayward, CA 94545 (speedlock triggers f. Rem. 1100 & 870 pumps)
Gilmore Pattern Works, P.O. Box 50234, Tulsa, OK 74150/918-245-7614 (wagner safe-T-Planer)
Glendo Corp., P.O. Box 1153, Emporia, KS 66801/316-343-1084 (Accu-Finish tool)
Gold Lode, Inc., 181 Gary Ave., Wheaton, IL 60187 (gold inlay kit)
Gopher Shooter's Supply, Box 278, Faribault, MN 55021 (screwdrivers, etc.)
Grace Metal Prod., 115 Ames St., Elk Rapids, MI 49629 (screw drivers, drifts)
Gunline Tools Inc., 719 No. East St., Anaheim, CA 92805
Gun-Tec, P.O. Box 8125, W. Palm Beach, FL 33407
Half Moon Rifle Shop, 490 Halfmoon Rd., Columbia Falls, MT 59912 (hex screws)
Hartford Reamer Co., Box 134, Lathrup Village, Mich. 48075
Paul Jaeger Inc., 211 Leedom St., Jenkintown, PA. 19046
Jeffredo Gunsight Co., 1629 Via Monserate, Fallbrook, CA 92028 (trap buttplate)
Jerrow's Inletting Service, 452 5th Ave., E.N., Kalispell, MT 59901
K&D Grinding Co., P.O. Box 1766, Alexandria, LA 71301/318-487-0823 (cust. tools f. pistolsmiths)
Kasenite Co., Inc., 3 King St., Mahwah, N.J. 07430 (surface hrdng. comp.)
J. Korzinek, RD #2, Box 73, Canton, PA 17724 (stainl. steel bluing)
LanDav Custom Guns, 7213 Lee Highway, Falls Church, VA 22046
John G. Lawson, 1802 E. Columbia Ave., Tacoma, WA 98404
Lea Mfg. Co., 237 E. Aurora St., Waterbury, Conn. 06720
Lightwood (Fieldsport) Ltd., Britannia Rd., Banbury, Oxfordsh. OX16 8TD, England
Lock's Phila. Gun Exch., 6700 Rowland Ave., Philadelphia, Pa. 19149
John McClure, 4549 Alamo Dr., San Diego, CA 92115 (electric checkering tool)
Marker Machine Co., Box 426, Charleston, Ill. 61920
Michaels of Oregon Co., P.O. Box 13010, Portland, Ore. 97213
Viggo Miller, P.O. Box 4181, Omaha, Neb. 68104 (trigger attachment)
Miller Single Trigger Mfg. Co., R.D. on Rt. 209, Millersburg, PA 17061
Frank Mittermeier, 3577 E. Tremont, N.Y., N.Y. 10465
Moderntools Corp, Box 407, Dept. GD, Woodside, N.Y. 11377
N&J Sales, Lime Kiln Rd., Northford, Conn. 06472 (screwdrivers)
Karl A. Neise, Inc., 5602 Roosevelt Ave., Woodside, N.Y. 11377
Palmgren Prods., Chicago Tool & Eng. Co., 8383 South Chicago Ave., Chicago, IL 60167 (vises, etc.)
Panavise Prods., Inc., 2850-29th St., Long Beach, CA 90806/213-595-7621
C. R. Pedersen & Son, Ludington, Mich. 49431
Richland Arms Co., 321 W. Adrian St., Blissfield, Mich. 49228
Riley's Supply Co., 121 No. Main St., Avilla, Ind. 46710 (Niedner buttplates, caps)
Ruhr-American Corp., So. Hwy #5, Glenwood, Minn. 56334
A. G. Russell, 1705 Hiway 71N, Springdale, AR 72764 (Arkansas oilstones)
Schaffner Mfg. Co., Emsworth, Pittsburgh, Pa. 15202 (polishing kits)
SGW, Inc. (formerly Schuetzen Gun Works), 624 Old Pacific Hwy. S.E., Olympia, WA 98503/206-456-3471
Shaw's, Rt. 2, Box 407-L, Escondido, CA 92025/714-728-7070
Shooters Specialty Shop, 5146 E. Pima, Tucson, AZ 85712/602-325-3346
Southern Blueing, 6027-B N.W. 31st Ave., Ft. Lauderdale, FL 33309 (gun blueing & repairs)
L. S. Starrett Co., 121 Crescent St. Athol, MA 01331
Texas Platers Supply Co., 2453 W. Five Mile Parkway, Dallas, TX 75233 (plating kit)
Timney Mfg. Co., 2847 E. Siesta Lane, Phoenix, AZ 85024
Stan de Treville, Box 33021, San Diego, Calif. 92103 (checkering patterns)
Twin City Steel Treating Co., Inc., 1114 S. 3rd, Minneapolis, Minn. 55415 (heat treating)
Will-Burt Co., 169 So. Main, Orrville, OH 44667 (vises)
Williams Gun Sight Co., 7389 Lapeer Rd., Davison, Mich. 48423
Wilson Arms Co., 63 Leetes Island Rd., Branford, CT 06405
Wisconsin Platers Supply Co., see: Texas Platers
W. C. Wolff Co., Box 232, Ardmore, PA 19003 (springs)
Woodcraft Supply Corp., 313 Montvale, Woburn, MA 01801

HANDGUN ACCESSORIES

A. R. Sales Co., P.O. Box 3192, South El Monte, CA 91733
Baramie Corp., 6250 E. 7 Mile Rd., Detroit, MI 48234 (Hip-Grip)
Bar-Sto Precision Machine, 633 S. Victory Blvd., Burbank, CA 91502
Behlert Custom Guns, Inc., 725 Lehigh Ave., Union, NJ 07083
Belt Slide, Inc., 1301 Brushy Bend Dr., Round Lake, TX 78664
Bingham Ltd., 1775-C Wilwat Dr., Norcross, GA 30093 (magazines)
C'Arco, P.O. Box 308, Highland, CA 92346 (Ransom Rest)
Central Specialties Co., 6030 Northwest Hwy., Chicago, Ill. 60631
D&E Magazines Mgf., P.O. Box 4579, Downey, CA 90242 (clips)
Bill Dyer, 503 Midwest Bldg., Oklahoma City, Okla. 73102 (grip caps)
Essex Arms, Box 345, Phaerring St., Island Pond, VT 05846 (45 Auto frames)
R. S. Frielich, 211 East 21st St., New York, NY 10010/212-777-4477 (cases)
Jafin Prods., Jacob & Tiffin Inc., P.O. Box 547, Clanton,, AL 35045 (Light Load)
Laka Tool Co., 62 Kinkel St., Westbury, L.I., NY 11590 (stainless steel 45 Auto parts)
Lee Custom Engineering, Inc., 46 E. Jackson St., Hartford, WI 53027
Lee's Red Ramps, 7252 E. Ave. U-3, Littlerock, CA 93543 (illuminated sights)
Lee Precision Inc., 4275 Hwy. U, Hartford, WI 53027 (pistol rest holders)
Kent Lomont, 4421 So. Wayne Ave., Ft. Wayne, IN 46807/219-694-6792 (Auto Mag only)
Los Gatos Grip & Specialty Co., P.O. Box 1850, Los Gatos, CA 95030 (custom-made)
Mascot rib sights (see: Travis R. Strahan)
Mellmark Mfg. Co., P.O. Box 139, Turlock, CA 95380 (pistol safe)
W. A. Miller Co., Inc., Mingo Loop, Oguossoc, ME 04964 (cases)
No-Sho Mfg. Co., 10727 Glenfield Ct., Houston, TX 77096
Pachmayr, 1220 S. Grand, Los Angeles, Calif. 90015 (cases)
Pacific Intl. Mchdsg. Corp., 2215 "J" St., Sacramento, CA 95818 (Vega 45 Colt comb. mag.)
Platt Luggage, Inc., 2301 S. Prairie, Chicago, Ill. 60616 (cases)
Sile Distributors, 7 Centre Market Pl., New York, NY 10013
Sportsmen's Equipment Co., 415 W. Washington, San Diego, Calif. 92103

Travis R. Strahan, Rt. 7, Townsend Circle, Ringgold, GA 30736/404-937-4495 (Mascot rib sights)
M. Tyler, 1326 W. Britton, Oklahoma City, Okla. 73114 (grip adaptor)
Whitney Sales, Inc., P.O. Box 875, Reseda, CA 91335
Dave Woodruff, Box 5, Bear, DE 19701 (relining and conversions)

HANDGUN GRIPS

Art Jewel Enterprises, Box 819, Berkeley, IL 60163
Beeman's Precision Airguns, Inc., 47 Paul Dr., San Rafael, CA 94903/415-472-7121 (airguns only)
Bingham Ltd., 1775-C Wilwat Dr., Norcross, GA 30093
Fitz, 653 N. Hagar St., San Fernando, CA 91340
Gateway Shooters' Supply, Inc., 10145-103rd St., Jacksonville, FL 32210 (Rogers grips)
The Gunshop, R. D. Wallace, 320 Overland Rd., Prescott, AZ 86301
Herrett's, Box 741, Twin Falls, Ida. 83301
Mershon Co., Inc., 1230 S. Grand Ave., Los Angeles, Calif. 90015
Mustang Custom Pistol Grips, 1334 E. Katella Ave., Anaheim, CA 92805/714-978-7474
Robert H. Newell, 55 Coyote, Los Alamos, NM 87544 (custom)
Rogers Grips (see: Gateway Shooters' Supply)
Jean St. Henri, 6525 Dume Dr., Malibu, CA 90265 (custom)
Schiermeier, Box 704, Twin Falls, ID 83301 (Thompson/Contender)
Sile Dist., 7 Centre Market Pl., New York, N.Y. 10013
Southern Gun Exchange, Inc., 4311 Northeast Expressway, Atlanta (Doraville), GA 30340 (Outrider brand)
Sports Inc., P.O. Box 683, Park Ridge, IL 60068 (Franzite)

HEARING PROTECTORS

AO Safety Prods., Div. of American Optical Corp., 14 Mechanic St., Southbridge, MA 01550 (ear valve)
Bausch & Lomb, 635 St. Paul St., Rochester, N.Y. 14602
David Clark Co., Inc., 360 Franklin St., Worcester, MA 01604
Hodgdon, 7710 W. 50 Hiway, Shawnee Mission, Kans. 66202
Norton Co., Safety Prods. Div., 16624 Edwards Rd., Cerritos, CA 90701 (Lee-Sonic ear valve)
Safety Direct, 23 Snider Way, Sparks, NV 89431 (Silencio)
Smith & Wesson, 2100 Roosevelt Ave., Springfield, MA 01101
Willson Safety Prods Div., P.O. Box 622, Reading, PA 19603 (Ray-O-Vac)

HOLSTERS & LEATHER GOODS

American Sales & Mfg. Co., P.O. Box 677, Laredo, Tex. 78040
Andy Anderson, P.O. Box 225, North Hollywood, CA 91603 (Gunfighter Custom Holsters)
Beeman Precision Airguns, Inc., 47 Paul Dr., San Rafael, CA 94903/415-472-7121 (airguns only)
Bianchi Holster Co., 100 Calle Cortez, Temecula, CA 92390
Edward H. Bohlin, 931 N. Highland Ave., Hollywood, CA 90038/213-463-4888
Bo-Mar Tool & Mfg. Co., P.O. Box 168, Carthage, TX 75633/214-693-5220
Boyt Co., Div. of Welch Sptg., Box 1108, Iowa Falls, Ia. 51026
Brauer Bros. Mfg. Co., 817 N. 17th, St. Louis, Mo. 63106
Browning, Rt. 4, Box 624-B, Arnold, MO 63010
J. M. Bucheimer Co., P.O. Box 280, Airport Rd., Frederick, MD 21701/301-662-5101
Cathey Enterprises, Inc., 9516 Neils Thompson Dr., Austin, TX 78758
Chace Leather Prods., 507 Alden St., Fall River, MA 02722
Cobra Ltd., 1865 New Highway, Farmingdale, NY 11735/516-752-8544
Colt's, 150 Huyshope Ave., Hartford, Conn. 06102
Daisy Mfg. Co., Rogers, Ark. 72756
G. Wm. Davis, P.O. Box 446, Arcadia, CA 91006
Eugene DeMayo & Sons, Inc., 2795 Third Ave., Bronx, N.Y. 10455
El Dorado Leather Co., 1045 Vernon Way, El Cajon, CA 92020
Ellwood Epps Northern Ltd., 210 Worthington St. W., North Bay, Ont. P1B 3B4, Canada (custom made)
The Eutaw Co., Box 608, U.S. Highway 176W, Holly Hill, SC 29059
Goerg Ent., P.O. Box 531, Renton, WA 98056/206-883-1529
Gunfighter (See Anderson)
Hoyt Holster Co., P.O. Box 69, Coupeville, WA 98239
Don Hume, Box 351, Miami, Okla. 74354
The Hunter Co., 3300 W. 71st Ave., Westminster, CO 80030
Jackass Leather Co., 7383 N. Rogers Ave., Chicago, IL 60626/312-338-2800
Jumbo Sports Prods., P.O. Box 280, Airport Rd., Frederick, MD 21701
George Lawrence Co., 306 S. W. First Ave., Portland, OR 97204
Leathercrafters, 710 S. Washington, Alexandria, VA 22314
S. D. Myres Saddle Co., P.O. Box 357, Millis, MA 02054/617-376-2315
Kenneth L. Null-Custom Concealment Holsters, R.D. #5, Box 197, Hanover, PA 17331 (see Seventrees)
Old West Inc. Leath. Prods., P.O. Box 2030, Chula Vista, CA 92012/714-429-8050
Pony Express Sport Shop Inc., 17460 Ventura Blvd., Encino, CA 91316
Ranger Leather Prods., Box 3198, East Camden, AR 71701
Red Head Brand Corp., 4949 Joseph Hardin Dr., Dallas, TX 75236/214-330-9134
Rickenbacker's, P.O. Box 532, State Ave., Holly Hill, SC 29059
Rogers Holsters, 10601 Theresa Dr., Jacksonville, FL 32216/904-641-9434
Roy's Custom Leather Goods, Hwy. 1325 & Rawhide Rd., Magnolia, AR 71753/501-234-1599
Safariland Leather Products, 1941 Walker Ave., Monrovia, Calif. 91016

Safety Speed Holster, Inc., 910 So. Vail, Montebello, Calif. 90640
Buddy Schoellkopf Products Inc., 4949 Joseph Hardin Dr., Dallas, TX 75236
Seventrees Systems Ltd., R.D. 5, Box 197, Hanover, PA 17331/717-632-6873 (see NULL)
Sile Distr., 7 Centre Market Pl., New York, N.Y. 10013
Smith & Wesson, 2100 Roosevelt Ave., Springfield, MA 01101
Torel, Inc., 1053 N. South St., Yoakum, TX 77995 (gun slings)
Triple-K Mfg. Co., 568 Sixth Ave., San Diego, CA 92101
Whitco, Box 1712, Brownsville, Tex. 78520 (Hide-A-Way)

HUNTING AND CAMP GEAR, CLOTHING, ETC.

Bob Allen Sportswear, P.O. Box 477, Des Moines, IA 50302
Eddie Bauer, 15010 NE 36th St., Redmond, WA 98052
L. L. Bean, Freeport, Me. 04032
Bear Archery R.R. 4, 4600 Southwest 41st Blvd., Gainesville, FL 32601/904-376-2327 (Himalayan backpack)
Bell Fatigue Co., P.O. Box 3484, Augusta, GA 30904 (camouflage suits)
Bernzomatic Corp., 740 Driving Pk. Ave., Rochester, N.Y. 14613 (stoves & lanterns)
Big Beam, Teledyne Co., 290 E. Prairie St., Crystal Lake, Ill. 60014 (lamp)
Browning, Rte. 1, Morgan, Utah 84050
Camouflage Mfg. Co., P.O. Box 5437, Pine Bluff, AR 71601
Camp Trails, P.O. Box 14500, Phoenix, Ariz. 85031 (packs only)
Camp Ways, 12915 S. Spring St., Los Angeles, CA 90061
Challanger Mfg. Co., Box 550, Jamaica, N.Y. 11431 (glow safe)
Cobra, Box 167, Brady, TX 76825 (Cobra 3-in-1 light)
Coleman Co., Inc., 250 N. St. Francis, Wichita, Kans. 67201
Converse Rubber Co., 55 Fordham Rd., Wilmington, MA 01887 (boots)
Dana Safety Heater, J. L. Galef & Son, Inc., 85 Chamber St., N.Y. N.Y. 10007
DEER-ME Prod. Co., Box 345, Anoka, Minn. 55303 (tree steps)
Dunham Co., P.O. Box 813, Brattleboro, VT 05301/802-254-2316 (boots)
Freeman Ind., Inc., 100 Marblehead Rd., Tuckahoe, N.Y. 10707 (Trak-Kit)
Game-Winner, Inc., 500 Peachtree Cain Tower, 229 Peachtree, N.E., Atlanta, GA 30303/404-588-0401 (camouflage suits)
Gander Mountain, Inc., Box 248, Wilmot, Wis. 53192
Gerry Mountain Sports, Inc. (see Colorado Sports)
Gokey, 94 E. 4th St., St. Paul, Minn. 55101
Gun Club Sportswear, Box 477, Des Moines, Ia. 50302
Gun-Ho Case Mfg. Co., 110 E. 10th St., St. Paul, Minn. 55101
Joseph M. Herman Shoe Co., Inc., Millis, MA 02054 (boots)
Herter's Inc., Waseca, Minn. 56093
Himalayan Industries, P.O. Box 5668, Pine Bluff, AR 71601
Bob Hinman Outfitters, 1217 W. Glen, Peoria, IL 61614
Hunting World, 16 E. 53rd St., New York, NY 10022
Kelty Pack, In., Box 3645, Glendale, Calif. 91201
Laacke & Joys, 1432 N. Water St., Milwaukee, WI 53202 (Wildwood prods.)
Peter Limmer & Sons Inc., Box 66, Intervale, NH 03845 (boots)
Marathon Rubber Prods. Co. Inc., 510 Sherman St., Wausau, WI 54401 (rain gear)
Marble Arms Corp., 420 Industrial Park, Gladstone, Mich. 49837
National Sports, 19 E. McWilliams St., Fond du Lac, WI 54935
Nimrod & Wayfarer Trailers, 500 Ford Blvd., Hamilton, O. 45011
Charles F. Orvis Co., Manchester, Vt. 05254 (fishing gear)
PGB Assoc., 310 E. 46th St., Suite 3E, New York, NY 10017/212-867-9560
Prime Leather Finishes Co., 205 S. Second St., Milwaukee, WI 53204 (leath. waterproofer; Boot n' Saddle Soap)
Ranger Mfg. Co., Inc., P.O. Box 3676, Augusta, GA 30904
Ranger Rubber Co., 1100 E. Main St., Endicott, NY 13760/607-757-4260 (boots)
Red Head Brand Corp., 4949 Joseph Hardin Dr., Dallas, TX 75236/214-330-9134
Red Wing Shoe Co., Rte. 2, Red Wing, Minn. 55066
Refrigiwear, Inc., 71 Inip Dr., Inwood, L.I., N.Y. 11696
Reliance Prod. Ltd., 1830 Dublin Ave., Winnipeg 21, Man. R3H 0H3 Can. (tent peg)
Royal Sporting Boots/Red Ball, 8530 Page Ave., St. Louis, MO 63114
Royal Sports Clothing, Washington, IN 47501
W. R. Russell Moccasin Co., 285 S.W. Franklin, Berlin, WI 54923
Buddy Schoellkopf Prods Inc., 4949 Joseph Hardin Dr., Dallas, TX 75236
Servus Rubber Co., 1136 2nd St., Rock Island, Ill. 61201 (footwear)
The Ski Hut-Trailwise, 1615 University Ave., P.O. Box 309, Berkeley, CA 94710
Snow Lion Corp., 2611-8th St., Berkeley, CA 94710/415-548-8650 (sleeping bags and parkas)
Stearns Mfg. Co., P.O. Box 1498, St. Cloud, MN 56301
Sterno Inc., 300 Park Ave., New York, NY 10022 (camp stoves)
Teledyne Co., Big Beam, 290 E. Prairie St., Crystal Lake, IL 60014
10-X Mfg. Co., 1745 S. Acoma St., Denver, CO 80223/303-778-0324
Thermos Div., KST Co., Norwich, Conn. 06361 (Pop Tent)
Norm Thompson, 1805 N.W. Thurman St., Portland, Ore. 97209
Utica Duxbak Corp., 1745 S. Acoma St., Denver, CO 80223/303-778-0324
Waffen-Frankonia, Box 6780, 87 Wurzburg 1, W. Germany
Weinbrenner Shoe Corp., Polk St., Merrill, WI 54452
Wenzel Co., 1280 Research Blvd., St. Louis, MO 63132
Woods Bag & Canvas Co., Ltd., 90 River St., P.O. Box 407, Ogdensburg, NY 13669/315-393-3520
Woodstream Corp., Box 327, Lititz, Pa. 17543 (Hunter Seat)
Woolrich Woolen Mills, Woolrich, Pa. 17779
Yankee Mechanics, RFD No. 1, Concord, NH 03301/603-225-3181 (hand winches)

KNIVES, AXES, HATCHETS, KNIFEMAKER'S SUPPLIES—HUNTING

A. W. Amoureux, 2311 Barrow, Anchorage, AK 99503 (cust. kniv.)
E. R. (Russ) Andrews II, ERA II Knives, P.O. Box 126, Harrisonville, MO 64701/816-884-4129 (custom)
W. E. Ankrom, 1260 N. Milford Rd., Highland, MI 48031 (cust. kniv.)
Ballard Cutlery, P.O. Box 97, Golf, IL 60029 (folders)
James Barbee, P.O. Box 1702, Fort Stockton, TX 79753 (cust. kniv.)
Jack Barnett, 1496 E. Caley Ave., Littleton, CO 80121 (benchmade, custom knives)
Jack Barrett, 2133 Peach Orchard Rd., Augusta, GA 30906/404-798-9840 (cust. knives)
Scott Barry, P.O. Box 354, Laramie, WY 82070 (cust. kniv.)
C. M. Barringer, 217-2nd Isle N., Port Richey, FL 33568/813-868-3777 (scrimshander)
L. L. Bean, Freeport, Maine 04032
Bear Archery, R.R. 4, 4600 Southwest 41st Blvd. Gainesville, FL 32601/904-376-2327
Beck Knives, 1504 Hagood Ave., Barnwell, SC 29812/803-259-5959 (custom, broch. $1)
Benchmark Knives, P.O. Box 998, Gastonia, NC 28052
William N. Bennett, 431 West King St., Jackson, TN 38301/901-427-5469 (cust. kkniv.)
W. F. Benton, 104 LaPine Dr., Eufaula, AL 36027/205-687-3438 (cust. kniv.)
Leslie L. Berryman, 39885 San Moreno Ct., Fremont, CA 94538/415-651-4781 (cust. kniv.)
Birt Custom Knives, P.O. Box 544, Bunker Hill, IN 46914 (ctlg. $1)
Paul W. Bizal, 10909 E. 56th Terr., Raytown, MO 64133 (cust. kniv.)
Keith W. Blalock, Jr., 1611 The Lane, Pleasanton, TX 78064 (cust. kniv.)
Bone Knife Co. Inc., 4900 Ave. A, Lubbock, TX 79404/806-765-6812
H. Gardner Bourne, 505 S. Huron, Columbus, OH 43204 (custom-knives)
Bowen Knife Co., P.O. Drawer 590, Blackshear, GA 31516
G. M. (Tim) Britton, Rte. 1, Box 141, Kinston, NC 28501/919-523-8631 (cust. kniv.)
Dennis Brooker, D. Brooker Cutlery & Engraving, 1526 Walnut, Des Moines, IA 50309/515-282-4575 (cust. kniv.)
Floyd E. Brown, 1940 83rd Ave. S.W., Miami, FL 33155 (custom knives)
L. E. "Red" Brown, Diamond "B" Knife Co., 3203 Del Amo Blvd., Lakewood, CA 90712 (custom-knives)
Stephen Brownfield, 259 Arapaho Central Park, Richardson, TX 75080/214-231-0970 (cust. kniv.)
Buck Knives, Inc., P.O. Box 1267; 1717 Magnolia Ave., El Cajon, CA 92022/714-449-1100
John W. Bugden, 106 So. 13th St., Murray, KY 42701 (cust. kniv.)
Camillus Cutlery Co., Main St., Camillus, NY 13031
Dick Campbell, 365 W. Oxford Ave., Englewood, CO 80110 (custom knives)
Canter's Custom Cutlery, Ronald Canter, 96 Bon Air Cir., Jackson, TN 38301/901-668-1780
Don Cantini, 3933 Claremont Pl., Weirton, WV 26062 (cust. kniv.)
Bob Cargill, 14401-136th Ave., Lockport, IL 60441/815-838-2969 (cust. kniv.)
Fred Carter, 2303 Dorothy, Wichita Falls, TX 76306 (cust. kniv.)
W. R. Case & Sons Cutlery Co., 20 Russell Blvd., Bradford, PA 16701
Frank and Mark Centofante Knives, P.O. Box 17587, Tampa, FL 33682/813-961-0637 (custom)
Challanger Mfg. Co., 118 Pearl St., Mt. Vernon, NY 10550
Charter Arms Corp., 430 Sniffens Lane, Stratford, CT 06497 (Skatchet)
John E. Chase, Case Custom Knives P.O. Drawer H, Aledo, TX 76008/817-441-8331
Cheatham, 2930 W. Marlette, Phoenix, AZ 85017 (custom knives)
D. E. (Lucky) Clark, Box 216 Woodlawn St., R.D. #1, Mineral Point, PA 15942 (cust. kniv.)
J. D. Clay, 4A Graysbranch Rd., Lloyd, KY 41156 (custom knives)
Gerald Click, 6830 S. Lakeshore Dr., Tempe, AZ 85283 (cust. kniv.)
Vernon W. Coleman, 141 Lakeside Pk. Dr., Hendersonville, TN 37075 (cust. kniv.)
A. J. Collins, K.K.K. Co., 1834 W. Burbank Blvd., Burbank, CA 91506/213-848-4905 (cust. kniv.)
Walter "Blackie" Collins, P.O. Box 10311, Rock Hill, SC 29730 (cust. kniv.)
Collins Brothers Div. (belt-buckle knife): see: Bowen Knife Co.
Michael Collins, Rte. 4, Batesville Rd., Woodstock, GA 30188 (custom-knives, scrimshander)
Cooper Knives, Box 1423, Burbank, CA 91507 (cust.)
Harold Corby, 1714 Brandonwood Dr., Johnson City, TN 37601 (custom knives)
Joseph G. Cordova, 1450 Lillie Dr., Bosque, NM 87068 (cust. kniv.)
Leonard Corlee, P.O. Box 143, Georgetown, GA 31754/912-234-5867 (cust. kniv.)
Jim Corrado, 1032 No. Columbian, Oak Park, IL 60302 (cust. kniv.)
Couchman's Custom Knives, Star Route, La Mesa, NM 88044/505-233-3137
Crawford Knives, Pat Crawford, 205 N. Center, West Memphis, AR 72301/501-735-4632 (custom; ctlg. $3)
John Culpepper, 2102 Spencer Ave., Monroe, LA 71202 (cust. kniv.)
Jim Cunningham, 1519 Madison, Memphis, TN 38104/901-272-1541 (cust. knives)
Custom Knifemaker's Supply, P.O. Box 308, Emory, TX 75440 (ctlg. 50¢)
Custom Purveyors, P.O. Box 886, Fort Lee, NJ 07024/201-886-0196
Dan Daggett, Rte. 1, Stewart, OH 45778 (cust. kniv.)
Dan-D Custom Knives, Box 2F, Del Norte, CA 81132 (ctlg. $1.00)
Art A. Darakis, RD #2, Box 165D Fredericksburg, OH 44627/216-695-4271 (custom knives)
Steve Davenport, 301 Meyer, Alvin, TX 77511 (cust. kniv.)

Davis Brothers Knives, P.O. Box 793, Camden, SC 29020 (cust.; ctlg. $1)
Davis Custom Knives, North 1405 Ash, Spokane, WA 99201
W. C. Davis, Rte. 2, Box 96, Raymore, MO 64083 (cust. kniv.)
J. R. Dennard, 907 Greenwood Pl., Dalton, GA 30720 (custom-knives)
D'Holder Custom Knives, 6808 N. 30th Dr., Phoenix, AZ 85017/602-242-4996
Julius S. Diana, Box 152, Carmichaels, PA 15320 (cust. kniv.)
Douglas M. Dent, Rt. 7, Box 463, So. Charleston, WV 25309 (cust. kniv.)
Dick Dorough Handmade Knives, Rt. 1, Box 210, Gadsden, AL 35901/205-442-5497
T. M. Dowell, 139 N.W., St. Helen's Pl., Bend, OR 97701 (TMD custom-knives, ctlg. $2)
Dragon Knives (see: Norman Levine)
Bill Duff, P.O. Box 217, 1488 Pioneer Way, Suite 5, El Cajon, CA 92022 (cust. kniv.)
Fain E. Edwards, 209 E. Mountain Ave., Jacksonville, AL 36265/205-435-4994 (cust. kniv.)
Brad Embry, P.O. Box 11931, Tampa, FL 33680/813-988-7230 (cust. kniv.)
Jim Ence, 145 So. 200 East, Richfield, UT 84701/801-896-6206 (cust. kniv.)
Mike England, 608 West 4th, Cordell, OK 73632/405-832-3770 (cust. knives)
Virgil England, Box 10197, Klatt Station, Anchorage, AK 99502 (cust. kniv.)
Tom Enos, Rt. 1 Box 66, Winter Garden, FL 32787/305-876-3041 (cust. kniv.)
Ensign Co., Gunnison, UT 84634 (cust. knives)
John D. Evans, 5414 Grissom Dr., Arlington, TX 76016 (cust. kniv.)
Eze-Lap Diamond Prods., Box 2229, 15164 Weststate St., Westminster, CA 92683/714-847-1555 (knife sharpeners)
Howard Faucheaux, P.O. Box 206, Loreauville, LA 70552 (cust. kniv.)
Vince Feragotti, RD #1, Beechwood Dr., Industry, PA 15052 (cust. kniv.)
Jimmy L. Fikes, 215 N. Main St., Orange, MA 01364/617-544-7160 (cust. kniv.)
L. C. Finger, Rte. 5, Box 97B, Weatherford, TX 76086 (cust. kniv.)
Fischer Custom Knives, Rt. 1, Box 170-M, Victoria, TX 77901
Don Fogg & Murad Sayen, River Forge custom knives, Rte. 152, Nottingham, NH 03290/603-679-8866
Allen Ford, 846 Thomas St., Roswell, GA 30075 (cust. kniv.)
Paul Fox, Rt. 1, Box 261-A, NC 28609 (cust. kniv.)
Heinrich H. Frank, 210 Meadows Rd., Whitefish, MT 59937/406-862-2681 (custom-knives)
Franklin Custom Knives, Mike Franklin, Rte. 41, Box M, Aberdeen, OH 45101/513-795-2571
Ron Frazier, Rt. 6, Box 217, Powhatan, VA 23139 (cust. kniv.)
W. C. Frazier, 1029 Kavanaugh St., Mansfield, LA 71052 (scrimshander)
A. J. Freiling, 3700 Niner Rd., Finksburg, MD 21048 (cust. kniv.)
Fuller & Hall Knives, P.O. Box 734, Livingston, AL 35470/205-652-2432 (custom)
John Fuller Custom Blades, 6156 Ridge Way, Douglasville, GA 30135/404-942-1155
W. T. Fuller, 400 S. 8th St., East Gadsden, AL 35903 (custom-knives)
Gault Present. Knives, Rt. 1, Box 184, Lexington, TX 78947 (ctlg. 50¢)
Rick Genovese, 2838 N. Prospect St., Colorado Springs, CO 80907/303-636-1588 (cust. kniv.)
Gerber Legendary Blades, 14200 S.W. 72nd St., Portland, OR 99223
Jean Gerry, 633-D Center St., Manchester, CT 06040 (cust. kniv.)
Wayne Goddard, 473 Durham Ave., Eugene, OR 97404 (custom knives)
Gordon Knives, Bill DeFreest, P.O. Box 573, Barnwell, SC 29812/803-259-3866 (cust.)
Charles W. Graham, Box 11, Eolia, MO 63344 (cust. kniv.)
Rendon Griffin, 9706 Cedardale, Houston, TX 77055 (cust. knives)
Gutman Cutlery Co., Inc., 900 S. Columbus Ave., Mt. Vernon, NY 10550
H & B Forge Co., Rte. 2, Box 24, Shiloh, OH 44878 (tomahawks)
Dr. Philip L. Hagen, Northport Shopping Center, Fargo, ND 58102 (cust. kniv.)
Robert J. Hajovsky, P.O. Box 21, Scotland, TX 76379 (cust. kniv.)
Lloyd A. Hale Handmade Knives, Rte. 2, Box 254-A, Lowell, AR 72745
Joe H. Hales, 1795 Dellwood Ave., Memphis, TN 38127/901-353-4144 (cust. kniv.)
Jim Hammond Handmade Knives Box 486, Arab, AL 35016/205-586-4151
Royal H. Hanson, 1977 S.W. Burdette Dr., Roseburg, OR 97470/503-679-6230 (cust. kniv.)
Jim Hardenbrook, JLH Custom Knives, 17988 Country Rd., G Cortez, CO 81321/303-565-8893
Phill Hartsfield, 13095 Brookhurst St., 13095 Brookhurst St., Garden Grove, CA 92642/714-636-7633 (cust. kniv.)
Don Hastings, P.O. Box 181, Palestine, TX 75801/214-729-7319 (cust. kniv.)
Rade Hawkins, P.O. Box H, Red Oak, GA 30272 (cust. kniv.)
J. A. Henckels Zwillingswerk, Inc., 1 Westchester Plaza, Elmsford, NY 10523/914-592-7370
Larry Hendricks, 9919 E. Apache Trail, Mesa, AZ 85207/602-986-9252 (cust. kniv.)
Wayne Hensley, 469 Hilltop Rd. S.W., Conyers, GA 30207/404-483-8938 (cust. kniv.)
Heritage Custom Knives, 2895 Seneca St., Buffalo, NY 14224
George Herron, 920 Murrah Ave., Aiken, SC 29801 (custom-knives, ctlg. $1)
Ron Hewitt, P.O. Box 632, Ludowici, GA 31316 (cust. knives)
Gil Hibben Knives, Inc., Rt. 1, Box 424, Branson, MO 65616/417-338-2727 (cust.)
Vernon W. Hicks, Rte. 1, Box 387, Bauxite, AR 72011 (cust. kniv.)
J. B. Hodge Handmade Pocketknives, 1100 Woodmont Ave., Huntsville, AL 35801/205-536-8388
Steve Hoel, P.O. Box 283, Pine, AZ 85544/602-476-4278 (cust. kniv.)
Donald B. Hoffmann, P.O. Box 174, San Miguel, CA 93451 (cust. kniv.)

Hoffritz, 515 W. 24th St., New York, NY 10011/212-924-7300
D'Alton Holder, 6808 N. 30th Dr., Phoenix, AZ 85017/602-242-4996 (cust. knives)
Jess Horn, Box 1274, Redding, CA 96001 (cust. kniv.)
Glen Hornby, 1317 Ehtel St., Glendale, CA 91207/213-244-1354 (cust. kniv.)
David M. Howie, P.O. Box 1662, Bay City, TX 77414 (cust. kniv.)
Arthur J. Hubbard, Hubbard Knife Works, 574 Cutlers Farm Rd., Monroe, CT 06468 (cust. kniv. ctlg $1)
Chubby Hueske, 4808 Tamarisk Dr., Bellaire, TX 77401 (custom-knives)
Jerry Hunt, 4606 Princeton Dr., Garland, TX 75042 (cust. kniv.)
Imel Custom Knives, 1616 Bundy Ave., New Castle, IN 47362/317-529-1651 (broch. $1)
Imperial Knife Associated Companies, 1776 Broadway, New York, NY 10019/212-757-1814
Indian Ridge Traders, Box 869, Royal Oak, MI 48068/313-399-6034 (mostly blades)
Dan Isaacs, 3701 Eureka, Sp. 59-A, Anchorage, AK 99503 (cust. kniv.)
Ron Isaacs, P.O. Box 3526, Kenai, AK 99611 (cust. kniv.)
Clifton James, Star Rt., Box 10, Atmore, AL 35611/205-368-5655 (cust. kniv.)
Jet-Aer Corp., 100 Sixth Ave., Paterson, NJ 07524 (G96 knives)
S. R. Jobs, 1513 Martin Chapel Rd., Murray, KY 42071 (cust. knives)
Gorden W. Johnson, 5426 Sweetbriar, Houston, TX 77060 (cust. kniv.)
Ruffin Johnson, 215 LaFonda, Houston, TX 77060/713-448-4407 (cust. kniv.; ctlg. $1)
Steve Johnson, P.O. Box 5. Manti, UT 84642/801-835-7941 (cust. kniv.)
LaDow (Doc) Johnston, 2322 W. Country Club Parkway, Toledo, OH 43614 (custom-knives scrimshaw)
KA-BAR Cutlery, Inc., 5777 Grant Ave., Cleveland, OH 44105
KaBar Knives, Collectors Division, 434 No. 9th St., Olean, NY 14760
Robert A. Kapela, 10060 Packard Rd., Temperance, MI 48182
Don Karlin, P.O. Box 668, Aztec, NM 87410 (cust. kniv.)
William L. Keeton, 4234 Lynnbrook Dr., Louisville, KY 40220/502-456-2378
Robert Kellog, P.O. Box 2006, West Monroe, LA 71291 (cust. kniv.)
Gary Kelly, 17485 S.W. Pheasant Lane, Aloha, OR 97005 (cust. kniv.)
Lance Kelly, 4226 Lamar St., Decatur, GA 30035 (custom-Made)
Kershaw Cutlery Co., 6024 Jean Rd., Suite-D, Lake Oswego, OR 97034/503-636-0111
Jon W. Kirk, 800 N. Olive, Fayetteville, AR 72701 (custom-knives)
W. Kneubuhler, P.O. Box 327, Pioneer, OH 43554 (custom-knives)
Michael T. Koval, P.O. Box 14130, Columbus, OH 43214/614-888-6486 (cust. kniv.)
Ron Lake, 123 East Park, Taylorville, IL 62568/217-824-2378 (custom knives)
Lakota Corp., 30916 Agoura Rd., Suite 311, Westlake Village, CA 91361
Milo J. Leach, 5377 W. Grand Blanc Rd., Swartz Creek, MI 48473/313-655-4850
Tommy Lee, Rt. 2, Box CE6, Gaffney, SC 29340/803-489-8302 (cust. knives, scrimshander)
Norman Levine, 915 Tascosa Dr., S.E., Huntsville, AL 35802/205-881-4755 (cust. kniv.)
Jimmy Lile Handmade Knives, Rte. 1, Box 56, Russellville, AR 72801
Ed Louchard, 158 Nimshew Stage, Chico, CA 95926 (cust. kniv.)
R. W. Loveless, P.O. Box 7836, Arlington Sta., Riverside, CA 92503 (custom-knives, ctlg. $2)
Ernest L. Lyle III, 4501 Meadowbrook Ave., Orlando, FL 32808 (cust. kniv.)
J. M. "Mickey" Maddox, 63 Spring Circle, Ringgold, GA 30736/404-935-5082 (cust. kniv.)
Clinton Manley, Rte. 1, Box 28, Zolfo Springs, FL 33890 (cust. kniv.)
Al Mar Knives, Inc., 5861 S.W. Benfield Ct., Lake Oswego, OR 97034/503-639-8554 (custom)
Marble Arms Corp., 420 Industrial Park, Gladstone, MI 49837
Jerry McAlpin, Box 71, Bullard, TX 75757 (cust. kniv.)
H. O. McBurnette, Jr., Rte. 4, Box 337, Piedmont, AL 36272 (custom knives)
C. O. "Mac" McClung, 748 N.W. 15th, Moore, OK 73160 (cust. kniv.)
Charles R. McConnell, 158 Genteel Ridge, Wellsburg, WV 26070 (cust. kniv.)
John McCormick, 9632 East 26th St., Tulsa, OK 74129 (cust. kniv.)
Harry McEvoy, 2155 Tremont Blvd. N.W., Grand Rapids, MI 49504 (cust. knives)
Daryl Meier, R.R. 4, Carbondale, IL 62901 (cust. kniv.)
Chris Miller, 1961 Southwest 36 Ave., Ft. Lauderdale, FL 33312 (cust. kniv.)
John T. Mims, 620 S. 28th Ave., Apt. 327, Hattiesburg, MS 39401 (custom-knives)
Jim Minnick, 144 N. 7th St., Middletown, IN 47356 (cust. kniv.)
Mitchell Custom Knives, 511 Ave. B, So. Houston, TX 77587
Wm. F. Moran, Jr., P.O. Box 68, Braddock Heights, MD 21744 (custom-knives, ctlg. 50¢)
C. H. Morris, 828 Meadow Dr., Atmore, AL 36502 (cust. kniv.)
Morseth Sports Equip. Co., 1705 Hiway 71N, Springdale, AR 72764 (custom-knives)
Naifeh Knives, Rte. 13, Box 380, Tulsa, OK 74107 (hand-crafted pocket knives)
Ivan F. Nealey, Anderson Dam, Mt. Home, ID 83647 (cust. kniv.)
Nolen Knives, Box 6216, Corpus Christi, TX 78411 (ctlg. 50¢)
R. D. Nolen, P.O. Box 2805, Estes Park, CO 80517 (cust. kniv.)
Normark Corp., 1710 E. 73th St., Minneapolis, MN 55423
Ogg Custom Knives, Robert Ogg, Rt. 1, Box 345, Paris, AR 72855/501-963-2767
Robert Oleson, 800 Keokuk St., Petaluma, CA 94952 (cust. kniv.)
Olsen Knife Co., Inc., 7 Joy St., Howard City, MI 49329
John Owens, 8755 S.W. 96th St., Miami, FL 33156 (cust. kniv.)

Howard Palmer, 2031 Tronjo Rd., Pensacola, FL 32503 (cust. kniv.)
Melvin M. Pardue, P.O. Box 14357, Tampa, FL 33690 (cust. knives)
W. C. Pass, P.O. Box 307, Merritt Island, FL 32952 (cust. kniv., ctlg. $1)
W. D. Pease, Rt. 1, Box 305, Ripley, OH 45167 (cust. kniv.)
Pendleton Knives, 2116 Broadmore Ave., San Pablo, CA 94806/415-758-0761 (cust.)
Pharris, 6247 Whitecliff Way, North Highlands, CA 95660/916-331-1544 (bowies)
Paul S. Phelps, 1306 Woodlawn Dr., Maryville, TN 37801/615-983-7402 (Pauls. handmade foldg. kniv.)
A. Pickens, 8229 C.R. 334, Ignacio, CO 81137/303-883-2303 (cust.-crafted ape kniv.)
Leon Pittman, Rt. 1, Box 46, Pendergrass, GA 30567 (cust. knives)
Plaza Cutlery Inc., South Coast Plaza #161 Costa Mesa, CA 92626/714-549-3932
James L. Poplin, P.O. Box 947, Washington, GA 30673/404-678-2729 (cust. kniv.)
Jim Pugh, 917 Carpenter St., P.O. Box 711, Azle, TX 76020 (cust. kniv.)
Aaron Pursley, Bear Paw Rte., Box 6-A, Big Sandy, MT 59520 (cust. kniv.)
Don Puterbaugh, 4062 Templeton Gap, Colorado Springs, CO 80907 (cust. kniv.)
Ramrod Knife & Gun Shop, Route 5, State Road 3 North, Newcastle, IN 47362 (custom-knives)
Randall-Made Knives, Box 1988, Orlando, FL 32802 (ctlg. 25¢)
Ratterree Knife Co., 2906 Hillsdale Ave., Charlotte, NC 28209/704-332-1607 (cust. kniv.)
Remote Survival Co., P.O. Box 523, New Haven, CT 06503 (custom knives)
Richardson Handmade Knives (see Neil/Sarah Schatz)
Rigid Knives, P.O. Box 816, Hwy. 290E., Lake Hamilton, AR 71951/501-525-1377 (custom-made)
Fred Rohn, 18005 Ventura Blvd., Encino, CA 91316/213-345-8611 (cust. kniv.)
Roman Eng. Prods. Co., 7727 W. Rascher Ave., Chicago, IL 60656 (cust. knives)
Richard Romano, 31 Arlington Rd., Windsor Lock, CT 06096 (cust. kniv.)
Ruana Knife Works, Box 574, Bonner, MT 59823 (ctlg. 50¢)
Ruko Sporting Goods, Inc., 195 Sugg Rd., Buffalo, NY 14225/716-632-0993
Joe Rundell, 6198 Frances Rd., Clio, MI 48420 (scrimshander)
A. G. Russell, 1705 Hiwy. 71 N., Springdale, AR 72764
Roger J. Russell, P.O. Box 7214, Spokane, WA 99207 (cust. kniv.)
SAM Enterprises, 1834 W. Burbank Blvd., Burbank, CA 91506 (Cooper cust. knives)
Lewis B. Sanchez, Cumberland Knife & Gun Works, 5661 Bragg Blvd., Fayetteville, NC 28303
Sanders, 2358 Tyler Lane, Louisville, KY 40205 (Bahco)
Jim Sasser, 1811 Santa Fe Dr., Pueblo, CO 81006 (cust. kniv.)
Neil and Sarah Schatz, Box 92, Sullivan, MO 63080/314-468-4203 (cust. kniv.)
Clifton Schenck, P.O. Box 1017, Bonners Ferry, ID 83805 (cust. kniv.)
Schmidt Knives, P.O. Box 598, 396 J.R. Road, Whitefish, MT 59937 (custom)
James A. Schmidt, RD 3, Eastern Ave., Ballston Lake, NY 12019 (cust. kniv.)
Herman Schneider, 24296 Via Quara, Laguna Niguel, CA 92677 (cust. kniv.)
Bob Schrimsher, Custom Knifemaker's Supply, P.O. Box 308, Emory, TX 75440
Maurice & Alan Schrock, 1708 S. Plum St., Pontiac, IL 61764 (cust. kniv.)
E. W. (Dubba) Schulenburg, 406 Sunset Blvd., Carrollton, GA 30117 (cust. kniv.)
Bob Schultz, 4062 Templeton Gap, Colorado Springs, CO 80907 (cust. kniv.)
John J. Schwarz, 41 Fifteenth St., Wellsburg, WV 26070 (custom-knives)
N. H. Schiffman Custom Knives, 963 Malibu, Pocatello, ID 83201
Jim Serven, 6153 Third St., Mayville, MI 48744/517-843-6539 (fold. hunters)
Robert G. Sharp, 2308 Vincent Ave. No., Minneapolis, MN 55411/612-522-0701 (cust. kniv.; broch. $1)
David Shaw, 2009 No. 450 East, Ogden, UT 84404 (cust. kniv.)
Shaw-Leibowitz, Rt. 1, Box 421, New Cumberland, WV 26047 (blade etchings)
George Sherwood, Box 735, Winchester, OR 97495 (engraver, scrimshander)
Corbet R. Sigman, Rt. 1, Box 212-A, Liberty, WV 25124
Silver Fox Knives, 4714-44th St., Dickinson, TX 77539 (custom)
Norman Simons, 12006 Newbrook, Houston, TX 77072 (cust. kniv.)
David Sites, 2665 Atwood Terr., Columbus, OH 43211 (cust. kniv.)
Ron Skaggs, 508 W. Central, Princeton, MI 48420 (scrimshander)
Skatchet, (see: Charter Arms)
Jim Small, 474 Foster St., Madison, GA 30650 (custom knives)
Smith & Wesson, 2100 Roosevelt Ave., Springfield, MA 01101
Adam Smith, Box 751, Woodbridge, Ont., L4L 1B5, Canada (cust. kniv.)
Cary Smith, 946 Marigney Ave., Mandeville, LA 70448 (cust. kniv.)
D. W. Smith, R.D. #1, Box 141, Franklin Rd., Mars, PA 16046 (cust. kniv.)
Jesse W. Smith Saddlery, E. 3024 Sprague, Spokane, WA 99201 (sheathmakers)
Jim Smith, 1608 Joann, Wichita, KS 67203 (cust. kniv.)
John T. Smith, 8404 Cedar Crest Dr., So. Haven, MS 38671 (custom-knives)
W. J. Sonneville, 1050 Chalet Dr. W., Mobile, AL 36608 (custom-knives)
Jim Sornberger, 5675 Meridian Ave., San Jose, CA 95118 (cust. kniv.)
Bernard Sparks, Box 32, Dingle, ID 83233 (custom-knives)
Chuck Stapel, Box 1617, Glendale, CA 91209/213-249-8337 (cust. kniv.)

Kelly Stephens, Rt. 3, 337B, Vine Grove, KY 40175/502-828-3630 (cust. kniv.)
Glen Sterns, 224½ Huron St., Toledo, OH 43605 (scrimshander)
Stone Knives, 610 No. Glenville Dr., Richardson, TX 75080/214-231-0970 (custom knives)
G. W. Stone, 259 Arapaho Central Park, Richardson, TX 75080 (cust. kniv.)
Swiss Army Knives, Inc., P.O. Box 846, Shelton, CT 06484 (Victorinox; folding)
Agee Taylor, Rt. 1, Box 56, Farmville, VA 23901 (cust. kniv.)
C. Gray Taylor, 134 Lana View Dr., Kingsport, TN 37664 (cust. kniv.)
Tekna, 3549 Haven Ave., Menlo Park, CA 94025/415-365-5112
Stephen Terrill, 908 S. Magnolia, Box 669, Lindsay, CA 93247 (cust. kniv.)
Bill Thomason, 167 Lower Dawnville Rd. NE, Dalton, GA 30720 (cust. knives)
Thompson/Center, P.O. Box 2405, Rochester, NH 03867
Danny Thornton, P.O. Box 334, Complex East, Hiway 160, Fort Mill, SC 29715/803-547-7383 (cust. kniv.)
Carolyn Tinker, 1699 N. Marengo Ave., Pasadena, CA 91103 (cust. kniv.)
Robert Tison, 1844 Barktram, Circle E, Jacksonville, FL 32207/904-725-3385 (handmade folding kniv.)
Pat Tomes, 41 Greenbriar Ave., Hampton, VA 23661 (cust. kniv.)
Dwight L. Towell, Rt. 1, Midvale, ID 83645 (custom knives)
Track Knives, 126 N. Wisconsin Ave., Whitefish, MT 59937 (custom knives)
Tru-Balance Knife Co., 2115 Tremont Blvd., Grand Rapids, MI 49504
R. A. Turnbull, 5722 Newburg Rd., Rockford, IL 61108/815-398-3799 (cust. kniv.)
Unique Inventions, Inc., 3727 W. Alabama St., Houston, TX 77027 (throwing knife)
H. J. Viele, 88 Lexington Ave., Westwood, NJ 07675/201-666-2906 (cust. kniv.)
Frank Vought, P.O. Box 62, Plattenville, LA 70393 (cust. kniv.)
W-K Knives, P.O. Box 327, Pioneer, OH 43554
A. F. Walters, 609 E. 20th St., Tifton, GA 31794 (cust. kniv.)
W. C. Ward, Rte. 6, Box 184-B, Clinton, TN 37716/615-457-3568 (cust. kniv.)
Buster Warenski, P.O. Box 214, Richfield, UT 84701 (cust. kniv.)
Frederick Weber, 401 W. Clinton St., Haldeon, NJ 07508 (cust. kniv.)
Donald Weiler, P.O. Box 1576, Yuma, AZ 85364 (cust. kniv.)
Charles L. Weiss, 18847 N. 13th Ave., Phoenix, AZ 85027 (cust. kniv.)
William H. Welch, WHW Knives, P.O. Box 7017, Fort Wayne, IN 46807/219-745-0411 (custom)
Wenoka Cutlery, 85 North Ave., Natick, MA 01760
Mike Wesolowski, 902-A Lohrman Lane, Petaluma, CA 94952 (cust. kniv.)
Western Cutlery Co., 1800 Pike Rd., Longmont, CO 80501
Walt Whinnery, Walts Cust. Leather, 1947 Meadow Creek Dr., Louisville, KY 40281/502-458-4361 (sheathmaker)
Weldon Whitley, P.O. Box 746, Jal, NM 88252 (cust. kniv.)
Horace Wiggins, 203 Herndon, Mansfield, LA 71502/318-872-2924; even. 872-4471 (custom knives)
W. C. Wilber, 400 Lucerne Dr., Spartanburg, SC 29302 (custom knives)
W. C. Williams, Rte. 2, Box 452, Atlanta, TX 75551/214-796-7260 (cust. kniv.)
Ronnie Wilson, P.O. Box 2012, Weirton, WV 26062 (custom-knives)
Art Wiman, P.O. Box 92, Plummerville, AR 72127 (cust. kniv.)
Bill Winn, Star Route, Gruver, TX 79040 (cust. kniv.)
Barry Wood, 650½ So. Venice Blvd., Venice, CA 90291 (cust. kniv.)
W. W. Wood, 731 Wood Ridge Dr., Cedar Hill, TX 75104 (cust. kniv.)
Tim Wright, 5831 S. Blackstone, Chicago, IL 60637 (cust. kniv.)
Wyoming Knife Co., 115 Valley Dr., Casper, WY 82601
Yancey Knife & Scrimshaw, Ann Yancey, P.O. Box 943, Estes Park, CO 80517/303-586-2153
Don Zaccagnino, P.O. Box Zack, Pahokee, FL 33476 (custom-knives)

LABELS, BOXES, CARTRIDGE HOLDERS

Milton Brynin, Box 162, Fleetwood Sta., Mount Vernon, NY 10552 (cartridge box labels)
E-Z Loader, Del Rey Products, P.O. Box 91561, Los Angeles, CA 90009
Jasco, J. A. Somers Co., P.O. Box 49751, Los Angeles, CA 90049 (cartridge box labels)
Peterson Label Co., P.O. Box 186, Redding Ridge, CT 06876 (cartridge box labels; Targ-Dots)
N. H. Schiffman, 963 Malibu, Pocatello, ID 83201 (cartridge carrier)

LOAD TESTING and PRODUCT TESTING, CHRONOGRAPHING, BALLISTIC STUDIES

Hutton Rifle Ranch, 1802 S. Oak Park Dr., Rolling Hills, Tucson, AZ 85710
Kent Lomont, 4421 S. Wayne Ave., Ft. Wayne, IN 46807/219-694-6792 (handguns, handgun ammunition)
Plum City Ballistics Range, Rte. 1, Box 29A, Plum City, WI 54761
Russell's Rifle Shop, Rte. 5, Box 92, Georgetown, TX 78626/512-778-5338 (load testing and chronographing to 300 yds.)
John M. Tovey, 4710 - 104th Lane NE, Circle Pines, MN 55014
H. P. White Laboratory, Inc., 3114 Scarboro Rd., Street, MD 21154/301-838-6550

MISCELLANEOUS

Accurizing Service, Herbert G. Troester, 2292 W. 1000 North, Vernal, UT 84078/801-789-2158

Action Sleeves, Alvin L. Davidson, 1215 Branson, Las Cruces, NM 88001
Adapters, Sage Industries, P.O. Box 2248, Hemet, CA 92343 (12-ga. shotgun; 38 S&W blank)
Adhesive Flannel, Forest City Prod., 722 Bolivar, Cleveland, OH 44115
Adjusta-Targ, Inc., 1817 Thackeray N.W., Massillon, OH 44646
Ammo Pouch, Creed Enterprises, P.O. Box 159, Coeur d'Alene, ID 83814
Archery, Bear, R.R. 4, 4600 Southwest 41st Blvd., Gainesville, FL 32601/904-376-2327
Arms Restoration, J. J. Jenkins Ent. Inc., 375 Pine Ave. No. 25, Goleta, CA 93017/805-967-1366
Barrel Band Swivels, Phil Judd, 83 E. Park St., Butte, Mont. 59701
Bedding Kit, Bisonite Co., P.O. Box 84, Kenmore Station, Buffalo, NY 14217
Bedding Kit, Fenwal, Inc., Resins Systems Div., 400 Main St., Ashland, MA 01721
Belt Buckles, Adina Silversmiths Corp., P.O. Box 348, 3195 Tucker Rd., Cornwell Heights, PA 19020/215-639-7246
Benchrest & Accuracy Shooters Equipment, Bob Pease Accuracy, P.O. Box 787, Zipp Road, New Braunfels, TX 78130/512-625-1342
Belt Buckles, Bergamot Brass Works, 42 N. Wisconsin, Darien, WI 53114
Belt Buckles, Just Brass Inc., 21 Filmore Place, Freeport, NY 11520 (ctlg. $2)
Belt Buckles, Sports Style Associates, 41 Jackson, Elmont, L.I., NY 11003
Belt Buckles, Pilgrim Pewter Inc., R.D. 2, Tully, NY 13159
Bootdryers, Baekgaard Ltd., 1855 Janke Dr., Northbrook, Ill. 60062
Bore Lamp, Spacetron, Inc., Box 84, Broadview, IL 60155 (Teenie-Genie)
Breech Plug Wrench, Swaine Machine, 195 O'Connell, Providence, R.I. 02905
Cannons, South Bend Replicas Inc., 61650 Oak Rd., S. Bend, IN 46614/219-289-4500 (ctlg. $4)
Cannons, A & K Mfg. Co., Inc., 1651 N. Nancy Rose Ave., Tucson, AZ 85712 (replicas)
Case Gauge, Plum City Ballistics Range, Rte. 1, Box 29A, Plum City, WI 54761
Chrome Brl. Lining, Marker Mach. Co., Box 426, Charleston, Ill. 61920
Clips, D&E Magazines Mfg., P.O. Box 4579, Downey, CA 90242 (handgun and rifle)
CO_2 Cartridges, Nittan U.S.A. Inc., 4901 Morena Blvd., Suite 307, San Diego, CA 92117/714-272-6113
Deer Drag, D&H Prods. Co., Inc., P.O. Box 22, Glenshaw, PA 15116/412-443-2190
Dryer, Thermo-Electric, Golden-Rod, Buenger Enterprises, Box 5286, Oxnard, CA 93030/805-985-9596
E-Z Loader, Del Rey Prod., P.O. Box 91561, Los Angeles, CA 90009
Ear-Valv, Sigma Eng. Co., 16624 Edwards Rd., Cerritos, CA 90701 (Lee-Sonic)
Firearms Consultant, Shelley Braverman, Four Mile Point, Athens, NY 12015
Flares, Colt Industries, Huyshope Ave., Hartford, Conn. 06102
Flares, Smith & Wesson Chemical Co., 2399 Forman Rd., Rock Creek, OH 44084
Game Hoist, Cam Gear Ind., P.O. Box 1002, Kalispell, MT 59901 (Sportsmaster 500 pocket hoist)
Game Hoist, Precise, 3 Chestnut, Suffern, NY 10901
Game Scent, Buck Stop Lure Co., Inc., 3015 Grow Rd. N.W., Stanton, MI 48888/517-762-5091
Game Scent, Pete Rickard, Box 1250, Cobleskill, NY 12043 (Indian Buck lure)
Gas Pistol, Penguin Ind., Inc., Airport Industrial Mall, Coatesville, PA 19320/215-384-6000
Golden-Rod, Buenger Enterprises, P.O. Box 5286, Oxnard, CA 93030 (Thermo-Electric Dryers)
Grip caps, Knickerbocker Enterprises, 16199 S. Maple Ln. Rd., Oregon City, OR 97045
Gun Bedding Kit, Fenwal, Inc., Resins System Div., 400 Main St., Ashland, MA 01721/617-881-2000
Gun Jewelry, Sid Bell Originals, R.D. 2, Tully, NY 13159
Gun Jewelry, Pilgrim Pewter Inc., R.D. 2, Tully, NY 13159
Gun Jewelry, Al Popper, 614 Turnpike St., Stoughton, Mass. 02072
Gun Jewelry, Sports Style Assoc., 41 Jackson, Elmont, L.I., NY 11003
Gun Record Book, B. J. Co., Bridge St., Bluffton, SC 29910
Gun Sling, Kwikfire, Wayne Prods. Co., P.O. Box 247, Camp Hill, PA 17011
Gun Slings, Torel, Inc., 1053 N. South St., Yoakum, TX 77995
Hat Saver Co., Inc., P.O. Box 307, Rosenberg, TX 77471
Hollow Pointer, Goerg Ent., P.O. Box 531, Renton, WA 98056/206-883-1529
Hugger Hooks, Roman Products, 15400 W. 44th Ave., Golden, CO 80401
Hunting Blinds, Sports Haven Inc., P.O. Box 88231, Seattle, WA 98188
Insect Repellent, Armor, Div. of Buck Stop, Inc., 3015 Grow Rd., Stanton, Mich. 48888
Insert Barrels, Sport Specialties, H. Owen, Box 5337, Hacienda Hts., CA 91745/213-330-0782
Light Load, Jacob & Tiffin Inc., P.O. Box 547, Clanton, AL 35045
Locks, Gun, Bor-Lok Prods., 105 5th St., Arbuckle, CA 95912
Locks, Gun, Master Lock Co., 2600 N. 32nd St., Milwaukee, WI 53245
Miniature Cannons, A & K Mfg. Co., 5146 E. Pima, Tucson, AZ 85712 (ctlg. $1)
Miniature Cannons, Karl J. Furr, 76 East-350 North, Orem, UT 84057 (replicas)
Miniature Guns, Charles H. Stoppler, 5 Minerva Place, New York, NY 10468
Monte Carlo Pad, Frank A. Hoppe Div., Penguin Ind., Airport Industrial Mall, Coatesville, PA 19320/215-384-6000
Muzzle-Top, Allen Assoc., 7502 Limekiln, Philadelphia, PA 19150 (plastic gun muzzle cap)

Patterning Data, Whits Shooting Stuff, P.O. Box 1340, Cody, WY 82414
Pell Remover, A. Edw. Terpening, 838 E. Darlington Rd., Tarpon Springs, FL 33589
Pockethoist, Cam-Gear Industries, Inc., P.O. Box 1002, Kalispell, MT 59901 (Sportsmaster 500)
Powderhorns, Kirk Olson, Ft. Woolsey Guns, P.O. Box 2122, Prescott, AZ 86302/602-778-3035
Powder Storage Magazine, C & M Gunworks, 2603 41st St., Moline, IL 61265
Practice Ammunition, Hoffman Prods., P.O. Box 853, Lake Forest, IL 60045
Pressure Testg. Machine, M. York, 5508 Griffith Rd., Gaithersburg, MD 20760
Ransom Handgun Rests, C'Arco, P.O. Box 308, Highland, CA 92346
Retriev-R-Trainer, Scientific Prods. Corp., 426 Swann Ave., Alexandria, VA 22301
Rifle Slings, Bianchi Leather Prods., 100 Calle Cortez, Temecula, CA 92390
Rifle Slings, Chace Leather Prods., 507 Alden St., Fall River, MA 02722
RIG, NRA Scoring Plug, Rig Prod. Co., Div. of Mittan, Inc., 21320 Deering Ct., Canoga Park, CA 91304/213-883-4700
Rubber Cheekpiece, W. H. Lodewick, 2816 N. E. Halsey, Portland, Ore. 97232
Saddle Rings, Studs, Fred Goodwin, Sherman Mills, ME 04776
Safeties, Williams Gun Sight Co., 7389 Lapeer Rd., Davison, Mich. 48423
Salute Cannons, Naval Co., R.D. 2, 4747 Cold Spring Creamery Rd., Doylestown, PA 18901
Sav-Bore, Saunders Sptg. Gds., 338 Somerset St., N. Plainfield, NJ 07060
Scrimshaw Engraving, C. Milton Barringer, 217-2nd Isle N., Port Richey, FL 33568
Sharpening Stones, Russell's Arkansas Oilstones, 1705 Hiway 71N., Springdale, AR 72764
Shell Shrinker Mfg. Co., P.O. Box 462, Fillmore, CA 93015
Shooter's Porta Bench, Centrum Industries, Inc., 443 Century, S.W., Grand Rapids, MI 49503/616-454-9424
Shooters Rubber Stamps, Craft Haven, 700 Sierra Dr., 70th & Vine, Lincoln, NB 68505
Shooting Coats, 10-X Mfg. Co., 1745 So. Acoma St., Denver, CO 80223/303-778-0324
Shooting Glasses, Willson Safety Prods. Division, P.O. Box 622, Reading, PA 19603
Shooting Ranges, Kory Shooting Equipment, 233 S. Wacker, Sears Tower, Suite 7130, Chicago, IL 60606
Shotgun Sight, bi ocular, Trius Prod., Box 25, Cleves, O. 45002
Shotshell Adapter, PC Co., 5942 Secor Rd., Toledo, OH 43623 (Plummer 410 converter)
Silver Grip Caps, Bill Dyer, P.O. Box 75255, Oklahoma City, Okla. 73107
Single Shot Action, John Foote, Foote-Shephard Inc., P.O. Box 6473, Marietta, GA 30065
Snap Caps, Edwards Recoil Reducer, 269 Herbert St., Alton, IL 62002
Sportsman's Chair, Custom Purveyors, P.O. Box 886, Fort Lee, NJ 07024
Springfield Safety Pin, B-Square Co., P.O. Box 11281, Ft. Worth, Tex. 76110
Springs, W. Wolff Co., Box 232, Ardmore, Pa. 19003
Stock pad, variable, Meadow Industries, Dept. 92, Meadow Lands, PA 15347
Supersound, Edmund Scientific Co., 101 E. Gloucester Pike, Barrington, NJ 08007 (safety device)
Swivels, Michaels, P.O. Box 13010, Portland, Ore. 97213
Swivels, Sile Dist., 7 Centre Market Pl., New York, N.Y. 10013
Swivels, Williams Gun Sight Co., 7389 Lapeer Rd., Davison, Mich. 48423
Tear Gas Pistol, Casady Eng. Associates, 560 Alaska Ave., Torrance, CA 90503
Tree Stand, Climbing, Amacker Prods., 219 Sussex, Monroe, LA 71203 (Deer Thief)
Trophies, Blackinton & Co., 140 Commonwealth, Attleboro Falls, Mass. 02763
Trophies, F. H. Noble & Co., 888 Tower Rd., Mundelein, IL 60060
Universal 3-shot Shotgun Plug, LanDav Custom Guns, 7213 Lee Highway, Falls Church, VA 22046
World Hunting Info., Jack Atcheson & Sons, Inc., 3210 Ottawa St., Butte, MT 59701
World Hunting Info., J/B Adventures & Safaris, Inc., 800 E. Girard, Suite 603, Denver, CO 80231/303-696-0261
World Hunting Info., Klineburger, 12 & East Pine, Seattle, WA 98122/206-329-1600
World Hunting Info., Wayne Preston, Inc., 3444 Northhaven Rd., Dallas, TX 75229

MUZZLE-LOADING GUNS, BARRELS OR EQUIPMENT

A&K Mfg. C., Inc., 1651 N. Nancy Rose Ave., Tucson, AZ 85712 (ctlg. $1)
Luther Adkins, Box 281, Shelbyville, IN 47176/317-392-3795 (breech plugs)
Anderson Mfg. Co., P.O. Box 3120, Yakima WA 98903
Armoury, Inc., Rte. 202, New Preston, CT 06777
Beaver Lodge, 9245 16th Ave. S.W., Seattle, WA 98106
John Bivins, Jr., 200 Wicklow Rd., Winston-Salem, NC 27106
Blue and Gray Prods., Inc., 817 E. Main St., Bradford, PA 16701
G. S. Bunch, 7735 Garrison, Hyattsville, Md. 20784 (flask repair)
Butler Creek Corp., Box GG, Jackson, WY 83001 (poly patch)
CAI, Conversion Arms, Inc., P.O. Box 449, Yuba City, CA 95991 (stainl. steel BP shotshell adaptors)
Cache La Poudre Rifleworks, 168 N. College, Ft. Collins, CO 80521/303-482-6913 (custom muzzleloaders)
Challanger Mfg. Co., 118 Pearl St., Mt. Vernon, NY 10550

R. MacDonald Champlin, P.O. Box 74, Wentworth, NH 03282 (custom muzzleloaders)
Chopie Mfg. Inc., 531 Copeland Ave., LaCrosse, WI 54601 (nipple wrenches)
Classic Arms Ltd., 20 Wilbraham St., Palmer, MA 01069/413-596-9691 (BP guns and kits)
Connecticut Valley Arms Co. (CVA), Saybrook Rd., Haddam, CT 06438 (kits also)
Earl T. Cureton, Rte. 2, Box 388, Willoughby Rd., Bulls Gap, TN 37711 (powder horns)
DJ Inc., 1310 S. Park Rd., Fairdale, KY 40118
Leonard Day & Co., 316 Burt Pits Rd., Northampton, MA 10160
Dixie Gun Works, Inc., P.O. Box 130, Union City, TN 38261
EMF Co., Inc., Box 1248, Studio City, CA 91604
Eagle Arms Co., 136 Westward Ho Dr., Northlake, IL 60164/312-562-2708
Euroarms of America, Inc., 14 W. Monmouth St., Winchester, VA 22601
The Eutaw Co., Box 608, U.S. Highway 176W, Holly Hill, SC 29059 (accessories)
Excam, Inc., 4480 E. 11th Ave., Hialeah, FL 33012
Ted Fellowes, Beaver Lodge, 9245 16th Ave. S.W., Seattle, Wash. 98106
Firearms Imp. & Exp. Corp., 4530 N.W. 135th St., Opa-Locka, FL 33054/305-685-5966
Marshall F. Fish, Rt. 22 N., Westport, NY 12993 (antique ML repairs)
Clark K. Frazier/Matchmate, RFD. 1, Rawson, OH 45881
C. R. & D. E. Getz, Box 88, Beavertown, PA 17813 (barrels)
Golden Age Arms Co., 14 W. Winter St., Delaware, OH 43015 (ctlg. $2)
A. R. Goode, 12845 Catoctin Furnace Rd., Thurmont, MD 21788/301-271-2228 (ML rifle bbls.)
Green River Forge, Ltd., P.O. Box 885, Springfield, OR 97477 (Forge-Fire flints)
The Flintlock Muzzleloading Gun Shop, 1238 S. Beach, Anaheim, CA 92804/714-821-6655
Harper's Ferry Arms Co., 256 E. Broadway, Hopewell, VA 23860 (guns)
Hopkins & Allen, #1 Melnick Rd., Monsey, NY 10952
International Arms, 23239 Doremus Ave., St. Clair Shores, MI 48080
JJJJ Ranch, Wm. Large, Rte. 1, State Route 243, Ironton, Ohio 45638/614-532-5298
Kern's Gun Shop, 319 E. Main St., Ligonier, PA 15658/412-238-7651 (ctlg. $1.50)
Art LeFeuvre, 1003 Hazel Ave., Deerfield, Ill. 60015 (antique gun restoring)
Les' Gun Shop (Les Bauska), Box 511, Kalispell, Mont, 59901
Lever Arms Serv. Ltd., 771 Dunsmuir, Vancouver, BC V6C 1M0, Canada
Log Cabin Sport Shop, 8010 Lafayette Rd., Lodi, OH 44254/216-948-1082 (ctlg. $3)
Loven Firearms Corp., Del Mar Dr., Brookfield, CT 06804
Lyman Products Corp., Rte. 147, Middlefield, CT 06455
McCann's Muzzle-Gun Works, 200 Federal City Rd., Pennington, NJ 08354/609-737-1707
McKeown's Guns, R.R. 4, Pekin, IL 61554/309-347-3559 (E-Z load rev. stand)
Judson E. Mariotti, Beauty Hill Rd., Barrington, NH 03825 (brass bullet mould)
Maurer Arms, 2366 Frederick Dr., Cuyahoga Falls, OH 44221 (cust. muzzleloaders)
Mountain State Muzzleloading Supplies, Box 154-1, Williamstown, WV 26187
Mowrey Gun Works, Box 28, Iowa Park, TX 76367
Muzzleloaders Etc., Inc., Jim Westberg, 9901 Lyndale Ave. S., Bloomington, MN 55420
Numrich Corp., W. Hurley, N.Y. 12491 (powder flasks)
Kirk Olson, Ft. Woolsey Guns, P.O. Box 2122, Prescott, AZ 86302/602-778-3035 (powderhorns)
Ox-Yoke Originals, 130 Griffin Rd., West Suffield, CT 06093 (dry lubr. patches)
Orrin L. Parsons, Jr., Central Maine Muzzle-Loading & Gunsmithing, RFD #1, Box 787, Madison, ME 04950
A. W. Peterson Gun Shop, 1693 Old Hwy. 441 N., Mt. Dora, FL 32757 (ML guns)
Richland Arms, 321 W. Adrian St., Blissfield, MI 49228
Rush's Old Colonial Forge, 106 Wiltshire Rd., Baltimore, MD 21221
Salish House, Inc., P.O. Box 27, Rollins, MT 59931
H. M. Schoeller, 569 So. Braddock Ave., Pittsburgh, Pa. 15221
Sharon Rifle Barrel Co., P.O. Box 106, Kalispell, MT 59901
Shiloh Products, 37 Potter St., Farmingdale, NY 11735 (4-cavity mould)
Shore Galleries, Inc., 3318 W. Devon Ave., Chicago, IL 60645/312-676-2900
Sile Distributors, 7 Centre Market Pl., New York, NY 10013
C. E. Siler Locks, Rt. 6, Box 5, Candler, NC 28715 (flint locks)
Ken Steggles, 17 Bell Lane, Byfield, Near Daventry, Northants NN11 6US, England (accessories)
T.E.S. Firearms Ltd., 2807 N. Prospect St., Colorado Springs, CO 80907 (underhammer target rifle)
Ten-Ring Precision, Inc., 1449 Blue Crest Lane, San Antonio, TX 78232/512-494-3063
Upper Missouri Trading Co., 3rd and Harold Sts., Crofton, NB 68730
R. Watts, 826 Springdale Rd., Atlanta, GA 30306 (ML rifles)
W. H. Wescomb, P.O. Box 488, Glencoe, CA 95232 (parts)
Thos. F. White, 5801 Westchester Ct., Worthington, O. 43085 (powder horn)
Williamson-Pate Gunsmith Serv., 117 W. Pipeline, Hurst, TX 76053/817-268-2887
York County Gun Works, R.R. #4, Tottenham, Ont. L0G 1W0, Canada (locks)

PISTOLSMITHS

Allen Assoc., 7502 Limekiln Pike, Philadelphia, PA 19150 (speed-cock lever for 45 ACP)

Bain and Davis Sptg. Gds., 559 W. Las Tunas Dr., San Gabriel, Cal. 91776
Lee Baker, 7252 East Ave. U-3, Littlerock, CA 93543/805-944-4487
Bar-Sto Precision Machine, 633 So. Victory Blvd., Burbank, CA 91502 (S.S. bbls. f. 45 Acp)
Behlert Custom Guns, Inc., 725 Lehigh Ave., Union, NJ 07083 (short actions)
F. Bob Chow, Gun Shop, 3185 Mission, San Francisco, Calif. 94110
Steven N. Brown, 8810 Rocky Ridge Rd., Indianapolis, IN 46217/317-881-2771 aft. 5 PM
J.E. Clark, Rte. 2, Box 22A, Keithville, LA 71047
Custom Gun Shop, 725 Lehigh Ave., Union, NJ 07083
Davis Co., 2793 Del Monte St., West Sacramento, CA 95691/916-372-6789
Day Arms Corp., 2412 S.W. Loop 410, San Antonio, TX 78227
Dominic DiStefano, 4303 Friar Lane, Colorado Springs, CO 80907 (accurizing)
Dan Dwyer, 915 W. Washington, San Diego, Calif. 92103
Ehresman Tool Co., Inc., 5425 Planeview Dr., Ft. Wayne, IN 46805 (custom)
Ken Eversull Gunsmith, Inc., P.O. Box 1766, Alexandria, LA 71301/318-442-0569
Giles' 45 Shop, Rt. 2, Box 847, Odessa, FL 33556
The Gunshop, R. D. Wallace, 320 Overland Rd., Prescott, AZ 86301
Gil Hebard Guns, Box 1, Knoxville, Ill. 61448
Lee E. Jurras & Assoc., Inc., P.O. Drawer F, Hagerman, NM 88232
Kart Sptg. Arms Corp., RD 2, Box 929-Broad Ave., Riverhead, NY 11901 (handgun conversions)
Lenz Firearms Co., 1480 Elkay Dr., Eugene, OR 97404
Kent Lomont, 4421 So. Wayne Ave., Ft. Wayne, IN 46807/219-694-6792 (Auto Mag only)
Mag-Na-Port Arms, Inc., 30016 S. River Rd., Mt. Clemens, MI 48043/313-469-6727
Rudolf Marent, 9711 Tiltree, Houston, TX 77075 (Hammerli)
Nu-Line Guns, 3727 Jennings Rd., St. Louis, MO 63121
Pachmayr Gun Works, 1220 S. Grand Ave., Los Angeles, Calif. 90015
L. W. Seecamp Co., Inc., Box 255, New Haven, CT 06502 (DA Colt auto conversions)
Silver Dollar Guns, P.O. Box 475, 10 Frances St., Franklin, NH 03235 (45 ACP)
Spokhandguns Inc., E. J. Christensen, East 1911 Sprague Ave., Spokane, WA 99202/509-534-4112
Sportsmens Equipmt. Co., 915 W. Washington, San Diego, Calif. 92103
Irving O. Stone, Jr., 633 S. Victory Blvd., Burbank, CA 91502
Victor W. Strawbridge, 6 Pineview Dr., Dover Pt., Dover, NH 03820
A. D. Swenson's 45 Shop, P.O. Box 606, Fallbrook, CA 92028
Dennis A. "Doc" Ulrich, 2511 S. 57th Ave., Cicero, IL 60650
Vic's Gun Refinishing, 6 Pineview Dr., Dover, NH 03820
Walters Industries, 6226 Park Lane, Dallas, TX 75225
Dave Woodruff, Box 5, Bear, DE 19701

REBORING AND RERIFLING

P.O. Ackley (see: Successo Dennis M. Bellm Gunsmithing, Inc.
Atkinson Gun Co., P.O. Box 512, Prescott, AZ 86301
Bain & Davis Sptg. Gds., 559 W. Las Tunas Dr., San Gabriel, Calif. 91776
Dennis M. Bellm Gunsmithing Inc., 2376 So. Redwood Rd., Salt Lake City, UT 84119
Charles P. Donnelly, Siskiyou Gun Works, 405 Kubli Rd., Grants Pass, OR 97526
Fuller Gun Shop, Cooper Landing, Alaska 99572
Bruce Jones, 389 Calla Ave., Imperial Beach, CA 92032
Les' Gun Shop, (Les Bauska), Box 511, Kalispell, MT 59901
Morgan's Cust. Reboring, 707 Union Ave., Grants Pass, OR 97526
Nu-Line Guns, 1053 Caulkshill Rd., Harvester, MO 63303/314-441-4500 (handguns)
Al Petersen, Box 8, Riverhurst, Saskatchewan, Canada S0H3P0
SGW, Inc. (formerly Schuetzen Gun Works), 624 Old Pacific Hwy. S.E., Olympia, WA 98503/206-456-3471
Sharon Gun Specialties, 14587 Peaceful Valley Rd., Sonora, CA 95370
Siegrist Gun Shop, 2689 McLean Rd., Whittemore, MI 48770
Snapp's Gunshop, 6911 E. Washington Rd., Clare, Mich. 48617
J. W. Van Patten, Box 145, Foster Hill, Milford, Pa. 18337
Robt. G. West, 27211 Huey Lane, Eugene, OR 97402

RELOADING TOOLS AND ACCESSORIES

Advance Car Mover Co., Inc., P.O. Box 1181, Appleton, WI 54911 (bottom pour lead casting ladles)
American Wad Co., 125 W. Market St., Morrison, IL 61270/815-772-7618 (12-ga. shot wad)
Anderson Mfg. Co., Royal, IA 51357 (Shotshell Trimmers)
Aurands, 229 E. 3rd St., Lewistown, Pa. 17044
B-Square Eng. Co., Box 11281, Ft. Worth, Tex. 76110
Bill Ballard, 830 Miles Ave., Billings, MT 59101 (ctlg. 50¢)
Ballistic Prods., Inc., 17610 19th Ave. No., Wayzata, MN 55391
Belding & Mull, P.O. Box 428, Philipsburg, Pa. 16866
Berdon Co., P.O. Box 70131, Seattle, WA 98107 (metallic press)
Blackhawk SAA East, K2274 POB, Loves Park, Ill. 61131/812-633-7784
Blackhawk SAA Mtn., Richard Miller, 1337 Delmar Parkway, Aurora, CO 80010/303-366-3659
Blackhawk SAA West, Box 285, Hiawatha, KS 66434
Bonanza Sports, Inc., 412 Western Ave., Faribault, Minn. 55021
Gene Bowlin, 3602 Hill Ave., Snyder, Tex. 79549 (arbor press)
Brown Precision Co., 5869 Indian Ave., San Jose, Calif. 95123 (Little Wiggler)

A. V. Bryant, 72 Whiting Rd., E. Hartford, CT 06118 (Nutmeg Universal Press)
C-H Tool & Die Corp., 106 N. Harding St., Owen, WI 54461/715-229-2146
CPM Industries Corp., 330 Elm St., Clyde, OH 43410
Central Products f. Shooters, 435 Route 18, East Brunswick, NJ 08816 (neck turning tool)
Camdex, Inc., 23880 Hoover Rd., Warren, MI 48089
Carbide Die & Mfg. Co., Box 226, Covina, CA 91724
Carter Gun Works, 2211 Jefferson Pk. Ave., Charlottesville, Va. 22903
Cascade Cartridge, Inc., (See Omark)
Catco-Ambush, Inc., P.O. Box 300, Corte Madera, CA 94926 (paper bullet patches)
Chevron Case Master, R.R. 1, Ottawa, IL 61350
Lester Coats, 416 Simpson St., No. Bend, Ore. 97459 (core cutter)
Container Development Corp., 424 Montgomery St., Watertown, WI 53094
Continental Kite & Key Co., Box 40, Broomall, PA 19008 (primer pocket cleaner)
Cooper-Woodward, Box 972, Riverside, Calif. 92502 (Perfect Lube)
D. R. Corbin Mfg. & Supply Inc., P.O. Box 758, Phoenix, OR 97535
Custom Products, 686 Baldwin St., Meadville, PA 16335/814-724-7045 (decapping tool, dies, etc.)
J. Dewey Mfg. Co., 125 Fenn Rd., Middlebury, CT 06762
Diverter Arms, Inc., P.O. Box 22084, Houston, TX 77027 (bullet puller)
Division Lead Co., 7742 W. 61st Pl., Summit, Ill. 60502
Eagle Products Co., 1520 Adelia Ave., So. El Monte, Cal. 91733
Edmisten Co. Inc., P.O. Box 1293, Hwy 105, Boone, NC 28607/704-264-1490
Efemes Enterprises, P.O. Box 122M, Bay Shore, NY 11706 (Berdan decapper)
W. H. English, 4411 S. W. 100th, Seattle, Wash. 98146 (Paktool)
Farmer Bros., 1102 Washington St., Eldora, IA 50627 (Lage)
Fitz, 653 N. Hagar St., San Fernando, CA 91340 (Fitz Flipper)
Flambeau Plastics, 801 Lynn, Baraboo, Wis. 53913
Forster Products Inc., 82 E. Lanark Ave., Lanark, Ill. 61046
Geo. M. Fullmer, 2499 Mavis St., Oakland, CA 94601 (seating die)
Gene's Gun Shop, 3602 Hill Ave., Snyder, Tex. 79549 (arbor press)
Goerg Enterprises, P.O. Box 531, Renton, WA 98056/206-833-1529
Gopher Shooter's Supply, Box 278, Faribault, MN 55021
Griffin Mfg. Co., P.O. Box 935, Brownwood, TX 76801
The Gun Clinic, 81 Kale St., Mahtomedi, Minn. 55115
Hart Products, Rob. W. Hart & Son Inc., 401 Montgomery St., Nescopeck, PA 18635
Henriksen Tool Co., Inc., P.O. Box 668, Phoenix, OR 97535
Hensley & Gibbs, Box 10, Murphy, Ore. 97533
Herter's Inc., RR1, Waseca, Minn. 56093
Richard Hoch, The Gun Shop, 62778 Spring Creek Rd., Montrose, CO 81401/303-249-3625 (custom schuetzen bullet moulds)
B. E. Hodgdon, Inc., 7710 W. 50 Hiway, Shawnee Mission, Kans. 66202
Hoffman Prods., P.O. Box 853, Lake Forest, IL 60045 (spl. gallery load press)
Hollywood Reloading, (see: Whitney Sales, Inc.)
Hornady (see: Pacific)
Hulme Firearm Serv., Box 83, Millbrae, Calif. 94030 (Star case feeder)
Independent Mach. & Gun Shop, 1416 N. Hayes, Pocatello, Ida. 83201
Ivy Armament, P.O. Box 10, Greendale, WI 53129
JASCO, Box 49751, Los Angeles, Calif. 90049
J & G Rifle Ranch, Box S80, Turner, MT 59542 (case tumblers)
Javelina Products, Box 337, San Bernardino, Cal. 92402 (Alox beeswax)
Neil Jones, 686 Baldwin St., Meadville, PA 16335 (decapping tool, dies)
Kexplore, 9450 Harwig #G, Houston, TX 77036
Kuharsky Bros. (see Modern Industries)
Lac-Cum Bullet Puller, Star Route, Box 240, Apollo, PA 15613/412-478-1794
Lage Uniwad Co., 1102 N. Washington St., Eldora, IA 50627 (Universal Shotshell Wad)
LanDav, 7213 Lee Highway, Falls Church, VA 22046 (X-15 bullet puller)
Lee Custom Engineering, Inc., 46 E. Jackson St. Hartford, WI 53027
Lee Precision, Inc., 4275 Hwy. U, Hartford, WI 53027
Leon's Reloading Service, 3945 No. 11 St., Lincoln, Neb. 68521
Lewisystems, Menasha Corp., 426 Montgomery St., Watertown, WI 53094
L. L. F. Die Shop, 1281 Highway 99 N., Eugene, Ore. 97402
Dean Lincoln, P.O. Box 1886, Farmington, NM 87401 (mould)
Ljutic Industries, 918 N. 5th Ave., Yakima, Wash. 98902
Lock's Phila. Gun Exch., 6700 Rowland, Philadelphia, Pa. 19149
Lyman Products Corp., Rte. 147, Middlefield, CT 06455
McKillen & Heyer Inc., 37603 Arlington Dr., Box 627, Willoughby, OH 44094/216-942-2491 (case gauge)
Paul McLean, 2670 Lakeshore Blvd., W., Toronto 14, Ont., Canada (Universal Cartridge Holder)
MEC, Inc. (see: Mayville Eng. Co.)
MTM Molded Prod., 5680 Webster St., Dayton, OH 45414
Magma Eng. Co., P.O. Box 881, Chandler, AZ 85224
Judson E. Mariotti, Beauty Hill Rd., Barrington, NH 03825 (brass bullet mould)
Marmel Prods., P.O. Box 97, Utica, MI 48087 (Marvelube, Marvelux)
Marquart Precision Co., Box 1740, Prescott, AZ 86301 (precision case-neck turning tool)
Mayville Eng. Co., 715 South St., Mayville, Wis. 53050 (shotshell loader)
Merit Gun Sight Co., P.O. Box 995, Sequim, Wash. 98382
Modern Industries, Inc., 613 W-11, Erie, PA 16501 (primer pocket cleaner)
Multi-Scale Charge Ltd., 3269 Niagara Falls Blvd., North Tonawanda, NY 14120
NL Industries Inc., Metal Div., P.O. Box 3618, Hightstown, NJ 08520/609-443-2209 (Lawrence Brand shot)
Normington Co., Box 6, Rathdrum, ID 83858 (powder baffles)
Ohaus Scale, (see: RCBS)
Omark-CCI, Inc., Box 856, Lewiston, Ida. 83501

Pacific Tool Co., P.O. Box 2048, Ordnance Plant Rd., Grand Island, NE 68801/308-384-2308
Pak-Tool Co., 4411 S.W. 100th, Seattle, WA 98146
Personal Firearms Record Book, Box 201, Park Ridge, Ill. 60068
Ferris Pindell, R.R. 3, Box 205, Connersville, IN 47331 (bullet spinner)
Plum City Ballistics Range, Rte. 1, Box 29A, Plum City, WI 54761
Ponsness-Warren, Inc., P.O. Box 8, Rathdrum, ID 83858
Marian Powley, Petra Lane, R.R.I. Eldridge, IA 52748
Precise Alloys Inc., 69 Kinkel St., Westbury, NY 11590 (chilled lead shot; bullet wire)
Quinetics Corp., 5731 Kenwick, San Antonio, TX 78238/516-684-8561 (kinetic bullet puller)
RCBS, Inc., Box 1919, Oroville, Calif. 95965
Redding Inc., 114 Starr Rd., Cortland, NY 13045
Reloaders Equipment Co., 4680 High St., Ecorse, MI 48229 (bullet puller)
Remco, 1404 Whitesboro St., Utica, N.Y. 13502 (shot caps)
Rifle Ranch, Rte. 5, Prescott, Ariz. 86301
Rochester Lead Works, Rochester, N.Y. 14608 (leadwire)
Rorschach Precision Prods., P.O. Box 1613, Irving, Tex. 75060
Rotex Mfg. Co. (see Texan)
Ruhr-American Corp., So. East Hwy. 55, Glenwood, Minn. 56334
SAECO Rel. Inc., P.O. Box 778, Carpinteria, Calif. 93013
SSK Industries, Rt. 1, Della Drive, Bloomingdale, OH 43910 (primer tool)
Sandia Die & Cartridge Co., Rte. 5, Box 5400, Albuquerque, NM 87123
Shassere, (Box 35865, Houston, TX 77096/713-780-7041 (cartridge case caddy/loading block)
Shiloh Products, 37 Potter St., Farmingdale, NY 11735 (4-cavity bullet mould)
Shooters Accessory Supply, see: D. R. Corbin
Sil's Gun Prod., 490 Sylvan Dr., Washington, Pa. 15301 (K-spinner)
Jerry Simmons, 715 Middlebury St., Goshen, Ind. 46526/219-533-8546 (Pope de- & recapper)
Smith & Wesson Ammunition Co., Inc., 2399 Forman Rd., Rock Creek, OH 44084
J. A. Somers Co., P.O. Box 49751, Los Angeles, CA 90049 (Jasco)
Sport Flite Mfg., Inc., 2520 Industrial Row, Troy, MI 48084/313-280-0648 (swaging dies)
D. E. Stanley, P.O. Box 833, Ringold, OK 74754 (Kake-Kutter)
Star Machine, Inc., 418 10th Ave., San Diego, CA 92101
T.E.S., Inc., 2807 N. Prospect St., Colorado Springs, CO 80907 (Vibra-Tek)
T&T Products, Inc., 6330 Hwy. 14 East, Rochester, MN 55901 (Meyer shotgun slugs)
Texan Reloaders, Inc., 444 Cip St., Watseka, IL 60970/815-432-5065
Trico Plastics, 590 S. Vincent Ave., Azusa, CA 91702
WAMADET, Silver Springs, Goodleigh, Barnstaple, Devon, England
Walker Mfg. Inc., 8296 So. Channel, Harsen's Island, MI 48028 (Berdan decapper)
Wammes Guns Inc., 236 N. Hayes St., Bellefontaine, OH 43311 (Jim's powder baffles)
Weatherby, Inc., 2781 Firestone Blvd., South Gate, Calif. 90280
Webster Scale Mfg. Co., Box 188, Sebring, Fla. 33870
Whits Shooting Stuff, P.O. Box 1340, Cody, WY 82414
Whitney Sales, Inc., P.O. 875, Reseda, CA 91335 (Hollywood)
L. E. Wilson, Inc., P.O. Box 324, 404 Pioneer Ave., Cashmere, WA 98815
Xelex, Ltd., P.O. Box 543, Renfrow K7V 4B1, Canada (powder)
Zenith Enterprises, 361 Flagler Rd., Nordland, WA 98358

RESTS—BENCH, PORTABLE, ETC.

Bill Anderson, 551 Fletcher, Wayne, PA 19087
Bausch & Lomb, 635 St. Paul St., Rochester, NY 14602 (rifle rest)
Jim Brobst, 299 Poplar St., Hamburg, PA 19526 (bench rest pedestal)
C'Arco, P.O. Box 2043, San Bernardino, CA 92401 (Ransom handgun rest)
Cole's Acku-Rite Prod., Box 364, Ellington, NY 14732
Cravener's Gun Shop, 1627 - 5th Ave., Ford City, PA 16226 (portable)
Decker Shooting Products, 1729 Laguna Ave., Schofield, WI 54476 (rifle rests)
The Gun Case, 11035 Maplefield, El Monte, Cal. 91733
Harris Engr., Inc., Barlow, KY 42024
Rob. W. Hart & Son, 401 Montgomery St., Nescopeck, Pa. 18635
Tony Hidalgo, 6 Capp St., Carteret, NJ 07008 (shooters stools)
North Star Devices, Inc., P.O. Box 2095, North St. Paul, MN 55109 (Gun Slinger)
Progressive Prods., Inc., P.O. Box 41, Holmen, WI 54636 (Sandbagger rifle rest)
Rec. Prods, Res., Inc., 158 Franklin Ave., Ridgewood, N.J. 07450 (Butts Pi-pod)
D. E. Stanley, P.O. Box 833, Ringold, OK 74754 (portable shooting rest)
Suter's, 332 Tejon, Colorado Springs, CO 80902
Tuller & Co., 29 Germania, Galeton, PA 16922 (Protector sandbags)
Wichita Arms, 333 Lulu, Wichita, KS 67211

RIFLE BARREL MAKERS

P.O. Ackley Rifle Barrels (see: David M. Bellm Gunsmithing Inc.)
Atkinson Gun Co., P.O. Box 512, Prescott, AZ 86301
Jim Baiar, 490 Halfmoon Rd., Columbia Falls, MT 59912/406-892-4409
Dennis M. Bellm Gunsmithing Inc., 2376 So. Redwood Rd., Salt Lake City, UT 84119
Ralph L. Carter, Carter's Gun Shop, 225 G St., Penrose, CO 81240/303-372-6240
Christy Gun Works, 875 57th St., Sacramento, Calif. 95819
Clerke Prods., 2219 Main St., Santa Monica, Calif. 90405
Cuthbert Gun Shop, 715 So. 5th, Coos Bay, Ore. 97420

B. W. Darr, Saeco-Darr Rifle Co., Ltd., P.O. Box 778, Carpinteria, CA 93013
Douglas Barrels, Inc., 5504 Big Tyler Rd., Charleston, W. Va. 25312
Douglas Jackalope Gun & Sport Shop, Inc., 1048 S. 5th St., Douglas, WY 82633
Federal Firearms Co., Inc., Box 145, 145 Thomas Run Rd., Oakdale, PA 15071
C. R. & D. E. Getz, Box 88, Beavertown, PA 17813
A. R. Goode, 12845 Catoctin Furnace Rd., Thurmont, MD 21788/301-271-2228
Half Moon Rifle Shop, 490 Halfmoon Rd., Columbia Falls, MT 59912/406-892-4409
Hart Rifle Barrels, Inc., RD 2, Lafayette, N.Y. 13084
Wm. H. Hobaugh, Box M, Philipsburg, MT 59858
David R. Huntington, RFD #1, Box 23, Heber City, UT 83032
Kogot, John Pell, 410 College Ave., Trinidad, CO 81082/303-846-9006 (custom octagon)
Gene Lechner, 636 Jane N.E., Albuquerque, NM 87123
Les' Gun Shop, (Les Bauska), Box 511, Kalispell, MT 59901
Marquart Precision Co., Box 1740, Prescott, AZ 86301
Nu-Line Guns, Inc., 1053 Caulkshill Rd., Harvester, MO 63303/314-441-4500
Numrich Arms, W. Hurley, N.Y. 12491
Al Petersen, The Rifle Ranch, Box 8, Riverhurst, Sask., Canada SOH3PO
Sanders Cust. Gun Serv., 2358 Tyler Lane, Louisville, Ky. 40205
SGW, Inc., D. A. Schuetz, 624 Old Pacific Hwy. S.E., Olympia, WA 98503/206-456-3471
Sharon Gun Specialties, 14587 Peaceful Valley Rd., Sonora, CA 95370/209-532-4139
Ed Shilen Rifles, Inc., 205 Metropark Blvd., Ennis, TX 75119
W. C. Strutz, Rte. 1, "Woodland", Eagle River, WI 54521
Titus Barrel & Gun Co., R.F.D. #1, Box 23, Heber City, UT 84032
Bob Williams, P.O. Box 143, Boonsboro, MD 21713
Wilson Arms, 63 Leetes Island Rd., Branford, CT 06405

SCOPES, MOUNTS, ACCESSORIES, OPTICAL EQUIPMENT

Aimpoint U.S.A., 29351 Stonecrest Rd., Rancho Palos Verdes, CA 90274 (electronic sight)
Alley Supply Co., Carson Valley Industrial Park, Gardnerville, NV 89410 (Scope collimator)
American Import Co., 1167 Mission, San Francisco, Calif. 94103
Anderson Mfg. Co., P.O. Box 3120, Yakima, WA 98903 (lens cap)
Armsport, Inc., 3590 N.W. 49th St., Miami, FL 33122/305-592-7850
B-Square Co., Box 11281, Ft. Worth, TX 76109 (Mini-14 mount)
Bausch & Lomb Inc., 1400 Goodman St., Rochester, NY 14602/716-338-6000
Beeman's Precision Airguns, Inc., 47 Paul Dr., San Rafael, CA 94903/415-472-7121
Bennett, 561 Delaware, Delmar, N.Y. 12054 (mounting wrench)
Lenard M. Brownell, Box 25, Wyarno, WY 82845/307-737-2468 (cust. mounts)
Browning Arms, Rt. 4, Box 624-B, Arnold, Mo. 63010
Maynard P. Buehler, Inc., 17 Orinda Highway, Orinda, Calif. 94563
Burris Co., 331 E. 8th St., Box 1747, Greeley, CO 80631
Bushnell Optical Co., 2828 E. Foothill Blvd., Pasadena, Calif. 91107
Butler Creek Corp., Box GG, Jackson Hole, WY 83001 (lens caps)
Kenneth Clark, 18738 Highway 99, Madera, Calif. 93637
Clearview Mfg. Co., Inc., 20821 Grand River Ave., Detroit, MI 48219 (mounts)
Clear View Sports Shields, P.O. Box 255, Wethersfield, CT 06107 (shooting/testing glasses)
Colt's, Hartford, Conn. 06102
Compass Instr. & Optical Co., Inc., 104 E 25th St., New York, N.Y. 10010
Conetrol Scope Mounts, Hwy 123 South, Seguin, TX 78155
D&H Prods. Co., Inc., P.O. Box 22, Glenshaw, PA 15116/412-443-2190 (lens covers)
Davis Optical Co., P.O. Box 6, Winchester, Ind. 47934
Del-Sports Inc., Main St., Margaretville, NY 12455/914-586-4103 (Kahles)
M. B. Dinsmore, Box 21, Wyomissing, PA 19610 (shooting glasses)
Eder Instrument Co., 5115 N. Ravenswood, Chicago, IL 60640 (borescope)
Flaig's, Babcock Blvd., Millvale, Pa. 15209
Fontaine Ind., Inc., 11552 Knott St., Suite 2, Garden Grove, CA 92641/714-892-4473 (traj. compensator dials)
Freeland's Scope Stands, Inc. 3734 14th, Rock Island, Ill. 61201
Griffin & Howe, Inc., 589 Broadway, New York, N.Y. 10012
H&H Assoc., P.O. Box 447, Strathmore, CA 93267 (target adj. knobs)
H. J. Hermann Leather Co., Rt. 1, Skiatook, OK 74070 (lens caps)
Herter's Inc., Waseca, Minn. 56093
J. B. Holden Co., 295 W. Pearl, Plymouth, MI 48170
The Hutson Corp., P.O. 1127, Arlington, Tex.76010
Hy-Score Arms Corp., 200 Tillary St., Brooklyn, N.Y. 11201
Interarms, 10 Prince St., Alexandria, VA 22313
Paul Jaeger, 211 Leedom St., Jenkintown, Pa. 19046 (Nickel)
Jana Intl. Co., Box 1107, Denver, Colo. 80201
Jason Empire Inc., 9200 Cody, P.O. Box 12370, Overland Park, KS 66212/913-888-0220
Jennison TCS (see Fontaine Ind., Inc.)
Kahles of America, Div. of Del-Sports, Inc. Main St., Margaretville, NY 12455/914-586-4103
Kesselring Gun Shop, 400 Pacific Hiway No., Burlington, WA 98283/206-724-3113
Kris Mounts, 108 Lehigh St., Johnstown, PA 15905
Kuharsky Bros. (see Modern Industries)
Kwik-Site, 5555 Treadwell, Wayne, MI 48185 (rings, mounts only)
LanDav, 7213 Lee Highway, Falls Church, VA 22046 (steel leverlock side mt.)

S. E. Laszlo House of Imports, 200 Tillary St., Brooklyn, NY 11201
Leatherwood Bros., Rte. 1, Box 111, Stephenville, TX 76401
T. K. Lee, 2830 S. 19th St., Off. #4, Birmingham, AL 35209 (reticles)
E. Leitz, Inc., Rockleigh, N.J. 07647
Leupold & Stevens Inc., P.O. Box 688, Beaverton, Ore. 97005
Jake Levin and Son, Inc., 9200 Cody, Overland Park, KS 66214
W. H. Lodewick, 2816 N.E. Halsey, Portland, OR 97232 (scope safeties)
Lyman Products Corp., Route 147, Middlefield, CT 06455
Mandall Shooting Supplies, 7150 E. 4th St., Scottsdale, AZ 85252
Marble Arms Co., 420 Industrial Park, Gladstone, MI 49837
Marlin Firearms Co., 100 Kenna Dr., New Haven, Conn. 06473
Robert Medaris, P.O. Box 309, Mira Loma, CA 91752/714-685-5666 (side mount f. H&K 91 & 93)
Modern Industries, Inc., 613 W-11, Erie, PA 16501
O. F. Mossberg & Sons, Inc., 7 Grasso Ave., North Haven, Conn. 06473
Normark Corp., 1710 E. 78th St., Minneapolis, Minn. 55423 (Singlepoint)
Numrich Arms, West Hurley, N.Y. 12491
Nydar, see: Swain Nelson Co.
PEM's Mounts, 6063 Waterloo, Atwater, PA 44201
Pachmayr Gun Works, 1220 S. Grand Ave., Los Angeles, Calif. 90015
Precise, 3 Chestnut, Suffern, NY 10901
Ranging Inc., 90 Lincoln Rd. North, East Rochester, NY 14445/716-385-1250
Ray-O-Vac, Willson Prod. Div., P.O. Box 622, Reading, PA 19603 (shooting glasses)
Redfield Gun Sight Co., 5800 E. Jewell Ave., Denver, Colo. 80222
S & K Mfg. Co., Box 247, Pittsfield, Pa. 16340 (Insta-mount)
Sanders Cust. Gun Serv., 2358 Tyler Lane, Louisville, Ky. 40205 (MSW)
Savage Arms, Westfield, Mass. 01085
Sears, Roebuck & Co., 825 S. St. Louis, Chicago, Ill. 60607
Sherwood Intl. Export Corp., 18714 Parthenia St., Northridge, CA 91324 (mounts)
W. H. Siebert, 22720 S.E. 56th Pl., Issaquah, WA 98027
Singlepoint (see Normark)
Southern Precision Inst. Co., 3419 E. Commerce St., San Antonio, TX 78219
Spacetron Inc., Box 84, Broadview, IL 60155 (bore lamp)
Stoeger Industries, 55 Ruta Ct., S. Hackensack, NJ 07606/201-440-2700
Strieter Corp., 2100 - 18th Ave., Rock Island, IL 61201/309-794-9800 (Swarovski, Habicht)
Supreme Lens Covers, Box GG, Jackson Hole, WY 83001 (lens caps)
Swain Nelson Co., Box 45, 92 Park Dr., Glenview, IL 60025 (shotgun sight)
Swift Instruments, Inc., 952 Dorchester Ave., Boston, Mass. 02125
Tasco, 1075 N.W. 71st, Miami, Fla. 33138
Ted's Sight Aligner, Box 1073, Scottsdale, AZ 85252
Thompson-Center Arms, P.O. Box 2405, Rochester, N.H. 03867 (handgun scope)
Tradewinds, Inc., Box 1191, Tacoma, Wash. 98401
John Unertl Optical Co., 3551-5 East St., Pittsburgh, Pa. 15214
United Binocular Co., 9043 S. Western Ave., Chicago, Ill. 60620
Verano Corp., Box 270, Glendora, CA 91740
Vissing (see: Supreme Lens Covers)
Weatherby's, 2781 Firestone, South Gate, Calif. 90280
W. R. Weaver Co., 7125 Industrial Ave., El Paso, Tex. 79915
Wide View Scope Mount Corp., 26110 Michigan Ave., Inkster, MI 48141
Williams Gun Sight Co., 7389 Lapeer Rd., Davison, Mich. 48423
Boyd Williams Inc., 8701-14 Mile Rd. (M-57), Cedar Springs, MI 49319 (BR)
Willrich Precision Instrument Co., 95 Cedar Lane, Englewood, NJ 07631/201-567-1411 (borescope)
Carl Zeiss Inc., 444 Fifth Ave., New York, N.Y. 10018 (Hensoldt)

SIGHTS, METALLIC

Accura-Site Co., Inc., Box 193, Neenah, WI 54956
B-Square Eng. Co., Box 11281, Ft. Worth, Tex. 76110
Beeman's Precision Airguns, Inc., 47 Paul Dr., San Rafael, CA 94903/415-472-7121 (airguns only)
Behlert Custom Sights, Inc., 725 Lehigh Ave., Union, NJ 07083
Bo-Mar Tool & Mfg. Co., Box 168, Carthage, Tex. 75633
Maynard P. Buehler, Inc., 17 Orinda Highway, Orinda, Calif. 94563
Christy Gun Works, 875 57th St., Sacramento, Calif. 95819
Jim Day, 902 N. Bownen Lane, Florence, SD 29501 (Chaba)
E-Z Mount, Ruelle Bros., P.O. Box 114, Ferndale, MT 48220
Freeland's Scope Stands, Inc., 3734-14th Ave., Rock Island, Ill. 61201
Paul T. Haberly, 2364 N. Neva, Chicago, IL 60635
Paul Jaeger, Inc., 211 Leedom St., Jenkintown, PA 19046
Lee's Red Ramps, 7252 E. Ave. U-3, Littlerock, CA 93543/805-944-4487 (illuminated sights)
Jim Lofland, 2275 Larkin Rd., Boothwyn, PA 19061
Lyman Products Corp., Rte. 147, Middlefield, Conn. 06455
Marble Arms Co., 420 Industrial Park, Gladstone, Mich. 49837
Merit Gunsight Co., P.O. Box 995, Sequim, Wash. 98382
Micro Sight Co., 242 Harbor Blvd., Belmont, Calif. 94002
Miniature Machine Co., 210 E. Poplar, Deming, NM 88030/505-546-2151
Modern Industries, Inc., 613 W-11, Erie, PA 16501
C. R. Pedersen & Son, Ludington, Mich. 49431
Poly Choke Co., Inc., P.O. Box 296, Hartford, CT 06101
Redfield Gun Sight Co., 5800 E. Jewell St., Denver, Colo. 80222
S&M Tang Sights, P.O. Box 1338, West Babylon, NY 11704
Schwarz's Gun Shop, 41 - 15th St., Wellsburg, W. Va. 26070
Simmons Gun Specialties, Inc., 700 Rodgers Rd., Olathe, Kans. 66061
Slug Site Co., Whitetail Wilds, Lake Hubert, MN 56469
Sport Service Center, 2364 N. Neva, Chicago, IL 60635
Tradewinds, Inc., Box 1191, Tacoma, WA 98401
Williams Gun Sight Co., 7389 Lapeer Rd., Davison, Mich. 48423

STOCKS (Commercial and Custom)

Abe and VanHorn, 5120¾ Huntington Dr., Los Angeles, CA 90032/213-227-4870
Adams Custom Gun Stocks, 13461 Quito Rd., Saratoga, CA 95070
Ahlman's Inc., R.R. 1, Box 20, Morristown, MN 55052
Don Allen, Rte. 1, Northfield, MN 55057 (blanks)
Anderson's Guns, Jim Jares, 706 S. 23rd St., Laramie, WY 82070
R. J. Anton, 874 Olympic Dr., Waterloo, IA 50701
Jim Baiar, 490 Halfmoon Rd., Columbia Falls, MT 59912
Joe J. Balickie, Custom Stocks, Rte. 2, Box 56-G, Apex, NC 27502
Bartas, Rte. 1, Box 129-A, Cato, Wis. 54206
Beeman's Precision Airguns, Inc., 47 Paul Dr., San Rafael, CA 94903/415-472-7121 (airguns only)
John Bianchi, 100 Calle Cortez, Temecula, CA 92390 (U. S. carbines)
Al Biesen, West 2039 Sinto Ave., Spokane, Wash. 99201
Stephen L. Billeb, Box 219, Philipsburg, MT 59858/406-859-3919
E. C. Bishop & Son Inc., Box 7, Warsaw, Mo. 65355
John M. Boltin, P.O. Box 1122, No. Myrtle Beach, SC 29582
Border Gun Shop, Garry Simmons, 2760 Tucson Hiway, Nogales, AZ 85621/602-281-0045 (spl. silueta stocks, complete rifles)
Brown Precision Co., P.O. Box 270W; 7786 Molinos Ave., Los Molinos, CA 96055/916-384-2506
Lenard M. Brownell, Box 25, Wyarno, WY 82845
E. J. Bryant, 3154 Glen St., Eureka, CA 95501
Jack Burres, 10333 San Fernando Road, Pacoima, CA 91331 (English, Claro, Bastogne Paradox walnut blanks only)
Calico Hardwoods, Inc., 1648 Airport Blvd., Windsor, Calif. 95492 (blanks)
Dick Campbell, 365 W. Oxford Ave., Englewood, CO 80110
Winston Churchill, Twenty Mile Stream Rd., Rt.1, Box 29B, Proctorsville, VT 05153
Crane Creek Gun Stock Co., 25 Shephard Terr., Madison, WI 53705
Reggie Cubriel, 15502 Purple Sage, San Antonio, TX 78255/512-695-8401 (cust. stockm.)
Dahl's Custom Stocks, Rt. 4, Box 187, Schofield Rd., Lake Geneva, WI 53147 (Martin Dahl)
Jack Dever, 8520 N.W. 90, Oklahoma City, OK 73132
Charles De Veto, 1087 Irene Rd., Lyndhurst, O. 44124
Bill Dowtin, P.O. Box 72, Celina, TX 75099
Gary Duncan, 1118 Canterbury, Enid, OK 73701 (blanks only)
David R. Dunlop, Rte. 1, Box 199, Rolla, ND 58367
Bob Emmons, 238 Robson Road, Grafton, OH 44044 (custom)
Reinhart Fajen, Box 338, Warsaw, MO 65355/814-438-5111
N. B. Fashingbauer, P.O. Box 366, Lac Du Flambeau, WI 54538/715-588-7116
Ted Fellowes, Beaver Lodge, 9245 16th Ave. S. W., Seattle, Wash. 98106
Clyde E. Fischer, Rt. 1, Box 170-M, Victoria, Tex. 77901
Jerry Fisher, 1244-4th Ave. W., Kalispell, MT 59901
Flaig's Lodge, Millvale, Pa. 15209
Donald E. Folks, 205 W. Lincoln St., Pontiac, IL 61764
Larry L. Forster, Box 212, Gwinner, ND 58040
Horace M. Frantz, Box 128, Farmingdale, N.J. 07727
Freeland's Scope Stands, Inc., 3734 14th Ave., Rock Island, Ill. 61201
Dale Goens, Box 224, Cedar Crest, N.M. 87008
Gary Goudy, 263 Hedge Rd., Menlo Park, CA 44025
Gould's Myrtlewood, 1692 N. Dogwood, Coquille, Ore. 97423 (gun blanks)
Charles E. Grace, 10144 Elk Lake Rd., Williamsburg, MI 49690
Rolf R. Gruning, 315 Busby Dr., San Antonio, Tex. 78209
The Gunshop, R. D. Wallace, 320 Overland Rd., Prescott, AZ 86301 (custom)
Half Moon Rifle Shop, 490 Halfmoon Rd., Columbia Falls, MT 59912
Harper's Custom Stocks, 928 Lombrano St., San Antonio, Tex. 78207
Harris Gun Stocks, Inc., 12 Lake St., Richfield Springs, N.Y. 13439
Hal Hartley, 147 Blairsfork Rd., Lenoir, NC 28645
Hayes Gunstock Service Co., 914 E. Turner St., Clearwater, Fla. 33516
Hubert J. Hecht, 55 Rose Mead Circle, Sacramento, CA 95831
Edward O. Hefti, 300 Fairview, College Sta., Tex. 77840
Herter's Inc., Waseca, Minn. 56093
Klaus Hiptmayer, Guncraft (Kelowna) Ltd., 1771 Harvey Ave., Kelowna, B.C. V1Y 6G4/604-860-8977
Richard Hodgson, 5589 Arapahoe, Unit 104, Boulder, CO 80301
Hollis Gun Shop, 917 Rex St., Carlsbad, N.M. 88220
Henry Houser, Ozark Custom Carving, 117 Main St., Warsaw, MO 65355
Jackson's, Box 416, Selman City, Tex. 75689 (blanks)
Paul Jaeger, 211 Leedom St., Jenkintown, Pa. 19046
JL Woods, Jim Jackson, 144 Colorado, Spearfish, SD 57783/605-642-2251 (blanks)
Johnson Wood Products, R.R. #1, Strawberry Point, IA 52076/319-933-4930 (blanks)
Monte Kennedy, P.O. Box 214, Kalispell, MT 59901
Don Klein, Box 277, Camp Douglas, WI 54618
LeFever Arms Co., Inc., R.D. 1, Lee Center-Stokes Rd., Lee Center, NY 13363/315-337-6422
Lenz Firearms Co., 1480 Elkay Dr., Eugene, OR 97404
Stanley Kenvin, 5 Lakeville Lane, Plainview, NY 11803/516-931-0321 (custom)
Philip D. Letiecq, AQ 18 Wagon Box Rd., P.O. Box 251, Story, WY 82842/307-683-2817
Al Lind, 7821 76th Ave. S.W., Tacoma, WA 98498 (cust. stockm.)
Bill McGuire, 1600 N. Eastmont Ave., East Wenatchee, WA 98801
Gale McMillan, 28638 N. 42 St., Box 7870 - Cave Creek Stage, Phoenix, AZ 85020/602-585-4684
Maurer Arms, 2366 Frederick Dr., Cuyahoga Falls, OH 44221
John E. Maxson, Box 332, Dumas, TX 79029/806-935-5990 (custom)

Leonard Mews, Spring Rd., Box 242, Hortonville, WI 54944
Robt. U. Milhoan & Son, Rt. 3, Elizabeth, W. Va. 26143
C. D. Miller Guns, Purl St., St. Onge, SD 57779
Nelsen's Gun Shop, 501 S. Wilson, Olympia, Wash. 98501
Oakley and Merkley, Box 2446, Sacramento, CA 95811 (blanks)
Jim Norman, Jim's Gunstocks, 11230 Calenda Road, San Diego, CA 92127/714-487-4173
Maurice Ottmar, Box 657, 113 E. Fir, Coulee City, WA 99115
Pachmayr Gun Works, 1220 S. Grand Ave., Los Angeles, CA 90015 (blanks and custom jobs)
Paulsen Gunstocks, Rte. 71, Box 11, Chinook, MT 59523 (blanks)
Peterson Mach. Carving, Box 1065, Sun Valley, Calif. 91352
Phillip Pilkington, P.O. Box 2284, University Station, Enid, OK 73701
R. Neal Rice, 5152 Newton, Denver, CO 80221
Richards Micro-Fit Stocks, P.O. Box 1066, Sun Valley, CA. 91352 (thumbhole)
Carl Roth, Jr., 4728 Pineridge Ave., Cheyenne, Wy. 82001
Matt Row, Lock, Stock 'N Barrel, 8972 East Huntington Dr., San Gabriel, CA 91775/213-287-0051
Royal Arms, Inc., 10064 Bert Acosta Ct., Santee, Calif. 92071
Sanders Cust. Gun Serv., 2358 Tyler Lane, Louisville, Ky. 40205 (blanks)
Saratoga Arms Co., R.D. 3, Box 387, Pottstown, Pa. 19464
Roy Schaefer, 965 W. Hilliard Lane, Eugene, OR 97404 (blanks)
Shaw's, Rt. 2, Box 407-L, Escondido, CA 92025/714-728-7070
Hank Shows, The Best, 1202 N. State, Ukaih, CA 95482
Walter Shultz, 1752 N. Pleasantview Rd., Pottstown, PA 19464
Sile Dist., 7 Centre Market Pl., New York, N.Y. 10013
Six Enterprises, 6564 Hidden Creek Dr., San Jose, CA 95120 (fiberglass)
Ed Sowers, 8331 DeCelis Pl., Sepulveda, CA 91343 (hydro-coil gunstocks)
Fred D. Speiser, 2229 Dearborn, Missoula, MT 59801
Sport Service Center, 2364 N. Neva, Chicago, IL 60635/312-889-1114 (custom)
Sportsmen's Equip. Co., 915 W. Washington, San Diego, Calif. 92103 (carbine conversions)
Keith Stegall, Box 696, Gunnison, Colo. 81230
Stinehour Rifles, Box 84, Cragsmoor, N.Y. 12420
Surf N' Sea, Inc., 62-595 Kam Hwy., Box 268, Haleiwa, HI 96712 (custom gunstocks blanks)
Swanson Cust. Firearms, 1051 Broadway, Denver, Colo. 80203
Talmage Enterpr., 43197 E. Whittier, Hemet, CA 92343
Brent L. Umberger, Sportsman's Haven, R.R. 4, Cambridge, OH 43725
John Vest, 6715 Shasta Way, Klamath Falls, OR 97601/503-884-5585 (classic rifles)
Weatherby's, 2781 Firestone, South Gate, Calif. 90280
Cecil Weems, Box 657, Mineral Wells, TX 76067
Frank R. Wells, 3019 W. Bartlett Pl., Tucson, AZ 85704 (custom stocks)
Western Gunstocks Mfg. Co., 550 Valencia School Rd., Aptos, CA 95003
Duane Wiebe, P.O. Box 497, Lotus, CA 95651
Bob Williams, P.O. Box 143, Boonsboro, MD 21713
Williamson-Pate Gunsmith Service, 117 W. Pipeline, Hurst, TX 76053/817-268-2887
Robert M. Winter, Box 484, Menno, S.D. 57045
Mike Yee, 4700-46th Ave. S.W., Seattle, WA 98116
Russell R. Zeeryp, 1601 Foard Dr., Lynn Ross Manor, Morristown, TN 37814

TARGETS, BULLET & CLAYBIRD TRAPS

Beeman's Precision Airguns, Inc., 47 Paul Dr., San Rafael, CA 94903/415-472-7121 (airgun targets, silhouettes and traps)
Caswell Equipment Co., Inc., 1221 Marshall St. N.E., Minneapolis, MN 55413
Cole's Acku-Rite Prod., Box 25, Kennedy, N.Y. 14747 (Site Rite targets)
Detroit Bullet Trap Co., 2233 N. Palmer Dr., Schaumburg, Ill. 60195/312-397-4070
Electro Ballistic Lab., 616 Junipero Serva Blvd., Stanford, CA 94305 (Electronic Trap Boy)
Ellwood Epps Northern Ltd., 210 Worthington St. W., North Bay, Ont. PIB 3B4, Canada (hand traps)
Gopher Shooter's Supply, Box 278, Faribault, MN 55021 (Lok-A-Leg target holders)
Kory Shooting Equipment, 233 S. Wacker, Sears Tower/Suite 7130, Chicago, IL 60606 (electric ranges)
Laporte S.A., B.P. 212, 06603 Antibes, France (claybird traps)
Laporte Equipment Inc., 70 rue Martin St., Granby, Queb. J2G 8B3, Canada (claybird traps)
MCM (Mathalienne de Construction de Mecanique), P.O. Box 18, 17160 Matha, France (claybird traps)
Millard F. Lerch, Box 163, 10842 Front St., Mokena, Ill. 60448 (bullet target)
National Target Co., 4960 Wyaconda Rd., Rockville, MD 20852
Outers Laboratories, Inc., Onalaska, Wis. 54650 (claybird traps)
Peterson Label Co., P.O. Box 186, Redding Ridge, CT 06876 (paste-ons)
Professional Tape Co., 355 E. Burlington Rd., Riverside, Ill. 60546 (Time Labels)
Recreation Prods. Res. Inc., 158 Franklin Ave., Ridgewood, NJ 07450 (Butts bullet trap)
Remington Arms Co., Bridgeport, Conn. 06602 (claybird traps)
Reproductions West, Box 6765, Burbank, CA 91510 (silhouette targets)
Rocky Mountain Target Co., P.O. Box 700, Black Hawk, SD 57718/605-787-5946 (Data-Targ)
Scientific Prod. Corp., 426 Swann Ave., Alexandria, VA 22301 (Targeteer)
Sheridan Products, Inc., 3205 Sheridan, Racine, Wis. 53403 (traps)
South West Metallic Silhouettes, P.O. Box 476, Uvalde, TX 78801
T-Magic Co., 33 Burnside Ave., East Hartford, CT 06108 (targets)
Time Products Co. (See Prof. Tape Co.)
Trius Prod., Box 25, Cleves, O. 45002 (claybird, can thrower)
Winchester-Western, New Haven, Conn. 06504 (claybird traps)

TAXIDERMY

Jack Atcheson & Sons, Inc., 3210 Ottawa St., Butte, MT 59701
Norris Brown, Box 189, 445 E. Kelly St., Jackson Hole, WY 83001
Jonas Bros., Inc., 1037 Broadway, Denver, CO 80203 (catlg. $2)
Knopp Taxidermy Studios, N. 6715 Division St., Spokane, WA 99208
Kulis Freeze-Dry Taxidermy, 725 Broadway Ave., Bedford, OH 44146
Mark D. Parker, 1233 Sherman Dr., Longmont, CO 80501/303-772-0214

TRAP & SKEET SHOOTERS EQUIP.

D&H Prods. Co., Inc., P.O. Box 22, Glenshaw, PA 15116/412-443-2190 (snap shell)
Creed Enterprises, P.O. Box 159, Coevr D'Alene, ID 83814 (ammo pouch)
Laporte S.A., B.P. 212, Pont de la Brague, 06603 Antibes, France (traps, claybird)
Laporte Equipment Inc., 70 rue Martin St., Granby, Queb. J2G 8B3, Canada (claybird traps)
MCM (Mathalienne de Construction de Mecanique), P.O. Box 18, 17160 Matha, France (claybird traps)
Wm. J. Mittler, 290 Moore Dr., Boulder Creek, CA 95006 (shotgun choke specialist)
Multi-Gauge Enterprises, 433 W. Foothill Blvd., Monrovia, CA 91061 (shotgun specialists)
William J. Nittler, 290 More Dr., Boulder Creek, CA 95006 (shotgun repairs)
Herb Orre, Box 56, Phillipsburg, OH 45354 (shotgun specialist)
Outers Laboratories, Inc., Route 2, Onalaska, WI 54650/608-783-1515 (trap, claybird)
Purbaugh Sporting Goods, 433 W. Foothill Blvd., Monrovia, CA 91016 (shotgun barrel inserts)
Remington Arms Co., Bridgeport, CT 06602 (trap, claybird)
Super Pigeon Corp., P.O. Box 428, Princeton, MN 55371 (claybird target)
Trius Products, Box 25, Cleves, OH 45002 (can thrower; trap, claybird)
Daniel Titus, 119 Morlyn Ave., Bryn Mawr, PA 19010 (hull bag)
Winchester-Western, New Haven, CT 06504 (trap, claybird)

TRIGGERS, RELATED EQUIP.

Ametek, Hunter Spring Div., One Spring Ave., Hatfield, PA 19440/215-822-2971 (trigger gauge)
M. H. Canjar Co., 500 E. 45th Ave., Denver, CO 80216 (triggers)
Central Specialties Co., 6030 Northwest Hwy., Chicago, IL 60631/312-774-5000 (trigger lock)
Custom Products, 686 Baldwin St., Meadville, PA 16335/814-724-7045 (trigger guard)
Dayton-Traister Co., 9322-900th West, P.O. Box 593, Oak Harbor, WA 98277 (triggers)
Electronic Trigger Systems, (Franklin C. Green), 530 W. Oak Grove Rd., Montrose, CO 81401
Flaig's, Babcock Blvd. & Thompson Run Rd., Millvale, PA 15209 (trigger shoe)
Gager Gage & Tool Co., 27509 Industrial Blvd., Hayward, CA 94545 (speedlock triggers f. Rem. 1100 and 870 shotguns)
Franklin C. Green, See Electronic Trigg. System
Bill Holmes, Rt. 2, Box 242, Fayetteville, AR 72701/501-521-8958 (trigger release)
Paul Jaeger, Inc., 211 Leedom St., Jenkintown, PA 19046
Michaels of Oregon Co., P.O. Box 13010, Portland, OR 97213 (trigger guards)
Miller Single Trigger Mfg. Co., R.D. 1 on Rte. 209, Millersburg, PA 17061
Viggo Miller, P.O. Box 4181, Omaha, NB 68104 (trigger attachment)
Ohaus Corp., 29 Hanover Rd., Florham Park, NJ 07932 (trigger pull gauge)
Pachmayr Gun Works, 1220 S. Grand Ave., Los Angeles, CA 90015 (trigger shoe)
Pacific Tool Co., P.O. Box 2048, Ordnance Plant Rd., Grand Island, NE 68801 (trigger shoe)
Richland Arms Co., 321 W. Adrian St., Blissfield, MI 49228 (trigger pull gauge)
Sport Service Center, 2364 N. Neva, Chicago, IL 60635 (release triggers)
Timney Mfg. Co., 2847 E. Siesta Lane, Phoenix, AZ 85024 (triggers)
Melvin Tyler, 1326 W. Britton Ave., Oklahoma City, OK 73114 (trigger shoe)
Williams Gun Sight Co., 7389 Lapeer Rd., Davison, MI 48423 (trigger shoe)